W9-ASV-283

Footprint Handbook
Peru, Bolivia
& Ecuador

ROBERT & DAISY KUNSTAETTER
BEN BOX

This is
Peru, Bolivia
& Ecuador

Imagine Peru, Bolivia and Ecuador and you automatically think of the Andes, the long, sinuous mountain chain that runs the full length of all three countries and forms the geographical and cultural spine of South America. Here, at over 3500 m, the first Incas rose from the freezing waters of Lake Titicaca. They named their capital Cuzco, 'Navel of the World', and built an empire that lasted until the Spanish came, saw, conquered and converted the natives.

But old habits die hard and today indigenous customs and beliefs are very much in evidence: in the beautiful and skilful *artesanía* (handicrafts); the spectacular festival costumes; the sacred temples and pyramids; or in the burying of a llama foetus under a new house to repel evil spirits. Often these ancient traditions were subsumed into the 'new' religion of the colonial masters.

It is the synthesis of ancient America and medieval Europe that is the essence of these countries. Thousands of years of empire-building, natural disasters, conquest, occupation and independence have all been played out, against the backdrop of those mighty mountains, the one constant in a continent of constant change.

There is more to these three countries than the Andes, however. To the east of the mountains spreads the vast Amazon Basin and each country has a claim to the tributaries that feed into the mighty river itself. The surrounding forest is home to some of the greatest diversity of wildlife on Earth. The western margin of Peru and Ecuador stands on the Pacific Ocean. In Peru the coastal lands are largely desert. Like Peru, Ecuador's coast offers good surf and terrific seafood, but also interesting national parks with good whale-watching. And way out in the ocean lie the Galápagos Islands, offering nature lovers the experience of a lifetime.

Robert & Daisy Kunstaetter
Ben Box

Best of
Peru, Bolivia & Ecuador

top things to do and see

❶ Cordillera Blanca

Beautiful and awe-inspiring, the snow-capped Cordillera Blanca attracts mountaineers, hikers, cyclists and rafters in their thousands. Here stand some of the highest mountains in South America, with 30 snow-crested peaks over 6000 m. Page 72.

❷ Colca Canyon

Come face to face with the magnificent Andean condor, the largest bird of prey in the world, in this canyon in Peru, one of the deepest in the world. It offers exceptional kayaking for those with a taste for profound adventure. Page 194.

❸ Lake Titicaca

The border between Peru and Bolivia divides the world's highest navigable lake, a superb destination for boat trips to islands rich in traditional culture. Ancient tombs and the pre-Hispanic city of Tiwanaku are within easy reach, and the celebrations of Puno and Copacabana are not to be missed. Page 210.

❹ Machu Picchu

The Inca mountain-top city is Peru's top attraction and deservedly so. It's the goal of many a hiker as well as countless tourists who prefer to go by luxury train, but its predominance is rivalled by many other archaeological sites and treks throughout Peru. Page 275.

❺ Manu and Tambopata Reserves

These protected areas in the steamy tropical forest of southern Peru are home to a huge diversity of wildlife. Rare birds and mammals, including jaguars, ocelots and giant otters, are fairly easy to spot due to a lack of hunting. Pages 331 and 334.

❻ Salar de Uyuni

Vast salt flats surrounded by stark volcanoes create some of South America's most iconic landscapes. Add to that flamingos sifting the waters of multi-coloured lakes, surreal deserts and high-altitude hot springs and you have one of Bolivia's most memorable attractions. Page 403.

❼ Jesuit missions

UNESCO has recognized six surviving Jesuit mission churches in Bolivia as World Heritage Sites. Not only the beautiful architecture and elaborate decoration survive, but also the baroque music that was written and played here. Page 469.

❽ Rurrenabaque

This is the starting point for tours upriver to community-based lodges in the jungles of the Parque Nacional Madidi, or downriver to gallery forests and wetlands of the pampas in Bolivia. Expect to see plenty of wildlife on boat trips and hikes. Page 480.

⑨ Quito

The capital's treasure trove of religious art and architecture is the heart of a vibrant city, offering many urban delights. It also provides access to outstanding areas nearby, such as Mindo and the cloudforests of Pichincha volcano, a nature lover's paradise. Page 494.

⑩ Otavalo

Best known for the largest craft market in South America, this Ecuadorean town is also home to a proud and prosperous indigenous people. They have made their name not only as successful weavers and traders, but also as symbols of cultural fortitude. Page 538.

⑪ Puerto López

A popular base for whale watching from June to September, this seaside town in Ecuador provides year-round access to the gorgeous Los Frailes beach and Parque Nacional Machalilla, which protects tropical forests, a marine ecosystem and Isla de la Plata. Page 633.

⑫ Galápagos Islands

Almost 1000 km from mainland Ecuador, the Galápagos Islands were the inspiration for Charles Darwin's theory of evolution and offer marine and terrestrial environments like nowhere else on Earth. A visit to this foremost wildlife sanctuary is an unforgettable experience. Page 672.

COLOMBIA

To Galápagos
Islands
←

⑩ Otavalo○
QUITO□ ⑨
ECUADOR
Baños○ ○Puyo
⑪ Puerto Riobamba
Lopéz○
Guayaquil○
Cuenca○

Tumbes○
Loja○
Vilcabamba○

Piura○

Jaén○
Chachapoyas○

Chiclayo○

Iquitos○

PERU

Trujillo○
Pucallpa○

Cordillera Blanca

①

Huaraz○

Pacific Ocean

La Oroya○

Huancayo○

LIMA□

Ayacucho○

Machu
Picchu ④
Abancay○   ○Cuzco

Manu
Biosphere
Reserve ◆

⑤   Puerto
Maldonado○

Tambopata
National
Reserve ◆

Pisco○
Ica○

Nazca○
Nazca Lines

②
Colca
Canyon

Juliaca
Puno○ ○ Lake
Titicaca

③

⑧
○Rurrenabaque

Trinidad○

Coroico○

Galápagos Islands

Charles Darwin
Teodoro Wolf

⑫ Pinta
Marchena
Genovesa

Santiago
Santa Cruz
Fernandina
San Cristóbal
Isabela
Floreana Española

Arequipa○

LA PAZ□

BOLIVIA

Cochabamba○

Oruro○

Lago
Poopó

Salar de
Uyuni

○Potosí

⑥ ○Uyuni

Tupiza○ Tarija○

CHILE

ARGENTINA

BRAZIL

Concepción

Santa Cruz

7

San Rafael

San José de Chiquitos

PARAGUAY

N

200 km
200 miles

Route
planner

The variety that Peru, Bolivia and Ecuador can offer the visitor is enormous. The obvious attractions in Peru are Machu Picchu, the Nazca Lines and the jungle reserves of Manu and Tambopata; while in Ecuador the colonial heritage of Quito and Cuenca, the Galápagos Islands and the Oriente jungle are the major draws. Bolivia's attractions include the Salar de Uyuni, Madidi National Park and the Jesuit missions of Chiquitania. But if you're on a tight schedule, how do you fit it all in? Seeing much of these countries by bus in the space of a few weeks is a forlorn hope. So you'll either need to concentrate on a small area or consider taking internal flights.

Two weeks

sacred Inca sites, colonial cities and the Galápagos Islands

The best option for a two-week visit is to limit yourself to one or two countries. As Peru is located in the middle, it is logical to combine it with a visit to either Bolivia or Ecuador. In Peru there are certain places that fit neatly into seven days of travelling. Southern Peru offers a short rewarding circuit covering the most popular sites in this region. You need at least four days, more if you plan to hike the Inca Trail, to see Cuzco and Machu Picchu, the crown jewels of the Inca Empire. Beautiful Titicaca, the highest navigable lake in the world, the elegant colonial city of Arequipa, nearby Colca Canyon, and the incredible Nazca Lines could all be combined with Cuzco for a 10-day tour.

You could then head from Lake Titicaca across the border to Copacabana and La Paz. Several interesting trips can be made from La Paz, including the ruins of the great pre-Inca city of Tiwanaku. From La Paz you can also mountain bike down the so-called 'world's most dangerous road' to the little town of Coroico, a popular resort in the subtropical valleys of the Yungas.

An alternative to Bolivia would be to fly from Lima to the beautiful colonial city of Quito, in Ecuador. One of Ecuador's great attractions is its relative compactness and

Right: Teleférico, La Paz
Opposite page: Arequipa, Peru

much of what you want to see is only a few hours by road from the capital. Just two hours north is Otavalo, home to one of the finest craft markets in all of Latin America, and a further few hours south are the spectacular Cotopaxi National Park, the lovely Quilotoa circuit and Baños, a popular spa town at the foot of an active volcano.

If you don't arrange a trip to the Amazon jungle from Cuzco (see below), it's easy to do so from Quito, to one of Ecuador's many excellent jungle lodges. You can also travel under your own steam to one of the main jungle towns and arrange a tour from there with a local agency. Tours can be organized from Puyo, Tena, Misahuallí, Coca, Macas and Baños, which is on the road from the highlands to the Oriente.

And then there are the unique Galápagos Islands, Ecuador's famed wildlife showcase. It's expensive to visit but well worth it. Galápagos tours range from four days up to 14 days, but seven days would be optimal, if you can afford it, to appreciate fully this once-in-a-lifetime experience.

One month
jungle wildlife reserves, Andean peaks and altiplano lakes

A month allows you the luxury of several further options for exploring more of Peru, Bolivia and Ecuador. With this amount of time you can visit Manu National Park or the Tambopata National Reserve in Peru's southeastern jungle, with wonderful opportunities for watchers of birds, butterflies and animals, and for plant lovers. Trips to the southeastern jungle can be booked in Cuzco, which is a jumping-off point for flights or the 11-hour overland journey.

Another option in Peru is to head for Huaraz, in the Cordillera Blanca, seven hours by paved road from Lima and one of the world's top climbing and trekking destinations.

Above: Cuenca, Ecuador
Right: Tambopata National Reserve, Peru
Opposite page: Laguna Colorada, Bolivia

There are several border crossings from northern Peru to the south of Ecuador. The easiest is from Piura to Loja, and an alternative adventurous route runs from Chachapoyas to Vilcabamba, on the fringes of Podocarpus National Park. Five hours north of Vilcabamba and Loja is Cuenca, a lovely colonial city and a great place to buy handicrafts. There are good road links north from Cuenca to Riobamba, with access to Chimborazo (Ecuador's highest summit) and the spectacular Devil's Nose train ride. Good roads from Riobamba continue north to Quito, and northeast to Baños and the Oriente jungle.

Alternatively, you could spend more time in Bolivia. If you're visiting during the dry season – April to October – take a trip north to Rurrenabaque, from where you can take a jungle or pampas tour and experience the amazing diversity of wildlife in Pilón Lajas Biosphere Reserve and Madidi National Park.

The altiplano landscape of southwest Bolivia is dramatically different but equally remarkable. Here is Oruro, home to world-famous Carnival celebrations. A train and bus service connects Oruro with Uyuni and Tupiza, starting points for tours of the Salar de Uyuni, a vast, blindingly white salt lake. South of the Salar is Reserva Eduardo Avaroa, with deserts, volcanoes, geysers and multi-coloured lakes, all higher than 4000 m above sea level.

The eastern lowlands of Santa Cruz form yet another markedly different region. Here the collection of Jesuit missions in Chiquitania is one of Bolivia's most fascinating colonial legacies.

Best
festivals

Q'Olloriti, Peru

The 'Snow Star' festival, a massive pilgrimage to a sanctuary at 4700 m, beneath the glaciers of Nevado Sinakara (south of Cuzco), takes place during the full moon before the June solstice. It is tough going, freezing cold and not for the faint-hearted. Nevertheless, tens of thousands of people trek up to the sacred ice to simultaneously honour an image of Christ and the *apus* (mountain gods) with music, dance and the sacrifice of their arduous journey. Page 262.

Semana Santa, Ayacucho, Peru

Many places in Peru make 'paintings' on the streets out of flower petals and coloured sawdust, to be trodden by the feet of participants in multitudinous religious parades. The most famous are the ones in Ayacucho, in the Peruvian Central Highlands, during the city's huge and impressive Semana Santa (Holy Week). The celebrations begin on the Friday before Palm Sunday and there are daily parades and nightly candlelit processions leading up to the solemn events of Good Friday. Page 304.

Alasitas, La Paz, Bolivia

This enchanting Feast of Plenty takes place every January in honour of Ekeko, the god of good fortune and abundance.

During Alasitas, everything under the sun can be bought in miniature: houses, trucks, tools, bolivianos, dollars, euros, computers and university diplomas – you name it. Have your purchase blessed by a *yatiri* (an Aymara priest) and the real thing will be yours within the year. Page 356.

Carnival in Oruro, Bolivia

Some 50 groups participate during the four days preceding Ash Wednesday, each with up to 700 dancers. Of the 18 different types of dances, the

Above: Carnival, Oruro
Left: Mama Negra, Latacunga
Opposite page: Ekeko at Alasitas, La Paz

most famous is La Diablada – dance of the devils – in which dancers wear grotesquely elaborate costumes and masks, some spewing fire. Participants dance as an act of devotion to the Virgen del Socavón, patroness of the miners. At the church, which marks the end of the gruelling 4-km parade, the most devout dancers approach the altar on their knees. Page 396.

Año Viejo, throughout Ecuador

On 31 December life-size puppets are built and displayed everywhere, depicting events of the year gone by. Children dressed in black are the old year's widows and beg for alms in the form of candy or coins. Just before midnight the Año Viejo's will is read and at the stroke of midnight the effigies are burned, wiping out the old year and all that it had brought with it. Page 514.

Mama Negra, Latacunga, Ecuador

Held on 23-25 September, and again around 11 November, this tumultuous parade features a man dressed as a black woman – the Mama Negra. He/she rides a horse, carries a doll and changes kerchiefs at every corner. Dancers pay homage to the Virgen de las Mercedes and commemorate the freedom achieved by black slaves who escaped the plantations and moved to this area during colonial times. Page 563.

The notorious North Yungas road to Coroico, Bolivia

When to go

Peru's high season in the highlands is from May to September, the best time for hiking and climbing. At this time the days are generally clear and sunny, though nights can be very cold at high altitude. During the wettest months in the highlands, November to April, some roads become impassable. April and May, at the tail end of the highland rainy season, is a beautiful time to see the Peruvian Andes. On the coast, high seasons are September and Christmas to February. The summer months from December to April are hot and dry, but from approximately May to October much of this area is covered with *la garúa*, a blanket of cloud and mist.

The best time to visit the jungle in **Peru** and **Bolivia** is during the dry season, from April to October. During the wet season, November to April, it is oppressively hot (40°C and above) and while it only rains for a few hours at a time, it is enough to make some roads impassable. These are also the months when mosquitoes and other biting insects are at their worst, so this is not a good time to visit the jungle. As for the rest of **Bolivia**, the altiplano does not receive much rain, so timing is not so crucial here, although hiking trails can get very muddy in the wet season. During the winter months of June and July, nights tend to be clearer but even colder than at other times. These are good months to visit the Salar de Uyuni, as the salt lake is very impressive under clear blue skies (but the mirror effect when it is flooded is also unforgettable).

Ecuador's climate is so varied and variable that any time of the year is good for a visit. Its high season is from June to early September, the best time for climbing and trekking. In the highlands, temperatures vary more with altitude than they do with the seasons. To the west of the Andes, June to September is dry and October to May is wet (but there is sometimes a short dry spell in December or January). To the east, October to February is dry and March to September is wet. The southern highlands are drier. In the Oriente, as in the rest of the Amazon Basin, heavy rain can fall at any time, but it is usually wettest from March to September. The Galápagos are hot from January to April, when heavy but brief showers are likely. May to December is the cooler misty season.

See the weather charts in individual cities for more detailed information on regional climates.

Festivals

Fiestas are a fundamental part of life for most South Americans, taking place throughout the continent with such frequency that it would be hard to miss one, even during the briefest of stays. This is fortunate, because arriving in any town or village during these inevitably frenetic celebrations is one of the great travelling experiences. Bolivia is especially well endowed with festivals year round, some lasting a week or more. See also Best festivals, page 10.

During the main festivals and public holidays most businesses such as banks and tour agencies close while supermarkets and street markets may be open. This depends a lot on where you are so enquire locally. Sometimes holidays that fall during midweek will be moved to the following Friday or Monday to make a long weekend, or some places will take a *día de puente* (bridging day) taking the Friday or Monday as a holiday before or after an official holiday on a Thursday or Tuesday. Cities may be very quiet on national holidays, but celebrations will be going on in the villages. Hotels are often full so it's worth booking in advance.

Invariably, fiestas involve drinking – lots of it. There's also non-stop dancing, which can sometimes verge on an organized brawl, and throwing of water (or worse). Not all festivals end up as massive unruly parties, however. Some are solemn and elaborate holy processions, often incorporating Spanish colonial themes into predominantly ancient pagan rituals. Below is a brief list of the most important festivals in each country. See also Festivals and public holidays, page 719.

Peru

Two of the major festival dates are **Carnaval**, which is celebrated in most of the Andes over the weekend before Ash Wednesday, and **Semana Santa** (Holy Week), which ends on Easter Sunday.

On **1 May Fiesta de la Cruz** is another important festival in much of the central and southern highlands and on the coast. In Cuzco, the entire month of **June** is one huge fiesta, culminating in **Inti Raymi**, on **24 June**, one of Peru's prime tourist attractions.

Bolivia

Carnaval, especially famous in Oruro, is celebrated throughout the country in **February** or **March**. There are parades with floats and folkloric dances, parties, much drinking and water throwing even in the coldest weather and nobody is

spared. Many related festivities take place around the time of Carnaval. Two weeks beforehand is **Jueves de Compadres** followed by **Jueves de Comadres**. In the altiplano Shrove Tuesday is celebrated as **Martes de Challa**, when house

ON THE ROAD
Day of the Dead (All Souls' Day)

Among the most important dates in the calendar in Latin America are 1 November, Todos Santos, and 2 November, the Día de los Difuntos or Finados (Day of the Dead).

Practices vary from place to place but the day is observed throughout Peru, Bolivia and Ecuador. In the Inca calendar, November was the eighth month and meant *ayamarca*, or land of the dead. The celebration is an example of the religious syncretism or adaptation in which pre-Hispanic practices blend with the rites of the Catholic Church.

According to ancient belief, the spirit visits its relatives at this time of the year and is fed in order to continue its journey in the afterlife. Relatives prepare for the arrival of the spirit days in advance. Bread dolls, called *guaguas de pan* in Ecuador and *t'anta wawas* in Bolivia, and bread figures of llamas or horses to provide transport for the dead are baked or bought. *Colada morada*, a sweet drink made from various fruits and purple corn is prepared in Ecuador.

Inside the home, families may construct an altar over which a black cloth is laid. This is adorned with the bread figures and the dead relative's favourite food and drink. Once the spirit has arrived and feasted with its living relatives, the entire ceremony is transported to the graveside in the local cemetery, where it is carried out again, along with many other mourning families.

Such elaborate celebrations are less common than in the past, and today most people commemorate Día de los Difuntos in more prosaic fashion; by visiting the cemetery and placing flowers at the graveside of their deceased relatives.

owners make offerings to Pachamama and give drinks to passers-by. **Carnaval Campesino** usually begins in small towns on Ash Wednesday, when regular Carnaval ends, and lasts for five days, until **Domingo de Tentación**. Palm Sunday (**Domingo de Ramos**) sees parades to the church throughout Bolivia; the devout carry woven palm fronds, then hang them outside their houses. **Semana Santa** in the eastern Chiquitania is very interesting, with ancient processions, dances, and games not found outside the region.

Ecuador

On **31 December** life-size puppets depicting the events of the previous year, the *años viejos*, are burnt after the reading of the old year's will. **Carnaval**, on Monday and Tuesday before Lent, is celebrated everywhere in the country (except Ambato) by throwing water at passers-by: be prepared to participate.

Improve your travel photography

Taking pictures is a highlight for many travellers, yet too often the results turn out to be disappointing. Steve Davey, author of Footprint's *Travel Photography*, sets out his top rules for coming home with pictures you can be proud of.

Before you go

Don't waste precious travelling time and do your research before you leave. Find out what festivals or events might be happening or which day the weekly market takes place, and search online image sites such as Flickr to see whether places are best shot at the beginning or end of the day, and what vantage points you should consider.

Get up early

The quality of the light will be better in the few hours after sunrise and again before sunset – especially in the tropics when the sun will be harsh and unforgiving in the middle of the day. Sometimes seeing the sunrise is a part of the whole travel experience: sleep in and you will miss more than just photographs.

Stop and think

Don't just click away without any thought. Pause for a few seconds before raising the camera and ask yourself what you are trying to show with your photograph. Think about what things you need to include in the frame to convey this meaning. Be prepared to move around your subject to get the best angle. Knowing the point of your picture is the first step to making sure that the person looking at the picture will know it too.

Compose your picture

Avoid simply dumping your subject in the centre of the frame every time you take a picture. If you compose with it to one side, then your picture can look more balanced. This will also allow you to show a significant background and make the picture more meaningful. A good rule of thumb is to place your subject or any significant detail a third of the way into the frame; facing into the frame not out of it.

This rule also works for landscapes. Compose with the horizon two-thirds of the way up the frame if the fore-ground is the most interesting part of the picture; one-third of the way up if the sky is more striking.

Don't get hung up with this so-called Rule of Thirds, though. Exaggerate it by pushing your subject out to the edge of the frame if it makes a more interesting picture; or if the sky is dull in a landscape, try cropping with the horizon near the very top of the frame.

Fill the frame

If you are going to focus on a detail or even a person's face in a close-up portrait, then be bold and make sure that you fill the frame. This is often a case of physically getting in close. You can use a telephoto setting on a zoom lens but this can lead to pictures looking quite flat; moving in close is a lot more fun!

Interact with people

If you want to shoot evocative portraits then it is vital to approach people and seek permission in some way, even if it is just by smiling at someone. Spend a little time with them and they are likely to relax and look less stiff and formal. Action portraits where people are doing something, or environmental portraits, where they are set against a significant background, are a good way to achieve relaxed portraits. Interacting is a good way to find out more about people and their lives, creating memories as well as photographs.

Focus carefully

Your camera can focus quicker than you, but it doesn't know which part of the picture you want to be in focus. If your camera is using the centre focus sensor then move the camera so it is over the subject and half press the button, then, holding it down, recompose the picture. This will lock the focus. Take the now correctly focused picture when you are ready.

Another technique for accurate focusing is to move the active sensor over your subject. Some cameras with touch-sensitive screens allow you to do this by simply clicking on the subject.

Leave light in the sky

Most good night photography is actually taken at dusk when there is some light and colour left in the sky; any lit portions of the picture will balance with the sky and any ambient lighting. There is only a very small window when this will happen, so get into position early, be prepared and keep shooting and reviewing the results. You can take pictures after this time, but avoid shots of tall towers in an inky black sky; crop in close on lit areas to fill the frame.

Bring it home safely

Digital images are inherently ephemeral: they can be deleted or corrupted in a heartbeat. The good news though is they can be copied just as easily. Wherever you travel, you should have a backup strategy. Cloud backups are popular, but make sure that you will have access to fast enough Wi-Fi. If you use RAW format, then you will need some sort of physical back-up. If you don't travel with a laptop or tablet, then you can buy a backup drive that will copy directly from memory cards.

Recently updated and available in both digital and print formats, Footprint's Travel Photography by Steve Davey covers everything you need to know about travelling with a camera, including simple post-processing. More information is available at www.footprinttravelguides.com

What to do

from birdwatching to whitewater rafting

Bird and wildlife watching

Peru Nearly 19% of all the bird species in the world and 45% of all neotropical birds are found in Peru. A birding trip is possible during any month as birds breed all year round. The peak in breeding activity occurs just before the rains come in October. The key sites, out of many, are the Manu Biosphere Reserve, Tambopata National Reserve, Abra Málaga, Iquitos, Paracas, Lomas de Lachay, the Colca Canyon, the Huascarán Biosphere Reserve and northern Peru, with its Tumbesian dry forest and Pacific slopes of the Andes. Before arranging your trip, see **www.perubirding routes.com** (in Spanish and English).

Bolivia The country has more than 40 well-defined ecological regions and the transition zones between them. On a trip to the Salar de Uyuni you will see Andean birdlife but also landscapes of unmatched, stark beauty. For lowland birds and animals, the main options are Rurrenabaque in the lowlands of the river Beni and the Parque Nacional Amboró, three hours west of Santa Cruz, containing ecosystems of the Amazon Basin, Andean foothills and the savannahs of the Chaco plain. For table-top mountains, forests, *cerrado*, wetlands and a stunning array of

wildlife, make the effort to get to Parque Nacional Noel Kempff Mercado.

Ecuador The Galápagos Islands are the top destination for reliably seeing wildlife close up, but a number of the species from the Galápagos may also be seen in the Parque Nacional Machalilla and on other parts of the coast. An added bonus on the mainland coast is the opportunity to watch whales from June to September. A huge number of bird species in a great variety of habitats and microclimates may easily be seen. There are five general regions: western lowlands and lower foothills; western Andes; inter-Andean forests and *páramos*; eastern Andes; and Oriente jungle. The **Jocotoco Foundation**, www.fjocotoco.org, specializes in buying up critical bird habitat in Ecuador.

Climbing

In **Peru**, the Cordillera Blanca, with Huaraz as a base, is an ice-climber's paradise. Over 50 summits are between 5000 and 6000 m and over 20 exceed 6000 m. There is a wide range of difficulty and no peak fees are charged (although national park entrance has to be paid in the Cordillera Blanca). The Cordillera Huayhuash, southeast of Huaraz, is a bit more remote, with fewer facilities, but has some of the most spectacular ice walls in Peru. In the south of the country, the Cordilleras Vilcabamba and Vilcanota are the main destinations, but Cuzco is not developed for climbing. Climbing equipment can be hired in Huaraz but the quality can be poor.

Some of the world's best mountaineering can be found in Bolivia. With a dozen peaks at or above 6000 m and almost a thousand over 5000 m, most levels of skill can find something to tempt them. The season is May to September, with usually stable conditions June to August. The Cordillera Real has 600 mountains over 5000 m, including six at 6000 m or above (Huayna Potosí is the most popular). Quimza Cruz, southeast of La Paz, is hard to get to but offers some excellent possibilities. The volcanic Cordillera Occidental contains Bolivia's highest peak, Sajama (6542 m). The Apolobamba range, northwest of La Paz, has many peaks over 5000 m.

Ecuador offers some exceptional high-altitude climbing, with 10 mountains over 5000 m, most with easy access. The four most frequently climbed are Cotopaxi, Chimborazo and Iliniza Norte. The other six – Iliniza Sur, Antisana, El Altar, Sangay, Carihuairazo and Cayambe – vary in degree of difficulty and/or danger. Sangay is technically easy, but extremely dangerous from the falling rocks being ejected from the volcano. Many other mountains can be climbed, and climbing clubs, guiding agencies and tour operators will give advice. There are two seasons: June to August for the western cordillera and December to February for the eastern cordillera. It is important to check on current volcanic activity and ice conditions.

Diving and snorkelling

The Galápagos Islands off the coast of Ecuador are well known for their distinctive marine environments and offer more than 20 dive sites. Each island contains a unique environment and many are home to underwater life forms found nowhere else. There are excellent specialized dive-tour boats and operators but you are not allowed to dive on an ordinary Galápagos cruise. Also note that conditions in the Galápagos are difficult and for experienced divers only. Snorkelling is highly recommended, however, and you will come face to face with all manner of marine creatures. A good option for novice divers is the Isla de la Plata in Machalilla National Park, on the coast of Ecuador.

Horse riding

In Ecuador horse riding is available in many popular resort areas including Otavalo, Baños and Vilcabamba. Throughout the country, haciendas also usually offer horse riding.

Mountain biking

This is a relatively new sport in Peru, but dedicated cyclists are beginning to open up routes which offer some magnificent possibilities. Peru has many kilometres of trails, dirt roads and single track, but very few maps to show you where to go. There is equipment for hire and tours in the Huaraz and Cuzco areas or join an organized group to get the best equipment and guiding.

In Bolivia, hard-core, experienced, fit and acclimatized riders can choose from a huge range of possibilities. Either take a gamble and figure it out from a map, or find a guide and tackle the real adventure rides. Some popular rides in the La Paz region, achievable by all levels of riders, are La Cumbre to Coroico, down the so-called world's most dangerous road; the Zongo Valley descent into the Yungas; Chacaltaya to La Paz, down from the (ex-) world's highest ski slope; and Hasta Sorata, to the trekking paradise of Sorata. If you plan on bringing your own bike and doing some hard riding, be prepared for difficult conditions, an almost complete absence of spare parts and very few good bike mechanics. There are now a number of operators offering guided mountain biking tours, but only a few rent good quality, safe machines. Choose a reputable company, guides who speak your language and only opt for the best US-made bikes.

Ecuador is growing in popularity as there are boundless opportunities in the Sierra, on coastal roads and in the upper Amazon Basin. Agencies which offer tours, rent equipment and help plan routes are in Quito (see page 517) and in other cities.

Parapenting/hang-gliding

Vuelo libre (parapenting) is popular. Flying from the coastal cliffs is easy and the thermals are good. In Peru, the best area is the Sacred Valley of Cuzco which has excellent launch sites, thermals and reasonable landing sites. Some flights in Peru have exceeded 6500 m. In Ecuador it can be done from several highland locations as well as Crucita on the coast. The season in the Sierra is May-October, with the best months being August-September.

Sandboarding and screeboarding

If you've always fancied tearing down a massive sand dune on a wooden board, then the southern coastal desert in Peru is the place for you. Just as much fun as snowboarding but without the cold or required technical expertise, sandboarding is a growing sport amongst warm-weather thrill-seekers. In Bolivia, screeboarding is offered in the recently deglaciated slopes of the Cordillera Real.

Surfing

Peru is a top international surfing destination. Its main draws are the variety of waves and the year-round action. The main seasons are September to February in the north and March to December in the south, though May is often ideal south of Lima. The biggest wave is at Pico Alto (sometimes 6 m in May), south of Lima, and the largest break is 800 m at Chicama, near Trujillo.

In Ecuador there are a few, select surfing spots, such as Mompiche, San Mateo, Montañita and Playas, near Guayaquil. Surf is best December to March, except at Playas where the season is June to September. In the Galápagos there is good surfing at Playa Punta Carola, outside Puerto Baquerizo Moreno on San Cristóbal.

Trekking

In Peru there are some fabulous circuits around the peaks of the Cordillera Blanca (eg Llanganuco to Santa Cruz, and the treks out of Caraz) and Cordillera Huayhuash. The Ausangate trek near Cuzco is also good. A second type of trek is walking among, or to, ruins. The prime example is the Inca Trail to Machu Picchu, but others include those to Vilcabamba (the Incas' last home) and Choquequirao, and the treks in the Chachapoyas region. The Colca and Cotahuasi canyons also offer superb trekking. Also see www.trekkingperu.org.

There are many opportunities for trekking in Bolivia, from gentle one-day hikes in foothills and valleys to challenging walks of several days from highlands to lowlands on Inca or gold-digger trails. The best known are: the Choro, Takesi and Yunga Cruz hikes, all of whose starting points can be reached from La Paz; the Illampu Circuit from Sorata; and the Apolobamba treks in the northwest. Various treks are outlined in the text, especially near La Paz and from Sorata.

In Ecuador, the varied landscape, diverse environments and friendly villages make travelling on foot a refreshing change from crowded buses. Hiking in the Sierra is mostly across high elevation *páramo*, through agricultural lands and past indigenous communities. There are outstanding views of glaciated peaks in the north and pre-Columbian ruins in the south. In the tropical rainforests of the Oriente, local guides are often required because of the difficulty in navigation and because you will be walking on land owned by local indigenous tribes. The Andean slopes are steep and often covered by virtually impenetrable cloud forests and it rains a lot. Many ancient trading routes head down the river valleys. Some of these trails are still used. Others may be overgrown and difficult to follow but offer the reward of intact ecosystems.

Volunteering

In Peru, the **Amauta Spanish School**, www.amautaspanish.com, offers volunteering opportunities. In Huanchaco, near Trujillo, **Otra Cosa Network**, www.otracosa.org, arranges a wide range of volunteer placements in the north of the country. Projects which aim to get children away from the street and into education include **Seeds of Hope**, Huaraz, www.seedsofhope.pe, and **Luz de Esperanza**, Huancayo, www.peruluzdeesperanza.com.

In Bolivia, see **www.manoamano bolivia.org**, based in Cochabamba. Volunteering opportunities are available in Sucre as well.

In Ecuador, 'voluntourism' attracts many visitors. Several language schools operate volunteering schemes in conjunction with Spanish classes. **Fundación Jatun Sacha**, www.jatun sacha.org, has many different sites at which volunteers can work, all in exceptional natural areas.

Whitewater rafting

Peru has some of the finest whitewater rivers in the world. Availability is almost year-round and all levels of difficulty can be enjoyed. Cuzco is probably the rafting capital and the Río Urubamba has some very popular trips. Further afield is the Río Apurímac, which has some of the best whitewater rafting, including a trip at the source of the Amazon. In the southeastern jungle, a trip on the Río Tambopata to the Tambopata Reserve involves four days of whitewater followed by two days of drifting through virgin forest, an excellent adventure which must be booked up in advance. Around Arequipa is some first-class, technical rafting in the Cotahuasi and Colca canyons and some less-demanding trips on the Río Majes. Other destinations are the Río Santa near Huaraz and the Río Cañete, south of Lima.

Ecuador is a whitewater paradise with dozens of accessible rivers, warm waters and tropical rainforest; regional rainy seasons differ so that throughout the year there is always a river to run. The majority of Ecuador's whitewater rivers share a number of characteristics. Plunging off the Andes, the upper sections are very steep creeks offering, if they're runnable at all, serious technical grade V, suitable for experts only. As the creeks join on the lower slopes they form rivers that are less steep, with more volume. Some of these rivers offer up to 100 km of continuous grade III-IV whitewater, before flattening out to rush towards the Pacific Ocean on one side of the ranges or deep into the Amazon Basin on the other. Of the rivers descending to the Pacific coast, the Blanco and its tributaries are the most frequently run. They are within easy reach of Quito, as is the Quijos on the eastern side of the Sierra. In the Oriente, the main rivers are the Aguarico and its tributary the Dué, the Napo, Pastaza and Upano.

Shopping tips

Artesanía (handicrafts) enjoy regional distinctiveness, especially in items such as textiles. Each region, or even village, has its own characteristic pattern or style of cloth, so the choice is enormous. Throughout the Andes, weaving has spiritual significance as well as a practical side. Reproductions of pre-Columbian designs can be found in pottery and jewellery and many people throughout the continent make delightful items in gold and silver. Musical instruments from Bolivia, Panama hats from Ecuador and all manner of ceramics are just some of the things you can bring home with you. Craft shops abound in Lima, Cuzco, La Paz, Quito and Cuenca, but many items are sold more economically where they are made, outside the big cities. Bargaining is expected when you are shopping for handicrafts and souvenirs, but remember that most items are made by hand, and people are trying to make a living, not playing a game. You want a fair price, not the lowest one.

Where to stay

from budget backpacker hostels to high-class haciendas

There is no uniform terminology for categories of accommodation in South America, but you should be aware of the generally accepted meanings for the following. *Hotel* is the generic term, much as it is in English. *Hospedaje* means accommodation, of any kind. *Pensión, alojamiento, casa de huéspedes* and *residencial* usually refer to more modest and economical establishments. A *posada* (inn) or *hostal* may be an elegant expensive place, while *hosterías* or haciendas usually offer upmarket rural lodgings.

The cheapest and nastiest hotels are found near bus and train stations and markets. In small towns, better accommodation can often be found around the main plaza. Be sure that taxi drivers take you to the hotel you want rather than the one that pays the highest commission. Always take a look at the room before checking in. Hotel owners will often attempt to rent out the worst rooms first; feel free to ask for a better room or bargain politely for a reduced rate if you are not happy. In cities, rooms away from the main street will be less noisy. Some hotels charge per room and not per person, so if you're travelling alone, it may be cheaper to share.

Air conditioning (a/c) is only really needed in the lowlands and jungle. If you want an air-conditioned room it will add about a third to the price. Upmarket hotels will usually have their own restaurant, while more modest places may only serve a simple breakfast. The electric showers in cheaper places should be treated with respect. Always wear rubber sandals to avoid an unwelcome morning shock.

Camping in all three countries is best suited to protected natural areas, to the grounds of hostels (for a fee), or next to private homes (with permission of the owner). It is not safe to camp on beaches, by towns and villages, or anywhere near cities. When in doubt, ask before you pitch your tent. Organized campsites and trailer parks are rare or non-existent.

Tip...
Take a torch or candles if travelling to more remote areas and jungle lodges where electricity may only be supplied during certain hours.

Peru

Accommodation is plentiful throughout the price ranges and finding a hotel room to suit your budget should not present any problems, especially in the main

Tip...
It's worth booking accommodation in advance during school holidays and local festivals, see pages 18 and 719.

tourist areas and larger towns and cities, except during the Christmas and Easter holidays, Carnival and at the end of July. Cuzco in June is also very busy.

All deluxe and first-class hotels charge 18% in state sales tax (IGV) and 10% service charges. Foreigners should not have to pay the sales tax on hotel rooms; check whether it has been included.

Student discounts are rare but for information on youth hostels see **Hostelling International Perú** ⓘ *www.hostellingperu.com.pe*.

Bolivia

In Bolivia, a *pensión* is a simple restaurant and may double as a place to sleep in smaller towns. Youth hostels or self-styled 'backpackers' are not necessarily cheaper than hotels. A number of mid-range *residenciales* are affiliated to **Hostelling International (HI)** ⓘ *www.hostellingbolivia.org*; some others just say they are. Another website listing hostels is www.boliviahostels.com, but they are not necessarily affiliated to HI.

Ecuador

Outside the provincial capitals and resorts, there are few higher-class hotels, although a number of very upmarket haciendas have opened their doors to paying guests. Some are in the **Exclusive Hotels & Haciendas of Ecuador group** ⓘ *www.ehhec.com*, but there are many other independent haciendas of good quality. Some are mentioned in the text.

Service of 10% and tax of 14% are added to bills at more upmarket hotels. Some cheaper hotels apply the 14% tax only, but check if it is included.

Price codes

Where to stay		Restaurants	
$$$$	over US$150	$$$	over US$12
$$$	US$66-150	$$	US$7-12
$$	US$30-65	$	US$6 and under
$	under US$30		

Price of a double room in high season, including taxes unless otherwise indicated.

Prices for a two-course meal for one person, excluding drinks or service charge.

Food
& drink
marinated ceviche, roast cuy and corn humitas

Peru

Peru is the self-styled gastronomic capital of South America and some of the cuisine is very innovative. Along the coast the best dishes are seafood based with the most popular being ceviche: raw white fish marinated in lemon juice. The staples of corn and potatoes are prevalent in highland cooking and can be found in a large and varied range of dishes. There is also an array of meat dishes with *lomo saltado* (stir-fried beef). Tropical cuisine revolves around fish and the common yucca and fried bananas.

Lunch is considered the main meal throughout Peru and most restaurants will serve one or two set lunches called the *menú ejecutivo* (US$2.50-4 for a three-course meal) or *menú económico* (US$2-3). A la carte meals normally cost US$5-8 but in top-class restaurants it can be up to US$80. Middle- and high-class restaurants may add 10% service, but not include the 18% sales tax in the bill (which foreigners do have to pay); this is not shown on the price list or menu, check in advance. Lower-class restaurants charge only tax, while cheap, local restaurants charge no taxes.

There are many *chifas* (Chinese restaurants) all over the country which offer good reasonably priced food.

Lager-type beers are the best, especially the **Cusqueña** and **Arequipeña** brands (lager) and **Trujillo Malta** (porter). In Lima only **Cristal** and **Pilsener** (not related to true **Pilsen**) are readily available, others have to be sought out. Look out for the sweetish *maltina* brown ale, which makes a change from the ubiquitous pilsner-type beers. The best wines are from Ica, Tacama and Ocucaje. Gran Tinto Reserva Especial and Viña Santo Tomas are reasonable and cheap. The most famous local drink is pisco which is a strong, clear brandy and forms the basis of the deliciously renowned *pisco sour*.

Bolivia

Bolivian cooking is usually tasty and *picante* (spicy). Recommended dishes include *sajta de pollo*, hot spicy chicken. Near Lake Titicaca fish becomes an important part of the local diet and trout, though not native, is usually delicious. Bolivian soups are usually hearty and warming. *Salteñas* are very popular meat pasties eaten as a mid-morning snack, the challenge is to avoid spilling the gravy all over yourself.

Bolivia's temperate and tropical fruits are excellent and abundant. Don't miss the luscious grapes and peaches in season (February-April). Brazil nuts, called *almendras* or *castañas*, are produced in the northern jungle department of Pando and sold throughout the country.

Most restaurants do not open early but many hotels include breakfast. Breakfast and lunch can also be found in markets, but eat only what is cooked in front of you. In *pensiones* and cheaper restaurants a basic lunch (*almuerzo*, usually finished by 1300) and dinner (*cena*) are normally available. The *comida del día* is the best value in any class of restaurant. Dishes cooked in the street are not safe.

There are several makes of local lager-type beer; **Paceña** and **Auténtica** are the best-selling brands. There are also microbrews in La Paz. Singani, the national spirit, is distilled from grapes, and is cheap and strong. *Chuflay* is singani and a fizzy mixer, usually 7-Up. *Chicha* is a fermented maize drink, popular in the highlands. Good wines are produced by several vineyards near Tarija (tours are available, see page 434). The hot maize drink, *api* (with cloves, cinnamon, lemon and sugar), is good on cold mornings. Bottled water (many brands with and without gas) is readily available but make sure the seal is unbroken. Tap, stream and well water should never be drunk without first being purified.

Ecuador

Ecuadorean cuisine varies extensively with region. The large cities have a wide selection of restaurants. Seafood plays an important role on the coast, particularly in the very popular ceviche (marinated raw fish, distinct from the Peruvian variety). Most Ecuadorean food is not spicy but every table has a small bowl of *ají* (hot pepper sauce).

Upmarket restaurants add 24% to the bill: 14% tax plus 10% service. All other places add the 14% tax, which is also charged on non-essential items in food shops. Tipping is not expected in the many cheaper places serving *almuerzos* and *meriendas* (set lunch and dinner).

The main beers available are **Pilsener** and **Club**. Argentine, Chilean and other imported wines can be found in major cities. The most popular local spirit is unmatured rum, called *aguardiente* (literally 'fire water'), also known as *puntas*, *trago de caña*, or just *trago*. There are many excellent fruit juices, including *naranjilla* and *tomate de arbol* (both tomato relatives), *maracuyá* (passion fruit), *guanábana* (soursop) and *mora* (blackberry), but ask whether juices are prepared with purified water. You can find good cappuccino and espresso in tourist centres and many upscale hotels and restaurants.

Menu reader

Peru

causa rellena entrée cold mashed potatoes with lemon juice, tuna or chicken salad and mayonnaise
ceviche raw white fish marinated in lemon juice, onion and hot pepper
cuy guinea pig
escabeche fried fish or chicken seasoned with pickled onions and hot peppers, served warm or cold
lomo saltado strips of beef stir fried with potatoes, onions, tomatoes and hot peppers
mazamorra morada a purple corn-flour pudding served as a snack or light dessert
palta rellena avocado filled with tuna or chicken salad
papa a la huancaína a starter: slices of cold boiled potato in a spicy creamy cheese sauce
rocoto relleno hot peppers stuffed with ground meat

Bolivia

ají de lengua ox-tongue with hot peppers, potatoes and *chuño* or *tunta*
chairo soup made with meat, vegetables and *chuño*

chuño dehydrated potatoes
fricase juicy pork
parrillada mixed grill
pique macho roast meat, sausage, chips, onion and pepper
sajta de pollo hot spicy chicken with onion, fresh potatoes and *chuño*
salteñas meat pasties
silpancho very thin fried breaded meat
tunta dehydrated potato

Ecuador

cuy guinea pig
encocadas dishes prepared in coconut milk
fritada fried pork
hornado roast pork
humitas tender ground corn steamed in corn leaves
llapingachos fried potato and cheese patties
locro de papas potato and cheese soup
patacones thick fried plantain chips
sopa de bola de verde plantain dumpling soup

This is Peru

Cuzco, capital of the Inca world, is now one of South America's premier tourist destinations, with its access to Machu Picchu and the Inca Trail, the Sacred Vilcanota Valley and a buzzing nightlife. On the border with Bolivia is Lake Titicaca, blessed with magical light and fascinating islands. But in Peru, the Egypt of the Americas, this is just the tip of the pyramid.

The coastal desert may seem uninhabitable, yet pre-Inca cultures thrived there. They left their monuments in sculptures etched into the surface of the desert, most famously at Nazca. Civilization builders welcomed gods from the sea and irrigated the soil to feed great cities of adobe bricks. After the Incas came the Spanish *conquistadores*, who left some of their own finest monuments. You can trek forever amid high peaks and blue lakes, cycle down remote mountainsides, look into bottomless canyons – deeper than any others on earth, or surf the Pacific rollers. There are enough festivals to brighten almost every day of the year, while the spiritual explorer can be led down mystical paths by a shaman.

East of the Andes the jungles stretch towards the heart of the continent with some of the richest biodiversity on earth. And, should you tire of nature, there is always Lima: loud, brash, covered in fog for half the year, but with some of the best museums, most innovative restaurants and liveliest nightlife in the country.

COLOMBIA

ECUADOR

Tumbes
Máncora
La Tina
Talara
San Ignacio
Piura
Sechura Desert
Jaén
Bayóvar

Pantoja
Puerto Arturo
Nuevo Andoas
Andoas
Leoncia Prado
Iquitos
Amazonas
Santa Rosa
Leticia
Tabatinga
Nauta
Sarameriza
Lagunas
Bretaña
Moyobamba
Sta Cruz
Yurimaguas
Chachapoyas
Tingo
Leymebamba
Celendín
Juanjuí
Tarapoto
Pampas de Sacramento
BRAZIL
Mórrope
Chiclayo
Pacasmayo
Puerto Chicama
Cajamarca
Cajabamba
Pucallpa
Abujao
Huanchaco
Huamachuco
Uchiza
Trujillo
Chimbote
Caraz
Yungay
Ganzo Azúl
Casma
Huaraz
Chavin de Huantar
Tingo María
Esperanza
Huarmey
Huánuco
Puerto Bermúdez
Patívilca
Barranca
Cerro de Pasco
Atalaya
Iñapari
Chancay
La Oroya
Junín
Tarma
Pto Prado
Iberia
Ancón
Manu Biosphere Reserve
Boca Manu
Puerto Maldonado
LIMA
Huancayo
Shintuya
Mazuko
Huancavelica
Ayacucho
Echarate
Machu Picchu
Pilcopata
Pacific Ocean
Cañete
Chincha Alta
Pisco
Ollantaytambo
Cuzco
Ayapata
Paracas
Ica
Andahuaylas
Tambobamba
Raqchi
Sta Rosa
Huacachina
Challa
Yauri
Ayaviri
Juliaca
Nazca
Nazca Lines
Cotahuasi
Chivay
Colca Canyon
Lake Titicaca
Puno
BOLIVIA
Ocoña
Arequipa
Desaguadero
Camaná
Mollendo
Moquegua
Ilo
Tacna
CHILE

Footprint picks

N

100 km
100 miles

Lima

Footprint picks

★ **Lima**, page 36
Historic buildings and the best food and nightlife in the country.

★ **Cordillera Blanca**, page 72
A region of jewelled lakes and dazzling mountain peaks.

★ **Huaca de la Luna**, page 104
The remains of the once-mighty Moche Empire.

★ **Chachapoyas**, page 146
Mysterious cities and cliff-side burial sites.

★ **Nazca Lines**, page 172
Vast, enigmatic drawings etched into miles of barren southern desert.

★ **Colca and Cotahuasi canyons**, pages 194 and 201
See the majestic Andean condor, rising on the morning thermals.

★ **Cuzco and the Sacred Valley**, pages 230 and 264
Colonial churches, pre-Columbian ruins and unforgettable Machu Picchu.

★ **Southern jungle**, page 331
Marvel at the diversity of habitats and wildlife.

Lima

★ Lima's colonial centre and suburbs, shrouded in fog which lasts eight months of the year, are fringed by the *pueblos jóvenes* which sprawl over the dusty hills overlooking the city. It has a great many historic buildings and some of the finest museums in the country and its food, drink and nightlife are second to none. Although not the most relaxing of South America's capitals, it is a good place to start before exploring the rest of the country.

Central Lima *Colour map 2, C2.*

the traditional heart of the city retains its colonial core

An increasing number of buildings in the centre are being restored and the whole area is being given a new lease of life as the architectural beauty and importance of the Cercado (as it is known) is recognized. Most of the tourist attractions are in this area. Some museums are only open 0900-1300 from January to March, and some are closed entirely in January.

☆Plaza de Armas (Plaza Mayor) and around

One block south of the Río Rímac lies the Plaza de Armas, or Plaza Mayor, which has been declared a World Heritage Site by UNESCO. Running along two sides are arcades with shops: Portal de Escribanos and Portal de Botoneros. In the centre of the plaza is a bronze fountain dating from 1650.

The **Palacio de Gobierno** ① *Mon-Fri 0830-1300, 1400-1730*, on the north side of the Plaza, stands on the site of the original palace built by Pizarro. The changing of the guard is at 1145-1200. The palace can be visited on a free 45-minute tour (Spanish and English); register two days in advance at the palace's tourist office (ask guard for directions).

The **Cathedral** ① *T01-427 9647, Mon-Fri 0900-1700, Sat 1000-1300; entry to cathedral US$3.65, ticket also including Museo Arzobispado US$11,* was reduced to rubble in the earthquake of 1746. The reconstruction, on the lines of the original, was completed 1755. Note the splendidly carved stalls (mid-17th century), the silver-covered altars surrounded by fine woodwork, mosaic-covered walls bearing the coats of arms of Lima and Pizarro and an allegory of Pizarro's commanders, the 'Thirteen Men of Isla del Gallo'. The remains of Francisco Pizarro, found in the crypt, lie in a small chapel, the first on the right of the entrance. The cathedral's **Museo de Arte Religioso** has sacred paintings, portraits, altar pieces and other items, as well as a café and toilets. Next to the cathedral is the **Archbishop's**

Finding your feet

All international flights land at Jorge Chávez airport in Callao, 16 km northwest of the centre; take a taxi into town. If arriving in the city by bus, most of the recommended companies have their terminals just south of the historic centre, many on Avenida Carlos Zavala. This is not a safe area so you should take a taxi to and from there. Downtown Lima is the historic centre of the city and retains many colonial buildings. Miraflores is 15 km south. It has a good mix of places to stay, parks, great ocean views, bookstores, restaurants and cinemas. From here you can commute to the centre by bus (45 minutes minimum) or taxi (30 minutes minimum). Neighbouring San Isidro is the poshest district, while Barranco, a little further out, is a centre for nightlife. Callao, Peru's major port, merges with Lima but is a city in its own right, with over one million inhabitants.

Getting around

Downtown Lima can be explored on foot by day; at night a radio taxi is safest. Buses, combis and *colectivos* provide an extensive public transport system but are not entirely safe. Termini are posted above the windscreens, with the route written on the side. There is also the Metropolitano rapid transit bus system and a limited metro service, neither of which is particularly useful for visitors. In most cases, taxis are the best way to travel between different districts. Bear in mind that Lima's roads are horribly congested at all times of day, so allow plenty of time to get from A to B and be patient. See also Transport, page 68.

Tip...

Several blocks, with their own names, make up a long street, a *jirón* (often abbreviated to Jr). Street corner signs bear both names, of the *jirón* and of the block. In the historic centre blocks also have their colonial names.

When to go

Only 12° south of the equator, one would expect a tropical climate, but Lima has two distinct seasons. The winter is May-November, when a *garúa* (mist) hangs over the city, making everything look grey. It is damp and cold. The sun breaks through around November and temperatures rise. Note that the temperature in the coastal suburbs is lower than the centre due to the sea's influence. Protect against the sun's rays when visiting the beaches.

Time required

A few days are enough to see the highlights; a full week will allow more in-depth exploration.

Weather Lima

January	February	March	April	May	June
26°C 20°C 2mm	26°C 20°C 1mm	26°C 20°C 0.5mm	24°C 17°C 0mm	22°C 15°C 0mm	20°C 15°C 4mm

July	August	September	October	November	December
19°C 15°C 3mm	18°C 13°C 9mm	19°C 13°C 1mm	20°C 14°C 1mm	22°C 16°C 0.5mm	24°C 18°C 0mm

Palace and museum ⓘ *T01-427 5790, Mon-Sat 0900-1700*, rebuilt in 1924, with a superb wooden balcony. Permanent and temporary exhibitions are open to the public.

Just behind the Municipalidad de Lima is **Pasaje Ribera el Viejo**, which has been restored and is now a pleasant place, with several good cafés with outdoor seating. Nearby is the **Casa Solariega de Aliaga** ⓘ *Unión 224, T01-427 7736, Mon-Fri 0930-1300, 1430-1745, US$11, knock on the door and wait to see if anyone will let you in, or contact in advance for tour operators who offer guided visits.* It is still occupied by the Aliaga family and is open to the public and for functions. The house contains what is said to be the oldest ceiling in Lima and is furnished entirely in the colonial style. The **Casa de la Gastronomía Nacional Peruana** ⓘ *Conde de Superunda 170, T01-426 7264, www. limacultura.pe, US$1, behind the Correo Central,* has an extensive permanent collection of objects and displays on Peruvian food, historic and regional. It also has temporary exhibitions on the same theme. All signs are in Spanish.

East of Plaza de Armas
The first two blocks of Calle Ancash, from Calle Carabaya (on the east side of the Palacio de Gobierno) to San Francisco church, have been designated the 'tourist circuit of the Calles

1 Lima

Pacific Ocean

➡ **Lima maps**
1 Lima, page 38
2 Lima centre, page 40
3 Miraflores, page 46

Where to stay		Restaurants
1 Albergue Juvenil Malka	4 Country Club & Libertador	8 Pay Purix	Restaurants
2 Chez Elizabeth	5 Garden	9 Sonesta El Olivar	1 Al Toke Pez
3 Costa del Sol Wyndham	6 Hostal Res Víctor		2 Antica Pizzería
	7 Mami Panchita		3 Antigua Taberna Queirola

El Rastro y Pescadería'. (These are the colonial names of these two blocks.) The circuit starts from **Desamparados railway station** (which now houses fascinating exhibitions on Peruvian themes) and includes the open-air **Museo de Sitio Bodega y Quadra** ① *Ancash 213, Tue-Sun 0900-1700, free* (which displays the foundations of an old building), the **Casa de la Literatura** ① *Ancash 207, www.casadelaliteratura.gob.pe, Tue-Sun 1000-1900, free* (with an exhibit about Peruvian identity and holds cultural events) and several historic houses. The area is fully pedestrianized.

At the end of the circuit is the baroque church of ☆**San Francisco** ① *1st block of Jr Lampa, corner of Ancash, T01-426 7377 ext 111, www.museocatacumbas.com, daily 0930-1645, guided tours only, US$2.75, students half price, US$0.40 children,* which was finished in 1674 and withstood the 1746 earthquake. The nave and aisles are lavishly decorated in Mudéjar style. The monastery is famous for the Sevillian tilework and panelled ceiling in the cloisters (1620). The catacombs under the church and part of the monastery are well worth seeing. The late 16th-century **Casa de Jarava** or **Pilatos** ① *Jr Ancash 390,* is opposite. Close by, **Casa de las Trece Monedas** ① *Jr Ancash 536,* still has the original doors and window grills. **Parque de la Muralla** ① *daily 0900-2000,* on the south bank of the Rímac, incorporates a section of the old city wall, fountains, stalls and street performers. There is a cycle track, toilets and places to eat both inside and near the entrance on Calle de la Soledad.

The **Palacio Torre Tagle** (1735) ① *Jr Ucayali 363, Mon-Fri during working hours,* is the city's best surviving example of secular colonial architecture. Today, it is used by the Foreign Ministry, but visitors are allowed to enter courtyards to inspect the fine Moorish-influenced wood-carving in balconies and wrought ironwork. At Ucayali 391 and also part of the Foreign Ministry is the Centro Cultural Inca Garcilaso, which holds cultural events. **Casa de la Rada**, or **Goyeneche** ① *Jr Ucayali 358,* opposite, is a fine mid 18th-century French-style town house which now belongs to a bank. The patio and first reception room are open occasionally to the public. **Museo Banco Central de Reserva** ① *Jr Ucayali at Jr Lampa, T01-613 2000 ext 2655, Tue-Fri 1000-1630, Wed 1000-1900, Sat-Sun 1000-1300, free, photography prohibited,* houses a large collection of pottery from the Vicus or Piura culture (AD 500-600) and gold objects from Lambayeque, as well as 19th- and 20th-century paintings: both sections are highly recommended. **San Pedro** ① *3rd block of Jirón Ucayali, Mon-Sat 0930-1145, 1700-1800,* finished by Jesuits in 1638, has marvellous altars with Moorish-style

SAN JUAN DE LURIGANCHO

Cerro San ▲ Cristóbal

Av Independencia

SANTA ANITA

Cerro El Agustino ▲

Av N Áyllón

Av Nicolás Arriola

Av Merino

ATE

To Puruchuco

Vía de Evitamiento

SAN BORJA

Museo de la Nación & Gran Teatro Nacional

Av Javier Prado Este

LA MOLINA

Hipódromo de Monterrico

MONTERRICO

Av Aviación

mos Av Primavera

Panamericana Sur

Av Alianza de Molina

Museo de Oro del Perú

El Tren Eléctrico ▬▬▬

Metropolitano bus line ▬▬▬

Terminal Lima Sur 🚉 Av Los Héroes
Atocongo

To Chorrillos

4 Chifa Titi
5 Como Agua Para Chocolate
6 Havanna
7 Pan de la Chola
8 San Antonio
9 Segundo Muelle

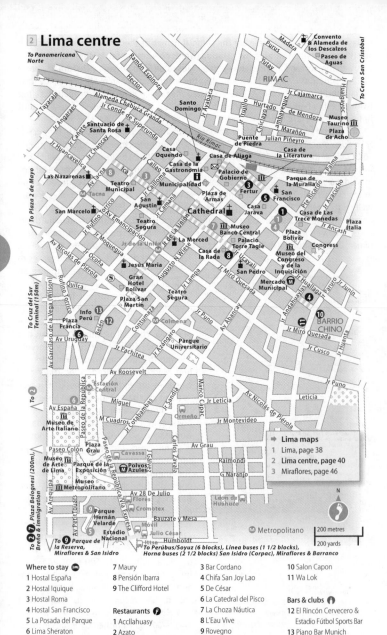

② Lima centre

Lima maps
→ 1 Lima, page 38
2 Lima centre, page 40
3 Miraflores, page 46

Where to stay
1 Hostal España
2 Hostal Iquique
3 Hostal Roma
4 Hostal San Francisco
5 La Posada del Parque
6 Lima Sheraton
7 Maury
8 Pensión Ibarra
9 The Clifford Hotel

Restaurants
1 Accllahuasy
2 Azato
3 Bar Cordano
4 Chifa San Joy Lao
5 De César
6 La Catedral del Pisco
7 La Choza Náutica
8 L'Eau Vive
9 Rovegno
10 Salon Capon
11 Wa Lok

Bars & clubs
12 El Rincón Cervecero &
Estadio Fútbol Sports Bar
13 Piano Bar Munich

balconies, rich gilded wood carvings in choir and vestry, and tiled throughout. Several Viceroys are buried here; the bell called La Abuelita, first rung in 1590, sounded the Declaration of Independence in 1821.

Between Avenida Abancay and Jr Ayacucho is **Plaza Bolívar**, where General José de San Martín proclaimed Peru's independence. The plaza is dominated by the equestrian statue of the Liberator. Behind lies the Congress building which occupies the former site of the Universidad de San Marcos and is now the **Museo del Congreso y de la Inquisición** ① *Plaza Bolívar, C Junín 548, near the corner of Av Abancay, T01-311 7777, ext 5160, www. congreso.gob.pe/museo.htm, daily 0900-1700, free.* The main hall, with a splendidly carved mahogany ceiling, remains untouched. The Court of Inquisition was held here from 1584; between 1829 and 1938 it was used by the Senate. In the basement there is a recreation *in situ* of the gruesome tortures. A description in English is available at the desk and students will offer to show round for a tip.

Behind the Congress is the Mercado Municipal (or Central) and the Barrio Chino, with many chifas and small shops selling oriental items. Block 700 of Ucayali is pedestrianized in `Chinese' style. The whole area is jam-packed with people.

West of Plaza de Armas

The 16th-century **Santo Domingo church and monastery** ① *T01-427 6793, monastery and tombs Mon-Sat 0900-1230, 1500-1800; Sun and holidays morning only, US$1.65,* is on the first block of Jr Camaná. The attractive first cloister dates from 1603. Beneath the sacristy are the tombs of San Martín de Porres, one of Peru's most revered saints, and Santa Rosa de Lima (see below). In 1669, Pope Clement presented the alabaster statue of Santa Rosa in front of the altar. Behind Santo Domingo is **Alameda Chabuca Granda**, named after one of Peru's greatest singers. In the evening there are free art and music shows and you can sample foods from all over Peru. A couple of blocks beyond Santo Domingo is **Casa de Osambela** or **Oquendo** ① *Conde de Superunda 298, T01-427 7987 (ask the caretaker if you can visit).* It is said that José de San Martín stayed here after proclaiming independence from Spain. The house is typical of Lima secular architecture with two patios, a broad staircase leading from the lower to the upper floor, fine balconies and an observation tower. It is now the Centro Cultural Inca Garcilaso de la Vega and headquarters of various academies. A few blocks west is **Santuario de Santa Rosa** ① *Av Tacna, 1st block, T01-425 1279, daily 0930-1300, 1500-1800, free to the grounds,* a small but graceful church and a pilgrimage centre, consisting of the hermitage built by Santa Rosa herself, the house in which she was born, a section of the house in which she attended to the sick, her well and other relics.

Due west of the Plaza de Armas is **San Agustín** ① *Jr Ica 251, T01-427 7548, daily 0830-1130, 1630-1900, ring for entry,* whose façade (1720) is a splendid example of churrigueresque architecture. There are carved choir stalls and effigies, and a sculpture of Death, said to have frightened its maker into an early grave. The church has been restored since the last earthquake, but the sculpture of Death is in storage. Further west, **Las Nazarenas church** ① *Av Tacna, 4th block, T01-423 5718, daily 0700-1200, 1600-2000,* is built around an image of Christ Crucified painted by a liberated slave in 1655. This is the most venerated image in Lima and is carried through the streets on a silver litter, along with an oil copy of El Señor de los Milagros (Lord of Miracles) encased in a gold frame (the whole weighing nearly a ton), on 18, 19 and 28 October and again on 1 November (All Saints' Day). *El Comercio* newspaper and local pamphlets give details of times and routes.

BACKGROUND
Lima

Lima, capital of Peru, is built on both sides of the Río Rímac, at the foot of Cerro San Cristóbal. It was originally named La Ciudad de Los Reyes, in honour of the Magi, at its founding by conquistador Francisco Pizarro in 1535. From then until the independence of the South American republics in the early 19th century, it was the chief city of Spanish South America. The name Lima, a corruption of the Quechua name Rimac (speaker), was not adopted until the end of the 16th century.

The Universidad de San Marcos was founded in 1551 and a printing press in 1595, both among the earliest of their kind in South America. Lima's first theatre opened in 1563, and the Inquisition was introduced in 1569 (it was not abolished until 1820). For some time the Viceroyalty of Peru embraced Colombia, Ecuador, Bolivia, Chile and Argentina. There were few cities in the Old World that could rival Lima's power, wealth and luxury, which was at its height during the 17th and early 18th centuries. The city's wealth attracted many freebooters and in 1670 a protecting wall 11 km long was built round it, then destroyed in 1869. The earthquake of 1746 destroyed all but 20 houses, killed 4000 inhabitants and ended the city's pre-eminence. It was only comparatively recently, with the coming of industry, that Lima began to change into what it is today.

Over the years the city has changed out of all recognition. The metropolitan area contains 8.6 million people, which equates to half the urban population of Peru and nearly one-third of the country's total population. Two-thirds of Peru's industries are located in the capital. Many of the hotels and larger businesses have relocated to the fashionable suburbs of Miraflores and San Isidro, thus moving the commercial heart of the city away from the Plaza de Armas. Modern Lima is seriously affected by chaotic traffic and smog for much of the year and is surrounded by poor grimy neighbourhoods. Many of these former squatters' camps of shacks in the desert have evolved into bustling working-class districts, home to millions of inhabitants and much of the city's commercial activity. They are generally not safe to visit on your own, but going accompanied by a local friend or guide can provide an eye-opening insight into the reality of life in Lima.

South of Plaza de Armas

The Jr de La Unión, the main shopping street, runs southwest from the Plaza de Armas. It has been converted into a pedestrian precinct which teems with life in the evening. In the two blocks south of Jr Unión, known as Calle Belén, several shops sell souvenirs and curios. **La Merced** ① *Unión y Miró Quesada, T01-427 8199, Mon-Sat 0800-1245, 1600-2000, Sun 0700-1300, 1600-2000; monastery daily 0800-1200 and 1500-1730*, is in Plazuela de la Merced. The first Mass in Lima was said here on the site of the first church to be built. The restored façade is a fine example of colonial Baroque. Inside are some magnificent altars and the tilework on some of the walls is noteworthy. A door from the right of the nave leads into the Monastery. The cloister dates from 1546.

Jr de la Unión leads to **Plaza San Martín**, which has a statue of San Martín in the centre. The plaza has been restored with colourful flower beds and is now a nice place to sit and relax. On its west side is the refurbished **Gran Hotel Bolívar** ① *Jr de la Unión 958, T01-619 7171, www.granhotelbolivar.com.pe*, which has a huge stained-glass dome over the entrance lobby. Its **El Bolivarcito** bar calls itself 'La Catedral del Pisco Sour'.

Further south, the **Museo de Arte Italiano** ① *Paseo de la República 250, T01-423 9932, Tue-Fri 0900-1900, Sat-Sun 1100-1700, US$1*, is in a wonderful neoclassical building, given to Peru on the centenary of its independence. Note the remarkable mosaic murals on the outside. It consists of a large collection of Italian and other European works of art and houses the **Instituto de Arte Contemporáneo**, which has many exhibitions.

Across Avenida 9 de Diciembre from here is the **Parque de la Exposición**, inaugurated for the Lima International Exhibition in 1872. **The Palacio de la Exposición**, built in 1868, now houses the **Museo de Arte de Lima** ① *Paseo Colón 125, T01-204 0000, www.mali.pe, Tue-Sun 1000-2000, Sat 1000-1700, US$2 minimum, US$4 suggested, children, students and over-65s US$1.35, guides US$1, bilingual guides available 1030-1600, signs in English*. There are more than 7000 exhibits, giving a chronological history of Peruvian cultures and art from the Paracas civilization up to today. It includes excellent examples of 17th- and 18th-century Cuzco paintings, a beautiful display of carved furniture, heavy silver and jewelled stirrups and also pre-Columbian pottery. The Filmoteca (movie club) is on the premises and shows films just about every night; see the local paper for details, or look in the museum itself.

The grounds now incorporate the **Gran Parque Cultural de Lima**. This large park has an amphitheatre, Japanese garden, food court and children's activities. Relaxing strolls through this green, peaceful and safe oasis in the centre of Lima are recommended. In the south of the park is the **Museo Metropolitano** ① *Av 28 de Julio, T01-433 7122, www.limacultura.pe, Tue-Sat 1000-2000, Sun from 1100, US$1.35, which* has audiovisual displays and temporary exhibitions about the history of Lima; it also hosts lectures and has a library.

In **Parque de la Reserva** ① *block 6 of Av Arequipa and Jr Madre de Dios opposite Estadio Nacional, Santa Beatriz, www.parquedelareserva.com.pe, Mon, Tue 0600-1300, Wed-Sun and holidays 0600-1300, 1500-2230*, is the **Circuito Mágico del Agua** ① *displays at 1915, 2015, 2130, US$1.50*, a display of 13 fountains, the highest reaching 80 m, enhanced by impressive light and music shows three times a night. It's great fun and very popular.

Inner suburbs

visit the major museums for an overview of Peru's history and culture

Rímac and Cerro San Cristóbal

The **Puente de Piedra**, behind the Palacio de Gobierno, is a Roman-style stone bridge built in 1610, crossing the Río Rímac to the district of the same name. On Jr Hualgayoc is the bullring in the **Plaza de Acho**, inaugurated on 20 January 1766, with the **Museo Taurino** ① *Hualgayoc 332, T01-482 3360, Mon-Sat 0800-1600, US$1, students US$0.50, photography US$2*. Apart from matador's relics, the museum contains good collections of paintings and engravings, some of the latter by Goya. There are two bullfight seasons: October to first week in December and during July.

The **Convento de Los Descalzos** ① *Alameda de Los Descalzos,Rímac, T01-481 0441, Wed-Sun 1000-1300, 1500-1800, US$1, guided tour only, 45 mins in Spanish (worth it)*, was founded in 1592. It contains over 300 paintings of the Cuzco, Quito and Lima schools which line the four main cloisters and two ornate chapels. The chapel of El Carmen was constructed in 1730 and is notable for its baroque gold leaf altar. The museum shows the life of the Franciscan friars during colonial and early republican periods. The cellar, infirmary, pharmacy and a typical cell have been restored.

Cerro San Cristóbal dominates downtown Lima. It can be visited on a one-hour minibus tour ① *Camaná y Conde Superunda, every 15 mins daily 1000-2100, US$3*, departing from in front of Santo Domingo. The tour includes a look at the run-down Rímac district, passes the Convento de los Descalzos (see above), ascends the hill through one of the city's oldest shanties with its brightly painted houses and spends about 20 minutes at the summit, where there is a small museum and café. There are excellent views on a clear day. The second half of the trip is a historical tour. **Urbanito** buses ① *T01-424 3650, www. urbanito.com.pe,* also include Cerro San Cristóbal on their three-hour tour of central Lima, departing from the Plaza de Armas (weekends and holidays only).

San Borja

☆**Museo de la Nación** ① *Javier Prado Este 2465, T01-613 9393 ext 2484, www.cultura. gob.pe. Tue-Sun 0900-1700, closed major public holidays. US$2.50, 50% discount with ISIC card.* Located in the huge **Banco de la Nación** building is the museum for the exhibition and study of the art and history of the aboriginal races of Peru. There are good explanations in Spanish and English on Peruvian history, with ceramics, textiles and displays of many ruins in Peru. It is arranged so that you can follow the development of Peruvian precolonial history through to the time of the Incas. A visit is recommended before you go to see the archaeological sites themselves. There are displays of the tomb of the Señor de Sipán, artefacts from Batán Grande near Chiclayo (Sicán culture), reconstructions of the friezes found at Huaca La Luna and Huaca El Brujo, near Trujillo, and of Sechín and other sites. 'Yuyanapaq' is a photographic record of the events of 1980-2000. Temporary exhibitions are held in the basement, where there is also a Ministerio de Cultura bookshop. The museum has a cafetería.

To get there, take a taxi from downtown Lima or Miraflores US$3.20. From Avenida Garcilaso de la Vega in downtown Lima take a combi with a 'Javier Prado/Aviación' window sticker. Get off at the 21st block of Javier Prado at Avenida Aviación. From Miraflores take a bus down Avenida Arequipa to Avenida Javier Prado (27th block), then take a bus with a 'Todo Javier Prado' or 'Aviación' window sticker.

Surco

Museo de Oro del Perú ① *Alonso de Molina 1100, Monterrico, Surco (between blocks 18 and 19 of Av Primavera), Lima 33, T01-345 1292, www.museoroperu.com.pe. Daily 1030-1800, closed 1 Jan, 1 May, 28 Jul, 25 Dec.US$11.55, children under 11 US$5.60; multilingual audioguides available.* This museum houses an enormous collection of Peruvian gold, silver and bronze objects, together with an impressive international array of arms and military uniforms from Spanish colonial times to the present day and textiles from Peru and elsewhere. Allow plenty of time to appreciate all that is on view. More than one hundred of its pieces can be seen in the **Sala Museo Oro del Perú**, in Larcomar (see below).

Breña and Pueblo Libre

Mateo Salado archaeological site ① *Corner of Avs Tingo María (Breña) and M H Cornejo (Pueblo Libre), T01-476 9887, tours Thu-Sun 0900-1600, US$3.35.* West of the centre, adjacent to Plaza de la Bandera, is this large administrative and ceremonial centre from the Ychma culture (AD 1100-1450) with five terraced pyramids made of rammed earth.

South of here, in the Pueblo Libre district is a trio of important museums, including the unmissable **Museo Larco de Lima**.

Museo Nacional de Antropología, Arqueología e Historia ① *Plaza Bolívar, Pueblo Libre (not to be confused with Plaza Bolívar in the centre), T01-463 5070, Tue-Sat 0900-1700, Sun and holidays 0900-1600, US$4, students US$1.20, guides available for groups;*

taxi from downtown US$3; from Miraflores US$4. The original museum of anthropology and archaeology has ceramics from the Chimú, Nazca, Mochica and Pachacámac cultures, a display on the Paracas culture, various Inca curiosities and works of art, and interesting textiles. **Museo Nacional de Historia** ① *T01-463 2009, Tue-Sat 0900-1700, Sun and holidays 0900-1600, US$3.65,* in a mansion occupied by San Martín (1821-1822) and Bolívar (1823-1826) is next door. It exhibits colonial and early republican paintings, manuscripts and uniforms.

To get there, take any public transport on Avenida Brasil with a window sticker saying 'Todo Brasil'. Get off at the 21st block called Avenida Vivanco. Walk about five blocks down Vivanco. The museum will be on your left. From Miraflores take bus SM 18 Carabayllo-Chorrillos, marked 'Bolívar, Arequipa, Larcomar', get out at block 8 of Bolívar by the Hospital Santa Rosa and walk down Avenida San Martín five blocks until you see a faded blue line marked on the pavement; turn left. The blue line is a pedestrian route (15 minutes) linking the Museo Nacional de Antropología, Arqueología e Historia to the Museo Larco de Lima.

☆**Museo Larco de Lima** ① *Av Bolívar 1515, T01-461 1312, www.museolarco.org, 0900-2200, 0900-1800 24 Dec-1 Jan, US$10.55 (half price for students, seniors US$8.75); texts in Spanish, English and French, disabled access, photography not permitted; taxi from downtown, Miraflores or San Isidro, 15 mins, US$4.* Located in an 18th-century mansion, itself built on a seventh-century pre-Columbian pyramid, this museum has a collection which gives an excellent overview on the development of Peruvian cultures through their pottery. It has the world's largest collection of Moche, Sicán and Chimú pieces. There is a Gold and Silver of Ancient Peru exhibition, a magnificent textile collection and a fascinating erotica section. Don't miss the storeroom with its vast array of pottery, unlike anything you'll see elsewhere. There is a library and computer room for your own research and a good café open during museum hours, see page 58. It is surrounded by beautiful gardens, and has a park outside.

To get there, take any bus to the 15th block of Avenida Brasil. Then take a bus down Avenida Bolívar. From Miraflores, take the SM 18 Carabayllo-Chorrillos (see above), to block 15 of Bolívar.

Southern suburbs

hotels, restaurants, bars and beaches

San Isidro, Miraflores and Barranco are the hub of the capital's social life, with numerous hotels, restaurants and night spots (see pages 51-62). There are also beaches further south and a number of sights worth seeing. Avenida Arequipa runs south for 52 blocks from downtown Lima to Parque Kennedy in Miraflores. Alternatively, the Vía Expresa, a six-lane urban freeway locally known as 'El Zanjón' (the Ditch) is the fastest route across the city.

San Isidro
To the east of Avenida La República, down Calle Pancho Fierro, is **El Olivar**, an olive grove planted by the first Spaniards which has been turned into a park. Some 32 species of birds have been recorded there. Between San Isidro and Miraflores is **Huallamarca** ① *C Nicolás de Rivera 201 and Av Rosario, T01-222 4124, Tue-Sun 0900-1700, US$1.75.* An adobe pyramid

of the Maranga (Lima) culture, it dates from about AD 100-500, but has later Wari and Inca remains. There is a small site museum. To get there, take bus 1 from Avenida Tacna, or minibus 13 or 73 to Choquechaca, then walk.

Miraflores

Parque Kennedy and the adjoining Parque Central de Miraflores are located between Avenida Larco and Avenida Mcal Oscar Benavides (locally known as Avenida Diagonal). The extremely well-kept park area has a small open-air theatre with performances Thursday to Sunday and an arts and crafts market most evenings of the week. To the north is the former house and now museum of the author **Ricardo Palma** ⓘ *Gral Suárez 189, T01-445 5836, http://ricardopalma.miraflores.gob.pe, Mon-Fri 0915-1245, 1430-1700, US$2.20, includes video and guided tour.*

At the southern end of Avenida Larco and running along the Malecón de la Reserva is the renovated **Parque Salazar** and the modern shopping centre called **Centro Comercial Larcomar**. Here you will find expensive shops, hip cafés and discos and a wide range of restaurants, all with a beautiful ocean view. The 12-screen cinema is one of the best in Lima and even has a 'cine-bar' in the 12th theatre. Don't forget to check out the Cosmic Bowling Alley with its black lights and fluorescent balls.

Tip...
To travel by public transport between Miraflores and central Lima, there is no shortage of Línea Azul buses along Avenida Arequipa. Buses to Barranco can be caught on Avenida Tacna, Avenida Wilson (also called Garcilaso de la Vega), Avenida Bolivia and Avenida Alfonso Ugarte.

100 metres
100 yards

Where to stay

1 Albergue Turístico Juvenil Internacional *D3*
2 Alemán *A3*
3 Antigua Miraflores *B1*
4 Belmond Miraflores Park *D1*
5 Blue House *C1*
6 Casa Andina *D2*
7 Casa Andina Private Collection *C3*
8 Casa Andina Select *C2*
9 Casa de Baraybar *A1*
10 Casa del Mochilero *A2*
11 Casa Rodas *B3*
12 Condor's House *A1*
13 El Carmelo *B1*
14 Explorer's House *A1*
15 Flying Dog *B2 , C2*
16 Friend's House *C1*
17 Hitchhikers B&B Backpackers *B1*
18 Hostal El Patio *C2*
19 HosteLima *A3*
20 Hotel de Autor *C1*
21 Inka Frog *A2*
22 José Antonio *C1*
23 JW Marriott *D1*
24 La Casa Nostra *D2*
25 La Castellana *C2*
26 Lion Backpackers *C3*
27 Loki Backpackers *A1*
28 Pariwana *B3*
29 Pirwa *A3*
30 San Antonio Abad *D3*
31 Señorial *D1*
32 Sipán *D2*
33 Sonesta Posadas del Inca *C2*
34 The Lighthouse *A2*

Restaurants

1 Ache & Amaz *D2*
2 Alfresco *B1*
3 AlmaZen *B2*
4 Café Café *B2*
5 Café de la Paz *B2, C2*
6 Café Tarata *C2*
7 Central *D1*
8 C'est si bon *A2*
9 Chef's Café *C2*
10 Chifa Internacional *D2*
11 El Kapallaq *D2*
12 El Parquetito *B2*
13 El Rincón Gaucho *D1*
14 Fiesta Gourmet *D2*
15 Govinda *D2*
16 Haiti *B3*
17 IK *A2*
18 La Estancia *C2*
19 La Gloria *B3*
20 La Lucha *B2*
21 La Preferida *D3*
22 Las Brujas de Cachiche *B1*
23 Las Tejas *C2*
24 La Tiendecita Blanca *B3*
25 Lobo del Mar – Octavio Otani *C1*
26 Madre Natura *A3*
27 Mama Olla *C2*
28 Manifiesto *B2*
29 Panchita *B3*
30 Pizza Street *B2*
31 Punto Azul *C2*
32 Rafael *C1*
33 Rosa Náutica *C1*
34 San Antonio *A3, D2*
35 Saqra *C2*

Bars & clubs

36 Media Naranja *B2*
37 Murphy's *C3*
38 The Old Pub *B2*
39 Treff Pub Alemán *C2*

➡ **Lima maps**
1 Lima, page 38
2 Lima centre, page 40
3 **Miraflores, page 46**

Ⓜ Metropolitano

A few hundred metres to the north is the famous ☆**Parque del Amor**, a great place for a stroll where, on just about any night, you'll see at least one wedding party taking photos.

Tip...

If you wish to walk down the paths or steps from Miraflores to the Costa Verde below, those below the Villena bridge and from Yitzah Rabin Park are said to be safest. Take care on any other descent.

Museo Arqueológico Amano ① *Retiro 160, 11th block of Av Angamos Oeste, Miraflores, T01-441 2909, www.fundacion museoamano.org.pe, by appointment only Mon-Fri 1500-1630, US$9 (photography prohibited), renovated in 2015,* has artefacts from the Chancay, Chimú and Nazca periods, which were owned by the late Mr Yoshitaro Amano. It has one of the most complete exhibits of Chancay weaving and is particularly interesting for pottery and pre-Columbian textiles, all superbly displayed and lit. To get there, take a bus or *colectivo* to the corner of Avenida Arequipa y Avenida Angamos and another one to the 11th block of Avenida Angamos Oeste. Taxi from downtown costs US$3.20; from Parque Kennedy, US$2.25.

Turn off Avenida Arequipa at 45th block to reach **Huaca Pucllana** ① *General Borgoño, 8th block s/n, T01-445 8695, www.miafloresperu.com/huacapucllana/, Wed-Mon 0900-1600, US$4.25, students US$2, includes 45-min tour in Spanish or English,* a pre-Inca site which is under excavation. Originally a Lima culture temple to the goddesses of sea and moon (AD 200-700), it became a Wari burial site (AD 700-900) before being abandoned. Ychsma occupation (AD 1000-1470) and subsequent looting followed. It has a small site museum with some objects from the site itself, a garden of traditional plants and animals and a souvenir shop (see Restaurants, page 58).

☆Barranco

The 45-minute walk south from Miraflores to Barranco along the Malecón is recommended in summer. This suburb was already a seaside resort by the end of the 17th century. There are many old mansions in the district, in a variety of styles, several of which are now being renovated, particularly on Calle Cajamarca and around San Francisco church. Barranco is quiet by day but comes alive at night (see Restaurants and Bars pages 60-62).

The attractive public library, formerly the town hall, stands on the plaza. It contains the helpful **municipal tourist office** ① *T01-719 2046.* Nearby is the interesting *bajada*, a steep path leading down to the beach. The **Puente de los Suspiros** (Bridge of Sighs) crosses the *bajada* to the earthquake-damaged La Ermita church (only the façade has been restored) and leads towards the Malecón, with fine views of the bay. A number of artists have their workshops in Barranco and there are several chic galleries.

The **Museo de Arte Contemporáneo de Lima (MAC Lima)** ① *Av Miguel Grau 1511, beside the municipal stadium, near Miraflores, T01-514 6800, www.maclima.pe, Tue-Sun 1000-1800, US$2, Sun US$0.35, with guided tour,* has permanent Latin American and European collections and holds temporary exhibitions. **MATE (Asociación Mario Testino)** ① *Av Pedro de Osma 409, T01-251 7755, www.mate.pe, Tue-Sat 1000-2000, Sun 1100-1800 , US$5.55, with audio tour (no other explanations),* is the world-renowned fashion photographer's vision of modern art, with a shop and excellent café/restaurant. Next door, by contrast, and equally important is the **Museo de Arte Colonial Pedro de Osma** ① *Av Pedro de Osma 423, T01-467 0141, www.museopedrodeosma.org, Tue-Sun 1000-1800, US$6.75, students half price, guided tours in English or Spanish, a* private collection of colonial art of the Cuzco, Ayacucho and Arequipa schools.

☆Pachacámac

T01-430 0168, http://pachacamac.cultura.pe, Tue-Sat 0900-1700, Sun 0900-1600; closed public holidays except by appointment, US$3.50, students US$1.75, guide US$7.

When the Spaniards arrived, Pachacámac in the Lurín valley was the largest city and ceremonial centre on the coast. A wooden statue of the creator-god, after whom the site is named, is in the new site museum (opened 2016). Hernando Pizarro was sent here by his brother in 1533 in search of gold for Inca emperor Atahualpa's ransom. In their fruitless quest, the Spaniards destroyed images and killed the priests. The ruins encircle the top of a low hill, whose crest was crowned with a **Temple of the Sun**, now partially restored. Slightly apart is the reconstructed **House of the Mamaconas,** where the 'chosen women' spun fine cloth for the Inca and his court. An impression of the scale of the site can be gained from the top of the Temple of the Sun, or from walking or driving the 3-km circuit, which is covered by an unmade road for cars and tour buses.

The site is large and it is expected that tourists will be visiting by vehicle (there are six parking areas). However, there are also combis from the Pan-American Highway (southbound) to Pachacámac for US$0.85 (the window sticker reads 'Pachacámac/Lurín'; let the driver know you want to get off at the ruins. A taxi from downtown will cost approximately US$5.50; pay extra for the driver to wait as you'll struggle to find a taxi back into the city.

Lima's beaches

Even though the water of the whole bay has been declared unsuitable for swimming, Limeños see the beach more as part of their culture than as a health risk. On summer weekends (December-April) the city's beaches get very crowded and lots of activities are organized. The beaches of **Miraflores**, **Barranco** and **Chorrillos** are popular, but the sand and sea here are dirty. It's much better to take a safe taxi south along the Circuito de Playas to Playa Arica (30 km south of Lima). There are many great beaches for all tastes between here and San Bartolo (45 km south). If you really want the height of fashion head to **Asia**, Km 92-104, where there are some 20 beaches with boutiques, hotels, restaurants and condos.

> **Warning...**
> Robbery is a serious threat on the beaches. Don't take any belongings of value with you and don't leave bags unattended at any time.

Tourist information

iPerú has offices at **Jorge Chávez international airport** (T01-574 8000, daily 24 hrs); **Casa Basadre** (Av Jorge Basadre 610, San Isidro, T01-421 1627/1227, Mon-Fri 0900-1800); and **Larcomar shopping centre** (La Rotonda nivel 2, stand 211-212, Miraflores, T01-445 9400, daily 1100-2100). The **Municipal tourist kiosk** is on Pasaje Escribanos, behind the Municipalidad, near the Plaza de Armas (T01-632 1542, www. visitalima.pe and www.munlima.gob.pe, daily 0900-1700); ask about guided walks in the city centre. There are 8 **kiosks in Miraflores**: Parque Central; Parque Salazar; Parque del Amor; González Prada y Av Petit Thouars; Av R Palma y Av Petit Thouars; Av Larco y Av Benavides; Huaca Pucllana (closed Sat pm); and Ovalo Gutiérrez. The **tourist police** (Jr Moore 268, Magdalena at the 38th block of Av Brasil, T01-460 1060/ T0800-22221, daily 24 hrs) are friendly and very helpful if you have your property stolen, English spoken. Also at Av España y Av Alfonso Ugarte; Colón 246, Miraflores, T01-243 2190, and at the airport. For English websites, see www.limaeasy.com and www. mirafloresperu.com and for an upmarket city guide see www.limainside.net.

Where to stay

If you are only staying a short time and want to see the main sites, central Lima is the most convenient place to stay. However, it is not as safe at night as the more upmarket areas of Miraflores, San Isidro and Barranco. All hotels in the upper price brackets charge 18% state tax and service on top of prices. In hotels foreigners pay no tax and the amount of service charge is up to the hotel. Neither is included in the prices below, unless otherwise stated. All those listed below have received good recommendations.

Lima has several international, high-class chain hotels: **JW Marriott**, www.marriott. com; **Lima Sheraton**, www.sheraton.com; **Sofitel Royal Park**, www.sofitel.com; **Swissôtel Lima**, www.lima.swissotel.com; **Westin**, www.starwoodhotels.com. All are recommended.

There are dozens of hostels in Lima offering dormitory accommodation and charging US$10-17 pp, usually including a simple breakfast, hot water in shared bathrooms, kitchen facilities, bar and living room. Double rooms with private bathrooms start at about US$30. Some hostels are linked to travel agents or adventure tour companies.

Central Lima

$$$ The Clifford Hotel
Parque Hernán Velarde 27, near 1st block of Av Petit Thouars, Sta Beatriz, T01-433 4249, www.thecliffordhotel.com.pe.
Nicely converted, republican town house in a quiet and leafy park. Rooms and suites, has a bar, café and conference room.

$$ La Posada del Parque
Parque Hernán Velarde 60, near 1st block of Av Petit Thouars, Sta Beatriz, T01-433 2412, www.incacountry.com.
A charmingly refurbished old house with a collection of fine handicrafts, in a safe area, comfortable rooms, breakfast 0830-0930, airport transfer 24 hrs for US$18 for 1-3 passengers (US$8 pp for larger groups), no credit cards, cash only. Always check the website for special offers and gifts. The owners speak good English. Excellent value. Gay friendly. Has an agreement with the nearby Lawn Tennis Club (Arenales 200 block) for guests to eat at the good-value **Set Point** restaurant and use the gym.

$$ Maury
Jr Ucayali 201, T01-428 8188.
Formerly an upmarket hotel in the historical centre, but past its heyday. Some non-smoking rooms, a/c, frigobar, restaurant, airport transfers, secure. The bar is reputed to be the home of the first-ever *pisco sour* (this is, of course, disputed!).

$$-$ Hostal Iquique
Jr Iquique 758, Breña, T01-433 4724.
Rooms on top floor at the back are best, from singles with shared bath to triples with private bath, well-kept if a bit noisy and draughty, use of kitchen, luggage storage, safe, airport pick up extra.

$ Hostal España
Jr Azángaro 105, T01-427 9196,
www.hotelespanaperu.com.
A long-standing travellers' haunt, rooms or dormitories, fine old building, motorcycle parking, laundry service, roof garden, good café, can be very busy.

$ Hostal Roma
Jr Ica 326, T01-427 7576,
Facebook: hostalromaperu.
Over 35 years in the business, rooms sleep 1-4, private or shared bath, hot water, often full, luggage deposit and safe box, motorcycle parking, airport transfers (**Roma Tours** arranges city tours, flight reservations). Next door is **Café Carrara**.

$ Hostal San Francisco
Jr Azángaro 127, T01-426 2735.
Dormitories with and without bathrooms, safe, Italian/Peruvian owners, good service, café.

$ Pensión Ibarra
Av Tacna 359, 1402 y 1502 (elevator to 14th/15th floors doesn't run all hours), no sign, T01-427 8603/1035,
pensionibarra@gmail.com.
Basic, economical, breakfast US$4, discount for longer stay, noisy, use of kitchen, balcony with views of the city, helpful owners

(2 sisters), hot water, full board available (good small café almost next door). Reserve in advance; taxis can't stop outside so book airport pick-up (US$18.50) for safe arrival.

Inner suburbs
San Miguel and Magdalena del Mar are on the seaward side of Pueblo Libre.

$$ Mami Panchita
Av Federico Gallessi 198 (ex-Av San Miguel), San Miguel, T01-263 7203,
www.mamipanchita.com.
Dutch-Peruvian owned, English, Dutch and Spanish spoken, includes breakfast and welcome drink, comfortable rooms with bath, hot water, living room and bar, patio, book exchange, airport transfers, 15 mins from airport, 15 mins from Miraflores, 20 mins from historical centre. Frequently recommended.

San Isidro

$$$$ Country Club
Los Eucaliptos 590, T01-611 9000,
www.hotelcountry.com.
Excellent, fine service, luxurious rooms, good bar and restaurant, buisness centre, gym, spa, golf, classically stylish with a fine art collection.

$$$$ Libertador Hotels Peru
Los Eucaliptos 550, T01-518 6300,
www.libertador.com.pe.
Overlooking the golf course, full facilities for the business traveller, large comfortable rooms in this relatively small hotel, jacuzzi, a/c, heating, fine service, good restaurant, airport transfers extra.

$$$$ Sonesta El Olivar
Pancho Fierro 194, T01-712 6000,
www.sonesta.com/Lima.
Excellent, one of the top 5-star hotels in Lima overlooking El Olivar park, modern, good restaurant and bar, terrace, gym, swimming pool, quiet, very attentive, popular.

$$$ Garden
Rivera Navarrete 450, T01-200 9800.
Good beds, a/c, heating, small restaurant, ideal for business visitors, convenient, good value.

$$ Chez Elizabeth
Av del Parque Norte 265, San Isidro, T9980 07557, http://chezelizabeth.typepad.fr.
Family house in residential area 7 mins' walk from Cruz del Sur bus station. Shared or private bathrooms, TV room, laundry, airport transfers.

$ Albergue Juvenil Malka
Los Lirios 165 (near 4th block of Av Javier Prado Este), San Isidro, T01-442 0162, www.youthhostelperu.com.
Dormitory style, 4-8 beds per room, also private doubles ($$), English spoken, laundry, climbing wall, nice café, airport transfer.

Miraflores

$$$$ Belmond Miraflores Park
Av Malecón de la Reserva 1035, T01-610 4000, www.miraflorespark.com.
An **Orient Express** hotel, excellent service and facilities, beautiful views over the ocean, top class. Rooftop, open-air, heated pool and spa which looks out over the ocean, open to the public when you buy a spa treatment.

$$$$ Casa Andina Private Collection
Av La Paz 463, T01-213 4300, www.casa-andina.com.
Top of the range hotel in this recommended Peruvian chain (see below), modern, wheelchair accessible, well-appointed large rooms with safe,. Fine food in **Alma** restaurant and good value café, **Sama**, first class service, bar, pool and gym.

$$$$ Hotel de Autor
Av 28 de Julio 562B, T01-396 2740, www.hoteldeautor.com.
Artistically decorated small hotel in a refurbished town house, in a courtyard off the street (no sign), 4 well-appointed

suites and pleasant common areas, personalized service, English spoken.

$$$$ Sonesta Posadas del Inca
Alcanfores 329, T01-241 7688, www.sonesta.com/Miraflores/.
Part of renowned chain of hotels, convenient location, a/c, restaurant, airport transfer extra.

$$$ Alemán
Arequipa 4704, T01-445 6999, www.hotelaleman.com.pe.
No sign, comfortable, quiet, garden, excellent breakfast, smiling staff.

$$$ Antigua Miraflores
Av Grau 350 at C Francia, T01-201 2060, www.antiguamiraflores.com.
A small, elegant hotel in a quiet but central location, excellent service, tastefully furnished and decorated, gym, good restaurant. Recommended.

$$$ Casa Andina
Av 28 de Julio 1088, T01-241 4050, www.casa-andina.com.
Also at Av Petit Thouars 5444, T01-447 0263, in Miraflores. The 'Classic' hotels in this chain have similar facilities and decor. Very neat, with many useful touches, comfortable beds, fridge, safe, laundry service, buffet breakfast, other meals available. Check website for discounts and for the more upmarket **Casa Andina Select** at Schell 452, T01-416 7500 ($$$$-$$$), with disabled facilities.

$$$ Casa de Baraybar
Toribio Pacheco 216, T01-652 2262, www.casadebaraybar.com.
1 block from the ocean, extra long beds, a/c or fan, colourful decor, high ceilings, 24-hr room service, laundry, airport transfers free for stays of 3 nights. Bilingual staff. Recommended.

$$$ José Antonio
28 de Julio 398 y C Colón and C Colón 328, T01-445 7743, www.hotelesjoseantonio.com.
Good in all respects, including the restaurant, large modern rooms, jacuzzis, swimming

pool, business facilities, helpful staff speak some English.

$$$ La Castellana
Grimaldo del Solar 222, T01-444 4662, www.castellanahotel.com.
Pleasant, good value, nice garden, safe, expensive restaurant, laundry, English spoken.

$$$ San Antonio Abad
Ramón Ribeyro 301, T01-447 6766, www.hotelsanantonioabad.com.
Secure, quiet, helpful, tasty breakfasts, 1 free airport transfer with reservation, justifiably popular, good value.

$$$ Señorial
José González 567, T01-445 0139, www.senorial.com.
90 rooms, with restaurant, room service, comfortable, nice garden, parking, good services.

$$$-$$ Casa Rodas
Tarapacá 250, T01-242 4872, www.casarodas.com.
Rooms for 2, 3 or 4, one with private bath, the rest with shared bath, good beds, helpful staff.

$$$-$$ Hostal El Patio
Diez Canseco 341, T01-444 2107, www.hostalelpatio.net.
Very nice suites and rooms, comfortable, English spoken, convenient, *comedor*, gay friendly. Very popular, reservations are essential.

$$$-$$ Inka Frog
Gral Iglesias 271, T01-445 8979, www.inkafrog.com.
Self-styled "Exclusive B&B", comfortable, nice decor, lounge with huge TV, rooftop terrace, good value.

$$ El Carmelo
Bolognesi 749, T01-446 0575, www.hostalelcarmelo.com.pe.
Great location a couple of blocks from the Parque del Amor, small restaurant downstairs

serving *criolla* food and ceviche, good value, comfortable, breakfast extra.

$$ La Casa Nostra
Av Grimaldo del Solar 265, T01-241 1718.
Variety of rooms (from singles to quad), all with private bath, good service, convenient, safe, tourist information. Popular.

$$ Sipán
Paseo de la República 6171, T01-241 3758, www.hotelsipan.com.
Very pleasant, on the edge of a residential area next to the **Vía Expresa** (which can be heard from front rooms). Economical meals available in restaurant, 24-hr room service, security box, secure parking. Airport transfers available.

$$-$ Albergue Turístico Juvenil Internacional
Av Casimiro Ulloa 328, San Antonio, T01-446 5488, www.limahostell.com.pe.
Dormitory accommodation or a double private room, basic cafeteria, travel information, laundry facilities, swimming pool often empty, extra charge for breakfast, safe, situated in a nice villa; 20 mins' walk from the beach. Bus No 2 or *colectivos* pass Av Benavides to the centre.

$$-$ Condor's House
Martín Napanga 137, T01-446 7267, www.condorshouse.com.
Award-winning, quiet hostel, 2 categories of dorm rooms with lockers, good bathrooms, also doubles, good meeting place, TV room with films, book exchange, *parrillada* prepared once a week, bar. Helpful staff.

$$-$ Explorer's House
Av Alfredo León 158, by 10th block of Av José Pardo, T01-241 5002, http://explorershouselima.com.
No sign, but plenty of indications of the house number, dorm with shared bath, or double rooms with bath, hot water, laundry service, Spanish classes, English spoken, very welcoming.

$$-$ Flying Dog
Diez Canseco 117, T01-445 6745,
www.flyingdogperu.com.
Also at Lima 457 and Olaya 280, all with
dorms, doubles, triples, quads. All are on or
near Parque Kennedy, with kitchen, lockers,
but all have different features. There are
others in Cuzco, Iquitos and Arequipa.

$$-$ Hitchhikers B&B Backpackers
Bolognesi 400, T01-242 3008,
www.hhikersperu.com.
Located close to the ocean, mixture of dorms
and private rooms with shared or private
bath, nice patio, parking, bicycles to borrow,
airport transfers. Also has a hostel in Cuzco.

$$-$ HosteLima
Cnel Inclán 399, T01-242 7034,
www.hostelima.com.
Private double rooms and brightly painted
dorms, close to Parque Kennedy, helpful
staff, safe, bar/restaurant and snack shop,
movie room, travel information.

$$-$ The Lighthouse
Cesareo Chacaltana 162, T01-446 8397,
www.thelighthouseperu.com.
Near Plaza Morales Barros, British/Peruvian
run, relaxed, small dorm or private rooms
with private or shared bath. Good services,
small indoor patio.

$$-$ Lion Backpackers
Grimaldo del Solar 139, T01-447 1827,
www.lionbackpackers.com.
Quiet hostel in a convenient location, private
and shared rooms (with lockers), all en suite,
those on upper floor are the nicest, clean
kitchen facilities, book exchange, helpful
owner and staff, bus terminal pick up.

$$-$ Loki Backpackers
José Galvez 576, T01-651 2966,
www.lokihostel.com.
In a quiet area, the capital's sister to the party
hostel of the same name in Cuzco, doubles
or dorms, good showers, cooked breakfast
extra, Fri barbecues, lockers, airport transfers.

$$-$ Pariwana
Av Larco 189, T01-242 4350,
www.pariwana-hostel.com.
Party hostel with doubles and dorms in the
heart of Miraflores, individual lockers with
power outlets so you can leave your gadgets
charging in a safe place. Always lots going
on here.

$$-$ Pirwa
Coronel Inclán 494, T01-242 4059,
www.pirwahostels.com.
Members of a chain of hostels in Peru (Cuzco,
Arequipa, Puno, Nazca), choice of dorms and
double rooms, lockers, transfers arranged,
bike rental.

$ Blue House
José González 475, T01-445 0476,
www.bluehouse.com.pe.
A true backpacker hostel, most rooms with
bath including a double, basic but good
value for the location, *terraza* with *parrilla*,
films to watch.

$ Casa del Mochilero
Cesareo Chacaltana 130A, T01-444 9089,
pilaryv@hotmail.com (casa-del-mochilero
on Facebook).
Ask for Pilar or Juan, dorms or double
room on terrace, all with shared bath,
breakfast and internet extra, hot water,
lots of information.

$ Friend's House
Jr Manco Cápac 368, T01-446 6248,
Friends.House.Miraflores.Lima.Peru
on Facebook.
Very popular, reserve in advance. Near
Larcomar shopping centre, dormitory
accommodation with shared bath and hot
water, plenty of good information and help,
family atmosphere. Highly recommended.
They have another branch at José González
427, T01-446 3521. Neither branch is signed,
except on the bell at No 427.

Barranco

$$$$ B
Sáenz Peña 204, T01-206 0800,
www.hotelb.pe.
Boutique hotel in an early 20th-century
mansion. Beautifully redesigned as a
luxury hotel in the original building and
a contemporary wing, eclectic design
features and a large collection of mostly
modern art, next to Lucía de la Puente
gallery and convenient for others, blog and
Facebook give cultural recommendations,
highly regarded Mediterranean/Peruvian
restaurant, cocktail bar, plunge pool, parking,
excellent service. 1 room for disabled
travellers. In **Relais y Châteaux** group.

$$$ Barranco 3B
Jr Centenario 130, T01-247 6915,
www.3bhostal.com.
Small, modern B&B, simple comfortable
rooms with fan.

$$-$ Barranco's Backpackers Inn
Mcal Castilla 260, T01-247 1326.
Ocean view, colourful rooms, all
en suite, shared and private rooms,
tourist information.

$$-$ Domeyer
Jr Domeyer 296, T01-247 1413,
www.domeyerhostel.net.
Private or shared rooms sleeping 1-3 people
in a historic house, secure, gay friendly.

$$-$2 Safe in Lima
Alfredo Silva 150, T01-252 7330,
www.safeinperu.com.
Quiet, Belgian-run *hostal* with family
atmosphere, single, double and triple
rooms, very helpful, airport pick-up US$28,
good value, reserve in advance, lots of
information for travellers.

$ The Point
Malecón Junín 300, T01-247 7997,
www.thepointhostels.com.
Rooms range from doubles to large
dormitories, all with shared bath, very
popular with backpackers (book in advance
at weekends), laundry, gay friendly,
restaurant, bar, party atmosphere most of
the time, but also space for relaxing, weekly
barbecues, travel centre.

Callao (near the airport)

$$$$ Costa del Sol Wyndham
Av Elmer Faucett s/n, T01-711 2000,
www.costadelsolperu.com.
Within the airport perimeter. Offers day rates
as well as overnights if you can't get into the
city. Good service, buffet breakfast, pool,
gym, spa, jacuzzi, but high-priced because
of lack of competition and expensive extras.

$$ Hostal Víctor
Manuel Mattos 325, Urb San Amadeo
de Garagay, Lima 31, T569 4662,
Facebook:hostelvictor.
5 mins from the airport by taxi, or phone
or email in advance for free pick-up, large
comfortable rooms, hot water, 10% discount
for Footprint book owners, American
breakfast (or packed breakfast for early
departure), evening meals can be ordered
locally, 2 malls with restaurants, shops,
cinemas, etc nearby, very helpful.

$$-$ Pay Purix
Av Japón (formerly Bertello Bolatti), Mz F,
Lote 5, Urb Los Jazmines, 1a Etapa, Callao,
T01-484 9118, www.paypurix.com.
3 mins from airport, can arrange pick-up
(taxi US$6, US$2 from outside airport).
Hostel with doubles and dorms, convenient,
English spoken, CDs, DVDs, games and use
of kitchen.

Restaurants

18% state tax and 10% service will be
added to your bill in middle- and upper-
class restaurants. Chinese is often the
cheapest at around US$5 including a
drink. For the rise of Peruvian cuisine,
see Gastronomic Lima, page 56.

Lima attracts terms such "gastronomic capital of South America", which is reflected in the fact that the **Mistura** festival (www.mistura.pe) each September attracts hundreds of thousands of visitors. There are several restaurants that are championed as the height of culinary excellence. They are often priced beyond the average traveller's budget, but a meal at one of these could celebrate a special occasion. At the heart of much of today's Peruvian gastronomy are traditional ingredients, from the coast, the Andes and the jungle. The star chefs all recognize the debt they owe to the cooks of the different regions. Their skill is in combining the local heritage with the flavours and techniques that they have learnt elsewhere, without overwhelming what is truly Peruvian.

Gastón Acurio is usually credited with being the forerunner of the evolution of Peruvian cuisine. He is also recognized for his community work. With **Astrid y Gastón Casa Moreyra** (Avenida Paz Soldán 290, San Isidro, www.astridygaston.com), Acurio and his wife Astrid have moved their flagship restaurant from Miraflores to this historic house in San Isidro. It has been completely remodelled and opened in 2014. Other ventures include ceviche at **La Mar** (Avenida Lar 770, Miraflores, T01-421 3365), *anticuchos* at **Panchita** (Avenida 2 de Mayo 298, Miraflores, T01-242 5957, see Facebook page) and his chain of **T'anta** cafés, eg behind the Municipalidad in the city centre, at Pancho Fierro 115 in San Isidro and in Larcomar.

Central (Santa Isabel 376, Miraflores, T01-446 9301, www.centralrestaurante.com.pe) presents Virgilio Martínez and award-winning, sophisticated recipes fusing Peruvian ingredients and molecular cuisine.

Manifiesto (Independencia 130, Miraflores, T01-249 5533, www.manifiesto.pe) is billed as "Tacna meets Italy", bringing together the birthplace and family roots of chef Giacomo Bocchio.

Central Lima

$$$ Wa Lok
Jr Paruro 864 and 878, Barrio Chino, T01-427 2656.
Good dim sum, cakes and fortune cookies (when you pay the bill). English spoken, very friendly. Also at Av Angamos Oeste 700, Miraflores, T01-447 1329.

$$$-$$ De César
Ancash 300, T01-428 8740. Open 0800-2300.
Old-fashioned atmosphere, apart from the 3 TVs, breakfasts, snacks, seafood, meat dishes, pastas, pizza, juices, coffees and teas. Good food.

$$ Chifa San Joy Lao
Ucayali 779.
A *chifa* with a good reputation, one of several on the pedestrianized part of the Barrio Chino.

$$ L'Eau Vive
Ucayali 370, also opposite the Torre Tagle Palace, T01-427 5612. Mon-Sat, 1230-1500 and 1930-2130.
Run by nuns, lunch *menú*, Peruvian-style in interior dining room, or à la carte in either of dining rooms that open on to patio, excellent, profits go to the poor, Ave María is sung nightly at 2100.

Rafael Osterling has two restaurants in the city: **Rafael** (San Martín 300, Miraflores, T01-242 4149, www.rafaelosterling.com), celebrated for its classic Peruvian dishes incorporating flavours from around the globe, especially the Mediterranean, and **El Mercado** (H Unanue 203, Miraflores, T01-221 1322), which concentrates on seafood, reflecting all the influences on Peruvian cooking.

At **IK** (Elias Aguirre 179, Miraflores, T01-652 1692, reservas@ivankisic.pe, see Facebook page), molecular gastronomy meets Peruvian ingredients at the late Ivan Kisic's restaurant.

Lima 27 (Santa Lucía 295 – no sign, T01-221 5822, www.lima27.com) is a modern restaurant behind whose black exterior you will find contemporary Peruvian cuisine. It's in the same group as **Alfresco** (Malecón Balta 790, T01-242 8960), **Cala on Costa Verde** (http://calarestaurante.com), and a new sandwich bar, **Manduca**, in Jockey Plaza.

Pedro Miguel Schiaffino's **Malabar** (Camino Real 101, San Isidro, T01-440 5200, http://malabar.com.pe) takes the Amazon and its produce as the starting point for its dishes, as does Schiaffino's **Amaz** (Av La Paz 1079, Miraflores, T01-221 9393). This eatery is in a group of four places under the Hilton Hotel. Also here is **Ache** (Avenida La Paz 1055, T01-221 9315, achecocinanikkei on Facebook) which specializes in Japanese fusion cuisine.

La Picantería (Moreno 388 y González Prada, Surquillo, T01-241 6676, www.picanteriasdelperu.com) serves excellent seafood, first-class ceviche, has a fish-of-the-day lunch menu and a good bar.

At **AlmaZen** (Federico Recavarrén 298 y Galvez, T01-243 0474) you will find one of the best organic slow-food restaurants in Latin America.

Beyond Lima there are many excellent innovative restaurants in Arequipa (see www.festisabores.com), Cuzco, Ayacucho and elsewhere. Don't forget that the regional cooking that provided inspiration for Peru's growing international fame is still very much alive and well, often in much more modest surroundings than the fine dining settings of the capital.

$$ Salon Capon
Jr Paruro 819.
Good dim sum, at this recommended *chifa*. Also has a branch at Larcomar shopping centre, elegant and equally recommended.

$$-$ Bar Cordano
Ancash 202 y Carabaya (in Calles El Rastro y Pescadería zone).
Historic tavern serving Peruvian food and drinks, great atmosphere, favoured by politicians.

$$-$ Rovegno
Arenales 456 (near block 3 of Arequipa), T01-424 8465.

Italian and Peruvian dishes, home-made pasta, also serves snacks and sandwiches and has a bakery. Good value.

$ Accllahuasy
Jr Ancash 400. Daily 0700-2300.
Around the corner from **Hostal España**. Good Peruvian dishes.

$ La Catedral del Pisco
Jr de la Unión 1100 esq Av Uruguay 114, T01-330 0079. Daily 0800-2200.
Comida criolla and drinks, including free Peruvian coffee (excellent) or *pisco sour* for Footprint Handbook owners! Live music at night, Wi-Fi.

Breña and Pueblo Libre

$$$ Café del Museo
At the Museo Larco, Av Bolívar 1515,
T01-462 4757. Daily 0900-2200,
seating inside and on the terrace.
Specially designed interior, selection of
salads, fine Peruvian dishes, pastas and
seafood, a tapas bar of traditional Peruvian
foods, as well as snacks, desserts and
cocktails. Highly regarded.

$$ Antigua Taberna Queirolo
Av San Martín 1090, 1 block from
Plaza Bolívar, T01-460 0441,
http://antiguatabernaqueirolo.com.
Mon-Sat 0930-2330, Sun 0930-1600.
Atmospheric old bar with glass-fronted
shelves of bottles, marble bar and old
photos, owns bodega next door. Serves
lunches, sandwiches and snacks, good for
wine, does not serve dinner.

$$ La Choza Náutica
Jr Breña 204 and 211 behind Plaza Bolognesi,
T01-423 8087, www.chozanautica.com.
Good ceviche and friendly service;
has 3 other branches.

$ Azato
Av Arica 298, 3 blocks from Plaza Bolognesi,
T01-423 0278. Open 1200-2300.
Excellent and cheap Peruvian dishes,
menú and à la carte.

San Isidro

$$$ Antica Pizzería
Av 2 de Mayo 732, T01-222 8437. 1200-2400.
Very popular, great ambience, excellent food,
Italian owner. Also in Barranco at Alfonso
Ugarte 242, www.anticapizzeria.com.pe.

$$$ Chifa Titi
Av Javier Prado Este 1212, Córpac,
T01-224 8189, www.chifatiti.com.
Regarded by many as the best Chinese
restaurant in Lima with over 60 years
in operation.

$$$-$$ Como Agua para Chocolate
Pancho Fierro 108, T01-222 0297.
Mon-Sat 1200-1600, 1800-2200.
Dutch-Mexican owned restaurant,
specializing in Mexican food as the name
suggests, also has a very amusing Dutch
night once a month, *menú* and à la carte.

$$$-$$ Segundo Muelle
Av Conquistadores 490, T01-717 9998,
www.segundomuelle.com. Daily 1200-1700.
Ceviches and other very good seafood
dishes, including Japanese, *menú* and
à la carte, popular.

Cafés

Havanna
Miguel Dasso 163, www.havanna.pe.
Mon-Sat 0700-2300, Sun 0800-2200.
Branch of the Argentine coffee and *alfajores*
chain, others in the city include **Larcomar**.

Miraflores
C San Ramón, known as **Pizza Street**
(across from Parque Kennedy), is a
pedestrian walkway lined with popular
outdoor restaurants/bars/discos that are
open until the wee small hours. Good-
natured touts try to entice diners and
drinkers inside with free offers.

$$$ El Kapallaq
Av Reducto 1505. On Facebook.
Mon-Fri 1145-1630 only.
Prize-winning Peruvian restaurant
specializing in seafood and fish, excellent
ceviches, also a few treats for meat eaters.

$$$ El Rincón Gaucho
Av Armendáriz 580, T01-447 4778
and Av Grau 540, Barranco.
Good grill, renowned for its steaks.

$$$ Huaca Pucllana
Gral Borgoño cuadra 8 s/n, alt cuadra
45 Av Arequipa, T01-445 4042,
www.resthuacapucllana.com.
Daily 1200-1600, 1900-2400.

Facing the archaeological site of the same name, contemporary Peruvian fusion cooking, very good food in an unusual setting, popular with groups.

$$$ La Gloria
Atahualpa 201, T01-445 5705,
www.lagloriarestaurant.com.
Mon-Sat 1300-1600, 2000-2400.
Popular upmarket restaurant serving Peruvian food, classic and contemporary styles, good service.

$$$ La Preferida
Arias Araguez 698, T01-445 5180, http://
restaurantelapreferida.com. Daily 0800-1700.
Seafood restaurant and tapas bar, with delicious ceviches, also has a branch in Monterrico.

$$$ La Trattoria
At Larcomar, T01-446 7002,
www.latrattoriadimambrino.com.
Italian cuisine, popular, good desserts. Has another branch, **La Bodega**, opposite entrance to Huaca Pucllana.

$$$ Las Brujas de Cachiche
Av Bolognesi 472, T01-447 1883,
www.brujasdecachiche.com.pe.
Mon-Sat 1200-2400, Sun 1230-1630.
An old mansion converted into bars and dining rooms, fine traditional food (menu in Spanish and English), live *criollo* music.

$$$ Rosa Náutica
T01-445 0149, www.larosanautica.com.
Daily 1200-2400.
Built on old British-style pier (Espigón No 4), in Lima Bay. Delightful opulence, fine fish cuisine, experience the atmosphere by buying a beer in the bar at sunset.

$$$ Saqra
Av La Paz 646, T01-650 88 84, www.saqra.pe.
Mon-Sat 1200-2400.
Colourful and casual, indoor or outdoor seating, interesting use of ingredients from all over Peru, classic flavours with a fun, innovative twist, inspired by street food and humble dishes, vegetarian options,

many organic products. Also good cocktail bar. Go with a group to sample as many dishes as possible.

$$$-$$ Chifa Internacional
Av Roosevelt (ex República de Panamá) 5915,
T01-445 3997, www.chifainternacional.com.
Mon-Fri 1230-1530, 1900-2330 (Fri until 0030),
Sat 1230-1600, 1900-0030, Sun 1200-2315.
Great *chifa* in San Antonio district of Miraflores.

$$$-$$ Punto Azul
San Martín 595, 01-T445 8078, Benavides
2711, T01-260 8943, with other branches
in San Isidro, Surco and San Borja, http://
puntoazulrestaurante.com. Tue-Fri 1100-
1600, Sat-Sun1100-1700 (San Martín 595
also open Mon-Sat 1900-2400).
Popular, well-regarded chain of seafood and ceviche restaurants.

$$ Café Tarata
Pasaje Tarata 260, T01-446 6330.
Mon-Sat 0830-2200.
Good atmosphere, family-run, good varied menu.

$$ El Parquetito
Lima 373 y Diez Canseco, T01-444 0490.
Daily 0900-0100.
Peruvian food from all regions, good *menú* and à la carte, serves breakfast, eat inside or out.

$$ La Estancia
Schell 385, 01-444 2558. Sun-Thu 0800-2200.
Café and restaurant, Peruvian dishes with a Mediterranean touch, salads, sandwiches, cocktails.

$$ Las Tejas
Diez Canseco 340, T01-444 4360.
Daily 1200-2400.
Good, typical Peruvian food, especially ceviche, *menú* and à la carte.

$$ Lobo del Mar – Octavio Otani
Colón 587, T01-242 1871.
Basic exterior hides one of the oldest *cevicherías* in Miraflores, excellent, a good selection of other seafood dishes.

$$ Mama Olla
Pasaje Tarata 248. Daily 0700-2400.
Charming café on a pedestrian walkway,
huge menu, also set meals, big portions.

$ Al Toke Pez
*Av Angamos Este 886, Surquillo, across
Paseo de la República from Miraflores.
Tue-Sun 1130-1530.*
Small popular economical ceviche bar, also
serves other seafood dishes, tasty, a real find.

$ Govinda
Schell 630.
Vegetarian, from Hare Krishna foundation,
lunch *menú* US$3.

$ Madre Natura
*Chiclayo 815, T01-445 2522, www.madre
naturaperu.com. Mon-Sat 0800-2100.*
Natural foods shop and eating place,
very good.

Cafés

Café Café
Martin Olaya 250, at the corner of Av Diagonal.
Very popular, good atmosphere, over
100 different blends of coffee, good
salads and sandwiches, very popular with
'well-to-do' Limeños. Also in Larcomar.

Café de la Paz
*Lima 351, middle of Parque Kennedy
and Pasaje Tarata 227, www.cafede
lapazperu.com. Daily 0800-2400.*
Good outdoor café right on the park,
expensive, great cocktails.

C'est si bon
Av Cdte Espinar 663. Daily 100-2100
Excellent cakes by the slice or whole,
best in Lima.

Chef's Café
Av Larco 375 and 763. Daily 0700-2400.
Nice places for a sandwich or coffee.

Haiti
*Av Diagonal 160, Parque Kennedy.
Mon-Thu 0700-0200, Fri-Sat 0700-0300.*
Great for people watching, good ice cream.

La Lucha
*Av Benavides y Olaya (under Flying Dog),
on Parque Kennedy, with small branches
between Olaya and Benavides, on Ovalo
Gutiérrez and at Larcomar.*
Excellent hot sandwiches, limited range,
choice of sauces, great juices, *chicha morada*
and *café pasado*. Good for a wholesome snack.

La Tiendecita Blanca
Av Larco 111 on Parque Kennedy.
One of Miraflores' oldest, expensive,
good people-watching, very good cakes,
European-style food and delicatessen.

Pan de la Chola
*Av La Mar 918, El-Pan-de-la-Chola on
Facebook. Tue-Sat 0800-2200, Sun 0900-1800.*
Café and bakery specializing in sourdough
bread, Peruvian cheeses, teas, juices
and sweets.

San Antonio
Av Angamos Oeste 1494.
Fashionable *pastelería* chain with hot
and cold lunch dishes, good salads,
inexpensive, busy. Other branches
at Rocca de Vergallo 201, Magdalena
del Mar, and Av Primavera 373, San Borja.

Barranco

$$$ Canta Rana
*Génova 101, T01-247 7274. Sun-Mon
1200-1700, Tue-Sat 1200-2200.*
Good ceviche, expensive, small portions,
but the most popular local place on Sun.

$$$ La 73
*Av Sol Oeste 176, casi San Martín, at the
edge of Barranco, T01-2470780. Mon-Sat
1200-2400, Sun 1200-2200.*
Mostly meat dishes, has a lunch menu,
look for the Chinese lanterns outside,
good reputation.

$$$ La Costa Verde
*Bajada Armendáriz al lado del Salvataje
on Barranquito beach, T01-247 1244,
www.restaurantecostaverde.com.
Mon-Sat 1300-2300, Sun buffet 1300-1600.*

Excellent fish and wine, expensive but considered one of the best.

$$$ Sóngoro Cosongo
Ayacucho 281, T01-247 4730, at the top of the steps down to Puente de Suspiros, www.songorocosongo.com. Mon-Sat 1200-2300, Sun from 2200.
Varied *comida criolla*, "un poco de todo".

$$$-$$ Tío Mario
Jr Zepita 214, on the steps to the Puente de Suspiros.
Excellent *anticuchería*, serving delicious Peruvian kebabs, always busy, fantastic service, varied menu and good prices.

$$ Las Mesitas
Av Grau 341, T01-477 4199. Open 1200-0200.
Traditional tea rooms-cum-restaurant, serving *comida criolla* and traditional desserts which you won't find anywhere else, lunch *menú* served till 1400, US$3.

Cafés

Expreso Virgen de Guadalupe
San Martín y Ayacucho.
Café and vegetarian buffet in an old tram, also seating in the garden, more expensive at weekends.

La Boteca
Grau 310-312.
Smart-looking café-bar.

Tostería Bisetti
Pedro de Osma 116, www.cafebisetti.com.
Coffee, cakes and a small selection of lunchtime dishes, service a bit slow but a nice place.

Bars and clubs

See also Entertainment (page 63) for a list of *peñas* offering live music and dancing.

Central Lima
The centre of town, specifically Jr de la Unión, has numerous nightclubs, but it's best to avoid the nightspots around the intersection of Av Tacna, Av Piérola and Av de la Vega, as these places are rough and foreigners will receive much unwanted attention. For the latest gay and lesbian nightspots, check out www.gayperu.com.

El Rincón Cervecero
Jr de la Unión (Belén) 1045, T01-428 1422, www.rinconcervecero.com.pe. Mon-Fri 1230-2400, Fri-Sat 1230-0030.
German-style pub, fun.

Estadio Fútbol Sports Bar
Jr de la Unión (Belén) 1049, T01-427 9609. Mon-Wed 1215-2300, Thu 1215-2400, Fri-Sat 1215-0300, Sun 1215-1800.
Beautiful bar with a disco, international football theme, good international and creole food.

Piano Bar Munich
Jr de la Unión 1044 (basement), T01-5737390. Mon-Sat from 1700.
Small and fun.

Miraflores

La Tasca
Av Diez Canseco 117, very near Parque Kennedy, part of the Flying Dog group and under one of the hostels (see Where to stay, above).
Spanish-style bar with cheap beer (for Miraflores). An eclectic crowd including ex-pats, travellers and locals. Gay-friendly. Small and crowded.

Media Naranja
Schell 130, at bottom of Parque Kennedy.
Brazilian bar with drinks and food.

Murphy's
Schell 619, T01-447 1082. Mon-Sat from 1600.
Happy hours every day with different offers, lots of entertainment, very popular.

The Old Pub
San Ramón 295 (Pizza St), www.oldpub.com.pe.
Cosy, with live music most days.

Treff Pub Alemán
Av Benavides 571-104, T01-444 0148 (hidden from the main road behind a cluster of tiny

houses signed 'Los Duendes'). *Mon-Thu 1200-0100, Fri-Sat 1800-0300, Sun 1900-0100.*
A wide range of German beers, plus cocktails, good atmosphere, darts and other games.

Barranco

Barranco is the capital of Lima nightlife. The following is a short list of some of the better bars and clubs. The pedestrian walkway Pasaje Sánchez Carrión, right off the main plaza, has watering holes and discos on both sides. Av Grau, just across the street from the plaza, is also lined with bars, including the **Lion's Head Pub** (Av Grau 268, p 2) and **Déjà Vu** at No 294. Many of the bars in this area turn into discos later on.

Ayahuasca
San Martín 130. Mon-Sat 2000-0300 (opens 1800 Thu-Fri).
In the stunning Berninzon House, which dates from the Republican era, a chilled out lounge bar with several areas for eating, drinking and dancing. Food is expensive and portions are small, but go for the atmosphere.

Barranco Beer Company
Grau 308, T01-247 6211, www.barranco beer.com. Sun-Wed 1100-2400, Thu 1100-0200, Fri-Sat 1100-0300.
Artisanal brewhouse.

El Dragón
N de Piérola 168, T01-221 4112.
Popular bar and venue for music, theatre and painting.

Juanitos
Av Grau, opposite the park. Daily 1600-0400.
Barranco's oldest bar, where writers and artists congregate, a perfect spot to start the evening.

La Noche
Bolognesi 307, at Pasaje Sánchez Carrión,T01-2471012. Mon-Sat 2000-0200. www.lanoche.com.pe.
A Lima institution. High standard live music, Mon is jazz night, all kicks off at around 2200.

La Posada del Angel
3 branches, Pedro de Osma 164 and 214, T01-247 0341, see Facebook. Mon-Sat 1900-0300.
These are popular bars serving snacks and meals.

La Posada del Mirador
Ermita 104, near the Puente de los Suspiros (Bridge of Sighs), see Facebook.
Beautiful view of the ocean, but you pay for the privilege.

Santos Café & Espirituosos
Jr Zepita 203, Bajada de Baños, just above the Puente de Suspiros, T01-247 4609, also on Facebook. Mon-Thu 1700-0100, Fri-Sat 1700-0300.
Favourite spot for trendy young professionals who want to drop a few hundred soles, relaxed, informal but pricey.

Sargento Pimienta
Bolognesi 757, www.sargentopimienta. com.pe. Tue-Sat from 2200.
Live music, always a favourite with Limeños.

Victoria
Av Pedro de Osma 135.
Upmarket pub in the beautiful Casa Cillóniz, serving up a selection of beers, cocktails, snacks and live music.

Entertainment

Theatre and concert tickets can be booked through **Teleticket** (T01-613 8888, Mon-Fri 0900-1900, www.teleticket.com.pe).
For cultural events, see **Lima Cultural** (www.limacultura.pe), the city's monthly arts programme.

Cinema
The newspaper *El Comercio* lists cinema information in the section called *Luces*. Mon-Wed reduced price at most cinemas. Most films are in English with subtitles and cost from US$7-8.75 in Miraflores and malls, US$3-4 in the centre. The best cinema chains in the city are **Cinemark, Cineplanet** and **UVK Multicines.**

Cinematógrafo de Barranco, *Pérez Roca 196, Barranco, T01-264 4374*. Small independent cinema showing a good choice of classic and new international films.
Filmoteca de Lima, Centro Cultural PUCP, *Camino Real 1075, San Isidro, T01-616 1616, http://cultural.pucp.edu.pe*.

Peñas
Del Carajo, *Catalino Miranda 158, Barranco, T01-247 7977, www.delcarajo.com.pe*. All types of traditional music.
La Candelaria, *Av Bolognesi 292, Barranco, T01-247 1314, www.lacandelariaperu.com. Thu-Sat 2000 onwards*. A good Barranco *peña* with a regular dance presentation and other shows.
La Estación de Barranco, *Pedro de Osma 112, T01-247 0344, www.laestaciondebarranco. com, Mon-Sat 1900-0300*. Good, family atmosphere, varied shows.
Las Brisas de Titicaca, *Héroes de Tarapacá 168, at 1st block of Av Brasil near Plaza Bolognesi, T01-715 6960, www.brisasdeltiticaca.com*. A Lima institution with lunch shows Fri-Sat 1300-1730, evening shows Tue-Wed 2100-0015, Thu 2145-0135, Fri-Sat 2200-0200.
Sachun, *Av del Ejército 657, Miraflores, T01-441 0123, www.sachunperu.com. Thu-Sat 2100-0300*. Great shows.

Theatre
El Gran Teatro Nacional, *corner of Avs Javier Prado and Aviación, San Borja*. Capable of seating 1500 people, it hosts concerts, opera, ballet and other dance as well as other events.
Teatro Municipal, *Jr Ica 377, T01-315 1300 ext 1767, see Facebook*. Completely restored after a fire, with full programmes and a theatre museum on Huancavelica.
Teatro Segura, *Jr Huancavelica 265, T01-427 9491*. Stages professional performances.

There are many other theatres in the city, some of which are related to cultural centres. All have various cultural activities; the press gives details of performances: **CCPUCP** (see Cinemas, above); **Instituto Cultural**

Peruano-Norteamericano (Jr Cusco 446, Lima Centre, T01-706 7000, central office at Av Angamos Oeste 160, Miraflores, www.icpna.edu.pe); **Centro Cultural Peruano Japonés** (Av Gregorio Escobedo 803, Jesús María, T01-518 7450, www.apj.org.pe).

Festivals

18 Jan Founding of Lima.
Mar/Apr Semana Santa, or Holy Week, is a colourful spectacle with processions.
28-29 Jul Independence, with music and fireworks in the Plaza de Armas on the evening before.
30 Aug Santa Rosa de Lima.
Mid-Sep Mistura, www.mistura.pe, a huge gastronomy fair in Parque Exposición, with Peruvian foods, celebrity chefs, workshops and more.
Oct The month of Our Lord of the Miracles; see Las Nazarenas church, page 41.

Shopping
Bookshops
Crisol, *Ovalo Gutiérrez, Av Santa Cruz 816, San Isidro, T01-221 1010, below Cine Planet*. Large bookshop with café, titles in English, French and Spanish. Also in **Jockey Plaza Shopping Center** (Av Javier Prado Este 4200, Surco, T01-436 0004, daily 1100-2300, and other branches, www.crisol.com.pe).
Epoca, *Av Cdte Espinar 864, Miraflores, T01-241 2951*. Great selection of books, mostly in Spanish.
Ibero Librerías, *Av Diagonal 500, T01-242 2798, Larco 199, T01-445 5520, in Larcomar, Miraflores, and other branches*. Stocks Footprint Handbooks as well as a wide range of other titles.

Camping equipment
It's better to bring all camping and hiking gear from home. Camping gas (the most popular brand is **Doite**) is available from any large hardware store or bigger supermarket. White gas (*bencina*) is available from hardware stores.

Alpamayo, *Av Larco 345, Miraflores at Parque Kennedy, T01-445 1671. Mon-Fri 1000-1930, Sat 1000-1300.* Sleeping mats, boots, rock shoes, climbing gear, water filters, tents, backpacks etc, very expensive but top quality equipment. Owner speaks fluent English and offers good information.

Altamira, *Arica 880, Parque Damert, behind Wong on Ovalo Gutiérrez, Miraflores, T01-445 1286.* Sleeping bags, climbing gear, hiking gear and tents.

Camping Center, *Av Benavides 1620, Miraflores, T01-242 1779, www.camping peru.com. Mon-Fri 1000-1800.* Selection of tents, backpacks, stoves, camping and climbing gear.

El Mundo de las Maletas, *Preciados 308, Higuereta-Surco, T01-449 7850. Daily 0900-2200 and CC Shopping Cente, Av La Mar 2275, San Miguel.* For suitcase repairs.

Tatoo, *CC Larcomar, locs 123-125B, T01-242 1938, www.tatoo.ws. Daily 1100-2150.* For top-quality imported ranges and own brands of equipment.

Todo Camping, *Av Angamos Oeste 350, Miraflores, near Av Arequipa, T01-242 1318. Mon-Fri 1000-2000, Sat 1000-1700.* Sells 100% deet, blue gas canisters, lots of accessories, tents, crampons and backpacks.

Handicrafts

Miraflores is a good place for high quality, expensive handicrafts; there are many shops on and around the top end of Av La Paz (starting at Av Ricardo Palma).

Agua y Tierra, *Diez Canseco 298 y Alcanfores, Miraflores, T01-444 6980. Mon-Fri 1000-2000.* Fine crafts and indigenous art.

Alpaca 859, *Av Larco 859, Miraflores, T01-447 7163.* Good quality alpaca and baby alpaca products.

Arte XXI, *Av La Paz 678, Miraflores, T01-447 9777, www.artemania-21.com.* Gallery and store for contemporary and colonial Peruvian paintings.

Artesanía Santo Domingo, *Plazuela Santo Domingo, by the church of that name, in Lima centre, T01-428 9860.* Good Peruvian crafts.

Centro Comercial El Alamo, *corner of La Paz y Diez Canseco, Miraflores. Artesanía* shops with good choice.

Dédalo, *Paseo Sáenz Peña 295, Barranco, T01-652 5400, http://dedaloarte.blogspot. co.uk.* A labyrinthine shop selling furniture, jewellery and other items, as good as a gallery. It also has a nice coffee shop and has cinema shows. Other branches on Parque Kennedy and at Larcomar.

Kuna by Alpaca 111, *Av Larco 671, Miraflores, T01-447 1623, www.kuna.com.pe. Daily 1000-2000.* High-quality alpaca, baby alpaca and vicuña items. Also in Larcomar (loc 1-07), Museo Larco, the airport, Jockey Plaza, at hotels and in San Isidro.

Kuntur Wasi, *Ocharán 182, Miraflores, opposite Sol de Oro hotel, T01-447 7173. Mon-Sat 1000-1900.* English-speaking owners are very knowledgeable about Peruvian textiles; often have exhibitions of fine folk art and crafts.

La Casa de la Mujer Artesana, *Juan Pablo Ferandini 1550 (Av Brasil cuadra 15), Pueblo Libre, T01-423 8840, www.casadelamujer artesana.com. Mon-Fri 0900-1230, 1400-1630.* A cooperative run by the Movimiento Manuela Ramos, excellent quality work mostly from *pueblos jóvenes*.

Las Pallas, *Cajamarca 212, Barranco, T01-477 4629, www.laspallas.com.pe. Mon-Sat 0900-1900.* Very high quality handicrafts, English, French and German spoken.

Luz Hecho a Mano, *Berlín 399, Miraflores, T01-446 7098. Mon-Fri 1100-1330, 1400-1700, Sat 1030-1700.* Lovely handmade handbags, wallets and other leather goods including clothing which last for years and can be custom made.

Museo de la Nación *(see page 44).* Often hosts specialist handicrafts markets presenting individual work from across Peru during national festivals. There are bargains in high-quality Pima cotton.

Jewellery

On Cs La Esperanza and La Paz, Miraflores, dozens of shops offer gold and silverware at reasonable prices.

Ilaria, *Av 2 de Mayo 308, San Isidro, T01-512 3530, www.ilariainternational.com. Mon-Fri 1000-1930.* Jewellery and silverware with interesting designs. There are other branches in Lima, Cuzco, Arequipa and Trujillo.

Maps

Instituto Geográfico Nacional, *Av Aramburú 1190, Surquillo, T01-475 9960, www.ign.gob.pe. Mon-Fri 0830-1645.* It has topographical maps of the whole country, mostly at 1:100,000, political and physical maps of all departments and satellite and aerial photographs. You may be asked to show your passport when buying these maps.

Lima 2000, *Av Arequipa 2625 (near the intersection with Av Javier Prado), T01-440 3486, www.lima2000.com.pe. Mon-Fri 0900-1800.* Has excellent street maps of Lima, from tourist maps, US$5.55, to comprehensive books US$18. Also has country maps (US$5.55-9.25), maps of Cuzco, Arequipa, Trujillo and Chiclayo and tourist maps of the Inca Trail, Colca area and Cordillera Blanca.

Markets

All are open 7 days a week until late(ish).

Feria Nacional de Artesanía de los Deseos y Misterios, *Av 28 de Julio 747, near junction with Av Arequipa and Museo Metropolitano.* Small market specializing in charms, remedies, fortune-telling and trinkets from Peru and Bolivia.

Mercado 1, *Surquillo, cross Paseo de le República from Ricardo Palma, Miraflores and go north 1 block.* Food market with a huge variety of local produce. C Narciso de la Colina outside has various places to eat, including **Heladería La Fiorentina** (No 580), for excellent ice creams.

Mercado Inca, *Av Petit Thouars, blocks 51-54 (near Parque Kennedy, parallel to Av Arequipa), Miraflores.* An unnamed crafts market area, with a large courtyard and lots of small flags.

This is the largest crafts arcade in Miraflores. From here to C Ricardo Palma the street is lined with crafts markets.

Parque Kennedy, the main park of Miraflores, hosts a daily crafts market from 1700-2300.

Polvos Azules, *on García Naranjo, La Victoria, just off Av Grau in the centre of town.* The 'official' black market, sells just about anything; it is generally cheap and very interesting; beware pickpockets.

Cycling

Bike Tours of Lima, *Bolívar 150, Miraflores, T01-445 3172, www.biketoursoflima.com. Mon-Fri 0930-1800, Sat-Sun 0930-1400.* Offer a variety of day tours through the city of Lima by bike, also bicycle rentals.

BikeMavil, *Av Aviación 4023, Surco, T01-449 8435, see Facebook page. Mon-Sun 1000-2000.* Rental service, repairs, tours, selection of mountain and racing bikes.

Buenas Biclas, *Domingo Elías 164, Miraflores, T01-241 9712, www.buenasbiclas.com. Mon-Fri 1000-2000, Sat 1000-1800.* Mountain bike specialists, knowledgeable staff, good selection of bikes, repairs and accessories.

Casa Okuyama, *Manco Cápac 590, La Victoria, T01-461 6435. Mon-Fri 0900-1300, 1415-1800, Sat 0900-1300.* Repairs, parts, try here for 28-in tyres, excellent service.

Cicloturismo Peru, *T99-9012 8105, www.cicloturismoperu.com.* Offers good-value cycling trips around Lima and beyond, as well as bike rental. The owner, Aníbal Paredes, speaks good English, is very knowledgeable and is the owner of **Mont Blanc Gran Hotel**.

Mirabici, *Parque Salazar, T01-673 3903. Daily 0800-1900.* Bicycle hire, US$7.50 per hr (tandems available); they also run bike tours 1000-1500, in English, Spanish and Portuguese. Bikes to ride up and down Av Arequipa can be rented on Sun 0800-1300, US$3 per hr, leave passport as deposit, www.jafibike.com.

Perú Bike, *Punta Sal 506, Surco, T01-260 8225, www.perubike.com. Mon-Fri 0930-1930, Sat 0930-1500.* Experienced agency leading tours, professional guiding, mountain bike school and workshop.

Diving

Peru Divers, *Av Defensores del Morro 175, Chorrillos, T01-251 6231, www.perudivers.com. Mon-Fri 0900-1700, call ahead.* Owner Lucho Rodríguez is a certified PADI instructor who offers certification courses, tours and a wealth of good information.

Hiking

Trekking and Backpacking Club, *Jr Huáscar 1152, Jesús María, Lima 11, T01-423 2515, T94-3866 794, www.angelfire.com/mi2/tebac.* Sr Miguel Chiri Valle, treks arranged, including in the Cordillera Blanca.

Paragliding

Aeroxtreme, *Trípoli 345, dpto 503, T01-242 5125, www,aeroxtreme.com, call ahead.* One of several outfits offering parapenting in Lima, US$70, 20 years' experience.
Andean Trail Perú, *T99-836 3436, www. andeantrailperu.com.* For parapenting tandem flights, US$53, and courses, US$600 for 10 days. They also have a funday for US$120 to learn the basics. Trekking, kayaking and other adventure sports arranged.

Textiles/cultural tours

Puchka Perú, *www.puchkaperu.com.* Web-based operator specializing in textiles, folk art and markets. Fixed-date tours involve meeting artisans, workshops, visit to markets and more. In association with Maestro Máximo Laura, world-famous weaver, http:// maximolauratapestries.com, whose studio in Urb Brisas de Santa Rosa III Etapa, Lima can be visited by appointment, T01-577 0952. See also Museo Máximo Laura in Cuzco.

Tour operators

Do not conduct business anywhere other than in the agency's office and insist on a written contract.
The Andean Experience Co, *Sáenz Peña 214, Barranco, T01-700 5100, www.andean-experience.com. Mon-Fri 0830-1815, Sat 0900-1200.* Offers tailor-made itineraries designed to match each traveller's personal interests, style and preferences to create ideal Peru trips.
Aracari Travel Consulting, *Schell 237, of 602, Miraflores, T01-651 2424, www.aracari. com. Mon-Sat 0800-1800.* Regional tours throughout Peru, also 'themed' and activity tours, has a very good reputation.
Coltur, *Av Reducto 1255, Miraflores, T01-615 5555, www.colturperu.com. Mon-Fri 0900-1800, Sat 0900-1200.* Very helpful, experienced and well-organized tours throughout Peru.
Condor Travel, *Armando Blondet 249, San Isidro, T01-615 3000, www.condortravel.com. Mon-Fri 0900-1800.* Highly regarded operator with tailor-made programmes, special interest tours, luxury journeys, adventure travel and conventional tourism. One-stop shopping with own regional network.
Dasatariq, *Av Reducto 1255, Miraflores, T01-447 2741, www.dasatariq.com.* Also in Cuzco. Well-organized, helpful, with a good reputation.
Domiruth Travel Service S.A.C, *Av Petit Thouars 4305, Miraflores, T01-610 6000, www.domiruth.com.* Tours throughout Peru, from the mystical to adventure travel. See also **Peru 4x4 Adventures**, part of Domiruth (Jr Rio de Janeiro 216-218, www. peru4x4adventures.com), for exclusive 4WD tours with German, English, Spanish, Italian and Portuguese-speaking drivers.
Ecocruceros, *Av Arequipa 4964, of 202, Miraflores, T01-226 8530, www.islaspalomino. com. Mon-Fri 0900-1900, Sat 0900-1300.* Daily departures from Plaza Grau in Callao (see page 37) to see the sea lions at Islas Palomino, 4 hrs with 30-40 mins wetsuit

swimming with guide, snack lunch, US$48 (take ID), reserve a day in advance.

Excursiones MYG, *T01-241 8091*. Offers a variety of tours in Lima and surroundings, including historic centre, nighttime, culinary tours, Caral, and further afield.

Explorandes, *C San Fernando 287, Miraflores, T01-200 6100, www.explorandes.com. Mon-Fri 0900-1750, Sat 0900-1200*. Award-winning company. Offers a wide range of adventure and cultural tours throughout the country. Also offices in Huaraz and Cuzco (see pages 81 and 253).

Fertur Peru Travel, *C Schell 485, Miraflores, T01-242 1900; and Jr Junín 211, Plaza de Armas, T01-427 2626; USA/Canada T1-877 247 0055 toll free, UK T020-3002 3811, www.fertur-travel.com. Mon-Fri 0900-1900, Sat 0900-1600*. Siduith Ferrer de Vecchio, CEO of this agency, is highly recommended for tour packages, up-to-date tourist information and also great prices on national and international flights, discounts for those with ISIC and youth cards. Other services include flight reconfirmations, hotel reservations and transfers to and from the airport or bus or train stations. Also in Cuzco at Simón Bolívar F23-317, T084-221304.

Il Tucano Peru, *Elías Aguirre 633, Miraflores, T01-444 9361, 24-hr number T01-975 05375, www.iltucanoperu.com. Mon-Fri 0900-1800*. Personalized tours for groups or individuals throughout Peru, also 4WD overland trips, first-class drivers and guides, outstanding service and reliability.

Info Perú, *Jr de la Unión (Belén) 1066, of 102, T01-425 0414, www.infoperu.com.pe. Mon-Fri 0900-1800, Sat 0930-1400*. Run by a group of women, ask for Laura Gómez, offering personalized programmes, hotel bookings, transport, free tourist information, sale of maps, books and souvenirs, English and French spoken.

InkaNatura Travel, *Manuel Bañón 461, San Isidro, T01-203 5000, www.inkanatura.com. Mon-Fri 0900-1800, Sat 0900-1300*. Also in Cuzco and Chiclayo, experienced company with special emphasis on both sustainable tourism and conservation, especially in Manu and Tambopata, also birdwatching, and on the archaeology of all of Peru.

Lima Mentor, *T01-243 2697, www.limamentor.com*. Contact through web, phone or through hotels. An agency offering cultural tours of Lima using freelance guides in specialist areas (eg gastronomy, art, archaeology, Lima at night), entertaining, finding different angles from regular tours. Half-day or full day tours.

Lima Tours, *N de Piérola 589 p 18, T01-619 6900, www.limatours.com.pe. Mon-Fri 0900-1745*. Very good for tours in the capital and around the country; programmes include health and wellness tours.

Peru For Less, *ASTA Travel Agent, Luis García Rojas 240, Urb Humboldt, T01-273 2486, US office: T1-877-269 0309, UK office: T+44-203-002 0571, Cuzco office: T084-254800, www.peruforless.com*. Will meet or beat any

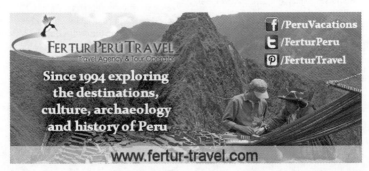

published rates on the internet from outside Peru. Good reports.

Peru Hop, *Av Larco 812, p 3, corner with San Martín, T01-242 2140, www.peruhop.com. Daily 0900-2100.* A hop-on, hop-off bus service from Lima to Cuzco via Paracas, Nazca, Arequipa, also to Puno and La Paz, daily departures, tours of places of interest, a variety of passes with different prices.

Peru Rooms, *Av Dos de Mayo 1545 of 205, San Isidro, T01-422 3434, www.perurooms.com.* Internet-based travel service offering 3- to 5-star packages throughout Peru, cultural, adventure and nature tourism.

Rutas del Peru SAC, *Av Enrique Palacios 1110, Miraflores, T01-445 7249, www.rutasdel peru.com.* Bespoke trips and overland expeditions in trucks.

Viajes Pacífico (Gray Line), *Av Paseo de la República 6010, p 7, T01-610 1911, www.graylineperu.com.* Tours throughout Peru and South America.

Viracocha, *Av Vasco Núñez de Balboa 191, Miraflores, T01-445 3986, peruviantours@vira cocha.com.pe. Mon-Fri 0900-1800, Sat 0900-1300.* Very helpful, especially for flights, adventure, cultural, mystical and birdwatching tours.

Open-top bus tours Mirabús (*Diagonal Oscar Benavides, block 3, T01-242 6699, www. mirabusperu.com, daily 0900-1900*), runs many tours of the city and Callao (from US$3.50 to US$30) – eg Lima half day by day, Lima by night, Costa Verde, Callao, Gold Museum, Miraflores, Pachacámac with Paso horses display and dance show, Caral. Similar services concentrating on the city are offered by **Turibus**, from Larcomar, *T01-230 0909, www.turibusperu.com.*

Private guides The MITINCI (Ministry of Industry Tourism, Integration and International Business) certifies guides and can provide a list. Most are members of **AGOTUR** (Asociación de Guías Oficiales de Turismo) (Av La Paz 678, Miraflores, for correspondence only), www.agotur.com). Book in advance. Most guides speak a foreign language.

Air

For details of flights see under destinations. A list of airlines is found in Getting around, page 711.

Jorge Chávez Airport (flight information T01-517 3500, www.lap.com.pe) is 16 km from the centre of Lima in Callao. It has all the facilities one would expect of an international airport. The **airport information desk** is by international Arrivals. **iPerú tourist information** desks at international arrivals, domestic departures and on the mezzanine (24 hrs). The airport has car hire offices, public telephones, **Global Net** and other ATMs, *casas de cambio* and a bank (note that exchange rates are substantially poorer than outside, **Forex** exchange kiosk with fair rates in **Outlet Shopping Centre**, left of the airport as you step out, Mon-Sat 1100-1900, do not take any luggage with you). Internet facilities are more expensive than in the city, but there is Wi-Fi at departure areas and all gates (10 mins free). Mobile phones can be hired in and outside international Arrivals. Smart shops, restaurants and cafés are plentiful. Purchase airline tickets at the airport, not across from it, were fake airline agents are located.

Transport from the airport *Remise* taxis are expensive (compare rates) and have desks outside both international and domestic Arrivals: **Taxi Green** (T01-484 4001, www.taxigreen.com.pe); **Mitsu** (T01-261 7788, www.mitsoo.net); and **CMV** (T01-219 0266). As a rough guide, these companies charge US$20-30 to the centre, US$22-42 to Miraflores and San Isidro, a bit more to Barranco. In the same place is the desk of

> **Tip…**
> Do not go to the airport's car park exit to find a taxi without an airport permit outside the perimeter. Although these are cheaper, they are not safe even by day, far less so at night.

Peruvian Shuttle (T01-373 5049, www. peruvian-shuttle.com), which runs private, shared and group transfers to the city: from US$6 pp shared, US$23-40 private. If you do not opt for one of these companies, taxi drivers await passengers in the entrance hall. Their fares vary little from the transport companies, although they will charge more at night.

Travelling by bus to/from the airport is not recommended, especially with luggage. Certainly, do not take the cheapest, stopping buses to the centre along Av Faucett as they are frequently robbed. If you must travel by public transport, avoid rush hour and travelling at night and pay more for a non-stop service. Combis to the centre (Av Abancay), lines '9',' C' or Roma 1', charge US$0.60,. Buses to Miraflores, line 'S' ('La S') or '18' and can be caught outside the airport on Av Faucett, US$0.85. Note that luggage is not allowed on public buses except very late at night or early in the morning.

Bus
Local Bus routes are shared by buses, combis (mid-size) and *colectivos* (mini-vans or cars). None is particularly safe; it is better to take a taxi (see below for recommendations). *Colectivos* run 24 hrs, although less frequently 0100-0600; they are quicker than buses and stop wherever requested. Buses and combis charge about US$0.40-0.45, *colectivos* a little more. On public holidays, Sun and from 2400 to 0500 every night, a small charge is added to the fare.

The **Metropolitano** (T01-203 9000, www.metropolitano.com.pe) is a system of articulated buses running on dedicated lanes north–south across the city from Naranjal in Comas to Estación Central (in front of the **Sheraton** hotel; estimated journey time 32 mins) and then south along the Vía Expresa/Paseo de la República to Matellini in Chorrillos (estimated journey time 32 mins); there are purpose-built stations along the route. The **Metropolitano** tends to be very crowded and is of limited use to visitors,

Tip...
In the weeks either side of 28/29 July (Independence), and of the Christmas/New Year holiday, it is practically impossible to get bus tickets out of Lima, unless you book in advance. Bus prices double at these times.

but can be handy for reaching Miraflores (use stations between Angamos and 28 de Julio) and Barranco (Bulevar is 170 m from the Plaza). There are two branches through downtown Lima, either via Av Alfonso Ugarte and Plaza 2 de Mayo, or via Jr Lampa and Av Emancipación. Fares are paid using a prepaid and rechargeable card (minimum S/5, US$1.45), available from every station; each journey costs S/2.50 (US$0.70). Services run Mon-Sat 0500-2300 with shorter hours on Sun and on some sections. There are express services Mon-Fri 0600-0900 and 1635-2115 between certain stations.

Long distance There are many different bus companies, but the larger ones are better organized, leave on time and do not wait until the bus is full, many are open 0700-about 2200. Leaving or arriving in Lima by bus in the rush hour can add an extra hour or more to the journey. All bus companies have their own offices and terminals in the centre of the city, many around Carlos Zavala, but this is not a safe area. Many north-bound buses also have an office and stop at the Terminal Plaza Norte (http://granterminalterrestre.com, Metropolitano Tomás Valle), not far from the airport, which is handy for those who need to make a quick bus connection after landing in Lima. Many south-bound buses are at the Terminal Terrestre Lima Sur, at Km 11-12 on the Panamericana Sur by Puente Atocongo (Metro Atocongo).

Cruz del Sur (T01-311 5050, www.cruzdel sur.com.pe) has its main terminal at Av Javier Prado 1109, La Victoria, with *Cruzero* and *Cruzero Suite* services (luxury buses) and *Imperial* service (quite comfortable buses and periodic stops for food and bathroom breaks, a reasonable option with a quality company) to most parts of Peru. Another terminal is at Jr Quilca 531, Lima centre, for *Imperial* services to Arequipa, Ayacucho, Chiclayo, Cuzco, Huancayo, Huaraz, and Trujillo. There are sales offices throughout the city, including at Terminal Plaza Norte.

Ormeño (www.grupo-ormeno.com.pe) and its affiliated bus companies depart from and arrive at Av Javier Prado Este 1057, Santa Catalina, T01-472 1710, but the terminal at Av Carlos Zavala 177, Lima centre, T01-427 5679, is the best place to get information and buy any Ormeño ticket. **Ormeño** offers *Royal Class* and *Business Class* service to certain destinations. These buses are very comfortable with bathrooms and hostess, etc.

Cial, República de Panamá 2460, T01-207 6900 ext 119, and Paseo de la República 646, T01-207 6900 ext 170, has national coverage.

Flores (T01-332 1212, www.floreshnos.pe) has departures to many parts of the country, especially the south from terminals at Av Paseo de le República 683, Av Paseo de le República 627 and Jr Montevideo 523. Some of its services are good quality.

Other companies include:

Cavassa, Raimondi 129, Lima centre, T01-431 3200, www.turismocavassa.com.pe. Also at Terminal Plaza Norte. Services to **Huaraz**.

Cromotex, Av Nicolás Arriola 898, Santa Catalina; Av Paseo de La República 659,

T01-424 7575, www.cromotex.com.pe. To **Cuzco** and **Arequipa**.

Ittsa, Paseo de la República 809, T01-423 5232, www.ittsabus.com. Also at Terminal Plaza Norte. Good service to the north, **Chiclayo**, **Piura**, **Tumbes**.

Julio César, José Gálvez 562, La Victoria, T01-424 8060, www.transportesjuliocesar. com.pe. Also at Terminal Plaza Norte. Good service to **Huaraz**; recommended to arrive in Huaraz and then use local transport to points beyond.

Línea, Paseo de la República 941-959, Lima centre, T01-424 0836, www.transporteslinea. com.pe. Also at Terminal Plaza Norte (T01-533 0739). Among the best services to destinations in the north.

Móvil, Av Paseo de La República 749, Lima centre (near the national stadium); Av Alfredo Mendiola 3883, Los Olivos, and Terminal Terrestre Lima Sur, T01-716 8000, www. moviltours.com.pe. To **Huaraz** and **Chiclayo** by *bus cama*, and **Chachapoyas**.

Oltursa, Aramburú 1160, San Isidro, T01-708 5000, www.oltursa.pe. A reputable company offering top-end services to **Nazca**, **Arequipa** and destinations in **northern Peru**, mainly at night.

Soyuz, Av México 333, T01-205 2370. To **Ica** every 7 mins, well organized. As PerúBus, www.perubus.com.pe, the same company runs north to **Huacho** and **Barranca**.

Tepsa, Javier Prado Este 1091, La Victoria; Av Gerardo Unger 6917, T01-617 9000, www. tepsa.com.pe. Also at Terminal Plaza Norte (T01-533 1524). Services to the north as far as **Tumbes** and the south to **Tacna**.

Transportes Chanchamayo, Av Nicolás Arriola 535, La Victoria, T01-265 6850, www. transporteschanchamayo.com. To **Tarma**, **San Ramón** and **La Merced**.

Transportes León de Huánuco, Av 28 de Julio 1520, La Victoria, T01-424 3893. Daily to **Huánuco**, **Tingo María**, **La Merced** and **Pucallpa**.

International Ormeño (see above) to **Guayaquil** (29 hrs with a change of bus at the border, US$56), **Quito** (38 hrs, US$75), **Cali** (56 hrs, US$131), **Bogotá** (70 hrs, US$141), **Caracas** (100 hrs, US$150), **Santiago** (54 hrs, US$102), **Mendoza** (78 hrs, US$159), **Buenos Aires** (90 hrs, US$148), **São Paulo** (90 hrs); a maximum of 20 kg is allowed pp. **Cruz del Sur** to **Guayaquil** (3 a week, US$85), **Buenos Aires** (US$201) and **Santiago** (US$130). **El Rápido** (Abtao 1279, La Victoria, T01-432 6380, www.elrapidoint.com.ar) to **Buenos Aires** Mon, Wed, Fri; connections in Mendoza to other cities in Argentina and Uruguay.

Car hire

Most companies have an office at the airport, where you can arrange everything and pick up and leave the car. It is recommended to test drive before signing the contract as quality varies. It can be much cheaper to rent a car in a town in the Sierra for a few days than to drive from Lima; also companies don't have a collection service. Cars can be hired from: **Paz Rent A Car**, Av Diez Canseco 319, of 15, Miraflores, T01-446 4395, T99-993 9853. **Budget**, T01-204 4400, www.budgetperu.com. Prices range from US$35 to US$85 depending on type of car. Make sure that your car is in a locked garage at night.

Metro

The 1st line of the **Tren Eléctrico** (www.linea uno.pe) runs from Villa El Salvador in the southeast of the city to Bayóvar in the northeast, daily 0600-2230. Each journey costs S/.1.50 (US$0.55); pay by swipe card S/.5 (US$1.75). Metro stations Miguel Grau, El Ángel and Presbitero Maestro lie on the eastern edge of the downtown area. Construction work has started on the next section.

Taxi

Taxis do not use meters although some have rate sheets (eg **Satelital**, T01-355 5555, http://3555555satelital.com). Agree the price of the journey beforehand and insist on being taken to the destination of your choice. At night, on Sun and holidays expect a surcharge of 35-50%. The following are taxi fares for some of the more common routes, give or take a sol. From downtown Lima to: Parque Kennedy (Miraflores), US$4; Museo de la Nación, US$3.75; San Isidro, US$3.75; Barranco, US$4.75. From Miraflores (Parque Kennedy) to: Museo de la Nación, US$2.75; Archaeology Museum, US$3.75; Barranco, US$4.80. By law, all taxis must have the vehicle's registration number painted on the side. They are often white or yellow, but can come in any colour, size or make. Licensed and phone taxis are safest, but if hailing a taxi on the street, local advice is to look for an older driver rather than a youngster.

There are several reliable phone taxi companies, which can be called for immediate service, or booked in advance; prices are 2-3 times more than ordinary taxis: to the airport, US$15; to suburbs, US$10. Try **Taxi Real**, T01-215 1414, www.taxireal.com; **Taxi Seguro**, T01-536 6956, www.taxiseguro lima.com; **Taxi Tata**, T01-274 5151, www.tata-taxis.com. If hiring a taxi by the hour, agree on price beforehand, US$7-9. **Note** Drivers don't expect tips; give them small change from the fare.

Train

Details of the service on the Central Railway to Huancayo are given on page 287.

Huaraz &
the cordilleras

★ Apart from the range running along the Chile-
Argentina border, the highest mountains in South
America lie along the Cordillera Blanca. This is an area
of jewelled lakes and snowy mountain peaks attracting
mountaineers and hikers in their thousands. Huaraz is the
natural place to head for: it has the best infrastructure
and the mountains, lakes and trails are within easy reach.
From town you can see more than 23 peaks over 5000 m,
of which the most notable is Huascarán (6768 m), the
highest mountain in Peru. Although the snowline is
receding, the Cordillera Blanca still contains the largest
concentration of glaciers found in the world's tropical
zone and the turquoise-coloured lakes, which form in the
terminal moraines, are the jewels of the Andes. Here also
is one of Peru's most important pre-Inca sites, at Chavín
de Huantar. Large multinational mining projects have
brought some prosperity as well as social change and
ecological damage to the area.

Essential Huaraz and the cordilleras

Finding your feet

Established in July 1975, Parque Nacional Huascarán includes the entire Cordillera Blanca above 4000 m, with an area of 3400 sq km. It is a UNESCO World Biosphere Reserve and part of the World Heritage Trust. Park fees are 10 soles (US$3) for one day and 20 soles (US$6) for three consecutive days (no overnight stays). Permits for 21 days (for trekking, camping and climbing) cost 65 soles (US$20). All permits must be bought at the national park office in Huaraz (Jr Federico Sal y Rosas 555, by Plazuela Belén, T043-422086, pnhuascaran@sernanp.gob.pe, Monday-Friday 0830-1300, 1430-1700), or at rangers posts at Llanganuco and Huascarán (for the Llanganuco–Santa Cruz trek), or at Collón for Quebrada Ishinca.

Warning...

Huaraz has its share of crime, especially since the arrival of mining and during the high tourist season. Women should not go to surrounding districts and sites alone. Muggings have taken place on the way to Laguna Churup, on the way to the Mirador Rataquenua, and also between the Monterrey thermal baths and Wilcawain ruins; do not walk this way.

Local guides are mandatory everywhere in the park except designated 'Recreation Zones' accessible by car. Tourists must hire a licensed tour operator for all activities and those operators may only employ licensed guides, cooks, arrieros and porters. Fees and regulations change frequently; always confirm details in Huaraz.

Getting around

The best way to explore the cordilleras is, of course, on foot (see Trekking and climbing in the cordilleras, page 82). However, there are also numerous buses and minivans daily between Huaraz and Caraz, and more limited services to settlements on the eastern side of the Cordillera Blanca. The bus journeys through the Cahuish tunnel (4516 m), Punta Olímpica tunnel (4700 m), and over Portachuelo de Llanganuco Pass (4767 m), are all spectacular.

When to go

The months of May to September are the dry season and best for trekking, although conditions vary from year to year. From November to April the weather is usually wet, views may be restricted by cloud, and paths are likely to be muddy.

Towards Huaraz and the cordilleras

high-altitude pass and plateau

North from Lima the Pan-American Highway parallels the coast and a series of roads branch off east for the climb up to Huaraz in the Callejón de Huaylas, gateway to Parque Nacional Huascarán. Probably the easiest route to Huaraz is the paved road that branches off the highway north of Pativilca, 203 km from Lima. The road climbs increasingly steeply to the chilly pass at 4080 m (Km 120). Shortly after, Laguna Conococha comes into view, where the Río Santa rises. A road branches off from Conococha to Chiquián (see page 94) and the Cordilleras Huayhuash and Raura to the southeast. After crossing a high plateau the main road descends gradually for 47 km until Catac, where another road branches east to Chavín and on to the Callejón de Conchucos on the eastern side of the Cordillera Blanca. Huaraz is 36 km further on. From Huaraz the road continues north between the towering Cordillera Negra, snowless and rising to 4600 m, and the snow-covered Cordillera Blanca.

The alternative routes to the Callejón de Huaylas are via the Callán pass from Casma to Huaraz (fully paved, see page 98), and from Chimbote to Caraz via the Cañón del Pato (partly paved, rough and spectacular; page 98).

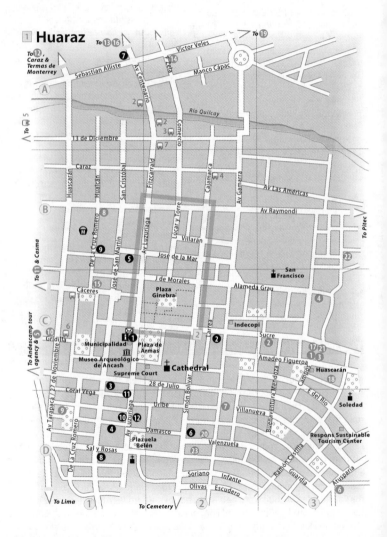

Huaraz

Located 420 km from Lima, Huaraz is the capital of Ancash department and the main town in the Cordillera Blanca, with a population of 115,000. It is expanding rapidly as a major tourist centre but is also a busy commercial hub, especially on market days. At 3091 m, it is a prime destination for hikers and a mecca for international climbers.

N

200 metres
200 yards

Where to stay
1 Albergue Churup *C3*
2 Alojamiento El Jacal *C3*
3 Alojamiento Soledad *C3*
4 Alpes Huaraz *C3*
5 Andescamp Hostel *C1*
6 Andino Club *D3*
7 Angeles Inn *D2*
8 Backpackers *B1*
9 Benkawasi *D1*
10 Casa Jaimes *C1*
11 Edward's Inn *B1*
12 El Patio *A1*
13 Hatun Wasi *A1*
14 Hostal Colomba *A2*
15 Hostal Quintana *C1*
16 Jo's Place *A1*
17 La Cabaña *C3*
18 La Casa de Zarela *C3*
19 Lodging House Ezama *A3*
20 Res NG *D2*
21 Res Sucre *C3*
22 San Sebastián *B3*
23 Suiza Peruana *D2*

Restaurants
1 Bistro de los Andes *C2*
2 Cafetería y Juguería *C2*
3 California Café *C1*
4 Chifa Jim Hua *D1*
5 Fuente de Salud *B1*
6 Huaraz Querido *D2*
7 Mi Comedia *A1*
8 Mi Comedia Gelatería *D1*
9 Panadería La Alameda *B1*
10 Panadería Salazar *D1*
11 Pizza Bruno *D1*
12 Sala de Estar *D1*

Transport
1 Sandoval/Chavín Express *C1*
2 Combis to Caraz *A1, A2*
3 Combis to Wilcawain *A2*
4 Julio César *B2*
5 Móvil Tours *A1*
6 Terminal de Transportistas Zona Sur *C1*
7 Trans Huandoy *A2*

Sights

Huaraz's setting, at the foot of the Cordillera Blanca, is spectacular. The town was almost completely destroyed in the earthquake of May 1970. The Plaza de Armas has since been rebuilt, but the new **Cathedral** is still under construction. **Museo Arqueológico de Ancash** ⓘ *Ministerio de Cultura, Plaza de Armas, Mon-Sat 0900-1700, Sun 0900-1400*, contains stone monoliths and *huacos* from the Recuay culture, well labelled. The main thoroughfare, Avenida Luzuriaga, is bursting at the seams with travel agencies, climbing equipment hire shops, restaurants, cafés and bars. A good district for those seeking peace and quiet is La Soledad, six blocks uphill from the Plaza de Armas on Avenida Sucre. Here, along Sucre and Jr Amadeo Figueroa, are many hotels and rooms for rent in private homes. The **Sala de Cultura SUNARP** ⓘ *Av Centenario 530, Independencia, T043-421301, Mon-Fri 1700-2000, Sat 0900-1300, free*, often has interesting art and photography exhibitions by local artists.

Around Huaraz

About 8 km to the northeast is **Willkawain** ⓘ *Tue-Fri 0830-1600, Sat-Sun 0900-1330, US$1.75, take a combi from 13 de Diciembre and Jr Cajamarca, US$0.50, 20 min, direct to Willkawain*. The ruins (AD 700-1100, Huari Empire) consist of one large three-storey structure with intact stone roof slabs and several small structures. About 500 m past Willkawain is Ichicwillkawain with several similar but smaller structures. A well-signed trail climbs from Wilkawain

➡ **Huaraz maps**
1 Huaraz, page 74
2 Huaraz centre, page 77

to Laguna Ahuac (Aguak Cocha, 4580 m); it's a demanding acclimatization hike (12 km return), with no services along the way.

North of Huaraz, 6 km along the road to Caraz at 2780 m, are the **Termas de Monterrey** ① *lower pool, US$0.85; upper pool (closed Mon for cleaning), US$1.35; tubs US$1.35 per person for 20 mins.* City buses run along Avenida Luzuriaga to Monterrey until 1900, US$0.22, taxi US$2-3. There are two pools here (the upper one is nicer), plus individual and family tubs, restaurants and hotels. Monterrey gets crowded at weekends and holidays.

Listings Huaraz *maps pages 74 and 77.*

Tourist information

The national park office (see Essential box, page 73) is principally administrative, with no information for visitors.

Indecopi
Av Gamarra 671, T043-423899, www.indecopi.gob.pe.
Government consumer protection office. Very effective but not always quick. Spanish only.

iPerú
Pasaje Atusparia, of 1, Plaza de Armas, T043-428812, iperuhuaraz@promperu.gob.pe. Mon-Sat 0900-1800, Sun 0900-1300.
Also at Jr San Martín cuadra 6 s/n, daily 0800-1100, and at Anta airport when flights arrive.

Policía de Turismo
Av Luzuriaga on Plaza de Armas, around the corner from iPerú, T043-421351, divtueco_huaraz@yahoo.com. Mon-Sat 0730-2100.
The place to report crimes and resolve issues with tour operators, hotels, etc. All female officers, limited English spoken.

Where to stay

Hotels fill up rapidly in high season (May-Sep), especially during public holidays and special events when prices rise (beware overcharging). Touts meet buses and aggressively 'suggest' places to stay. Do not be put off your choice of lodging; phone ahead to confirm.

$$$$-$$$ Andino Club
Pedro Cochachín 357, some way southeast of the centre (take a taxi after dark), T043-421662, www.hotelandino.com.
Swiss-run hotel with very high standards, excellent restaurant, variety of rooms including panoramic views, balcony, fireplace, jacuzzi and sauna.

$$$ El Patio
Av Monterrey, 250 m downhill from the Monterrey baths, T043-424965, www.elpatio.com.pe.
Very colonial-style with lovely gardens, comfortable rooms, singles, doubles and triples, some with balconies, also 4 lodges with fireplaces. Meals on request, bar.

$$$ Hostal Colomba
Francisco de Zela 210, just off Centenario across the river, T043-421501, www.huarazhotel.com.
Lovely old hacienda, family-run, garden with playground and sports, safe parking, gym and well-equipped rooms sleeping 1-6, comfortable beds, restaurant.

$$$ The Lazy Dog Inn
30 mins' drive from Huaraz (US$10 by taxi), close to the boundary of Huascarán National Park, 3.1 km past the town of Marian, close to the Quebrada Cojup, T943-789330, www.thelazydoginn.com.
Eco-tourism lodge actively involved in community projects (see www.andeanalliance.org), water recycling systems and composting toilets. Beautifully designed in warm colours, great location gives access to several mountain valleys.

Organizes horse riding and hiking trips.
Excellent home-cooked breakfast and dinner
included. Canadian owned, English spoken.
Recommended.

Huaraz centre

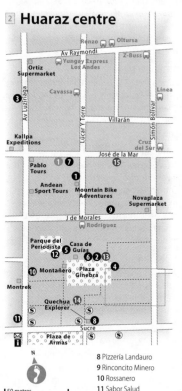

50 metres

50 yards

Where to stay 🛏
1 Oscar's Hostal

Restaurants 🍴
1 Café Andino &
   Familia Meza Lodging
2 Chilli Heaven
3 Créperie Patrick
4 El Horno Pizzería Grill
5 Encuentro
6 Maialino
7 Pizza B&B
8 Pizzería Landauro
9 Rinconcito Minero
10 Rossanero
11 Sabor Salud
12 Trivio

Bars & clubs 🍸
13 '13 Buhos'
14 Amadeus
15 Taberna Tambo

➡ **Huaraz maps**
1 Huaraz,
   page 74
2 **Huaraz centre,**
   page 77

$$$-$$ San Sebastián
Jr Italia 1124, T043-426960,
www.sansebastianhuaraz.com.
Elegant, modern hotel, comfortable beds with
duvets, parking available, helpful, good views.

$$ Suiza Peruana
Jr Federico Sal y Rosas 843, T043-425263,
www.suizaperuana.com.
Comfortable rooms, nice design, great views,
elevator, garage, 24-hr service.

$$-$ Albergue Churup
Jr Amadeo Figueroa 1257, T043-424200,
www.churup.com.
13 rooms with private bath or 2 dorms with
shared bath, hot water, fire in sitting room on
4th floor, cafetería, use of kitchen 1800-2200,
lots of information, laundry, book exchange,
English spoken, Spanish classes, adventure
travel tours, extremely helpful. Airport
transfers and free pick-up from bus.

$$-$ Edward's Inn
Bolognesi 121, T043-422692.
With or without bath, nice garden, laundry,
breakfast extra, insist on proper rates in low
season, popular. Edward speaks English and
has 30 years' experience trekking, climbing
and guiding in the area. He also rents gear.

$$-$ Hatun Wasi
Jr Daniel Villayzán 268, T043-425055.
Family-run hotel next to **Jo's Place**.
Spacious rooms, with hot water, pleasant
roof terrace, ideal for breakfasts, with
great views of the Cordillera.

$$-$ La Casa de Zarela
J Arguedas 1263, T043-421694,
www.lacasadezarela.hostel.com.
Hot water, use of kitchen, laundry facilities,
popular with climbers and trekkers, owner
Zarela who speaks English organizes groups
and is very knowledgeable.

$$-$ Residencial NG
Pasaje Valenzuela 837, T043-421831,
www.residencialng.com.
Breakfast, hot water, good value, helpful,
has restaurant.

$ Alojamiento El Jacal
Jr Sucre 1044, T043-424612.
With or without shower, hot water, helpful family, garden, laundry facilities.

$ Alojamiento Soledad
Jr Amadeo Figueroa 1267, T043-421196, www.lodgingsoledad.com.
Simple breakfast, private and shared bath, abundant hot water, use of kitchen, family home and atmosphere, trekking information and tours.

$ Alpes Huaraz
Jr Ladislao Meza 112, up a cobblestone street past the San Francisco church, T043-428896, www.hostalalpeshuaraz.com.
Rooms with private bath, hot water, fireplace, kitchen, terrace with views, garden, tour agency, friendly atmosphere, good value.

$ Andescamp Hostel
Jr Huáscar 615, T043-423842, www.andescamphostel.com.
Hostel with dorms and private rooms, some with bath, and snack bar. Tour agency, see What to do, page 81.

$ Angeles Inn
Av Gamarra 815, T043-422205, solandperu@yahoo.com.
No sign, look for **Sol Andino** travel agency in same building (www.solandino.com), laundry facilities, garden, hot water, owners Max and Saul Angeles are official guides, helpful with trekking and climbing, rent equipment.

$ Backpackers
Av Raimondi 510, T043-421773.
Breakfast not included. Dorms or private room with bathroom. Spacious, hot showers, good views, energetic staff, a real bargain, but heavy traffic outside.

$ Benkawasi
Parque Santa Rosa 928, 10 mins from centre, T043-423150, http://huarazbenkawasi.com.
Doubles, also rooms for 3, 4 and dorm, hot water, breakfast US$5, laundry, games room, pick-up from bus station. Owner Benjamín

Morales also has a lodge at Playa Tortugas near Casma (arranges downhill biking from Huaraz).

$ Casa Jaimes
Alberto Gridilla 267, T043-422281, 2 blocks from the main plaza, www.casajaimes.com.
Dormitory with hot showers, laundry facilities, has maps and books of the region. Noisy but otherwise good.

$ Familia Meza
Lúcar y Torre 538, behind Café Andino (enquire here, see Restaurants, below), T043-421203.
Shared bath, hot water, laundry facilities, popular with trekkers, mountaineers and bikers.

$ Hostal Quintana
Mcal Cáceres 411, T043-426060, www.hostal-quintana.com.
English, French, Italian and Spanish spoken, mountain gear rental, 2 of the owner's sons are certified guides and can arrange itineraries, laundry facilities, café popular with trekkers.

$ Jo's Place
Jr Daniel Villayzan 276, T043-425505.
Safe, hot water at night, nice mountain views, garden, terrace, English owner, warm atmosphere, popular.

$ La Cabaña
Jr Sucre 1224, T043-423428.
Shared and double rooms, hot showers, laundry, popular, safe for parking, bikes and luggage, English and French spoken, good value.

$ Lodging House Ezama
Mariano Melgar 623, Independencia, T043-423490, 15 mins' walk from Plaza de Armas (US$0.50 by taxi).
Light, spacious rooms, hot water, safe, helpful.

$ Oscar's Hostal
La Mar 624, T043-422720, cvmonical@hotmail.com.
Hot water, cheap breakfast next door, good beds, cheaper in low season, helpful.

$ Residencial Sucre
Sucre 1240, T043-422264,
filibertor@terra.com.pe.
Private house, kitchen, laundry facilities, hot water, English, German and French spoken, mountaineering guide, Filiberto Rurush, can be contacted here.

Restaurants

$$$ Créperie Patrick
Luzuriaga 422.
Excellent crêpes, fish, quiche, spaghetti and good wine.

$$$ Pizza Bruno
Luzuriaga 834. Open from 1600-2300.
Best pizza, excellent crêpes and pastries, good service, French owner Bruno Reviron also has a 4WD with driver for hire.

$$$-$$ Mi Comedia
Av Centenario 351, T043-587954.
Open 1700-2300.
Wood-oven pizzas, rustic European style, very good service.

$$$-$$ Trivio
Parque del Periodista. Lunch and dinner.
Creative food, good coffee, nice view.

$$ Bistro de los Andes
Plaza de Armas 2nd floor, T043-426249.
Great food, owner speaks English, French and German. Plaza branch has a nice view of the plaza. Wide range of dishes and breakfasts.

$$ Chilli Heaven
Parque Ginebra, T043-396085.
Run by a British biker, specializing in spicy food (Mexican, Indian, Thai), book exchange.

$$ El Horno Pizzería Grill
Parque Ginebra, T043-424617.
Good atmosphere, fine grilled meats and nice location, very popular.

$$ Fuente de Salud
J de la Mar 562.
Vegetarian, also meat and pasta dishes, serves good soups and breakfast.

$$ Huaraz Querido
Bolívar 981. Lunch only.
Very popular place for great ceviche and other fish dishes.

$$ Maialino
Parque Ginebra, T940-241660.
Popular for Italian and local dishes, cosy, welcoming, set meal for lunch and dinner costs US$2.50.

$$ Pizza B&B
La Mar 674, beside laundry of same name.
Excellent traditional sauces for pizza and pasta, and desserts.

$$ Pizzería Landauro
Sucre, on corner of Plaza de Armas.
Closed 1200-1800 and Sun.
Very good for pizzas, Italian dishes, sandwiches, breakfasts, nice atmosphere.

$$ Rinconcito Minero
J de Morales 757.
Breakfast, lunch, vegetarian options, coffee and snacks.

$$ Sabor Salud
Luzuriaga 672, upstairs.
Pizzeria with vegetarian and Italian food.

$$-$ Chifa Jim Hua
Teófilo de Castillo 556. Mon-Sat 0900-1500, 1800-2400, Sun 1800-2200.
Large, tasty portions, economical *menú*.

$$-$ Encuentro
Parque del Periodista and Julian de Morales 650, www.restaurantencuentro.com.
Opens 0700.
Breakfast, lunch and dinners, very busy, good.

$$-$ Sala de Estar
Luzuriaga 923, upstairs. Tue-Sun 1700-2300.
Pasta dishes, home-made desserts, fruit juices and drinks. Good creative meals.

Cafés

Café Andino
Lúcar y Torre 538, 3rd floor, T043-421203, www.cafeandino.com.

Peruvian/American-owned café-restaurant-bar with book exchange and extensive lending library in many languages. A great place to relax and meet other travellers, warmly recommended. Owner Chris Benway also runs **La Cima Logistics**, www. lacimalogistics.com, for custom outfitting in Cordilleras Blanca and Huayhuash.

Cafetería y Juguería
Sucre 806.
Cheap café just above the Plaza. Serves excellent yogurt and honey drinks, among other treats.

California Café
28 de Julio 562, T043-428354, http://huaylas. com/californiacafe/california.htm.
Excellent breakfast, great coffee and chocolate cake, book exchange. Californian owner is a good source of information on trekking in the Cordillera Huayhuash and security issues.

Mi Comedia Gelatería
Jr San Martin 1213.
"The best home-made *gelato* this side of Milan."

Panadería La Alameda
Juan de La Cruz Romero 523 near market.
Excellent bread and sweets.

Panadería Salazar
Av Luzuriaga 944.
Good bakery and café, cheap, pleasant atmosphere, good for a snack.

Rossanero
Luzuriaga entre Sucre y J de Morales, 2nd floor.
'Sofa-cafe' with extensive menu, ice cream, reasonable prices.

Bars and clubs

13 Buhos Bar
Parque Ginebra.
Afternoon, evening and nightspot, very popular, owner makes his own craft beer. Good music, games, nice ambience.

Amadeus
Parque Ginebra.
Bar-disco.

Taberna Tambo
José de la Mar 776. Open 1000-1600, 2000-early hours.
Folk music daily, disco, full on, non-stop dance mecca. Very popular with both locals and gringos.

Festivals

3 May Patron saints' day, **El Señor de la Soledad**, celebrations last a week.
Jun **Semana del Andinismo**, international climbing week.
Jun **San Juan** and **San Pedro** are celebrated throughout the region during the last week of Jun.
Aug **Inkafest**, mountain film festival, dates change each year.

Shopping

Clothing
For local sweaters, hats, gloves and wall hangings at good value, try Pasaje Mcal Cáceres, off Luzuriaga; the stalls off Luzuriaga between Morales and Sucre; Bolívar cuadra 6, and elsewhere. **Last Minute Gifts** (Lucar Y Torre 530, 2nd floor) sells hats, clothing, souvenirs and jewellery.

Markets
The central market offers various canned and dry goods, as well as fresh fruit and vegetables. Beware pickpockets in this area. There are also several supermarkets in town (map, page 77), do not leave valuables in your bags while shopping.

What to do

Try to get a recommendation from someone who has recently returned from a tour or trek. All agencies run conventional tours to Llanganuco (US$12 per person, very long day) and Chavín (8-10 hrs, US$14 per person), entry tickets not included. Many hire equipment.

Horse riding
Posada de Yungar, *Yungar (about 20 km from Huaraz on the Carhuaz road), T043-421267/967-9836.* Swiss-run. Ask for José Flores or Gustavo Soto. US$4.50 per hr on good horses; good 4-hr trip in the Cordillera Negra.
Sr Robinson Ayala Gride, *T043-423813.* Contact him well in advance for half-day trips; enquire at **El Cortijo** restaurant, on Huaraz-Caraz road, Km 6.5. He is a master *paso* rider.

Mountain biking
Mountain Bike Adventures, *Lúcar y Torre 530, T043-424259, www.chakinaniperu.com.* Contact Julio Olaza. US$60 pp for day trip, all inclusive, various routes, excellent standard of equipment. Julio speaks excellent English and also runs a book exchange, sells topo maps and climbing books.

Trekking and climbing
Trekking tours cost US$50-70 pp per day, climbing US$100-140 pp per day. Many companies close in low season.
Active Peru, *Gamarra 699 y Sucre, T043-423339, www.activeperu.com.* Offers classic treks, climbing, plus standard tours to Chavín and Llanganuco, among others, good in all respects, Belgian owner speaks Dutch, German and English.
Alpa-K, *Parque Ginebra 30-B, above Montañero, www.alpa-k.org.* Owner Bertrand offers tours throughout Peru and has a B&B ($) on the premises. French, Spanish and some English spoken.
Andean Footsteps, *Cra Huaraz-Caraz Km 14, Paltay, and Jr José Olaya 103, Huaraz, T943-318820.* British/Peruvian operation (Yvonne Danson and David Maguiña), specializing in treks, climbs and tours with a commitment to using local personnel and resources. Local projects are sponsored.
Andean Kingdom, *Parque Ginebra next to Casa de Guías, T043-425555, www.andeankingdom.com.* Free information, maps, climbing wall, rock and ice climbing, including multi-day courses, treks, equipment rental, English and some Hebrew

spoken, can be very busy. The company has a Refugio de Montaña, **Hatun Machay ($)**, near the excellent rock-climbing site of Hatun Machay in the Cordillera Negra, with kitchen facilities and heating, transport arranged.
Andescamp, *Jr Huáscar 615, T043-423842, or T943-563424, www.andescamphostel.com.* Popular agency and hostel (see Where to stay, page 78), especially with budget travellers. Only qualified guides used for climbing trips. Variety of treks, mountaineering expeditions and courses, rafting, paragliding and other adventure sports.
Cordillera Blanca Adventures, *run by the Mejía Romero family, Los Nogales 108, T043-421934, www.cordillerablanca.org.* Experienced, quality climbing/trekking trips, good guides/equipment.
Explorandes, *Gamarra 835, T043-421960, www.explorandes.com.*
Galaxia Expeditions, *Parque del Periodista, T043-425355, www.galaxia-expeditions.com.* Usual range of tours, climbing, hiking, biking, equipment hire, etc. Go to the office to buy tours direct, do not buy from unscrupulous sub-contractors.
Huascarán, *Jr Pedro Campos 711, Soledad, T043-424504, www.huascaran-peru.com.* Contact Pablo Tinoco Depaz, one of the brothers who run the company. Good 4-day Santa Cruz trip. Good food and equipment, professional service, free loan of waterproofs and *pisco sour* on last evening.
Kallpa, *José de la Mar y Luzuriaga, p 2, T043-427868.* Organizes treks, rents gear, arranges arrieros and mules, very helpful.
Montañero, *Parque Ginebra 30-B, T043-426386, www.trekkingperu.com/i-trekking.htm.* Run by veteran mountain guide Selio Villón. German, French and English spoken.
Monttrek, *Luzuriaga 646, upstairs, T043-421124, monttrek@terra.com.pe.* Good trekking/climbing information, advice and maps, ice and rock climbing courses (at Monterrey), tours to Laguna Churup and the 'spectacular' Luna Llena tour; also hire mountain bikes, run ski instruction and trips, and river rafting. Helpful, conscientious

ON THE ROAD
Trekking and climbing in the cordilleras

The Cordillera Blanca offers popular backpacking and trekking, with a network of trails used by the local people and some less well-defined mountaineers' routes. Most circuits can be hiked in five days. Although the trails are easily followed, they are rugged with high passes, between 4000 m and 5000 m, so backpackers should be fit, acclimatized to the altitude and able to carry all equipment. Essential items are a tent, warm sleeping bag, stove, and protection against wind and rain. The weather is unreliable and you cannot rule out rain and hail storms even in the dry season. Less stamina is required if you hire mules to carry equipment.

Safety The height of the Cordillera Blanca and the Callejón de Huaylas ranges and their location in the tropics create conditions different from the Alps or even the Himalayas. Fierce sun makes the mountain snow porous and glaciers move more rapidly. Deglaciation is rapidly changing the face of the Cordillera. Older maps do not provide a reliable indication of the extent of glaciers and snow fields (according to some studies 15% of the range's glaciers have disappeared since the 1970s), so local experience is important. If the national park rules prohibiting independent treks or climbs have been lifted, move in groups of four or more, reporting to the Casa de Guías (see opposite) or the office of the guide before departing, giving the date at which a search should begin, and leaving your embassy's telephone number, with money for the call. International recommendations are for a 300 m per day maximum altitude gain. Be wary of agencies wanting to sell you trips with very fast ascents (but ask around if this is what you want).

It is imperative that all climbers carry adequate insurance (it cannot be purchased locally). Be well prepared before setting out on a climb. Wait or cancel your trip when the weather is bad. Every year climbers are killed through failing to take weather conditions seriously. Climb only when and where you have sufficient experience.

Rescue services, while better than in the past, may not be up to international standards. In the event of an emergency try calling the Casa de Guías, T043-427545 or 421811; Edson Ramírez at the national park office, T944-627946 or T943-626627; or the Police, T105. Satellite phones can be rented through the Casa de Guías and some agencies, ask around. There is cell-phone coverage in some (but not all) parts of the Cordillera Blanca.

Personal security and responsibility Before heading out on any trekking route, always enquire locally about crime levels. The Cordillera Blanca is generally safe, but muggings are not unknown. On all treks in this area, respect the locals' property,

guides. Next door in the Pizzería is a climbing wall, good maps, videos and slide shows. For new routes/maps contact Porfirio Cacha Macedo, 'Pocho', at Monttrek or at Jr Corongo 307, T043-423930.

Peruvian Andes Adventures, *José Olaya 532, T043-421864, www.peruvianandes.com.* Run by Hisao and Eli Morales, professional, registered mountain and trekking guides. All equipment and services for treks

leave no rubbish behind, do not give sweets or money to children who beg and remember your cooking utensils and tent would be very expensive for a *campesino*, so be sensitive and responsible. Along the most popular routes, campers have complained that campsites are dirty, toilet pits foul and that rubbish is not taken away by groups. Do your share to make things better.

Information Casa de Guías, Plaza Ginebra 28-g in Huaraz, T043-421811. Monday-Saturday 0900-1300, 1600-1800. This is the climbers' and hikers' meeting place. It has a full list of all members of the Asociación de Guías de Montaña del Perú (AGMP) throughout the country and has useful information, books, maps, arrangements for guides, *arrieros*, mules, etc. It also operates as an agency and sells tours. Notice board, postcards and posters for sale. A useful trekking guidebook for the Cordillera Blanca and other regions is *Trekking Peru* by Robert and Daisy Kunstaetter (also see www.trekkingperu.org).

Guides, arrieros and porters The Dirección de Turismo issues qualified guides and *arrieros* (muleteers) with a photo ID. Note down the name and card number in case you should have any complaints. Most guides are hired in Huaraz or, to a lesser extent, in Caraz. Prices apply across the region, with some minor variations in the smaller towns: *arriero*, US$18 per day; donkey or mule, US$8 per day; trekking guides US$40-70 per day (more for foreign guides); climbing guides US$90-200 per day (more for foreign guides), depending on the difficulty of the peak; cooks US$30-40 per day; all subject to change. You are required to provide or pay for food and shelter for all *arrieros*, porters, cooks and guides. Associations of *arrieros*: Humacchuco-Llanganuco (for porters and cooks), T943-786497, victorcautivo@hotmail.com. Pashpa Arrieros, T043-830540/83319. Musho Arrieros, T043-230003/814416. Collon Arrieros (for llama trekking), T043-833417/824146.

of 3-15 days, climbing technical and non-technical peaks, or just day walks. Vegetarians catered for.
Quechua Explorer, *Sucre 705 of 4*, T043-422886, www.quechuaexplorer.com. Hiking, mountaineering, rock and ice climbing, rafting, biking, cultural and ecological tourism, experienced and friendly guides.
Quechuandes, *Av Luzuriaga 522*, T943-562339, www.quechuandes.com. Trekking,

mountaineering, rock climbing, ice climbing, skiing, mountain biking and other adventure sports, guides speak Spanish, Quechua, English and/or French. Animal welfare taken seriously with weight limits of 40 kg per donkey.

Respons Sustainable Tourism Center, *Jr Eulogio del Rio 1364, Soledad, T956-125568, www.respons.org*. Sustainable tourism initiatives, community based, with trekking, homestays, tours, volunteering and other responsible travel ideas.

Guides For details of the Casa de Guías, see page 83.

Aritza Monasterio, *through Casa de Guías*. Speaks English, Spanish and Euskerra.

Augusto Ortega, *Jr San Martín 1004, T043-424888*. The only Peruvian to have climbed Everest.

Christopher Benway, *La Cima Logistics, cafeandino@hotmail.com*. Makes custom arrangements for climbing and trekking trips.

Filiberto Rurush Paucar, *Sucre 1240, T043-422264 (Lodging Casa Sucre)*. Speaks English, Spanish and Quechua.

Genaro Yanac Olivera, *T043-422825*. Speaks good English and some German, also a climbing guide.

Hugo Sifuentes Maguiña, *Siex (Sifuentes Expeditions), Jr Huaylas 139, T043-426529*. Trekking, rock climbing and less adventurous tours.

Koky Castañeda, *T043-427213, or through Skyline Adventures, or Café Andino*. Speaks English and French, UIAGM Alpine certified.

Max, Misael and Saul Angeles, *T043-456891/422205 (Sol Andino agency)*. Speak some English, know Huayhuash well.

Máximo Henostrosa, *T043-426040*. Trekking guide with knowledge of the entire region.

Ted Alexander, Skyline Adventures, *Pasaje Industrial 137, Cascapampa, Huaraz, T043-427097, www.skyline-adventures.com*. US outward bound instructor, very knowledgeable.

Tjen Verheye, *Jr Carlos Valenzuela 911, T043-422569*. Belgian and speaks Dutch, French, German and reasonable English,

runs trekking and conventional tours and is knowledgeable about the Chavín culture.

Camping gear The following agencies are recommended for hiring gear: **Andean Kingdom**, **Galaxia Expeditions**, **Monttrek**, **Kallpa** and **Montañero**. Also **Skyline**, **Andean Sport Tours** (Luzuriaga 571, T043-421612), and **MountClimb** (Jr Mcal Cáceres 421, T043-426060, mountclimb@yahoo.com). Casa de Guías rents equipment and sells dried food. Check all camping and climbing equipment very carefully before taking it. Quality varies and some items may not be available, so it's best to bring your own. All prices are standard, but not cheap, throughout town. All require payment in advance, passport or air ticket as deposit and rarely give any money back if you return gear early. Many trekking agencies sell screw-on camping gas cartridges. White gas (*bencina*) is available from *ferreterías* on Raymondi below Luzuriaga and by Parque Ginebra.

Tour operators

Chavín Tours, *José de la Mar, T043-421578, www.chavintours.com.pe*. All local tours, long-standing agency with its head office in Lima.

Pablo Tours, *Luzuriaga 501, T043-421145, www.pablotours.com*. For all local tours, also with many years of operation.

Transport

Air LC Peru flies daily to/from **Lima**, 1 hr.

Bus Many of the companies have their offices along Av Raymondi and on Jr Lúcar y Torre. Some recommended companies are: **Cavassa**, Jr Lúcar y Torre 446, T043-425767; **Rodríguez**, J de Morales 650, T043-429253; **Cruz del Sur**, Bolívar Mz C Lote 12, T043-728726; **Empresa 14**, Fitzcarrald 216, T043-421282, terminal at Bolívar 407; **Julio César**, Prol Cajamarca s/n, cuadra 1, T043-396443; **Móvil**, Av Confraternidad Internacional Oeste 451, T043-422555; **Oltursa**, Av Raymondi 825, T043-423717; **Z-Buss**, Av Raymondi, T043-428327.

Long distance To **Lima**, 7-8 hrs, US$17-30 (**Móvil** prices), large selection of ordinary service and luxury coaches throughout the day. To **Casma** via the Callán pass and Pariacoto (150 km, fully paved), 4 hrs, US$9, best to travel by day and sit on the left for views. **Transportes Huandoy**, Fitzcarrald 261, T043-427507 (terminal at Caraz 820), daily at 0800, 1000 and 1300. **Yungay Express**, Raymondi 930, T043-424377, 3 a day; they continue to Chimbote, 185 km. To Chimbote, Yungay Express, daily, US$12, 7 hrs via Caraz and the Cañon del Pato (sit on the right for the most exciting views). **Línea** (Simón Bolívar 450, T043-726666), **Móvil** and **Empresa 14** (see above) go via Pativilca (160 km, 4 hrs; total journey, 7 hrs); most continue to **Trujillo**, 8-9 hrs at night, US$17-30.

Within the Cordillera Blanca Several buses and frequent minivans run daily, 0500-2000, between Huaraz and **Caraz**, 1¼ hrs, US$2, from the parking area by the bridge on Fitzcarrald, no luggage racks, you might have to pay an extra seat for your bag. To **Chavín**, 110 km, 2 hrs (sit on left side for best views), US$6: **Sandoval/Chavín Express**, Mcal Cáceres 338, 3 a day. Also **Trans Río Mosna**, Mcal Cáceres 265, T043-426632, 3 a day; buses go on to **Huari**, 4 hrs, US$7.50.

To **Chacas**, US$7, and **San Luis**, an unforgettable ride via the 4700-m-high Punta Olímpica tunnel, US$8, at 0700 with **Virgen de Guadalupe**, Caraz 607. **Renzo**, Raymondi 821, T043-425371, runs to Chacas daily (0615, 1400), **Piscobamba** and **Pomabamba** (0630, best, and 1900). **Los Andes**, same office as **Yungay Express**, T043-427362, daily 0630 to **Yungay**, US$1, **Lagunas de Llanganuco**, US$7, **Yanama**, US$7, **Piscobamba**, US$8 and **Pomabamba**, US$9, 8 hrs. This route is also served by **La Perla de Alta Mayo**, daily 0630, 8 hrs to Pomabamba, US$9. To **Sihuas**, also **Sandoval/Chavín Express**, Tue/Fri 0800; **Perú Andino**, 1 a week, 8 hrs, US$11.

Colectivos to **Recuay**, US$0.75, and **Catac**, US$0.85, daily at 0500-2100, from Gridilla, just off Tarapacá (Terminal de Transportistas Zona Sur). To **Chiquián** for the Cordillera Huayhuash, 120 km, 3½ hrs, with **Trans El Rápido**, Bolognesi 216, T043-422887, at 1345, or **Chiquián Tours**, on Tarapacá behind the market. To **Huallanca** (Huánuco) on the paved road through Conococha, Chiquián, Aquia to Huansala, then by good dirt road to Laguna Pachacoto and Huallanca to La Unión (paving under way). Departs Huaraz twice a day, 1st at 1300, with **Trans El Rápido**, as before, US$8. Frequent daily service from Huallanca to **Huánuco**.

Taxi Standard fare in town is about US$1, more at night; radio taxis T043-421482 or 422512.

Chavín and the Callejón de Conchucos

don't miss this pre-Inca fortress temple

From Huaraz it is possible to make a circuit by road, visiting Chavín de Huantar, Huari, San Luis, Yanama and Yungay, but bear in mind that the road north of Chavín is gravel and rough in parts and the bus service is infrequent.

South of Huaraz

South of Huaraz is **Olleros**, from where the spectacular and relatively easy three- to four-day hike to Chavín, along a pre-Columbian trail, starts. Some basic meals and food supplies are available; for guides and prices, see Trekking and climbing in the cordilleras, above. Alternatively, if you're travelling by road to Chavín, head south from Huaraz on the main road for 38 km to **Catac** (two basic hotels and a restaurant), where a paved road branches east for Chavín.

Further south, the Pumapampa valley is a good place to see the impressive *Puya raimondii* plants. A 14-km gravel road leads from Pachacoto to a park office at 4200 m, where you can spend the night. Walking up the road from this point, you will see the gigantic plants, whose flower spike can reach 12 m in height and takes 100 years to develop. The final flowering (usually in May) is a spectacular sight. Another good spot, and less visited, is the **Queshque Gorge**, which is easy to find by following the Río Queshque from Catac.

From Catac to Chavín is a magnificent journey. The road passes Lago Querococha, and there are good views of the Yanamarey peaks. At the top of the route the road cuts through a huge rock face, entering the Cahuish tunnel at 4516 m. The tunnel has no light and is single lane with a small stream running through it. Cyclists must have powerful lights so that trucks and buses can see them. On the other side of the tunnel, the road descends into the Tambillo valley, then the Río Mosna gorge before Chavín.

☆Chavín de Huantar *Colour map 2, B2.*

Tue-Sun 0900-1600, US$3.50, students half price, guided tours in Spanish for groups available for an extra charge. You will receive an information leaflet in Spanish at the entrance.

Chavín de Huantar, a fortress temple, was built about 800 BC. It is the only large structure remaining of the Chavín culture, which, in its heyday, is thought to have held influence from Cajamarca and Chiclayo in the north to Ayacucho and Ica in the south. In 1985, UNESCO designated Chavín a World Heritage Trust Site. The site is in good condition despite the effects of time and nature but becomes very crowded in high season. In order to protect the site some areas are closed to visitors. All the galleries open to the public have electric lights. The guard is also a guide and gives excellent explanations of the ruins.

The main attractions are the marvellous carved stone heads (*cabezas clavas*), the designs in relief of symbolic figures and the many tunnels and culverts, which form an extensive labyrinth throughout the interior of the pyramidal structure. The carvings are in excellent condition, and the best are now in the Museo Nacional Chavín. The famous Lanzón dagger-shaped stone monolith of 800 BC is found inside one of the temple tunnels.

Just north of the ruins, the town of Chavín, painted colonial yellow and white, has a pleasant plaza with palm and pine trees. There are a couple of good, simple hotels and restaurants here and a local fiesta in mid July. The **Museo Nacional Chavín** ① *1 km north of town and 1.6 km from the site, Tue-Sun, 0900-1700, US$3.50,* has a comprehensive collection of items gathered from several deposits and museums, including the Tello obelisk dating from the earliest period of occupation of Chavín (c 100 BC), and many impressive *cabezas clavas*.

Chavín to Huari

The road north from Chavín descends into the Mosna river canyon. The scenery is quite different from the other side of the Cordillera Blanca, very dry and hot. After 8 km it reaches **San Marcos**, the town that has been most heavily impacted by the huge **Antamina** gold mine. Hotels may be full with mine workers and public safety is a concern, so press on for 32 km to Huari.

Huari is perched on a hillside at 3150 m and has various simple hotels ($ Huagancu 2, Jirón Sucre 335, T043-630434, clean and good value) and restaurants. The fiesta of **Nuestra Señora del Rosario** takes place on 7 October, with festivities during the first two weeks of the month. There is a spectacular two- to three-day walk from Huari to Chacas via Laguna Purhuay inside Parque Nacional Huascarán. Alberto Cafferata of Caraz writes: "The Purhuay area is beautiful. It has splendid campsites, trout, exotic birds and, at its north end, a 'quenual' forest with orchids. This is a microclimate at 3500 m, where the animals, insects and flowers are more like a tropical jungle, fantastic for ecologists and photographers." A pleasant alternative for those who don't want to do the longer walk to Chacas is a day walk to Laguna Purhuay, starting at the village of Acopalca; a taxi from Huari to Acopalca costs US$3.50, to Puruhuay, US$14. The lake has a visitor centre, food kiosk and boat rides.

San Luis to Huaraz

From Huari the road climbs to the Huachacocha pass at 4350 m and descends to **San Luis** at 3130 m, 60 km from Huari. Here you'll find the $ **Hostal Puñuri** (Ramón Castilla 151, T043-830408, with bath and hot water), a few basic restaurants, shops and a market.

Beyond San Luis there are a few options to take you back to Huaraz. The first is via **Chacas**, 10 km south of San Luis on a paved road. It has a fine church and celebrates the **Virgen de la Asunción** on 15 August, with bullfights, a famous carrera de cintas and fireworks. There are hostels ($), shops, restaurants and a small market. ☆A spectacular paved road and 4700-m-high tunnel through **Punta Olímpica** connect Chacas with Carhuaz in the Callejón de Huaylas north of Huaraz. Alternatively, it is a three-day hike west from Chacas to Marcará via the Quebradas Juytush and Honda (lots of condors to be seen). Quebrada Honda is known as the Paraíso de las Cascadas because it contains at least seven waterfalls.

The second road route heads some 20 km north of San Luis, to where a road branches left to **Yanama**, 45 km from San Luis, at 3400 m. It has a good comfortable hotel, Andes Lodge Peru ① T043-943 847423, www.andeslodgeperu.com, $$, full board available, excellent food and services, fabulous views. The village retains many traditional features and is beautifully surrounded by snow-capped peaks. There are superb views from the ruins above the town, reachable on a day hike. From Yanama the road continues west via the Portacheulo de Llanganuco pass to Yungay (see page 89).

North of San Luis

A longer circuit to Huaraz can be made by continuing from San Luis for 62 km to **Piscobamba**, which has a couple of basic hotels, a few shops and small restaurants. Beyond Piscobamba by 22 km is **Pomabamba**, worth a visit for some very hot natural springs (the furthest are the hottest). There are various hotels ($) near the plaza and restaurants. Pomabamba is also the terminus of one the variations of the **Alpamayo Trek**, see page 64.

From Pomabamba a dusty road runs up the wooded valley crossing the puna at Palo Seco, 23 km. The road then descends steeply into the desert-like Sihuas valley, passing through the village of Sicsibamba. The valley is crossed half an hour below the small town of **Sihuas**, a major connection point between the Callejón de Conchucos, Callejón de Huaylas, the upper Marañón and the coast. It has a few $ hotels and places to eat.

From Sihuas it is also possible to travel in the other direction, via Huancaspata, Tayabamba, Retamas and Chahual to Huamachuco along a road which is very poor in places and involves crossing the Río Marañón twice. Using this route, it is possible to travel from Cuzco to Quito through the Andes entirely by public transport. This journey is best undertaken in this direction, but it can take over two days (if it's not impassable) in the wet season.

Where to stay

Chavín

$$$ Tambo Konchukos
10kms north of Chavin, T043-709772.
A small ecolodge attached to a farm researching traditional Andean farming practices. Offers a variety of activities, rooms have wood burning stoves, restaurant serves Andean cuisine.

$$-$ La Casona
Wiracocha 130, Plaza de Armas, T043-454116, www.lacasonachavin.com.pe.
In a renovated house with attractive courtyard, single, double and triple rooms, some with balcony overlooking Plaza or courtyard, nice breakfast, laundry, parking.

$$-$ R'ikay
On 17 de Enero 172N, T043-454068.
Set around 2 patios, modern, best in town, variety of room sizes, hot water, restaurant does Italian food in the evening. Recommended.

$ Inca
Wiracocha 170, T043-754021.
Rooms are cheaper without bath, good beds, hot water on request, nice garden.

Restaurants

Chavín

$$-$ Chavín Turístico
Middle of 17 de Enero.
The best in town, good *menú* and à la carte, delicious apple pie, nice courtyard, popular. Also run a *hostal* nearby.

$$-$ La Portada
Towards south end of 17 de Enero.
In an old house with tables set around a pleasant garden.

$ La Ramada
Towards north end of main street, 17 de Enero.
Regional dishes, also trout and set lunch.

Transport

Chavín

It is much easier to get to Chavín (even walking!) than to leave the place by bus. All buses to **Huaraz** (2 hrs from Chavín), originate in Huari or further afield. They pass through Chavín at irregular hours and may not have seats available. Buying a ticket at an agency in Chavín does not guarantee you will get a seat or even a bus. **Sandoval/ Chavín Express** goes through around 1200, 1600 and 1700 daily, **Río Mosna** at 0430 and then 4 between 1600-2200. There are also services to **Lima**, 438 km, 12 hrs, US$14, with **Trans El Solitario** and **Perú Andino** daily, but locals prefer to travel to Huaraz and then take one of the better companies from there.

In the other direction, buses from Huaraz or Lima (such as **El Solitario,** which passes through Chavín at 1800) go on to **Huari**, with some going on to **San Luis**, a further 61 km, 3 hrs; **Piscobamba**, a further 62 km, 3 hrs; and **Pomabamba**, a further 22 km, 1 hr. The other way to reach places in the Callejón de Conchucos is to hop on and off the cars and combis that leave regularly from Chavín's main plaza, every 20 mins and 30 mins respectively, to **San Marcos**, 8 km, and **Huari**, 38 km.

Huari

Terminal Terrestre at Av Circunvalación Baja. Bus to **Huaraz**, 4 hrs, US$5.50, **Sandoval/ Chavín Express** 3 a day. Also runs to **San Luis** and **Lima**.

San Luís to Huaraz

There are daily buses between Yanama and **Yungay** over the 4767-m Portachuelo de Llanganuco (3 hrs, US$7.50), stopping at Vaquería (at the end of the Santa Cruz valley trek) 0800-1400, US$4, 2 hrs.

North of San Luís

Pomabamba

To **Piscobamba**, combis depart hourly, 1 hr, US$1.50; also combis to Sihuas (see below). **El Solitario** has a service to Lima on Sun, Mon and Thu at 0800, 18 hrs, US$15, via San Luis (4 hrs, US$5), Huari (6 hrs, US$7.50) and Chavín (9 hrs, US$9); **La Perla del Alto Mayo** goes from Pomabamba to Lima via **Yungay** and **Huaraz** on Wed, Thu, Sat, Sun, 16 hrs.

Sihuas

To **Pomabamba**, combi from Av 28 de Julio near the market at 1100, 4 hrs, US$7 (returns 0200). To **Huaraz**, via Huallanca,

with **Cielo Azul**, daily at 0830, 10 hrs, US$11. To **Tayabamba**, for the Marañón route north to Huamachuco and Cajamarca: **Andía** passes through from Lima on Sat and Sun at 0100, **La Perla del Alta Mayo** passes through Tue, Thu 0000-0200; also **Garrincha** Wed, Sun around 0800; all 8 hrs, US$11, the beginning of a long wild ride. To **Huacrachuco**, **Andía** passes through Wed, Sat 0100. To **Chimbote**, **Corvival** on Wed, Thu and Sun morning, 9 hrs, US$9; **La Perla del Alta Mayo** Tue, Thu, Sun. To **Lima** (19 hrs, US$20) via Chimbote, **Andía** Tue, Sun 0200, Wed, Sat 1600; and 3 other companies once or twice a week each.

Callejón de Huaylas

hike to beautiful mountain lakes

Carhuaz and Mancos *Colour map 2, B2.*

Carhuaz is a friendly, quiet mountain town with a pleasant plaza. There is very good walking to thermal baths or up the Ulta valley. Market days are Wednesday and Sunday (the latter is much larger). The local fiesta of **Virgen de las Mercedes**, 14-24 September, is rated as among the best in the region. From Carhuaz it is 14 km to Mancos at the foot of Huascarán. The village has a dormitory at **La Casita de mi Abuela**, some basic shops and restaurants. After Mancos, the main road goes to **Yungay** (8 km north, 30 minutes).

☆Yungay *Colour map 2, B2.*

The town of Yungay was completely buried by a massive mudslide during the 1970 earthquake; a hideous tragedy in which 20,000 people lost their lives. The earthquake and its aftermath are remembered by many older residents of the Callejón de Huaylas. The original site of Yungay, known as Yungay Viejo, is desolate and haunting; it has been consecrated as a *camposanto* (cemetery). The new settlement is on a hillside just north of the old town. It has a pleasant plaza and a concrete market, good on Wednesday and Sunday. The **Virgen del Rosario** fiesta is celebrated on 17 October, and 28 October is the anniversary of the founding of the town. The tourist office is on the corner of the Plaza de Armas. The main road continues 12 km north of Yungay to Caraz.

Lagunas de Llanganuco

The Lagunas de Llanganuco are two lakes nestling 1000 m below the snowline beneath Huascarán and Huandoy. From Yungay, the first you come to is Laguna Chinancocha (3850 m), the second Laguna Orconcocha (3863 m). The park office is situated before the lakes at 3200 m, 19 km from Yungay. Accommodation is provided for trekkers who want to start the Santa Cruz Valley trek from here (see below). From the park office to the lakes takes about five hours (a steep climb). The last section is a nature trail, Sendero María Josefa (sign on the road); it takes 1½ hours to walk to the western end of Chinancocha where there is a control post, descriptive trail and boat trips on the lake. Walk along the road beside the lake to its far end for peace and quiet among the quenual trees, which provide shelter for 75% of the birdlife found in the park.

Caraz *Colour map 2, B2.*

This pleasant town at 2290 m is a good centre for walking and parasailing and is the access point for many excellent treks and climbs. Tourist facilities are expanding as a more tranquil alternative to Huaraz, and there are great views of Huandoy, Huascarán and surrounding summits in July and August. In other months, the mountains are often shrouded in cloud. In addition to its many natural attractions, Caraz is also developing a lively cultural scene. Events are organized by **Caraz Cultura** ⓘ *contact Ricardo Espinosa, T991-996136, carazcultura@gmail.com.* On 20 January is the fiesta **Virgen de Chiquinquirá.** In the last week of July is **Semana Turística.**

The **Museo Arqueológico Municipal** is on San Martín, half a block up from the plaza. The ruins of **Tumshukaiko** are 1.5 km from the Plaza de Armas in the suburb of Cruz Viva, to the north before the turn-off for Parón. There are seven platforms from the Huaraz culture, dating from around 2000-1800 BC, but the site is in poor shape.

☆Treks around Caraz

Caraz has a milder climate than Huaraz and is more suited to day trips. A good day walk goes from Caraz by the lakes of Miramar and Pampacocha to Huaripampa, where you can get a pickup back to Caraz. A longer full-day walk with excellent views of Huandoy and Huascarán follows the foothills of the Cordillera Blanca east along the main Río Santa valley, from Caraz south through the villages of Chosica and Ticrapa. It ends at Puente Ancash on the Caraz–Yungay road, from where frequent transport goes back to Caraz.

Laguna Parón From Caraz a narrow, rough road goes east 32 km to beautiful Laguna Parón ⓘ *US$3.50*, in a cirque surrounded by several, massive snow-capped peaks, including Huandoy, Pirámide Garcilazo and Caraz. The gorge leading to it is spectacular. It is a long day's trek for acclimatized hikers (25 km) up to the lake at 4150 m, or a four-to five-hour walk from the village of Parón, which can be reached by combi (U$2.50). Camping is possible. There is no trail around the lake and you should not attempt it as it is slippery and dangerous, particularly on the southern shore; tourists have been killed here.

Santa Cruz Valley One of the best known treks in the area is the beautiful three- to five-day route from Vaquería, over the 4750 m Punta Unión pass, to Quebrada Santa Cruz and the village of Cashapampa. It can be hiked in either direction. Starting in Cashapampa, you climb more gradually to the pass, then down to Vaquería or the Llanganuco lakes beyond. Along this 'clockwise' route the climb is gentler, giving more time to acclimatize, and the pass is easier to find although, if you start in Vaquería and finish in Cashapampa you ascend for one day rather than three in the other direction. You can hire an *arriero* and mule in Cashapampa; see box, page 82, for prices. Campsites are at Llamacorral and Taullipampa before Punta Unión, and Quenoapampa (or Huaripampa) after the pass. You can end the hike at Vaquería on the Yanama–Yungay road and take a minibus or, better, an open truck from there (a beautiful run). Or end the walk a day later with a night at the Yuraccorral campsite at the Llanganuco lakes, from where cars go back to Yungay. This trek is very popular and offered by all tour agencies in Huaraz and Caraz.

☆Puyas raymondii at Winchos

A large stand of *Puya raimondii* can be seen in the Cordillera Negra southwest of Caraz. Beyond Pueblo Libre is a paved road which heads west via Pamparomás and Moro to join the Panamerican highway south of Chimbote. The *Puya raymondii* plants are located at a place called **Winchos**, after 45 km (1½ hours). There are far-reaching views of the

Cordillera Blanca and west to the Pacific. The plants are usually in flower May or October. Take warm clothing, food and water. You can also camp near the puyas and return the following day. The most popular way to visit is to rent a bike (US$18 per day), travel up by public transport (see below), and then ride back down in four or five hours. Or form a group (eg via the bulletin board at Pony's Expeditions, Caraz) and hire a car which will wait for you (US$60 for five). From Caraz, a minibus for Pamparomás leaves from Ramón Castilla y Jorge Chávez around 0830, two hours, US$3 (get there at about 0800 as they often leave early). From the pass (El Paso) or El Cruce it is a short walk to the plants. Return transport leaves between 1230 and 1300. If you miss the bus, you can walk back to Pueblo Libre in four hours, to Caraz in six to eight hours, but it is easy to get lost and there are not many people to ask directions along the way.

Listings Callejón de Huaylas

Tourist information

Caraz

The **tourist office** (Plaza de Armas, next to the municipality, T043-391029 ext 143), has limited information. There are 3 ATMs in the centre.

Where to stay

Carhuaz

$$ pp Casa de Pocha
1.5 km out of town towards Hualcán, at foot of Nevado Hualcán, ask directions in town, T943-613058 (mob 1800-2000), www. socialwellbeing.org/lacasadepocha.htm.
Including breakfast and dinner, country setting, entirely solar and wind energy powered, hot water, sauna and pool, home-produced food (vegetarian available), horses for hire, camping possible, many languages spoken. Book in advance.

$$ El Abuelo
Jr 9 de Diciembre 257, T043-394456, www.elabuelohotel.com.
Modern, comfortable 3-star, laundry, restaurant, large garden with organic fruit and veg, parking, credit cards accepted. Knowledgeable owner is map-maker, Felipe Díaz.

$ Hostal Señor de Luren
Buin 549, 30 m from Plaza de Armas, T043-668806.

Hot water, safe motorcycle parking, very hospitable.

$ 4 family-run *hospedajes* operate as part of a community development project. All have private bath and hot water. The better 2 are: **Hospedaje Robri** (Jr Comercio 935, T043-394505), and **Alojamiento Las Torresitas** (Jr Amazonas 603, T043-394213).

Yungay

$ Complejo Turístico Yungay (COMTURY)
Prolongación 2 de Mayo 1012, 2.5 km south of the new town, 700 m east of main road in Aura, the only neighbourhood of old Yungay that survived, T043-788656.
Nice bungalows, pleasant country setting, hot water, fireplace, restaurant with regional specialities, camping possible.

$ Hostal Gledel
Av Arias Graziani, north past plaza, T043-793048.
Owned by Sra Gamboa, who is hospitable and a good cook, shared bath, hottish water, no towels or soap, cheap meals prepared on request, nice courtyard.

$ Hostal Sol de Oro
Santo Domingo 7, T043-493116.
Most rooms with bath, hot water, comfortable, breakfast and dinner on request, good value, best in town.

Lagunas de Llanganuco

$$$$-$ Llanganuco Mountain Lodge
Lago Keushu, Llanganuco Valley, close to Huascarán park entrance (booking office in Huaraz: Gamarra 699), T943-669580, www.llanganucomountainlodge.com.
2 luxury rooms, 2 standard rooms and 10-bed dormitory. Room rate is seasonal and full board with a packed lunch, dorm beds can be with or without meals, modern, camping area, excellent food in restaurant, helpful staff, fine views and limitless possibilities for trekking (equipment rental and logistics), British-owned.

Caraz

$$$-$$ Los Pinos Lodge
Parque San Martín 103 (also known as Plazuela de la Merced), T043-391130, www.lospinoslodge.pe.
Nice comfortable rooms, patio, gardens, parking, cosy bar, tourist information. Recommended. Also have a nearby annex nearby called **Caraz Backpacker** ($).

$$$-$$ O'Pal Inn
Km 265.5, 5 min south of Caraz, T043-391015, www.opalsierraresort.com.
Scenic, family bungalows, suites and rooms, swimming pool, includes breakfast, restaurant, games room.

$$-$ La Alameda
Av Noé Bazán Peralta 262, T043-391177, www.hostallaalameda.com.
Comfortable rooms, hot water, ample parking, pleasant gardens.

$ Caraz Dulzura
Sáenz Peña 212, about 12 blocks from the city centre, T043-392090, www.hostalcarazdulzura.com.
Modern building in an old street, hot water, comfortable, airy rooms, restaurant and bar.

$ Chavín
San Martín 1135 just off the plaza, T043-391171.

Get a room overlooking the street, many others have no window. Warm water, breakfast extra, guiding service, tourist info.

$ Hostal La Casona
Raymondi 319, 1 block east from the plaza, T043-391334.
With or without bath, hot water, lovely little patio, noisy at night.

$ La Perla de los Andes
Daniel Villar 179, Plaza de Armas, next to the cathedral, T043-392007.
Comfortable rooms, hot water, helpful, average restaurant.

$ San Marco
San Martín 1133, T043-391558.
Comfortable rooms with private or shared bath, hot water, patio.

Restaurants

Carhuaz

$$ La Bicharra
Just north of Carhuaz on main road, T943-780893.
Innovative North African/Peruvian cooking, lunch only, busy at weekends, call ahead to check if they are open on weekdays.

Yungay

$$ Alpamayo
Av Arias Graziani s/n. Lunchtime only.
At north entrance to town, good for local dishes.

$ Café Pilar
On the main plaza.
Good for juices, cakes and snacks.

Caraz

$$ Venezia
Av Noé Bazán Peralta 231, T043-784813.
Good home-made pasta, Italian owner.

$$-$ Entre Panes
Daniel Villar 211, half a block from the plaza. Closed Tue.

Variety of excellent sandwiches, also meals.
Good food, service and atmosphere.

$$-$ La Punta Grande
D Villar 595, 10 mins' walk from centre.
Closes 1700.
Best place for local dishes.

$$-$ La Terraza
Jr Sucre 1107, T043-301226.
Good *menú* as well as pizza, pasta, juices,
home-made ice cream, sandwiches, sweets,
coffee and drinks.

$ Jeny
Daniel Villar on the plaza next to the Cathedral.
Local fare at reasonable prices, ample variety.

Cafés

Café de Rat
Sucre 1266, above Pony's Expeditions.
Breakfast, vegetarian dishes, good pizzas,
drinks and snacks, darts, travel books,
nice atmosphere.

El Turista
San Martín 1117. Open in morning and
evening only.
Small, popular for breakfast, ham omelettes
and ham sandwiches are specialities.

Heladería Caraz Dulzura
D Villar on the plaza.
Home-made ice cream.

Panificadora La Alameda
D Villar y San Martín.
Good bread and pastries, ice cream, popular
with locals. The excellent *manjar blanco* for
which the town earned its nickname 'Caraz
dulzura' is sold here and at several other
shops on the same street.

Bars and clubs

Caraz

Airu Resto Bar
At Los Pinos Lodge, Parque San Martín.
Open 1800-2200.
Serves wines and piscos.

Shopping

Caraz
There's fresh food in the market. Some
dried camping food is available from
Pony's Expeditions, who also sell
Camping Gaz canisters and white gas.

What to do

Caraz
Agencies in Caraz arrange treks in the
Cordillera Huayhuash, as well as more
local destinations.
Apu-Aventura, *Parque San Martín 103,*
5 blocks west of plaza, T043-391130, www.
apuaventura.pe. Range of adventure sports
and equipment rental.
Pony's Expeditions, *Sucre 1266, near*
the Plaza de Armas, T043-391642, www.
ponyexpeditions.com. Mon-Sat 0800-2200.
English, French, Italian and Quechua spoken.
Owners Alberto and Aidé Cafferata
are knowledgeable about treks and
climbs. They arrange local tours, offer
accommodation at **Pony's Lodge** (**$$**)
and **Backpacker Los Ponys** (**$**), trekking,
transport for day excursions, and rental of
a 4WD vehicle with driver (US$125 per day
plus fuel). Also maps and books for sale,
equipment hire and mountain bike rental
(US$18 for a full day). Well organized and
reliable. Highly recommended.

Transport

Carhuaz
All transport leaves from the main plaza.
To **Huaraz**, *colectivos* and buses leave 0500-
2000, US$1, 40 mins. To **Caraz**, 0500-2000,
US$1, 1 hr. Buses from Huaraz to **Chacas** in
the Cordillera Blanca, 87 km, 4 hrs, US$5.75,
pass through Carhuaz about 40 mins after
leaving Huaraz. The road works its way
up the Ulta valley to the pass at Punta
Olímpica from where there are excellent
views. The dirt road is not in good condition
due to landslides (can be closed in the wet
season). **Renzo** daily buses pass through

en route to **San Luis** (see page 87), a further 10 km, 1½ hrs.

Yungay

Buses and *colectivos* run all day to **Caraz**, 12 km, US$0.50, and **Huaraz**, 54 km, 1½ hrs, US$1. To the **Llanganuco lakes**, combis leave when full, especially 0700-0900, from Av 28 de Julio 1 block from the plaza, 1 hr, US$2.50. To **Yanama**, via the Portachuelo de Llanganuco Pass, 4767m, 58 km, 3½ hrs, US$5; stopping at María Huayta (for the Llanganuco–Santa Cruz trek), after 2 hrs, US$3. To **Pomabamba**, via Piscobamba, **Trans Los Andes**, daily at 0700-0730, the only company with a ticket office in Yungay; **Transvir** and **La Perla de Alta Mayo** buses coming from Huaraz, stop in Yungay at 0730 if they have room, 6-7 hrs, US$6. After passing the Llanganuco lakes and crossing the Portachuelo the buses descend to Puente Llacma, where it is possible to pick up buses and combis heading south to San Luis, Chacas and Huari.

Caraz

To **Lima**, 470 km, daily, US$11-30, 10-11 hrs via Huaraz and Pativilca, 9 companies: **El Huaralino** (T996-896607), **Huaraz Buss** (T943-469736), **Zbuss** (T043-391050), **Cooperativa Ancash** (T043-391126), all on Jr Cordova, also **Rochaz** (Pasaje Olaya, T043-794375), **Cavassa** (Ctra Central, T043-392042), **Yungay Express** (Av Luzuriaga, T043-391492), **Móviltours** (east end of town, www.moviltours.com.pe) and **Rodríguez** (Daniel Villar, T043-635631).

To **Chimbote**, Yungay Express, via Huallanca, Casma and Cañon del Pato, 3 daily, US$9, 7 hrs, sit on right for best views. To **Trujillo**, via Casma with **Móviltours**. To **Huaraz**, combis leave from a terminal on the way out of town, where the south end of C Sucre meets the highway, daily 0400-2000, 1¼ hrs, US$2, no luggage racks, you might have to pay an extra seat for your bag. To **Yungay**, 12 km, 15 mins, US$0.70. To **Huallanca** and **Yuramarca** (for the Cañón del Pato), combis and cars leave from Córdova y La Mar, 0700-1600, US$2.50. To **Cashapampa** (for the Santa Cruz valley) *colectivo*/minibus from Ramón Castilla y Jorge Chávez, Caraz, leave when full from 0600 to 1530, 1½ hrs, US$2. To **Parón** (for the walk to Laguna Parón), *colectivos* leave from Ramón Castilla y Jorge Chávez, close to the market, 1 hr, US$2.

Cordillera Huayhuash

remote mountains just waiting to be explored

The Cordillera Huayhuash, lying south of the Cordillera Blanca, has azure trout-filled lakes interwoven with deep quebradas and high pastures around the hem of the range. It is perhaps the most spectacular cordillera for its massive ice faces that seem to rise sheer out of the puna's contrasting green. You may see tropical parakeets in the bottom of the gorges and condors circling the peaks. The area offers fantastic scenery and insights into rural life.

The cordillera is approached from four points: **Chiquián** in the north is a town of narrow streets and overhanging eaves; **Oyón**, with links to Cerro de Pasco, lies to the southeast; **Churín** is to the south, and **Cajatambo**, a small market town with a beautiful 18th-century church and a lovely plaza, lies to the southwest. Note that the road out of Cajatambo is not for the faint-hearted. For the first three to four hours it is no more than a bus-width, clinging to the cliff edge.

☆Huayhuash trekking circuit

The complete circuit is very tough; allow 10 to 12 days. There are up to eight passes over 4600 sm, depending on the route. Fees are charged by every community along the way, adding up to about US$80 for the entire circuit; take soles in small denominations and insist on getting a receipt every time. A half-circuit is also possible, and there are many other options. The trail head is at **Cuartel Huain,** between Matacancha and the **Punta Cacanan Pass** (which marks the continental divide at 4700 m).

Listings Cordillera Huayhuash

Where to stay

There are various hotels ($) and some good restaurants around the plaza in Cajatambo. The following are all in Chiquián:

$ Hostal San Miguel
Jr Comercio 233, T043-447001.
Nice courtyard and garden, clean, many rooms, popular.

$ Hotel Huayhuash
28 de Julio 400, T043-447049.
Private bathroom, hot water, restaurant, laundry, parking, modern, great views, information and tours.

$ Los Nogales de Chiquián
Jr Comercio 1301, T043-447121, http:// hotelnogaleschiquian.blogspot.com.
Traditional design, with private or shared bath, hot water, cafeteria, parking. Recommended.

Restaurants

$ El Refugio de Bolognesi and Yerupajá
Tarapacá, Chiquián.
Both offer basic set meals.

$ Panificadora Santa Rosa
Comercio 900, on the plaza, Chiquián.
For good bread and sweets, has coin-operated phones and fax.

Transport

Coming from Huaraz, the road is now paved beyond Chiquián to Huansala, on the road to Huallanca (Huánuco). Private vehicles can sometimes be hired in Chiquián or Llamac (less likely) to take you to the trailhead at Cuartel Huain; otherwise you'll have to walk.

Chiquián

To **Huaraz**, buses leave the plaza at 0500 daily, US$1.75, except **Trans El Rápido**, Jr Figueredo 216, T043-447049, at 0500 and 1330, US$3.65. Also *colectivo* to Huaraz 1500, 3 hrs, US$2.45 pp. There is also a connection from **Chiquián to Huallanca** (Huánuco) with buses from Lima in the early morning and combis during the day, which leave when full, 3 hrs, US$2.50. From Huallanca there are regular combis on to **La Unión**, 1 hr, US$0.75, and from there transport to **Huánuco**.

Cajatambo

Buses to **Lima** daily at 0600, US$9, with **Empresa Andina** (office on plaza next to Hostal Cajatambo), **Tour Bello** (1 block off the Plaza) and **Turismo Cajatambo** (Jr Grau 120; or Av Carlos Zavala 124 corner of Miguel Aljovin 449, Lima, T01-426 7238).

North
coast

The north of Peru has been described as the Egypt of South America, as it is home to many ruined pre-Inca treasures. Many tourists pass through without stopping on their way to or from Ecuador, missing out on one of the most fascinating parts of the country. Along a seemingly endless stretch of desert coast lie many of the country's most important pre-Inca sites: Chan-Chán, the Moche pyramids, Túcume, Sipán, Batán Grande and El Brujo. The main city is Trujillo, while Chiclayo is more down to earth, with one of the country's largest witchdoctors' markets. The coast is also famous for its deep-sea fishing, surfing and the unique reed fishing boats at Huanchaco and Pimentel. Inland lies colonial Cajamarca, scene of Atahualpa's last stand. Further east, where the Andes meet the jungle, countless unexplored ancient ruins await the more adventurous traveller.

Best for
Archaeology ▪ Seafood ▪ Surfing

Huacho and around

The Pan-American Highway is four-lane (several tolls, about US$2.65) to Km 101. Here it by-passes both **Huacho** and **Puerto Huacho**, 19 km to the west. There are several hotels in Huacho. The beaches south of the town are clean and deserted.

☆Caral

25 km east of the Panamericana (Km 184); after 18.5 km, a track leads across the valley to the ruins (30 mins), though the river may be impassable Dec-Mar. Information: Proyecto Especial Caral, T01-205 2500 (Lima), www.caralperu.gob.pe. Daily 0900-1600. US$4, US$7 per group; all visitors must be accompanied by an official guide and not stray from the marked paths.

A few kilometres before Barranca, a signed turning to the east at Km 184 leads up the Supe valley to the UNESCO World Heritage Site of Caral. This ancient city, 26 km from the coast, dates from about 2600 BC. Many of the accepted theories of Peruvian archaeology have been overturned by Caral's age and monumental construction. It appears to be the oldest city in South America (a claim disputed by the Miravalles site, in the department of Cajamarca). The dry desert site lies on the southern fringes of the Supe valley, along whose flanks are 32 more ruins, 19 of which have been explored. Caral covers 66 ha and contains eight significant pyramidal structures. To date seven have been excavated by archaeologists from the University of San Marcos, Lima, who are undertaking careful restoration on the existing foundations to re-establish the pyramidal tiers.

It is possible to walk around the pyramids on marked paths. A viewpoint provides a panorama of the whole site. Allow at least two hours for your visit. Handicrafts are sold in the car park. You can stay or camp at the **Casa del Arqueólogo**, a community museum in Supe (at the turn-off to Caral), which provides information on the Caral culture and the progress of the excavations.

Barranca to Huarmey

Barranca is by-passed by the Highway but is an important transport hub for the region so you may find yourself there to change buses. Some 4 km beyond the turn-off to Huaraz at Pativilca, beside the Panamericana, are the well-preserved ruins of the Chimú temple of **Paramonga** ① *US$1.80; caretaker may act as guide.* Set on high ground with a view of the ocean, the fortress-like mound is thought to be of Huari origin and resembles a llama when seen from above.

Between Pativilca and Chimbote the mountains come down to the sea. The road passes by a few very small protected harbours in tiny rock-encircled bays, such as **Huarmey**, with a fine beach and active hostel.

☆Sechín

5 km north of Casma, off the road to Huaraz. Daily 0800-1700 (photography best around midday). US$1.80 (children US$0.35, students US$1.40); ticket also valid for the Max Uhle Museum by the ruins and other sites in the Casma Valley. Mototaxi from Casma, US$2.85 each way for 2 passengers, US$8.55 return including wait.

This archaeological site in the Nepeña Valley, north of Casma, is one of the most important ruins on the Peruvian coast. It consists of a large square temple completely faced with about 500 carved stone monoliths narrating, it is thought, a gruesome battle in graphic detail. The style is unique in Peru for its naturalistic vigour. The complex as a whole is associated with the pre-Chavín Sechín culture, dating from about 1600 BC. Three sides of the large stone temple have been excavated and restored, but you cannot see the earlier adobe buildings inside the stone walls because they were covered up and used as a base for a second storey, which has been completely destroyed.

Casma and around *Colour map 2, B2.*

Sechín is accessed from the city of Casma (population 22,600), which has a pleasant Plaza de Armas, several parks and two markets including a good food market. While safer than Chimbote, you should still take care if staying in Casma. Tortugas, ten minutes away, is a better option and is a pleasant place to spend a day at the seaside and enjoy the seafood.

Chimbote to Callejón de Huaylas *Colour map 2, B2.*

The port of Chimbote (population 296,600) serves the national fishing industry; the smell of its fishmeal plants is overpowering. If that's not enough to put you off staying here, the city is also unsafe. Take extensive precautions; always use taxis from the bus station, and avoid staying overnight if possible.

Just north of Chimbote, a road branches northeast off the Pan-American Highway and goes up the Santa valley following the route of the old Santa Corporation Railway which used to run as far as **Huallanca** (not to be confused with the town southeast of Huaraz), 140 km up the valley. At Chuquicara, three hours from Chimbote (paved – very rough thereafter), is **Restaurante Rosales**, a good place to stop for a meal (you can sleep here, too, but it's very basic). There are also places to stay and eat at Huallanca, and fuel is available. At the top of the valley by the hydroelectric centre, the road goes through the very narrow and spectacular **Cañón del Pato**. You pass under tremendous walls of bare rock and through almost 40 tunnels, but the flow of the river has been greatly reduced by the hydroelectric scheme. After this point the road is paved to the Callejón de Huaylas and south to Caraz and Huaraz. For bus services along this route, see Transport, in Listings section below.

A faster route to Huaraz, paved and also very scenic, branches off the Pan-American Highway at **Casma**. It climbs to **Pariacoto**, with basic lodging, and crosses the Cordillera Negra at the **Callán Pass** (4224 m). The descent to Huaraz offers great views of the Cordillera Blanca. This beautiful trip is worth taking in daylight; sit on the right for the best views. The road has many dangerous curves requiring caution. For bus services along this route, see Transport, opposite.

An alternative road for cyclists (and vehicles with a permit) is the 50-km private road known as the 'Brasileños', used by the Brazilian company Odebrecht which has built a water channel from the Río Santa to the coast. The turn-off at Km 482 on the Pan-American Highway is 35 km north of the Santa turning and 15 km south of the bridge in Chao. It is a good all-weather road via Tanguche. Permits are obtainable from the Chavimochic HQ at San José de Virú, US$7.50, or from the guard at the gate on Sunday.

> **Tip...**
>
> If arriving in Chimbote from Caraz via the Cañón del Pato there is usually time to make a connection to Casma or Trujillo/Huanchaco and avoid overnighting in Chimbote. If travelling to Caraz from Chimbote, take the **Línea** 0600 service or earlier from Trujillo to make the 0830 bus up the Cañón del Pato. If overnighting is unavoidable, head south to Casma for the night, but buy your ticket to Caraz the day before.

Where to stay

Barranca to Huarmey

$ Jaime Crazy
Manuel Scorza 371 y 373, Sector B-8, Huarmey, T043-400104, JaimeCrazyPeru on Facebook.
A hostel offering trips to beaches, archaeological sites, farming communities, volunteering and all sorts of activities.

Casma and around
Hotel prices are higher in Jan and Feb.

$$ Hostal El Farol
Túpac Amaru 450, Casma, T043-411064, www.elfarolinn.com.
Very nice, rooms and suites, swimming pool, pleasant garden, very good restaurant, parking, information.

$$ Hostal Gabriela
Malecón Grau Mz 6, Lt 18, Tortugas, T043-631302, misateinversiones@gmail.com.
Pleasant 10-room hotel, lounge with ocean views, good restaurant with extensive menu, seafood, local and international dishes.

$$ Tarawasi
1a Línea Sur, Centro, Tortugas, T043-782637, tarawasitortugas@hotmail.com.
Small family-run *hospedaje*, pleasant atmosphere, 2 terraces with ocean views, good restaurant serves Peruvian and Mediterranean food.

$ El Dorado
Av Garcilazo de la Vega Mz J, Lt 37, 1 block from the Panamericana, Casma, T043-411795, http://eldoradocasma.blogspot.com.
With fan, pool, restaurant and tourist information.

$ Las Dunas
Luis Ormeño 505, Casma, T043-711057.
An upgraded and enlarged family home, welcoming.

Chimbote to Callejón de Huaylas
There are plenty of hotels in Chimbote, so try to negotiate a lower rate.

$$ Cantón
Bolognesi 498, T043-344388.
Modern, higher quality than others, has a good but pricey *chifa* restaurant.

$$ Ivansino Inn
Av José Pardo 738, T043-321811.
Includes breakfast, comfortable, modern.

$ Hostal El Ensueño
Sáenz Peña 268, 2 blocks from Plaza Central, T043-328662.
Cheaper rooms without bath, very good, safe, welcoming.

$ Hostal Karol Inn
Manuel Ruiz 277, T043-321216.
Hot water, good, family-run, laundry, *cafetería*.

$ Residencial El Parque
E Palacios 309, on plaza, T043-345572.
Converted old home, hot water, nice, secure.

Restaurants

Huacho and around
Good restaurants in Huacho include **Cevichería El Clásico** (C Inca s/n, daily 1000-1800), and **La Estrella** (Av 28 de Julio 561).

Casma and around
The best restaurants are at **Hostal El Farol** and at the hotels in Tortugas. Cheap restaurants are on Huarmey. The local ice cream, **Caribe**, is available at Ormeño 545.

$$ Tío Sam
Huarmey 138.
Specializes in fresh fish, good ceviche.

What to do

Casma and around
Akela Tours, *Lima A3-3, T990-283145, Facebook: akelatours.* Good tours of Sechín,

trips to the desert and beaches, sandboarding; run by Monika, an archaeologist.

Sechín Tours, *Hostal Monte Carlo, Casma, T043-411421, renatotours@yahoo.com*. Organizes tours in the local area. The guide, Renato, only speaks Spanish but has knowledge of local ruins.

Transport

Huacho and around
AméricaMóvil (Av Luna Pizarro 251, La Victoria, Lima, T01-423 6338; in Huacho T01-232 7631) and **Zeta** (Av Abancay 900, Lima, T01-426 8087; in Huacho T01-239 6176) run every 20-30 mins **Lima–Huacho**, daily 0600 to 2000, 2½ hrs, US$6 (more expensive at weekends).

Caral
Empresa Valle Sagrado Caral buses to the site leave the terminal in Barranca (Berenice Dávila, cuadra 2), US$2.75 shared, or US$35 private service with 1½ hrs at the site. A taxi from Barranca to the ruins costs US$10 one way. Tours from Lima usually allow 1½ hrs at Caral, with a 3-hr journey each way, stopping for morning coffee and for lunch in Huacho on the return. If you don't want to go back to Lima, you'll have to get to Barranca to continue your journey.

Barranca to Huarmey
Bus companies have their offices in Barranca, so buses tend to stop there (opposite El Grifo service station at the end of town) rather than at Pativilca or Paramonga. To **Lima**, 3½ hrs, US$7.50. To **Casma**, 155 km, several daily, 2½ hrs, US$6. To **Huaraz**, take a minibus from C Lima in Barranca to the gas station in Pativilca where you can catch a bus, *colectivo* or truck along the paved road to Huaraz. From Barranca buses run only to Paramonga port (3 km off the Highway, about 15 mins from Barranca); from there you can get a taxi to the **Paramonga ruins**, US$9; otherwise it's a 3-km walk along the Panamericana.

Casma and around
América Express and **Tres Estrellas** run frequent services from **Lima** to **Chimbote** (see Chimbote below) stopping in Casma, 370 km, 6 hrs, US$11-18; other companies going to Chimbote or Trujillo might drop you off by the highway. In the other direction, many of the buses to **Lima** stop briefly opposite the petrol station, block 1 of Ormeño or, if they have small offices, along blocks 1-5 of Av Ormeño.

To **Chimbote**, 55 km, it is easiest to take the **Los Casmeños** *colectivos*, which depart when full from between the Plaza de Armas and Banco de la Nación, 45 mins, US$2.15. To **Trujillo** and Chiclayo, it is best to go first to Chimbote bus station and then take an **América Express** bus.

To **Huaraz,** 150 km via **Pariacoto**, 4 hrs, US$9, with **Transportes Huandoy** (Ormeño 166, T043-712336) daily 0700, 1100 and 1400, or **Yungay Express** (by the Ovalo near the Repsol petrol station) daily 0600, 0800 and 1400; also *colectivos* from the same Ovalo, US$11, 3 hrs.

Chimbote
The bus station is 4 km south of town on Av Meiggs. Under no circumstances should you walk to the centre: minibus, US$0.50, taxi US$1.50. There are no hotels near the terminal; some companies have ticket offices in the centre.

To/from **Lima**, 420 km, 5½ hrs, US$15-20, frequent service with many companies, eg hourly with **América Express**, several daily with **Tres Estrellas**. To **Trujillo**, 130 km, 2 hrs, US$6, **América Express** every 20 mins till 2100, these continue to **Chiclayo**.

To **Huaraz,** most companies, with the best buses, go the 'long way round': down the Panamericana to Pativilca, then up the main highway, 7 hrs, US$14; the main companies start in Trujillo and continue to **Caraz**. The fastest route, however, is via Pariacoto, 5 hrs, US$11, with **Trans Huandoy** (Etseturh, T043-354024) at 0600, 1000 and 1300, and **Yungay Express** at 0500, 0700 and 1300. Alternatively, you can travel to **Caraz** via the Cañón del Pato, 6 hrs, US$12, with **Yungay Express** at 0830; sit on the left-hand-side for the best views.

a colonial city with ancient archaeology on its doorstep

The capital of La Libertad Department, 548 km from Lima, Trujillo disputes the title of second city of Peru with Arequipa. It has an urban population of over 1.5 million, but the compact colonial centre has a small-town feel. The greenness surrounding the city is a delight against the backcloth of brown Andean foothills and peaks. Founded by Diego de Almagro in 1534 as an express assignment ordered by Francisco Pizarro, it was named after the latter's native town in Spain. Nearby are some of Peru's most important Moche and Chimú archaeological sites and a stretch of the country's best surfing beaches.

Sights

The focal point is the pleasant and spacious **Plaza de Armas**, whose buildings, and many others in the vicinity, are painted in bright pastel colours. The prominent sculpture represents agriculture, commerce, education, art, slavery, action and liberation, crowned by a young man holding a torch depicting liberty. Fronting it is the **Cathedral** ① *daily 0700-1230, 1700-2000*, dating from 1666, with religious paintings and sculptures displayed next door in the **museum** ① *Mon-Fri 0900-1300, 1600-1900, Sat 0900-1300, US$1.45*. Also on the Plaza are the **Hotel Libertador**, the colonial-style Sociedad de Beneficencia Pública de Trujillo and the Municipalidad. The **Universidad de La Libertad**, second only to that of San Marcos at Lima, was founded in 1824. The colonial-style **Casa Urquiaga (or Calonge)** on the plaza now houses the **Banco Central de Reserva** ① *Pizarro 446, Mon-Fri 0930-1500, Sat-Sun 1000-1330, free 30-min guided tour; take passport*, which contains valuable pre-Columbian ceramics. Another beautiful colonial mansion is **Casa Bracamonte (or Lizarzaburu)** ① *Independencia 441*, which houses the Seguro Social de Salud del Perú and has occasional exhibitions. Opposite the Cathedral on Independencia, is the **Casa Garci Olguín** (Caja Nuestra Gente), recently restored but boasting the oldest façade in the city and Moorish-style murals. Near the Plaza de Armas is the spacious 18th-century **Palacio Iturregui**, now occupied by the **Club Central** ① *Jr Pizarro 688, restricted entry to patio, daily 0830-1000, US$1.85*, an exclusive social club with a private collection of ceramics. **Casa Ganoza Chopitea** ① *Independencia 630*, which now houses a pizzeria (see Restaurants, below), is considered architecturally the most representative of the viceroyalty in the city. It combines baroque and rococo styles and is also known for the pair of lions that adorn its portico.

Other mansions still in private hands include **Casa del Mayorazgo de Facalá** ① *Pizarro 314 (Scotiabank), another entrance on Bolognesi, Mon-Fri 0915-1230*. **Casa de la Emancipación** ① *Jr Pizarro 610 (Banco Continental), Mon-Sat 0900-1300, 1600-2000*, is the building where independence from Spain was planned and was the first seat of government and congress in Peru. The **Casa del Mariscal de Orbegoso** now houses the **Museo de la República** ① *Orbegoso 553, daily 0930-2000*. It is owned by the BCP bank and holds temporary exhibitions. **Museo Haya de la Torre (Casa del Pueblo)** ① *Orbegoso 664, Mon-Sat 0900-1300, 1600-2000*, is a small, well-presented museum about the life of the founder of the APRA party who was one of the leading 20th-century socialists in the Americas. He was born in the house, which now holds a cinema club once a week.

> **Warning...**
> The city is generally safe, but take care beyond the inner ring road, Avenida España, as well as at bus stops, terminals, ATMs and internet cafés.

One of the best of the many churches is the 17th-century **La Merced** ⓘ *Pizarro 550, daily 0800-1200, 1600-2000*, with picturesque moulded figures below the dome. The church and monastery of **El Carmen** ⓘ *Colón y Bolívar, Mass Sun 0700-0730*, has been described as the 'most valuable jewel of colonial art in Trujillo', but is rarely open except for Mass. **La Compañía** ⓘ *near Plaza de Armas*, is now an auditorium for cultural events.

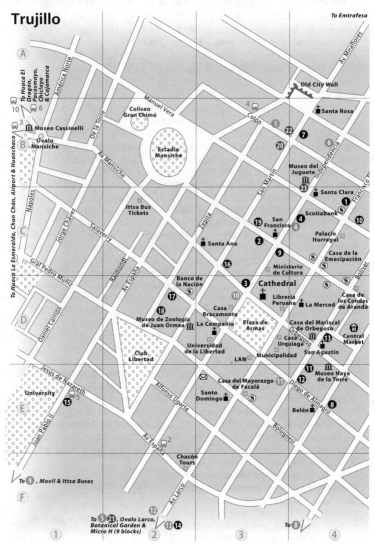

Trujillo

Museo de Arqueología ① *Junín 682 y Ayacucho, Casa Risco, T044-249322, Mon-Fri 0830-1430, US$1.85*, houses a large and interesting collection of thematic exhibits. The **Museo del Juguete** ① *Independencia 705 y Junín, Mon-Sat 1000-1800, Sun 1000-1300, US$1.85, children US$0.70*, is a toy museum containing examples from prehistoric times to 1950, collected by painter Gerardo Chávez. Downstairs is the Espacio Cultural Angelmira with a

N

200 metres
200 yards

To Huamachuco

Where to stay
1 Bona Nit &
  Munay Wasi Hostel *B3*
2 Casa de Clara *F6*
3 Chan Chán Inn *A5*
4 Colonial *C4*
5 El Gran Marqués *F2*
6 El Mochilero *B4*
7 Gran Bolívar *B5*
8 Hostal El Centurión *F4*
9 Kallpa *F1*
10 Libertador *D3*
11 Los Conquistadores *E3*
12 MD Hotel *F2*
13 Res Vanini *F2*
14 Turismo *D5*

Restaurants
1 Asturias, Demarco,
  Oviedo & Romano *C4*
2 Café Amaretto *C3*
3 Café van Gogh *D3*
4 Casona Deza *C4*
5 Cevichería Puerto Mori *B4*
6 Chelsea *B5*
7 Dulcería Doña Carmen *B4*
8 El Chileno *E4*
9 El Celler de Cler *C3*
10 El Kluv *C4*
11 El Mochica *E4*
12 Fitopán *E4*
13 Juguería San Agustín *D4*
14 Mar Picante *F2*
15 Pizzería Pizzanino *E1*
16 Rincón de Vallejo *C3*
17 Sabor Supremo *D2*
18 Sal y Pimienta *D2*
19 Trujillo Señorial *C3*

Bars & clubs
20 Canana *B3*
21 El Boticario *F2*
22 El Estribo *B4*
23 Juguete *C4*

Transport
1 Buses to Huaca del Sol y
  de la Luna *D6*
2 Combi A to Chan Chán &
  Huanchaco *E2, E5*
3 Combis A & B; & Micros B, H
  & H-Corazón: to Chan Chán
  & Huanchaco *B1*
4 Combi B & Micro B: to
  Chan Chán &
  Huanchaco *A4, B3*
5 Micro H to Chan Chán &
  Huanchaco *E1*
6 El Dorado *B1*
8 Oltursa & Flores *A5*
9 Ormeño *A5*
10 Turismo Díaz *B1*
11 Cruz del Sur *A4*

Buses

To Ovalo Grau & Micro H (5 blocks), Southern
Bus Terminal, CIAL, Línea, Chimbote & Lima

Av España
La Unión
Plazuela
El Retreo
Pizarro
Estete
El Carmen
Museo de
Arqueología
Old City Wall
San Lorenzo
Mercado
Mayorista
Junín
Ayacucho
Galvez
Suárez
Zela
Gamarra
Grau
España
Simch Roca
Lloque Yupanqui
Atahualpa
Av Los Incas
Huayna Cápac
Nicaragua
Moche
Cahuide
Ejército
Amazonas

café bar ⓘ *daily 0900-2300*; in a restored *casona*; it's worth a visit. **Museo de Zoología de Juan Ormea** ⓘ *Jr San Martín 368, T044-205011, Mon-Fri 0900-1800, US$0.70*, has interesting displays of Peruvian animals.

Gerardo Chávez also opened the **Museo de Arte Moderno** ⓘ *Av Industrial, 3.5 km from centre, T044-215668, Mon-Fri 0800-1300, 1345-1745, Sat-Sun 0800-1500, US$3, students half price*, which has some fine exhibits, a peaceful garden and friendly staff. The basement of the **Cassinelli garage** ⓘ *Av N de Piérola 607, T044-231801, behind a petrol station, daily 1000-1300, 1430-1800, US$2.45*, contains a private collection of Mochica and Chimú pottery which is recommended. There is also a **botanical garden** ⓘ *Mon-Sat 0800-1700, free*, about half a block beyond the Ovalo Larco, southwest of the city centre.

★Huacas del Sol and de la Luna

Information: Proyecto Huaca de la Luna, Jr San Martín 380, Trujillo, T044-221269, www. huacas.com. Daily 0900-sunset (last entry 1600); access by 1-hr guided tour only (English, French or Spanish); groups can be up to 25 people and quite rushed. US$4 (students US$2, children US$0.40), booklet in English or Spanish US$2.85; all tickets are sold at the Museo Huacas de Moche – see below.

A few kilometres south of Trujillo are the huge and fascinating Moche pyramids, the Huaca del Sol and the Huaca de la Luna. Until the Spaniards destroyed a third of it in a vain search for treasure, Huaca del Sol was the largest man-made structure in the western hemisphere, at 45 m high. It consisted of seven levels, with 11 or 12 phases of construction over the first six centuries AD. Today, about two thirds of the pyramid have been lost and it is closed to the public.

Huaca de la Luna, 500 m away, received scant attention until extensive polychrome moulded decorations were uncovered in the 1990s. The colours on these remarkable geometric patterns and deities have faded little and it is now possible to view impressive friezes of the upper four levels on the northern exterior wall of the *huaca*. The highest mural is a 'serpent' which runs the length of the wall; beneath it are several levels of repeated motifs depicting victorious warriors, 'felines', 'fishermen' holding fish and huge 'spider/crab' images. Combined with intricate, brightly painted two-dimensional motifs in the sacrificial area atop the huaca, and with new discoveries in almost every excavation, Huaca de la Luna is now a truly significant site well worth visiting.

The **Templo Nuevo**, or Plataforma III, represents the period 600 to 900 AD and has friezes in the upper level showing the so-called Rebellion of the Artefacts, in which weapons take on human characteristics and attack their owners. Also visit the **Museo Huacas de Moche** ⓘ *5 mins' walk from Huaca de la Luna, www.huacasdemoche.pe, daily 0900-1600, US$1, students US$0.75, children US$0.40*, the site museum. Three halls display objects found in the *huacas*, including beautiful ceramics, arranged thematically around the Moche culture, the cermonial complex, daily life, the deities of power and of the mountains and priests who worshipped them. Food is available on Sunday at the nearby town of Moche.

The **visitor centre** ⓘ *T044-834901*, has a café showing videos and a souvenir shop and good toilets. In an outside patio, craftsmen reproduce ceramics in designs from northern Peru.

Chan Chán

5 km from Trujillo centre. Daily 0900-1600. Site may be covered up if rain is expected. Tickets cost US$3.80 (US$2 with ISIC card), children US$0.35, and are valid for Chan Chán, Huaca El

Dragón and Huaca La Esmeralda for 2 days. Official guides, US$10, wait by the souvenir shops; toilets here too.

The imperial city of the Chimú domains was once the largest adobe city in the world. The vast, crumbling ruins consist of 10 great compounds built by Chimú kings, with perimeter walls up to 12 m high surrounding sacred enclosures with usually only one narrow entrance. Inside, rows of storerooms contained the agricultural wealth of the kingdom, which stretched 1000 km along the coast from near Guayaquil to the Carabayllo Valley, north of Lima. The Incas almost certainly copied this system and used it in Cuzco where the last Incas continued building huge enclosures. The Chimú surrendered to the Incas around 1471 after 11 years of siege.

Most of the compounds contain a huge walk-in well which tapped the ground water, raised to a high level by irrigation further up the valley. Each compound also included a platform mound which was the burial place of the king, his women and his treasure, presumably maintained as a memorial.

The dilapidated city walls enclose an area of 28 sq km containing the remains of palaces, temples, workshops, streets, houses, gardens and a canal. What is left of the adobe walls bears either well restored or modern fibreglass fabrications of moulded decorations showing small figures of fish, birds, fishing nets and various geometric motifs. Painted designs have been found on pottery unearthed from the debris of a city ravaged by floods, earthquakes and *huaqueros* (grave looters). The **Ciudadela de Nik-An** (formerly called Tschudi) is the part that visitors see.

The **site museum** ① *on the main road, 100 m before the turn-off, daily 0830-1630, US$1,* has objects found in the area, with displays and signs in Spanish and English.

The partly restored temple, **Huaca El Dragón** ① *daily 0930-1630 (in theory); combis from Huayna Cápac y Los Incas, or Av España y Manuel Vera marked 'Arco Iris/La Esperanza', taxi US$2,* is on the west side of the Pan-American Highway in the district of La Esperanza. It dates from Huari to Chimú times (AD 1000-1470) and is also known as **Huaca Arco Iris** (rainbow), after the shape of friezes which decorate it.

The poorly preserved **Huaca La Esmeralda** is at Mansiche, between Trujillo and Chan Chán, behind the church and near the Mall Aventura shopping centre. Buses to Chan Chán and Huanchaco pass the church at Mansiche.

☆ El Brujo
3 km from Magdalena de Cao. Daily 0900-1600. US$4 (US$2 with ISIC card, children US$0.35). Shops and toilets at the entrance. See www.fundacionwiese.com.

A complex collectively known as El Brujo, 60 km north of Trujillo, is considered one of the most important archaeological sites on the north coast. Covering 2 sq km, it was a ceremonial centre for up to 10 cultures, including the Moche. Excavations here will, no doubt, continue for many years. Trujillo travel agencies run tours and there is a trail system for exploring the site.

Huaca Cortada (or El Brujo) has a wall decorated with stylized figures in high relief. Huaca Prieta is, in effect, a giant

> **Warning...**
> There are police at the entrance to the site, but it is a 25-minute walk from there to the ticket office. If you're not on a tour, you are advised to take one of the vehicles that wait at the entrance as it is not safe to walk to the ticket office. On no account should you walk beyond Chan Chán to Buenos Aires beach, nor walk on the beach itself, as there is serious risk of robbery and of being attacked by dogs.

rubbish tip dating back 5000 years, which once housed the original inhabitants of the area. It was first investigated by the US archaeologist Junius Bird in the late 1940s, leading him to establish the chronology of prehistoric Peru that prevails today and cementing the place of this unremarkable *huaca* in Peruvian history.

Huaca Cao Viejo has extensive friezes, polychrome reliefs up to 90 m long, 4 m high and on five different levels. The mummy of a tattooed, pregnant woman, La Señora de Cao, dating from AD 450, was found here. Her mausoleum, with grave goods, can be visited in an excellent purpose-built museum. In front of Cao Viejo are the remains of one of the oldest Spanish churches in the region. It was common practice for the Spaniards to build their churches near these ancient sites in order to counteract their religious importance.

☆Huanchaco

An alternative to Trujillo is this fishing and surfing village, full of hotels, guesthouses and restaurants. It is famous for its narrow pointed fishing rafts, known as *caballitos* (little horses) *de totora*, made of totora reeds and depicted on the pottery of Mochica, Chimú and other cultures. Unlike those used on Lake Titicaca, they are flat, not hollow, and ride the breakers rather like surfboards. You can see fishermen returning in their reed rafts at about 0800 and 1400 when they stack the boats upright to dry in the fierce sun. Fishermen offer trips on their *caballitos* for US$1.75; be prepared to get wet. Groups should contact Luis Gordillo (El Mambo, T044-461092). Overlooking Huanchaco is a huge church (1535-1540), whose belfry has extensive views. **El Quibishi**, at the south end of the beach, is the main *artesanía* market and also has a food section.

Puerto Chicama

Surfers claim that **Puerto Chicama** (**Malabrigo**), 70 km north of Trujillo (turn off the Panamericana at Paiján) is the best surf beach in Peru, with the longest left-hand point-break in the world. The best waves are from March to October (high point May/June). The town has a 1-km-long fishing pier, huge, abandoned warehouses and the remains of a railway to Casa Grande cooperative left over from the town's sugar-exporting days. There are a few *hospedajes* and simple places to eat in town itself (shop early by the market for fresh seafood), but the best places to stay and eat are in Distrito El Hombre, the clifftop south of town (eg **Chicama**, Arica 625); avoid the shacks that line the beach.

Pacasmayo and around *Colour map 2, B1.*

Pacasmayo, 102 km north of Trujillo, is the port for the next oasis north. It has a nice beachfront with an old Customs House and a very long pier. Away from the front Pacasmayo is a busy commercial centre. Resort El Faro is 1 km away, with surfing at the point and kite- and windsurfing closer to town. There are maritime festivals at New Year and Semana Santa. Some 20 km further north on the Panamericana is the main road connection from the coast to Cajamarca (see page 140) at a junction called Ciudad de Dios.

Santuario y Reserva Nacional Calipuy

These two adjacent highland nature reserves are home to impressive stands of *Puya raimondii* and the largest herd of guanaco in Peru, respectively. Both reserves (sncalipuy@sernanp.gob.pe, rncalipuy@sernanp.gob.pe) reach elevations above 4000 m and are not easy to get to, but well worth the effort. Entry is free. Access is either through Chao (more direct), along the Panamericana south of Virú, or the regional centre of Santiago de Chuco, which has simple places to stay and eat, see Transport (page 116).

Tourist information

Useful websites include http://trujilloperu.xanga.com.

Gobierno Regional de la Libertad
Dirección de Turismo, Av España 1800,
T044-296221.
Information on regional tourism.

Indecopi
Santo Toribio de Mogrovejo 518,
Urb San Andrés II etapa, T044-295733,
sobregon@indecopi.gob.pe.
For tourist complaints.

iPerú
Jr Independencia 467, of 106, T044-294561,
iperutrujillo@promperu.gob.pe. Mon-Sat
0900-1800, Sun 0900-1300. Also at Huaca de
La Luna, daily 0900-1300.

Municipalidad de Trujillo
Sub-Gerencia de Turismo, Av España 742,
T044-244212, anexo 119,
sgturismo@munitrujillo.gob.pe.

Tourist police
Independencia 572, in the Ministerio de
Cultura building, policia_turismo_tru@
hotmail.com. Mon-Sat 0800-2000.
Provide useful information and can help with
reports of theft, some staff speak English.

Where to stay

Trujillo

$$$$ Casa Andina Private Collection
Av El Golf 591, Urb Las Flores del Golf III,
T01-213 9739, www.casa-andina.com.
Large multi-storey luxury hotel, part of a
nationwide chain, located outside the centre.
All facilities.

$$$$ Libertador
Independencia 485, Plaza de Armas,
T044-232741, www.libertador.com.pe.
Modern hotel in historic building, lovely place
to stay. Comfortable rooms, excellent service,
swimming pool in a flower-filled patio, sauna,
cafetería and restaurant, breakfast extra,
excellent buffet lunch on Sun.

$$$ El Gran Marqués
Díaz de Cienfuegos 145-147, Urb La Merced,
T044-481710, www.elgranmarques.com.
Price includes breakfast, modern, minibar,
pool, sauna, jacuzzi, restaurant.

$$$ Gran Bolívar
Bolívar 957, T044-222090,
www.granbolivarhotel.net.
In converted 18th-century house,
restaurant and room service, café, bar,
laundry, gym, parking.

$$$ Kallpa
Díaz de las Heras s/n, Urb Vista Hermosa,
T044-281266, www.kallpahotel.pe.
A smart boutique hotel, welcoming, English
spoken, below usual boutique hotel prices.

$$$ Los Conquistadores
Diego de Almagro 586, T044-481650,
www.losconquistadoreshotel.com.
An elegant modern hotel with good service,
1 block from Plaza de Armas.

$$ Colonial
Independencia 618, T044-258261,
www.hostalcolonial.com.pe.
Attractive but small rooms, hot showers,
basic breakfast, good restaurant, especially
for set lunch. Recommended.

$$ Hostal El Centurión
Paraguay 304, Urb El Recreo, T044-201526,
www.hostalelcenturion.com.
About 20 mins' walk from the Plaza, modern,
good rooms, well kept, safe but no a/c,
simple restaurant, good service.

$$ MD Hotel
Larco 384, Urb San Andrés, T044-200777,
mdhotelsac@hotmail.com.
Rooms with frigobar and windows that you
can open for fresh air (many hotels in the
centre don't have these), hospitable.

$$-$ Residencia Vanini
Av Larco 237, outside Av España, T044-200878, kikacarmelavanini@hotmail.com.
Youth hostel in a converted private house, nice garden, basic rooms, some with bath.

$ Bona Nit
Colón 257, T044-298530, www.bonanithostal.com.
Well located hostel, rooms with fan and frigobar, includes breakfast, good value.

$ Casa de Clara
Cahuide 495, T044-243347, http://trujilloperu.xanga.com.
Friendly backpackers' *hostal*, hot water, good food, helpful, information, lodging packages with meals and tours, laundry service, use of kitchen with permission and charge for gas, meeting place and lots going on, many languages spoken (see Clara Bravo and Michael White, Tour guides, page 114). Restaurants nearby. Good economy option.

$ Chan Chán Inn
Av Ejército 307, T044-791515, chanchaninn@hotmail.com.
Close to several bus terminals so noisy, includes breakfast, popular with backpackers, café, laundry, money exchange, information.

$ El Mochilero
Independencia 887, T044-297842, Elmochilerotrujilloperuoficial on Facebook.
A variety of basic dorms and rooms, only one with bath, electric showers, breakfast available, fridge for guests' use. Tours arranged, information.

$ Munay Wasi Hostel
Jr Colón 250, T044-231462, www.munaywasihostel.com.
Family-run hostel within Av España, private and shared rooms (US$10 pp with breakfast), shared bath, book exchange, tourist information, fully equipped kitchen.

El Brujo

$ Hospedaje Jubalu
Libertad 105, Magdalena de Cao, T995-670600.
With hot water. There's no internet in town and limited shopping.

Huanchaco

$$$-$$ Bracamonte
Los Olivos 160, T044-461162, www.hotelbracamonte.com.pe.
Comfortable, modern, contemporary decor, pool and garden, secure, good restaurant offers lunch *menú* and some vegetarian dishes, English spoken, laundry service, games room, garage. Highly recommended.

$$$-$$ Qhamar
Av Circunvalación 140, Urb. El Boquerón, T044-462366, www.qhamarhotel.com.
Modern quiet hotel away from the centre. All rooms with sea view, a bit small but bright and comfortable. Small swimming pool, pool table, table football, bar, garden, airport pickup available.

$$ Hostal Huanchaco
Larco 185 on Plaza, T044-461272.
With hot water, pool, good but pricey cafeteria, video, pool table.

$$ Hostal Huankarute
La Rivera 312, T044-461705, www.hostalhuankarute.com.
On the seafront, with small pool, bar, sun terrace, bicycle rental; some rooms larger, more luxurious and more pricey, all with ocean view.

$$ Las Palmeras
Av Larco 1150, sector Los Tumbos, T044-461199, www.laspalmerasdehuanchaco.com.
Rooms with terrace, hot water, dining room, pool and gardens. Rooms on top floor with sea view cost more than ground floor rooms with pool view. Basic breakfast.

$$ Residencial Sol y Mar
La Rivera 400, T044-461120.

Ample rooms, large pool, garden, terrace, event room, no breakfast but café next door.

$ Casa Amelia
Av Larco 1150, T044-46135,
www.casaamelia.net.
Small quiet hostel with a big garden and homely atmosphere, kitchen facilities, 2 terraces, book exchange, good surfing information, parking, Dutch run.

$ Casa Fresh
Av La Rivera 322, T945-917150,
www.casafresh.pe.
Popular seafront hostel, basic rooms, roof bar/terrace with great views over the Huanchaco surf spot. Noisy weekend disco next door. Frequently organizes activities, has a collection of instruments to play and is connected to a surf school and tour agency.

$ Frogs
C El Pescador 308, Los Tumbos,
www.frogsperu.com.
Located in a quiet area, big bright rooms, some with with sea view. Yoga area, terrace with hammocks and bean bags, sunset views, bar, pool table, ping pong, ample kitchen facilities and TV room. Popular meeting place, organize daily activities, Peruvian-German owned, opened in 2015.

$ Hospedaje My Friend
Los Pinos 533, T044-461080.
Dorm rooms with bath upstairs, hot water, TV room, information. Tours arranged but service is erratic. Popular with surfers, good meeting place, restaurant/bar open 0800-2230.

$ La Casa Suiza
Los Pinos 308, T044-639713,
www.lacasasuiza.com.
This Huanchaco institution has a variety of rooms with/without bath, breakfast US$3, BBQ on the roof, book exchange.

$ McCallum Lodging
Los Ficus 460, T044-626923, http://
mccallumlodginghouse.wordpress.com.

Private rooms and dorms, hot water, hammocks, home-cooked meals available and recipes shared, laundry, baggage and surfboard storage, family atmosphere, highly considered by locals and tourists.

$ Ñaylamp
Av Larco 1420, northern end of
seafront in El Boquerón, T044-461022,
www.hostalnaylamp.com.
Rooms set around a courtyard with patios and garden, others have sea view, dorms, hammocks, good beds, hot water, kitchen facilities, camping, tents for hire, laundry, safe, Italian food, good breakfasts.

Puerto Chicama
The following are in Distrito El Hombre (several close out of season).

$$$ Chicama Surf Resort
T044-576206, www.chicamasurf.com.
Exclusive, with surfing classes, boats to the waves, spa, restaurant, infinity pool, open all year.

$$ Hostal Los Delfines
T943-296662.
Owner is Tito Venegas. Guests can use well-equipped kitchen, rooms with balcony, hot water, spacious.

$$ Iguana Inn
C Progreso, Pto Malabrigo, T04-57622,
www.hoteliguanainn.com.
Good mid-range option, well equipped rooms with fridge and coffee/tea maker.

$ Hostel El Hombre
C Arica 803, T044-576077.
Legendary surfers' hangout and meeting spot. Basic rooms. Owner Doris prepares food.
In town there are several cheaper places; **Hostal El Naipe**, Tacna 395, is arguably the best.

Pacasmayo

$$$ El Faro
Urb La Perla, T044-311802,
www.elfaropacasmayo.com.

Well known surf resort on the coast, simple rooms, large pool, good restaurant, bar, surfboard and other gear rentals, organizes tours.

$$ El Mirador
Aurelio Herrera 10,
www.perupacasmayo.com.
Variety of rooms and prices, all with private bath, fan and safe box. Well located, popular and good value.

$$ Libertad
Leoncio Pardo 1-D, T044-521937,
http://hotellibertad.pe/pacasmayo/.
2 km from beach by petrol station, with breakfast, Wi-Fi and internet, safe, restaurant/bar, parking, efficient and nice.

$ Duke Kahanamoku
Ayacucho 44, T044-521889.
Backpakers' surfing place, with classes and board rental, breakfast extra, hot water, free internet.

Restaurants

A speciality is *shambar*, a thick minestrone made with pork. On sale everywhere is *turrón*, a nougat-type sweet. All along Pizarro are restaurants to suit all tastes and budgets. On the west side of the central market at Grau y Ayacucho are several small, cheap restaurants.

Trujillo

$$$ El Celler de Cler
Independencia 588, upstairs.
Open 1830-0100.
One of the best restaurants of Trujillo, located in an old colonial house in the centre, some seating on a nice little balcony. Peruvian and international dishes, mostly meat, no fish.

$$$-$$ El Mochica
Bolívar 462.
Good typical food with live music on special occasions.

$$ Café van Gogh
Independencia No 533. Open 0830-2130.
Small quiet restaurant half a block from Plaza de Armas. Very good coffee, vegetarian dishes and crêpes.

$$ Mar Picante
Húsares de Junín 412, T044-20846.
Very good local seafood in a family-run restaurant.

$$ Chelsea
Estete 675, T044-257032.
Daily 1145-1645, 1700-0100.
Restaurant/bar. Buffet Criollo US$8.70, special shows on Fri (live music, fee US$3.50) and Sat (Marinera dance show, US$5.25). Recommended.

$$ Demarco
Pizarro 725.
Popular at midday for lunchtime *menús* and for its cakes and desserts, good service.

$$ Pizzería Pizzanino
Av Juan Pablo II 183, Urb San Andrés, opposite University.
Good for pizzas, pastas, meats, desserts, evening only.

$$ Romano
Pizarro 747.
International food, good *menú*, breakfasts, coffee, excellent milkshakes, cakes.

$$-$ Cevichería Puerto Mori
Estete 482, T044-346752.
Very popular, they serve only good seafood. At the same location are 2 more fish restaurants, but not of the same quality.

$ Asturias
Pizarro 741.
Nice café with a reasonable *menú*, good pastas, cakes and sandwiches.

$ Juguería San Agustín
Bolívar 526.
Good juices, good *menú*, sandwiches, ice creams, popular, excellent value. Also at Av Larco Herrera y Husares de Junín.

$ Oviedo
Pizarro 737.
With soups, vegetarian options, good salads and cakes, helpful.

$ Rincón de Vallejo
Orbegoso 303.
Good *menú*, typical dishes, very crowded at peak times. 2nd branch at Av España 736.

$ Sabor Supremo
Diego de Almagro 210, T044-220437.
Menú and à la carte vegetarian food, vegan on special request.

$ Sal y Pimienta
Zepita 366.
Very popular for economical lunch, close to buses for Huanchaco and Chan Chán.

$ Trujillo Señorial
Gamarra 353, T044-204873.
Mon-Sat 1300-1530.
Restaurant and hotel school, good *menú*, food nicely presented, good value.

Cafés

Café Amaretto
Gamarra 368.
Smart, good selection of real coffees, "brilliant" cakes, sweets, snacks and drinks.

Casona Deza
Independencia 630. Tue-Sun 1600-2300.
Comfortable café/bar selling home-made pasta and pizza and good coffee in an old mansion.

Dulcería Doña Carmen
San Martín 814.
Serves local specialities such as *alfajores*, *budín*, *king kong*, etc.

El Chileno
Ayacucho 408.
Café and ice cream parlour, popular.

El Kluv
Junín 527 (next to Metro Market).
Italian-owned, fresh, tasty pizzas at noon and in the late afternoon.

Fitopán
Bolívar 406, www.fitopan.com.
Good selection of breads, also serves lunches. Has 3 other branches.

El Brujo

$ Café Antojitos
At entrance to Plaza de Armas, Magdalena de Cao.
Run by a women's cooperative, specializing in sugar-based snacks.

$ El Brujo
Plaza de Armas, Magdalena de Cao.
Best place to eat in town and accustomed to providing meals for tourists.

Huanchaco
There are about 30 restaurants on the beachfront. Recommended on Av Larco are **Estrella Marina** at No 740, **Los Herrajes** at No 1020, and **Lucho del Mar** at No 750; all $$. Many close in the low season and at night.

$$$ Big Ben
Av Larco 1884, El Boquerón, T044-461378, www.bigbenhuanchaco.com.
Daily 1200-1700.
Seafood and international cuisine, very good.

$$$ Club Colonial
La Rivera 514, on the beachfront, T044-461015. Daily 1100-2300.
A smart restaurant and bar, French-speaking Belgian owner.

$$$ El Mochica
Av Larco 700, T044-461963. Open 0900-2300.
Same owners and good quality as the restaurant in Trujillo.

$$$ Huanchaco Beach
Av Larco 800, T044-461484. Open 1200-1700.
One of the best quality in town, popular with tours.

$$$-$$ El Sombrero
Av Larco 510, T044-462283, www.restaurant elsombrero.com. Open 1100-2300.

Smart restaurant serving good ceviche and seafood, most tables have great sea view. Has another branch at Av Mansiche 267, Trujillo.

$$ Casa Tere
Plaza de Armas, T044-461197.
For best pizzas in town, also pastas, burgers and breakfasts.

$$ La Barca
Raimondi 117, T044-461855.
Very good seafood, well-run, popular.

$ La Esquina
Jr Unión 120. Open 1200-2200.
Small place serving very good barbecued fish.

$ Otra Cosa
Av Victor Larco 1312. Open 0800-2200.
Dutch-Peruvian vegetarian restaurant serving a variety of dishes including falafel, burritos and *menú*. Good organic coffee, fruit salads, juices and the best Dutch apple pie in Peru.

Cafés

Argolini
Av Rivera 400.
Convenient for people staying in the Los Pinos/Los Ficus area for fresh bread, cakes, ice cream, coffee and juices.

Chocolate
Av Rivera 752. Daily 0830-1800.
Swiss management, serves breakfast, also some vegetarian food, coffee and cakes.

Trujillo

Bar/Café Juguete
Junín y Independencia. Until midnight.
An old-style café serving good coffee as well as alcohol. Has a pasta restaurant attached.

Canana
San Martín 788, T044-232503.
Bars and restaurant, disco, live music at weekends (US$1.50-3), video screens (also has travel agency). Recommended, but take care on leaving.

El Boticario
Av Larco 962, T044-639346. Open from 2000 .
A small but very elegant upmarket bar with great service and original cocktails. You have to go well dressed but it's worth it.

El Estribo
San Martín 809, T044-204053.
A club playing a wide variety of genres and attracting a mixed crowd.

Huanchaco

Jungle Bar Bily
Av Larco 420. Open 1000-0200.
Well known popular cocktail bar, happy hour 1800-2200. Also a good restaurant.

Sabes?
Av Larco 920, http://sabesbar.com. Open 1900-0200.
Well established British-owned pub, good pizzas and cocktails (happy hour 1900-2100), pool table and tranquil atmosphere. Popular with tourists and trujillanos alike.

Festivals

End Jan **National Marinera Contest**.
Last week of Sep **Festival Internacional de La Primavera**.
Both festivals have cultural events, parades, beauty pageants and Trujillo's famous **Caballos de Paso**.

Huanchaco
1st week of May **Festival del Mar**, a celebration of the disembarkation of Taycanamo, the leader of the Chimú period. A procession is made in Totora boats.
29 Jun **San Pedro**, patron saint of fishermen. His statue is taken out to sea on a huge totora-reed boat. There are also surf competitions.
Carnival and **New Year** are also popular celebrations.

Shopping

Trujillo
Bookshops
Librería Peruana, *Pizarro 505, just off the Plaza.* Has the best selection in town, plus postcards; ask for Sra Inés Guerra de Guijón.

There are also 3 branches of **SBS:** on Jr Bolívar 714; in Mall Aventura, Av Mansiche block 20, and in Plaza Real Mall, Prol Av César Vallejo (behind UPAO University), California (take taxi or green California micro A).

Handicrafts
120 Artesanía por Descubrir, *Las Magnolias 403, California, www.tienda120.blogspot.com.* Art gallery designs and handmade crafts, near Real Plaza.
APIAT, *Av España y Zela.* The largest craft market in the city, good for ceramics, totora boats, woodwork and leather, competitive prices.
Artesanía del Norte, *at Dulcería La Libertad, Jr Pizarro 758, and at the Huacas del Sol y de la Luna, www.artesaniadelnorte.com.* Sells items mostly designed by the owner, Mary Cortijo, using traditional techniques.
Trama Perú, *Pizarro 754, T044-243948, www.tramaperu.com. Daily 1000-2200.* High-quality, hand-made art objects, authorized Moche art replicas.

Markets
Mercado Central, *Gamarra, Ayacucho and Pasaje San Agustín.*
Mercado Unión, *between Av Santa and Av Perú.* A little safer than others; also repairs shoes, clothes and bags.

What to do

Trujillo
City tours
Mirabus, *tickets from Travelers Tours, Pizarro 561, T044-232889, US$4.50, departs from Plaza de Armas at 1000, 1200, 1500, 1700 in summer, 1200 and 1700 in winter.* 1 hr ride through the colonial centre in a double-decker bus.

Horse shows
Asociación de Criadores de Caballo de Passo, *Vía de Evitamiento Km 569, Buenos Aires, T948-315056, open 1330-1430, US$9.* These horses, typical of northern Peru, have been bred for their special gait which makes them more comfortable to ride. In the show they dance to the sounds of *marinera.* An on-site restaurant offers good lunches.

Tour operators
Prices vary and competition is fierce so shop around for the best deal. Few agencies run tours on Sun and often only at fixed times on other days. Groups are usually large. City tours, 2-2½ hrs for US$3.50 pp. To Chan Chán, El Dragón and Huanchaco, 4-4½ hrs for US$8-9 pp. To Huacas del Sol and de la Luna, 2½-3 hrs for US$8-9 pp. To El Brujo, 4-5 hrs for US$27-34 pp. Prices do not include entrance fees.
Chacón Tours, *Av España 106-112, T044-255212. Sat afternoon and Sun morning.* Recommended for flights etc, not local tours.
Colonia Tours, *Independencia 618 (Hotel Colonial), T044-255826.* Local tours including Chan Chán, Las Huacas and El Brujo.
Domiruth, *Diego de Almagro 539, T044-299 0952, www.domiruth.com.* For airline tickets.
North Perú Tours, *Francisco Pizarro 478, of 201, T044-310423, www.north-peru.com.* Organizes tours around Trujillo and throughout northern Peru.

Tour guides
Many hotels work on a commission basis with taxi drivers and travel agencies. If you decide on a guide, make your own direct approach and always agree what is included in the price. The tourist police (see Tourist information, see page 107) has a list of guides; average cost US$7 per hr. Beware of cowboy outfits herding up tourists around the plazas, especially Plaza de Armas, and bus terminals for rapid, poor quality tours. Also beware scammers offering surfing or salsa lessons and party invitations.

Alfredo Ríos Mercedes, *T949-657978, riosmercedes@hotmail.com*. Speaks English.
Clara Bravo and Michael White, *Cahuide 495, T044-243347, http://trujilloperu. xanga.com, microbewhite@yahoo.com*. Clara is an experienced tourist guide who speaks Spanish, English, German and understands Italian and runs small group tours daily: archaeological tour US$20 for 6 hrs, city tour US$7 pp, US$53 per car to El Brujo, with extension to Sipán, Brüning Museum and Túcume possible (tours in Lambayeque involve public transport, not included in cost). Clara works with **Michael White**, who provides transport and is very knowledgeable about tourist sites.
Henry Valiente, *T949-547132, ysaac_hnr9@ hotmail.com*. An experienced English-speaking guide.
Jannet Rojas Sánchez, *Alto Mochica Mz Q 19, Trujillo, T949-344844*. Speaks English, enthusiastic. Also works for **Guía Tours** (Av Nicolas De Pierola 1208, T998-460330).
Luis Ocas Saldaña, *Jr José Martí 2019, T954-042086, guianorteperu@hotmail.com*. Very knowledgeable, helpful, covers all of northern Peru.
William Alvarado, *T947-006070, william_alvarado_gotur@hotmail.com*. An experienced English-speaking guide.

Volunteering
There are many social and volunteer projects in Trujillo, but not all are recommendable. Try to get a personal recommendation from other volunteers before signing up.
Supporting Kids in Peru, *www.skipperu.org*. Works with poor children and their families in Trujillo.

Huanchaco
Language classes
Sam Owen, *T967-992775, skypispanish@ gmail.com*. Originally from Wales and married to a Peruvian, he offers unique and very practical Spanish lessons.

Surfing
There are plenty of surf schools. Equipment rental is US$8.75/day; single lesson, about US$15 for 2 hrs.
Indigan, *Deán Saavedra 582 (next to soccer field), T044-462591*. Jhon and Giancarlos Urcía for lessons, surf trips and rentals. Also offer lodging at their home.
Muchik, *Av Larco 650, T044-462535, www. escueladetablamuchik.com*. Instructors Chicho and Omar Huamanchumo are former surf champions. They arrange trips to other surf sites and also offer repairs. Recommended.

Volunteering
Fairmail, *www.fairmail.info*. An innovative social enterprise that teaches poor kids to use a camera, sells their photo-art and returns the profits to them.

Trujillo
Air The **airport** is west of the city; access to town is along Av Mansiche. Taxi to city hotels, US$6-8.
To **Lima**, 1 hr, several daily flights with **LATAM** and **Avianca/TACA**.

Bus Local Micros (small buses with 25 or more seats) and combis (up to 15 passengers) on all routes within the city cost US$0.50-0.60; *colectivos* (6 passengers) charge US$0.50 and tend to run on main avenues starting from Av España. In theory, they are not allowed in the city centre. For transport to the archaeological sites, see below.
To **Huanchaco**, there are 2 combi routes (A and B; both take 25 mins), run by the **Caballitos de Totora** company (white and black), and 4 micros (A, B, H and H-Corazón;

Tip...
On Friday to Sunday nights the better bus services must be pre-booked two to three days in advance.

45-60 mins), run by **Transportes Huanchaco** (red, yellow and white). They run 0500-2030, every 5-10 mins, US$0.75. The easiest place to pick up any of these combis or micros is Ovalo Mansiche, 3 blocks northwest of Av España in front of the Cassinelli museum. Combi A takes the southerly route on Av España, before heading up Av Los Incas. Combi B takes the northerly route on Av España.

Long distance The **Terminal Terrestre de Trujillo** (TTT), or Terrapuerto, is to the southeast of the centre, at Km 558 on the Panamericana Norte, beyond Ovalo La Marina. It was completed in 2014 but bus companies continue to operate from their private terminals as well. Always ask where the bus leaves from when buying your ticket. On arrival, take a taxi from the terminal and insist on being taken to your hotel of choice.

To **Lima**, 561 km, 9-10 hrs in the better class buses, average fare US$22-32; 10 hrs or more in the cheaper buses, US$11-16. There are many bus companies doing this route, among those recommended are: **Cruz del Sur** (Amazonas 437, between Av Ejército and Miraflores, T044-720444), the only one with a morning service from Lima to Trujillo at 0800; **Turismo Díaz** (TTT); **Línea** (Av América Sur 2857, T044-297000), 3 levels of service; **Flores** (Av Ejército 346, T044-208250); **Ittsa** (TTT and Av Juan Pablo 1110, T044-284644), frequent service, good value; **Móvil** (TTT, T044-245523 and Av América Sur 3959, T044-286538); **Oltursa** (TTT, T044-263055; note different stations for buses to Lima and Máncora), 3 *bus cama* services to Lima; **Ormeño** (Av El Ejército 233, T044-259782) .

To **Puerto Chicama**, combis from Santa Cruz terminal (Av Santa Cruz, 1 block from Av America Sur), US$2, 1½ hrs; also **Dorado** buses (Av N de Piérola 1062, T044-291778), US$2, via Chocope (US$0.75) and Paiján (US$0.60). Small **Pakatnamú** buses leave when full, 0400-2100 (from Av N de Piérola 1092, T044-206594), to **Pacasmayo**, 102 km, 1¼ hrs, US$5.50.

Warning…
Solo cyclists should not cross the desert as muggings have occurred. Take the safer, inland route to Piura via Olmos. In the desert, there is no water, fuel or accommodation. Do not attempt this alone.

To **Chiclayo**, 4 hrs from Trujillo, from US$5.50, several companies, including **Emtrafesa** (Av Túpac Amaru 185, T044-471521) and **Ittsa** (see above), both hourly. To **Jaén**, 9 hrs. To **Piura**, 6 hrs, US$15 (Ittsa's 1330, or **Línea**'s 1415 buses are good choices). **Ittsa** also goes to **Talara**, 2200, 9 hrs, US$16.

Direct buses to **Huaraz**, 319 km, via Chimbote and Casma (169 km), with **Línea** and **Móvil**, 8 hrs, US$17-30. There are also several buses and *colectivos* to **Chimbote**, with **América Express** (from Av La Marina 315), 135 km, 2 hrs, US$6, departures every 30 mins from 0530 (ticket sales from 0500); leave Trujillo before 0600 to make a connection to Huaraz from 0800 in Chimbote (see page 100). Ask Clara Bravo and Michael White (see Tour guides, above) about transport to Caraz avoiding Chimbote: a worthwhile trip via the Brasileños road and Cañon del Pato.

To **Cajamarca**, 300 km, 7-8 hrs, US$10-27, with **Línea, Turismo Díaz** and **Emtrafesa** at 2145. To **Huamachuco**, 170 km, 5-6 hrs, see page 138.

Taxi Taxis in town charge US$1 within Av España and US$1.20 within Av América; always use official taxis, which are mainly black, or cooperative taxis, which have the company logo on the side (eg **Sonrisas**, T044-233000). Beware of overcharging; check fares with locals.

Huacas del Sol and de la Luna

There are combis every 15 mins from Ovalo Grau in Trujillo and, less safe, from Galvez y Los Incas, but they drop you a long walk from the site. Taxis charge about US$5; there are few at the site so ask your driver to wait.

Chan Chán

Take any transport between Trujillo and Huanchaco (see above) and ask to get out at the turn-off, US$0.50; then get onward transport from the entrance to the ticket office, US$1. Do not walk from the turn-off to the ticket office. A taxi from Trujillo to the site is US$5; from Huanchaco, US$3.

El Brujo

The complex can be reached by taking one of the regular buses from Trujillo to Chocope, US$1.25, every 10 mins, 1 hr, and then a *colectivo* to Magdalena de Cao, US$0.75 (leave when full), 15 mins, then a mototaxi taking up to 3 people to the site, US$7.50 including 1½-hr wait. Unless you particularly like Peruvian public transport, it is more convenient to go on a tour.

Huanchaco

From Huanchaco, micro A goes to the 28 de Julio/Costa Rica junction in Trujillo where it turns west along Prolongación César Vallejo, passing the UPAO university and Plaza Real shopping centre, continuing to the Av El Golf (the terminus for the return to Huanchaco on almost the same route). On other routes from Huanchaco to Trujillo centre, ask the *cobrador* to let you off near C Pizarro on Av España. To reach the **Línea, Móvil Tours** and southern bus terminals in Trujillo, take micro H from Huanchaco; it also goes to Ovalo Grau where you can catch buses to the Huacas del Sol and de la Luna. For **Cruz del Sur, Ormeño and Flores bus services**, take combi or micro B from Huanchaco.

Puerto Chicama

Buses stop just off Plaza Central, opposite the Comisaria.

Santuario y Reserva Nacional Calipuy

Buses from Terminal Santa Cruz in Trujillo to **Santiago de Chuco**, US$6, 4 hrs. Private 4WD from Santiago de Chuco to the reserves, about US$85 return. To hire a 4WD in Trujillo to the reserves via Chao, contact Manuel Rubio, T948-312400, about US$150 for 1 day, US$215 for 2.

Chiclayo and around *Colour map 2, B1.*

witches' brews and Moche treasures

Lambayeque Department, sandwiched between the Pacific and the Andes, is a major agricultural zone, especially for rice and sugar cane. It boasts a distinctive cuisine and musical tradition, and an unparalleled ethnographic and archaeological heritage. Excavations at the region's adobe pyramid cities are uncovering fabulous treasures.

Chiclayo

Since its foundation in the 16th century, Chiclayo has grown to become a major commercial hub with a population of 800,000. Its witchcraft market is famous, but it is best known for the spectacular cache of prehispanic archaeological treasures found on its doorstep.

On the Plaza de Armas is the 19th-century neoclassical **Cathedral**, designed by the English architect Andrew Townsend. The private **Club de la Unión** is on the Plaza at the corner of Calle San José. Continue five blocks north on Balta, the busiest commercial street, to the **Mercado Modelo**, one of northern Peru's liveliest and largest daily markets. Don't miss the market stalls off Calle Arica on the south side, where ritual paraphernalia used by traditional curers and diviners (*curanderos*) are sold: herbal medicines, folk charms, curing potions and exotic objects, including dried llama fetuses, to cure all manner of real and imagined illnesses. At **Paseo Artesanal Colón**, south of the Plaza, shops sell handicrafts in a quiet, custom-built open-air arcade. Other relaxing spots are the **Paseo de las Musas**, with its gardens and imitation Greek statues, and **Paseo Yortuque**, with 80 fiberglass statues representing the history of the area.

Chiclayo

N

100 metres
100 yards

Where to stay 🛏
1 Alfonso Ugarte *B2*
2 Costa del Sol *C3*
3 Embajador *A3*
4 Gran Hotel Chiclayo *B1*
5 Hosp Concordia *C3*
6 Hosp San Eduardo *C3*
7 Inti *B2*
8 Paraíso *A3*
9 Pirámide Real *C3*
10 Santa Rosa *B2*
11 Sicán *C2*
12 Sol Radiante *C2*
13 Sunec *C2*

Restaurants 🍴
1 Balta 512 *C3*
2 Boulevar *B2*
3 Café 900 *C3*
4 Café Astoria *C2*
5 D'Onofrio *C3*
6 El Huaralino *C1*
7 Fiesta *B1*
8 Hebrón *C3*
9 Kaprichos *A3*
10 La Panadería *B2*
11 La Parra *C3*
12 La Plazuela *B1*
13 Las Américas *B3*
14 Roma *C3*
15 Tradiciones *C2*

Transport 🚌
1 Brüning Express to Lambayeque *B1*
2 Cial *C1*
3 Civa *C3*
4 Colectivos to Lambayeque *A2*
5 Colectivos to Puerto Etén *A3*
6 Cruz del Sur *C3*
7 Emtrafesa *C3*
8 Línea *C2*
9 Móvil *C1*
10 Oltursa *B1*
11 Tepsa *C2*
12 Transportes Chiclayo *B1*

Monsefú and the coast

The traditional town of **Monsefú**, southwest, is known for its music and handicrafts; there's a good market, four blocks from the plaza. The stalls open when potential customers arrive (see also Festivals, page 124).

Beyond Monsefú are three ports serving the Chiclayo area. **Pimentel**, 8 km from Chiclayo, is a beach resort which gets very crowded on Sundays and during the summer (US$4 to rent a chair and sunshade). Most of the seafront has been bought up by developers, but the main plaza is an oasis of green. There are several seafood restaurants (**El Muelle de Pimentel**, Rivera del Mar cuadra 1, T074-453142, is recommended). You can walk along the restored pier for US$0.75. Sea-going reed boats (*caballitos de totora*) are used by fishermen and may be seen from the pier returning late morning or afternoon on the beach.

The surfing between Pimentel and the Bayovar Peninsula is excellent, reached from Chiclayo (14.5 km) by a road branching off from the Pan-American Highway. Nearby **Santa Rosa** has little to recommend it, other than to see the realities of fishing life, and it is not safe to walk there from Pimentel. The most southerly port, 24 km by road from Chiclayo, is **Puerto Eten**, a quaint place with some wooden buildings on the plaza. Its old railway station has been declared a national heritage monument. The adjacent roadstead, Villa de Eten, is a centre for panama hat-making, but is not as picturesque.

☆ Lambayeque

About 12 km northwest of Chiclayo is Lambayeque, a good base from which to explore the Chiclayo area. Its narrow streets are lined by colonial and Republican houses, many retaining their distinctive wooden balconies and wrought-iron grillwork over the windows, although many are in very bad shape. On Calle 2 de Mayo don't miss **Casa de la Logia o Montjoy**, whose 67-m-long balcony is said to be the longest in the colonial Americas. It has been restored and can be visited (free). At 8 de Octubre 345 is **Casona Descalzi** ① *T074-283433, daily 1100-1700*, which is well preserved as a good restaurant. It has 120 carved iguana heads on the ceiling. **Casona Iturregui Aguilarte**, at No 410, is, by contrast, seriously neglected. Also of interest are the 16th-century **Complejo Religioso Monumental de San Francisco de Asís** and the baroque church of the same name, which stands on Plaza de Armas 27 de Diciembre.

The reason most people visit is to see the town's two museums. The older of the two is the **Brüning Archaeological Museum** ① *daily 0900-1700, US$2.75, a guided tour costs an extra US$10*, in a modern building, which specializes in Mochica, Lambayeque/Sicán and Chimú cultures. Three blocks east is the more recent **Museo de las Tumbas Reales de Sipán** ① *Av Juan Pablo Vizcardo y Guzmán 895, T074-283977, www. museotumbasrealessipan.pe, Tue-Sun 0900-1700, US$3.55, mototaxi from plaza US$0.60*, shaped like a pyramid. The magnificent treasure from the tomb of the 'Old Lord of Sipán', and a replica of the Lord of Sipán's tomb are displayed here (see below). A ramp from the main entrance takes visitors to the third floor, from where you descend, mirroring the sequence of the archaeologists' discoveries. There are handicrafts outside and in the museum shop, also a branch of **Arte y Joyas Arqueológicas del Perú** ① *T9-8512 2539, ciecsipanarqueojoyas@gmail.com (also at Museo Amano in Lima and Museo Inkariy, Urubamba Km 53, Cuzco)*, selling jewellery inspired by pre-Inca and Inca art. There is also a **tourist office** ① *Tue-Sun 1000-1400*.

At Lambayeque the Pan-American Highway branches off the older road for 190 km, heading north across the **Sechura Desert**, a large area of shifting sands separating the oases of Chiclayo and Piura. If you're travelling this route, stop off in **Mórrope**, 20 km north of Lambayeque, to see one of the earliest churches in northern Peru. **San Pedro de Mórrope** (1545), an adobe and *algarrobo* structure on the plaza, contains the tomb of the cacique Santiago Cazusol.

Sipán

Turn-off is well signposted in the centre of Pomalca. Daily 0900-1700. Tombs and museum, US$3.50; guide at site US$10 (may not speak English). To visit the site takes about 3-4 hrs. There are comedores outside the site.

At this imposing complex a short distance east of Chiclayo excavations since 1987 in one of three crumbling pyramids have brought to light a cache of funerary objects considered to rank among the finest examples of pre-Columbian art. Peruvian archaeologist Walter Alva, former leader of the dig, continues to probe the immense mound that has revealed no less than 16 royal tombs filled with 1800-year-old offerings worked in precious metals, stone, pottery and textiles of the Moche culture (circa AD 1-750). In the most extravagant Moche tomb El Señor de Sipán was discovered, a priest clad in gold (ear ornaments, breast plate, etc), with turquoise and other valuables.

In another tomb were found the remnants of what is thought to have been a priest, sacrificed llama and a dog, together with copper decorations. In 1989 another richly appointed, unlooted tomb contained even older metal and ceramic artefacts associated with what was probably a high-ranking shaman or spiritual leader, called 'The Old Lord of Sipán'. Three tombs are on display, with replicas of the original finds. **Museo de Sitio Huaca Rajada** ① *daily 0900-1700, US$2.85*, concentrates on the finds at the site, especially Tombs 14, 15 and 16 containing 'Priest-Warriors', the decorative techniques of the Moche and the roles that archaeologists and local communities play in protecting these precious discoveries. You can wander around the previously excavated areas of the Huaca Rajada to get an idea of the construction of the burial mound and adjacent pyramids. For a good view, climb the large pyramid across from the excavated Huaca Rajada.

Ventarrón

A 4000-year-old temple, Ventarrón, was uncovered about 20 km from Sipán in 2007 by Walter Alva; his son, Ignacio, is now in charge of the dig. It predates Sipán by some 2000 years and shows at least three phases of development. Its murals, which appear to depict a deer trapped in a net, are claimed to be the oldest in the Americas and there is evidence of cultural exchange with as far away as the Amazon. A project to build a site museum and improve access is underway; until then, entry with guide is US$4 (some speak English), open 0800-1700, allow one to two hours to visit the site.

Chaparrí Reserve

75 km from Chiclayo, for day visits T074-433194, www.chaparri.org. US$10.50 entry to the reserve; groups of 10 accompanied by a local guide. Mototaxi from Chongoyape to Chaparrí, US$15.

East from Pomalca, just before Chongoyape, is the turning to the Chaparrí private ecological reserve, 34,000 ha, set up and run by the Comunidad Muchik Santa Catalina de Chongoyape. Visitors can go for the day or stay at the **EcoLodge Chaparrí** (see Where to stay, page 123). All staff and guides are locals, which provides work and helps to prevent littering. There are no dogs or goats in the area so the forest is recuperating; it contains many bird and mammal species of the dry forest, including white-winged guan and spectacled bear. There is a Spectacled Bear Rescue Centre where bears rescued from captivity live in semi-wild enclosures. The Tinajones reservoir is good for birdwatching.

Túcume

T074-835026, www.museodesitiotucume.com. Daily 0830-1630. US$4.50, students US$1, children US$0.30, plus guide US$15. Mototaxi from highway/new town to ruins, US$0.75. Allow at least 3 hrs to visit the whole site and museum.

About 35 km north of Chiclayo, not far from the Panamericana and Túcume Nuevo, lie the ruins of this vast city built over 1000 years ago. A short climb to the two *miradores* on **Cerro La Raya** (or **El Purgatorio**) offers the visitor an unparalleled panoramic vista of 26 major pyramids, platform mounds, walled citadels and residential compounds flanking a ceremonial centre and ancient cemeteries. One of the pyramids, Huaca Larga, where excavations are still being undertaken, is the longest adobe structure in the world, measuring 700 m long, 280 m wide and over 30 m high. There is no evidence of occupation at Túcume before the Sicán or Lambayeque people who developed the site AD 1000-1375. Thereafter the Chimú conquered the region, establishing a short reign until the arrival of the Incas around 1470. The Incas built on top of the existing structure of **Huaca Larga** using stone from Cerro La Raya.

Among the other pyramids which make up this huge complex are: **Huaca El Mirador** (90 m by 65 m, 30 m high), **Huaca Las Estacas**, **Huaca Pintada** and **Huaca de las Balsas**, which is thought to have housed people of elevated status such as priests. A walkway leads around the covered pyramid and you can see many mud reliefs including fishermen on rafts.

> **Tip...**
> There is a pleasant dry forest walk to Huaca I, with shade and the chance to do some bird- and lizard-watching.

Apart from the miradores, not much of the site is open to view, as lots of archaeological study is still going on. However, a site museum displays many objects found here, including miniature offerings relating to the prehispanic gods and mythology of Lambayeque, items relating to the last Inca governor of Túcume and a room detailing the history of the region from pre-Columbian times to the present. There is also a shop.

The town of **Túcume Viejo** is a 20-minute walk beyond the site. Look for the side road heading towards a park, opposite which is the ruin of a huge colonial church made of adobe and some brick. The surrounding countryside is pleasant for walks through mango trees and fields of maize. **Fiesta de la Purísima Concepción**, the festival of the town's patron saint, takes place eight days prior to Carnival in February, and also in September.

☆Ferreñafe

The colonial town of **Ferreñafe**, 20 km northeast of Chiclayo, is worth a visit, especially for the **Museo Nacional Sicán** ⓘ *Av Batán Grande cuadra 9, T074-286469, Museo-Nacional-Sican-109965152373661 on Facebook, Tue-Sun 0900-1700, US$4, students half price, good explanations in Spanish, café and gift shop.* This excellent museum on the outskirts of town houses objects of the Sicán (Lambayeque) culture from near Batán Grande. To get there, take a mototaxi from the centre, five minutes, US$1.75, or, from Chiclayo, catch a combi from Avenida N de Piérola towards Batán Grande; these pass the museum every 15-20 minutes, taking 40 minutes, US$1.

Sicán (El Santuario Histórico Bosque de Pómac)

20 km beyond Ferreñafe along the road to Batán Grande (from the Panamericana another entrance is near Túcume), dalemandelama@gmail.com. Daily 0900-1700. US$4; a guide

(Spanish only) can be hired with transport, US$12, or horses for hire US$7. Food and drinks are available at the visitor centre, and camping is permitted.

El Santuario Histórico Bosque de Pómac includes the ruins of Sicán. Visiting is not easy because of the arid conditions and distances involved: it is 10 km from the visitor centre to the nearest *huaca* (pyramid). A two-hour guided tour of the area includes at least two *huacas*, some of the most ancient carob trees and a mirador that has a beautiful view across the emerald-green tops of the forest with the enormous pyramids dramatically breaking through.

Sicán has revealed several sumptuous tombs dating to AD 900-1100. The ruins comprise some 12 large adobe pyramids, arranged around a huge plaza, measuring 500 m by 250 m, with 40 archaeological sites in total. The city of the Sicán (or Lambayeque culture) was probably moved to Túcume (see above), 6 km west, following 30 years of severe drought and then a devastating El Niño-related flood in AD 1050-1100. These events appear to have provoked a rebellion in which many of the remaining temples on top of the pyramids were burnt and destroyed. The forest itself has good birdwatching possibilities.

Olmos and around

On the old Pan-American Highway 885 km from Lima, Olmos is a tranquil place surrounded by endless lemon orchards and vineyards; there are several hotels and a **Festival de Limón** in the last week in June. A paved road runs east from Olmos over the Porculla Pass, branching north to Jaén and east to Bagua Grande (see page 160). Olmos is the best base for observing the critically endangered white-winged guan, a bird thought extinct for 100 years until its rediscovery in 1977. The **Barbara d'Achille breeding centre** ① *0900-1700, US$1.75*, for the white-winged guan can be visited. The old Pan-American Highway continues from Olmos to Cruz de Caña and Piura.

Listings Chiclayo and around *map page 117*.

Tourist information

Chiclayo

Indecopi
Los Tumbos 245, Santa Victoria, T074-206223, aleyva@indecopi.gob.pe. Mon-Fri 0800-1300, 1630-1930.
For complaints and tourist protection.

iPerú
Palacio Municipal, C San José 823, T074-205703, iperuchiclayo@promperu.gob.pe. Mon-Sat 0900-1800, Sun 0900-1300.
Also in Lambayeque at Museo de las Tumbas Reales de Sipán, Tue-Sun 1000-1400. There are tourist kiosks on the Plaza and on Balta.

Tourist police
Av Sáenz Peña 830. Daily 24 hrs.

Very helpful and may store luggage and take you to the sites themselves.

Ferreñafe

Mincetur
On the Plaza de Armas, T074-282843, citesipan@mincetur.gob.pe.
Helpful.

Where to stay

Chiclayo

$$$ Costa del Sol
Balta 399, T074-227272, www.costadelsolperu.com.
Non-smoking rooms, smart, small pool, sauna, jacuzzi, Wi-Fi, ATM. **Páprika** restaurant, good value Sun buffets, vegetarian options.

$$$ Gran Hotel Chiclayo
(Casa Andina Select)
Villareal 115, T511-2139739,
www.casa-andina.com.
Large, modern hotel for corporate and leisure guests, pool, safe car park, changes dollars, jacuzzi, entertainments, restaurant. Now operated by **Casa Andina**.

$$$ Inti
Luis Gonzales 622, T074-235931,
www.intihotel.com.pe.
More expensive rooms with jacuzzi, family rooms available, welcome cocktail, airport transfer included, parking, safe and fridge in room, restaurant, helpful staff.

$$$ Sunec
Izaga 472, T074-205110,
www.sunechotel.com.pe.
Modern hotel in a central location, parking and small pool.

$$ Embajador
7 de Enero 1388, 1½ blocks from Mercado Modelo, T074-204729,
https://hotelchiclayoembajador.com.
Modern, bright, good facilities, 20 mins' walk from centre, small comfortable rooms, small restaurant, excellent service, free pick-up from bus office, tours arranged.

$$ Paraíso
Pedro Ruiz 1064, T074-228161,
www.hotelesparaiso.com.pe.
Modern rooms with fan, restaurant, 24-hr cafeteria, meeting rooms, parking, very good service.

$ Alfonso Ugarte
Alfonso Ugarte 1193, T074-222135.
No meals, small but comfortable double and single rooms.

$ Hospedaje Concordia
7 de Enero Sur 235, Urb San Eduardo, T074-209423.
Rooms on 2nd floor bigger than 3rd, modern, pleasant, no meals, laundry service, view of Parque San Eduardo.

$ Hospedaje San Eduardo
7 de Enero Sur 267, Urb San Eduardo, T074-208668.
No meals, colourful decor, modern bathrooms, fan, Wi-Fi, public phone, quiet, hot water.

$ Pirámide Real
MM Izaga 726, T074-224036.
Compact and spotless, good value, no meals, safe in room, fan, very central.

$ Santa Rosa
L González 927, T074-224411.
Rooms with windows are bright and spacious, best at rear. Hot water, fan, laundry, good value.

$ Sicán
MM Izaga 356, T074-208741,
hsican@hotmail.com.
With breakfast, hot water, fan, comfortable, restaurant and bar, laundry, parking, welcoming and trustworthy.

$ Sol Radiante
Izaga 392, T074-237858.
Hot water, comfortable, pleasant, family-run, laundry, tourist information. Pay in advance.

Lambayeque

$$$ Hostería San Roque
2 de Mayo 437, T074-282860,
www.hosteriasanroque.com.
In a fine, extensive colonial house, beautifully refurbished, helpful staff, bar, swimming pool, lunch on request. Single, double, triple, quad rooms and dorm for groups of 6, $.

$ Hostal Libertad
Bolívar 570, T074-283561,
www.hostallibertad.com.
1½ blocks from plaza, big rooms, fridge, secure.

$ Hostal Real Sipán
Huamachuco 664, opposite Brüning Museum.
Modern, an option if arriving late at night.

Mórrope

$$-$ La Casa del Papelillo
San Pedro 357, T955-624734,
lacasadelpapelillo@gmail.com,
www.airbnb.es/rooms/89079.
3 rooms in a remodelled 19th-century home,
1 with private bath, includes breakfast,
communal areas, cultural events, discounts
for community volunteer work. Owner
Cecilia is knowledgeable and helpful.

Chaparrí Reserve

$$$$ EcoLodge Chaparrí
T984-676249 or in Chiclayo T074-452299,
www.chaparrilodge.com.
A delightful oasis in the dry forest,
6 beautifully decorated cabins (more
being built) and 5 double rooms with
shared bath, built of stone and mud, nice
and cool, solar power. Price is for 3 meals
and a local guide for one day, first-class
food. Sechuran foxes in the gardens;
hummingbirds bathe at the pool about
0600 every day. Recommended.

Túcume

$$ pp Los Horcones
T951-831705, www.loshorconesdetucume.com.
Closed Feb-Mar.
Rustic luxury in the shadow of the pyramids,
adobe and algarrobo rooms set in lovely
garden with lots of birdlife, pool. Good food,
pizza oven, breakfast included. Note that if
rice is being grown nearby in Jan-May there
can be a serious mosquito problem.

Olmos

$$$ Los Faiques
9 km from old Panamericana on road to
Salas, can arrange a taxi from Chiclayo
or take Salas combi from Chiclayo, T979-
299932, www.losfaiques-salas.com.
Very pretty place in a quiet forest setting,
buffet breakfast, dinner on request.

$ El Remanso
San Francisco 100, T074-427158,
elremansolmos@yahoo.com.
Like a hacienda, with courtyards, small pool,
whitewashed rooms, colourful bedding,
flowers and bottled water in room, hot
water (supposedly). Price is full board, good
restaurant. Charming owner. There are
several other places to stay in town.

Restaurants

Chiclayo
For delicious, cheap ceviche, go to the
Nativo stall in the Mercado Central, a local
favourite. For ice cream, try **D'Onofrio**
(Balta y Torres Paz). **La Panadería** (Lapoint
847), has a good choice of breads, including
integral, snacks and soft drinks.

$$$ El Huaralino
La Libertad 155, Santa Victoria.
Wide variety, international and creole,
but mixed reports of late.

$$$ Fiesta
Av Salaverry 1820 in 3 de Octubre suburb,
T074-201970, www.restaurantfiesta
gourmet.com.
Gourmet local dishes, excellent food and
service, beautifully presented, daily and
seasonal specials, fabulous juices, popular
business lunch place.

$$$ Sabores Peruanos
Los Incas 136. Tue-Sun 1200-1700.
Great Peruvian seafood and meat dishes.

$$ Balta 512
Balta 512, T074-223598.
First-class local food, usually good breakfast,
popular with locals.

$$ Boulevar
Colón entre Izaga y Aguirre.
Good, friendly, *menú* and à la carte.

$$ Hebrón
Balta 605.
For more upmarket than average chicken,
but also local food and *parrilla*, good salads.

Also does an excellent breakfast and a good buffet at weekends.

$$ Kaprichos
Pedro Ruíz 1059, T074-232721.
Chinese, delicious, huge portions.

$$ Las Américas
Aguirre 824. Daily 0700-0200.
Good service.

$$ Roma
Izaga 706. Open all day.
Wide choice, breakfasts, snacks and meals.

$$ Tradiciones
7 de Enero Sur 105, T074-221192.
Daily 0900-1700.
Good variety of local dishes, including ceviche, and drinks, pleasant atmosphere and garden, good service.

$$ Vichayo Restobar
Los Alamos 230, Urb Santa Victoria,
T074-227664. Wed-Sun.
Excellent fish and seafood dishes.

$ Café 900
MM Izaga 900, www.cafe900.com.
Appealing atmosphere in a remodelled old house, good food, popular with locals, sometimes has live music.

$ Café Astoria
Bolognesi 627. Daily 0800-1200, 1530-2100.
Breakfast, good-value *menú*.

$ La Parra
Izaga 746.
Chinese and creole *parrillada*, very good, large portions, cheerful.

$ La Plazuela
San José 299, Plaza Elías Aguirre.
Good food, seats outside.

Lambayeque

A Lambayeque speciality is the 'King Kong', a giant *alfajor* biscuit filled with *manjar blanco* and other sweets. San Roque brand (www.sanroque.com.pe), sold throught Peru, is especially good.

$$ Casona Descalzi
Address above. Lunch only.
Good menu, including traditional northern dishes.

$$ El Cántaro
2 de Mayo 180. Lunch only.
For traditional local dishes, à la carte and a good *menú*.

$$ El Pacífico
Huamachuco 970, T074-283135. Lunch only.
Renowned for its enormous plates of *arroz con pato* and *causa norteña*.

$$ El Rincón del Pato
A Leguía 270. Lunch only.
Offers 40 different duck dishes.

$$-$ Sabor Norteño
Bolívar 440.
One of the few restaurants open in the early evening.

$ Café Cultural La Cucarda
2 de Mayo 263, T074-284155. Evening only.
Small alternative café, decorated with antiques, delicious pastries, pies and cakes. Recommended.

Festivals

6 Jan Reyes Magos in Mórrope, Illimo and other towns, a recreation of a medieval pageant in which pre-Columbian deities become the Wise Men.
4 Feb Túcume devil dances.
14 Mar and 14 Sep El Señor Nazareno Cautivo, in Lambayeque and Monsefú, whose main celebration of this festival is 14 Sep.
Mar/Apr Holy Week, traditional Easter celebrations and processions in many villages.
2-7 Jun Divine Child of the Miracle, Villa de Eten.
27-31 Jul Fexticum in **Monsefú**, traditional foods, drink, handicrafts, music and dance.
5 Aug Pilgrimage from the mountain shrine of **Chalpón** to **Motupe**, 90 km north of Chiclayo; the cross is brought down from a cave and carried in procession through the village.

24 Dec-1 Jan Christmas and **New Year** processions and children dancers (*pastorcitos* and *seranitas*) can be seen in many villages, including **Ferreñafe**, **Mochumi**, **Mórrope**.

What to do

Chiclayo
Tour operators

Lambayeque's museums, Sipán and Túcume can easily be visited by public transport (see below). Local operators run 3-hr tours to Sipán; Túcume and Lambayeque (5 hrs); Sicán is a full-day tour including Ferreñafe and Pómac. There are also tours to Zaña and coastal towns.

InkaNatura, *Manuel María Izaga 730, of 203, T979-995024, www.inkanatura.net. Mon-Fri 0915-1315, 1515-1915, Sat 0915-1315.* Historical and nature tours throughout northern Peru. Good service.

Julio Porras, *T979-710768, julio.porras.guide@gmail.com.* Julio organizes tours in an around Chiclayo. He knows the area well and speaks fluent English.

Sicán (El Santuario Histórico Bosque de Pómac)
Horse riding

Rancho Santana, *Pacora, T979-712145, www.cabalgatasperu.com.* Relaxing tours on horseback, half-day (US$15.50), 1-day (US$22.50) or 3-day tours to Santuario Bosque de Pómac, Sicán ruins and Túcume, Swiss-run (Andrea Martin), good horses. Also $ a bungalow, a double room and camping (tents for hire) at the ranch with safe parking for campervans. Frequently recommended.

Transport

Chiclayo
Air José Abelardo Quiñones González **airport** 1 km from town, T074-233192; taxi from centre US$4. Arrive 2 hrs before flight; be prepared for manual search of hand luggage; no restaurant or bar in departure lounge.

Daily flights to/from **Lima** and **Piura** with **LATAM** (MM Izaga 770) and **StarPerú**

(MM Izaga 459, T074-225204), direct or via **Trujillo**.

Bus Local Combis to **Monsefú** cost US$0.75 from Bolognesi y Sarmiento, or Terminal Epsel (Av Castañeda Iparraguirre s/n). Combis to **Pimentel** leave from Av L Ortiz y San José, US$1.10. *Colectivos* to **Lambayeque**, US$0.75, 25 mins, leave from Pedro Ruíz at the junction with Av Ugarte; also **Brüning Express** combis from Vicente de la Vega entre Angamos y Av L Ortiz, every 15 mins, US$0.50, or **Trans Lambayeque** *colectivo* from Plaza Elias Aguirre, US$0.90. Combis to **Sipán** leave from terminal Epsel, US$1, 1 hr. To **Chongoyape** for Chaparrí Reserve, take a public bus from Leoncio Prado y Sáenz Peña (1¼ hrs, US$1.50), then a mototaxi to **Chaparrí**, US$10. Combis to Tucumé leave from Av Leguía, 15 m from Angamos, US$1, 45 mins. *Colectivos* to the centre of Ferreñafe leave from Terminal Epsel every few mins, or from 8 de Octubre y Sáenz Peña, 40 mins, U$1. Combis to **Batán Grande** depart from Av N de Piérola, and pass the museum in Ferreñafe every 15-20 mins, 40 mins, US$1.

Long distance There is no central terminal; most buses stop outside their offices on Bolognesi. To **Lima**, 770 km, US$25-36, with **Civa** (Av Bolognesi 714, T074-223434); **Cruz del Sur** (Bolognesi 888, T074-225508); **Ormeño** (Haya de la Torre 242, 2 blocks south of Bolognesi, T074-234206); **Ittsa** (Av Bolognesi 155, T074-233612); **Línea** (Bolognesi 638, T074-222221), *especial* and *bus cama* service; **Móvil** (Av Bolognesi 195, T074-271940), goes as far as Tarapoto; **Oltursa** (ticket office at Balta e Izaga, T074-237789, terminal at Vicente de la Vega 101, T074-225611); **Tepsa** (Bolognesi 504-36 y Colón, T074-236981) and **Transportes Chiclayo** (Av L Ortiz 010, T074-223632). Most companies leave from 1900 onwards.

To **Trujillo**, 209 km, with **Emtrafesa** (Av Balta 110, T074-600660), every 15 mins, 4 hrs, US$5.50, and **Línea**. To **Piura**, 4 hrs, US$5.50, **Transportes Chiclayo** leave

15 mins throughout the day; also **Línea** and **Emtrafesa** and buses from the **Cial/ Flores** terminal (Bolognesi 751, T074-239579). To **Sullana**, US$8.50. To **Tumbes**, US$9, 9-10 hrs; with **Cial**, **Cruz del Sur** or **El Dorado**. To **Cajamarca**, 260 km, US$9-20, eg **Línea**, 4 a day; others from Tepsa terminal (Bolognesi y Colón, eg **Días**, T074-224448). To **Chachapoyas**, US$13.50-25, with **Civa**, 1730 daily, 10-11 hrs; **Transervis Kuelap** (Tepsa station), 1830 daily; **Móvil**, at 2000. To **Jaén**, US$7.75-9.60, many companies; **Móvil** charges US$11.55-15.50. To **Tarapoto**, 18 hrs, US$25-29, with **Móvil**, also Tarapoto Tours (Bolognesi 751, T074-636231). To **Guayaquil**, with **Civarun** at 1825, *semi-cama* US$34.75, *cama* US$42.50, also **Super Semería**, US$25, 12 hrs, via Piura, Máncora, Tumbes; they also go to Cuenca.

Taxi Mototaxis are a cheap way to get around: US$1 anywhere in city. Chiclayo to Pimentel, US$6, 20 mins. Taxi *colectivos* to Eten leave from Mariscal Nieto and José Quiñones.

Lambayeque
Some major bus lines have offices in Lambayeque and can drop you off there. There are numerous combis between Lambayeque and **Chiclayo** (see above). Combi to **Túcume**, US$1.25, 25 mins.

Piura and around *Colour map 2, A1.*

a proud and historic city

Piura was founded in 1532, three years before Lima, by the conquistadors left behind by Pizarro. The city has public gardens and two well-kept parks, Cortés and Pizarro (also called Plaza de las Tres Culturas); the latter has a statue of the man himself. Old buildings are kept in repair and new buildings blend with the Spanish style of the old city. Three bridges cross the Río Piura to Castilla: the oldest is the pedestrian-only Puente San Miguel from Calle Huancavelica; another is from Calle Sánchez Cerro, and the newest is from Avenida Panamericana Norte at the west end of town.

Sights
On the **Plaza de Armas** is the **cathedral** ① *daily 0800-1200, 1700-2030*, with a gold-covered altar and paintings by Ignacio Merino. A few blocks away is **San Francisco** ① *Mon-Sat 0900-1200, 1600-1800*, where the city's independence from Spain was declared on 4 January 1821, nearly eight months before Lima. **Casa Museo Grau** ① *C Tacna 662, opposite the Centro Cívico, T073-326541, Mon-Fri 0800-1300, 1500-1800, Sat-Sun 0800-1200, US$0.70*, is the birthplace of Admiral Miguel Grau, hero of the War of the Pacific with Chile. The museum contains a model of the *Huáscar*, the largest Peruvian warship in the War of the Pacific, which was built in Britain. It also contains interesting old photographs. The small **Museo Municipal Vicús** ① *Sullana, near Huánuco, Tue-Sat 0900-1645, Sun 0900-1300*, includes a Sala de Oro (closed weekends, US$1.45) with 60 gold artefacts from the local Vicús culture and an art section.

Catacaos
Twelve kilometres southwest of Piura, Catacaos is famous for its *chicha*, *picanterías* (local restaurants, some with music) and for its crafts, including tooled leather, gold and silver filigree jewellery, wooden articles

Tip...
The winter climate, May to September, is very pleasant although nights can be cold and the wind piercing; December to March is very hot.

and straw hats (expensive). The town has splendid celebrations during Holy Week. About 2 km south of Catacaos is the **Narihuala archaeological site** ⓘ *Tue-Sun 0830-1630, US$0.70, children will guide you for a tip, mototaxi from Catacaos US$1.80*, which consists of deteriorated adobe pyramids of the Tallán culture (AD 900-1400) and a site museum.

Piura

Where to stay 🛏
1 California
2 Costa del Sol
3 El Príncipe
4 Hosp Pacífico
5 Hostal Los Jardines
6 Ixnuk
7 Las Arenas
8 Los Portales
9 Sol de Piura

Restaurants 🍴
1 Alex Chopp's
2 Carburmer -
 Picantería La Santitos
3 Don Parce
4 D'Pauli
5 El Chalán
6 Ganímedes
7 Juguería La Floresta
8 La Pera Madura
9 La Tomasita
10 Romano
11 Urius

Paita and around

Paita, 50 km from Piura, is the major fishing port for the area and is flanked on three sides by a towering, sandy bluff. Looming over Paita is a small colonial fortress built to repel pirates, who attacked it frequently. Several colonial buildings survive. Bolívar's mistress, Manuela Sáenz, lived the last 24 years of her life in Paita, after being exiled from Quito. She supported herself until her death in 1856 by weaving, embroidering and making candy, after refusing the fortune left her by her husband. Nearby beaches include **Colán**, to the north, with various hotels, restaurants and a long sandy beach (beware the stingrays); and less developed **Yasila**, a fishing village to the south.

Listings Piura and around *map page 127.*

Tourist information

iPerú
Ayacucho s/n y C Libertad, edif Serpost, in a lane off the Plaza de Armas, T073-320249, iperupiura@promperu.gob.pe. Mon-Sat 0900-1800, Sun 0900-1300; there's another office in Arrivals at the airport.
Very helpful staff.

Where to stay

$$$$-$$$ Costa del Sol
Av Loreto 649, T073-302864, www.costadelsolperu.com.
Centrally located, part of the Peruvian first class hotel chain, pool, restaurant.

$$$$-$$$ Los Portales
Libertad 875, Plaza de Armas, T073-321161, www.losportaleshoteles.com.pe.
Elegantly refurbished *casona* in the heart of the city, luxurious suites and rooms, includes welcome cocktail, the city's social centre pleasant terrace, nice pool.

$$$ Ixnuk
Ica 553, T073-322205, www.ixnuk.com.
Modern hotel with bright ample rooms, a/c, fridge, airport transfers.

$$$-$$ El Príncipe
Junín 930, T073-324868.
Comfortable suite and rooms with a/c, fridge, airport transfers.

$$ Las Arenas
Loreto 945, T073-305554.
Older well maintained hotel in a central location, variety of rooms, a/c, cheaper with fan, small pool, IYHF discounts.

$$ Sol de Piura
Tacna 761, T073-332395, www.soldepiura.com.
Centrally located modern hotel, comfortable rooms with a/c, fridge, airport transfers.

$$-$ Hostal Los Jardines
Av Los Cocos 436, Urb Club Grau, T073-326590, www.hotellosjardines.com.
Not far from the centre, rooms with ceiling fan, ageing but OK, parking, good value.

$ California
Jr Junín 835, upstairs, T073-328789.
Shared or private bath, own water-tank, mosquito netting on windows, roof terrace.

$ Hospedaje Pacífico
Apurimac 717, T073-303061.
Simple comfortable rooms with fan, the newer ones on the top floors are the nicest, no breakfast, good value.

Restaurants

$$$ Carburmer – Picantería La Santitos
Libertad 1001, T073-309475. Daily 1100-1900.
Very good fish, regional dishes and pizza in a renovated colonial house.

$$$ La Tomasita
Tacna 853, T073-321957. Daily 1100-1730.
Very good *picantería* serving regional dishes
including ceviche, *arroz con cabrito* (goat)
and *seco de chavelo* (sun-dried meat). A/c.

$$$-$$ Don Parce
Tacna 642, T073-300842. Daily 0700-2100.
Upmarket restaurant serving varied
international food. *Menú* Mon-Sat.

$$ Alex Chopp's
Huancavelica 538, T073-322568.
Daily 1200-2400.
A la carte dishes, seafood, fish, and
especially beer.

$$ Urius
Sánchez Cerro 210, T073-332581, www.
uriusrestaurante.com. Daily 0700-1600.
Upmarket dining, regional and international
dishes à la carte and a more economical
menú. Part of a cooking school.

$$-$ Romano
Ayacucho 580, Mon-Sat 0730-2300,
and El Otro Romano, Ayacucho 673.
Tue-Sun 0900-1600.
Popular with locals, extensive menu,
excellent set meal. Recommended.

$ Ganímedes
Apurímac 468-B. Mon-Sat 0800-2230,
Sun 0800-2100.
A popular vegetarian restaurant serving set
lunch. Pizza and à la carte from 1800, bakery
with a wide selection of bread and sweet
and savoury pastries.

Cafés and snack bars

D'Pauli
Lima 541. Mon-Sat 0900-1400, 1600-2130.
Sweets, cakes and sandwiches.

El Chalán
Several branches including Tacna 520 on Plaza
de Armas, Grau 173, Grau 452 and others.
Sandwiches, sweets, fruit salad and very
good ice cream,

Juguería La Floresta
Cusco 965. Mon-Sat 0900-1400, 1600-2200.
A selection of fresh fruit juices and natural
food products.

La Pera Madura
Arequipa 168, next to Teatro Municipal,
no sign. Daily 1700-2300.
For turkey sandwiches, *tamales* and other
local specialities.

Catacaos
Among the town's *chicha picanterías*, **Chayo**
(Jr San Francisco 497) is very good.

What to do

City tours, visits to craft towns, beaches,
adventure sports (including surfing and
sandboarding) and nature tours in the Piura
highlands and desert are all available.

Canechi Tours, *C Tacna 349, p2, T073-311327,*
www.canechitours.com.
Dry Forest Expeditions, *Jr Huancavelica 878,*
p2, T073-618391, www.dryforestexpeditions.com.
Piura Tours, *C Arequipa 978, T073-326778,*
piuratours@speedy.com.pe. The manager
Mario speaks good English.

Transport

Air Capitán Guillermo Concha airport is
in Castilla, 10 mins from the centre by taxi
(US$1.80-2.50). It has gift shops and car rental
agencies (see below). 8 daily flights to **Lima**
with **Avianca/TACA** (Centro Comercial Real
Plaza), **LATAM** (Centro Comercial Open Plaza)
or **Peruvian Airlines** (Libertad 777).

Bus Local *Colectivos* have their stops near
the Piura stations; they leave as they fill up.
To **Catacaos**, *colectivos* from Jr Loreto 1292,
1 block from Ovalo Bolognesi, US$0.90,
20 mins. To **Paita**, **Trans Dora** (T968-158086)
from Prolongación Sánchez Cerro, next to
Club de Tiro, every 20 mins, 1 hr, US$1.50;
also from **Terminal Gechisa** (Prolongación
Sánchez Cerro, opposite Proyecto Chira,
T073-399322) and *colectivos* from Av Loreto

block 12, by Jr Tumbes. Transfer in Paita for **Colán** and **Yacila**. To Chulucanas, **Trans Dora** from Prolongación Sánchez Cerro, next to Club de Tiro, every 30 mins, US$1.15, 45 mins; also from **Terminal El Bosque** in Castilla. To **Huancabamba**, with **San Pedro y San Pablo** (T073-349271), from **Terminal El Bosque**, Castilla, at 0730, 1330, 1830, 6 hrs; also **Civa** (T073-397991) from same terminal at 1030, 1800; and **Turismo Express Norte** (073-344330) from **Terminal Castilla**, at 0730, 1400, 1830.

Long distance Most long-distance bus companies are clustered along Av Sánchez Cerro, blocks 11-13, and Av Loreto, blocks 11-14; the latter is in a more pleasant area and closer to the centre. Some regional services run from **Terminal Gechisa**, Prolongación Sánchez Cerro (the road to Sullana), west of the city.

To **Lima**, 973 km, 14-15½ hrs, US$30-48. Most buses stop at the major cities on route: **Cruz del Sur** (Av Circunvalación 160, T073-337094); Oltursa (Bolognesi 801, T073-326666); **ITTSA** (Sánchez Cerro 1142, T073-333982); **Tepsa** (Loreto 1195, T073-306345); **Flores** (Av Loreto cuadra 12), 8 daily; several others.

To **Chiclayo** and **Lambayeque**, 209 km, 4 hrs, from US$5.50, with **Trans Chiclayo** (Sánchez Cerro 1121, T073-308455), every 30 min; **Línea** (Sánchez Cerro 1215, T073-303894, www.linea.pe), hourly; several others. To **Trujillo**, 7 hrs, 420 km, US$12.50-15, **Línea** at 1330 and 2300; to travel by day **ITTSA** at 0900 or change in Chiclayo; several others in the afternoon and around 2300.

To **Sullana**, 38 km, 30 mins, US$0.50, frequent service from **Terminal Gechisa**

0500-2200. To **Ayabaca**, 6 hrs, with **Transporte Vegas** (Panamericana C1 Lt10, Urb San Ramón, T073-308729) at 0730, 0830 and 1400, or **El Poderoso Cautivo** (Sullana Norte 7, Urb San Ramón, T073-309888) at 0730, 0840 and 1500.

To **Tumbes**, 282 km, 4½ hrs, US$7-8.50, **El Dorado** (Sánchez Cerro 1119, T073-325875), every 1-2 hrs; several others originating in cities to the south eg **Cruz del Sur, Cial** (Bolognesi 817, T073-304250), **CIVA** (Av Loreto 1401, T073-345451) and **Emtrafesa** (Los Naranjos 255, T073-337093, also to Chiclayo and Trujillo); also *colectivos*, US$12. To **Máncora**, 187 km, US$5.50, 3 hrs, with **Eppo** (Av Panamericana 243, behind CC Real Plaza, T073-304543, www.eppo.com.pe), every 30 mins; or buses to Tumbes or Ecuador; *colectivos* from Terminal Gechisa, US$11. To **Cajamarca**, 467 km, US$18, 10 hrs, at 1900 with **Dias** (Av Loreto 1485, T073-302834), also to Lima at 1500.

To Ecuador To **Guayaquil** via Tumbes, US$15-20, 9 hrs, with **CIFA**, from the same terminal as **Dias** (Av Loreto 1485, T073-324144), at 0720, 1950, 2100, 2330; also **Super Semeria** (from the same terminal), at 2200, and **CIVA**, from Av Loreto 140, at 2040. To **Loja** via Macará, with **Transportes Loja**, from the same terminal as Ronco (Av Loreto 1241, T073-33260), at 0900 and 2100, US$15, 8-9 hrs; or with **Unión Cariamanga**, from Dias terminal, at 2000. To **Cuenca**, US$16, 10 hrs, with **Azuay**, from Ronco terminal, T962-647002), at 2100; or **Super Semeria**, from **Dias terminal**, at 2030.

Car hire Ramos, T073-348668; and **Vicus**, T073-342051, both outside the airport, several others.

beach resorts and nature reserves en route to the border

Sullana to La Tina

The Pan-American Highway forks at **Sullana,** 38 km north of Piura. Built on a bluff over the fertile Chira valley, the city is neither clean nor safe, so there is no reason to stop here. To the east the Panamericana crosses the Peru–Ecuador border at La Tina (see below) and continues via Macará to Loja and Cuenca. The excellent paved road is very scenic and is the best option if you want to visit the southern or central highlands of Ecuador.

Border at La Tina–Macará The border crossing is problem-free and both sides are open 24 hours. Immigration, customs and other services are on either side of the international bridge. On the Peruvian side, there is one *hospedaje* and several eating places on the road down to the bridge. On the Ecuadorean side, Macará is a small city with all services, 2.5 km past the bridge. There are no money changers or ATMs right at the bridge, only at the park in Macará where vehicles leave for the border.

Sullana to Máncora

The second branch of the Pan-American Highway is the coastal road which goes from Sullana northwest towards the Talara oilfields, and then follows the coastline to Máncora and Tumbes. This is the more frequently used route to Ecuador. From Talara, the Panamericana goes a few kilometres inland but the old Panamericana gives access to lovely beaches and fishing towns that are a peaceful alternative to Máncora.

Máncora

Máncora, a resort stretching along the Pan-American Highway, is popular with young Limeños, Chileans and Argentines and also as a stop-off for travellers, especially surfers, on the Peru-Ecuador route. Development here has been rapid and haphazard. The resort is crowded and noisy during the December-February high season; beaches can get dirty; drugs and scams (many involving mototaxis) abound, and safety is a concern. Enquire locally about which sections of Máncora are currently safe. There is one bank and various ATMs in Máncora. **Vichayito,** 7 km south of Máncora, is accessed from Km 1150 or from Las Pocitas and is a lovely beach well suited to swimming, kite-surfing (April to November) and diving. Separated by a headland from Vichayito is **Las Pocitas**, a stretch of beautiful beach with rocks, behind which little pools (or *pocitas*) form at low tide. It is another alternative to Máncora, just 4 km away, for those looking for tranquillity.

Punta Sal to Tumbes

At Km 1187, 22 km north of Máncora, is the turn-off for **Punta Sal**, marked by a large white arch (El Arco) over the road (2 km). Punta Sal boasts a 3-km-long white sandy beach and a more upmarket clientèle than Máncora, with accommodation (and prices) to match. There is no town centre and no banks, ATMs or restaurants independent of hotels, so it is very quiet in the low season.

Zorritos, 62 km north of Punta Sal and 27 km south of Tumbes, is an important fishing centre with a good beach. At **Caleta La Cruz**, 16 km southwest of Tumbes, is the only part of the Peruvian coast where the sea is warm all year. It was here that Pizarro landed in 1532. There are regular *colectivos*, US$0.30 each way, from Tumbes.

Tumbes and around *Colour map 2, A1.*

The most northerly Peruvian city is Tumbes, 265 km north of Piura. Few tourists stop here since international buses take you directly north to Ecuador or south to the beaches or Piura.

The most striking aspect of the town itself is its bright and cheery modern public buildings: the **Malecón Benavides**, a long promenade beside the Tumbes river, has rainbow-coloured archways and a monstrous statue called El Beso (the Kiss); the Plaza de Armas sports a large structure of many colours, and even the **cathedral**, built in 1903 and restored in 1985, has green and pink stripes. Calles Bolívar and San Martín (Paseo de la Concordia) make for a pleasant wander, and there is a small artisans' market at the top end of San Martín (approaching Plaza Bolognesi). On Calle Grau, there are the tumble-down colonial houses, many of which are no longer in use.

☆ Tumbes provides access to important protected areas, administered by Sernanp ① *Panamericana Norte 1739, Tumbes, T072-526489; Los Cocos H-23, Urb Club Grau, Piura, T072-321668*, which, due to the latitude, are rich in fauna and flora found nowhere else in Peru. The best time to visit the parks is the dry season, April to December. On the coast, the **Santuario Nacional los Manglares de Tumbes** protects 3000 ha of Peru's remaining 4750 ha of mangrove forest. Inland, the **Parque Nacional Cerros de Amotape** protects 90,700 ha of varied habitat, but principally the best preserved area of dry forest on the west coast of South America. Adjoining it is the **Zona Reservada de Tumbes** (75,000 ha), which protects dry equatorial forest and tropical rainforest. The Río Tumbes crocodile, which is a UN Red-data species, is found at the river's mouth, where there is a small breeding programme, and in its upper reaches.

> **Tip...**
> There is an Ecuadorean Consulate in Tumbes at Bolívar 129, piso 3, Plaza de Armas, T072-525949, consultum@speedy.com.pe, Monday-Friday 0800-1300.

Border with Ecuador The best way to cross this border is on one of the international buses that run between Peru (Piura, Máncora or Tumbes) and Ecuador (Huaquillas, Machala, Guayaquil or Cuenca). If travelling from further south in Peru, do not take a bus all the way to the border; change to an Ecuador-bound bus in Piura, Máncora or Tumbes. Formalities are only carried out at the new bridge, far outside the border towns of **Aguas Verdes** (Peru) and **Huaquillas** (Ecuador). There are two border complexes called CEBAF (**Centro Binacional de Atención Fronteriza**), open 24 hours on either side of the bridge. Both complexes have Peruvian and Ecuadorean immigration officers so you get your exit and entry stamps in the same place. If crossing with your own vehicle however, you may have to stop at both border complexes for customs.

If you do not take one of the international buses then the crossing is hot, harrowing and transport between the two sides via the new bridge and border complex is inconvenient and expensive (see Transport, below). Travellers often fall victim to thefts, muggings, shakedowns by minor officials and countless scams on both sides. Never leave your baggage unattended and do your own arithmetic when changing money. Those seeking a more relaxed crossing to or from Ecuador should consider La Tina–Macará or Namballe–La Balsa.

Tourist information

Máncora

iPerú
Av Piura 250. Thu-Sun 1000-1700.
See also www.vivamancora.com.

Tumbes

iPerú
Malecón III Milenio, p3, T072-506721.
Mon-Sat 0900-1800, Sun 0900-1300,
iperutumbes@promperu.gob.pe.

Where to stay

Máncora

There are at least 50 hotels in and around Máncora, heavily booked in high season (Dec-Mar) when prices can increase by 100% or more. Many hotels have even higher rates for Christmas, New Year, Easter and Independence Day holidays when the resort is full to bursting. The main strip of the Panamericana is known as Av Piura from the bridge for the first couple of blocks, then Av Grau to the end of town. The better hotels are at the southern end of town, with a small concentration of mid-range hotels just over the bridge. Hotels to the left look onto the beach directly in front of the best surf and often have beach entrances as well as road entrances. They are the most popular with tourists and are all noisy at night from nearby discos, which last until around 0200 Mon-Thu and 0600 Fri-Sun.

When checking into any hotel, expect to pay up front and make sure you get a receipt or you are likely to be asked to pay again the next time the receptionist sees you. Take every precaution with your valuables, theft is common. Mosquitoes are bad at certain times of the year, so take plenty of bug spray.

Máncora town

$$$ Don Giovanni
Pje 8 de Noviembre s/n, T073-258525,
www.dongiovannimancora.com.
3-storey Indonesian-style beachfront hotel, includes breakfast, restaurant and ice cream parlour, kitesurfing classes available.

$$ Del Wawa
Beachfront, T073-258427,
www.delwawa.com.
This relaxed and spacious Spanish-owned hotel is popular with serious surfers and kitesurfers. Hotel service poor, rooms noisy, food average, but great location and nice restaurants round the corner.

$$ Kon Tiki
Los Incas 200, T073-258138,
www.kontikimancora.com.
On hill with lighhouse, great views, cabins with thatched roofs, hammocks, kitchen facilities, bar. Transport to/from bus station provided. Advance booking required.

$$ Las Olas
Beachfront, T073-258099,
www.lasolasmancora.com.
Smart, cabin-style rooms, top floor rooms have best view of ocean, hammocks and gardens, includes breakfast.

$$ Punta Ballenas Inn
Km 1164, south of Cabo Blanco bridge at
the south entrance to town, T072-630844,
www.puntaballenas.com.
Lovely setting on beach, garden with small pool, expensive restaurant.

$$-$ Kokopelli Beachpackers
Av Piura 209, T073-258091,
www.hostelkokopelli.com.
Popular hostel 3 mins' walk from beach, with pool, bar, good food, good meeting place, lots of facilities. Rooms for 2, 4 or 8, mixed or female only, all with bath, hot water.

$$-$ Laguna Surf Camp
T01-99 401 5628, www.vivamancora.com/
lagunacamp.
50 m from the sea, thatched roofs, cabins
sleeping up to 6 people (US$11 pp), also
cabins around small communal area with
hammocks, pool and restaurant. Good surf
lessons, helpful staff.

$$-$ Loki del Mar
Av Piura 262, T073-258484,
www.lokihostel.com.
In the **Loki** group of hostels, seafront,
bright white and modern muti-storey
building, doubles with private bath or
dorms with 4-6 beds and lockable closets,
bar, restaurant, pool, lots of activities.
Be ready for loud music and parties.
Advance booking required.

$ Casa del Turista
Av Piura 224, T073-258126.
Family-run, TV, roof terraces giving sea views,
good value and location. Recommended.

Quebrada Cabo Blanco
Crossing the bridge into Máncora, a dirt track
leads downhill to the right, to the Quebrada
Cabo Blanco, signed to **La Posada Youth
Hostel**. The many hotels at the end of the
track are badly lit for guests returning at
night (robberies have occurred) but are
relatively quiet and relaxing.

$$ Kimbas Bungalows
T073-258373, www.kimbas
bungalowsmancora.com.
Relaxed spot with charming thatched
bungalows, Balinese influences, nice garden
with hammocks, pool, some rooms have
hot water, good value. Recommended.

$$ La Posada
T073-258328, http://hostellaposada.com.
IYHF affiliated hostel, dorms (US$20 pp),
camping (US$12 pp) and rooms with private
bath, fan, garden with hammocks, pool,
cooking facilities, parking,

Las Pocitas and Vichayito
There are over 40 hotels in this area, south
of Máncora. Most are more upmarket than
those in town.

$$$$ Arennas
Antigua Panamericana Norte, Km 1213,
T073-258240, www.arennasmancora.com.
Smart, luxury pool or beachfront suites,
all modern facilities, with central bar and
restaurant serving imaginative dishes,
beautiful pool, palm-lined beach frontage,
very romantic.

$$$ Las Pocitas
Antigua Panamericana Norte, Km 1215,
T998-139711, www.laspocitas.pe.
Great location, rooms with ocean views,
lovely palm-lined beach, terrace, pool,
restaurant and bar.

$$$ Máncora Beach Bungalows
Antigua Panamericana Norte, Km 1215, Lima
T01-201 2060, www.mancora-beach.com.
Comfortable rooms with ceiling fan, terrace
and hammocks, good restaurant, good value
for this price range.

$$$ Puerto Palos
Antigua Panamericana Norte, 2 km south
of Máncora (10 mins by mototaxi, US$2),
T073-258199, www.puertopalos.com.
Variety of rooms, fan, suites have a/c.
Excellent, nice pool overlooking ocean,
hammocks, sunbeds, umbrellas, good
restaurant. Friendly and hospitable.

$$ Marcilia Beach Bungalows
Antigua Panamericana Norte, Km 1212,
T994-685209, www.marciliadevichayito.com.
Nice rustic bamboo cabins with ocean views,
includes breakfast, family-run.

Punta Sal to Tumbes
There is a huge resort of the Colombian
Royal Decameron group in Punta Sal,
www.decameron.com.

$$$$ Punta Sal
Panamericana Norte, Km 1192, Punta Sal Chica,
T072-596700/540088, www.puntasal.com.pe.

A beautiful complex of bungalows along a fine sandy beach, with pool, bar decorated with photos of big game fishing, fine restaurant. Most deals are all-inclusive, but massages and whale-watching trips are extra. Good food and service.

$$$-$ Waltako Beach Town
Panamericana 1199, Canoas de Punta Sal, T998-141976, www.waltakoperu.com.
Thatched cabins for 2, 4 or 6 people, with kitchenette, porch and hammock. Camping on the beach if you bring your own tent. Restaurant and bar, bicycles, quad bikes and horses for hire. Volunteers welcomed for conservation and reforestation work.

$$ Hospedaje El Bucanero
At the entrance to Playa Punta Sal, set back from the beach, T072-540118, www.elbucaneropuntasal.com.
The most happening place in Punta Sal, popular with travellers, rates rise in high season, a variety of rooms, pool, restaurant, bar and gardens.

$$ Huá
On the beach at the entrance to Playa Punta Sal, T072-540023, www.hua-puntasal.com.
A rustic old wooden building, pleasant terrace overlooking ocean, hammocks, quiet, restful, good food, friendly service.

$$-$ Las Terrazas
Opposite Sunset Punta Sal, T072-507701.
One of the more basic and cheaper hotels in Punta Sal in operation since 1989, restaurant has sea view, some rooms better than others, those with own bath and sea view twice the price. Helpful owners.

$ Hospedaje Orillas del Mar
San Martín 496, Cancas.
A short walk from Punta Sal Chica beaches, this is the best of the basic *hostales* lining the beach and Panamericana.

$ Hostal Grillo Tres Puntas
Panamericana Norte, Km 1235, Zorritos, T072-794830, www.casagrillo.net.

On the beach, rustic bamboo cabins, quiet and peaceful. Great food prepared by Spanish chef-owner, León, who breeds Peruvian hairless dogs. Lukewarm showers, Wi-Fi in dining area, camping possible on the beach.

Tumbes
Note that Av Tumbes is still sometimes referred to by its old name of Teniente Vásquez. At holiday times it can be very difficult to find a room.

$$$ Costa del Sol
San Martín 275, Plazuela Bolognesi, T072-523991, www.costadelsolperu.com.
The only high-class hotel in town, minibars, a/c, good restaurant, garden, pool, excellent service. Parking for an extra fee. Rooms which look onto the Plaza Bolognesi are noisy.

$$ Lourdes
Mayor Bodero 118, 3 blocks from main plaza, T072-522966.
Welcoming place. Narrow corridor leading to cell-like rooms which are plushly decorated with a mixture of antique and modern furniture. Good bathrooms, fans in each room.

$$-$ Asturias
Av Mcal Castilla 307, T072-522569.
Comfortable, hot water, a/c or fan, restaurant, bar and laundry. Accepts credit cards.

$ Hostal Tumbes
Filipinas s/n, off Grau, T072-522203, or T972-852954.
Small, dark, basic but cleanish rooms with fans and bath. Good cheap option.

Máncora
Máncora is packed with restaurants: plenty of sushi, pizza and grills. Most are pricey; the cheaper places are north along Av Piura.

$$$ Pizzería Mamíferos
Av Piura 346. Tue-Sun 1800-2300.
Wood-fired pizzas and lasagne.

$$$-$$ Josil
Av Piura, near The Birdhouse. Closed Sun.
Very good sushi bar.

$$$-$$ Tao
Av Piura. Closed Wed.
Good Asian food and curries.

$$ Angela's Place/Cafetería de Angela
*Av Piura 396, www.vivamancora.com/
deangela. Daily 0800-2300.*
A great option for a healthy breakfast or
lunch and heaven for vegetarians and
whole-food lovers: home-made bread,
yoghurts, fresh fruit, etc.

$$ Don César
*Hard to find, ask around or take a mototaxi.
Closed Sun.*
Good fresh seafood, very popular with locals.

$ The Birdhouse
Av Piura.
This small open-air commercial centre
incorporates **Green Eggs and Ham**,
open daily 0730-1300 for great breakfasts
(US$3.35), including waffles, pancakes or
eggs and bacon, plus juice or coffee. Directly
underneath is **Papa Mo's** milk bar, with
comfy seats next to the sand and a selection
of drinks.

$ Café La Bajadita
Av Piura.
Has an impressive selection of delicious
home-made desserts and cakes.

Tumbes

There are cheap restaurants on the Plaza
de Armas, Paseo de la Concordia and near
the markets.

$$-$ Budabar
Grau 309, on Plaza de Armas, T072-525493.
One of a kind chill-out lounge offering
traditional food and comfy seating with
outdoor tables and cheap beer, popular
in the evenings.

$$-$ Chifa Wakay
Huáscar 413. Evenings only.
A large, well-ventilated smart restaurant
offering the usual *chifa* favourites.

$$-$ Classic
Tumbes 185.
Look for it almost under the bridge over the
river, heading south. Popular for local food.

$$-$ Los Gustitos
Bolívar 148.
Excellent *menús* and à la carte. Popular, good
atmosphere at lunchtime.

$ Cherry
San Martín 116. Open 0800-1400, 1700-2300.
Tiny café offering an amazing selection
of cakes and desserts, also fresh juices,
shakes, sandwiches, hot and cold drinks
and traditional *cremoladas* (fruit juice with
crushed ice).

$ Sí Señor
Bolívar 119 on the plaza.
Good for snacks, cheap lunch menus.

What to do

Máncora

Surfing on this coast is best Nov-March;
boards and suits can be hired from several
places on Av Piura, US$10 per day. Many
agencies on Av Piura offer day trips to
Manglares de Tumbes, as well as private
transport in cars and vans.
Iguanas Trips, *Av Piura 306, T073-632762,
www.iguanastrips.com.* Run by Ursula Behr,
offers a variety of adventure tourism trips,
horseriding and camping in the nearby
national parks and reserve zones.
Samana Chakra, *in the eponymous hotel,
T073-258604, www.samanachakra.com.*
Yoga classes, US$5 per hr.
Surf Point Máncora, *on the beach next
to Hostal del Wawa.* Surf lessons US$17.50
per hr, kitesurfing (season Mar-Sep) US$50
per hr. Surfboard, body-board and paddle-
board rentals.

Transport

Sullana

Bus Several bus companies including **Ormeño** share a Terminal Terrestre outside the centre. It's best to take a taxi or mototaxi to and from the terminal. To **Tumbes**, 244 km, 4-5 hrs, US$8, several buses daily. To **Chiclayo** and **Trujillo** (see under Piura). To **Lima**, 1076 km, 14-16 hrs, several buses daily, most coming from Tumbes, luxury overnight via Trujillo with **Ittsa** (T073-503705), also with **Ormeño** and **Tepsa** (José de Lama 236, T073-502120). To **Máncora**, **Eppo**, frequent, 2½ hrs, US$4.50.

To the international bridge at **La Tina** (see page 131), shared taxis leave when full from the Terminal Terrestre La Capullana, off Av Buenos Aires, several blocks beyond the canal, US$5.40 per person, 1¾ hrs. Once on the Ecuador side, buses leave frequently from Macará for Loja, so even if you are not taking the through bus (see Piura, page 126), you can still go from Sullana to Loja in a day.

Máncora

Bus To **Sullana** with **Eppo**, every 30 mins, 0400-1830, US$4.50, 2½ hrs; to **Piura**, US$5.50, 3 hrs; also *colectivos* to Piura, 2 hrs, US$11. To **Tumbes** (and points in between), minibuses leave when full, US$5.50, 1½ hrs. Several companies to **Lima**, US$28-70, 18 hrs. To **Chiclayo**, **Tran Chiclayo**, US$17.50, 6 hrs. To **Trujillo**, US$25, 9 hrs.

To Ecuador To **Machala** (US$14, 5 hrs) and **Guayaquil** (US$17.50, 8 hrs), with **CIFA** and **Super Semería** at 0800, 1100 and 1300; Guayaquil direct at 2300 and 2330; several others, see Piura Transport. To **Cuenca**, **Super Semería** at 2300, US$20; or **Azuay** at 2330.

Punta Sal

Taking a taxi from Máncora to Punta Sal is the safest option, 20 mins, US$14; mototaxi 40 mins, US$10.

Tumbes

Air Daily flights to and from **Lima** with **LATAM** (Bolognesi 250).

Bus Daily to and from **Lima**, 1320 km, 18-20 hrs, depending on stopovers, US$34-45 regular fare, or US$60 with **Cruz del Sur VIP** (Tumbes Norte 319, T072-896163). **Civa** (Av Tumbes 518, T072-525120) has several buses daily. Cheaper buses usually leave 1600-2100, more expensive ones 1200-1400. Except for the luxury service, most buses to Lima stop at major cities en route. Tickets to anywhere between Tumbes and Lima sell quickly, so if arriving from Ecuador you may have to stay overnight. Piura is a good place for connections in the daytime.

To **Sullana**, 244 km, 3-4 hrs, US$8, several buses daily. To **Piura**, 4-5 hrs, 282 km, US$7-8.50, with **El Dorado** (Piura 459, T072-523480) every 1-2 hrs; **Trans Chiclayo** (Tumbes 466, T072-525260) and **Cruz del Sur**. *Colectivos* **Tumbes/Piura** (Tumbes N 308, T072-525977) are a faster option, 3½ hrs, US$12 pp, leave when full. To **Chiclayo**, 552 km, 7-8 hrs, US$9, several each day with **Cruz del Sur**, **El Dorado** and others. To **Trujillo**, 769 km, 10-11 hrs, from US$15, with **Ormeño** (Av Tumbes s/n, T072-522228), **Cruz del Sur**, **El Dorado**, **Emtrafesa** (Tumbes Norte 596, T072-522894).

To Ecuador **CIFA** (Av Tumbes 958) runs to **Machala**, US$4, and **Guayaquil**, 5 hrs, 4 a day, luxury bus at 1000, US$8.50. For other options, see Piura Transport. If you cannot cross on an international bus (the preferred option), then take a taxi from Tumbes to the new international bridge and border complex beyond Aguas Verdes, 17 km, US$12, and from there to **Huaquillas** across the border, US$2.50-5. See Border with Ecuador, page 132.

Northern
highlands

Leaving the Pacific coast behind, you climb in a relatively short time up to the Sierra. It was here, at Cajamarca, that the defeat of the Incas by the Spaniards began, bringing about cataclysmic change to this part of the world. But, unlike this well-documented event, the history of the Incas' contemporaries and predecessors has to be teased out of the stones of their temples and fortresses, which are shrouded in cloud in the 'Eyebrow of the Jungle'.

Trujillo to Cajamarca

don't miss the extensive ruins at Marca Huamachuco

The main route from the coast to Cajamarca is via Ciudad de Dios, a junction some 20 km north of Pacasmayo (see page 106) on the Panamericana. The 175-km paved road branches off the highway soon after it crosses the Río Jequetepeque. Terraced rice fields and mimosas may often be seen in bloom, brightening the otherwise dusty landscape. The old road (now paved) via Huamachuco and Cajabambais longer and higher but more interesting, passing over the bare puna before dropping to the Huamachuco valley.

Huamachuco and around *Colour map 2, B2.*

This colonial town is located at 3180 m, 181 km from Trujillo. It was on the royal Inca Road and has the largest main plaza in Peru, with fine topiary and a controversial modern **cathedral**. On Sundays there is a colourful **market**, with dancing in the plaza. **Museo Municipal Wamachuko** ① *Sucre 195, Mon-Sat 0900-1300, 1500-1900, Sun 0900-1200, free,* displays artefacts found at nearby **Cerro Amaru** and **Marca Huamachuco** (see below). The extensive Huari ruins of **Wiracochapampa** are 3 km north of town (45 minutes' walk), but much of the site is overgrown. There are good thermal baths at **El Edén** with several open air pools, 45 minutes by combi via Sausacocha.

☆**Marca Huamachuco** ① *Access along a poor road, off the road to Sanagorán, 5 km from Huamachuco (there is an archway at the turn-off). Daily 0900-1700; a minimum of 2 hrs is needed, or 4 hrs to really explore. US$1. Carry all food and drink with you. Mototaxi* from Huamachuco to the turn-off, US$2, or combi to Sanagorán. These hilltop pre-Inca fortifications rank in the top 10 archaeological sites in Peru. They are 3 km long, dating back to at least 300 BC though many structures were added later. Its most impressive features are: El Castillo, a remarkable circular structure with walls up to 8 m high located at the highest point of the site, and El Convento complex, five circular structures of varying sizes towards the northern end of the hill. The largest one has been partially reconstructed.

Cajabamba

Cajabamba is a small market town and a useful stop-over point between Huamachuco and Cajamarca. A thermal bath complex, **La Grama**, is 30 minutes by combi (US$1) from Cajabamba, with a pool, very hot individual baths and an adjoining small *hostal*.

Listings Trujillo to Cajamarca

Where to stay

Huamachuco

$$ Real
Bolívar 250, T044-441402,
www.hotelrealhuamachuco.com.
Modern, sauna, majority of fittings are wood, pleasant with good service.

$$ Santa María
Grau 224, T044-348334.
An enormous, sparsely furnished edifice offering the best-quality rooms in town, with restaurant.

$$-$ Hostal Santa Fe
San Martín 297, T044-441019,
www.actiweb.es/luisnv83/.
Good value, hot water, parking, restaurant.

$ Hostal Huamachuco
Castilla 354, on the plaza, T044-440599.
With private or shared hot showers, small rooms but large common areas, good value, has parking.

Cajabamba

$ Hostal Flores
Leoncio Prado 137, Plaza de Armas,
T076-551086.
With electric shower, cheaper without bath, clean but rooms are gloomy, nice patio; no breakfast.

Restaurants

Huamachuco

$$-$ Bull Grill
R Castilla 364.
Smart place specializing in meat dishes, with a cool bar at the back.

$ Café Somos
Bolognesi 665.
Good coffee, large turkey/ham sandwiches and excellent cakes.

$ Doña Emilia
Balta 384, on Plaza de Armas.
Good for breakfast and snacks.

$ El Viejo Molino
R Castilla 160.
Specializes in local cuisine, such as *cuy* (guinea pig).

Cajabamba

$ Cafetería La Otuscana
Grau 929. Daily 0730-2200.
Good bakery, sweets and sandwiches.

$ Don Lucho
Jr Leoncio Prado 227.
Good local trout and other à la carte dishes.

Festivals

Huamachuco

1st weekend of Aug **El Chaku**, in which vicuñas in the area are rounded up and shorn.

14 Aug **Founding of Huamachuco**, celebrated for many days before and after the date. Spectacular fireworks and amazing, aggressive male dancers called *turcos*, bull-fighting in one of the largest rings in Perú.

Transport

Huamachuco

Bus To/from **Trujillo**, 170 km, 5-6 hrs, US$9-15 (see page 101): the best service is **Fuentes** (J Balta 1090, Huamachuco, T044-441090 and Av R Palma 767, Trujillo, T044-204581); **Tunesa** (Suárez 721, T044-441157). To **Cajabamba**, with **Trans Los Andes** (Pje Hospital 109), 3 combis a day, 2 hrs, US$7.50.

Cajabamba

Bus Several companies run buses and combis to **Cajamarca**, 127 km, US$7.50-8, 3 hrs.

Cajamarca and around   *Colour map 2, B2.*

follow in Atahualpa's fateful footsteps

Cajamarca is an attractive colonial town surrounded by lovely countryside. It was here in 1532 that Pizarro ambushed and captured Atahualpa, the Inca emperor. This was the first showdown between the Spanish and the Incas and, despite being greatly outnumbered, the Spanish emerged victorious. Change has come fast to Cajamarca: the nearby Yanacocha gold mine (www.yanacocha.com.pe) has brought new wealth to the town but also major ecological disruption and social problems. The city is also the hub of tourism development for the whole Circuito Turístico Nororiental, which encompasses Chiclayo, Cajamarca and Chachapoyas.

City centre

The **Plaza de Armas**, where Atahualpa was executed, has a 350-year-old fountain, topiary and gardens. The **Cathedral** ⓘ *daily 0800-1000, 1600-1800*, opened in 1776 and is still missing its belfry, but the façade has beautiful baroque carving in stone. On the opposite side of the plaza is the 17th-century church of **San Francisco** ⓘ *Mon-Fri 0900-1200, 1600-1800*, older than the Cathedral and with more interior stone carving and elaborate altars. The attached **Museo de Arte Colonial** ⓘ *entrance is behind the church on Amalia Puga y Belén, Mon-Sat 1430-1800, US$1*, is filled with colonial paintings and icons. The guided tour of the museum includes entry to the church's spooky catacombs.

The group of buildings known as **Complejo Belén** ⓘ *Tue-Sat 0900-1300, 1500-1800, Sun 0900-1300. US$5 (valid for more than 1 day and for the Cuarto de Rescate; see below), guided tour for all the sites, US$2.85-8.50*, comprises the tourist office and Institute of Culture, two museums and the beautifully ornate church of Belén, considered the city's finest. The arches, pillars and walls of the nave are covered in lozenges (rombos), a design picked out in the gold tracery of the altar. Look up to see the inside of the dome, where eight giant cherubs support an intricate flowering centrepiece. The carved pulpit has a spiral staircase and the doors are intricately worked in wood. In the same courtyard is the **Museo Médico Belén**, which has a collection of medical instruments. Across the street on Junín and Belén is a maternity hospital from the colonial era, now the **Archaeological and Ethnological Museum**. It has a range of ceramics from all regions and civilizations of Peru.

To the east, the **Cuarto de Rescate (Ransom Chamber)** ⓘ *entrance at Amalia Puga 750, Tue-Sat 0900-1800, Sun 0900-1300,* is the room where Atahualpa was held prisoner. A red line on the wall is said to indicate where Atahualpa reached up and drew a mark, agreeing to have his subjects fill the room to that height, once with gold and twice with silver.

You can also visit the stone altar set high on **Santa Apolonia hill** ⓘ *US$0.60, take bus marked Santa Apolonia/Fonavi, or micro A,* from where Atahualpa is said to have surveyed his subjects. There is a road to the top, or you can walk up from Calle 2 de Mayo, using the steep stairway. The view is worth the effort, especially at sunrise (but go in a group).

Around the city centre are many fine old houses, with garden patios and 104 elaborately carved doorways. Look out for the **Bishop's Palace**, across the street from the Cathedral; the **palace of the Condes de Uceda**, at Jr Apurímac 719 (now occupied by BCP bank, photography prohibited); and the **Casa Silva Santiesteban** (Junín y 2 de Mayo).

The Universidad Nacional de Cajamarca maintains an experimental arboretum and agricultural station, the **Museo Silvo-agropecuario** ⓘ *Km 2.5 on the road to Baños del Inca,* with a lovely mural at the entrance.

Cajamarca

Where to stay	10 La Casona del Inca	6 El Pez Loco
1 Cajamarca	11 Los Balcones de	7 El Zarco
2 Costa del Sol	La Recoleta	8 Heladería Holanda
3 El Cabildo		9 Om-Gri
4 El Cumbe Inn	**Restaurants**	10 Pascana
5 El Ingenio	1 Bella's Café Lounge	11 Pizzería El Marengo
6 El Portal del Marqués	2 Casa Club	12 Pizzería Vaca Loca
7 Hosp Los Jazmines	3 Cascanuez	13 Querubino
8 Hostal Becerra	4 De Buena Laya	14 Salas
9 Hostal Perú	5 Don Paco	15 Sanguchón.com

100 metres
100 yards

Around Cajamarca

☆**Los Baños del Inca** ① *6 km from Cajamarca. Daily 0500-2000, T076-348385, www. ctbinca.com.pe, entry US$0.70, baths US$1.75-2.10, sauna US$3.50, massage US$7. Combis marked Baños del Inca cost US$0.20, 15 mins; taxis US$2.30.* These sulphurous thermal springs are where Atahualpa bathed to try to cure a festering war wound; his bath is still there. The water temperature is at least 72° C, and the main baths are divided into five categories, all with private tubs and no pool (take your own towel; soaps are sold outside); many of the facilities are open to men- or women-only at certain times. Obey the instructions and only spend 20 minutes maximum in the water. The complex is renewed regularly, with gardens and various levels of accommodation (see Where to stay, below). A nice 13-km walk downhill from the Baños del Inca will bring you **Llacanora** after two hours, a typical Andean village in beautiful scenery.

Ventanillas Head north from the baños to the **Ventanillas de Otusco** ① *8 km from Cajamarca, daily 0800-1800, US$1.10, combi US$0.20,* part of an old pre-Inca cemetery that has a deteriorating gallery of secondary burial niches. There are good day walks in this area and local sketch maps are available. From Otusco, a road leads 20 km to **Ventanillas de Combayo** ① *occasional combis on Mon-Sat; more transport on Sun when a market is held nearby, 1 hr.* These burial niches are more numerous and spectacular than those at Otusco, being located in an isolated, mountainous area and distributed over the face of a steep, 200-m-high hillside.

Cumbe Mayo This site, 20 km southwest of Cajamarca, is famous for its extraordinary, well-engineered pre-Inca channels, running for 9 km across the mountain tops at 3600 m. This hydraulic irrigation system is said to be the oldest man-made construction in South America. The sheer scale of the scene is impressive, backed by the huge rock formations known as Los Frailones ('big monks') and others. On the way to Cumbe Mayo is the Layzón ceremonial centre. It is possible to walk from Cajamarca to Cumbe Mayo in three to four hours, although you're advised to take a guide or join a tour group. The trail starts from the hill of Santa Apolonia (see above) and goes straight through the village and up the hill. At the top of the mountain, leave the trail and take the road to the right to reach the canal. The walk is not difficult and you do not need hiking boots, but it is cold (best weather May to September). Take warm clothing and a good torch. The locals use the trail to bring their goods to market. There is no bus service to Cumbe Mayo; taxi US$15. Guided tours run from 0830 to 1400 and are recommended in order to see all the pre-Inca sites.

Porcón The rural cooperative, with its evangelical faith expressed on billboards, is a popular excursion, 30 km northwest of Cajamarca. It is a tightly organized community, with carpentry, bakery, cheese and yoghurt-making, zoo and vicuñas. A good guide helps to explain everything. If you're not taking a tour, contact **Cooperativa Agraria Atahualpa Jerusalén** ① *Chanchamayo 1355, Fonavi 1, T076-825631.* At Km 8 along the road to Porcón is **Huambocancha**, a town specializing in stone sculptures. Combis run from Cajamarca market, US$0.75, 30 minutes.

Kuntur Wasi ① *21 km north of Chilete, site museum in San Pablo US$1.75, ruins US$2.50.* Some 93 km west of Cajamarca is the mining town of Chilete, near which is **Kuntur Wasi**, a site devoted to a feline cult. It consists of a pyramid and stone monoliths. There are two basic *hostales* in Chilete, with very limited facilities.

Tourist information

Information is available from: **iPerú** (Jr Cruz de Piedra 601, T076-365166, iperucajamarca@ promperu.gob.pe, Mon-Sat 0900-1800, Sun 0900-1300); **Dirección Regional de Turismo** and **Ministerio de Cultura,** in the Conjunto Monumental de Belén (Belén 631, T076-362601, Mon-Fri 0900-1300, 1500-1730), and the **Sub-Gerencia de Turismo** (Av Alameda de los Incas, Complejo Qhapac Ñan, opposite UNC university on the road to Baños del Inca, T076-363626, www.municaj.gob.pe). The **University tourist school** (Del Batán 289, T076-361546, Mon-Fri 0830-1300, 1500-2200) also offers free advice and leaflets.

Where to stay

$$$$ Costa del Sol
Cruz de Piedra 707, T076-362472,
www.costadelsolperu.com.
On the Plaza de Armas, part of a Peruvian chain, with airport transfer, welcome drink; restaurant, café and bars, pool, spa, casino, business centre.

$$$ El Ingenio
Av Vía de Evitamiento 1611-1709,
T076-368733, www.elingenio.com.
Colonial style buildings 1½ blocks from El Quinde shopping mall. With restaurant, solar-powered hot water, spacious, quiet and relaxed, generous breakfast.

$$ Cajamarca
Dos de Mayo 311, T076-362532,
hotelcajamarca@gmail.com.
3-star in beautiful colonial mansion, sizeable rooms, hot water, food excellent in **Los Faroles** restaurant.

$$ El Cabildo
Junín 1062, T076-367025.
Includes breakfast, in historic monument with patio and modern fountain, full

of character, elegant local decorations, comfortable, breakfast served.

$$ El Cumbe Inn
Pasaje Atahualpa 345, T076-366858,
www.elcumbeinn.com.
Includes breakfast and tax, comfortable, variety of rooms, hot water, evening meals on request, small gym, will arrange taxis, very helpful.

$$ El Portal del Marqués
Del Comercio 644, T076-368464,
www.portaldelmarques.com.
Attractive converted colonial house, laundry, safe, parking, leased restaurant **El Mesón del Marqués** has good lunch *menú*. Casino with slot machines.

$$ La Casona del Inca
2 de Mayo 458-460, Plaza de Armas,
T076-367524, www.casonadelinca.pe/
turismo.html.
Upstairs, old building, traditional style, some rooms overlooking plaza, some with interior windows, good beds, breakfast in café on top floor, tours, laundry.

$$ Los Balcones de la Recoleta
Amalia Puga 1050, T076-363302,
http://hostalbalcones.jimdo.com.
Beautifully restored 19th-century house, central courtyard full of flowers, some rooms with period furniture, internet.

$ Hospedaje Los Jazmines
Amazonas 775, T076-361812,
www.hospedajelosjazmines.com.pe.
In a converted colonial house with courtyard and café, 14 rooms with hot water, all profits go to disabled children, guests can visit the project's school and help.

$ Hostal Becerra
Del Batán 195, T076-367867.
With hot water, modern, pleasant, will store luggage until late buses depart.

$ Hostal Perú
Amalia Puga 605, on Plaza, T076-365568.
With hot water, functional rooms in old
building around central patio used by
El Zarco restaurant, wooden floors,
credit cards taken.

Los Baños del Inca

$$$$-$$$ Laguna Seca
Av Manco Cápac 1098, T076-584300,
www.lagunaseca.com.pe.
In pleasant surroundings with thermal
streams, private hot thermal baths in
rooms, swimming pool with thermal water,
restaurant, bar, health spa with a variety of
treatments, disco, horses for hire.

$$$ Hacienda Hotel San Antonio
2 km off the Baños road (turn off at Km 5),
T076-348237, Facebook: Hacienda-Hotel-
San-Antonio-258452027710.
An old hacienda, wonderfully restored, with
open fireplaces and gardens, 15 mins walk
along the river to Baños del Inca, riding on
caballos de paso, own dairy produce, fruit and
vegetables, catch your own trout for supper;
try the *licor de sauco*.

$$-$ Los Baños del Inca
See page 142, T076-348385.
Various accommodation: bungalows for
2 to 4 with thermal water, fridge; **Albergue
Juvenil**, not IYFH, hostel rooms with bunk
beds or double rooms, private bath, caters
to groups, basic. Camping possible.
Restaurant offers full board.

See page 142

Restaurants

$$$ Pascana
Av Atahualpa 947.
Well-known and recommended as the best
in town, near the Qhapac Ñan Municipality.
Their **Taberna del Diablo** is the top disco
in town.

$$$ Querubino
Amalia Puga 589, T076-340900.

Mediterranean-style decoration, a bit
of everything on the menu, including
pastas, daily specials, breakfasts, cocktails,
coffees, expensive wines otherwise
reasonable, popular.

$$ Casa Club
Amalia Puga 458-A, T076-340198.
Daily 0800-2300.
Menú, including vegetarian, and extensive
selection à la carte, family atmosphere, slow
but attentive service.

$$ Don Paco
Amalia Puga 390, T076-362655.
Opposite San Francisco. Typical, including
Novo Andino, and international dishes, tasty
food, desserts, drinks.

$$ El Pez Loco
San Martín 333.
Recommended for fish dishes.

$$ Om-Gri
San Martín 360, near the Plaza de Armas.
Opens 1300 (1830 Sun).
Good Italian dishes, small, informal,
French spoken.

$$ Pizzería El Marengo
Junín 1201.
Good pizzas and warm atmosphere,
T368045 for delivery.

$$ Salas
Amalia Puga 637, on the main plaza,
T076-362867. Open 0800-2200.
A Cajamarca tradition: fast, attentive service,
excellent local food (try their *cuy frito*), best
tamales in town, very popular.

$$-$ De Buena Laya
2 de Mayo 343.
With a rustic interior, popular with *hostales*,
offers Novo Cajamarquino cuisine; lunchtime
menú US$3.50.

$$-$ El Zarco
Jr Del Batán 170, T076-363421.
Sun-Fri 0700-2300.
Breakfast, good vegetarian dishes, excellent
fish, also has short *chifa* menu, very popular.

$ Pizzería Vaca Loca
San Martín 330.
Popular, best pizzas in town.

Cafés

Bella's Café Lounge
Junín 1184, T076-345794.
For breakfasts, sandwiches, great desserts
and coffee from Chanchamayo, Wi-Fi,
a place to linger, check emails and relax,
owner Raul speaks English. Popular with
visitors to the city.

Cascanuez
Amalia Puga 554.
Great cakes, extensive menu including
humitas, breakfasts, ice creams and coffees,
highly regarded.

Heladería Holanda
Amalia Puga 657 on the Plaza de Armas,
T076-340113.
Dutch-owned, easily the best ice creams in
Cajamarca, 50 flavours (but not all on at the
same time); try *poro poro, lúcuma* or *sauco,*
also serves coffee. 4 branches, including at
Baños del Inca. Ask if it is possible to visit
their factory.

Sanguchón.com
Junín 1137.
Best burgers in town, sandwiches, also
popular bar.

Festivals

Feb **Carnaval**. Cajamarca's pre-Lent
festivities are spectacular and regarded
as among the best in the country; they
are also perhaps the most raucous.
Mar **Palm Sun**. The processions in Porcón,
16 km to the northwest, are worth seeing.
24 Jun **San Juan** in Cajamarca, Chota,
Llacanora, San Juan and Cutervo.
Jul Agricultural fair is held at Baños del Inca
Oct **Festival Folklórico** in Cajamarca on
the 1st Sun.

Shopping

Handicrafts
Specialities including gilded mirrors and
cotton and wool saddlebags (*alforjas*). Items
can be made to order. The **Mercado Central**
at Amazonas y Apurímac is colourful and
worth a visit for *artesanía*. There are also
stalls at the Belén complex (Belén and/or
2 de Mayo) and along the steps up to Santa
Apolonia hill. Other options for a good
range of local crafts are the **Feria Artesenal**
(Jr El Comercio 1045, next to the police
office) and **El Molino** (2 de Mayo).

What to do

Agencies around the Plaza de Armas offer
trips to local sites and further afield, trekking
on Inca trails, riding *caballos de paso* and
handicraft tours. Prices are roughly as
follows: Cumbe Mayo, US$6.50-8.50, 4-5 hrs
at 0930; Porcón, US$6.50-8.50, 4-5 hrs
at 0930; Otusco, US$4.50-7, 3-3½ hrs at
1530; city tour, US$7, 3 hrs at 0930 or 1530.
Kuntur Wasi is a full day trip. There are also
2 day/3 night tours to Kuélap and Cutervo
National Park.

Cumbemayo Tours, *Amalia Puga 635 on the
plaza, T076-362938.* Standards tours, guides
speak English and French.
Mega Tours, *Amalia Puga 691 on the
plaza, T076-341876, www.megatours.org.*
Conventional tours, full day and further
afield, ecotourism and adventures.

Transport

Air The airport is 5 km from town; taxi US$8.
There are flights to/from **Lima**, with **LC Peru**
(Comercio 1024, T076-361098), Sun-Fri, and
LATAM (Cruz de Piedra 657).

Bus Buses in town charge US$0.35. Bus
companies have their own ticket offices
and terminals; many are on Av Atahualpa
blocks 2-6, a 20-min walk from the Plaza
de Armas.

To **Lima**, 870 km, 12-14 hrs, US$27-53, many daily with **Civa** (Ayacucho 753, T076-361460), **Cruz del Sur** (Atahualpa 606, T076-361737) and **Línea** (Atahualpa 318, T076-363956), **Móvil** (Atahualpa 405, T076-340873), **Tepsa** (Sucre y Reina Forje, T076-363306) and **Turismo Días** (Av Evitamiento s/n, T076-344322), including several luxury services.

To **Trujillo**, 295 km, 7 hrs, US$10-27, regular buses daily 0900-2230, with **Emtrafesa** (Atahualpa 315, T076-369663), **Línea** and **Turismo Días**; most continue to Lima via Chimbote. To **Chiclayo**, 265 km, 6 hrs, US$9-20, several buses daily with **Línea** and **Turismo Días**; you have to change buses to go on to Piura and Tumbes. To **Celendín**, 107 km, 3½ hrs, US$6, usually a 2 a day with **CABA** (Atahualpa 299, T076-366665), **Royal Palace's** (Reina Forje 130, T076-343063) and **Rojas** (Atahualpa 309, T076-340548). To **Chachapoyas**, 336 km, 11-12 hrs, US$18, with **Virgen del Carmen** (Atahualpa 333A, T983-915869), at 0500, via **Leymebamba**, US$11.55, 9-10 hrs; the route follows a paved road through beautiful countryside.

Taxi US$2 within city limits. Mototaxis, US$0.75. Radio taxi: **El Sol**, T076-368897, 24 hrs; **Taxi Super Seguro**, T076-507090.

★ Chachapoyas region

uncover the mysteries of a once-mighty empire

Cajamarca is a convenient starting point for the trip east to the department of Amazonas, which contains the archaeological riches of the Chachapoyans. Here lie the great pre-Inca cities of Vilaya (not yet developed for tourism) and the immense citadel of Kuélap, among many others. It is also an area of great natural beauty with waterfalls, notably Gocta, cliffs and caves. The road is paved but prone to landslides in the rainy season. It follows a winding course through the mountains, crossing the wide and deep canyon of the Río Marañón at Balsas. The road climbs steeply with superb views of the mountains and the valleys below. The fauna and flora are spectacular as the journey alternates between high mountains and low forest.

Celendín *Colour map 2, B2.*

East from Cajamarca, this is the first town of note, with a pleasant plaza and cathedral that is predominantly blue. The fascinating local market on Sunday is held in three distinct areas. From 0630 till 0730 there's a **hat market** by the Alameda, between Ayacucho and 2 de Mayo at Jorge Chávez,

> Tip...
> The **Multired** ATM beside the **Banco de la Nación** on 2 de Mayo in Celendín may not accept all foreign cards; take cash.

at which you can see hats at every stage of production. Then, at 0930 the **potato market** takes place at 2 de Mayo y Sucre, and, at the other end of town, there's a **livestock market** on Túpac Amaru. The **Virgen del Carmen** festival takes place from 16 July to 3 August. The most popular local excursion is to the hot springs and mud baths at **Llanguat**, 20 km away (US$2.75 by limited public transport).

Leymebamba and around *Colour map 2, B2.*

There are plenty of ruins – many of them covered in vegetation – and good walking possibilities around this pleasant town at the source of the Utcubamba River. **La Congona**, a Chachapoyan site, is well worth the effort, with stupendous views. It consists of three hills: on the vegetation-covered conical hill in the middle, the ruins are clustered in a small area, impossible to see until you are right there. The other hills have been levelled. La Congona is the best preserved of three sites in this area, with 30 round stone houses (some with evidence of three storeys) and a watch tower. The two other sites, **El Molinete** and **Cataneo**, are nearby. All three sites can be visited in a day but a guide is advisable. It is a brisk three hours' walk from Leymebamba, first along the rough road to Fila San Cristóbal, then a large trail. The road starts at the bottom of Jr 16 de Julio.

In 1996 six burial chullpas were discovered at **Laguna de los Cóndores**, a spectacular site in a lush cloudforest setting. The chullpas contained 219 mummies and vast quantities of ceramics, textiles, woodwork, quipus and everyday utensils from the late Inca period, now housed in the excellent ☆**Museo Leymebamba** ① *outside San Miguel, on the road to Celendín, T041-816803, www.museoleymebamba.org, daily 0800-1700, entry US$5.75.* It is beautifully laid-out and very informative, and the collection of mummies and quipus is superb. To get there from Leymebamba, walk to the village of 2 de Mayo, ask for the trail to San Miguel, then take the footpath uphill; the road route is much longer (taxi from Leymebamba US$2.75, mototaxi US$2).

It is also possible to visit Laguna de los Cóndores itself; the trip takes 10 to 12 hours on foot and horseback from Leymebamba. An all-inclusive tour for the three-day muddy trek can be arranged at Leymebamba hotels (ask for Sinecio or Javier Farge) or with Chachapoyas operators, US$70 per person.

Around Yerbabuena

The road to Chachapoyas follows the Utcubamba River north. In the mountains rising from the river at **Yerbabuena** (important Sunday market, basic *hospedaje*) are a number of archaeological sites. Before Yerbabuena, a road heads east to **Montevideo** (basic *hospedaje*) and beyond to the small village of **San Pedro de Utac**, where you can hike up to the impressive but overgrown ruins of Cerro Olán.

On the other side of the river, west of Yerbabuena, are burial chullpas from the Revash culture (AD 1250), entry US$3. They are reached from either **San Bartolo** (30-45 minutes' walk, horses can be rented) or along a trail starting past **Puente Santo Tomás** (1½ to two hours' walk).

The town of **Jalca Grande** (or La Jalca), at 2800 m, is reached along a road going east at **Ubilón**, north of Yerbabuena. Jalca Grande has the remains of a Chachapoyan roundhouse, a stone church tower, a small **museum** with ceramics and textiles, and one very basic *hospedaje*.

Tingo to Kuélap *Colour map 2, B2.*

Situated at the junction of the Tingo and Utcubamba rivers, 40 km north of Leymebamba and 37 km south of Chachapoyas, Tingo (altitude 1800 m) is the access point for Kuélap. A road climbs steeply from Tingo to Nuevo Tingo and Choctámal, where it divides. The right branch provides access to the southern part of Gran Vilaya; the left branch climbs east to Lónguita, María, Quizango and Kuélap. It is also possible to walk to Kuélap from María (two to 2½ hours), Choctámal (four to five hours) and Tingo, although this last is a strenuous, five-hour uphill slog and only fit hikers should try to ascend and descend in one day on foot. Take waterproofs, food and drink, and start early as it gets very hot. In the rainy season it is advisable to wear boots; at other times it is hot and dry. Take all your water with you as there is nothing on the way up. See also Transport, page 155. A cable car from Nuevo Tingo to Kuélap is scheduled to start operation in 2017; price US$6.

☆Kuélap

Daily 0800-1700. US$6, guides available for US$9 per group (Rigoberto Vargas Silva has been recommended). The ticket office at the car park has a small but informative Sala de Interpretación.

Kuélap is a spectacular pre-Inca walled city at 3000 m which was re-discovered in 1843. It was built continuously from AD 500 up to Inca times and is said to contain three times more stone than the Great Pyramid at Giza in Egypt. The site lies along the summit of a mountain crest, more than 1 km in length. The massive stone walls, 585 m long by 110 m wide at their widest, are as formidable as those of any pre-Columbian city. Some reconstruction has taken place, mostly of small houses and walls, but the majority of the main walls on all levels are original, as is the inverted, cone-shaped main temple. The structures have been left in their cloudforest setting, the trees covered in bromeliads and moss, the flowers visited by hummingbirds.

Chachapoyas *Colour map 2, B2.*

The capital of the Amazonas Region was founded in 1538 and retains its colonial character. The city's importance as a crossroads between the coast and jungle began to decline in the late 1940s, but archaeological and ecological tourism have grown gradually since the 1990s and have brought increasing economic benefits to the region.

The cathedral, with a lovely modern interior, stands on the spacious Plaza de Armas. **Ministerio de Cultura Museum** ① *Ayacucho 904, T041-477045, Mon-Fri 0800-1300, 1500-1700, free,* contains a small collection of artefacts and mummies, with explanations in Spanish. The **Museo Santa Ana** ① *Jr Santa Ana 1054, T041-790988, Mon-Fri 0900-1700, US$2,* has colonial religious art and prehispanic ceramics and textiles. Jr Amazonas, pedestrianized from the Plaza de Armas uphill to Plaza Burgos, makes a pleasant stroll.

Around Chachapoyas

Huancas ① *Autos leave from Jr Ortiz Arrieta 370 in Chachapoays, daily 0600-1800, 20 mins, US$1.15, or 2-hr walk.* Huancas is a small village to the north of Chacha where rustic pottery is produced. Walk uphill from the plaza to the **mirador** ① *1 km, US$0.70,* for magnificent views into the deep canyon of the Río Sonche, with tumbling waterfalls. There are crafts on sale here. At **Huanca Urco**, 5 km from Huancas, past the large prison complex, are ruins, remains of an Inca road and another mirador with fine views to Gocta waterfall in the distance.

Levanto Due south of Chachapoyas, Levanto was built by the Spaniards in 1538, directly on top of the previous Chachapoyan structures, as their first capital of the area. Nowadays Levanto is an unspoilt colonial village overlooking the massive canyon of the Utcubamba River. On a clear day, Kuélap can be seen on the other side of the rift. A 30-minute walk from Levanto towards Chachapoyas will bring you to the overgrown ruins of **Yalape**, which seems to have been a massive residential complex, extending over many hectares. Local people can guide you to the ruins.

Mendoza and around

A paved road heads east from Chachapoyas, reaching Mendoza after 2½ hours. The town is the centre of the coffee-producing region of Rodríguez de Mendoza. Close by are the caves at Omia, the Tocuya thermal baths, Mirador Wimba and the Santa Natalia waterfall. Also of interest is the Guayabamba Valley, where there is an unusually high incidence of fair-skinned people. It is a worthwhile four-hour hike from Mendoza to Huamanpata, a very pretty valley surrounded by forest; there's a lake here in the wet season, but this reduces down to a river in drier months. Robert Cabrerra (T949-305401) has cabins and camping, and he offers two-day tours from US$35 per person; contact him well in advance.

Lamud and around

At Km 37 on the Chachapoyas–Pedro Ruiz road an unpaved road leads to the village of **Luya** where it divides. One branch goes north to **Lamud**, a convenient base for several interesting sites, such as San Antonio and Pueblo de los Muertos. **EcoMuseo Molino de Piedra San José** ① *1 km north of Lamud, daily 0900-1600*, has a fascinating display of traditional rural life with demonstrations of milling, baking, weaving, etc. Also worth visiting is the **Quiocta cave** ① *30 mins by car from Lamud, then a 10-min walk, US$2, 0800-1600, closed*

Tip...
South of the road from Chachapoyas to Mendoza, in the district of Soloco, is Parjugsha, Peru's largest cave complex, about 300 m deep and with some 20 km of galleries (10 km have been explored and connected). Spelunking experience is essential.

Chachapoyas

To Museo Santa Ana & Capilla de la Virgen Asunta

Jr Santa Ana

Quebrada Santa Lúcia

To ⑫

Jr Libertad ⑨

To ⑧

④

A

Santo Domingo

To ①

Pje D Reina

⑪

Jr Salamanca

⑦

Pol

⑤ Isamax ③

Ⓜ

⑤ S

Ministerio de Cultura

③ ②

iPerú

⑩

Plaza de Armas

⑧

Jr Chincha Alta

Cathedral

⑤

Banco de la Nación ⑥

⑥ ②

④

⑩

B

⑨

GH Bus Tickets

Jr Ortiz Arrieta

Jr Triunfo

Jr 2 de Mayo

Jr Amazonas

Jr Ayacucho

Jr Recreo

④

⑦

Jr Unión

To Pedro Ruiz

Jr Junín

Jr Grau

① ②

To ⑬

To Terminal Terrestre (6 blocks)

③

N

200 metres
200 yards

Where to stay 🛏
1 Aventura Backpackers Lodge *A1*
2 Belén *A1*
3 Casa Vieja *A1*
4 Casona Monsante *B2*
5 Casona Revash *B2*
6 Chachapoyas Backpackers *B2*

7 El Dorado *A1*
8 Las Orquídeas *A1*
9 Posada del Arriero *B1*
10 Puma Urco *B2*
11 Rumi Huasi *A2*
12 Vista Hermosa *A1*
13 Xalca *B1*

Restaurants 🍴
1 Batán del Tayta *B2*
2 Dulcería Santa Elena *B2*
3 El Edén *A2*
4 El Tejado *A1*
5 Fusiones *A1*
6 Heladería San Antonio *B2*
7 Matalaché *B3*
8 Panadería Café San José *B2*
9 Paraíso de las Pizzas *A1*
10 Romana *B1*

Transport 🚌
1 Civa *A2*
2 GH Bus *A3*
3 Móvil Tours *B3*
4 Star Bus & Transervis Kuelap *B3*

Thu. The cave is 560 m long, 23 m deep, and has four chambers with stalactites and stalagmites and a stream running through it. There are petroglyphs at the mouth, and partly buried human remains. Tours to the cave can be arranged in Chachapoyas or through the Lamud tourist office.

The second road from Luya goes south and west to Cruzpata for access to **Karajía** ⓘ *2½ hrs' walk from Luya or 30 mins from Cruzpata, US$2, take binoculars*, where remarkable, 2.5-m-high sarcophagi are set into an impressive cliff-face overlooking the valley. Other sites nearby include **Chipuric**, 1½ hours' walk from Luya, and **Wanglic**, a funeral site with large circular structures built under a ledge in a lush canyon with a beautiful waterfall nearby: a worthwhile excursion (1½ hours). Ask for directions in Luya, or take a local guide (US$10 a day). The road to Luya and Lamud is unpaved; see Chachapoyas Transport, page 155, for how to get there.

☆Gocta

Access from San Pablo de Valera or Cocachimba. Entry fee US$4, guides (compulsory), US$15 for up to 15 passengers.

South of Pedro Ruíz is the spectacular **Gocta waterfall**, one of the highest in the world at 771 m. (The upper waterfall is 231 m; the lower waterfall is 540 m.) From Chachapoyas, take the Pedro Ruiz road for 35 km to Cocahuayco (about 18 km before Pedro Ruiz) where there are two roads up to Gocta, along either bank of the Cocahuayco River. The first turn-off leads to the village of **San Pablo de Valera** at 1934 m (6 km from the main road, 20 minutes by car). From here, it is a one- to 1½-hour walk to a mirador, and then 30 to 60 minutes to the base of the upper falls, 6.3 km in total. The second turn-off, 100 m further along the main road, leads to the village of **Cocachimba** at 1796 m (5.3 km from the main road, 20 minutes). From here, it is a 1½- to 2½-hour walk (5.5 km) to the base of the lower waterfall, of which there is an impressive view. Both routes go through about 2 km of lovely forest; the San Pablo trail is somewhat flatter. A path connecting both banks starts on the San Pablo side at the mirador. This is a much smaller trail, quite steep and not signposted past the mirador. There is a suspension footbridge over the main river before the trail joins the Cocachimba trail about three quarters of the way to the base of the lower falls. To see both sides in one day you need to start very early, but this is a great way to get the full experience. Each community offer similar services: horses can be hired for US$12 (they can only go part of the way); rubber boots and rain ponchos are available for US$1.20 (it is always wet by the falls). The best time to visit is during the dry season from May to September; in the wet season the falls are more spectacular, but it is cold, rainy and the trails may be slippery.

Several more waterfalls in this area are increasingly accessible, including **Yumbilla**, which is 895 m (124 m higher than Gocta) in eight tiers. For more information about expeditions to Yumbilla, other falls and related projects, see the Florida-based NGO, **Amazon Waterfalls Association** ⓘ *www.amazonwaterfalls.org*.

Tip…
If you start the hike at San Pablo and finish at Cocachimba, arrange transport to return to San Pablo at the end of the day. Or, if you are staying in Cocachimba, arrange transport to San Pablo to begin the hike. The ride is about 30 minutes.

Tourist information

Chachapoyas

iPerú
On the Plaza de Armas, T041-477292,
iperuchachapoyas@promperu.gob.pe.
Mon-Sat 0900-1800, Sun 0900-1300.

Mendoza

For information on the area, ask for Michel
Ricardo Feijoó Aguilor in the Mendoza
municipal office, mifeijoo@gmail.com; he can
help arrange guides and accommodation.
A recommended guide is Alfonso Saldana
Pelaez, fotoguiaalsape@gmail.com.

Gocta

Community tourist information is available
in both San Pablo, T041-631163, daily 0800-
1730, and Cocachimba, T041-630569,
daily 0800-1730.

Where to stay

Celendín

$$-$ Hostal Celendín
Unión 305, Plaza de Armas, T076-555041,
hcgustavosd1@hotmail.com.
Some rooms with plaza view, central patio
and wooden stairs, hot water, pleasant,
has 2 restaurants: **Rinconcito Shilico** (2 de
Mayo 816), and **Pollos a la brasa Gusys**.

$ Hostal Imperial
Jr Dos de Mayo 568, 2 blocks from the plaza,
T076-555492.
Large rooms, good mattresses, hot water,
Wi-Fi, parking, decent choice.

$ Loyer's
José Gálvez 410, T076-555210.
Patio with wooden balcony all round,
nice, singles, doubles and family rooms.

$ Maxmar
Dos de Mayo 349, T076-555330.
Cheaper without bath, hot shower extra,
basic, parking, good value, helpful owners.

$ Mi Posada
Pardo 388, next to Atahualpa bus,
T074-979-758674.
Includes breakfast, small cheerful rooms,
family atmosphere.

$ Raymi Wasi
Jr José Gálvez 420, T976-551133.
With electric shower, cheaper without, large
rooms, has patio, quiet, parking, good value,
restaurant and karaoke.

Leymebamba and around

$$$$-$$$ Kentitambo
Across the road from Museo Leymebamba,
T971-118273, www.kentitambo.com.
Accommodation in 3 comfortable cabins,
lovely grounds with hummingbirds, meals
made from local produce. **Kentikafe** offers
sandwiches, cake, tea and coffee.

$$ La Casona
Jr Amazonas 223, T041-630301,
www.casonadeleymebamba.com.
Nicely refurbished old house with balcony,
attractive common area, simple rooms with
solar hot water, arrange tours and horses.

$ La Petaca
Jr Amazonas 426, on the plaza, T999-020599.
Good rooms with hot water, breakfast
available, café, helpful.

Tingo to Kuelap

$$$ Estancia Chillo
5 km south of Tingo towards Leymebamba,
T041-630510/979-340444.
On a 9-ha farm, dinner and breakfast
included, with bath, hot water, transport,
horse riding. Friendly family, a lovely country
retreat. Reported overpriced but negotiable.

$$ Choctámal Marvelous Spatuletail Lodge
3 km from Choctámal towards Kuélap at Km 20, T041-941-963327, www.marvelousspatuletail.com.
Book in advance. Heated rooms, hot showers, hot tub, telescope for star-gazing. Meals US$8-10. Offers horse riding and a chance to see the endangered marvellous spatuletail hummingbird.

$ Albergue León
Along the south bank of the Río Tingo, just upriver from the highway, T941-715685, hildegardlen@yahoo.es.
Basic, private or shared bath, electric shower, guiding, arrange horses, run by Lucho León who is knowledgeable.

$ Albergue Tingo
On the main highway, just north of the Río Tingo, T941-732251.
Adequate rooms with electric shower, restaurant.

Walking towards Kuélap from Tingo, the last house to the right of the track (**El Bebedero**) offers very basic rooms with bed, breakfast and dinner, helpful. It may be fully booked by archaeologists, but **Gabriel Portocarrero**, Kuélap's caretaker, runs a hostel just below the ruins, basic, friendly. **Sra Juanita** (T989-783432), offers basic rooms in the home of archaeologist Arturo Ruiz Estrada, with shared bath, cold water, breakfast. The village of **María**, 2½ hrs from Kuélap on the vehicle road to Choctámal has 10 *hospedajes*, some with bath and hot water; meals available. All these places are in the $ range.

Chachapoyas

$$$ Casa Vieja
Chincha Alta 569, T041-477353, www.casaviejaperu.com.
Converted old house with lovely courtyard, very nicely decorated, all rooms different, comfy beds, family atmosphere, good service, living room and *comedor* with open fire, includes breakfast, good café, Wi-Fi and library. Repeatedly recommended.

$$$ Xalca
Jr Grau 940, T041-479106, www.laxalcahotel.com.
Built in colonial style with central patio, large comfortable rooms, parking, good service.

$$ Casona Monsante
Amazonas 746, T041-477702, www.lacasonamonsante.com.
Converted colonial house with patio, orchid garden, comfortable rooms decorated with antiques.

$$ Las Orquídeas
Ayacucho 1231, T041-478271, www.hostallasorquideas.com.
Converted home, pleasantly decorated rooms, large garden.

$$ Posada del Arriero
Grau 636, T041-478945, www.posadadelarriero.net.
Old house with courtyard nicely refurbished in modern style, rooms are a bit plain, helpful.

$$ Puma Urco
Amazonas 833, T041-477871, www.hotelpumaurco.com.
Comfortable rooms, includes breakfast, TV, frigobar, **Café Café** next door, hotel and café receive good reports, run tours with **Turismo Explorer**.

$$-$ Casona Revash
Grau 517, Plaza de Armas, T041-477391, www.hostalrevash.com.
Traditional house with patio, stylish decor, steaming hot showers, breakfast available, helpful owners, good local information, popular. Operate tours and sell local crafts.

$ Aventura Backpackers Lodge
Jr Amazonas 1416, T959-555939, Facebook: AventuraBackpackersLodge.
Dorms with bunk beds, use of kitchen, good value.

$ Belén
Jr Ortiz Arrieta 540, Plaza de Armas,
T041-477830, www.hostalbelen.com.
With hot water, nicely furnished, pleasant
sitting room overlooking the Plaza, good value.

$ Chachapoyas Backpackers
Jr Dos de Mayo 639, T041-478879,
www.chachapoyasbackpackers.com.
Simple 2- and 3-bed dorms with shared bath,
electric shower, a good budget option, same
owners as **Turismo Explorer** tour operator.
Lovely family-run place. Recommended.

$ El Dorado
Ayacucho 1062, T041-477047,
ivvanovt@hotmail.com.
With bathroom, electric shower, helpful staff,
a good economical option.

$ Rumi Huasi
Ortiz Arrieta 365, T041-791100.
With and without bath, electric shower,
small rooms, simple and good.

$ Vista Hermosa
Puno 285, T041-477526.
Pleasant ample rooms, some have balconies,
electric shower, good value.

Levanto

$ Levanto Marvelous Spatuletail Lodge
Behind the church, T041-478838,
www.marvelousspatuletail.net.
2 circular buildings with tall thatched roofs,
4 bedrooms with 2 external bathrooms can
accommodate up to 12 people, hot shower,
lounge with fireplace and kitchen, meals
US$8-10, must book ahead.

Lamud and around

$$$ Tambo Sapalanchan
500 m north of Lamud, T987-936003,
tambosapalanchan@gmail.com.
Comfortable bungalows overlooking
attractive farmland, restaurant.

$ Hostal Kuélap
Garcilaso de la Vega 452, on the plaza, Lamud.
With or without bath or hot water, basic.

Gocta
San Pablo

$ Hospedaje Las Gardenias
T941-718660.
Basic rooms with shared bath, cold water,
economical meals available.

$ Hotel Gocta Camping
T941-718660.
Camping with hot showers and lovely views
at the site of a hotel under construction.

Cocachimba

$$$ Gocta Andes Lodge
Cocachimba, T041-630552 (Tarapoto
T042-522225), www.goctalodge.com.
Beautifully located lodge overlooking the
waterfall, ample rooms with balconies, lovely
terrace with pool, restaurant. Packages
available with other hotels in the group.

$ Hospedaje Gallito de la Roca
T041-630048.
Small simple rooms with or without bath,
hot water, economical meals available.

$ Hospedaje Las Orquídeas
T041-631265.
Simple rooms in a family home, shared bath,
cold water, restaurant.

Restaurants

Celendín

$$-$ La Reserve
José Gálvez 313.
Good quality and value, extensive menu,
from Italian to *chifa*.

$ Carbón y Leña
2 de Mayo 410.
For chicken, *parrillas* and pizzas.

$ Juguería Carolin
Bolognesi 384. Daily 0700-2200.

One of the few places open early, for juices, breakfasts and *caldos*.

Chachapoyas

$$$ Batán del Tayta
La Merced 604. Closed Sun.
Excellent innovative local cuisine, generous portions. Recommended.

$$ El Tejado
Santo Domingo 424. Daily for lunch only, but hours vary.
Excellent upscale *comida criolla*. Large portions, attentive service, nice atmosphere and setting. Good-value *menú ejecutivo* on weekdays.

$$ Paraíso de las Pizzas
Chincha Alta 355. Open till 2200.
Good pizzas and pastas, family-run.

$$-$ Romana
Amazonas 1091. Daily 0700-2300.
Choice of set meals and à la carte, good service.

$ El Edén
Grau by the market. Sun-Thu 0700-2100, Fri 0700-1800.
Simple vegetarian, a variety of dishes à la carte and economical set meals.

$ Matalaché
Ayacucho 616. Daily 0730-1530, 1800-2230.
Famous for their huge *milanesa* (breaded beef); also serves *menú*.

Cafés

Dulcería Santa Elena
Amazonas 800. Daily 0900-2230.
Old-fashioned home-made desserts.

Fusiones
Ayacucho 952, Plaza de Armas. Mon-Sat 0730-1130, 1600-2100.
Breakfast, fair-trade coffee, juices, snacks, Wi-Fi, book exchange, volunteer opportunities, occasional live music.

Heladería San Antonio
2 de Mayo 521 and Amazonas 856.
Good home-made ice cream; try the *lúcuma* and *guanábana* flavours.

Panadería Café San José
Ayacucho 816. Mon-Sat 0630-2200.
Bakery and café, good breakfasts, sweets and snacks.

What to do

Chachapoyas
The cost of full-day trips depends on season (higher Jul-Sep), distance, number of passengers and whether meals are included. Several operators have daily departures to Kuélap (US$15-19, 3 hrs each way in vehicle, including lunch stop on return, 3 hrs at the site; note that tour prices and travel times will change once the cable car is operational); Gocta, US$13.50-15; Quiocta and Karajía, US$19-27, and Museo de Leymebamba and Revash, US$31-39. All-inclusive trekking tours to Gran Vilaya cost about US$46-50 pp per day.

Amazon Expedition, *Jr Ortiz Arrieta 508, Plaza de Armas, T041-798718, http://amazon expedition.com.pe.* Day tours and multi-day treks.

Andes Tours, *at Casona Revash.* Daily trips to Kuélap and Gocta, other tours to ruins, caves and trekking. Also less-visited destinations, combining travel by car, on horseback and walking.

Cloudforest Expeditions, *Jr Puno 368, T041-477610, www.kuelapnordperu.com.* Tours to ruins, trek to Yumbilla, English and German spoken.

Nuevos Caminos, at **Café Fusiones**, *T041-479170, www.nuevoscaminostravel.com.* Alternative community tourism throughout northern Peru, volunteer opportunities.

Turismo Explorer, *Jr Grau 509, T041-478162, www.turismoexplorerperu.com.* Daily tours to Kuélap, Gocta and other destinations, trekking tours including Laguna de los Cóndores and other archaeological sites, transport, good service.

Vilaya Tours, *T941-708798, www.vilayatours. com*. All-inclusive treks to off-the-beaten-path destinations throughout northern Peru. Run by Robert Dover, a very experienced and knowledgeable British guide, book ahead.

Transport

Celendín
Bus To **Cajamarca**, 107 km, 3½ hrs, with **Royal Palace's** (Jr Unión y José Gálvez, by Plaza de Armas), 1400 daily; also **CABA**, 2 a day, and **Rojas**, 3 a day. Cars to Cajamarca leave when full from Ovalo Agusto Gil, Cáceres y Amazonas, 2½ hrs, US$9 pp. They also go from the same place to **Chachapoyas**, 6 hrs, US$18 pp. **Virgen del Carmen** (Cáceres 112 by Ovalo A Gil, T076-792918) to Chachapoyas, daily at 0900, US$11.55, via **Leymebamba**, 6 hrs, US$7.75.

Leymebamba and around
To **Chachapoyas** (fills quickly, book ahead), 2½-3 hrs, cars US$7.75, combis US$4, best with **Raymi Express**, at 0500, 0600, 0630, 1200, 1400; several other companies. To **Celendín**, US$7.75, and **Cajamarca**, US$11.55, 8 hrs, service originating in Chachapoyas.

Tingo to Kuélap
The easiest way to visit Kuélap is on a tour from Chachapoyas (see above) or by hiring a vehicle with driver (US$45 per vehicle, or US$54 with wait). Alternatively, **Trans Roller's** combis or cars depart from the Terminal Terrestre in Chachapoyas at 0400 to **Tingo** (US$3.10, 1 hr), **Choctámal** (US$4.50, 1½ hrs), **Lónguita** (US$5, 2 hrs), **María** (US$6, 2½ hrs) and **Kuélap**, US$8, 3 hrs (only if they have enough passengers). Note that the car returns from Kuélap straight away (around 0700), so you will have to spend the night in the area (see Where to stay). There is also additional transport in combis or cars to María with **Sr José Cruz** (Grau 331) at 0530 (returns from María at 0800) and to Lónguita with **Trans Shubet** (Pasaje Reyes, off Grau) around 1400-1500. Cars bound

for Magdalena with **Brisas del Utcubamba** (Grau 332, Chachapoyas) and transport going to/from Yerbabuena or Leymebamba also pass through **Tingo**.

Chachapoyas
Air There are 3 flights a day to/from **Tarapoto** in a 9-seater aircraft.

Bus Regional The Terminal Terrestre, a regional transport terminal, is 9 blocks from the Plaza de Armas, at Jr Triunfo, block 1. For services to **Tingo**, **Choctámal** and **Kuélap**, see above. To **Leymebamba**, 83 km, 3 hrs, US$4 (reserve ahead), the best service is with **Raymi Express**, at 0930, 1200, 1400, 1600, 1700; several other companies. For **Revash**, to **Santo Tomás**, **Comité Santo Tomás** at 1000, 1300, 1500 (return at 0300, 0400, 0500), US$4.30, 3 hrs; get off at **Cruce de Revash** (near Puente Santo Tomás), US$4.30, 2½ hrs; or with the same company to **San Bartolo** at 1400 (return 0600), US$4.30, 3 hrs. To **Jalca Grande**, 2 combis depart Mon-Fri from 1330 onwards, US$4.30, 3 hrs (return 0300-0400). To **Levanto**, cars daily 1200-1300, US$2.90. To **Mendoza** (86 km), **Guayabamba**, US$7.75, 2½ hrs, also combis US$6. To **Luya** and **Lamud**, cars 0400-1800, US$2.85; there are cars from Luya to Cruzpata, 0600-1700, US$3, 1 hr.

Also from the Terminal Terrestre, to **Pedro Ruiz** (for connections to Chiclayo, Jaén, or Tarapoto), cars depart as they fill 0600-2200, US$3.85, 1 hr; combis every 2 hrs 0600-1800, US$2; and **Diplomáticos** vans, as they fill 0500-1900. To **Bagua Grande** (for connections to Jaén), cars US$8.50, 2 hrs; combis/vans with **Evangelio Poder de Dios**, US$6. This company also goes to **Moyobamba** (for connections to Tarapoto), at 0700, US$9.75, 5 hrs. To **Celendín** (8-9 hrs, US$11.55) and **Cajamarca** (11-12 hrs, US$18) with **Amazonas Express**, at 0530 and 1930 daily; **Virgen del Carmen**, at 1900 to Celendín and 1930 to Cajamarca; also with **Transportes Karlita**.

Long distance The recommended companies serving Chachapoyas are:

MóvilTours (Libertad 464, T041-478545), GH Bus (tickets from Jr Grau entre Triunfo y Amazonas, T041-479200; station at C Evitamiento, take a taxi) and Transervis Kuélap (Jr Unión 330, T041-478128). To Lima (20-22 hrs, US$44-52) with Móvil Tours at 1300; with GH Bus at 1030. To Chiclayo (9 hrs, US$15-25) at 1930 with Móvil Tours or GH Bus; Tue and Sat at 1900, other days at 2000 with Transervis Kuélap. Other options to Chiclayo are Civa (Salamanca y Ortiz Arrieta, T041-478048) at 1815 and Star Bus (Jr Unión 330) at 1930. To Trujillo (12 hrs, US$23-29), at 1930 with Móvil Tours or GH Bus.

Gocta

The easiest way to get to Gocta is with a tour from Chachapoyas; in high season there are also tours from Pedro Ruiz. A taxi from Chachapoyas costs US$30, or US$38 with 5-6 hrs' wait. A taxi from Pedro Ruiz costs US$2 pp (there are seldom other passengers to share) or US$10 for the vehicle. Sr Fabier, T962-922798, offers transport service to San Pablo; call ahead to find out when he will be in Pedro Ruiz. A mototaxi from Pedro Ruiz (5 Esquinas, along the road to Chachapoyas, 4 blocks from the highway) costs US$6, beware of overcharging and dress warmly; it is windy and cold. Arrange return transport ahead or at the tourist offices in San Pablo or Cocachimba, as it is difficult to get transport back from Cocahuayco to either Chachapoyas or Pedro Ruiz.

Chachapoyas to the Amazon

look out for birdlife on this dramatic journey to the jungle

From Chachapoyas the road heads north through the beautiful Utcubamba canyon for one hour to a crossroads at Pedro Ruíz, which has two hotels, other lodgings and some basic restaurants. From here, you can return to the coast, head to Jaén for Ecuador, or continue east to Tarapoto and Yurimaguas, making the spectacular descent on a paved road from high Andes to jungle.

☆Pedro Ruiz to Moyobamba

In the rainy season, the road east of Pedro Ruiz may be subject to landslides. This is a very beautiful journey, first passing Laguna Pomacochas, then leading to where the high Andes tumble into the Amazon Basin before your eyes. The descent from the heights of the Abra Patricia Pass to the Río Afluente at 1400 m is one of the best birdwatching areas in northern Peru. ECOAN ⓘ T041-816814, www.ecoanperu.org, has two private bird reserves: 20 minutes east of Pedro Ruiz before Pomacochas, protecting the marvelous spatuletail hummingbird (*Loddigesia mirabilis*), US$10, 0600-1800; and at Km 364.5 aimed at conserving the critically endangered long-whiskered owlet (*Xenoglaux loweryi*) and other rare species. Further along, Nueva Cajamarca (reported unsafe), Rioja (198 km, with several hotels) and Moyobamba are growing centres of population, with much forest clearance beside the road.

Moyobamba *Colour map 2, B2.*

Moyobamba, capital of the San Martín Region, is a pleasant town in the attractive Río Mayo valley. The area is renowned for its orchids: there is a **Festival de la Orquídea** over three days around 1 November. Among several places to see the plants is **Orquideario Waqanki** ⓘ *www.waqanki.com, daily 0700-1800, US$0.55*, where the orchids have been placed in trees. Just beyond are **Baños Termales San Mateo** ⓘ *5 km southeast, daily 0600-2200, US$0.55*, which are worth a visit. Boat trips can be taken from **Puerto Tahuishco**, the town's harbour, a pleasant walk north of the centre.

Morro de Calzada ① *13.5 km west of Moyobamba via Calzada, combi to the Calzada turnoff, US$0.55, mototaxi to the start of the trail US$2.50*, is an isolated outcrop in white sand forest that is good for birdwatching. A path through forest leads to a lookout at the top (1½ hours), but enquire about safety beforehand.

Tarapoto and around *Colour map 2, B2.*

Tarapoto, the largest commercial centre in the region, with a population of 120,000, is a very friendly place. It stands at the foot of the forested hills of the **Area de Conservación Regional Cordillera Escalera** (149,870 ha), which is good for birdwatching and walking. Next to the conservation area and within easy reach of town is the 9-ha **El Amo del Bosque Sector** ① *Urawasha, 5 km walk (9 km by car) from town, T042-524675 (after 1900)*, where the knowledgeable owner, Sr José Macedo, offers guided tours, and 20-ha **Wayrasacha** ① *6-km walk (10 km by car) from the city, T042-522261*, run by Peruvian-Swiss couple César Ramírez and Stephanie Gallusser, who offer day trips, overnight stays in a basic shelter and volunteer opportunities (English and French spoken).

Lamas

Off the main road, 22 km northwest of Tarapoto, Lamas is a small hill town with a Quechua-speaking native community, descendants of the Chancas people from the distant central highlands. Lamas is known as 'la ciudad de los tres pisos' (the city of three storeys). On the top level is a lookout with good views, a hotel-restaurant and a *recreo turístico*. The main town occupies the middle level, where there is a small **Museo Los Chankas** ① *Jr San Martín 1157, daily 0830-1300, 1430-1800, US$1.15*, with ethnological and historical exhibits. Uphill from the museum is **El Castillo de Lamas** ① *Mon-Sat 0900-1230, 1400-1800, Sun 0930-1830, US$2*, an art gallery and café set in an incongruous medieval castle. On the lower level is the neighbourhood of **Wayku**, where the native Chancas live. Lamas' **Easter** celebrations draw many Peruvian visitors, as do the **Fiestas Patronales** in honour of Santa Rosa de Lima in the last week in August.

Tarapoto to Yurimaguas

From Tarapoto it is 129 km to Yurimaguas on the Río Huallaga (see page 309), along a spectacular paved road. The road climbs through lush country reaching the 50-m **Ahuashiyacu Falls** ① *US$1.15*, within the **Cordillera Escalera** conservation area after 15 km. This is a popular place with locals. Tours are available or there's transport from La Banda de Shilcayo, a Tarapoto neighbourhood. Past Ahuashiyacu, the road climbs to a tunnel – stop at the police control for good birdwatching (mototaxi US$6) – after which you descend through beautiful forest perched on rocky cliffs to Pongo de Caynarachi (several basic comedores), where the flats start. From Yurimaguas launches go to Iquitos (see page 321).

Listings Chachapoyas to the Amazon

Tourist information

Moyobamba

See www.moyobamba.net.

Dirdetur
Jr San Martín 301, T042-562043.
Mon-Fri 0800-1300, 1430-1730.
Has leaflets and map, English spoken.

Oficina Municipal de Información
Jr Pedro Canga 262, at Plaza, T042-562191 ext 541. Mon-Fri 0800-1300, 1430-1715.
No English spoken.

Tarapoto

Dircetur
Jr Angel Delgado Morey, cuadra 1,
T042-522567.

Oficina Municipal de Información
Jr Ramírez Hurtado, at plaza, T042-526188.
Mon-Sat 0800-1300, 1500-2000,
Sun 0900-1300.

Where to stay

Moyobamba

$$$ Puerto Mirador
Jr Sucre, 1 km from centre, T042-562050,
www.hotelpuertomirador.com.
Buffet breakfast, lovely grounds, views
overlooking river valley, pool, good
restaurant, credit cards accepted.

$$ Orquídea del Mayo
Jr San Martín 432, T042-561049,
orquideadelmayohostal@hotmail.com.
Modern comfortable rooms with bath,
hot water.

$$ Río Mayo
Jr Pedro Canga 415, T042-564193.
Central, modern comfortable rooms,
frigobar, small indoor pool, parking.

$$-$ El Portón
Jr San Martín 449, T042-562900.
Pleasant modern rooms with fan, hot water,
nice grounds with hammocks, kitchen facilities.

$ Cobos
Jr Pedro Canga 404, T042-562153.
Private bath, cold water, simple but good.

$ La Cueva de Juan
Jr Alonso de Alvarado 870, T042-562488,
lacueva870@hotmail.com.
Small courtyard, private bath, hot water,
central but reasonably quiet, good value.

Lamas

$ Hospedaje Girasoles
Opposite the mirador in the upper part of
town, T042-543439, stegmaiert@yahoo.de.

Breakfast available, nice views, pizzeria and
friendly, knowledgeable owners.

Tarapoto and around

There are several $ *alojamientos* on Alegría
Arias de Morey, cuadra 2, and cheap basic
hotels by the bus terminals.

$$$ Puerto Palmeras
Cra Belaúnde Terry, Km 614, T042-524100.
Private reserve outside town. Large, modern
complex, popular with families, lots of
activities and entertainment. Nice rooms,
helpful staff, good restaurant, pleasant
grounds with pool, mountain bikes,
horses and small zoo, airport transfers.

$$$ Puma Rinri Lodge
Cra Shapaja–Chasuta, Km 16, T042-526694,
www.pumarinri.com.
Lodge/resort hotel on the shores of the
Río Huallaga, 30 km east of Tarapoto.
Offers a variety of all-inclusive packages.

$$ Huingos Lodge
Prolongación Alerta cuadra 6, Sector Takiwasi,
T042-524171, www.huingoslodge.com.
Nice cabins in lovely grounds by the Río
Shilcayo. Fan, electric shower, frigobar,
kitchen facilities, hammocks, HI-affiliated,
mototaxi from bus stations US$1.55-2.

$$ La Patarashca
Jr San Pablo de la Cruz 362, T042-528810,
www.lapatarashca.com.
Very nice hotel with large rooms, cheaper
without a/c, rustic, restaurant, electric
shower, large garden with hammocks,
tours arranged.

$$ Luna Azul
Jr Manco Capac 276, T042-525787,
www.lunaazulhotel.com.
Modern, central, includes breakfast and
airport transfers, with bath, hot water,
a/c or fan, frigobar.

$$-$ El Mirador
Jr San Pablo de la Cruz 517, 5 blocks
uphill from the plaza T042-522177,
www.elmiradortarapoto.blogspot.com.

With bath, electric shower, fan, Wi-Fi, laundry facilities, breakfast available, hammocks on rooftop terrace with good views, tours arranged. Family-run and very welcoming.

$ San Antonio
Jr Jiménez Pimentel 126, T042-525563.
Rooms with private bath, hot water and fan, good value.

Restaurants

Moyobamba

$$-$ Kikeku
Jr Pedro Canga 450, next to casino. 24 hrs.
Good *chifa*, also *comida criolla*, noisy.

$ El Avispa Juane
Jr Callao 583. Mon-Sat 0730-1600,
Sun 0800-1500.
Regional specialities, menu Mon-Sat and snacks, popular.

$ La Buena Salud
25 de Mayo 227, by market. Sun-Fri 0800-1500.
Vegetarian set meals, breakfast and fruit juices.

Helados La Muyuna
Jr Pedro Canga 529.
Good natural jungle fruit ice cream.

Tarapoto
There are several restaurants and bars around Jr San Pablo de la Cruz on the corner of Lamas – a lively area at night.

$$$-$$ Chalet Venezia
Jr Alegría Arias de Morey 298.
Tue-Sun 1200-2300.
Upmarket Italian/Amazonian fusion cuisine, wine list, elegant, interior or terrace seating.

$$$-$$ Real Grill
Jr Moyobamba on the plaza. Daily 0830-2400.
Regional and international food. One of the best in town.

$$-$ Chifa Cantón
Jr Ramón Castilla 140. Mon-Fri 1200-1600,
Sat-Sun 1200-2400.
Chinese, very popular and clean.

$ El Manguaré
Jr Moyobamba corner Manco Cápac.
Mon-Sat 1200-1530.
Good set meals or à la carte, good service.

Cafés

Café Plaza
Jr Maynas corner Martínez, at the plaza.
Daily 0730-2300.
Breakfast, coffee, snacks, juices, Wi-Fi, popular.

Helados La Muyuna
Jr Ramón Castilla 271. Sun-Thu 0800-2400,
Fri 0800-1700, Sat 1830-2400.
Good natural ice cream, fruit salads and drinks made with jungle fruits.

Transport

Pedro Ruíz
Bus Many buses on the **Chiclayo–Tarapoto** and **Chiclayo–Chachapoyas** routes pass through town. Bus fare to Chiclayo, US$11.50-19; to Tarapoto, US$11.50-15.50. Cars or combis are more convenient for Chacha or Bagua. To **Jaén**, **Trans Fernández** bus from Tarapoto passes Pedro Ruiz about 1400-1500, or take a car to Bagua Grande and transfer there.

Car, combi and van To **Chachapoyas**, cars US$4, combis US$2, 1 hr. To **Bagua Grande**, cars US$4.75, combis US$4, 1 hr. To **Moyobamba**, cars US$10.70, 4 hrs. To **Nueva Cajamarca**, cars US$9.75, combis US$7.75, 3-3½ hrs. From Nueva Cajamarca it's a further 20 mins to **Rioja** by car, US$1.15, or combi, US$0.75. From Rioja to **Moyobamba**, 21 km, 20 mins, car US$1.15, combi, US$0.75.

Moyobamba
Bus The bus terminal is 12 blocks from the centre on Av Grau (mototaxi US$0.55). No services originate in Moyobamba; all buses are en route to/from Tarapoto. Several companies head west to **Pedro Ruiz** (US$9, 4 hrs), **Jaén** (US$9, 7 hrs), **Chiclayo** (US$15-US$23, 12 hrs). To reserve a seat on a long-haul bus, you may have to pay the fare to the final destination even if you get off sooner.

Car, combi and van Empresa San Martín (Benavides 276) and **ETRISA** (Benavides 244) run cars (US$1.15) and vans (US$0.75) to **Rioja**, 20 mins; to **Nueva Cajamarca**, 40 mins (US$2, US$1.55) and **Tarapoto**, 2 hrs (US$7.75, US$4); combis cost about 50% less on all routes. To **Chachapoyas**, Evangelio Poder de Dios (Grau 640), at 1500, US$9.75, 5 hrs.

Tarapoto

Air Taxi to town, US$3; mototaxi US$1.15. To **Lima**, daily with **LATAM** (Ramírez Hurtado 183, on the plaza, T042-529318), **Avianca/ TACA, Peruvian Airlines** and **Star Perú** (San Pablo de la Cruz 100, T042-528765). **Star Perú** to **Iquitos** daily (Mon, Wed, Fri via Pucallpa), **LATAM** to Iquitos Mon, Thu.

Bus Buses depart from Av Salaverry, blocks 8-9, in Morales; mototaxi from centre, US$1.15, 20 mins.
   To **Moyobamba**, 116 km, US$3.85, 2 hrs; to **Pedro Ruiz**, US$11.50-15.50 (companies going to Jaén or Chiclayo), 6 hrs; to **Chiclayo**, 690 km, 15-16 hrs, US$25-29;

and **Lima**, US$46-52, *cama* US$64, 30 hrs. For **Chachapoyas**, go to Moyobamba and take a van from there (see above). To **Jaén**, US$13.50-15.50, 9-10 hrs, with **Fernández**, 4 a day. To **Piura** US$23, 16 hrs, with **Sol Peruano**, at 1200. To **Tingo María**, US$27, and **Pucallpa**, US$35, Mon, Wed, Fri 0500, Tue, Thu, Sat 0830, **Transamazónica** and **Transmar** alternate days; there have been armed holdups on this route.

Car, combi and van To Lamas, cars from Av Alfonso Ugarte, cuadra 11, US$1.45, 30 mins. To **Moyobamba**, cars with **Empresa San Martín** (Av Alfonso Ugarte 1456, T042-526327) and **ETRISA** (Av Alfonso Ugarte 1096, T042-521944); both will pick you up from your hotel, US$7.70, 2 hrs; combis with **Turismo Selva** (Av Alfonso Ugarte, cuadra 11), US$4, 2½ hrs. To **Yurimaguas**, **Gilmer Tours** (Av Alfonso Ugarte 1480), frequent minibuses, US$5.75, 2½ hrs; cars with **Empresa San Martín**, US$7.75, 2 hrs; **Turismo Selva** vans, US$4, 8 daily.

Bagua Grande and further west
This is the first town of note heading west from Pedro Ruiz. It has several hotels but is hot, dusty and unsafe; Pedro Ruiz or Jaén are more pleasant places to spend the night. From Bagua Grande the road follows the Río Chamaya, climbing to the Abra de Porculla (2150 m) before descending to join the old Pan-American Highway at Olmos (see page 121). From Olmos you can go southwest to Chiclayo, or northwest to Piura.

Jaén Colour map 2, B2.
Some 50 km west of Bagua Grande, a road branches northwest at Chamaya to **Jaén**, a convenient stopover en route to the jungle or Ecuador. It is a modern city surrounded by rice fields, with a population of about 100,000. The **Museo Hermógenes Mejía Solf** ⓘ *2 km south of centre, T976-719590, Mon-Fri 0800-1400, mototaxi US$0.60*, displays pre-Columbian artefacts from a variety of cultures. Newly discovered temples at Monte Grande and San Isidro, close to Jaén, are revealing more finds, dating back possibly to 3500 BC.

San Ignacio to the border
A road runs north for 109 km to **San Ignacio** (only the first 55 km are paved), a pleasant town with steep streets in the centre of a coffee-growing area. The nearby hills offer excursions to waterfalls, lakes, petroglyphs and ancient ruins. West of San Ignacio is the **Santuario Tabaconas-Namballe** ⓘ *Sernanp, Huancabamba s/n, Sector Santiago,*

downhill from the centre in San Ignacio, T968-218439, a 32,125-ha reserve at 1700-3800 m protecting the spectacled bear, mountain tapir and several ecosystems including the southernmost Andean *páramo*. From San Ignacio the unpaved road, being widened, runs 45 km through green hills to **Namballe**. The border is 15 minutes from Namballe at **La Balsa** (taxi or mototaxi, US$1.15), which has a simple lodging and *comedor*, a few small shops and money changers. To leave Perú, head directly to immigration (daily 0830-1300, 1500-2000; ask for the officer at his house if he is not at his desk). To enter Peru, visit immigration first, then get a stamp from the PNP (police), and return to immigration. *Rancheras* (open-sided buses) run from La Balsa to Zumba at 1200, 1700 and 1915 (US$1.75, 1¾ hours) and from Zumba to La Balsa at 0800, 1430 and 1700. From Zumba there is onward transport to Vilcabamba and Loja. There are Ecuadorean military controls before and after Zumba (keep your passport to hand), but in general this crossing is relaxed and straightforward.

Listings Chachapoyas to Ecuador

Where to stay

Bagua Grande

$$-$ Río Hotel
Jr Capac Malku 115, www.riohotel baguagrande.blogspot.com.
A good choice if you can't avoid staying in Bagua Grande.

Jaén

$$ Casa del Sol
Mcal Castilla 140, near Plaza de Armas, T076-434478, hotelcasadelsol@hotmail.com.
Modern confortable rooms with frigobar, parking, suites with jacuzzi.

$$ El Bosque
Mesones Muro 632, T076-431184, hoteleraelbosque@speedy.com.pe.
On main road by bus terminals. Quiet rooms at back, gardens, frigobar, hot water, pool, restaurant.

$$ Prim's
Diego Palomino 1341, T076-431039, www.primshotel.com.
Includes breakfast, good service, comfortable, hot water, a/c or fan, frigobar, Wi-Fi, friendly, small pool.

$ Danubio
V Pinillos 429, T076-433110.

Older place, nicely refurbished, many different rooms and prices, some cheaper rooms have cold water only, fan, good.

San Ignacio to the border

$ Gran Hotel San Ignacio
Jr José Olaya 680 at the bottom of the hill, San Ignacio, T076-356544, granhotel-sanignacio@hotmail.com.
Restaurant for breakfast and good lunch *menú*, modern comfortable rooms, upmarket for here.

$ Hostal Maldonado
Near the plaza, Namballe, T076-830011 (community phone).
Private bath (cheaper without), cold water, basic.

$ La Posada
Jr Porvenir 218, San Ignacio, T076-356180.
Simple rooms which are cheaper without bath or hot water, restaurant.

$ Sol de la Frontera
1 km north of Namballe, 4 km from La Balsa, T976-116781, T01-247 8881 in Lima, www.hotelsoldelafrontera.com.
British-run by Isabel Wood. Comfortable rooms in bungalows, bathtubs, gas water heaters, continental breakfast, set in 2.5 ha of countryside. A good option if you have your

own vehicle or bring some food. Meals only available for groups with advance booking. Camping and campervans.

Restaurants

Jaén

$$-$ La Cabaña
San Martín 1521. Daily 0700-0000.
Daily specials at noon, à la carte in the evening, popular.

$$-$ Lactobac
Bolívar 1378 at Plaza de Armas. Daily 0730-0000.
Variety of à la carte dishes, snacks, desserts, good *pollo a la brasa*. Very popular.

$ Ebenezer
Mcal Ureta 1360. Sun-Thu 0700-2130, Fri 0700-1600.
Simple vegetarian restaurant serves economical midday *menú* and à la carte.

$ Gatizza
Diego Palomino 1503. Mon-Sat 0830-1800.
Tasty and varied *menú*.

Transport

Bagua Grande
Many buses pass through **Bagua Grande** en route to/from Chiclayo, Tarapoto or Chachapoyas. Cars to **Jaén** from Mcal Castilla y Angamos at the west end of town, US$4, combis US$2.50, 1 hr. From R Palma 308 at the east end of town, cars leave to **Pedro Ruiz**, US$4.60, combis US$4, 1 hr; to **Chachapoyas**, US$9.75, combis US$5.75, 2½ hrs.

Jaén
Bus, car and combi Terminals are strung along Mesones Muro, blocks 4-7, south of centre; there are many ticket offices, so always enquire where the bus actually leaves from. To **Chiclayo**: US$7.75-15.50, 6 hrs, many companies, **Móvil** more expensive than others. Cars to Chiclayo from Mesones Muro, cuadra 4, US$27, 5 hrs. To **Lima**, with **Móvil** at 1500, 16 hrs, *bus cama* US$46, *semi-cama* US$38.50; with **Civa** (tickets from Mcal Ureta 1300 y V Pinillos; terminal at Bolívar 935), 1700, US$35-42. Service to Lima also goes through **Trujillo**. To **Piura** via Olmos, with S**ol Peruano**, at 2200, US$15.50, 8 hrs. To **Tarapoto**, 490 km, US$13.50-15.50, 9-10 hrs, with **Fernández**, 4 a day. To **Moyobamba**, US$11.50-13.50, 7 hrs, same service as Tarapoto, likewise to **Pedro Ruiz,** US$6-7.75, 3½ hrs. To **Bagua Grande**, cars from Mesones Muro cuadra 6, 0400-2000, US$4, 1 hr; combis from cuadra 9, US$2.50. To **Chamaya,** cars from Mesones Muro, cuadra 4, 0500-2000, US$1, 15 min. To **San Ignacio** (for Ecuador), cars from Av Pacamuros, cuadra 19, 0400-1800, US$7.75, 2 hrs; combis from cuadra 17 and 20, US$4.60, 3 hrs.

San Ignacio to the border
Bus From San Ignacio to **Chiclayo**, with **Civa** (Av San Ignacio 386), daily at 1830, US$11.55, 10-11 hrs; with **Trans Chiclayo** (Av San Ignacio 406), 1945 daily. To **Jaén**, from *óvalo* at south end of Av Mariano Melgar. To **Namballe** and **La Balsa** (border with Ecuador), cars leave from Sector Alto Loyola at north end of town, way above the centre, US$6 to Namballe, US$6.55 to La Balsa, 1½ hrs.

South
coast

The Pan-American Highway runs all the way south from Lima to the Chilean border. This part of Peru's desert coast has its own distinctive attractions. The most famous, and perhaps the strangest, are the mysterious Nazca Lines, whose origin and function continue to puzzle scientists the world over. But Nazca is not the sole archaeological resource here: remains of other pre-Columbian civilizations include outposts of the Inca empire itself. Pisco and Ica are the main centres before Nazca. The former, which is near the famous Paracas marine reserve, is named after the latter's main product, the pisco grape brandy and a number of places are well known for their bodegas.

South from Lima
vineyards, seabirds and a forgotten valley

Beyond the beaches which are popular with Limeños the road passes near several towns, including Cañete and Chincha, with its Afro-Peruvian culture. The Paracas peninsula, near Pisco, is one of the world's great marine bird reserves and was home to one of Peru's most important ancient civilizations. Further south, the Ica valley, with its wonderful climate, is home to that equally wonderful grape brandy, pisco. Most beaches have very strong currents and can be dangerous for swimming; if unsure, ask locals.

Cañete and Quebrada de Lunahuana
About 150 km south of Lima, on the Río Cañete, is the prosperous market centre of **San Vicente de Cañete**. All the main services are within a few blocks of the plaza. A paved road runs inland, mostly beside the Río Cañete, through Imperial and Nuevo Imperial to **Lunahuaná** (40 km). This town is located 8 km beyond the Inca ruins of **Incawasi**, which used to dominate the valley. In the week **Lunahuaná** is very quiet, but on Sunday the town is full of life, with pisco tastings from the valley's bodegas, food and handicrafts

for sale in the plaza and lots of outdoor activities. Throughout February and March you may still be able to see traditional methods of treading the grapes to the beat of a drum.

☆Upper Cañete Valley

Beyond Lunahuaná the road ascending the Cañete Valley leaves the narrow flood-plain and runs 41 km, paved, through a series of gorges to the San Jerónimo bridge. A side road heads to Huangáscar and the village of Viñac, where **Mountain Lodges of Peru** has its **Viñak-Reichraming Lodge** (see Where to stay, page 166). The road beyond Huangáscar, from which you can see extensive areas of pre-Columbian agricultural terracing, is impassable from January to mid-March.

The main road carries on to the market towns of **Yauyos** (basic accommodation, 5 km off the road) and Llapay, a good base in the middle of the valley. Beyond Llapay, the Cañete valley narrows to an exceptionally tight canyon; the road squeezes between rock and rushing water. Near Alís, the road forks. The eastern branch climbs steeply to a 4600-m pass then drops down to Huancayo (see page 289), while the northern branch follows the Río Cañete deeper into the **Reserva Paisajística Nor Yauyos-Cochas** ① *contact Juan Carlos Pilco (pilco_traveler@hotmail.com) or the Sernanp regional office: RPNYC, Av Francisco Solano 107, San Carlos, Huancayo, T064-213064.* After the attractive village of **Huancaya,** the valley is transformed into one of the most beautiful upper valleys in all Peru, on a par with Colca. The river passes through high Andean terrain and descends through a series of absolutely clear, turquoise pools and lakes, interrupted by cascades and white water rapids. Culturally, the valley is fascinating for its dying indigenous languages and traditional ways of life, including perhaps the best pre-Columbian terracing anywhere in Peru.

Pisco and around *Colour map 2, C3.*

The largest port (population 82,250) between Callao and Matarani, Pisco is located a short distance west of the Pan-American Highway and 237 km south of Lima. In August 2007, an earthquake of 7.9 on the Richter scale struck the coast of Peru south of Lima, killing 519 people and injuring 1366; 58,500 homes were destroyed. In Pisco itself almost half of the buildings were destroyed. In October 2011, another earthquake, this time measuring 6.9 on the Richter scale, occurred just off the coast of Ica, leaving one dead, 1705 homeless and 515 damaged or destroyed houses.

Criollo culture is celebrated at local festivals (see page 170) in **Chincha Alta**, 35 km north of Pisco, where African slave labour once allowed the great haciendas to thrive. Chincha is also a good place to sample locally produced wine and pisco.

From Pisco to the sierras

A 317-km paved road goes up the Pisco valley from the suburb of San Clemente to Ayacucho in the sierra, with a branch to Huancavelica. At Castrovirreyna it reaches 4600 m. The scenery on this journey is superb. The road passes one of the best-preserved Inca ruins in coastal Peru after 38 km: **Tambo Colorado** ① *see www.facebook.com/TamboColorado for details of a French research project here,* includes buildings where the Inca and his retinue would have stayed. Many of the walls retain their original colours. On the other side of the road are the public plaza, the garrison and the messengers' quarters. The caretaker will act as a guide and has a small collection of items found on the site. You can visit Tambo Colorado on a guided tour from Pisco (US$15, minimum two people) or travel independently by taxi, bus or *colectivo* (see Transport, page 171).

Paracas National Reserve

Daily 1100-1500. US$1.75 pp. Tours (recommended) cost US$9 in a bus with 20 people.

Down the coast from Pisco is the bay of **Paracas**, sheltered by the Paracas peninsula to the south and west. The peninsula, a large area of coast to the south and the Ballestas Islands are protected as a national reserve, with the highest concentration of marine birds in the world.

> **Tip...**
> Paracas means 'sandstorm' in Quechua; these can last for up to three days, especially in August. The wind gets up every afternoon, peaking at around 1500.

Paracas can be reached by the coast road from San Andrés, passing the fishing port and a large proportion of Peru's fishmeal industry. Alternatively, go down the Pan-American Highway for 14.5 km past the Pisco turning and take the road to Paracas across the desert. In town is the **Museo Histórico de Paracas** ⓘ *Av Los Libertadores Mz JI Lote 10, T955-929514*, with exhibits from the pre-Columbian culture of the region.

The entrance to the reserve is at the south end of town on the main road. Just inside the reserve is the **Julio C Tello** site museum (named after the Peruvian archaeologist who first researched the Paracas culture). It was rebuilt following the 2007 earthquake and reopened in 2016. Tours follow a route through the reserve, including to a *mirador* overlooking **La Catedral** rock formation, which collapsed in 2007. Longer tours venture into the deserts to the south. The tiny fishing village of **Lagunilla** is 5 km from the museum across the neck of the peninsula. Eating places there are poor value (watch out for prices in dollars), but almost all tours stop for lunch here. About 14 km from the museum is the pre-Columbian image known as '**El Candelabro**' (the candelabra), which has been traced into the hillside. It's at least 50 m long and is best seen from the sea; sit on the left side of the boat.

> **Warning...**
> It's advisable to see the peninsula as part of a tour from either Pisco or Paracas: it is not safe to walk alone and it is easy to get lost.

☆Trips to the **Islas Ballestas** leave from the jetties in Paracas town. The islands are spectacular, eroded into numerous arches and caves which give the islands their name (*ballesta* means archer's bow) and provide shelter for thousands of seabirds. You will see, close up, guano birds, pelicans, penguins, hundreds of inquisitive sea lions and, if you're lucky, dolphins swimming in the bay. Birdlife here includes some very rare species. The book *Las Aves del Departamento de Lima* by Maria Koepcke is useful. Most boats are speedboats with life jackets, some are very crowded; wear warm clothing and protect against the sun. The boats pass Puerto San Martín and the Candelabra en route to the islands.

Ica *Colour map 2, C3.*

Ica, 70 km southeast of Pisco, is Peru's chief wine centre and is also famous for its *tejas*, a local sweet of *manjarblanco*. It suffered less damage than Pisco in the 2007 earthquake, but one side of the Plaza de Armas did collapse. The **Museo Regional** ⓘ *Av Ayabaca, block 8 (take bus 17 from the Plaza de Armas, US$0.50), T056-234383 Mon-Wed 0800-1900, Thu-Sun 0900-1800, US$4, students US$2.15, tip guides US$4-5*, has mummies, ceramics, textiles and trepanned skulls from the Paracas, Nazca and Inca cultures. There's also a good, well-displayed collection of Inca quipus and clothes made of feathers. Behind the building is a scale model of the Nazca Lines with an observation tower, which is useful for orientation before visiting the lines themselves. The kiosk outside sells copies of motifs from ceramics and textiles.

Huacachina

From Ica, take a taxi for US$1.75 or colectivo from Bolívar block 2, return from behind Hotel Mossone, US$0.75.

....

About 5 km from Ica, round a palm-fringed lake amid amazing sand dunes, is the oasis and summer resort of Huacachina, a popular hang-out for people seeking a change from the archaeology and chill of the Andes. Plenty of cheap hostels and bars have opened, playing pop and grunge as opposed to pan-pipe music. Paddleboats can be rented, and sandboarding on the dunes has become a major pastime. For the inexperienced, note that sandboarding can be dangerous.

☆Bodegas around Ica

Local wine *bodegas* that you can visit include **La Caravedo** ⓘ *Panamericana Sur 298, T01-9833 4729*, with organic production and sophisticated presentation, and **El Carmen**, on the right-hand side when arriving from Lima, which has an ancient grape press made from a huge tree trunk. **El Catador** ⓘ *Fondo Tres Esquinas 102, Subtanjalla, 10 km outside Ica, T056-962629, elcatadorcristel@yahoo.es, daily 1000-1800, US$1.50, combi from the 2nd block of Moquegua, every 20 mins, US$0.75, taxi takes 10 mins, good tours in Spanish,* has a shop selling wines, pisco and crafts associated with winemaking. In the evening there's a restaurant-bar with dancing and music. El Catador is best visited during harvest from late February to early April. Near El Catador is **Bodega Alvarez**, whose owner, Umberto Alvarez, is very hospitable. The town of Ocucaje is a popular excursion from Ica for tours of the **Ocucaje winery** ⓘ *Ctra Panamericana Sur, Km 335.5, T01-251 4570, www.ocucaje.com,* which makes wines and pisco.

Listings South from Lima

Tourist information

Cañete and Quebrada de Lunahuana
For information on Cañete town, see www.municanete.gob.pe, or the Oficina de Turismo's Facebook page. There's a **tourist office** in Lunahuaná in the Municipalidad, opposite the church, T01-284 1006, daily.

Ica
Dircetur (Av Grau 148, T056-238710). Some tourist information is also available at travel agencies.

Where to stay

Cañete and Quebrada de Lunahuana
There are places to stay in San Vicente de Cañete, and a range of options in and around Lunahuaná, from large family resorts and *casas de campo* to campsites, plus many *restaurantes campestres*. Note that prices may rise at weekends and holidays.

Upper Cañete Valley
For details of accommodation in Huancaya, call T01-810 6086/7, or see www.huancaya.com.

$$$ Viñak-Reichraming Lodge
Mountain Lodges of Peru, T01-421 6952, www.refugiosdelperu.com (see page 254).
A wonderful place to relax or go horse riding or walking, with superb views and excellent food. Prices are per person for full board.

$ Hostal Llapay
Llapay.
Basic but very friendly, will open at any hour, restaurant.

Pisco

$$ Posada Hispana Hostal
Bolognesi 222, T056-536363,
www.posadahispana.com.
Some rooms with loft and bath, also
rooms with shared bath, hot water, can
accommodate groups, comfortable,
breakfast extra, **Café de la Posada** on site,
information service, English, French, Italian
and Catalan spoken.

$$-$ El Candelabro
Callao y Pedemonte, T056-532620,
www.hoteleselcandelabro.com.
Modern and pleasant, with restaurant.
All rooms have bath and fridge.

$$-$ Hostal San Isidro
San Clemente 103, T056-536471,
http://sanisidrohostal.com.
With or without bath, hot water, safe,
welcoming, nice pool and cafeteria, pizzeria,
free laundry facilities, games room, English
spoken, parking. Breakfast not included, free
coffee in mornings, use of kitchen. Arranges
dune buggy tours and other excursions.

$$-$ San Jorge Residencial
Jr Barrio Nuevo 133, T056-532885,
Facebook: Hotel-San-Jorge-
Residencial-684121474997837.
Smart and modern. Hot water, secure
parking, breakfast is served in the restaurant,
also lunch and dinner, swanky and spacious,
café/bar in garden.

$ Hostal Los Inkas Inn
Prol Barrio Nuevo Mz M, Lte 14, Urb San Isidro,
T056-536634.
Affordable rooms and dorms with private
bath, fan, safes, rooftop games area,
small pool.

$ Hostal Tambo Colorado
Av Bolognesi 159, T056-531379,
www.hostaltambocolorado.com.
Welcoming, helpful owners are
knowledgeable about the area, hot
water, small café/bar, use of kitchen.

Paracas

**$$$$ Hotel Paracas Luxury Collection
Resort**
Av Paracas 173, T056-581333,
www.libertador.com.pe.
The famous Hotel Paracas has been
reincarnated as a resort, with spa, pools,
excellent rooms in cottages around the
grounds, access to beach, choice
of restaurants, bar, kayaking.

$$$$ La Hacienda Bahía Paracas
Lote 25, Urb Santo Domingo, T01-213 1000,
www.hoteleslahacienda.com.
Next to **Doubletree** but not connected,
rooms and suites, some with access straight
to pool, spa, choice of restaurants, bar.

**$$$$-$$$ Doubletree Guest Suites
Paracas**
Lote 30-34, Urb Santo Domingo on the
outskirts, T01-617 1000, www.doubletree.com.
Low rise, clean lines and a comfortable
size, built around a lovely pool, on beach,
water sports, spa, all mod cons and popular
with families.

$$$ El Mirador
At the turn-off to El Chaco, T056-545086,
www.elmiradorhotel.com.
Hot water, good service, boat trips
arranged, meals available, large pool,
tranquil gardens, relaxing.

$$$ Gran Palma
Av Principal Mz D lote 03, half block from plaza,
T01-665 5932, www.hotelgranpalma.com.
Central, convenient for boats, best rooms
have sea view, buffet breakfast on the terrace.

$$ Brisas de la Bahía
Av Principal, T056-531132,
www.brisasdelabahia.com.
Good, family-run *hostal*, convenient position
for waterfront and bus stops, ask for a back
room, good breakfast.

$$ Los Frayles
Av Paracas Mz D lote 5, T056-545141,
www.hostallosfrayles.com.

Variety of simple, well-kept rooms, ocean view, breakfast extra, roof terrace, tourist information, transfers to/from bus arranged.

$$ Mar Azul
Alan García Mz B lote 20, T056-534542, www.hostalmarazul.com.
Family-run *hostal* overlooking the sea, although most rooms face away from ocean, comfortable, hot water, breezy roof terrace with sea view for breakfast (included), helpful owner Yudy Patiño. Also **Ballestas Expeditions** for local tours.

$$ Santa María
Av Paracas s/n, T056-545045, www.hostalsantamariaparacas.com.
Smart rooms, hot water, no view. **El Chorito** restaurant, mainly fish and seafood. Also has **Santa María 2**, round the corner in lovely converted house (same contact numbers), not all rooms have view but has rooftop terrace. **Santa María 3**, under construction on the approach road, will have more facilities and pool.

$ Backpackers House
Av Los Libertadores, beside museum, T056-635623, www.paracasbackpackers house.com.pe.
Rooms with and without bath, private and dorms, at high season prices rise to $$-$. Good value, comfortable, tourist information.

$ Hostal El Amigo
El Chaco, T056-545042, hostalelamigo@hotmail.com.
Simple, hot water, no food, no internet but very helpful staff.

Ica
Hotels are fully booked during the harvest festival and prices rise. Many hotels are in residential neighbourhoods; insist taxis go to the hotel of your choice.

$$$$-$$$ Las Dunas
Av La Angostura 400, T056-256224, www.lasdunashotel.com.

Lima office: Av Vasco Núñez de Balboa 259, Lima, T01-213 5000. Variety of rooms and suites. Prices are reduced on weekdays. Packages available. Complete resort with restaurant, swimming pool, many sporting activities and full-day programmes.

$$$ Villa Jazmín
Los Girasoles Mz C-1, Lote 7, Res La Angostura, T056-258179, www.villajazmin.net.
Modern hotel in a residential area near the sand dunes, 8 mins from the city centre, solar heated water, restaurant, buffet breakfast, pool, tours arranged, airport and bus transfers, helpful staff, tranquil and very good.

$$ Princess
Santa Magdalena D-103, Urb Santa María, T056-215421, www.hotelprincess.com.pe.
Taxi ride from the main plaza, small rooms, hot water, frigobar, pool, tourist information, helpful, peaceful, very good.

$ Arameli
Tacna 239, T056-239107.
1 block from the Plaza de Armas, is a nice place to stay, good value, café on 3rd floor.

Huacachina

$$$ Mossone
East end of the lake, T056-213630, www.dmhoteles.pe.
Faded elegance, hacienda-style with a view of the lagoon, full board available, good buffet breakfast, large rooms, bilingual staff, lovely courtyard, bicycles and sandboards, large, clean swimming pool.

$$ Hostal Huacachinero
Av Perotti, opposite Hostal Salvatierra, T056-217435, http://elhuacachinero.com.
Spacious rooms, sparsely furnished but comfortable beds, nice atmosphere, pool, outside bar and restaurant, parking, offers tours and buggy rides.

$$ Hostería Suiza
Malecón 264, T056-238762, hostesuiza@terra.com.pe.

Overlooking lake, lovely grounds, quiet, safe parking.

$ Carola del Sur (also known as Casa de Arena II)
Av Perotti s/n, T056-237398.
Basic rooms, popular, small pool, restaurant/bar, hammocks, access to Casa de Arena's bigger pool, noisy at night, pressure to buy tours.

$ Casa de Arena
Av Perotti s/n, T056-215274.
Basic rooms and dorms, thin walls, bar, small pool, laundry facilities, board hire, popular with backpackers but grubby, check your bill and change carefully, don't leave valuables unattended, disco next door.

$ Desert Nights
Run by Desert Adventures
(see What to do, below).
Good reputation, English spoken, food available.

$ Hostal Rocha
T056-222256, kikerocha@hotmail.com.
Hot water, with or without bath, family-run, kitchen and laundry facilities, board hire, small pool, popular with backpackers, but a bit run-down.

$ Hostal Salvatierra
T056-232352, http://salvaturgroup.galeon.com.
An old building, with or without bath, not on waterfront, charming, pool, relaxing courtyard, rents sandboards, good value.

Restaurants

Pisco

$$-$ As de Oro
San Martín 472, T056-532010. Closed Mon.
Good food, not cheap but always full at lunchtime, swimming pool.

$ Café Pirata
Callao 104, T056-534343.
Mon-Sat 0630-1500, 1800-2200.
Desserts, pizzas, coffee and lunch menu.

$ Chifa Lisen
Av San Martín 325, T056-535527.
Daily 1230-1530, 1800-2200.
Chinese food and delivery.

Paracas

There are several eating places on the Malecón by Playa El Chaco, all with similar menus and prices (in our **$$** range), vegetarian options and open for breakfast, including **Bahía; Brisa Marina** (varied menu, mainly seafood), and **Johnny y Jennifer.** Better value *menús* are available at lunchtime on the main road, eg at Lobo Fino. Higher quality food within walking distance of the centre can be found at the **Hotel Paracas'** restaurant and trattoria, **$$$**, both of which are open to the public.

Ica

$$-$ Anita
Libertad 133, Plaza de Armas.
Local dishes, breakfast, à la carte a bit expensive for what's offered, but set menus at US$4.50 are good value.

$ Carne y pescao
Av Juan José Elías 417, T056-228157.
Seafood and, at night, grilled chicken and *parrilladas*.

$ D'lizia
Lima 155, Plaza de Armas, T056-237733,
www.delizia.com.pe.
Also in the Patio de comidas at Plaza Vea mall and in Urb Moderna. Modern and bright, for breakfasts, lunches, sandwiches, snacks, ice cream, cakes and sweets, juices and drinks.

$ Plaza 125
C Lima 125, T056-211816.
On the plaza, regional and international food as well as breakfast, good-value set lunches.

$ Tejas Helena
Cajamarca 137.
Sell the best *tejas* and locally made chocolates.

Huacachina

$ La Casa de Bamboo
Av Perotti s/n, next to Hostería Suiza,
T056-776649.
Café-bar, English breakfast, marmite, Thai curry, falafel, vegetarian and vegan options, book exchange, games.

$ Moroni
T056-238471. Open 0800 till late.
Only restaurant right on the lake shore, serving a variety of Peruvian and international foods.

Festivals

Cañete and Quebrada de Lunahuana
Feb A festival of adventure sports is held in Lunahuaná.
1st weekend of Mar **Fiesta de la Vendimia** (grape harvest) in Lunahuaná.
Last week of Aug **Cañete festival**, with regional music and dancing.

Pisco and around
End Feb **Verano Negro**. Famous festival in Chincha Alta celebrating black and criollo culture.
Nov **Festival de las Danzas Negras** is held in El Carmen, 10 km south of Chincha Alta.

Ica
Early Mar **Festival Internacional de la Vendimia** (wine harvest).
Oct The image of **El Señor de Luren** draws pilgrims from all Peru to a fine church in Parque Luren on the 3rd Mon, when there are all-night processions; celebrations start the week before.

What to do

Cañete and Quebrada de Lunahuana
Several agencies in Lunahuaná offer rafting and kayaking on the Río Cañete, especially at the anexo of San Jerónimo: Nov-Apr rafting is at levels IV-V; May-Oct is low water, levels I-II only.

Paracas
There are agencies all over town offering trips to the Islas Ballestas, the Paracas reserve, Ica, Nazca and Tambo Colorado.
A 2-hr boat tour to the islands costs US$13-15 pp, including park entrance fee and tax, departure 0800. Usually, agencies will pool 40 clients together in 1 boat. An agency that does not pool clients is **Huacachina**, based in Ica, with an office in Paracas, T056-215582, www.huacachinatours.com. Do not book tours on the street.
Zarcillo Connections, *Independencia A-20, Paracas, T056-536636, www.zarcillo connections.com*. With long experience for trips to the Paracas National Reserve, Tambo Colorado, trekking and tours to Ica, Chincha and the Nazca Lines and surrounding sites. Agent for **Cruz del Sur** buses. Also has its own hotel, **Zarcillo Paradise**, in Paracas.

Ica
Agencies offer city tours, trips to the Nazca Lines, Paracas and Islas Ballestas, plus dune buggies and sandboarding.
AV Dolphin Travel, *C Municipalidad 132, of 4, T056-256234, www.av-dolphintravelperu.com.*
Desert Travel, *Lima 171, inside Tejas Don Juan on Plaza, T056-227215, desert_travel@hotmail.com.*
Ica Desert Trip, *Bolívar 178, T056-237373, www.icadeserttrip.com.* Roberto Penny Cabrera (speaks Spanish and English) offers 1-, 2- and 3-day trips off-road into the desert, archaeology, geology, etc. 4 people maximum, contact by email in advance. Take toilet paper, something warm for the evening, a long-sleeved loose cotton shirt for daytime and long trousers. Recommended, but "not for the faint-hearted".

Huacachina
Dune buggies do white-knuckle, rollercoaster tours for US$20 (plus a small municipal fee); some start at 1000 but most between 1600 and 1700 to catch the sunset, 2½ hrs.
Desert Adventures, *Huacachina, T056-228458, www.desertadventure.net.* Frequently

recommended for sandboarding and camping trips into the desert by 4WD and buggies, French, English and Spanish spoken. Also to beaches, Islas Ballestas and Nazca Lines flights. Has **Desert Nights** hostel (see Where to stay, above).

Cañete and Quebrada de Lunahuana
Soyuz bus runs between Lima and **Cañete** every 7 mins, US$5. There are combis between Cañete and **Lunahuaná**, US$2.75.

Upper Cañete Valley
Cars run from the Yauyos area to **Huancayo**, US$7.50. Ask locally where and when they leave. Public transport between villages is scarce and usually goes in the morning. When you get to a village you may have to wait till the early evening for places to open up.

Pisco
Air Capitán RE Olivera airport is being redeveloped from a military base into an international hub. The main buildings were inaugurated in Mar 2016 and full operations were expected sometime in 2017. **Aerodiana** (Av Casimiro Ulloa 227, San Antonio, Lima, T01-447 6824, www.aerodiana.com.pe) offers Nazca overflights from Pisco.

Bus Buses drop passengers at San Clemente on Panamericana Sur (**El Cruce**); many bus companies and tour agencies have their offices here. It's a 10-km taxi ride from the centre, US$8, or US$10 to Paracas. *Colectivos* leave from outside Banco Continental (plaza) for El Cruce when full, US$2.

To **Lima**, 242 km, 4 hrs, US$7.50. The best company is **Soyuz**, every 7 mins from El Cruce. **Ormeño** has an office in Pisco plaza and will take you to El Cruce to meet their 1600 bus. **Flores** is the only company that

goes into Pisco town, from Lima and Ica, but buses are poor and services erratic. To **Ica**, US$1.25, 45 mins, 70 km, with **Ormeño**; also *colectivos*. To **Nazca**, 210 km, take a bus to Ica and then change to a *colectivo*. To **Ayacucho**, 317 km, 8-10 hrs, US$12-20, several buses daily leave from El Cruce; book in advance and take warm clothing as it gets cold at night. To **Huancavelica**, 269 km, 12-14 hrs, US$12, with **Oropesa**, coming from Ica. To **Arequipa**, US$17, 10-12 hrs, 2 daily.

To **Tambo Colorado**, buses depart from near the plaza in Pisco at 0800, US$2.50, 3 hrs; also *colectivos*, US$2 pp. Alight 20 mins after the stop at Humay; the road passes right through the site. For buses back to Pisco in the afternoon, wait at the caretaker's house.

Taxi To **Paracas** about US$3; combis when full, US$1.75, 25 mins. To **Tambo Colorado**, US$30 (return).

Paracas
Cruz del Sur has 2 direct buses a day to its Paracas terminal, regular bus from US$9, luxury services US$30-35 from **Lima**, US$15 to **Nazca**. Agencies in Paracas sell direct transfers between Paracas and Huacachina, with **Pelican Perú**, at 1100 daily, US$7, comfortable and secure.

Ica
Bus All bus offices are on Lambayeque blocks 1 and 2 and Salaverry block 3. To **Pisco**, US$1.25, 45 mins, 70 km, with **Ormeño**; also *colectivos*. To **Paracas junction**, US$1.15. To **Lima**, 302 km, 4 hrs, US$21-34, on upmarket buses, several daily including **Soyuz** (Av Manzanilla 130), every 7 mins, 0600-2200, and **Ormeño** (Lambayeque 180). To **Nazca**, 140 km, 2 hrs, several buses (US$3.50) and *colectivos* (US$5) daily, including **Ormeño**, **Flores**, 4 daily, and **Cueva** (José Elias y Huánuco), hourly 0600-2200; buses to **Arequipa** follow this route.

mysterious and unmissable drawings in the desert

Set in a green valley amid a perimeter of mountains, Nazca's altitude puts it just above any fog which may drift in from the sea. Nearby are the mysterious, world-famous Nazca Lines and numerous other ancient sites.

Nazca town *Colour map 2, C3.*

Nazca town lies 140 km south of Ica via the Pan-American Highway (444 km from Lima) and is the tourist centre for visiting the Nazca Lines. **Museo Antonini** ① *Av de la Cultura 600, eastern end of Jr Lima (10-min walk from the plaza or short taxi ride), T056-523444, cahuachi@terra.com.pe or CISRAP@numerica.it, daily 0900-1900 (ring the bell), US$6 including guide,* houses the discoveries of Professor Orefici and his team from the huge pre-Inca

Tip...
There is a small market at Lima y Grau, the Mercado Central at Arica y Tacna and a Raulito supermarket at Grau 245.

city at Cahuachi (see page 174), which, Orefici believes, holds the key to understanding the Nazca Lines. Many tombs survived the *huaqueros* (tomb robbers), and there are displays of mummies, ceramics, textiles, amazing *antaras* (pan pipes) and photos of the excavations. In the garden is a pre-Hispanic aqueduct. Recommended.

The **Maria Reiche Planetarium** ① *Hotel Nazca Lines, T056-522293, show daily usually at 1915 in English, 2000 in Spanish, US$7 (students half price),* offers introductory lectures every night about the Nazca Lines, based on Reiche's theories, which cover archaeology and astronomy. The show lasts about 45 minutes, after which visitors are able to look at the moon, planets and stars through telescopes.

Viktoria Nikitzhi, a colleague of Maria Reiche, gives one-hour lectures about the Nazca Lines at **Dr Maria Reiche Center** ① *Av de los Espinales 300, 1 block from Ormeño bus stop, T965-888056, viktorianikitzki@hotmail.com, US$5.* She also organizes tours in June and December (phone in advance to confirm times or to ask about volunteer work).

Just south of town are the **Paredones ruins and aqueduct** ① *US$3.55 (including El Telar Geoglyphs, Acueductos de Cantayoc, Las Agujas Geoglyphs and Acueductos de Ocongalla).* The ruins, also called Cacsamarca, are Inca on a pre-Inca base but are not well preserved. However, the underground aqueducts, built 300 BC-AD 700, are still in working order and worth seeing. A 30-minute to one-hour walk through Buena Fe (or organize a taxi from your hotel) will bring you to the Cantayoc, Las Agujas and El Telar sites, which consist of markings in the valley floor and ancient aqueducts descending in spirals into the ground. The markings consist of a triangle pointing to a hill and a telar (cloth) with a spiral depicting the threads. Climb the mountain to see better examples.

★Nazca Lines

Cut into the stony desert above the Ingenio valley north of Nazca are the famous Nazca Lines, thought to have been etched onto the Pampa Colorada sands by three different groups: the Paracas people (900-200 BC), the Nazcas (200 BC-AD 600) and the Huari settlers from Ayacucho (about AD 630); see Origins of the Lines, below. There are large numbers of lines, not only parallels and geometrical figures, but also recognizable designs, including a dog, an enormous monkey, birds (one with a wing span of over 100 m), a spider and a tree. They are best seen from the air (see What to do, page 178), but three of the huge designs – the Hands, the Lizard and the Tree – can also be viewed from the mirador, 17 km north of Nazca on the Pan-American Highway, paid for by Maria Reiche in 1976. (Travellers suggest the view from the hill 500 m back to Nazca is better.) The mirador is included on most tours; otherwise hire a taxi-guide to take you (US$5-8 per person), or you can hitch, but there is not always much traffic. Go early as the site gets very hot and busy by mid-morning. In January 1994 Maria Reiche also opened a small site **museum** ① *Km 421, 5 km from town, US$1; take micro from in front of Ormeño terminal (US$0.75, frequent).*

Tip...
Maria Reiche's book, *Mystery on the Desert*, is on sale in Nazca for US$10 (proceeds to conservation work). Another good book is *Pathways to the Gods: the mystery of the Nazca Lines*, by Tony Morrison (Michael Russell, 1978).

Origins of the Lines The Nazcas had a highly developed civilization which reached its peak about AD 600. Their polychrome ceramics, wood carvings and adornments of gold are on display in many of Lima's museums. The Paracas people represented an early phase of the Nazca culture, renowned for their superb technical quality and stylistic variety in weaving and pottery. The Nazcas were succeeded by the Huari Empire, in conjunction with the Tiahuanaco culture, which dominated much of Peru from AD 600-1000.

The German expert, Dr Maria Reiche, who studied the Lines for over 40 years, mostly from a step ladder, maintained that they represent some sort of vast astronomical pre-Inca calendar. Other theories abound: that the Lines are the tracks of running contests (Georg A von Breunig, 1980, and English astronomer Alan Sawyer); that they were used for ritualized walking (Anthony Aveni); that they represent weaving patterns and yarns (Henri Stierlin) and that the plain is a map of the Tiahuanaco Empire (Zsoltan Zelko). Johan Reinhard

Nazca

Where to stay		
1 Alegría	10 Oro Viejo	Travel Service
2 Casa Andina Classic	11 Paredones Inn	4 Kañada
3 Hosp Flores	12 Posada de Don Hono	5 La Choza
4 Hostal Alegría	13 Posada Guadalupe	6 La Taberna
5 La Encantada	14 Sol de Nasca	7 Los Angeles
6 Maison Suisse		8 Mamashana &
7 Majoro	**Restaurants** 🍴	Vía La Encantada
8 Nasca	1 Chifa Guang Zhou	9 Panadería
9 Nazca Lines	2 Coffee Break	10 Rico Pollo
	3 El Huarango &	

N

200 metres
200 yards

proposes that the Lines conform to fertility practices throughout the Andes, in common with the use of straight lines in Chile and Bolivia. William H Isbell proposed that the Lines are the equivalent of pyramid-building in other parts of Peru in the same period, with the added purpose of controlling population growth through mass labour.

Another theory, based on the idea that the Lines are best seen from the air, is that the ancient Nazcas flew in hot-air balloons (Jim Woodman, 1977, and, in part, the BBC series *Ancient Voices*). A related idea is that the Lines were not designed to be seen physically from above, but from the mind's eye of the flying shaman. Both theories are supported by pottery and textile evidence which shows balloonists and a flying creature emitting discharge from its nose and mouth. There are also local legends of flying men. The depiction in the desert of creatures such as a monkey or killer whale suggests the qualities needed by the shaman in his spirit journeys.

After six years' work at La Muña and Los Molinos near Palpa (43 km north of Nazca) using photogrammetry, Peruvian archaeologist Johny Isla and Markus Reindel of the Swiss-Liechtenstein Foundation deduced that the lines on both the Palpa and Nazca plains were offerings dedicated to the worship of water and fertility, two elements which also dominate on ceramics and on the engraved stones of the Paracas culture. Isla and Reindel believe that the Palpa lines predate those at Nazca and that these lines and drawings are themselves scaled-up versions of the Paracas drawings. This research proposes that the Nazca culture succumbed not to drought, but to heavy rainfall, probably during an El Niño event.

In all probablility, there was no single, overriding significance to the Lines for the people who made them. Some of the theories attached to them may capture parts of their meaning, and, no doubt, more theories and new discoveries will be tested to cast fresh light on the puzzle.

Other sights

Overlooking Nazca town to the east is **Cerro Blanco**, the highest sand dune in the world at 2078 m. Tours to the dune start very early in the morning and involve a three-hour hike to the summit. Descents can be made on dune buggies, or by sandboarding or parapenting.

The Nazca area is dotted with over 100 ancient cemeteries, where the dry, humidity-free climate has perfectly preserved invaluable tapestries, cloth and mummies. At **Chauchilla** ① *30 km south of Nazca, last 12 km a sandy track, US$3, huaqueros* ransacked the tombs and left bones, skulls, mummies and pottery shards littering the desert. A tour takes about two hours and usually includes a visit to a small family gold-processing shop where very old-fashioned techniques are still used.

One hour west of the Nazca Lines along a rough dirt track. **Cahuachi** ① *US$3.50 entry, US$17 pp on a tour, US$12-15 in private taxi*, is a Nazca ceremonial site comprising some 30 pyramids. Less than 5% of the site has been excavated so far, some of which has been reconstructed. Some believe it could be larger than Chan Chán, making it the largest adobe city in the world (see also Museo Antonini, above). Some 4 km beyond Cahuachi is a site called **El Estaquería**, thought to have been a series of astronomical sighting posts; more recent research suggests the wooden pillars were used to dry dead bodies and therefore it may have been a place of mummification.

On the coast west of Nazca, **Reserva Nacional de San Fernando** was established in 2011 to protect migratory and local land and oceanic wildlife, such as the Humboldt penguin, sea lions, the Andean fox, dolphins and whales. Condors and guanacos may also be seen, which is unusual for the coast. San Fernando is located in the highest part of the Peruvian coastal desert, where the Nazca Plate lifts the continental plate, generating moist accumulation in the ground with resulting seasonal winter flora and a continental wildlife corridor between the high coastal mountains and the sea. Full-day and two-day/one-night tours are offered by some agencies in town.

Towards Cuzco: Sondondo Valley

Two hours out of Nazca on the paved road to Abancay and Cuzco is the **Reserva Nacional Pampas Galeras** at 4100 m, which has a vicuña reserve and an interesting Museo del Sitio. There's also a military base and park guard here. Entry is free. At Km 155 is **Puquio**, an uninspiring commercial centre which provides access to **Andamarca** and the surrounding villages of the splendid **Sondondo Valley** in the south of the department of Ayacucho. Sondondo offers limitless ancient terraced slopes, a very good chance to see condors, *Puyas raimondii*, small friendly villages and great walking opportunities. This off-the-beaten-path area has modest infrastructure but is gradually opening up to tourism. Beyond Puquio, it's another 185 km to **Chalhuanca**. Fuel is available in both towns. There are wonderful views on this stretch, with lots of small villages, valleys and alpacas.

☆Puerto Inca

10 km north of Chala. Taxi, US$8, or colectivo towards Nazca as far as the turn-off at Km 610, about US$6.

On the coast southwest of Nazca, near the fishing village of **Chala**, are the large pre-Columbian ruins of **Puerto Inca**. This was the port for Cuzco. The site is in excellent condition: the drying and store houses can be seen as holes in the ground (be careful where you walk). On the right side of the bay is a cemetery; on the hill, a temple of reincarnation, and the Inca road from the coast to Cuzco is clearly visible. The road was 240 km long, with a staging post every 7 km so that, with a change of runner at every post, messages could be sent in 24 hours. The site is best appreciated when the sun is shining.

Listings Nazca and around *map page 173.*

Tourist information

iPerú is located at the airport (iperunasca@ promperu.gob.pe, daily 0700-1300, 1400-1600). The **tourist police** are at Av Los Incas cuadra 1, T056-522105. The ordinary police are at Av Los Incas, T056-522105 (T105 for emergencies).

Where to stay

If arriving by bus, beware of touts who tell you that the hotel of your choice is closed, or full. If you phone or email, the hotel should pick you up at the bus station free of charge, day or night.

$$$ Casa Andina Classic
Jr Bolognesi 367, T01-213 9739,
www.casa-andina.com.
This recommended chain of hotels' Nazca property, offering standardized services in distinctive style. Bright, modern decor, central patio with palm trees, pool, restaurant.

$$$ Maison Suisse
Opposite airport, T056-522434,
www.nazcagroup.com.

Comfortable, safe car park, expensive restaurant, pool, suites with jacuzzi, good giftshop, shows video of Nazca Lines. Also has camping facilities. Its packages include flights over Nazca Lines.

$$$ Majoro
Panamericana Sur Km 452, T056-522490, www.hotelmajoro.com.
A charming old hacienda about 5 km from town past the airstrip so quite remote, beautiful gardens, pool, slow and expensive restaurant, quiet and welcoming, good arrangements for flights and tours.

$$$ Nazca Lines
Jr Bolognesi 147, T056-522293.
With a/c, rather dated rooms with private patio, hot water, peaceful, restaurant, safe car park, pool (US$9-10.50 pp includes sandwich and drink). Can also arrange package tours which include 2-3 nights at the hotel plus a flight over the lines and a desert trip.

$$$-$$ Oro Viejo
Callao 483, T056-521112, www.hoteloroviejo.net.
Has a suite with jacuzzi and comfortable standard rooms, nice garden, swimming pool, restaurant and bar. Recommended.

$$$-$$ Puerto Inka
2 km along a side road from Km 610 Panamericana Sur south of Nazca (reservations T054-778458), www.puertoinka.com.pe.
Bungalows on the beautiful beach, hammocks outside, indoor games room, disco, breakfast extra, great place to relax, kayaks, boat hire, diving equipment rental, pleasant camping US$5, low season discounts, used by tour groups, busy in summer.

$$ Alegría
Jr Lima 166, T056-522497, www.hotelalegria.net.
Rooms with hot water, cafeteria serving breakfast, pool, garden, English, Hebrew, Italian and German spoken, laundry facilities, book exchange, restaurant, ATM, parking, bus terminal transfers. OK but can be noisy

from disco and traffic. Also has a tour agency where guests are encouraged to buy tours (see What to do), flights and bus tickets.

$$ La Encantada
Callao 592, T056-522930, www.hotellaencantada.com.pe.
Pleasant modern hotel with restaurant, laundry and parking.

$$ Paredones Inn
Jr Lima 600, T056-522181.
1 block from the Plaza de Armas, modern, colourful rooms, great views from roof terrace, laundry service, bar, suites with minibar, microwave, jacuzzi, helpful staff.

$$ Posada de Don Hono
Av María Reiche 112, T056-506822, laposadadedonhono1@hotmail.com.
Small rooms and nice bungalows, good café, parking.

$ Hospedaje Flores
Grau 550, T056-521040.
Pleasant, family-run place, hot water, Wi-Fi, parking.

$ Hostal Alegría
Av Los Incas 117, opposite Ormeño bus terminal, T056-522497.
Basic, hot water, hammocks, nice garden, camping, restaurant.

$ Nasca
C Lima 438, T056-522085, marionasca13@hotmail.com.
Hot water, with or without bath, laundry facilities, newer annexe at the back, nice garden, safe motorcycle parking.

$ Posada Guadalupe
San Martín 225, T056-522249.
Family run, lovely courtyard and garden, hot water, with or without bath, good breakfast, relaxing. (Touts selling tours are nothing to do with hotel.)

$ Sol de Nasca
Callao 586, T056-522730.
Some rooms with hot showers, restaurant, don't leave valuables in luggage store.

Restaurants

There's a *panadería* at Bolognesi 387.

$$$-$$ Vía La Encantada
Bolognesi 282 (website as hotel above).
Modern, stylish with great food – fish, meat or vegetarian, good-value lunches.

$$-$ La Choza
Bolognesi 290.
Nice decor with woven chairs and thatched roof, all types of food, live music at night. Single women may be put off by the crowds of young men hanging around the doors handing out flyers.

$$-$ La Taberna
Jr Lima 321, T056-521411.
Excellent food, live music, popular with gringos, it's worth a look just for the graffiti on the walls.

$$-$ Mamashana
Bolognesi 270.
Rustic style with a lively atmosphere, for breakfast, grills, pastas and pizzas.

$ Chifa Guang Zhou
Bolognesi 297, T056-522036.
Very good.

$ Coffee Break
Bolognesi 219. Sun-Fri 0700-2300.
For real coffee and good pizzas.

$ El Huarango
Arica 602.
National and international cuisine. Relaxed family atmosphere and deliciously breezy terrace.

$ Kañada
Lima 160, nazcanada@yahoo.com.
Cheap, good *menú*, excellent *pisco sours*, nice wines, popular, display of local artists' work, email service, English spoken, helpful.

$ Los Angeles
Bolognesi 266.
Good, cheap, try the *sopa criolla*, and the chocolate cake.

$ Rico Pollo
Lima 190.
Good local restaurant with great chicken dishes.

Festivals

29 Aug-10 Sep Virgen de la Guadalupe festival.

What to do

Land-based tours
All guides must be approved by the Ministry of Tourism and should have an official identity card. Touts (*jaladores*) operate at popular hotels and the bus terminals using false ID cards and fake hotel and tour brochures. They are rip-off merchants who overcharge and mislead those who arrive by bus. Only conduct business with agencies at their office, or phone or email the company you want to deal with in advance. Some hotels are not above pressurising guests to purchase tours at inflated prices. Taxi drivers usually act as guides, but most speak only Spanish. Do not take just any taxi on the plaza for a tour; always ask your hotel for a reputable driver.
Air Nasca Travel, *Jr Lima 185, T056-521027.* Guide Susi recommended. Very helpful and competitive prices. Can do all types of tours around Nazca, Ica, Paracas and Pisco.
Algería Tours, *Lima 186, T056-523431, http:// alegriatoursperu.com.* Offers inclusive tours. Guides with radio contact and maps can be provided for hikes to nearby sites. Guides speak English, German, French and Italian. They also offer adventure tours, such as mountain biking from 4000 m in the Andes down to the plain, sandboarding, and more.
Félix Quispe Sarmiento, 'El Nativo de Nazca'. He has his own museum, Hantun Nazca, at Panamericana Sur 447 and works with the Ministerio de Cultura to offer tours off the beaten track. Can also arrange flights. Knowledgeable. Ask for him at Kañada restaurant.

Fernández family, *Hotel Nasca (see above)*. Local tours; ask for the hotel owners and speak to them direct.

Huarango Travel Service, *Arica 602, T056-522141, huarangotravel@yahoo.es*. Tours around Ica, Paracas, Huacachina, Nazca and Palpa.

Mystery Peru, *Simón Bolívar 221, T01-435 0051, T956-691155, www.mysteryperu.com*. Owned by Enrique Levano Alarcón, based in Nazca with many local tours, also packages throughout Peru.

Nazca Perú 4x4, *Bolognesi 367 (in Casa Andina), T056-522928, or T975-017029*. Tubular 4WD tours to San Fernando National Reserve and other off-the-beaten-track locations.

Sightseeing flights

Small planes take 3-5 passengers to see the Nazca Lines. Flights last 30-35 mins and are controlled by air traffic personnel at the airport to avoid congestion. The price for a flight is around US$130 pp plus US$10 airport tax. Most tours include transport to the airport; otherwise it's US$5 by taxi or US$0.25 by bus. It is best to organize a flight with the airlines themselves at the airport. They will weigh you and select a group of passengers based on weight, so you may have to wait a while for your turn. Make sure you clarify everything before getting on the plane and ask for a receipt. Also let them know in advance if you have any special requests.

Aero Diana, *Av Casimiro Ulloa 227, San Antonio, Lima, T01-447 6824, www.aerodiana. com.pe*. Daily flights over the Lines.

Aero Paracas, *T01-641 7000, www. aeroparacas.com*. Daily flights over the Lines.

Alas Peruanas, *T056-522444, http://alas peruanas.com, or through Hotel Alegría*. Experienced pilots offer flights over the Nazca Lines as well as 1-hr flights over the Palpa and Llipata areas, where you can see more designs and other rare patterns (US$130 pp, minimum 3); Nazca and Palpa combined, US$250. See the website for promotional offers. All **Alas Peruanas** flights include the BBC film of Nazca.

Transport

Air The airport caters only for sightseeing flights.

Bus It is worth paying extra for a good bus; there are reports of robbery on the cheaper services. Over-booking is common.

To **Lima**, 446 km, 7 hrs, several buses and *colectivos* daily, US$23-26. **Ormeño** (T056-522058) *Royal Class* at 0530 and 1330 from Hotel Nazca Lines, normal service from Av Los Incas, 6 a day; **Civa** (Av Guardia Civil, T056-523019), normal service at 2300; **Cruz del Sur** (Lima y San Martín, T056-720440), via Ica and Paracas, luxury service, US$39-55. To **Ica**, with **Ormeño**, 2 hrs, US$3.50, 4 a day. For **Pisco** (210 km), 3 hrs, buses stop 5 km outside town (see under Pisco, Transport, page 171), so change in Ica for direct transport into Pisco.

To **Arequipa**, 565 km, 9 hrs, US$19-22.50, or US$28-52 for *bus cama* services: **Ormeño**, from Av Los Incas, Royal Class at 2130, 8 hrs, also **Cruz del Sur** and **Oltursa** (Av los Incas 103, T056-522265), reliable, comfortable and secure on this route. Delays are possible out of Nazca because of drifting sand across the road or because of mudslides in the rainy season. Travel in daylight if possible. Book your ticket the previous day.

To Cuzco, 659 km, via **Chalhuanca** and **Abancay** (13 hrs), with **Ormeño**, US$50, and **Cruz del Sur**, 2015, 2100, US$50-70. The highway from Nazca to Cuzco is paved and is safe for bus travellers, drivers of private vehicles and motorcyclists.

Warning...
Be aware that fatal crashes by planes flying over the Lines do occur. Some foreign governments advise tourists not to take these flights and some companies will not provide insurance for passengers until safety and maintenance standards are improved.

Arequipa &
the far south

The colonial city of Arequipa, with its guardian volcano, El Misti, is the ideal place to start exploring southern Peru. It is the gateway to two of the world's deepest canyons, Colca and Cotahuasi, whose villages and terraces hold onto a traditional way of life and whose skies are home to the magnificent condor. From Arequipa there are routes to Lake Titicaca and to the border with Chile.

Arequipa *Colour map 2, C4.*

beautiful buildings and fascinating museums in the 'White City'

The city of Arequipa (population one million) stands in a beautiful valley 1011 km from Lima, at the foot of the perfect cone of El Misti volcano (5822 m), guarded on either side by the mountains Chachani (6057 m), and Pichu-Pichu (5669 m). The city has fine Spanish buildings and many old and interesting churches built of sillar, a pearly white volcanic stone almost exclusively used in the construction of Arequipa. The city was re-founded on 15 August 1540 by an emissary of Pizarro, but it had previously been occupied by Aymara peoples and the Incas. It is the main commercial centre for the south and is a busy place. Arequipeños resent the general tendency to believe that everything is run from Lima. It has been declared a World Cultural Heritage Site by UNESCO.

City centre

Plaza de Armas The elegant Plaza de Armas is faced on three sides by arcaded buildings with many restaurants, and on the fourth by the massive **Cathedral**, founded in 1612 and largely rebuilt in the 19th century. It is remarkable for having its façade along the whole length of the church (entrances on Santa Catalina and San Francisco 0700-0900, 1700-1900). Inside is the fine Belgian organ and elaborately carved wooden pulpit. The Cathedral has a **museum** ① *www.museocatedralarequipa.org.pe, Mon-Sat 0900-1630, US$3*, which outlines the history of the building, its religious objects and art and the bell tower. Behind the Cathedral is an alley with handicraft shops and places to eat.

☆**Santa Catalina Convent** ① *Santa Catalina 301, T054-2212132, www.santacatalina. org.pe. Mon, Wed, Fri-Sun 0800-1700 (last admission 1600), Tue and Thu 0800-2000, US$11.50,*

1-hr tour US$6 for group up to 4, many guides speak English or German. This is by far the most remarkable sight, opened in 1970 after four centuries of mystery. It is a complete miniature walled colonial town of over 2 ha in the middle of the city, where about 450 nuns lived in total seclusion, except for their women servants. The few remaining nuns have retreated to one section of the convent, allowing visitors to see a maze of cobbled streets and plazas bright with geraniums and other flowers, cloisters and buttressed houses. These have been painted in traditional white, orange, deep red and blue. The convent has been beautifully refurbished, with period furniture, paintings of the Cuzco school and fully equipped kitchens. On Tuesday and Thursday evenings the convent is lit with torches, candles and blazing fireplaces: very beautiful. There is a good café, which sells cakes, sandwiches, baked potatoes and a special blend of tea.

☆**Museo Santuarios Andinos** ⓘ *La Merced 110, T054-286614, ext 105. Mon-Sat 0900-1800, Sun 0900-1500, US$6 includes a 20-min video in English; 40-min guided tour US$3, discount with university student card (not ISIC).* This museum contains the frozen Inca mummies of child sacrifices found on Mount Ampato. To the Incas, Nevado Ampato was a sacred god, who claimed the highest tribute: human sacrifice. The mummy known as 'Juanita', found in 1995, is particularly fascinating as both the body and the Inca textiles it is wearing are so well preserved; it reveals a huge amount of information about Inca life and ritual practices. From January to April, Juanita is often jetting round the world and is replaced by other child sacrifices unearthed in the mountains.

Monasterio de Santa Teresa ⓘ *Melgar 303, T054-281188, www.museocarmelitas.com, Tue-Sat 0900-1700, Sun 0900-1300, US$6, multilingual guides available (tip suggested).* Smaller, less known, but as impressive as Santa Catalina, is the Monastery of Santa Teresa, dating to 1710. This living monastery is the home of Carmelite nuns and one of Arequipa's hidden treasures. Housed in one cloister the **Museo de Arte Virreinal**, which also includes an exhibit about the techniques and materials used in colonial art. If you

Essential Arequipa

Getting around

Arequipa is the main commercial centre and transport hub for the south, with flights and long-distance buses to/from Lima and other major cities. In the city the main places of interest and the hotels are within walking distance of the Plaza de Armas. The centre is known as Cercado; the Río Chili, spanned by six bridges, separates it from the suburbs to the west, among them the colonial district of Yanahuara. If you are going to the suburbs, take a bus or taxi. Traffic can be chaotic, making the city noisy; perhaps a planned public transit system will help.

When to go

The climate in Arequipa is delightful, with a mean daytime temperature in the low 20s. The sun shines on 360 days of the year and average annual rainfall is just 100 mm.

Safety

There have been reports of taxi drivers colluding with criminals to rob both tourists and locals. Ask hotels, restaurants, etc, to book a safe taxi for you. Theft can be a problem in the market area and the park at Selva Alegre at quiet times. Be very cautious walking anywhere at night. The police are conspicuous, friendly, courteous and efficient, but their resources are limited.

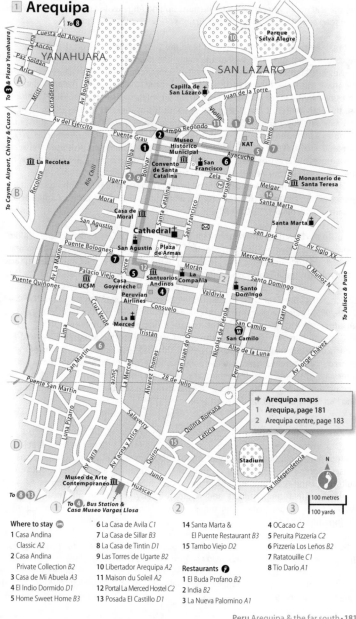

1 Arequipa

YANAHUARA

SAN LÁZARO

Parque Selva Alegre

To 8

Cuesta del Ángel

Paz Soldán

Ancón

Arica

Cortaderas

Misti

Av Bolognesi

Av del Ejército

La Recoleta

Recoleta

Río Chili

Puente Grau

Campo Redondo

Capilla de San Lázaro

Juan de la Torre

Violín

KAT

Rivero

Ayacucho

Museo Histórico Municipal

Convento de Santa Catalina

San Francisco

Zela

Jerusalén

Melgar

Santa Marta

Monasterio de Santa Teresa

Bolívar

Villalba

Ugarte

Santa Catalina

Moral

Santa Marta

San José

Casa de Moral

San Agustín

Cathedral

San Agustín

Puente Bolognesi

Av La Marina

Puente Quiñones

Plaza de Armas

Palacio Viejo

UCSM

Casa Goyeneche

Peruvian Airlines

La Merced

Santuarios Andinos

La Compañía

Morán

Valdivia

Santo Domingo

Santo Domingo

Mercaderes

Colón

Av Siglo XX

O Muñoz N

Consuelo

Tristán

San Camilo

San Camilo

Alto de la Luna

Pizarro

Perú

Av Jorge Chávez

To Juliaca & Puno

Cruz Verde

Lima

San Juan

Puente San Martín

Luna Pizarro

Sucre

La Merced

Álvarez Thomas

28 de Julio

San Juan de Dios

Nicolás de Piérola

Quinta Romaña

Leticia

Salaverry

Stadium

Museo de Arte Contemporáneo

Av Tacna y Arica

Quiroz

Junín

Huáscar

La Parra

Av Independencia

To 8 13

To 4, Bus Station & Casa Museo Vargas Llosa

To Cayma, Airport, Chivay & Cuzco

To 9 & Plaza Yanahuara

A

B

C

D

1

2

3

N

100 metres

100 yards

➡ Arequipa maps
1 Arequipa, page 181
2 Arequipa centre, page 183

Where to stay 🛏
1 Casa Andina Classic *A2*
2 Casa Andina Private Collection *B2*
3 Casa de Mi Abuela *A3*
4 El Indio Dormido *D1*
5 Home Sweet Home *B3*
6 La Casa de Ávila *C1*
7 La Casa de Sillar *B3*
8 La Casa de Tintin *D1*
9 Las Torres de Ugarte *B2*
10 Libertador Arequipa *A2*
11 Maison du Soleil *A2*
12 Portal La Merced Hostel *C2*
13 Posada El Castillo *D1*
14 Santa Marta & El Puente Restaurant *B3*
15 Tambo Viejo *D2*

Restaurants 🍴
1 El Buda Profano *B2*
2 India *B2*
3 La Nueva Palomino *A1*
4 OCacao *C2*
5 Peruita Pizzería *C2*
6 Pizzería Los Leños *B2*
7 Ratatouille *C1*
8 Tío Darío *A1*

are there at noon, you can listen to the nuns singing Angelus and other prayers. Sweets, rose soap and other things made by the nuns are sold at the gift shop.

Colonial houses Arequipa is said to have the best preserved colonial architecture in Peru, apart from Cuzco. As well as the many fine churches, there are several seignorial houses with large carved tympanums over the entrances. Built as single-storey structures, they have mostly withstood earthquakes. They have small patios, no galleries, flat roofs and small windows, disguised by superimposed lintels or heavy grilles. Good examples are the 18th-century **Casa Tristán del Pozo**, or **Gibbs-Ricketts house** ① *San Francisco 108, Mon-Fri 0900-1800, Sat 0900-1200*, with its fine portal and puma-head waterspouts. It houses a bank and art gallery. **Casa de Moral** ① *Moral 318 y Bolívar, Mon-Sat 0900-1700, Sun 0900-1300, US$1.80, US$1 for students*, also known as Williams house is now a bank and has a museum. **Casa Goyeneche** ① *La Merced 201 y Palacio Viejo*, is also a bank office, but the guards will let you view the courtyard and fine period rooms.

The oldest district of Arequipa is **San Lázaro**, a collection of tiny climbing streets and houses quite close to the **Hotel Libertador**, where you can find the ancient **Capilla de San Lázaro** ① *daily 0900-1700, US$1.80.*

Arequipa's churches Among the many fine churches is **La Compañía** ① *General Morán y Alvarez Thomas*, whose main façade (1698) and side portal (1654) are striking examples of the florid Andean *mestizo* style. To the left of the sanctuary is the **Capilla San Ignacio de Loyola** or **Capilla Real** (Royal Chapel) ① *Mon-Sat 0900-1300, 1500-1800, Sun 0900-1300, Mass daily 1200, US$1.50*, with a beautiful polychrome cupola. Also well worth seeing is the church of **San Francisco** ① *Zela 103, Mon-Sat 0715-0900, 1500-2000, Sun 0715-1245, 1800-2000*. There are religious art **museums** ① *Mon-Sat 0900-1200, 1500-1800, US$1.80*, on either side of it, and also at the convent and at Templo de la Tercera Orden.

Opposite San Francisco is the interesting **Museo Histórico Municipal** ① *Plaza San Francisco 407, Mon-Sat 0800-1600, Sun 0900-1300, US$3*, with scale models of the façades of Arequipa's churches, much war memorabilia, some impressive photos of the city in the aftermath of several notable earthquakes, and some items from the important pre-Inca Chiribaya culture (AD 800-1350) which extended from southern Peru to northern Chile and had its centre in Ilo, on the coast.

Beyond the city centre

La Recoleta ① *Jr Recoleta 117, T054-270966. Mon-Sat 0900-1200, 1500-1700. US$3.* This Franciscan monastery, built in 1647, stands on the other side of the river. A seldom-visited gem, it contains a variety of sights, including several cloisters, a religious art museum and a pre-Columbian art museum with ceramics and textiles produced by cultures of the Arequipa area. Most impressive however is the museum of Amazon exploration featuring artifacts and photos of early Franciscan missionaries in the Amazon. The library, containing many antique books, is open for supervised visits during museum hours.

☆**Casa Museo Vargas Llosa** ① *Av Parra 101, south of the centre, T054-283574. Tours Tue-Sun at 1000, 1030, 1400 and 1430 (3-10 visitors). US$3.* The birthplace of Peru's Nobel laureate in literature, Mario Vargas Llosa (1936-) is now an innovative, modern museum. In holographic displays the writer himself tells you about the highlights of his life and career; during the 90-minute tour, you even get to meet some of the characters in his

N

50 metres
50 yards

Where to stay 😴
1 Casa Andina Select *B1*
2 Casablanca Hostal *B1*
3 Casa de Melgar *A2*
4 Cazorla Hostel *A1*
5 Hostal Santa Catalina *A1*
6 Hostal Solar *A2*
7 La Casa de Margott *A2*
8 La Casona de Jerusalén *A1*
9 La Posada del Cacique *A2*
10 Le Foyer *A1*
11 Los Andes B&B *B1*

Restaurants 🍴
1 Bóveda San Agustín *B1*
2 Café Capriccio *B1, B2*
3 Café Valenzuela *B2*
4 Chicha *B1*
5 Crepísimo, Chaqchao &
  Alianza Francesa *A1*
6 El Asador *A1*
7 El Turko & Paladar 1900 *B2*

8 Entre Libros y Café *A2*
9 Hatunpa *A1*
10 Istanbul *B1*
11 La Alemana *B1*
12 La Canasta *B2*
13 La Trattoria del
   Monasterio *A1*
14 Pura Fruta *A1*
15 Sandwichería Mamut *B2*
16 Zig Zag *B2*

Bars & clubs 🍸
17 Casona Forum &
   Déjà Vu *A1*
18 Farren's *B1*
19 Museo del Pisco *B1*

novels. Vargas Llosa's private library is now found at the **Biblioteca Regional** ⓘ *San Francisco 308, Mon-Sat 0830-2030*.

Other sights Museo de Arte **Contemporáneo Arequipa** ⓘ *Tacna y Arica 201, T054-221068, Mon-Fri 0900-1400, US$1.50*, in the old railway station, is dedicated to painting and photography from 1950 onwards. The building is surrounded by gardens. **Museo de Arqueología Universidad Católica de Santa María UCSM** ⓘ *Cruz Verde 303, T054-221083, Mon-Fri 0830-1600, donations welcome*, has a small collection of textiles, ceramics and mummies, tracing the region's history from pre-Columbian times to the Republican era.

Yanahuara
In the district of Yanahuara, northwest of the centre across Puente Grau, is the mestizo-style church of **San Juan Bautista** ⓘ *Plaza de Yanahuara, open Sun and for mass Mon-Sat 0700, Sun 0700 and 1100*, completed in 1750, with a magnificent churrigueresque façade, all in sillar. On the same plaza is a *mirador* through whose arches there is a fine view of El Misti with the city at its feet, a popular spot in the late afternoon. Yanahuara has many fine restaurants.

Around Arequipa
Some 3 km beyond the southwestern suburb of **Tingo**, beside the Río Sabandía on the Huasacanche road, is **La Mansión del Fundador** ⓘ *daily 0900-1700, US$4.50*. Originally owned by the founder of Arequipa, Don Garcí Manuel de Carbajal, it has been restored as a museum with original furnishings and paintings; it also has a cafetería and bar.

About 8 km southeast of Arequipa is the **Molino de Sabandía** ⓘ *US$3, ring bell for admission; taxi US$7*. This was the first stone mill in the area, built in 1621. It has been fully restored, and the guardian diverts water to run the grinding stones when visitors arrive. Adjoining Sabandía is the

Inca site of **Yumina** ⓘ *free, taxi US$7.50 or take a bus to Characato or Sabandía from Av La Paz by Mercado Siglo XX*, with many Inca terraces which are still in use.

Climbing El Misti and Chachani

At 5822 m, El Misti volcano offers a relatively straightforward opportunity to scale a high peak. There are three routes for climbing the volcano; all take two days. The northeast route starts from the Aguada Blanca reservoir, reached by 4WD, from where a four-hour hike takes you to the Monte Blanco camp at 4800 m. Then it's a five- to six-hour ascent to the top. Two hours takes you back down to the trail. The southwest route involves taking a 4WD vehicle to the trailhead at Pastores (3400 m), followed by a hike of five or six hours to a camp at 4700 m. A five-hour climb takes you to the summit, before a three-hour descent to the trail. A southern route (Grau) also starts at 3400 m, with a camp at 4610 m, followed by a five-hour hike to the summit and a two-hour descent.

Climbing Chachani (6057 m), northwest of El Misti, is also popular. This peak retains its icy covering longer than El Misti, though this is fast disappearing.

Remember that both summits are at a very high altitude and that this, combined with climbing on scree, makes it hard going for the untrained. Great care must be taken on the unstable rock left by deglaciation; serious accidents have occurred. Be prepared for early starts, and take plenty of water, food and protection against the weather. Favoured months are May to September. Always contact an experienced guiding agency or professional guide in Arequipa as you should never climb alone (see What to do, page 191).

Listings Arequipa *maps pages 181 and 183.*

Tourist information

Indecopi
Hipólito Unanue 100-A, Urb Victoria, T054-212054, mlcornejo@indecopi.gob.pe.

iPerú
Portal de la Municipalidad 110, on the south side of Plaza de Armas, T054-223265, iperuarequipa@promperu.gob.pe. Mon-Sat 0900-1800, Sun 0900-1300, also in the airport Arrivals hall, at flight times.

Municipal tourist office
Portal de la Municipalidad 112 next to iPerú. Mon-Fri 0830-1600.

Tourist police
Jerusalén 315, T054-201258. Daily 24 hrs. Very helpful dealing with complaints or giving directions.

Where to stay

There are several economical *hostales* along Puente Grau and Ayacucho, near Jerusalén. Hostel chains include: **Flying Dog** (www.flyingdogperu.com), **The Point** (www.thepointhostels.com), **Pirwa** (www.pirwahostels.com) and **Wild Rover** (www.wildroverhostels.com).

$$$$ Casa Andina Private Collection
Ugarte 403, T054-226907, www.casa-andina.com.
Luxury hotel in a restored 18th-century mansion, former Casa de la Moneda. 5 large suites in colonial building, 36 rooms in modern extension off 2nd courtyard. Gourmet restaurant, room service, business centre, roof terrace with views.

$$$$ Libertador Arequipa
Plaza Simón Bolívar, Selva Alegre, T054-215110, www.libertador.com.pe.
Large comfortable rooms, good service, swimming pool (cold), gardens, good meals, pub-style bar, cocktail lounge, squash court.

$$$ Casa Andina Classic
Jerusalén 603, T054-202070,
www.casa-andina.com.
Part of the attractive **Casa Andina** chain,
with breakfast, comfortable and colourful,
central, modern, good restaurant, parking.

$$$ Casa Andina Select
Portal de Flores 116, T054-412930,
www.casa-andina.com.
Remodelled 5-storey building on Plaza de
Armas, modern rooms, buffet breakfast,
restaurant, small pool, gym, caters to
business travellers.

$$ Casablanca Hostal
Puente Bolognesi 104, a few metres from
the Plaza de Armas, T054-221327, www.
casablancahostal.com.
Super stylish *hostal*, lovely minimalist rooms
in a colonial building. Ambient lighting,
rooms with exposed stone walls, most
with balcony.

$$ Casa de Melgar
Melgar 108, T054-222459,
www.lacasademelgar.com.
18th-century building, excellent rooms, solar
hot water, courtyard, good breakfast buffet.

$$ Casa de Mi Abuela
Jerusalén 606, T054-241206,
www.lacasademiabuela.com.
An Arequipa tradition, in the same family
for several generations, suites with bathtub
and rooms, small swimming pool, rooms
at the back are quieter and overlook the
garden, English spoken, parking, restaurant
and piano bar, buffet breakfast or evening
snacks on patio or in beautiful gardens, tour
operator. Warmly recommended.

$$ Hostal Solar
Ayacucho 108, T054-241793,
www.hostalsolar.com.
Colonial building, newer rooms in back
are bright, good breakfast served in nice
patio, sun lounge on roof, very secure,
multilingual staff.

> **Tip...**
> On arrival, do not believe taxi drivers who
> say the hotel of your choice is closed or
> full in order to take you to another hotel
> which pays them commission. Instead,
> phone your preferred hotel in advance,
> or ring the doorbell and check.

$$ La Casa de Avila
San Martín 116, Vallecito, T054-213177,
www.casadeavila.com.
Rooms around spacious, sunny garden,
computers for guests' use, can arrange
airport/bus station pick-up, recommended
Spanish courses held in the garden and
other activities.

$$ La Casa de Margott
Jerusalén 304, T054-229517,
www.lacasademargott.com.
Family-run in a refurbished 19th-century
house, bright with a massive palm tree in
patio, spacious, convenient, small bar/café,
security box, heaters in fancier rooms.

$$ La Casa de Tintin
Urbanización San Isidro F1, Vallecito,
T054-284700, www.hoteltintin.com.
20 mins' walk, 5 mins by taxi from the Plaza
de Armas, Belgian/Peruvian-owned, garden,
terrace, sauna, massage, laundry service, café
and bar, very pleasant and comfortable.

$$ Las Torres de Ugarte
Ugarte 401A, T054-283532.
Round the corner from Santa Catalina
convent, some rooms are bungalow style
in colonial part at the back, roof terrace,
safe, luggage store, reflexology.

$$ Maison du Soleil
Pasaje Violín 102, Plazoleta Campo
Redondo, San Lázaro, T054-212277,
www.maisondusoleil.com.pe.
Nice hotel in a quiet, pleasant location,
comfortable rooms, lovely common areas
and terrace, includes buffet breakfast,
attentive service, **Arthur** restaurant features
molecular cuisine and offers cooking lessons.

$$ Posada El Castillo
Pasaje Campos 105, Vallecito, T054-201828,
www.posadaelcastillo.com.
Dutch/Peruvian-owned, in an old house
decorated with utensils found in the
renovation, 5 mins by taxi from city centre.
Variety of rooms and suites, some with
balcony and view of El Misti, wonderful
breakfast in annexe, pool, lovely gardens,
a good choice.

$$ Santa Marta
Santa Marta 207, T054-243925,
www.hostalsantamarta.com.
Pleasant, comfortable hotel with nice patio,
modern rooms in back, arrange airport and
bus terminal transfers.

$$-$ La Casona de Jerusalén
Jerusalén 306, T054-205453,
lacasonadejerusalen@hotmail.com.
Centrally located colonial house, ample
bright rooms with or without bath, private
bath rooms include breakfast, terrace,
English, German and italian spoken,
renovated in 2016.

$ Cazorla Hostel
Ugarte 202, p2, T054-226111,
www.cazorlahostel.com.
Nice hostel in a central location, private
rooms with bath and 8-10-bed dorms, buffet
breakfast included, kitchen facilities, terrace.

$ El Indio Dormido
Av Andrés Avelino Cáceres B-9,
T054-427401, http://members.
tripod.com/h_indio_dormido/.
Close to bus terminals, kitchen,
cafeteria, parking, laundry,
TV room, very helpful, family-run.

$ Home Sweet Home
Rivero 509A, T054-405982, www.
homesweethome-peru.com.
Family-run, Cathy, who runs a travel agency
speaks Spanish, English, French, very helpful,
warm and inviting atmosphere, substantial
fresh breakfast included. Private or shared

bath, hot water all day, simple rooms, kitchen
and laundry facilities.

$ Hostal Santa Catalina
Santa Catalina 500, T054-243705,
www.hostalsantacatalinaperu.com.
On busy corner, simple rooms arranged
around a courtyard, private or shared bath,
kitchen facilities, security box, roof terrace
with great views, helpful staff.

$ La Casa de Sillar
Rivero 504, T054-284249,
www.lacasadesillar.com.
Nice refurbished 17th Century stone house,
comfortable rooms, private or shared
bath, nice patio with plants, ample kitchen
facilities, terrace with views, tour operator.

$ La Posada del Cacique
Jerusalén 404, T054-202170,
posadadelcacique@ yahoo.es.
Well maintained, good value and
helpful, with roof terrace.

$ Le Foyer
Ugarte 114, T054-286473, www.hlefoyer.com.
Nicely refurbished old house, pleasant
common areas, colourfully decorated, private
rooms and US$9 pp in dorm, book exchange,
arrange tours, popular.

$ Los Andes Bed & Breakfast
La Merced 123, T054-330015,
www.losandesarequipa.com.
Good value, kitchen use, hot water, large
rooms with waxed wood floors and
minimalist decor, TV rooms, pleasant
roof terrace.

$ Lula's B&B
In Cayma, T054-272517, www.bbaqpe.com.
Same owners as **Ari Quipay** language school,
Lula (Peruvian) and her husband (Swiss)
speak Spanish, English, German and French,
with airport/bus terminal pick-up, modern,
charming, quiet, meals available.

$ Tambo Viejo
Av Mariscal Cáceres 107, IV Centenario,
T054-288195, www.tamboviejo.com.

5 blocks south of the plaza near the rail station.12-room guesthouse, quiet, English and Dutch spoken, walled garden, choice of 8 fresh breakfasts (extra), vegetarian restaurant, safe deposit, coffee shop, bar, book exchange (2 for 1), money changed, tourist information for guests, luggage store extra, tours and volcano climbs arranged, discounts for long stays. For a small fee, you can use the facilities if passing through. Free pick-up from bus terminal 0700-2300 (call when arriving), US$20 for airport pick-up.

Restaurants

Arequipa is proud of its gastronomy. Typical dishes, many of them spiced with the hot *rocoto* pepper, accompanied by a glass of local *chicha* or an Arequipeño wine, are available in *picanterías* and at San Camilo market. There are also regional sweets and excellent chocolate, see Shopping below. AGAR, the local gastronomy association, organizes a yearly event, see Festivals, page 189.

$$$ Chicha
Santa Catalina 210,Casona Santa Catalina int 105, T054-287360. Mon-Sat 1200-2300, Sun 1200-1800.
The menu of mostly local and fusion dishes is created by Gastón Acurio, fine dining in a historic building opposite Santa Catalina. In the same patio and also with an Acurio menu is **Tanta**, serving breakfast and snacks.

$$$ La Trattoria del Monasterio
Santa Catalina 309, T054-204062, www. latrattoriadelmonasterio.com. Mon-Sat 1200-1600, 1900-2300, Sun 1200-1600.
A fusion of Italian and Arequipeño styles and ingredients, in a cloister in Convento de Santa Catalina.

$$$ Paladar 1900
San Francisco 227. Mon-Sat 1200-2400, Sun 1200-2300.
Stylish, contemporary design in a lovely refurbished old house. Peruvian-Mediterranean fusion cuisine, interesting and tasty.

$$$ Salamanto
Urbanización León XXIII, H-11, Cayma, T054-340607, www.salamanto.com. Mon-Sat 1900-2330.
Gourmet Peruvian cuisine, the menu changes every 3 months, bar, good service, popular among foreigners. Also **El Molle Café** next door (Tue-Sat 1200-2330, Sun 1230-1600).

$$$ Zig Zag
Zela 210, T054-206020, www.zigzag restaurant.com. Daily 1200-2400.
Lovely atmosphere and decor in a colonial house with arched ceilings, gourmet European/Peruvian fusion cuisine, specializes in meat (alpaca is recommended) and fish cooked on volcanic rock. Also offer a choice of set meals at midday. Delicious, very popular, book in advance. Recommended.

$$$-$$ La Nueva Palomino
Pje Leoncio Prado 122, Yanahuara, T054-252393. Daily 1130-1730.
An Arequipa institution that has been in the same family for 3 generations, a very popular, large *picantería*, with a wide selection of local dishes, such as *rocoto relleno*, *cuy chactado* and *chupe de camarones*, accompanied by *chicha arequipeña*, made with purple corn, large portions. Expect queues at weekends. Recommended.

$$$-$$ Tío Darío
Pje del Cabildo 100, 2 blocks from the Yanahuara church, T054-270473. Daily 1100-1630.
Very good ceviche and other seafood specialities with an Arequipeño touch, also meat dishes, outdoor seating in pleasant gardens with views.

$$ Bóveda San Agustín
Portal San Agustín 127-129, T054-243596. Daily 0700-2300.
Attractive bar downstairs, with an upstairs balcony overlooking the

Plaza de Armas. Good breakfasts, lunches and evening specials.

$$ Crepísimo
Santa Catalina 208, at Alianza Francesa, T054-206620, www.crepisimo.com. Daily 0800-2400.
Over 100 different sweet and savoury crepes with traditional and Peruvian flavours, plus salads, sandwiches, *menú* at lunch, great coffee and juices, drinks, magazines and board games, pleasant ambiance. Very tasty, recommended.

$$ Pizzería Los Leños
Jerusalén 407, T054-281818. Daily 1700-2300.
The first wood-fired pizza in the city, plus pasta, original flavours with a touch of Peruvian home cooking, pleasant atmosphere and music.

$$-$ Gonzalette El Asador
Zela 201-B. Mon-Sat1730-2400, and Villa Hermosa 1009, Av Aviación. Sat-Sun and holidays 1100-1700.
Good value for alpaca steaks, *parrillada*, pleasant atmosphere, good music.

$$-$ Hatunpa
Ugarte 208. Mon-Sat 1230-2130.
Small place serving tasty dishes prepared with Andean native potatoes with a choice of toppings, warm personalized service, very popular.

$$-$ Peruita Pizzería
Palacio Viejo 321A, T054-212621. Mon-Fri 1230-1500, 1730-2230, Sat 1730-2230.
Set lunch at midday and à la carte in the evening, very good wood-fired pizza and Italian dishes, Italian run.

$ El Buda Profano
Bolívar 425. Daily 1200-2200.
Tasty vegan sushi bar, soups, drinks, cultural events, English spoken.

$ El Puente
Santa Marta 207-A, Mon-Sat 0830-1700, and Bello Horizonte C-11B, across Puente Quiñones, behind Umacollo stadium, daily 0830-1800.
A choice of tasty vegetarian dishes, good value.

$ El Turko
San Francisco 223-25. Sun-Thu 0800-2400, Fri and Sat 0800-0600.
Bright café/bar selling kebabs, coffee, recommended breakfasts and good sandwiches.

$ India
Bolívar 502. Mon-Sat 1200-2100.
Very small restaurant serving tasty Indian cuisine, prepared by an Indian cook, many vegetarian dishes.

$ Istanbul
San Francisco 231. Mon-Wed 0900-2400, Thu-Sat 0900-0200, Sun 1100-2400.
Middle Eastern fast food, including a delicious falafel and other vegetarian dishes Also good coffee. In the same group as El Turko.

$ Ratatouille
Puente Bolognesi 214, T958-794192, http://ratatouillearequipa.wix.com/home.
French/Peruvian-owned, colourful, serves typical Mediterranean dishes, as the name implies, based on fresh produce, good value, popular.

$ Sandwichería Mamut
Mercaderes 111. Daily 0900-2100.
Very tasty giant sandwiches with classic and typical Peruvian flavours and many different dressings.

Cafés

Café Capriccio
Mercaderes 121. Daily 0800-2200.
Not that cheap, but excellent coffee, cakes, etc. Very popular with local business people. **Capriccio Gourmet**, on Santa Catalina 120, San Francisco 135 and at several shopping centres, is also good.

Café Valenzuela
Morán 114 and other locations.
Mon-Sat 0800-2200, Sun 1630-2030.
Fantastic coffee (also sells beans and ground coffee), locals' favourite.

Chaqchao
Santa Catalina 204, p2, T054-234572.
Daily 1100-2100.
Coffee, pizza, desserts, organic chocolate. At 1500 and 1800 they offer fun chocolate-making classes (US$21), reserve ahead.

Entre Libros y Café
Jerusalén 307. Mon-Sat 0930-2100 .
Coffee from various regions of Peru, juices, fraps, sandwiches, library, books for sale, musical and other cultural events.

La Alemana
San Francisco 137 and at shopping centres.
Mon-Thu 0800-2400, Fri-Sat 0800-0300.
Wide choice of sausages, plus very good *empanadas* and sandwiches. Good value and popular.

La Canasta
Jerusalén 115 in courtyard, no sign.
Mon-Sat 0830-2000.
Excellent baguettes twice daily, also serves breakfast and delicious apple and brazil nut pastries, courtyard seating.

OCacao
Palacio Viejo 205 A. Mon-Fri 0900-2130,
Sat 1000-2130.
Small café run by a Belgian *chocolatier*: coffee, sweets, excellent truffles and bonbons.

Pura Fruta
Mercaderes 131 and Av Trinidad Morán 205,
Cayma. Mon-Sat 0800-2200, Sun 0900-1400.
A great variety of fruit juices and smoothies, coffee, frappés, yoghurt, salads, sandwiches, desserts.

Bars and clubs

Casona Forum
San Francisco 317, www.casonaforum.com.
Huge complex incorporating the **Retro Bar** (live music Tue-Sat from 1930), **Zero** pool bar for rock music, **Club Latino** for salsa dancing, Club de los 80 (Thu-Sat from 2200) for 1980s music and lovely views, and **Forum**, an underground club with imitation waterfall and plants (Thu-Sat from 2200).

Déjà Vu
San Francisco 319-B. Daily 1900-0300.
Popular rooftop bar, hosts DJ electronic music evenings and live music, weekend drinks specials. During the day (1100-1800), **La terraza@Deja Vu** fish restaurant ($$) operates in the terrace, lovely setting and food.

Farren's
Pasaje Catedral 107.
Good meeting place, great music.

Museo del Pisco
Moral 229A. Daily 1200-2400.
Bar where you can learn about the pisco culture and history, also tastings and mixology classes.

Festivals

A full list of the region's many festivals is available locally from **iPerú**, see Tourist information, above.

10 Jan Sor Ana de Los Angeles y Monteagudo, festival for the patron saint of Santa Catalina monastery.
Mar-Apr Semana Santa celebrations involve huge processions every night, culminating in the burning of an effigy of Judas on Easter Sun in the main plazas of Cayma and Yanahuara, and the reading of his will, containing criticisms of the city authorities.
27 Apr The celebration of the apostle Santiago.
May Is known as the **Mes de Las Cruces**, with ceremonies on hilltops throughout the city.

3 Aug A procession through the city bearing the images of Santo Domingo and San Francisco.

6-31 Aug **Fiesta Artesanal del Fundo El Fierro** is a sale and exhibition of *artesanía* from all parts of Peru, taking place near Plaza San Francisco.

6-17 Aug Celebration of the city's anniversary on 15th, many events including a mass ascent of El Misti.

Oct-Nov FestiSabores, www.festisabores. com, gastronomic festival held at Plaza Yanahuara for 4 days around the last weekend in Oct. A good place to sample the local food, wine, pisco and music; check www.festisabores.com for exact dates.

2 Nov **Day of the Dead** celebrations in cemeteries.

Dec Hay Festival, www.hayfestival.org/ arequipa, week-long cultural festival, offshoot of the UK literary festival.

Shopping

The central San Camilo market, between Perú, San Camilo, Piérola and Alto de la Luna, is worth visiting.

Alpaca goods, textiles and crafts

Claustros de La Compañía, *Morán 140*. Handicrafts shopping centre in a colonial setting, containing many alpaca knitwear outlets including a factory outlet in the 2nd patio.

Fundo del Fierro, large handicraft market behind the old prison on Plaza San Francisco; it's worth a visit.

El Ekeko, *at Patio del Ekeko, Mercaderes 141, www.elekeko.pe*. A variety of crafts, T-shirts, Panama hats, gourmet foodstuffs.

Ilaria, *at Patio del Ekeko*. Fine jewellery.

Kuna by Alpaca 111, *at Patio del Ekeko, www.kuna.com.pe or www.incalpaca.com*. High-quality alpaca and wool products. Also at Casona Santa Catalina, Santa Catalina 210, Local 1-2; in **Hotel Libertador** and at the airport. Shops in Lima, Cuzco and Puno.

Tip...

You may find painted and unpainted souvenir condor feathers for sale in the markets in both Arequipa and Cuzco. Condors are being killed for this trade. It is illegal in Peru to sell or purchase condor feathers and the crime carries a sentence of four years in prison.

La Comercial, *Mercaderes 236 (no sign), opposite Teatro Municipal*. Recommended for knitted goods, bags, etc.

Michell y Cia, *Juan de la Torre 101, www. michell.com.pe*. Factory outlet, excellent place for alpaca and other wool yarn in huge variety of colours, also a clearance room for baby and adult alpaca yarn. Alpaca and pima cotton garments also for sale at **Sol Alpaca**, Casona Santa Catalina, Santa Catalina 210. 1920s machinery on display. Branches in Lima and Cuzco.

Millma's Baby Alpaca, *Pasaje Catedral 112 and 117, also at Santa Catalina 225, millmas@ hotmail.com*. 100% baby alpaca goods, run by Peruvian family, high quality, beautiful designs, good prices.

Bookshops

Librería El Lector, *San Francisco 213*. Wide selection, including Peruvian authors, book exchange in various languages (2 for 1), stocks *Footprint*.

Librerías San Francisco has branches at *Portal de Flores 138, San Francisco 102-106 and San Francisco 133-135*. Books on Arequipa and Peru, some in English, also expensive regional topographical maps.

SBS Book Service, *San Francisco 125, T054-205317*. Has a good selection of travel books, etc.

Shopping centres

There are several international style malls in the suburbs of Cayma, Paucarpata, Cerro Colorado and others.

Patio del Ekeko, *Mercaderes 141*. A commercial centre with upmarket restaurants and shops, cinema and **Museo de Arte Textil** upstairs (Mon-Sat 1000-2030, Sun 1000-1530).

Sweets

Antojitos de Arequipa, *Morán 129*. An Arequipa institution. Sells traditional sweets. Also at Jerusalén 120, Portal de Flores 144, the airport and all shopping centres.
La Ibérica, *Jerusalén 136, www.laiberica.com. pe*. Another Arequipa stalwart since 1909. Top-quality chocolate, but expensive. Outlets at Mercaderes 102, Morán 112, Portal de Flores 130, the airport and all shopping centres.

What to do

City tours

A cheap tour of the city can be made in a *Vallecito* city bus, 1½ hrs for US$0.50. It is a circular route which goes down Jerusalén and San Juan de Dios. There are 4 guides' associations, one of which (**Adegopa**, Morán 118, Claustros de la Compañía, tienda 11, http://adegopa.org) offers free promotional tours. **Panoramic bus tours** are offered by several companies (eg www.bus tour.com.pe, www.tahuantinsuyotravel.com), US$10 for 2 hrs, US$13 for 4 hrs. Most depart from Portal San Agustín, Plaza de Armas, several times daily. **Free walking tours** are offered daily at 1000 and 1500 by tourism students from the Universidad Nacional San Agustín UNSA; contact the Municipal Tourist office at Plaza de Armas; also with **Free Walking Tour Peru**, T9989-59566, www.fwtperu.com, depart Plaza San Francisco at 1145, tips expected.

Climbing, cycling, rafting and trekking

Be wary of agencies offering climbing trips with very fast ascents.
Beinhart Peru, *T994 402236, www.beinhart-peru.de.vu (in German)*. Custom tailored multi-day or week cycling and trekking expeditions for small groups. Run by Klaus Hartl a very dynamic guide, German, English and Czech spoken.

Carlos Zárate Aventuras, *Jerusalén 505-A, T054-202461, www.zarateadventures.com/en*. Run by Carlos Zárate of the Asociación de Guías de Montaña de Perú. Good family-run business that always works with qualified mountain guides. A specialist in mountaineering and exploring, with a great deal of information and advice and some equipment rental. Carlos also runs trips to one of the supposed sources of the Amazon, Nevado Mismi, as well as trekking in the Cotahuasi canyon, climbing tougher peaks such as Ampato and Coropuna, rock climbing and rafting.
Colca Trek, *Jerusalén 401 B, T054-206217, www.colcatrek.com.pe*. Knowledgeable and English-speaking Vlado Soto is one of the best guides for the Cotahuasi Canyon and is recommended for climbing, trekking and mountain biking in the Colca Canyon. He also rents equipment and has topographical maps.
Cusipata, *Jerusalén 402-A, T054-203966, www. cusipata.com*. Recommended as a very good local rafting operator, very popular half-day trips. Also 6-day trips on the Río Colca. May-Dec, Río Chili 1-day kayak courses, also trekking and mountain bike tours.
Expediciones y Aventuras, *Rivero 504 at La Casa de Sillar, T958 314821, www. expedicionesyaventuras.com*. Family-run adventure sports operator led by Gustavo Rondón. Experienced guides for rafting, kayaking, biking, climbing, trekking, sand-boarding, body-boarding and horse riding tours. Innovative 4WD routes and camping tours to Colca, Valle de los Volcanes, Cotahuasi, protected areas and the coast; very helpful.
Naturaleza Activa, *Santa Catalina 211, T988 227723, naturactiva@yahoo.com*. Experienced guides, knowledgeable, climbing, trekking and mountain biking.
Sacred Road Tours, *Jerusalén 400 AB2, T054-212332, www.sacredroad.com*. Arranges hiking, climbing, biking, and rock climbing in Colca Canyon

and elsewhere, experienced guides led by Arcadio Mamani, equipment available.
Volcanyon Travel, *Las Condes D2, Cayma, T958 021556,www.volcanyontravel.com; main office in Cuzco.* Trekking and some mountain bike tours in the Colca Canyon, also volcano climbing.

Language classes
Centro de Intercambio Cultural Arequipa (CEICA), www.ceica-peru.com; **Escuela de Español Ari Quipay (EDEAQ)**, www.edeaq. com; **Instituto Cultural Peruano Alemán**, www.icpa.org.pe; **Llama Education**, www. arequipaspanish.com; **Spanish School Arequipa**, www.spanishschoolarequipa. com; **Carlos Rojas**, rojasnuezcarlosmiguel@ yahoo.com.pe; **Silvana Cornejo**, silvanacor@ yahoo.com.

Tour operators
Many agencies on Jerusalén, Santa Catalina and around Plaza de Armas sell air and bus tickets and offer tours of Colca, Cotahuasi, Toro Muerto and the city. Prices vary greatly so shop around; check carefully what is included in the cheapest tours and that there are enough people for the tour to run. Travel agents frequently work together to fill buses. Many tourists prefer to contract tours through their hotel. If a travel agency puts you in touch with a guide, make sure he/she is official. The following have been recommended as helpful and reliable:
Andina Travel Service, *Jerusalén 309-A, T054-285477.* Good 1- to 4-day tours of Colca Canyon, climbing and other adventure sports, guide Gelmond Ynca Aparicio is very enthusiastic.
Colca Explorer, *Mariscal Benavides 201, Selva Alegre (north of the centre), T054-282488, www.colca-explorer.com.* Agency associated with **Amazonas Explorer** in Cuzco, with many options in Colca and southern Peru: from classic local tours to horse riding, mountain biking, fishing in remote lakes, climbing, treks and visiting alpaca farms on the altiplano.

Colca Journeys, *C Rodríguez Ballón 533, Miraflores (northeast of the centre), T973-901010, www.colcajourneys.com.* Specializes in and operates tours to the Colca Valley and Cotahuasi Valley.
Giardino Tours, *at Casa de Mi Abuela (see above), T054-221345, www.giardinotours.com.* Professional company offering tours and transport, has own properties in Arequipa, Colca (eg delightful **La Casa de Mamayacchi** in Coporaque) and Valle de Los Volcanes, community tourism options, good information.
Kuntur Adventure and Tourism (KAT), *Jerusalén 524B, T054-281864, www.katperu tours.com.* Offers a variety of standard and adventure tours including Colca. Run by Gerardo Pinto, very knowledgeable and helpful, English and German spoken.
Land Adventure, *Residencial La Peña A-20, Sachaca (southwest of the centre), 947 376345, www.landadventures.net.* 'Sustainable' tour operator with good guides for communities in Colca, trekking (including a 5-day Salkantay trek and Lares), climbing, downhill biking; private tours only.
Pablo Tour, *Jerusalén 400-AB-1, T054-203737, www.pablotour.com.* Family-run agency, has connections with several *hostales* in Cabanaconde and knows the area well, 3-day mixed tours in the Colca Canyon with mountain biking, trekking and rafting, also climbing and sandboarding, free tourist information, topographical maps for sale, bus and hotel reservation service. Son Edwin Junco Cabrera can sometimes be found in the office; he speaks fluent French and English and is very helpful.
Tierra Ětnica, *Jerusalén521B, T054-286927, www.tierraetnica.com.* Gastronomic tours, community tourism in Colca, rock climbing.
Vita Tours, *Jerusalén 302, T054-284211, www.vitatours.com.pe.* Tours in the Arequipa area, including to the coast, and in the Colca Canyon where they have a hotel, **La Casa de Lucila in Chivay**.

Volunteering

Paz Holandesa, *Villa Continental, Calle 4, No 101, Paucarpata, T054-432281, www. pazholandesa.com*. Dutch foundation dedicated to helping the impoverished (see their website if you are interested in volunteering). Also has a travel clinic for tourists, Dutch and English spoken, 24-hr service, highly recommended.

Volunteers Peru, *www.volunteersperu.org*. Runs social projects in a home for abandoned girls in the city and teaching English in Cotahuasi.

Transport

Taking a taxi from the airport or bus terminals to your hotel is recommended.

Air Rodríguez Ballón airport is 7 km from the centre, T054-434834. 2 desks offer hotel reservations; also car rentals. Take a taxi to/from your hotel, 30 mins. Airport taxis charge US$7-9 to the centre; other taxis charge US$4-6 to/from the centre; best to use a radio taxi company listed below. The stop for local buses and combis (eg 'Río Seco', 'Cono-Norte' or 'Zamacola') is about 500 m from the airport, but this is not recommended with luggage.

To **Lima**, 1 hr 30 mins, several daily with Avianca/TACA (Centro Comercial Real Plaza, Av del Ejército, Cayma), **LATAM** (Santa Catalina 118-C) and **Peruvian Airlines** (La Merced 202-B). **LATAM** also serves **Juliaca**, 30 mins. **Avianca/TACA** and **LATAM** also serve **Cuzco**, 1 hr from Arequipa. **Peruvian Airlines** also serves **Tacna**. **Amaszonas** (La Merced 121-B, www.amaszonas.com) sells tickets between Cuzco and **La Paz**, Bolivia.

Bus There are 2 terminals at Av Arturo Ibáñez Hunter, south of the centre, 30 mins by city bus (not recommended with luggage, US$0.50), or 20 mins by taxi, US$2.50-3.60. The older **Terminal Terrestre**, T054-427792, has shops and places to eat. The newer **Terrapuerto**, across the car park, T054-

Tip...
Theft is a serious problem in the bus station area. Take a taxi to and from the bus station and do not wander around with your belongings.

348810, has a travel agency (T054-427852, daily 0600-1400, 2000-2300), which gives information and makes hotel reservations. Most luxury class services leave from the Terrapuerto. Terminal tax is US$0.55-.90. Some companies have offices in both terminals. Flores, with frequent service to Lima and throughout southern Peru, is in both terminals and also has a private terminal nearby at Av Forga y Av Los Incas. Note that buses may not depart from the terminal where you bought your ticket.

To **Lima**, 1011 km, 15-18 hrs, standard services US$18-29, luxury US$36-56. **Cruz del Sur** (T054-427375), **Enlaces** (T054-430333), **Tepsa** (T054-608079), **Ormeño** (T054-424187), Oltursa (T01-708-5000) are recommended. The road is paved but drifting sand and breakdowns may prolong the trip.

To **Nazca**, 566 km, 9-11 hrs, US$19-22.50 (US$30-52 on luxury services), several buses daily, mostly at night; most buses continue to Ica (US$30-42) and Lima. Also US$12 to **Chala**, 400 km, 6 hrs. Note that some companies charge a full fare to Lima for intermediate destinations. To **Moquegua**, 213 km, 4 hrs, US$6.50-12, several buses and *colectivos* daily. To **Tacna**, 320 km, 6-7 hrs, US$9-11, hourly with **Flores**, direct luxury service without stopping in **Moquegua**, US$16.

To **Cuzco**, all buses go via Juliaca, US$11-46, 10-11 hrs. Most companies go overnight (eg **Enlaces, Cial, Cruz del Sur, Oltursa** and **Ormeño**), but Flores and others travel in daytime, at 0715 and 1230.

To **Juliaca**, US$5.50 normal, US$7 *semi-cama*, US$9-27 cama, 5 hrs with **Julsa** (T054-430843), hourly 0300-2400, with **Flores**, 6-8 daily; some buses continue to Puno. To **Puno**, 297 km, 5-6 hrs, US$7-11, hourly with **Julsa**, 4 daily with **Flores**, at 0800 with **Cruz del Sur** (US$21-27), several others. **4M Express** (La Merced 125 Int 111, T054-452296, www.4m-express.com) offers a **tourist service** to Puno with stops at Pampa Cañahuas (vicuña observation), Vizcachani (rock formations) and Lagunillas (flamingo and other bird observation) daily at 1245, 6 hrs, US$30-35 (high season), includes bilingual guiding, snack and hotel pickup in Arequipa. They offer a similar service from Chivay to Puno and Cuzco (see Colca transport, page 200), so you don't necessarily have to travel via Arequipa. To **Puerto Maldonado** via Juliaca, US$21-36, 17-18 hrs, at 1530 with **Julsa, Power, Wayra** (T959-390512) or **Mendivil** (T974-210329); more frequent departures from Juliaca.

To Chivay, with Andalucía (Terrapuerto, T959 448412) at 0930*, 1500, 2400*, Reyna (Terminal Terrestre, T958 793712) at 0100*, 0830, 1100*,and Trans Milagros (T054-298090) at 0330*, 0530, 1400*, US$4, 3 hrs; those with an asterisk (*) continue to **Cabanaconde**, US$5.50, a further 56 km, 2 hrs. **4M Express** provide private transport between Arequipa and Chivay on request and tour vans will also take extra passengers, pickup starting 0300, arrange with a tour operator.

Taxi From US$1 for trips around town. Companies include: **Alo 45**, T054-454545; **Taxitel**, T054-266262; Real T054-426161; **Turismo Arequipa**, T054-458888.

★ Colca Canyon

watch condors cruising above this spectacular canyon

The Colca Canyon is deep: twice as deep as the Grand Canyon. The Río Colca descends from 3650 m above sea level at Chivay to 3287 m at Cabanaconde. In the background looms the grey, smoking mass of Sabancaya (5976 m), one of the most active volcanoes in the Americas, and its more docile neighbours, Ampato (6265 m) and Hualca Hualca (6025 m). Unspoiled Andean villages lie on both sides of the canyon, inhabited by the Cabana and Collagua peoples, and some of the extensive pre-Columbian terraced fields are still in use. High on anyone's list when visiting the canyon is an early-morning trip to the Cruz del Cóndor to see these majestic birds at close quarters.

Arequipa to Chivay

From Arequipa there are two routes to **Chivay**, the first village on the eastern edge of the canyon. The old dirt route goes through Cayma and then runs north between Misti and Chachani to the altiplano. The newer paved route is longer but quicker. It goes through Yura, following the railway. The two routes join at Cañahuas, one of the access points to Reserva Nacional Salinas y Aguada Blanca, where you will have to purchase or show your tourist ticket. Both routes afford fine views of the volcanoes Misti, Chachani, Ampato and Sabancaya; if you're lucky, you can see herds of vicuñas near the road. Cyclists should use the Yura road, as it's in better condition and has less of a climb at the start. At Cañahuas, you can change buses to/from Juliaca or Chivay if you want to bypass Arequipa; the road from Cañahuas to Puno via Patahuasi, Imata and Juliaca is paved and has a daily tourist transport service (see Transport, page 200). It can be cold in the morning, reaching 4825 m in the Pata Pampa pass, but the views are worth it.

Essential Colca Canyon

Finding your feet

To enter the canyon you must buy a tourist ticket for US$25 (valid for 10 days) at a checkpoint on the road to Chivay; you may be required to show this ticket at Mirador Cruz del Cóndor. It is not always possible to join a tour in Chivay; it is best to organize it in Arequipa and travel with a group. Prices generally do not include the Colca entry ticket, meals other than breakfast nor entry to the baths. From Arequipa a one-day tour to the mirador costs US$20-25. It departs Arequipa at 0300-0330, arrives at the Cruz del Cóndor at 0730-0830, followed by an expensive lunch stop at Chivay and back to Arequipa by 1800-1900. For many, especially for those with altitude problems, this is too much to fit into one day (the only advantage is that you don't have to sleep at high altitude). Two-day tours are about US$25-35 per person with an overnight stop in Chivay or Yanque; more expensive tours range from US$45 to US$90. Most agencies will have a base price for the tour and then different prices depending on which hotel you pick.

Trekking

There are many hiking possibilities in the area, with *hostales* or camping for longer treks. Make sure to take enough water, or purification tablets, as it gets very hot and there is not a lot of fresh water available. Sun protection is also a must. Ask locals for directions as there are hundreds of confusing paths going into the canyon. In Cabanaconde trekking and adventure sports can be organized quite easily at short notice. Buy food for longer hikes in Arequipa. Topographical maps are available at the **Instituto Geográfico Nacional** in Lima, and at **Colca Trek** or **Pablo Tour** in Arequipa. Economical trekking tours from Arequipa cost US$45-55 for two days, US$55-65 for three days; entry tickets and lunch on the last day are not included. Agencies pool their passengers and the tour quality is often poor. A private three-day trekking tour for two passengers costs about US$450 per person.

When to go

Conditions vary annually, but January to April is the rainy season, which makes the area green with lots of flowers. This is not the best time to see condors, however, or to go hiking as some treks are impossible if it rains heavily (this is very rare). May to December is the dry, cold season when there is more chance of seeing the birds.

Time required

Allow at least two to three days to appreciate the Colca Canyon fully, more if you plan on doing some trekking.

Chivay and around

Chivay (3650 m) is the gateway to the canyon, and its road bridge is the main link between the north and south sides (others are at Yanque and Lari). Crossing the river at Chivay going west to follow the canyon on the north side, you pass the villages of **Coporaque**, **Ichupampa** (a footbridge crosses the river between the two villages), **Lari**, **Madrigal** and **Tapay**.

In Chivay, the **Maria Reiche Planetarium and Observatory** ① *in the grounds of the Casa Andina hotel, 6 blocks west of the Plaza between Huayna Capac and Garcilazo, www.casa-andina.com, US$5.70, discounts for students*, makes the most of the Colca's clear Southern Hemisphere skies with a powerful telescope and two 55-minute presentations per day at 1830 (Spanish) and 2000 (English). There is a Globalnet ATM close to the plaza. The hot springs of **La Calera** ① *US$4.30 to bathe, half price to visit, regular colectivos (US$0.30), taxi (US$1.70) or a 1-hr walk from town,* are 4 km away and are highly recommended after a hard day's trekking.

Beyond the baths, the road continues northeast to **Tuti**, which has a small handicrafts shop and is the starting point for the trek to **Nevado Mismi** (5598 m). After Tuti is **Sibayo** (*pensión* and grocery store) from where a long circuit leads back to Arequipa, passing through **Puente Callalli**, **Chullo** and **Sumbay**. This is a little-travelled road, but the views, with vicuña, llamas, alpacas and Andean duck are superb.

Chivay to Cruz del Cóndor

From Chivay, the main road goes west along the south side of the Colca Canyon. The first village encountered is **Yanque** (8 km, excellent views), with an interesting church containing superbly renovated altar pieces and paintings; there's a museum on the opposite side of the plaza. A large thermal swimming pool is 20 minutes' walk from the plaza, beside the renovated colonial bridge that leads to the villages of Coporaque and Ichupampa on the other side of the canyon (US$0.75). The road west continues paved to **Achoma** and **Maca** (footbridge to Madrigal on the north side), which barely survived an earthquake in 1991. Then comes the tiny village of **Pinchollo**. From here it is a 30-minute walk on a dirt track to the **Hatun Infiernillo** geyser.

The Mirador at **Cruz del Cóndor**, where you may be asked to show your tourist ticket, overlooks the deepest point of the canyon. The view is wonderful and condors can be seen rising on the morning thermals (0900, arrive by 0800 to get a good spot) and sometimes in the late afternoon (1600-1800). Camping here is officially forbidden, but if you ask the tourist police in Chivay they may help. **Milagros'** 0630 bus from Chivay stops here very briefly at around 0800 (ask the driver), or try hitching with a tour bus at around 0600. Buses from Cabanaconde stop at about 0700 (**Andalucía**) or 0830 (**Reyna**); they leave Cabanaconde's plaza 30 minutes earlier.

Cabanaconde

From the Mirador it is a 20-minute ride in tourist transport or 40 minutes by local bus on a paved road to Cabanaconde at 3287 m. You can also walk: three hours by the road, or two hours via a short cut following the canyon. This is the last village in the Colca Canyon, friendly, smaller and less touristy than Chivay. The views are superb and condors can be seen from the hill just west of the village, a 15-minute walk from the plaza. You'll also see agricultural terraces, arguably the most attractive in the valley, to the south of the village. Cabanaconde is an excellent base for visiting the region, with interesting trekking, climbing, biking and horse riding.

Treks around Cabanaconde

Two hours below Cabanaconde is **Sangalle**, an 'oasis' of palm trees and swimming areas where there are three campsites with basic bungalows and toilets. It's a beautiful spot, recommended. (It's three to 4½ hours back up; ask for the best route in both directions. Horses can be hired to carry your bag, US$5.85.)

A popular hike involves walking east on the Chivay road to the Mirador de Tapay (before Cruz del Cóndor), then descending to the river on a steep track (four hours, take care). Cross the bridge to the village of San Juan de Chuccho on the north bank, where you can stay and eat at a basic family hostel, of which there are several. From here, pass **Tapay** (also possible to camp here, minivan to Cabanaconde at 0400 and 1100) and the small villages of Cosñirhua and Malata, all the time heading west along the north side of the Río Colca (take a guide or ask local directions). After about three hours' walking, cross another bridge to the south bank of the Río Colca, follow signs to Sangalle, spend the night and return to Cabanconde on the third day. This route is offered by many Arequipa and local agencies.

Another nice hike, which can be combined with the one above, goes west past the stadium to Mirador de Achachihua, then steeply downhill to a road and, along it to a pedestrian or a car bridge over the Río Colca (three to four hours). Before crossing, look for geysers upstream from the pedestrian bridge. On the north side, continue on the road for about 30 minutes. At a hairpin bend where the road turns northeast, go left and follow a large trail northwest, cross a pedestrian bridge over the Río Huaruro, just ahead is **Llahuar** (30 minutes from the road) with nice rustic thermal baths next to the Colca River and two places to stay. Minivans from Tapay to Cabanaconde pass the Llahuar turnoff around 0500 and 1200. From Llahuar, you can continue steeply uphill to the villages of Llatica and Fure and the Fure and Huaruro Falls (five to six hours). From Fure you can reach the Tapay–Cabanaconde road.

Listings Colca Canyon

Tourist information

Tourist information and a map are available in Arequipa from the **Autoridad Autónoma del Colca** (Puente Grau 116, T054-203010, Mon-Fri 0900-1700, Sat 0900-1200). In Chivay, there is a very helpful **tourist office** in the Municipalidad on the west side of the plaza (closed at weekends). The tourist police, also on the plaza, can give advice about local guides. There's a traveller's **Medical Center** (**TMC**) (Ramón Castilla 232, T054-531037). There's also a friendly tourist information office in Cabanaconde (T054-280212) that is willing to give plenty of advice, if not maps. It's a good place to find trekking guides and muleteers (US$25 a day mule and guide).

Where to stay

Note that only the fancier hotels and *hostales* have Wi Fi and it is very slow.

Chivay and around

$$$ Casa Andina
Huayna Cápac s/n, Chivay, T054-531020, www.casa-andina.com.
Attractive cabins with hot showers and a cosy bar/dining area, a member of the recommended hotel chain, heating, parking.

$$$ Pozo del Cielo
C Huáscar B-3, Sacsayhuaman–Chivay, T054-531041 (Alvarez Thomas 309, Arequipa, T054-346547), www.pozodelcielo.com.pe.
Very comfortable option, located over the Puente Inca from Chivay amid pre-Inca terraces. Warm rooms, good views, good service and restaurant.

$$ Colca Inn
Salaverry 307, Chivay, T054-531111, www.hotelcolcainn.com.
Good mid-range option, modern, decent restaurant, basic breakfast included or US$2.50 for buffet breakfast, some rooms with heaters, nice views from upper rooms. Also run the more upmarket **Hotel Colcallacta**.

$$ La Casa de Mamayacchi
in Coporaque, 6 km from Chivay on the opposite side of the river, T054-531004, www.lacasademamayacchi.com, reservations through Giardino Tours in Arequipa.
Part of the hotel is in an original Inca structure, nice rooms with heaters, lovely dining area, terraced garden, multi-day packages including transport.

$$ Posada del Colca
Salaverry 325, Chivay, T054-531040,
laposadadelcolca@hotmail.com,
also on Facebook.
Central, good rooms.

$ Hospedaje Restaurant Los Portales
Arequipa 603, Chivay, T054-531101,
losportalesdechivay@hotmail.com,
also on Facebook.
Good value, though beds have rather
'floppy' mattresses. Restaurant downstairs.

$ La Casa de Lucila
M Grau 131, Chivay, T054-531109,
http://vitatours.com.pe.
Small, refurbished, comfortable house, guides
available, reserve ahead in high season.

$ La Pascana
Puente Inca y C Siglo XX 106, Chivay,
T054-531001, hrlapascana@hotmail.com.
Excellent value on the northwest corner of
the Plaza. Spacious en suite rooms overlook
a pleasant garden, hot water, parking and a
good restaurant.

$ Rumi Wasi
Sucre 714, 6 blocks from plaza
(3 mins' walk), Chivay.
Good rooms, hot water, helpful.

Chivay to Cruz del Cóndor

$$$$ Colca Lodge
Across the river from Yanque, T054-
531191 (office: Mariscal Benavides 201,
Selva Alegre, Arequipa, T054-202587),
www.colca-lodge.com.
Very relaxing, with beautiful hot springs
beside the river, spend at least a day to make
the most of the activities on offer. Day passes
available. Rooms heated with geothermal
energy, solar-heated water.

$$$$ Las Casitas del Colca
Av La Curiña s/n, Yanque, T996 998355,
www.lascasitasdelcolca.com.
Luxury cottages made of local materials
with underfloor heating and plunge pools.
Has a gourmet restaurant, bar, vegetable

garden and farm, offers cookery and
painting courses, the spa offers a variety
of treatments, swimming pool.

$$$ Collahua
Av Collahua cuadra 7, Yanque (office:
Mercaderes 212, Galerías Gamesa, Arequipa,
T054-226098), www.hotelcollahua.com.
Modern bungalows just outside Yanque,
with heating, solar-powered 24-hr hot
water and plush rooms, restaurant.

$$$ Eco Inn
Lima 513, Yanque, T054-837112,
www.ecoinnhotels.com.
Perched high on a bluff with incredible
views over the valley and restored Uyo
Uyo ruins. Large, comfortable rooms in
cabins, restaurant open from 0530 for buffet
breakfast, Wi-Fi in lobby and restaurant.

$$ Tradición Colca
Av Colca 119, Yanque, T054-781178
(office: C Argentina 108, Urb Fecia
JL Bustamante y Rivero, T054-424926),
www.tradicioncolca.com.
Adobe construction, gas stove, garden spa,
massages, sauna. Restaurant, bar, games
room, observatory and planetarium (free for
guests), horse riding from 2 hrs to 2 days,
hiking tour to Ullu Ullu, bike rentals, travel
agency in Arequipa.

$ Casa Bella Flor Sumaq Wayta Wasi
Cuzco 303, Yanque, T054-774505,
www.casabellaflor.com.
Charming small lodge run by Sra Hilde
Checca, flower-filled garden, tasteful rooms,
good meals (also open to non-residents).
Hilde's uncle, Gregorio, guides visitors to
pre-Columbian sites.

$ Hospedaje Refugio del Geyser
C Melgar s/n, behind municipality,
Pinchollo, T959-007441.
Basic with good local information.

$ Rijchariy Colca Lodge
On the track leading down to the footbridge
over the river, Yanque, T054-764610.
Great views, garden, comfortable, restaurant.

Cabanaconde

$$ Kuntur Wassi
C Cruz Blanca s/n, on the hill above the plaza,
T054-233120, www.arequipacolca.com.
Excellent 3-star, restaurant with fine
traditional meals. Creative design, with
rooms with heaters spaced between rock
gardens and waterfalls. Viewing 'tower'
and conference centre above. Owners
Walter and María very welcoming and
knowledgeable about treks.

$$ La Casa de Santiago
Grau, 3 blocks from the plaza, T941 414048,
www.lacasadesantiago.com.
Upmarket small *hostal*, with views of the
mountains and a large garden.

$$ Posada del Conde
C San Pedro, T054-440197,
pdelconde@yahoo.com.
Smart hotel and lodge. Cheaper in low
season, with hot shower, comfortable beds,
good food. Local guides and horses for hire.

$ Hostal Valle del Fuego
1 and 2 blocks from the plaza on C Grau y
Bolívar, T054-668910, www.valledelfuego.com.
Rooms with comfortable beds and dorms
(US$7 pp, breakfast extra), laundry facilities,
restaurant. Can arrange guides, pack
animals, bike rentals. The Junco family have
plenty of information and work with related
establishments, including: **Pablo Tour** in
Arequipa, where you can make reservations
and get a Colca map; **Oasis Paraíso** in
Sangalle (discounts for clients of Valle del
Fuego and related hotels); **Casa de Pablo
Club** at the end of the street, and **La Casa de
Santiago** (see above). They usually meet the
incoming buses. Popular.

$ La Posada de San Felipe
At Anglican Church, Camino al Mirador
Achachihua, 4 blocks from the Plaza,
T983 855648.
Nice ample rooms with bath and reliable hot
water, quiet location.

$ Pachamama Home
San Pedro 209, T054-767277,
www.pachamamahome.com.
Backpacker hostel, rooms with and without
bath, family atmosphere, hot water, lots of
information, good bar/pizzería **Pachamama**
next door, try the Colca Sour, made from a
local cactus. You can help with teaching and
activities for village children.

$ Virgen del Carmen
Av Arequipa s/n, 5 blocks up from the plaza.
Hot showers, may even offer you a
welcoming glass of *chicha*.

Trekking around Cabanaconde
Sangalle has 3 campsites with basic
bungalows and toilets. In San Juan de
Chuccho, **Hostal Roy** and **Casa de Rebelino**
($) are both good. US$2 will buy you a decent
meal. Llahuar hostels ($) fill up, reserve ahead,
Llahuar Lodge, T956 271333, llahuar.lodge@
hotmail.com, rustic cabins with shared
cold shower, nice camping area above hot
pools (US$3pp), good meals; next door and
more economical is **Casa de Virginia**, T973
559851, rooms with shared bath with solar
hot shower, camping (US$2.30 pp) meals on
request, use of pools at Llahuar Lodge.

Restaurants

Chivay and around
Several restaurants serve buffet lunches
for tour groups, US$5 pp, also open to the
general public. Of the few that open in the
evening, most have folklore shows and are
packed with tour groups. When walking in
the valley meals and drinks can be taken in
any of the larger lodges. For local cheeses
and dairy products, visit **Productos del Colca**
(Av 22 de Agosto), in the central market.

$$ El Balcón de Don Zacarías
Av 22 de Agosto 102 on plaza, T054-531108.
Breakfast, the best lunch buffet in town,
à la carte menu, *Novo Andino* and
international cuisine.

$$ Yaraví
Plaza de Armas 604.
Arequipeña food, vegetarian options and the most impressive coffee machine in town.

$$-$ McElroys's Irish Pub
On the plaza.
Warm bar, good selection of drinks (sometimes including expensive Guinness), sandwiches, pizza, pasta and music. Accepts Visa.

$ Innkas Café-Bar
Plaza de Armas 706.
Coffee, sandwiches, *menú*, pizzas, pool table, good atmosphere.

Cabanaconde

$$-$ Casa de Pablo Club
C Grau.
Excellent fresh juices and *pisco sour*, cable TV (football!), small book exchange and some equipment hire.

$ Café de Mirko
At Plaza de Armas. Opens early.
Small café serving coffee, herbal teas and snacks.

$ Rancho del Colca
On plaza.
Mainly vegetarian.

Festivals

There are numerous festivals in the Colca region, many of which last several days and involve traditional dances and customs.

2-3 Feb Virgen de la Candelaria, celebrated in Chivay, Cabanaconde, Maca and Tapay.
Feb Carnaval in Chivay.
3 May Cruz de la Piedra in Tuti.
13 Jun San Antonio in Yanque and Maca.
14 Jun San Juan in Sibayo and Ichupampa.
21 Jun Anniversary of Chivay.
29 Jun San Pedro y San Pablo in Sibayo.
14-17 Jul La Virgen del Carmen in Cabanaconde.
25 Jul Santiago Apóstol in Coporaque.

26 Jul-2 Aug Virgen Santa Ana in Maca.
15 Aug Virgen de la Asunta in Chivay.
8 Dec Immaculada Concepción in Yanque and Chivay.
25 Dec Sagrada Familia in Yanque.

What to do

It is not always possible to join a tour in Chivay; it is best to organize it in Arequipa and travel with a group. In Cabanaconde trekking and adventure sports can be organized quite easily at short notice. See also Essential Colca Canyon, page 195.

Chivay
Ampato Adventure Sports, *Av Siglo XX 417, 2 blocks from the bus station, T054-489156, www.ampatocolca.com.* Offer information and rent good mountain bikes.
Pedro Samayani, *T958 034023, pedroscolca@ hotmail.com.* Local guide offers tours throughout the Colca area.
Zacarías Ocsa Osca, *T949 494866, zacariasocsa@hotmail.com.* Local trekking guide offers Colca tours and more unusual routes such as Mismi, Inca road from Chivay to Apurimac, a 5-day tour to 3 canyons and llama trekking.

Cabanaconde
Local guides charge US$15 pp per day to Sangalle, US$20 pp per day to Llahuar, minimum 3 passengers. A muleteer with 1 mule charges US$25 per day.
Agotour Colca, *T951 526615 (Alejandro Maque).* An association of regional guides.
Chiqui Travel & Expeditions, *Plaza de Armas s/n, next to the Municipalidad, T958-063602, cazador55555@hotmail.com.* Edizon Gomosio, private guide, professional and reliable, organizes trekking, biking and horse riding, can also arrange for pack animals and make reservations.

Transport

Bus The bus station in Chivay is 3 blocks from the main plaza, next to the stadium for service to Arequipa, Cabanaconde and Pinchollo. Vans and *colectivos* leave from the terminal behind the market to other villages in the area.

See Arequipa Transport, page 193, for service originating there. To **Arequipa**, buses start at the Plaza de Armas in **Cabanaconde**, US$5.50, 5 hrs; **Reyna** at 0700 and 1400, **Andalucía** at 0815 and 0900 and **Trans Milagros** at 1130 and 2200; they pass **Cruz del Cóndor** (20 mins, US$2.20), then **Chivay** 2 hrs after departure; Chivay–Arequipa US$4, 3 hrs. Tour buses take extra passengers if they have room, enquire with tour operators. **4M Express** (see below) offers private transport to Arequipa on request. **Chivay** to/from **Cabanaconde**, 56 km, US$1.45, 2 hrs, through buses from/to Arequipa; also hourly minibuses depart half a block from the Chivay terminal. To **Cuzco**, take the **4M Express** tourist service (see

below) or a regular bus to Cañahuas and change there for a bus to Juliaca, then carry on to Cuzco. Note, however, there are no bus stations in Cañahuas, it is cold and buses to Juliaca are often full.

Tourist service 4M Express, www.4m-express.com, has several routes departing from Hotel La Pascana on Chivay's plaza, all stop at places of interest along the way and include a snack. To **Puno** Terminal Terrestre, daily 1315, US$50, 7 hrs, stopping at Patapampa lookout, Chucura Volcano and Lagunillas (birdwatching). To **Cuzco**, direct route along a paved road via Tuti, Sibayo and Sicuani, Mon, Wed and Fri at 0700, US$65 (lunch extra), 10½ hrs, stopping at Castillos de Callalli rock formations, Yauri rock forest, Laguna de Langui (25 km long), Sicuani (lunch break) and dropping off at 4M's private station.

★ Cotahuasi Canyon

how low can you go?

At its deepest, at Ushua (just below the village of Quechualla), the Cotahuasi Canyon measures 3354 m from rim to river, making it 163 m deeper than the Colca Canyon and the deepest canyon in the world. From this point, the only way along the canyon is by kayak, and it is through kayakers' reports that the area has come to the notice of tourists. The Reserva Paisajística Cañón de Cotahuasi protects the extensive Cotahuasi drainage, from the icy summits of Solimana and Huanzo (5445 m) to where it joins the Río Ocoña at 950 m. The canyon is very dry, especially from April to October when the contrast between the desert slopes and the green irrigated oases along the wider sections of the river valley and on the hanging valleys of its tributaries is particularly striking. Grapes, organic kiwicha (amaranth) and quinoa for export, avocados, citrus and other fruits are grown here. The side canyons are very impressive in their own right.

Despite the arid climate and rugged geography, the canyon has been populated for centuries. There are a number of pre-Inca and Inca remains perched on terraces cut into the vertical canyon walls and segments of Inca trade routes from the coast to the highlands can still be seen. The area has several thermal baths, waterfalls, impressive rock formations, cacti and *Puya raimondii* bromeliad forests, and amazing views. There is a good *turismo vivencial* programme with homestays in many villages.

Towards Cotahuasi: Río Majes Valley

Southwest of Arequipa, a paved road branches off the Pan-American to the impressive Siguas Canyon and on to the agricultural valley and canyon of the Río Majes, a rafting destination. At the linear roadside town of **Corire** are several hotels and restaurants serving excellent freshwater shrimp.

Nearby is the world's largest field of petroglyphs at **Toro Muerto** ① *6.5 km from Corire, US$1.45, van from the plaza in Corire to La Candelaria Mon-Fri 0700, returning 1400, US$0.60, or taxi, US$14 incl 2-hr wait, tours available from Arequipa.* Access to the UNESCO World Heritage Site is signposted off the main road 1.5 km south of Corire, where a road turns east to the village of La Candelaria, 2 km from the main road. One block above the plaza is the archaeological site's office where the entry fee is collected. From here it is 3 km on a dirt road to the site entrance which provides the only shade in the area; the immense field of 5000 sculpted rocks in the desert lies beyond. The sheer scale of the 5-sq-km site is awe-inspiring and the view is wonderful. The higher you go, the more interesting the petroglyphs, though some have been ruined by graffiti. Don't believe the guides who, after the first few rocks, say the others are all the same. The designs range from simple llamas to elaborate human figures and animals. There are several styles which are thought to be Wari (AD 700-1100), Chuquibamba (AD 1000-1475) and Inca in origin. An extensive review of the designs is found in *Memorias del Arqueólogo Eloy Linares Málaga* (Universidad Alas Peruanas, 2011). Take plenty of water, sunglasses and sun cream. At least an hour is needed to visit the site.

From Corire an unpaved road follows the Río Majes to Camaná on the coast. Upriver from Corire, the paved road goes past a park with dinosaur prints to the regional centre of **Aplao**, which has a small museum containing Wari cultural objects from the surrounding area. A side road to the north leads to **Andagua** (several places to stay) in the fascinating **Valle de los Volcanes**, while the main road continues northwest to **Chuquibamba** (several places to stay and eat) in a scenic terraced valley, where the paving ends. Beyond Chuquibamba, the road climbs steeply to traverse the *puna* between Nevado Coropuna (6425 m) and Nevado Solimana (6093 m). The views are awe-inspiring, so it is well worth the effort to travel this route by day.

Cotahuasi and the upper canyon

From Mirador Allhuay (3950 m) at the rim of the Cotahuasi Canyon, the road, now paved, winds down to the peaceful colonial town of **Cotahuasi**, nestled in a sheltered hanging valley at 2680 m, beneath Cerro Huinao. Its streets are narrow, with whitewashed houses. The Río Cotahuasi flows 1500 m below the town at the bottom of its great canyon.

Following the Río Cotahuasi to the northeast up the valley, you come to **Tomepampa** (10 km), a small town at 2700 m, with painted houses and a colonial church. The attractive hot springs of **Luicho** ① *16.5 km from Cotahuasi, daily 0330-2130, US$1.80, 1 simple room for rent*, are a short walk from the road, across a bridge. There are three pools (33° to 38°C). The paved road ends at **Alca**, 20 km from Cotahuasi, at 2750 m, with several simple places to stay and eat. Above it are the small ruins of Kallak, Tiknay and a 'stone library' of rock formations. All these places are connected by hourly mini-buses from Cotahuasi (see Transport). **Puyca** ① *23 km beyond Alca, bus from Alca at 0530, return at 1200, 1½ hrs, US$2.50, www.canyoncotahuasi.com*, is the last village of any significance in the valley, hanging on a hillside at 3560 m. Locals can guide you on treks in the area, and horses can be hired. Nearby, at 3700 m, are the extensive Wari ruins of Maucallacta (20-minute walk), the most important in the Cotahuasi area. Beyond is **Churca** ① *24 km from Puyca, van from Alca at 0530, return at 1200, 2-3 hrs, US$3.20*, from where you can walk to Lauripampa at about 4000 m in 20 minutes to see a vast prairie of *Puya raimondii* plants. On the opposite side of the river from Churca is Chincayllapa from where you can drive to the Occoruro geysers at 4466 m, also reached in a full-day walk from Puyca.

Downstream from Cotahuasi

A rough, narrow road follows the Río Cotahuasi downriver for 28 km to Mayo. At Km 13 is the access to the powerful, 150-m **Cataratas de Sipia** ① *2 km from the road, bus from Terminal Terrestre Tue-Thu and Sat 0630, Mon and Sun 0630 and 1330, Fri 0630 and 1400, US$1.45, 30 mins (return 2½-3 hrs later)*. A good trail leads from the road to several lookouts over the three-tiered falls, which are the most visited attraction in the canyon; take care near the edge, especially if it is windy. The best light is at midday. You can also get an overview of the falls from the road, continuing past the turnoff to the top of the hill.

Listings Cotahuasi Canyon

Tourist information

Tourist information is available from **CONSETUR** (www.cotahuasituristico.com), represented in Cotahuasi by **Purek Tours** (C Arequipa 103, daily 0900-1300, 1400-2000). A map of Cotahuasi may be available at **iPerú** in Arequipa. See also www.municipiolaunion.com. There are no ATMs in Cotahuasi but **Banco de la Nación** (C Cabildo) changes US$ cash.

Where to stay

Río Majes Valley

$ Hostal Willy's
Av Progreso opposite the market, Corire, T054-472046 and Progreso y Morán, at the Plaza, Aplao, T959-476622.
Both modern buildings with comfortable rooms, no breakfast.

$ La Casa de Mauro
La Central, 12 km north of Aplao (combi service), T054-631076, www.star.com.pe/lacasademauro.
Simple cabins and camping (US$5.50 per tent) in a lovely rural setting, restaurant with 60 different shrimp dishes, run by the friendly Zúñiga family, rafting, trekking and conventional tours.

$ Montano
Ramón Castilla s/n, Corire, T054-472122.
Best rooms are at the back away from the road, some rooms are small, no breakfast, good value.

Cotahuasi and the upper canyon
For information about homestays in the towns outside Cotahuasi, contact CONSETUR (see above).

$$ Valle Hermoso
Tacna 108-110, Cotahuasi, T054-581057, www.hotelvallehermoso.com.
Nice and cosy, includes breakfast, beautiful views of the canyon, comfortable rooms, large garden, meals with home-grown fruit and veg require advanced notice.

$ Casa Primavera
Main street, Tomepampa, T954-734056.
Family-run hostel with a flower-filled courtyard, some rooms with private bath, price includes breakfast, other meals on request, kitchen facilities, common areas, good value.

$ Don Justito
Arequipa110, ½ block below the plaza, Cotahuasi, T973-698053.
Ample functional rooms with and without bath, plenty of solar heated water, popular, good value economy option.

$ El Mirador
Centenario 100-A, Cotahuasi, T054-489417.
Pleasant rooms, great views, no breakfast.

$ Hatun Huasi
Centenario 309, Cotahuasi, T054-581054, www.hatunhuasi.com.
Popular *hostal* with a variety of rooms, nice small garden and common areas, parking, breakfast extra, helpful owner Catalina Borda speaks some English. Recommended.

Restaurants

Cotahuasi and the upper canyon

There are many tiendas well-stocked with fruit, vegetables and local wine.

$$-$ Buen Sabor
C Arequipa, up from the plaza, Cotahuasi.
A la carte Peruvian dishes, caters to tourists.

$ La Chocita Cotahuasina
Av Independencia, ½ block from the church, Cotahuasi. Open 0700-2100, closed Wed.
Good set meals, pleasant patio seating.

What to do

Several tour operators in Arequipa, including:
Amazonas Explorer, *in Cuzco, www. amazonas-explorer.com.* Can organize 5-day kayaking expeditions on the Cotahuasi for experienced kayakers only.
Cotahuasi Trek, *www.cotahuasitrek.com.* Run 4-day trips to Cotahuasi, taking in the main attractions. They can also organize adventure activities.

Río Majes Valley

La Casa de Mauro Tours, *see Where to stay, T959-362340, www.star.com.pe/ lacasademauro.* Pancho Zúñiga offers rafting, trekking and 4WD tours in the Majes, Cotahuasi and Colca areas.
Majes Tours, *T983 785995, www.majes toursarequipa.com.* Eva Nazarit Mina runs 1-3-day tours which include Toro Muerto and combine walking, cycling, rafting and kayaking.

Cotahuasi and the upper canyon

Purek Tours, *C Arequipa 103, Cotahuasi, T054-698081, cotahuasitours@gmail.com.* Biking, horse riding and 2- to 3-day trekking tours.

Transport

Río Majes Valley

Empresa Del Carpio buses to **Corire** and **Aplao** leave from the Terrapuerto in **Arequipa** about every 1½ hrs 0430-1900, 3-4 hrs, US$4.30; to **Chuquibamba** at 0515 and 1615, return 0500 and 1200, US$7.50, 6-7 hrs. For **Toro Muerto**, ask to be let out at the turnoff to La Candelaria. Cotahuasi-bound buses from Arequipa stop at the plaza in Corire (near the Del Carpio station), at the highway in Aplao and at the terminal in Chuquibamba. To **Camaná** on the coast (transfer here for Nazca and Lima), van from Aplao at 0800, passes Corire 0830, US$5.40, 2 hrs; returns from Camaná at 0400-0500. To **Andagua**, **Reyna** from Arequipa at 1600, via Corire and Aplao, return about 1500. There is a daily minivan from Andagua to **Chacas**.

Cotahuasi and the upper canyon

Destinations along the canyon are connected Mon-Sat 0600-1800 by hourly combis from Cotahuasi, fewer on Sun. Cotahuasi has a modern bus station (terminal fee US$0.35) 10 mins' walk from the plaza. Buses daily from **Arequipa** Terminal Terrestre, 10-11 hrs, US$11: **Cromotex** at 1700 and 1800; **Reyna** at 1630; they stop for refreshments in Chuquibamba, about halfway. Both companies continue to **Tomepampa** and **Alca;** buses leave Alca for Arequipa around 1400 (you can get off at Cotahuasi). Return Cotahuasi to Arequipa, **Cromotex** at 1800 and 1900, **Reyna** at 1700. From **Lima**, Trans López (Sebatián Barranca 158, La Victoria, T01-332 1015), Sun at 0900, US$36, 20 hrs (passes Chuquibamba Mon 0500-0630); return Cotahuasi to Lima Tue 0700. This is the only public transport daytime option to/from Cotahuasi, offering magnificent views; you can board in Corire, Aplao or Chuquibamba.

From Arequipa, the main road to the coast goes southwest for 37 km to Repartición where it divides. One branch goes west from here for 54 km through a striking arid landscape before dividing again: northwest to the Majes and Cotahuasi areas (see above) or southwest to Camaná (170 km from Arequipa) on the coast. The second branch from Repartición goes south and, in 15 km, divides south to Mollendo and southeast towards Moquegua.

Moquegua and around *Colour map 3, B1.*

This city lies 213 km from Arequipa in the narrow Moquegua river valley and enjoys a sub-tropical climate. The old centre, a few blocks above the Pan-American Highway, has winding, cobbled streets and 19th-century buildings. The Plaza de Armas, with its mix of ruined and well-maintained churches, colonial and republican façades and fine trees, is one of the most interesting small-city plazas in the country. Within the ruins of Iglesia Matriz is the **Museo Contisuyo** ① *Jr Tacna 294, on the Plaza de Armas, T053-461844, www. museocontisuyo.com, Wed-Mon 0800-1300, 1430-1730, Tue 0800-1200, 1600-2000, US$0.50,* which focuses on the cultures that thrived in the Moquegua and Ilo valleys, including the Huari, Tiahuanaco, Chiribaya and Estuquiña, who were conquered by the Incas. Artefacts are well displayed and explained in Spanish and English.

A highly recommended excursion is to **Cerro Baúl** (2590 m) ① *30 mins by colectivo, US$2,* a tabletop mountain with marvellous views and many legends, which can be combined with the pleasant town of Torata, 24 km northeast.

One of the most breathtaking stretches of the **Carretera Binacional** from Ilo to La Paz runs from Moquegua to Desaguadero at the southeastern end of Lake Titicaca. The road is fully paved and should be travelled in daylight. It skirts Cerro Baúl and climbs through zones of ancient terraces to its highest point at 4755 m. On the altiplano there are herds of llamas and alpacas, lakes with waterfowl, strange mountain formations and snow-covered peaks. At Mazo Cruz there is a PNP checkpoint where all documents and bags are checked. Approaching Desaguadero the Cordillera Real of Bolivia comes into view.

Tacna *Colour map 3, B2. See map, page 206.*

Thanks to its location, only 36 km from the Chilean border and 56 km from the international port of Arica, Tacna has free-trade status. It is an important commercial centre, and Chileans come here for cheap medical and dental treatment. Around the city the desert is gradually being irrigated to produce olives and vines; fishing is also important. Tacna was in Chilean hands from 1880 to 1929, when its people voted by plebiscite to return to Peru. Above the city (8 km away, just off the Panamericana Norte) is the **Campo de la Alianza**, scene of a battle between Peru and Chile in 1880. The cathedral, designed by Eiffel, faces the Plaza de Armas, which contains huge bronze statues of Admiral Grau and Colonel Bolognesi. They stand at either end of the Arca de los Héroes, the triumphal arch which is the symbol of the city. The bronze fountain in the Plaza is said to be a duplicate of the one in the Place de la Concorde (Paris) and was also designed by Eiffel. The **Parque de la Locomotora** ① *knock at the gate under the clocktower on Jr 2 de Mayo for entry, daily 0700-1700, US$0.30,* near the city centre, has a British-built locomotive, which was used in the War of the Pacific. There is a very good railway museum at the station.

Border with Chile

It is 56 km from Tacna to the Chilean city of Arica. The border post is 30 minutes from Tacna at Santa Rosa, open 0800-2300 Sunday to Thursday and 24 hours on Friday and Saturday. You need to obtain a Peruvian exit stamp at Santa Rosa before proceeding a short distance to the Chilean post at Chacalluta where you will get a Chilean entrance stamp. Formalities are straightforward and should take about 30 minutes in total. All luggage is X-rayed in both directions. No fruit or vegetables are allowed across the border. If you need a Chilean visa, get it from the Chilean consulate in Tacna (Presbítero Andía block 1, T052-423063, Monday-Friday 0800-1300). Money-changers can be found at counters in the international bus terminal; rates are much the same as in town. Remember that Peruvian time is one hour earlier than Chilean time from March to October; two hours earlier from September/October to February/March (varies annually).

Crossing by bus It takes one to two hours to travel from Tacna to Arica, depending on waiting time at the border. Buses charge US$2.50, and *colectivo* taxis, which carry five passengers, charge US$7.50 per person. All leave from the international terminal in Tacna throughout the day, although *colectivos* only leave when full. As you approach

Tacna

To Bus Station, Panamericana Norte & Alto de la Alianza

To Panamericana Norte & Stadium

Chilean Consulate

Presbitero Andía

Zarumilla

Museo Ferroviario

Julio Mac Lean

Mercado 2 de Mayo

2 de Mayo

Teatro Municipal

Touring y Automóvil Club

OGD Tur Tacna

Modesto Basadre

Centro Cultural Micula

Francisco de Zela

Scotiabank

Casa de la Cultura

BCP

San Martín

Cathedral

Plaza de Armas

Callao

Simón Bolívar

Parque de la Locomotora

Av Bolognesi

Mercado Central

Av Grau

Av Restauración

To Panamericana Sur, Airport & Arica

N

400 metres
400 yards

Where to stay	Restaurants
1 Copacabana	1 Café Zeit
2 Dorado	2 Cusqueñita
3 El Mesón	3 Da Vinci
4 Gran Hotel Tacna	4 Fu-Lin
5 Hostal Anturio	5 Il Pomodoro
6 Hostal Bon Ami	6 Koyuki
7 La Posada del Cacique	7 Un Limón
8 Roble 18 Residencial	8 Verdi

the terminal you will be grabbed by a driver or his agent and told that the car is "just about to leave". This is hard to verify as you may not see the *colectivo* until you have filled in the paperwork. Once you have chosen a driver/agent, you will be rushed to his company's office where your passport will be taken from you and the details filled out on a Chilean entry form. It is then 30 minutes to the Peruvian border post at Santa Rosa. The driver will hustle you through all the exit procedures. A short distance beyond is the Chilean post at Chacalluta, where again the driver will show you what to do. It's a further 15 minutes from Chacalluta to Arica's bus terminal. A Chilean driver is more likely to take you to any address in Arica.

Crossing by private vehicle Those leaving Peru by car must buy *relaciones de pasajeros* (official forms, US$0.45) from the kiosk at the border or from a bookshop; you will need four copies. At the border, return your tourist card to immigration (Migraciones), visit the PNP (police) office, return the vehicle permit to the SUNAT/Aduana office and finally depart through the checkpoints.

Listings South to Chile *map page 206.*

Tourist information

Moquegua

Dircetur
Ayacucho 1060, T053-462236.
Mon-Fri 0800-1630.
The regional tourist office.

Tacna

Dircetur
Blondell 50, p 2, T052-246944, www.
turismotacna.com. Mon-Fri 0730-1530.
Provides a city map and regional information.

Immigration
Av Circunvalación s/n, Urb El Triángulo,
T052-243231.

iPerú
San Martín 491, Plaza de Armas, T052-
425514. Mon-Sat 0830-1800, Sun 0830-1300,
iperutacna@promperu.gob.pe.
Also in the Arrivals hall at the airport
(usually open when flights are scheduled
to arrive), at the Terminal Terrestre
Internacional (Mon-Sat 0830-1500)
and at the border (Fri-Sat 0830-1600).

OGD Tur Tacna
Deústua 364, of 107, T052-242777.

Tourist police
Pasaje Calderón de la Barca 353, inside the
main police station, T052-414141 ext 245.

Where to stay

Moquegua
Most hotels do not serve breakfast.

$ Alameda
Junín 322, T053-463971.
Includes breakfast, large comfortable
rooms, welcoming.

$ Hostal Adrianella
Miguel Grau 239, T053-463469.
Hot water, safe, helpful, tourist information,
close to market and buses, bit faded.

$ Hostal Carrera
Jr Lima 320-A (no sign), T053-462113.
With or without bath, solar-powered hot
water (best in afternoon), laundry facilities
on roof, good value.

$ Hostal Plaza
Ayacucho 675, T053-461612.
Modern and comfortable, good value.

Tacna

$$$ Gran Hotel Tacna
Av Bolognesi 300, T052-424193,
www.granhoteltacna.com.
Disco, gardens, safe car park. The pool is
open to non-guests who make purchases
at the restaurant or bar. English spoken.

$$ Copacabana
Arias Aragüez 370, T052-421721,
www.copahotel.com.
Good rooms, also has a restaurant and pizzería.

$$ Dorado
Arias Aragüez 145, T052-415741,
www.doradohoteltacna.com.
Modern and comfortable,
good service, restaurant.

$$ El Mesón
H Unanue 175, T052-425841,
www.mesonhotel.com.
Central, modern, comfortable, safe.

$ Hostal Anturio
28 de Julio 194 y Zela, T052-244258.
Cafeteria downstairs, breakfast extra,
good value.

$ Hostal Bon Ami
2 de Mayo 445, T052-244847.
With or without bath, hot water best
in afternoon, simple, secure.

$ La Posada del Cacique
Arias Aragüez 300-4, T052-247424.
Antique style in an amazing building
constructed around a huge spiral staircase.

$ Roble 18 Residencial
H Unanue 245, T052-241414,
roble18@gmail.com.
1 block from Plaza de Armas. Hot water,
English, Italian, German spoken.

Restaurants

Moquegua

$ Moraly
Lima y Libertad. Mon-Sat 1000-2200, Sun
1000-1600.
The best place for meals. Breakfast, lunches,
menú US$1.75.

Tacna

$$ DaVinci
San Martín 596 y Arias Araguez, T052-744648.
Mon-Sat 1100-2300, bar Tue-Sat 2000-0200.
Pizza and other dishes, nice atmosphere.

$$ Il Pomodoro
Bolívar 524 y Apurimac. Closed Sun evening
and Mon lunchtime.
Upscale Italian serving set lunch on
weekdays, pricey à la carte in the evening,
attentive service.

$ Cusqueñita
Zela 747. Daily 1100-1600.
Excellent 4-course lunch, large portions, good
value, variety of choices. Recommended.

$ Fu-Lin
Arias Araguez 396 y 2 de Mayo.
Mon-Sat 0930-1600.
Vegetarian Chinese.

$ Koyuki
Bolívar 718. Closed Sun evening.
Generous set lunch daily, seafood and
à la carte in the evening. Several other
popular lunch places on the same block.

$ Un Limón
Av San Martín 843, T052-425182.
Ceviches and variety of seafood dishes.

Cafés

Café Zeit
Deústua 150, CafeZeit on Facebook.
German-owned coffee shop, cultural
events and live music as well as quality
coffee and cakes.

Verdi
Pasaje Vigil 57.
Café serving excellent *empanadas* and
sweets, also set lunch.

Festivals

Moquegua

25 Nov *Día de Santa Catalina*.
The anniversary of the founding
of the colonial city.

Transport

Moquegua

Bus All bus companies are on Av Ejército,
2 blocks north of the market at Jr Grau,
except **Ormeño** (Av La Paz casi Balta). To
Lima, US$30-42, 15 hrs, many companies
with executive and regular services. To
Tacna, 159 km, 2 hrs, US$6, hourly buses
with **Flores** (Av del Ejército y Andrés Aurelio
Cáceres). To **Arequipa**, 3½ hrs, US$7.50-12,
several buses daily. *Colectivos* for Tacna and
Arequipa leave when full from Av del Ejercito
y Andrés Aurelio Cáceres; they charge
almost double the bus fare – negotiate.
To **Desaguadero** and **Puno**, San Martín-
Nobleza, 4 a day, 6 hrs, US$12; *colectivos* to
Desaguadero, 4 hrs, US$20, with **Mily Tours**
(Av del Ejército 32-B, T053-464000).

Tip...

If you're travelling to **La Paz**, Bolivia,
the quickest and cheapest route is via
Moquegua and Desaguadero; it involves
one less border crossing than via Arica
and Tambo Colorado. There is a **Bolivian
Consulate** in Tacna (Avenida Bolognesi
175, Urb Pescaserolli, T052-245121,
Monday-Friday 0830-1630).

Tacna

Air The airport (T052-314503) is at Km 5
on the Panamericana Sur, on the way to the
border. To go from the airport directly to
Arica, call the bus terminal (T052-427007)
and ask a *colectivo* to pick you up on its way
to the border, US$7.50. Taxi from airport to
Tacna centre US$5-6.

To **Lima**, 1½ hrs; daily flights with **LATAM**
(Apurímac 101, esq Av Bolognesi, T01-213

Tip...

Bus passengers' luggage is checked at
Tomasiri, 35 km north of Tacna. Do not
carry anything on the bus for anyone else.
Passports may be checked at Camiara, a
police checkpoint some 60 km from Tacna.
There is also a post where any fruit will be
confiscated in an attempt to keep fruit fly
out of Peru.

8200) and **Peruvian Airlines** (Av Bolognesi
670, p2, T052-412699), also to **Arequipa**.

Bus There are 2 bus stations (T052-427007;
local tax US$0.50) on Hipólito Unánue, 1 km
from the plaza (*colectivo* US$0.35, taxi US$1
minimum). One terminal is for international
services (ie Arica), the other for domestic;
both are well organized, with baggage
stores. It is easy to make connections to the
border, Arequipa or Lima. To **Moquegua,**
2 hrs, US$6, and **Arequipa**, 6 hrs, frequent
buses with **Flores** (Av Saucini behind the
Terminal Nacional, T052-426691), **Trans
Moquegua Turismo** and **Cruz del Sur**. Ask at
the **Flores** office about buses along the Vía
Costanera to Ilo. To **Nazca**, 793 km, 12 hrs,
several buses daily, en route to Lima (fares
US$3 less than to Lima). Several companies
daily to **Lima**, 1239 km, 21-26 hrs, US$26-62
bus-cama with **Oltursa** or Civa; **Cruz del Sur**
(T052-425729) charges US$43.

Buses to **Desaguadero**, **Puno** and
Cuzco leave from Terminal Collasuyo
(Av Internacional, Barrio Altos de la Alianz,
T052-312538); taxi to centre US$1. **San
Martín–Nobleza** in early morning and at
night to **Desaguadero**, US$22, and **Puno**,
US$18, 8-10 hrs.

Train The station is at Av Albaracín y 2 de
Mayo. Following 5 years of interruption,
service along the cross-border line to
Arica was resumed in 2016 with 4 trains
running daily.

Lake
Titicaca

★ Straddling Peru's southern border with Bolivia are the sapphire-blue waters of mystical Lake Titicaca, a huge inland sea which is the highest navigable lake in the world. Its shores and islands are home to the Aymara and Quechua, who are among Peru's oldest peoples. Here you can wander through traditional villages where Spanish is a second language and where ancient myths and beliefs still hold true. Paved roads climb from the coastal deserts and oases to the high plateau in which sits Lake Titicaca (Arequipa-Yura-Santa Lucía-Juliaca-Puno; Moquegua-Desaguadero-Puno). The steep ascents lead to wide open views of pampas with agricultural communities, desolate mountains, small lakes and salt flats. It is a rapid change of altitude, so be prepared for some discomfort and breathlessness.

Best for
Boat trips ▪ Festivals ▪ Handicrafts ▪ Local customs ▪ Scenery

Located on the northwest shore of Lake Titicaca at 3855 m, Puno is capital of its region and Peru's folklore centre, with a vast array of handicrafts, festivals and costumes and a rich tradition of music and dance. The city has a noticeable vitality, helped by the fact that students make up a large proportion of the 100,000-strong population. Puno gets bitterly cold at night: from June to August the temperature at night can fall to -25°C, but is generally not below -5°C.

Sights

The **Cathedral** ① *daily 0730-1200, 1500-1800, Sat until 1900,* completed in 1657, has an impressive baroque exterior, but an austere interior. Across the street from the Cathedral is the **Balcony of the Conde de Lemos** ① *Deústua y Conde de Lemos, art gallery open Mon-Fri 0830-1230, 1330-1730,*

> **Tip...**
> The Bolivian consulate in Puno is at Jr Aymaraes G-5, Urbanización APROVI, T051-205-5400, Monday-Friday 0800-1800.

where Peru's Viceroy stayed when he first arrived in the city. The **Museo Carlos Dreyer** ① *Conde de Lemos 289, Mon-Sat 0900-1900, US$5.40 includes 45-min guided tour,* has eight halls with archaeological and historical artefacts from pre-Inca to republican times.

The heart of the tourist scene is along Jirón Lima, between the Plaza de Armas and Plaza Pino, where it becomes a pedestrian mall. Many restaurants, cafés, bars, several hotels and other services are concentrated here and in the nearby streets.

A short walk up Independencia leads to the **Arco Deústua**, a monument honouring those killed in the battles of Junín and Ayacucho. Nearby is a *mirador* giving fine views over the town, the port and the lake beyond. The walk from Jr Cornejo following the Stations of the Cross up a nearby hill, with fine views of Lake Titicaca, has been recommended, but be careful and don't go alone; the same applies to any of the hills around Puno, including Huajsapata and Kuntur Wasi; the latter is patrolled 0800-1200 and 1600-1800.

From the Plaza de Armas Avenida Titicaca leads 12 blocks east to the lakeshore and port. From its intersection with Avenida Costanera towards the pier, one side of the road is lined with the kiosks of the **Artesanos Unificados de Puno**, selling crafts. Closer to the port are food kiosks. On the opposite side of the road is a shallow lake where you can hire **pedal boats** ① *US$2.15 for up to 3 passengers for 20 mins.* At the pier are the ticket counters for transport to the islands. The **Malecón Bahía de los Incas**, a lovely promenade along the waterfront, extends to the north and south; it has a sundial and is a pleasant place for a stroll and for birdwatching.

The **Yavari** ① *Av Sesquicentenario 610, Huaje, T051-369329, www.yavari.org, daily 0900-1700, free but donations welcome,* the oldest ship on Lake Titicaca, is berthed near the entrance to the **Sonesta Posada del Inca** hotel; you have to go through the hotel to get to it. Alternatively, a boat from the port costs US$2 return, with wait. The ship was built in England in 1862 and was shipped in kit form to Arica, then by rail to Tacna and by mule to Lake Titicaca, a journey that took six years. The *Yavari* was finally launched on Christmas Day 1870. Berthed near the Yavari, is the *MS Ollanta*, which was built in Hull (UK) and sailed the lake from 1926 to the 1970s. Another old ship moored near the port is the **MN Coya**, built in Scotland and launched on the lake in 1892.

☆Sillustani

32 km from Puno off the road to Juliaca. Daily 0830-1730. US$3.60. Tours from Puno, US$15-18, last about 3-4 hrs, and usually stop at a Colla house on the way, to see local products.

Near Puno are the chullpas (pre-Columbian funeral towers) of Sillustani in a beautiful setting on a peninsula in Lake Umayo. The scenery is barren, but impressive. John Hemming writes: "Most of the towers date from the period of Inca occupation in the 15th century, but they are burial towers of the Aymara-speaking Colla tribe. The engineering involved in their construction is more complex than anything the Incas built – it is defeating archaeologists' attempts to rebuild the tallest 'lizard' chullpa."

Artefacts found in the tombs can be seen at the Museo Carlos Dreyer in Puno (see above). Handicraft sellers wait at the exit. There is a small community at the foot of the promontory.

Tip...
Photography at Sillustani is best in the afternoon light, though this is when the wind is strongest.

Puno

Where to stay
1 Casa Andina Private Collection Puno *A4*
2 Casa Andina Tikarani *B2*
3 Casona Colón Inn *Puno centre*
4 Conde de Lemos *C2*
5 El Buho *Puno centre*
6 Hacienda Plaza de Armas *C2*
7 Hacienda Puno *Puno centre*
8 Hostal Imperial & Los Uros *B3*
9 Hostal Italia *B2*
10 Hostal Los Pinos *B2*
11 Hostal Margarita *B2*
12 Hostal Pukara *Puno centre*
13 Inka's Rest *B3*
14 Intiqa *B2*
15 Libertador Lago Titicaca *A4*
16 Plaza Mayor *Puno centre*
17 Posada Don Giorgio *B2*
18 Posada Luna Azul *C2*
19 Sonesta Posadas del Inca *A4*
20 Tayka & Vylena Hostels *C1*
21 Tierra Viva Puno Plaza *Puno centre*

Restaurants
1 Cafetería Mercedes *Puno centre*
2 Casa del Corregidor *C2*
3 Chifa Nan Hua *B2*
4 IncAbar *Puno centre*
5 La Casona *Puno centre*
6 La Cayma *Puno centre*
7 La Estancia *Puno centre*
8 La Hostería *Puno Centre*
9 Loving Hut *C3*
10 Machupizza *Puno centre*
11 Mojsa *C2*

There are more chullpas from the Lupaca and Colla kingdoms (AD 1100-1450) in **Cutimbo** ① *turn-off at Km 17 on the Puno–Moquegua road, daily 0830-1730, US$3*, where rock art and Inca ruins are also to be found.

☆Península de Capachica

The Península de Capachica encloses the northern side of the Bahía de Puno and is a great introduction to Lake Titicaca. The scenery is very pretty, with sandy beaches, pre-Inca terracing, trees and flowers. It is also good for hiking and mountain biking, and sailing boats can be hired. Some visitors consider the view of the sunset from Capachica's Auki Carus hill to be even better than that from Taquile (see page 222). At the eastern end of the peninsula, the pretty farming villages of **Llachón**, **Santa María** and **Ccotos** have become a focus of community-based tourism. There are currently six organizations, each with a dozen or more families and links to different tour operators in Puno, Cuzco or abroad. Visitors share in local activities and 70% of all produce served is from the residents' farms. Throughout the peninsula the dress of the local women is very colourful, with four-cornered hats called *monteras*, matching vests and colourful *polleras*. Off the east coast of the peninsula is the island of **Ticonata**, whose community tourism association offers accommodation in round houses and various activities. It's a short boat ride from Ccotos, or from Amantaní (see page 222); motorboats from Puno take 3½ hours.

Puno centre

☆Western shore: Chucuito to the border

Anybody interested in religious architecture should visit the villages along the western shore of Lake Titicaca. An Inca sundial can be seen near the village of **Chucuito** ① *19 km from Puno, vans from Jr La Oroya 195 y Banchero Rossi, US$0.55, 25 mins*, which has houses with carved stone doorways and two interesting colonial churches: 16th-century Santo Domingo, the first in the region, and 17th-century La Asunción. Also here is the Inca Uyo, a fertility plaza filled with stone phalli. A lookout affords good views of the lake. Further south is the larger town of **Acora** (34 km), which provides access to a lovely peninsula with luxury hotels and the Charcas beaches. The important commercial centre of **Ilave** is 55 km from Puno.

Juli ① *80 km, colectivo from Puno, US$1.60; returns from outside Juli market at Ilave 349*, has some fine examples of

12 Pizzería/Trattoria El Buho *Puno centre*
13 Ricos Café *C2, centre*
14 Tradiciones del Lago *Puno centre*
15 Tulipan's *Puno centre*
16 Ukukus *Puno centre*

Bars & clubs 🎵
17 Positive *Puno centre*

religious architecture. **San Pedro** on the plaza is the only functioning **church** ① *Mon, Wed-Sat 0800-1700, Tue for Mass only at 0700, Sun for Mass at 0730, 1100 and 1800, free, donations appreciated*. It contains a series of paintings of the saints, with the Via Crucis scenes in the same frame, and gilt side altars above which some of the arches have baroque designs. **San Juan Letrán** and **La Asunción** ① *both daily 0830-1730, US$3*, are now museums containing paintings by artists from the Cuzco School of Art and from Italy. San Juan has two sets of 17th-century paintings of the lives of St John the Baptist and St Teresa, contained in sumptuous gilded frames, as well as intricate *mestizo* carving in pink stone. The nave at La Asunción is empty, but its walls are lined with unlabelled paintings. The original murals on the walls of the transept can be seen. Its fine bell tower was damaged by earthquake or lightning. Outside is an archway and atrium which date from the early 17th century. Needlework, other weavings, handicrafts and antiques are offered for sale in town.

A further 20 km along the lake, atop a hill, is **Pomata** ① *bus from Juli US$0.90, US$3 from Puno*, whose red sandstone church of **Santiago Apóstol** ① *daily 0800-1200, 1300-1800, US$0.70 (if guardian is not there, leave money on table)*, has a striking exterior and beautiful interior, with superb carving and paintings.

Past Pomata, the road south along the lake divides; one branch continues straight towards the Bolivian border at Desaguadero, via **Zepita**, where the 18th-century Dominican church is worth a visit. **Desaguadero** is a bleak place with simple restaurants and accommodation. Friday is the main market day, when the town is packed. There is a smaller market on Tuesday but at other times it is deserted.

The other branch of the road from Pomata follows the lakeshore to the border crossing to **Bolivia** at Kasani near **Yunguyo**. Vans depart from Yunguyo to Punta Hermosa, where you can catch a boat to Anapia in Lago Menor. There are three different routes across the border from Puno. Remember that Peruvian time is one hour behind Bolivian time and that US citizens need a visa for Bolivia. These can be obtained at the Yunguyo border crossing or in advance from the Bolivian consulate in Puno, see Tip, page 211; consular visas take about 48 hours. For the third border crossing, see page 226.

Listings Puno and around *map page 212.*

Tourist information

Useful websites include www.munipuno. gob.pe (the municipal site) and www. titicaca-peru.com (in Spanish and French).

Dircetur
Ayacucho 684, T051-364976, dircetur@dirceturpuno.gob.pe.
Also has a desk at the Terminal Terrestre.

Indecopi
Jr Ancash 146, T051-363667.
Consumer protection bureau.

iPerú
Jr Lima y Deústua, near Plaza de Armas, T051-365088, iperupuno@promperu.gob.pe.

Mon-Sat 0900-1800, Sun 0900-1300.
Helpful English- and French-speaking staff, good information and maps.

Tourist police
Jr Deústua 588, T051-352303. 24 hrs.
Report any scams, such as unscrupulous price changes, and beware touts.

Where to stay

There are over 200 places to stay including a number of luxury hotels in and around the city. Prices vary according to season. Many touts try to persuade tourists to go to a hotel not of their own choosing. Be firm.

$$$$ Casa Andina Private Collection Puno
Av Sesquicentenario 1970, T051-363992, www.casa-andina.com.
This recommended chain's luxury lakeshore property.

$$$$ Libertador Lago Titicaca
on Isla Esteves linked by a causeway 5 km northeast of Puno (taxi US$3), T051-367780, www.libertador.com.pe.
Modern hotel with every facility, built on a Tiahuanaco-period site, spacious, good views, bar, restaurant, disco, good service, parking.

$$$$ Sonesta Posadas del Inca
Av Sesquicentenario 610, Huaje, 5 km from Puno on the lakeshore, T051-364111, www.sonesta.com/laketiticaca/.
62 rooms with heating, facilities for the disabled, local textile decorations, good views, **Inkafé** restaurant has an Andean menu, folklore shows.

$$$ Hacienda Plaza de Armas
Jr Puno 419, T051-367340, www.hhp.com.pe.
Tastefully decorated modern hotel overlooking the Plaza de Armas, small comfortable rooms, all with bathtub or jacuzzi, heater, safety box, restaurant.

$$$ Hacienda Puno
Jr Deústua 297, T051-356109, www.hhp.com.pe.
Refurbished colonial house, with buffet breakfast, rooms and suites with good bathrooms, restaurant with local specialities, comfortable.

$$$ Intiqa
Jr Tarapacá 272, T051-366900, www.intiqahotel.com.
Built around a sunny courtyard. Stylish, rooms have heaters, dinner available, professional staff.

$$$ Plaza Mayor
Deústua 342, T051-368728, www.plazamayorhotel.com.

Comfortable, well-appointed, good big beds, buffet breakfast, heating, restaurant.

$$$ Tierra Viva Puno Plaza
Jr Grau 270, 1 block from plaza, T051-368005, www.tierravivahoteles.com.
Regional decor, heating, all rooms non-smoking, central, business centre.

$$$-$$ Casona Colón Inn
Tacna 290, T051-351432, www.coloninn.com.
Colonial style, good rooms, some with bathtub, heating, good service. **Le Bistrot** serves international and Peruvian cuisine.

$$ Casa Andina Tikarani
Independencia 185, T051-367803, www.casa-andina.com.
A central option. Heating, non-smoking rooms, business centre.

$$ Conde de Lemos
Jr Puno 681, T051-369898, www.condelemosinn.com.
Convenient, comfy suites and rooms with bathtubs, heating, elevator, 1 room has wheelchair access, restaurant.

$$ El Buho
Lambayeque 142, T051-366122, www.hotelbuho.com.
Nice carpeted rooms, most with bathtubs, heating, discount for Footprint book owners, travel agency for trips and flights, parking extra.

$$ Hostal Imperial
Teodoro Valcarcel 145, T051-352386, www.hostalimperial.com.
Basic but big rooms, good hot showers, safety box, helpful, stores luggage, comfortable.

$$ Hostal Italia
Teodoro Valcarcel 122, T051-367706, www.hotelitaliaperu.com.
2 blocks from the train station. Cheaper in low season, good restaurant, small rooms, staff helpful.

$$ Hostal Pukara
Jr Libertad 328, T051-368448, www.pukaradeltitikaka.com.

Excellent, English spoken, helpful service, heating, central, quiet, free coca to drink in evening, American breakfast included, dining room on top floor, lots of stairs.

$$ Posada Don Giorgio
Tarapacá 238, T051-363648, Facebook: Posada-Don-Giorgio-Puno-199808310121923.
Comfortable large rooms, nicely decorated, traditional architecture, heater extra.

$$ Posada Luna Azul
Cajamarca 242, T051-364851, www.posadalunaazul.com.
Comfortable carpeted rooms, heating, parking, luggage storage.

$$ pp MN Yavari
Muelle del Hotel Sonesta Posadas del Inca, T051-369329 (in Lima T01-255 7268), reservasyavari@gmail.com.
B&B is available on board this historic ship in 3 twin bunk rooms with shared bath. Dinner served on request downstairs in the Victorian saloon.

$ Hostal Los Pinos
Tarapacá 182, T051-367398, hostalpinos@hotmail.com.
Family-run, helpful, breakfast available, cold rooms, heater on request, reliable hot water, laundry facilities, small book exchange, tours organized, good value.

$ Hostal Margarita
Jr Tarapacá 130, T051-352820.
Large building, family atmosphere, cold rooms, private or shared bath, heaters on request, helpful owner, tours can be arranged.

$ Hostal Vylena
Jr Ayacucho 503, T051-351292, hostalvylena20@hotmail.com.
Functional rooms, hot water during limited hours, breakfast available, luggage storage, economical.

$ Inka's Rest
Pasaje San Carlos 158, T051-368720.
Several sitting areas, heating, double or twin rooms with private or shared bath

and US$9 pp in dorm, cooking and laundry facilities, a place to meet other travellers, reserve ahead.

$ Los Uros
Teodoro Valcarcel 135, T051-352141.
Private or shared bath, breakfast available, quiet at back, small charge to leave luggage, laundry, heating costs extra.

$ Tayka Hostel
Jr Ayacucho 515, T051-351427, www.taykahostel.com.
Simple lodging, private rooms include breakfast, shared rooms (US$9 pp) do not, electric showers, luggage storage.

Península Capachica
Families offer accommodation on a rotational basis and, as the community presidents change each year, the standard of facilities changes from year-to-year and from family to family. To be assigned to a family, go to the **Centro Artesanal** in Llachón. All hosts can arrange boat transport to Amantaní. Among those who offer lodging ($ per bed, meals extra) are: **Tomás Cahui Coila** (Centro Turístico Santa María Llachón, T951-691501); **Primo Flores** (**Villa Santa María Tours**, T951-821392, primopuno@hotmail.com); **Valentín Quispe** (**Asociación de Turismo Solidario Llachón,** T951-821392, llachon@yahoo.com). But do recognize that there are other families who accept guests.

Western shore: Chucuito to the border

$$$$ Castillo del Titicaca
Playa de Charcas, 45 min from Puno, T950-308000, www.castillo.titicaca-peru.com.
Exclusive 5-room hotel on a rocky promontory overlooking the lake and surrounded by extensive terraced gardens. Luxurious apartments and rooms, 1 inside a castle, restaurant with lake views, full board. Belgian manager Christian Nonis is known for his work on behalf of the people of Taquile.

$$$$ Titilaka Lodge
Comunidad de Huencalla s/n, on a private peninsula near Chucuito, T01-700 5111 (Lima), www.titilaka.com.
Luxury boutique hotel in Relais et Châteaux group offering all-inclusive packages in an exclusive environment on the edge of the lake. Plenty of activities available on land and on the water; works with local Uros communities.

$$$ Taypikala
Sandia s/n, Chucuito and at Panamericana Sur Km 18, T051-792266, www.taypikala.com.
2 upmarket hotels near the lakeshore, suites with jacuzzi, fridge and fireplace, and heated rooms with bathtub and safety box; restaurant, pool, spa, water sports, gym, meditation and yoga areas.

$$ Las Cabañas
Jr Tarapacá 538, Chucuito, T951-751196, www.chucuito.com.
Rooms and ample cottages in nice grounds, breakfast included, other meals available. Owned by Sr Juan Palao, a knowledgeable local historian, busy at weekends, events held here; will collect you from Puno if you phone in advance.

$ Hostal Isabel
San Francisco 110, near Plaza de Armas, Yunguyo, T951-794228.
With or without bath, nice rooms and courtyard, electric shower, parking, friendly. A few other cheap places to stay.

$ Sra Nely Durán Saraza
Chucuíto Occopampa, T951-586240.
2 nice rooms, 1 with lake view, shared bath, breakfast and dinner available, very welcoming and interesting.

Restaurants

Tourist restaurants, all offering alpaca, trout, *cuy* and international dishes, are clustered along Jr Lima.

$$$-$$ La Casona
Lima 423, p2, T051-351108, www.lacasona-restaurant.com. Daily 1200-2130.
Upmarket tourist restaurant serving a wide choice of international dishes.

$$$-$$ Mojsa
Lima 635 p 2, Plaza de Armas, www.mojsarestaurant.com.
Good international and *Novo Andino* dishes, also has an arts and crafts shop.

$$$-$$ Tradiciones del Lago
Lima 418, T051-368140, www.tradiciones delago.com. Daily 1000-2100.
Popular tourist restaurant serving a great variety of à la carte dishes.

$$ IncAbar
Lima 348, T051-368031. Open for breakfast, lunch and dinner.
Interesting dishes in creative sauces, fish, pastas, curries, café and couch bar, nice decor.

$$ La Estancia
Libertad 137. Daily 1100-2200.
Grilled meat and à la carte Peruvian dishes, large portions, very popular.

$$ La Hostería
Lima 501, T051-365406.
Good set meal and à la carte dishes including local fare like alpaca and *cuy*, pizza, also breakfast.

$$ Tulipan's
Lima 394. Mon-Sat 1100-2100, Sun 1630-2030.
Sandwiches, juices and a lunchtime menu are its staples. One of the few places in Puno with outdoor seating in a pleasant colonial courtyard, a good option for lunch.

$$-$ Chifa Nan Hua
Arequipa 378. Daily 1200-2200.
Tasty Chinese, big portions.

$$-$ La Cayma
Libertad 216, T051-634226. Open 1200-2200, closed Sat.
Good pizza, Peruvian and international dishes, tasty set lunch, pleasant atmosphere, good service.

$$-$ Loving Hut
Pje Choquehuanca 188. Mon-Sat 1130-1530.

Daily choice of very tasty, creative vegan dishes and salad bar.

$$-$ Machupizza
Tacna 279 and at Arequipa 409, T951-390652. Mon-Sat 1800-2200.
Tasty pizza and other Italian dishes, good value, popular with locals.

$$-$ Pizzería/Trattoria El Buho
Lima 349 and at Jr Libertad 386, T051-356223. Open 1800 onwards.
Excellent pizza, lively atmosphere.

$ Ukukus
Libertad 216 and Pje Grau 172, T051-367373/369504.
Good combination of Andean and *Novo Andino* cuisine as well as pizzas and some Chinese *chifa* style.

Cafés

Cafetería Mercedes
Jr Arequipa 144.
Good menú, bread, cakes, snacks, juices.

Casa del Corregidor
Deústua 576, aptdo 2, T051-365603.
In restored 17th-century building, sandwiches, good snacks, coffee, good music, great atmosphere, nice surroundings with patio. Also has a Fairtrade store offering products directly from the producers.

Ricos Café
Jr Arequipa 332 and Jr Moquegua 334. Mon-Sat 0600-2130, Sun 1500-2130.
Café and bakery, great cakes, excellent coffees, juices and pastries, breakfasts and other dishes.

Bars and clubs

Dómino
Libertad 443.
Happy hour Mon-Thu 2000-2130.
"Megadisco", good.

Pachas
Lima 370.
Innovative bar.

Platinum
Libertad 521.
Club, popular with local youth.

Positive
Lima 382.
Drinks, large-screen TV, modern music, occasional heavy metal groups.

Festivals

1st 2 weeks in Feb Fiesta de la Virgen de la Candelaria. On the 1st Sun, some 100 communities compete in an indigenous dance contest. The dances include *llameritos*, *wifala* and *ayarachis*. The following Sun and Mon colourfully attired dancers participate in a contest of *mestizo* folk dances such as *diablada*, *morenada*, *llamerada*, *caporales* and *saya*. A large procession takes place on 2 Feb, the main day. The nighttime festivities on the streets are better than the official functions in the stadium. The dates of the festival until 2020 are posted on www.titicaca-peru.com.
Mar/Apr Good Fri. A candlelit procession through darkened streets.
3 May Festividad de las Cruces. Celebrated with masses, a procession and the Alasitas festival of miniatures.
29 Jun Colourful festival of **San Pedro**, with a procession at Zepita (see page 214).
4-5 Nov Pageant dedicated to the founding of Puno and the emergence of Manco Cápac and Mama Ocllo from the waters of Lake Titicaca.

Shopping

Puno is the best place in Peru to buy alpaca wool articles; bargaining is appropriate. There are numerous outlets selling alpaca garments, paintings and other handicrafts in the centre. You will be hassled to buy along Jr Lima, so keep your wits about you.

Markets
Along the avenue leading to the port is the large **Mercado Artesanal Asociación de Artesanos Unificados** (daily 0900-1800).

Closer to the centre are **Mercado Coriwasi** (Ugarte 150, daily 0800-2100) and **Central Integral de Artesanos del Perú** (**CIAP**; Jr Deústua 792, Mon-Sat 0900-1900). The **Mercado Central**, in the blocks bound by Arbulú, Arequipa, Oquendo and Tacna, has all kinds of food, including good cheeses as well as a few crafts. Beware pickpockets. **Súper Mico** (Jr Arbulú 119, opposite the market, daily 0800-2100) has a good selection of dried fruits, nuts and cereals.

What to do

To avoid paying above the odds for a tour by a *jalagringo*, ask to their ID card. Only use agencies with named premises, compare prices and only hand over money at the office, never on the street or in a hotel.

Agencies organize trips to the Uros floating islands (see page 221, ½ day from US$5.50), the islands of Taquile (full day including Uros from US$11, US$21 on a fast boat) and Amantaní (2 days, see page 222), as well as to Sillustani (½ day from US$9) and other places. The standard tour is 2 days, 1 night, visiting the Uros, staying in either Taquile or Amantaní and then visiting the other island the next day (from US$27 pp). Choose an agency that allows you to pay direct for your lodging so you know that the family is benefiting. Make sure that you settle all details before embarking on the tour. Some agencies pool tourists. We have received good reports on the following:

All Ways Travel, *Casa del Corregidor, Deústua 576, p 2, T051-353979, and at Tacna 287, of 106, T051-355552, www.titicacaperu.com*. Good quality tours, very helpful, kind and reliable, speak German, French, English and Italian, towards the upper end of the price range. Among their tours is a unique cultural tour to the islands of Anapia and Yuspique in Lake Wiñaymarka, beyond the straits of Tiquina.
CEDESOS, *Centro para el Desarrollo Sostenible (Centre for Sustainable Development), Jr Moquegua 348 Int p 3, T051-367915, www.cedesos.org*. A non-profit NGO which offers

interesting tours of Capachica peninsula (see page 213) with overnight stops in family homes, going to the less visited islands where there are few tourists.
Cusi Expeditions, *Jr T Varcarcel 155, T051-369072, reservascusi@terra.com.pe*. Experienced operator that owns most of the standard tour boats to the islands. You will very likely end up on a Cusi tour so it's best to buy from them directly to get the best price and the most accurate information.
Edgar Adventures, *Lima 328, T051-353444, www.edgaradventures.com*. English, German and French spoken, very helpful and knowledgeable, work with organized groups. Constantly exploring new areas, lots of off-the-beaten-track tours, eg kayaking tour of Llachón. Community-minded, promote responsible tourism. Consistently recommended.
Kontiki Tours, *Jr Melgar 188, T051-353473, www.kontikiperu.com*. Large receptive tour agency specializing in special interest excursions.
Nayra Travel, *Lima 419, of 105, T051-337934, www.nayratravel.com*. Small agency run by Lilian Cotrado and her helpful staff, traditional local tours and a variety of options in Llachón. Can organize off-the-beaten track excursions for a minimum of 2 people. Recommended.
Pirámide Tours, *Jr Rosendo Huirse 130, T051-366107, www.titikakalake.com*. Sells out of the ordinary and classic tours, flexible, personalized service, modern fast launches, very helpful, works only via internet, overseas clients.
Titikaka Explorers, *Jr Puno 633 of 207, T051-368903, www.titikaka-explorer.com*. Good service, helpful, works with organized groups.

Transport

Air The regional airport is in Juliaca (see Transport page 228). Airport transfers from/to **Puno** US$5.60 pp with **Camtur** (Jr Tacna 336, of 104, T951-967652) and **Rossy Tours** (Jr Tacna 308, T051-366709); many hotels also offer an airport transfer. Taxi from Puno to the airport, about US$25-28. Alternatively, take regular public transport to Juliaca (see below) and then a taxi to the airport from there, but allow extra time for the minibuses to drive around Puno picking up passengers before leaving.

Boat Boats to the islands (see page 224) leave from the terminal at the harbour; *trici-taxi* from centre, US$1. There are also boats to Llachón, Sat 1000, US$1.80, 3½ hrs.

To Bolivia Crillon Tours, Camacho 1223, La Paz, T+591 2-233 7533, www.titicaca.com, run luxury services by bus and hydrofoil between La Paz and Puno, with onward tours to Cuzco and Machu Picchu. Similar services, by catamaran, are run by **Transturin** (Jr Puno 633, of 3, Puno, www.transturin.com).

Bus Local Small buses and vans for Juliaca, Ilave and towns on the lakeshore as far as Desaguadero and Yunguyo, leave from the **Terminal Zonal** (Av Costanera 451; taxi to the centre, US$1.80). To **Juliaca**, 44 km, 1 hr, vans US$1.25, also from **Terminal Fátima** (Jr Ricardo Palma 225); they all go to the *Salida a Cuzco*, outside the centre of Juliaca; for long-distance bus services to Juliaca, see below. To **Yunguyo**, hourly 0600-1900, 2½ hrs, US$2.90; if there are enough passengers, they may continue to the border at Kasani, US$3.60. To **Desaguadero**, hourly vans 0600-1900, 2½ hrs, US$3.60 (taxi US$33).

Long distance All long-distance buses leave from the **Terminal Terrestre** (1 de Mayo 703 y Victoria, by the lake, T051-364733). It has a tourist office. Platform tax, US$0.35. Taxi to the centre, US$1.80.

To **Juliaca**, 44 km, 1 hr, US$1 (see also Local bus, above); buses go to their own terminals in Juliaca. To **Puerto Maldonado**, several daily from Juliaca (see below). To **Arequipa**, 5-6 hrs via Juliaca, 297 km,

US$7-11, hourly with **Julsa**, 4 daily with **Flores**, at 1500 with **Cruz del Sur** (city office at Jr Lima 394, T051-368524, US$21-27), several others. **Tourist service** with 3 stops (see Arequipa transport, page 194 for details), with **4M Express**, www.4m-express.com, from the Terminal Terrestre at 0600, 6 hrs, US$27-35 includes bilingual guiding, snack and hotel dropoff in Arequipa. The same company offers service with 3 stops direct to **Chivay** on the **Colca Canyon** (see Transport, page 200), without going to Arequipa, from the Terminal Terrestre at 0600, US$50, 7 hrs. To **Moquegua**, 5 hrs, US$9-18, and **Tacna**, 7 hrs, US$11-18. To **Lima**, 1011 km, 21-24 hrs, US$36-57, all buses go through Arequipa, sometimes with a change of bus (see Arequipa Transport, page 194).

To **Cuzco**, 388 km, 6-7 hrs, there are 3 levels of service, all via Juliaca: Regular, stopping in Juliaca, US$7-12; Direct, US$15-27, from Terminal Terrestre with **Tour Perú** (city office at Jr Tacna 285, www.tourperu.com.pe) at 0800 and 2200, with **Cruz del Sur** at 2200 and with **Transzela** (www.transzela.com.pe) at 0815 and 2200; Tourist service with 5 stops (Pucará, La Raya, Sicuani for lunch, Raqchi and Andahuaylillas), US$45-50 (includes lunch, may or may not include entry tickets), 10 hrs. Several companies offer the tourist service; all depart from the Terminal Terrestre (except Turismo Mer): **Inka Express** (Terminal Terrestre and Jr Tacna 346, T051-365654), leaves 0700; **Turismo Mer** (Jr Tacna 336, T051-367223, www.turismomer.com) leaves from private terminal at Av Costanera 430, past the Terminal Zonal, at 0730; **Wonder Perú** (Terminal Terrestre and Jr Tacna 344, T051-353388) leaves 0715. In high season, reserve 2 days ahead.

To **Bolivia** (see page 214) To **Copacabana** (via **Kasani border**), US$5.40-7, 3½ hrs, departures at 0700 or 0730 and 1430; continuing to **La Paz**, US$10-12.50 (from Puno), 10 hrs (including border and lunch stops); most services involve transferring to a Bolivian company in Copacabana. All companies have offices at the Terminal

Tip...
Try to travel between Puno and Cuzco by day, for safety as well as for the views.

Terrestre from where they leave; some also have offices in the centre; some provide hotel pick-up. The better companies include: **Tour Peru** (Jr Tacna 285, of 103, T951-604189, www.tourperu.com.pe); **Panamericano** (Jr Tacna 245, T051-354001); **Huayruro Express** (Jr Arequipa 624, T051-366009), and **Titicaca** (Jr Tacna 285, of 104, T051-363830, www. titicacabolivia.com), which also has a 0600 departure. **Litoral**, at the Terminal Terrestre, is cheaper, but thefts have been reported on its night buses. To **La Paz**, direct via Desaguadero with **Tour Peru** at 0700, US$16, 5 hrs.

Taxi 3-wheel trici-taxis cost about US$0.25 per km and are the best way to get around town.

Train The train station is 3 blocks from Pl Pino. The railway runs from Puno to Juliaca (44 km), where it divides, to Cuzco (381 km) and Arequipa (279 km; no passenger service). *Andean Explorer* (La Torre 224, T051-369179, www.perurail.com, Mon-Fri 0700-1200, 1500-1800, Sat 0700-1500) runs services from Puno to **Cuzco,** US$169, or from Cuzco to Puno, US$289; both US$5 less in low season. Departures Mon, Wed, Fri (Apr-Oct) and Sat at 0800, arriving in Cuzco at about 1800; try to sit on the right-hand side for the views. The train stops at La Raya. In high season buy tickets several days in advance; passport required.

Península Capachica

Boat There is only 1 weekly public boat between Puno and Llachón, departing Puno Fri 0900, returning to Llachón Sat 1000, US$1.80 each way, 3½ hrs. The daily 0800 boat from Puno to Amantaní may drop you off at Colata (at the tip of the peninsula), a 1-hr walk from Llachón; confirm details in advance. Returning to Puno, you can try to flag down the boat from Amantaní which passes Colata between 0830 and 0930. In Santa María (Llachón), boats can be hired for trips to **Amantaní** (US$29 return, 40 mins) and **Taquile** (US$32 return, 50 mins), minimum 10 passengers. If there is demand, passenger service costs US$1.80 pp, one way.

Road Vans run daily 0700-1600 from Av Costanera y Jr Lampa in Puno to **Capachica**, 1½ hrs, US$1.45, where you get another van to **Llachón**; these leave when full, 30 mins, US$1; by mototaxi costs US$5.40, by taxi US$7.

Western shore
Minibuses to **Puno** depart from Jr Cusco esq Arica, 1 block from Plaza 2 de Mayo, in Yunguyo, hourly 0600-1900, 2½ hrs, US$2.90. Don't take a taxi from Yunguyo to Puno without checking its reliability first; the driver may pick up an accomplice to rob passengers.

The islands

witness traditional life on the lake when the tour boats go home

The Uros
US$3 to land, 5 km northeast of Puno.

Of the estimated 80 Uros or 'floating islands' in Puno Bay, only about 15 are regularly visited by tourists. There are two kinds of Uros people; those close to the city of Puno and easily accessible to tourism, and those on islands that remain relatively isolated. On the more far-flung islands, reached via narrow channels through the reed beds, the Uros do not like to be photographed and continue to lead relatively traditional lives outside the monetary economy. They hunt and fish and depend on trade with the mainland for other essentials. They also live off the lake's plants, the

Tip...
The Uros people cannot live from tourism alone, so it is better to buy their handicrafts or pay for services rather than just to tip them.

most important of which are the reeds they use for their boats, houses and the very foundations of their islands.

Visitors to the floating islands will encounter more Uros women than men. These women wait every day for the tour boats to sell their handicrafts, while most of the men are out on the lake, hunting and fishing, although you may see some men building or repairing boats or nets. They glean extra income from tourists offering overnight accommodation in reed houses, selling meals and providing Uro guides for two-hour tours. Organized tour parties are usually given a boat-building demonstration and the chance to take a short trip in a reed boat. Some islanders will also greet boatloads of tourists with a song and will pose for photos. The islanders, who are very friendly, appreciate gifts of pens, paper, and other items for their two schools. This form of tourism on the Uros Islands is now well-established and, whether it has done irreparable harm or will ultimately prove beneficial, it takes place in superb surroundings. Take drinking water as there is none on the islands.

Taquile
US$3 to land, 37 km east of Puno. Contact Munay Taquile, the island's community-based travel agency, Titicaca 508, Puno, T051-351448, www.titicaca-taquile.com.

Isla Taquile is just 1 km wide but 6-7 km long. It has numerous pre-Inca and Inca ruins, and Inca terracing. The sunset from the highest point of the island (3950 m) is beautiful. Full-day tours usually include a stop in Taquile along with Uros, and two-day tours to Amantaní also stop here either on the way there or back. This means there are lots of people on the island around midday. For a more authentic experience, get a tour that stays overnight in Taquile, or go independently to have time to explore the island's six districts or *suyos* and to observe the daily flurry of activity around the boatloads of tourists: demonstrations of traditional dress and weaving techniques, the preparation of trout to feed the hordes. When the boats leave, the island breathes a gentle sigh and people slowly return to their more traditional activities.

On Sunday, people from all the districts gather for a meeting in the main plaza after Quechua mass. There is an (unmarked) **museum of traditional costumes** on the plaza and a co-operative shop that sells exceptional woollen goods; they are not cheap, but of very fine quality. Each week different families sell their products. Other shops on the plaza sell postcards, water and dry goods. If you are staying over, you are advised to bring some food with you, particularly fruit, bread and vegetables, as well as water, plenty of small-value notes, candles, a torch, toilet paper and a sleeping bag. Take precautions against sunburn and take warm clothes for the cold nights.

☆Amantaní
US$3 to land, 44 km northeast of Puno.

Another island worth visiting is Amantaní. It is very beautiful, peaceful and arguably less spoiled and friendlier than Taquile. There are three docks; the one on the northwest shore is closest to Pueblo de Amantaní, the main village. There are seven other villages on the island and ruins on both of its peaks, **Pacha Tata** (4115 m) and **Pacha Mama** (4130 m), from which there are excellent views. There are also temples. On the northwest shore, 30 minutes from the Pueblo, is the **Inkatiana,** a throne carved out of stone, eroded from flooding. The residents make

> **Tip...**
> There are four docks at the island, so if you have trouble walking up many steps at high altitude, ask to be taken to a landing stage which requires less climbing.

beautiful textiles and sell them quite cheaply at the Cooperativa de Artesanos. They also make basketwork and stoneware. The people are Quechua speakers, but understand Spanish. Islanders arrange dances for tour groups for which visitors are invited to dress up in local clothes and join in. Small shops sell water and snacks.

Listings The islands

Where to stay

The iPerú office in Puno has a list of families offering accommodation in their homes.

The Uros
Accommodation costs from US$14 pp with simple meals extra or US$60 pp full board including tour. **René Coyla Coila** (T951-743533), is an official tour guide who can advise on lodgings. Some families you can contact are: **Elsa Coila Coila** (Isla Aruma Uros, T951-607147); **Cristina Suaña** (Kantati Uros, T951-695121); **Luis Carvajal** (Qhanan Pacha, T951-835264); and **Silverio Lujano** (**Kamisaraki Inn Lodge**, Kamisaraki, T951-049493).

Taquile
The Community Tourism Agency **Munay Taquile** (T051-351448, www.titicaca-taquile.com) can arrange accommodation on the island. Someone will approach you when you get off the boat if you don't have anything booked in advance. Rates are from US$9 pp for bed only, from US$21 pp full board, or US$43 pp including transport and guiding. Some families have become popular with tour groups and so have been able to build bigger and better facilities (with showers and loos), classified as Albergue Rural or Hotel Rural. As a result, families with more basic accommodation (Casa Rural) are often losing out on valuable tourist income. Instead of staying in the busy part of the island around the main square, consider staying with the Huayllano community on the south side of the island; contact **Alipio Huatta Cruz** (T951-668551 or T951-615239) or arrange a visit with **All Ways Travel**, see page 219.

Amantaní
The **Presidente del Comité Turístico de Amantaní** is Gerardo Yanarico (T951-848548). Rates are US$11-30 pp full board, or from US$29 pp including a tour. If you are willing to walk to more distant communities, you might get a better price and you are helping to share the income. Options include: **$$ Kantuta Lodge** (T051-630238, 951-636172, www.kantutalodge.com), run by Richard Cari and family, full board; **Hospedaje Ccolono** (Occosuyo, T951-675918); **Eduardo Yucra Mamani (Jatari**, Comunidad Pueblo, T951-664577); or **Victoriano Calsin Quispe** (T051-360220/363320).

Restaurants

Taquile
There are many small restaurants around the plaza and on the track to the Puerto Principal, including Gerardo Huatta's **La Flor de Cantuta**, on the steps, and **El Inca** on the main plaza. Meals are generally fish, rice and chips, omelette and *fiambre*, a local stew. Meat is rarely available and drinks often run out. Breakfast consists of pancakes and bread.

Amantaní
The artificially low price of tours allows families little scope for providing anything other than basic meals, so take your own supplies.

Festivals

Taquile
Jun-Aug The principal festivals are **2-7 Jun** and the **Fiesta de Santiago 25 Jul-2 Aug**, with many dances in between.

Amantaní

15-20 Jan Pago a la Tierra or
San Sebastián is celebrated on the hills of
the island. The festivities are very colourful,
musical and hard-drinking.
9 Apr Aniversario del Consejo
(the local council).
8-16 Aug Feria de Artesanías.

Transport

Purchasing one-way tickets gives you more
flexibility if you wish to stay longer on
the islands, but joining a tour is the most
convenient way to visit, especially as it will
include transport between your hotel and
the port. 2-day tours to Uros, Amantaní and
Taquile, including simple lodging and meals,
start at US$27.

The Uros
Asociación de Transporte los Uros (T051-
368024, aeuttal@hotmail.com, daily 0800-
1600) runs motorboats from Puno to the
islands, daily 0630-1630 or whenever there

are 10 people, US$3.60. Agencies charge
US$5.50-7 for a ½-day tour.

Taquile
Operaciones Comunales Taquile (T051-
205477, daily 0600-1800) has boats at 0730
and 0800 in high season, stopping at the
Uros on the way, returning at 1400 and
1430; in low season only 1 boat travels, US$7
return. Organized tours cost US$21-25.

Amantaní
Transportes Unificados Amantaní (T051-
369714, daily 0500-1800) has 2 boats daily
at 0815, 1 direct, the 2nd stopping at Uros;
they return at 0800 the next day, 1 direct
to **Puno**, the 2nd stopping at **Taquile** and
continuing to Puno at 1200. Rates are US$7.50
Puno to Amantaní direct one way; US$11
return including stops at **Uros** and Taquile;
US$3 Amantaní to Taquile one way. If you
stop in Taquile on the way back, you can
choose to continue to Puno at 1200 with
the Amantaní boat or take a Taquile boat
at 1400 (also 1430 in high season).

North of Puno

routes to Cuzco, the jungle and Bolivia

Heading north from Puno, the road crosses a range of hills to another coastal plain,
which leads to Juliaca. This town is the main transport hub for journeys north to
Cuzco or the jungle, west to Arequipa or east along the unspoiled northern shores
of the lake.

Juliaca *Colour map 3, B2.*
Freezing cold at night, hygienically challenged and less than safe, Juliaca, 289 km
northeast of Arequipa, is not particularly attractive. As the commercial focus of an area
bounded by Puno, Arequipa and the jungle, it has grown very fast into a noisy chaotic
place with a large, impermanent population of over 100,000, lots of contraband and more
trici-taxis than cars. Monday, market day, is the most disorganized of all.

Lampa
The unspoiled friendly little colonial town of **Lampa**, 31 km northwest of Juliaca along an old
road to Pucará, is known as the 'Pink City'. Being so close to Juliaca, it is a fine alternative place
to stay for those seeking tranquility. It has a splendid church, **La Inmaculada** ⓘ *daily 0900-
1200, 1400-1600, US$3.60*, containing a copy of Michelangelo's 'Pietà' cast in aluminium, many
Cuzqueña school paintings and a carved wooden pulpit. A plaster copy of the 'Pietà' and a
mural depicting local history can be seen in the Municipalidad. **Kampac Museo** ⓘ *Jr Alfonso*

Ugarte 462 y Ayacucho, T951-820085, daily 0700-1800, US$1.80, a small private museum featuring an eclectic collection of sculptures and ceramics from a number of Peruvian cultures; the owner, Profesor Jesús Vargas, can be found at the shop opposite. Lampa has a small Sunday market and celebrates a fiesta of **Santiago Apóstol** on 6-15 December. There is a fine colonial bridge just south of the town and La Cueva del Toro cave with petroglyphs at Lensora, 4 km past the bridge. The Tinajani rock formations and stands of *Puya raimondii* plants south of Ayaviri (see below) can also be accessed from Lampa.

Juliaca to Cuzco

The road Puno–Juliaca–Cuzco is fully paved. There is much to see on the way, but neither the regular daytime buses nor the trains make frequent stops. Tourist buses stop at the most important attractions, but to see these and other sights at a more relaxed pace, you will need to take local transport from town to town, or use your own car. There are plenty of places to stay and eat en route.

The road and railway cross the altiplano, gradually climbing. Along the way is **Pucará**, 65 km northwest of Juliaca, which has pre-Inca ruins, a museum and produces ceramic bulls which are placed on roofs throughout the region. Accessed from **Ayaviri** (33 km from Pucará), whose speciality is a mild, creamy cheese, are the Tinajani rock formations, stands of *Puya raimondii* plants and Laguna Orurillo. Knitted alpaca ponchos and pullovers and miniature llamas are made in **Santa Rosa** (42 km from Ayaviri), which has access to Nuñoa where more *Puyas raimondii* can be seen.

At **La Raya** (4350 m), the highest pass between Juliaca and Cuzco, there is a crafts market by the railway. Trains stop here so passengers can admire the scenery. Up on the heights breathing may be a little difficult, but the descent along the Río Vilcanota is rapid. At **Aguas Calientes**, 10 km from La Raya along the railway, are steaming springs reaching 40°C, with thermal pools for bathing; the beautiful deposits of red ferro-oxide in the middle of the green grass is a startling sight. At **Maranganí**, the river is wider and the fields greener, with groves of eucalyptus trees.

Located 38 km beyond La Raya pass at 3690 m is **Sicuani**, the main city in eastern Cuzco and a good base from which to visit the easternmost attractions of the region. It is an important commercial and agricultural centre and a transport hub. Excellent llama and alpaca wool products and skins are sold next to the pedestrian walkway and at the Saturday market. Around Plaza Libertad there are several hat shops. The tourist office (see Tourist information) has an excellent display of traditional outfits from all the districts of Canchis, which are among the most colourful in Cuzco. For information about places between Sicuani and Cuzco, see Raqchi and around, page 261.

Puno to the jungle

A branch of the Interoceanic Highway, fully paved, runs together with the Juliaca–Cuzco road, before branching north across the vast alpaca-grazed altiplano. **Azángaro** (73 km from Juliaca) has the Templo de Tintiri, an adobe colonial church rich in art. Beyond is the cold regional centre of **Macusani**, 192 km from Juliaca, at 4400 m. The dramatic road then descends past the mining supply towns of **Ollachea** (with simple accommodation and eateries, a waterfall, thermal baths and pre-Inca ruins) and **San Gabán** (with petroglyphs and waterfalls) to **Puente Iñambari** (or Loromayo), where it converges with the other branches of the Interoceánica from Cuzco and Puerto Maldonado (see page 334). **Mazuko** (360 km from Juliaca), another mining town, is 5 km north of the junction. This off-the-beaten-path route through the **Cordillera Carabaya** connects Lake Titicaca and the southern jungle (see Transport below).

This is an excellent area for those who want to explore. Along the way are rock formations, petroglyphs and the glaciated summits of Allin Cápac surrounded by lakes and valleys ideal for trekking. Richar Cáceres (T942-989821) in Macusani, is a recommended English-speaking mountaineer and guide, who is knowledgeable about the area.

Further east, leading north from the northeastern shore of Titicaca near Huancané, another road goes towards the jungle. At **Putina**, 92 km from Juliaca, are **thermal baths** ① *Tue-Sun 0400-2100, US$0.70.* Vicuñas can be seen at Picotani nearby, and *Puya raimondii* plants at Bellavista, 5 km from town. The road then crosses the beautiful Cordillera Apolobamba to **Sandia** (125 km from Putina), **San Juan del Oro** (80 km from Sandia) and **Putina Punco**, 40 km ahead. Beyond lies the remote **Parque Nacional Bahuaja-Sonene** ① *Sernanp, Libertad 1189, Puno, T051-363960,* with restricted access requiring a Sernamp permit (US$54). It is difficult to reach the park from this side and involves paddling a canoe through serious rapids; access is easier from the Río Tambopata side, see page 334.

Huancané to Bolivia

A paved road goes northeast from Juliaca across the *puna* for 56 km to **Huancané** (altitude 3825 m), which has a massive adobe church by its attractive plaza and good birdwatching possibilities nearby in the **Reserva Nacional del Titicaca**, where the road crosses the Río Ramis. Nearby, a road goes north to Putina and the jungle, see above. East of Huancané, the shore of Titicaca is beautiful, with terraced hills rising above coves on the lake. There are many Inca and pre-Inca ruins as well as pre-Inca roads to follow. In the warmer coves, where the climate is tempered by the lake, people lead traditional lives based on fishing and subsistence farming. There is access from the shore to idyllic **Isla Suasi** (www.islasuasi.pe) and to the Bolivian border. Lodging and eateries in the towns along this route are generally basic; there are also water shortages.

Puno–La Paz via Tilali and Puerto Acosta The most remote route to Bolivia is along the northeast shore of the lake, via Huancané, **Tilali** (Peru) and **Puerto Acosta** (Bolivia). There are no Peruvian immigration facilities at this border, only customs controls, so make sure you get an exit stamp at Migraciones in Puno (Ayacucho 280, T051-357103, Monday-Friday 0800-1300, 1500-1900), post-dated by a couple of days. From Juliaca there are minibuses to Tilali, the last village in Peru; these may continue to the border on market days (Wednesday and Saturday). At other times you may have to walk 3 km from Tilali to the frontier and then a further 10 km to Puerto Acosta in Bolivia. Try hitching to **Puerto Acosta** in order to catch the bus from there to **La Paz** daily at about 1400 (Bolivian time), more frequent service on Sunday, five hours, US$6. If you are in a hurry and miss the bus in Puerto Acosta, ask the truck to drop you off 25 km further into Bolivia at Escoma, from where there are frequent minivans to La Paz.

Listings North of Puno

Tourist information

Juliaca
Information is available from **Dircetur** (Jr Noriega 191, p 3, T051-321839, Mon-Fri 0730-1530) and **iPerú** (at the airport,

iperupunoapto@promperu.gob.pe, open when flights arrive).

Juliaca to Cuzco
The **Sicuani tourist information office** (at the Municipio, Plaza de Armas, T084-

509257, Mon-Fri 0800-1300, 1430-1800) has
pamphlets and very helpful staff.

Where to stay

Juliaca
The town has water problems in dry season.

$$$-$$ Hotel Don Carlos
*Jr 9 de Diciembre 114, Plaza Bolognesi,
T051-323600, www.hotelesdoncarlos.com.*
Comfortable, modern facilities, heater, good
service, breakfast, restaurant and room
service. Also has **Suites Don Carlos** (Jr M
Prado 335, T051-321571).

$$ Royal Inn
*San Román 158, T051-321561,
www.royalinnhoteles.com.*
Rooms and suites with heater and bathtub,
good restaurant ($$-$).

$$ Sakura
*San Román 133, T322072,
hotelsakura@hotmail.com.*
Quiet, basic rooms in older section with
shared bath.

$$-$ Hostal Luquini
*Jr Brasesco 409, Plaza Bolognesi,
T051-321510.*
Comfortable, patio, helpful staff,
reliable hot water in morning only,
motorcycle parking.

$ Yurac Wasi
Jr San Martín 1214.
Near Terminal Terrestre, good simple
economical rooms, private or shared bath.

Lampa

$$ La Casona
*Jr Tarapacá 271, Plaza de Armas, T999-
607682, patronatolampa@yahoo.com.*
Lovely refurbished 17th-century house,
nice ample rooms with heaters and duvets,
advanced booking required, tours arranged.

$ Hospedaje Estrella
*Jr Municipalidad 540, T980-368700,
juanfrien@hotmail.com.*
Appealing rooms, with or without private
bath, solar hot water, very friendly, breakfast
available, parking.

Huancané to Bolivia

$$$$ Hotel Isla Suasi
*T051-351102 (office), T941-741347,
www.islasuasi.pe.*
The hotel is the only house on this tiny,
tranquil, private island. There are beautiful
terraced gardens, best Jan-Mar. The non-
native eucalyptus trees are being replaced by
native varieties. You can take a canoe around
the island to see birds and the island has
vicuñas, a small herd of alpacas and vizcachas.
The sunsets from the highest point are
beautiful. Facilities are spacious, comfortable
and solar-powered, price includes buffet
breakfast, guided walk, birdwatching, canoe
tour and sauna. Transport costs US$100 pp
return, either by land from the airport or by
private boat from Puno, including stops in
Uros and Taquile, or a combination of the two.

Restaurants

Juliaca

$$ El Asador
Unión 113. Daily 1200-0100.
Regional dishes, chicken, grill and pizza,
good food and service, pleasant atmosphere.

$ Delycia's
M Núñez 168. Closed Fri evening and Sat.
Good vegetarian set lunch with small
salad bar.

$ Nuevo Star
Bolívar 121. Daily 0600-2000.
Decent set meals.

$ Ricos Pan
Jr San Román y Jorge Chávez.
Good bakery with café, popular.

Shopping

Juliaca

La Dominical, *near the exit to Cuzco.
Held on Sun.* A woollens market.
Las Calceteras, *Pl Bolognesi.*
Handicrafts gallery.
Túpac Amaru market, *on Moquegua
7 blocks east of railway line.* Cheap.

Transport

Juliaca

Air Manco Cápac airport, remodelled
in 2014, is small but well organized. To/
from **Lima**, 1¾ hrs, 4-5 a day with **LATAM**
(T051-322228 or airport T051-324448) via
Arequipa (30 mins), **Cuzco** and direct; and
1-2 a day direct with **Avianca/TACA**. Beware
over-charging for ground transportation.
If you have little luggage, regular taxis and
vans stop just outside the airport parking
area. Taxi from Plaza Bolognesi, US$2.75; taxi
from airport to centre US$3.60, or less from
outside airport gates. For transfers to/from
Puno, see page 219.

Bus Local To **Puno**, minibuses leave
when full from Jr Brasesco near Plaza
Bolognesi throughout the day, US$1.25, 1 hr.
To **Capachica**, they leave when full from
Cerro Colorado market, 0500-1700, US$2,
1½ hrs. To **Lampa**, cars (US$1.25) and vans
(US$0.90) leave when full from the Mercado
Santa Bárbara area, eg **El Veloz** (Jr Huáscar
672 y Colón) or **Ramos** (2 de Mayo y Colón),
others nearby, 30 mins. Vans to **Pucará**
(US$1.25, 45 min), **Ayaviri** (US$1.80, 1½ hrs)
and **Azángaro** depart from Terminal Virgen
de Las Mercedes (Jr Texas, corner San Juan
de Dios); they also stop at Paseo Los Kollas
by the exit to Cuzco to pick up passengers.
To **Sicuani**, take a bus bound for Cuzco (see
below) or **Chasquis** vans leave when full
from 8 de Noviembre 1368, by Paseo de
Los Kollas, US$5.40, 2½-3 hrs. Minibuses for
Moho via **Huancané** depart when full 0500-
1800 from Jr Moquegua y Circunvalación,

north of Mercado Tupac Amaru, US$2.15,
1½ hrs. Minibuses for **Conima** and **Tilali**
depart when full from Jr Lambayeque y
Av Circunvalación Este, also near the market,
US$3.60, 3 hrs; these continue to the Bolivian
border on market days.

Long distance The Terminal Terrestre is
at the east end of San Martín (cuadra 9, past
the Circunvalación). To **Lima**, US$38 normal,
US$43-70 *cama*, 20-22 hrs; with **Ormeño**
1630, 2000, **Flores** or **Civa** at 1500, several
others. To **Cuzco**, US$5.40 normal, US$9
semi-cama, US$12.50-17 *cama*, 5-6 hrs, with
Power (T051-322531) every 2 hrs, 0530-2330,
Flores at 1200 and 1700, several others. To
Arequipa, US$5.50 normal, US$7 semi-
cama, US$9-27 *cama*, 4-5 hrs, with **Julsa**
(T051-331952) hourly 0300-2400, with **Flores**
6-8 daily, several others. To **Moquegua**
(7 hrs) and **Tacna** (8-9 hrs), US$9-11 *semi-
cama*, US$12.50-15 *cama*, most depart
1930-2030, with **San Martín** also at 0745. To
Puerto Maldonado along the Interoceanic
Highway, US$14-27, 12 hrs; several companies
leave from the Terminal Terrestre and then
pick up passengers at private terminals
around M Nuñez cuadra 11, 'El Triángulo', by
the exit to Cuzco: **Santa Cruz** (M Núñez y
Cahuide, T051-332185) at 0900, 1400, 1800
and 1900; **Julsa** (Ferrocarril y Cahuide, T051-
326602); **Wayra** at 2030; **ITSA** at 1730 and
1830; **Aguilas** at 1800. To **Macusani**, **Alianza**
(Av Ferrocarril y Cahuide) 1300, 1700, 1815,
US$3.50, 3 hrs; **Jean** (M Núñez y Pje San José),
0845, 1330, 1800; also minibuses from Pje San
José, leave when full, US$4.25.

Juliaca to Cuzco
Sicuani

The bus terminal is in the newer part of town,
which is separated from the older part and
the Plaza by 3 bridges, the middle one has
a pedestrian walkway. To **Juliaca**, Chasquis
vans leave when full, US$5.40, 2½-3 hrs. To
Cuzco, 137 km, US$3.60, 3 hrs. (The Sicuani
terminals in Cuzco are at Av Huayruropata,
Wanchaq, near Mercado Tupac Amaru.)

Puno to the jungle

From Macusani to **Juliaca**, US$3.50, 3 hrs; also minibuses US$4.25. Vans go as they fill from Macusani to San Gabán; some continue to Puente Iñambari.

Border with Bolivia

Puno–La Paz via Yunguyo and Copacabana

The most frequently travelled route is along the southwest coast of Titicaca, from Puno to La Paz via **Yunguyo** (Peru) and **Copacabana** (Bolivia). The border villages on either side are called Kasani. This route is very scenic and involves crossing the Straits of Tiquina on a launch (there are barges for the vehicles) between Copacabana and La Paz. Almost all the tourist class bus services use this route.

Peruvian immigration (daily 0700-1830, Peruvian time) is five minutes' drive from **Yunguyo** and 500 m from the Bolivian immigration post (daily 0800-2000, Bolivian time). Minibuses from the Terminal Zonal in Puno to Yunguyo may continue to the border at Kasani if there are enough passengers; there are also shared taxis (US$0.40 per person) and private taxis (US$2.50) from Yunguyo (Jr Titicaca y San Francisco, one block from Plaza de Armas) to Kasani, five minutes. Minibuses (US$0.50) and taxis (US$3 or US$0.60 per person) run from Kasani to Copacabana (8 km, 15 minutes).

There is one ATM at Plaza 2 de Mayo in Yunguyo and money changers on the Peruvian side of the border, compare rates before changing.

Puno–La Paz via Desaguadero

A more direct route between Puno and La Paz is via the bleak town of **Desaguadero** (same name on both sides of the border), on the southwest coast of the lake. The Carretera Binacional, which joins La Paz with Moquegua and the Pacific port of Ilo, goes through Desaguadero, see page 214, but there is no need to stop here, as all roads to Desaguadero are paved and, if you leave La Paz, Moquegua or Puno early enough, you should be at your destination before nightfall. This particular border crossing allows you to stop at the ruins of Tiahuanaco in Bolivia along the way. The **Peruvian border office** is open daily 0700-1930; the Bolivian office, daily 0800-2030 (both local time). It is easy to change money on the Peruvian side where there are many changers by the bridge.

Cuzco

⭐ Cuzco stands at the head of the Sacred Valley of the Incas and is the jumping-off point for the Inca Trail and famous Inca city of Machu Picchu. It's not surprising, therefore, that this is the prime destination for the vast majority of first-time visitors to Peru. The ancient Inca capital is said to have been founded around AD 1100, when the Sun sent his son, Manco Cápac, and the Moon sent her daughter, Mama Ocllo, to find a suitably fertile place to found their kingdom. The Spanish transformed the navel of the Inca civilization into a jewel of colonial achievement.

In more recent times Cuzco has developed into a major commercial and tourism centre of 450,000 inhabitants, most of whom are Quechua. Colonial churches, monasteries and convents and extensive pre-Columbian ruins are interspersed with countless hotels, bars and restaurants that cater to the over one million tourists who visit every year. Almost every central street has remains of Inca walls and doorways; the perfect Inca stonework now serves as the foundations for more modern dwellings. This stonework is tapered upwards (battered); every wall has a perfect line of inclination towards the centre, from bottom to top. The curved stonework of the Temple of the Sun, for example, is probably unequalled in the world.

Best for
Colonial architecture ▪ Festivals ▪ Inca archaeology ▪ Museums

Finding your feet

Respect the altitude: rest for several hours after arrival; eat lightly; don't smoke; avoid alcohol; drink plenty of water, and remember to walk slowly. There are too many sights in the city to see on a single visit; limit yourself to the highlights or to areas of particular interest. Note that many churches close to visitors on Sunday, and photography inside churches is generally not allowed.

Tip...
The best place for an overall view of the Cuzco Valley is from the top of the hill of Sacsayhuaman.

Getting around

The **airport** is to the southeast of the city; the road into the centre passes close to Wanchac station, at which **trains** from Puno arrive. The **bus terminal** is near the Pachacútec statue in Ttio district. If transport has not been arranged by your hotel on arrival, you are advised to travel by taxi from the airport, train or bus stations. You are also strongly advised to take a taxi when returning to your hotel at night. During the day, the centre of Cuzco is quite small and easy to explore on foot. Agencies offer guided tours of the city and surrounding archaeological sites, but visiting independently is not difficult. There are regular buses from Cuzco to villages and towns throughout the region.

Visitors' tickets

A combined entry ticket, called *Boleto Turístico de Cusco (BTC)*, is available to most of the main sites of historical and cultural interest in and around the city, and costs as follows: 130 soles (US$38.25) for sites for 10 days; or 70 soles (US$25) for either the included city museums (valid for two days); or Sacsayhuaman, Qenqo, Puka Pukara and Tambo Machay (one day); or Pisac, Ollantaytambo, Chinchero and Moray (two days). The BTC can be bought at **iCusco** (Portal Mantas 117-A, Monday-Saturday 0900-1200, 1400-1800) and **Cosituc** (Avenida El Sol 103, of 102, Galerías Turísticas, T084-261465, daily 0800-1800, www.cosituc.gob.pe), or at any of the sites included in the ticket. For students with an ISIC card the 10-day BTC costs 70 soles (US$25), only available at the Cosituc office upon presentation of the ISIC card. Take your ISIC card when visiting the sites, as some officials may ask to see it.

Two other combined entry tickets apply to churches and religious museums, and can be purchased at any of the included sites. The *Circuito Religioso Arzobispal (CRA)* costs 30 soles (US$11 for 30 days) and includes the Cathedral, Museo Arzobispal, San Blas and San Cristóbal. The *Ruta del Barroco Andino (RBA)* costs 25 soles (US$7.35 for seven days) and includes La Compañía in Cuzco and churches in Adahuaylillas, Huaro and Canincunca.

Machu Picchu entrance tickets are sold electronically at www.machupicchu.gob.pe, and at the Cuzco ticket office (C Garcilaso, s/n, next to Museo de Historia Regional, T084-582030, Monday-Saturday 0700-1930) on the machupicchu.gob.pe website.

Security

Police patrol the streets and stations, but still be vigilant. On no account walk back to your hotel after dark from a bar or club: strangle muggings and rapes do occur. Pay for the club's doorman to call you a taxi, and make sure that it is licensed. You should also take care at San Pedro market (otherwise recommended), in the San Cristóbal area and at out-of-the-way ruins. Also take precautions during Inti Raymi. Always go to the police when robbed, even though reporting it takes time.

Sights Colour map 3, A1.

Inca stones, colonial churches and 21st-century crowds

Since there are so many sights to see in Cuzco city, not even the most ardent tourist would be able to visit them all. Those with limited time, or who want a whistle-stop tour, should visit the cathedral, Qoricancha, La Compañía de Jesús, San Blas, La Merced, San Cristóbal (for the view) and Sacsayhuaman. If you visit one museum make it the Museo Inka, which has the most comprehensive collection.

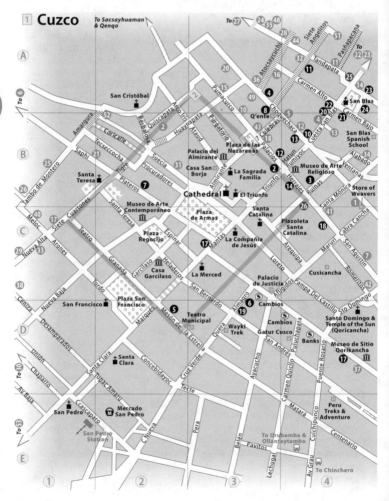

Cuzco

City centre

Plaza de Armas The heart of the city in Inca days was Huacaypata (the Place of Tears) and Cusipata (the Place of Happiness), divided by a channel of the Saphi River (no longer visible). Today, Cusipata is Plaza Regocijo and Huacaypata is the Plaza de Armas. This was the great civic square of the Incas, flanked by their palaces, and was a place of solemn parades and great assemblies. Around Plaza de Armas are colonial arcades and four great churches. To the northeast is the early 17th-century baroque **Cathedral** ⓘ *US$9 or CRA ticket, daily 1000-1800*. It was built on the site of the Palace of Inca Wiracocha

Where to stay 🛏
1 Albergue Casa Campesina *B4*
2 Albergue Municipal *B2*
3 Amaru Colonial *B5*
4 Amaru Hostal *B4*
5 Andenes al Cielo *B4*
6 Andenes de Saphi *A1*
7 Casa Andina Koricancha *C4*
8 Casa Andina Private Collection Cusco *C5*
9 Casa Andina San Blas *B5*
10 Casa Cartagena *A3*
11 Casa de la Gringa *A4*
12 Casa Elena *B4*
13 Casa San Blas & Tika Bistro *B4*
14 Casona Les Pleiades *A4*
15 El Arqueólogo & Divina Comedia Restaurant *A3*
16 El Grial *A3*
17 El Mercado *C1*
18 El Monasterio *B3*
19 Estrellita *C5*
20 Flying Dog Hostel *A3*
21 Hitchhikers B&B Backpackers Hostel *B2*
22 Hosp El Artesano de San Blas *A4*
23 Hosp Inka *A4*
24 Hostal Casa de Campo *A3*
25 Hostal El Balcón *B1*
26 Hostal Killipata *B1*
27 Hostal Kuntur Wasi *A3*
28 Hostal Pakcha Real *A4*
29 Hostal Qorichaska *C1*
30 Hostal Quipu *D1*
31 Hostal Suecia *B2*
32 Hostal Tikawasi *A4*
33 Hostal Wayras *C1*
34 Hostería de Anita *B4*
35 La Encantada *A3*
36 Los Apus Hotel & Mirador *A3*
37 Maison de la Jeunesse *D4*
38 Mamá Simona Hostel *C1*
40 Niños/Hotel Meloc *C1*
41 Novotel *C4*
42 Palacio del Inka Luxury Collection *C4*
43 Palacio Nazarenas *B3*
44 Pensión Alemana *A3*
46 Pirwa Backpackers San Blas *A5*
47 Pirwa Garcilaso *D6*
48 Quinua Villa Boutique *A3*
49 Rumi Punku *A3*
50 Sonesta Posadas del Inca *E6*
51 The Blue House *A4*
52 The WalkOn Inn *B2*
53 Tu Casita *E1*

Restaurants 🍴
2 A Mi Manera *B3*
3 Baco *B4*
4 Blue Alpaca *A3*
5 Café Cocla *D2*
6 Café El Ayllu *D3*
7 Café Morena *B2*
8 Café Punchay *A3*
9 El Paisa *E5*
10 Jack's Café *B4*
11 Juanito's Sandwich Café *A4*
12 Justina *B3*
13 Kuska...fé *B4*
14 La Bodega 138 *B4*
15 La Chomba *C5*
16 La Cusqueñita *E6*
17 La Valeriana *D4, C3*
18 Le Soleil *C4*
19 Los Toldos *D3*
20 Macondo *A4*
21 Pachapapa *B4*
22 Panadería El Buen Pastor *A4*
23 Tacomanía *A4*
24 The Meeting Place *A4*

Bars & clubs 🍸
25 Km 0 (Arte y Tapas) *A4*
26 Museo del Pisco *B4*

N

100 metres
100 yards

ON THE ROAD
Inca society

Cuzco was the capital of the Inca empire – one of the greatest planned societies the world has known – from its rise during the 11th century to its death in the early 16th century. (See John Hemming's *Conquest of the Incas* and B C Brundage's *Lords of Cuzco* and *Empire of the Inca*.) It was solidly based on other Andean civilizations which had attained great skill in textiles, building, ceramics and working in metal. Immemorially, the political structure of the Andean *indígena* had been the *ayllu*, the village community; it had its divine ancestor, worshipped household gods, was closely knit by ties of blood to the family and by economic necessity to the land, which was held in common. Submission to the *ayllu* was absolute, because it was only by such discipline that food could be obtained in an unsympathetic environment.

All the domestic animals, the llama and alpaca and the dog, had long been tamed, and the great staple crops, maize and potatoes, established. What the Incas did – and it was a magnificent feat – was to conquer enormous territories and impose upon the variety of *ayllus*, through an unchallengeable central government, a willing spiritual and economic submission to the State. The common religion, already developed by the classical Tiwanaku culture, was worship of the Sun, whose vice-regent on earth was the absolute Sapa Inca. Around him, in the capital, was a religious and secular elite which never froze into a caste because it was open to talent. The elite was often recruited from chieftains defeated by the Incas; an effective way of reconciling local opposition. Even the idol-gods of conquered peoples were brought to Cuzco, at once a form of homage and captivity.

The mass of the people were subjected to rigorous planning. They were allotted land to work, for their group and for the State; set various tasks (the making of textiles, pottery, weapons, ropes, etc) from primary materials supplied by the functionaries, or used in enlarging the area of cultivation by building terraces on the hill-sides. Their political organization was simple but effective. The family, and not the individual, was the unit. Families were grouped in units of 10, 100, 500, 1000, 10,000 and 40,000, each group with a leader. The Sapa Inca crowned the political edifice; his four immediate counsellors were those to whom he allotted responsibility for the northern, southern, eastern and western regions (*suyos*) of the empire.

Equilibrium between production and consumption must depend heavily upon statistical information. This the Incas raised to a high degree of efficiency by means of their *quipus*: a decimal system of recording numbers by knots in cords. Seasonal variations were guarded against by creating a system of state barns in which provender could be stored during years of plenty, to be used in years of scarcity. Statistical efficiency alone required that no one should be permitted to leave their home or their work. The loss of personal liberty was the price paid by the masses for economic security. In order to obtain information and to transmit orders quickly, the Incas built fine paved pathways along which couriers sped on foot. The whole system of rigorous control was completed by the greatest of all their monarchs, Pachacútec, who also imposed a common language, Quechua, as a further cementing force.

(Kiswarcancha). The high altar is solid silver and the original altar *retablo* behind it is a masterpiece of Andean woodcarving. The Cathedral contains two interesting paintings: the first is the earliest surviving painting of the city, depicting Cuzco during the 1650 earthquake; the second, at the far right-hand end of the church, is a local painting of the Last Supper replete with Peruvian details, including *cuy* and *chicha*. In the sacristy are paintings of all the bishops of Cuzco. The choir stalls, by a 17th-century Spanish priest, are a magnificent example of colonial baroque art. The elaborate pulpit is also notable. Much venerated is the crucifix of El Señor de los Temblores, the object of many pilgrimages and viewed all over Peru as a guardian against earthquakes.

The tourist entrance to the Cathedral is through the church of **La Sagrada Familia** (also known as Jesús, María y José; 1733), which stands to the left of the Cathedral as you face it. Its gilt main altar has been renovated. The far simpler **El Triunfo**, on the right of the Cathedral, was the first Christian church in Cuzco, built on the site of the Inca Roundhouse (the Suntur Huasi) in 1536. It has a statue of the Virgin of the Descent that is reputed to have helped the Spaniards repel Manco Inca when he besieged the city in 1536.

On the southeast side of the plaza is the beautiful **La Compañía de Jesús** ① *US$5, or RBA ticket, Mon-Sat 0900-1730, Sun 0900-1130, 1300-1730*, built in the 17th century on the site of the Palace of the Serpents (Amarucancha), residence of Inca Huayna Capac. Its twin-towered exterior is extremely graceful, and the baroque interior is rich in fine murals and paintings, with a resplendent altar decorated in gold leaf. Outside the church, look for the **Inca stonework** in the Callejón Loreto, running southeast past La Compañía de Jesús from the main plaza, with the walls of the Acllahuasi (see below) on one side, and the **Amarucancha** on the other.

Santa Catalina and around The church, convent and museum of **Santa Catalina** ① *Arequipa at Santa Catalina Angosta, Mon-Sat 0830-1730, Sun 1400-1700*, were built upon the foundations of the *Acllahuasi*, where Inca women chosen for their nobility, virtue and beauty were housed in preparation for ceremonial and domestic duties. The convent is a closed order, but the church and museum are worth visiting. Guided tours by English-speaking students (tip expected) will point out the church's ornate gilded altarpiece and beautifully carved pulpit and the museum's collection of Cuzqueño art.

Around the corner, **Museo Machupicchu** (Casa Concha) ① *Santa Catalina Ancha 320, T084-255535, Mon-Sat 0900-1700, US$7*, features objects found by Hiram Bingham during his initial excavations of Machu Picchu in 1912, which were returned by Yale University to the Peruvian government in 2010.

If you continue down Arequipa from Santa Catalina you come to Calle Maruri. Between this street and Santo Domingo is **Cusicancha** ① *US$1.75, Mon-Fri 0715-1300, 1400-1600, sometimes open at weekends*, an open space showing the layout of the buildings as they would have been in Inca times.

Santo Domingo and Qoricancha ① *Mon-Sat 0800-1730, Sun 1400-1700 (closed holidays), Museo Qoricancha US$3.60; church free, multi-lingual guides charge US$11 for a 40-min tour.* This is one of the most fascinating sights in Cuzco. Behind the walls of a 17th-century Catholic church are the remains of Qoricancha, a complex that formed the centre of the vast Inca society. Its Golden Palace and Temple of the Sun were filled with such fabulous treasures of gold and silver that it took the Spanish three months to melt it all down.

The first Inca, Manco Cápac, is said to have built the temple when he left Lake Titicaca and founded Cuzco with Mama Ocllo. However, it was the ninth Inca, Pachacútec, who transformed it. When the Spaniards arrived, the complex was awarded to Juan Pizarro, the younger brother of Francisco, who willed it to the Dominicans when he was fatally wounded in the Sacsayhuaman siege. The Dominicans ripped much of the complex down to build their church. The baroque cloister has since been excavated to reveal four of the original chambers of the great Inca Temple of the Sun – two on the west have been partly reconstructed in a good imitation of Inca masonry. The finest stonework is in the celebrated curved wall beneath the west end of Santo Domingo. This can be seen (complete with a large crack from the 1950 earthquake) when you look out over the Solar Garden. Excavations have revealed Inca baths below here and more Inca retaining walls. Another superb stretch of late Inca stonework is in Calle Ahuacpinta outside the temple, to the east, or left as you enter.

Around the corner from the site (but not part of it), **Museo de Sitio Qorikancha** (formerly Museo Arqueológico) ① *Av El Sol, Mon-Sat 0900-1800, Sun 0800-1400, entrance by BTC*, contains a limited collection of pre-Columbian items, Spanish paintings of imitation Inca royalty dating from the 18th century, and photos of the excavation of Qoricancha.

Southwest of the Plaza de Armas The church of La Merced ① *Plazoleta Espinar, C Mantas, church Mon-Sat 0700-0800, 1700-2000, Sun 0700-1300, 1800-2000; monastery*

2 **Around Plaza de Armas**

→ **Cuzco maps**
1 Cuzco, page 232
2 Around Plaza de Armas, page 236

and museum *Mon-Sat 0800-1230, 1400-1730, US$2*, was first built in 1534 and rebuilt in the late 17th century. Attached is a very fine monastery with an exquisite cloister. Inside the church are buried Gonzalo Pizarro, half-brother of Francisco, and the two Almagros, father and son. The church is most famous for its jewelled monstrance, which is on view in the monastery's museum during visiting hours.

Museo de Historia Regional ① *in the Casa Garcilaso, C Garcilaso y Heladeros, daily 0800-1700, entrance by BTC*, tries to show the evolution of the Cuzqueño school of painting. It also contains Inca agricultural implements, colonial furniture and paintings.

San Francisco ① *on Plaza San Francisco, 3 blocks southwest of the Plaza de Armas, daily 0900-1800*, is an austere church reflecting many indigenous influences.

☆Two blocks south of here, **San Pedro market** is popular with tourists but has only been slightly sanitized for their benefit. It remains a working market and is a pleasant and reasonably safe place to purchase local produce and crafts. In front of the market, the church of **San Pedro** was built in 1688. Its two towers were made from stones brought from an Inca ruin.

☆**Calle Hatun Rumiyoc** This street, running northeast from the Plaza de Armas, contains some of the most imposing Inca masonry in Cuzco, including the famous 'Stone of 12 angles' (halfway along its second block, on the right-hand side going away from the Plaza). The huge stone has been precisely cut into a 12-sided polygon in order for it to fit perfectly with the surrounding stones.

The **Museo de Arte Religioso** ① *Hatun Rumiyoc y Herrajes, daily 0800-1800, US$3.60 or CRA ticket*, is housed in the **Palacio Arzobispal**, which was built on the site of the palace occupied in 1400 by the Inca Roca. The museum contains a collection of colonial paintings and furniture, including the paintings by the indigenous master, Diego Quispe Tito, of a 17th-century Corpus Christi procession that used to hang in the church of Santa Ana.

☆**San Blas** The San Blas district, uphill from the centre to the northeast, is now firmly on the tourist map, thanks to its shops, galleries and good-value hotels and restaurants. Its main sight is the small, simple church of **San Blas** ① *Plazoleta San Blas, Carmen Bajo, daily 0800-1800, US$3.60 or CRA ticket*, which has a beautiful *mestizo* pulpit, carved from a single cedar trunk; well worth seeing. **Museo Máximo Laura** ① *Carmen Alto 133, T084-227383, http:// museomaximolaura.com, Mon-Sat 0930-*

2000, Sun 1330-2000, displays 24 prize-winning exhibits by this celebrated textile artist, with workshop, gallery and shop.

☆**Museo Inka** ⓘ *Cuesta del Almirante 103, T084-237380, Mon-Sat 0800-1830. US$4.* The impressive **Palacio del Almirante**, just north of the Plaza de Armas, houses the Museo Inka, run by the Universidad San Antonio de Abad. The museum exhibits the development of culture in the region from pre-Inca, through Inca times to the present day, with displays of textiles, ceramics, metalwork, jewellery, architecture and technology. Don't miss the collection of miniature turquoise figures and other offerings to the gods. Weaving demonstrations are given in the courtyard.

☆**Museo de Arte Precolombino** ⓘ *Pl de las Nazarenas 231, daily 0900-2200, US$7, US$3.50 with student card; under same auspices as the Larco Museum in Lima, MAP Café (see Restaurants, page 246).* Housed in the **Casa Cabrera** on the northwest side of the Plaza de las Nazarenas, this beautiful museum is set around a spacious courtyard and contains many superb examples of pottery, metalwork (largely in gold and silver), woodcarvings and shells from the Moche, Chimú, Paracas, Nazca and Inca cultures. There are some vividly rendered animistic designs, giving an insight into the way Peru's ancient people's viewed their world and the creatures that inhabited it. Every exhibit carries explanations in English and Spanish. Highly recommended.

Elsewhere on the plaza, the **Convento de las Nazarenas** is now a hotel. You can see the Inca-colonial doorway with a mermaid motif, but ask permission to view the lovely 18th-century frescos inside.

☆**Sacsayhuaman**
30-min walk from Plaza de las Nazarenas. Daily 0700-1730. Entry with BTC ticket. Students offer free guided tours; give them a tip.

There are some magnificent Inca walls in this ruined ceremonial centre, on a hill in the northern outskirts. The massive rocks weighing up to 130 tons are fitted together with absolute perfection. Three walls run parallel for over 360 m and there are 21 bastions. Sacsayhuaman was thought for centuries to be a fortress, but the layout and architecture suggest a great sanctuary and temple to the Sun, which rises exactly opposite the place previously believed to be the Inca's throne; this was probably an altar, carved out of the solid rock, with broad steps leading to it from either side. The hieratic, rather than the military, hypothesis was supported by the discovery in 1982 of the graves of priests, who would have been unlikely to be buried in a fortress. The precise functions of the site, however, will probably continue to be a matter of dispute as very few clues remain, owing to its steady destruction.

The site survived the first years of the conquest. Pizarro's troops had entered Cuzco unopposed in 1533 and lived safely at Sacsayhuaman, until the rebellion of Manco Inca in 1536 caught them off guard. The bitter struggle that ensued became the decisive military action of the conquest: Manco's failure to hold Sacsayhuaman cost him the war and the empire. The destruction of the hilltop site began after the defeat of Manco's rebellion. The outer walls still stand, but the complex of towers and buildings was razed to the ground. From then until the 1930s, Sacsayhuaman served as a kind of unofficial quarry of pre-cut stone for the inhabitants of Cuzco.

Tip...
Since it is cold in Cuzco and many hotels have no heating, ask for an *estufa*, a heater which some places will provide for an extra charge.

The site can be reached in 30 minutes by walking up Pumacurco from Plaza de la Nazarenas, or from the church of **San Cristóbal**, just north of the centre. The church was built by Cristóbal Paullu Inca to honour his patron saint. North of San Cristóbal, you can see the 11 doorway-sized niches of the great Inca wall of the **Palacio de Colcampata**, which was the residence of Manco Inca before he rebelled against the Spanish and fled to Vilcabamba.

Beyond Sacsayhuaman

Take a guide to the sites and visit in the morning for the best photographs. Entry by BTC ticket; carry it with you as there are roving ticket inspectors. To get there take the Pisac bus or the Señor del Huerto city bus up to Tambo Machay (US$0.70).

Along the road from Sacsayhuaman to Pisac, past a radio station, is the temple and amphitheatre of **Qenqo**, which has some of the finest examples of Inca stone carving *in situ*, especially inside the large hollowed-out stone that houses an altar. On the same road is **Puka Pukara**, known as the Red Fort, but more likely to have been a *tambo*, or post-house; it's worth coming here for the wonderful views alone. Nearby is the spring shrine of **Tambo Machay**, which is in excellent condition. Water still flows by a hidden channel out of the masonry wall, straight into a little rock pool traditionally known as the Inca's bath. You can visit the sites on foot, a pleasant walk of at least half a day through the countryside; enquire about safety beforehand, take water and sun protection, and watch out for dogs. Alternatively, catch a bus up, and walk back.

Listings Cuzco *maps pages 232 and 236.*

Tourist information

iPerú is the most reliable source of information. Their main office and information desk is at the airport (T084-237364, daily 0600-1700). There is also an iPerú desk on Plaza de Armas (Portal de Harinas 177 at BCP Traveller Point, T084-252974, Mon-Fri 0900-1900, Sat-Sun 0900-1300) and a kiosk next to La Compañía church (Mon-Sat 0900-1300, 1400-1800). Another source of information is **iCusco/Dircetur** (Portal Mantas 117-A, next to La Merced church, T084-222032, Mon-Sat 0800-2000, Sun 0800-1330). See also www.aboutcusco.com and www.cuscoonline.com.

The **tourist police** (Plaza Túpac Amaru, Wanchac, T084-512351/235123) will prepare a *denuncia* (report for insurance purposes) for you. (These are available from the Banco de la Nación.) **Indecopi** (Urbanización Constancia Mz A-11-2, Wanchac, T084-252987, toll-free 24-hr T0800-44040,

paragon@indecopi.gob.pe) is the consumer protection bureau.

Where to stay

Cuzco has hundreds of hotels in all categories but the more expensive ones should nonetheless be booked several months in advance, particularly for the week around Inti Raymi, when prices are greatly increased. Prices given are for the high season in Jun-Aug. When there are fewer tourists, hotels may drop their prices by as much as half. Always check for discounts. Be wary of unlicensed hotel agents for medium-priced hotels who are often misleading about details; their local nickname is *jalagringos* (gringo pullers), or *piratas*. Many places will store your luggage when you go trekking, but always check valuables and possessions before and after depositing them with hotel/hostel staff.

International chain hotels in Cuzco include **Best Western** (www.bestwestern.com), **JW Marriott** (www.marriott.com), **Novotel** (www.novotel.com) and **Sonesta** (www.sonesta.com).

Around the Plaza de Armas

$$$$ Inkaterra La Casona
Pl Las Nazarenas 113, T084-234010, www.inkaterra.com.
A private, colonial-style boutique hotel in a converted 16th-century mansion, built on the site of Manco Cápac's palace. 11 exclusive suites, all facilities, concierge service with activities and excursions, highly regarded and the height of luxury.

$$$$ The Fallen Angel Guest House
Pl Las Nazarenas 221, T084-258184, www.fallenangelincusco.com.
A 4-room luxury hotel above the restaurant of the same name. Each suite is decorated in its own lavish style (with living room, dining room, bathroom, feather duvets, heating), very comfortable and a far cry from the usual adaptation of colonial buildings elsewhere in the city. With all amenities, excellent service.

$$$ Andean Wings
Siete Cuartones 225, T084-243166, www.andeanwingshotel.com.
In a restored 17th-century house, intimate suites, some with jacuzzi, are individually designed (one is accessible for the disabled), spa, restaurant and bar.

$$$ Casa Andina Classic – Cusco Plaza
Portal Espinar 142, T084-231733, www.casa-andina.com.
40-room hotel near plaza, ATM and safe deposit box. Equally recommendable are **Casa Andina Koricancha** (San Agustín 371, T084-252633), **Casa Andina Catedral** (Santa Catalina Angosta 149, T084-233661), and the **Casa Andina San Blas** (Chihuampata 278, San Blas, T084-263694), all of which are in the same vein.

$$$ Loreto Boutique Hotel
Pasaje Loreto 115, T084-226352, www.loretoboutiquehotel.com.
Great location; 12 spacious rooms with original Inca walls, upgraded to boutique status. Laundry service, will help organize travel services including guides and taxis, free airport pick-up.

$$$ Marqueses
Garcilaso 256, T084-264249, www.hotelmarqueses.com.
Spanish colonial style, with 16/17th-century style religious paintings and 2 lovely courtyards. Rooms have heavy curtains and some are a little dark; luxury rooms have bath and shower. Buffet breakfast.

$$$ Sonesta Posadas del Inca
Portal Espinar 108, T084-22706; and Av el Sol 954, T084-581200; www.sonesta.com.
Includes buffet breakfast, warmly decorated rooms with heating, safe, some rooms on 3rd floor have view of Plaza, very helpful, English spoken, restaurant with Andean food, excellent service.

$$$ Tierra Viva Cusco Plaza
Suecia 345, T084-245858, www.tierravivahoteles.com.
Boutique hotel in the former residence of Gonzalo Pizarro. Rooms and suites have comfortable beds, heating, minibar, safe, with excellent breakfast. Exemplary service, airport transfers.

$$ EcoPackers Hostel
Santa Teresa 375, T084-235460, www.ecopackersperu.com.
Ecologically friendly, well-regarded *hostal* in a colonial *casona*, double rooms with en suite or dorms for 4-18 people, communal kitchen, games room, bar, large-screen TV room, garage for bicycles or motorcycles.

$$ Pariwana
Mesón de la Estrella 136, T084-233751, www.pariwana-hostel.com.
Variety of rooms in a converted colonial mansion with courtyard, from doubles with bath to dorms sleeping 14, also girls only dorm, restaurant, bar/lounge, English spoken, lots of activities.

$$-$ Hostal Resbalosa
Resbalosa 494, T084-224839,
www.hostalresbalosa.com.
Private or shared bath, hot water all day,
ask for a room with a view, dorm beds,
laundry facilities, full breakfast extra.

$$-$ Pirwa Hostels
T084-244315, www.pirwahostelscusco.com.
This chain of hostels offers a range of rooms
from private doubles with bath to dorms, in
colonial buildings, lockers, 24-hr reception:
Pirwa Posada del Corregidor (Portal de
Panes 151, Pl de Armas) and Pirwa Garcilaso
(Av Garcilaso 210, Wanchac) are the B&B
branches; **Pirwa Backpackers San Blas**
(Tandapata 670), and **Pirwa Backpackers
Colonial** (Pl San Francisco 360).

$$-$ The Point
Mesón de la Estrella 172, T084-506698,
www.thepointhostels.com.
Dormitory accommodation, also has
doubles and singles, hot showers,
good party atmosphere.

$ El Procurador del Cusco
Coricalle 425, Prolongación Procuradores,
T084-243559, http://hostelprocuradordel
cusco.blogspot.com.
Youth hostel. Price includes use of the basic
kitchen and laundry area, with or without
bath, basic rooms, but upstairs is better,
helpful, good value.

$ Hostal Royal Frankenstein
San Juan de Dios 260, 2 blocks from
the Plaza de Armas, T084-236999,
www.hostal-frankenstein.net.
Eccentric place but a frequent favourite,
with private or shared bath, hot water, safe,
kitchen, includes breakfast, small charge
for computer, heater and laundry, medical
services, German-owned, German and
English spoken.

Beyond the Plaza, including San Blas

$$$$ Casa Andina Private Collection Cusco
Plazoleta de Limacpampa Chico 473,
T084-232610, www.casa-andina.com.
The most upmarket and comfortable in
this group, in a 16th-century mansion with
4 courtyards, enriched oxygen available in
the rooms, plus a gourmet restaurant serving
local cuisine and a bar with an extensive
pisco collection.

$$$$ Casa Cartagena
Pumacurco 336, T084-224356,
www.casacartagena.com.
In a converted monastery and national
heritage building, super-deluxe facilities
with Italian design and colonial features,
4 levels of suite, **La Chola** restaurant,
extensive complimentary Qoya spa, enriched
oxygen system, and all services to be
expected in a Luxury Properties group hotel.

$$$$ El Mercado
C Siete Cuartones 306, T084-582640,
www.elmercadotunqui.com.
On the site of a former market close to
the Plaza de Armas, owned by **Mountain
Lodges of Peru**, superior rooms and suites,
restaurant, bar, helpful staff.

$$$$ El Monasterio (Belmond)
C Palacios 136, Plazoleta Nazarenas,
T084-604000, www.monasteriohotel.com.
5-star, beautifully restored Seminary of San
Antonio Abad (a Peruvian National Historical
Landmark), including the baroque chapel,
spacious comfortable rooms with all facilities
(some rooms offer an oxygen-enriched
atmosphere), very helpful staff (buffet
breakfast open to non-residents, will fill you
up for the rest of the day), good restaurants,
lunch and dinner à la carte, business centre.

$$$$ Palacio del Inka Luxury Collection
Plazoleta Santo Domingo 259, T084-231961,
www.libertador.com.pe.

5-star, good, especially the service, warm and bright, **Inti Raymi** restaurant, excellent, live music in the evening.

$$$$ Palacio Nazarenas (Belmond)
Plazoleta Nazarenas 144, T084-582222, www.palacionazarenas.com.
Boutique hotel in a beautifully restored former convent. Outdoor swimming pool, spa, history booklet and cooking classes.

$$$$-$$$ Casa San Blas
Tocuyeros 566, just off Cuesta San Blas, T084-237900, www.casasanblas.com.
An international-standard boutique hotel with bright, airy rooms decorated with traditional textiles. Breakfast, served in the **Tika Bistro** downstairs. Pleasant balcony with good views, attentive service.

$$$$-$$$ Quinua Villa Boutique
Pasaje Santa Rosa A-8, parallel to Tandapata, T084-242646, www.quinua.com.pe.
A beautiful living museum, 5 different apartments, each with a different theme and kitchen, low season discounts.

$$$ El Arqueólogo
Pumacurco 408, T084-232522, www.hotelarqueologo.com.
Helpful, French and English spoken, heating extra, will store luggage, garden, cafeteria and kitchen. Same group as **Vida Tours** (Ladrillo 425, T084-227750, www.vidatours.com). Traditional and adventure tourism.

$$$ La Encantada
Tandapata 354, T084-242206, www.encantadaperu.com.
Good beds, rooftop spa, fabulous views of the city. Swiss-Peruvian owned.

$$$ Los Apus Hotel & Mirador
Atocsaycuchi 515 y Choquechaca, San Blas, T084-264243, www.losapushotel.com.
Includes airport transfer, full of character, very clean and smart, central heating, disabled facilities, 2 restaurants, 4th floor terrace.

$$$ Pensión Alemana
Tandapata 260, San Blas, T084-226861, www.hotel-cuzco.com.
Colonial-style modern building. Swiss-owned, welcoming, comfortable, discount in low season.

$$$ Rumi Punku
Choquechaca 339, T084-221102, www.rumipunku.com.
An Inca doorway leading to a sunny courtyard, comfortable rooms, helpful staff, safe, spa (US$15 per day).

$$$-$$ Amaru Hostal Group
Cuesta San Blas 541, T084-225499, www.amaruhostal.com.
Private or shared bath. Price includes airport/train/bus pick-up. Oxygen, kitchen for use in the evenings, book exchange. Rooms around a pretty courtyard, good beds, pleasant, relaxing, some same price category and services at: **Amaru Colonial** (Chihuampata 642, San Blas, T084-223521, www.amaruhostal2.com), and **Hostería de Anita** (Alabado 525-5, T084-225933, www.hosteriadeanita.com), safe, quiet, good breakfast.

$$$-$$ Andenes al Cielo
Choquechaca 176, T084-222237, www.andenesalcielo.com.
At the foot of the San Blas district, 15 rooms and a penthouse in renovated historic home, most expensive rooms have fireplaces, all with either balconies or patios, heating. Buffet breakfast, rooftop patio, safe deposit box, free airport pick up.

$$$-$$ Casona Les Pleiades
Tandapata 116, T084-506430, www.casona-pleiades.com.
Small guesthouse in renovated colonial house, cosy and warm, generous hosts, hot water, video lounge and book exchange, café, free airport pickup with reservation, lots of info, low season discounts.

$$$-$$ Hostal Casa de Campo
Tandapata 298 (at the end of the street), T084-244404, www.hotelcasadecampo.com.

Some of the top rooms have a *lot* of steps up to them, hot water, includes bus/airport/rail transfer with reservations, 10% discount for Footprint book owners, safe deposit box, sun terrace, quiet, relaxing, all rooms have great views, Dutch and English spoken, take a taxi after dark.

$$$-$$ Hostal El Balcón
Tambo de Montero 222, T084-236738, www.balconcusco.com.
Warm atmosphere, very welcoming, quiet, laundry, meals on request, English spoken, wonderful views, beautiful garden.

$$$-$$ Hostal Tikawasi
Tandapata 491, T084-231609, www.tikawasi.com.
Includes heating, family-run, lovely garden overlooking the city. Stylish, modern rooms with good views, comfortable beds.

$$ Albergue Casa Campesina
Av Tullumayo 274, T084-233466, www.hotelescbc-cusco.com/casacam/.
Private or shared bath, lovely place, funds support the **Casa Campesina** organization (www.cbc.org.pe), which is linked to local *campesina* communities (see also **Store of Weavers** under Shopping, page 251).

$$ Andenes de Saphi
Saphi 848, T084-227561, www.andenesdesaphi.com.
Set around 3 Inca terraces. Rooms nicely decorated with animal themes. Common room, laundry services, bright reception area.

$$ Casa Elena
Choquechaca 162, T084-241202, www.casaelenacusco.com.
French/Peruvian hostel, very comfortable, helpful staff, good choice.

$$ El Grial
Carmen Alto 112, T084-223012, www.hostalelgrial.com.
Family-run, 2 star hostel, in a 17th-century building, coffee shop, laundry service.

$$ Hostal Kuntur Wasi
Tandapata 352-A, San Blas, T084-227570, www.hospedajekunturwasi.com.
Great views, cheaper without bath, use of basic kitchen and laundry (both extra), owner speaks a bit of English and is very helpful and welcoming, a pleasant place to stay.

$$ Hostal Qorichaska
Nueva Alta 458, T084-228974, www.qorichaskaperu.com.
Rooms are clean and sunny, the older ones have traditional balconies. Also has dorms, mixed and men or women only. Laundry service. A good choice.

$$ Hostal Quipu
Fierro 495, T084-236179, www.hostalquipu.com.
Small pleasant rooms with private bath and reliable hot water, sunny patio, modern kitchen facilities, helpful staff, good value.

$$ Hostal Suecia
Suecia 332, T084-233282, www.hostalsuecia1.com.
Central location in a beautiful colonial building, private bath, hot showers, laundry.

$$ Niños/Hotel Meloc
Meloc 442, T084-231424, www.ninoshotel.com.
Modern decor in colonial building. Hot water, excellent breakfast extra, restaurant, laundry service, luggage store, English spoken, run as part of the Dutch foundation **Niños Unidos Peruanos** and all profits are invested in projects to help street children. Also has **Niños 2/Hotel Fierro** (C Fierro 476, T084-254611), with all the same features.

$$-$ Casa de La Gringa
Tandapata y Pasñapacana 148, T084-241168, www.casadelagringa.com.
Uniquely decorated rooms, lots of art and colour, 24-hr hot water, kitchen, common areas, heaters, safe homely feeling. See also **Another Planet**, page 257.

$$-$ Flying Dog Hostel
Choquechaca 469, T084-253997,
www.flyingdogperu.com.
Shared and private rooms and family
suites, bar, living room with TV and DVD,
buffet breakfast.

$$-$ Hostal Loki
Cuesta Santa Ana 601, T084-243705,
www.lokihostel.com/en/cusco.
Huge bustling hostel in a restored viceroy's
residence on the steep Cuesta Santa Ana,
dorms and rooms set around a beautiful
courtyard, comfortable beds, hot water.
A great meeting place.

$$-$ Mamá Simona Hostel
Ceniza 364, San Pedro, near the market,
T084-260408, www.mamasimona.com.
Traditional old house with rooms around
a courtyard, doubles (heating extra) and
dorms, duvets, shared bathrooms, hot water,
towel rental, includes breakfast, laundry
service, helpful.

$$-$ The WalkOn Inn
Suecia 504, T084-235065,
www.walkoninn.com.pe.
2 blocks from the Plaza, dorms and rooms
with private or shared bathrooms, breakfast
extra, laundry service, airport/bus station
pick-up available.

$ Albergue Municipal
Quiscapata 240 (between Resbalosa and
Arcoiris), T984-252506.
Youth hostel. Dormitories and double rooms
with shared bath, great views, small cooking
facilities, laundry, luggage store, very clean,
pleasant and good value.

$ Estrellita
Av Tullumayo 445, parte Alta, T084-234134.
Most rooms with shared bath, 2 with private
bath, basic but excellent value, safe parking
available for bikes.

$ Hitchhikers B&B Backpackers Hostel
Saphi 440, T084-260079,
www.hhikersperu.com.

Located close to the plaza, mixture of dorms
and 1- to 3-bed private rooms with private
or shared bath, includes breakfast, hot water,
kitchen, lockers.

$ Hospedaje El Artesano de San Blas
Suytuccato 790, San Blas, T084-263968,
elartesano2015@hotmail.com.
Many bright and airy rooms overlooking
courtyard, quiet, taxis leave you at Plaza
San Blas, then it's a steep walk uphill for
5-10 mins.

$ Hospedaje Inka
Suytuccato 848, San Blas,T084-231995,
http://hospedajeinka.weebly.com.
Taxis leave you at Plaza San Blas, walk steeply
uphill for 5-10 mins, or phone the *hostal.*
Private or shared bath. Wonderful views,
spacious rooms, very helpful owner, Américo.

$ Hostal Killipata
Killichapata 238, just off Tambo de Montero,
T084-236668, hostalkillipata@hotmail.com.
Family-run lodging with variety of room
sizes, private or shared bath, good showers,
hot water and fully equipped kitchen.
Breakfast is extra.

$ Hostal Pakcha Real
Tandapata 300, San Blas, T084-237484,
www.hostalpakchareal.com.
Family-run, hot water, relaxed, with or
without bath. Breakfast included, laundry
facilities extra. Airport/train/bus pick-up, but
call ahead if arriving late.

$ Hostal Wayras
Nueva Alta 451, T084-237930,
wayrashouse@hotmail.com.
Small quiet place, best rooms on top floor,
cheaper with shared bath, solar hot water,
small kitchen, attentive owner.

$ Maison de la Jeunesse
Av El Sol, Cuadra 5, Pasaje Grace, Edif San
Jorge (down a small side street opposite
Museo Sitio de Qoricancha), T084-235617,
hostellingcusco@hotmail.com.
Double rooms with bath or a bed in a dorm
with shared bath; TV and video room,

lockers, cooking facilities and hot water. Affiliated to HI (www.hihostels.com).

$ The Blue House
Kiskapata 291 (parallel and above Tandapata), T084-242407.
Cosy family *hostal*, good value. Reductions for longer stays, includes breakfast, hot shower, views.

$ Tu Casita
C Hospital 787(entrance down an alley near San Pedro market), T984-754519, tucasitacusco@gmail.com.
Dorms, shared bath, 2 kitchens, balcony. Friendly owner Delcy.

Restaurants

Around the Plaza de Armas
There are many good cheap restaurants on Procuradores, Plateros and Tecseccocha.

$$$ A Mi Manera
Triunfo 393, T084-222219.
Imaginative *Novo Andino* cuisine with open kitchen. Great hospitality and atmosphere.

$$$ Chicha
Plaza Regocijo 261, p 2 (above El Truco), T084-240520. Daily 1200-2400.
Specializes in regional dishes created by restaurateur Gastón Acurio (see box, page 56), Peruvian cuisine of the highest standards in a renovated colonial house, at one time the royal mint, tastefully decorated, open-to-view kitchen, bar with a variety of *pisco sours*, good service.

$$$ Cicciolina
Triunfo 393, 2nd floor, T084-239510. Reservations required for dinner.
Sophisticated cooking focusing largely on Italian/Mediterranean cuisine, impressive wine list. Good atmosphere, great for a special occasion.

$$$ El Truco
Plaza Regocijo 261, T084-235295. Open 0900-0100.

Excellent local and international dishes, buffet lunch 1200-1500.

$$$ Fallen Angel
Plazoleta Nazarenas 221, T084-258184. Sun from 1500.
International and *Novo Andino* gourmet cuisine, great steaks, genuinely innovative interior design, worth checking out their events.

$$$ Fusi Chicken and Grill
Av El Sol 106, T084-233341. Open 1100-2300.
In the La Merced commercial centre, 2nd floor. *Novo Andino* and international cuisine in a chic contemporary setting, fine wines.

$$$ Greens Organic
Santa Catalina Angosta 135, upstairs, T084-254753.
Exclusively organic, but not wholly vegetarian, ingredients in fusion cuisine, very good.

$$$ Incanto
Santa Catalina Angosta 135, T084-254753. Daily 1100-2400.
Under same ownership as **Inka Grill** and with the same standards, restaurant has Inca stonework and serves Italian dishes (pastas, grilled meats, pizzas), and desserts, accompanied by an extensive wine list. Also Peruvian delicatessen.

$$$ Inka Grill
Portal de Panes 115, Pl de Armas, T084-262992.
Specializing in *Novo Andino* cuisine, also home-made pastas, wide vegetarian selection, live music, excellent coffee and home-made pastries 'to go'.

$$$ Kión
Triunfo 370, T084-431862. Open 1100-2300.
Traditional *chifa* and regional flavours using Chinese techniques.

$$$ Limo
Portal de Carnes 236, T084-240668.
On 2nd floor of a colonial mansion overlooking the Plaza de Armas, Peruvian

cuisine of the highest standard, with strong emphasis on fish and seafood, fine pisco bar, good service and atmosphere.

$$$ MAP Café
In Museo de Arte Precolombino,
Plaza de las Nazarenas 231, T084-242476.
Open 1100-1500 and 1830-2200.
Haute cuisine approach to traditional dishes using Andean crops, innovative children's menu, minimalist design and top-class service.

$$$ Papacho's
Portal de Belén 115, upstairs, off Plaza de Armas, T084-245359. Daily 1200-2400.
Gastón Acurio's upmarket US-style diner with a Peruvian twist. Emphasis on burgers.

$$$ Tunupa
Portal Confiturias 233, p 2, Pl de Armas.
Large restaurant, small balcony overlooking Plaza, international, Peruvian and *Novo Andino* cuisine, good buffet US$15, nicely decorated, cocktail lounge, live music and dance at 1930 and 2130.

$$$ Tupananchis
Portal Espinar 180-184, T084-231198.
Tasty *Novo Andino* and fusion cuisine in a sophisticated atmosphere.

$$$-$$ Café Morena
Plateros 348B, T084-437832.
Mon-Sun 1200-2200.
Modern takes on Peruvian food in a nicely decorated setting, generous portions, good service. Recommended.

$$ Pucará
Plateros 309. Mon-Sat 1230-2200.
Peruvian and international food (no language skills required as a sample plate of their daily menu is placed in the window at lunchtime), nice atmosphere.

$$ Sara
Santa Catalina Ancha 370, T084-261691.
Vegetarian-friendly organic café bistro, stylish and modern setting, menu includes

both traditional Peruvian dishes as well as pasta and other international dishes.

$$ Víctor Victoria
Tecseccocha 466, T084-252854.
Daily 0700-2200.
Set lunch with salad bar, Peruvian dishes and a few vegetarian options.

$ El Encuentro
Tigre 130. Daily 0800-2200.
Breakfast, economical *menú* and à la carte. Good vegetarian food, very busy at lunchtime.

Cafés

Café Cocla
Mesón De La Estrella 137.
Excellent coffee, also sells organic coffee beans, works with several cooperatives in the Cuzco region.

Café El Ayllu
Almagro 133, and Marqués 263.
Classical/folk music, good atmosphere, superb range of milk products, wonderful apple pastries, good selection for breakfast, great juices, quick service. A Cuzco institution.

Café Halliy
Plateros 363.
Popular meeting place, especially for breakfast, good for comments on guides, has good snacks and 'copa Halliy' (fruit, muesli, yoghurt, honey and chocolate cake), also good vegetarian *menú* and set lunch.

Café Perla
Santa Catalina Ancha 304, on the plazoleta.
Extensive menu of light meals, sandwiches, desserts and coffee, including beans for sale roasted on the premises. Popular.

Dolce Vita
Santa Catalina Ancha 366. Open 1000-2100.
Delicious Italian ice cream.

Dos por Tres
Marquez 271.
Popular for over 20 years, great coffee and cakes.

La Bondiet
Heladeros 118, 0730-2300.
Upmarket French café with a good
selection of sweet and savoury pastries,
empanadas, good sandwiches, juices and
coffee. A local favourite.

Museo del Café
*Espaderos 136, around a beautifully restored
colonial courtyard.*
Coffee, snacks, sweets and a chance get to
know the coffee making process. Coffee
accessories for sale.

Yajúú! Juice Bar
Portal Confitería 249. Daily 0700-2300.
Fresh inexpensive juices and smoothies as
well as sandwiches.

Beyond the Plaza, including San Blas

$$$ Baco
Ruinas 465, T084-242808.
Wine bar and bistro-style restaurant, same
owner as Cicciolina. Specializes in BBQ and
grilled meats, also veggie dishes, pizzas
and good wines. Unpretentious and comfy,
groups welcome.

$$$ Le Soleil
*C San Agustin 275, in La Lune hotel, T084-
240543, www.restaurantelesoleilcusco.com.
Closed Wed.*
Excellent restaurant using local products to
make classic French cuisine.

$$$ Pachapapa
*Plazoleta San Blas 120, opposite church of San
Blas, T084-241318.*
A beautiful patio restaurant in a colonial
house, good Cusqueña and other dishes,
at night diners can sit in their own, private
colonial dining room, attentive staff.

$$$-$$ Divina Comedia
*Pumacurco 408, T084-437640.
Daily 1200-1500, 1800-2200.*
An elegant restaurant just 1 block
from the Monasterio hotel, diners

are entertained by classical piano
and singing. Friendly atmosphere with
comfortable seating, perfect for a special
night out, reasonable prices.

$$ Blue Alpaca
*Choquechaca 278, T084-233565.
Daily 1100-2200.*
Variety of national and international dishes,
many vegetarian options, hearty alpaca
burgers, lunch and dinner *menú*.

$$ El Paisa
Av El Sol 819, T084-501717. Open 0900-1700.
Typical northern Peruvian dishes including
ceviche and goat.

$$ Jack's Café
*Choquechaca y Cuesta San Blas,
T084-254606.*
Excellent varied menu, generous portions,
relaxed atmosphere, can get very busy at
lunchtime, expect a queue in high season.

$$ Justina
Palacios 110. Mon-Sat from 1800.
Good value, good quality pizzería,
with wine bar. It's at the back of a patio.

$$ Kushka...fé
*Choquechaca 131-A and Portal Espinar 159.
Daily 0700-2300.*
Great food in a nice setting, English spoken.

$$ La Bodega 138
Herrajes 138, T084-260272.
Excellent pizza, good salads and pasta.
Warm and welcoming. Craft beer.

$$ La Cusqueñita
Tullumayo 227 y Av Garcilaso.
A traditional *picantería* serving Cuzco
specialities, live music and dance show daily.

$$ Los Toldos
Almagro 171, T084-229829 (deliveries).
Grilled chicken, fries and salad bar,
also *trattoria* with home-made pasta
and pizza, delivery.

\$\$ Macondo
Cuesta San Blas 571, T084-227887.
Interesting restaurant with an imaginative
menu, good food, well-furnished,
gay friendly.

\$\$ Tacomanía
Tandapata 917. Dinner only.
Serving tacos cooked to order with freshly
made Mexican fillings.
Owned by Englishman Nick Garret.

\$ Café Punchay
Choquechaca 229, T084-261504.
German-owned vegetarian restaurant, with
a variety of pasta and potato dishes, good
range of wines and spirits, projector for
international sports and you can bring a
DVD for your own private movie showing.

\$ La Chomba
Tullumayo 339. Lunch only.
Large portions of traditional Peruvian food.
Popular with locals, good for tourists seeking
a genuine experience.

Cafés

Juanito's Sandwich Café
7 Angelitos 638, San Blas.
Great grilled veggie and meaty burgers and
sandwiches, coffee, tea and hot chocolate.
Juanito himself is a great character and the
café stays open late.

La Valeriana
*Av El Sol 576, and Mantas near
Plaza de Armas.*
Good coffee and pastries.
Try the *lúcuma* cupcakes.

Panadería El Buen Pastor
Cuesta San Blas 579.
Very good bread, *empanadas* and pastries,
proceeds go to a charity for orphans and
street children.

Qucharitas
Procuradores 385 and Plaza San Francisco 138.
Ice cream made right in front of you, with a
wide variety of flavours and toppings.

The Meeting Place
Plazoleta San Blas 630.
Good coffee, waffles and pastries. Supports
various social projects. Popular.

Bars and clubs

Bars

Indigo
Tecseccocha 2, p 2, T084-260271.
Lounge, cocktail bar and serves Asian and
local food. A log fire keeps out the night-
time cold.

Km 0 (Arte y Tapas)
Tandapata 100, San Blas.
Mediterranean themed bar tucked in behind
San Blas, good snacks and tapas, with live
music every night (around 2200).

Los Perros Bar
Tecseccocha 436. Open 1100-0100.
Great place to chill out on comfy couches,
excellent music, welcoming, good coffee,
tasty meals available (including vegetarian),
book exchange, English and other
magazines, board games.

Museo del Pisco
*Santa Catalina Ancha 398, T084-262709,
www.museodelpisco.org. Daily 1100-0100.*
A bar where you can sample many kinds
of pisco; tapas-style food served.

Norton's Pub
Santa Catalina Angosta 116. Daily 0700-0300.
On the corner of the Plaza de Armas, fine
balcony, microbrews, sandwiches and light
meals, cable TV, English spoken, pool, darts,
motorcycle theme. Very popular.

Paddy's Pub
*Triunfo 124 on the corner of the plaza.
Open 1000-0100.*
Irish theme pub, deservedly popular,
good grub.

Clubs

El Garabato Video Music Club
Plateros 316. Daily 1600-0300.
Dance area, lounge for chilling, bar, live shows 2300-0030 (all sorts of styles) and large screen showing music videos.

Mama Africa
Portal de Panes 109.
Cool music and clubber's spot, good food with varied menu, happy hour till 2300, good value.

Mythology
Portal de Carnes 298, p 2.
Mostly an early '80s and '90s combination of cheese, punk and classic, popular.

Temple
Tecseccocha y Tigre. Open 2100-0600.
A big nightclub set in a covered courtyard with large bar and pool table. Live bands some nights.

Ukuku's
Plateros 316. Entry US$1.35.
Very popular, good atmosphere, good mix of music including live shows nightly.

Entertainment

Centro Qosqo de Arte Nativo, *Av El Sol 604, T084-227901.* Regular nightly folklore show from 1900 to 2030, entrance on BTC ticket.
La Esencia, *Limacpampa Chico 400, upstairs, T984-169134, www.facebook. com/laesenciacusco.* Nightly music, storytelling, theatre or movies. Serves tea and light snacks.
Teatro Municipal, *C Mesón de la Estrella 149 (T084-226203 for information 0900-1300 and 1500-1900).* Plays, dancing and shows, mostly Thu-Sun. They also run classes in music and dancing Jan-Mar which are great value.

Festivals

Feb or Mar   Carnival in Cuzco is a messy affair with flour, water, cacti, bad fruit and animal manure being thrown about in the streets.

Easter Mon   El Señor de los Temblores (Lord of the Earthquakes). Procession starting at 1600 outside the Cathedral. A large crucifix is paraded through the streets, returning to the Plaza de Armas around 2000 to bless the tens of thousands of people who have assembled there.

2-3 May   Vigil of the Cross takes place at all mountaintops with crosses on them, a boisterous affair.

Jun   Corpus Christi (Thu after Trinity Sun). All the statues of the Virgin and the saints from Cuzco's churches are paraded through the streets to the Cathedral. The Plaza de Armas is surrounded by tables with women selling *cuy* (guinea pig) and a mixed grill called *chiriuchu* (*cuy*, chicken, tortillas, fish eggs, water-weeds, maize, cheese and sausage) and lots of Cusqueña beer.

24 Jun   The pageant of **Inti Raymi**. The Inca festival of the winter solstice, is enacted in Quechua at 1000 at the Qoricancha, moving on to Sacsayhuaman at 1300. Tickets for the stands can be bought a week in advance from the Emufec office (Santa Teresa 142), US$100-140, less if bought Mar-May. Travel agents can arrange the whole day for you, with meeting points, transport, reserved seats and packed lunch. Those who try to persuade you to buy a ticket for the right to film or take photos are being dishonest. On the night before Inti Raymi, the Plaza de Armas is crowded with processions and food stalls. Try to arrive in Cuzco 15 days before Inti Raymi.

28 Jul   Peruvian Independence Day. Prices shoot up during these celebrations.

Aug   On the last Sun is the **Huarachicoy** festival at Sacsayhuaman, a spectacular re-enactment of the Inca manhood rite, performed in dazzling costumes by boys from a local school.

8 Sep Day of the Virgin is a colourful procession of masked dancers from the church of Almudena, at the southwest edge of Cuzco, near Belén, to the Plaza de San Francisco. There is also a splendid fair at Almudena, and a free bull fight on the following day.

1 Nov All Saints' Day, celebrated everywhere with bread dolls and traditional cooking.

8 Dec Day of the Immaculate Conception. Churches and museums close at 1200.

24 Dec Santuranticuy, 'the buying of saints', with a big crafts market in the plaza, very noisy until early hours of the 25th. This is one of the best festivals with people from the mountains coming to celebrate Christmas in Cuzco.

Shopping

Arts and crafts

In the Plaza San Blas and the surrounding area, authentic Cuzco crafts still survive. A market is held on Sat. Many leading artisans welcome visitors. Among fine objects made are Biblical figures from plaster, wheatflour and potatoes, reproductions of pre-Columbian ceramics and colonial sculptures, pious paintings, earthenware figurines, festive dolls and wood carvings.

Cuzco is one of the great weaving centres of Peru and excellent textiles can be found at good value. Be very careful of buying gold and silver objects and jewellery in and around Cuzco. Do not buy condor feathers, painted or unpainted, as it is illegal to sell or purchase them. Condors are being killed for this trade. The prison sentence is 4 years.

Agua y Tierra, *Cuesta San Blas 595, T084-236466*. Excellent quality crafts from rainforest communities and Ayacucho.

Factoría La Vicuñita, *Saphi 818, T084-233890*. Huge selection of alpaca clothing, textiles, ceramics, rugs and jewellery. They can show you how to distinguish between fake and real alpaca items.

Mendívil, *Plaza San Blas 619 and Hatunrumiyoc 486*. Known for its long-

necked statues of saints. Also sells a wide assortment of other crafts.

Mercado Artesanal, *Av El Sol, block 4*. Good for cheap crafts.

Pedazo de Arte, *Plateros 334B*. A tasteful collection of Andean handicrafts, many designed by Japanese owner Miki Suzuki.

Seminario, *inside Museo de Arte Precolombino, Plaza Nazarenas*. Sells the ceramics of Seminario-Behar (see page 267), plus cotton, basketry, jewellery, etc.

Books and maps

Centro de Estudios Regionales Andinos Bartolomé de las Casas, *Limacpampa Grande 571, T084-234073, www.cbc.org.pe*. Mon-Sat 1100-1400, 1600-1900. Good books on Peruvian history, archaeology, etc.

Jerusalem, *Heladeros 143, T084-235428*. 1030-1400,1630-1830. English and Spanish books, maps, guidebooks, postcards, book exchange (2 for 1). Helpful owner.

Maratón, *Av de la Cultura 1020, across the street from San Antonio Abad university, T084-225387*. Wide selection of IGN topographical maps, of interest to trekkers and cyclists.

SBS Librería Internacional, *Av El Sol 864, T084-248106, www.sbs.com.pe*. Mon-Fri 0900-2030, Sat 0930-1330, 1600-2000. Good selection of books and maps.

Camping equipment

For renting equipment, check with tour agencies. Check the equipment carefully as it is common for parts to be missing or damaged. A deposit is asked, plus credit card, passport or plane ticket. White gas (*bencina*), US$3 per litre, can be bought at hardware stores. Stove spirit (*alcohol para quemar*) is available at some pharmacies; cooking gas canisters can be found at hardware stores and camping shops.

Camping Rosly, *Procuradores 394, T084-248042*. New and second-hand gear sales and rentals; repairs. Owner speaks English.

Tatoo, *Espinar 144, T084-236703, www.tatoo.ws*. High-quality hiking, climbing and

Fabrics and alpaca clothing

Alpaca Golden, *Portal de Panes 151, T084-262914, alpaca.golden@terra.com.pe.* Also at Plazoleta Nazarenas 175. Designer, producer and retailer of fine alpaca clothing.

The Center for Traditional Textiles of Cuzco, *Av El Sol 603, T084-228117, www.textilescusco.org.* A non-profit organization that seeks to promote, refine and rediscover the weaving traditions of the Cuzco area. Tours of workshops, weaving classes, you can watch weavers at work. Also run 3-day weaving courses. Over 50% of the price goes direct to the weaver. Recommended.

Hilo, *Carmen Alto 260, T974-222294.* Fashionable items designed individually and handmade on-site. Run by Eibhlin Cassidy, she can adjust and tailor designs.

Josefina Olivera, *Portal Comercio 173, Plaza de Armas. Daily 1100-2100.* Sells old textiles and weavings, expensive but worth it to save pieces being cut up to make other item.

Kuna by Alpaca 111, *Plaza Regocijo 202, T084-243233, www.kuna.com.pe.* High-quality alpaca clothing with outlets also in hotels **Mariott** and **Palacio del Inka**.

Store of Weavers (Asociación Central de Artesanos y Artesanas del Sur Andino Inkakunaq Ruwaynin), *Av Tullumayo 274, T084-233466.* Store run by 6 local weaving communities, some of whose residents you can see working on site. All profits go to the weavers themselves.

Food and natural products

Choco Museo, *Garcilaso 210, 2nd floor, also in Ollantaytambo,T084-244765, www.chocomuseo.com.* Offers chocolate-making classes and runs trips to their cocoa plantation.

The Coca Museum, *Plaza San Blas 618, T084-501020, daily 0800-2000.* Shop/museum offers a free tour and sells coca-based products. Information about the history and nutritional value of coca; also about cocaine production.

La Cholita, *Los Portales Espinar 142B.* Special chocolates made with local ingredients.

San Isidro, *San Bernardo 134. Mon-Sat 0900-1300, 1600-2000.* Excellent local dairy products (great natural yoghurt and a variety of cheeses), honey and jams.

Jewellery

Cusco Ink, *Choquechaca 131.* Tattoo and piercing studio. Also sells Peruvian clothing and jewellery including a wide variety of gauges.

Esma Joyas, *in the courtyard at Triunfo 393.* Handmade jewellery with interesting designs distinct from other local options.

Ilaria, *Portal Carrizos 258, T084-246253.* Branches in hotels **Monasterio**, **Palacio del Inka** and at the airport. Recommended for jewellery and silver.

Inka Treasure, *Triunfo 375, T084-262914.* With branches at Plazoleta Nazarenas 159 and Portal de Panes 163. Also at the airport and the airport in Juliaca. Fine jewellery including goldwork, mostly with pre-Columbian designs, and silver with the owner's designs. Tours of workshops at Av Circunvalación, near Cristo Blanco. The stores also incorporate the work of famed jeweller Carlos Chakiras.

Spondylus, *Plazoleta San Blas 617 and Cuesta San Blas 505, T084-235227.* A good selection of interesting gold and silver jewellery and fashion tops with Inca and pre-Inca designs.

Markets

Wanchac (Av Garcilaso, southeast of centre) and **San Pedro Market** (see page 237) sell a variety of goods. **El Molino**, beyond the Terminal Terrestre, sells everything under the sun at knock-down prices, but quality is not guaranteed and there are no tourist items; it's fascinating but crowded, so go there by *colectivo* or taxi and don't take valuables.

Music

Sabino Huamán, *Tandapata 370, T984-296440.* Shop and workshop featuring traditional Andean instruments. With advance notice, he can help you create your own custom pan pipe. Recommended for anyone interested in Andean music.

What to do

There are many travel agencies in Cuzco. The sheer number and variety of tours on offer is bewildering and prices for the same tour can vary dramatically. In general you should only deal directly with the agencies themselves. Do not deal with guides who claim to be employed by agencies listed below without verifying their credentials. Be sure to ask whatever questions you may have in advance. Doing so by email offers the advantage of getting answers in writing but it may also be worth visiting a prospective operator in person to get a feeling for their organization. Competition among agencies can be fierce, but remember that the cheapest option is often not the best. For the latest information, consult other travellers returning from trips. Student discounts are only obtainable with an ISIC card.

City tours cost about US$10-15 for 4 hrs; check what sites are included and that the guide is experienced. Open sightseeing bus tour, about 1 hr, US$7; tickets sold from the Western Union office on Plaza de Armas (C del Medio, T979-340615). Various 'free' walking tours of Cuzco meet at the Plaza de Armas around midday, the guides expect a minimum tip, ask how much in advance.

In general visitors to Cuzco are satisfied with their tours. Independent travellers should keep in mind, however, that you can do any trek and visit any archaeological site on your own, except for the Inca Trail to Machu Picchu. Visiting independently requires more time, effort and greater language skills than taking a package tour, but it opens the door to a wealth of authentic experiences beyond the grasp of mass tourism.

For a list of recommended Tour operators for Manu, see page 340.

Cultural tours

Faces of Cusco, *Portal de Carnes 216, Plaza de Armas, T084-225745, www.faces ofcusco.com*. Cultural tours including the San Pedro Market, chocolate making, salsa dancing, cocktail classes, pisco and craft beer tasting. A good place to hang out and meet people. Friendly owner Vinay is a good source of information.

Milla Tourism, *Urb Lucrepata E16, T084-231710, www.millaturismo.com. Mon-Fri 0800-1300, 1500-1900, Sat 0800-1300*. Mystical tours to Cuzco's Inca ceremonial sites such as Pumamarca and the Temple of the Moon. Guide speaks only basic English. They also arrange cultural and environmental lectures and courses.

Inca Trail and general tours

Only a restricted number of agencies are licensed to operate **Inca Trail** trips. **Sernanp** (Oswaldo Baca 402, T084-229297, www. sernanp.gob.pe) verifies operating permits (see Visitors' tickets, above, for Dirección de Cultura office). Unlicensed agencies will sell Inca Trail trips, but pass clients on to the operating agency. This can cause confusion and booking problems at busy times, so book your preferred dates as early as possible in advance. Note also that many companies offer treks as alternatives to the trails to Machu Picchu. These treks are unregulated, so it is up to clients to ensure that the trekking company does not employ the sort of practices (such as mistreating porters, not clearing up rubbish) which are now prohibited on the trails to Machu Picchu. See Essential Inca Trail, page 282.

Action Valley Adventure Park, *C Santa Teresa 325, Plaza Regocijo, T954-777400, www.actionvalley.com*. Paragliding, rafting, bungee jumping and other tours and adventure activities.

Amazon Trails Peru, *Tandapata 660, T084-437374, or T984-714148, www.amazontrails peru.com*. Trekking tours around the area, including the Inca Trail, Salkantay and Choquequirao. Also well-equipped and well-guided trips to Manu.

Amazonas Explorer, *see under Rafting, mountain biking and trekking, below.* Run a high-quality 5-day/4-night Inca Trail trek, every Tue, Mar-Nov.

Andean Treks, *US company, no Cuzco storefront,* www.andeantreks.com. Manager Tom Hendrickson uses high-quality equipment and satellite phones. Organizes itineraries, from 2 to 15 days with a wide variety of activities in this area and further afield.

Andina Travel, *Plazoleta Santa Catalina 219, T084-251892,* www.andinatravel.com. Eco-agency with more than 10 years' experience operating all local treks and biking trips, notably the Lares Valley and Inca Trail. Has a reputation in Cuzco for local expertise and community projects.

Big Foot, *Triunfo 392 (oficina 213), T084-233836,* www.bigfootcusco.com. Tailor-made hiking trips, especially in the remote corners of the Vilcabamba and Vilcanota mountains; also the Inca Trail.

Chaska, *Garcilaso 265 p 2, of 6, T084-240424,* www.chaskatours.com. Dutch-Peruvian company offering cultural, adventure, nature and esoteric tours. They specialize in the **Inca Trail**, but also llama treks to Lares, treks to Choquequirao.

Culturas Peru, *Tandapata 354A, T084-243629,* www.culturasperu.com. Swiss/Peruvian company offering adventure, cultural, ecological and spiritual tours. Also specialize in alternative Inca trails.

Destinos Turísticos, *Portal de Panes 123, oficina 101-102, Plaza de Armas, T084-228168,* www.destinosturisticosperu.com. The owner speaks Spanish, English, Dutch and Portuguese and specializes in package tours from economic to 5-star budgets. Advice on booking jungle trips and renting mountain bikes. Very helpful.

EcoAmerica Peru, *C Marquez 259, of 8, 2nd floor, T999-705538,* www.ecoamerica peru.com. Associated with **America Tours** (La Paz, Bolivia). Owned by 3 experienced consultants in responsible travel, conservation and cultural heritage. Specializes in culture, history, nature, trekking, biking and birding tours. Knowledgeable guides, excellent customer service for independent travellers, groups or families. Also sell tours and flights to Bolivia.

Enigma Adventure, *C Fortunato L Herrera 214, Urb Magisterial 1a Etapa, T084-222155,* www.enigmaperu.com. Run by Spaniard Silvia Rico Coll. Well-organized, innovative trekking expeditions including a luxury service, Inca Trail and a variety of challenging alternatives. Also cultural tours to weaving communities, Ayahuasca therapy, climbing and biking.

Explorandes, *Paseo Zarzuela Q-2, Huancaro, T084-238380 ext 116,* www.explorandes.com. Experienced high-end adventure company. Arrange a wide variety of mountain treks; trips available in Peru and Ecuador, book

through website also arranges tours across Peru for lovers of orchids, ceramics or textiles. Award-winning environmental practices.

Fertur Peru Travel, *C Simón Bolívar No F23 317, T084-221304, www.fertur-travel.com.* Cuzco branch of the Lima tour operator, see page 67.

FlashpackerConnect Adventure Travel, *T+1-507-304 0075, www.flashpackerconnect.com.* Specializing in small group tours/treks to off-the-beaten track locations including the Inca Trail and Rainbow Mountain.

Gatur Cusco, *Puluchapata 140 (a small street off Av El Sol 3rd block), T084-245121, www.gaturcusco.com.* Esoteric, ecotourism, and general tours. Owner Dr José (Pepe) Altamirano is knowledgeable in Andean folk traditions. Excellent conventional tours, bilingual guides and transportation. Guides speak English, French, Spanish and German. They can also book internal flights.

Habitats Peru, *Condominio La Alborada B-507, Wanchac, T084-246271, www.habitats peru.com.* Birdwatching and mountain biking trips offered by Doris and Carlos. They also run a volunteer project near Quillabamba.

Hiking Peru, *Mantas 113, T984-651414, www.hikingperu.com.* 8-day treks to Espíritu Pampa; 7 days/6 nights around Ausangate; 4-day/3-night Lares Valley Trek.

Inca Explorers, *C Peru W-18, Ttio, T084-241070, www.incaexplorers.com.* Specialist trekking agency for small group expeditions in socially and environmentally responsible manner. Also 2-week hike in the Cordillera Vilcanota (passing Nevado Ausangate), and Choquequirao to Espíritu Pampa.

InkaNatura Travel, *Ricardo Palma J1, T084-243408, www.inkanatura.com.* Offers tours with special emphasis on sustainable tourism and conservation. Knowledgeable guides.

Inkayni Tours, *Triunfo 392, of 214, T084-232817, www.inkayniperutours.com.* Offers trips and treks to Machu Picchu, city tours in Cuzco and alternative treks, such as Salkantay, Lares, Huchuy Qosqo.

Llama Path, *Cuichipunco 257, T084-265134, www.llamapath.com.* A wide variety of local tours, specializing in Inca Trail and alternative treks, involved in environmental campaigns and porter welfare. Many good reports.

Mountain Lodges of Peru, *T084-243636 (North America T1-877-491-5261, Europe T+44-0-800-014-8886), www.mountainlodgesofperu.com.* Offer a series of lodges on the Santa Teresa trek to Machu Picchu. They also have 5- or 7-day guided tours going from lodge to lodge from Lamay to Ollantaytambo via the Lares Valley (www.laresadventure.com) with flexible options for activities, which are at Soraypampa (**Salkantay Lodge and Adventure Resort**), Huayraccmachay (**Wayra Lodge**), Collpapampa (**Colpa Lodge**) and Lucmabamba (**Lucma Lodge**).

Peru Treks & Adventure, *Av Pardo 540, T084-222722, www.perutreks.com.* Professional, high-quality tour operators specializing in trekking and cultural tours in the Cuzco region. They pride themselves on good treatment of porters and support staff and have been consistently recommended for professionalism and customer care; a portion of profits go to community projects.

Q'ente, *Choquechaca 229, p 2, T084-222535, www.qente.com.* Their Inca Trail service is recommended. Also private treks to Salkantay, Ausangate, Choquequirao, Vilcabamba and Q'eros. Horse riding to local ruins costs US$35 for 4-5 hrs. Very good, especially with children.

Sky Travel, *Santa Catalina Ancha 366, interior 3-C, T084-240141, www.skyperu.com.* English spoken. General tours around city and Sacred Valley. Inca Trail with good-sized double tents and a dinner tent (the group is asked what it would like on the menu 2 days before departure). Other trips include Vilcabamba and Ausangate (trekking).

Southamerica Planet, *Garcilaso 210, of 201 T084-241424, www.southamericaplanet.com.* Peruvian/Belgian-owned agency offering the Inca Trail, other treks around Cuzco and packages within Peru, as well as Bolivia and Patagonia.

THE BEST PRICES EVER !

ALL DEPARTURES 100% GUARANTEED

CULTURE & HERITAGE:

Our immersion tours cover all bases in Peru, complete with a knowledgeable and local guide to help along the way. Our 12 day trips take clients around our beautiful country from bustling cities, mountains, lakes and canyons, to rural communities to taste traditional food, and to live a-day-in-the-life of the local people; finishing in the mysterious citadel of Machu Picchu.

THE BEST IN TREKS & ADVENTURE:

Our professional and experienced staff plan everything from start to finish while allowing our visitors to have time to explore themselves. Our world class chefs ensure that everyone is energized at family-style meals with restaurant quality cuisine. We supply our porters with footwear, clothes and anything else that they need to ensure that they are comfortable whilst assisting our clients with their needs.

SPECIALLY SELECTED ACCOMMODATION

Whatever the accommodation, we always aim to supply the best. In our hotels, our clients experience a quality establishment for an affordable price. During homestays, the families are welcoming and accommodating to any needs. On our treks, our camping equipment is of a good standard, and we always offer added extras for anyone wanting some further comfort.

Valencia Travel Cusco offers the best in tours and Inca Trail Trek to Machu Picchu packages for the most memorable experience!

VALENCIA TRAVEL CUSCO

USA / CANADA: 1 - (888) 803 8004
Sales Service: 1 - (917) 983 2727
Customer Service: 1 - (860) 856 5858

e. info@valenciatravelcusco.com
w. www.valenciatravelcusco.com

Tanager Tours, *T084-237254, Lima T01-669 0825, www.tanagertours.com*. Specializes in birdwatching tours throughout Peru but all will also arrange other tours. Owners live in Cuzco but currently no office. Most of their tours are arranged via the internet and they contact clients at their accommodation.

T'ika Trek, *no storefront, UK T07768-948366, www.tikatrek.com*. UK contact Fiona Cameron lived for many years in Peru and is a keen hiker and biker. With over 10 years in the Cuzco tourism business, Fiona provides high-quality personalized tours all over Peru as well as to the Galápagos Islands (Ecuador). Focus is on small groups and families.

Trekperu, *Av República de Chile B-15, Parque Industrial, Wanchac, T084-261501, www.trekperu.com*. Experienced trek operator as well as other adventure sports and mountain biking. Offers 'culturally sensitive' tours. Cusco Biking Adventure includes support vehicle and good camping gear (but providing your own sleeping bag).

United Mice, *Av Pachacútec 424 A-5, T084-221139, www.unitedmice.com*. Inca Trail and alternative trail via Salkantay and Santa Teresa, well-established and reputable. Good guides who speak languages other than Spanish. Discount with student card, good food and equipment. City and Sacred Valley tours and treks to Choquequirao.

Valencia Travel Cusco, *Portal Panes 123, Centro Comercial Ruisenores, Of 306-307, T084-255907, www.valenciatravelcusco.com*. Specialize in adventure trails, both the classics and the roads less travelled, and immersion homestays.

Wayki Trek, *Quera 239, T084-224092, www.waykitrek.net*. Budget travel agency recommended for their Inca Trail service. Owner Americo Aguilar knows the area very well. Treks to several almost unknown Inca sites and interesting variations on the 'classic' Inca Trail with visits to porters' communities. Also treks to Ausangate, Salkantay and Choquequirao.

Language courses

Academia Latinoamericana de Español, www.latinoschools.com; **Acupari**, www.acupari.com; **Amauta Spanish School**, C San Agustín 249, www.amautaspanish.com; **Amigos Spanish School**, www.spanishcusco.com; **Fair Services Spanish School**, www.fairservices-peru.org; **San Blas Spanish School**, www.spanishschoolperu.com.

Rafting, mountain biking, paragliding and trekking

When looking for an adventure operator please consider more than just the price of your tour. Competition between companies in Cuzco is intense and price wars can lead to compromises in safety. Check the quality of safety equipment (lifejackets, etc) and ask about the number and experience of rescue kayakers and support staff. On large and potentially dangerous rivers like the Apurímac and Urubamba (where fatalities have occurred), this can make all the difference. Always use a licensed operator.

Amazonas Explorer, *Av Collasuyo 910, T084-252846, www.amazonas-explorer.com*. Experts in rafting, standup paddleboarding, catamaran sailing, mountain biking, horse riding and hiking. Owner Paul Cripps has great experience. Also offer the classic Inca Trail and alternatives. All options are at the higher end of the market. Highly recommended.

Apumayo, *Jr Ricardo Palma Ñ-II, Santa Mónica, Wanchac, T084-246018, www.apumayo.com*. Mon-Sat 0900-1300, 1600-2000. Urubamba rafting (from 0800-1530 every day); 3- to 4-day Apurímac trips. Also mountain biking to Maras and Moray in Sacred Valley, or from Cuzco to the jungle town of Quillabamba. This company also offers tours for disabled people, including rafting.

Apus Perú, *Cuichipunco 366, T084-232691, www.apus-peru.com*. Conducts most business by internet, specializes in alternatives to the Inca Trail, strong commitment to sustainability, well organized. Associated with **Threads of Peru** NGO which helps weavers.

Pachatusan Trek, *Villa Union Huancaro G-4, B 502, T084-231817, www.pachatusantrek.com.* Offers a wide variety to treks, as alternatives to the Inca Trail, professional and caring staff, "simply fantastic".

River Explorers, *Urb Kennedy, Av Los Brillantes B36, T084-431116, www.riverexplorers.com.* An adventure company offering mountain biking, trekking and rafting trips (on the Apurímac, Urubamba and Tambopata). Experienced and qualified guides with environmental awareness.

Terra Explorer Peru, *T084-237352, Urb Santa Ursula D4, Wanchac, www.terraexplorerperu. com.* Offers a wide range of trips from high-end rafting in the Sacred Valley and expeditions to the Colca and Cotahuasi canyons, trekking the Inca Trail and others, mountain biking, kayaking (including on Lake Titicaca) and jungle trips. All guides are bilingual.

Shamans and mystical plant experiences

San Pedro and Ayahuasca have been used since before Inca times, mostly as a sacred healing experience. If you choose to experience these plants, only do so under the guidance of a reputable agency or shaman and always have a friend with you who is not partaking. If the medicine is not prepared correctly, it can be highly toxic and dangerous. Never buy from someone who is not recommended; never buy off the streets, and never try to prepare the plants yourself.

Another Planet, *Tandapay y Pasñapakana 148, San Blas, T084-241168, www.another planetperu.org.* Run by Lesley Myburgh, who operates mystical and adventure tours in and around Cuzco, and is an expert in San Pedro cactus preparation. She arranges San Pedro sessions for healing in the garden of her house outside Cuzco. Tours meet at **Casa de la Gringa**, see page 243.

Etnikas Travel & Shamanic Healing, *Av la Cultura 2122 and Recoleta 674, T084-244516, www.etnikas.com.* A shamanic centre offering travel for mind, body and spirit. Offers ayahuasca sessions in their proper ceremonial context. Expensive but serious in their work.

Sumac Coca Travel, *San Agustín 245, T084-260311, www.sumaccoca.com.* Mystical tourism, offering Ayahuasca and San Pedro ceremonies, and also more conventional cultural tourism. Professional and caring.

Private guides

As most of the sights do not have any information or signs in English, a good guide can really improve your visit. Either arrange this before you set out or contract one at the sight you are visiting. A tip is expected at the end of the tour. Tours of the city or Sacred Valley cost US$50 for half-day, US$65 full day plus transport and entrance fees; a guide to Machu Picchu charges US$80 per day. A list of official guides is held by **Agotur Cusco** (C Heladeros 157, Of 34-F, p 3, T084-233457). See also www.leaplocal.org.

Transport

Air The airport is at Quispiquilla, near the bus terminal, 1.6 km from centre, airport information T084-222611/601. There are plans to build a new airport at Chinchero, 23 km northwest of the city (see page 267). The airport can get very busy; check in at least 2 hrs before your flight. Flights may be delayed or cancelled during the wet season, or may leave early if the weather is bad. The Arrivals area has mobile phone rentals, ATMs, LAC Dollar money exchange, an Oxyshot oxygen sales stand, an **iPerú** office, phone booths, restaurant, cafeteria and a Tourist Protection Bureau desk. Hotel representatives and travel agents operate at the airport offering transport to particular hotels for arriving visitors without prior bookings; take your time to choose a hotel at a price you can afford. If you already have a booking, taxis and tourist minibuses meet new arrivals and (should) take you to the hotel of your choice: be insistent. A taxi to and from the airport costs US$5-7 (US$11 from the official taxi desk. *Colectivos* cost US$0.30 between Plaza San Francisco and the airport car park.

To **Lima**, 55 mins, over 30 daily flights with **Avianca/TACA, Star Perú, LATAM** and **Peruvian Airlines**. To **Arequipa**, 30 mins daily with **LATAM** and **Avianca**. To **Juliaca** (for Puno), 1 hr daily with **LATAM**. To **Puerto Maldonado**, 30 mins, with **LATAM** and **Star Perú**. To **La Paz**, Peruvian Airlines and **Amaszonas** (www.amaszonas.com), 1 hr, daily.

Bus Long distance The busy, often crowded Terminal Terrestre is on Av Vallejo Santoni, block 2 (Prolongación Pachacútec). *Colectivo* from centre US$0.50 (not safe with luggage), taxi US$2-3. Platform tax US$0.50.

To **Lima,** US$35-65, a long ride (20-24 hrs) and worth paying for a comfortable bus. The route is via **Abancay** (US$7, 5 hrs) and **Nazca** (US$30, 13 hrs) on the Panamerican Highway. It is paved, but floods in the wet season often damage large sections. At night, take a blanket or sleeping bag to ward off the cold. Better companies to Lima include: **Molina**, daily at 2000; **Cruz del Sur** at 1400 and 1800; **Móvil Tours** at 0900 and 1700 and **Oltursa** at 1600. **Bredde** has most frequent service (5 daily) to Abancay; others include **Expreso Sánchez** and **Celajes**. **Los Chankas** to Abancay at 0730, 1930 and 2000 continues to **Andahuaylas** (US$13.50, 9 hrs) and **Ayacucho** (US$25, 16 hrs).

To **Juliaca**, 344 km, US$5 normal, US$9 semi-cama, US$12.50-17 cama, 5-6 hrs, with **Power** every 2 hrs, 0400-2300; several others. The road is fully paved, but after heavy rain buses may not run. To **Puno**, 388 km, 6-7 hrs; there are 3 levels of service, all via Juliaca: regular, stopping in Juliaca, US$7-12; direct, US$15-27, with **Tour Perú** (www.tourperu.com.pe), **Cruz del Sur** or **Transzela** (www.transzela.com.pe); and tourist service with 5 stops (Andahuaylillas church, Raqchi, Sicuani for lunch, La Raya and Pucará), US$45-50 (includes lunch, may or may not include entry tickets; ask), 10 hrs.

Tip...
If you're prone to travel sickness, take precautions on the way from Cuzco to Abancay; there are many curves but the scenery is magnificent.

Several companies offer the tourist service; all leave from private terminals: **Inka Express** at 0700 from Av 28 de Julio 211, 5th stop Urb Ttio, T084-247887; **Turismo Mer** at 0700 from Av La Paz A-3, Urb El Ovalo, Wanchac, T084-245171, www.turismomer.com.pe; and **Wonder Perú** at 0700 from Av 28 de Julio R2-1, Urb Ttio, Wanchac. In high season, reserve 2 days ahead. **Note** It is advisable to travel by day on the Juliaca-Puno-Cuzco route, for safety as well as the views.

To **Arequipa (via Juliaca)**, 521 km, 10-11 hrs, with **Cruz del Sur** at 2000 and 2030, US$37-47; **Cromotex** at 2000, US$11-36; **Flores** at 0645 and 2030, US$11; **Power** at 0500 and 1700, US$11; many others, mostly at night. A tourist service direct to **Chivay** on the **Colca Canyon** is offered by **4M Express** (Av 28 de Julio, Urbanización Ttio, Wanchac, T054-452296, www.4m-express.com), Tue, Thu and Sat at 0700, US$65 (lunch extra); see Colca Canyon Transport, page 200, for details.

To **Puerto Maldonado**, **Móvil** at 1000 and 2100, US$18-30, 10-11 hrs; also **Transportes Iguazú, Machupicchu, Palomino** and **Mendivil**, several daily, see page 342.

To the **Sacred Valley** There are 2 routes to Urubamba and Ollantaytambo: 1 via Pisac and Calca, the other via Chinchero. It is worth going on one and returning on the other. To **Pisac** (32 km, 1 hr, US$1.50), **Calca** (50 km, 1½ hrs, US$1.50) and **Urubamba** (72 km via Pisac and Calca, 2 hrs, US$1.50), *colectivos* and minibuses from C Pututi near Av la Cultura (see map, page 232), leave when full 0600-1800. Buses returning from Pisac are often full; last one back leaves around 2000. Taxis charge about US$20 one way to Pisac.

To **Chinchero** (23 km, 45 min US$2), **Urubamba** (50 km via Chinchero, 1½ hrs,

US$1.50), **Ollantaytambo** (70 km via Chinchero and Urubamba, 2 hrs, US$3.50-5), *colectivos* and minibuses from C Pavitos near Av Grau (see map, page 232). Taxi to Ollantaytambo US$22 one way.

Taxi In Cuzco taxis are recommended when arriving by air, train or bus. They have fixed prices but you have to stay alert to overpricing (always agree on the price in advance): in the centre US$1.50 in town (50% more after 2100 or 2200). Safer and more expensive are radio-dispatched taxis with a sign on the roof, including **Aló Cuzco** T084-222222, **Ocarina** T084-255000, and many others. Trips to **Sacsayhuaman**, US$10; ruins of **Tambo Machay** US$15-20 (3-4 people); day trip US$50-85.

Train PeruRail uses Estación Wanchac (Av El Sol, T084-238722). The ticket office is open Mon-Fri 0700-1700, Sat, Sun and holidays 0700-1200, and offers direct information and sales for all PeruRail services.

There are also **PeruRail** offices at Portal de Carnes 214, open daily 0700-2200, and Plaza Regocijo 202, same hours (take your passport or a copy when buying tickets). You can also buy tickets on www.perurail.com, at Lima airport (kiosk in domestic departures) or through a travel agent.

The *Andean Explorer* to Puno leaves Wanchac at 0800, Mon, Wed, Fri (Apr-Oct) and Sat, arriving at Puno around 1800; sit on the left for views. The train makes a stop to view the scenery at La Raya. Always check whether the train is running in the rainy season, when services may be cancelled. Cuzco to Puno costs US$289, Puno to Cuzco US$169; both US$5 less in low season. Meals are served on the train. When arriving in Cuzco, a tourist bus meets the train to take visitors to hotels whose touts offer rooms.

Trains to **Machu Picchu** and the **Sacred Valley** leave from Poroy, 7.5 km east of the centre, see page 276.

Upper Vilcanota Valley
head upstream to avoid the crowds

The main road from Cuzco to Lake Titicaca and Arequipa follows the Río Vilcanota upstream to La Raya, the border with the neighbouring department of Puno. Along the route are archaeological sites, fascinating colonial churches, beautiful lakes and the majestic Ausangate massif, where you can do some serious high-altitude trekking.

Southeast of Cuzco
Between the villages of Saylla and Oropesa are the extensive **Tipón ruins** ⓘ *5-km climb from village, daily 0800-1630, entry only with BTC; take a combi to Oropesa, then a taxi*, which include baths, terraces, irrigation systems, possibly an agricultural laboratory and a temple complex, accessible from a path leading from just above the last terrace. **Oropesa**, whose church contains a fine ornately carved pulpit, is the national 'Capital of Bread'; try the delicious sweet circular loaves known as *chutas*.

Paucartambo and around
At **Huambutío**, north of the village of Huacarpay, the road divides, with one branch leading northwest to Pisac and the other heading north to **Paucartambo**, on the eastern slope of Andes. This remote town, 80 km east of Cuzco, has become a popular tourist destination with basic accommodation. In the Centro Cultural is the Museo de los Pueblos, with exhibits on the history, culture, textiles and society of the region, including the famous **Fiesta de la Virgen del Carmen** (Mamacha Carmen; 16 July). This is a major

attraction, with masked dancers enacting rituals and folk tales. In the dry season, you can travel 44 km from Paucartambo, to **Tres Cruces**, along the Pilcopata road, turning left after 25 km. Come here for the sunrise in June and July, when peculiar climactic conditions make it appear that three suns are rising. Tour agencies in Cuzco can arrange transport and lodging.

Piquillacta
Daily 0800-1630, entry only with BTC. Buses to Urcos will drop you near the entrance.

Further on from Huacarpay are the extensive pre-Inca ruins of Piquillacta (which translates as the City of Fleas). This was an administrative centre at the southern end of the Huari Empire. The whole site is surrounded by a wall encompassing many enclosed compounds with buildings of over one storey; it appears that the walls were plastered and finished with a layer of lime.

Andahuaylillas to Urcos
Buses from Cuzco to Urcos leave when full from Av de la Cultura y Pje Carrasco, opposite the Hospital Regional, US$1, 1 hr, passing Andahuaylillas en route.

Andahuaylillas, 32 km southeast of Cuzco, has a lovely shady plaza and beautifully restored early 17th-century **church** ① *daily 0730-1730, on RBA ticket or US$5.50*. It's known as the 'Andean Sistine Chapel', due to its fabulous frescoes. There's also a splendid doorway and a gilded main altar. The next village, **Huaro**, also has a church whose interior is entirely covered with colourful frescoes. Urcos, meanwhile, is a chaotic commercial centre and transport hub; beware overcharging for everything here.

Cordillera Vilcanota
A spectacular road from Urcos crosses the Eastern Cordillera to Puerto Maldonado in the jungle (428 km, see page 334). Some 82 km from Urcos, near the base of Nevado Ausangate, is the town of **Ocongate**, a friendly regional centre with most services and a good place to prepare for trekking. Beyond Ocongate, **Tinqui** is a smaller, colder town with basic places to stay and eat; it's the starting point for hikes around Ausangate, which, at 6384 m, is the loftiest peak in the Vilcanota range. From Mahauyani, 12 km beyond Tinqui, a wide trail runs 8.5 km up to the sanctuary of Señor de Q'Olloriti at 4700 m, where a massive festival is held each June. Above the Christian sanctuary are the glaciers of Nevado Cinajara, the original object of devotion and still considered a sacred site. There is good trekking in the area and few visitors outside the festival.

Continuing east, some 47 km after passing the snow line on the Hualla-Hualla pass, at 4820 m, the super-hot thermal baths of **Marcapata** ① *173 km from Urcos, US$0.20*, provide a relaxing break. Beyond this point, what is arguably the most spectacular road in Peru descends the eastern flank of the Andes towards Puerto Maldonado (see page 334).

☆**Ausangate Trek** ① *entry US$3.50 at Tinqui plus US$3.50 at each of 3 communities along the route.* The hike around the mountain of Ausangate is spectacular. There are two popular routes requiring three to six days. It is hard going, with a pass over 5000 m and camping above 4000 m, so you need to be fit and acclimatized. Temperatures in high season (April-October) can drop well below zero at night. It is recommended to take a guide and/or *arriero*. *Arrieros* and mules can be hired in Tinqui: US$12 per day for a guide, US$10 per mule, more for a saddle horse. *Arrieros* also expect food. Make sure you sign a contract with full details. Buy supplies in Cuzco or Ocongate. Maps are available at the IGN in Lima or **Maratón** in Cuzco (see Shopping, above). Cuzco agencies and **Hostal Ausangate** (see Where to Stay, below) run tours from about US$120. Bring your own warm sleeping bag. **Miguel Pacsi** (T984-668360, mpacsi1@hotmail.com) has been recommended as a private guide and can help with logistics.

Q'eswachaka

At Combapata (50 km from Urcos) a paved road climbs west for 16 km, through a region of large highland lakes, to the cold regional centre of **Yanaoca** at 3950 m. Yanaoca has simple places to stay and eat, and provides access to the village of Quehue, 20 km further south. Near the village an Inca bridge spans the upper Río Apurímac at Q'eswachaka. The bridge, a UNESCO World Heritage Site, is 15 m long and is made entirely of straw, woven and spliced to form cables which are strung across the chasm. The bridge is rebuilt each year in June, during a unique and spectacular four-day event. Cuzco operators offer tours during the festival or you can go on your own at any time of the year, although it's not safe to cross the bridge between December and June.

Raqchi and around

Continuing on the main road to Sicuani, **Tinta**'s church has a brilliant gilded interior and an interesting choir vault. **Raqchi** is the scene of the region's great folklore festival and also the site of the **Viracocha Temple** ⓘ *daily 0800-1600, US$5.50, take a bus from Cuzco towards Sicuani, US$3.50*. John Hemming wrote: "What remains is the central wall, which is adobe above and Inca masonry below. This was probably the largest roofed building ever built by the Incas. On either side of the high wall, great sloping roofs were supported by rows of unusual round pillars, also of masonry topped by adobe. Nearby is a complex of barracks-like buildings and round storehouses. This was the most holy shrine to the creator god Viracocha, being the site of a miracle in which he set fire to the land – hence the lava flow nearby. The landscape is extraordinary, blighted by huge piles of black volcanic rocks."

Listings Upper Vilcanota Valley

Where to stay

Andahuaylillas to Urcos
These are all in Andahuaylillas; the 1 decent hostal in Urcos (**$ El Amigo**, C Carpintero y Jr César Vallejo, T084-307064) is often full.

$ Hostal Chiss
C Quispicanchis 216, T984-857294.
Economical accommodation in a family home with kitchen and washing facilities, private or shared bath, electric shower, some mattresses are poor. Effusively friendly owner, Sr Ladislao Belota.

$ Hostal El Nogal
Plaza de Armas, T084-771164.
Small place with 3 warm bright rooms, shared bath, electric shower, restaurant.

Cordillera Vilcanota

$ Hostal Ausangate
On the right-hand side as you enter Tinqui from Ocongate, T974-327538, Cuzco T084-227768, ausangate_tour@outlook.com.
Basic rooms with shared bath, cold water, meals available. Sr Cayetano Crispín, the owner, is knowledgeable and can arrange guides, mules, etc. A reliable source of trekking and climbing information.

$ Hostal Siesta
C Libertad, Ocongate, T996-030606.
Pleasant rooms with shared bath, patio, very clean and good value. Helpful owner Sr Raúl Rosas changes US$ at fair rates.

Jun Confirm all dates locally. **Q'eswachaka**, during the 1st weekend of the month, is a 4-day festival centred on the reconstruction of the Inca rope bridge; **Q'Olloriti**, the multitudinous Snow Star Festival, is held at a sanctuary at 4700 m near Ocongate and Tinqui. It lasts 3 days starting Trinity Sun; several Cuzco agencies offer tours; on the 2nd or 3rd weekend the folklore dance festival in Raqchi draws participants from all over Peru.

Paucartambo
Buses to Paucartambo leave from the *Paradero Control* in the San Jerónimo neighbourhood of Cuzco at 0800, 0900 and 1500, US$3.25, 3 hrs; also vans from the same location, every half-hour 0600-1800, US$4.25.

Cordillera Vilcanota
Buses to **Ocongate** (some continue to **Tinqui**) leave from a small terminal on Av Tomasatito Condemayta, corner of the Coliseo Cerrado in Cuzco, every 30 mins, 0430-1800, 3 companies, US$3.25, 3 hrs.

Cuzco to Choquequirao

stunning views from a 'lost city'

West of Cuzco a road heads towards Abancay (see page 1480) for access to Ayacucho and the central highlands, or Nazca and the coast. About 100 km from Cuzco is the exciting descent into the Apurímac canyon, near the former Inca suspension bridge that inspired Thornton Wilder's *The Bridge of San Luis Rey*.

☆Choquequirao
Entry US$13.50, students US$6.75.

Choquequirao is another 'lost city of the Incas', built on a ridge spur almost 1600 m above the Apurímac at 3100 m. It is reckoned to be a larger site than Machu Picchu, but the buildings are more spread out. The main features of Choquequirao are the **Lower Plaza**, considered by most experts to be the focal point of the city. The **Upper Plaza**, reached by a huge set of steps or terraces, has what are possibly ritual baths. A beautiful set of slightly curved agricultural terraces run for over 300 m east-northeast of the Lower Plaza.

The **usnu** is on a levelled hilltop, ringed with stones and giving awesome 360° views. The **Ridge Group**, still shrouded in vegetation, is a large collection of unrestored buildings some 50-100 m below the usnu. The **Outlier Building**, thought to be the priests' residence, is isolated and surrounded on three sides by sheer drops of over 1.5 km into the Apurímac Canyon. It has some of the finest stonework in Choquequirao. The **Llama Terraces** are 200 m below and west of the Lower Plaza, a great set of agricultural platforms beautifully decorated with llamas in white stone. East of the Lower Plaza are two other very large and impressive groups of terraces built on nearly vertical slopes.

Part of what makes Choquequirao so special is its isolation. At present, the site can only be reached on foot, a tough and exceptionally rewarding trek which attracts fewer than 50 hikers a day in high season and far fewer at other times. Sadly, there are plans to build a cable car to Choquequirao which would convert it into a mass tourism alternative to Machu Picchu, although construction had not yet begun in early 2017.

Tip...
Some tours allow insufficient time at Choquequirao (at least one full day is highly recommended), so enquire before you sign up.

The route to Choquequirao begins in (San Pedro de) **Cachora**, a village on the south side of the Apurímac, reached by a side road from the Cuzco–Abancay highway, shortly after Saywite. Take an Abancay-bound bus from Cuzco, four hours to the turn-off called Ramal de Cachora, where cars wait for passengers, then it's a 30-minute descent from the road to Cachora village. From the village you need at least a day to descend to the Río Apurímac then another day or two to climb up to Choquequirao, depending on your condition and how much weight you are carrying. Horses can be hired to carry your bags. Allow one or two days at the site. The route is well signed and in good condition, with several nice campsites (some with showers) en route.

You can either return to Cachora the way you came or continue two to four days from Choquequirao to Yanama, and then on to either Huancacalle (see page 284) or to Totora, Santa Teresa and Machu Picchu (see page 275). These treks are all long and demanding. Cuzco agencies offer all-inclusive trekking tours to Choquequirao; some continue to Yanama and Santa Teresa, fewer to Huancacalle.

Listings Cuzco to Choquequirao

Where to stay

$$ Casa de Salcantay
200 m below the Plaza, Cachora,
T984-281171, www.salcantay.com.
Price includes breakfast, dinner available if booked in advance, very nice comfortable rooms, fantastic views. Dutch/Peruvian-run, Dutch, English, German spoken. Very helpful owners Jan and Giovana can organize treks.

$$ Los Tres Balcones
Jr Abancay, Cachora, www.choquequirau.com.
Hostel designed as start and end-point for the trek to Choquequirao. Breakfast included, comfortable, hot showers, restaurant and pizza oven, camping. They run an all-inclusive 5-day trek to Choquequirao. May be closed when there is no group, book in advance.

$ Casa Nostra
500 m below Cachora off the road to Capuliyoc,
T958-349949, www.choquequiraohotel.com.
Rooms with private bath and dorms, includes breakfast, other meals available, superb views, Italian/Peruvian-run by Matteo and Judith. Treks to Choquequirao organized.

$ Hospedaje Salcantay
1 block above the Plaza, Cachora,
T958-303055.
Simple rooms with clean shared bathrooms, warm water, large yard, good value.

Transport

From Cuzco take any bus towards Abancay; **Bredde** has 5 daily, 0600-2030, US$7, 4 hrs, to **Ramal de Cachora**. *Colectivos* from Ramal de Cachora to **Cachora** village, US$1.80, 30 mins, beware overcharging. *Colectivos* also run all day from Prolongación Núñez in Abancay to Cachora, US$3.50, 1½ hrs. **Note** when travelling to Cachora, avoid changing vehicles in Curahuasi, where drivers have attempted to hold up tourists.

Sacred Valley
of the Incas

★ As the Río Vilcanota (in places called the Río Urubamba) flows north and west, it waters the agricultural heartland that provided the context for the great city of Cuzco. Here the Incas built country estates, temples, fortresses and other monumental works and, in the process, it became their 'Sacred Valley'. The name conjures up images of ancient, god-like rulers who saw the landscape itself as a temple; their tributes to this dramatic land survive in places such as Machu Picchu, Ollantaytambo, Pisac and countless others. For the tourist, the most famous sights are now within easy reach of Cuzco and draw massive crowds, but there remains ample scope for genuine exploring, to see lost cities in a less 21st-century setting. If archaeology is not your thing, there are markets to enjoy, birds to watch, trails for mountain-biking and a whole range of hotels to relax in.

Best for
Inca ruins ▪ Markets ▪ Trekking ▪ Rafting ▪ Relaxing

The road from Cuzco that runs past Sacsayhuaman and on to Tambo Machay (see page 239) climbs up to a pass, then continues over the pampa before descending into the densely populated Vilcanota valley. This road then crosses the river by a bridge at Pisac and follows the north bank to the end of the paved road at Ollantaytambo. It passes through Calca, Yucay and Urubamba, which can also be reached from Cuzco by the beautiful, direct road through Chinchero, see page 267.

☆Pisac Colour map 3, A1.

Pisac, 30 km north of Cuzco, has a traditional Sunday morning **market**, at which local people sell their produce in exchange for essential goods. It is a major draw for tourists who arrive in their droves throughout the day. Pisac has other, somewhat less crowded but more commercial markets every second day. Each Sunday at 1100 there is a Quechua Mass in the church on the plaza, where there is also a small, interesting **Museo Folklórico**. Elsewhere, the **Museo Comunitario Pisac** ⓘ *Av Amazonas y Retamayoc K'asa, museopisac@gmail.com, 0800-1300, 1400-1700, closed Sat, free but donations welcome,* has a display of village life, created by the people of Pisac. At dusk you will hear, if not see, the *pisaca* (partridges), after which the place is named. There are many souvenir shops on Bolognesi. Local fiesta: 15 July.

High above the town on the mountainside is Pisac's superb **Inca fortress** ⓘ *1½- to 2-hr walk from the plaza (1 hr descent), daily 0800-1630, you must show your BTC multi-site ticket to enter; combi US$0.75, taxi US$7 each way from near the bridge.* Walking up, although tiring, is recommended for the views and location. It's at least one hour uphill all the way, starting from the plaza and continuing past the Centro de Salud and a control post. The path goes through working terraces, giving the ruins a context. The first group of buildings is Pisaqa, with a fine curving wall. Climb then to the central part of the ruins, the Intihuatana group of temples and rock outcrops in the most magnificent Inca masonry. Here are the Reloj Solar ('Hitching Post of the Sun') – now closed because thieves stole a piece from it, palaces of the moon and stars, solstice markers, baths and water channels. From Intihuatana, a path leads around the hillside through a tunnel to Q'Allaqasa, the military area. At this point, a large area of Inca tombs in holes in the hillside can be seen across the valley. The end of the site is Kanchisracay, where the agricultural workers were housed. Road transport approaches from the Kanchisracay end; the drive up from town takes about 20 minutes. Even if you're going by car, do not rush as there is a lot to see and a lot of walking to do.

☆Calca and Huchuy Cuzco

The second village on the road from Pisac towards Urubamba is Lamay, which has warm spring nearby that are highly regarded for their medicinal properties. Next is **Calca**, 18 km beyond Pisac at 3000 m, which has basic hotels and eating places around its large plaza and a bus terminal along the highway. The **Fiesta de la Vírgen Asunta** is held here on 15-16 August.

Dramatically located at 3700 m on a flat esplanade on the opposite side of the river are the impressive ruins of a small Inca town, **Huchuy Cuzco** ⓘ *access from either Calca or Lamay (7 km southeast), then either by road or 3 hrs hiking on a good steep trail, entry US$8.* The views are magnificent. The ruins themselves consist of extensive agricultural terraces with high retaining walls and several buildings made from finely wrought stonework and adobe mud bricks. A lovely one- or two-day trek leads to Huchuy Cuzco from Tambo Machay, the route once taken by the Inca from his capital to his country estate.

Valle de Lares

The Valle de Lares is renowned for its magnificent mountains, lakes and small villages, which make it perfect for trekking and mountain biking, although parts are undergoing rapid development. One route starts near an old hacienda in Huarán (6 km west of Calca at 2830 m), crosses two passes over 4000 m and ends at the hot springs near Lares. From this village, transport runs back to Calca. Alternatively, you can add an extra day and continue to Ollantaytambo, or start in Lares and finish in Yanhuara (between Urubamba and Ollantaytambo). Several agencies in Cuzco offer trekking and biking tours to the region (see page 256).

Yucay

About 3 km east of Urubamba, Yucay has two grassy plazas divided by the restored colonial church of Santiago Apóstol, with its oil paintings and fine altars. On the opposite side from Plaza Manco II is the adobe palace built for Sayri Túpac (Manco's son) when he emerged from Vilcabamba in 1558.

Urubamba *Colour map 3, A1.*

Like many places along the valley, Urubamba is in a fine setting at 2863 m with snow-capped peaks in view. The main road along the valley skirts the town, and the bridge

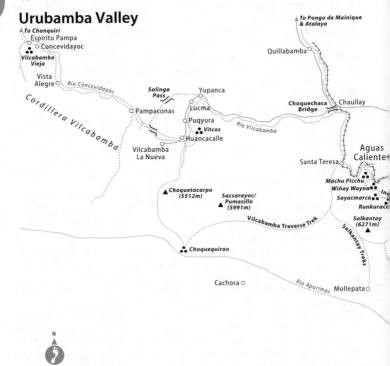

Urubamba Valley

for the road to Cuzco via Chinchero is just to the east. The large market square is one block west of the main plaza. Calle Berriózabal, on the west edge of town, is lined with pisonay trees. There are many pottery studios in town, including **Seminario-Bejar Ceramic Studio** ① *Berriózabal 405, T084-201002, www.ceramicaseminario.com*. Pablo Seminario and his workshop have researched pre-Columbian techniques and designs and now use them in their distinctive pottery. The tour of the of the workshops is highly recommended.

Chinchero
Church and archaeological site daily 0800-1600, BTC ticket (see page 231).

Chinchero (3762 m) is southeast of Urubamba along the more direct (western) road to Cuzco. It is a friendly town with an attractive church built on an Inca temple. The church has been restored to reveal the full glory of its interior paintings: ceiling, beams and walls are covered in beautiful floral and religious designs. Excavations have revealed many Inca walls and terraces around the town's plaza. Groups from Cuzco come to visit the church, ruins and several touristy textile centres in the town. Much of the area's character will change when the new airport for Cuzco is built nearby.

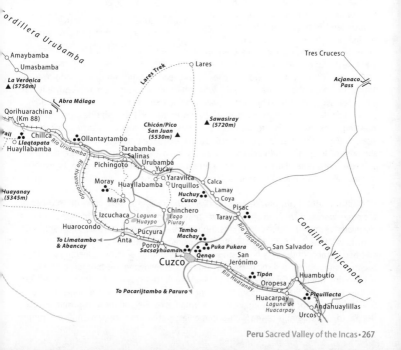

☆Moray and around
9 km by road west of Maras, BTC ticket (see page 231).

The remote but beautiful site of Moray comprises three 'colosseums', used by the Incas, according to some theories, as a sort of open-air crop nursery; it is known locally as the 'laboratory of the Incas'. The great depressions contain no ruined buildings, but are lined with fine terracing. Each level is said to have its own microclimate. It is a very atmospheric place which, many claim, has mystical power, and the scenery is absolutely stunning.

The most interesting way to get to Moray from Urubamba is via **Tarabamba**, 6 km west, where a bridge crosses the Río Urubamba. Turn right after the bridge to reach **Pichingoto**, a tumbled-down village built under an overhanging cliff. Just over the bridge and before the town to the left of a small, walled cemetery is a salt stream. Follow the footpath beside the stream to Salineras, a small village below which are a mass of terraced **Inca salt pans** ① *entry US$3, taxi from Urubamba, US$11.* There are over 5000 *salineras* and they are still in operation. The village of Maras is about 45 minutes beyond the salt pans, from where it's 9 km by unmade road or 5 km through the fields to Moray; ask in Maras for the best walking route. Tour companies in Cuzco offer cycle trips to Moray; see Transport, page 274, for further details on how to get there. There are no hotels at all in the area, so take care not to get stranded. If you're walking to the salt pans and Moray, take water as this side of the valley can be very hot and dry.

Ollantaytambo *Colour map 3, A1.*
The attractive but touristy town of Ollantaytambo is located at 2800 m at the foot of some spectacular Inca ruins and terraces and is built directly on top of an original Inca town. A great many visitors arrive by road from Cuzco to see the ruins and take the train from here to Machu Picchu.

> **Tip...**
> Traffic around Ollantaytambo train station is chaotic every evening; take care not to be run over on Avenida Ferrocarril.

Entering Ollantaytambo from the east, the road is built along the long Wall of 100 Niches. Note the inclination of the wall, which leans towards the road. Since it was the Incas' usual practice to build their walls leaning towards the interior of the building, it has been deduced that the road, much narrower then, was built inside a succession of buildings. The road leads into the Plaza de Armas. The Inca town, or *Llacta*, on which the present-day town is based, can clearly be seen behind the north side of the plaza, where the original Inca *canchas* (blocks of houses) are almost entirely intact and still occupied. The road out of the plaza leads across a bridge to the colonial church with its enclosed *recinto*. Beyond are Plaza Araccama and the entrance to the archaeological site

☆Ollantaytambo temple fortress ① *Daily 0800-1600; if possible arrive at 0800, before the other tourists. Admission by BTC visitor's ticket, which can be bought at the site. Guides are available at the entrance.* After crossing the great high-walled trapezoidal esplanade known as 'Mañariki', visitors to Ollantaytambo are confronted by a series of 16 massive, stepped terraces of the very finest stonework. These flights of terraces leading up above the town are superb, and so are the curving terraces following the contours of the rocks overlooking the river. Ollantaytambo was successfully defended by Manco Inca's warriors against Hernando Pizarro in 1536. Manco Inca built the wall above the site and another wall closing the Yucay valley against attack from Cuzco. Beyond these imposing terraces lies the so-called Temple of Ten Niches. Immediately above this are six monolithic upright

blocks of rose-coloured rhyolite, the remains of what is popularly called the Temple of the Sun. The temple was started by Pachacútec, using Colla *indígenas* from Lake Titicaca – hence the similarities of the monoliths facing the central platform with the Tiahuanaco remains. The massive, highly finished granite blocks at the top are worth the climb to see. The Colla are said to have deserted halfway through the work, which explains the many unfinished blocks lying about the site.

There are more Inca ruins in the small area behind the church, between the town and the temple fortress. Most impressive of these is the so-called Baño de la Ñusta (bath of the princess) carved from the bedrock. Some 200 m behind the bath, along the face of the mountain, are some small ruins known as Inca Misanca, believed to have been a small temple or observatory. A series of steps, seats and niches have been carved out of the cliff. There is a complete irrigation system, including a canal at shoulder level, some 6 inches deep, cut out of the sheer rock face.

On the west side of the main ruins, a two-dimensional 'pyramid' has been identified in the layout of the fields and walls of the valley. A fine 750 m wall aligns with the rays of the winter solstice on 21 June. It can be appreciated from a high point about 3.5 km from Ollantaytambo.

Listings Pisac, Urubamba and Ollantaytambo

Tourist information

Tourist information is available on the main plaza in Pisac (daily 0800-1700), the bus terminal in Urubamba (Mon-Fri 0745-1630) and the Municipio in Ollantaytambo (T084-204030, ext 207, Mon-Fri 0800-1300, 1400-1700, Sat-Sun 0800-1300).

Where to stay

Pisac

$$$ Melissa Wasi
15 mins walk from Pisac Plaza, close to the river, T084-797589, www.melissa-wasi.com.
A family-run bed and breakfast with rooms and small bungalows. Very homely, English spoken.

$$$ Royal Inka Pisac
Carretera Ruinas Km 1.5, T084-263276, www.royalinkahotel.pe.
Converted hacienda with olympic-size swimming pool (US$3.50 per day), sauna and jacuzzi for guests only, very pleasant, provides guides. This chain also has **Royal Inkas I** and **II** in Cuzco.

$$$-$$ Paz y Luz
T984-216293, www.pazyluzperu.com.
10-15 mins' walk from Pisac Plaza, close to the river.
American-owned, pleasant garden, nicely designed rooms, breakfast included. Diane Dunn offers healing from many traditions (including Andean), sacred tours, workshops and gatherings.

$$$-$$ Pisac Inn
At the corner of Pardo on the Plaza, T084-203062, www.pisacinn.com.
Bright and charming local decor, pleasant atmosphere, private and shared bathrooms, hot water, sauna and massage. Good breakfast, the **Cuchara de Palo** restaurant serves meals using local ingredients, plus pizza and pasta, café.

$$ Hostal Varayoc
Mcal Castilla 380, T942-338130, luzpaz3@hotmail.com.
Renovated hotel around a colonial courtyard. Decor is smart, modern private bathrooms. Ask to see the guinea pig house.

$ Residencial Beho
Intihuatana 114, T084-203001.

Ask for room in main building, good breakfast available.

Valle de Lares

$$$ The Green House
Km 56.8 Huarán, T941-299944,
www.thegreenhouseperu.com.
A charming retreat, only 4 rooms, breakfast included, comfortable lounge, restaurant, small kitchen for guests, beautiful garden, restricted internet. No children under 10. Information on walks and day trips in the area. Activities include hiking, biking, horse riding and rafting. Intimate, beautiful and relaxing.

Yucay

$$$$-$$$ Sonesta Posadas del Inca Sacred Valley
Plaza Manco II de Yucay 123, T084-201107,
www.sonesta.com.
Converted 300-year-old monastery is like a little village with plazas, chapel, 88 comfortable, heated rooms, price includes buffet breakfast. Lots of activities can be arranged, canoeing, horse riding, mountain biking, etc. **Inkafe** restaurant is open to all, serving Peruvian, fusion and traditional cuisine with a US$15 buffet.

$$$ La Casona de Yucay
Plaza Manco II 104, T084-201116,
www.hotelcasonayucay.com.
This colonial house was where Simón Bolívar stayed during his liberation campaign in 1824. With heating, 2 patios and gardens, **Don Manuel** restaurant and bar.

Urubamba

$$$$ Casa Andina Private Collection Sacred Valley
Paradero 5, Yanahuara, between Urubamba and Ollantaytambo, T984-765501,
www.casa-andina.com.
In its own 3-ha estate, with all the facilities associated with this chain, plus **Valle Sagrado Andean Cottage** for family and long-stay accommodation, 'Sacred

Spa', gym, planetarium, good restaurant, adventure options.

$$$$ Río Sagrado (Belmond)
Km 76 Ctra Cuzco–Ollantaytambo,
T084-201631, www.belmond.com.
4 km from Urubamba, set in beautiful gardens overlooking the river with fine views. Rooms and villas, **Mayu Wilka** spa, restaurant and bar, offers various packages.

$$$$ Sol y Luna
Fundo Huincho, west of town, T084-608930,
www.hotelsolyluna.com.
Award-winning bungalows and suites set off the main road in lovely gardens, pool, excellent gourmet restaurant, wine tastings, spa, handicrafts shop. Also has **Wayra** lounge bar and dining room, open to non-guests, for freshly cooked, informal lunches. Entertainment includes paso fino horse shows, contemporary arts and circus shows (open to all). Arranges adventure and cultural activities and traditional tours. Profits go to **Sol y Luna** educational association, www.colegiosolyluna.com.

$$$$ Tambo del Inka
Av Ferrocarril s/n, T084-581777,
www.luxurycollection.com/vallesagrado.
A resort and spa on the edge of town, in gardens by the river. Completely remodelled with a variety of rooms and suites, fitness centre, swimming pools, **Hawa** restaurant, bar, business facilities and lots of activities arranged.

$$$ Casa Colibrí
2.5 km from town on road to Ollantaytambo,
T084-205003, www.casacolibriecolodge.com.
Delightful, spacious rooms and casitas made of local stone, wood and adobe, set in beautiful gardens to attract bees, butterflies and hummingbirds. Very restful, hammocks, meditation room, excellent homegrown food, swings and table tennis, popular with couples, families and yoga groups.

$$ Las Chullpas
Querocancha s/n, 3 km from town,
T084-201568, www.chullpas.pe.

Very peaceful, excellent breakfast, vegetarian meals, English spoken, natural medicine, treks, riding, mountain biking, camping US$3 with hot shower. Mototaxi from town US$2.50, taxi (ask for Querocancha) US$4.

$$ Urubamba Homestay
C Pisagua s/n, T084-201562, www.urubambahomestay.com.
3 rooms with bath in a private home, includes breakfast, roof terrace, gardens, support community projects. British-run by Keith and Joan Parkin.

$$-$ Tambo del Sol
Av La Convención 113-B, T084-201352
Ample modern rooms with bathtubs, beautiful garden, parking, good value.

$ Hospedaje Buganvilla
Jr Convención 280, T084-205102, bukanvilla@hotmail.com.
Sizable rooms with hot water, breakfast on request, quiet, bright, lovely gardens, lively owners Raul and Mónica, good value, very pleasant.

$ Hospedaje Los Jardines
Jr Convención 459, T084-201331, www.hospedajelosjardines.blogspot.co.uk.
Attractive guesthouse with comfortable rooms, hot water, non-smoking, delicious breakfast US$3.25 extra (vegans catered for), safe, lovely garden, laundry. **Sacred Valley Mountain Bike Tours** also based here.

Chinchero

$$$ La Casa de Barro
Miraflores 147, T084-306031, www.lacasadebarro.com.
Modern hotel, with heating, bar, restaurant serving 'fusion' food using organic local produce, tours arranged.

$$ Mi Piuray
C Garcilaso 187, T084-306029, www.hospedajemipiuraycusco.com.
Simple rooms around a patio with flowers, private or shared bath, electric showers,

kitchen facilities, meals on request, knowledgeable owner.

Ollantaytambo
There are many hotels but they are often full, so it's best to book ahead in high season.

$$$$ Pakaritampu
C Ferrocarril 852, T084-204020, www.pakaritampu.com.
Modern, well-appointed rooms, buffet breakfast, restaurant and bar, laundry, safe and room service. Adventure sports can be arranged. Lunch and dinner are extra. Excellent quality and service, but room 8 is next to the railway station car park.

$$$$-$$$ El Albergue Ollantaytambo
Within the railway station gates, T084-204014, www.elalbergue.com.
Owned by North American artist Wendy Weeks. Also has **Café Mayu** in the station and a very good restaurant using ingredients from their own organic farm. Characterful rooms, rustic elegance, some larger than others, safety boxes, lovely gardens and a eucalyptus steam sauna. Books and crafts for sale. Private transport arranged to nearby attractions and Cuzco airport.

$$$ Apu Lodge
Calle Lari, T084-797162, www.apulodge.com.
On the edge of town, great views of the ruins and surrounding mountains. Run by Scot Louise Norton, good service, quiet, nice garden, good buffet breakfast, can help organize tours and treks.

$$$ Hostal Sauce
C Ventiderio 248, T084-204044, www.hostalsauce.com.pe.
Smart, simple decor and views of the ruins from 3 of the 6 rooms as well as from the dining room, food from own farm.

$$$ Sol Ollantay
C Ventiderio s/n by the bridge between the 2 plazas, T084-204130, www.hotelsol ollantaytambo.com.

Tastefully renovated with good views from most rooms, hot water.

$$$-$$ Picaflor Tambo
Larricalle s/n, T084-436758, www.picaflortambo.com.
6 comfortable rooms set around a courtyard, charming, a good choice.

$$$-$$ Tika Wasi
C Convencion s/n, T084-204166.
Great location close to the archaeological site, garden, good service and comfortable rooms decorated in 'Inca style'.

$$ Casa de Wow
C Patacalle 840, T084204010, www.casadewow.com.
Dorms, kitchen facilities, balcony with great view of ruins, English spoken. Organizes tours.

$$ Full Moon Lodge
Cruz Esquina s/n, T989-362031, http://fullmoonlodgeperu.com.
Quiet place away from the centre, rooms with private bath set around a large garden with hammocks, also has camp site on Av Estudiantil (US$5 pp). Offers San Pedro experiences.

$$ Hostal Iskay II
Patacalle 722, T084-434109, www.hostaliskay.com.
In the Inca town. Great location but car access is difficult. Only 7 rooms, hot water, free tea and coffee, use of kitchen. Good reports.

$$ Hostal K'uychipunku
K'uychipunku 6, T084-204175, www.kuychipunkuhostal.com.
Close to Plaza Araccama, hot water, modern, some rooms with view, courtyard.

$$ Las Orquídeas
Av Ferrocarril 406, T084-204032, www. lasorquideasollantaytambo.com.
Hot water, fairly small but nice rooms, flower-filled patio, discounts for 2 or more nights.

$ Hospedaje El Tambo
C Horno, north of the plaza, T984-489094, www.hostaleltambo.com.

Once past the door you emerge into a lovely garden full of fruit trees and flowers. Small basic rooms for up to 4 people, shared bath downstairs in the courtyard, hot water, breakfast available, good value. Friendly owner.

$ Hostal Chaska Wasi
Plaza de Armas, T084-204045.
Private rooms and dorms, hammocks, hot showers, free hot drinks, laundry, popular. Owner Katy is very friendly.

$ Hostal Plaza Ollantaytambo
Beside the police station on Plaza de Armas, T084-436741, hostalplazaollantaytambo@gmail.com.
Small modern rooms with private bath and reliable hot water. Variable service, all a bit improvised but great location and value.

Restaurants

Pisac

$$$ Mullu
Plaza de Armas 352, T084-203073, and Mcal Castilla 375, T084-203182. Tue-Sun 0900-1900.
Café/restaurant with Peruvian and Asian fusion menu. Has a gallery promoting local artists.

$$$-$$ Cuchara de Palo
In Pisac Inn on Plaza de Armas, T084-203062.
Gourmet restaurant using local ingredients to make traditional Peruvian food. Pleasant, cosy atmosphere.

$$ Sapos Lounge
Espinar y Arequipa, T994-647979. Tue-Sun 1500-2300.
Good pizza and drinks, produce from a local organic farm. Good nightlife spot.

Cafés

Blue Llama Café
Corner of the plaza opposite Pisac Inn, T084-203135.
Cute, colourful café with a huge range of teas, good coffee, breakfasts, daily *menús*, and board games.

Horno Colonial San Francisco
Mcal Castilla 572.
Good wholemeal bread and
cheese *empanadas*.

Ulrike's Café
C Pardo 613, T084-203195. Daily 0800-2100.
Has possibly the best apple crumble with
ice cream, excellent coffee, smoothies and
many international dishes. Good value
3-course daily *menú*. Book exchange.

Urubamba

$$$ El Huacatay
*Arica 620, T084-201790, www.elhuacatay.com.
Mon-Sat 1230-2130.*
A small restaurant with a reputation for fine,
creative fusion cuisine (local, Mediterranean,
Asian). Lovely garden setting.

$$$ El Maizal
*Av Conchatupa, the main road before the
bridge, T984-705211. Daily 1200-1600.*
Country-style restaurant, buffet service
with a variety of *Novo Andino* and
international choices, beautiful gardens,
caters to tour groups.

$$$ Tunupa
*On road from Urubamba to Ollantaytambo,
on riverbank, T974-782163. Open 1200-1500.*
Buffet lunch US$15. Same owners as Tunupa
in Cuzco, colonial-style hacienda, excellent
food and surroundings, pre-Columbian and
colonial art exhibitions.

$$$ Tres Keros
*Av Señor de Torrechayoc, T084-201701.
Novo Andino* cuisine, try the lamb chops.

$$$-$$ Paca Paca
*Av Mcal Castilla 640, T084-201181.
Tue-Sun 1300-2100.*
Varied selection of dishes including Peruvian
fusion, also pizza, pleasant inviting atmosphere.

$$-$ Guyin
*Comercio 453, T084-608838 for delivery.
Daily 1600-2300.*

Pizza, pastas and grill. Popular with
local expats.

$$-$ Pizza Wasi
*Av Mcal Castilla 857, Plaza de Armas, T084-
434751 for delivery. Daily 1200-2300.*
Good pizzas and pastas. Mulled wine
served in a small restaurant with nice
decor, good value.

$ El Edén
*Av Mcal Castilla 960, T984-850095.
Mon-Sat 0900-2100.*
Pastries, sandwiches, coffee and juices. Jams
and bread to go. Some gluten-free products.

Ollantaytambo
There are restaurants all over town offering
menú turístico, pizzas, pastas, juices and
hot drinks.

$$$ Papa's
*C Horno at the plaza, T974-787191.
Daily 1100-2100.*
Restaurant and lounge serving Tex-Mex, local
dishes, pizzas, soups, salads, and desserts.

$$$-$$ Puka Rumi
*Av Ventiderio s/n, next to Heart's Café,
T084-204151. Daily 0700-2100.*
Serves a variety of international dishes, pizza,
salads, upmarket *menú*.

$$ Coffee Tree
Plaza de Armas, T084-436734.
Good coffee and a variety of Peruvian
and international dishes. Popular.

$$ Heart's Café
*Av Ventiderio s/n, T084-436726, www.
livingheartperu.org. Open 0700-2100.*
International and Peruvian dishes including
vegetarian, box lunch and takeaway
available, good coffee. All profits to
education and self-help projects in the
Sacred Valley. Popular, tasty food but
disappointing service.

$$ Huatakay
*Ancopacha, 5 mins before town on the main
road, T984-397305. Daily 0600-2100.*

Large restaurant serving *menú* and regional specialities à la carte. Pleasant setting, small camping area on the grounds, US$7 per tent.

$$ Il Piccolo Forno
C del Medio 120. Tue-Sun 1200-2100.
Very good Italian food and take-away pizza, as well as home baked bread, pies and cookies. Gluten free options.

$$ La Esquina
C Principal at the corner of Plaza de Armas. Mon-Sat 0700-2100.
Variety of international dishes, wide selection of pastries and sweets, popular.

$ Doña Eva
C Ollantay facing the market. Sun-Fri 0700-2100, Sat 0700-1900.
Economical *menú* and à la carte, one of the few unpretentious places in town, popular with locals and travellers alike.

Festivals

Urubamba
May-Jun Harvest months, with many processions following ancient schedules. Urubamba's main festival, **El Señor de Torrechayoc**, takes place around 20 May.
8 Sep Chinchero celebrates the **Day of the Virgin**.

Ollantaytambo
6 Jan **Bajada de Reyes Magos** (Epiphany) is celebrated with dancing, a bull fight, local food and a fair.
End-May/early-Jun **Fiesta del Señor de Choquekillca**, patron saint of Ollantaytambo, has his festival 50 days after Easter, with several days of dancing, weddings, processions, masses, feasting and drinking.
Jun **Ollanta-Raymi**. A colourful festival on the Sun following Inti Raymi.
29 Oct The town's anniversary, with lots of dancing in traditional costume and many local delicacies for sale.

What to do

Urubamba
Perol Chico, *5 km from Urubamba at Km 77, T950-314065/950-314066, www.perolchico.com.* Dutch/Peruvian-owned and operated stables offering 1- to 11-day horse riding trips. Good horses, riding is Peruvian paso style.

Ollantaytambo
Awamaki, *C La Convención across from the church, T084-436744, www.awamaki.org.* Cultural tours and artisan workshops (dying, weaving, woodcarving) which can be integrated with homestays in local communities. Also adventure tours, volunteering, Spanish and Quechua classes.

Transport

Pisac
To **Urubamba**, US$1, 1 hr. To **Cuzco**, 32 km, 1 hr, US$1.50, last one back leaves around 2000; these buses are often full. There are also *colectivos* and minibuses; all leave from C Amazonas near the main bridge.

Urubamba
The Terminal is on the main road, 3 blocks west of the centre. To **Calca**, US$0.50, 30 mins; and **Pisac**, US$1, 1 hr. To **Cuzco**, by bus, US$1.50, 1½ hrs via Chinchero or 2 hrs via Pisac; by van US$2; by car US$2.50. Frequent vans to **Ollantaytambo**, US$0.50, 30 mins, all leave when full throughout the day.

Moray and around
Any bus between Urubamba and Cuzco via Chinchero passes the clearly marked turning to Maras; from the junction taxi *colectivos* charge US$2.50 pp to Maras, or you can walk all the way from here to Moray (see page 268). There is also public transport from Chinchero to Maras until 1700. A taxi to Moray and the salt pans (from where you can walk back to the Urubamba–Ollantaytambo road) costs US$25, including 1-hr wait.

Ollantaytambo

Bus Vans leave all day for Urubamba from the produce market, 1 block east of the main plaza, US$0.50, 30 mins. Vans to Cuzco leave frequently from Av Ferrocarril above the railway station and from the main Plaza near the information centre, US$3.50, 1½ hrs. Taxi to Cuzco, US$22.

Train Ollantaytambo is the point of departure for most trains to Machu Picchu (see Transport, page 280). The station is a 10- to 15-min walk from the Plaza, longer in the early evening when Av Ferrocarril is clogged with vehicles. There are **Perú Rail** and **Inca Rail** ticket offices outside the station and you must have a ticket to be allowed onto the platform unless you are staying at El Albergue Hotel.

Machu Picchu Colour map 3, A1.

iconic and unmissable

★There is a tremendous feeling of awe on first witnessing Machu Picchu. The ancient citadel (42 km from Ollantaytambo by rail) straddles the saddle of a high mountain (2380 m) with steep terraced slopes falling away to the fast-flowing Vilcanota river snaking its hairpin course far below in the valley floor. Towering overhead is Huayna Picchu, and green jungle peaks provide the backdrop for the whole majestic scene. Machu Picchu is a complete Inca city. For centuries it was buried in jungle, until Hiram Bingham stumbled upon it in 1911. It was then explored by an archaeological expedition sent by Yale University. The ruins require at least a day to explore. Take time to appreciate not only the masonry, but also the selection of large rocks used for foundations, the use of water in the channels below the Temple of the Sun and the beauty of the surrounding mountains.

Main site

The **main entrance** to the ruins is set at the eastern end of the extensive **terracing** that must have supplied the crops for the city. Above this point to the south is the final stretch of the Inca Trail leading down from **Intipunku** (Sun Gate). From the **Watchman's Hut** you get the perfect view of the city (the one you've seen on all the postcards), laid out before you with Huayna Picchu rising above the furthest extremity. The main path into the ruins comes to a **dry moat**; from here a long staircase goes to the upper reaches of the city, past quarries on the left and roofless buildings on the right which show the construction methods used. Above the main plazas are the **Temple of the Three Windows,** the **Principal Temple** and the **Sacristy**. These buildings were clearly of great importance, given the fine stonework involved. Beyond the Sacristy is the **Intihuatana** or 'hitching-post of the sun', one of the highlights of Machu Picchu. Carved rocks (*gnomons*) such as this are found at all major Inca sites and were the point to which the sun was symbolically 'tied' at the winter solstice, before being freed to rise again on its annual ascent towards the summer solstice. Below the Intihuatana is the **Main Plaza** and, at its northern end a small plaza fronted by the **Sacred Rock**. The outline of this gigantic, flat stone echoes that of the mountains behind it. Southeast of the Main Plaza to the left are several groups of closely packed buildings that were probably **living quarters** and workshops; also in this area are the **Condor Temple** and a cave called **Intimachay**. A short distance to the south is a series of **ceremonial baths**, probably used for ritual bathing. The uppermost, **Principal Bath**, is the most elaborate. Next to it is the **Temple of the Sun**, or Torreón, which was almost certainly used for astronomical purposes. Underneath the Torreón is the Tomb

Essential Machu Picchu

Getting there

The easiest way to get to Machu Picchu is by train from Poroy (near Cuzco) or Ollantaytambo to Aguas Calientes, from where you can walk or catch a bus to the ruins. Santa Teresa provides alternative access for those who have travelled by road from Ollantaytambo. The most strenuous but rewarding way to Machu Picchu is to hike one of the Inca trails (see page 281).

Tickets

The entrance fee for Machu Picchu is 152 soles (US$45), or 77 soles (US$23) for Peruvians, citizens of other Andean Community nations, students with ISIC card, and visitors under age 18. An afternoon-only ticket costs 10% less. To climb Huayna Picchu you have to buy a ticket that includes site entry and the climb for 200 soles (US$59), specifying whether you are going to arrive 0700-0800 or 1000-1100 (only 400 people are allowed up at one time). It is wise to reserve your ticket online in advance at www.machupicchu.gob.pe. You can also pay online (unless you need to show an ISIC card) with Visa or at branches of **Banco de la Nación**; **Centro Cultural de Machu Picchu** (Avenida Pachacútec cuadra 1) in Aguas Calientes; Dirección Regional de Cultura in Cuzco (C Garcilaso s/n, Mon-Sat, 0700-1930); AATC (C Nueva Baja 424) in Cuzco; offices of **PeruRail** and **Inca Rail** in Cuzco, and **Hotel Monasterio** in Cuzco. Other websites offer tickets for sale at an inflated price. The only place to buy tickets without a previous online reservation is at Dirección Regional de Cultura (see above). Do not buy (fake) tickets on the street in Cuzco.

On arrival

The site is open from 0600 to 1600. Officially, only 2500 visitors are allowed entry each day, but there may be more in high season, April through August. It is best to arrive early, although it is not possible to walk up to the ruins before the first buses arrive. You can deposit your luggage at the entrance for a small fee. Guides are available at the site, US$80 for one to 10 people. Site wardens are also informative. The **Sanctuary Lodge** is located next to the entrance, with a self-service restaurant and the only toilets on the site.

Regulations

In an attempt to mitigate crowding, the authorities announced new regulations in 2014, but these had not been implemented by early 2017. They would require that all visitors be accompanied by a guide, that they follow one of three established routes without turning back and that they limit stops at certain places to three to five minutes. There has also been talk of limiting entry to morning-, or afternoon-only tickets.

Advice and precautions

Take your own food, if you don't want to pay hotel prices, and take plenty of drinking water. Note that food is not officially allowed into the site and drink can only be carried in canteens/water bottles, not disposable containers. Toilets are only at the entrance. Take insect repellent and wear long clothes. Also take protection against the sun and rain.

or Palace of the Princess, which combines a natural cave-like opening with fine masonry. Across the stairway from the Torreón is the group of buildings known as the **Royal Sector**.

Around Machu Picchu

Huayna Picchu ⓘ *Access to the main path daily 0700-0800 and 1000-1100; latest return time 1500; max 200 people per departure. Check on www.machupicchu.gob.pe or with the Ministerio de Cultura in Aguas Calientes or Cuzco for current departure times and to sign up for a place.* The mountain overlooking the site (on which there are also ruins) has steps to the top for a superlative view of the whole site, but it is not for those who are afraid of heights, and you shouldn't leave the path. The climb takes up to 90 minutes but the steps are dangerous after bad weather. Another trail to Huayna Picchu is via the Temple of the Moon, which consists of two caves, one above the other, with superb Inca niches inside. To reach the Temple of the Moon, take the marked trail to the left of the path to Huayna Picchu. It is in good shape, although it descends further than you think it should and there are very steep steps on the way. After the Temple it is safest to return to the main trail to Huayna Picchu, instead of taking a difficult shortcut. The round trip takes about four hours. Before doing any trekking around Machu Picchu, check with an official which paths may be used, or which are one-way.

Other sights and trails The famous Inca bridge is about 45 minutes along a well-marked trail south of the Royal Sector. The bridge (on which you cannot walk) is spectacularly sited, carved into a vertiginous cliff-face. East of the Royal Sector is the path leading up to **Intipunku** on the Inca Trail (60 minutes, fine views; see page 281). Climbing Machu Picchu mountain is another excellent and generally less crowded option which gives a completely different view of the site and surrounding valleys. The route is steep and takes up to three hours; a ticket for the site and the mountain costs 140 soles (US$50). There are two daily departures, 0700-0800 and 0900-1000, maximum 400 people per departure but they are seldom fully booked.

Aguas Calientes

The terminus of the tourist rail service to Machu Picchu, Aguas Calientes (official name Machu Picchu Pueblo) has grown from a handful of tin shacks along the railway in the 1980s, into an international resort village with countless multi-storey luxury hotels, restaurants advertising four-for-one happy hours, persistent massage touts and numerous services for the over one million tourists who visit every year. Although it is not to every traveller's taste, it may be worth spending the night here in order to visit the ruins early in the morning. Avenida Pachacútec leads from the plaza to the **thermal baths** ⓘ *at the upper end of town, daily 0500-2000, US$3.50,* which have a communal pool smelling of sulphur that's best early in the morning. There are showers for washing *before* entering the baths; take soap and shampoo, and keep an eye on valuables. The **Museo Manuel Chávez Ballón y Jardín Botánico** ⓘ *near the bridge to Machu Picchu, 25-min walk from town, daily 0900-1600, US$8,* displays objects found at Machu Picchu and local plants. There is also a **Butterfly House** ⓘ *access from Camping Municipal, see below, US$3.50.*

Tourist information

iPerú
Av Pachacútec, by the plaza, Aguas Calientes,
T084-211104.
Provides tourist information Mon-Sat
0900-1300, 1400-1800, Sun 0900-1300.

Where to stay

Machu Picchu

$$$$ Machu Picchu Sanctuary Lodge
Reservations as for the Hotel Monasterio in
Cuzco, which is under the same management
(Belmond), T084-211038, www.belmond.com.
Comfortable, good service, helpful staff, food
well-cooked and presented. Electricity and
water 24 hrs a day, prices are all-inclusive,
restaurant for residents only in the evening,
but the buffet lunch is open to all. Usually
fully booked well in advance, but try Sun
night when other tourists find Pisac market
a greater attraction.

Aguas Calientes

$$$$ Casa Andina Classic
Av Imperio de los Incas E-34, T084-582950,
www.casa-andina.com.
Luxury chain hotel, rooms with heating
and safety boxes, restaurant serving
Novo Andino cuisine.

$$$$ Casa del Sol
Av Imperio de los Incas 608, on the railroad,
T951-298695, www.casadelsolhotels.com.
5-storey hotel with lift/elevator, different room
categories with river or mountain views, nice
restaurant, beautiful spa. Shower service and
changing room available after check out.

$$$$ Inkaterra Machu Picchu Pueblo
Km 104, 5 mins walk along the railway
from town, T084-211122. Reservations from
C Andalucía 174, Miraflores, Lima, T01-610
0400, or Plaza las Nazarenas 113 p2, in
Cuzco, T084-234010, www.inkaterra.com.

Beautiful colonial-style bungalows in village
compound surrounded by cloudforest, lovely
gardens with a lot of steps between the
public areas and rooms, spa, pool, excellent
restaurant, offer tours to Machu Picchu,
several guided walks on and off the property.
Good baggage service to coordinate with
train arrivals and departures. Also has the
Café Inkaterra by the railway line.

$$$$ Sumaq Machu Picchu
Av Hermanos Ayar Mz 1, Lote 3, T084-211059,
www.sumaqhotelperu.com.
Award-winning 5-star hotel on the edge of
town, between railway and road to Machu
Picchu. Suites and luxury rooms with heating,
restaurant, bar, spa.

$$$ Gringo Bill's
Colla Raymi 104, T084-211046,
www.gringobills.com.
Pretty rooms, good beds, balconies, train-
station pickup (on foot), lot of coming and
going, good restaurant, breakfast from 0500,
packed lunch available.

$$$ La Cabaña
Av Pachacútec 805, near thermal
baths, T084-211048, www.la
cabanamachupicchu.com.
Variety of rooms, café, laundry service,
helpful, popular with groups.

$$$ Presidente
Av Imperio de los Incas, at the old station,
T084-211034, www.hostalpresidente.com.
Adjoining **Hostal Machu Picchu**, see below,
more upmarket but little difference.

$$$ Wiracocha Inn
C Wiracocha 206, T084-211088,
www.wiracochainn.com.
Rooms and higher-priced suites, restaurant,
helpful, popular with groups.

$$$-$$ Rupa Wasi
Huanacaure 105, T084-211101,
www.rupawasi.net.

Charming 'eco-lodge' up a small alley off Collasuyo, laid back, comfortable, great views from the balconies, purified water available, organic garden, good breakfasts, half-board available, excellent restaurant, **The Tree House**, and cookery classes.

$$$-$$ Terrazas del Inca
Wiracocha M-18-4, T084-771529, www.terrazasdelinca.com.
Includes breakfast, safety deposit box, helpful.

$$ Hostal El Místico
Av Pachacútec 814, near thermal baths, T084-211051, www.elmisticomachupicchu.com.
Good breakfast, quiet, new-wave-ish, comfortable.

$$ Hostal Machu Picchu
Av Imperio de los Incas 135, T084-211095 sierrandina@gmail.com.
Functional, quiet, Wilber, the owner's son, has travel information, hot water, nice balcony over the Urubamba, grocery store.

$$ Hostal Pirwa
C Túpac Inka Yupanki 103, T084-244315, www.pirwahostelscusco.com.
In the same group as in Cuzco, Lima and elsewhere.

$$ Imperio de los Inkas
Av Pachacútec 602, T084-211105, www.hostalimperiodelosinkas.com.
Functional, quiet, family-owned *hostal*, group rates, good value.

$$ Jardines de Mandor
4 km from Aguas Calientes along the railway to Estacíon Hidroeléctrica, T940-188155, www.jardinesdemandor.com.
Relaxed rural lodging with simple rooms and a lovely garden. Camping possible, meals available, a delightful contrast to the buzz of Aguas Calientes.

$ Hostal Quilla
Av Pachacútec 705, T084-211009, namdo_28@hotmail.com.
Adequate functional rooms, small terrace, pizzeria downstairs.

$ Las Bromelias
Colla Raymi 102, just off the plaza, T084-211145.
Rooms with private bath and hot water, some are small, family-run, good value.

Camping
See **Jardines de Mandor**, above. There is also a campsite (US$6 per tent) in a field by the river, just below the former Puente Ruinas station. It has toilets and cold showers. There's an unpleasant smell from the nearby garbage-processing plant. Do not leave your tent and belongings unattended.

Restaurants

Aguas Calientes
The town is packed with eating places which double as bars, many of them are similar-looking *pizzerías*. Tax is often added as an extra to the bill. Simple economical set meals are served upstairs at the produce market, clean and adequate, daily 0600-1900. See also **The Tree House** restaurant at Rupa Wasi, above.

$$$ Café Inkaterra
On the railway, just below the Machu Picchu Pueblo Hotel.
US$15 for a great lunch buffet with scenic views of the river.

$$$ Chullpi
Av Imperio de los Incas 140, T084-211350
Traditional Peruvian food with good service.

$$ Indio Feliz
C Lloque Yupanqui, T084-211090.
Great French cuisine, excellent value and service, set 3-course meal for US$20, good *pisco sours*, great atmosphere.

$$ Inka Wasi
Av Pachacútec 112, T984-110301.
Very good choice, has an open fire, full Peruvian and international menu available.

$$ Pueblo Viejo
Av Pachacútec 6th block (near plaza), T084-211072.

Good food in a spacious but warm environment. Price includes use of the salad bar.

$$ Toto's House
Av Imperio de los Incas, on the railway line across from the craft market.
Same owners as **Pueblo Viejo**. Good value and quality *menú*, buffet from 1130-1500.

Cafés

La Boulangerie de Paris
Jr Sinchi Roca by the footbridge. Open 0500-2100.
Coffee, sandwiches, quiche and great French pastries.

Transport

Bus Buses leave **Aguas Calientes** for Machu Picchu as they fill (long queues) daily 0530-1500, 25 mins, US$24 return, US$12 single, children US$12, valid 48 hrs. The bus stop and ticket office in Aguas Calientes is on Malecón Hermanos Ayar y Av Imperio de los Incas. Tickets can also be bought in advance at **Consettur** in Cuzco (Av Infancia 433, Wanchaq, T084-222125, www.consettur. com), which saves additional queuing when you arrive in Aguas Calientes. Buses return from the ruins to Aguas Calientes daily 0700-1730. The walk up from Aguas Calientes takes 1-2 hrs following a poor path and crossing the motor road (take care). The road is also in poor condition and landslides can cause disruptions.

Train 2 companies operate services to Machu Picchu, terminating at the station in Aguas Calientes (Av Imperio de los Incas): **PeruRail** (Av Pachacútec, Wanchac Station, T084-581414, www.perurail.com) runs trains from Poroy (near Cuzco), from Urubamba and from Ollantaytambo. **Inca Rail** (Portal de Panes 105, Plaza de Armas, Cuzco, T084-581860, www.incarail.com) runs trains from Ollantaytambo only. **Note** Services

Tip...
Make sure your train ticket for the return to Cuzco has your name on it (spelt absolutely correctly), otherwise you will have to pay for any changes.

may be disrupted in the rainy season, especially Jan-Feb.

There are 4 classes of **PeruRail** tourist train: **Vistadome** (recommended, US$92 one-way from Poroy, US$75 from Urubamba or Ollantaytambo); **Expedition** (US$100 one-way from Poroy, US$63 from Ollantaytambo); and the luxurious **Belmond Hiram Bingham** service with meals, drinks and entertainment (US$475 one way from Poroy, US$795 round trip). Vistadome and Expedition services are more frequent from Ollantaytambo than from Poroy or Urubamba. Seats can be reserved even if you're not returning the same day. These trains have toilets, video, snacks and drinks for sale.

You must have your original passport to travel on the trains to Machu Picchu. Tickets for all trains may be bought at Wanchac station and Portal de Carnes 214, Plaza de Armas, in Cuzco, at travel agencies, or via **PeruRail**'s website, www.perurail.com.

Inca Rail has 4 trains a day from Ollantaytambo to Machu Picchu, 0640, 0720 (budget service), 1115 and 1636, returning 0830, 1430, 1612 and 1900, US$60 one way economy class, US$135 one way first class. Carriages have a/c and heating, snacks and drinks served. In high season (1 Apr-31 Oct, Christmas and New Year) a 1st class service is added to the 0640, 1115 and 1636 trains and an exclusive Inca Princess carriage can also be added (US$300 return). The above are high-season fares; they are slightly cheaper in low season and at less convenient hours and all are subject to change; see company websites.

Tourists may not travel on the local trains to Machu Picchu, except from Santa Teresa, see page 285.

☆The most impressive way to reach Machu Picchu is via the centuries-old Inca Trail that winds its way from the Sacred Valley near Ollantaytambo, taking three to five days. What makes this hike so special is the stunning combination of Inca ruins, unforgettable views, magnificent mountains, exotic vegetation and extraordinary ecological variety. This, the most famous trek in South America, is extremely popular and limited to 500 hikers a day (including guides and porters) and fully booked many months in advance. It can only be done with a licensed tour operator or licensed private guide (the majority of trekkers sign up with an operator); independent trekking is not permitted. The Inca Trail is rugged and steep and you should be in reasonable physical shape. For most hikers, the magnificent views compensate for any weariness, but it is cold at night and weather conditions change rapidly.

The Classic Trail

The trek to Machu Picchu begins either at Km 82, **Piscacucho**, or at Km 88, **Qorihuayrachina**, at 2600 m. In order to reach Km 82 hikers are transported by their tour operator in a minibus on the road that goes from Ollantaytambo to Quillabamba. At Phiry the road divides; the left branch follows the north shore of the Río Vilcanota and ends at Km 82, where there is a bridge. Equipment, food, fuel and field personnel reach Km 82 (depending on the tour operator's logistics) for the Sernanp staff to weigh each bundle before the group arrives. Since many groups leave every day, it is convenient to arrive early. Km 88 can only be reached by train, which is slower than a bus, but you start your walk nearer to Llaqtapata and Huayllabamba.

The walk to **Huayllabamba**, following the Río Cusichaca, needs about three hours and isn't too arduous. Huayllabamba is a popular camping spot for tour groups, but there is another camping place about an hour ahead at **Llulluchayoc** (3200 m). A punishing 1½-hour climb further is **Llulluchapampa**, an ideal meadow for camping. If you have the energy to reach this point, it will make the second day easier because the next stage, the ascent to the first pass, **Warmiwañuska** (Dead Woman's Pass) at 4200 m, is tough; 2½ hours.

Afterwards take the steep path downhill to the **Pacaymayo** ravine. Beware of slipping on the Inca steps after rain. Tour groups usually camp by a stream at the bottom (1½ hours from the first pass). Camping is no longer permitted at **Runkuracay**, on the way up to the second pass. This is a much easier climb to 3900 m, with magnificent views near the summit in clear weather. **Chaquicocha** camp (3600 m) is about 30 minutes past the ruins at **Sayacmarca** (3500 m), about an hour beyond the top of the second pass.

A gentle two-hour climb on a fine stone highway leads through an Inca tunnel to the third pass. Near the top there's a spectacular view of the entire Vilcabamba range, and another campsite. You descend to Inca ruins at **Phuyupatamarca** (3650 m), well worth a long visit.

From there steps go downhill to the magnificent ruins of **Wiñay-Wayna** (2700 m), with impressive views of the cleared terraces of Intipata. There is a campsite here that gets crowded and dirty. After Wiñay-Wayna there is no water and no camping till after Machu Picchu, near Aguas Calientes (see Where to stay, page 279). The path from this point goes more or less level through jungle for two hours before it reaches the steep staircase up to

Essential Inca Trail

Equipment

Take strong footwear, rain gear and warm clothing, extra snacks, water and water-purification supplies, insect repellent, plastic bags, a good sleeping bag and a torch/flashlight. Equipment is provided by tour agencies, but always check what is included. Maps are available from Cuzco bookshops. On most tours, porters will take the heavy gear; you should carry a day-pack for your water, snacks, etc.

Tours

Tour operators must be licensed. **Sernanp** (Avenida José Gabriel Cosio 308, Urb Magisterial, 1 etapa, T084-229297, www.sernanp.gob.pe) verifies operating permits. Unlicensed agencies will sell Inca Trail trips, but pass clients on to the operating agency. This can cause booking problems at busy times. There have been many instances of disappointed trekkers whose bookings did not materialize. Don't wait to the last minute, and check your operator's cancellation fees. Tour operators in Cuzco include transport to the start, equipment and food, as part of the total price for all treks. Prices start at about US$600 per person for a four-day/three-night trek on the Classic Inca Trail and rise according to the level of service given. If the price is significantly lower the company may be cutting corners. Operators pay US$15 per day for each porter and other trail staff; porters are not permitted to carry more than 20 kg. Groups of up to four independent travellers who do not wish to use a tour operator are allowed to hike the trails if they contract an independent, licensed guide to accompany them, but it's hard to find a guide.

Tickets

Current advice is to book your preferred dates as early as possible, several months to a year in advance, depending on the season, then confirm nearer the time. Don't wait to the last minute. Check your operator's cancellation fees before booking. Tickets cost US$86; students and children under 15, US$43. This is the price for all hiking trails (Km 82 or Km 88 to Machu Picchu, Salkantay to Machu Picchu, and Km 82 or Km 88 to Machu Picchu via Km 104) except for the Camino Real de los Inkas (from Km 104 to Wiñay-Wayna and Machu Picchu), for which the fee is US$65 (US$33 for students and children). Tickets can only be purchased by tour operators or guides on behalf of clients. They are non-refundable and cannot be changed. No tickets are sold at the entrance to any of the routes.

When to go

July and August is the height of the tourist season but the Trail is booked to capacity for most of the year. Check conditions in the rainy season from December to March; the weather may be cloudy and the paths are very slippery and difficult in the wet. The Trail is closed each February for cleaning and repair.

Time required

Four days would make a comfortable trip (though much depends on the weather). Allow a further day to see Machu Picchu when you have recovered from the hike. Alternatively, you can take a five-day tour. The first two days of the Trail involve the stiffest climbing.

Regulations and precautions

Littering is banned, as is carrying plastic water bottles (canteens only may be carried). Groups must use approved campsites only. You cannot take backpacks into Machu Picchu; leave them at the entrance. Leave all your valuables in Cuzco and keep everything inside your tent, even your shoes. Security has, however, improved in recent years. Always take sufficient cash to tip porters and guides at the end (S/.50-100 each).

the **Intipunku**, where there's a fine view of Machu Picchu, especially at dawn, with the sun alternately in and out, clouds sometimes obscuring the ruins, sometimes leaving them clear. Groups try to reach Machu Picchu as early as possible to avoid the crowds, but this is usually a futile endeavour and requires a pre-dawn start as well as walking along the edge of the precipice in the dark.

Camino Real de los Inkas and other options

The **Camino Real de los Inkas** starts at Km 104, where a footbridge gives access to the ruins of Chachabamba and the trail, which ascends above the ruins of Choquesuysuy to connect with the main trail at Wiñay-Wayna. This first part is a steady, continuous ascent of three hours (take water). Many people recommend this short Inca Trail. It can be extended into a three-night trek by starting from Km 82, trekking to Km 88, then along the Río Urubamba to Pacaymayo Bajo and Km 104, from where you can join the Camino Real de los Inkas. Alternatively, good day hiking trails from Aguas Calientes run along the banks of the Urubamba.

Salkantay treks

Two treks involve routes from **Salkantay**: one, known as the **High Inca Trail** joins the classic trail at Huayllabamba, then proceeds as before on the main Trail through Wiñay Wayna to Machu Picchu. To get to Salkantay, you have to start the trek in Mollepata, three hours northwest of Cuzco in the Apurímac valley. (**Ampay** buses run to Mollepata from Arcopata on the Chinchero road, or you can take private transport). Salkantay to Machu Picchu this way takes three nights.

The second Salkantay route, known as the **Santa Teresa Trek**, takes four days and crosses the 4500-m Huamantay Pass to reach the Santa Teresa valley, which you follow to its confluence with the Vilcanota. The goal is the town of Santa Teresa (see page 284).

There was talk in 2017 that trekking permits would be introduced on the Salkantay treks, but no official announcement by the close of this edition.

Inca Jungle Trail

This route is offered by several tour operators in Cuzco and combines hiking with cycling and other activities. On the first day you cycle downhill from the Abra Málaga pass on the Ollantaytambo–Quillabamba highway to Santa María at 2000 m. This involves three to four hours of riding on the main road with speeding vehicles inattentive to cyclists; it's best to pay for good bikes and back-up on this section. Some agencies also offer white-water rafting in the afternoon. The second day is a hard 11-km trek from Santa María to Santa Teresa. It involves crossing three adventurous bridges and bathing in the hot springs at Santa Teresa. The third day is a six-hour trek from Santa Teresa to Aguas Calientes. Some agencies offer zip-lining near Santa Teresa as an alternative. The final day is a guided tour of Machu Picchu.

Vilcabamba and around

discover the last refuge of the Incas

Santa María

A paved road runs from Ollantaytambo to Santa María, sometimes called Puente Chaullay, an important crossroads with basic places to stay and eat. This is a very beautiful journey, with snowy peaks on either side of the valley. The climb to the **Abra Málaga pass** (4350 m), west of Ollantaytambo, is steep with many tight curves – on the right is a huge glacier. Soon on the left, Nevado Verónica begins to appear in all its huge and snowy majesty. After endless zig-zags and breathtaking views, you reach the pass. The descent to the Vilcanota valley around Santa María shows hillsides covered in lichen and Spanish moss. From Santa María, roads run to Quillabamba in the lowlands to the north; to Lucma, Pucyura, Huancacalle and Vilcabamba to the west, and to Santa Teresa to the south.

Huancacalle and around

West of Santa Maria, the tranquil little village of **Huancacalle** is the best base for exploring the last stronghold of the Incas, including the nearby ruins of **Vitcos**, which were the palace of the last four Inca rulers from 1536 to 1572. **Yurac Rumi**, the sacred white rock of the Incas is also here. It is 8m high and 20 m wide and covered with intricate carvings. The 7-km loop from Huancacalle to Vitcos, the Inca terraces at Rosaspata, Yurac Rumi and back to Huancacalle makes a nice half-day hike. Several excellent longer treks begin or end in Huancacalle: from Choquequirao to Vilcabamba Vieja (Espíritu Pampa, see below), and to Machu Picchu via Santa Teresa.

Towards Vilcabamba Vieja

The road continues west from Huancacalle, 5 km up to the chilly little village of **Vilcabamba**; there's no regular transport but you can hike through the pleasant countryside. There is a mission here run by Italians, with electricity and running water, where you may be able to spend the night; ask for '*La Parroquia*'.

Beyond Vilcabamba the road runs a further 12 km to **Pampaconas**, start of the trail to the **Vilcabamba Vieja** ruins **at Espíritu Pampa**, a vast pre-Inca site with a neo-Inca overlay set in deep jungle at 1000 m. This is where the last Incas held out against the Spanish for nearly 40 years. From Huancacalle a trip to Espíritu Pampa will take three or four days on foot. Give yourself at least a day at the site to soak up the atmosphere before continuing to **Chuhuanquiri** for transport back to Quillabamba and Cuzco. It is advisable to take local guides and mules, and to enquire in Cuzco and Huancacalle about public safety along the route. Distances are considerable and the going is difficult. The best time of year is May to November. Outside this period it is dangerous as the trails are very narrow and can be thick with mud and very slippery. There are no services along the route; bring all food and supplies including plenty of insect repellent, and take all rubbish with you back to Cuzco for disposal.

Santa Teresa

South of Santa María, this relaxed little town provides alternative access to Machu Picchu (via Estación Hidroeléctrica; see Transport, below) for those who do not wish to ride the train from Cuzco or Ollantaytambo, and makes a good base for activities in the area. Santa Teresa is located at the confluence of the Ríos Sacsara, Salkantay and Vilcanota, and its lower elevation at 1600 m creates a warm climate that is a pleasant change from the chill of Cuzco and trekking at high altitude. Many tour groups and independent travellers pass through or spend the night en route to or from Machu Picchu, and several popular treks go through here (see page 281). There are plenty of hotels, restaurants and most services. The **Colcamayo Thermal Baths** ① *2 km from town along the Río Vilcanota, Wed, Thu, Sat-Mon 0500-2300, Tue and Fri 1600-2300, US$1.75,* have crystal-clear warm pools in a pretty setting and an ice-cold

Tip...
Many Cuzco agencies sell 'Machu Picchu By Car' tours that go through Santa Teresa. You can also reach it by road on your own.

waterfall; free camping nearby. There are several zip-lines around town, including **Cola de Mono** (www.canopyperu.com), which is part of various tour itineraries.

Where to stay and eat

Huancacalle
Huancacalle has a few basic shops and eateries, although these are not always open; there's a better selection in Pucyura, 2 km north.

$ Sixpac Manco
Huancacalle, T971-823855.
A good simple *hostal*, with shared bath, electric shower, large garden, meals on request. It is managed by the Cobos family, who are very knowledgeable about the area and can arrange for guides and pack animals for trekking.

Santa Teresa
There is a **tourist information office** in the Municipio, Mon-Sat 0800-1700.

$ Casa de Judas
Av Calixto Sánchez by the Plaza, T974-709058.
Rooms with private bath and dorm, solar hot water, good value economy option.

$ Hospedaje El Sol
Av Av Calixto Sánchez, T989-606591, https://hospedajesol.com.
Rooms of various sizes, all with private bath and hot water.

$ Hostal Yacumama
C Julio Tomás Rivas, T974-290605.
Rooms with private bath, hot water, breakfast available, restaurant next door.

Transport

Santa María
To reach Santa María from Cuzco, take a Quillabamba-bound van from Av Antonio Lorena by an unnamed street 3 blocks uphill (west) of C Almudena, in the Santiago district, US$9, 4 hrs to Santa María. Cars leave Santa María as they fill throughout the day for **Santa Teresa**, US$3.50, 45 min. There are also vans from Santa María to **Cuzco** and **Quillabamba** (US$1.75, 1 hr).

Huancacalle
Take a van to Quillabamba (US$9, 5 hrs to Quillabamba, see Santa María, above). Then take a *colectivo* from Quillabamba to Huancacalle, 3 daily, US$5.50, 2½ hrs. When travelling from Huancacalle to Cuzco you can get off the *colectivo* at Santa María and catch Cuzco-bound transport from there, but from Cuzco to Huancacalle you should go all the way to Quillabamba because *colectivos* are usually full on route to Huancacalle.

Santa Teresa
From Santa Teresa market, vans leave for the **Estación Hidroeléctrica** at 0530-0700 and 1200-1430, US$1.75, 30 mins, to meet the local train which runs to Aguas Calientes, US$20 for tourists, 40 min. There are **PeruRail** ticket offices at Santa Teresa market (daily 0500-0720, 1000-1200, 1300-1600, plus 1900-2100 on Wed and Sun; confirm current train schedules here) and at the Estación Hidroeléctrica (daily 0630-0745, 1220-1630), which is not much more than a railway siding. You can also walk 11 km along the tracks from Estación Hidroeléctrica to Aguas Calientes, a pleasant 3- to 4-hr hike with great views and many birds, but mind the passing trains.

Central highlands

The Central Andes have many remote mountain areas with small typical villages, while larger cities of the region include Ayacucho and Huancayo. The vegetation is low, but most valleys are cultivated. Secondary roads are often in poor condition, sometimes impassable in the rainy season; the countryside is beautiful with spectacular views and the people are friendly. Three paved roads, from Lima, Pisco and Nazca, connect the central highlands to the coast. Huancayo lies in a valley which produces many crafts; the festivals are very popular and not to be missed.

Lima to Huancayo

ride the rails into the hills

The Central Highway more or less parallels the course of the Central Railway between Lima and Huancayo (335 km). With the paving of roads from Pisco to Ayacucho and Nazca to Abancay, there are now more options for getting to the Sierra and the views on whichever ascent you choose are beyond compare. You can also reach the central highlands from Cuzco (via Abancay and Andahuaylas) and from Huaraz (via La Unión and Huánuco), so Lima is not the sole point of access overland.

Marcahuasi
3 hrs' walk from San Pedro de Casta. Entry US$4, pack donkey US$8, horse US$10.

Up the Santa Eulalia valley, 40 km beyond **Chosica** (a chaotic town, 45 km east of Lima), is Marcahuasi, a table mountain about 3 km by 1 km at 4000 m, near the village of **San Pedro de Casta**. There are three lakes, a 40-m-high Monumento a la Humanidad and other mysterious lines, gigantic figures, sculptures, astrological signs and megaliths. Their origin is a mystery, although a widely accepted theory is that the formations are the result of wind erosion. The trail to Marcahuasi starts south of the village of San Pedro and climbs southeast. It's three hours' walk to the *meseta*; guides are advisable in misty weather. At shops in San Pedro you can buy everything for the trip, including bottled

ON THE ROAD
☆Central Railway

Constructed in the late 19th and early 20th centuries, this is the second-highest railway in the world and is a magnificent feat of engineering, with 58 bridges, 69 tunnels and six zigzags, passing beautiful landscapes. It's a great way to travel to the central highlands. The main line runs from **Lima**, via La Oroya, to Huancayo, and is run as an irregular tourist service, operated mostly on national holidays by **Ferrocarril Centro Andino** (Avenida José Gálvez Barrenechea 566, piso 5, San Isidro, Lima, T01-226 6363, www.ferrocarrilcentral.com.pe). The train leaves Lima at 0700, reaching Huancayo 11 hours later; the return journey begins at 0700 or 1800, three or four days later; see the website for the next departure date. There are *turístico* (US$80 single, US$125 return) and *clásico* fares (US$40 single, US$70 return), sold online and by Lima and Huancayo agencies. Coaches have reclining seats and heating; there's also a restaurant, tourist information, toilets and a nurse with first aid and oxygen.

Beyond Huancayo trains run on a narrow gauge (3 ft) line 120 km to **Huancavelica**. They depart from a small station in the Huancayo suburb of Chilca (15 mins by taxi from the centre, US$2) three to four times a week, either as *Expreso* (*Tren Macho*; US$3), or *Autovagón*. Enquire locally about schedules, as they are constantly changing. This authentic Andean train journey on the *Tren Macho* takes seven long, uncomfortable hours and navigates 38 tunnels and 15 bridges. There are fine views as it passes through typical mountain villages where vendors sell food and crafts. In some places, the train has to reverse and change tracks.

water. Take all necessary camping equipment for the trek. Tourist information is available at the municipality on the plaza and tours can be arranged with travel agencies in Lima.

Towards La Oroya

For a while, beyond Chosica, each successive valley looks greener and lusher, with a greater variety of trees and flowers. Between Río Blanco and **Chicla** (Km 127, 3733 m), Inca contour-terraces can be seen quite clearly. After climbing up from **Casapalca** (Km 139, 4154 m), there are glorious views of the highest peaks and of mines at the foot of a deep gorge. The road ascends to the Ticlio Pass, before the descent to **Morococha** and **La Oroya**. A large metal flag of Peru can be seen at the top of Mount Meiggs; this is not by any means the highest peak in the area, but through it runs the Galera Tunnel, 1175 m long, in which the Central Railway reaches its greatest altitude, 4782 m.

La Oroya (3755 m) is the main smelting centre for the region's mining industry. It stands at the fork of the Yauli and Mantaro rivers. Any traveller, but asthmatics in particular, should beware the pollution from the heavy industry, which can cause breathing difficulties. For destinations to the east and north of La Oroya, see page 308.

Jauja and around

The town of Jauja, founded 1535, 80 km southeast of La Oroya at 3400 m, was Pizarro's provisional capital until the founding of Lima. It has a colourful Wednesday and Sunday market. The **Museo Arqueológico Julio Espejo Núñez** ⓘ *Jr Cusco 537, T064-361163, Mon and Wed 1500-1900, Sun 0900-1200, 1400-1700, donations welcome, knock on door of La Casa del Caminante opposite where the creator and curator lives*, is a quaint but endearing mix of relics from various Peruvian cultures, including two mummies, one still wrapped in the original shroud. The **Cristo Pobre** church is supposedly modelled on Notre Dame and is something of a curiosity. On a hill above Jauja there is a fine line of Inca storehouses, and, on hills nearby, the ruins of Huajlaasmarca, with hundreds of circular stone buildings from the Huanca culture. There are also ruins near the **Laguna de Paca** ① *3.5 km from Jauja; colectivos from the Terminal, US$0.50*. The western shore is lined with restaurants, many of which offer weekend boat trips, US$1.

On the road south to Huancayo is **Concepción** at 3251 m, with a market on Sunday. From Concepción a branch road (6 km) leads to the **Convent of Santa Rosa de Ocopa** ① *Wed-Mon 0900-1200 and 1500-1800, 45-min tours start on the hour, US$1.25; colectivos from the market in Concepción, 15 mins, US$0.50*, a Franciscan monastery set in beautiful surroundings. It was established in 1725 in order to train missionaries for the jungle. It contains a fine library with over 25,000 volumes, a biological museum and a large collection of paintings.

Listings Lima to Huancayo

Tourist information

Jauja
Subgerencia de Turismo (at the Municipalidad on the Plaza, T064-362075, Mon-Fri 0800-1300, 1400-1700), has pamphlets and general information.

Where to stay

Marcahuasi
Locals in San Pedro de Casta will put you up ($); ask at tourist information at the municipality. The best hotel in town is the $ **Marcahuasi**, just off the plaza. Rooms with private or shared bath; it also has a restaurant. There are 2 other restaurants in town.

Jauja

$ Hatun Wasi
Jr Junín 1072, T064-362416.
Modern multi-storey hotel, good simple rooms, solar hot water after 1100, no breakfast, good value.

$ Hostal María Nieves
Jr Gálvez 491, behind school, 1 block from Plaza de Armas, T064-362543.
Safe, helpful, large breakfast available, hot water on request, small patio, parking. Family run, older place but well cared for.

Restaurants

Towards La Oroya

$$ El Tambo
2 km before town on the road from Lima.
Good trout and frogs legs, local cheese and *manjar*; recommended as the best in and around town; buses on the Lima route stop here.

Jauja

$ Quickly's
Jr Junín 1100. Sun-Fri 0900-2300, Sat 1700-2300.
Menú for lunch, à la carte and sandwiches at night. Clean and friendly.

$ Yuraq Wasi
Jr Bolognesi 535. Sun-Fri lunch only.
Selection of tasty *menús*, pleasant garden seating, good service, a 'find' for Jauja.

Transport

Most buses on the Lima–La Oroya route are full when they pass through Chosica.

Marcahuasi
Bus *Colectivos* for Chosica leave from Av Grau, **Lima**, when full, between 0600 and 2100, US$1. Minibuses to San Pedro de

Casta leave **Chosica** from Parque Echenique, opposite market, 0900 and 1500, 4 hrs, US$3.50; return 0700 and 1400.

Towards La Oroya
Bus To **Lima**, 4½ hrs, US$8. To **Jauja**, 80 km, 1½ hrs, US$2. To **Tarma**, 1½ hrs, US$2.50. To **Cerro de Pasco**, 131 km, 3 hrs, US$3. To **Huánuco**, 236 km, 6 hr, US$7.50. Buses leave from Zeballos, adjacent to the train station. *Colectivos* also run on all routes.

Jauja
Air Francisco Carle airport is located just outside Jauja. **LC Peru** has 2 daily flights from **Lima**, 45 mins; price includes transfer to Huancayo.

Bus The old train station serves as the bus station. To **Lima**, US$15, or with **Cruz del Sur** (Pizarro 220), direct, 6 hrs, US$22-29 *bus cama*. To **Huancayo**, 44 km, 1 hr, US$2.25; combis to Huancayo from 25 de Abril y Ricardo Palma, 1¼ hrs, US$2.50. To **Cerro de Pasco**, with **Turismo Central**, 5 hrs, US$6. **Turismo Central** also goes to **Huánuco**, 8 hrs, US$15. To **Tarma**, US$3, hourly buses from Junín y Tarma, about 10 blocks north of the centre. Also *colectivos* to Tarma from the same corner.

Huancayo and the Mantaro Valley   *Colour map 2, C3.*
a nexus of traditional crafts and culture

Huancayo is the capital of the Junín Region and the main commercial centre for central inland Peru, with a population of over half a million. The city lies in the Mantaro Valley at 3271 m, surrounded by villages that produce their own original crafts and celebrate festivals all year round. People flock in from far and wide to the important festivals in Huancayo, with an incredible range of food, crafts, dancing and music.

Sights
The weekly Sunday market gives a little taste of Huancayo at festival time; it gets going after 0900. Jiron Huancavelica, 3 km long and four stalls wide, sells clothes, fruit, vegetables, hardware, handicrafts and traditional medicines and goods for witchcraft. There is also an impressive daily market behind the railway station and a large handicrafts market on Plaza Huanamarca, between Ancash and Real, offering a wide selection. However, in general, it is better to go to the villages themselves for local handicrafts. The **museum** ① *at the Salesian school, Pje Santa Rosa 229, north of the river in El Tambo, Mon-Fri 0900-1300, 1500-1800, Sat 0900-1200, US$1.75,* has a good collection of ceramics from various cultures, as well as stuffed animals and miscellaneous curiosities. The **Parque de Identidad Wanka** ① *on Jr San Jorge in the Barrio San Carlos northeast of the city, daily 0800-2000, entry free,* is a mixture of surrealistic construction interwoven with native plants and trees and the cultural history of the Mantaro Valley. It also has restaurants and craft stalls. On a hillside on the outskirts of town are the impressive, eroded sandstone towers of **Torre-Torre**; take a bus to Cerrito de la Libertad and walk up.

☆Mantaro Valley
The whole Mantaro Valley is rich in culture. Near the small town of Huari are the ruins of **Warivilca** ① *5 km from Huancayo, daily 1000-1200, 1500-1700 (museum mornings only), US$1.75, take a micro for Chilca from Av Ferrocaril,* with the remains of a pre-Inca temple of the Huanca tribe. The Museo de Sitio on the plaza houses deformed skulls and the modelled, painted pottery of successive Huanca and Inca occupations of the shrine.

East of the Río Mantaro, the villages of **Cochas Chico** and **Cochas Grande** ① *11 km north of Huancayo, micros from the corner of Huancas and Giráldez, US$0.50*, are famous for *mate burilado*, or gourd carving. You can buy samples cheaply direct from manufacturers such as Pedro Veli or Eulogio Medina; ask around. There are beautiful views of the Valle de Mantaro and Huancayo from here.

Hualahoyo, near Cochas, has a little chapel with 21 colonial canvases. **San Agustín de Cajas** (8 km north of Huancayo) makes fine hats, and **San Pedro** (10 km) makes wooden chairs. **Hualhuas** (12 km) is known for its fine alpaca weavings which you can watch being made. The weavers take special orders, and small items can be finished in a day; negotiate a price.

Where to stay		
1 El Marquez *A2*	8 Presidente *C2*	4 Café París *A2*
2 Hosp Piccolo *B2*	9 Samay *A3*	5 Chifa Centro *B2*
3 Kiya *B2*	10 Turismo *B2*	6 Chifa Xu *B2*
4 La Casa de La Abuela *A3*		7 Detrás de la Catedral *B2*
5 Las Lomas *B3*	**Restaurants** 🍴	8 Donatelo's *B2*
6 Los Balcones *A2*	1 A La Leña *B2*	9 El Olímpico *B2*
7 Perú Andino *A3*	2 Becot Crepes *B2*	10 Govinda *A2*
	3 Café Koky *B2*	11 Inca *A2*

12 La Cabaña *B3*	
13 La Pérgola *A2*	
14 Mass *B2*	
15 Pizzería Antojitos *B2*	
Bars & clubs 🍸	
16 Galileo *B1*	

The town of **San Jerónimo** is renowned for the making of silver filigree jewellery. It has a Wednesday market and a fiesta on the third Saturday in August. There are ruins two to three hours' walk above San Jerónimo, but seek advice before hiking to them.

Between Huancayo and Huancavelica, **Izcuchaca** is the site of a bridge over the Río Mantaro. On the edge of town is a fascinating pottery workshop whose machinery is driven by a water turbine. There is also a small shop. It's a nice hike to the chapel on a hill overlooking the valley (one to 1½ hours each way).

> **Tip...**
> In Izcuchaca many locals are enthusiastic about renting a room to a gringo traveller for a night; you may well make a friend for life.

Huancayo to Ayacucho via Huanta

There is a fully paved route to Ayacucho from Huancayo which involves not so much climbing for cyclists. Cross the pass into the Mantaro valley on the road to **Quichuas**. Then to **Anco** and **Mayocc** (lodging). From here the road crosses a bridge after 10 km and in another 20 km reaches **Huanta** in the picturesque valley of the same name. Huanta celebrates the **Fiesta de las Cruces** during the first week of May. Its Sunday market is large and interesting. The area is notable as the site of perhaps the oldest known culture in South America, dating from 20,000 years ago. Evidence was found in the cave of **Pikimachay**, 24 km from Ayacucho, off the road from Huanta. The remains are now in Lima's museums.

Listings Huancayo and Mantaro Valley *map page 290.*

Tourist information

The regional office is in Jauja (see above). For city information contact **DIRCETUR** at the train station (T064-222575). **Indecopi** (Pje Comercial 474, El Tambo, T064-245180, abarrientos@indecopi.gob.pe) is the consumer protection office.

Where to stay

Huancayo
Prices may rise in Holy Week. The Plaza de Armas is called Plaza Constitución.

$$$ Presidente
*C Real 1138, T064-231275, http://huancayo.
hotelpresidente.com.pe.*
Helpful, classy, safe, serves breakfast, restaurant, convention centre.

$$$ Turismo
*Ancash 729, T064-231072, http://turistases.
hotelpresidente.com.pe/.*

Restored colonial building, same owner as Presidente, with more atmosphere, elegant, rooms quite small, Wi-Fi extra, quiet. Restaurant ($$-$) serves good meals, fine service.

$$$-$$ El Marquez
*Puno 294, T064-219202,
www.elmarquezhuancayo.com.*
Good value, efficient, popular with local business travellers, safe parking.

$$ Kiya
*Giráldez 107, T064-214955,
www.hotelkiya.com.pe.*
Comfortable although ageing, hot water, helpful staff. Spectacular view of Plaza.

$ Hospedaje Piccolo
Puno 239.
With hot water, good beds, well-kept.

$ La Casa de la Abuela
*Prolongación Cusco 794 y Gálvez, T064-234383,
www.incasdelperu.org/casa-de-la-abuela.*

Doubles with or without private bath and dorms, 10-min walk from town. Hot shower, breakfast, laundry facilities, meals available, sociable staff, owner speaks English, good meeting place, games room, free pickup from bus station if requested in advance. Discount for Footprint readers.

$ Las Lomas
Giráldez 327, T064-237587.
Central location, basic rooms, hot water, good value, can arrange tours.

$ Los Balcones
Jr Puno 282, T064-214881.
Comfortable rooms, restaurant, hot water, helpful staff, elevator (practically disabled-accessible). View of the back of the Cathedral.

$ Peru Andino
Pasaje San Antonio 113-115, near Parque Túpac Amaru, in 1st block of Francisco Solano (left side of Defensoría del Pueblo), 10-15 mins' walk from the centre (if taking a taxi, stress that it's Pasaje San Antonio), T064-223956.
Hot showers, several rooms with bath, laundry and kitchen facilities, breakfast and other meals on request, safe area, cosy atmosphere, run by Sra Juana and Luis, who speak some English, organize trekking and mountain bike tours, bike hire, Spanish classes. Can pick up guests at Lima airport with transfer to bus station.

$ Samay
Jr Florida 285 (cdra 9 de Giráldez), T064-365259.
Hostel with shared bath, quiet (unless the little football field next door is being used), breakfast, laundry and kitchen facilities, garden, nice terraces on 3rd floor, helpful staff.

Huancayo to Ayacucho

$ Hostal Recreo Sol y Sombra
Quichuas.
Charming, small courtyard, helpful, basic.

Restaurants

Huancayo

Breakfast is served in Mercado Modelo from 0700. Better, more expensive restaurants serve typical dishes for about US$6, drinks can be expensive. Lots of cheap restaurants along Av Giráldez, and a large food court in Real Plaza mall.

$$ Detrás de la Catedral
Jr Ancash 335 (behind Cathedral as name suggests), T064-212969.
Pleasant atmosphere, excellent dishes. Charcoal grill in the corner keeps the place warm on cold nights. Considered by many to be the best in town.

$$ El Olímpico
Giráldez 199.
Long-established, one of the more upscale establishments offering Andean and *comida criolla*; the real reason to go is the owner's model car collection displayed in glass cabinets.

$$ La Cabaña
Av Giráldez 675, T064-223303.
Daily 0900-2400.
Pizzeria, restaurant and bar, pastas, grill, juices and ice cream, wide variety of dishes, excellent atmosphere, Wi-Fi, home delivery US$2.

$$ Pizzería Antojitos
Puno 599.
Attractive, atmospheric pizzería with live music some nights.

$$-$ Chifa Xu
Giráldez 208.
Good food at reasonable prices, always a bustling atmosphere.

$ A La Leña
Ancash on Plaza Constitución.
Good rotisserie chicken and salads, popular.

$ Chifa Centro
Giráldez 238, T064-217575. Another branch at Av Leandra Torres 240.
Chinese food, good service and atmosphere.

$ Donatelo's

Puno 287.

Excellent pizza and chicken place, with good atmosphere, popular.

$ Govinda

Jr Cusco 289.

Vegetarian restaurant and café, good service, sells natural products. Nice tranquil atmosphere with no blaring TV, good concert videos instead.

$ La Pérgola

Puno 444, overlooking the plaza.

An oldie with a pleasant atmosphere, 4-course *menú*.

$ Mass

Real 549 and on block 10 of Real.

A clean place for *pollo a la brasa* with good fast service.

Cafés

Becot Crepes

Av Real 471.

Savoury and sweet crêpes to go, tasty and cheap.

Café Koky

Ancash y Puno, Ancash 235, and Real Plaza Mall. Daily 0700-2300, lunch 1230-1530.

Good for breakfasts, lunches, sandwiches, capuccino and pastries, fancy atmosphere, free Wi-Fi.

Café París

Puno 254 and Arequipa 265.

Sofá-café and restaurant, good food and atmosphere, many sweets, *menú* at midday.

Inca

Puno 530.

Popular *fuente de soda*, with coffee, Peruvian food, desserts, milkshakes.

Huancayo

Galileo Disco-Pub

Paseo La Breña 376.

Live music Wed through Sat, good atmosphere.

There are so many festivals in the Mantaro Valley that it is impossible to list them all. Nearly every day of the year there is some sort of celebration in one of the villages.

1-6 Jan **New Year** celebrations; also **La Huaconada** dance festival in Mito.
20 Jan **San Sebastián y San Fabián,** recommended in Jauja.
Feb There are carnival celebrations for the whole month, with highlights including **Virgen de la Candelaria** and **Concurso Nacional de Huaylash**.
Mar-Apr **Semana Santa**, with impressive Good Fri processions.
3-8 May **Fiesta de los Shapis** in Chupaca.
May **Fiesta de las Cruces** throughout the whole month.
15 Jun **Virgen de las Mercedes.**
24 Jun **San Juan Bautista.**
29 Jun **Fiesta Patronal.**
16 Jul **Virgen del Carmen.**
24-25 Jul **Santiago.**
4 Aug **San Juan de Dios.**
16 Aug **San Roque.**
30 Aug **Santa Rosa de Lima.**
8 Sep **Virgen de Cocharcas.**
15 Sep **Virgen de la Natividad.**
23-24 Sep **Virgen de las Mercedes.**
29 Sep **San Miguel Arcángel.**
4 Oct **San Lucas.**
28-30 Oct Culmination of month-long celebrations for **El Señor de los Milagros.**
1 Nov **Día de Todos los Santos.**
3-13 Dec **Virgen de Guadalupe.**
8 Dec **Inmaculada Concepción.**
25 Dec **Navidad** (Christmas).

All crafts are made outside Huancayo in the many villages of the Mantaro Valley, or in Huancavelica. The villages are worth a visit to learn how the items are made.

Huancayo
Tour operators
American Travel & Service, *Plaza Constitución 122, of 2 (next to the Cathedral), T064-211181, T964-830220.* Wide range of classical and more adventurous tours in the Mantaro Valley and the central jungle. Transport and equipment rental possible. Most group-based day tours start at US$8-10 pp.

Hidden Perú, *no storefront, T964-164979, andinismo_peru@yahoo.es, Facebook: Eco Mountain trek – Peru.* Marco Jurado Ames is a mountain guide who organizes adventure and cultural trips in the Andes and Amazon Basin, for 1-12 days with trekking in the Mantaro valley, Huaytapallana and Pariacaca ranges; mountain biking, walking and mountaineering in Cuzco and Huaraz.

Incas del Perú, *Av Giráldez 675, T064-223303, www.incasdelperu.org.* Jungle, biking and hiking trips throughout the region as well as day trips to the Mantaro Valley. Also arranges flight/train tickets and language and volunteer programmes (Spanish for beginners, US$50 for 5 days or US$185 per week, including accommodation at **Hostal La Casa de La Abuela** and all meals at La Cabaña); also home-stays and weaving, traditional music, Peruvian cooking and lots of other things. Very popular and recommended.

Peruvian Tours, *Plaza Constitución 122, p 2, of 1, T064-213069. Next to the Cathedral and American Travel & Service.* Classic tours of the Mantaro valley, plus day trips up to the Huaytapallana Nevados above Huancayo, plus long, 16-hr excursions to Cerro de Pasco and Tarma.

Transport

Huancayo
For train services, see Central Railway, page 287.

Bus **Terminal Terrestre Huancayo** for buses to most destinations is 3 km north of the centre in the Parque Industrial. **Terminal Los Andes** (also known as **Terminal Centro-Selva**; Av Ferrocarril 151, T064-223367) serves mainly the central highlands and the jungle. Some companies have their own terminal in the centre, including **Turismo Central** (Jr Ayacucho 274, T064-223528). Most buses to the Mantaro Valley leave from several places around the market area, and from Av Ferrocarril. Buses to **Hualhuas** and **Cajas** leave from block 3 of Pachitea. Buses to **Cochas** leave from Amazonas y Giráldez.

There are regular buses to **Lima**, 6-7 hrs on a good paved road, US$13-25 with **Oltursa**. Other recommended companies with frequent service include **Etucsa**, **Turismo Central**, **Mega Bus** (Ancash 385, T064-225432) and **Cruz del Sur** (Terminal Los Andes). Travelling by day is recommended for the fantastic views and for safety, although most major companies go by night (take warm clothing).

To **Ayacucho**, 319 km, 9-10 hrs, US$13 with **Molina** (C Angaraés 334, T064-224501), 3 a day, recommended; 1 a day with **Turismo Central** (via Huanta) US$10-22; also **Ticllas** and **Etucsa** from Terminal Terrestre, US$5-10. There are 2 routes: one via Huanta, mostly paved; and the other via Huancavelica, partly paved with the remainder in poor condition, very difficult in the wet. Take warm clothing.

To **Huancavelica**, 147 km, 3 hrs, US$5. Many buses daily, including **Transportes Yuri** (Ancash 1220), 3 a day. The road is paved and offers a delightful ride, much more comfortable than the train (if you can find a driver who will not scare you to death). Shared taxis from Av Real cuadra 12, US$8 (US$10 on weekends), negotiable.

To **Cerro de Pasco**, 255 km, 5 hrs, US$7.50. Several departures. Alternatively, take a bus to La Oroya, about every 20 mins from Terminal Los Andes, or a shared taxi, US$5, 2 hrs. From La Oroya there are regular buses and *colectivos* to Cerro, US$8. The road to La Oroya and on to Cerro is paved and in good condition. To **Huánuco**, 7 hrs, **Turismo Central**, twice daily, US$20, good service.

To **Tarma**, **Lobato** and **America** from Terminal Los Andes, 5 hrs, US$10; some continue to **La Merced**. Also **Turismo Central** to La Merced, US$19. Minibuses and cars from outside the terminal, to Tarma US$6, to La Merced US$12, 3 hrs.

To **Yauyos**, cars at 0500 from Plaza de los Sombreros, El Tambo, US$7.50. It is a poor road with beautiful mountain landscapes before dropping to the valley of Cañete; cars go very fast.

To **Jauja**, 44 km, 1 hr. *Colectivos* and combis leave every few mins from Terminal Los Andes, US$2.50. Taxi to Jauja US$15, 45 mins.

To **Tingo María** and **Pucallpa**, daily with **Turismo Central**, US$27.

Huancavelica *Colour map 2, C3.*

a colonial mountain town

Huancavelica is a friendly and attractive town at 3676 m, surrounded by huge, rocky mountains. It was founded in the 16th century by the Spanish to exploit rich deposits of mercury and silver, but it remains predominantly an indigenous town. There are beautiful mountain walks in the surrounding area.

Sights

The Cathedral, located on the Plaza de Armas, has an altar considered to be one of the finest examples of colonial art in Peru. Also very impressive are the five other churches in town, although most are closed to visitors. The church of San Francisco, for example, has no less than 11 altars. The **Ministerio de Cultura** ① *Plazoleta San Juan de Dios, Arica y Raimondi, T064-453420*, is a good source of information on festivals, archaeological sites, history, etc. It also runs courses and lectures on music and dancing, and has a small but interesting **Museo Regional** ① *T064-753420, Mon-Sat 0830-1300, 1430-1800,* with exhibits of archaeology, anthropology and popular art.

Bisecting the town is the Río Ichu. South of the river is the main commercial centre. On the hillside north of the river are the **San Cristóbal thermal baths** ① *Av Escalinata y 28 de Abril, daily 0600-1700, US$0.50 for private rooms, water not very hot (26º C), US$0.30 for the hot public pool, also hot showers, take a lock for the doors*. The pedestrian walkway up to the baths on Av Escalinata is full of figures illustrating the village festivals of the region and their typical characters. There are also thermal baths in Secsachaca, 1 km from town. The Potaqchiz hill, just outside the town, gives a fine view; it's about one hour walk up from San Cristóbal.

Huancavelica to Ayacucho

The fully paved route from Huancavelica to Ayacucho (247 km) is one of the highest continuous roads in the world. The journey is a cold one but spectacular, as the road rarely drops below 4000 m for 150 km, with great views and many lakes en route. It goes via Santa Inés (4650 m), which is located 78 km south of Huancavelica on the main Pisco–Ayacucho road.

Out of Huancavelica the road climbs steeply with switchbacks between herds of llamas and alpacas grazing on rocky perches. Around Pucapampa (Km 43) is one of the highest habitable altiplanos (4500 m), where the rare and highly prized ash-grey alpaca can be seen. Snow-covered mountains are passed as the road climbs to 4853 m at the Abra Chonta pass, 23 km before Santa Inés. By taking the turn-off to Huachocolpa at Abra Chonta and continuing for 3 km you'll reach one of the highest drivable passes in the world, at 5059 m. Nearby are two lakes (Laguna Choclacocha) which can be visited in 2½ hours. The Abra de Apacheta at 4750 m is 52 km beyond Santa Inés, on the main road 98 km from Ayacucho. The rocks here are all the colours of the rainbow, and running through this fabulous scenery is a violet river. You can combine a tour to Santa Inés with the trip to Ayacucho (eg with Paccari Tours, see below).

A more adventurous route to Ayacucho is via Lircay and Julcamarca, along dirt roads with beautiful scenery all the way; see Transport, below, for bus services and accommodation options.

Listings Huancavelica

Tourist information

Dircetur
*Jr Victoria Garma 444, upstairs,
T064-452938. Mon-Sat.*
Very helpful.

Where to stay

$$$ Presidente
*Plaza de Armas, T064-452760, http://
huancavelica.hotelpresidente.com.pe.*
Lovely colonial building, higher-priced suites available, heating, parking, safe, laundry, buffet breakfast, very good restaurant (small and old-fashioned) and café.

$ Ascención
*Jr Manco Capac 481 (Plaza de Armas),
T064-453103.*
Very comfortable, wooden floors, with or without bath, hot water, good value.

$ La Portada
Virrey Toledo 252, T064-453603.
Large rooms with private bath or small, basic rooms with shared bath with extra charge for TV. Lots of blankets, unlimited coca tea, helpful staff, good value, secure metal doors.

$ Montevideo
Av Malecón Santa Rosa 168, T967-980638.
Clean basic rooms. 4th floor terrace has great views of the river and *malecón*.

$ Victoria
Virrey Toledo 133, next to the plaza.
Basic, functional, modern and clean.

Restaurants

$$ Los Farolitos
*Jr Arica 202, Plazoleta San Juan de Dios.
Mon-Sat 0800-2200.*
Restaurant, café and bar serving good food, juices and drinks. Small place with tables on the pedestrian street, nice atmosphere. Recommended.

$$-$ Roma II
*Manco Capac 580, T064-452608.
Open 1800-2300.*
Pizzas, smells delicious, friendly staff, delivery available.

$ Chifa El Mesón
Manchego Muñoz 153, T064-453570.
Very popular, standard *chifa* fare, delivery available.

$ Frutas
Manchego 279.
Clean modern place serving fruit salads, juices and sandwiches.

$ Joy Campestre
Av de los Incas 870.
Comida criolla and regional dishes served in a leisurely country environment.

$ Killa Café
Virrey Toledo, on Plaza de Armas opposite the Cathedral, evenings only.
Good coffee, sandwiches and wine, no noisy TV, free Wi-Fi, paintings for sale, nice and cosy.

$ Los Portales
Virrey Toledo 158, on Plaza de Armas.

Good breakfast, sandwiches and coffee, giant fruit extracts (try the apple extract).

Festivals

4-8 Jan Fiesta de los Reyes Magos y los Pastores.
2nd Sun in Jan Fiesta del Niño Perdido.
20 Jan-mid Mar Pukllaylay Carnavales, celebration of the first fruits from the ground (harvest).
Mar/Apr Semana Santa (Holy Week).
End May-Jun Toro Pukllay festival.
May and Aug Fiesta de Santiago in all communities.
22-28 Dec Los Laijas or Galas (scissors dance). This event is on UNESCO's World Heritage list.

Shopping

Huancavelica is a major craft centre, with a wide variety of goods produced in surrounding villages. Handicraft sellers congregate on the 4th block of Victoria Garma and under Plaza Santa Ana (*sótano*). Most handicrafts are transported directly to Lima, but you can still visit craftsmen in neighbouring villages.

What to do

Cielo Azul, *Jr Manuel Ascencio Segura 140, on the plaza (former municipal tourism office)*, *T967-718802*. City tours and many others, US$10-30 pp for a group of 6.
Paccari Tours, *Av Ernesto Morales 637, T978-978828, www.paccaritours.com*. Offers city tours (also by bike), visits to Uchkus Inkañan archaeological site, boating on one of the lakes, alpaca herding on the Puna, and historic mine tours. Owner Daniel Páucar is very helpful.
Willka Tours, *Jr Carabaya 199, T967-758007, www.willkatours.com*. Variety of local tours.

Transport

Bus There is a Terrapuerto bus terminal in Ascensión, next to the Esalud Hospital II in the west end of town. Many bus companies also have offices on, and leave from the east end of town, around Parque M Castilla (Santa Ana), between Manchego and O'Donovan.

To **Huancayo**, 147 km, 5 hrs, US$4, paved road, **Transportes Ticllas** (Manchego 686, T064-452787). Also shared taxis all day from Av Machego y González Prada and from the Terrapuerto, US$8 Mon-Thu, US$10 Fri-Sun, 3½ hrs. Most buses to Huancayo go on to Lima, 445 km, 13 hrs, minimum, US$14; there are several a day including **Molina** (Manchego 608, T064-454244). The other route is via **Pisco**, 269 km, 12 hrs, US$12, and **Ica**, US$13, 1730 daily, with **Oropesa** (Manchego 612, T064-369082), continuing to Lima. Buy your ticket 1 day in advance. The road is poor until it joins the Ayacucho–Pisco road, beyond which it is paved. Most of the journey is done at night; be prepared for sub-zero temperatures in the early morning as the bus passes snowfields, then for temperatures of 25-30°C as the bus descends to the coast.

Train Station at Av Ferrocarril s/n, T064-452898. To **Huancayo**, 3-4 times a week (see Central Railway, page 287).

Huancavelica to Ayacucho

There is no direct transport from Huancavelica to Ayacucho, other than with **Molina** which passes through from Huancayo daily between 2230 and 2400, US$13. Otherwise you have to go to **Rumichaca** just beyond Santa Inés on the Pisco–Ayacucho road, with **San Juan Bautista**, 0430, 4 hrs, then take a minibus to Ayacucho, 3 hrs. Rumichaca has only a couple of foodstalls and some filthy toilets.

The alternative route to Ayacucho is to take a taxi or *colectivo* from Huancavelica with **Transportes 5 de Mayo** (Av Sebastián Barranca y Cercado) to the small village of **Lircay**, US$7.55, 2½ hrs. The village has an unnamed *hostal* ($) at Sucre y La Unión, with bath and hot water (much better than **Hostal El Paraíso**, opposite). **Transportes**

5 de Mayo continues from Lircay Terminal Terrestre hourly from 0430 to Julcamarca, 2½ hrs, US$6, where there is a colonial church and the very basic **Hostal Villa Julcamarca**, near the plaza (no tap water).

From Julcamarca plaza, take a minibus to Ayacucho, US$4, 2 hrs.

The final, slow option to Ayacucho is to take the train to Izcuchaca, stay the night and continue by *colectivo* from there (see page 291).

Ayacucho and around Colour map 2, C3.

indigenous handicrafts and colonial churches

☆The city of Ayacucho, the capital of its department, is famous for its hugely impressive Semana Santa celebrations, its splendid market and, not least, its plethora of churches – 33 of them no less – giving the city its alternative name La Ciudad de las Iglesias. A week can easily be spent enjoying Ayacucho and its hinterland. The climate is lovely, with warm, sunny days and pleasant balmy evenings. It is a hospitable, tranquil place, where the inhabitants are eager to promote tourism. It also boasts a large, active student population. Ayacucho is a large city but the interesting churches and colonial houses are all fairly close to the Plaza Mayor. Barrio Santa Ana is further away to the south; you can take a taxi or walk.

The decisive Battle of Ayacucho was fought on the Pampa de Quinua (see page 301), on 9 December 1824, bringing Spanish rule in Peru to an end. In the middle of the festivities, the Liberator Simón Bolívar decreed that the city be named Ayacucho, 'Place of the Souls', instead of its original name, Huamanga.

Sights

Plaza Mayor The city is built round the Plaza Mayor, with the Cathedral, Municipalidad, Universidad Nacional de San Cristóbal de Huamanga (UNSCH) and various colonial mansions facing on to it. The **Cathedral** ① *open for Mass Mon-Sat 1730, Sun 1000 and 1730,* built in 1612, has superb gold-leaf altars. It is beautifully lit at night. On the north side of the Plaza Mayor, at Portal de la Unión 37, is the **Casona de los Marqueses de Mozobamba del Pozo**, also called Velarde-Alvarez. Recently restored as the Centro Cultural de la UNSCH, it hosts frequent artistic and cultural exhibitions; see the monthly Agenda Cultural. Jr Asamblea is pedestrianized for its first two blocks north of the plaza; on a parallel street is **Santo Domingo** (1548) ① *9 de Diciembre, block 2, Mass daily 0630-0730.* Its fine façade has triple Roman arches and Byzantine towers.

South of the plaza Jr 28 de Julio is pedestrianized for two blocks south of the plaza. A stroll down 28 de Julio leads to the prominent **Arco del Triunfo** (1910), which commemorates victory over the Spaniards. Through the arch is the church of **San Francisco de Asís** (1552) ① *28 de Julio, block 3, daily for morning Mass.* It has an elaborate gilt main altar and several others. Across 28 de Julio from San Francisco is the **Mercado de Abastos Carlos F Vivanco**, the packed

Tip...
For a moving insight into the recent history of this region and the violence surrounding the Sendero Luminoso campaign, visit **Museo de la Memoria de ANFASEP** (Asociación Nacional de Familiares de Secuestrados Detenidos y Desaparecidos del Perú), Prolongación Libertad 1229 (cuadra 14), in the north of the city, T066-317170, Mon-Sat 0900-1300, 1500-1800, US$0.70.

Ayacucho

To ❼, Museo de la Memoria & Terrapuerto (bus station)

To ❶❽

To Pisco & Lima

To Combis for Julcamarca, Huari, Quinua & Huanta

Mercado Artesanal Shosaku Nagase

Quinua

Libertad

Garcilaso de la Vega

Manco Capac

9 de Diciembre

Asamblea

Pie Cáceres

Los Andes

Miller

Cruz del Sur

Directur

Av Mariscal Cáceres

9 de Diciembre

⑩ ✉
Santo Domingo ❷
⑰ ❸
⑪ ❹

Bellido

Tres Máscaras

Sol

❺
⑯
①
③
San Agustín

LAN & LC Perú

⑮ ⑧
⑨

Callao

Prefectura ❻

Plaza Mayor

iPerú
Municipalidad
✚ Cathedral

Cuzco

④

Lima

⑩
⑪
❼ ❸
⑫
⑫

Tourist Police

Buena Muerte

Arequipa

To Barrio Belén

La Compañía de Jesús
Centro Turístico Cultural San Cristóbal

⑭

San Martín

❻

La Merced

Río Alameda

To Airport & Cuzco

Libertad

Grau

28 de Julio

Casona Jáuregui

❾
Arco del Triunfo

Av Ramón Castilla

Nazareno

Carlos F Vivanco

❷

Santa Clara de Asis

Mercado de Abastos Carlos F Vivanco

San Francisco de Asís

Huatatas

2 de Mayo

S J de Dios

❺

Mercado 12 de Abril

C Chorro

Raymondi

Museo Andrés A Cáceres (Casona Vivanco)

N

Santa Teresa

San Cristóbal

To Barrio Santa Ana

100 metres
100 yards

Where to stay 🛏

1 Ayacucho Hotel Plaza
2 Crillonesa
3 El Condeduque
4 Florida
5 Grau
6 Hostal 3 Máscaras
7 Internazionale
8 Marcos
9 San Francisco de Paula
10 Santa Rosa
11 Universo
12 ViaVia Café Ayacucho

5 La Italiana
6 La Miel
7 Las Tinajas
8 Los Manglares
9 Mamma Mia
10 Mía Pizza
11 Nino
12 Portal 1
13 Retablo
14 Salud y Vida & Wambar
15 Wallpa Sua

Restaurants 🍴

1 Cabo Blanco
2 Chifa Wa Lin
3 Frutimix
4 La Casona

Bars & clubs 🍸

16 Punto Caliente
17 Toto's Night & Tupana Wasy

central market. As well as household items and local produce, look out in particular for the stalls dedicated to cheese, breads and fruit juices. West of the market, **Santa Clara de Asís** ① *Jr Grau, block 3, open for Mass 0600-0800*, is renowned for its beautifully delicate coffered ceiling and for housing an image of Jesús Nazareno, patron of Huamanga. It is open for the sale of sweets and cakes made by the nuns; go to the door at Nazareno 184, which is usually open.

One block east of Jr 28 de Julio, the 16th-century church of **La Merced** ① *2 de Mayo, open for Mass 0600-0800 and 1700-1900*, is the second oldest in the city. The high choir is a good example of the simplicity of churches in the early period of the Viceroyalty. **Casona Jáuregui**, opposite, is also called **Ruiz de Ochoa** after its original owner. Its outstanding feature is its doorway, which has a blue balcony supported by two fierce beasts with erect penises.

On the fifth block of 28 de Julio is the late 16th-century **Casona Vivanco**, which houses the **Museo Andrés A Cáceres** ① *Jr 28 de Julio 508, Mon-Fri 0900-1300, 1500-1700, US$0.70*. The museum has baroque painting, colonial furniture, republican and contemporary art, and exhibits on Mariscal Cáceres' battles in the War of the Pacific. Further south still, on a pretty plazuela, is **Santa Teresa** (1683) ① *28 de Julio, block 6, daily Mass 0600-0800, usually 1600*, with its monastery. The nuns here sell sweets and crystallized fruits and a *mermelada de ají*, made to a recipe given to them by God; apparently it is not *picante* (spicy). **San Cristóbal** ① *Jr 28 de Julio, block 6, rarely open*, was the first church to be founded in the city (1540), and is one of the oldest in South America. With its single tower, it is tiny compared with Santa Teresa, see above.

Barrio Santa Ana For a fascinating insight into Inca and pre-Inca art and culture, a visit to Barrio Santa Ana is a must. Here, about 200 families have workshops making *artesanías*: textiles, retablos, ceramics and work in stone. Their work is distributed through the galleries in the barrio. A good grasp of Spanish is essential to appreciate the galleries fully. Note that the galleries in the barrio are closed on Sunday. Visit **Julio Gálvez** ① *Plazoleta Santa Ana 120, T066-314278*, for remarkable jewellery and sculptures in alabaster (*piedra de huamanga*). Also see Handicrafts, page 304.

North of Ayacucho

A good road north from Ayacucho leads to Huari ① *22 km from Ayacucho, daily 0800-1700, US$1;* vans leave from Paradero a Huari Quinua (Jr Ciro Alegría, 3ra cuadra), when full from 0700, 40 mins, US$1.50; or take a tour. This site dates from the 'Middle Horizon' (AD 600-1000), when the Huari culture spread across most of Peru. This was the first urban walled centre in the Andes. The huge irregular stone walls are up to 3-4 m high, and rectangular houses and streets can be made out. The most important activity here was artistic: ceramics, gold, silver, metal and alloys such as bronze, which was used for weapons and for decorative objects. The ruins now lie in an extensive *tuna* cactus forest (don't pick the fruit). There is a museum at the site.

Vans to Huari continue to **Quinua** ① *37 km northeast of Ayacucho, a further 25 mins, US$0.75, or US$1.50; ask the driver to go all the way to the 'Obelisco' for an extra US$0.75.* This village has a charming cobbled main plaza and many of the buildings have been restored. There is a small market on Sunday. The village's handicrafts are recommended, especially its ceramics; San Pedro Ceramics, at the foot of the hill, and Mamerto Sánchez (Jr Sucre) should be visited, but there are many others. Most of the houses have miniature ceramic churches on the roof. The **Fiesta de la Virgen de Cocharcas** is celebrated around

8th September. Nearby, on the **Pampa de Quinua** (part of a 300-ha Santuario Histórico), a 44-m-high obelisk commemorates the Battle of Ayacucho in 1824. A reenactment of the battle is held on 9 December, with college students playing the roles of Royalist and South American soldiers.

Trips of about six hours can be arranged to Huari, La Quinua village and the Santuario Histórico for US$15 per person (minimum three people).

Vilcashuamán and around

Full-day tours to these sites cost US$23 pp for 8 passengers, departing 0500. Alternatively, travel by van from Terminal Zona Sur, Av Cuzco 350 (daily 0200-1600, return 0700-1700, 4 hrs, US$4.50) and stay overnight in one of the 3 basic but clean hotels ($).

The Inca ruins of **Vilcashuamán** are 120 km to the south of Ayacucho. Vilcashuamán was an important Inca provincial capital at the crossroads where the main road from Cuzco to the central coast met the empire's north–south highway. There are several monumental Inca buildings, including an intact *usnu*, a flat-topped pyramid which was used for religious ceremonies. The village of Vischongo is one hour from Vilcashuamán; it has a market on Wednesday. Other attractions in the area include **Intihuatana**, Inca baths of fine masonry, near a lake about one hour uphill from the village, and Puya Raimondi plants at Titankayuq, one hour's walk from Vischongo.

Listings Ayacucho and around *map page 299.*

Tourist information

Dirección Regional de Industria y Turismo (Dircetur)
Asamblea 481, T066-312548.
Mon-Fri 0730-1430.
Friendly and helpful.

iPerú
Jr Cusco 108, T066-318305, iperuayacucho@prompéru.gob.pe. Mon-Sat 0900-1800, Sun 0900-1300.
Very helpful. Also has an office at the airport, open mornings only.

Tourist police
Arequipa cuadra 1, T066-312055.

Where to stay

$$$ Ayacucho Hotel Plaza
Jr 9 de Diciembre 184, T066-312202, www.dmhoteles.pe.
Spacious and elegant in a colonial *casona*, comfortable rooms, some suites have balconies overlooking the plaza. With restaurant, bar, cafetería, games room, conference rooms, parking. Helpful staff, organizes tours.

$$$-$$ Internazionale
Urb María Parado de Bellido Mz O, Lt 1, Emadi, T066-314701, www.internazionalehotel.pe.
Business-orientated, 5 mins drive from the centre, modern, junior suites with jacuzzi and roof terrace with great view of the city. Restaurant, helpful staff.

$$$-$$ ViaVia Café Ayacucho
Portal Constitución 4, Plaza de Armas, T066-312834, www.viaviacafe.com/en/ayacucho.
Single, double and triple rooms with private bath, solar hot water 24 hrs, TV room, Spanish, Dutch and English spoken. The attached **ViaVia** restaurant and travellers' café overlooks the Plaza, offering international and Peruvian food, a lunch *menú*, lounge and live music Fri-Sat. Has a 2nd property, **Via Via Alameda** (Alameda Valdelirios 720), slightly cheaper, with bar-restaurant, ice cream parlour.

$$ San Francisco de Paula
*Jr Callao 270, T066-312353, www.
hotelsanfranciscodepaula.com.*
A bit like a museum with hallways filled with
handicrafts and a nice patio, mirador (terrace
with views), restaurant, parking, popular
choice. Comfortable rooms and some suites
with jacuzzi.

$$ Santa Rosa
*Jr Lima 166, T066-314614,
www.hotelsantarosa.com.pe.*
Lovely colonial courtyard in building with
historical associations, roof terrace, warm
rooms, attentive staff, car park, computers
for guests, cash only, good restaurant with
good value *menú*.

$$ Universo
*Jr Grau 101, 1 block from the plaza,
T066-313888.*
Modern rooms, parking, laundry, meeting
room, tour desk, helpful.

$ Crillonesa
*C Nazareno 165, T066-312350,
hotelcrillonesa@outlook.com.*
Good rooms, hot water, laundry facilities,
great views from roof terrace, near produce
market but reasonably quiet, volunteer
opportunities. Good value, warmly
recommended. Owner Carlos Manco is
very friendly, helpful and has loads of
information. He will act as a local tour
guide and knows everyone.

$ El Condeduque
*Jr Asamblea 159, T066-316231,
elcondeduquehotel@hotmail.com.*
Ample rooms with private bath, hot water,
nice common areas, good central location,
includes breakfast, good value.

$ Florida
Jr Cuzco 310, T066-312565.
Small, central location, pleasant, quiet,
patio with flowers, electric showers,
no breakfast.

$ Hostal 3 Máscaras
*Jr 3 Máscaras 194, T066-312921,
www.hoteltresmascaras.galeon.com.*
Newer rooms with bath better, but with
less character, than the old ones without,
nice colonial building with patio, hot water,
breakfast extra, car park.

$ Marcos
9 de Diciembre 143, T066-316867.
Comfortable, modern, in a cul-de-sac half
a block from the Plaza, quiet, hot water,
laundry, includes breakfast in the cafetería.

Restaurants

Ayacucho has its own regional gastronomy,
a speciality is *cuy chactado* (fried guinea
pig). For a cheap, healthy breakfast, try
maca, a drink of maca tuber, apple and
quinoa, sold outside the market opposite
Santa Clara, 0600-0800.

$$ Las Flores
*Jr José Olaya 106, Plaza Conchopata,
east of city in the 'gourmet neighbourhood',
T066-316349. Daily 1100-1900.*
Specializes in *cuy chactado*. Taxi US$1.50
from centre.

$$ Las Tinajas
*Portal Independencia 65, T066-310128.
Open 1200-2400.*
Chicken grill and bar, large balcony
overlooking the main square, very
popular with locals, good service.

$$ Mamma Mia
Jr 28 de Julio 262.
Excellent pizza, elegant and cosy, located on
Plaza More, a nice spot where there are other
restaurants and cafés, boutiques, jewellers
and 4 karaoke pubs.

$$-$ La Casona
Jr Bellido 463. Open 0800-2230.
Dining under the arches and in dining room,
regional specialities, try their *puca picante*,
mondongo and *cuy*, and a wide menu.

$$-$ Los Manglares
Av 26 de Enero 415, T066-315900.
Open 1030-1600.
The best-established *cevichería* of several on this avenue, also does home delivery.

$$-$ Nino
Jr 9 de Diciembre 205, on small plaza opposite Santo Domingo church, T066-814537.
Daily 1700-2300.
Quaint decor, terrace and garden; serves chicken and *parrillas*, including take-away.

$ Cabo Blanco
Av Maravillas 198, close to Shosaku Nagase market (see Shopping). Open 0800-1800.
Ceviches, seafood and fish dishes, small place with personal service. Also serves, beers, wines and cocktails.

$ Chifa Wa Lin
Asamblea 257.
Very popular Chinese, variety of *menús* said to be the best in town.

$ La Italiana
Jr Bellido 486, T066-317574. Daily 1700-2300.
Pizzeria with a huge wood-burning oven for all to see.

$ Mía Pizza
Av Mcal Cáceres 1045, T066-313273.
Open 1800-0200.
Pizzas *a la leña*, pastas and karaoke (also has a bar to get you in the mood for singing). Good atmosphere, like an old tavern.

$ Retablo
Jr Asamblea 219, T066-528453.
Chicken, meat, burgers and more in a large modern locale. Always full with locals, good value.

$ Salud y Vida
San Martín 439, Mon-Sun 0700-1600.
Vegetarian *menú*, generous portions, good service. Lunches are better than breakfasts.

$ Wallpa Sua
Jr Garcilazo de la Vega 240.
A good chicken place, also with *parrillas*.

$ Wambar
San Martín 403, upstairs. Daily.
Generous portions of grilled chicken with native Andean potatoes and *quapchi*.
Live music Sat-Sun.

Cafés

Centro Turístico Cultural San Cristóbal
28 de Julio 178.
Has some expensive cafés including **Lalo's** (café, pizza delivery service and bar) and **Café Express** (coffee specialists) as well as other restaurants and some interesting craft shops. There are tables in the pleasant courtyard.

El Mestizo
Upstairs at Portal Unión 37, Plaza Mayor. Mon-Sat 0800-2300.
Restaurant, café and art gallery serving regional specialities, vegetarian and international dishes. Tranquil atmosphere in a colonial *casona*.

Frutimix
Portal Independencia 56, and Jr 9 de Diciembre 427.
Shakes, frapps (Baileys, chocolate or frapuccino), modern and tasty.

La Miel
Portal Constitución 11-12, on the Plaza. Daily 1000-2300.
Good coffee, hot drinks, juices, shakes, cakes and snacks, also ice creams.

Bars and clubs

Punto Caliente
Jr Asamblea 187. Daily from 1830 until the night is over.
Music, drinks, pizzas and karaoke, modern and upscale.

Tupana Wasy
Jr 9 de Diciembre 213, 3rd floor.
Live contemporary and traditional Andean music. On the 2nd floor is **Toto's Night**, another pub.

Festivals

The area is well known for its festivals throughout the year. Almost every day there is a celebration in one of the surrounding villages; check with the tourist office.

Feb Carnaval. Reported to be a wild affair.
Mar/Apr Semana Santa begins on the Fri before Holy Week. There follows one of the world's finest Holy Week celebrations, with candle-lit nightly processions, floral 'paintings' on the streets, daily fairs (the biggest on Easter Sat), horse races and contests among peoples from all over central Peru. Prices double and all accommodation is fully booked for months in advance. Many people offer beds in their homes during the week. Look out for notices on the doors and in windows of transport companies.
25 Apr Anniversary of the founding of Huamanga province.
1-2 Nov Todos Los Santos and Día de los Muertos.
9 Dec Reenactment of the Battle of Ayacucho on the Pampa de Quinua.

Shopping

Handicrafts

Ayacucho is a good place to buy local crafts including filigree silver, which often uses *mudéjar* patterns. Also look out for little painted nativity scenes, carvings in local alabaster, harps, or the pre-Inca tradition of carving dried gourds. The most famous goods are carpets and retablos. In both weaving and retablos, scenes of recent political strife have been added to more traditional motifs. For carpets, go to Barrio Santa Ana (see page 300). Also recommended is **Familia Pizarro** (Jr Perú 102, Barrio Belén), who produce textiles, *piedra huamanga* (sculptures in local alabaster) and carnival masks of good quality; all pieces are individually made. They also have rooms for visitors to stay and take classes. Edwin Pizarro (T966-180666) creates amazing altar-pieces.

Markets

Mercado 12 de Abril, *Chorro y San Juan de Dios*. For fruit and vegetables.
Shosaku Nagase, *Jr Quinua y Av Maravillas, opposite Plazoleta de María Parado de Bellido*. A large handicraft market.

What to do

A&R Tours, *Jr 9 de Diciembre 130, T066-311300, www.viajesartours.com. Daily 0800-2000.* Offers tours in and around the city.
Fly Travel, *Jr 9 de Diciembre 118, T066-313282*. Offers tours along 2 main circuits. To the north: Wari-Quinua-Huanta; south: Vilcashuamán-Cangallo.
Morochucos Rep's, *Jr 9 de Diciembre 136, T066-317844, www.morochucos.com*. Dynamic company in business for over 30 years, with tours locally and to other parts of Peru, flight, train and bus tickets.
Urpillay Tours, *28 de Julio 262 (Plaza More), of 8, T066-315074, urpillaytours@ terra.com*. All local tours and flight tickets.
Wari Tours, *Lima 138, T066-311415*. Local tours.
Willy Tours, *Jr 9 de Diciembre 209, T066-314075*. Personal guides, also handles flight and bus tickets.

Transport

Air The airport is to the east of the city along Av Castilla. Taxi from airport to city centre, US$3.

To/from **Lima**, 55 mins, with **LATAM** (Jr 9 de Diciembre 107), daily; **LC Peru** (Jr 9 de Diciembre 119, T066-312151), 2 daily; **StarPerú** (Portal Constitución 17, T066-316676).

Bus Long distance Bus terminal **Terrapuerto "Libertadores de América"** (Av Javier Pérez de Cuéllar s/n, T066-312666) is 10 mins northwest of centre. All bus companies are here, and **Cruz del Sur** also has its own terminal in the centre (Av Mcal Cáceres 1264, T066-312813).

To **Lima**, 8 hrs on a good paved road, via Ica, several companies US$14-22, including

Expreso **Molina** (Jr 9 de Diciembre 459, T066-312984), 7 daily, 5 in the evening; **Cruz del Sur,** US$26 *regular*, US$37 *suite* and *VIP* services; **Tepsa,** US$37, presidencial; **Internacional Palomino** (Jr Manco Cápac 216, T066-313899), morning service, US$13-26; **Los Chankas** (Jr Manco Cápac 450, T066-401943), at 2000 hrs, US$10-16. For **Pisco**, 332 km, take an Ica/Lima bus and get out at San Clemente (10 mins from Pisco), 5 hrs, same fare as Ica; then take a bus or van.

To **Cuzco**, with **Los Chankas**, vans at 0720 to Andahuaylas, US$9, transfer there; buses at 2000 direct to Cuzco, US$18, some continue to Puerto Maldonado. Also **Señor De Huanca** (Pasaje Cáceres 166).

To **Huancayo**, 319 km, 9-10 hrs, US$10-13, 3 daily with **Molina**, also **Turismo Central** (Jr Manco Cápac 513, T066-317873), US$13 at 2030. The views are stunning.

For **Huancavelica**, **Expreso Molina** at 2100, US$13, 3 hrs, continuing to Huancayo, you must pay the full fare to there; also **Turismo Central** at 2030.

Ayacucho to Cuzco

stop to stretch your legs on the journey to Cuzco

Beyond Ayacucho are two highland towns, Andahuaylas and Abancay, which are possible stopping or bus-changing places on the road to Cuzco. The road towards Cuzco climbs out of Ayacucho and crosses a wide stretch of high, treeless *páramo* before descending through Ocros to the Río Pampas. It then climbs up to Chincheros, 158 km from Ayacucho, and Uripa, which has a good Sunday market. Ayacucho to Andahuaylas is 261 km on a paved road. It's in good condition when dry, but landslides may occur in the wet. The scenery is stunning. Daytime buses stop for lunch at Chumbes, which has a few restaurants, a shop selling fruit, bread and *refrescos*, and some grim toilets.

Andahuaylas

Andahuaylas is about 80 km further on, at 3000 m in a fertile valley. It offers few exotic crafts, but beautiful scenery, great hospitality and a good market on Sunday. On the north side is the Municipalidad, with a small **Museo Arqueológico**, which has a collection of pre-Columbian objects, including mummies. A worthwhile excursion is to the **Laguna de Pacucha** ⓘ *colectivo from Av Los Chankas y Av Andahuaylas, at the back of the market, US$1, 40 mins*. On the shore is the town of Pacucha, which has a family-run *hostal* (\$) on the road from the plaza to the lake and various places to eat. A road follows the north shore of the lake and climbs to **Sóndor** ⓘ *8-10 km from Pacucha, US$0.65; taxi from Andahuaylas, US$10, or colectivo towards Argama.* This Inca archaeological site at 3300 m has various buildings and small plazas leading up to a conical hill with concentric stone terracing and, at the summit, a large rock or *intihuatana*. Sóndor Raymi is celebrated here each year on 18-19 June. With any form of public transport, you will have to walk back to Pacucha, unless you are very lucky.

Abancay

Nestled between mountains in the upper reaches of a glacial valley, the town of Abancay is first glimpsed when you are many kilometres away. It is capital of the department of Apurimac, an important mining area. **Santuario Nacional de Ampay** ⓘ *5 km north of town on a paved road (take a colectivo to Tamburco and ask the driver where to get off), US$1.50,* has two lakes called Ankasccocha (3200 m) and Uspaccocha (3820 m), a glacier (receding rapidly) on Ampay mountain at 5235 m and a forest of endemic *Intimpa* trees (*Podocarpus glomeratus*). It's a two-day trek to the glacier, with overnight camping.

Saywite
3 km from the main road, Km 49 from Abancay. US$4, students US$2.

Beyond the town of Curahuasi, 126 km before Cuzco, is the large carved rock of Saywite. It is a UNESCO World Heritage Site. The principal monolith is said to represent the three regions of jungle, sierra and coast, with the associated animals and Inca sites of each. It is fenced in, but ask the guardian for a closer look. It was defaced, allegedly, when a cast was taken, breaking off many of the animals' heads. Six further archaeological areas stretch away from the stone and its neighbouring group of buildings.

Listings Ayacucho to Cuzco

Tourist information

Abancay
Information is available from the **tourist office** (Lima 206, daily 0800-1430) or **Dircetur** (Av Arenas 121, p1, T083-321664 in Abancay).

Where to stay

Andahuaylas

$ El Encanto de Apurímac
Jr Ramos 401 (near Los Chankas and other buses), T083-723527.
With hot water, very helpful.

$ El Encanto de Oro
Av Pedro Casafranca 424, T083-423066, www.encantodeoro.4t.com.
Modern, comfy, hot water, laundry service, restaurant, organizes trips on request. Reserve in advance.

$ Las Américas
Jr Ramos 410, T083-721646.
Near buses, bit gloomy in public areas, rooms are fine if basic, cheaper without bath, hot water, helpful.

$ Sol de Oro
Jr Juan A Trelles 164, T083-721152.
Good value, good.

Abancay

$$-$ Turistas
Av Díaz Barcenas 500, T083-321017, www.turismoapurimac.com.
The original building is in colonial style, rooms a bit gloomy, breakfast not included. Newer rooms on top floor (best) and in new block are more expensive, including breakfast. Good restaurant ($$), wood panelled bar, parking.

$ Hostal Arenas
Av Arenas 192, T083-322107.
Well-appointed rooms, good beds, hot showers, helpful service, restaurant.

$ Imperial
Díaz Barcenas 517, T083-321538.
Great beds, hot water, spotless, very helpful, parking, good value, cheaper without bath or breakfast.

Restaurants

Andahuaylas

$ El Dragón
Jr Juan A Trellas 279.
A recommended *chifa* serving huge portions, excellent value (same owner as **Hotel El Encanto de Apurímac**).

$ Il Gatto
Jr G Cáceres 334.
A warm pizzeria, with wooden furniture, pizzas cooked in a wood-burning oven.

$ Nuevo Horizonte
Jr Constitución 426.
Vegetarian and health food restaurant, breakfast.

Abancay

$ Focarela Pizzería
Díaz Bárcenas 521, T083-322036.
Simple but pleasant decor, pizza from a wood-burning oven, fresh, generous toppings, popular (ask for *vino de la casa!*).

$ Pizzería Napolitana
Díaz Barcenas 208.
Wood-fired clay oven, wide choice of toppings.

What to do

Abancay
Apurimak Tours, *at Hotel Turistas, see Where to stay.* Run local tours and 1- and 2-day trips to Santuario Nacional de Ampay: 1-day, 7 hrs, US$40 per person for 1-2 people (cheaper for more people). Also a 3-day trip to Choquequirao including transport, guide, horses, tents and food, just bring your sleeping-bag, US$60 pp. The hotel can also put you in touch with Carlos Valer, a very knowledgeable and kind guide.

Transport

Andahuaylas
To Ayacucho, with **Los Chankas** (Av José María Arguedas y Jr Trelles, T083-722441) 6 hrs, at 0600 and 1800 or 1840 (bus from Cuzco). To **Abancay**, 138 km, paved, 3-4 hrs, with **Señor de Huanca** (Av Martinelli 170, T083-721218), 3 a day, US$6, or **Los Chankas** at 0630, US$7.50. To **Cuzco**, with **San Jerónimo** (Av José María Arguedas 425, T083-801767), via Abancay, 1800 or 1830, also 1900 Sun, US$22, or **Los Chankas**. To **Lima**, buses go via Ayacucho or Pampachiri and Puquio, US$20. On all night buses, take a blanket.

Abancay
The Terminal Terrestre is on Av Pachacútec, on the west side of town. Taxi to centre, US$1, or it's a steep walk. All buses leave from Terminal Terrestre but several companies have offices on or near the El Olivo roundabout at Av Díaz Bárcenas y Gamarra; others are on Av Arenas.

To **Cuzco**, 195 km, 4½ hrs, US$14-18, with **Bredde** (Gamarra 423, T083-321643), 5 a day; **Molina** (Gamarra 422, T083-322646), 3 a day; **San Jerónimo**, at 2130; **Los Chankas** (Díaz Bárcenas 1011, El Olivo, T083-321485) and several others. To Lima, Oltursa, US$66, or Tepsa US$71; several others. The scenery en route is dramatic, especially as it descends into the Apurímac valley and climbs out again. To Andahuaylas, **Molina** at 2330; **San Jerónimo** at 2130; **Señor de Huanca** (Av Arenas 198, T083-322377), 3 a day; also Los Chankas.

A paved road heads north from La Oroya towards Cerro de Pasco and Huánuco. Just 25 km north of La Oroya a branch turns east towards Tarma, then descends to the little-visited jungles of the Selva Central. This is a really beautiful run. North of La Oroya the road crosses the great heights of the Junín pampa and the mining zone of Cerro de Pasco, before losing altitude on its way to the Huallaga Valley. On this route you can connect by road to the Cordillera Blanca via La Unión.

☆Selva Central

Founded in 1534, **Tarma** (60 km from La Oroya) has a charming Plaza de Armas and is notable for its Semana Santa celebrations (see Festivals, below) and its locally made fine flower-carpets. The town is noisy and dirty, mainly of interest as a transport hub, but the surrounding countryside is beautiful. Around 8 km from Tarma, the small town of **Acobamba** has *tapices* made in San Pedro de Cajas which depict the Crucifixion. There are festivities during May. About 2 km beyond the town is the **Santuario de Muruhuay**, which has a venerated picture painted on the rock behind the altar.

Beyond Tarma the road is steep and crooked but there are few places where cars cannot pass one another. In the 80 km from Tarma to La Merced the road runs between great overhanging cliffs as it drops 2450 m and the vegetation changes dramatically from temperate to tropical. The first town in Chanchamayo Province is **San Ramón**, 11 km before La Merced. It has several hotels ($$$-$) and restaurants, and there are regular combis and *colectivos* between the two towns. **La Merced** lies in the fertile Chanchamayo valley. Asháninka *indígenas* can usually be found around the central plaza selling bows, arrows, necklaces and trinkets. There is a festival in the last week of September. There are several hotels ($$-$) and restaurants.

About 25 km from La Merced along the road to **Oxapampa**, a road turns northeast to Villa Rica, centre of an important coffee-growing area. From here, a poor dirt road continues northeast to **Puerto Bermúdez**. This authentic jungle town, at the geographic centre of Peru, has grown up along the now seldom-used airstrip. It lies on the Río Pichis, an affluent of the Pachitea, and is a great base for exploring further into the Selva Central, with trips upriver to the Asháninka community. Tours are arranged by **Albergue Humboldt** (see Where to stay, below). To go further downriver to Pucallpa, there is road transport via Ciudad Constitución, about US$20 over two stages.

Pampas de Junín

The road north from La Oroya runs up the Mantaro Valley through canyons to the wet and mournful Junín pampa at over 4250 m, one of the world's largest high-altitude plains. An obelisk marks the battlefield where the Peruvians under Bolívar defeated the Spaniards in 1824. Blue peaks line the pampa in a distant wall. This windswept sheet of yellow grass is bitterly cold and the only signs of life are the youthful herders with their sheep and llamas. The road follows the east shores of Lago Junín. The town of **Junín** lies some distance south of the lake and has the desolate feel of a high *puna* town, bisected by the railway; it has several basic hotels. The **Junín National Reserve** ① *US$5, ticket from Sernanp in Junín, Jr San Martín 138, T064-344146*, protects one of the best birdwatching sites in the central Andes where the giant coot and even flamingos may be spotted. It is easiest to visit from the village of Huayre, 5 km south of Carhuamayo, from where it is a 20-minute walk down to the lake. Fishermen are usually around to take visitors out on the lake.

Cerro de Pasco and around *Colour map 2, B3.*

This long-established mining centre, 130 km from La Oroya, is not attractive, but is nevertheless very friendly. Copper, zinc, lead, gold and silver are mined here, and coal comes from the deep canyon of Goyllarisquisga, 42 km north of Cerro de Pasco. It is the highest coal mine in the world and its name translates as the 'place where a star fell'. The town is sited between Lago Patarcocha and the huge abyss of the mine above which its buildings and streets cling precariously. Nights are bitterly cold here at 4330 m. Southwest of Cerro de Pasco by 40 km is **Santuario Huayllay (Bosque de Piedras)** ① *information from Sernanp in Junín, US$1; camping permitted; minibuses to Huallay depart from Cerro de Pasco's terminal throughout the day, about 1 hr, US$1; last return 1800.* These unique weathered limestone formations at 4100-4600 m are in the shape of a tortoise, elephant, alpaca, and more. They can be explored on 11 tourist circuits through the rock formations. The village of **Huallay** is 6 km southwest of the sanctuary; it has a municipal hostel and other hotels. A festival of sports and music is held here on 6-8 September.

Huánuco and around

The Central Highway from Cerro de Pasco continues northeast another 528 km to Pucallpa, the limit of navigation for large Amazon river boats. The first part of this road has been rebuilt into an all-weather highway, and the sharp descent along the nascent **Río Huallaga** is a tonic to travellers suffering from *soroche*. The road drops 2436 m in the 100 km from Cerro de Pasco to Huánuco, most of it in the first 32 km. From the bleak high ranges the road plunges below the tree line offering great views. The only town of any size before Huánuco is **Ambo**. Huánuco itself is an attractive Andean town on the Upper Huallaga with an interesting market. Situated between the highlands and jungle at 1894 m, it has a particularly pleasant climate.

Located 5 km west of Huánuco on the road to La Unión is **Kótosh** ① *US$0.75, including a guide (in Spanish); taxi from Huánuco, US$5 including a 30-min wait.* Investigations suggest that this archaeological site, at an altitude of 1912 m, was occupied for over 2000 years. Six distinct phases of occupation have been identified, the oldest of which dates back some 4000 years. The Temple of Crossed Hands dates from 2000 BC and was once regarded as the 'oldest temple in the Americas'.

La Unión and around

From Huánuco, a spectacular but poor dirt road leads to **La Unión**, capital of Dos de Mayo district. It's a fast-developing town with a couple of simple hotels ($) and restaurants, but electricity can be a problem and it gets very cold at night. On the pampa above La Unión are the Inca ruins of ☆**Huánuco Viejo** (or **Huánuco Pampa**) ① *2½ hrs' walk from La Unión, entry US$1.50; taxi from La Unión, US$6.50-9.50 with wait,* a great temple-fortress with residential quarters. The site has examples of very fine Inca stonework comparable with anything to be seen in Cuzco. It is the only major Inca settlement on the royal highway not to have been built over by a colonial or modern town.

> **Tip...**
> One of the finest stretches of the Royal Inca Road, or Capaq Ñan, runs from Huanuco Viejo to the **Callejón de Conchucos**. Some tour operators in Huaraz (page 80) offer this trek.

Tourist information

Selva Central

There is a **tourist office** on the plaza in Tarma (Arequipa 259, T064-321010, Mon-Fri 0800-1300, 1500-1800) is very helpful; see also www.tarma.info. In La Merced, visit **Dircetur** (Pardo 110, San Ramón, T064-331265).

Huánuco and around

The **tourist office** is on the plaza (Gen Prado 716, T062-512980). A website giving local information is www.webhuanuco.com.

Where to stay

Selva Central
Tarma

$$$ Hacienda Santa María
2 km out of town at Vista Alegre 1249, Sacsamarca, T064-321232.
A beautiful (non-working) 17th-century hacienda, beautiful gardens and antique furniture. Includes breakfast. Excellent guides for local day trips.

$$$ Los Portales
Av Castilla 512, T064-321411, www.losportaleshoteles.com.pe.
On the edge of town, hot water, heating, 1950s building with old furnishings, includes breakfast, good restaurant.

$$$-$$ Hacienda La Florida
6 km from Tarma, T064-341041, www.haciendalaflorida.com.
18th-century working hacienda owned by German-Peruvian couple Inge and Pepe, who also arrange excursions. Variety of rooms sleeping 1-4, adjoining family rooms, dorm for groups and an independent house; all with hot water, meals available, lots of home-grown organic produce. Also camping for US$5.

$$ Los Balcones
Jr Lima 370, 064-323600.
Good location near the plaza, all rooms are non-smoking, some with balcony and frigobar, indoor parking.

$$ Normandie
Beside the Santuario de Muruhuay, Acobamba, T064-341028, Lima T01-365 9795, www.hotelnormandie.com.pe.
Rooms with hot water, bar, restaurant, tours offered.

$ Hospedaje Residencial El Dorado
Huánuco 488, T064-321914, www.hospedajeeldoradotarma.com.
Hot water, rooms set round a patio, 1st floor better, breakfast available, safe, welcoming, secure parking. Older place but well cared for.

$ Tampu Wasi
Jr Amazonas 798, T064-321744, and Jr Huánuco 235, T064-323128.
Rooms with private bath, electric shower, parking. Nice place, good value.

Puerto Bermúdez

$ Albergue Cultural Humboldt
By the river port (La Rampa), T063-963-722363, http://alberguehumboldt.free.fr.
The owner, Basque writer Jesús, has created a real haven for backpackers, with maps, library and book exchange. Rooms sleep 1-3, or there are hammocks and tents. Meals available, Spanish and Peruvian food. Jesús arranges tours, from day trips to camping and trekking in primary forest.

Pampas de Junín

Carhuamayo is the best place to stay when visiting the reserve. **Gianmarco** (Maravillas 454) and **Patricia** (Tarapacá 862) are the best of several basic *hostales*. There are numerous restaurants along the main road.

Cerro de Pasco and around

$ Hostal Arenales
Jr Arenales 162, near the bus station,
T063-723088.
Modern, TV, hot water in the morning.

$ Señorial
Jr San Martín 1, in the district of San Juan,
5 mins north of Cerro by taxi, T063-422802,
hotelsenorial@hotmail.com.
The most comfortable in town, hot water,
fine view across the mine pit.

$ Welcome
Av La Plata 125, opposite the entrance to the
bus station, T063-721883.
Some rooms without window,
hot water 24 hrs.

Huánuco and around

$$$ Grand Hotel Huánuco
(Inka Comfort)
Jr D Beraún 775, T062-514222,
www.grandhotelhuanuco.com.
With restaurant, pool, sauna, gym
and parking.

$ El Roble
Constitución 629, T062-512515.
Without bath, cheap and good value.

$ Hostal Miraflores
Valdizán 560, T062-512848,
www.granhostalmiraflores.com.
Hot water, private bathroom, quiet, safe,
laundry service.

$ Imperial
Huánuco 581, T062-518737.
With hot showers, quiet and helpful.

$ Las Vegas
28 de Julio 940, on Plaza de Armas,
T062-512315.
Small rooms, hot water, restaurant
next door. Good.

Selva Central
Tarma

$ Chavín
Jr Lima 270 at Plaza de Armas.
Daily 0730-2230.
Very good quality and variety in set meals
(weekdays only), also à la carte.

$ Chifa Roberto Siu
Jr Lima 569 upstairs.
A good option for Chinese food, popular
with locals.

$ Comedor Vegetariano
Arequipa 695. Open 0700-2100,
but closed Fri after lunch and Sat.
Vegetarian, small and cheap,
sells great bread.

Cerro de Pasco and around

$ Los Angeles
Jr Libertad, near the market.
Excellent *menú* for US$1.50. Recommended.

$ San Fernando
Bakery in the plaza. Opens at 0700.
Great hot chocolate, bread and pastries.

Huánuco and around

$ Chifa Men Ji
28 de Julio, block 8.
Good prices, nice Chinese food.

$ Govinda
Prado 608.
Reckoned to be the best vegetarian
restaurant in town.

$ La Olla de Barro
Gral Prado 852, close to main plaza.
Serves typical food, good value.

$ Pizzería Don Sancho
Prado 645.
Best pizzas in town.

Festivals

Selva Central

Mar/Apr The **Semana Santa** celebrations at Tarma are spectacular, with a very colourful Easter Sun morning procession in the main plaza. Accommodation is hard to find at this time, but you can apply to the Municipalidad for rooms with local families.

Pampas de Junín

6 Aug Colourful ceremony to commemorate the **Batalla de Junín** (1824), which was fought on the nearby Pampas de Junín, marking a decisive victory in favour of the independence of Peru and South America. The town fills with visitors, prices rise and hotel rooms are scarce.

Huánuco and around

20-25 Feb Carnaval Huanuqueño.
3 May La Cruz de Mayo.
16 Jul Fiesta de la Virgen del Carmen.
12-18 Aug Tourist week.
28-29 Oct Fiesta del Señor de Burgos, the patron of Huánuco.
25 Dec Fiesta de los Negritos.

La Unión and around

27 Jul Fiesta del Sol. Major annual festival at Huánuco Viejo. Lodgings in La Unión are almost impossible to find at this time.

Transport

Selva Central
Tarma

Bus Most buses and vans leave from the Terminal Terrestre at the west end of Jr Lima. Some companies also have private terminals. Beware overcharging by *colectivo* drivers. To **Lima**, 231 km (paved), 6 hrs, US$15, with the following companies: **Transportes Junín** (Amazonas 669; in Lima at Av Nicolás Arriola 198, T01-224 9220), 6 a day, with *bus cama* at night; **Trans La Merced**, 3 a day; **Trans Los Canarios** (Jr Amazonas

694), 2 daily starting in Tarma; **Transportes Chanchamayo** (Callao 1002, T064-321882), 2 a day, en route from Chanchamayo. To **Jauja**, US$2, and **Huancayo**, US$3, from the stadium, 0800-1800, every 1½ hrs; also **Trans Los Canarios** about 1 per hr, 0500-1800, and **Trans Junín** at 1200 and 2400; *colectivos* depart when full from Callao y Jauja, 2 hrs, US$4, and 3 hrs, US$6, respectively. To **Cerro de Pasco**, **Empresa Junín** (Amazonas 450), 4 a day, 3 hrs, US$2.50; also *colectivos* when full, 2 hrs, US$4. To **La Oroya, buses** leave from opposite the Terminal, 1 hr, US$1.50, while *colectivos* leave from petrol station on Av Castilla block 5, 45 mins, US$2. To **San Ramón**, US$1.75, 1½ hrs, with **Trans Junín**, 4 a day, continuing to La Merced, US$2.75, 2 hrs; vans US$1.75, and *colectivos*, US$4, depart from the stadium to La Merced. Combis and *colectivos* run along Jr Huánuco by the Mercado Modelo to **Acobamba** and up to **Muruhuay**, 15 mins, US$0.30 and US$0.45 respectively.

Chanchamayo

Air Flights leave from San Ramón. There is a small airstrip where **Aero Montaña**, T064-331074 has air taxis that can be chartered (*viaje especial*) to the jungle towns, with a maximum of 3 people, but you have to pay for the pilot's return to base. Flights cost US$250 per hr. **Puerto Bermúdez** takes 33 mins. You can also just go to the air base, across the river, on the east side of town.

Bus Many buses go to La Merced from **Lima**: **Expreso Satipo**, **Junín**, **La Merced** and **Chanchamayo** each have several buses during the day, US$8 *regular*, US$11 *cama* upper level, US$12.50 *cama* lower level, 7-8 hrs. To **Tarma, with Transportes Angelitos/San Juan**, hourly, 2½ hrs, US$1.75, or *colectivos*, just over 1 hr, US$4. To **Puerto Bermúdez**, **Empresa Transdife** and **Villa Rica** have 4WD pick-ups between 0400 and 0600 and may pick up passengers at their hotels. You must purchase tickets in advance, the vehicles get very full, US$14 in front,

US$8 in the back (worth spending the extra money), 8-10 hrs or more.

Cerro de Pasco and around
Bus There is a large bus station. To **Lima** several companies including **Carhuamayo** and **Transportes Apóstol San Pedro,** hourly 0800-1200, plus 4 departures 2030-2130, 8 hrs, US$8. If there are no convenient daytime buses, you could change buses in La Oroya. Buses leave when full, about every 20-30 mins, to **Carhuamayo** (1 hr, US$1), **Junín** (1½ hrs, US$1) and **La Oroya** (2½ hrs, US$2); *colectivos* also depart with a similar frequency, 1½ hrs, US$2.50, to La Oroya. To **Tarma, Empresa Junín,** at 0600, 1500, 3 hrs, $2.50; *colectivos* also depart hourly, 1½ hrs, US$4. To **Huancayo,** various companies leave throughout the day, 5 hrs, US$4. To **Huánuco,** buses and cars leave when full, about half hourly, 2½ hrs and 1½ hrs, US$2 and US$4 respectively.

Huánuco and around
Air The airport (T062-513066) is served by flights from **Lima,** with **StarPerú** and **LCPeru** (2 de Mayo 1355, T062-518113), daily, 55 mins.

Bus To **Lima,** US$18-25, 8 hrs, with **León de Huánuco** (Malecón Alomía Robles 821), 3 a day; also **Bahía Continental** (Valdizán 718), recommended, and **Transportes El Rey.** The majority of buses of all companies leave 2030-2200, most also offer a bus at 0900-1000. A *colectivo* to Lima, costing US$23, leaves at 0400, arriving at 1400; book the night before at Gen Prado 607, 1 block from

Tip...
The route to Tingo María and Pucallpa has many checkpoints, and robberies can occur. Travel by day and check on the current situation regarding safety.

the plaza; recommended. To **Cerro de Pasco,** 3 hrs, US$2, *colectivos* under 2 hrs, US$4; all leave when full from the Ovalo Carhuayna on the north side of the city, 3 km from the centre. To **Huancayo,** 7 hrs, US$6, with **Turismo Central** (Tarapacá 530), at 2100. *Colectivos* run to **Tingo María,** from block 1 of Prado close to Puente Calicanto, 2½ hrs, US$5; also **Etnasa,** 3-4 hrs, US2. For **Pucallpa,** take a *colectivo* to Tingo María, then a bus from there.

To **La Unión, Turismo Unión,** daily 0730, 7 hrs, US$5; also **Turismo Marañón,** daily 0700; this is a rough road operated also by **El Niño** *colectivos* (Aguilar 530), which leave when full, US$7.15.

La Unión and around
Bus To **Huánuco with Turismo Unión** (Jr Comercio 1224), daily at 0600, US$8, 7 hrs; also **Turismo Marañón** (Jr Comercio 1309), daily at 0700 (no afternoon/ evening departures), and El Niño *colectivos* (Jr Comercio 12, T062-515952), 5 hrs. To **Huallanca** (for access to Huaraz and the Cordillera Blanca), combis leave from the market, about hourly, when full and follow the attractive Vizcarra valley, 1 hr, US$2. **El Rápido** runs to **Huaraz** 0400, 4½ hrs, US$8, or change in Huallanca.

Amazon Basin

The Amazon Basin covers a staggering 4,000,000 sq km, but despite the fact that 60% of Peru is covered by this green carpet of jungle, less than 6% of its population lives here, meaning that much of Peru's rainforest is still intact. It is home to 2000 species of fish, 300 mammal species, over 10% of the world's 8600 bird species and, together with the adjacent Andean foothills, 4000 butterfly species. This incredible biological diversity is coupled with acute ecological fragility: petroleum exploitation, gold mining and colonization from the highlands are perennial threats.

The principal means of communication in the jungle is by its many rivers, the most important being the Amazon, which rises high up in the Andes as the Marañón, then joins the Ucayali to become the longest river in the world. The two major tourist areas in the Peruvian Amazon are the northern and southern jungles. Wildlife-viewing in these two areas is quite different. Northeastern Peru is dominated by flood plains and vast rivers, with much of the land regularly submerged. There are chances of seeing manatees, giant otters and pink and grey Amazonian dolphins. The Southern Amazon has faster-running rivers and rapids unsuited to dolphins and manatees, but a huge variety of habitats mean there are more bird species here. Moreover, in protected areas such as Manu and Tambopata, tapir, giant anteaters, otters and primates are fairly easy to spot due to the lack of hunting pressure.

Best for
Ecotourism ▪ River trips ▪ Wildlife watching

experience the transition from Andes to Amazon

Huánuco to Tingo María

The journey to Tingo María from Huánuco, 135 km, is very dusty but gives a good view of the jungle. Some 25 km beyond Huánuco the paved road begins a sharp climb to the heights of Carpish (3023 m). A descent of 58 km brings it to the Río Huallaga again; it then continues along the river to Tingo María. Landslides along this section are frequent and construction work causes delays. Although this route is reported to be relatively free from terrorism, robberies do occur and it is advisable to travel only by day.

Tingo María

Tingo María is situated on the Río Huallaga, in the Ceja de Montaña (literally 'eyebrow of the mountain'). The Cordillera Azul, the front range of the Andes, covered with jungle-like vegetation to its top, separates this transition zone from the jungle lowlands to the east. The meeting here of highlands and jungle makes the landscape extremely striking. Tingo María is isolated for days in the rainy season. Annual rainfall here is

> **Warning...**
> Tingo María and Pucallpa are a main narco-trafficking centre and although the towns are generally safe, it is not safe to travel at night. Always keep to the main routes.

2642 mm, but the altitude prevents the climate from being oppressive. Bananas, sugar cane, cocoa, rubber, tea and coffee are grown, but the main crop of the area is coca, grown on the *chacras* (smallholdings) in the countryside, and sold legitimately and otherwise in Tingo María.

The mountain that can be seen from all over the town is called La Bella Durmiente (the Sleeping Beauty). A small university outside the town, beyond the **Hotel Madera Verde**, has a little **museum-cum-zoo** ⓘ *free but a small tip is appreciated*; it also maintains botanical gardens in the town. About 6.5 km from Tingo, on a rough road, is a fascinating cave, the **Cueva de las Lechuzas** ⓘ *US$1 for the cave, take a torch, and do not wear open shoes; to get there, take a motorcycle-taxi from town, US$1.75*, crossing the Río Monzón by new bridge. There are many oilbirds in the cave and many small parakeets near the entrance.

Pucallpa *Colour map 2, B3.*

Pucallpa, 255 km by road from Tingo María, is a rapidly expanding jungle town on the Río Ucayali, navigable by vessels of 3000 tons from Iquitos, 533 nautical miles away. Different 'ports' are used depending on the level of the river; they are all just mud banks without any facilities (see Transport, below). The economy of the area includes sawmills, plywood factories, oil refinery, fishing and boat building. Large discoveries of oil and gas are being explored. The town is hot and dusty between June and November and muddy from December to May. **Museo Regional in the Parque Natural de Pucallpa** ⓘ *Cra Federico Basadre Km 4.2, Mon-Fri 0800-1630, Sat and Sun 0900-1730, park entry US$1.10*, has examples of Shipibo ceramics, as well as some delightful pickled snakes and other reptiles.

Lago Yarinacocha

Northeast of Pucallpa, 20 mins by colectivo or bus along Jr Ucayali, US$0.50, or 15 mins by taxi.

The main attraction in this area is **Lago Yarinacocha**, an oxbow lake linked to the Río Ucayali by a canal at the northern tip of its west arm. River dolphins can be seen here.

Puerto Callao, also known as **Yarinacocha** or **Yarina**, is the main town at the southern tip, reached by road from Pucallpa. There are a number of restaurants and bars here and it is popular at weekends. From the town, a road continues along the western arm to **San José**, **San Francisco** and **Santa Clara** (bus US$0.75). The area is populated by the Shipibo people, who make ceramic and textile crafts. The area between the eastern arm of the lake and the Río Ucayali has been designated a reserve and incorporates the beautifully located **Jardín Botánico Chullachaqui** ① *free, reached by boat from Puerto Callao to Pueblo Nueva Luz de Fátima, 45 mins, then a 1-hr walk.* For more information ask at Moroti-Shobo on the Plaza de Armas in Puerto Callao.

Listings From Huánuco to Pucallpa

Tourist information

Tingo María

The **tourist office** is at Av Ericson 158, T062-562310, perucatapress@gmail.com. The **municipality** (Alameda Perú 525, T062-562058) also provides information, and the tourist police has an office in the municipal offices.

Pucallpa

Tourist information is available from **Dircetur** (Jr 2 de Mayo 111, T061-575110, Mon-Fri 0730-1300, 1330-1515) and from **Gobierno Regional de Ucayali** (GOREU; Raimondi block 220, T061-575018).

Where to stay

Tingo María

$$$-$$ Madera Verde
Av Universitaria s/n, out of town on the road to Huánuco, near the University, T062-562047.
Wooden chalets, cabins and rooms in beautiful surroundings, breakfast included, restaurant, 2 swimming pools, butterfly farm, free entry to wildlife rescue centre.

$$ Albergue Ecológico Villa Jennifer
Km 3.4 Carretera a Castillo Grande, 10 mins from Tingo María, T962-603509, www.villajennifer.net.
Danish-Peruvian owned, includes breakfast, 2- to 4-night packages, US$50-90, and tours to local sites, pool, mini-zoo, birdwatching, restaurant, laundry service, phone ahead

to arrange bus station pick-up. Rooms are surrounded by local flora, with lots of birdlife.

$$ Nueva York
Av Alameda Perú 553, T062-562406, joferjus@hotmail.com.
Central and noisy, cheaper without bath and TV, laundry, good value, restaurant.

Pucallpa

$$$ Sol del Oriente
Av San Martín 552, T061-575154.
Price includes breakfast and airport transfer, a/c, pool, mini-zoo, good restaurant, bilingual guides.

$$$-$$ Grand Hotel Mercedes
Raimondi 610, T061-575120, www.granhotelmercedes.com.
Pucallpa's first hotel, still family-run, with some refurbished rooms, modern facilities with old-fashioned ambiance, includes breakfast, hot water, a/c, fridge, pool, restaurant.

$$ Antonio's
Jr Progreso 545, T061-573721, www.antonioshotel.com.pe.
A variety of rooms and prices, garden, pool, jacuzzi, parking, airport pick-up.

$$ Komby
Ucayali 360, T061-571562, http://kombypucallpa.com.
Cold water, fan or a/c, ample rooms, pool, very noisy street but back rooms are quiet, good value, free airport pick-up.

$$-$ Arequipa
Jr Progreso 573, T061-571348,
www.hostal-arequipa.com.
Good, a/c or fan, breakfast, comfortable, safe,
restaurant, pool.

$ Barbtur
Raimondi 670, T061-572532.
Cheaper without bath, central, good beds,
cold water, friendly but noisy.

Lago Yarinacocha

$$$ pp Yarina Ecolodge (Pandisho Amazon Ecolodge)
North of the village of 11 de Agosto,
towards the northern tip of the eastern
shore of the west arm, T061-799214,
www.amazon-ecolodge.com (in Pucallpa,
Pasaje Bolívar 261, T961-994227).
Full board, good resort with cabins by the
lakeshore, includes packages of varying
length and rainforest expeditions. Also has
a lodge in Pacaya-Samiria, Amazon Green.

Restaurants

Pucallpa

$$-$ C'est si bon
Jr Independencia 560 y Pasaje Zegarra,
Plaza de Armas. Daily 0800-2400.
Chicken, snacks, drinks, sweets; ice cream.

$$-$ La Favorita
Jr Adolfo Morey e Inmaculada, T061-563712.
Daily 0800-1600.
Regional and home cooking, good set meals
Mon-Sat and *parrilladas* on Sun, popular.

Shopping

Pucallpa
Many Shibipo women carry and sell their
products around Pucallpa and Yarinacocha.
For local wood carvings visit the workshop
of **Agustín Rivas** (Jr Tarapacá 861/863, above
a small restaurant; ask for it), whose work is
made from huge tree roots. **Artesanías La**

Anaconda (Pasaje Cohen by Plaza de Armas)
has a good selection of indigenous crafts.

Festivals

Pucallpa
Local festivals are **Carnival** in **Feb**, San Juan
on **24 Jun**, and the Ucayali regional fair in **Oct**.

What to do

Pucallpa
Usko Ayar Amazonian School of Painting,
Jr LM Sánchez Cerro 465-467, T958-623871,
see Facebook page. Located in the house of
artist and healer Pablo Amaringo, who died
in 2009, the renowned school provides art
classes for local people and is dependent
upon selling their art. It welcomes overseas
visitors for short or long stays to study
painting and learn Spanish and/or to teach
English to Peruvian students.

Transport

Tingo María
Air To/from **Lima** Mon-Fri, 1 hr 10 mins,
with **LCPerú** (Av Raymiondi 571, Rupa Rupa,
T062-561672).

Bus To **Huánuco**, 119 km, 3-4 hrs, US$2 with
Etnasa (not recommended due to theft and
drug-trafficking); instead take a micro, US$2,
or *colectivo*, US$5, 2 hrs, several daily. Direct
buses continue to Lima, 10 hrs, with **Turismo
Central** (Raimondi cuadra 9, T062-562668;
in Lima at Av N Arriola 515, La Victoria,
T01-472 7565, www.turismocentral.com.pe);
Transmar (Av E Pimentel 147, T062-564733;
in Lima at Av 28 de Julio 1511 and Av N
Arriola 197, T01-265 0190, www.transmar.
com.pe); **GM Internacional** (Av Raimondi
740, T062-561895; in Lima at Av 28 de Julio
1275, T01-715 3122, www.gminternacional.
com.pe), and **Bahía Continental**
(recommended, T01-424 1539), US$18-30.
    To **Pucallpa**, 5 hrs, US$15 with **Ucayali
Express** *colectivos* (Raimondi y Callao) and
Selva Express (Av Tito Jaime 218, T062-
562380). Buses take 7-8 hrs, US$9.

Pucallpa

Air To **Lima** and **Iquitos**, daily 1 hr, with **LATAM** (Jr Tarapacá 805, T061-579840), **Peruvian** (Independencia 324, T061-505655) and **Star Perú** (7 de Junio 865, T061-590585). Airport taxis charge US$6 to town; other taxis charge US$3.

Bus There are regular bus services to **Lima**, several companies, 18-20 hrs (longer in the rainy season, Nov-Mar), including **Transmar** (Av Raimondi 793, T061-579778); fares range from US$17.50 *regular* to US$43 for top level *bus cama*. To **Tingo María**, bus US$9, 7-8 hrs, bound for Lima, also **Etposa** (7 de Junio 843) at 1700; or by combi, 5 hrs, US$15, with **Turismo Ucayali** (7 de Junio 799, T061-593002) and **Selva Express** (Jr 7 de Junio 841, T061-579098). Take blankets as the crossing of the Cordillera at night is bitterly cold.

Ferry Boats to all destinations dock around Puerto Inmaculada, 2 blocks downriver from the Malecón Grau, at the bottom of Jr Inmaculada, unless the water level is very high, in which case they dock at Puerto Manantay, 4 km south of town. A mototaxi to any of the ports costs US$0.75 from the Plaza de Armas; taxis charge US$3.

To **Iquitos** down the Ucayali and Amazon rivers, 3-4 days, longer if the water level is low when larger boats must travel only by day, hammock US$40, berth US$140 double. **Henry** is a large company with departures Mon, Wed, Fri and Sat from Puerto Henry at the bottom of Jr Manco Capac, by Jr Arica; their newer boats, *Henry 6* and *7*, have some cabins with private bath. Another good boat is *Pedro Martín 2* sailing from Puerto Inmaculada. You must ask around for the large boats to Iquitos. Departure times are marked on chalk boards on the deck. Schedules seem to change almost hourly. Do not pay for your trip before you board the vessel, and only pay the captain. Some boat captains may allow you to live on board for a couple of days before sailing. Bottled drinking water can be bought in Pucallpa, but not cheaply. See also River, page 713.

Yurimaguas and Pacaya-Samiria

explore the waterways and wetlands

The Río Huallaga winds northwards for 930 km from its source to the confluence with the Marañón. The Upper Huallaga is a torrent, dropping 15.8 m per km between its source and Tingo María. In contrast, the Lower Huallaga moves through an enervation of flatness. Its main port, Yurimaguas, lies below the last rapids and only 150 m above the Atlantic Ocean yet is distant from that ocean by over a month's voyage. Between the Upper and Lower rivers lies the Middle Huallaga, the third of the river that is downstream from Tingo María and upstream from Yurimaguas.

Yurimaguas *Colour map 2, A2.*

Yurimaguas is connected by road with the Pacific coast, via Tarapoto (120 km) and Moyobamba (see page 156). It's a very relaxed jungle town and, as the roadhead on the lower Río Huallaga, is an ideal starting point for river travel in the Peruvian Amazon. A colourful

Tip...
There are several banks with ATMs in town and **Casa de Cambio Progreso** (Progreso 117) changes US$ cash.

Mercado Central is open every morning, full of fruit and jungle animals, many, sadly, for the pot. The town's patron saint, La Santísima Virgen de las Nieves, is celebrated from 5 to 15 August each year, which coincides with tourism week. Excursions in the area include the gorge of Shanusi and the lakes of Mushuyacu and Sanango.

☆Reserva Nacional Pacaya-Samiria

SERNANP, Jorge Chávez 930/942, Iquitos, T065-223555, Mon-Fri 0700-1300, 1500-1700. Entry US$2 for 1 day, US$23 for 3 days, US$46 for 7 days, payable at the ranger stations.

Northeast of Yurimaguas, this vast reserve is bounded by the rivers Marañón and Ucuyali, narrowing to their confluence near the town of Nauta. At 2,080,000 ha, it is the country's second-largest protected area. The reserve's waterways and wetlands provide habitat for several cats (including puma and jaguar), manatee, tapir, river dolphins, giant otters, black cayman, boas, 269 species of fish and 449 bird species. Many of the animals found here are in danger of extinction. There are 208 population centres in the area of the reserve, 92 within the park, the others in the buffer zone. Five native groups plus colonos live in the region.

The reserve can only be visited with an authorized guide arranged through a tour operator or a local community tourism association. Native guides generally speak only Spanish and native tongues. Most of the reserve is off-limits to tourists, but eight areas have been set up for visitors. These have shelters or camping areas; conditions are generally simple and may require sleeping in hammocks. Trips are mostly on the river and often include fishing. Four circuits are most commonly offered. All are rich in wildlife.

The basin of the Yanayacu and Pucate rivers is the most frequently visited area and includes Laguna El Dorado, an important attraction. This area is accessed from **Nauta** on the Marañón, 1½-2 hours by paved road from Iquitos. It's three hours by *peque peque* or 1½ hours by *deslizador* from Nauta to the reserve. Note that Nauta has pirate guides, so it's best to arrange a tour with an operator.

The middle and lower Samiria is accessed from **Leoncio Prado** (which has a couple of *hospedajes*), 24 hours by *lancha* from Iquitos along the Marañón. Several lakes are found in this area.

The lower Pacaya, mostly flooded forest, is accessed from **Bretaña** on the Canal de Puinahua, a shortcut on the Ucayali, 24 hours by *lancha* from Iquitos. This area is less frequently visited than others.

The Tibilo-Pastococha area in the western side of the park, also in the Samiria basin, is accessed from **Lagunas**, on the Río Huallaga. It's 10-12 hours by *lancha* or three hours by *deslizador* from Yurimaguas, 17 hours by *deslizador* from Nauta and 48 hours by *lancha* from Iquitos. All river traffic from Yurimaguas to Iquitos stops here.

Another way of visiting the reserve is on a cruise, sailing along the main rivers on the periphery of the park. These tours are offered by some Iquitos operators.

Listings Yurimaguas and Pacaya-Samiria

Tourist information

Yurimaguas
Ask for information at the **Municipalidad Provincial de Alto Amazonas** (Plaza de Armas 112-114, T065-351213), or see www.yurimaguas.net.

Pacaya-Samiria Reserve
General information and a list of authorized community associations and operators is found on the reserve's web page, at the reserve office in Iquitos and at iPerú in Iquitos.

Where to stay

Yurimaguas

$$$-$$ Río Huallaga
*Arica 111, T065-353951, http://
hotelriohuallaga.com.*
Pleasant modern hotel overlooking the
river, safety box, pool, bar, cinema, rooftop
restaurant with lovely views.

$$-$ Hostal Luis Antonio
*Av Jaúregui 407, T352062, hostal_luis_
antonio@hotmail.com (also on Facebook).*
Cold water, small pool, a/c at extra cost,
breakfast, very helpful.

$$-$ Posada Cumpanama
*Progreso 403, T065-352905, http://
posadacumpanama.blogspot.com.*
Rooms cheaper with shared bath,
breakfast extra, tastefully decorated,
pool, very pleasant.

$ Hostal Akemi
*Jr Angamos 414, T065-352237,
www.hostalakemi.com.*
Decent rooms with hot water, cheaper
without a/c, some with frigobar, restaurant,
pool, helpful owner, good value.

$ Hostal El Caballito
Av Jaúregui 403, T065-352427.
Cold water, small bathroom, fan, pleasant,
good value.

$ Hostal El Naranjo
*Arica 318, T065-352650, www.
hostalelnaranjo.com.pe.*
A/c or fan, hot water, frigobar, small pool,
with restaurant.

Pacaya-Samiria Reserve

$$$$ Pacaya Samiria Amazon Lodge
*www.pacayasamiria.com.pe; office at Urb Las
Palmeras 09, Iquitos, T065-225769.*
Hatuchay hotel group. Beautifully designed
lodge on a hill overlooking the Marañón,
just inside the reserve but close to road
and town. All buildings in indigenous style,
with balconies and en suite bathrooms,

restaurant, bar. Community visits and
specialist birdwatching trips included in the
price, but boat trips (also included) can be
long. Camping trips can be arranged deeper
inside the reserve. Packages start at US$520
pp for 3-day/2-night programme.

**$$$ Ecological Jungle Trips &
Expeditions Tours**
*www.ecologicaljungletrips.com;
office at Putumayo 163 p 2, Iquitos,
T965-783409/942-643020.*
Delfín Lodge, 2½ hrs from Nauta on the
Río Yarapa, is the base for tours to Pacaya-
Samiria, 10 rooms. Programmes from 3 days
to 7 days, tailored according to the interests
of the guests.

$ Basic places in Nauta include **Nauta Inn**
(Manuel Pacaya by Laguna Sapi Sapi, T065-
411025) and **Plaza Inn** (Marañón 365, T65-
411735, with bath, some rooms with a/c).

$ Basic places in Lagunas include **Eco**
(Jr Padre Lucero, near cemetery, T065-
503703); **Hostal Paraíso Verde** (Carrión
320, ½ block from the plaza, T941 809988,
www.hostalparaisoverde.com, with fan and
electric shower); **Samiria** (Jr José Cárdenas,
near the market).

What to do

Yurimaguas
Huayruro Tours, *Río Huallaga Hotel,
Yurimaguas; also at Alfonso Aiscorbe 2 in
Lagunas, T065-401186, www.peruselva.com.*
Tours to lakes, day and multi-day trips to
Pacaya-Samiria.

Pacaya-Samiria
Community associations in many of the
villages around the reserve run tours.
Community tours cost about US$70 pp
per day, compared to US$80 minumum for
agency tours arranged in Iquitos. Make sure
you know exactly what is included (park fees,
lodging, food, transport, guide), what the
trip involves (canoeing, walking, hunting,
fishing) and the type of accommodation. In

the community of San Martín de Tipishca in the Samiria Basin are **Asiendes** (Asociación Indígena en Defensa de la Ecología Samiria), T965-861748, asiendesperu@hotmail.com (asiendes.peru on Facebook) and **Casa Lupuna**. 5 associations operate in Lagunas; a tour operator is **Huayruro Tours** (see above). In Bretaña, the **Gallán family** offer tours.

Transport

Yurimaguas

Bus The road to Tarapoto is paved. To Lima, with **Paredes Estrella** (Mariscal Cáceres 220), 0830 daily, 32-34 hrs, US$38.50, via **Tarapoto** (US$4), **Moyobamba** (US$7.75, 5-6 hrs), **Pedro Ruiz** (US$17.50), **Chiclayo** (US$27) and

Trujillo (US$33). Also **Ejetur**, 0500 to Lima. Faster than the bus to Tarapoto are: **Gilmer Tours** (C Victor Sifuentes 580), frequent mini-buses, US$5.75, 2½ hrs; cars (eg **San Martín**) US$7.75; and combis (**Turismo Selva**, Mcal Cáceres 3rd block) US$4.

Ferry There are 6 docks in all. To **Iquitos**, *lanchas* from Embarcadero La Boca, 3 days/2 nights, best is **Eduardo/Gilmer** (Elena Pardo 114, T065-352552; see under Iquitos, Transport). To **Lagunas** for Pacaya Samiria Reserve, from Embarcadero Abel Guerra at 0900, US$11.55, 10 hrs. Also *rápidos* to Lagunas and Nauta (1½ hrs by *colectivo* from Iquitos, US$4), see Iquitos Transport, page 330.

unique jungle city and gateway to the Amazon

☆Iquitos stands on the west bank of the Amazon and is the chief town of Peru's jungle region. Some 800 km downstream from Pucallpa and 3646 km from the mouth of the Amazon, the city is completely isolated except by air and river. Its first wealth came from the rubber boom in the late 19th century and early 20th century, but now the main economic activities are logging, commerce and petroleum. The atmosphere of the city is completely different from the rest of Peru: hot, dirty, colourful, noisy and congested with the tens-of-thousands of mototaxis and motorcycles that fill the streets. Iquitos is the main starting point for tourists wishing to explore Peru's northern jungle. Here you can experience the authentic Amazon, from the lively streets of the city to the pink dolphins and Victoria regia water lilies of the river and its waterways.

Sights

The incongruous **Iron House/Casa de Fierro** stands on the Plaza de Armas, designed by Eiffel for the Paris exhibition of 1889. It is constructed entirely of iron trusses and sheets, bolted together and painted silver and was supposedly transported from Paris by a local rubber baron. It now houses a pharmacy. Of special interest in the city are the older buildings, faced with *azulejos* (glazed tiles). They date from the rubber boom of 1890 to 1912, when rich merchants imported tiles from Portugal and Italy and ironwork from England to embellish their homes. The **Casa de Barro** on the Plaza (house of the controversial rubber baron Fitzcarrald), is now a bank. **Museo Amazónico** ⓘ *Malecón Tarapacá 386, T065-234221, Mon-Sat 0800-1300, 1430-1730, Sun 0800-1230, free, some guides speak English, tip expected*, in the Prefectura, has displays of native art and sculptures by Lima artist Letterstein. Also worth visiting is the **Museo de Culturas Indígenas Amazónicas** ⓘ *Malecón Tarapacá 332, T065-235809, daily 0800-1930, US$5.25*, the private museum of Dr Richard Bodmer, who owns the **Casa Morey** hotel (see page 324).

It celebrates cultures from the entire Amazon region; ask here about historic Amazonian boats, such as **Barco Ayapua** ⓘ *Plaza Ramón Castilla, T065-236072, US$5*, an early 20th-century vessel from the rubber boom era, fully restored for visits, expeditions and short

Iquitos

Where to stay
1 Casa Linda
2 Casa Morey
3 El Dorado Isabel
4 El Dorado Plaza
5 El Sitio
6 Flying Dog Hostel
7 Green Track Hostel
8 Hostal El Colibrí
9 La Casa Fitzcarraldo
10 La Casona
11 Las Amazonas Inn
12 Marañón
13 Royal Inn
14 Samiria Jungle
15 Sol del Oriente
16 Victoria Regia

Restaurants
1 Antica Pizzería
2 Ari's Burger
3 Chef Paz
4 Chez Maggy Pizzería
5 Comedor Vegetariano
6 El Carbón
7 El Sitio
8 Fitzcarraldo
9 Helados Giornatta
10 Helados La Muyuna
11 Huasaí
12 La Gran Maloca
13 La Quinta de Abtao
14 María's Café
15 Mitos y Cubiertos
16 Norma Mía
17 Panadería Tívoli
18 Yellow Rose of Texas

Bars & clubs
19 Amazon Bistro
20 Arandú
21 Ikaro
22 Karma
23 Noa Noa

trips. The waterfront by Malecón Maldonado, known as 'Boulevard', is a pleasant place for a stroll and gets busy on Friday and Saturday evenings.

Belén, the picturesque, lively waterfront district, is an authentic part of Amazon river life, but is not safe at night. Most of its huts were originally built on rafts to cope with the river's 10 m change of level during floods from January to July; now they're more commonly built on stilts. Arrive by 0700 to see people arriving with their forest fruits and fish to sell in the Belén market. On Pasaje Paquito are bars serving local sugar cane rum and places where shamans buy medicinal plants and other items for their ceremonies. The main plaza has a bandstand made by Eiffel. In the high season canoes can be hired on the waterfront for a tour of Belén, US$3 per hour. To get there take a mototaxi to Los Chinos and walk down to the port.

Around Iquitos

There is a pleasant beach, with white sand and palms, at **Tipishca** on the Río Nanay, reached in 20 minutes by boat from Puerto de Santa Clara near the airport; it gets quite busy at weekends. **Santa Rita**, reached from Puerto de Pampa Chica, on a turnoff from the airport road, is quieter. Also near the airport is the village of **Santo Tomás** ① *turn left just before the airport, then take another left 300 m further on, then it's about 4 km to the village; mototaxi from Iquitos US$5*. It has a nice lake for swimming and renting canoes; beaches appear when the river is low, from July to September. The restaurants at the lake are very basic, so it's best to take your own food.

Pilpintuhuasi Butterfly Farm ① *near the village of Padre Cocha, T065-232665, www. amazonanimalorphanage.org, Tue-Sun 1000-1600, guided tours at 0930, 1100, 1330 and 1500, US$7.75, students US$4, includes guided tour*, has butterflies, a small, well-kept zoo and a rescue centre, run by Austrian biologist Goody. (Next door is another butterfly farm run by Goody's ex-husband.) To get there catch a *colectivo* from Bellavista to Padre Cocha (20 minutes), then walk 15 minutes from there. If the river is high, speedboats can reach Pilpintuhuasi directly from Iquitos, US$25 return including waiting time; pay at the end.

The **Centro de Rescate Amazónico Acobia** ① *Km 4.5 on the road to Nauta, http://gonzalomatosuria.blogspot.com/p/fundacion-iquitos-centro-de-rescate_20.html, daily 0900-1500, US$6.75, must show ID*, is where orphaned and injured manatees are nursed until they can be released. It's a good place to see this endangered species. Further along the road to Nauta are several *balnearios*.

Allpahuayo-Mishana Reserve

SERNANP, Jorge Chávez 930/942, Iquitos, T065-223555, Mon-Fri 0700-1300, 1500-1700, reserve fees US$8.50, students US$6.25.

On the Río Nanay, some 25 km south of Iquitos by the Nauta road or two hours by boat from Bellavista, this reserve protects the largest concentration of white sand jungle (varillales) in Peru. Part of the Napo ecoregion, it has one of the highest levels of biodiversity in the Amazon basin. Among several endangered species are two primates and several endemic species. The area is rich in birds: 475 species have been recorded. Within the reserve at Km 25 is **Zoocriadero BIOAM**, a good birdwatching circuit in land belonging to the Instituto Nacional de Innovación Agraria (INIA). Just beyond is the **Jardín de Plantas Medicinales y Frutales** ① *Km 26.8, daily 0800-1600, guiding 0800-1000*; with over 2400 species of medicinal plants. At Km 28, **El Irapay interpretation centre** ① *Mon-Sat 0830-1430*, has a trail to Mishana village by the river.

Border with Brazil and Colombia

Lanchas and *rápidos* make the journey downriver to the tri-border. Details on exit and entry formalities seem to change frequently, so when leaving Peru, check in Iquitos first at **Immigration** ① *Mcal Cáceres 18th block, T065-235371, Mon-Fri 0800-1615*, or with the Capitanía at the port. Boats stop in Santa Rosa for Peruvian exit formalities. Santa Rosa has six simple hotels (**Bellavista**, ½ block past immigration, with private bath, **Diana** and **Las Hamacas** are reported better than the others, price around US$15 for a double). All other details are given in the Brazil chapter. **Consulates in Iquitos**: Brazil ① *Sargento Lores 363, T065-235151, cg.iquitos@itamaraty.gov.br. Mon-Fri 0800-1400*, visas issued in two days; **Colombia** ① *Calvo de Araújo 431, T065-231461, http://iquitos.consulado.gov.co, Mon-Fri 0800-1400*.

Listings Iquitos and around *map page 322.*

Tourist information

iPerú (Jr Napo 161, of 4, T065-236144, iperuiquitos@promperu.gob.pe, Mon-Sat 0900-1800, Sun 0900-1300) also has a desk at the airport, open at flight times. If arriving by air, go to this desk first to get a list of hotels, a map and advice about the touts outside the airport. Both www.iquitosnews.com and www.iquitostimes.com have articles, maps and information. If you have a complaint about service, contact **Indecopi** (Putumayo 464, T065-243490, Mon-Fri 0830-1630); to report a crime, contact the **tourist police** (Sargento Lores 834, T065-242081).

Where to stay

Information on jungle lodges is given under What to do, below, as many work closely or exclusively with particular tour operators. Around Peruvian Independence Day (27 and 28 Jul) and Easter, Iquitos can get crowded and flight prices rise at this time.

$$$$ El Dorado Plaza
Napo 258 on main plaza, T065-222555, www.grupo-dorado.com.
Good accommodation and restaurant, bar, business-type hotel, pool, prices include service, small breakfast, welcome drink and transfer to/from airport. Also owns **$$$ El Dorado Isabel**, Napo 362, T065-232574.

$$$$ Samiria Jungle
Ricardo Palma 159, T065-223232, www.samiriajunglehotel.com.
Modern upmarket hotel, includes airport transfers, large suites and rooms, frigobar, bathtub, restaurant, bar, pool, meeting rooms.

$$$ Casa Morey
Raymondi y Loreto, Plaza Ramón Castilla, T065-231913, www.casamorey.com.
Boutique hotel in a beautifully restored historic rubber-boom period mansion. Great attention to detail, includes airport transfers, ample comfortable rooms, pool, good library.

$$$ Sol del Oriente
Av Quiñónez Km 2.5 on the way to the airport, T065-260317.
Airport transfers, pool, internet in hall, nice gardens, deco a bit kitsch.

$$$ Victoria Regia
Ricardo Palma 252, T065-231983, www.victoriaregiahotel.com.
Free map of city, safe deposit boxes in rooms, good restaurant, indoor pool.

$$$-$$ La Casa Fitzcarraldo
Av La Marina 2153, T065-601138, http://casafitzcarraldo.com/.
Prices vary according to room. Includes breakfast and airport transfer, with Wi-Fi, satellite TV, minibar, 1st-class restaurant, treehouse, pool in lovely gardens, captive

animals. The house is the home of Walter Saxer, the executive-producer of Werner Herzog's famous film, lots of movie and celebrity memorabilia.

$$$-$$ Marañón
Fitzcarrald y Nauta 289, T065-242673, http://hotelmaranon.com.
Multi-storey hotel, spotless comfortable rooms, a/c, convenient location, small pool.

$$ Royal Inn & Casino
Aguirre 793, T065-224244, www.royalinncasinohotel.com.
Modern, comfortable, frigobar and, bidet, airport transfer, good.

$$-$ Casa Linda
Napo 818, T065-231533, http:// residenciacasalinda.com.
Good hotel in a quiet area, rooms with a/c, private bath, hot water, frigobar.

$$-$ Flying Dog Hostel
Malecón Tarapacá 592, T065-223755, www.flyingdogperu.com.
Nice old house, pleasant 4 bed dorms and private rooms with bath and a/c or fan, clean kitchen, lockers.

$$-$ Hostal El Colibrí
Raymondi 200, T065-241737, hostalelcolibri@hotmail.com.
1 block from Plaza and 50 m from the river so can be noisy, nicely refurbished house, a/c or fan, hot water, secure, good value, breakfast extra, helpful staff.

$$-$ La Casona
Fitzcarald 147, T065-234 394, www. hotellacasonaiquitos.com.pe.
In building dating from 1901, now modernized, hot water, fan or a/c, kitchen facilities, small patio, pool, popular with travellers. Opposite, at Fitzcarald 152, is **Hostal La Casona Río Grande**, with smaller rooms, fan. Transport to either from the airport with advance reservation.

$ El Sitio
Ricardo Palma 541, T065-234932.
Fan, private bath, cold water, good value.

$ Green Track Hostel
Ricardo Palma 516, T950-664049, www.greentrack-hostel.com.
Pleasant hostel, dorms with a/c or fan, private rooms with and without bath, free pick up with advanced booking, terrace, Brazilian breakfast, English spoken, helpful owners, tours arranged to Tapiche Reserve (see below).

$ Las Amazonas Inn
Ricardo Palma 460, T065-225367, las_amazonas_inn_iquitos@yahoo.es.
Simple rooms with electric shower, a/c, kitchen facilities, breakfast available, friendly owner.

Restaurants

Local specialities include palm heart salad (*chonta*), or *a la Loretana* dish on menus; also try *inchicapi* (chicken, corn and peanut soup), *cecina* (fried dried pork), *tacacho* (fried green banana and pork, mashed into balls and eaten for breakfast or tea), *juanes* (chicken, rice, olive and egg, seasoned and wrapped in bijao leaves and sold in restaurants) and the *camu-camu*, an acquired taste, said to have one of the highest vitamin C concentrations in the world. Avoid eating endangered species, such as paiche, caiman or turtle, which are sometimes on menus.

For a good local breakfast, go to the Mercado Central, C Sargento Lores, where there are several kiosks outside, popular and cheap. Try the local drink *chuchuhuasi*, made from the bark of a tree, which is supposed to have aphrodisiac properties (for sale at Arica 1046), and *jugo de cocona*, and the alcoholic *cola de mono* and *siete raices* (aguardiente mixed with the bark of 7 trees and wild honey), sold at **Musmuqui** (Raymondi 382), Mon-Sat from 1900.

$$$ Al Frío y al Fuego
On the water, go to Embarcadero Turístico (El Huequito) and a boat will pick you up, T065-224862. Mon 1830-2300, Tue-Sat 1130-1600 and 1830-2300, Sun 1130-1600.

Good upscale floating restaurant with regional specialities.

$$$ Fitzcarraldo
Malecón Maldonado 103 y Napo.
Smart, typical food, also pizza, good pastas and salads.

$$$ La Gran Maloca
Sargento Lores 170, opposite Banco Continental. Closes 2000 on Sun, other days 2300.
A/c, high class regional food.

$$$-$$ Chef Paz
Putumayo 468, T065-241277. Mon-Sat 0800-midnight.
Excellent food including fish, shellfish, meat dishes, local specialities and their own jungle sushi.

$$ Ari's Burger
Plaza de Armas, Próspero 127.
Medium-priced fast food, breakfasts, popular with tourists but questionable hygiene.

$$ Yellow Rose of Texas
Putumayo 180. Open 24 hrs so you can wait here if arriving late at night.
Varied food including local dishes, Texan atmosphere, good breakfasts, lots of information, also has a bar, Sky TV and Texan saddle seats.

$$-$ Antica Pizzería
Napo 159. Sun-Thu 0700-2400, Fri-Sat 0700-0100.
"The best pizza in town" and Italian dishes, pleasant ambiance especially on the upper level.

$$-$ Chez Maggy Pizzería
Raymondi 177. Daily 1800-0100.
Wood-fired pizza and home-made pasta.

$$-$ La Quinta (5ta) de Abtao
Abtao 527. Closed Mon.
Small place serving ceviche of river fish and other dishes using local ingredients. Very good. Also does a good value lunch menu.

$ Comedor Vegetariano
Morona y Arica.
Small restaurant with a lot of vegetarian choices, US$3.35.

$ El Carbón
La Condamine 115. Open 1900-2300 only.
Grilled meats, salads, regional side dishes such as *tacacho* and *patacones*.

$ El Sitio
Sargento Lores 404. Mon-Sat 1930-2230.
A simple place for *anticuchos* for all tastes including vegetarian, popular.

$ Huasaí
Fitzcarrald 131. Open 0715-1615, closed Mon.
Varied and innovative menu, popular, good food and value, go early.

$ Mitos y Cubiertos
Napo 337, by the Plaza. Mon-Sat midday only.
Generous lunches, good value.

Cafés

Helados Giornatta
Próspero, on Plaza de Armas.
Specializes in ice creams flavoured with fruits from the rainforest.

Helados La Muyuna
Jr Próspero 621 and on Napo near Malecón.
Good natural jungle fruit ice cream.

María's Café
Nauta 292. Tue-Sun 0800-1230.
Breakfasts, sandwiches, burgers, coffee and cakes, with desserts of the day.

Norma Mía
La Condamine 153.
Doña Norma has been making delicious cakes for over 30 years, also sells ice cream.

Panadería Tívoli
Ricardo Palma, block 3.
A variety of good bread and sweets.

Bars and clubs

Amazon Bistro
Malecón Tarapacá 268.
Upscale French bistro/bar on the waterfront, drinks, snacks, breakfasts and meal of the day. Trendy and popular. Live music at weekends.

Arandú
Malecón Maldonado.
Good views of the river.

El Pardo
Cáceres y Alzamora.
Huge place with live music; you dance along with 5,000 others. Bands play salsa, cumbia and música tropical. Only beer for sale; dirty toilets.

Ikaro
Putumayo 341.
Good Spanish rock music. Also has internet.

Karma
Napo 138.
Cocktails and rock music, has a happy hour.

Noa Noa
Pevas y Fitzcarrald.
Popular disco with cumbia and Latin music.

Festivals

5 Jan Founding of Iquitos.
Feb-Mar **Carnival.**
Jun Tourist week is the 3rd week.
24 Jun **San Juan**, the most important festival.
28-30 Aug **Santa Rosa de Lima**.
8 Dec **Immaculate Conception**
(**La Purísima**), celebrated in Punchana, near the docks, Bellavista and Nanay.

Shopping

Handicrafts
Hammocks in Iquitos cost about US$12.
Mercado Artesanal Anaconda, by the waterfront at Napo is good for Amazon handicrafts, but be sure not to buy items that contain animal products. Also try the **Asociación de Artesanos El Manguaré**, which has kiosks on Jr Nauta, block 1.
Mercado Artesanal de Productores (4 km from the centre in the San Juan district, on the road to the airport; take a *colectivo*) is the cheapest in town with more choice than elsewhere.

For jungle clothing and equipment, visit **Comisesa** (Arica 348), and **Mad Mick's Trading Post** (Putumayo 163, top floor, next to the Iron House).
La Restinga, *Raymondi 254, T065-221371, larestinga@gmail.com.* This association sells T-shirts, books and soaps made by children. It also runs literacy workshops in Belén on Tue and Thu from 1430-1800, at which you can volunteer.

What to do

Jungle tours
Agencies arrange 1-day or longer trips to places of interest with guides speaking some English. Take your time before making a decision and don't be bullied by the hustlers at the airport (they get paid a hefty commission). You must make sure your tour operator or guide has a proper licence (check with **iPerú**). Do not go with a company which does not have legal authorization; there are many unscrupulous people about. Find out all the details of the trip and food arrangements before paying (a minimum of US$50 per day). Several companies have their own lodges, providing various levels of accommodation in the heart of the jungle (see below). All prices are negotiable, except tours run by **Muyuna**, **Heliconia Lodge** and **Explorama** (see below), who do not give commissions.

River cruises
There are several agencies that arrange river cruises in well-appointed boats. Most go to the Pacaya-Samiria region, very few towards Brazil. In addition to the vessels of **Aqua** and **Delfín** (see below), other options include **La Amatista** of the Dorado hotel group,

the **Aquamarina**, **Arapaima** and **Queen Violeta** group and **Estrella Amazónica**. Contact a company like **Rainforest Cruises** (www.rainforestcruises.com), for options. Alternatively, speed boats for river trips can be hired by the hour or day at the **Embarcadero Turístico**, at the intersection of Av de la Marina and Samánez Ocampo in Punchana. Prices vary greatly, usually US$15-20 per hr, US$80 for speedboat, and are negotiable.

Shaman experiences

Iquitos is an important place for ayahuasca tourism. There are legitimate shamans as well as charlatans. **Karma Café** (Napo 138; see above) is the centre of the scene in town. See also the work of Alan Shoemaker (**Soga del Alma**, Rómulo Espinar 170, Iquitos 65, alanshoemaker@hotmail.com), who holds an International Amazonian Shamanism Conference every year.

Tour operators and jungle lodges

Amazon Yarapa River Lodge, *Av La Marina 124, www.yarapa.com.* On the Río Yarapa, award-winning in its use of ecofriendly resources and its work with local villages. Flexible and responsible. Its field laboratory is associated with Cornell University. Arranges trips to Pacaya-Samiria.

Aqua Expeditions, *Iquitos 1167, T065-601053, www.aquaexpeditions.com.* Luxury river cruises of 3, 4, or 7 nights on the *M/V Aria* (from US$2835 pp) and the *M/V Aqua* (from US$2685 pp), both designed by famous Peruvian architect Jordi Puig to look like floating town houses rather than boats, with massive picture windows in each a/c suite. Amazing food with local delicacies on the gourmet tasting menu, good shore excursions with knowledgeable local guides.

Chullachaqui Eco Lodge, *Raymondi 138, Iquitos, T965-705919, http://amazoniantrips. com/chullachaqui-eco-lodge/.* 1 hr by speed boat up the Amazon on the Río Tapira. Thatched timber cabins, basic accommodation, private bath, communal

dining room, hammock room, insect screens, tours with naturalist guides to see river dolphins and other wildlife.

Cumaceba Amazonia Tours, *Putumayo 184 in the Iron House, T065-232229, www. cumaceba.com.* Overnight visits to Cumaceba Lodge, 35 km from Iquitos, and tours of 1-4 nights to the Botanical Lodge on the Amazon, 80 km from Iquitos, birdwatching tours, ayahuasca ceremonies.

Curuhuinsi Eco Adventure Tours & Expeditions, *T965-013225, www.facebook. com/CuruhuinsiEcoAdventureToursExpeditions.* **Gerson Pizango** is a local, English-speaking and award-winning guide who will take you to his village 2½ hrs by boat, from where you can trek and camp or stay and experience village life. Expert at spotting wildlife and knowledgeable about medicinal plants, he offers interesting and varied expeditions benefitting the community. In the village, accommodation is in a hut by the riverside where there are pink and grey dolphins. A private room with mosquito net costs US$50-70 pp per day depending on length of trip and size of party, includes food, water, camping gear, boots, raincoats, torches, binoculars, fishing rods, machetes.

Dawn on the Amazon, *Malecón Maldonado 185 y Nauta, T065-223730, www. dawnontheamazon.com.* Offers a variety of day tours around Iquitos on the luxurious 20 passenger *Dawn on the Amazon III* (US$199 pp). Also offer custom-made cruises for several days. Their wooden vessels are decorated with carvings of jungle themes. Also has a good bar/restaurant in town.

Delfín, *Av Abelardo Quiñones Km 5, San Juan Bautista, T065-262721, www.delfinamazon cruises.com.* Luxury cruises in the Delfín I and Delfín II (the cheaper of the 2), 3- and 4-night expeditions to Pacaya-Samiria, with daily activities including kayaking, bird- and wildlife-watching, fresh organic food, from US$2400 pp. Under same ownership as **Al Frío y al Fuego** restaurant in town.

Explorama Tours, *by the riverside docks on Av La Marina 340, T065-252530, www.*

explorama.com. The biggest and most established operator, with over 40 years' experience. Frequently recommended. Their lodges are:

Ceiba Tops, 40 km (1½ hrs) from Iquitos, a comfortable resort with 75 a/c rooms with electricity, hot showers, pool with hydromassage and beautiful gardens. The food is good and, as in all Explorama's properties, is served communally. There are attractive walks and other excursions, a recommended jungle experience for those who want their creature comforts, US$340 pp for 1 night/2 days.

Explorama Lodge at Yanamono, 80 km from Iquitos, 2½ hrs from Iquitos, has palm-thatched accommodation with separate bathroom and shower facilities connected by covered walkways, cold water, no electricity, good food and service. US$455 for 3 days/2 nights.

Explornapo Lodge at Llachapa on the Sucusai creek (a tributary of the Napo), is in the same style as Explorama Lodge, but is further away from Iquitos, 160 km (4 hrs), and is set in 105,000 ha of primary rainforest, so is better for seeing wildlife, US$1,120 for 5 days/4 nights. Nearby is the impressive canopy walkway 35 m above the forest floor and 500 m long, 'a magnificent experience and not to be missed'. It is associated with the Amazon Center for Tropical Studies (ACTS), a scientific station, only 10 mins from the canopy walkway. Close to Explornapo is the ReNuPeRu medicinal plant garden, run by a curandero.

Explor Tambos, 2 hrs from Explornapo, offer more primitive accommodation, 8 shelters for 16 campers, bathing in the river.

Heliconia Lodge, Ricardo Palma 242; contact T01-421 9195, www.heliconialodge. com.pe. On the Río Amazonas, 80 km downriver from Iquitos, surrounded by rainforest, islands and lagoons, this is a beautiful place for resting, birdwatching, looking for pink dolphins, jungle hikes.

Organized packages 3 days/2 nights, US$282. Good guides, food and flexible excursions according to guest's requirements. The lodge has hot water, electricity for 5 hrs each day and a traditionally rustic yet comfortable design. Same management has bungalows 15 km from Iquitos on a lake.

Muyuna Amazon Lodge, Putumayo 163, ground floor, T065-242858/T065-993 4424, www.muyuna.com. 140 km upstream from Iquitos on the Río Yanayacu, before San Juan village. 1- to 5-night packages available. 2 nights/3 days is US$340 pp all-inclusive for 2-10 people. Trusted guides, high-quality accommodation, good food and service; very well organized, flexible and professional. Amenities are constantly updated with new ecological considerations. Birdwatching and camping trips into the forest. This area is less spoilt than some other parts of the forest downstream. **Centro de Rescate Amazónico** (see page 323) has released manatees here. Highly recommended.

Paseos Amazónicos Ambassador, *Pevas 246, T065-231618, www.paseos amazonicos.com*. Operates the **Amazonas Sinchicuy Lodge**, 1½ hrs from Iquitos on the Sinchicuy river, 25 mins by boat from the Amazon. The lodge consists of several wooden buildings with thatched roofs on stilts, cabins with bathroom, no electricity but paraffin lamps are provided, good food, and plenty activities, including visits to local villages. Recommended. They also have Tambo Yanayacu and Tambo Amazónico lodges, organize visits to Pacaya Samiria and run local tours.

Tapiche Reserve, *Ricardo Palma 516, T065-600805/950-664049, office at Green Track Hostel (see above), www.tapichejungle.com*. On the Río Tapiche, a tributary of the Ucayali, 11 hrs up river from Iquitos. Fully screened wood cabins with thatched roofs, custom designed trips according to the visitor's interests, 4-day/3-night and 5-day/4-night tours offered.

Transport

Air Francisco Secada Vigneta airport, T065-260147 is southwest of the city; a taxi to the airport costs US$10; *mototaxi* (motorcycle with 2 seats), US$3.25. Most buses from the main road outside the airport go through the centre of town, US$0.75. To **Lima**, daily, with **LATAM** (direct or via Tarapoto), **Peruvian Airlines** and **Star Perú** (direct or via Tarapoto, also daily to Pucallpa) and Avianca/TACA. The military **Grupo Aéreo 42** fly occasionally to Santa Rosa.

Bus To **Nauta**, **Trans del Sur** from Libertad y Próspero, daily 0530-1900, US$3.10, 2 hrs; also vans from Av Aguirre cuadra 14 by Centro Comercial Sachachorro, which leave when full, US$4, 1½ hrs.

Ferry For general hints on river travel, see page 713. For information about boats, go to the corresponding ports of departure for each destination, except for speed boats to the Brazil/Colombian border which have their offices clustered on Raymondi block 3. When river levels are very high departures may be from alternative places.

Lanchas leave from Puerto Henry and Masusa, 2 km north of the centre, a dangerous area at night. The 1st night's meal is not included. Always deal directly with boat owners or managers, avoid touts and middle-men. All fares are negotiable. If arriving in Iquitos on a regular, slow boat, take extreme care when disembarking. Things get very chaotic at this time and theft and pickpocketing is rife. Some of the newer boats have CCTV to deter theft. *Deslizadores* or *rápidos* leave from Embarcadero Turístico or Nauta (see below).

To **Pucallpa**, 4-5 days upriver along the Amazon and Ucayali (can be longer if the water level is low), larger boats must travel only by day, hammock US$40, berth US$140 double. **Henry** (T065-263948) is a large company with 4 departures per week from Puerto Henry; *Henry 5, 6* and *7* have some cabins with bath. Another good boat is *Pedro Martín 2* from Puerto Masusa.

To **Yurimaguas** by *lancha*, 3-4 days upriver along the Amazon, Marañón and Huallaga, hammock space US$40, berth US$119-134 double. The **Eduardo/Gilmer** company, T065-960404, with 8 boats is recommended, sailing from Puerto Masusa several times a week, except Sun; *Eduardo I* and *Gilmer IV* have berths with bath for US$192. By *rápido* from Nauta, with **Rápido NR** (C Puerto Principal, Nauta, T953-998980), 20 hrs navigation upstream, US$40 includes a meal, snack and overnight lodging in Lagunas; all basic. The reverse, downstream, journey is 12 hrs, US$38, no overnight in Lagunas.

To **Santa Rosa** (on the border with Brazil and Colombia), the most convenient way to travel is by *rápido*, 8-10 hrs downriver, US$60, from the **Embarcadero Turístico** (always confirm departure point in advance) at 0530 Tue-Sun; be at the port 0445 for customs check, board 0500-0530. (In the opposite direction, boats leave Santa Rosa Tue-Sun at 0400 and take 10-12 hrs upstream; if you're coming from Brazil or Colombia get your immigration entry stamp the day before.) *Rápidos* carry life jackets and have bathrooms; a simple breakfast and lunch are included in the price. Luggage limit is 15 kg. Purchase tickets in advance from company offices in Iquitos: **Golfinho** (Raymondi 378, T065-225118, www.transportegolfinho.com) and **Transtur** (Raymondi 384, T065-221356). *Lanchas* to Santa Rosa, which may continue to Islandia, leave from the Puerto Pesquero or Puerto Masusa (enquire at T065-250440), Mon-Sat at 1800, 2-3 days downriver, US$31 in hammock, US$50 in cabin; in the other direction they depart Santa Rosa Mon-Sat at 1200.

To reach the border with Ecuador you go to **Pantoja**, 5-7 days upriver on the Napo, a route requiring plenty of time, stamina and patience. There are irregular departures once or twice a month, US$38, plus US$3 per day for a berth if you can get one; for details call **Radio Moderna** in Iquitos (T065-250440), or T065-830055 (a private phone in Pantoja village). The vessels are usually cargo boats that carry live animals, some of which are slaughtered en route. Crowding and poor sanitation are common. Once in Pantoja, there is no public transport to **Nuevo Rocafuerte** (Ecuador), so you must hire a private boat, US$60. To shorten the voyage, or to visit the jungle towns along the way, go to **Indiana**, daily departures from **Muelle de Productores** in Iquitos, US$5, 45 mins,

Tip...
There is no Ecuadorean consulate in Iquitos; if you need a visa, get it in Lima or your home country.

then take a mototaxi to **Mazán** on the Río Napo. From Mazán, there are *rápidos* to **Santa Clotilde**, US$31 includes a snack, 4-5 hrs, information from **Familia Ruiz** in Iquitos (T065-251410).

Southern jungle

Peru's premier wildlife-watching destination

★The southern *selva* is mostly in Madre de Dios department, which contains the Manu National Park (2.04 million ha), the Tambopata National Reserve (254,358 ha) and the Bahauja-Sonene National Park (1.1 million ha). The forest of this lowland region (altitude 260 m) is technically called Sub-tropical Moist Forest, which means that it receives less rainfall than tropical forest and is dominated by the floodplains of its meandering rivers. The most striking features are the former river channels that have become isolated as oxbow lakes. These are home to black caiman and giant otter and a host of other species. Other rare species living in the forest are jaguar, puma, ocelot and tapir. There are also howler monkeys, capybara, macaws, guans, currasows and the giant harpy eagle.

As well as containing some of the most important flora and fauna on Earth, the region also harbours gold-diggers, loggers, hunters, drug smugglers and oil-men, whose activities have endangered the unique rainforest. Moreover, the construction of the Interoceánica, a road linking the Atlantic and Pacific oceans via Puerto Maldonado and Brazil, will certainly bring more uncontrolled colonization in the area, as seen so many times before in the Brazilian Amazon.

☆Manu Biosphere Reserve

Few other reserves on the planet can compare with Manu for the diversity of life forms; it holds over 1000 species of birds and covers an altitudinal range from 200 m to 4100 m above sea-level. Giant otters, jaguars, ocelots and 13 species of primates abound in this pristine tropical wilderness; uncontacted indigenous tribes are present in the more remote areas, as are indigenous groups with limited access.

The reserve is one of the largest conservation units on Earth, encompassing the complete drainage of the Manu River. It is divided into the **Manu National Park** (1,692,137 ha), which only government-sponsored biologists and anthropologists may visit with permits from the Ministry of Agriculture in Lima; the **Reserved Zone** (257,000 ha) within the national park, which is set aside for applied scientific research and ecotourism; and the **Cultural Zone** (92,000 ha), which contains acculturated native groups and colonists along the Alto Madre de Dios and its tributaries, where the locals still employ their traditional way of life. Among the ethnic groups in the Cultural Zone are the Mashco-Piro and the Yine, while the Harakmbut are in the Reserved Zone. Associated with Manu are other areas protected

Essential Manu

Access

The Multi-Use Zone of Manu Biosphere Reserve is accessible to anyone and several lodges exist in the area. The Reserved Zone is accessible by permit only, available from the Manu National Park office in Cuzco; entry is strictly controlled and visitors must visit the area under the auspices of an authorized operator with an authorized guide. Permits are limited and reservations should be made well in advance. There is very little permanent accommodation in the Reserved Zone but several companies have tented safari camp infrastructures, some with shower and dining facilities, but all visitors sleep in tents. The entrance fee to the Reserved Zone is 150 soles pp (about US$55) and is included in package tour prices.

Tours to Manu usually enter by road, overnighting in a lodge in the cloudforest, and continue by boat (the route is described below). It is this journey from the highlands down through the various strata of habitat that sets it apart from many other visits to the jungle. At the end of the tour, passengers either return overland or fly back to Cuzco from Puerto Maldonado. There is an airstrip at Diamante, near Boca Manu, but there are no regular flights from Cuzco. Ask the tour operators in Cuzco if your tour will go overland or by air.

When to go

The climate is warm and humid, with a rainy season from November to March and a dry season from April to October. Cold fronts from the South Atlantic, called friajes, are characteristic of the dry season, causing temperatures to drop to 15-16°C during the day and to 13°C at night. Always bring a sweater at this time. The best time to visit is during the dry season when there are fewer mosquitoes and the rivers are low, exposing the beaches. This is also a good time to see birds nesting and to view animals at close range, as they stay close to the rivers and are easily seen. A pair of binoculars is essential and insect repellent is a must.

Tip...
It is not possible to arrange trips to the Reserved Zone of the national park from Itahuania, owing to park regulations. All arrangements, including permits, must be made in Cuzco.

---

by conservation groups, or local people (for example the Blanquillo Reserved Zone) and some cloudforest parcels along the road. The **Nahua-Kugapakori Reserved Zone**, set aside for these two nomadic native groups, is the area between the headwaters of the Río Manu and headwaters of the Río Urubamba, to the north of the alto Madre de Dios.

Cuzco to Manu and Puerto Maldonado via Pilcopata and Itahuania
Cuzco to Pilcopata The arduous 255 km trip over the Andes from Cuzco to Pilcopata takes about eight to 12 hours by bus or truck, or 10 hours to two days in the wet season. The road is in places hair-raising and breathtaking, and the scenery is magnificent. From Cuzco you climb up to the Huancarani pass (very cold at night) then drop to Paucartambo in the eponymous river valley. The road then ascends to a second pass (also cold at night), after which it goes down to the cloudforest and then the rainforest, reaching **Pilcopata** at 650 m on the border between the departments of Cuzco and Madre de Dios.

Pilcopata to Itahuania After Pilcopata, the route passes through **Atalaya**, the first village on the Alto Madre de Dios River and tourist port for hiring boats to Boca Manu;

there are basic lodgings and restaurants here. The route continues to **Salvación**, where the park office and entrance are situated, plus some basic *hostales* and restaurants.

The road, which bypasses the previous port of **Shintuya**, continues as far as **Itahuania**, currently the starting point for river transport. The road is scheduled to continue to Nuevo Edén, 11 km away downriver, and to Diamante, so the location of the river port will be determined by road-building progress. Eventually, the road will go all the way to Boca Colorado. As it is, rain often disrupts wheeled transport.

Itahuania to Puerto Maldonado via Boca Colorado Cargo boats leave Itahuania for the gold-mining centre of Boca Colorado on the Río Madre de Dios, via Boca Manu (see below), but only when the boat is fully laden (see Transport, page 342). Very basic accommodation can be found in Boca Colorado, but it is not recommended for lone women travellers. From Colorado you can take a *colectivo* to Puerto Carlos, cross the river, then take another *colectivo* to Puerto Maldonado: 4½ hours in all.

Boca Manu and around
Boca Manu is the connecting point between the rivers Alto Madre de Dios, Manu and Madre de Dios. It has a few houses and some food supplies. It is also the entrance to the Manu Reserved Zone and to go further you must be part of an organized group. The park ranger station is located in Limonal. You need to show your permit here. Camping is allowed if you have a permit.

Upstream on the Río Manu you pass the **Manu Lodge** on the Cocha Juárez after three or four hours (see www.manuperu.com for information on this lodge). You can continue to Cocha Otorongo in 2½ hours and Cocha Salvador, a further 30 minutes. The latter is the biggest lake with plenty of wildlife. From here it is two to three hours to Pakitza, the entrance to the National Park Zone, only accessible to biologists with a special permit.

Between Boca Manu and Boca Colorado is **Blanquillo**, a private reserve of 10,000 ha. Bring a good tent with you and all food if you want to camp and do it yourself, or alternatively accommodation is available at the **Tambo Blanquillo** (full board or accommodation only). Wildlife is abundant, especially macaws and parrots at the macaw lick near **Manu Wildlife Centre**. There are occasional boats to Blanquillo from Shintuya; six to eight hours.

Cuzco to Puerto Maldonado via Mazuko
This route is Cuzco–Urcos–Quincemil–Mazuko–Puerto Maldonado; it has been upgraded as part of the Interoceánica highway and its susceptibility to bad weather has declined. The changing scenery en route is magnificent.

Quincemil, 240 km from Urcos on the road to Mazuko, is a centre for alluvial gold-mining with many banks. Hunt Oil is building a huge oil and gas facility here; its exploration controversially overlaps the Amarakaeri Communal Reserve.

Puente Iñambari is the junction of three sections of the Interoceanic Highway, from Cuzco, Puerto Maldonado and Juliaca (see Puno to the jungle, page 225). However, this is only a small settlement and transport stops 5 km further north at **Mazuko**. In the evenings, Mazuko is a hive of activity as temperatures drop and the buses arrive.

The Highway beyond Mazuko cuts across lowland rainforest, large areas of which have been cleared by migrants engaged in small-scale gold mining. Their encampments of plastic shelters, shops and prostibars now line the Highway for several kilometres. A worthwhile stop on the route is the **Parador Turístico Familia Méndez** ① *Km 419, 45 mins from Puerto Maldonado,* which prepares local dishes from home-grown ingredients and has a trail network in the surrounding forest.

Puerto Maldonado *Colour map 2, C5.*

Puerto Maldonado is an important base for visiting the southeastern jungles of the Tambopata Reserve or departing for Bolivia or Brazil. It overlooks the confluence of the rivers Tambopata and Madre de Dios and, because of the gold mining and timber industries, the immediate surrounding jungle is now cultivated. A bridge, as part of the Interoceánica highway, has been built across the Río Madre de Dios; even before its completion, business activity in the town was growing fast.

> **Tip...**
> Try the locally grown Brazil nuts (*castañas*) sold in the markets and shops of Puerto Maldonado. Many inhabitants of the Madre de Dios Region are involved in their production. The harvest is from December to February, and the crop tends to be good on alternate years.

Jungle tours from Puerto Maldonado

The beautiful and tranquil **Lago Sandoval** ⓘ *entry US$9.50; boat hire from the Madre de Dios port, US$25 (minimum 2 people), plus petrol costs*, is a one-hour boat ride along the Río Madre de Dios, and then a 5-km walk into the jungle; parts of the first 3 km are on a raised wooden walkway, but boots are advisable. You must go with a guide, which can be arranged by the boat driver. Don't pay the boat hire fee until you're safely back at port.

Trips can also be made to **Lago Valencia**, 60 km from Puerto Maldonado near the Bolivian border (four hours there, eight hours back). It is an oxbow lake with lots of wildlife and many excellent beaches and islands within an hour's boat ride. Mosquitoes are voracious, though. If you're camping, take food and water.

☆Tambopata National Reserve
Sernanp, Av 28 de Julio 482, Puerto Maldonado, T082-573278.

The Tambopata National Reserve (TNR) lies between the rivers Madre de Dios, Tambopata and Heath. The area was first declared a reserve in 1990 and is a very reasonable alternative for those who do not have the time or money to visit Manu. It is a close rival in terms of seeing wildlife and boasts some superb oxbow lakes. Other highlights are the famous clay licks or *collpas*, where macaws and parrots gather to eat minerals which allow them to digest otherwise toxic seeds and fruits. There are a number of lodges here which are excellent for lowland rainforest birding. If you're not visiting the reserve as part of a lodge package, it is quite easy to arrange a boat and guide from Puerto Maldonado (see Tour operators, page 341), travelling up the Tambopata river or down the Madre de Dios.

Bahuaja Sonene National Park
Sernanp, Libertad 1189, Puno, T051-363960, daranibar@sernanp.gob.pe, fee US$54 for 7-day visit.

The Bahuaja-Sonene National Park, declared in 1996, stretches from the Heath River across the Tambopata, incorporating the Santuario Nacional Pampas del Heath. There are no facilities in the park. Visits only with tour operators who offer seven-day rafting trips along the Río Tambopata, down river from Putina Punco, in the department of Puno, camping on the shore of the river and finishing at the Tambopata Research Centre (TRC). It is an adventurous trip involving paddling through grade III and IV rapids. Sernanp has a list of authorized operators, it includes **Amazonas Explorer** and **River Explorers**, see Cuzco operators, page 252. There are lodges in the park's buffer zone, **InkaNatura** has a lodge on the Río Heath, the **Heath River Wildlife Center** ① www.inkanatura.com.

Río Las Piedras

Lying to the northeast of, and running roughly parallel to the Río Manu, this drainage runs some 700 km from rainforest headwaters in the Alto Purús region. The lower, more easily accessible section of the river, closer to Puerto Maldonado and outside state protection, runs through rich tropical forests, very similar to those in the Manu and Tambopata areas. Close to 600 species of birds, at least eight primate species and some of the Amazon's larger mammals – giant otter, jaguar, puma, tapir and giant anteater –are all present. Hunting pressure has resulted in wildlife being shier than in Manu or Tambopata, but this remains an excellent wildlife destination. See www.arbioperu.org and www.relevantfilms.co.uk/propied/las-piedras/.

To Iberia and Iñapari

Daily public transport runs to **Iberia** and **Iñapari** on the border with Brazil. No primary forest remains along the road, only secondary growth and small chacras (farms). There are picturesque caseríos (settlements) that serve as processing centres for the brazil nut.

Iberia, Km 168, has a few simple hotels, including **Casa Blanca** ($, José Aldamis 848, T972-702204), with private bath, cold water, fan and a small garden. It's a small, quiet frontier town.

Iñapari, at the end of the road, Km 235, is connected by a suspension bridge to Brazil.

Crossing to Brazil Public transport stops near immigration in Iñapari for exit stamps, open 0930-1300, 1500-1930 daily (Brazilian side 0830-1200, 1400-1830). Brazilian entry stamps are given by Polícia Federal just outside Assis Brasil. The only exchange facilities at the border are in Iñapari but rates are better in Puerto Maldonado. There is a paved road with frequent shared taxis (expensive) and a bus service from Assis Brasil to Brasiléia, where you can cross to Cobija, Bolivia, or carry on to Rio Branco and further into Brazil.

Listings Southeastern jungle

Tourist information

Manu Biosphere Reserve

Amazon Conservation Association (ACCA)
C Cesar Vallejo K-6, Urb Santa Mónica, Wanchaq, Cuzco, T084-222329, www.amazonconservation.org; also at Jr Cusco 499, T082-573543, Puerto Maldonado.
An NGO whose mission is to protect biodiversity by studying ecosystems and developing conservation tools while suporting local communities.

Asociación Peruana para la Conservación de la Naturaleza (APECO)
Parque José Acosta 187, p 2, Magdalena del Mar, Lima, T01-264 5804, apeco@apeco.org.pe.

Manu National Park Office
Av Cinco los Chachacomos F2-4, Larapa Grande, San Jerónimo, Cuzco, T084-274509, www.visitmanu.com. Mon-Fri.
Issues permits for the Reserved Zone.

Perú Verde
Ricardo Palma J-1, Santa Mónica, Cuzco, T084-226392, www.peruverde.org.
This is a local NGO that can help with information and has free video shows

about Manu National Park and Tambopata National Reserve. Friendly and helpful, with information on research in the jungle area of Madre de Dios.

Pronaturaleza
Doña Juana 137, Urb Los Rosales, Santiago de Surco, Lima, T01-271 2662; also in Puerto Maldonado at Jr Cajamarca cuadra 1 s/n, T082-571585, www.pronaturaleza.org.

Puerto Maldonado
There are tourist offices at the airport and at **Dircetur** (Urb Fonavi; take a mototaxi to the 'Posta Médica', which is next door).

Where to stay

Manu Biosphere Reserve
Lodges in Manu
Most jungle lodges are booked as package deals for 3 days, 2 nights, or longer, with meals, transport and guides; see websites for offers.

Amazon Yanayacu Lodge
Cahuide 824, Punchana, T062-250822.
About 1 hr by boat above Diamante village on the southern bank of the Madre de Dios, close to a small parrot *collpa* (mineral lick). Using local river transport to arrive at the lodge rates are very reasonable, prices depend on length of stay. The lodge also offers several different itineraries in Manu.

Amazonia Lodge
On the Río Alto Madre de Dios just across the river from Atalaya, T084-816131, www.amazonialodge.com; in Cuzco at Matará 334, p 3, T084-231370.
An old tea hacienda run by the Yabar Calderón family, famous for its bird diversity and fine hospitality, a great place to relax, meals included, birding or natural history tours available, contact Santiago in advance and he'll arrange a pick-up.

Casa Machiguenga
Near Cocha Salvador, upriver from Manu Lodge. Contact Manu Expeditions or Apeco NGO, T084-225595.

Machiguenga-style cabins run by local communities with NGO help.

Erika Lodge
On the Alto Madre de Dios, 25 mins from Atalaya.
Offers basic accommodation and is cheaper than the other, more luxurious lodges. Contact **Manu Adventures** (see page 341).

Manu Learning Centre
Fundo Mascoitania.
A 600-ha reserve within the cultural zone, see **Crees Tours**, What to do, page 340.

Manu Wildlife Center
2 hrs down the Río Madre de Dios from Boca Manu, near the Blanquillo macaw lick.
Book through **Manu Expeditions** (www.manuexpeditions.com), which runs it in conjunction with the conservation group **Peru Verde**. 22 double cabins, with private bathroom and hot water. Also canopy towers for birdwatching and a tapir lick.

Pantiacolla Lodge
30 mins downriver from Shintuya.
Owned by the Moscoso family. Book through **Pantiacolla Tours** (see page 341).

Cuzco to Manu and Puerto Maldonado via Pilcopata and Itahuania

$ Hospedaje Manu
Boca Colorado, on street beside football field.
Cell-like rooms, open windows and ceilings but comfy mattresses and mosquito netting.

$ Sra Rubella in Pilcopata.
Very basic but friendly.

$ Yine Lodge
Next to Boca Manu airport.
A cooperative project run between **Pantiacolla Tours** and the Yine community of Diamante, who operate their own tours into their community and surroundings. Also **$ Hostal** in Boca Manu run by the community. Basic accommodation.

Cuzco to Puerto Maldonado

Accommodation is available in Quincemil at $ **Hotel Toni**, friendly, clean, cold shower, good meals. There are more options in Mazuko; $ **Hostal Valle Sagrado** is the best.

Puerto Maldonado

New hotels catering for business travellers are springing up.

$$$ Don Carlos
Av León Velarde 1271, T082-571029,
www.hotelesdoncarlos.com.
Nice view over the Río Tambopata, a/c, restaurant, airport transfers, good.

$$$ Wasaí Lodge & Expeditions
Plaza Grau 1, T082-572290,
www.wasai.com.
In a beautiful location overlooking the Madre de Dios, with forest surrounding cabin-style rooms, shower, small pool with waterfall, good restaurant (local fish a speciality). They can organize local tours and also have a lodge on the Río Tambopata (see page 339).

$$$-$$ Cabañaquinta
Cuzco 535, T082-571045,
www.hotelcabanaquinta.com.
A/c or fan, frigobar, laundry, free drinking water, good restaurant, lovely garden, very comfortable, airport transfer. Request a room away from the Interoceanic Highway.

$$ Anaconda Lodge
600 m from airport, T982-611039,
www.anacondajunglelodge.com.
With private or shared bath, Swiss/Thai-owned bungalows, hot showers, swimming pool, Thai restaurant or Peruvian food and pizza if you prefer, tours arranged, has space for camping, very pleasant, family atmosphere.

$$ Paititi Hostal
G Prada 290 y Av León Velarde, T082-574667,
see Facebook page.
All mod-cons, executive and standard rooms. Reserve in advance.

$$ Perú Amazónico
Jr Ica 269, T082-571799,
peruamazonico@hotmail.com.
Modern, comfortable and good.

$ Amarumayo
Libertad 433, 10 mins from the centre,
T082-573860.
Comfortable, with pool and garden, good restaurant.

$ Hospedaje El Bambú
Jr Puno 837, T082-793880.
Basic and small but well-kept rooms with fan, family atmosphere, breakfast and juices not included in price but served in dining room. A good budget option.

$ Hospedaje Español
González Prada 670, T082-572381.
Comfortable, set back from the road, in a quiet part of town.

$ Tambopata Hostel
González Prado 161, T082-574201,
www.tambopatahostel.com.
The only real backpacker hostel in town, dorm beds, hammocks or camping. Nice atmosphere, they also organize local tours.

Around Puerto Maldonado

Most jungle lodges are booked as package deals for 3 days, 2 nights, or longer, with meals, transport and guides; see websites below for offers.

Lodges on the Río Madre de Dios

Casa de Hospedaje Mejía
T082-571428; contact Ceiba Tours, L Velarde 420, Puerto Maldonado, T082-573372,
turismomejia@hotmail.com.
Attractive but basic rustic lodge close to Lago Sandoval, full board can be arranged, canoes are available.

Eco Amazonia Lodge
On the Madre de Dios, 1 hr down-river from Puerto Maldonado. Office at Av 26 de Diciembre 435, T082-573491; also Enrique Palacios 292, Miraflores, Lima, T01-242 2708,

and Garcilazo 210, of 206, Cuzco, T084-236159, www.ecoamazonia.com.pe.
Basic bungalows and dormitories, good for birdwatching, has its own Monkey Island with animals taken from the forest.

El Corto Maltés
Billinghurst 229, Puerto Maldonado, T082-573831, www.cortomaltes-amazonia.com.
On the Madre de Dios, halfway to Sandoval which is the focus of most visits. Hot water, huge dining room, well run.

Estancia Bello Horizonte
20 km northeast of Puerto Maldonado, Loreto 252, T082-572748, www.estancia bellohorizonte.com.
In a nice stretch of forest overlooking the old course of the Madre de Dios, now a huge *aguajal* (swamp) populated with macaws. A small lodge with bungalows for 30 people, with private bath, hot water, pool. Transport, all meals and guide (several languages offered) included, US$220 for 3 days/2 nights. The lodge belongs to **APRONIA**, an organization that trains and provides employment for orphaned children. Suitable for those wanting to avoid a river trip.

Inkaterra Reserva Amazónica Lodge
45 mins by boat down the Madre de Dios. Contact: Inkaterra, Andalucía 174, Miraflores L18, Lima, T01-610 0400; Plaza Nazarenas 167 p 2, Cuzco T084-245314, www.inkaterra.com.
Tastefully redecorated hotel in the jungle with suites and bungalows, solar power, good food in huge dining room supported by a big tree. Jungle tours in its own 10,000 ha plus a new canopy walk; also tours to Lago Sandoval.

Sandoval Lake Lodge
1 km beyond Mejía on Lago Sandoval. Book through InkaNatura.
Usual access is by canoe after a 3-km walk or rickshaw ride, huge bar and dining area, electricity, hot water. InkaNatura also has a lodge on the Río Heath, the Heath River Wildlife Center, about 4½ hrs from Puerto Maldonado by boat, but journey times

depend on river levels. Just 10 mins from the lodge is a macaw and parrot clay lick. In the vicinity you can visit both jungle and savannah and in the latter are many endemic bird species. InkaNatura runs tours which combine both lodges.

Lodges on the Tambopata
Lodges on the Tambopata are reached by vehicle to Bahuaja port, 15 km upriver from Puerto Maldonado by the community of Infierno, then by boat. Over 15 small lodges and *casas de hospedaje* along the Tambopata river are grouped together under the names: **Tambopata Ecotourism Corridor** and **Tambopata Homestays**. See lodge websites for prices of packages offered.

Explorers Inn
58 km from Puerto Maldonado (2½ hrs up the Río Tambopata; 1½ hrs return); office at Terminal Terrestre, p2, of 111, T082-573029, www.explorersinn.com.
Just before the La Torre control post, adjoining the TNR, in the part where most research work has been done, this is one of the best places in Peru for seeing jungle birds (580 plus species have been recorded) and butterflies (1230 plus species). There are also giant river otters, but you probably need more than a 2-day tour to benefit fully from the location. Tours through the adjoining community of La Torre. The guides are biologists and naturalists undertaking research in the reserve. They provide interesting wildlife-treks, including to the macaw lick (*collpa*).

> **Tip…**
> Some of the lodges along the Tambopata river offer guiding and research placements to biology and environmental science graduates. For more details contact **TReeS**, www.tambopata.org.uk).

Posada Amazonas Lodge
1½ hrs by vehicle and boat upriver from Puerto Maldonado; book through Rainforest Expeditions, San Francisco de Paula Ugariza 813, Of 201, San Antonio-Miraflores, Lima, T01-241 4880/T01-997 903650, www.perunature.com.

A collaboration between the tour agency and the local native community of Infierno. Attractive rooms with cold showers, visits to Lake Tres Chimbadas, with good birdwatching including the Tambopata *collpa*. Offers trips to a nearby indigenous primary healthcare project where a native healer gives guided tours of the medicinal plant garden. Service and guiding is very good. The **Tambopata Research Centre**, the company's more intimate, but comfortable lodge, is about 6 hrs further upriver. Rooms are smaller than Posada Amazonas, with shared showers, cold water. The lodge is next to the famous Tambopata macaw clay lick. 2 hrs from Posada Amazonas, Rainforest Expeditions also has the **Refugio Amazonas**, close to Lago Condenados. It is the usual stopover for those visiting the *collpa*. 3 bungalows accommodate 70 people in large, kerosene-lit, en suite rooms with mosquito nets, well-designed and run, atmospheric. There are many packages at the different lodges and lots of add-ons.

Tambopata Eco Lodge
On the Río Tambopata; reservations office at Nueva Baja 432, Cuzco, T084-245695; operations office Jr Gonzales Prada 269, Puerto Maldonado, T082-571726, www.tambopatalodge.com.

Rooms with solar-heated water, good guides, excellent food. Trips go to Lake Condenado, some to Lake Sachavacayoc, and to the Collpa de Chuncho, guiding mainly in English and Spanish, naturalists programme provided.

Wasaí Lodge and Expeditions
Río Tambopata, 120 km (3 hrs by speedboat) upriver from Puerto Maldonado; contact Las Higueras 257, Residencial Monterrico, La Molina, Lima 12, T01-436 8792, or Plaza Grau 1, Puerto Maldonado, T082-572290, www.wasai.com.

Kayaking, zip-line, fishing, photography tours, mystic tours, wildlife observation, volunteering, etc. Also tours to the Colllpa de Chuncho and Lago Sandoval. Guides in English and Spanish.

Lodges on the Río Las Piedras

Amazon Rainforest Conservation Centre
Contact Pepe Moscoso, Jr Los Cedros B-17, Los Castaños, Puerto Maldonado, T082-573655.

Roughly 8 hrs upriver, overlooking a beautiful oxbow lake, Lago Soledad, which has a family of giant otters. Comfortable bungalows, with bath and hot water. Activities include a viewing platform 35 m up an ironwood tree, a hide overlooking a macaw lick, and walks on the extensive trail network. Most trips break the river journey half way at Tipishca Lodge (same website as above).

Las Piedras Biodiversity Station
T082-573922.

A small lodge in a 4000-ha concession of 'primary' rainforest 90 km up the Río Las Piedras. Visitors camp en route to the lodge. 20 beds in 10 rooms, central dining-room, shared bath, no electricity, library, guiding in English/Spanish. Minimum package is for 4 days/3 nights. Birdwatching trips cost more.

Restaurants

Puerto Maldonado

$$-$ Burgos's
26 de Diciembre 135.
Serves traditional dishes and has a good set lunch menu.

$$-$ El Hornito/Chez Maggy
On the plaza.
Cosy, good pizzas, busy at weekends.

$$-$ Kuskalla
Av 26 de Diciembre 195.
Peruvian/Brazilian fusion food with views of the Madre de Dios and Tambopata rivers.

$ D'Kaoba
Madre de Dios 439.
Serves the most delicious *pollos a la brasa* in town.

$ El Asadero
Arequipa 246, east side of Plaza.
Popular *menú* at lunchtime, great sandwiches later in the day, cool bar in the evening.

Gustitos del Cura
Loreto 258, Plaza de Armas.
Thu-Tue 0800-2300.
Ice cream and juice parlour run by the APRONIA project for homeless teenagers, offering unusual flavours.

Bars and clubs

Puerto Maldonado

Casa de la Cerveza
on the plaza adjoining El Hornito.
Nearest thing to a pub in Puerto Maldonado.

El Witite
Av León Velarde 153. Fri and Sat.
A popular disco playing latin music.

T-Saica
Loreto 335.
An atmospheric bar with live music at weekends.

What to do

Beware of pirate operators on the streets of Cuzco who offer trips to the Reserved Zone of Manu and end up halfway through the trip changing the route "due to emergencies", which, in reality means they have no permits to operate in the area. Some unscrupulous tour guides will offer trips to see the uncontacted tribes of Manu; on no account make any attempt to view these very vulnerable people.

The following companies in Cuzco organize trips into the Multiple Use and Reserved Zones. Contact them for more details.

Amazon Trails Peru, *Tandapata 660, San Blas, Cuzco, T084-437374, or T984-714148, www.amazontrailsperu.com.* Well-organized tours to the national park and Blanquillo clay lick, with knowledgeable guides, good boatmen and cooks, small groups, guaranteed departure dates. Runs 2 lodges in Manu. Also offers trekking in the Cuzco area.
Bonanza Tours, *Suecia 343, Cuzco, T084-507871, www.bonanzatoursperu.com.* 3- to 8-day tours to Manu with local guides, plenty of jungle walks, rafting, kayaking and camp-based excursions with good food. Tours are high quality and good value.
Crees Tours, *Urb Mcal Gamarra B-5, Zona 1, Cuzco, T084-262433, and 7/8 Kendrick Mews, London SW7 3HG, T+44 (0)20-7581 2932, www.crees-manu.org.* Tours from 4 days/3 nights to 9 days/8 nights to the Manu Learning Centre, a lodge accommodating 24 guests, 45 mins from Atalaya by boat. The lodge has all en suite rooms with hot showers; food is produced locally in a bio-garden. All tours spend the 1st night at the **Cock of the Rock Lodge**, on the road from Paucartambo to Atalaya. Tours are associated with the **Crees Foundation** (www.crees-foundation.org), a fully sustainable organization which works with immigrant and indigenous communities to reduce poverty and protect biodiversity in the rainforest.
Expediciones Vilca, *Plateros 359, Cuzco, T084-244751.* Offers tours at economical prices.
Greenland Peru, *Celasco Astete C-12, Cuzco, T084-246572, www.greenlandperu.com.* Fredy Domínguez is an Amazonian and offers good-value trips to Manu with comfortable accommodation and transport and excellent food cooked by his mother. Experienced, knowledgeable and enthusiastic, and he speaks English.
InkaNatura, *Ricardo Palma J1, Cuzco; also in Lima at Manuel Bañón 461, San Isidro, T01-203 5000, www.inkanatura.com.* Tours to **Manu Wildlife Centre** (see page 336) and to **Sandoval Lake Lodge** in Tambopata (see below) with emphasis on sustainable tourism

and conservation. Knowledgeable guides. They also run treks in Cuzco area.

Manu Adventures, *Plateros 356, Cuzco, T084-261640, www.manuadventures.com.* This company operates one of the most physically active Manu programmes, with options for a mountain biking descent through the cloudforest and 3 hrs of whitewater rafting on the way to **Erika Lodge** on the upper Río Madre de Dios. Jungle specialists.

Manu Expeditions and Birding Tours, *Jr Los Geranios 2-G, Urb Mariscal Gamarra, 1a Etapa, Cuzco, T084-225990, www.manuexpeditions. com.* Owned by ornithologist Barry Walker, 3 trips available to the reserve and **Manu Wildlife Center**, page 336.

Oropéndola, *Av Circunvalación s/n, Urb Guadalupe Mz A Lte 3, Cuzco, T084-241428, www.oropendolaperu.org.* Guide Walter Mancilla Huamán is an expert on flora and fauna. 5-, 7- and 9-day tours from US$800 pp plus park entrance. Good reports of attention to detail and to the needs of clients.

Pantiacolla Tours SRL, *Garcilaso 265, interior, p 2, of 12, Cuzco, T084-238323, www.pantiacolla.com.* Run by Marianne van Vlaardingen and Gustavo Moscoso. They have tours to the **Pantiacolla Lodge** (see Where to stay, page 336) and also 8-day camping trips. Pantiacolla has started a community-based ecotourism project, called the **Yine Project**, with the people of Diamante in the Multiple Use Zone.

Puerto Maldonado
Boat hire
Boat hire can be arranged through the Capitanía del Puerto (Río Madre de Dios, T082-573003).

Guides
All guides should have a carnet issued by the **Ministry of Tourism (DIRCETUR)**, which also verifies them as suitable for trips to other places and confirms their identity. Check that the carnet has not expired. Reputable guides are **Hernán Llave Cortez**, **Romel Nacimiento** and the **Mejía** brothers, all of whom can be contacted on arrival at the airport, if available. Also recommended are: **Carlos Borja Gama** (www.carlosexpeditions. com), a local guide offering specialist birdwatching and photography trips as well as traditional jungle tours; he speaks several languages; **Víctor Yohamona** (T982-686279, victorguideperu@hotmail.com) who speaks English, French and German.

Local tour operators
See **Ceiba Tours**, under **Casa de Hospedaje Mejía**, page 337.

Transport

Tour companies usually use their own vehicles for the overland trip from Cuzco to Manu, but it is possible to do it independently.

Cuzco to Manu and Puerto Maldonado via Pilcopata and Itahuania

Road and river From the Coliseo Cerrado in Cuzco 3 buses run to **Pilcopata** Mon, Wed, Fri, returning same night, US$10. They are fully booked even in low season. The best are **Gallito de las Rocas**; also **Unancha** from C Huáscar near the main plaza. Trucks to Pilcopata run on same days, returning Tue, Thu, Sat, 10 hrs in wet season, less in the dry. Only basic supplies are available after leaving Cuzco, so take all camping and food essentials, including insect repellent. Transport can be disrupted in the wet season because the road is in poor condition, although improvements are being made. A *camioneta* service between Pilcopata and **Salvación** connects with the buses, Mon, Wed, Fri. The same *camionetas* run **Itahuania–Shintuya–Salvacion** regularly, when there are sufficient passengers, usually once a day, also 2 trucks a day. On Sun, there is no traffic.

To reach **Boca Manu** you can hire a boat in Atalaya, several hundred dollars for a *peke peke*, more for a motorboat. It's cheaper to wait or hope for a boat going empty up to Boca Manu to pick up passengers, when the fare will be US$15 per passenger. Itahuania–Boca Manu in a shared boat is US$7.50; a private, chartered boat would be over US$100. From Itahuania, cargo boats leave for **Boca Colorado** on the Río Madre de Dios, via Boca Manu, but only when the boat is fully laden; about 6-8 a week, 9 hrs, US$20.

To reach Puerto Maldonado from Boca Colorado, catch a *colectivo* from near the football field for Puerto Carlos, 1 hr, US$5, for the ferry across the river, 10 mins, US$1.65; *colectivos* then run to Puerto Maldonado, 3 hrs, US$10, on a rough road until the Carretera Interoceánica; in Puerto Maldonado, contact **Turismo Boca Colorado** (Tacna 342, T082-573435).

Cuzco to Puerto Maldonado: via Urcos and Mazuko

Bus The *Interoceánica* is paved all the way. There are many daily buses, US$18-30 (*económico* or *semi-cama*), 10-11 hrs, from the Terminal Terrestre in **Cuzco** with **Transportes Iguazú** (one of the cheapest, less reliable, no toilet), **Mendivil**, **Machupicchu**, **Palomino** and **Móvil Tours** (one of the better companies, T082-795785). All are on Av Tambopata, blocks 3 and 5 in Puerto Maldonado. There are also frequent *colectivos* from Mazuko to Puerto Maldonado. Several buses also run daily along the Interoceanic Highway from Arequipa and Juliaca, crossing the altiplano and joining the Cuzco–Puerto Maldonado section at Puente Iñambari, 5 km from Mazuko. There is regular traffic from Mazuko to Puerto Maldonado, including *colectivos*, 3 hrs, US$11.

Puerto Maldonado

Air To **Lima**, daily with **LATAM** (León Velarde 503), **Avianca/TACA** (2 de Mayo 312) and **Star Perú** (León Velarde 505) via Cuzco. Mototaxi from town to airport, US$2.25, taxi US$3.50, 8 km.

Bus and boat For **Boca Manu** and **Itahuania** take a *colectivo* to **Boca Colorado** (see above) and then take a cargo boat (no fixed schedule). From Itahuania there is transport to Pilcopata and Cuzco. To **Iberia**, 2½ hrs, US$6.50, and **Iñapari**, 3½ hrs, US$8.50, daily combis from Jr Ica y Jr Piura; recommended companies are **Turismo Imperial** and **Turismo Real Dorado**. To **Juliaca**, via Mazuko, San Gabán and Macusani, US$14-27, 12 hrs, with **Santa Cruz** (T951-298980) at 0600, 1330, 1630 and 1830; **Julsa** at 1530; **Mendivil** at 1600; **Wayra** at 1700; the last 3 continue to **Arequipa**, US$21-36, 17-18 hrs. Other companies on this route are **Aguilas** and **ITSA**. For all routes, ask around the bus offices for *colectivo* minibuses.

Motorcycle hire Scooters and mopeds can be hired from **Las Anclas**, G Prado 380, T983-766618, English and German spoken. Passport and driver's licence must be shown.

This is
Bolivia

Like its luminescent sky, Bolivia remains largely unpolluted and, in an age of rampant Disneyfication, stands out for its authenticity. There are over 17 million hectares of protected natural areas, but isolation is what best protects the intense and often bizarre beauty of Bolivia's landscapes. For the same reason, the cultural integrity of its peoples remains intact. Even though Evo Morales' government is bringing municipalities closer together, paving roads and building communal facilities, it takes time and patience to travel from one place to the next.

No matter how far you travel in Bolivia, no matter how close you think you are to figuring it out, it will catch you off guard. Amazing new experiences will leave you humbled and in awe of this remarkable country. These are just a few of the author's favourites, gathered on journeys around the country: a guide playing his charango in a cathedral-like cave near Torotoro; listening to the choir practise baroque music in San José de Chiquitos; bathing in hot springs at Laguna Blanca and not wanting to get out because the air is almost zero; gliding down the river Yacuma being watched by countless caiman and cackled at by family after family of prehistoric hoatzin.

From the shores of Titicaca, the world's highest navigable lake, to the 'Lost World' table-lands of Noel Kempff Mercado National Park, following the footsteps of dinosaurs, bandits and revolutionaries, there are endless opportunities for off-the-beaten path exploration. Along the way are rest-stop cities and towns where travellers can indulge in creature comforts and recount tall tales of their adventures.

Footprint
picks

1 **La Diablada festival, Oruro**, page 396
2 **Copacabana**, page 377
3 **Coroico**, page 390
4 **Salar de Uyuni**, page 403
5 **Chiquitano missions**, page 469
6 **Madidi National Park**, page 480

BRAZIL

Assis
Brasil
Brasiléia
Cobija
Puerto
Rico
Riberalta
Guayaramerín

Puerto
Pardo
Puerto Heath

PERU

El Chorro

San Joaquín
Magdalena

*Parque
Nacional
Madidi*
Reyes

Sta Ana
de Yacuma

*Pilón Lajas
Biosphere
Reserve*

San Javier

*Parque Nacional
Noel Kempff Mercado*

Rurrenabaque
San Borja
Yucumo
San Ignacio
de Moxos

Casarebe
Perserancia

*Lake
Titicaca*
Carabuco
Guanay
Sorata
Caranavi

Trinidad
Caimanes

San
Pablo

*Baia
Grande*

Copacabana
Tiwanaku
Coroico
Chulumani

LA PAZ

Villa
Tunari

Puerto
Villarroel

San Javier

San Ignacio
de Velasco

Concepción

San Rafael

Santa Ana

San Matías

Cochabamba

*Parque
Nacional
Sajama*

Totora

*Parque
Nacional
Torotoro*

Buena
Vista

San
Ramón

San
Miguel

San José
de Chiquitos

Tambo
Quemado

Oruro

Huanuni

Aiquile

*Parque
Nacional
Amboró*

Montero

Santa Cruz
de la Sierra

Roboré

Quijarro/
Puerto
Suárez

Sacabaya
Challapata
Samaipata

*Lago
Poopó*

La Higuera

Abapó

*Parque
Nacional
Kaa-Iya*

Sabaya

Sucre

Tarabuco

Llica

Potosí

Monteagudo

Camiri

Boyuibe

*Salar de
Uyuni*
Colchane

Uyuni
Cerdas

Camargo

Hito Villazón

Villamontes

Ibibobo

PARAGUAY

Chiguana

San
Vicente

Tupiza

Tarija

Yacuiba

Pocitos

Fortín Infante
Rivarola

*Reserva Fauna Andina
Eduardo Avaroa*

*Laguna
Colorada*

Hito
Cajones

*Laguna
Verde*

Villazón

Bermejo

CHILE

ARGENTINA

N

100 km
100 miles

La Paz

Footprint picks

★ **La Diablada festival, Oruro**, page 396

Dance with the devil at Bolivia's world-renowned carnival.

★ **Copacabana**, page 377

Picturesque little town on beautiful Lake Titicaca.

★ **Coroico**, page 390

A first-class place to relax after the famous downhill ride with stunning scenery and good walks.

★ **Salar de Uyuni**, page 403

The largest and highest salt lake in the world – one of the great Bolivian trips.

★ **Chiquitano missions**, page 469

Remarkable colonial churches in a sparsely populated plain.

★ **Madidi National Park**, page 480

Possibly the world's most bio-diverse region with pristine jungle and abundant wildlife.

La Paz

The minute you arrive in La Paz, the highest seat of government in the world, you realize this is no ordinary place. El Alto airport is at a staggering 4061 m above sea level. The sight of the city, lying hundreds of metres below, at the bottom of a steep canyon and ringed by snow-peaked mountains, takes your breath away – literally – for at this altitude breathing can be a problem.

The Spaniards chose this odd place for a city on 20 October 1548, to avoid the chill winds of the plateau, and because they had found gold in the Río Choqueyapu, which runs through the canyon. The centre of the city, Plaza Murillo, is at 3636 m, about 400 m below the level of the altiplano and the sprawling city of El Alto, perched dramatically on the rim of the canyon.

Weather La Paz

January	February	March	April	May	June
15°C 4°C 137mm	15°C 4°C 83mm	15°C 3°C 82mm	15°C 2°C 32mm	15°C -2°C 8mm	14°C -4°C 10mm

July	August	September	October	November	December
14°C -4°C 6mm	15°C -3°C 30mm	16°C -1°C 28mm	16°C 2°C 40mm	17°C 2°C 50mm	16°C 4°C 77mm

Best for
Markets ▪ Museums ▪ Tours

Essential La Paz

Finding your feet

La Paz has the highest commercial **airport** in the world, high above the city at El Alto. A taxi from the airport to or from the centre takes between 30 minutes and one hour.

Orientation

The city's main street runs from **Plaza San Francisco** as Avenida Mariscal Santa Cruz, then changes to Avenida 16 de Julio (more commonly known as El Prado) and ends at **Plaza del Estudiante**. The business quarter, government offices, central university (UMSA) and many of the main hotels and restaurants are in this area. Banks and exchange houses are clustered on Calle Camacho, between Loayza and Colón, not far from **Plaza Murillo**, the traditional heart of the city. From the Plaza del Estudiante, Avenida Villazón splits into Avenida Arce, which runs southeast towards the wealthier residential districts of **Zona Sur**, in the valley, 15 minutes away; and Avenida 6 de Agosto which runs through **Sopocachi**, an area full of restaurants, bars and clubs. Zona Sur has shopping centres and some of the best restaurants and bars in La Paz (see pages 363 and 366).

Getting around

There are three main **bus terminals**: the bus station at Plaza Antofagasta, the cemetery district for Sorata, Copacabana and Tiwanaku, and Minasa bus station in Villa Fátima for the Yungas, including Coroico, and northern jungle.

A system of cable cars (*teleféricos*) is under construction. Three lines were in operation at the time of writing, the red line, between El Alto and Vita, west of the main bus station, the yellow line from Ciudad Satélite (El Alto) to Sopocachi and Obrajes, and the green line, which continues from Obrajes to Calacoto (Zona Sur). There are three types of city bus: *puma katari* (a fleet of new buses with defined stops), *micros* (small, old buses) and faster, more plentiful minibuses. *Trufis* are fixed-route collective taxis, with a sign with their route on the windscreen. Taxis come in three types: regular honest taxis, fake taxis and radio taxis, the safest, which have a dome light and number.

When to go

The weather is cool all year; locals say that the city experiences all the seasons in one day. The sun is strong, but the moment you go into the shade, the temperature falls. From December to March, the summer, it rains most afternoons, making it feel colder than it actually is. Temperatures are even lower in winter, June-August, when the sky is always clear.

It is good to visit La Paz at any time. The two most important festivals, when the city gets particularly busy, are **Alasitas** (four weeks starting 24 January) and **Festividad del Señor del Gran Poder** (end May/early June). See Festivals, page 367.

Safety

La Paz is in general a safe city, but like any metropolis it is not crime-free. Areas where you must take care are around Plaza Murillo and the Cemetery neighbourhood where local buses serve Copacabana and Tiwanaku. **Tourist police** (T222 5016) now patrol these bus stops during the daytime, but caution is still advised. Also beware of fake police who work the main bus terminal. **Warning for ATM users**: scams to get card numbers and PINs have flourished, especially in La Paz. The tourist police post warnings in hotels. See also Safety, page 727.

Time required

Two to three days to acclimatize to the altitude and see the city's highlights; one to two weeks for excursions and treks.

La Paz 1

La Paz maps
1 La Paz, page 350
2 La Paz centre, page 353
3 Sopocachi, page 355

To ① ② ⑬, Bus Station, El Alto, Airport,
Titicaca, Tiwanaku & Oruro

Plaza Riosinio
Museo Costumbrista
& other museums

Museo de Instrementos Musicales

Teatro Municipal

Where to stay 🛏
1 Adventure Brew B&B *A2*
2 Adventure Brew
  Hostel *A2*
3 Arthy's Guesthouse *A2*
4 Bacoo *A3*
5 Casa Prado *C4*
6 El Rey Palace *D4*
7 Estrella Andina *B2*
8 Europa *C4*
9 Hostal República *B4*
10 La Joya *B1*
11 Onkel Inn 1886 *C3*
12 Rosario & Tambo
   Colonial Restaurant *B2*
13 Tambo de Oro *A3*
14 Wild Rover
   Backpackers Hostel *B4*

🚠 Teleférico station

Restaurants 🍴
1 Alexander Coffee *C4*
2 Café Urbano *C4*
4 Ken-Chan *D4*
5 Paladar *C6*
6 Potokos *A6*
7 Vienna *D4*
8 Wist'u Piku *D4*

Bars & clubs 🍸
9 Etno Café *A3*

N

100 metres
100 yards

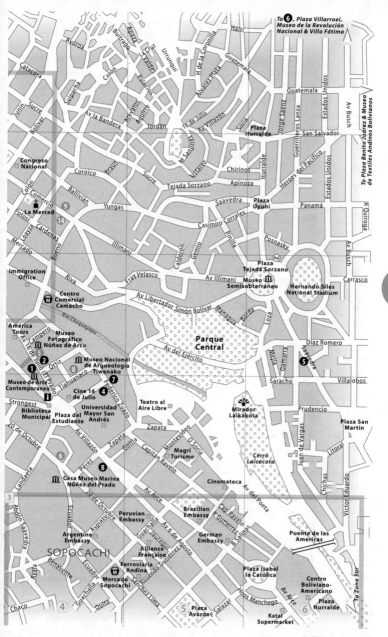

To 6, Plaza Villarroel,
Museo de la Revolución
Nacional & Villa Fátima

To Plaza Benito Juárez & Museo
de Textiles Andinos Bolivianos

Haití

Ayaroa
Bullrain
La Paz
Cruz
Plaza
Urrunqui
H. de la Cornilla
Guatemala

Catacora
Colón
Palacios
Alvarez Plata
Guatemala

Junín
Suipacha
Ant. Ferreros
Aguirre
16 de Julio
Sota
Jorge Sáenz
Guerrilleros Lanza
San Salvador
Estados Unidos
Av Busch

Sucre
Av la Bandera
Jordán
M. Santinez
Av Villazón
Plaza
Iturralde
Heroes del Pacífico
Estados Unidos

Bolívar
Chirinos
Iturralde

Congreso
Nacional
Coroico
Braud
Sucre
Tejada Sorzano
Apinoza
Saavedra
Plaza
Uyuni
Panamá

Colón
Comercio
Ballivián
Yungas
Casimiro Corrales
Pinilla
Posnasky
R Quiroga
Av Busch

La Merced
Potosí
Loayza
Cárdenas
Illimani
Gemio
Plaza
Tejada Sorzano
Carrasco

Mercado
Bueno
Riva
Fray Velasco
Av Illimani
Museo
Semisubterráneo
Hernando Siles
National Stadium
Díaz Romero

Immigration
Office
Centro
Comercial
Camacho
Av Libertador Simón Bolívar
Managua
Borda
Loza

América
Tours
Av 16 de Julio
El Prado
Campero
Río Choqueyapu
Parqué
Central
Av del Ejército
Melía
Guarani
Saavedra
Villalobos

Museo
Fotográfico
Núñez de Arco
Ortiz
Tiahuanaco
Museo Nacional
de Arqueología
Tiwanaku
Av del Poeta
Saracho
Prudencio

Museo de Arte
Contemporáneo
Federico Zuazo
Cine 16
de Julio
Teatro al
Aire Libre
Mirador
Laikakota
Plaza San
Martín

Strongest
Biblioteca
Municipal
Plaza del
Estudiante
Universidad
Mayor San
Andrés
Zapata
Montevideo
O'Sofia
Cerro
Laicacota
Juan de Vargas
Chichas
Litoral

20 de Octubre
Av Villazón
Goitia
Capitán Ravelo
Zapata

Landaeta
Pérez
Av Arce
Magri
Turismo
Cinemateca
Av del Poeta

Casa Museo Marina
Núñez del Prado
20 de Octubre
Av 6 de Agosto
Brazilian
Embassy
Cap Ravelo
F Gutiérrez
Puente de las
Americas
Victor Eduardo

Peruvian
Embassy
Guachalla
Tumusla
German
Embassy
B Salinas

Argentine
Embassy
Ricardo
Aspiazu
Alliance
Française
Rosendo Gutiérrez

SOPOCACHI
Ecuador
Guachalla
Quiro
Ferroviaria
Andina
Mercado
Sopocachi
Sánchez Lima
Plaza Isabel
la Católica
Av Arce
Centro
Boliviano-
Americano
Plaza
Iturralde

Chaco
Abdón Saavedra
Ávila
Benavente
Plaza
Avaroa
Salazar
Hnos Manchego
Ketal
Supermarket
To Zona Sur

the centre has lively markets and some worthwhile museums

There are few colonial buildings left in La Paz; probably the best examples are in Calle Jaén (see below). Late 19th- and early 20th-century architecture, often displaying European influence, can be found in the streets around Plaza Murillo, but much of La Paz is modern. The Plaza del Estudiante (Plaza Franz Tamayo), or a bit above it, marks a contrast between old and new styles, between the commercial and the more elegant. El Prado itself is lined with high-rise blocks dating from the 1960s and 1970s.

Around Plaza Murillo

Plaza Murillo Three blocks north of El Prado, this is the traditional centre. Facing its formal gardens are the **Cathedral**, the **Palacio Presidencial** in Italian Renaissance style, known as the **Palacio Quemado** (burnt palace) twice gutted by fire in its stormy 130-year history, and, on the east side, the **Congreso Nacional**. In front of the Palacio Quemado is a statue of former President Gualberto Villarroel who was dragged into the plaza by a mob and hanged in 1946. Across from the Cathedral on Calle Socabaya is the **Palacio de los Condes de Arana** (built 1775), with beautiful exterior and patio. It houses the **Museo Nacional de Arte** ⓘ *T02-240 8600, www.mna.org.bo, Tue-Fri 0930-1230, 1500-1900, Sat 1000-1730, Sun 1000-1330, US$2.15.* It has a fine collection of colonial paintings including many works by Melchor Pérez Holguín, considered one of the masters of Andean colonial art, and which also exhibits the works of contemporary local artists. Calle Comercio, running east-west across the Plaza, has most of the stores and shops. West of Plaza Murillo, at Ingavi 916, in the palace of the Marqueses de Villaverde is the **Museo Nacional de Etnografía y Folklore** ⓘ *T02-240 8640, www.musef.org.bo, Mon-Fri 0900-1230, 1500-1900, Sat 0900-1630, Sun 0900-1430, US$3, filming costs US$6.* Various sections show the cultural richness of Bolivia by region through textiles and other items. It has a videoteca.

Calle Jaén Northwest of Plaza Murillo is Calle Jaén, a picturesque colonial street with a café, craft shops, good views and four museums (known as **Museos Municipales** ⓘ *Tue-Fri 0930-1230, 1500-1900, Sat 1000-1700, Sun 0900-1330, US$1.50 each*), housed in colonial buildings. **Museo Costumbrista Juan de Vargas** ⓘ *on Plaza Riosinio, at the top of Jaén, T02-228 0758, US$0.60,* has miniature displays depicting incidents in the history of La Paz and well-known Paceños, as well as miniature replicas of reed rafts used by the Norwegian Thor Heyerdahl, and the Spaniard Kitin Muñoz, to prove their theories of ancient migrations. **Museo del Litoral Boliviano** ⓘ *T02-228 0758,* has artefacts of the War of the Pacific, and interesting selection of old maps. **Museo de Metales Preciosos** ⓘ *T02-228 0329,* is well set out with Inca gold artefacts in basement vaults, also ceramics and archaeological exhibits, and **Museo Casa Murillo** ⓘ *T02-228 0553,* the erstwhile home of Pedro Domingo Murillo, one of the martyrs of the La Paz independence movement of 16 July 1809, has a good collection of paintings, furniture and national costumes. In addition to the Museos Municipales and also in a colonial house is the **Museo de Instrumentos Musicales** ⓘ *C Jaén 711 e Indaburo, T02-240 8177, Tue-Fri 0930-1230, 1500-1900; Sat-Sun*

Tip...

Travellers arriving in La Paz, especially when flying directly from sea level, may experience mild altitude sickness. If your symptoms are severe, consult a physician. See Health, page 720.

1000-1300 US$1.40, founded by Ernesto Cavour and based on 30 years of research. The International Charango Association is based here and lessons are available.

Museo Tambo Quirquincho ⓘ *C Evaristo Valle, south of Jaén, Plaza Alonso de Mendoza, T02-239 0969, Tue-Fri, 0930-1230, 1500-1900, Sat-Sun, 0900-1300, US$1.20*, displays modern

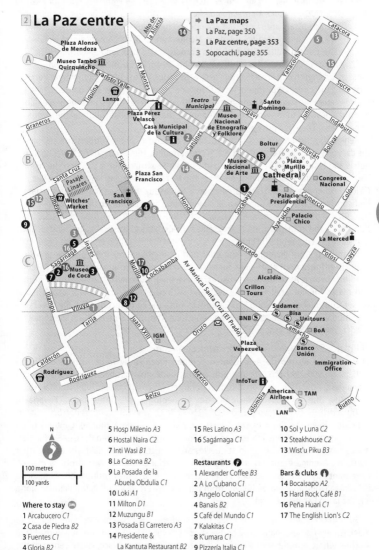

La Paz centre

➡ **La Paz maps**
1 La Paz, page 350
2 La Paz centre, page 353
3 Sopocachi, page 355

N

| 100 metres |
| 100 yards |

painting and sculpture, carnival masks, silver, early 20th-century photography and city plans, and is recommended.

Plaza San Francisco up to the cemetery district

☆**Church and monastery of San Francisco** ⓘ *Plaza San Francisco, open for Mass at 0700, 0900, 1100 and 1900, Mon-Sat, and also at 0800, 1000 and 1200 on Sun.* At the upper end of Avenida Mcal Santa Cruz, this church and monastery, dating from 1549, is one of the finest examples of colonial religious architecture in South America and well worth seeing. The **Centro Cultural Museo San Francisco** ⓘ *Plaza San Francisco 503, T02-231 8472, Mon-Sat 0900-1800, US$2.80, allow 1½-2 hrs, free guides available but tip appreciated, some speak English and French*, offers access to various areas of the church and convent including the choir, crypt (open 1400-1730), roof, various chapels and gardens. Fine art includes religious paintings from the 17th, 18th and 19th centuries, plus visiting exhibits and a hall devoted to the works of Tito Yupanqui, the indigenous sculptor of the Virgen de Copacabana. There is a pricey but good café at entrance.

Behind the San Francisco church a network of narrow cobbled streets rise steeply up the canyon walls. Much of this area is a ☆**street market**. Handicraft shops, travel agencies, hotels and restaurants line the lower part of **Calle Sagárnaga** (here you find the highest concentration of tourists and pick-pockets). The **Mercado de Brujas**, 'witchcraft market', on Calles Melchor Jiménez and Linares, which cross Santa Cruz above San Francisco, sells charms, herbs and more gruesome items like llama foetuses. The small **Museo de la Coca** ⓘ *Linares 906, T02-231 1998, www.cocamuseum.com, Mon-Sat 1000-1900, Sun 1000-1600, US$2.15*, is devoted to the coca plant, its history, cultural significance, medical values and political implications. A guidebook in English is available and there's a shop selling coca products.

Further up, from Illampu to Rodríguez and in neighbouring streets, is the produce-based **Rodríguez market** ⓘ *daily, but best on Sun morning*. Turning right on Max Paredes, heading north, is **Avenida Buenos Aires**, where small workshops turn out the costumes and masks for the Gran Poder festival, and with great views of Illimani, especially at sunset. Continuing west along Max Paredes towards the **cemetery district**, the streets are crammed with stalls selling every imaginable item. Transport converges on the cemetery district. See also Safety, page 727.

El Prado, Sopocachi, Miraflores and Zona Sur

El Prado The **Museo de Arte Contemporáneo Plaza** ⓘ *Av 16 de Julio 1698, T02-233 5905, daily 0900-2100, US$2.20*, in a 19th-century house that has been declared a national monument, exhibits a selection of contemporary art from national and international artists.

Nearby, the ☆**Museo Nacional de Arqueología** or **Tiahuanaco (Tiwanaku)** ⓘ *Tiwanacu 93 entre Bravo y F Zuazo, T02-233 1633, www.minculturas.gob.bo*, just off El Prado (down the flight of stairs near the Maria Auxiliadora church), contains good collections of the arts and crafts of ancient Tiwanaku and items from the eastern jungles. It also has an exhibition of gold statuettes and objects found in Lake Titicaca. Further north, on Avenida Camacho, is the **Centro Comercial Camacho**, with produce market, restaurants, gym and an area for entertainment. To the east, the continuation of Camacho is Avenida Libertador Simón Bolívar, from where there are views of Mount Illimani; along it is the large **Parque Central**.

☆**Sopocachi** To the south of Plaza del Estudiante, Sopocachi is a combination of older stately homes (many now house shops or offices) and high-rise buildings. **Plaza Avaroa**, where a number of the city's cultural activities take place, is the centre of the neighbourhood. Uphill from Plaza Avaroa is the smaller **Plaza España**, near which is a station on the yellow line of the ☆ **Teleférico**, and next to it **El Montículo**, a lovely park with more great views of the city. From Plaza España, Avenida Ecuador leads north towards San Pedro and downtown. Along it is the **Casa Museo Marina Núñez del Prado** ① *Ecuador 2034, T02-242 4175, www.bolivian.com/cmnp, daily 0930-1300, Tue-Fri 1500-1900 (may be closed afternoons and weekends), US$0.75, students US$0.30*, which houses an excellent collection of Marina Núñez's sculptures in the family mansion.

Miraflores Downhill from Plaza Avaroa along Calle Pedro Salazar, at the intersection with Avenida Arce, is **Plaza Isabel La Católica**. Avenida Arce leads to the Zona Sur, the continuation of Salazar leads to Miraflores via the **Puente de las Américas**, which offers more excellent views of Illimani.

In the residential district of Miraflores, east of the centre, on Plaza Tejada Sorzano, outside the Hernán Siles national football stadium is the **Museo Semisubterráneo**,

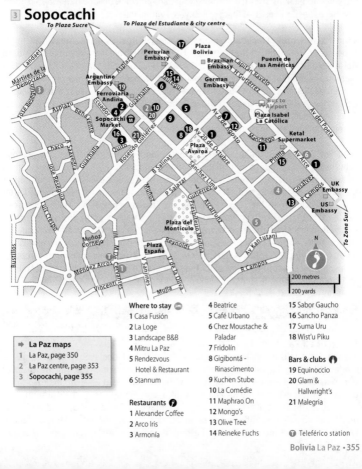

3 Sopocachi

Where to stay 😴
1 Casa Fusión
2 La Loge
3 Landscape B&B
4 Mitru La Paz
5 Rendezvous Hotel & Restaurant
6 Stannum

➡ La Paz maps
1 La Paz, page 350
2 La Paz centre, page 353
3 Sopocachi, page 355

Restaurants 🍴
1 Alexander Coffee
2 Arco Iris
3 Armonía
4 Beatrice
5 Café Urbano
6 Chez Moustache & Paladar
7 Fridolín
8 Gigibontá - Rinascimento
9 Kuchen Stube
10 La Comédie
11 Maphrao On
12 Mongo's
13 Olive Tree
14 Reineke Fuchs
15 Sabor Gaucho
16 Sancho Panza
17 Suma Uru
18 Wist'u Piku

Bars & clubs 🍸
19 Equinoccio
20 Glam & Hallwright's
21 Malegria

🚡 Teleférico station

ON THE ROAD

Tiny treats

One of the most intriguing items for sale in Andean markets is Ekeko, the god of good fortune and plenty and one of the most endearing of the Aymara folk legends. He is a cheery, avuncular little chap, with a happy face, a pot belly and short legs. His image, usually in plaster of Paris, is laden with various household items, as well as sweets, confetti and streamers, food, and with a cigarette dangling cheekily from his lower lip. Believers say that these statues only bring luck if they are received as gifts. The Ekeko occupies a central role in the festival of Alasitas, the Feast of Plenty, which takes place in La Paz or a month starting 24 January. Everything under the sun can be bought in miniature: houses, trucks, buses, suitcases, university diplomas; you name it, you'll find it here. The idea is to have your mini-purchase blessed by a *yatiri*, an Aymara priest, and the real thing will be yours within the year.

a sunken garden full of replicas of statues and artefacts from Tiwanaku, but difficult to get to because of the traffic. At the north end of Avenida Busch are Plaza Villarroel and **Museo del la Revolución Nacional** ① *Tue-Fri 0930-1200, 1500-1800, Sat-Sun 1000-1200, US$0.15*, a memorial of the 1952 revolution and a mausoleum with tombs of former presidents. East of Avenida Busch, on Calles Cuba and Guatemala, are Plaza Benito Juárez and the **Museo de Textiles Andinos Bolivianos** ① *Plaza Benito Juárez 488, T02-224 3601, Mon-Sat 0930-1200, 1500-1800, Sun 1000-1230, US$1.25*, with good displays of textiles from around the country, detailed explanations and a knowledgeable owner.

Zona Sur The Zona Sur, in the valley 15 minutes south of the city, includes the wealthier suburbs of La Paz. Home to some of the diplomatic and expat community, it has shopping centres, supermarkets stocked with imported items, a few exclusive hotels, and some of the smartest restaurants and bars of the city. **Obrajes** is the first suburb reached after a steep descent from the city; here is the link station between the yellow andgreen Teleférico lines. The green line ends in the district of **Calacoto**, at the entrance to **Irpavi**. Nearby is **Megacenter**, the largest shopping centre in the city, with cinema, restaurants, pubs, bowling and ice skating. The Zona Sur is also reached from the centre on any minibus (US$0.40) or *trufi* (US$0.50) marked Calacoto, San Miguel, Achumani or Chasquipampa.

Just before Calacoto the road splits, the right branch leads to the districts of **Mallasa** and **Río Abajo**, favourite spots for weekend outings among *paceños*, see below.

Excursions from La Paz

day trips, and treks once you've acclimatized

South of La Paz

Beyond Calacoto is the **Valle de la Luna**, or 'Valley of the Moon' (US$7), with impressive eroded hills; the climate in this valley is always much warmer than in the city. For transport details see page 374. About 3 km from the bridge at Calacoto the road forks, get out of the minibus at the turning and walk a few minutes east to the Valle entrance, or get out at the football field which is by the entrance. Take good shoes and water, but do not go alone, armed robbery has occurred. Just past the Valle de la Luna is **Mallasa** where horses and motorcycles can be rented and there are several small roadside restaurants and cafés and the **Hotel Oberland** (see page 362). To the south of the city are dry hills of many colours, topped by the **Muela del Diablo**, a striking outcrop reached through El Pedregal neighbourbood (take minibus 288); **Gravity Bolivia** (see page 370) offers cycling tours here.

El Alto

Sprawled around the rim of the canyon is El Alto, Bolivia's second-largest city (after Santa Cruz, La Paz is third). Its population (848,840) is mostly indigenous migrants from the countryside and its economic and political influence has grown rapidly. Of interest in El Alto are 'cholets' or 'nueva arquitectura andina', glitzy and colourful mansions of the new rich; a blend of modern architecture and traditional Aymara styles. See Shopping, Markets, below, for details of the ☆**Feria 16 de Julio**, the largest market in the department of La Paz.

El Alto is connected to La Paz by the ☆**Teleférico** and by a motorway (toll US$0.25) as well as by a road to Obrajes and the Zona Sur. Minibuses from Plaza Eguino leave regularly for Plaza 16 de Julio, El Alto; more leave from Plaza Pérez Velasco for La Ceja, the edge of El Alto. Intercity buses to and from La Paz always stop at El Alto in an area called Terminal, off Avenida 6 de Marzo, where transport companies have small offices. If not staying in La Paz, you can change buses here and save a couple of hours. If going to La Paz terminal, this can be a slow business as bags and boxes are unloaded in El Alto. There is accommodation nearby, but the area is not safe, especially at night. See Transport, page 374, for full details.

Trekking and climbing near La Paz

Three so-called 'Inca Trails' link the altiplano with the Yungas, taking you from the high Andes to the subtropics, with dramatic changes in weather, temperature and vegetation. Each has excellent sections of stonework and they vary in difficulty from relatively straightforward to quite hard-going. In the rainy season going can be particularly tough. For details of how to reach the starting point of each trail, see Transport sections on page 374.

Takesi Trail Start at **Ventilla**, walk up the valley for about three hours passing the village of **Choquekhota** until the track crosses the river and to the right of the road, there is a falling-down brick wall with a map painted on it. The Takesi and **Alto Takesi** trails start here, following the path to the right of the wall. The road continues to Mina San Francisco. In the first hour's climb from the wall is excellent stone paving which is Inca or pre-Inca, depending on who you believe, either side of the pass at 4630 m. There are camping possibilities at **Estancia Takesi** and near the village of **Kakapi** where there is an *albergue*. Be prepared for bridges to be washed away periodically. You also have to pass the unpleasant mining settlement of **Chojlla**. Between Chojlla and Yanacachi is a gate where it is necessary to register and often pay a small 'fee'. **Yanacachi** has a couple of places to stay, several good hikes and an orphanage you can help at. The **Fundación Pueblo** ⓘ *on the plaza, T02-212 4413, www.fundacionpueblo.org*, has information; they organize clean-ups of the trail each year. Buy a minibus ticket on arrival in Yanacachi or walk 45 minutes down to the La Paz–Chulumani road for transport.

The trek can be done in one long day, especially if you organize a jeep to the start of the trail, but is more relaxing in two or three days. If you take it slowly, though, you'll have to carry camping kit. Hire mules in Choquekhota for US$10 per day plus up to US$10 for the muleteer.

A two- to three-day alternative is from Mina San Francisco to El Castillo and the village of Chaco on the La Paz–Chulumani road. This trek is called **La Reconquistada** and has the distinction of including a 200-m disused mining tunnel (torch essential).

Choro Trail (La Cumbre to Coroico) Immediately before the road drops down from La Cumbre to start the descent to Las Yungas, there is a good dirt road leading up to the *apacheta* (narrow pass) where the trail starts properly. Cloud and bad weather are normal at La Cumbre (4660 m): you have to sign in at the Guardaparque post on the way to the pass. The trail passes **Samaña Pampa** (small shop, sign in again, camping), **Chucura** (pay US$1.50 fee, another shop, camping), **Challapampa** (camping possible, US$1.20, small shop), the **Choro bridge** and the **Río Jacun-Manini** (fill up with water at both river crossings). At **Sandillani** is a lodge ($$-$). There is good paving down to **Villa Esmeralda**, after which is **Chairo** (lodging and camping), then to **Yolosa**. It takes three days to trek from La Cumbre to Chairo, from where you can take a truck to Puente Yolosita, the turn-off for Cocoico on the new road. From Puente Yolosita trucks run uphill to Coroico when they fill, US$0.80, 15 minutes.

Huayna Potosí Huayna Potosí (6088 m) is normally climbed in two days, with one night in a basic shelter at 5300 m or camped on a glacier at 5600 m. Acclimatization and experience on ice are essential, and the mountain is dangerous out of season. There are four shelters: a community-run shelter 10 minutes up from the pass, one by the lake, very cold; **Refugio Huayna Potosí** at 4780 m, with toilets and shower, run by the tour operator of the same name, and a basic shelter at 5300 m owned by the same operator. Average cost is US$185 per person for a two-day tour for three people including all equipment except sleeping bag; US$215 for three days. Private three-day tours run about US$100 more. **Refugio Huayna Potosí** charges US$150 for two days, US$170 for three days with exclusive use of its base camp. Park entrance fee of US$2.10 is not included. The starting point for the normal route is at **Zongo**. See Climbing, hiking and trekking, page 368, for tour operators.

Listings La Paz *maps pages 350, 353 and 355.*

Tourist information

Gobierno Municipal de La Paz (www. lapaz.bo) has information centres at:

Plaza del Estudiante
Lower end of El Prado between 16 de Julio and México, T02-237 1044. Mon-Fri 0830-1200, 1430-1830.
Very helpful, English and French spoken.

El Prado InfoTur
Mariscal Santa Cruz y Colombia, T02-265 1677, Facebook: LaPazMaravillosa. Mon-Fri 0830-1230, 1430-1830, Sat-Sun 0930-1300.

Bus terminal
T228 5858. Mon-Fri 0830-1200, 1430-1900, Sat-Sun 1000-1400, holidays 0800-1200, 1600-2000.

Plaza Pérez Velasco
Opposite San Francisco, under the pedestrian walkway. Mon-Fri 0830-1200, 1430-1900.

Tomás Katari
Av Bautista y José María Aliaga, by the cemetery. Mon-Fri 0900-1700, Sat-Sun 1000-1800.
Specifically for tourists going to and from Tiwanaku and Titicaca, has luggage store. They also have information booths at the Plaza Alonso de Mendoza, Angelo Colonial on C Linares, at the Casa de la Cultura and Parque Metropolitano Laikacota.

See also www.turismolapaz.com and http://lapaz.metro-blog.com. For news and information pick up a copy of the free *Bolivian Express* magazine, www. bolivianexpress.org.

Boltur (Boliviano de Turismo)
Plaza Murillo 551, T2-218 5999 and 9011 05296, www.boltur.gob.bo. Mon-Fri 0830-1230, 1430-1830, Sat 1000-1200.
State tourism agency, offering a limited number of tours throughout the country.

Tourist Police
Plaza Stadium, Edif Olimpya, Miraflores, next to Love City Chinese restaurant, T800-140081. Mon-Fri 0830-1800, Sat 0830-1200.
For police report for insurance claims after theft. Officers are on call for emergencies outside office hours.

El Alto

Unidad de Turismo
Av Bolivia, C 1, Plaza de la Cruz (also at arrivals in airport and at El Alto bus terminal area), T02-283 3341. Mon-Fri 0800-1200, 1400-1800.

Where to stay

Around Plaza Murillo

$$$$ Presidente
Potosí 920 y Sanjines, T02-240 6666, www.hotelpresidente.com.bo.
The "highest 5-star in the world". Excellent service, comfortable, heating, 2 good restaurants, gym and sauna, pool, all open to non-residents, bar. See also **Urban Rush**, under What to do, page 371.

$$$ Casa de Piedra
Sanjinés 451, T02-290 6674, http://casadepiedrahb.com.
In a historic *posada* in the centre, wooden floors, beautiful ceilings above the inner balcony, objets d'art, 16 rooms with heating and all facilities, includes buffet breakfast, restaurant open 0700-2300, airport transfers extra.

$$$ Gloria
Potosí 909, T02-240 7070, www.hotelgloria.com.bo.
Modern rooms and suites, good central location, includes buffet breakfast, good service, runs **Gloria Tours** (www.gloriatours. com.bo) and also owns **Gloria hotels in Coroico, Copacabana and Urmiri** (resort 2 hrs from La Paz). Recommended.

$$-$ Hostal República
Comercio 1455, T02-220 2742, www.hostalrepublica.com.

Old house of former president, with and without bath, also apartment for 5, good café, quiet garden, book ahead and ask for room on upper floor.

$$-$ Residencial Latino
Junín 857, T02-228 5463, www.residenciallatino.com.
Centrally located hotel, simple rooms with private bath, those with shared bath have no TV, basic breakfast included, heating, book exchange.

$ Adventure Brew Bed & Breakfast
Av Montes 533, T02-291 5896, www.theadventurebrewhostel.com.
Mostly private rooms with bath, cheaper in dorms for 4 or 8, includes buffet breakfast, use of kitchen, 1 free beer from microbrewery every night, rooftop bar with great views and spa, nightly BBQs, good value, popular meeting place.

$ Adventure Brew Hostel
Av Montes 503, T02-291 5896, www.theadventurebrewhostel.com.
More economical than the B&B above, 8-bed dorm with bath and 8- to 20-bed dorms with shared hot showers, includes buffet breakfast and a free beer every night, rooftop terrace with great views of the city and Illimani, basement bar, pool table, travel agency and bank, lively young crowd, convenient to the bus station, associated with **Gravity Bolivia** (see What to do, page 370).

$ Arthy's Guesthouse
Montes 693, T02-228 1439, http://arthyshouse.tripod.com.
Shared bath, warm water, safe, no breakfast, helpful, popular with bikers, English spoken, 2400 curfew.

$ Bacoo
Calle Alto de la Alianza 693, T02-228 0679, www.bacoohostel.com.
Some rooms with private bath, cheaper in 6- to 18-bed dorms, restaurant and bar, garden, ping-pong and pool, arrange tours.

$ Hospedaje Milenio
Yanacocha 860, T02-228 1263,
www.hospedajemilenio.blogspot.com.
Economical, shared bath, electric shower,
basic, family house, homely and welcoming,
popular, helpful owner, quiet, kitchen,
breakfast extra, security boxes, great value.

$ Loki
Av América 120, esq Plaza Alonso de
Mendoza, T245 7300, www.lokihostel.com.
Members of a chain of popular party hostels.
Private double rooms and 4- to 10-bed
dorms, TV room, computer room, bar
(meals available), tour operator.

$ Posada El Carretero
Catacora 1056, entre Yanacocha y Junín,
T228 5271, El-Carretero on Facebook.
Very economical single and double rooms
(cheaper with shared bath), also dorms,
hot showers, kitchen facilities, terrace,
helpful staff, good atmosphere and value.

$ Tambo de Oro
Armentia 367, T02-228 1565.
Near bus station, private or shared bath,
hot showers, good value if a bit run down,
safe for luggage.

$ Wild Rover Backpackers Hostel
Comercio 1476, T02-211 6903,
http://wildroverhostels.com.
Party chain hostel in renovated colonial-style
house with courtyard and high-ceilings,
dorms with 4-10 beds with shared bath,
Irish bar, TV room, book exchange, breakfast
included, other meals available, helpful staff
speak English.

Plaza San Francisco up to the cemetery district

$$$$-$$$ La Casona
Av Mcal Santa Cruz 938, T02-290 0505,
www.lacasonahotelboutique.com.
Boutique hotel in beautifully restored former
San Francisco convent dating to 1860, nice
rooms (those in front get street noise), suites
have jacuzzi, includes buffet breakfast (0700-

1000 or continental breakfast 0300-0700)
and some museum entry fees, heating, safe
box, terrace and cupola with nice views, very
good restaurant.

$$$ Rosario
Illampu 704, T02-245 1658,
www.gruporosario.com.
Tasteful rooms, buffet breakfast included,
good restaurant also serves dinner, stores
luggage, no smoking, very helpful staff.
Highly recommended. **Turisbus** travel agency
downstairs (see Tour operators, page 371),
Cultural Interpretation Centre explains
items for sale in nearby 'witches' market'.

$$ Estrella Andina
Illampu 716, T02-245 6421,
juapame_2000@hotmail.com.
Cheaper in low season, all rooms have a
safe and are decorated individually, includes
buffet breakfast, English spoken, family-run,
comfortable, tidy, helpful, roof terrace, game
room, pool table, computer room, heaters,
money exchange, very nice. Also owns **$ Cruz
de los Andes** (Aroma 216, T02-245 1401), same
style but shares premises with a car garage.

$$ Hostal Naira
Sagárnaga 161, T02-235 5645,
www.hostalnaira.com.
Comfortable but pricey, rooms around
courtyard, some are dark, price includes
good buffet breakfast in **Café Banais**,
restaurant, safety deposit boxes.

$$ La Posada de la Abuela Obdulia
C Linares 947, T02-233 2285,
http://hostalabuelaposada.com.
Very pleasant inn, rooms for 2-4 people
around a courtyard in an early 20th-century
building, café, computer room, terrace with
city view.

$$ Milton
Illampu 1126-1130, T02-236 8003,
www.hotelmiltonbolivia.com.
Popular hotel with psychedelic 1970s-style
wallpaper in many rooms, restaurant,
excellent views from roof.

$$-$ Onkel Inn 1886
Colombia 257, T02-249 0456,
www.onkelinn.com.
Hostel in a remodelled 19th-century house,
private rooms and 6- to 9-bed dorms, all
with private bath. Jacuzzi, laundry facilities,
café and bar, pool table, computer room.
HI affiliated. Also in Copacabana.

$$-$ Sagárnaga
Sagárnaga 326, T02-235 0252,
www.hotel-sagarnaga.com.
Rooms on the ground floor with smaller beds
are cheaper, solar hot water, includes buffet
breakfast, 2 ATMs, English spoken, *peña*,
popular with tour groups, helpful owner.

$ Arcabucero
C Viluyo 307 y Linares, T02-231 3473,
arcabucero-bolivia@hotmail.com.
Price rises in high season, pleasant new
rooms in converted colonial house, excellent
value but check the beds, breakfast extra,
kitchen facilities.

$ Fuentes
Linares 888, T02-231 3966,
www.hotelfuentes.com.bo.
Private or shared bath, hot water, variety
of rooms and prices, nice colonial style,
comfortable, includes simple breakfast,
sauna, good value, family-run.

$ Inti Wasi
Murillo 776, T02-236 7963,
intiwasi.bolivia@gmail.com.
Central economical hostel, private rooms and
4-bed dorms all with shared bath, kitchen
facilities, terrace, medical services, taxi and
travel agency, good value, gets crowded.

$ La Joya
Max Paredes 541, T02-245 3841,
www.hotelajoya.com.
Modern and comfy, private or shared bath and
4-bed dorm, includes simple breakfast, lift,
area unsafe at night but provides transfers.

$ Muzungu Hostel
Illampu 441, T02-2451640,
muzunguhostel@hotmail.com.
Rooms with 1-4 beds, with and without
bath and cheaper rate for dorms, several
common areas, good restaurant (closed
Sun) and bar, breakfast and 1 drink per day
included, ping pong table.

El Prado, Sopocachi, Miraflores and Zona Sur

$$$$ Casa Grande
Av Ballivián 1000 y C 17, T02-279 5511, and
C 16 8009, T02-277 4000, both in Calacoto,
www.casa-grande.com.bo.
Beautiful, top-quality suites, those on C 16
are under a greenhouse dome, buffet
breakfast, business centre, gym, pool and spa,
airport transfers at night only, restaurants,
ice cream parlour, very good service.

$$$$ Europa
Tiahuanacu 64, T02-231 5656,
www.hoteleuropa.com.bo.
Next to the Museo Nacional de Arqueología.
Excellent facilities and plenty of frills,
health club, several restaurants, parking.
Recommended.

$$$$ Stannum
Av Arce 2631, Torre Multicine, p 12,
T02-214 8393, www.stannumhotels.com.
Boutique hotel on the 12th floor of an office
building with lovely views of Illimani and
the city, above mall and cinema complex.
Comfortable rooms with minimalist decor,
includes breakfast, bathtub, heating, a/c,
fridge, restaurant, bar, business centre, gym,
spa, airport transfers, no smoking anywhere
on the premises.

$$$ Casa Fusión
Miguel de Cervantes 2725, Sopocachi,
T02-214 0933, www.casafusion.com.bo.
Lovely hotel with modern comfortable
rooms, predominantly white, good
fittings, includes buffet breakfast, heating,
meeting room, cafeteria, bakery, good
value, no smoking. Near Plaza España
Teleférico station.

$$$ Casa Prado
Av 16 de Julio (El Prado) 1615,
entre Campero y Ortiz, T02-231 2094,
www.casapradolapaz.com.bo.
'Boutique'-style hotel in a renovated old
building, plain rooms and suites with
colourful furnishings, simple breakfast
included, airport transfer arranged.

$$$ El Rey Palace
Av 20 de Octubre 1947, Sopocachi,
T02-241 8541 or toll free T800-100013,
www.reypalacehotel.com.
Large suites and rooms with heating, buffet
breakfast included, excellent restaurant,
business centre, parking.

$$$ La Loge
Pasaje Medinacelli 2234, Sopocachi, T02-242
3561, www.lacomedie-lapaz.com/es/loge.
Above, and owned by, **La Comedie** restaurant,
elegant apart-hotel rooms, a good option.

$$$ Mitru La Paz
6 de Agosto 2628, Edif Torre Girasoles,
Sopocachi, T02-243 2242,
www.hotelmitrulapaz.com.
Modern hotel on the 1st 3 floors of the
highest building in La Paz (37 storeys).
Includes breakfast and complimentary hot
drinks, comfortable, bright ample rooms
and suites most with bathtubs, heating, safe
boxes, fridge, parking, convenient location
for Sopocachi dining, excellent value for its
price category, helpful staff. Recommended.

$$ Rendezvous
Sargento Carranza 461, side street at the end
of Sánchez Lima, Sopocachi, T02-291 2459,
www.rendezvouslapaz.com.
Delightful rooms in small hotel above the
restaurant of the same name (see below),
family atmosphere, roof terrace with good
view, communal area with DVD library,
kitchen, safe, garden. Recommended.

$$-$ Landscape B&B
Reseguín 1945 entre Aspiazu y
Harington, Sopocachi, T7066 0542,
Facebook: landscape.bolivia.

Like a family home, use whatever you like
except the washing machine (laundry
service provided), 5 rooms, Private or shared
bath, with breakfast, popular. Also has
another house at Reseguín 1981 and an
apartment in the city centre.

South of La Paz

$$$ Oberland
Av Florida, C 2, Mallasa, 12 km from La Paz
centre, T02-274 5040, www.h-oberland.com.
A Swiss-owned, chalet-style restaurant
(excellent, not cheap) and hotel (also good)
with rooms and suites and older resort
facilities, lovely gardens, spa, sauna, covered
pool (open to public – US$4.30-5.70 – very hot
water), volleyball, tennis. Welcomes camping
with or without vehicle. Recommended.

$$$-$$ Allkamari
Near Valle de las Animas, 30 mins from
town on the road to Palca, T02-277 2711,
www.boliviamistica.com.
Reservations required, cabins for up to 8 in a
lovely valley between the Palca and La Animas
canyons, a place to relax and star-gaze, $ pp
in dorm, solar heating, breakfast and jacuzzi
included, other meals on request, lots of
packages available, horse and bike rentals,
massage, acupuncture and other therapies,
shamanic rituals, taxi from Calacoto US$7, bus
No 42 from the cemetery to within 1 km.

$$-$ Colibrí Camping
C 4, Jupapina, near Mallasa, 30 mins from La
Paz, T7629 5658, http://colibricamping.com.
Cabins, teepee, tents and sleeping bags
for hire or set up your own tent for
US$11 pp, nice views, details about
transport on their website.

El Alto

$$-$ Alexander Palace
Av Jorge Carrasco 61 y C 3, Ceja,
Zona 12 de Octubre, T02-282 3376,
www.alexanderpalacehotel.com.bo.
Modern, heated rooms, with buffet
breakfast, restaurant, parking, disco, karaoke.

$ Orquídea
C 15-B, Ciudad Satélite, T02-282 6487.
Comfortable heated rooms, private or
shared bath, electric showers, includes
simple breakfast, good value. Better than
others in the area. 2nd, more expensive ($$),
location in Ciudad Satélite, Av Satélite 632,
T02-2812283, www.hotelesorquidea.com,
includes buffet breakfast.

Restaurants

Around Plaza Murillo

$$ La Kantuta
In Hotel Presidente, Potosí 920, T02-240 6666.
Daily 0600-2300.
Excellent food, good service, lunch buffet
1200-1500. **La Bella Vista** on the top floor
is fancier, open 1200-1500, 1900-2300.

Cafés

Alexander Coffee
Potosí 1091.
Part of a chain (see below), sandwiches,
salads, coffee, pastries.

Wist'u Piku
Comercio 1057, half a block from Plaza Murillo;
also at 6 de Agosto 2048, near the university,
and 20 de Octubre 2463, Sopocachi and other
locations. Mon-Sat 0700-2230, Sun 0830-2030.
A Cochabamba chain, now in other cities,
with a variety of *empanadas* and other
Bolivian snacks, fruit juices and *api*
(a warm corn-flour drink).

Plaza San Francisco up to the cemetery district

$$$-$$ Steakhouse
Psje Tarija 243B, T02-214 8864,
www.4cornerslapaz.com. Daily 1200-2300.
Good cuts of meat, large variety of sauces and
a great salad bar in a modern environment.

$$$-$$ Tambo Colonial
In Hotel Rosario (see page 360).
Daily 0630-0930, 1800-2130.

Excellent local and international cuisine, good
salad bar, buffet breakfast open to the public.

$$ Pizzería Italia
Illampu 809, T02-246 3229. Daily 1000-2300.
Thin-crust pizza, and pasta.

$$-$ A Lo Cubano
Sagárnaga 357, entre Linares y Illampu,
T02-245 1797. Mon-Sat 1200-2400.
Almuerzo for US$4.30, but it runs out fast,
also other choices of good Cuban food,
good value. Live music Sat night.

$$-$ Angelo Colonial
Linares 922, T02-215 9633.
Mon-Sat 0730-2300. Sun 0900-2300.
Breakfast, many vegetarian options, good
music, internet, can get busy with slow
service. 2nd location and *hostal* at Av Mariscal
Santa Cruz 1058.

$$-$ Kalakitas
Sagárnaga 363, T7756 0 770.
Mon-Sat 1200-2400.
Small, brightly decorated Mexican restaurant,
good food, drinks, also breakfast, popular.

$$-$ Sol y Luna
Murillo 999 y Cochabamba, T02-211 5323,
www.solyluna-lapaz.com. Daily 0900-0100.
Dutch run, breakfast, *almuerzo* and
international menu, coffees and teas, full
wine and cocktail list, live music Mon and
Thu, movies, Wi-Fi, guide books for sale,
book exchange, salsa lessons.

Cafés

Banais
Sagárnaga 161, same entrance as
Hostal Naira. Daily 0700-2200.
Coffee, sandwiches and juices, buffet
breakfast, set lunch, à la carte dishes in $$
range, laid-back music and computer room.

Café del Mundo
Sagárnaga 324. Daily 0630-2100.
Swedish-owned, breakfasts, pancakes, waffles,
sandwiches, coffees, teas and chocolate.

K'umara

Pasaje Tarija casi Linares. Daily 0800-2000.
Small café serving breakfasts, cereals, juices, sandwiches, omelettes, soups and drinks, organic produce, Wi-Fi.

El Prado, Sopocachi, Miraflores and Zona Sur

Restaurants listed are in Sopocachi unless noted otherwise.

$$$ Chalet la Suisse

Av Muñoz Reyes 1710, Cota Cota, T02-279 3160, www.chaletlasuisse.com. Mon-Fri 1200-1430, 1900-0030, Sat 1900-0030, Sun 1200-1530, booking is essential on Fri.
Serves excellent fondue, steaks, seafood.

$$$ Gustu

C 10 No 300, Calacoto, T02-211 7491, www.restaurantgustu.com. Mon-Sat 1200-1500, 1830-2300.
Upmarket restaurant with remarkable food and cookery school. Part of the Nordic cuisine pioneers, aimed at stimulating Bolivian gastronomy and giving opportunities to vulnerable people through the **Melting Pot Foundation**, www.meltingpot-bolivia.org. Also has a street food tour, Suma Phayata.

$$$-$$ La Comédie

Pasaje Medinacelli 2234, T02-242 3561, www.lacomedie-lapaz.com. Mon-Fri 1200-1500, 1900-2300, Sat 1900-2300.
'Art café restaurant', contemporary, French menu, good salads, wine list and cocktails.

$$$-$$ Maphrao On

Hnos Manchego 2586, near Plaza Isabel La Católica, T02-243 4682. Sun-Mon 1900-2200, Tue-Sat 1200-1600, 1900-2400.
Thai and Southeast Asian food, warm atmosphere, good music.

$$$-$$ Rendezvous

Sargento Carranza 461, end of Sánchez Lima, T02-291 8459, www.rendevouzlapaz.com. Mon-Sat 1800-2300.
Classic French cuisine and Mediterranean food, excellent variety and quality.

$$$-$$ Sabor Gaucho

F Guachalla 319 entre Av 6 de Agosto y 20 de Octubre, and Pinilla 273 entre Av 6 de Agosto y Arce, T02-244 0844, www.elsaborgaucho.com. Daily 1200-2400, Pinilla location till 1600 on Sun.
Argentine meat dishes, excellent *parrillada*, also has salad bar, wine list, good service.

$$$-$$ Sancho Panza

Av Ecuador 738 y Gutiérrez, T02-242 6490. Tue-Sat 1200-2300.
Mediterranean and Spanish tapas, *tablas* and daily specials, also good-value set lunches (no credit cards or US dollars).

$$ Beatrice

Guachalla 510 y Ecuador, opposite Sopocachi market, www.beatricepastas.com. Open 1100-2200, Sun 1100-1700, closed Tue.
Excellent home-made pasta, good value and very popular with locals.

$$ Chez Moustache

F Guachalla esq Av 20 de Octubre, at Alliance Française, Chez-Moustache on Facebook. Mon-Fri 1100-1530, 1900-2300, Sat 1900-2300
French restaurant with good food, extensive wine list and fun atmosphere.

$$ Ken-Chan

Bat Colorados 98 y F Suazo, p 2 of Japanese Cultural Centre, T02-244 2292. Tue-Sun 1130-1500, 1800-2200.
Japanese restaurant with wide variety of dishes, popular.

$$ Mongo's

Hnos Manchego 2444, near Plaza Isabel La Católica, T02-244 0714. Tue-Sat 1200-1500, 2000-0300. Live music Tue-Wed (cover US$4) salsa lessons Tue, club after midnight.
Excellent Mexican fare and steaks, open fires, bar (cocktails can be pricey), popular with gringos and locals.

$$ Paladar

Av Saavedra 1984, Edif Cristembo, Miraflores, T02-224 1520, and in San Miguel. Open 1200-1630, Mon-Sat in Miraflores, Tue-Sun in San Miguel.

Brazilian dishes, daily specials, popular and good value.

$$ Reineke Fuchs
Pje Jauregui 2241, Sopocachi, T02-244 2979, www.reinekefuchs.com. Mon-Fri 1200-1500 and from 1900, Sat from 1900 only. Also Av Montenegro y C 18, San Miguel, T02-277 2103. Mon-Fri from 1800, Sat and Sun from 1200, and at Centro Comercial Camacho, Av Camacho y Bueno, daily 1200-2230.
German-style bar/restaurant, microbrews and many imported German beers, also set lunch from US$5.

$$ Suma Uru
Av Arce 2177 in Real Plaza Hotel, T02-244 1111. Daily 24 hrs.
Almuerzo Mon-Fri for US$9 and excellent buffet on Sun 1200-1500, US$13.60. Friendly to backpackers.

$$-$ Potokos
Costa Rica 1346, T02-224 4306, Potokos on Facebook. Only Sat-Sun 1200-1630.
Potosino food, traditional dishes, very good.

$$-$ Vienna
Federico Zuazo 1905, T02-244 1660, www.restaurantvienna.com. Mon-Fri 1200-1400, 1830-2200, Sun 1200-1430.
Excellent Austrian, international and local food, great atmosphere and service, live piano music, popular.

$ Armonía
Av Ecuador 2286, above bookstore, T02-2418458. Mon-Sat 1200-1430.
Nice varied vegetarian buffet with organic produce from proprietors' farm. Recommended.

$ Olive Tree
Campos 334, Edif Iturri, T02-243 1552. Mon-Fri 1130-2200.
Good salads, soups and sandwiches, attentive service.

Cafés

Alexander Coffee
Av 16 de Julio 1832, El Prado, also at 20 de Octubre 2463 Plaza Avaroa, Av Arce 2631 (Multicine), Av Montenegro 1336, San Miguel, and at the airport (16 branches in all). Daily 0730-2300; Fri-Sat till 0130 at Av Arce and Av Montenegro.
Excellent coffee, smoothies, muffins, cakes and good salads and sandwiches, Wi-Fi.

Arco Iris
F Guachalla 554 y Sánchez Lima, Sopocachi. Also in Achumani, C 16 by the market. Mon-Sat 0700-2015.
Bakery and handicraft outlet of **Fundación Arco Iris** (www.arcoirisbolivia.org), which works with street children, good variety of breads, pastries, meats and cheeses.

Café Urbano
16 de Julio 1615, El Prado; and 20 de Octubre 2331, Sopocachi, T02-242 2009. Mon-Sat 0700-2300, Sun 1000-2200.
Excellent sandwiches and coffee, pancakes, breakfasts, Wi-Fi.

Fridolín
Av 6 de Agosto 2415; and Prolongación Montenegro, San Miguel. Mon-Sat 0700-2200.
Empanadas, tamales, savoury and sweet (Austrian) pastries, coffee, breakfast, Wi-Fi.

Gigibontá-Rinascimento
20 de Octubre 927, Plaza Avaroa and Claudio Aliaga 1202, San Miguel, see gigibonta.bolivia on Facebook. Sun-Wed 1100-2100, Thu-Sat 11-2200
Authentic Italian ice creams, delicious flavours.

Kuchen Stube
Rosendo Gutiérrez 461, Sopocachi, T02-2424089. Daily 0900-2100.
Excellent cakes, coffee and German specialities, breakfast, also *almuerzo* Mon-Fri, US$5.

Bars and clubs

The epicentre for nightlife in La Paz is currently Plaza Avaroa in Sopocachi. Clubs are clustered around here and crowds gather Fri and Sat nights.

Around Plaza Murillo

Etno Café
Jaén 722, T02-228 0343. Mon-Sat 1930-0300.
Small café/bar with cultural programmes including readings, concerts, movies, popular, serves artisanal and fair trade drinks (alcoholic or not).

Plaza San Francisco up to the cemetery district

Hard Rock Café
Santa Cruz 399 e Illampu, T02-211 9318. Daily 2100-0400. Cover US$5.80.
Turns into nightclub around 2400, popular with locals and tourists, especially on Sun.

The English Lion's
Sagárnaga 189, T02-2231682. Daily 0800-0300.
English-style pub serving breakfast from 0800, sandwiches, fish and chips, bangers and mash, sports channels, music, party atmosphere at night with 2 for 1 drinks.

El Prado, Sopocachi, Miraflores and Zona Sur

Equinoccio
Sánchez Lima 2191, Sopocachi. Thu-Sat 2130-0330, cover charge US$3.60, or more for popular bands.
Top venue for live rock music and bar.

Glam
Sánchez Lima 2237, T7061 6000. Thu-Sat from 2100.
Good place to go dancing, live salsa on Fri, electronic music on Sat.

Hallwrights
Sánchez Lima 2235, T6706 3699. Mon-Sat 1700-2400.
The only wine bar in La Paz.

Malegria
Pje Medinacelli 2282. Thu-Sat 2130-0300.
Bar and club, good pizza, varied music for dancing. Live *saya* (Afrobolivian dance) performances Thu at 2200 and 2300. Popular with Bolivians and foreigners of all ages.

Entertainment

For current information on cinemas and shows, check *La Prensa* or *La Razón* on Fri, or visit www.laprensa.com.bo or www. la-razon.com. Also look for *Bolivian Express* (in English) and *Mañana*, both free monthly magazines with listings of concerts, exhibits, festivals, etc.

Cinemas
Films mainly in English with Spanish subtitles cost around US$5-6, some cinemas have 2 for the price of 1 promotioons on Wed. See www.cinecenter.com.bo, http:// megacenter.irpavi.com and www.multicine. com.bo; the latter, in Sopocachi, has the most comfortable halls. **Cinemateca Boliviana**, Oscar Soria (prolong Federico Zuazo) y Rosendo Gutiérrez, T02-244 4090, www. cinematecaboliviana.org. Municipal theatre with emphasis on independent productions.

Peñas
Bocaisapo, *Indaburo 654 y Jaén, T7774 3456. Tue-Thu 2030-0200, Fri-Sat 2030-0300.* Live music in a bar; no cover charge, popular. **Peña Huari**, *Sagárnaga 339, T02-231 6225. Daily 1900-2200.* Good shows of traditional music and dance at 2000 (if there are at least 8 clients), also serves food and drink.

Theatre
Teatro Municipal Alberto Saavedra Pérez, *Sanjinés e Indaburo, T02-240 6183,* has a regular schedule of plays, opera, ballet and classical concerts. The National Symphony Orchestra is very good and gives inexpensive concerts. Next door is the **Teatro Municipal de Cámara**, which shows dance, drama, music and poetry. **Casa Municipal de la Cultura 'Franz Tamayo',**

almost opposite Plaza San Francisco, hosts a variety of exhibitions, paintings, sculpture, photography, etc, mostly free. Free monthly guide to cultural events at information desk at entrance. The **Palacio Chico**, *Ayacucho y Potosí, Mon-Fri 0900-1230, 1500-1900*, in old Correo, operated by the Secretaría Nacional de Cultura, also has free exhibitions (good for modern art), concerts and ballet.

Festivals

24 Jan (continuing for 4 weeks), **Alasitas** (see Tiny treats, page 356), in Parque Central up from Av del Ejército, also in Plaza Sucre/San Pedro, recommended.
Feb/Mar Carnaval.
End May/early Jun Festividad del Señor del Gran Poder, the most important festival of the year, with a huge procession of costumed and masked dancers on the 3rd Sat after Trinity.
Jul Fiestas de Julio, a month of concerts and performances at the Teatro Municipal, with a variety of music, including the University Folkloric Festival.
8 Dec Festival around **Plaza España**, colourful and noisy.
31 Dec New Year's Eve, fireworks displays; view from higher up.
See page 719 for national holidays and festivals outside La Paz.

Shopping

Camping equipment
Ayni Sport Bolivia (Jiménez 806). Rents and sometimes sells camping equipment and mountain gear (trekking shoes, fleeces, climbing equipment etc). **Camping Bolivia** (Edif Handal Center, No 9, Av Mcal Santa Cruz y Socabaya, T6557 5899). Outdoor equipment. **Tatoo Bolivia** (Illampu 828, T02-245 1265, www.tatoo.ws). Tatoo clothing plus outdoor equipment including backpacks, shoes, etc. English spoken. For camping stove fuel enquire at **Emita Tours** on Sagárnaga.

Handicrafts
Behind San Francisco church is the **Mercado Artesanal** with many handicraft stalls. Above Plaza San Francisco (see page 354), up C Sagárnaga, are booths and small stores with interesting local items of all sorts. The lower end of Sagárnaga is best for antiques. On Linares, between Sagárnaga and Santa Cruz, high-quality alpaca goods are priced in US$. Also in this area are many places making fleece jackets, gloves and hats, but shop around for value and service. **Galería Doryan** (Sagárnaga 177), is an entire gallery of handicraft shops; includes: **Comart Tukuypaj** (also at Linares 958, T02-231 2686 and Galería Centro de Moda, Local 4B, C 21, Calacoto, www.comart-tukuypaj.com), high-quality textiles from an artisan community association; and **Tejidos Wari** (unit 12), for high-quality alpaca goods, will make to measure, English spoken. **Alpaca Style** (C 22 No 14, Achumani, T02-271 1233). Upmarket shop selling alpaca and leather clothing. **Arte y Diseño** (Illampu 833, T7128 0696). Makes typical clothing to your own specifications in 24 hrs. The shop at Illampu 857 sells *tejidos* (material) by the metre. **Artesanía Sorata** (Sagárnaga 303 y Linares, T02-245 4728, and Sagárnaga 363, www.artesaniasorata.com). Specializes in dolls, sweaters and weavings. **Ayni** (Illampu 704, www.aynibolivia.com). Fairtrade shop in Hotel Rosario, featuring Aymara work. **Jiwitaki Art Shop** (Jaén 705, T7725 4042, Mon-Fri 1100-1300, 1500-1800). Run by local artists selling sketches, paintings, sculptures, literature, etc. **LAM** shops on Sagárnaga and Linares. Good quality alpaca goods. **Millma** (Sagárnaga 225, T02-231 1338, and Claudio Aliaga 1202, Bloque L-1, San Miguel, closed Sat afternoon and Sun). High-quality alpaca knitwear and woven items and, in the San Miguel shop, a permanent exhibition of ceremonial 19th and 20th century Aymara and Quechua textiles (free). **Mistura**, Sagárnaga 163, www.misturabolivia.com. Clothing, hats, bags, wine and other produce, jewellery and scents, high-end design incorporating traditional features.

Mother Earth (Linares 870, T02-239 1911, daily 0930-1930). High-quality alpaca sweaters with natural dyes. **Toshy** on Sagárnaga. Top-quality knitwear.

Jewellery

Good jewellery stores with native and modern designs include **King's** (Loayza 261, between Camacho and Mercado also at Torre Ketal, C 15, Calacoto).

Maps

IGM (head office at Estado Mayor, Av Saavedra 2303, Miraflores, T02-214 9484, Mon-Thu 0900-1200, 1500-1800, Fri 0900-1200, take passport to buy maps. Also office in Edif Murillo, Final Rodríguez y Juan XXIII, T02-237 0116, Mon-Fri 0830-1230, 1430-1830), some stock or will get maps from HQ in 24 hrs. **Librería IMAS** (Av Mcal Santa Cruz entre Loayza y Colón, Edif Colón, T02-235 8234). Ask to see the map collection. Maps are also sold in the Post Office on the stalls opposite the Poste Restante counter.

Markets

In addition to those mentioned in the Plaza San Francisco section (page 354), the 5-km sq **Feria 16 de Julio, El Alto** market is on Thu and Sun (the latter is bigger). The best way to get there is on the red line of the Teleférico, the terminus is by the market. Alternatively, take any minibus that says La Ceja and get off at overpass after toll booth (follow crowd of people or tell driver you're going to La Feria), or take 16 de Julio minibus from Plaza Eguino. Arrive around 0900; most good items are sold by 1200. Goods are cheap, especially on Thu. Absolutely everything imaginable is sold here. Be watchful for pickpockets, just take a bin liner to carry your purchases. **Mercado Sopocachi**, Guachalla y Ecuador, a well-stocked covered market selling foodstuffs, kitchen supplies, etc, closes 1400 on Sun. Produce also available at **Centro Comercial Camacho** near El Prado.

Musical instruments

Many shops on Pasaje Linares, the stairs off C Linares, also on Sagárnaga/Linares, for example **Walata 855**.

City tours

The red and yellow lines of the **Teleférico** give a spectacular overview of La Paz (see Transport). **Sightseeing**, www.lapazcitytour. net, city tours on a double-decker bus, 2 circuits, downtown and Zona Sur with Valle de la Luna (1 morning and 1 afternoon departure to each), departs from Plaza Isabel La Católica and can hop on at Plaza San Francisco, tour recorded in 7 languages, US$8.60 for both circuits, daily at 0900 and 1500 (city), 1030 and 1330 (Zona Sur). City tours also with **Gloria Tours**; for walking tours see **La Paz On Foot, Magri Turismo** and **Red C & P**; for El Alto market and wrestling cholitas tours, see Andean Secrets and **Red C & P**; and for La Paz pub crawl tours, see **Red C & P**; all under Tour operators, below.

Climbing, hiking and trekking

Guides must be hired through a tour company. There is a mountain rescue group, **Socorro Andino Boliviano**, contact Jenaro Yupanqui, T7158 1118 or 02-239 5891. **Altitud 6000**, *Sagárnaga 389, T02-245 3935, www.altitud6000.com. Mon-Sat 1000-1230, 1400-1830.* Climbing tours in Bolivia, Argentina, Chile, Ecuador and Peru. Well organized, very good guides and excellent food.
Andean Base Camp, *Illampu 1037, T02-246 3782. Mon-Sat 1500-2100.* Climbing and trekking, equipment rentals, Swiss staff, good reports.
Andean Summits, *Muñoz Cornejo 1009 y Sotomayor, Sopocachi, T02-242 2106, www. andeansummits.com. Mon-Fri 0900-1200, 1500-1900.* For mountaineering and other trips off the beaten track, contact in advance.
Bolivian Mountain Guides, *Sagárnaga 348, T7758 0433, www.bolivianmountainguides.*

com. Mon-Fri 0800-2000, Sat-Sun 0900-1900. For private climbs and treks in the Cordillera and around La Paz.

Bolivian Mountains, *Rigoberto Paredes 1401 y Colombia, p 3, San Pedro, T02-249 2775, www.bolivianmountains.com (in UK T01273-746545)*. High-quality mountaineering with experienced guides and good equipment, not cheap.

Climbing South America, *Linares 940, T02-297 1543, www.climbingsouthamerica.com. Mon-Fri 0900-1900, Sat 0900-1300*. Climbing, trekking, hiking and multi-activity trips, 4WD and cultural tours, Australian-run.

Refugio Huayna Potosí, *Sagárnaga 398, T02-231 7324, www.huayna-potosi.com. Mon-Fri 0900-1900, Sat 0900-1500*. Climbing and trekking tours, run 2 mountain shelters on Huayna Potosí and a climbing school. Check equipment before using.

Football

Popular and played on Wed and Sun at the **Siles Stadium** in Miraflores (Micro A), which is shared by both La Paz's main teams, Bolívar and The Strongest. There are reserved seats.

Golf

Mallasilla, *T02-274-5124*. is the world's highest golf course, at 3318 m. Non-members can play here on weekdays, US$85.

Language schools

Instituto Exclusivo (IE), *Av 20 de Octubre 2315, Edif Mechita, T02-242 1072, www.instituto-exclusivo.com*. Spanish lessons for individual and groups (US$9.25 per hr), accredited by Ministry of Education.

Tour operators

America Tours, *Av 16 de Julio 1490 (El Prado), Edif Avenida pb, No 9, T02-237 4204, www.america-ecotours.com. Mon-Fri 0900-1800*. Ecotourism and adventure trips in Bolivia and Peru. Specialists in the Amazon jungle and pampas, Lake Titicaca and Salar de Uyuni. Highly professional and recommended.

Andean Secrets, *Av Saavedra 1135 (at Hotel Tópaz), Miraflores, T7729 4590, www.andean-secrets.com. Mon-Fri 1500-1900, Sat 0900-1730, Sun 1000-1400*. Mountain guide Denys Sanjines specializes in the Cordillera Quimsa Cruz. She also arranges visits to El Alto to see the Wrestling Cholitas. Arrange hotel pick-up, go on your own or book through a Red C&P tour (see below).

Barracuda Biking Company, *Linares 971, of 5, T7672 8881, www.barracudabiking.com. Mon-Fri 1000-1900, Sat 1000-1400*. Bike trips to Coroico at a lower price than the upmarket companies.

Crillon Tours, *Camacho 1223, T02-233 7533, http://crillontours.com. Mon-Fri 0900-1200, 1430-1830, Sat 0900-1200*. A company with over 50 years' experience. Trips throughout Bolivia, including the Yungas, Sajama and Lauca, community and adventure tourism, tours combining Bolivia and Peru. Fixed departures and luxury camper service to Salar de Uyuni (www.uyuni.travel). Full details of their Lake Titicaca services on page 383. ATM for cash. Recommended.

Deep Rainforest, *Av América 121, T02-215 0385, www.deep-rainforest.com. Mon-Sat 1000-1400, 1500-1900, Sun 1000-1900*. Off-the-beaten-track trekking, canoe trips from Guanay to Rurrenabaque, rainforest and pampas trips.

Enjoy Bolivia, *Plaza Isabel La Católica, Edif Presidente Bush, of 2, T02-243 5162, www.enjoybolivia.org. Mon-Thu 0900-1900, Fri 0900-1800*. Wide selection of tours and transport service. Transfers to bus terminal and airport (US$20), van service to Oruro (US$108 shared between 4-8 passengers). Attentive service.

Fremen Tours, *Av 20 de Octubre 2396, Edif María Haydee, p 10, T02-242 1258, www.andes-amazonia.com. Mon-Fri 0900-1230, 1430-1830, Sat 0900-1200*. Customized tours and special interest travel throughout Bolivia, including Salar de Uyuni and Reina de Enín riverboat.

Gloria Tours, *Potosí 909, T02-240 7070, www.gloriatours.com.bo. Mon-Fri 0900-1230, 1430-1900, Sat 0900-1300*. Good service for ½ to full-day city tours, excursions further afield and tours throughout Bolivia. See **Hotel Gloria**, page 359.

Gravity Bolivia, *Linares 940, p 1, between Tarija and Sagárnaga, T02-231 0218, after hours T7721 9634, www.gravitybolivia.com (book on website). Mon-Fri 0900-1700.* A wide variety of mountain-biking tours throughout Bolivia, including the world-famous downhill ride to Coroico. They offer a zip-line at the end of the ride, or independently (www.ziplinebolivia.com). Also more challenging bike rides, including single-track and high-speed dirt roads, with coaching and safety equipment, and customized bike tours. They have cycle spares, very knowledgeable service. Also offer a ride and river tour from La Paz to Rurrenabaque and run **ScreeRush** on some of the world's highest scree slopes near Huyana Potosí. Book in advance at the office or by phone (T7721 9634), until 1900. Recommended.

Kanoo Tours, *Illampu 828 entre Sagárnaga y Santa Cruz, T02-246 0003, www.kanootours.com. Mon-Fri 1000-1800.* Also at **Adventure Brew Hostel** (open Sat). Sells **Gravity Bolivia** tours (see above), Vertical Route in Yungas (www.verticalroutebolivia.com), plus Salar de Uyuni, Rurrenabaque jungle trips and Peru.

La Paz On Foot, *Indaburo 710 y Jaén, T7154 3918 and at Prol Posnanski, 400 Miraflores, T022-224 8350, www.lapazonfoot.com.* Walking city tours, walking and sailing trips on Titicaca, tours to Salar de Uyuni, multi-day treks in the Yungas and Apolobamba and regional tours focused on Andean food and biodiversity, which also include Peru, northern Chile and Argentina. Also works with the **Tarapari Biodiversity Garden and Guesthouse** in Chulumani, www.tarapari.org, see page 392. Recommended.

Lipiko Tours, *Pedro Salazar, Edif Santa Martha, p13, Sopocachi, T7910 3555, http://lipiko.com. Mon-Fri 0900-1700, Sat 0900-1300.* Tailor-made tours for all budgets, 4WD tours, trekking, climbing and adventure sport, trips to Amazon and national parks. Also runs trips to Peru, Chile and Argentina.

Magri Turismo, *Capitán Ravelo 2101, T02-244 2727, www.magriturismo.com. Mon-Fri 0830-1215, 1430-1830, Sat 0900-1200.* Recommended for tours throughout Bolivia, flight tickets. Own **La Estancia** hotel on the Isla del Sol. They also have a city walking tour led by shoeshine boys.

Moto Andina, *Urb La Colina N°6 C 25, Calacoto, T7129 9329, www.moto-andina.com (in French).* Motorcycle tours of varying difficulty in Bolivia, contact Maurice Manco.

Mundo Quechua, *Av Circunvalación 43, Achumani, Zona Sur, T02-279 6145, www.mundoquechua.com.* Daily tours to the Cordillera Real, private transport in and around La Paz, custom made climbing, trekking and 4WD tours throughout Bolivia. Has an office in Uyuni, see **Atacama Mística/Mundo Quechua** on page 409. Also extensions to Peru and Argentina. English, French and Portuguese spoken, good service.

Peru Bolivian Tours, *C23 No 7875, Edif Magnolia, PB of 1, Calacoto, T02-279 9501, www.perubolivian.com. Mon-Fri 0900-1230, 1430-1830, Sat 0900-1200.* More than 20 years' experience, arranges special programmes throughout Bolivia and Peru.

Pure! Bolivia, *Lisimaco Gutiérrez 481 y 20 de Octubre, Sopocachi, T02-243 4455 (6701 1344 24 hrs), info@bolivia-pure.com.* Member of the **Pure! Travel Group**, www.pure-travelgroup.com. Offering tailor-made, conventional, special interest and adventure tours in Bolivia.

Red C&P, *Linares 940, upstairs, T7628 5738, www.redcapwalkingtours.com. Mon-Fri 0900-1830.* La Paz walking tours daily at 1100 and 1400 from Plaza San Pedro, 2½ hrs, US$3, look for the guide with a red cap; they also offer pub crawl tours Tue-Sat 2100, US$16, local food tours (4 hrs of tasting and learning about local dishes US$30), extended tours off the beaten track and, on Thu and Sun, to El Alto market with option to see Wrestling Cholitas (extra cost, see Andean Secrets, above).

Topas Travel, *Carlos Bravo 299 (behind Hotel Plaza), T02-211 1082, www.topas.bo. Mon-Fri 0900-1700, Sat 0900-1200.* Joint venture of **Akhamani Trek** (Bolivia), **Topas** (Denmark) and the Danish embassy, offering trekking, overland truck trips, jungle trips and climbing, English spoken, restaurant and *pensión*.

Transturin, *C20, Calacoto, T02-242 2222, also C6 Nº100, Achumani, T02-218 9600, www.transturin.com. Mon-Fri 0900-1900.* Full travel services with tours in La Paz and throughout Bolivia. Details of their Lake Titicaca services on page 383.

Tupiza Tours, *Villalobos 625 y Av Saavedra, Edif Girasoles, ground floor, Miraflores, T02-224 5254, www.tupizatours.com. Mon-Fri 0900-1300, 1500-1900.* La Paz office of the Tupiza agency, also have an office in Tarija. Specialize in the Salar de Uyuni, Reserva Avaroa and southwest Bolivia, but also offer tours around La Paz and throughout the country.

Turisbus, *Av Illampu 704, T02-245 1341, also C 10 y Av Costanera 501, Calacoto, www.grupo rosario.com. Mon-Fri 0900-1200, 1500-2000, Sat 1600-1900.* Lake Titicaca and Isla del Sol, Salar de Uyuni, Rurrenbaque, trekking and Bolivian tours. Also airport transfers (US$12 pp), city tours and tours and tickets to Puno and Cuzco.

Turismo Balsa, *Av 6 de Agosto y Pinilla, Pje Pascoe 3, Sopocachi, T02-244 0620, www. turismobalsa.com.* City and tours throughout Bolivia. Owns **Hotel Las Balsas**, in beautiful lakeside setting at Puerto Pérez on Lake Titicaca, T02-289 5147, 72 km from La Paz, with excellent restaurant.

Urban Rush, *T7629 7222, www.urbanrush bolivia.com.* Go to **Hotel Presidente**, 17th floor, 1300-1800 for abseiling or rap jumping from one of the tallest buildings in La Paz, US$25 for 1 jump, US$34 for 2, US$13 for each extra jump.

Air

La Paz has the highest commercial **airport** in the world, at El Alto (4061 m); T02-215 7300, www.sabsa.aero. **Cotranstur** minibuses, T02-231 2032, white with 'Cotranstur' and 'Aeropuerto' written on the side and back, go from Plaza Isabel La Católica, stopping all along El Prado and Av Mcal Santa Cruz to the airport, 0610-2130, US$0.55 (allow about 1 hr), best to buy an extra seat for your luggage, departures every 4 mins. Shared transport from Plaza Isabel La Católica, US$4 pp, carrying 4 passengers, also private transfers from **Enjoy Bolivia** and **Turisbus**, see Tour operators, above and page 369. Radio-taxi is US$8-10 to centre and Sopocachi, US$11-15 to Zona Sur. Prices are displayed at the airport terminal exit. There is an **Info Tur** office in arrivals with a *casa de cambio* next to it (dollars, euros and cash, poor rates; open 0530-1300, 1700-0300, closed Sun evening). Several ATMs in the departures hall. There are also food outlets and shops (prices of handicrafts in the duty-free area are ridiculously high). The international and domestic departures hall is the main concourse, with all check-in desks. There are separate domestic and international arrivals. For details of air services, see under destinations.

great walks
great guides
great memories

882-B Calle Linares
La Paz Bolivia
+591-71543918
lapazonfoot.com

Bus

City buses There are 3 types of city bus: the modern *puma katari*, with 3 lines along different routes, mostly from El Alto through the centre to the Zona Sur, US$0.25-0.30 depending on route, US$0.42-0.50 at night, for frequent use you can buy a card for US$2.85, which can then be topped up; additional lines will be added (www.lapazbus.bo); *micros* (small, old buses), which charge US$0.25 a journey; and minibuses (small vans), US$0.25-0.40 depending on the journey. *Trufis* are fixed-route collective taxis, with a sign with their route on the windscreen, US$0.50 pp in the centre, US$0.60 outside.

Long distance For information, T02-228 5858. Buses to: **Oruro**, **Potosí**, **Sucre**, **Cochabamba**, **Santa Cruz**, **Tarija**, **Uyuni**, **Tupiza** and **Villazón**, leave from the main terminal at Plaza Antofagasta (micros 2, M, CH or 130), see under each destination for details. Taxi to central hotels should be US$1.50-2.50 and US3-4 to hotels in Sopocachi and Zona Sur. Take Taxi Terminal, or Taxi Magnífico for best service. The terminal (open 0400-2300) has a tourist booth by the main entrance, ATMs, internet, a post office, **Entel**, restaurant, luggage store and travel agencies. Touts find passengers the most convenient bus and are paid commission by the bus company. To **Oruro** van service with **Enjoy Bolivia**, see Tour operators, page 369, US$13 pp shared, US$90 private. To **Copacabana**, several bus companies (tourist service) pick-up travellers at their hotels (in the centre) and also stop at the main terminal, tickets from booths at the terminal (cheaper) or agencies in town. They all leave about 0800 (**Titicaca Bolivia** also at 1400), 3½ hrs, US$3.60-4.50 one way, return from Copacabana about 1330. When there are not enough passengers for each company, they pool them. **Diana Tours**, T02-235 0252, **Titicaca Bolivia**, T02-246 2655, **Turisbus**, T02-245 1341 (more expensive),

many others. You can also book this service all the way to Puno, US$7.

Public buses to **Copacabana**, **Tiwanaku**, **Desaguadero** (border with Peru) and **Sorata**, leave from the Cemetery district. To get there, take any bus or minibus marked 'Cementerio' going up C Santa Cruz. On Plaza Reyes Ortiz are **Manco Capac**, and **2 de Febrero** for **Copacabana** and **Tiquina**. From the Plaza go up Av Kollasuyo and at the 2nd street on the right (Manuel Bustillos) is the terminal for minibuses to **Achacachi**, **Huatajata** and **Huarina**, as well as **Trans Unificada** and **Flor del Illampu** minibuses for **Sorata**. Several micros (20, J, 10) and minibuses (223, 252, 270, 7) go up Kollasuyo. Taxi US$2 from downtown, US$4.30 from Zona Sur. Buses to **Coroico**, the **Yungas and northern jungle** leave from Terminal Minasa in Villa Fátima (25 mins by micros B, V, X, K, 131, 135, or 136, or *trufis* 2 or 9, which pass Pérez Velasco coming down from Plaza Mendoza, and get off at Minasa terminal, Puente Minasa). See Safety, page 349.

International buses From main bus terminal: to **Puno** and **Cuzco**, luxury and indirect services, see under Lake Titicaca, page 384. Also **Bolivia Hop**, www.boliviahop.com, which runs a hop-on, hop-off service from La Paz to Cuzco or Arequipa and on to Lima, via Copacabana and Puno, daily 0700, daily except Sat at1700 from Copacabana, packages start at US$39. Direct to Cuzco, 12 hrs with **Litoral**, US$23 via Desaguadero and Puno (5 hrs, US$8). To **Lima**, **Ormeño** daily at 1430, US$90, 27 hrs; **Nuevo Continente** at 0830, US$88, 26 hrs, via Desaguadero, change to **Cial** in Puno. To **Buenos Aires**, US$102, 2 a week with **Ormeño**, T02-228 1141, 54 hrs via Santa Cruz and Yacuiba; via Villazón with **Río Paraguay**, 3 a week, US$75, or **Trans Americano**, US$85. Alternatively, go to Villazón and change buses in Argentina. To **Arica** via the frontier at Tambo Quemado and Chungará, **Pullmanbus** at 0630 (good), **Cuevas** at 0700, **Zuleta** at 0600, **Nuevo Continente** at 1230 except Sat, **Litoral**, T02-228 1920, Sun-Thu 1230, US$26.

The main route to **Chile** is via Tambo Quemado (see page 397), but an alternative route, on which there are no trucks, is to go by good road direct from La Paz via Viacha to **Santiago de Machaco** (130 km, petrol); then 120 km on a very bad road to the border at **Charaña** (basic **Alojamiento Aranda**; immigration behind railway station). From Visviri, on the Chilean side of the frontier (no services), a regular road runs to Putre. A motorized railway car also runs from Viacha to Charaña on Mon and Thu at 0800 (4 hrs, US$4.30), returning Tue and Fri at 1200. There is no train service on the Chilean side.

Cable car

Teleférico A system of 3 lines of cable cars (www.miteleferico.bo) joining neighbourhoods along the edge of the altiplano, including El Alto, with the centre of the city and the Zona Sur, was inaugurated in 2014. The lines are: **Línea Roja** (red line) from Zona 16 de Julio, El Alto, to the old train station, 3 blocks above Plaza Eguino, in an area known as Vita in the northwest of the city, via Av Entre Ríos in the cemetery district; **Línea Amarilla** (yellow line) from Parque Mirador, Ciudad Satélite in Al Alto, to Curva de Holguín, Av Libertador at the border between Sopocachi and Alto Obrajes, via Av Buenos Aires and Plaza España in Sopocachi; **Línea Verde** (green line) from Curva de Holguín to Zona Sur: Calle 12 and 13 in Calacoto, entrance to Irpavi, via Alto Obrajes and Calle 17 de Obrajes. Each ride costs US$0.45, but for frequent use you can buy a card for US$2.10, which can then be topped up. There are long queues at rush hour (especially 1800-2000) and on the red line Sun 1300-2000). 2 new lines are nearing completion in 2017 and additional ones are planned.

Car hire

Imbex, C15 esquina Los Sauces, Calacoto, T02-212 1010, www.imbex.com. Wide range of well-maintained vehicles; Suzuki jeeps from US$60 per day, including 200 km free for 4-person 4WD. Also office in Santa Cruz, T03-311001. Recommended. **Petita Rent-a-car**, Valentín Abecia 2031, Sopocachi Alto, T02-242 0329, www.rentacarpetita.com. Recommended for personalized service and well-maintained 4WD jeeps, minimum rental 1 week. Their vehicles can also be taken outside Bolivia. Also offer adventure tours (English spoken).

Taxi

Taxis are often, but not always, white. Taxi drivers are not tipped. There are 3 types: **standard taxis**, which may take several passengers at once (US$0.45-1.75 for short trips within city limits), **fake taxis**, which have been involved in robberies, and **radio taxis**, which take only one group of passengers at a time. Since it is impossible to distinguish between the first two, it is best to pay a bit more for a radio taxi, especially at night. These have a dome light, a unique number (note this when getting in) and radio communication (eg **Servisur**, T02-279 9999; Taxi Terminal at the bus station; **Taxi Magnífico**; **Taxi Diplomático**, T02-222 4343). They charge US$1.50-2.50 in the centre, more to suburbs and at night.

> Tip...
> Taxi ranks outside malls, cinemas, etc operate with radio taxis and are more expensive than the ones you flag down on the street, but are good places to find the safer option. Especially avoid taking ordinary cabs in the cemetery district, where robberies have been reported.

Train

Ferroviaria Andina (FCA), www.fca.com.bo, Mon-Fri 0800-1600. Sells tickets for the **Oruro–Uyunui–Tupiza–Villazón** line; see schedule and fares under Oruro Transport (page 402). Tickets for *ejecutivo* class sold up to 2 weeks in advance, for *salón* 1 week. Must show passport to buy tickets. Every 2nd Sun, FCA runs a **tourist train** from El Alto to **Guaqui**, with a 1½-hr stop at Tiwanaku and 2 hrs at Guaqui. The station is at C 8, 3 blocks from Av 6 de Marzo, by Cuartel Ingavi, departs 0800, returns 1320, arrives in El Alto 1915, US$11.50 *ejecutivo*, US$3 *salón*, tickets from office in Sopocachi, as above. Confirm all details in advance.

South of La Paz

For **Valle de la Luna**, Minibuses 231, 273 and 902 can be caught on C México, the Prado or Av 6 de Agosto. Alternatively take Micro 11 ('Aranjuez' large bus) or ones that say 'Mallasa' or 'Mallasilla' along the Prado or Av 6 de Agosto, US$0.75, and ask driver where to get off. You can also catch these minibuses and micros at Curva de Holguín, the southern terminus of the yellow line of the Teleférico. Most of the local travel agents organize tours to the **Valle de la Luna**. Some are a brief, 5-min stop for photos in a US$15 tour of La Paz and surroundings, but longer tours and cycling trips are also available.

Takesi Trail

Take a **Líneas Ingavi** bus from C Gral Luis Lara esq Venacio Burgoa near Plaza Líbano, San Pedro, going to **Pariguaya** (2 hrs past Chuñavi), several daily, US$3.55, 2 hrs. On Sun, also minibuses from C Gral Luis Lara y Boquerón, hourly 0700-1500. To **Mina San Francisco**: hire a **jeep** from La Paz; US$85, takes about 2 hrs. **Veloz del Norte** (T02-221 8279) leaves from Ocabaya 495 in Villa Fátima, T02-221 8279, 0900 daily, and 1400 Thu-Sun, US$3.55, 3½ hrs, continuing to Chojlla. From **Chojlla** to La Paz daily at 0500, 1300 also on Thu-Sun, passing **Yanacachi** 15 mins later. You can also catch a bus to La Paz from La Florida on the main Yungas road, US$3.55.

Choro Trail

To the *apacheta* pass beyond **La Cumbre**, take a **taxi** from central La Paz for US$20, 45 mins, stopping to register at the Guardaparque hut. Buses from Villa Fátima to Coroico and Chulumani pass La Cumbre. Tell driver where you are going, US$3. The trail is signed.

Huayna Potosí

The mountain can be reached by transport arranged through tourist agencies (US$100) or the *refugio*, **taxi** US$45. **Minibus** Trans Zongo, Av Chacaltaya e Ingavi, Ballivián, El Alto, daily 0600, 2½ hrs, US$2 to Zongo, check on return time. Also minibuses from the Ballivián area that leave when full (few on Sun). If camping in the Zongo Pass area, stay at the site near the white house above the cross.

Around La Paz
& Lake Titicaca

Within striking distance of La Paz are an enormous variety of landscapes, extraordinary historical sites and potential for adventure. The most popular excursion is to the remarkable site of Tiwanaku, 72 km west of the city. Rising out of the vast flatness of the altiplano are the remains of pyramids and temples, of a great civilization that predated the Incas by a thousand years.

No visit to Bolivia would be complete without seeing the sapphire-blue waters of mystical Lake Titicaca and its beautiful islands. Covering 8000 sq km, Titicaca is the highest navigable lake in the world at over 3800 m above sea level.

Tiwanaku *Colour map 3, B2.*

Bolivia's best-known archaeological site is a 'must see' excursion

☆This remarkable archaeological site, 72 km west of La Paz, near the southern end of Lake Titicaca, takes its name from one of the most important pre-Columbian civilizations in South America. It is the most popular excursion from La Paz, with good facilities for the visitor.

The site
The site is open 0900-1700, US$12, including entry to museums. Allow 4 hrs to see the ruins and village. See also Transport, page 377.

Many archaeologists believe that Tiwanaku existed as early as 1200 BC, while the complex visible today probably dates from the eight to the 10th centuries AD. The site may have been a ceremonial complex and political centre, the nucleus of an empire which is thought to have covered most of Bolivia, southern Peru, northern Chile and northwest Argentina. It was also a hub of trans-Andean trade. The demise of the Tiwanaku civilization remains a mystery, but heading the list of theories is that some form of major change in the climate, most probably drought, meant that the area's extensive system of raised

Best for
Archaeology ■ Cycling ■ Islands ■ Trekking ■ Wildlife

Essential Around La Paz and Lake Titicaca

Getting around

Tiwanaku village, Copacabana, Sorata and other towns in the area are all linked by bus from La Paz. A paved road runs from La Paz to the southeastern shore of the lake. One branch continues north along the eastern shore, another branch goes to the Straits of Tiquina (114 km El Alto–San Pablo) and Copacabana. A third road goes to Guaqui and Desaguadero on the southwestern shore. Ferries cross the Straits of Tiquina and go to islands in the lake. See also Transport, below.

When to go

Cool all year; rainy season December to March.

Time required

One day for Tiwanaku, two to four days for Copacabana or Sorata, two to three weeks for the more remote areas.

fields (*sukakollu*), which at one stage were capable of sustaining many thousands of people, failed to feed the population and, more importantly, the elites. As a result, some time around 1000-1100 AD the main culture collapsed and disappeared. The Pumapunku section, 1 km south of the main complex, may have been a port, as the waters of the lake used to be much higher than they are today. The raised field system is once again being used in parts locally.

Kalasasaya One of the main structures is the Kalasasaya, meaning 'standing stones', referring to the statues found in that part: two of them, the Ponce monolith (centre of inner patio) and the Fraile monolith (southwest corner), have been re-erected.

Puerta del Sol In the northwest corner is the Puerta del Sol, originally at Pumapunku. Its carvings are thought to be either a depiction of the creator god, or a calendar. The motifs are exactly the same as those around the Ponce monolith.

Templo Semisubterráneo This is a sunken temple whose walls are lined with faces, all different. According to some theories they depict states of health, the temple being a house of healing; another theory is that the faces display all the ethnicities of the world.

Akapana Originally a pyramid (said to have been the second largest in the world, covering over 28,000 sq m), the Akapana still has some ruins on it.

Pumapunku A natural disaster may have put a sudden end to the construction at Pumapunku before it was finished; some of the blocks weigh 100 to 150 tonnes.

Museums There is a small **Museo Lítico** at the ticket office, with several large stone pieces and, at the site, the **Museo Regional Arqueológico**, contains a well-illustrated explanation of the raised field system of agriculture. Many other artefacts are in the **Museo Nacional de Arqueología** in La Paz.

Tiwanaku village

Nearby Tiwanaku village, with several basic hotels and eateries, still has remnants from the time of independence and the 16th-century church was built using pre-Columbian masonry. In fact, Tiwanaku for a long while was the 'quarry' for the altiplano. For the **Willkakuti**, winter solstice festival on 21 June, there is an all-night vigil and colourful dances. There is also a colourful local festival on the Sunday after Carnaval.

Transport

Tours to Tiwanaku cost US$10-12, not including entry fee or lunch.

If not on a tour take any **micro** marked 'Cementerio' in La Paz, get out at Plaza Félix Reyes Ortiz, on Mariano Bautista (north side of cemetery), go north up Aliaga, 1 block east of Asín to find Tiwanaku micros, US$2, 1½ hrs, every 30 mins, 0600 to 1500. Tickets can be bought in advance. **Taxi** costs US$30-55 return (shop around), with 2 hrs at site. Some **buses** go on from Tiwanaku to Desaguadero; virtually all Desaguadero buses stop at the access road to Tiwanaku, 20-min walk from the site. Return buses (last back 1700) leave from south side of the Plaza in village. Minibuses (vans) to **Desaguadero**, from José María Asín y P Eyzaguirre (Cemetery district) US$2, 2 hrs, most movement on Tue and Fri when there is a market at the border.

Note When returning from Tiwanaku (ruins or village) to La Paz, do not take an empty minibus. We have received reports of travellers being taken to El Alto and robbed at gun point. Wait for a public bus with paying passengers in it.

Lake Titicaca *Colour map 3, B2.*

superb views, altiplano life and trips on the lake

Lake Titicaca is two lakes joined by the Straits of Tiquina: the larger, northern lake (Lago Mayor, or Chucuito) contains the Islas del Sol and de la Luna; the smaller lake (Lago Menor, or Huiñamarca) has several small islands. The waters are a beautiful blue, reflecting the hills and the distant cordillera in the shallows of Huiñamarca, mirroring the sky in the rarified air and changing colour when it is cloudy or raining. A boat trip on the lake is a must.

La Paz to Copacabana

The main road from La Paz to Copacabana reaches the east side of the Straits of Tiquina at **San Pablo** (clean restaurant in blue building, toilets at both sides of the crossing). On the west side is San Pedro, the main Bolivian naval base, from where a paved road goes to Copacabana and the border. Vehicles are transported across on barges, US$5. Passengers cross separately, US$0.20 (not included in bus fares) and passports and visas may be checked (do not leave your documents on the bus or in your hotel in La Paz). Expect delays during rough weather, when it can get very cold.

★Copacabana

A popular little resort town on Lake Titicaca, 158 km from La Paz by paved road, Copacabana (population 5515, altitude 3850 m) is set on a lovely bay and surrounded by scenic hills. **Centro de Información Turística** ① *16 de Julio y 6 de Agosto, T7251 6220, Mon-Sat 0800-1330, 1600-1900*, English spoken, provides pamphlets and maps of Copacabana and Isla del Sol. Next door, the **Red de Turismo Comunitario** ① *6 de Agosto y 16 de Julio, T7729 9088, Mon-Sat 0800-1230, 1300-1900*, can arrange tours to nearby communities. There are four unreliable ATMs in town, best take some cash.

At major holidays (Holy Week, 3 May, and 6 August), the town fills with visitors. It can also be busy at weekends and in the high season (June-August).

Copacabana has a heavily restored, Moorish-style **basilica** ① *open 0700-2000; minimum 5 people at a time to visit museum, Tue-Sat 1000-1100, 1500-1600, Sun 1000-1100, US$1.50, no* *photos allowed*. It contains a famous 16th-century miracle-working Virgen Morena (Black Madonna), also known as the Virgen de Candelaria, one of the patron saints of Bolivia. The basilica is clean, white, with coloured tiles decorating the exterior arches, cupolas and chapels. It is notable for its spacious atrium with four small chapels; the main chapel has one of the finest gilt altars in Bolivia. There are 17th- and 18th-century paintings and statues in the sanctuary. Vehicles decorated with flowers and confetti are blessed in front of the church at weekends and other special days (eg Semana Santa).

On the headland which overlooks the town and port, **Cerro Calvario**, are the Stations of the Cross (a steep 45-minute climb – leave plenty of time if going to see the sunset). On the hill behind the town is the **Horca del Inca**, two pillars of rock with another laid across them; probably a solar calendar, the Inti Watana, now covered in graffiti. There is a path marked by arrows; boys will offer to guide you, but fix a price in advance.

Hiking around Copacabana

There are many great hikes in the hills surrounding Copacabana. North of town is the **Yampupata Peninsula**. It is a beautiful 17-km (six-hour) walk to the village of Yampupata at the tip of the peninsula, either via **Sicuani** on the west shore or **Sampaya** on the east shore, both picturesque little towns. There are also minibuses from Copacabana to Yampupata, where you can hire a motorboat or rowboat to Isla del Sol or Isla de la Luna; boats are also available from Sampaya to Isla de la Luna (US$21 for a motorboat, US$14 for a rowing boat).

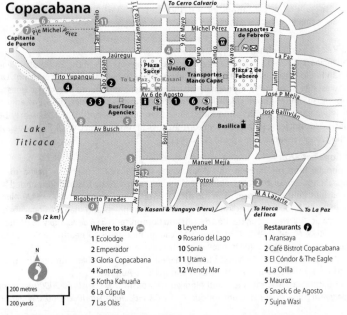

Copacabana

Where to stay 🛏		Restaurants 🍴
1 Ecolodge	8 Leyenda	1 Aransaya
2 Emperador	9 Rosario del Lago	2 Café Bistrot Copacabana
3 Gloria Copacabana	10 Sonia	3 El Cóndor & The Eagle
4 Kantutas	11 Utama	4 La Orilla
5 Kotha Kahuaña	12 Wendy Mar	5 Mauraz
6 La Cúpula		6 Snack 6 de Agosto
7 Las Olas		7 Sujna Wasi

☆Isla del Sol

The site of the main Inca creation myth (there are other versions) is a place of exceptional natural beauty and spiritual interest. Legend has it that Viracocha, the creator god, had his children, Manco Kapac and Mama Ocllo, spring from the waters of the lake to found Cuzco and the Inca dynasty. **La Roca Sagrada** (sacred rock) at the island's northwest end is worshipped as their birthplace. Near the rock are the impressive ruins of **Chincana**, the labyrinth, a 25-minute walk from the village of **Challapampa**, with a basic **Museo de Oro** ⓘ *US$1.45 includes landing fee and entry to Chincana*. Challampa is beautifully set along two sandy bays, separated by an isthmus. Near the centre of the island is the community of Challa on a secluded bay with an **ethnographic museum** ⓘ *US$2.15, includes trail fees*. Towards the south end of the island is the **Fuente del Inca**, a spring reached by Inca steps, Las Mil Gradas, leading up from the lake and continuing up to Yumani. The village is spread out along a steep slope between the port and a ridge 200 m above. Near the southeast tip of the island, 2 km from the spring, are the ruins of **Pilcocaina** ⓘ *US$0.75 include landing fees*, the Temple of the Sun, a two-storey building with false domes and nice views over the water. You must pay the fees even if you don't visit the museums or ruins. Keep all entry tickets, you may be asked for them at other locations. Several restored pre-Columbian roads cross the island from north to south.

The three communities are along the east shore of the island. All have electricity (Yumani also has internet), accommodation and simple places to eat. The island is heavily touristed and gets crowded in high season. Touts and beggars can be persistent, especially in Yumani. Tour operators in Copacabana offer half- and full-day 'tours' (many are just transport, see page 384) but an overnight stay at least is recommended to appreciate fully the island and to enjoy the spectacular walk from north to south (or vice-versa), about 11 km, at a comfortable pace. In a day trip, you will barely have time for a quick look at Chincana and you will see Pilcocaina from the boat. Note that it is a steep climb from the pier to the town of Yumani. Local guides are available in Challapampa and Yumani.

Isla de la Luna Southeast of Isla del Sol is the smaller Isla de la Luna (or Coati), which may also be visited. The community of Coati is located on the west shore, the ruins of the Inca **Palacio de Iña Kuyu** ⓘ *US$1.45 community fee for ruins and landing*, on the east shore.

Border with Peru

West side of Lake Titicaca The road goes from La Paz 91 km west to the former port of **Guaqui** (passports may be inspected at the military checkpoint here and at other spots along the road). The road crosses the border at **Desaguadero**, 22 km further west, and runs along the shore of the lake to Puno. Bolivian immigration is just before the bridge, open 0800-2030 (0700-1930 Peruvian time, one hour earlier than Bolivia). Get an exit stamp, walk 200 m across the bridge then get an entrance stamp on the other side. Peruvian visas should be arranged in La Paz. There are a few hotels and restaurants on both sides of the border; very basic in Bolivia, slightly better in Peru. Money changers on the Peruvian side give reasonable rates. Market days are Friday and Tuesday, otherwise the town is dead.

Via Copacabana From Copacabana a paved road leads 8 km south to the frontier at Kasani, then to Yunguyo, Peru. Do not photograph the border area. For bus services on this route, see page 385, and What to do, page 384. The border is open 0800-1930 Bolivian time (0700-1830 Peruvian time). International tourist buses stop at both sides of the border; if using local transport walk 300 m between the two posts. Do not be fooled into paying any unnecessary charges to police or immigration. Going to Peru, money can be changed at the Peruvian side of the border. Coming into Bolivia, the best rates are at Copacabana.

East side of Lake Titicaca From Huarina, a road heads northwest to Achacachi (Sunday market; fiesta 14 September). Here, one road goes north across a tremendous marsh to **Warisata**, then crosses the altiplano to Sorata (see below). At Achacachi, another road runs roughly parallel to the shore of Lake Titicaca, through **Ancoraimes** (Sunday market, the church hosts a community project making dolls and alpaca sweaters, also has dorms), **Carabuco** (with a colonial church), **Escoma** (which has an Aymara market every Sunday morning) to **Puerto Acosta**, 10 km from the Peruvian border. It is a pleasant, friendly town with a large plaza and several simple places to stay and eat. The area around Puerto Acosta is good walking country. From La Paz to Puerto Acosta the road is paved as far as Escoma, then good until Puerto Acosta (best in the dry season, approximately May to October). North of Puerto Acosta towards Peru the road deteriorates and should not be attempted except in the dry season. There is a smugglers' market at the border on Wednesday and Saturday, the only days when transport is plentiful. There is a Peruvian customs post 2 km from the border and 2 km before Tilali, but Peruvian immigration is in Puno.

Listings Lake Titicaca map page 378.

Where to stay

La Paz to Copacabana

$$ Hotel Titicaca
Between Huatajata and Huarina, Km 80 from La Paz, T02-289 5180 (in La Paz T02-290 7000).
Beautiful views, sauna, pool, good restaurant. It's very quiet during the week.

$ Máximo Catari's Inti Karka Hotel
On the lakeshore, T7197 8959, erikcatari@hotmail.com.
Rooms are cheaper with shared bath. Also restaurant, open daily, average prices.

Copacabana

$$$ Gloria Copacabana
Av 16 de Julio, T02-862 2094, La Paz T02-240 7070, www.hotelgloria.com.bo.
On the lakeshore. Full board available, bar, café and restaurant with international and vegetarian food, gardens, mini-golf, racquetball, parking. Same group as **Gloria** in La Paz.

$$$ Rosario del Lago
Rigoberto Paredes y Av Costanera, T02-862 2141, reservations La Paz T02-244 1756, www.hotelrosario.com/lago.
Comfortable rooms with lake views, beautifully furnished, good restaurant, small museum, **Turisbus** office (see Transport, page 384), parking. Efficient and attentive service.

$$ Ecolodge
2 km south along the lakeshore, T02-862 2500 (or T02-245 1626, Hostal Copacabana, La Paz).
Small comfortable cabins in a quiet out-of-the-way location, nice grounds. Only breakfast available, solar hot water, helpful owner.

$$ Las Olas
lake-end of Pje Michel Pérez past La Cúpula, T7250 8668, www.hostallasolas.com.
Tastefully decorated suites, each in its own style. All have kitchenettes, heaters, lovely grounds and views, outdoor solar-heated jacuzzi, a special treat. Warmly recommended.

$$ Utama
Pje Michel Pérez, T02-862 2013, www.utamahotel.com.
Comfortable rooms, hot water, good showers, restaurant, book exchange.

$$ Wendy Mar
Av 16 de Julio, opposite Gloria, T02-862 2124, www.hotelwendymar.com.

Very clean, light rooms in pastel colours, large modern building, conveniently placed, terrace, cheaper in low season.

$$-$ La Cúpula
Pje Michel Pérez 1-3, 5 mins' walk from centre, T6708 8464, www.hotelcupula.com.
Variety of rooms and prices from suite with jacuzzi to comfortable rooms with shared bath, reliable hot water, sitting room with TV and video, fully equipped kitchen, library, book exchange, attentive service, excellent restaurant ($$ with vegetarian options, great breakfast). Popular, advance booking advised. Highly recommended.

$$-$ Leyenda
Av Costanera y Germán Busch, T7067 4097, hostel.leyenda@gmail.com.
Lakeshore hotel with eclectic decor, rooms elaborately decorated with local motifs, electric shower.

$ Emperador
C Murillo 235, T02-862 2083.
Very economical, even cheaper without bath, electric showers, newer rooms at the back, popular, helpful, tours arranged.

$ Kantutas
Av Jaúregui esq Bolívar, on Plaza Sucre, T02-862 2093, hostalkantutas@entel.bo.
Good rooms, a decent option in the middle price range, convenient location for transport, includes breakfast.

$ Kotha Kahuaña
Av Busch 15, T7652 3760, juandediosab@gmail.com.
Very economical, cheaper without bath, simple kitchen facilities, quiet, hospitable, basic but good value.

$ Sonia
Murillo 253, T7196 8441.
Rooms are cheaper without bath, good beds, big windows, roof terrace, laundry facilities, breakfast in bed on request, very helpful, good value. Recommended.

Isla del Sol
La Posada del Inca, a restored colonial hacienda, owned by **Crillon Tours**, is only available as part of a tour with Crillon, see page 383. **Magri Turismo** also owns a hotel on the island, **La Estancia** (www.ecolodge-laketiticaca.com). See page 370. See also **Transturin's** overnight options on page 383.

Yumani
The majority of *posadas* are in the south of the island, most in the upper part of Yumani. For those unable to walk a long way up the steps there are *hostales* and *cabañas* between Yumani port and higher up the village. Quality varies; ignore the touts and shop around for yourself. Please conserve water, it is hauled up the steep hill by donkeys.

$$ Palla Khasa
600 m north of town on the main trail to Challapampa, T7321 1585, pallakhasalodge@gmail.com.
Includes good breakfast, nice cabins, large rooms, good beds, restaurant with fine views, nice location and grounds, family-run, solar electricity, changes US$ and other currencies. Book in advance.

$ Casa de la Luna
Halfway down from Inti Kala towards Hostal Imperio del Sol, T7190 8040.
More expensive than some, spacious rooms, breakfast included, also has a restaurant.

$ Hostal Utama
Almost at the top of the hill, T7300 3268.
In a pleasant location, rooms with or without bath, breakfast and restaurant, small garden, helpful and good value.

$ Inti Kala
At the top of the hill, T7197 3878, javierintikala@hotmail.com.
With bath, electric shower, terrace, lake views, serves breakfast in dining area.

$ Mirador del Inca
Access from the port along the steps to the south of the main Inca steps, at the same level as the Fuente del Inca.
Simple but nice hostel with lake views, cheaper rooms with shared bath, electric showers, breakfast extra.

$ Templo del Sol
At the top of the hill, T7351 8970.
Comfortable rooms, cheaper without bath, electric shower, great views, comfy beds, meals available on request, good value.

Challa
Located mid-island on the east shore, about 200 m below the main north-south trail. Most hostels are on the beach, the town is uphill.

$ Inca Beach
On the beach, T7353 0309.
Simple rooms with bath, electric shower, kitchen and laundry facilities, meals available, nice common area, camping possible, good value.

$ Qhumpuri
On hillside above beach, T7472 6525.
Simple 2-room units with nice views, private toilet, shared electric shower, tasty meals available.

Challapampa

$ Cultural
1 block from beach, T7190 0272.
Clean rooms, cheaper without bath, nice terrace, does not include breakfast, helpful owners, good value.

$ Manco Kapac
By the dock, T7128 8443.
Basic clean rooms, shared bath, electric shower, camping possible, does not include breakfast.

$ Mirador del Sol
At north end of southern bay, past the docks, T7370 6536.
Simple rooms with great views, shared bath, electric shower, no breakfast.

Camping
Camping is permitted along the beach of the northern bay.

La Paz to Copacabana
Huatajata

$$-$ Inti Raymi
Next to Inca Utama hotel, Huatajata.
With fresh fish and boat trips. There are other restaurants of varying standard, most lively at weekends and in the high season.

Copacabana
Excellent restaurants at hotels **Rosario del Lago** and **La Cúpula**. Many touristy places on Av 6 de Agosto toward the lakeshore, all similar.

$$ Café Bistrot Copacabana
Cabo Zapana y 6 de Agosto, upstairs.
Daily 0730-2100.
Varied menu, international dishes, vegetarian options, French and English spoken.

$$-$ La Orilla
Av 6 de Agosto, close to lake.
Daily 1000-2200 (usually).
Warm, atmospheric, tasty food with local and international choices.

$$-$ Mauraz
Av 6 de Agosto, 1 block from Plaza Sucre toward the lake. Open 0730-2230.
A good choice for food (pizza, fast food, breakfasts) and drinks, has a happy hour, music.

$ Aransaya
Av 6 de Agosto 121.
Good restaurant and café serving local dishes, including trout.

$ El Cóndor & The Eagle
Av 6 de Agosto, 1 block from Plaza Sucre toward the lake, upstairs in Residencial París.
Only open for breakfast, good food, sandwiches, cakes, teas and coffee, friendly, English spoken.

$ Snack 6 de Agosto
Av 6 de Agosto, 2 branches.
Good trout, big portions, some vegetarian dishes, serves breakfast.

$ Sujna Wasi
Jaúregui 127. Daily 0730-2300.
Serves breakfast, vegetarian lunch, wide range of books on Bolivia, slow service.

Isla del Sol
Yumani

$$ Las Velas
Yumani, near the top of the hill behind a eucalyptus grove, follow the signs.
Great views, especially at sunset, take a torch for the way back. Lovely candle-lit atmosphere, small choice of excellent meals, all freshly prepared, slow service, but worth the wait.

Festivals

Copacabana
Note At these times hotel prices quadruple.
24 Jan Alacitas, held on Cerro Calvario and at Plaza Colquepata, is when miniature houses, cars and the like are sold and blessed.
1-3 Feb Virgen de la Candelaria, massive procession, dancing, fireworks, bullfights.
Mar/Apr Easter, with candlelight procession on Good Friday.
2-5 May Fiesta del Señor de la Cruz de Colquepata, very colourful with dances in typical costumes.
21 Jun Aymara New Year, celebrated throughout the Titicaca region.
4-6 Aug La Virgen de la Candelaria, processions, dancing, fireworks; coincides with Bolivian Independence Day. Very popular, advance hotel bookings required.

What to do

Lake Titicaca
Crillon Tours, *La Paz, see page 369.* A very experienced company which runs a hydrofoil service on Lake Titicaca with excellent bilingual guides. Tours stop at their Andean Roots cultural complex at Inca Utama. The **Inca Utama Hotel and Spa ($$$)** has a health spa based on natural remedies and Kallawaya medicine; the rooms are comfortable, with heating, electric blankets, good service, bar, restaurant, Wi-Fi, reservations through **Crillon Tours** in La Paz. Crillon is Bolivia's oldest travel agency and is consistently recommended. Also at **Inca Utama** is an observatory (*alajpacha*) with 2 telescopes and retractable roof for viewing the night sky, an altiplano museum, a floating restaurant and bar on the lake (**La Choza Náutica**), a 252-sq-m floating island and examples of different altiplano cultures. Health, astronomical, mystic and ecological programmes are offered. The hydrofoil trips include visits to Andean Roots complex, Copacabana, Islas del Sol and de la Luna, Straits of Tiquina and the Cocotoni community. See Isla del Sol, Where to stay, for **La Posada del Inca**. Crillon has a sustainable tourism project with Urus-Iruitos people from the Río Desaguadero area on floating islands by the Isla Queweya. Trips can be arranged to/from Puno and Juli (bus and hydrofoil excursion to Isla del Sol) and from Copacabana via Isla del Sol to Cuzco and Machu Picchu. Other combinations of hydrofoil and land-based excursions can be arranged (also highland, Eastern lowland, jungle and adventure tours). See http://crillontours.com and www.uyuni.travel for details. All facilities and modes of transport connected by radio.

Transturin, *www.transturin.com, see also page 371.* Run catamarans on Lake Titicaca, either for sightseeing or on the La Paz-Puno route. The catamarans are more leisurely than the hydrofoils of **Crillon** so there is more room and time for on-board meals and entertainment, with bar, video and sun deck. From their dock at Chúa, catamarans run full-day and 2-day/1-night cruises starting either in La Paz or Copacabana. Puno may also be the starting point for trips. Overnight cruises involve staying in a cabin on the catamaran, moored at the Isla del Sol, with lots of activities. On the island,

Transturin has the Inti Wata cultural complex which has restored Inca terraces, an Aymara house, the underground Ekeko museum and cultural demonstrations and activities. There is also a 30-passenger totora reed boat for trips to the Pilcocaina Inca palace. All island-based activities are community-led and for catamaran clients only. Transturin runs through services to Puno without many of the formalities at the border. Transturin also offers last-minute programmes in Puno, Cuzco and La Paz, if booked 6 days prior to departure only. You can book by phone or by email, but ask first, as availability depends on date.

Turisbus, *www.gruporosario.com/turisbus-tours, see La Paz, Tour operators page 371 and Hoteles Rosario, La Paz, and Rosario del Lago, Copacabana.* Offer full-day guided tours in the fast launches *Titicaca Explorer I* (28 passengers) and *II* (8 passengers) to the Isla del Sol, and 2-day tours with an overnight at **Hotel Rosario del Lago** and the option to include Isla de la Luna.

Copacabana

Copacabana town is filled with tour agencies, all offering excursions to floating islands on imitation reed vessels, and tours to Isla del Sol (see Transport, below). Kayak and pedal-boat rentals on the beach, US$3 per hr.

Transport

La Paz to Copacabana: Huatajata
Boat Máximo Catari (see Where to stay, above) and Paulino Esteban (east end of Huatajata, T7196 7383) arrange trips to the islands in Lago Huiñamarca for US$15 per hr.

Bus La Paz–Huatajata, US$1, frequent minibuses from Bustillos y Kollasuyo, Cementerio district, daily 0400-1800, continuing to Tiquina.

Copacabana
If arriving in Bolivia at Copacabana and going to La Paz, it is best to arrive in the city before dark.

Bus To/from **La Paz**, US$2.15 plus US$0.30 for Tiquina crossing, 4 hrs, throughout the day with **Manco Capac**, 2 de Febrero. Both have offices on Copacabana's main plaza (but leave from Plaza Sucre) and in La Paz at Plaza Reyes Ortiz, opposite entrance to cemetery. Buy ticket in advance at weekends and on holidays. Tourist bus services are run by **Trans Titicaca** (www.titicacabolivia.com), **Vicuña Travel**, **Diana Tours** and others, daily from Plaza Sucre, 16 de Julio y 6 de Agosto, US$3.50-4.50. **Trans Titicaca** takes you to the main bus terminal, the others to Sagárnaga e Illampu in the tourist district, but they will not drop you off at your hotel. (See also Border with Peru via Copacabana, below.)

Isla del Sol
Boat Boat companies have ticket booths at the beach, by the bottom of Av 6 de Agosto; there are also agencies selling boat and bus tickets along Av 6 de Agosto. All departures are at 0830, unless otherwise noted, and boats arrive back at Copacabana around 1730. The crossing from Copacabana to Yumani takes about 1½ hrs, to Challpampa 2 hrs. Return tickets are only valid on the same day, get a one way fare if you plan to stay overnight. **Andes Amazonía** run full-day trips Copacabana–Challapampa–Yumani–Copacabana, US$5. If you wish to walk, you can be dropped off at Challapampa around 1030-1100 and picked up at Yumani at 1530 (boats leave punctually, so you will have to walk quickly to see the ruins in the north and then hike south to Yumani and down to the pier). They also have a 1330 departure to Yumani, returning 1600, with a 10-min stop at Pilcocaina on the way back. **Unión Marinos**, run Copacabana–Challapampa–Copacabana, US$4.25 (US$3.50 one way); they depart for Challapampa at 0830 and 1330. **Titicaca Tours** run Copacabana–Coati (Isla de la Luna)–Yumani–Copacabana, US$5.65 return, US$4.25 Copacabana–Coati–Yumani, US$2.80 Copacabana–Yumani; they leave for Coati and Yumani at 0830, with a stop for 1 hr at Coati; they depart at 1330

for Yumani only. They depart from Yumani at 1530. Wilka boats also run from Challa to Copacabana Wed, Sat, Sun at 0700, returning 1330, US$2.80 one way.

From **Yampupata** to Yumani by motorboat, US$15 per boat (US$5 pp by rowing boat). To **Isla de la Luna** from the village of Sampaya, US$21 for a motorboat, US$14 for a rowing boat. **Taxi** Copacabana–Sampaya US$11.50 or take Yampupata transport and get out at the turn-off, 4 km before the village.

Border with Peru
West side of Lake Titicaca
Bus Road paved all the way to Peru. Buses from La Paz to Guaqui and Desaguadero depart from J M Asín y P Eyzaguirre, Cementerio, from 0500, US$1.50, shared taxi US$3, 2 hrs. From Desaguadero to **La Paz** buses depart 4 blocks from bridge, last vehicle 2000.

Via Copacabana
Bus Several agencies go from La Paz to **Puno**, with a change of bus and stop for lunch at Copacabana, or with an open ticket for continuing to Puno later. They charge US$8 and depart La Paz 0800, pick-up from hotel. From Copacabana they continue to the Peruvian border at Kasani and on to Puno, stopping for immigration formalities and changing money (better rates in Puno). Both **Crillon Tours** (page 383) and **Transturin** (page 383) have direct services to Puno without a change of bus at the border. From Copacabana to Puno, with connection to Cuzco, **Trans Titicaca** (www.titicacabolivia.com) at 0900, 1330, 1830 and other agencies at 1330, offices on 6 de Agosto, US$4-5, 3 hrs. Also **Turisbus** (www.gruporosario.com) to Puno from Hotel Rosario del Lago at 1330, US$9, and services La Paz–Copacabana–Cuzco–Machu Picchu. Also **Bolivia Hop**, www.boliviahop.com, hop-on, hop-off service La Paz–Copacabana–Puno–Cuzco 4 days a week. To go to **Cuzco**, you will have to change in Puno where the tour company arranges connections, which may involve a long wait, check details (US$14-22 La Paz–Cuzco). In high season, book at least a day in advance. It is always cheaper, if less convenient, to buy only the next segment of your journey directly from local bus companies and cross the border on your own. *Colectivo* taxi Copacabana (Plaza Sucre)–**Kasani** US$0.55 pp, minivan US$0.45, 15 mins, Kasani–**Yunguyo**, where Peruvian buses start, US$0.30 pp.

East side of Lake Titicaca
Bus **La Paz** (Reyes Cardona 772, Cancha Tejar, Cementerio district, T02-238 2239)–**Puerto Acosta**, 5 hrs, US$4, Tue-Sun 0500. Transport past Puerto Acosta only operates on market days, Wed and Sat, and is mostly cargo trucks. Bus Puerto Acosta–La Paz at about 1500. There are frequent minivans to La Paz from **Escoma**, 25 km from Puerto Acosta; trucks from the border may take you this far.

Cordillera north of La Paz
go trekking and biking in wonderful mountain scenery

Sorata *Colour map 3, B2.*
This beautiful colonial town (population 2523, altitude 2700 m), 163 km from La Paz along a paved road, is nestled at the foot of Mount Illampu; all around it are views over steep lush valleys. The climate is milder and more humid than the altiplano. Nearby are some challenging long-distance treks and mountain-bike adventures, as well as great day-hikes. The town has a charming plaza, with views of the snow-capped summit of Illampu on a clear day. The main fiesta is 14 September.

Tip...
There is no ATM in Sorata, so do take enough cash.

A popular excursion is to **San Pedro cave** ⓘ *0800-1700, US$3, toilets at entrance*, beyond the village of San Pedro. The cave has an underground lake (no swimming allowed) and is lit. It is reached either by road, a 12 km walk (three hours each way), or by a path high above the Río San Cristóbal (about four hours, impassable during the rainy season and not easy at any time). Get clear directions before setting out and take sun protection, food, water, etc. Taxis and pick-ups from the plaza, 0600-2200, US$11 with a 30-minute wait. The **Mirador del Iminapi** (above the community of Laripata) offers excellent views of town and the Larecaja tropical valleys. It is a nice day-walk or take a taxi, 20 minutes, US$11 return.

Trekking and climbing from Sorata

Sorata is the starting point for climbing **Illampu** and **Ancohuma**. All routes out of the town are difficult, owing to the number of paths and the very steep ascent. Experience and full equipment are necessary. You can hire trekking guides and mules (see What to

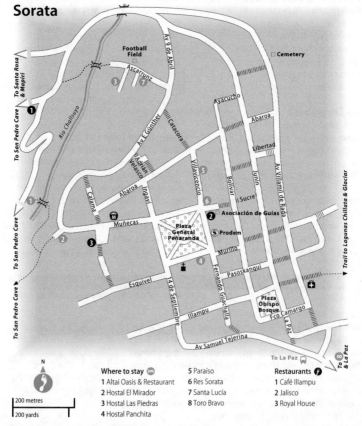

Sorata

N

| 200 metres |
| 200 yards |

Where to stay 🛏
1 Altai Oasis & Restaurant
2 Hostal El Mirador
3 Hostal Las Piedras
4 Hostal Panchita
5 Paraíso
6 Res Sorata
7 Santa Lucía
8 Toro Bravo

Restaurants 🍴
1 Café Illampu
2 Jalisco
3 Royal House

do, page 388). The three- to four-day trek to **Lagunas Chillata and Glaciar** is the most common and gets busy during high season. Laguna Chillata can also be reached by road or on a long day-hike with light gear, but mind the difficult navigation and take warm clothing. Laguna Chillata has been heavily impacted by tourism (remove all trash, do not throw it in the pits around the lake) and groups frequently camp there. The ☆**Illampu Circuit**, a six- to seven-day high-altitude trek (three passes over 4000 m, one over 5000 m) around Illampu, is excellent. It can get very cold and it is a hard walk, though very beautiful with nice campsites. Some food can be bought in Cocoyo on the third day. You must be acclimatized before setting out. Another option is the **Trans-Cordillera Trek**, 10-12 days from Sorata to Huayna Potosí, or longer, all the way to Illimani at the opposite (south) end of the Cordillera Real. Some communities charge visitors fees along the way.

☆Cordillera Apolobamba

The Area Protegida Apolobamba forms part of the Cordillera Apolobamba, the north extension of the Cordillera Real. The range itself has many 5000-m-plus peaks, while the conservation area of some 560,000 ha protects herds of vicuña, huge flocks of flamingos and many condors. The area adjoins the Parque Nacional Madidi (see page 480).

This is great trekking country and the four- to six-day **Charazani to Pelechuco** (or vice versa) mountain trek is one of the best in the country (see Footprint's *Bolivia Handbook* for details). It passes traditional villages and the peaks of the southern Cordillera Apolobamba.

Charazani is the biggest village in the region (3200 m), with hot springs (US$0.75). Its three-day fiesta is around 16 July. There are some cheap *alojamientos*, restaurants and shops. **Pelechuco** (3600 m) is a smaller village, also with cheap *alojamientos*, cafés and shops. The road to Pelechuco goes through the Area Protegida, passing the community of Ulla Ulla, 5 km outside of which are the reserve's HQ at La Cabaña. Visitors are welcome to see the orphaned vicuñas. There are economical community hostels at the villages of Lagunillas and Agua Blanca. Basic food is available in the communities. For information, contact **SERNAP** ⓘ *www.sernap.gob.bo*.

Listings Cordillera north of La Paz *map page 386.*

Where to stay

Sorata

$$ Altai Oasis
T02-213 3895, www.altaioasis.com.
At the bottom of the valley in a beautiful setting, a 15-min steep downhill walk from town, or taxi US$2. Cabins, rooms with bath (cheaper with shared bath), dorms and camping (US$5 pp). Very good restaurant ($$), bar, lovely grounds, pool, peaceful, very welcoming, family-run by the Resnikowskis, English and German spoken. Warmly recommended.

$ Hostal El Mirador
Muñecas 400, T7350 5453.

Cheaper with shared bath, hot water, kitchen, laundry facilities, terrace.

$ Hostal Las Piedras
Just off Ascarrunz, T7191 6341, laspiedras2002@yahoo.de.
Rooms with and without bath, good mattresses, electric shower, very nice, good breakfast with home-made products available, very helpful, English and German spoken. Recommended.

$ Hostal Panchita
On plaza, T02-213 4242.
Simple rooms, shared bath, electric shower, sunny courtyard, washing facilities, does not include breakfast, good value.

$ Paraíso
Villavicencio 117.
With electric shower, basic rooms, terrace, breakfast available.

$ Residencial Sorata
On plaza, T02-213 6672.
Cheaper without bath, electric shower, restaurant, large but scruffy grounds, poor beds, a bit run-down overall but still adequate.

$ Santa Lucía
Ascarrunz, T02-213 6686.
Rooms are cheaper with shared bath, electric shower, carpeted rooms, patio, does not include breakfast, not always open.

$ Toro Bravo
Below petrol station at entrance to town, T7725 5255.
With electric shower, ample grounds and rooms (upstairs rooms are better), small pool, restaurant, a bit faded but good value.

Restaurants

Sorata
There are several $$-$ Italian places on the plaza, all quite similar.

$$-$ Café Illampu
15 mins' walk on the way to San Pedro cave. Closed Tue and Dec-Mar.
Excellent sandwiches, bread and cakes, camping possible. Offers tours with own 4WD vehicle, Swiss-run, English and German spoken.

$$-$ Jalisco
On plaza.
Mexican and Italian dishes, sidewalk seating.

$ Royal House
Off Muñecas by the market.
Decent set lunch, friendly.

Festivals

Sorata
14 Sep Fiesta Patronal del Señor de la Columna, is the main festival.

What to do

Sorata
Guides for trekking
It may be cheaper to go to Sorata and arrange trekking there than to book a trek with an agency in La Paz. Buy necessary foods and supplies in La Paz, Sorata shops have basic items.
Asociación de Guías, *Sucre 302 y Guachalla, leave message at Residencial Sorata (T02-213 6672).* Hires guides, porters and mules. Prices vary: guides approximately US$30 per day, mules US$15 per day. Porters take maximum 2 mules, remember you have to feed your guide/porter.
Eduardo Chura, *T7157 8671, guiasorata@ yahoo.com.* Is an independent local trekking guide.

Mountain biking
Sorata is an increasingly popular destination for mountain biking, especially for long-distance routes from the mountains and gold-mining communities above Sorata, down to the town of Consata and then on to Mapiri in the lowlands. From Mapiri the route continues by jeep or boat to Guanay, from where you can return to La Paz, or carry on by boat to Rurrenabaque. See **Gravity**, page 370, for a company offering this adventure.

Transport

Sorata
Bus Minibuses throughout the day 0400-1800 from **La Paz** with **Trans Unificada** (C Manuel Bustillos 683 y Av Kollasuyo in the Cementerio district, T02-238 1693); also **Perla del Illampu** (Manuel Bustillos 615, T02-238 0548), US$2.50, 3½ hrs. Booking recommended on Fri. In Sorata they leave from C Samuel Tejerina, near the exit to La Paz. To or from **Copacabana** and **Peru**, change buses at Huarina but they are often full so start early and be prepared for a long wait.

Jeep, boat and motorcycle Jeeps run from La Paz (C Chorolque y Tarapacá, T02-245 0296, often full), via Sorata to **Santa Rosa** (US$15, 13 hrs), on the road to **Mapiri** and **Guanay**, a rough route with interesting vegetation and stunning scenery. Onward transport can be found in Santa Rosa. From Guanay private boats may be arranged to **Rurrenabaque**, and vehicles run to Caranavi and thence to Coroico. Sorata–Coroico by this route is excellent for off-road motorcycling. (See also Mountain biking, above.)

If travelling by public transport it is easier to go La Paz–Coroico–Caranavi–Guanay–Santa Rosa–Sorata–La Paz, than vice versa.

Cordillera Apolobamba
Charazani
Bus From C Reyes Cardona 732, off Av Kollasuyo, Cemetery district, **La Paz**, daily with **Trans Altiplano**, 0600-0630, 7 hrs, US$3.50, very crowded. Return to La Paz at 1800; also has 0900 on Sat and 1200 Mon and Fri.

Pelechuco
Bus From **La Paz Trans Provincias del Norte** leaves daily 0600-0700 from Ex Tranca de Río Seco in El Alto, passing through Qutapampa, Ulla Ulla and Agua Blanca to Pelechuco, 10-12 hrs, US$5, sometimes on sale 24 hrs before departure at the booking office in C Reyes Cardona. Return to La Paz between 0300 and 0400 most days.

The Yungas
a 3500-m drop to the green subtropical forest in 70 km

☆Only a few hours from La Paz are the subtropical valleys known as the Yungas. These steep, forested slopes, squeezed in between the Cordillera and the Amazon Lowlands, provide a welcome escape from the chill of the capital. They have become a centre for adrenaline sports including mountain biking, zip-lines, rappelling, a via ferrata, paragliding and more. Many tourists enjoy these on a day-trip from La Paz but the area deserves a longer visit. The warm climate of the Yungas is also ideal for growing citrus fruit, bananas, coffee and especially coca.

La Paz to the Yungas
The roads from La Paz to Nor- and Sud-Yungas go via **La Cumbre**, a pass at 4725 m about one hour northeast of the city. The road out of La Paz circles cloudwards over La Cumbre; all around are towering snow-capped peaks. The first village after the pass is **Unduavi**, where there is a checkpoint, a petrol station and roadside stalls. Beyond Unduavi an unpaved road branches right 75 km to Chulumani and the Sud-Yungas (see below). Beyond Sud-Yungas, to the southeast, are the **Yungas de Inquisivi**, see Quime, page 395. The paved road continues to Cotapata, where it again divides: right is the old unpaved road to Yolosa, the junction 8 km from Coroico (this is the popular cycling route). To the left, the new paved road goes via Chuspipata and Puente Yolosita, where an unpaved road climbs steeply to Coroico. Between Yolosita and Yolosa (see below) is **Senda Verde** ① *T7472 2825, www.sendaverde.com, open 1000-1700, 1-hr tours at 1000, 1100, 1200 and 1500, US$14.50,* an animal refuge, ecolodge ($$) and restaurant with opportunities for volunteering. In addition, from Puente Villa on the Unduavi–Chulumani road, an unpaved road runs to Coripata and Coroico. For the La Cumbre–Coroico hike (Choro), see page 358.

☆All roads to Coroico drop some 3500 m to the green subtropical forest in 70 km. The best views are in May to June, when there is less chance of fog and rain. The old road, the so-called '**World's Most Dangerous Road**', is steep, twisting, clinging to the side of sheer cliffs, and it is slippery in the wet. It is a breathtaking descent (best not to look over the edge if you don't like heights) and its reputation for danger is more than matched by the beauty of the scenery. It

Tip...
The road is especially dangerous when it is raining (mid-December to mid-February), be sure the bike is in top shape and be extra cautious.

passes through **Parque Cotapata** ① www.sernap.gob.bo, and there is a community tax of US$3.55 to enter. Many tourists go on a mountain-bike tour: it is your responsibility to choose top-quality bikes (with hydraulic disc brakes) and a reputable company which offers bilingual guides, helmet, gloves, vehicle support throughout the day (see La Paz, Tour operators, page 369). Many bike companies take riders back to La Paz the same day, but Coroico is worth more of your time. In **Yolosa**, at the end of the bike ride, is a three-segment zip-line (total 1555 m) operated by **Gravity Bolivia** (see page 370 and www.ziplinebolivia.com; T02-231 3849 or book through La Paz agencies).

★Coroico Colour map 3, B2.

The little town of Coroico (population 2903, altitude 1750 m), capital of the Nor-Yungas region, is perched on a hill amid beautiful scenery. The hillside is covered with orange and banana groves and coffee plantations. Coroico is a first-class place to relax with several good walks. A colourful four-day festival is held 19-22 October. On 2 November, All Souls' Day, the cemetery is festooned with black ribbons.

A good walk is up to the waterfalls, starting from **El Calvario**. Follow the stations of the cross by the cemetery, off Calle Julio Zuazo Cuenca, which leads steeply uphill from the plaza. Facing the chapel at El Calvario, with your back to the town, look for the path on your left. This leads to the falls which are the town's water supply (Toma de Agua) and, beyond, to two more falls. **Cerro Uchumachi**, the mountain behind El Calvario, can be climbed following the same stations of the cross, but then look for the faded red and white antenna behind the chapel. From there it's about two hours' steep walk to the top (take water). A third walk goes to the pools in the **Río Vagante**, 7 km off the road to Coripata; it takes about three hours. With the Yungas so close to La Paz, you get the chance to see the production of crops which cannot be grown at high altitude and some farms welcome visitors to their fruit, coffee or coca leaf plantations. In the interests of personal safety, women in particular should not hike alone in this area. There are two ATMs on the plaza and the hospital is the best in the Yungas.

Caranavi Colour map 3, B2.

From the junction at Puente Yolosita, the paved road follows the river 11 km to Santa Bárbara, then 65 km to Caranavi (population 21,883, altitude 600 m), an uninspiring town 156 km from La Paz. From here the road continues towards the settled area of the Alto Beni, at times following a picturesque gorge. Market days are Friday and Saturday. There is a range of hotels and alojamientos and buses from La Paz (Villa Fátima) to Rurrenabaque pass through. Beyond Caranavi, 70 km, is **Guanay** at the junction of the Tipuani and Mapiri rivers (see also under Sorata, page 385).

Sud-Yungas

The capital of Sud-Yungas is **Chulumani,** a small town (population 3650), 124 km from La Paz, with beautiful views. There are many birds in the area and good hiking. The Fiesta de San Bartolomé (24 August) lasts 10 days and there is a lively market every weekend. There is no ATM in Chulumani, take cash. **Irupana** is a friendly little colonial village (altitude 1900 m, irupana.bolivia on Facebook), is 31 km east of Chulmani (minibus or shared taxi US$2) and has a lovely location, delightful climate, more good walking and birdwatching, and a couple of very nice places to stay.

Listings The Yungas

Tourist information

Coroico
A good independent website is www.coroico.info.

Gobernación
Corner of the main plaza.

Chulumani
Tourist office
In the main plaza. Open irregular hours, mostly weekends.

Where to stay

Coroico
Hotel rooms are hard to find at holiday weekends and prices are higher.

$$$-$$ El Viejo Molino
1 km on road to Santa Bárbara, T02-243 0020, www.hotelviejomolino.com.
Upmarket hotel and spa, offers massage, pool, gym, games room, rafting and other tours, restaurant with set menu lunch and dinner.

$$$-$$ Gloria
C Kennedy 1, T02-289 5554, www.hotelgloria.com.bo.
Traditional resort hotel, full board, pool, restaurant with set lunches and à la carte, internet, transport from plaza at extra charge.

$$ Esmeralda
On the edge of town, C Julio Suazo 10 mins uphill from plaza (see website for transport), T02-213 6017, www.hotelesmeraldacoroico.com.
Most rooms include breakfast, cheaper in dorms, prices rise at weekends, hot showers, satellite TV and DVD, book exchange, good buffet restaurant, sauna, garden,

pool, camping, can arrange local tours and transport to/from La Paz, free pick-up from Coroico bus stop or Plaza.

$$ Sol y Luna
Carretera Apanto Alto, 15-20 mins beyond Hotel Esmeralda, T7156 1626, www.solyluna-bolivia.com.
Excellent accommodation in fully equipped cabins, apartments and rooms with and without bath, splendid views, restaurant (vegetarian specialities), camping US$6.50 pp (not suitable for cars), garden, pool, hot tub US$13, shiatsu massage and yoga available, good value, Sigrid (owner) speaks English, French, German, Spanish.

$$-$ Bella Vista
C Héroes del Chaco 7 (2 blocks from main plaza), T02-213 6059, www.coroicobellavista.blogspot.com.
Beautiful rooms and views, includes breakfast, cheaper without bath, racquetball court, terrace, bike hire, restaurant.

$$-$ Hostal Kory
At top of steps leading down from the plaza, T02-243 1234/7156 4050, info@hostalkory.com.
Rooms with and without bath, electric showers, restaurant, huge pool, terrace, good value but basic, helpful.

$ Don Quijote
500 m out of town, on road to Coripata, T02-213 6007.
Economical, electric shower, pool, quiet, nice views.

$ El Cafetal
Miranda, next to the hospital, a 10-min walk from town, T7193 3979, http://elcafetal.coroico.info.

Rooms with and without bath, very nice, great views, pool, restaurant with excellent French/Indian/vegetarian cuisine, French-run, a good choice.

$ Los Tunqui Eye
Iturralde 4043, T7350 0081.
Simple rooms with and without bath, hot water, good value.

$ Matsu
1 km from town on road to El Calvario (call for free pick-up, taxi US$2), T7069 2219, ecolodgematsu@hotmail.com.
Economical, has restaurant, pool, views, quiet, helpful.

$ Residencial de la Torre
Julio Zuazo Cuenca, ½ block from plaza, T02-289 5542.
Welcoming place with courtyard, cheap sparse rooms, no alcoholic drinks allowed.

Sud-Yungas
Chulumani
Chulumani suffers from water shortages, check if your hotel has a reserve tank.

$$ Monarca
Av Circunvalación, T7673 6121, velezdimopolus@hotmail.com.
Good hotel, largest in the area, with pool, gardens, restaurant, parking.

$$ San Bartolomé
T02-244 1111, plaza@plazabolivia.com.bo.
Comfortable rooms and cabins in a rural setting, pool, sports field, games room, mini-golf, restaurant and bar.

$ Country House
400 m out of town on road to cemetery, T7528 2212, La Paz T02-274 5584, countryhouse.chulumani on Facebook.
Rooms with hot water, lovely tranquil setting, pool and gardens, library, video room, restaurant, bar, family-run. Enthusiastic owner Xavier Sarabia is hospitable and offers hiking advice and tours, English spoken.

$ Tarapari
On the outskirts, 10 mins' walk from centre, T7651 5088.
Guesthouse in a biodiversity garden, butterfly sanctuary and organic coffee farm, 3 rooms, shared bath, price is per person, breakfast included, use of kitchen extra, also tours, workshops and treks. Base of **La Paz on Foot**'s Sud Yungas tours (see www. lapazonfoot.com and page 370).

Irupana

$ Nirvana Inn
Uphill at the edge of town past the football field, T02-213 6154.
Comfortable cabins on beautiful grounds with great views, pool, sauna, parking, flower and orchid gardens lovingly tended by the owners. Includes breakfast, other meals on request.

Coroico

$$ Bamboos
Iturralde y Ortiz.
Good Mexican food and pleasant atmosphere, live music some nights with cover charge. Happy hour 1800-1900.

$$-$ Carla's Garden Pub and Pastelería Alemana Back-stube
Pasaje Adalid Linares, 50 m from the main plaza, T7207 5620. Wed-Sun 1200-2230.
Sandwiches, snacks, pasta and international food, vegetarian options, German dishes, coffee, groups catered for. Lots of music, live music at weekends. Garden, hammocks, games, book exchange, terrace with panoramic views, nice atmosphere, tourist information.

$ Pizzería Italia
2 with same name on the plaza.
Daily 1000-2300.
Pizza, pasta, snacks.

Chulumani

There are a couple of other places around the plaza, all closed Mon. Basic eateries up the hill by bus stops.

$ La Cabaña Yungeña
C Sucre 2 blocks below plaza. Tue-Sun.
Simple set lunch and dinner.

What to do

Coroico
Coffee production
Café Munaipata, *Camino a Carmen Pampa Km 4, T7204 2824, www.cafemunaipata.com.* Visits to a finca producing high-altitude coffee. Recommended. They also have an outlet in the San Pedro district of La Paz, T02-249 0356.

Cycling
CXC, *T7157 3015, cxc_mtb@yahoo.com.* Contact 2 days in advance by phone or email. Good bikes, US$25 for 6 hrs including packed lunch, a bit disorganized but good fun and helpful, English and German spoken.

Horse riding
El Relincho, *Don Reynaldo, 100 m past Hotel Esmeralda (enquire here).* Rides from 2 hrs to 2 days; average price US$30 for 4 hrs.

Language classes
Siria León Domínguez, *T7195 5431.* US$6.50 per hr, also rents rooms, makes silver jewellery and gives language classes in Coroico and La Paz, excellent English.

Transport

Coroico
Bus From La Paz all companies are at Minasa terminal, Puente Minasa, in Villa Fátima: minibuses and buses (less often) leave throughout the day US$3-4.50, 2½ hrs on the paved road: **Turbus Totaí, Palmeras, Yungueña** and several others. Services return to La Paz from the small terminal down the hill in Coroico, across from the football field. All are heavily booked at weekends and on holidays.

To **Rurrenabaque**: take a pick-up from the small mirador at Pacheco y Sagárnaga that go to **Puente Yolosita**, 15 mins, US$0.70. Here you can try to catch a bus, but they are usually full. Ask at **Turbus Totaí** or others in the Coroico terminal if you can reserve a seat to Rurre (US$9). There are also *trufis* (US$3.25) and trucks from Yolosita to **Caranavi**, where La Paz–Rurre buses pass through in the evening, often full. After Caranavi the road goes to Sapecho and then Yucumo, from where *trufis* go to Rurre. Caranavi–Rurre 12 hrs minimum, US$7, **Flota Yungueña**, at 1800-1900, **Turbus Totaí** 2100-2200, and others. See also **Gravity** and **Deep Rainforest**, La Paz (page 370). For Guanay to **Sorata** via **Mapiri** and **Santa Rosa**, see page 388.

Sud-Yungas
Bus From **La Paz** to Chulumani, several companies from Virgen del Carmen y San Borja, Villa Fátima, leave when full, US$4, 4 hrs: eg **San Cristóbal** and 24 de Agosto, both also go to Irupana. In Chulumani most buses leave from the top of the hill by the petrol station; minibuses and taxis to local villages from plaza.

Southwest Bolivia

The mining town of Oruro, shimmering salt flats, coloured lakes and surrealistic rock formations combine to make this one of the most fascinating regions of Bolivia. Add some of the country's most celebrated festivals and the last hideout of Butch Cassidy and the Sundance Kid and you have the elements for some great and varied adventures. The journey across the altiplano from Uyuni to San Pedro de Atacama is a popular route to Chile and there are other routes south to Argentina.

Oruro and around   *Colour map 3, B3. See map, page 398.*

dancing devils and old tin mines

★The mining town of Oruro (population 264,943) is the gateway to the altiplano of southwest Bolivia. It's a somewhat drab, dirty, functional place which explodes into life once a year with its famous carnival, symbolized by La Diablada (see box, page 396). To the west is the national park encompassing Bolivia's highest peak, Sajama.

Although Oruro became famous as a mining town, there are no longer any working mines of importance. It is, however, a railway terminus and the commercial centre for the mining communities of the altiplano, as well as hosting the country's best-known carnival (see La Diablada, page 396).

Sights

The Plaza 10 de Febrero and surroundings are well maintained and several buildings in the centre hint at the city's former importance. The **Museo Simón Patiño** ⓘ *Soria Galvarro 5755, Mon-Fri 0830-1130, 1430-1800, Sat 0900-1500, US$1*, which was built as a mansion by the tin baron Simón Patiño, is now run by the Universidad Técnica de Oruro in the Casa de Cultura and contains European furniture and temporary exhibitions.

There is a view from the Cerro Corazón de Jesús, near the church of the Virgen del Socavón, which is five blocks west of Plaza 10 de Febrero at the end of Calle Mier. The **Museo Sacro, Folklórico, Arqueológico y Minero** ⓘ *inside the Church of the Virgen del Socavón, T02-525 0616, entry via the church daily 0900-1145, 1500-1800, US$1.50, guided tours every 45 mins*, contain religious art, clothing and jewellery and, after passing through old mining tunnels and displays of mining techniques, a representation of El Tío (the god of the underworld).

Museo Antropológico Eduardo López Rivas ⓘ *south of centre on Av España y Urquidi, T02-527 4020, daily 0800-1200, 1400-1800, US$0.75, guide mandatory, getting there: take*

Essential Southwest Bolivia

Getting around

The only airport serving the region is at Uyuni, with flights to/from La Paz (expensive). The area can also be reached along roads from Potosí and Tarija, both of which have flights to/from La Paz and Cochabamba. Tarija also has flights from Santa Cruz. Tupiza is reached from Potosí, Tarija or Argentina. The road from La Paz to Oruro is a dual carriageway, which has paved connections to Cochabamba and Chile and from Oruro to Potosí. From Potosí to Uyuni there is a good paved road. Another excellent paved road runs from Oruro to Uyuni and work is in progress to extend it as far as Tupiza. Tupiza to Villazón is also paved. Travel times in the area have been reduced and train travel is losing importance in the face of improved bus service.

Safety

Getting stranded out on the altiplano or, worse yet on the *salar* itself, is dangerous because of extreme temperatures and total lack of drinking water. It is best to visit this area with a tour operator. Travellers with their own vehicle should be aware that the edges of the *salares* are soft and only established entry points or ramps (*terraplenes*) should be used to cross onto or off the salt. The intersalar route (Oruro–Coipasa–Uyuni) should only be attempted following extensive local inquiry or after taking on a guide to avoid becoming lost or bogged.

When to go

The altiplano can be bitterly cold at night, especially in the drier months of May to September. Sunny days can be dazzling and warm and protection against the sun is needed. The rainy season is November to March, when travel can be disrupted. The high season is June to August, but in the wet season there is a popular market for rapid tours to see the Salar de Uyuni as a mirror, in and out in a day.

Time required

Except at carnival time, Oruro itself requires a day or two, but once you head south into the *salares*, the minimum you should spend is four days. Most tours of the Salar de Uyuni area are this long, but you can easily extend this for further exploration. If you continue to Tupiza or start there, add another two or three days, but bear in mind the time required for transport into and out of the region.

micro A heading south or any trufi going south. It has a unique collection of stone llama heads as well as impressive carnival masks. The **Museo Mineralógico y Geológico** ① *part of the University, T02-526 1250, Mon-Sat 0800-1200, 1400-1900, US$0.70, getting there: take micro A south to the Ciudad Universitaria,* has mineral specimens and fossils. **Casa Arte Taller Cardozo Velásquez** ① *Junín 738 y Arica, east of the centre, T02-527 5245, http://catcarve. blogspot.co.uk, Mon-Sat 1000-1200, 1500-1800, US$1,* features contemporary Bolivian painting and sculpture displayed in the Cardozo Velásquez home, a family of artists.

There are thermal baths outside town at **Obrajes** ① *23 km from Oruro, minibuses leave from Caro y Av 6 de Agosto, US$1, 45 mins; baths open 0700-1800, US$1.50, Oruro office: Murgía 1815 y Camacho, T02-525 0646.*

Quime

North of Oruro, 2½ hours by bus (233 km, four hours south of La Paz) is the junction at Konani, where there are a few places to eat. From here a beautiful road, mostly paved, runs over the altiplano to the **Tres Cruces pass** (over 5000 m) before dropping a spectacular

ON THE ROAD

★La Diablada

If you are in Bolivia in the period before Lent, you should make every effort to visit Oruro to witness one of South America's most distinctive festivals. Starting on the Saturday before Ash Wednesday, Los Carnavales de Oruro include the famous **Diablada** ceremony in homage to the miraculous Virgen del Socavón, patroness of miners, and in gratitude to Pachamama, the Earth Mother. The carnival is especially notable for its fantastically elaborate and imaginative costumes. The Diablada was traditionally performed by indigenous miners, but several other guilds have taken up the custom.

The **Sábado de Peregrinación** starts its 5 km route through the town at 0700, finishing at the Sanctuary of the Virgen del Socavón, and continues into the early hours of Sunday. There the dancers invoke blessings and ask for pardon.

At dawn on Sunday, **El Alba** is a competition of all participating musicians at Plaza del Folklore near the Santuario, an amazing battle of the bands. The **Gran Corso** or **La Entrada** starts at 0800 on the Sunday, a more informal parade along the same route.

Monday is **El Día del Diablo y del Moreno** in which the Diablos and Morenos, with their bands, bid farewell to the Virgin. Arches decorated with colourful woven cloths and silverware are set up on the road leading to the Santuario, where a Mass is held. In the morning, at Avenida Cívica, the Diablada companies participate in a play of the Seven Deadly Sins. This is followed by a play about the meeting of the Inca Atahualpa with Pizarro. On Tuesday, **Martes de Chall'a**, families get together, with ch'alla rituals to invoke ancestors and unite with Pachamama. The Friday before Carnaval,

---

2000 m to Quime (founded 1887, population 3000), a town in the Yungas de Inquisivi at the southern edge of the Cordillera Quimsa Cruz. It can also be reached along scenic secondary roads from Chulumani in Sud-Yungas and Cochabamba. It's an increasingly popular escape from La Paz, to relax or hike in the *cordillera*. Excursions include to Aymara mining communities and waterfalls and mountain-biking trips, including a downhill from Tres Cruces. The main festival is 24-25 July (Apóstol Santiago). There are basic services, modem internet in the Biblioteca Municipal in the Alcaldía at the Plaza, but no ATMs.

☆Parque Nacional Sajama
Park HQ in Sajama village, T02-513 5526 (in La Paz SERNAP T02-242 6268, or 252 8080), www.biobol.org, US$4.25 payable to community of Sajama.

A one-day drive to the west of Oruro, Parque Nacional Sajama was established in 1939. Covering 100,230 ha, it contains the world's highest forest, consisting mainly of the rare queñual tree (*Polylepis tarapacana*) which grows up to an altitude of 5500 m. The scenery is wonderful with views of several volcanoes, including Sajama – Bolivia's highest peak at 6542 m – Parinacota and Pomerape (jointly called Payachatas). The road is paved and leads across the border into the Parque Nacional Lauca in Chile. You can trek in the park, with or without porters and mules, but once you move away from the Río Sajama or its major tributaries, lack of water is a problem. There is basic accommodation in Sajama village (see below) as well as a more comfortable and expensive option at **Tomarapi** on the north side of the mountain; see page 400.

traditional miners' ceremonies are held at mines, including the sacrifice of a llama. Visitors may only attend with advance permission.

Preparations for Carnaval begin four months before the actual event, on the first Sunday of November, and rehearsals are held every Sunday until one week before Carnaval, when a plain clothes rehearsal takes place, preceded by a Mass for participants. In honour of its syncretism of ancestral Andean traditions and Catholic faith, the Oruro Carnaval has been included on UNESCO's Heritage of Humanity list.

Seating Stands are erected along the entire route. Tickets are for Saturday and Sunday, there is no discount if you stay only one day. Some stands have a cover for shade or rain. A prime location is around Plaza 10 de Febrero where the companies perform in front of the authorities. Along Avenida 6 de Agosto a sought-after location is by TV cameras, where performers put on their best. Seats cost US$35-70.

Where to stay During Carnaval, accommodation costs as much as five times more than normal and must be booked well in advance. Hotels charge for Friday, Saturday and Sunday nights. You can stay for only one night, but you'll be charged for three. Locals also offer places to stay in their homes, expect to pay at least US$12 per person per night.

Transport When demand is at its peak, posted prices are ignored and buses from La Paz charge three or more times the usual fare. Buses fill quickly starting Friday and tickets are not sold in advance. Many agencies in La Paz organize day-trips for the Saturday parade. They leave around 0430 and return late. Trips in 2016 cost US$150 and up (much more for seats on the plaza) for transport, breakfast, box lunch, drinks and seats for the parade.

Sajama village In Sajama village (population 500, altitude 4200 m), visitors are billeted in basic family-run *alojamientos* on a rotating basis (about US$4.50 per person). All are basic to very basic, especially the sanitary facilities; no showers or electricity, solar power for lighting only. *Alojamientos* may provide limited food, so take your own supplies. It can be very windy and cold at night; a good sleeping bag, gloves and hat are essential. Crampons, ice axe and rope are needed for climbing the volcanoes and can be hired in the village. Maps are hard to find. Local guides charge US$50-70 per day. Pack animals can be hired for US$10 per day including guide. Good bathing is available at the Manasaya thermal complex, 6 km northwest of the village (entry US$4.25). Many villagers sell alpaca woollen items.

By road to Chile

The shortest and most widely used route from La Paz to Chile is the road to **Arica** via the border at **Tambo Quemado** (Bolivia) and **Chungará** (Chile). From La Paz take the highway south towards Oruro. Immediately before Patacamaya (see above), turn right at a green road sign to Puerto Japonés on the Río Desaguadero, then on to Tambo Quemado.

Bolivian **customs and immigration** are at Tambo Quemado, where there are a couple of very basic places to stay and eat. Border control is open daily 0800-2000. Shops change bolivianos, Chilean pesos and US dollars. From Tambo Quemado there is a stretch of about 7 km of 'no-man's land'

Tip...
Take extra petrol (none available after Chilean border until Arica), food and water.

before you reach the Chilean frontier at Chungará. Here the border crossing, which is set against the most spectacular scenic backdrop of Lago Chungará and Volcán Parinacota, is thorough but efficient; open 0800-2000. Expect a long wait at weekends and any day behind lines of lorries. Drivers must fill in 'Relaciones de Pasajeros', US$0.25 from a kiosk at border, giving details of driver, vehicle and passengers. Do not take any livestock, plants, fruit, vegetables, coca or dairy products into Chile.

An alternative crossing from Oruro: several bus companies travel southwest to Iquique, via the border posts of **Pisiga** (Bolivia) and **Colchane** (Chile). The road is paved

Oruro

Where to stay 🛏
1 El Lucero *A3*
2 Flores Plaza *C2*
3 Gran Sucre *D2*
4 Repostero *D3*
5 Res Gran Boston *C3*
6 Samay Wasi *D2*
7 Villa Real San Felipe *D2*

Restaurants 🍴
1 Ardentia *C2*
2 Café Sur *D2*
3 Govinda *D2*
4 La Casona *C2*
5 Las Retamas *D1*
6 Nayjama *D3*
7 Panadería Doña Filo *D2*
8 Sergio's *C2*

from Oruro to Toledo (32 km) and from Opoquari to Pisiga via Huachachalla (about 100 km). The rest of the 170-km road in Bolivia is due to be paved; on the Chilean side it's paved all the way to Iquique, 250 km. There is also service from Oruro to Arica via Patacamaya and Tambo Quemado.

South of Oruro

Salar de Coipasa and around Reached via the Oruro–Pisiga–Iquique road (turn off at **Sabaya**), is the **Salar de Coipasa**, 225 km from Oruro. It is smaller and less visited than the Salar de Uyuni, and has a turquoise lake in the middle of the salt pan surrounded by mountains with gorgeous views and large cacti.

Coipasa is northwest of the Salar de Uyuni and travel from one to the other is possible with a private vehicle along the impressive **Ruta Intersalar**. Along the way are tombs, terracing and ancient irrigation canals at the archaeological site of **Alcaya** ⓘ *US$1.25*, gradually being developed by the local community. It is near **Salinas de Garci Mendoza**, locally known as Salinas (SalinasDeGarciMendoza on Facebook), a pleasant colonial town with basic services and places to stay and eat and a petrol station.

At the edge of the Salar de Uyuni is **Coquesa** (lodging available), which has a mirador and tombs with mummies (US$1.25 entry to each site). Nearby are the towering volcanic cones of Cora Cora and Tunupa. Access to the north end of the Salar de Uyuni is at **Jirira**, east of Coquesa, with a salt hotel (see **Posada Doña Lupe**, Where to stay, below) and airstream camper vans run by **Crillon Tours** (www.uyuni.travel).

Listings Oruro and around *map page 398.*

Tourist information

Oruro

Tourist office
Bolívar y Montes 6072, Plaza 10 de Febrero, T02-525 0144. Mon-Fri 0800-1200, 1430-1830.
Helpful and informative.

The **Prefectura** and the **Policía de Turismo** jointly run information booths in front of the **Terminal de Buses** (T02-528 7774, Mon-Fri 0800-1200, 1430-1830, Sat 0830-1200); and opposite the **railway station** (T02-525 7881), same hours.

Quime

Info Tur office
Av Bolívar, near Avaroa, 2 blocks from Plaza Principal, T02-213 5644, or 6813 0384, Turismo Quime Bolivia on Facebook.
Not open all the time, but very helpful.

Where to stay

Oruro

$$ Flores Plaza
Adolfo Mier 735 at Plaza 10 de Febrero, T02-525 2561, www.floresplazahotel.com.
Comfortable carpeted rooms, central location.

$$ Gran Sucre
Sucre 510 esq 6 de Octubre, T02-525 4100, hotelsucreoruro@entelnet.bo.
Refurbished old building (faded elegance), rooms and newer suites, heaters on request, internet in lobby, helpful staff.

$$ Samay Wasi
Av Brasil 232 opposite the bus terminal, T02-527 6737, www.hotelessamaywasi.com.
Carpeted rooms, discount for IYHF members, has a 2nd branch in Uyuni (Av Potosí 965).

$$ Villa Real San Felipe
San Felipe 678 y La Plata, south of the centre, T02-525 4993.

Quaint hotel, nicely furnished but small rooms, heating, buffet breakfast, sauna and whirlpool, restaurant, tour operator.

$$-$ Repostero
Sucre 370 y Pagador, T02-525 8001.
Hot water, parking, restaurant serves set lunch. Renovated carpeted rooms are more expensive but better value than their old rooms.

$ El Lucero
21 de Enero 106 y Brasil, opposite the terminal, T02-527 9468, www.hotelbernal-lucero.com.bo.
Multi-storey hotel, reliable hot water, front rooms noisy, good value.

$ Residencial Gran Boston
Pagador 1159 y Cochabamba, T02-527 4708.
Refurbished house, rooms around a covered patio, cheaper with shared bath, good value.

Quime

There are various other basic, slightly cheaper *alojamientos* in town (eg of the Helguero family, in an old house, nice, clean; also Santiago).

$ Hostal Rancho Colibrí
4 steep blocks uphill from main plaza (ask directions or see website, it's not easy to spot), http://ranchocolibri.wordpress.com.
8 simple rooms with shared bath, breakfast extra but has a fully equipped kitchen, most guests do their own cooking. Ask for printed information on the area (website is helpful).

$ Quime
Close to Plaza Principal.
Big, basic place with shared bath, a couple of more expensive rooms have bath, TV, windows on to corridor, private rooms in a smaller block.

Parque Nacional Sajama

$$ Tomarapi Ecolodge
North of Sajama in Tomarapi community, near Caripe, ecotomarapi@yahoo.es (see

tomarapi on Facebook), represented by Millenarian Tourism & Travel, Av Sánchez Lima 2193, La Paz, T02-241 4753, www. boliviamilenaria.com.
Including full board (good food) and guiding service with climbing shelter at 4900 m, helpful staff, simple but comfortable, with hot water, heating.

South of Oruro

$ Alojamiento Paraíso
Sabaya.
Take a sleeping bag, shared bath, cold water, meals on request or take own food. Sells petrol.

$ Doña Wadi
Salinas de Garci Mendoza, C Germán Busch, near main plaza, T02-513 8015.
Shared bath, hot water, basic but clean, meals available.

$ Posada Doña Lupe
Jirira.
Partly made of salt, hot water, cheaper without bath, use of kitchen but bring your own food, no meals available, caters to tour groups, pleasant, comfortable.

$ Zuk'arani
On a hillside overlooking Salinas de Garci Mendoza and the salar, T02-513 7086, zukarani@hotmail.com.
2 cabins for 4, with bath, hot water, cheaper in rooms with shared bath, hot water, meals on request.

Restaurants

Oruro

$$ Nayjama
Aldana 1880.
Good regional specialities, very popular for lunch, huge portions.

$$-$ Las Retamas
Murguía 930 esq Washington.
Mon-Sat 0930-2330, Sun 0930-1430.

Excellent quality and value for set lunches ($), Bolivian and international dishes à la carte, very good pastries at **Kuchen Haus**, pleasant atmosphere, attentive service, a bit out of the way but well worth the trip. Recommended.

$ Ardentia
Sorria Galvarro y Junín, open 1900-2200.
Home cooking, tasty pasta and meat dishes.

$ Govinda
6 de Octubre 6071. Mon-Sat 0900-2130.
Excellent vegetarian.

$ La Casona
Pres Montes 5970, opposite Post Office. Closed midday.
Salteñas in the morning. Good *pizzería* at night.

$ Sergio's
La Plata y Mier, at Plaza 10 de Febrero.
Very good pizza, hamburgers, snacks; also pastries in the afternoon, good service.

Cafés

Café Sur
Arce 163 entre Velasco y 6 de Agosto, near train station. Tue-Sat.
Live entertainment, seminars, films, good place to meet local students.

Panadería Doña Filo
6 de Octubre esq Sucre. Closed Sun.
Excellent savoury snacks and sweets, takeaway only.

Bars and clubs

Oruro

Bravo
Montesinos y Pagador. Open 2100-0300.
Varied music.

Imagine
6 de Octubre y Junín. Open 2200-0400.
Latin and other music.

Shopping

Oruro
Camping equipment
Camping Oruro, *Pagador 1660, T02-528 1829, camping_oruro@hotmail.com.*

Crafts
On Av La Paz the blocks between León and Belzu are largely given over to workshops producing masks and costumes for Carnaval.
Artesanías Oruro, *A Mier 599, esq S Galvarro.* Lovely selection of regional handicrafts produced by 6 rural community cooperatives; nice sweaters, carpets, wall-hangings.

Markets
C Bolívar is the main shopping street.
Global, *Junín y La Plata.* A well-stocked supermarket.
Irupana, *S Galvarra y A Mier.* Sells natural food and snacks.
Mercado Campero, *V Galvarro esq Bolívar.* Sells everything, also *brujería* section for magical concoctions.
Mercado Fermín López, *C Ayacucho y Montes.* Sells food and hardware.
Mercado Kantuta, *Tacna entre Beni y D, north of the bus terminal; take minibus from northeast corner of Plaza 10 de Febrero.* A *campesino* market on Tue and Fri.

What to do

Oruro
Asociación de Guías Mineros, *contact Gustavo Peña, T02-523 2446.* Arranges visits to San José mine, US$7-10.
Freddy Barrón, *T02-527 6776, lufba@hotmail.com.* Custom-made tours and transport, speaks German and some English.

Transport

Oruro
Bus Bus terminal 10 blocks north of centre at Bakovic and Aroma, T02-527 5070/9554, US$0.25 terminal use fee, luggage store,

ATMs. Micro 2 to centre, or any saying 'Plaza 10 de Febrero'. To **Challapata** and **Huari**: several companies go about every hour, US$1, 1¾ hrs, and Huari, US$1.25, 2 hrs, last bus back leaves Huari about 1630. You can also take a bus to Challapata and a shared taxi from there to Huari, US$0.30. Daily services to: **La Paz** (along a 4-lane motorway) at least every hour 0400-2200, US$4-5.35, 3-4 hrs; also tourist van service with **Enjoy Bolivia**, see La Paz Tour operators, page 369. **Cochabamba**, US$4.50-5.75, 4 hrs, frequent. **Potosí**, US$5.50-7.50, 5 hrs, several daily. **Sucre**, all buses around 2000, US$9-12, 9 hrs. **Tarija**, 2 departures at 2030, US$14.50, 14 hrs. **Uyuni**, several companies, all depart 1900-2100, US$7 regular, US$10.75 semi-cama, 7-8 hrs. **Todo Turismo**, offers a tourist bus departing from La Paz at 2100, arrange ahead for pick-up in Oruro at midnight, US$28, office Rodríguez 134 entre 6 de Agosto y Bakovic, T02-511 1889. To **Tupiza**, via Potosí, **Boquerón** at 1230, **Illimani** at 1630 and 2000, US$13, 11-12 hrs, continuing to Villazón, US$14.50, 13-14 hrs. **Santa Cruz, Bolívar** at 2000, US$12, bus cama at 2130, US$17, 11 hrs. To **Pisiga** (Chilean border), **Trans Pisiga**, Av Dehene y España, T02-526 2241, at 2000 and 2030, or with Iquique bound buses, US$5, 4-5 hrs. **International buses** (US$2 to cross border): to **Iquique** via Pisiga, US$17, 8 hrs, buses leave around 1200 coming from Cochabamba. **Arica** via Patacamaya and Tambo Quemado, several companies daily around 1100-1300 and 2300, US$25 normal, US$30 semi-cama, US$37 cama, 8 hrs, some continue to Iquique, 12 hrs.

Train The station is at Av Velasco Galvarro y Aldana, T02-527 4605, ticket office Mon-Fri 0800-1200, 1430-1800, Sun 0830-1120, 1530-1800. Tickets for ejecutivo class are sold up to 4 weeks in advance, 1 week for salón. Tickets can also be purchased in La Paz, see page 373. **Ferroviaria Andina** (FCA, www.fca. com.bo), runs services from Oruro to **Uyuni**, **Tupiza** and **Villazón**. **Expreso del Sur** runs Tue and Fri at 1530, arriving in Uyuni at 2220, and **Wara Wara** on Sun and Wed at 1900, arriving in Uyuni at 0220.

    Fares Expreso del Sur to **Uyuni**, Ejecutivo US$15, Salón US$7.50; **Tupiza**, 12½ hrs: US$30, US$13.50; **Villazón**: 15½ hrs, US$34.75, US$15.75. **Wara Wara del Sur** to **Uyuni**: Ejecutivo US$13.50, Salón US$6; **Tupiza**, 13½-14 hrs: US$22.50, US$10 respectively; **Villazón**, 17 hrs: US$27.50, US$12.50.

Quime

Bus To get to Quime, take any bus from La Paz to Oruro or Cochabamba and get out at Konani, 2-3 hrs, US$2 (likewise get out at Konani coming from Oruro or Cochabamba). Change to a bus, minibus or taxi (wait till full) to Quime, 1½ hrs, US$3.75. Direct buses from La Paz to Quime, 5 hrs, are **Inquisivi** from the bus terminal (T282 4734) and **Apóstol Santiago** from El Alto (T259 7544), US$3.75. All transport stops on the Alameda in town.

Parque Nacional Sajama

Bus To get to the park, take a La Paz–Oruro bus and change at Patacamaya. Minivans from Patacamaya to Sajama Sun-Fri 1200, 3 hrs, US$2.75. Sajama to **Patacamaya** Mon-Fri 0600, some days via **Tambo Quemado**, confirm details and weekend schedule locally. From Tambo Quemado to Sajama about 1530 daily, 1 hr, US$0.75. Or take a La Paz–Arica bus, ask for Sajama, try to pay half the fare, but you may be charged full fare.

South of Oruro

Bus To **Coipasa** ask if **Trans Pisiga** (see above) is running a fortnightly service. If not, you can take one of the buses for Iquique and get off at the turn-off, but it's difficult to hire a private vehicle for onward transportation in this sparsely populated area. Salinas de Garci Mendoza from **Oruro**, **Trans Cabrera**, C Tejerina y Caro, daily except Sat (Mon, Wed Fri, Sun 1900, Tue, Thu 0830, Sun also at 0730). Return to Oruro same days, US$3.40, 7 hrs. Also **Trans Thunupa**, daily 1800, 1900, office at Tarapacá 1144 entre Caro y Montesinos, T7231 6471.

shimmering salt flats and luminous lakes

★Crossing the Salar de Uyuni, the largest and highest salt lake in the world, is one of the great Bolivian trips. Driving across it is a fantastic experience, especially during June and July when the bright blue skies contrast with the blinding-white salt crust. Further south, and included on most tours of the region, is the Reserva Eduardo Avaroa (REA, see page 405) with the towering volcanoes, multicoloured lakes with abundant birdlife, weird rock formations, thermal activity and endless *puna* that make up some of most fabulous landscapes in South America. For information on the north shore of the *salar*, see South of Oruro, page 399.

The Salar de Uyuni contains what may be the world's largest lithium deposits and the Bolivian government has announced plans to build large-scale extraction facilities. A pilot plant has been operating (away from usual tourist routes) and concern has been expressed about the impact of more extensive lithium mining.

Uyuni

Uyuni (population 18,000, altitude 3670 m) lies near the eastern edge of the Salar de Uyuni and is one of the jumping-off points for trips to the salt flats, volcanoes and lakes of southwest Bolivia. Still a commercial and communication centre, Uyuni was, for much of the 20th century, important as a major railway junction.

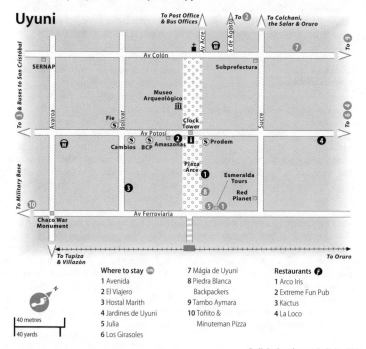

Uyuni

Where to stay
1 Avenida
2 El Viajero
3 Hostal Marith
4 Jardines de Uyuni
5 Julia
6 Los Girasoles
7 Mágia de Uyuni
8 Piedra Blanca Backpackers
9 Tambo Aymara
10 Toñito & Minuteman Pizza

Restaurants
1 Arco Iris
2 Extreme Fun Pub
3 Kactus
4 La Loco

Essential Salar de Uyuni

Finding your feet

The Salar de Uyuni and Reserva Eduardo Avaroa (REA) are best visited on a tour, these generally start in Uyuni or Tupiza. Uyuni is reached by air from La Paz; by bus from La Paz, Oruro or Potosí; or by train from Oruro. Tupiza is reached by air on a flight La Paz–Tarija and a bus from there; by bus from La Paz, Oruro, Potosí, Tarija or Salta (Argentina); or by train from Oruro. Special arrangements are required to drive to the Salar de Uyuni from Oruro via the Salar de Coipasa (intersalar route), to drive across the Salar de Uyuni and to access it from San Pedro de Atacama (Chile). Villages along the Salar perimeter are reached by infrequent buses.

Tip...

There are ATMs of Banco FIE and BNB in Uyuni and Banco FIE and Banco Unión in Tupiza, but they may not always have funds. To be sure, take cash.

Getting around

Travel is in 4WD Landcruisers, cramped on the back seat, but the staggering scenery makes up for it.

Safety

Getting stranded out on the altiplano or, worse yet on the *salar* itself, is dangerous because of extreme temperatures and total lack of drinking water. It is best to visit this area with a tour operator. Travellers with their own vehicles should be aware that the edges of the *salares* are soft and only established entry points or ramps (*terraplenes*) should be used to cross onto or off the salt. The intersalar route (Oruro–Coipasa–Uyuni) should only be attempted following extensive local inquiry or after taking on a guide to avoid becoming lost or bogged.

When to go

The temperature in the *salares* fluctuates greatly. In direct sun it can reach 30°C in summer (December to April), but it can fall well below freezing at night, with record low temperatures of -30°C registered in the winter (June to September). The average temperature is 6°C.

During the rainy season (December to April), water can cover part or all of the *salar* turning it into an immense mirror. The *salar* is beautiful with a few millimetres of water on its surface. If there is too much water, however, driving on it is not possible, it can only be admired from the shore and tour routes must be altered. After the rains, the intense solar radiation and the wind dry the surface and a pure white crust is formed. Beneath this layer, the salt is still wet. As the surface crust cracks, the salt crystallizes as it dries up, forming polygons on the surface. *Ojos de agua* are round holes that allow you to see water welling up from under the salt crust.

Two monuments dominate Avenida Ferroviaria: one of a railway worker, erected after the 1952 Revolution, and the other commemorating those who died in the Chaco War. **Museo Arqueológico y Antropológico de los Andes Meridionales** ⓘ *Arce y Potosí, Mon-Fri 0830-1200, 1400-1800, Sat-Sun 0900-1300, US$0.35*, is a small museum with local artefacts. The market is at Potosí y Bolívar and the town's fiesta is 11 July. There is a Railway Cemetery outside town with engines from 1907 to the 1950s, now rusting hulks. **Pulacayo**, 25 km from Uyuni on the road to Potosí, is a town at the site of a 19th-century silver mine. The train cemetery here is more interesting with Bolivia's first locomotive and the train robbed by Butch Cassidy and the Sundance Kid.

Trips to the Salar de Uyuni

Trips to the Salar de Uyuni originating in Uyuni enter via the *terraplén* (ramp) at **Colchani**, which has a **Museo de la Llama y de la Sal** selling souvenirs. Tours include stops to see traditional salt-mining techniques and the Ojos del Agua, where salt water bubbles to the surface of the salt flat, perhaps a call at a salt hotel (see Where to stay, page 408) and a visit to the **Isla Incahuasi** ① *entry US$4.30*. This is a coral island, raised up from the ocean bed, covered in tall cacti. There is a walking trail with superb views, a café, basic lodging and toilets. If on an extended tour (see below), you may leave the *salar* by another *terraplén*, eg Puerto Chuvica in the southwest. Some tours also include **Gruta de la Galaxia** ① *entry US$2.80*, an interesting cave at the edge of the *salar*. Private star- and sunrise-watching *salar* tours go for a few hours to an area flooded year round, where you can appreciate the mirror effect.

San Cristóbal

The original village of San Cristóbal, southwest of Uyuni, was relocated in 2002 to make way for a huge open-pit mine, said to be one of the largest silver deposits in South America. The original church (1650) had been declared a national monument and was therefore rebuilt in its entirety. Ask at the Fundación San Cristóbal Office for the church to be opened as the interior artwork, restored by Italian techniques, is worth seeing. The fiesta is 27-28 July.

Reserva Nacional de Fauna Andina Eduardo Avaroa (REA)

SERNAP office in Quetena Chico, T7237 8318 and at Colón y Avaroa, Uyuni, T02-693 2225, www. boliviarea.com or www.biobol.org, Mon-Fri 0830-1230, 1430-1800; entry to reserve US$21 (not included in tour prices; pay in bolivianos) Entry fees charged by communities can add up to US$32, depending which places are visited. Park ranger/entry points are near Laguna Colorada, Lagunas Verde and Blanca, close to the Chilean border, and at Sol de Mañana, near Quetena Chico. There is public transport from Uyuni into the region, but rarely more than 1 bus a week, with several hours rough travelling. If travelling independently, note that there are countless tracks and no signposts.

In the far southwest of Bolivia, in the López region, is the 714,745-ha Reserva Nacional Eduardo Avaroa (REA). There are two access routes from Uyuni: one via the *salar* and one from Tupiza. This is one of Bolivia's prime attractions and tour vehicles criss-cross the *puna* every day, some on the route from Uyuni to San Pedro de Atacama (Chile). Roads are still unmarked rugged tracks, however, and may be impassable in the wet season. ☆**Laguna Colorada** at 4278 m, 346 km southwest of Uyuni, is just one of the highlights of the reserve, its shores and shallows encrusted with borax and salt, an arctic white counterpoint to the flaming red, algae-coloured waters in which the rare James flamingos, along with the more common Chilean and Andean flamingos, breed and live. **Laguna Verde** (lifeless because it is laden with arsenic) and its neighbour **Laguna Blanca**, near the Chilean border, are at the foot of Volcán Licancábur, 5868 m. Between Lagunas Colorada and Verde there are thermal pools at Laguna Blanca (blissful water, a challenge to get out into the bitter wind – no facilities) and at Polques ① *entry US$0.85*, on the shores of Río Amargo/Laguna Salada by the Salar de Chalviri. A *centro comunal* at Polques has a dining room, changing room and toilets.

All these places are on the 'classic' tour route, across the Salar de Uyuni to **San Juan**, which has a museum of local *chullpas*, and is where most tour companies stop (there are plenty of lodgings). Other tours stop at **Culpina K**.

> **Tip...**
> Be prepared for the altitude, intense solar radiation and lack of drinking water.

Then you go to the Salar de Chiguana, Mirador del Volcán de Ollagüe, Cinco Lagunas, a chain of small, flamingo-specked lagoons, the much-photographed Arbol de Piedra in the Siloli desert, then Laguna Colorada (spend the second night here: Hospedaje Laguna Colorada, the newer and better $ Don Humberto in Huayllajara, and Campamento Ende). From Colorada you go over the Cuesta del Pabellón, 4850 m, to the **Sol de Mañana** geysers (not to be confused with the Sol de Mañana entry point); the **Desierto de Dalí**, a pure sandy desert as much Daliesque for the spacing of the rocks, with snow-covered peaks behind, as for the shape of the rocks themselves; and **Laguna Verde** (4400 m).

Jurisdiction of the reserve belongs to the villages of **Quetena Chico** and **Quetena Grande**, to the east of Laguna Colorada. The villagers run lodging in the reserve: Quetena Chico runs *hospedajes* at Laguna Colorada. Quetena Grande runs **La Cabaña** at Hito Cajones (see below). In Quetena Chico is the reserve's visitors centre, **Centro Ecológico Ch'aska** ① *daily 0730-1800*, with informative displays about the region's geology, vulcanology, fauna, flora and human history; a worthwhile stop. The village has two cheap *hospedajes* (**Piedra Preciosa** and **Hostal Quetena**, hot water extra), and places to eat. With the exception of Quetena Chico, *alojamientos* in the villages on the tour routes cannot be booked. You turn up and search for a room. All provide kitchen space for the tour's cook or independent traveller to prepare meals, take your own stove, though.

Sadly, lakes in the reserve are gradually drying up, most noticeably Laguna Verde. This has been attributed to global climate change but the real reason may be massive underground water consumption by Bolivian, Chilean and Argentine mines.

From Tupiza Tour operators in Tupiza (see page 415) run trips to the REA and Salar de Uyuni and go to places not included on tours from Uyuni. These may include the beautiful **Lagunas Celeste** and **Negra** below Cerro Uturunco, which is near Quetena Chico; the **Valle de las Rocas**, 4260 m, between the villages of **Alota** and **Villa Mar** (a vast extension of rocks eroded into fantastic configurations, with polylepis trees in sheltered corners); **Ciudad Roma** rock formations near the village of **Guadalupe**; and isolated communities in the *puna*. The high-altitude scenery is out of this world. An alternate access to this area from the south is from **Villazón**, along a wide gravel road.

Crossing into Chile

There is a REA ranger station near Lagunas Blanca and Verde: if going from Bolivia, have your park entry receipt at hand, if crossing from Chile pay the entry fee here. Alongside is a *refugio*, **La Cabaña**; US$7 per person in comfortable but very cold dorms, solar-powered lighting, hot water seldom works, cooking facilities (in high season book in advance – tour agencies can do this).

There is good climbing and hiking in the area with outstanding views. You must register at the ranger station before heading out and they may insist that you take a guide (eg to climb Licancábur, US$100 for guide plus US$30 for transport unless it is part of your tour).

From the ranger station it's 5 km to the border at **Hito Cajones** (on the Chilean side called Hito Cajón), 4500 m. Bolivian immigration open 0800-2100, charges US$2 in any currency. If you plan to cross to Chile here, you should first go to the immigration office in Uyuni (see above). There are no services or facilities at the border. A further 6 km along a good dirt road into Chile is the intersection with the fully paved road from San Pedro de Atacama to **Paso de Jama**, the border between Chile and Argentina. From here it's 40 km (2000 m downhill) to San Pedro. Chilean customs and immigration are just outside San Pedro and can take 45 minutes at busy times. See Transport, below.

Tourist information

Uyuni

Dirección de Turismo Uyuni
At the clock tower, T02-693 2060, or 6794 5797.
Mon-Sat 0800-1200, 1430-1830, Sun 0900-1200.

Subprefectura de Potosí
Colón y Sucre. Mon-Fri 0800-1200, 1430-1830,
Sat 0800-1200.
Departmental information office, the place
to file complaints in writing.

Where to stay

Uyuni

Many hotels fill early, reservations are advised
in high season. Be conservative with water
use, this is a very dry area, water is scarce and
supplied at limited hours (better hotels have
reserve tanks).

$$$ Jardines de Uyuni
Av Potosí 113, T02-693 2989,
www.jardinesdeuyuni.com.
Tastefully decorated, comfortable, heating,
open fire in the lounge, small pool, parking.

$$$ Mágia de Uyuni
Av Colón 432, T02-693 2541,
www.hostalmagiauyuni.com.
Nice ample rooms and suites upstairs with
heating, cheaper in older colder rooms
downstairs (ask for a heater), parking.

$$$-$$ Los Girasoles
Santa Cruz 155, T693 3323,
www.girasoleshotel.hostel.com.
Buffet breakfast, bright and warm (especially
2nd floor), comfortable, nice decor, heaters,
cheaper in old section, internet extra.

$$$-$$ Tambo Aymara
Camacho s/n y Colón, T02-693 2227,
www.hoteltamboaymara.com.
Lovely colonial-style modern hotel, large
comfortable rooms, heating, Belgian/
Bolivian-owned, operate their own tours.

$$-$ Toñito
Av Ferroviaria 60, T02-693 3186,
www.tonitouyuni.com.
Spacious rooms with good beds, solar-
powered showers and heating in new wing,
cheaper in old section with electric showers,
parking, book exchange, tours.

$ Avenida
Av Ferroviaria 11, near train station,
T02-693 2078.
Simple but well maintained, cheaper with
shared bath, hot water (shared showers
0700-2100), long patio with laundry facilities,
family-run, helpful, good value, popular and
often full.

$ El Viajero
Cabrera 334 y 6 de Agosto, near bus terminals,
T02-693 3549.
Basic rooms, cheaper with shared bath,
electric shower, parking.

$ Hostal Marith
Av Potosí 61, T02-693 2174.
Basic, cheaper with shared bath and in
dorm, electric showers from 0830, patio
with laundry facilities, tours (have salt
hotel at Atulcha near the *salar*).

$ Julia
Ferroviaria 314 y Arce, T02-693 2134,
www.juliahoteluyuni.com.
Spacious rooms, cheaper with shared bath,
electric showers, internet extra.

$ Piedra Blanca Backpackers
Av Arce 27, T7643 7643, www.piedra
blancabackpackers.hostel.com.
Warm, comfortable, private rooms, some
with bath, and dorms, luggage store extra,
has Wi-Fi in common areas, simple breakfast.

**Salar de Uyuni and Reserva Eduardo
Avaroa**
These *hoteles de sal* are generally visited on
tours, seldom independently.

$$$$-$$$ Luna Salada
5 km north of Colchani near the edge of the salar, T7121 2007, La Paz T02-277 0885, www.lunasaladahotel.com.bo.
Lovely salt hotel, comfortable rooms, hot water, ample common areas with fabulous views of the *salar*, salt floors, skylights make it warm and cosy, reserve ahead.

$$$$-$$$ Palacio de Sal
On the edge of the salar, near the ramp outside Colchani, T6482 0888, www.palaciodesal.com.bo.
Book through **Hidalgo Tours** (Potosí, T02-622 9512). Spacious, luxury salt hotel, decorated with large salt sculptures, heating, sauna, lookout on 2nd storey with views of the *salar*.

$$$ Mallku Cueva
Outside Villa Mar, along the route from Tupiza to the reserve, T02-693 2989, www.hotelesrusticosjardines.com.
Nicely decorated upmarket hotel with all services, including Wi-Fi. Run by **Hidalgo Tours**, see What to do, below.

$$$ Tayka
Uyuni office: Sucre 7715 entre Uruguay y México, T02-693 2987, La Paz T02-241 3065, www.taykahoteles.com.
A chain of 4 upmarket hotels in Salar de Uyuni-REA area, operating in conjunction with local communities. The hotels have comfortable rooms with bath, hot water, heating and restaurant, price includes breakfast, discounts in low season. The **Hotel de Sal** (salt hotel) is in Tahua, on the north shore of the *salar*; the **Hotel de Piedra** (stone hotel) is in San Pedro de Quemes, on the south shore of the *salar*; the **Hotel del Desierto** (desert hotel) is in Ojo de Perdiz in the Siloli Desert, north of Laguna Colorada; the **Hotel de los Volcanes** (volcanoes hotel) is in San Pablo de López, between Uturunco Volcano and Tupiza.

San Cristóbal

There are also a couple of inexpensive *alojamientos* in town.

$$ Hotel San Cristóbal
In centre, T7264 2117.
Purpose-built and owned by the community. The bar is inside a huge oil drum, all metal furnishings. The rest is comfortable if simple, hot water, good breakfast, evening meal extra.

Restaurants

Uyuni
Plaza Arce has various tourist restaurants serving mostly mediocre pizza.

$$-$ Kactus
Bolívar y Ferrovaria. Daily 0830-2200.
Set lunches and international food à la carte, also sells pastries and whole-wheat bread, slow service.

$$-$ La Loco
Av Potosí y Camacho, T693 3105. Mon-Sat 1600-0200 (food until about 2130), closed Jan-Feb.
International food with a Bolivian and French touch, music and drinks till late, open fire, popular, reserve in Jul-Aug. Also run a small exclusive guesthouse: **La Petite Porte** ($$$ www.hotel-lapetiteporte-uyuni.com), which has a good reputation.

$ Arco Iris
Plaza Arce. Daily 1600-2230.
Good Italian food, pizza, and atmosphere, occasional live music.

$ Extreme Fun Pub
Potosí 9.
Restaurant/pub, pleasant atmosphere, good service, videos, friendly owner is very knowledgeable about Bolivia.

$ Minuteman
Pizza restaurant attached to Toñito Hotel (see above).
Good pizzas and soups, also serves breakfast.

What to do

Uyuni
Tour operators
See also Booking a tour, page 404.

Always check the itinerary, the vehicle, group numbers, the menu (especially vegetarians), what is included in the price. The most popular trips are three to four days: Salar de Uyuni, Reserva Eduardo Avaroa, and back to Uyuni or on to San Pedro de Atacama (Chile); or Tupiza to Uyuni, San Pedro de Atacama or back to Tupiza. There are also one- to two-day tours and five-day tours which include additional attractions or climbing a volcano. Prices per person start at US$50 for a day tour, US$100 for a three-day tour and US$190 for four days plus park fee of Bs 150 (US$21) and entry fees to some attractions (total of up to US$32). The cheapest tours are not recommended and usually involve crowding, insufficient staff and food, poor vehicles (fatal accidents have taken place) and accommodation. The best value is at the mid- to high-end, where you can assemble your own tour for four or five passengers, with driver, cook and good equipment. Private star- and sunrise-watching tours cost US$150-250, for two or three hours, for one or two passengers.

Three factors often lead to misunderstandings: 1) agencies pool clients when there are not enough passengers to fill a vehicle. 2) Agencies all over Bolivia sell *salar* tours, but booking from far away may not give full information on the local operator. 3) Many drivers work for multiple agencies and will cut tours short. If the tour seriously fails to match the contract and the operator refuses any redress, complaints can be taken to the Subprefectura de Potosí in Uyuni (see below) but don't expect a quick refund. Try to speak to travellers who have just returned from a tour before booking your own, and ignore touts on the street and at the rail or bus stations. For tour operators, see Uyuni, page 408 and Tupiza, page 415.

Andes Travel Office (ATO), *in Hotel Tambo Aymara (see above), T02-693 2227, tamboaymara@gmail.com.* Upmarket private tours, Belgian/Bolivian-owned, English and French spoken, reliable.

Atacama Mística/Mundo Quechua, *Av Ferroviaria, www.atacamamistica.cl, www.mundoquechua.com.* Chilean-Bolivian company, daily tours with transfer to San Pedro de Atacama.

Creative Tours, *Sucre 362, T02-693 3543, www.creativetours.com.bo.* Long-established company, partners in the **Tayka** chain of hotels, see above. Premium tours in

the region and throughout the country, with another office in Cochabamba and representatives in the main cities.

Esmeralda, *Av Ferroviaria y Arce, T02-693 2130, www.esmeraldatoursuyuni.com*. At the more economical end of market, tours from 1 to 4 days.

Hidalgo Tours, *Av Potosí 113 at Hotel Jardines de Uyuni, www.salardeuyuni.net*. Well-established *salar*/REA operator, also runs **Palacio de Sal** and **Mallku Cueva** hotels (see above); also in Potosí.

Mammut, *Peú y Sucre, T7240 4720*. 1-, 2- and 3-day tours to the salt flats and Reserva Eduardo Avaroa, transfers to San Pedro de Atacama and express service to La Paz, Tupiza and other cities. Spanish-speaking guides.

Red Planet, *Sucre entre Potosí y Av Ferroviaria, T7240 3896, http://redplanetexpedition.com*. Tours to the *salar*, 1, 2 and 3 days, also from Potosí, transport from La Paz for groups. English-speaking guides.

San Cristóbal

Llama Mama, *T7240 0309*. 60 km of exclusive bicycle trails descending 2-3 or 4 hrs, depending on skill, 3 grades, all-inclusive, taken up by car, with guide and communication.

Transport

Uyuni

Air To/from **La Paz**, **Amazonas** (Potosí y Arce, T02-693 3333) and **Boa**, 2 daily each, US$90-173 (the most expensive in Bolivia), also **TAM** 3 times a week.

Bus Most offices are on Av Arce and Cabrera. To **La Paz**, US$13.75-19.50, 11 hrs, daily at 2000 (La Paz–Uyuni at 1900) with **Panasur**, www.uyunipanasur.com, **Cruz del Norte**, and **Trans Omar**, www.transomar. com; or transfer in Oruro. Tourist buses with **Todo Turismo**, Cabrera 158, T02-693 3337, www.todoturismo.bo, daily at 2000, US$34 (La Paz office, Av Uruguay 102, Edif Paola, p1 of 6, opposite the bus terminal, T02-211 9418, daily to Uyuni at 2100), note this service does not run if the road is poor during the rainy

season. **Oruro**, several companies 2000-2130, US$7-10.75, 7 hrs; **Todo Turismo** (see above), US$20. To **Potosí** several companies around1000 and 1900, US$6, 3-4 hrs, spectacular scenery. The road from Potosí to Uyuni is paved. To **Sucre**, **6 de Octubre** and **Emperador** at 1000, US$8.35-11.75, 7 hrs; or transfer in Potosí. To **Tupiza** US$8, 8 hrs, via **Atocha**, several companies daily at 0600 and 2030 (from Tupiza at 1000 and 1800). A paved road Uyuni–Tupiza was under construction in 2017. To **Villazón** on the Argentine border, 3 daily, US$9.50-12, 7 hrs, or go via Potosí and change buses there to travel on paved roads. For **Tarija** change in Potosí or Tupiza. Regional services to villages in **Nor-** and **Sud-Lípez** operate about 3 times a week, confirm details locally. To **Pulacayo** take any bus for Potosí.

Car and train A road and railway line run south from Oruro, through Río Mulato, to Uyuni (323 km, each about 7 hrs). The road is sandy and, after rain, very bad, especially south of Río Mulato. The train journey is more comfortable. **Expreso del Sur** train leaves for **Oruro** on Thu and Sun at 0005, arriving 0700. **Wara Wara del Sur** leaves on Tue and Fri at 0145, arriving 0910 (prices for both under Oruro, page 402). To **Atocha**, **Tupiza** and **Villazón Expreso del Sur** leaves Uyuni on Tue and Fri at 2240, arriving, respectively, at 0450, 0400 and 0705. **Wara Wara** leaves on Mon and Thu at 0250, arriving 0500, 0835 and 1205. The ticket office (T02-693 2153) opens Mon-Fri 0900-1200, 1430-1800, Sat-Sun 1000-1100, and 1 hr before the trains leave. It closes once tickets are sold – get there early or buy through a tour agent (more expensive).

Advance preparations are required to drive across the *salar* and REA. Fuel is not easily available in the Lípez region, so you must take jerrycans. A permit from the Dirección General de Substancias Controladas in La Paz is required to fill jerrycans; you will be authorized to fill only two 60 l cans. Fuel for vehicles with foreign plates may be considerably more expensive than for those with local plates.

Crossing into Chile

The easiest way is to go to San Pedro de Atacama as part of your tour to the *salar* and REA (see above). **Colque Tours** (www.colquetours.com) runs 1 minibus daily from near the ranger station at Hito Cajones to San Pedro de Atacama, departing 1000, US$10, 1 hr including stop at immigration. At other times onward transport to San Pedro must be arranged by your agency, this costs US$10-15 for shared service if it is an add-on to your tour, or US$120-160 per vehicle for private service. The ranger station may be able to assist in an emergency. From Uyuni to **Avaroa** and on to **Calama**, **Centenario**, Cabrera y Arce, Sun, Mon, Wed, Thu at 0330, transfer at the border to **Frontera** (daily from Calama to Ollagüe) or Atacama, Thu, Mon 2000. To Avaroa, 4½ hrs; to Calama, another 4 hrs, US$21 in total; allow 2 hrs at the border (all times minimum).

If driving your own vehicle, from **Colchani** it is about 60 km across to the southern shore of the *salar*. Follow the tracks made by other vehicles in the dry season. The salt is soft

Tip...
Chile is one hour ahead of Bolivia from mid-October to March. Chile does not allow coca, dairy produce, tea bags, fruit or vegetables to be brought in.

and wet for about 2 km around the edges so only use established ramps. It is 20 km from the southern shore to Colcha K military checkpoint. From there, a poor gravel road leads 28 km to San Juan then the road enters the Salar de Chiguana, a mix of salt and mud which is often wet and soft with deep tracks which are easy to follow; 35 km away is Chiguana, another military post, then 45 km to the end of this *salar*, a few kilometres before border at Ollagüe. This latter part is the most dangerous; very slippery with little traffic. Or take the route that tours use to Laguna Colorada and continue to Hito Cajones. **Atacama Mística** of Uyuni will let you follow one of their groups if you arrange in advance. There is no fuel between Uyuni and Calama (Chile) if going via Ollagüe, but expensive fuel is sold in San Pedro de Atacama. Keep to the road at all times; the road is impassable after rain.

Tupiza and the far south *Colour map 3, C3.*

last hideout of Butch Cassidy and the Sundance Kid

☆Set in a landscape of colourful, eroded mountains and stands of huge cacti (usually flowering December-February), Tupiza, 200 km south of Uyuni, is a pleasant town (population 25,709) with a lower altitude (2975 m) and milder climate, making it a good alternative for visits to the Reserva Eduardo Avaroa and the *salar*.

Several Tupiza operators offer *salar*, REA and local tours. Beautiful sunsets over the fertile Tupiza valley can be seen from the foot of a statue of Christ on a hill behind the plaza.

There are two ATMs in Tupiza, beside Tu Pizza restaurant and at Banco FIE. Don't rely on them, though; take cash. There is a public hospital on Calle Suipacha, opposite the bus terminal.

Around Tupiza

Circuitos Bioculturales There is good hiking around Tupiza but be prepared for sudden changes of climate including hailstorms, and note that dry gullies are prone to flash flooding. The routes are very scenic and the villages are tranquil. You can arrange to spend a couple of days relaxing there. A worthwhile excursion is to **Quebrada Palala**, with the nearby 'Stone Forest'. Here is the hamlet of **Torre Huayco**, part of a community tourism project, Circuitos Bioculturales. **Oploca**, a small town 17 km northwest of Tupiza with a lovely colonial church, is also part of the project, as is **Chuquiago**, 30 km south of Tupiza, along the rail line. Each has a small *eco-albergue* ($ pp, with breakfast, simple comfortable rooms, kitchen) and guides. A circuit can be done in one to three days by bicycle, horse, trekking, jeep, or a combination of these (US$35-50 per day, ask tour operators in Tupiza).

Butch Cassidy and the Sundance Kid tours Tupiza is the base for Butch Cassidy and the Sundance Kid tours. The statue in the main plaza is to **José Avelino Aramayo** (1809-1882), of the 19th-century mining dynasty. Butch and Sundance's last holdup was of an Aramayo company payroll at Huaca Huañusca on 4 November 1908. They are believed by some (see *Digging Up Butch and Sundance*, by Anne Meadows, Bison Books, 2003) to have died soon afterwards at the hands of a military patrol in **San Vicente**, a tiny mining camp at 4500 m, but no grave in the San Vicente cemetery has yet to be positively identified as theirs. There is a small museum with local artifacts but no lodging or other services. Visits can be arranged by Tupiza agencies.

South to the Argentine border
Villazón The Argentine border is at Villazón (population 44,645, altitude 3443 m), 81 km south of Tupiza. At Plaza 6 de Agosto are the municipal museum about the Chicha culture

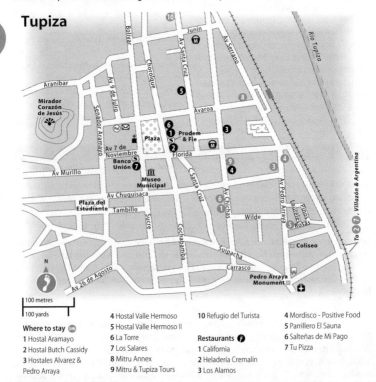

Tupiza

Where to stay		Restaurants
1 Hostal Aramayo	4 Hostal Valle Hermoso	10 Refugio del Turista
2 Hostal Butch Cassidy	5 Hostal Valle Hermoso II	
3 Hostales Alvarez &	6 La Torre	1 California
Pedro Arraya	7 Los Salares	2 Heladería Cremalín
	8 Mitru Annex	3 Los Alamos
	9 Mitru & Tupiza Tours	4 Mordisco - Positive Food
		5 Parrillero El Sauna
		6 Salteñas de Mi Pago
		7 Tu Pizza

and tourist information office. Of traditional villages in the surroundings, those to the west, like Berque, are known for their pottery, rock art is found in Yanalpa, to the east, and San Pedro in the centre, has colonial haciendas. Many *casas de cambio* on Avenida República de Argentina, leading to the border, change US dollars, pesos and euros, all at poor rates. There are banks and three ATMs near the main plaza. Tour operators are near the old bus terminal. The border area must not be photographed.

Border with Argentina Migración Conjunta, a joint immigration complex, is on the Argentine side of the international bridge, open 0700-2100 Bolivian time (0800-2200 Argentine standard time, see below); longer hours during July and December school holidays, 0600-2200 Bolivian time (0700-2300

Tip...
Change all your bolivianos in Villazón as there is nowhere to do so in La Quiaca or beyond.

Argentine standard time). Exit and entry stamps for both countries are issued at the corresponding booths in the same complex. If entering Argentina, you have to proceed to a customs control after getting your entry stamp; there is no customs control entering Bolivia. Queuing begins at 0600 and there may be long delays, especially entering Argentina. Allow several hours if crossing with your own vehicle. The border is four blocks along Avenida República de Argentina from Plaza 6 de Agosto, Villazón's main square, five blocks from the old bus station (taxi US$0.70) and 10 blocks from the train station. A new Villazón bus station, 3 km from the border, was not yet operating in early 2017. The border is 10 blocks from La Quiaca (Argentina) bus terminal (taxi US$1.50). Taxis do not cross the bridge. Entering Bolivia, boys offer to wheel your bags uphill to the bus or train station, US$1-1.50 (but they will ask for more). The Argentine consulate is at Plaza 6 de Agosto 111, T02-597 2011, Monday-Friday 0800-1500. **Note** Argentine time is one hour later than Bolivia, two hours when Buenos Aires adopts daylight saving.

Listings Tupiza and the far south *map page 412.*

Where to stay

Tupiza
Most hotels have Wi-Fi, but it's very slow.

$$-$ Mitru
Av Chichas 187, T02-694 3001,
www.hotelmitru.com.
Pleasant ample grounds with heated pool, nice atmosphere, a variety of rooms and prices, the more expensive rooms have king-size beds, a/c, heating and hairdryers, cheaper in older section with private bath and even cheaper with shared bath. All include good buffet breakfast with bread made on the premises, reliable solar hot water, parking, luggage store, book exchange. Very helpful and knowledgeable, popular, reserve ahead in high season. Warmly recommended.

$ Hostal Alvarez
Av P Arraya 492, T02-694 5327.
Near the bus and train stations, good small 10-room hostel, brighter rooms on 2nd storey, cheaper with shared bath, extra charge for a/c and breakfast.

$ Hostal Aramayo
Av Chichas 230, T02-694 2184,
http://hotelaramayo.com.
Nice centrally located 24-room hotel, most rooms with private bath, pleasant common areas. Opened in 2016.

$ Hostal Butch Cassidy
Av José Luis San Juan s/n, the main road in Chajrahuasi, T7183 6651.
Modern 12-room hostel, private and shared bath, parking, on the opposite bank of the

river from town, can be cold in the winter when it is windy. Opened in 2016.

$ Hostal Pedro Arraya
Av P Arraya 494, T02-694 2734,
www.hostalpedroarraya.com.
Convenient to bus and train stations, small rooms, cheaper with shared bath, hot water, breakfast available, laundry facilities, terrace, family-run.

$ Hostal Valle Hermoso
Av Pedro Arraya 478, T02-694 3441,
www.vallehermosotours.com.
Breakfast available, private or shared bath, cheaper in dorm. TV/breakfast room, book exchange, motorbike parking. 2nd location, **Valle Hermoso II**, Av Pedro Arraya 585, near the bus station, 3 simple rooms with bath, several dorms with bunk beds, same prices as No 1.

$ La Torre
Av Chichas 220, T02-694 2633,
www.latorretours-tupiza.com.
Lovely refurbished house, newer rooms at back, comfortable, cheaper with shared bath and no TV, great service, good value. Recommended.

$ Los Salares
C Ecuador s/n, Zona Chajrahuasi,
behind petrol station, T02-694 5813,
www.lossalares.hostel.com.
Nice small hotel with 9 rooms, 1 without bath (cheaper), kitchen facilities, parking, on the opposite bank of the river from town, can be cold in the winter when it is windy, curfew at 2200.

$ Mitru Annex
Avaroa 20, T02-694 3002,
www.hotelmitru.com.
Nicely refurbished older hotel, buffet breakfast, cheaper with shared bath, good hot showers, use of pool and games room at **Hotel Mitru** (see above).

$ Refugio del Turista
Av Santa Cruz 240, T02-694 3155,
www.hotelmitru.com.

Refurbished home with garden, shared bath, reliable hot water, well-equipped kitchen, laundry facilities, use of pool and games room at **Hotel Mitru,** parking and electric outlet for camper vans, popular budget option, good value.

Villazón
Hotels in Villazón do not have Wi-Fi.

$ Center
Plaza 6 de Agosto 125, T02-596 5472.
Rooms with private or shared bath, includes simple breakfast, parking.

$ Grand Palace
C 25 de Mayo 52 T02-596 5333.
Simple rooms with private or shared bath, no breakfast.

$ Olimpo
Av República Argentina 116 y Chorolque,
T02-597 2219,olimpograngranhotel@gmail.com.
Among the better hotels in town, private or shared bath, heating, includes simple breakfast, restaurant, parking.

Restaurants

Tupiza
Several touristy pizza places on C Florida are mediocre to terrible, also watch your belongings here.
　　The best options are just outside town (all $$-$), they serve grilled meat and good regional specialities like *picante de cabrito* (spicy goat) but open only Sat or Sun midday – go early. These include: **La Campiña**, in Tambillo Alto, 45 mins' walk north along the river; and **La Estancia**, 2 km north in Villa Remedios. There are food stalls upstairs in the market but mind the cleanliness.

$ California
Cochabamba 413, 2nd floor.
Set lunches, hamburgers and snacks in the evening when service is slow.

$ Los Alamos
Av Chichas 157. Open 0800-2400.

Local and international dishes, good atmosphere, average food, good juices, large portions, popular with tourists.

$ Parrillero El Sauna
Av Santa Cruz entre Avaroa y Junín.
Tue-Sun from 1700.
Very good *parrilladas* with Argentine meat, salad buffet.

$ Tu Pizza
Sucre y 7 de Noviembre, on Plaza.
Mon-Sat 1830-2300.
Cute name, variety of pizzas, very slow service.

Heladería Cremalín
Cochabamba y Florida, on Plaza.
Ice cream, juices and fruit shakes.

Mordisco – Positive Food
Chichas 189, next to Hotel Mitru.
Open 0730-0930, 1630-2200.
Small snack bar serving sandwiches, wraps and salads with a choice of healthy ingredients, fruit juices; box breakfasts and lunches available.

Salteñas de Mi Pago
Cochabamba, on Plaza. Tue-Sun 0900-1300.
Tasty *salteñas* every morning.

Villazón
Restaurants are clustered 2 blocks around the main plaza.

$$-$ Rincón Salteño
C Suipacha 135. Open 1100-2300.
Good Argentine style *parrillada* and a variety of pizzas.

What to do

Tupiza
Tour operators in Tupiza run trips to the REA and Salar de Uyuni and go to places not included on tours from Uyuni.

Tours on offer include 1-day jeep tours US$35 pp for group of 5; horse riding 3-, 5- and 7-hr tours, the latter includes lunch, US$10 per hr, multi-day tours US$70 per day; 2-day San Vicente plus colonial town of

Portugalete US$80 pp (plus lodging); Salar de Uyuni and REA, 4 days with Spanish-speaking guide, US$190 pp for a group of 5, US$230 pp in high season, plus Bs150 (US$21) park fee and US$32 total entry fees to attractions. Add US$23 pp for English-speaking guides. 5-day tours are also available.

La Torre Tours, *in Hotel La Torre (see above). Salar/REA tours and local trips on jeep, bicycle, walking or horse riding.*

Tupiza Tours, *in Hotel Mitru (see above), www.tupizatours.com.* Highly experienced and well organized for *salar*/REA and local tours. Also offer 1-day 'triathlon' of horse riding, biking and jeep, US$50 pp for group of 5, a good way to see the area if you only have 1 day; trekking tours, Butch Cassidy tours; Paseos Bioculturales, and extensions to the Uyuni tour. Have offices in La Paz and Tarija, and offer tours in all regions of Bolivia. Highly recommended.

Valle Hermoso Tours, *in Hostal Valle Hermoso 1 (see above), www.vallehermoso tours.com.* Offers similar tours on horse or jeep, as do several other agencies and most Tupiza hotels.

Villazón
Aventuras del Sur, *C 20 de Mayo 544, T02-5973224, carlosalvarez_26@hotmail.es.* Jeep, cycling and walking tours to communities around Villazón, also Salar and REA tours.
Imperio Inca, *C Suipacha 546, T02-5965744, www.imperinca.com.* Tours throughout Bolivia, also in Argentina, Chile and Peru.

Transport

Tupiza
Bus There is a small, well-organized bus terminal at the south end of Av Pedro Arraya. To **Villazón** several buses daily, USUS2.50-3, 2 hrs; also from opposite the terminal: vans (minibuses), US$3.50, 1½ hrs, and shared taxis (*expresos* or *rapiditos*), US$3-3.50, 1 hr, leave when full; taxi US$30. To **Potosí**, several companies (**Oglobo** and **Expreso Tupiza** are best) around 1000 and

2100, US$5-10, 6 hrs; vans and *rapiditos*, 3-4 per day, US$8-15 (according to demand), 5 hrs, might require a transfer in Cotagaita; taxi US$120. To **Sucre**, **Expreso Villazón** at 1500, **Trans Illimani** at 2030 (more comfortable but known to speed) 6 de Octubre (with *bus cama*), US$9-14, 8-9 hrs; or transfer in Potosí. To **Tarija**, several around 1930-2030, US$9.50-15, 5-6 hrs (change here for **Santa Cruz**), **Juárez**, has regular service at 2000 and a recommended more comfortable bus with loo at 1200; also for daytime travel, **Narváez** at 0900. A good option for reaching Tupiza is to take a flight to Tarija (cheaper than to Uyuni) and a bus from there. To **Uyuni**, several companies around 1000 and 1800, US$8, 8 hrs; a paved road is under construction in 2017. To **Oruro**, **Trans Illimani** at 1300, 1800, US$13, 12 hrs; continuing to **Cochabamba**, US$19, 17 hrs. To **La Paz** several at 1200 and 1730-2030, US$19-25, 16-17 hrs. Agent for the Argentine company **Balut** at terminal sells tickets to Jujuy, Salta, Buenos Aires or Córdoba (local bus to the border at Villazón, then change to Balut), but beware overcharging or buy tickets directly from local companies once in Argentina.

Train Train station ticket office, T02-694 2529, open Mon-Sat 0800-1100, 1530-1730, and early morning half an hour before trains arrive. To **Villazón**: **Expreso del Sur** Wed and Sat at 0410; **Wara Wara** Mon and Thu at 0905. To **Atocha**, **Uyuni** and **Oruro**: **Expreso del Sur** Wed and Sat at 1825; **Wara Wara** Mon and Thu at 1905. Fares are given under Oruro, page 402.

Villazón

Bus Bus terminal is near the plaza, 5 blocks from the border. Taxi to border, US$0.70

or hire a porter, US$1, and walk. A new terminal, 2.6 km northeast of the centre, on Av Tumulsa by the ring-road was not yet operating in early 2017. To **La Paz**, several companies, US$15-23, *bus cama* US$23, depart **Villazón** 0830-1000 and 1500-1900 (eg Illimani *bus cama* at 1500 and 1900). To **Tupiza**, several daily buses, vans and cars, see Tupiza Transport, above. To **Potosí** several buses between 0800-0900 and 1830-1900, US$6-10, 8 hrs; vans US$8, 7 hrs; cars (*rapiditos*) US$9-15 (according to demand), 6 hrs. To **Uyuni**, at 0900, 1100 and 1500, US$9.50-12, 7 hrs, or go via Potosí and change buses there to travel on paved roads. To **Tarija**, at 0900, 2000 and 2100, US$9.50-13, 6 hrs, change here for **Santa Cruz**. To **Sucre**, at 1100, 1500 and 2030, US$10-14, 11 hrs. Tickets for buses in **Argentina** are sold in Villazón but beware of scams and overcharging. Buy only from company offices, never from sellers in the street and allow extra time for border formalities. Safer still, cross to La Quiaca and buy onward tickets there.

Car The road north from Villazón through Tupiza, Potosí and Sucre, to Cochabamba or Santa Cruz is paved. 2 scenic roads lead to Tarija, 1 from Villazón (about 40% paved) and one from Tupiza (about 50% paved). There is also a good gravel road from Villazón to Uyuni.

Train Station about 1 km north of border on main road, T02-597 2565, ticket sales Mon-Sat 0800-1100, 1530-1730. To **Tupiza**, **Atocha**, **Uyuni** and **Oruro**: **Expreso del Sur** Wed and Sat at 1530; **Wara Wara** Mon and Thu at 1530. Fares are given under Oruro, page 402.

Central &
southern highlands

This region boasts two World Cultural Heritage Sites, Sucre, the white city and Bolivia's official capital, and the mining city of Potosí, the source of great wealth for colonial Spain and of indescribable hardship for many Bolivians. In the south, Tarija is known for its fruit and wines, and for its traditions which set it apart from the rest of the country.

Sucre and around *Colour map 3, C3. See map, page 419.*
a white colonial masterpiece and the world's largest palaeontological site

Sucre is sometimes referred to as La Ciudad Blanca, owing to the tradition that all buildings in the centre are painted in their original colonial white. This works to beautiful effect and in 1991 UNESCO declared the city a World Heritage Site.

With a population of 338,281, there are two universities, the older dating from 1624. Founded in 1538 as La Plata, it became capital of the Audiencia of Charcas in 1559. Its name was later changed to Chuquisaca before the present name was adopted in 1825 in honour of the second president of the new republic. From 1825 to 1899 Sucre was the only capital of Bolivia; it remains the constitutional capital as it is home to Bolivia's judicial branch although La Paz is the administrative one. *La capitalidad* remains an emotionally charged issue among *sucrenses*, who strive to see Sucre regain its status as the only capital.

Sights
Plaza 25 de Mayo Plaza 25 de Mayo is large, spacious, full of trees and surrounded by elegant buildings. Among these are the **Casa de la Libertad** ⓘ *T04-645 4200, Tue-Sat 0900-1230, 1430-1800, US$2.15 with tour; US$5.80 video.* Formerly the Assembly Hall of the Jesuit University, where the country's Declaration of Independence was signed, this house contains a famous portrait of Simón Bolívar by the Peruvian artist Gil de Castro, admired for its likeness. Also on the plaza are the beautiful 17th-century **cathedral** and **Museo Eclesiástico** ⓘ *Ortiz 61, T04-645 2257, Mon-Fri 1000-1200, 1500-1700, US$1.45.* Worth seeing are the famous jewel-encrusted Virgin of Guadalupe, 1601, and works by Viti, the first great painter of the New World, who studied under Raphael.

Best for
Colonial history ▪ Fossils ▪ Textiles ▪ Wine

Essential Sucre

Finding your feet

Sucre's airport, 5 km northwest of town, has regular services to and from La Paz, Santa Cruz, Cochabamba and Tarija. Access by road to Potosí is straightforward and quite quick. To get elsewhere by road takes time, but there are daily bus services to all major cities. The bus terminal is on the northern outskirts of town, 3 km from the centre. See also Transport, page 425.

When to go

Sucre has a pleasant climate. In winter, May-August, days are sunny and mild, nights are cold (temperatures can drop below freezing in June to July). December-March there is rain, but also many sunny days.

Safety

Caution is advised after 2200 and in market areas.

Time required

Two or three days but many visitors stay longer for a period of language study or volunteering.

South of the plaza Visits to **San Felipe Neri** ① *entrance through school, Ortiz 165 y Azurduy, T04-645 4333, Mon-Sat 1400-1800, US$1.45 (extra charge for photos)*, include the neoclassical church with its courtyard, the crypt and the roof (note the penitents' benches), which offers fine views over the city. The monastery is used as a school. Diagonally opposite is the church of **La Merced** ① *T04-645 1338*, which is notable for its gilded central and side altars. The **Museo Universitario Charcas** ① *Bolívar 698, T04-645 3285, Mon-Fri 0800-1200, 1400-1800, Sat 0800-1200, US$0.50, photos extra*, has anthropological, archaeological and folkloric exhibits, and colonial collections and presidential and modern-art galleries.

East of the plaza San Lázaro (1538) ① *Calvo y Padilla, Mass daily 0700, Sun also 1900*, is regarded as the first cathedral of La Plata (Sucre). On the nave walls are six paintings attributed to Zurbarán; it has fine silverwork and alabaster in the baptistery. San Miguel, San Francisco and San Lázaro are only open during Mass. The **Monasterio de Santa Clara** ① *Calvo 212, Mass daily 0730, museum open Mon-Fri 1400-1800, Sat 1400-1730, US$2, good guided tours in Spanish*, displays paintings by Bitti, sculptures, books, vestments, some silver and musical instruments (including a 1664 organ). Small items made by the nuns are on sale. The excellent **Museo de Arte Indígena ASUR (Museo Téxtil Etnográfico)** ① *Pasaje Iturricha 314, opposite Casa Kolping in La Recoleta, T04-645 6651, www.asur.org.bo, Mon-Fri 0900-1200, 1430-1830, Sat 0930-1200, 1400-1800, US$3, English and French-speaking guides*, displays regional textiles and traditional techniques, shop sells crafts. Near the main plaza is the **Museo Nacional de Etnografía y Folklore (MUSEF)** ① *España 74 y San Alberto, T04-645 5293, www.musef.org.bo, Tue-Fri 0930-1230, 1430-1830, Sat 0930-1230, free*, with an impressive display of masks and an exhibition on the Uru-Chipaya culture.

North of the plaza San Miguel ① *Arenales 10, T04-645 1026, Mass Mon-Sat 0800 and 1915, Sun 1100, no shorts, short skirts or short sleeves allowed*, completed in 1628, has been restored and is very beautiful with Moorish-style carved and painted ceilings, alfarjes (early 17th century), pure-white walls and gold and silver altar. Some early sculpture can be seen in the sacristy. Nearby **Santa Mónica** ① *Arenales y Junín*, is one of the finest gems of Spanish architecture in the Americas, but has been converted into the theatre and hall for the Colegio Sagrado Corazón. Near the Mercado Central, **San Francisco** (1581)

ⓘ *Ravelo y Arce, Mass daily 0700 and 1900, Sun also 1030 and 1700*, has altars coated in gold leaf and 17th-century ceilings; one of its bells summoned the people of Sucre to struggle for independence.

Four blocks northwest of Plaza 25 de Mayo is the **Corte Suprema de Justicia** ⓘ *Luis Paz Arce 352, Mon-Fri 1000-1200, 1500-1800, free*, the seat of Bolivia's national judiciary

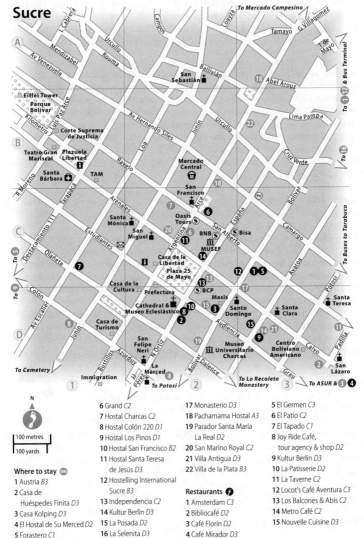

Sucre

100 metres
100 yards

Where to stay 🛏
1 Austria *B3*
2 Casa de Huéspedes Finita *D3*
3 Casa Kolping *D3*
4 El Hostal de Su Merced *D2*
5 Forastero *C1*
6 Grand *C2*
7 Hostal Charcas *C2*
8 Hostal Colón 220 *D1*
9 Hostal Los Pinos *D1*
10 Hostal San Francisco *B2*
11 Hostal Santa Teresa de Jesús *D3*
12 Hostelling International Sucre *B3*
13 Independencia *C2*
14 Kultur Berlin *D3*
15 La Posada *D2*
16 La Selenita *D3*
17 Monasterio *D3*
18 Pachamama Hostal *A3*
19 Parador Santa María La Real *D2*
20 San Marino Royal *C2*
21 Villa Antigua *D3*
22 Villa de la Plata *B3*

Restaurants 🍴
1 Amsterdam *C3*
2 Bibliocafé *D2*
3 Café Florín *D2*
4 Café Mirador *D3*
5 El Germen *C3*
6 El Patio *C2*
7 El Tapado *C1*
8 Joy Ride Café, tour agency & shop *D2*
9 Kultur Berlin *D3*
10 La Patisserie *D2*
11 La Taverne *C2*
12 Locot's Café Aventura *C3*
13 Los Balcones & Abis *C2*
14 Metro Café *C2*
15 Nouvelle Cuisine *D3*

and what remains of the city's official status as capital of Bolivia. To enter you must be smartly dressed and leave your passport with the guard; guides can be found in the public relations office. The nearby **Parque Bolívar** contains a monument and a miniature of the Eiffel Tower and Arc de Triomphe in honour of one of Bolivia's richest 20th-century tin barons, Francisco Argandoña, who created much of Sucre's splendour. At the downhill-end of the park is the **Fuente del Bicentenario**, where a **sound and light show** ⓘ *Thu-Sun 1900-2100*, is displayed. The **obelisk** opposite the Teatro Gran Mariscal in Plazuela Libertad, was erected with money raised by fining bakers who cheated on the size and weight of their bread. Also on this plaza is the Hospital Santa Bárbara (1574).

Around Sucre

North of Sucre Some 3 km north of Sucre is ☆**Cal Orcko**, considered the world's largest palaeontological site, where tracks from eight types of dinosaur have been identified (inside the Fancesa cement works, not open to the public). Nearby is **Parque Cretácico** ⓘ *T04-645 7392, http://parquecretacicosucre.com, Mon-Fri 0900-1700, Sat 1000-2000, Sun 1000-1700, US$4.35, children US$0.75*, crowded at weekends, with fibreglass dinosaurs, recorded growls, a 30-minute guided tour and binoculars through which (for an extra US$0.30) you can look at the prints on Cal Orcko, 300 m away. The **Sauro Tours** bus leaves daily 0930, 1200, 1430 from corner of cathedral, US$1.75 return, or take Micros 4 or H from Calle Arenales y Junín.

South of Sucre Southeast of the city, at the top of Dalence is **La Recoleta**, a lookout with arches, offering good views over the city. Here, within the Franciscan convent of La Recoleta is the **Museo de la Recoleta** ⓘ *Plaza Pedro de Anzúrez, T04-645 1987, Mon-Fri 0830-1200, 1430-1730, Sat 1500-1700, US$1.45 for entrance to all collections, guided tours only*, notable mainly for the beauty of its cloisters and gardens; the carved wooden choir stalls above the nave of the church are especially fine (see the martyrs transfixed by lances). In the grounds is the Cedro Milenario, a 1400-year-old cedar. Behind Recoleta monastery a road flanked by Stations of the Cross ascends an attractive hill, **Cerro Churuquella**, with large eucalyptus trees on its slopes, to a statue of Christ at the top.

About 5 km south on the Potosí road is the **Castillo de la Glorieta** ⓘ *Tue-Sat 0900-1630, US$2.50, US$1.25 to take photos, take Micro 4 marked Liceo Militar*. The former mansion of the Argandoña family, built in a mixture of contrasting European styles with painted ceilings, is in the military compound. Ask to see the paintings of the visit of the pope, in a locked room.

Tarabuco *Colour map 3, C3.*

Tarabuco, 64 km southeast of Sucre (altitude 3295 m), is best known for its colourful indigenous market on Sunday. The local people wear their traditional dress of conquistador-style helmets, multicoloured ponchos, *chuspas* (bags for carrying coca leaves) and the elaborate *axsu*, an overskirt worn by women. The market starts around 0930-1000 and is very popular with tourists. ☆**Textiles** are sold in a purpose-built market on Calle Murillo. Next to the market is a small museum, **Incapallay** ⓘ *Murillo 52, T04-646 1936, www.incapallay.org, Sun 0930-1400*, run by a weavers' association. The market is not held at Carnaval (when all Tarabuco is dancing in Sucre), Pujllay, Easter Sunday or All Saints' Day. The Pujllay independence celebration on the third Sunday in March is very vibrant. No one sleeps during this fiesta but basic accommodation is available if arranged in advance.

map page 419.

Tourist information

Sucre

Tourist office
Dirección de Turismo de la Alcaldía
(Argentina 65, p 2, Casa de la Cultura,
T04-643 5240, Mon-Fri 0800-1200, 1400-
1800), some English spoken; also have
kiosks at the airport, bus terminal, **Plazuela
Libertad** (Destacamento 111 y Arenales)
and **La Recoleta** (Polanco e Iturrichia).
Another **tourist office** (Estudiantes 25,
T04-644 7644, Mon-Fri 0900-1200, 1500-
1830) is staffed by university students and
open only during term.

Where to stay

Sucre

$$$ La Posada
Audiencia 92, T04-646 0101,
www.hotellaposada.com.bo.
Smart, colonial-style, good restaurant.
Recommended.

$$$ Parador Santa María La Real
Bolívar 625, T04-691 1920,
www.parador.com.bo.
Tastefully restored and upgraded colonial
house, bathtub, safety box, frigobar, heating.
It has a shop, spa and restaurant.

$$$ Refugio Andino Bramadero
30 km from the city towards Ravelo, details
from Raul y Mabel Cagigao, Avaroa 472,
T04-645 5592, bramader@yahoo.com,
or Restaurant Salamandra (Avaroa 510,
good food, 24 hrs, see Facebook).
Cabins or rooms, well-furnished, full board,
drinks and transport included, excellent
value, owner Raúl can advise on hikes and
astronomy, book in advance. Recommended.

$$$ Sky Hacienda
In Mosoj Llacta, by Yotala, 19 km south of
Sucre along the road to Potosí, T04-643 0045,
www.skyhacienda.com.
Upmarket hotel in a rural setting, nice
views from the rooms with heating, jacuzzi,
restaurant, nice patio and garden, pool, horse
riding, bicycles, minimum stay 2 nights, no
children under 12. Transfers to airport and
bus station are extra.

$$$ Villa Antigua
Calvo 237, T04-644 3437,
www.villaantiguahotel.com.
Tastefully restored colonial house with
garden, internet room, gym, large rooftop
terrace has great views, some suites with
kitchenette, airport transfers.

$$$-$$ Monasterio
Calvo 140, T04-641 5222, www.
hotelmonasteriosucre.com.
Beautiful 16th-century house with colonial
and neoclassic architecture. Elegant common
areas, heated rooms and suites, restaurant
serves international dishes, quiet terrace,
airport transfers.

$$ Casa Kolping
Pasaje Iturricha 265, La Recoleta, T04-642
3891, www.casakolpingsucre.com.bo.
Pleasant, lovely location with nice views,
good **Munay Pata** restaurant ($$-$),
internet lounge, wheelchair access, parking.
Part of the Kolping International network,
www.kolping.net.

$$ El Hostal de Su Merced
Azurduy 16, T04-644 2706,
www.desumerced.com.
Beautifully restored colonial building, lots
of character, owner and staff speak French
and English, good breakfast buffet, sun
terrace, restaurant. Airport transfer US$7.50.
Recommended.

$$ Hostal Santa Teresa de Jesús
San Alberto 431, T04-645 4189,
www.santateresahostal.com.
Refurbished colonial house, restaurant,
comfortable, garage. Recommended.

$$ Independencia
Calvo 31, T04-644 2256,
www.independenciahotel.com.
Historic colonial house, opulent salon, spiral stairs, lovely garden, comfortable, some rooms with bathtub, café, attentive service.

$$ La Selenita
J Mostajo 145, T7285 9993,
www.laselenita.com.
Pleasant guesthouse with 4 cabins for 2-3 persons, 2 types of breakfast with home-made bread and jam available, nice gardens, quiet, panoramic views of the colonial city, French/Belgian-run.

$$ San Marino Royal
Arenales 13, T04-645 1646, www.sanmarinoroyalhotel.com.bo.
Nicely converted colonial house, frigobar, cafeteria, $$$ for suite.

$$-$ Austria
Av Ostria Gutiérrez 506, by bus station, T04-645 4202, www.hostalaustria.com.bo.
Hot showers, good beds and carpeted rooms, cafeteria, parking, cheaper with shared bath and no breakfast, parking extra.

$$-$ Hostelling International Sucre
G Loayza 119 y Ostria Gutiérrez, T04-644 0471, www.hosteltrail.com/hostels/hisucre.
Functional hostel 1½ blocks from bus terminal, cheaper without bath and in dorms, breakfast available, garden, internet extra, parking, Spanish language classes, discount for HI members.

$$-$ Kultur Berlin "Sleep"
Avaroa 326, T646 6854, http://kulturberlin.com.
Associated with the Kultur Berlin café and the Insituto Cultural Boliviano-Alemán, imaginatively designed, spotless rooms with solar hot water, some with kitchenette. Recommended.

$ Casa de Huéspedes Finita
Padilla 233 (no sign), T04-645 3220, delfi_eguez@hotmail.com.
Some rooms with bath, good breakfast, hot water, heaters, tasty lunch, garden, terrace, also apartments with fully equipped kitchens for longer stays. Good value and recommended.

$ Forastero
Destacamento 111 No 394, T04-643 5407, or 7944 8788.
Comfortable rooms with and without bath, good hot showers, common areas, kitchen facilities, restaurant **Rinconcito Tupiceño** in nice garden.

$ Grand
Arce 61, T04-645 2461.
Older hotel but well maintained, comfortable (ask for room 18), ground floor at the back is noisy, some rooms dark, electric showers, good-value lunch in **Arcos** restaurant, Wi-Fi in patio.

$ Hostal Charcas
Ravelo 62, T04-645 3972, hostalcharcas@yahoo.com.
Cheaper without bath or TV, good value, huge breakfast extra, hot showers, at times runs bus to Tarabuco on Sun.

$ Hostal Colón 220
Colón 220, T04-645 5823.
Very nice guesthouse, cheaper with shared bath, laundry, helpful owner speaks English and German and has tourist information, coffee room.

$ Hostal los Pinos
Colón 502, T04-645 5639.
Comfortable, hot showers, garden, quiet, peaceful, parking.

$ Hostal San Francisco
Av Arce 191 y Camargo, T04-645 2117.
Colonial building, electric showers, breakfast available, quiet, patio, good value.

$ Pachamama Hostal
Arce 450, T04-645 3673, hostal_pachamama@hotmail.com.
Simple rooms with bath, electric shower, pleasant patio, parking, good value.

$ Villa de la Plata
Arce 369, T04-645 6849,
villadelaplata888@gmail.com.
Good-value apartments with kitchenette,
discounts for long stays, popular.

Restaurants

Sucre
Sausages and chocolates are among the
locally produced specialities.

$$ El Huerto
Ladislao Cabrera 86, San Matías, T04-645
1538. Daily 1130-1600 and Thu-Sun 1830-2100.
International food with salad bar, good
almuerzo, in a beautiful garden. Take a taxi
there at night.

$$ El Tapado
Olañeta 165 y Loa, T04-643 8778.
Daily, all day.
Extensive breakfast and dinner menu, llama
dishes, sandwiches, micro brews, parties in
the patio on Fri and Sat night.

$$ La Taverne
In the Alliance Française, Arce 35. Mon-Sat
1200-1500, 1800-2230, Sun 1900-2200.
Lovely terrace seating, weekly lunch specials,
international food, also regular cultural events.

$$-$ El Germen
San Alberto 231. Mon-Sat 0800-2200.
Mostly vegetarian, set lunches, excellent
breakfast, German pastries, book exchange,
German magazines. Recommended.

$$-$ Los Balcones
Plaza 25 de Mayo 34, upstairs.
Open 1200-2400.
Good food, popular with locals, set lunch
with salad bar, views over plaza.

$$-$ Nouvelle Cuisine
Avaroa 537. Daily 1100-2300.
Excellent *churrasquería* (grill), good value.

Cafés

Abis
Plaza 25 de Mayo 32.

Tip…
Llama meat contains parasites, so make
sure it has been properly cooked, and be
especially careful of raw salads as many
tourists experience gastrointestinal upsets.

Belgian-owned café and *heladería*,
with coffees, breakfasts, sandwiches,
light meals, ice cream.

Amsterdam
Bolivar 426. Mon-Fri from 1200, Sun from 1530.
Drinks, snacks and meals, book exchange,
Wi-Fi, live music Wed-Thu. Dutch-run, works
with a programme for migrant children.

Bibliocafé
N Ortiz 50, near plaza. Open 1200-1500,
1800-0200, Sun 1900-2400.
Pasta and light meals. Music and drinks, Wi-Fi.

Café Florín
Bolívar 567. Daily 0730-0200,
weekends to 0300.
Breakfast, sandwiches, snacks and
international meals ($$), large portions,
microbrews. Sunny patio, Wi-Fi, tour
bookings, cosy atmosphere, Dutch-run.

Café Mirador
Pasaje Iturricha 297, La Recoleta.
Open 0930-2000.
Very good garden café, fine views, good
juices, snacks and music, popular.

El Patio
San Alberto 18.
Small place for delicious *salteñas/empanadas*.

Joy Ride Café
N Ortiz 14, www.joyridebol.com.
Daily 0730-2300.
Great international food and drink, music,
Wi-Fi, very popular, upstairs lounge shows
films, also cultural events. Joy Ride has a
new hostel ($) at Avaroa 431, T04-645 0035.

Kultur Berlin "Eat & Drink"
Avaroa 326, T646 6854, http://kulturberlin.com.
German, Bolivian and international dishes,
themed evenings and other events.

La Patisserie
Audiencia 17. Open 0830-1230, 1530-2030.
French-owned, popular for crêpes, salads
and puddings.

Locot's Café Aventura
*Bolívar 465, T04-691 5958. Mon-Sat 0800-
2400, Sun 1100-2300.*
Bar serving international and Mexican food,
live music and theatre, Wi-Fi, also offer many
types of adventure sports: mountain biking,
hiking, riding, paragliding.

Metro Café
Calvo y España on Plaza 25 de Mayo.
A variety of coffees, sandwiches, breakfasts,
pastries, desserts, juices; delicious and
good service.

Bars and clubs

Sucre

Mitos
*F Cerro 60, near Junín, Disco-Mitos
on Facebook. Thu-Sat 2100-0300.*
Disco, popular with travellers.

Stigma
Bolívar 128 y Camargo, www.stigmasucre.com.
Varied music, young crowd.

Festivals

Sucre
24-26 May Independence celebrations,
most services, museums and restaurants
closed on 25.
8 Sep Virgen de Guadalupe, 2-day fiesta.
21 Sep Día del Estudiante, music around
main plaza.
**Oct/Nov Festival Internacional de la
Cultura**, 2nd week, shared with Potosí.

Shopping

Sucre
Handicrafts
ASUR (opposite Casa Kolping in La Recoleta)
sells weavings from around Tarabuco
and from the Jalq'a. More expensive,

but of higher quality than elsewhere.
Artesanías Calcha (Arce 103, opposite San
Francisco church) is recommended and
has a knowledgeable proprietor. Several
others nearby. **Bolsa Boliviana** (Calvo 64),
non-profit, has many nice items, especially
bags. **Casa de Turismo** (Bustillos 131) groups
several craft shops and tour operators under
one roof. **Centro Cultural Masis** (Bolívar
591, T04-645 3403, www.losmasis.com),
teaches local youth traditional music and
culture and has items for sale; visitors are
welcome at events and exhibitions. **Inca
Pallay** (Audiencia 97 y Bolívar, T04-646
1936, www.incapallay.org), a not-for-profit
association and Fairtrade shop, sells textiles
by Tarabuco and Jalq'a weavers, clothing,
gifts, bags and household items; also in
Tarabuco and La Paz. Artisans sell their wares
at the **La Recoleta** lookout. **Chocolates
Para Tí** (Arenales 7, Audiencia 68, at the
airport and bus terminal), is one of the best
chocolate shops in Sucre. **Taboada** (Arce y
Arenales, Daniel Campos 82, at airport and
bus terminal, www.taboada.com.bo) is also
very good for chocolates.

Markets
The central market is colourful with some
stalls selling *artesanía*, but beware of theft .

What to do

Sucre
Language classes
**Academia Latinoamericana de
Español**, *Dalence 109, T04-643 9613,
www.latinoschool.com.* Professional,
good extracurricular activities, US$180
for 20 hrs per week, US$350 with home
stay (US$300 for private teacher).
Alianza Francesa, *Aniceto Arce 35, T04-645
3599, www.sucre.alianzafrancesa.org.bo.*
Spanish and French classes.
Bolivian Spanish School, *Kilómetro 7 No 250,
T04-644 3841, www.bolivianspanishschool.
com.* Near Parque Bolívar, pleasant school,
good value, excellent teachers.

Centro Boliviano Americano, *Calvo 301, T04-644 1608, www.cbasucre.org*. Recommended for language courses. These centres run cultural events, have libraries and branches in La Paz.

Continental Spanish School, *Olañeta 224, T04-643 8093, www.schoolcontinental.com*. Good teachers and fun activities.

Fox Academy, *Av Destacamento Chuquisaca 134, T04-644 0688, www.foxacademysucre. com*. Spanish and Quechua classes, US$5 per hr, non-profit, proceeds go to teaching English to children, volunteering arranged.

Instituto Cultural Boliviano-Alemán (**ICBA, Goethe Institute**), *Bolívar 609, T04-645 2091, www.icba-sucre.edu.bo*. Spanish, German, Portuguese and Quechua courses, US$7.50 pp per lesson; also has an Ecomuseum.

Sucre Spanish School, *Calvo 350, T04-643 6727, www.sucrespanishschool.com*. US$6.50 per hr, friendly and flexible, home stays or lodging at Kultur Berlin, can arrange tours and volunteering.

Tour operators

Bolivia Specialist, *N Ortiz 30, T04-643 7389, www.boliviaspecialist.com*. Dutchman Dirk Dekker's agency for local hikes, horse riding and 4WD trips, tours in Bolivia and Peru; also bus and plane tickets and information.

Candelaria Tours, *JJ Pérez 301 y Colón, T04-644 0340, www.candelariatours.com*. Hikes around Sucre, tours to weaving communities, English spoken.

Cóndor Trekkers, *Calvo 102 y Bolívar, T7289 1740, www.condortrekkers.org*. Not-for-profit trekking company using local guides supported by volunteers, city walks and treks around Sucre, proceeds go to social projects, first-aid carried.

Joy Ride Tourism, *N Ortiz 26, at corner of Plaza, T04-645 7603, www.joyridebol.com*. Mountain- and motorbiking, hiking, climbing, horse riding, paragliding, tours to Potosí and Salar de Uyuni.

L y D, *final Panamá 127 y Comarapa, Barrio Petrolero, T04-642 0752, turismo_lyd@hotmail. com*. Lucho and Dely Loredo and son Carlos

(who speaks English) offer custom-made tours using private or public transport, to regional communities and attractions, and further afield.

Oasis Tours, *Arce 95, of 2, T04-643 2438, www.oasistours-bo.com*. City walking tour, indigenous communities, Chataquila, Inca trail. Also sell bus tickets and have their own office in Uyuni for *salar* trips. Very helpful owner.

Seatur, *Plaza 25 de Mayo 25, T04-646 2425*. Local tours, hiking trips, English, German, French spoken.

Transport

Sucre

Air Juana Azurduy de Padilla airport is 5 km northwest of town (T04-645 4445). **BoA** direct flights to Santa Cruz and to Cochabamba for connections. **TAM** daily to **La Paz**, **Santa Cruz** and **Cochabamba**, less frequently to **Tarija** and **Yacuiba**. Ecojet, direct to Cochabamba, **Santa Cruz and Tarija**. Airport tax US$1.60. Micros 1, 3, 7, A and F go from entrance to Av Hernando Siles, a couple of blocks from main plaza, US$0.20, 25 mins. Taxi US$3.50.

Bus Bus terminal is on north outskirts of town, 3 km from centre on Ostria Gutiérrez, T04-644 1292; taxi US$1.15; Micro A or 3. Daily to/from **La Paz** several companies at 1700-2000, 12 hrs, regular US$12.75, *semi-cama* US$17.75, *cama* US$25.50. To **Cochabamba**: several companies daily at 1830-1930, 9 hrs via Aiquile; at 2100 via Oruro, 12 hrs, US$9.65, *semi-cama* US$12.50, *cama* US$19.50. To **Potosí**: frequent departures between 0630 and 1800, US$3-6, 3 hrs. Shared taxis with pick-up service: **Cielito Lindo**, at Casa de Turismo, Bustillos 131, T04-643 2309, **Cielito Express**, T04-643 1000 and **Expreso Dinos**, T04-643 7444, both outside the bus terminal, 2½ hrs, US$7 pp. To **Oruro**: 2000-2200, 4 companies via Potosí, 8 hrs, US$9-12, *cama* US$17.75. To **Tarija**: 4 companies, at 1500-1600, 14 hrs, US$14 via Potosí. To **Uyuni**: direct at 0830, **6 de Octubre**, 7 hrs,

Emperador 0700, 1230, with change and long wait in Potosí, US$8.35-11.75. Or catch a bus to Potosí and change; try to book the connecting bus in advance. To **Villazón** via Potosí and Tupiza: at 1330, 1730, **6 de Octubre** (with bus cama), 11 hrs, US$10-14; to **Tupiza**, 8-9 hrs, US$9-14. To **Santa Cruz**: many companies 1600-1730, 15 hrs, US$13.75; *semi-cama* US$18, *cama* US$24.

To Tarabuco Minivans leave when full from C Túpac Yupanqui (Parada de Tarabuco), daily starting 0630, US$1, 1¼ hrs

on a good paved road. To get to the Parada take a micro "C" or "7" from the Mercado Central. Also buses to Tarabuco from Av de las Américas y Jaime Mendoza, same fare and times. Tourist bus from the cathedral on Sun at 0830, US$5 round-trip, reserve at **Oasis Tours** (address above); also **Real Audiencia**, depart San Alberto 181 y España, T04-644 3119, at 0830, return 1330; you must use the same bus you went on. Shared taxi with **Cielito Lindo** (see Transport to Potosí above), Sun at 0900, US$5 return.

one of the most beautiful, saddest and fascinating places you'll ever experience

Potosí is the highest city of its size in the world (population 175,562, altitude 3977 m). It was founded by the Spaniards on 10 April 1545, after they had discovered indigenous mine workings at Cerro Rico (4824 m), which dominates the city. Immense amounts of silver were once extracted. In Spain *'es un Potosí'* (it's a Potosí) is still used for anything superlatively rich.

By the early 17th century Potosí was the largest city in the Americas, but over the next two centuries, as its lodes began to deteriorate and silver was found elsewhere, Potosí became little more than a ghost town. It was the demand for tin – a metal the Spaniards ignored – that saved the city from absolute poverty in the early 20th century, until the price slumped because of over-supply. Mining continues in Cerro Rico (mainly tin, zinc, lead, antimony and wolfram) to this day.

Sights

Plaza 10 de Noviembre and around Large parts of Potosí are colonial, with twisting streets and an occasional great mansion with its coat of arms over the doorway. The city, which has a population of 175,562, is a UNESCO World Heritage Site. Some of the best buildings are grouped round the Plaza 10 de Noviembre. The old Cabildo and the Royal Treasury – Las Cajas Reales – are both here, converted to other uses. The massive cathedral faces Plaza 10 de Noviembre.

West of the plaza The ☆**Casa Nacional de Moneda (Mint)** ⓘ *C Ayacucho, T02-622 2777, www.bolivian.com/cnm, Tue-Sat 0900-1230, 1430-1830, Sun 0900-1230, entry US$3, plus US$3 to take photos, US$6 for video, entry by regular, 2-hr guided tour only (in English or French if there are 10 or more people, at 0900, 1030, 1430 and 1630)*, is near the plaza. Founded in 1572, rebuilt 1759-1773, it is one of the chief monuments of civil building in Hispanic America. Thirty of its 160 rooms are a museum with sections on mineralogy, silverware and an art gallery in a splendid salon on the first floor. One section is dedicated to the works of the acclaimed 17th- to 18th-century religious painter Melchor Pérez de Holguín. Elsewhere are coin dies and huge wooden presses which made the silver strips from which coins were cut. The smelting houses have carved altarpieces from Potosí's ruined churches. You can't fail to notice the huge, grinning mask of Bacchus over an archway between two principal courtyards. Erected in 1865, its smile is said to be ironic and aimed at the departing Spanish. Wear warm clothes; it's cold inside.

Potosí has many outstanding colonial churches. Among its baroque churches, typical of 18th-century Andean or 'mestizo' architecture, are the Jesuit **Compañia de Jesús church and bell-gable** ⓘ *Ayacucho entre Bustillos y Oruro*, whose beautiful façade hides the modern tourist office building, and whose tower has a **mirador** ⓘ *0800-1200, 1400-1800, 30 mins later Sat-Sun, US$1.40*.

Further west, the **Convento y Museo de Santa Teresa** ⓘ *Santa Teresa y Ayacucho, T02-622 3847, http://museosantateresa. blogspot.co.uk, only by guided tour in Spanish or English, Mon-Sat 0900-1230, 1500-1800; Sun 0900-1200, 1500-1800, museum is closed Tue and Sun morning; US$3, US$1.50 to take photos, US$25 for video*, has an impressive amount of giltwork inside and an interesting collection of colonial and religious art.

South of the plaza Another interesting church, **San Francisco** ⓘ *Tarija y Nogales, T02-622 2539, Mon-Fri 0900-1100, 1430-1700, Sat 0900-1100, US$2.15*, has a fine organ and is worthwhile for the views from the tower and roof, the museum of ecclesiastical art and an underground tunnel system.

Three blocks east, the **Museo del Ingenio de San Marcos** ⓘ *La Paz 1565 y Betanzos, T02-622 6717, 1000-1500, US$1.40; textiles museum and shop Mon-Sat 1430-2200; restaurant 1000-1530, 1830-2200*, is a well-preserved example of the city's industrial past, with machinery used in grinding down the silver ore. It also has cultural activities and an exhibition of Calcha textiles.

North of the plaza On the north side of the Plaza 6 de Agosto, the **Teatro Omiste** has an imposing façade.

To the east are the churches of **La Merced** ⓘ *Hoyos y Millares, US$1.40 for museo sacro and mirador, US$0.70 for mirador only (with café)*, with great views of Cerro Rico and the city, and **San Martín** ⓘ *Hoyos, T02-622 3682, Mon-Sat 1000-1200, 1500-1830, free*, which has an uninviting exterior, but is beautiful inside. It is normally closed for fear of theft so ask the German Redemptorist Fathers to show you around; their office is just to the left of the church.

Directly north of the plaza, the **Museo Universitario** ⓘ *C Bolívar 54 y Sucre, T02-622 7310, Mon-Fri 0800-1200, 1400-1800, US$0.70*, displays archaeology, fossils, costumes,

The airport, 6 km out of town on the Sucre road, has scheduled flights to La Paz and Cochabamba with BoA. The bus terminal (Nueva Terminal) is on Avenida de las Banderas at the north end of the city. Frequent buses go to Oruro and La Paz and there are good roads to Uyuni, Sucre and Tarija. Cochabamba is a long bus ride with connections on to Santa Cruz. See also Transport, page 432.

When to go

Bring warm clothes at any time of year; the average temperature is 9°C and there are 130 sub-zero nights a year. The dampest months are October to March.

Time required

Two to three days to visit the city.

Tip...
Take it easy on arrival; remember Potosí is even higher than La Paz.

musical instruments and some good modern Bolivian painting. Guided tour to the mirador (tower) offers great views, US$0.70. Nearby is the church of **San Agustín** ⓘ *Bolívar y Quijarro, open only for Mass*, which has crypts and catacombs (much of the city was interconnected by tunnels in colonial times), and **San Lorenzo** (1728-1744) ⓘ *Héroes del Chaco y Bustillos, Mass 0700-1000*, with a rich portal and fine views from the tower.

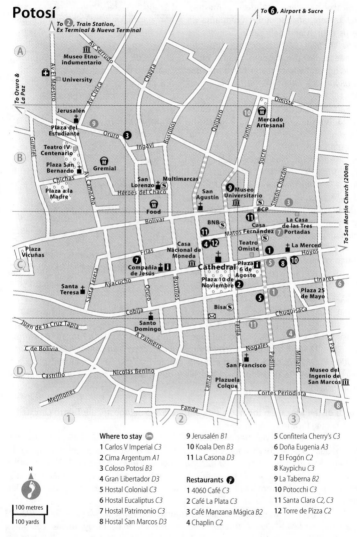

Potosí

Where to stay
1 Carlos V Imperial *C3*
2 Cima Argentum *A1*
3 Coloso Potosí *B3*
4 Gran Libertador *D3*
5 Hostal Colonial *C3*
6 Hostal Eucaliptus *C3*
7 Hostal Patrimonio *C3*
8 Hostal San Marcos *D3*
9 Jerusalén *B1*
10 Koala Den *B3*
11 La Casona *D3*

Restaurants
1 4060 Café *C3*
2 Café La Plata *C3*
3 Café Manzana Mágica *B2*
4 Chaplin *C2*
5 Confitería Cherry's *C3*
6 Doña Eugenia *A3*
7 El Fogón *C2*
8 Kaypichu *C3*
9 La Taberna *B2*
10 Potocchi *C3*
11 Santa Clara *C2, C3*
12 Torre de Pizza *C2*

Further north, the fascinating **Museo Etno-indumentario** ① *Av Serrudo 152, T02-622 3258, Mon-Fri 0930-1200, 1430-1800, Sat 0930-1200, US$1.40, includes tour*, displays in detail the dress, customs and histories of Potosí department's 16 provinces.

City centre architecture In Potosí, 2000 colonial buildings have been catalogued. Among the better preserved examples is the **house of the Marqués de Otavi**, now the BNB bank, on Junín between Matos and Bolívar. Next to **Hotel Gran Libertador**, on Millares between Nogales and Chuquisaca, is a doorway with two rampant lions in low relief on the lintel. The **Casa de las Tres Portadas** (house of the three arches), on Bolívar near La Paz, is a *hostal*.

☆Mine tours

For many, the main reason for being in Potosí is to visit the mines of Cerro Rico. The state mines were closed in the 1980s and are now worked as cooperatives by small groups of miners in conditions which are, if anything, more dangerous than in colonial times. An estimated 14,000 miners work in 49 cooperatives, some 800 are children. *The Devil's Miner* is a recommended documentary film about child labour in the mines, shown regularly by Potosí agencies and Sucre cafés.

A tour to the mines and ore-processing plant involves meeting miners and seeing them at work first-hand. Mine entrances are above 4000 m and temperatures inside can reach 40ºC, with noxious dust and gasses. You should be acclimatized, fit and have no heart or breathing problems, such as asthma. Tours last up to five hours and their difficulty varies; you can ask for a shorter, less gruelling, visit if you wish. Not all tours visit the processing plant.

Guided tours are conducted by former miners; by law all guides have to work with a tour agency and carry an ID card issued by the Prefectura. Essential equipment is provided: helmet, lamp and usually protective clothing but large-size boots may not be available. Wear old clothes and take a torch and a handkerchief or mask to filter the dusty air. The smaller the tour group, the better. Some are as large as 20 people, which is excessive. Tours cost about US$10.50-13 per person and include transport. Many agencies say they give part of their proceeds to miners but such claims are difficult to verify. You can also contribute directly, for example by taking medicines to the health centre (*Posta Sanitaria*) on Cerro Rico. Saturday and Sunday are the quietest days (Sunday is the miners' day off). **Note** Tourists are not allowed to buy dynamite to give to miners.

Museo Histórico Minero Diego Huallpa ① *by Mina Pailaviri on Cerro Rico, city buses P, Q, 70 and others, T02-623 1143, Mon-Sat 0900-1200, 1430-1800, Sun 0900-1500, US$10*, has exhibits of minerals and mining techniques, two-hour visits include mine tunnels with mannequins instead of real miners.

Tarapaya

A good place to freshen up after visiting the mines (or to spend a day relaxing) is Tarapaya, 21 km on the road to Oruro, where there are **thermal baths** ① *public pools US$0.50 and private baths US$1.20 per hr (see complejorecreacional.detarapaya on Facebook), and cabins for rent ($) and camping, US$4.25*. On the other side of the river from Tarapaya is a 60-m-diameter crater lake, which has a temperature of 30-34ºC; take sun protection. Below the crater lake are boiling ponds, not fit for swimming. **Balneario Miraflores** (25 km) ① *pools US$0.35, private baths US$2.80*, has hotter water than Tarapaya, but is not as clean. Minibuses run to both *balnearios* from outside Chuquimia market on Avenida Universitaria, 0600-1800, US$0.75; taxi US$9. The last vehicle back to Potosí from Miraflores is at 1800.

South of Potosí

A paved road runs south of Potosí. At Ingenio Cucho (Km 38) the road splits. One branch continues south to Cotagaita, Tupiza and Villazón. The other road goes east to the next valley then south to Camargo and the Valle de Cinti to El Puente, where it climbs to the altiplano before descending eventually to Tarija. Both branches are paved.

The tranquil colonial town of **Camargo** (population 14,200, altitude 2406 m) is surrounded by vineyards and fruit orchards, 186 km south of Potosí. Straddling the Río Chico and flanked by crumbling red sandstone cliffs on one side and rolling hills on the other, the town has a very pretty setting. The church is by the main **Plaza 6 de Agosto**. The bus terminal and a small market are along Avenida Chuquisaca, closer to **Plazuela Avaroa**. The main market is at the opposite end of town past the main plaza. Also along Avenida Chuquisaca is the **Alcaldía**, where you can get information about the area. Places to stay include **Hostal Plaza** ($$ Grau 13, T04-629 2977, hostalplaza.camargo@outlook. es, modern, family-run, very hospitable) and **Villa Sofía** ($ Potosí 17, T04-629 2047, www. hostalvillasofia.com, old house and new sections, big garden, family-run, very nice). Many shops sell excellent fruit preserves, singani and wine. Many vineyards nearby can be visited and there is **Museo Etno Antropológico de Cinti** ① *Comunidad El Chical, just south of Camargo, T04-629 2092, US$1.50, with toilets.*

The main road runs south from Camargo, between the Río Chico and towering red cliffs, 42 km to **Villa Abecia**, a lovely small town surrounded by vineyards and fruit orchards on the banks of the Río Grande ($$-$ **Hostal Cepas de Mi Abuelo**, near the plaza, T7299 0111, is a delightful hotel with traditional linen and home-made and home-grown produce). Beyond Villa Abecia is **Las Carreras**, in the far southern reaches of the department of Chuquisaca, where a small bodega, **La Casa de Barro**, is denominated a **Museo de Sitio Vivo**, with its vines clambering over molle and chañar trees. Next is **El Puente**, where the road turns east and crosses the Río San Juan de Oro into the department of Tarija. From here it climbs steeply along cacti-covered slopes with beautiful views to the **Altiplano de Tarija**, a high plateau at about 3500 m. After the **Falda la Queñua** tunnel is a vertiginous 1900-m descent to the flat valley north of Tarija.

Listings Potosí *map page 428.*

Where to stay

Unless otherwise stated hotels have no heating.

$$$ Coloso Potosí
Bolívar 965, T02-622 2627,
www.potosihotel.com.
Comfortable modern rooms with frigobar, heating, bath tubs and nice views. Small indoor pool, sauna, parking.

$$$-$$ Cima Argentum
Av Villazón 239, T02-622 9538,
www.hca-potosi.com.
Modern comfortable rooms and suites all with safe. Warm and bright, heating, frigobar.

$$$-$$ Hostal Patrimonio
Matos 62, T02-622 2659,
www.hostalpatrimonio.com.
Bright, warm, modern hotel. Heating, frigobar and safe in each room, sauna and jacuzzi (suites each have their own).

$$ Hostal Colonial
Hoyos 8, T02-622 4809, www.
hostalcolonialpotosi.com.
Older place but well located, breakfast extra, carpeted, heating, bathtubs, frigobar.

$$ Hotel Gran Libertador
Millares 58, T02-622 7877, www.
hotelgranlibertador.com.

Colonial-style hotel, good buffet breakfast, cafeteria, comfortable rooms, central heating, quiet, helpful, parking.

$$-$ Jerusalén
Oruro 143, T02-622 4633,
http://hoteljerusalen.es.tl.
HI affiliated, private rooms and dorms, near Mercado Gremial, family-run, money exchange, book exchange, common and TV room, laundry service, café.

$ Carlos V Imperial
Linares 42, T02-623 1010.
Cheaper rooms without bath, hot water, kitchen facilities.

$ Hostal Eucaliptus
Linares 88A, T7240 1884, part of Koala Tours (see below).
Pleasant bright rooms, cheaper with shared bath, heating, good breakfast, 350 m from the main plaza.

$ Hostal San Marcos
La Paz 1626 y Periodista, T02-623 001.
Colonial house, nice comfortable rooms, heating, cooking facilities.

$ Koala Den
Junín 56, T02-622 6467, papaimilla@ hotmail.com (Koala-Den on Facebook).
Private rooms with bath and breakfast (cheaper in dorm), heating, TV and video, use of kitchen, popular and often full.

$ La Casona
Chuquisaca 460, T02-623 0523, www.hotelpotosi.com.
Cheaper with shared bath and in dorm, courtyard, kitchen facilities.

Restaurants

$$ 4060 Café
Hoyos y Sucre. Open 1600-late, food until 2300.
Restaurant/bar serving good meals, varied menu, large portions, nice atmosphere, heating. Recommended.

$$ El Fogón
Frías 58 y Oruro. Daily 1200-2300.
Restaurant/grill, good food and atmosphere.

$$-$ Kaypichu
Millares 16. Tue-Sun 0700-1300, 1700-2300.
Breakfast, vegetarian options, *peña* in high season.

$$-$ La Taberna
Junín 12, open all day.
Bolivian and international food, set lunch and à la carte in the evening, good service.

$$-$ Potocchi
Millares 24, T622 2759. Open 0800-2230.
International and local dishes, can accommodate special diets with advance notice, *peña* in high season.

$ Doña Eugenia
Santa Cruz y Ortega. Open 0900-1300.
Typical food such as the warming *kalapurca* soup with corn and meat (be careful it is hot) and *chicharrón de cerdo*, pork crackling.

$ Torre de Pizza
Matos 14. Open 0700-2200.
Pizza, pasta, vegetarian options, also breakfast, family-run, attentive service.

Cafés

Café La Plata
Tarija y Linares at Plaza 10 de Noviembre. Mon-Sat 1000-2200.
Upmarket place for coffee, sweets and drinks. Nice atmosphere, English and French spoken.

Café Manzana Mágica
Oruro 239.
Meat-free meals only, a popular, small café.

Chaplin
Matos y Quijarro. Mon-Fri 0830-1200.
Breakfasts and excellent *tucumanas* (fried *empanadas*).

Confitería Cherry's
Padilla 8. Open 0800-2230.
Small economical place, good cakes, breakfast.

Santa Clara
Quijarro 32 y Matos, also Sucre 33 y Bolívar and other locations. Mon-Sat 0700-2300. Popular with locals for afternoon snacks.

Festivals

Potosí is sometimes called the 'Ciudad de las Costumbres', especially at Corpus Cristi, Todos Santos and Carnaval, when special sweets are prepared, families go visiting friends, etc.

End May/beginning Jun Fiesta de Manquiri: on 3 consecutive Sat llama sacrifices are made at the cooperative mines in honour of Pachamama.
Jan/Feb Carnaval Minero, 2 weeks before Carnaval in Oruro, includes **Tata Ckascho**, when miners dance down Cerro Rico and El Tío (the Dios Minero) is paraded.
Aug San Bartolomé, or **Chutillos**, is held from the middle of Aug, with the main event being processions of dancers on the weekend closest to the 24-26 Aug; Sat features Potosino, and Sun national, groups. Costumes can be hired in the *artesanía* market on C Sucre. Hotel and transport prices go up by 30% for the whole of that weekend. **10 Nov Fiesta Aniversiario de Potosí**.

Shopping

Mercado Artesanal, *Sucre y Omiste. Mon-Sat 0830-1230, 1430-1830.* Sells handwoven cloth and regional handicrafts. There are several craft shops on C Sucre between Omiste and Bustillos.
Mercado Central, *Bustillos y Bolívar.* Sells mainly meat and some produce.
Mercado Gremial, *between Av Camacho and Oruro.* For household goods.

What to do

All agencies offer mine tours (see page 429), trips to the Salar de Uyuni and REA (see page 405) and trekking at Kari Kari lakes, the artificial water sources for the city and mines.

Claudia Tours, *Ayacucho 7, T02-622 5000, www.turismoclaudia.com.* City tours, mines and trekking; also in Uyuni, Av Ferroviaria opposite Hotel Avenida.
Hidalgo Tours, *La Paz 113, T02-622 9512, www.salardeuyuni.net; also in Uyuni.* Specialized services in Potosí and to Salar de Uyuni. Guide Efraín Huanca has been recommended for mine tours. Pioneering tour operator for the Uyuni salt flats and the lagoons, having the first salt hotel in the world, the **Palacio de Sal**; see page 408.
Koala Tours, *Ayacucho 3, T02-622 2092, koalabolivia@hotmail.com.* Owner Eduardo Garnica speaks English and French. Their mine tours are popular and have been recommended.
Silver Tours, *Quijarro 12, T02-622 3600, www.silvertours.8m.com.* Economical mine tours.
Sin Fronteras, *Ayacucho 17 y Bustillos, T02-622 4058, frontpoi@entelnet.bo.* Owner Juan Carlos Gonzales speaks English and French and is very helpful. Also hires camping gear.
Turismo Potosí, *Lanza 12 y Chuquisaca, T02-622 8212.* Guide and owner Santos Mamani has been recommended.

Transport

Air The airport, Capitán Nicolás Rojas, is 6 km from Potosí on the road to Sucre. **BoA** flies to **La Paz** (5 per week, US$51-57) and **Cochabamba** (3 per week).

Bus Large modern bus terminal (Nueva Terminal, use fee US$0.30) with ATMs, luggage store, information office, tourist police and food court. **Note** it is far from the centre: taxi US$2; city buses F, I, 150, US$0.20, but there are no city buses or taxis late at night; not safe to go out on the street, try to arrive by day or wait inside until morning. Daily services: **La Paz** several companies 1900-2230, US$9-13, 10 hrs by paved road; *bus cama* US$18.25 (departures from La Paz 1830-2030). To travel by day, go to **Oruro**, **San Miguel** and others, all day, US$5.40-7.50, 5 hrs. Buses to **Uyuni** leave from either side of the railway line at Av Toledo y Av Universitaria, 1000-1200 and 1800-2000, US$6, 3-4 hrs on a new road, superb scenery; book in advance. **Cochabamba** several companies 1830-2030, US$9-13, *bus cama* US$18.75, 10 hrs. **Sucre** frequent service 0630-1800, US$3-6, 3 hrs; also shared taxis from behind the old bus terminal, **Cielito Lindo**, T02-624 3381, 2½ hrs, US$7 pp, drop-off at your hotel. For **Santa Cruz** change in Sucre or Cochabamba. **Tupiza** several companies (**Oglobo** and **Expreso Tupiza** are best) around 0730 and 2000, US$5-10, 6 hrs; continuing to **Villazón**, US$6-10, 8 hrs. Also vans (*minibuses*) and cars

(*rapiditos*), 3-4 per day, US$8-15 (according to demand), 5 hrs to Tupiza, might require a transfer in Cotagaita; taxi US$120; to Villazón vans US$8, 7 hrs; cars (*rapiditos*) US$9-15, 6 hrs. **Tarija** several companies 1800-1830, US$10.35-13.60, 8 hrs, spectacular journey. To go by day take a bus to **Camargo**, 5 hrs, US$6, then change. Camargo buses leave from offices outside main terminal.

Train Station is at Av Sevilla y Villazón, T02-622 3101, www.fca.com.bo. A 25-passenger railcar to **Sucre** leaves on Tue, Thu, Sat 0800, 6 hrs, US$3.60; confirm details in advance.

Tarija and around Colour map 3, C4.

an easy-going city with shady parks and flower-filled plazas

☆This pleasant city on the banks of the Río Guadalquivir, with streets and plazas planted with flowering trees, is blessed with plenty of sun and a spring-like climate almost all year-round. Tarija is known for the fruit and wines of the fertile Valle Central in which it sits.

Founded 4 July 1574 by Capitán Luis de Fuentes y Vargas, Tarija declared itself independent of Spain in 1807, and in 1825 it opted to join Bolivia. With a population of 234,422, the city has a strong cultural heritage which sets it apart from the rest of the country. Since 2005 it has experienced an economic boom thanks to the development of natural gas in the department.

Sights

The oldest and most interesting church in the city is the **Basílica de San Francisco** ① *corner of La Madrid y Daniel Campos, 0700-1000, 1800-2000, Sun 0630-1200, 1800-2000*. It is beautifully painted inside, with praying angels depicted on the ceiling and the four evangelists at the four corners below the dome. The library is divided into old and new sections, the old containing some 15,000 volumes, the new a further 5000. To see the library, go to the door at Ingavi O-0137. Behind the church is the **Museo Fray Francisco Miguel de Mari** ① *Colón 641, entre La Madrid e Ingavi, T664 4909, www.franciscanosdetarija.com, Mon-Fri 0900-1200, 1500-1700, US$2.15*, with colonial and contemporary art collections, colonial books, the oldest of which is a 1501 Iliad, 19th-century photograph albums and other items.

The **Casa Dorada** ① *Ingavi 370 entre Trigo y Sucre, http://casadelaculturatarija.com, guided tours Mon-Fri at 0900, 1000, 1100, 1500, 1600, and 1700, Sat 0900, 1000, 1100, US$0.70*, begun in 1886, is also known as the Maison d'Or and is now part of the Casa de la Cultura. It belonged to importer/exporter Moisés Navajas and his wife Esperanza Morales and has been beautifully restored inside and out.

Tarija's **Museo de Arqueología y Paleontología** ① *Trigo 402 y Lema, T04-663 6680, Mon-Fri 0800-1200, 1500-1800, Sat 0900-1200, 1500-1800, US$0.45*, contains a palaeontological collection (fossils, remains of several Andean elephants of the Pleistocene), as well as smaller mineralogical, ethnographic and anthropological collections. The outskirts of the city can be a good place to look for **fossils**, but report any finds to the university.

Finding your feet

Daily scheduled flights to La Paz, Cochabamba and Santa Cruz. There are paved roads to Potosí, where good connections can be made elsewhere, and Bermejo on the Argentine border. Roads west to Tupiza and east to the Chaco for the route to Santa Cruz are being improved – slowly.

Getting around

Note that blocks west of Calle Colón have a small O before number (oeste), and all blocks east have an E (este); blocks are numbered from Colón outwards. All streets north of Avenida Las Américas are preceded by N (norte).

When to go

The best time to visit is from January onwards, when the fruit is in season, but September, after the spring rains begin, is also nice. The months when most rain falls are October to March.

Time required

Two to three days in the city and surroundings, but if travelling onwards overland, allow another day to get to your next destination.

Immigration

Calle Ingavi esq Rojas 789, Barrio El Molino, T04-664 3450, Monday-Friday 0830-1230, 1430-1830. Visa renewals in 48 hours.

Valle Central

The Valle Central, which surrounds Tarija, offers many opportunities for excursions in pleasant countryside at about 1800 m. As well as the fossil deposits, there are vineyards and bodegas (wineries), riverside beaches, waterfalls and colonial towns. It is this zone which inspires the nickname Andalucía of Bolivia because of its fruit and berry production, vegetables, ham cured Serrano-style, goat's cheese, preserves and honey. You can buy local produce at **Las Duelas Calamuchita** ① *opposite the sports field in village of Calamuchita near Valle de la Concepción, T04-666 8943, daily 0900-1700*, a shop and small winery, selling mostly artisanal wines and singani from nine producers, wine-tasting and regional preserves, ham and other items. In Tarija itself **La Vinoteca** ① *Ingavi O-0731 y Gral Trigo, Mon-Sat 0900-1200, 1500-1900*, sells wine at bodega prices, cheese and ham, and **La Rotisería** ① *Gral Trigo y Bolívar*, is good for meats, cheeses and wines (see http://tarijaaromasysabores.com).

☆Wineries

Tarija is proud of its **wine** and **singani** (clear brandy) production, the best in Bolivia. There are two distinct wine-producing regions near Tarija. The first is in the Valle de Cinti, which can easily be reached from Tarija. The best option is to take a tour (see What to do, page 439), which provides transport and allows you to visit several different bodegas on the same day. The same applies to the second region, south of town in the Valle Central. See box, opposite, for a selection of wine producers. The main centres for wine are Santa Ana and Valle de la Concepción.

North of Tarija

About 15 km north of the centre is the charming town of **San Lorenzo**. Just off the plaza is the **Museo Méndez** ① *Mon-Sat 0900-1230, 1500-1830, minimum US$0.30 entry*, the house of the independence hero Eustaquio Méndez, 'El Moto'. The small museum exhibits his weapons, his bed and his 'testimonio'. At lunchtime on Sunday, many courtyards serve cheap meals. Minibuses from Domingo Paz y J M Saracho leave every five minutes, US$0.75. The road to San Lorenzo passes **Tomatitas** (5 km), now almost a suburb of Tarija,

ON THE ROAD
Tarija wineries

Aranjuez, *T04-664 2552, gcomercial@vinosaranjuez.com*. Bodega at Avenida Dr A Baldivieso E-1976, Barrio Aranjuez, across the river within walking distance of town. One of the smallest, produces only wine.

Bodega Magnus, *T04-611 2462 (bodega)*. A relatively new winery which is open to tourists, concentrating on reds and rosé, in Valle de la Concepción.

Campos de Solana, *15 de Abril E-0259 entre Suipacha y Méndez (tienda), T04-664 8482, www.camposdesolana.com.* Increasingly recognized for their selection of fine wines (the Malbec is highly regarded), as well as the popular Casa Real brand of singani (same company, same shop but different bodega, T04-664 5498, http://casa-real. com). The Campos de Solana bodega is in El Portillo, 6 km on road to Bermejo and the Casa Real bodega (T6737 0868, visitas@casa-real.com) is in Santa Ana, about 15 km off the road to Bermejo.

Casa Vieja, *Trigo casi Corrado (shop), T04-666 2605, www.lacasavieja.info, Mon-Sun 1000-1600*. A traditional *bodega artesanal*, small-scale winery, located in Valle de la Concepción, 25 km from Tarija. Interesting and recommended. It also has a popular restaurant overlooking the vines, open daily for lunch (dishes US$3-7) and, on Sunday, live music and roast suckling pig (*chancho a la cruz*), US$10.

Kohlberg, *Av Francisco Lazcano, Barrio San Jorge No 1, T04-666 6366, http://kohlberg. com.bo*. Bodega La Cabaña in Santa Ana, 15 km from town off the road to Bermejo. The first industrial winery and now the largest. Specializes in table wines, their Syrah is well regarded.

La Concepción, *Colón entre 15 de Abril y La Madrid (shop), T04-664 5040, T04-666 3787 (bodega), 7870 9646, www.laconcepcion.bo*. Wines (try their Cabernet Sauvignon) and Rujero singani, bodega in Valle de Concepción.

a popular picnic and river-bathing area, from where a good day trip is to the waterfalls at **Coimata**. **Rincón de la Victoria**, 14 km from Tarija, has a similar setting.

There is a challenging one- to two-day **Camino del Inca** from Pujzara in **Reserva de Sama** to **Pinos Sud**, from where public transport can take you back to the city. For information contact **SERNAP** ⓘ *Av Jaime Paz 1171, T04-665 0850*, or the NGO **Prometa** ⓘ *Alejandro del Carpio 659, T04-664 3873, www.prometa.org.bo*.

To Argentina
The quickest route is via Bermejo, which is easily reached from Tarija; 210 km all paved, the views are also spectacular (sit on the right). **Bermejo** (population 21,500, altitude 415 m) is well supplied with places to sleep and eat and there are many *casas de cambio* (including in the bus terminal); it's very hot. Immigration here normally takes about 30 minutes.

An international bridge crosses the river from Bermejo to **Aguas Blancas**, Argentina. Bolivian immigration and customs are by the bridge, which is used by through buses and private vehicles. You can also cross the river by launch (US$0.65), which takes you directly to the Argentine immigration post, by the Aguas Blancas bus stop. Bermejo's bus terminal is the opposite end of town from the international bridge (taxi immigration-terminal US$3). Another option is the road to Villazón (see page 412), which is the shortest route to Argentina, 189 km, but it's a tiring trip along a winding, scenic mountain road. A third option, from Tarija to the Yacuiba/Pocitos border (see page 468), is 290 km away.

Tip...
Remember, Bolivia is one or two hours behind Argentina, depending on the time of year.

Listings Tarija and around

Tourist information

Tarija
See the website www.tarija.thusside.nl for constantly updated information on the region.

Dirección de Turismo
Ingavi y Gral Trigo, T04-667 2633. Mon-Fri 0800-1200, 1500-1900, also at airport.
Helpful, and they provide a city and departmental map.

Dirección Municipal de Turismo
C 15 de Abril y Mcal Sucre, T04-663 3581. Mon-Fri 0800-1200, 1430-1830.
Helpful, city map, some English spoken; also has a booth at the Terminal de Buses, T04-666 7701, 0700-1100, 1430-2200. The municipal office is in the Alcaldía, on the south side of the Plaza Luis de Fuentes, which also contains the Patio del Cabildo, where events and concerts are held.

Valle Central

Información Turística
Plaza Principal, Valle de la Concepción, T04-667 2854. Mon-Sat 0800-1600.
Offer maps and pamphlets.

Where to stay

Tarija
Some hotels may offer low-season discounts, May-Aug.

$$$$-$$$ Los Parrales Resort
Urbanización Carmen de Aranjuez Km 3.5, T04-664 8444, www.losparraleshotel.com.

Large luxury hotel offering fine views over the city and surrounding hills. Includes buffet breakfast, pool, spa, gym, Wi-Fi in communal areas. Non-guests can pay to use the pool and other facilities.

$$$ Altiplano
Belgrano 1640 entre Lazcano y Gral Sosa, T04-666 3550, www.altiplanohotel.com.
A high-standard B&B owned by a couple from New Zealand, a bit of a walk from the centre, cosy elegant, contemporary design with traditional fabrics, delightful rooms, very comfortable, good breakfast, thoughtful service with attention to detail. Warmly recommended.

$$$ Terravina
Bolívar E 525 entre Santa Cruz y Junín, T04-666 8673, terravinatarija@gmail.com.
Modern boutique hotel with a wine theme, rooms with fridge and heating and fully furnished 1- and 2-bedroom apartments, 2 rooms on the ground floor are equipped for disabled guests, includes buffet breakfast.

$$ Hostal Carmen
Ingavi O-0784, T04-664 3372, www.hostalcarmentarija.com.
Older place but well maintained, excellent buffet breakfast, hot water, heating, airport transfers available. Often full, advance booking advised, very helpful, good value. Recommended.

$$ Mitru Tarija
Avaroa 450, entre Isaac Attie y Delgadillo, T04-664 3930, www.hotelmitrutarija.com.

Modern hotel built around a central garden, convenient, large comfortable rooms with a/c, heating, frigobar and safe, also family rooms, light and airy, includes buffet breakfast, in the same group as, and with the same high standards as the Mitru hotels in Tupiza and La Paz.

$ Alojamiento Familiar
Rana S-0231 y Navajas, T04-664 0832.
Shared bath, hot shower, cheap, helpful, close to bus terminal, traffic noise.

$ Hostel Casa Blanca
Ingavi 645 entre Juan Misael Saracho y Ballivian, T04-664 2909, luiszilvetiali@gmail.com (see also Facebook HostelCasaBlancaTarija).
Good cheap option, popular with foreign travellers, conveniently placed 3 blocks from the main plaza, English spoken, lots of information, café.

$ Residencial Rosario
Ingavi O-0777, T04-664 2942.
Simple rooms, cheaper with shared bath, hot water, good budget option, family atmosphere, helpful.

Valle Central

$ Hostería Valle d'Vino
Verdiguera y 6 de Julio, Valle de la Concepción, T04-665 1056, www.valledivinotarija.com.
Hostel with private rooms with bath and dorms, breakfast extra, idiosyncratic place with the small **Infiernillo Bodega** with wine for sale and weekend fiestas, a museum with a mish-mash of items from flat irons and stoves to fossils and animal skins, a 'tunnel of love' and other oddities (tour of the property US$1.50).

To Argentina

$ París
La Paz y Tarija, Bermejo, T04-696 1022.
Central hotel with bath and a/c, cheaper with fan, electric shower, includes breakfast, parking.

$ Querubines
Tarija 209, Bermejo, T04-696 1882, www.querubineshotel.com.
Also central, plain rooms with bath and a/c breakfast included, parking.

Restaurants

Tarija
Many restaurants (and much else in town) close between 1400 and 1600.

$$$-$$ Don Pepe Rodizio
D Campos N-0138, near Av Las Américas.
Stylish restaurant serving tasty daily set lunch, all-you-can-eat *rodizio* at weekends for US$10.

$$$-$$ El Fogón del Gringo
La Madrid O-1053, Plaza Uriondo. Mon-Sat 1900-2300, Fri-Sun also 1200-1430.
Upmarket *parrillada* includes excellent salad bar.

$$$-$$ Plaza Mayor
La Madrid entre Trigo y Campero, ½ block from Cathedral.
Mid-sized restaurant serving good Tarijeña food and wine, pleasant atmosphere.

$$$-$$ Sabores del Río
Av Jaime Paz 2313 esq Romero, T04-665 2686.
A very good fish restaurant not far from the entrance to the airport.

$$ El Marqués
La Madrid entre Trigo y Sucre, on the main plaza, www.elmarquesrestaurant.com.
In the beautiful historic Casa El Marqués de Tojo, specializing in international food, seafood and fish, caters for events, popular.

$$ Guten
15 de Abril y Colón, Plaza Sucre, T04-6676445.
Limited menu of meat and fish dishes with a German touch, pasta and a snack menu, desserts, also bar, sports TV screens, low-key, good for a light meal.

$$ La Taberna Gattopardo
La Madrid y Sucre, on main plaza. Daily 0800-2100.

Pizza, *parrillada* with Argentine beef, local wines, deserts, snacks, excellent salads, popular meeting place, Wi-Fi.

$ Club Social
Sucre 508 y 15 de Abril.
In a traditional setting on the main plaza, serves good-value, local *almuerzo* and meat dishes, also has a *hostal*, **La Estrella**.

$ El Patio
Sucre N-0458. Mon-Sat.
Good set lunch with small salad bar, pleasant seating in patio, also great *tucumanas al horno*.

$ Guadalquivir
Oruro entre O'Connor y Carlos Paz, on Parque Bolívar opposite the monument.
Economical restaurant offering daily *almuerzos* and a salad buffet, open every day.

$ Miiga Comida Coreana
Cochabamba 813 y Ballivian.
Open every night except Tue.
Sushi with salmon and a small but tasty range of Korean dishes. Also has a disco.

Cafés

DeliGelato
Colón N-0421, Plaza Sucre. Daily until 2130.
Good ice cream.

Nobu
Gral Trigo on the main plaza.
Serving coffee, juices and cakes.

Nougat Café-Bar
Gral Trigo corner 15 de Abril. Daily 0800-2400.
Well-decorated European-style café. Breakfast, à la carte dishes, snacks and sweets, Wi-Fi.

Panificadora Sofía
Avaroa entre Sucre y Gral Trigo.
Nice fancy bakery with Middle-Eastern pastries, a variety of breads and a café.

Tarija
Tarija is known for its fiestas.
Feb/Mar **Carnaval Chapaco** is lively and colourful; **Compadres and Comadres**, celebrated on the Thu preceding carnival, are an important part of the tradition.
Apr **Abril en Tarija**, cultural events are held throughout the month.
15 Aug-14 Sep **La Virgen de Chaguaya**, a 45-km pilgrimage from the city to the Santuario Chaguaya, south of El Valle. For less devoted souls, Línea P *trufi* from Plaza Sucre, Tarija, to Padcaya, US$1; bus to Chaguaya and Padcaya from terminal daily, 0700, returns 1700, US$1.35.
16 Aug-1st week Sep **San Roque**, Tarija's main festival. *Chunchos*, male devotees of the saint wearing tall, brightly stripped turbans, veils, colourful shawls and calf-length robes, carry the image of San Roque and dance to the tunes of unusual instruments. These processions take place throughout the 1st week of Sep. A different church is visited every day and on the main day, the 1st Sun, the procession with the richly dressed saint's statue goes to all the churches and ends in the church of San Roque. No alcohol is consumed.
Dec Christmas is the time of the Adoraciones, when children dance around a pole to the music of *tambores y quenas* (drums and flutes).

Around Tarija
Feb/Mar **Fiesta de la Vendimia**, Valle de la Concepción, 25 km from Tarija, is a week-long wine vintage festival. 10 days before La Vendimia is the Encuentro El Arte y El Vino, with music, theatre, painting, sculpture, workshops for children. The artworks remain with the Municipio.
Mar/Apr **Easter week**, communities such as San Lorenzo and Padcaya welcome visitors with colourful arches and flowers to **La Pascua Florida** processions.
2nd Sun in Oct The flower festival commemorates the **Virgen del Rosario**

(celebrations in the surrounding towns are recommended, eg San Lorenzo and Padcaya).

Shopping

Tarija
Handicrafts
Artesanías Bolivia, *Sucre 952 entre D Paz y Corrado, T04-664 6947.* For local handicrafts and musical instruments.

Local produce and wine
See Valle Central, page 434, for shops selling local produce and wine.
La Rotisería, *Gral Trigo y Bolívar.* For meats, cheeses and wines.
La Vinoteca, *Ingavi O-0731 y Gral Trigo. Mon-Sat 0900-1200, 1500-1900.* Sells wine at bodega prices, cheese and ham.

Markets
The main market is in the block between Domingo Paz, Sucre, Bolívar and Trigo. In early 2017 it was being rebuilt and was due for completion the same year. On Sun there is a Mercado Campesino on La Loma de San Juan. There is also a **book market** on Ingavi entre JM Saracho y Campero. The wholesale market is on the road heading north out of town towards San Lorenzo.

What to do

Tarija
Tour operators
There are several tour operators in the city, offering wine tours, tours of surroundings (Campiña and Chapaca), city tours, and the Camino del Inca.

Bolivian Wine Tours, *Méndez entre Avaroa y Av Las Américas, T7187 1626/7022 5715, info@ bolivianwinetours.com.* Speciality tours to vineyards and wine cellars (bodegas) in the Valle Central and Valle de Cinti, focusing not only on the production of high-altitude wines but also on local culture. Ask here also about trips to the Reserva Biológica Cordillera de Sama and the Camino del Inca and to the Valle de Cóndores, a hard, 1½-day walk from Rosillas, near Padcaya, to see condors.
Educación y Futuro, *at the Ecosol shop, Virgino Lema y Suipacha, Plazuela Sucre, T04-666 4973, www.educacionyfuturo.com.* An NGO giving information on homestays with rural families, cheese making and guided trekking in the Valle de Los Cóndores.
Sur Bike, *Ballivián 601 e Ingavi, T7619 4200.* Bike rentals US$16.50 per day.
Tupiza Tours, *at Hotel Mitru, T7052 4503, www.tupizatours.com.* A branch of the Tupiza operator offering local tours to wineries and surroundings. Also innovative 'salt and wine' private trips of 3 or more days combining Tarija and its attractions with Tupiza, Reserva Avaroa and Salar de Uyuni; tours can start or end in Potosí, San Pedro de Atacama, Villazón, Tupiza or Tarija.
VTB, *Ingavi 784 entre Ballivian y R Rojas, at Hostal Carmen (see Where to stay, above), T04-664 4341, www.vtbtourtarija.com.* All tours include a free city tour; 4- to 6-hr trips including bodegas, US$23 pp; comprehensive 10-hr 'Tarija and surroundings in 1 Day', US$35; you can also try your hand at excavation with a palaeontology specialist! Good vehicles, recommended.
Viva Tours, *Bolívar 251, entre Sucre y Daniel Campos, Edif Ex Hansa p 2, of 6, T04-663 8325, auriventur@hotmail.com.* Vineyard tours US$30 with lunch.

Transport

Tarija
Air BoA (General Trigo 327 entre V Lema y A del Carpio, T04-665 4004) flies to **Cochabamba**, **La Paz** and **Santa Cruz**, with connections to other Bolivian cities. **TAM** (La Madrid O-0470 entre Trigo y Campero, T04-664 2734), to **La Paz** (US$45-65), **Sucre**, **Santa Cruz** or **Yacuiba**, depending on day of week. **Amaszonas** (Trigo y Lema, T04-667 6800) has daily flights to **Santa Cruz**; also to **Salta** (Argentina) Mon, Wed and Fri. **Ecojet** (La Madrid 590 esq Colón, T04-611 3427),

daily to **Santa Cruz** early morning with return same day.

Bus To **La Paz** several buses at 0700-0800 and 1700 (935 km) 13 hrs, US$18.70-25, via Potosí and **Oruro** (US$14.50); check which company operates the best buses. To **Potosí**, several additional departures 1630-1800, 8 hrs, US$10.35-13.60. To **Camargo**, from La Parada del Norte (Carretera a Tomatitas, past the wholesale market), US$7, 2½ hrs.

To **Sucre** at 1630 and 1800, US$14. To **Potosí** *trufis* run a faster service than buses (6 hrs), US$15, likewise to Sucre. To **Tupiza**, several companies around 1930-2100, 5-6 hrs, US$9.50-15; **Diamante** at 1930; **Juárez** has 2 buses at 2100, a regular one and a recommended more comfortable bus (with loo, good service, US$15); for daytime service, Narváez at 0900. To **Villazón,** 3 daily, US$9.50-1300, 6 hrs. To **Santa Cruz** via Villamontes, several companies at 1830, US$18.70-27, 17 hrs. To get to Villamontes in daylight, take a **La Guadalupana** or **La Entreriana** *trufi* from Parada del Chaco (east end of Av Las Américas) to **Entre Ríos**, US$3, 1½ hrs, some continue to Villamontes (spectacular route), mostly in daylight. Entre Ríos to Villamontes can take up to 8 hrs.

To Argentina: to **Villazón**, several companies daily, 1930-2030, 8 hrs, US$6.40. To **Bermejo**, shared taxis (*trufis*) eg 7 de Diciembre del Sur, El Fronterizo, leave when full from opposite the bus station and go as fast as they are allowed, 3 hrs, US$7; bus US$4, 4½ hrs. To **Salta**: **Juárez**, Sun, Thu 1900, take photocopy of passport when booking, US$36, no change of bus at border, and **Dragón Rojo**, C Sucre N-0235, T04-666 5014, US$36, daily, 2000, transfer to shared taxis or a different bus once in Argentina. Buses to **Yacuiba** US$8, up to 11 hrs via Villamontes, most depart in the evening. There is an alternative route via Caraparí, further south, which also crosses the Serranía de Aguaragüe, which is shorter.

Taxi Within the city centre, journeys start at about US$0.55.

Valle Central
From Tarija to **Valle de la Concepción**, micros run from Corrado entre Trigo y Campero, all day to 1800, US$0.85 pp. Taxis leave from Corrado y JM Saracho.

North of Tarija
From Tarija to **San Lorenzo**, from Domingo Paz y JM Saracho, US$0.85, all day.

Cochabamba &
central Bolivia

Set in a bowl of rolling hills at a comfortable altitude (2570 m), Cochabamba enjoys a wonderfully warm, dry and sunny climate. Its parks and plazas are a riot of colour, from the striking purple of the bougainvillea to the subtler tones of jasmine, magnolia and jacaranda.

Markets, colonial towns and archaeological sites are all close by. Conquering Cerro Tunari is a challenge for all adventurers. Further afield, the dinosaur tracks and great scenery at Torotoro National Park are worth the trip. The paved lowland route to Santa Cruz de la Sierra has much more transport than the rough old road over the mountains via Comarapa and Samaipata. Both offer access to Carrasco and Amboró national parks.

Cochabamba and around Colour map 3, B3. See map, page 443.

eat, drink and be merry in this appealing city

☆Bolivia's fourth largest city (population 650,038) was founded in 1571 and in colonial times it was the 'breadbasket' of Bolivia, providing food for the great mining community of Potosí. Today it is an important commercial centre. Many visitors particularly enjoy La Cancha market, one of the largest in Bolivia, as well as Cochabamba's very good dining and nightlife.

Sights
At the heart of the old city is the arcaded **Plaza 14 de Septiembre** with the **Cathedral** ⓘ *Mon-Fri 0800-1000, 1500-1800, Sat-Sun 0800-1200*, dating from 1701, but much added to. Of the colonial churches nearby, the **Convent and Museum of Santa Teresa** ⓘ *Baptista y Ecuador, T04-422 1252, guided tours only Mon-Fri 1430, 1530, 1630, US$2.50, camera US$3 extra*, original construction 1760-1790, has a lovely courtyard, a Sala Capitular with painted walls, many other paintings and a beautiful Coro (being restored in 2016). There are spectacular views from the roof.

Best for
Fossils ▪ Inca ruins ▪ Markets ▪ Nightlife

Essential Cochabamba and central Bolivia

Finding your feet

Neither airport, nor bus station are far from the centre. Buses and taxis serve both.

Getting around

The city is divided into four quadrants based on the intersection of Avenida Las Heroínas running west to east, and Avenida Ayacucho running north to south. In all longitudinal streets north of Heroínas the letter N (Norte) precedes the four numbers. South of Heroínas the numbers are preceded by S (Sur). In all transversal streets west of Ayacucho the letter O (Oeste) precedes the numbers and all streets running east are preceded by E (Este). The first two numbers refer to the block, 01 being closest to Ayacucho or Heroínas; the last two refer to the building's number. See also Transport, page 449.

Safety

Do not venture into any of the hills around town on foot (including San Sebastián,

La Coronilla and San Pedro with the Cristo de la Concordia, although at the Cristo itself there are usually plenty of people about). At night take only radio taxis (marked with stickers on the back doors). Take usual precautions with your belongings in markets, on public transport and other crowded places. In the main towns in the coca-growing region of Chapare tourists are reasonably safe, but don't go off the beaten track alone. See also Safety, page 727.

When to go

The rainy season is December-March. At this time roads to outlying areas can become difficult.

Time required

Three or four days for the city and a day excursion, of which there are a few. There are other two-day trips and Torotoro requires three to four days. Stopping on the overland route to Santa Cruz can add a couple more days to a visit to this region.

Museo Arqueológico ⓘ *Jordán E-199 y Aguirre, T04-425 0010, www.museo.umss. edu.bo, Mon-Fri 0800-1800, Sat 0800-1200, US$3.50, guided tours in English at no extra cost, Mon-Fri from 1300,* is part of the Universidad de San Simón. The museum displays some 40,000 artefacts including Amerindian hieroglyphic scripts, mummies, and pre-Inca textiles, through to the colonial era. There is a lot to appreciate, but descriptions are only in Spanish and the presentation is a bit dated. **Casona Santiváñez** ⓘ *Santiváñez O-0156, Mon-Fri 0900-1200, 1430-1800, free,* has a nice colonial patio (open 1700-1845), and exhibition of paintings and historic photographs.

From Plaza Colón, at the north end of the old town, the wide **Avenida Ballivián** (known as **El Prado**) runs northwest to the wealthy modern residential areas; along it you can find restaurants and bars. Also in the north is the Patiño family's **Palacio Portales** ⓘ *Av Potosí 1450, T04-448 9666, Mon-Fri 1500-1830, Sat-Sun 1000-1200, entry US$2; guided tours in Spanish Tue-Fri 1500, 1530, 1630, 1730, 1800, in English or French 1600, 1700, 1830, Sat in Spanish at 1000, 1100, 1200, English or French 1030, 1130; the gardens are open Tue-Fri 1500-1830, Sat-Sun 1000-1200, no charge.* Built in French Renaissance style, furnished from Europe and set in 10 ha of gardens inspired by Versailles, the Patiño mansion was finished in 1927 but never occupied. It is now the **Centro Cultural Simón I Patiño** ⓘ *http://portal. fundacionpatino.org,* with an excellent art gallery in the basement. To get there, take a taxi (five minutes from the centre) or micro G from Avenida San Martín. Next to Palacio

Cochabamba

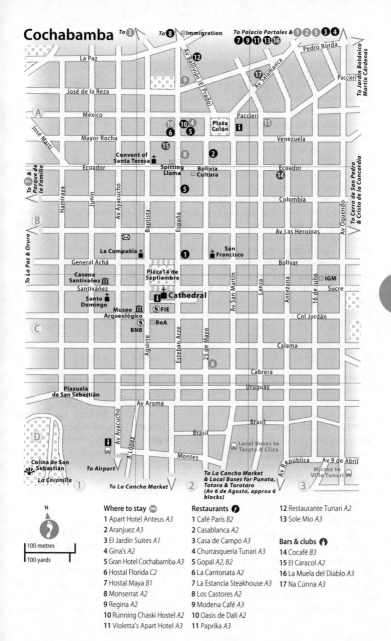

Where to stay
1 Apart Hotel Anteus A3
2 Aranjuez A3
3 El Jardín Suites A1
4 Gina's A2
5 Gran Hotel Cochabamba A3
6 Hostal Florida C2
7 Hostal Maya B1
8 Monserrat A2
9 Regina A2
10 Running Chaski Hostel A2
11 Violetta's Apart Hotel A3

Restaurants
1 Café París B2
2 Casablanca A2
3 Casa de Campo A3
4 Churrasquería Tunari A3
5 Gopal A2, B2
6 La Cantonata A2
7 La Estancia Steakhouse A3
8 Los Castores A2
9 Modena Café A3
10 Oasis de Dalí A2
11 Paprika A3
12 Restaurante Tunari A2
13 Sole Mio A3

Bars & clubs
14 Cocafé B3
15 El Caracol A2
16 La Muela del Diablo A3
17 Na Cúnna A3

Portales is the interesting **Museo de Historia Natural Alcide d'Orbigny** ⓘ *Av Potosí 1458 y Buenos Aires, T04-448 6969, Mon-Fri 0900-1200, 1500-1800, US$0.65*, named after the famous 19th-century French naturalist. It houses well-presented natural history collections of international importance.

East of the centre is **Cerro de San Pedro**, at the top of which stands an enormous statue of **Cristo de la Concordia**. A modern **cable car** ⓘ *Tue-Sat 1000-1800, Sun 0900-1800, US$1.50 return*, will whizz you to the top from the east end of Heroínas. Steps up to the statue are reasonably safe in daylight hours, but if you go in the afternoon, take a taxi, US$1.50. The 34.2-m, 2200-ton statue, finished in 1994, is claimed to be the biggest depiction of Christ in the world. It gives a 360° view over the city and its bowl-like setting. North of Cerro de San Pedro is the **Jardín Botánico Martín Cárdenas** ⓘ *Av Gral Galindo y R Rivera, Mon-Fri 0930-1630, Sat-Sun 1000-1630*, with over 250 species of cactus and pleasant tree-lined avenues.

To the south of the old town lie the bus terminal and former train station and one of the best markets in Bolivia. The huge and fascinating **Mercado La Cancha** ⓘ *between Aguirre, Punata, República and Pulacayo*, is open all week but best on Wednesday and Saturday when it is packed with *campesinos* and trading spills over into surrounding streets. It has four main sections and various offshoots, with a vast array of foodstuffs and local goods. Souvenirs can be found mainly in the San Antonio section, Avenida Esteban Arze y Punata, but you can find things of interest everywhere inside.

The **Parque de la Familia**, ⓘ *entre Av Rafael Urquidi y Puente Cobija, in the Costanera district, 5 min by taxi from the centre, Tue-Fri 1500-2200, show at 2000, Sat-Sun 1000-2300, shows at 2000 and 2130*, is an interesting park with 20-metre-high dancing fountains, a Bolivian culture show projected with music on a wall of water, and places to eat and meet.

Parque Nacional Tunari
SERNAP office, Av Atahuallpa 2367, T04-445 2534, www.sernap.gob.bo, see also www.biobol.org.

Despite the proximity of this national park (300,000 ha, just outside Cochabamba), it remains a beautiful unspoilt natural area and a good place for trekking and acclimatization to altitude. There are traditional communities, *kewiña* forests, llamas and alpacas above 4000 m and even the occasional condor. The highest point in the park, **Cerro Tunari** (5035 m), offers magnificent views, even as far as Illimani. The peak can be climbed in a day trip, but it is easy to get lost and a guide is required. Access to Cerro Tunari is from Tawa Cruz reached by taxi from Quillacollo (see below), or take a tour with a Cochabamba operator (see page 448) or **Berghotel Carolina** (see Where to stay, below). Another park entrance, which does not provide access to Cerro Tunari, is along a marked trail from Avenida Circunvalación in the north of Cochabamba, but it is not recommended because armed attacks on visitors have taken place here.

West of Cochabamba
Quillacollo Thirteen kilometres west of the city, Quillacollo has a Sunday produce market and a famous festival (see page 447). Take any micro or *trufi* marked "Quillacollo" along Avenida Heroínas. Some 8 km beyond town is the turn-off to the beautiful **Hacienda Pairumani** ⓘ *Mon-Fri 1500-1600, Sat 0900-1100, T04-401 0470, http://portal. fundacionpatino.org*, centre of the Patiño agricultural foundation. Also known as **Villa Albina**, it was built in 1925-1932, furnished from Europe and inhabited by Patiño's wife, Albina. From the main square of Quillacollo take *trufi* 211 with a red flag marked "Iskaypata".

Tourist information

Cochabamba

Centro de Información Turística Virtual (CITV)
Plaza Colón 448, T04-466 2277.
Mon-Fri 0800-1200, 1430-1830.
This is the municipal office and the best option. Other offices at the bus station (Mon-Fri 0730-1130, 1730-2230) and Jorge Wilstermann airport (Mon-Fri 0800-1200, 1430-1630). There is a kiosk behind the cathedral (Pasaje Catedral, Esteban Arze y Sucre, Mon-Fri 0900-1200, 1430-1800).

Immigration office
Av J Rodríguez entre C Sanata Cruz y C Potosí, T04-450 7080.

Tourist police
Plaza 14 de Septiembre, north side, T04-450 3880.

Where to stay

Cochabamba
However attractive their prices, places to stay south of Av Aroma and near the bus station are unsafe at all times.

$$$ Apart Hotel Anteus
Potosí 1365, T04-424 5067,
www.hotelanteus.com.
Very nice hotel in a good residential area, a few steps from supermarket and shopping area. Comfortable rooms and common areas, includes buffet breakfast.

$$$ Aranjuez
Av Buenos Aires E-0563, T04-428 0076,
www.aranjuezhotel.com.
The most beautiful of the luxury hotels with a nice garden and lots of style, 4-star, small, good restaurant and bar, small swimming pool. Recommended.

$$$ Gran Hotel Cochabamba
Plaza de la Recoleta E-0415, T04-448 9520,
www.granhotelcochabamba.com.
One of the best hotels in Cochabamba, pool, tennis courts, business centre, airport transfers, parking.

$$ El Jardín Suites
C Baptista 722 casi La Paz, T04-452 3821,
danielwestlopez@yahoo.com.
Very good location just behind the Prado. Large clean rooms with private bath and frigobar, well-equipped common kitchen.

$$ Gina's
México 346 entre España y 25 de Mayo, T04-422 2925.
Has a variety of rooms for 1-5 persons, includes simple breakfast, safe box in rooms, convenient location in the heart of the city.

$$ Monserrat
España 0342, T04-452 1011,
http://hotelmonserrat.com.
Older-style hotel near many bars and restaurants, helpful, good service, convenient, cafetería, buffet breakfast.

$$ Regina
Reza 0359, T04-425 4629,
www.hotelreginabolivia.com.
Excellent spacious and efficient hotel, with breakfast, restaurant.

$$ Violetta's Apart Hotel
Lanza 0464, T04-452 0257, www.violettas.com.
Good central hotel, comfortable rooms and furnished apartments, transfers available.

$ Hostal Florida
25 de Mayo S-0583, T04-425 7911.
Cheaper with shared bath, hot water, noisy, popular with backpackers, safe deposit box, breakfast.

$ Hostal Maya
Colombia 710 y Suipacha, T04-425 9701.
Includes breakfast, private bath, hot water.

$ Running Chaski Hostel
España 449 casi México, T04-425 0559,
www.runningchaski.com.bo.

Good hostel in the nightlife zone, private rooms with bath, and dorms for girls only and mixed, each dorm has bathroom and lockers with electric sockets. Kitchen, movie room, balcony with views, garden with hammocks, lots of information and activities.

Parque Nacional Tunari

$$$ Berghotel Carolina
Pairumani, at the foot of the Cerro Tunari, T7213 0003, www.berghotelcarolina.com.
Arranges private transport, 45 mins from Cochabamba, 25 mins from Plaza Bolívar in Quillacollo. Mountain lodge with 5 comfortable rooms with private bath and 2 with shared bath, restaurant, bar, living room with fireplace, sauna and large terrace. Organizes guided 2-day walking tours with tent to the Laguna Cajón (4100 m), Cerro Tunari and other peaks in Parque Tunari. Walking trails start right from the lodge.

Quillacollo

$$ El Poncho Eco Center
Quillacollo Marquina, T04-439 2283, www.elponcho.org.
Ecological cabins in a lovely setting, camping, restaurant, pool and various outdoor activities.

Restaurants

Cochabamba
North of the Río Rocha on the Pasaje Boulevard de la Recoleta and Av Pando is a group of restaurants and bars.

$$$-$$ Casa de Campo
Pasaje Boulevard de la Recoleta 618, T04-424 3937. Mon-Sun 1230-0200.
One of the best in town. Large menu of mostly local dishes, all-in-one price, very popular, half-portions available, also has *peña*, book at weekend evenings.

$$$-$$ Churrasquería Tunari
Pasaje Boulevard de la Recoleta, T04-448 8153. Tue-Sat 1830-2300, Fri-Sat also 1200-1500, Sun 1200-1500 only.

The most delicious meat you can find in Cochabamba.

$$$-$$ La Estancia Steakhouse
Pasaje Boulevard de la Recoleta 786, T04-424 9262. Mon-Sun 1200-1500, 1800-2330.
Best steak in town, salads and international food in this traditional restaurant.

$$$-$$ Restaurante Tunari
Av Ballivián 676 y La Paz, T04-452 8588. Mon-Sat 0930-2230, Sun 0930-1530.
Family-run restaurant specializing in local meat dishes (half-portions available), good filling food, also sandwiches.

$$ La Cantonata
España y Mayor Rocha 409, T04-425 9222. Mon-Sat 1200-1430, 1830-2330, Sun 1200-1500, 1900-2230.
Pleasant Italian restaurant with good food and service, no smoking. Recommended.

$$ Sole Mio
Av América 826 y Pando, T04-428 3379. Tue-Fri 1730-0000, Sat-Sun also 1200-1430.
A smart Neapolitan pizza restaurant with wood-burning pizza oven, delicious, also good for desserts. Attentive service.

$$-$ Paprika
Chuquisaca 688 y Antezana. Mon-Sun 1130-0030.
Nice atmosphere, good international food, cocktails and desserts.

$ Gopal
España 250, and Mayor Rocha 375 near Plaza Colón. Mon-Sat 1100-1400.
Bolivian Hare-Krishna, vegetarian buffet lunch. In the same garden is **Café Fragmentos** (Mon-Wed 1600-0000, Thu 1500-0200, Fri-Sat 1730-0230, Sun 1700-2400), for juices, coffee, teas, breakfasts and light meals, cocktails and wines.

Cafés
There are several cafés at the junction of the Pasaje Catedral and Esteban Arze.

Café París
Bolívar, corner of Plaza 14 de Septiembre.
Serves good coffee and crêpes,
traditional atmosphere.

Casablanca
25 de Mayo entre Venezuela y Ecuador.
Attractive, buzzing, good food, mostly pastas,
pizzas and Mexican, and a wide selection of
coffee, popular for wine and cocktails in the
evening, indoor games and music.

Los Castores
Ballivián 790 y Oruro, several other branches.
Open 0745-1330.
Popular, good for *salteñas*, 4 different kinds
including an extra spicy variety.

Modena Café
Beni 508 esquina Potosí, in La Recoleta.
Variety of coffees, sweet and savoury snacks,
drinks and ice cream.

Oasis de Dalí
España 428.
Great music, good food, nice atmosphere,
try the *café helado* (ice coffee).

Bars and clubs

Cochabamba
The main nightlife district is on España,
Ecuador, Mayor Rocha and Av Ballivian
(El Prado) with lots of bars and a few
restaurants. Wander around and see what
takes your fancy.

Cocafé
Ecuador y Antezana 279.
Friendly, family atmosphere, snacks, good
place for foreigners to meet. Street musicians
always pass by to show off their skills.

El Caracol
Mayor Rocha entre Baptista y España.
High ceilings, Mediterranean-themed dishes,
desserts, lots of drinks and coffees.

La Muela del Diablo
Potosí 1392 y Portales, next to Palacio
Portales. Mon-Fri 1100-2330,
Sat 1800-0100.
Bolivian rock music, theatre groups, German
beer, variety of wines, pastas, good pizzas
and desserts.

Na Cúnna
Av Salamanca 577. Tue-Thu 1900-2400,
Fri-Sat 1900-0230.
Irish pub and restaurant, live music.
They also serve Guinness.

Entertainment

Cochabamba
Art galleries
There are several art galleries in the centre,
such as **Salón Municipal de Verano** (Plaza 14
de Septiembre) and **Galería Walter Terrazas**
(Av Heroínas y España, T04-422 7561).

Theatre and cinema
For cinema, see www.cinecenter.com.bo.
mARTadero, *Av 27 de Agosto entre Ollantay
y Ladislao Cabrera, micros/trufis P, Q, and 212
to Plaza de los Arrieros, T04-458 8778, www.
martadero.org. Daily 1500-1800.* Cultural and
artistic centre for local and international
artists, exhibitions, and events, in a
refurbished slaughterhouse.
Teatro Achá, *España 280 entre Heroínas
y Bolívar, T04-425 8054.* The city's oldest
cultural centre, with monthly presentations.
Teatro Hecho a Mano, *Av Uyuni 635 entre
Puente Recoleta y Potosí, T04-448 5528,
Hecho-a-Mano on Facebook.* Theatre school.

Festivals

Cochabamba
Feb **Carnaval** is celebrated 15 days before
Lent. Rival groups (*comparsas*) compete in
music, dancing, and fancy dress, culminating
in **El Corso de Corsos** on the last Sat of the
Carnaval; crowded, go very early to buy seats.
14 Sep **Día de Cochabamba**.

Quillacollo
14-15 Aug **Fiesta de la Virgen de Urkupiña**
(www.urcupina.com), in Quillacollo. There's
plenty of transport from Cochabamba, hotels

are all full. Be there before 0900 to be sure of a seat, as you are not allowed to stand in the street. The 1st day is the most colourful with all the groups in costumes and masks, parading and dancing in the streets till late at night. Many groups have left by the 2nd day and dancing stops earlier. The 3rd day is dedicated to the pilgrimage.

Shopping

Cochabamba
Camping gear, maps, etc
Camping Oruro, *Sucre entre 25 de Mayo y San Martín in Shoping Sucre*. Good quality outdoor gear.
IGM, *16 de Julio S-237, T04-425 5503, Mon-Thu 0800-1200, 1430-1800, Fri 0800-1200*. Sells topographic maps of Cochabamba department.
The Spitting Llama, *España N-615 y Ecuador, T04-489 4540, www.thespittingllama.com*. Travel shop.

Handicrafts
Artesanos Andinos, *Pasaje Catedral, T04-450 8367*. An artisans' association selling textiles.
Fotrama, *Bolívar 0349, entre San Martín y 25 de Mayo*. High-quality alpaca clothing.

What to do

Adventure sports and tours
Cochabamba is growing in popularity for parapenting, with several outfits offering tandem jumps starting at US$50, as well as courses.
AndesXtremo, *La Paz 138 entre Ayacucho y Junín, T04-452 3392, www.andesxtremo.com*. Adventure sports company specializing in parapenting, also offers climbing, rafting and trekking, good value, professional staff. Recommended.
Bolivia Cultura, *Ecuador 342 entre 25 de Mayo y España, T04-452 7272, www.boliviacultura. com*. Tours to Torotoro. They run year-round tours for 3 and 4 days to all the major sites and can arrange longer trips. Tours also to other local destinations.

Bolivia Motors, *no storefront, T 6740 1468, www.boliviamotors.com*. Reliable motorcycle tours and rentals, Kiwi owned and operated.
Creative Tours, *no storefront, T04-403 2941, www.creativetoursbolivia.com*. Offer good Salar de Uyuni trips, tours based at the hotels of the Ruta Tayka (see page 408), river cruises on the *Reina de Enín*, and **Hotel El Puente** in the tropics of Cochabamba.
D'Orbigny Travel, *Pasaje de la Promotora 344 entre España y Heroínas, T04-451 1367*. Run by an enthusiastic Bolivian couple, sell flight tickets and excursions in Cochabamba department and throughout Bolivia.
El Mundo Verde Travel, *no storefront, T6534 4272, www.elmundoverdetravel.com*. Great for local information, regional experts offer tours to Torotoro, Pico Tunari, Inkallajta and Chimboata village. Also rafting, zip-lines, jungle trips in Chapare and throughout Bolivia; day trips and adventure tours. Dutch/Bolivian-run, very enthusiastic and informative. Also 4WD tours to **Samaipata**. English, Dutch and Spanish spoken. Warmly recommended.

Language classes
There are many qualified language teachers in the city.
Beyond Bolivia, *www.beyondsouth america.com*. Dutch organization which offers Spanish/Portuguese language classes, homestays and recommended volunteer programmes and internships.
Bolivia Sostenible, *Julio Arauco Prado 230, Zona Las Cuadras, T04-423 3786, www. boliviasostenible.org*. Offers homestays and paid placements for volunteers.
Centro de Idiomas Kori Simi, *Lanza 727, entre La Paz y Chuquisaca, T04-425 7248, www. korisimi.com*. Spanish and Quechua school run by staff from Switzerland, Germany and Bolivia, also offers activity programme, homestays and volunteer placements.
Juntucha, *T7976 1679, info@juntucha.org*. Spanish school run by a Dutchman, funds are donated to a charity, www.casadelaalegria.nl.
Runawasi, *Maurice Lefebvre 0470, Villa Juan XXIII, Av Blanco Galindo Km 4.5, T04-424 8923,*

www.runawasi.org. Spanish, Quechua and Aymara, also has accommodation.

Volunteer Bolivia, *Ecuador E-0342, T04-452 6028, www.volunteerbolivia.org*. Bolivian/US-run organization which offers language classes, homestays and a recommended volunteer programme.

Transport

Cochabamba

Air Jorge Wilstermann airport, T04-412 0400; modern, with places to eat, *casas de cambio* and ATMs. Airport bus is Micro B from Heroínas y Ayacucho, US$0.40; taxis from airport to centre US$4. Arrive 2 hrs ahead for international flights. Cochabamba is an air transport hub with several daily flights to/from **La Paz** (35 mins) and **Santa Cruz** (40 mins) with **Amaszonas**, Av Libertador Bolívar 1509, Edif El Solar, PB, T04-479 4200, **Boliviana de Aviación**, Jordán 202 y Nataniel Aguirre, T04-414 0873 or 901-105010, and **TAM** Militar, Buenos Aires entre Av Santa Cruz y América, T04-441 1545. **Ecojet**, Plazuela Constitución 0879 entre 16 de Julio y Chuquisaca, T04-412 3700, to **Sucre**, **Tarija**, **Trinidad** and other northern cities. **TAM** has flights to **Trinidad**, with connections to other northern cities.

Bus *Micros* and *colectivos*, US$0.30; *trufis*, US$0.30. Anything marked 'San Antonio' goes to the market. *Trufis* C and 10 go from bus terminal to the city centre.

Regional *Trufis* leave from Av Barrientos y Manuripi, or Barrientos y Guayaramerin, south of La Cancha, for **Tarata**, US$1. From Av Barrientos y Av 6 de Agosto, for **Cliza**, US$0.85. From Av 6 de Agosto y Av República to **Punata**, US$1.15, and **Totora**, US$2 (minibus). Av Oquendo y 9 de Abril (be careful in this area), to **Villa Tunari**, US$4.50, 4-5 hrs, from 0400 to 2000; **Puerto Villarroel**, US$7, 6 hrs (from 0800 when full, daily).

Long distance The main bus terminal is on Ayacucho y Tarata (T04-422 0550). To **Santa Cruz**, almost hourly 0600-2130, 12 hrs; **Trans Copacabana** *semi-cama*, 2130, US$13; **Bolívar** *bus-cama*, US$18.50; all via the paved lowland road through Villa Tunari. See next page. To/from **La Paz** almost hourly 0500-2200, 7 hrs, *semi-cama* US$10.50, *bus-cama* US$15. To **Oruro**, 0500-2200, 4 hrs, *semi-cama* US$5.75, *bus-cama* US$10. To **Potosí**, departures 1900-2130 *semi-cama* US$13, *bus-cama* US$19 with **Bolívar** and **Trans Copacabana**, 10 hrs. Daily to **Sucre**, 8 hrs, several companies (**Bolívar** and **Trans Copacabana** at 1900-2130), *semi-cama* US$12.50, *bus-cama* US$20. To **Sucre** by day; go to Aiquile by bus (several from Av 6 de Agosto entre Av República y Av Barrientos, US$4, none before 1200) or **Ferrobús**, then a bus at 0200-0300 passing en route to Sucre, or Fri and Sun, 2000.

Taxi About US$1 from anywhere to the plaza, more expensive to cross the river; double after dark.

Beyond Cochabamba

caves, canyons, waterfalls, wildlife and stunning scenery

☆Parque Nacional Torotoro

Entry US$4.50 for foreigners, payable at the Dirección de Turismo, Calle Cochabamba, Main Plaza, T7227 0968, T04-413 5736, open 0730-1200, 1400-1700, all visitors must register here. SERNAP office on Calle del Olvido, 3 blocks southwest of the plaza, next to Rosas T'ika.

In the department of Potosí, but best reached from Cochabamba (136 km), is **Torotoro**, a small village, set amid dramatic rocky landscape in the centre of the Parque Nacional Torotoro, covering an area of 21,744 ha.

Attractions in the park include caves, canyons, waterfalls, ruins, rock paintings, fossils and thousands of incredible fossilized dinosaur tracks, some of which can be seen by the

Río Torotoro just outside the village. Near the community of **Wayra K'asa**, about 8 km northwest of Torotoro, **Umajalanta cave**, the largest in Bolivia, has many stalactites, stalagmites and a lake with endemic blind fish; 7 km have been explored and are open to caving. Head torch and helmet are required and for hire at the entrance, US$1; it's not recommended for claustrophobics. Beyond the cave, 21 km from Torotoro village, is **Ciudad de Itas**, in the community of Ovejerías, a circular walk on top of and within an unusual rock formation with caves (some resemble gothic cathedrals) and rock paintings. The **Cementerio de Tortugas** (turtle cemetery) is 3.5 km southeast of the town, with fossilized remains of sea turtles (Cheloniidae family). Other sites of interest include the **Cañón de Torotoro** for birdwatching, **Vergel** for bathing and **Chiflon Q'aqa** for rappelling.

Tours or day trips must be organized by the **Asociación de Guías (Guiaventura)** ⓘ *Main Plaza across from the Oficina de Turismo, T7435 9152, open 0730-1130, 1330-1630. You can reserve a guide in advance, otherwise the person at the desk will phone for a guide; guides charge US$14.50 per route for 1 to 6 people (a little more to Itas)*. 4WD tours are also offered by **El Mundo Verde Travel** ⓘ *www.elmundoverdetravel.com*, which can also provide transport from Sucre, and other Cochabamba agencies.

Cochabamba to Santa Cruz: the lowland road

Villa Tunari The lowland road from Cochabamba through Villa Tunari to Santa Cruz is partly paved and prone to landslides after heavy rain. Villa Tunari is a relaxing place and holds an annual Fish Fair the first weekend of August, with music, dancing and food. The Facebook page, villatunarituristica, has a lot of information. At **La Hormiga** ⓘ *contact through El Mundo Verde, see page 448*, Rolando Mamani leads jungle walks, with good chance of seeing monkeys, birds, insects and snakes, about which he educates local farmers.

Parque Ecoturístico Machía Just outside Villa Tunari, Parque Ecoturístico Machía is managed by **Inti Wara Yassi** ⓘ *T04-413 6572, www.intiwarayassi.org, entrance of US$0.90 payable to the municipality, donations welcome, open Tue-Sun 0930-1600 (not open when raining)*. This 36-ha park includes a well-signposted 3-km interpretive trail and other trails through semi-tropical forest. The park is run by an animal rescue organization that operates two other parks, one about halfway between Santa Cruz and Trinidad and another near Rurrenabaque. Contact them for volunteer opportunities.

☆**Parque Nacional Carrasco** ⓘ *Information from SERNAP, Av Atahuallpa 2367, T04-445 6633 www.sernap.gob.bo*. Southeast of Villa Tunari, this park covers 622,600 ha between 300 and 4500 m. It has 11 ecological life zones, superb birdwatching and many rivers, waterfalls, canyons and pools.

Access is from Villa Tunari, Totora and Monte Punku – Sehuencas; taking a guide is advised. From the park entrance 20 km from Villa Tunari, a cable car takes you across the Río San Mateo for a 2½-hour walking circuit to the **Cavernas de Repechón** (oilbird caves) and bat caves. Guides may be hired from the **Kawsay Wasi community** ⓘ *T7939 0894, www.tusoco.com*. Julián (T7480 9714) and Sebastián (T6852 1150) are recommended.

Cochabamba to Santa Cruz: the highland road

The 500-km highland road from Cochabamba to Santa Cruz is very scenic. Some sections are unpaved and the newer lowland route is preferred by most transport. Between Monte Punku (Km 119) and Epizana is the turn-off to Pocona and Inkallajta. It is 13 km from Pocona as far as the village of Collpa, then take the left fork for a further 10 km; see Transport, below. Tours are offered by Cochabamba operators.

The ruins of ☆**Inkallajta** (1463-1472, rebuilt 1525), on a flat spur of land at the mouth of a steep valley, are the largest Inca archaeological site in Bolivia and the main structure may have been the largest roofed Inca building anywhere. There are several good camping sites near the river and some basic facilities and services.

The highland Cochabamba-Santa Cruz road continues to **Epizana**, junction for the road to Sucre (being paved in 2016) via the beautiful colonial village of **Totora** (14 km) and the more modern town of **Aiquile**.

Past Epizana the road from Cochabamba goes on, unpaved, to **Pojo**, Comarapa and Samaipata (see page 461).

Listings Beyond Cochabamba

Where to stay

Parque Nacional Torotoro

$$ Eco-albergue Ujalanta
In the community of Wayra K'asa, T6742 2461, ecoalbergue.umajalanta@gmail.com.
Comfortable rooms and cabins with private bath, built in rustic style using local materials and administered by the local community. Great location, spectacular views, includes breakfast, other meals available.

$$ El Molino
1.5 km from the village,T04-243 633, T7647 5999, www.elmolinotorotoro.com.
Beautiful Spanish-style country house surrounded by mountains and a river, comfortable rooms with private bath, nice common areas including facilities for events, fireplace, bar, pool table, indoor patio. All-inclusive 2- to 4-day tours from Cochabamba arranged.

$$ Villa Etelvina
C Sucre, 15-min walk from plaza, T7073 7807, www.villaetelvina.com.
Bungalow for 4 with private bath, cheaper in rooms with shared bath, includes breakfast, other meals available, beautiful garden, parking, Wi-Fi, can arrange tours and activities.

$ El Vergel
Arteche y Charcas, T6747 6325, Sr Eduardo Santiváñez.
Rooms with and without bath, with breakfast and Wi-Fi.

$ Hostal Asteria
Guadalupe y El Olvido, T7208 2130.
Colonial-style hotel, rooms with private bath, restaurant serving all meals, beautiful patio, parking.

$ Hostal Las Hermanas
C Cochabamba, ½ block from the plaza, T7221 1257.
Basic rooms, cheaper with shared bath, Doña Lily serves delicious food and is very attentive.

$ Hostal Santa Bárbara
Calle Santa Bárbara, T7278 1307.
A nice house in the centre of town, cheaper with shared bath, meals on request, parking.

$ Hostal Urkupiña
Charcas y Cochabamba, near plaza, T6852 3191, franz77230964@gmail.com.
Single, double and family rooms with private bath, hot water, parking. Breakfast extra in **Restaurant El Dinosaurio** which also serves good meals, including vegetarian options.

Villa Tunari

$$$-$$ Victoria Resort
Km 156 on the road to Santa Cruz, 4 km before Villa Tunari on the right, T04-413 6538, www.victoria-resort.com.
Modern, *cabaña* style, 500 m from the main road in the middle of the forest, quiet, large pool, breakfast buffet.

$$ El Puente Jungle Hotel
Av de la Integración, 4 km from town,
bgT04-458 0085, www.hotelelpuente.com.bo
(or book in advance through Creative Tours,
see page 409).
Cabins from 2 persons to family-size
surrounded by tropical vegetation, with
breakfast and bath, pool, zip-line, stream
and natural swimming pools, nature treks.
Very good restaurant.

$$ Los Tucanes Casa de Campo
On the mainroad after the 2nd bridge,
T04-413 6506, www.lostucaneshotel.com.
Clean rooms with a/c, 2 pools,
buffet breakfast.

Totora

$$-$ Casa de Huéspedes Villa Eva
On main road, Totora, T7437 1530.
Well-furnished country house with large
living room, fully equipped kitchen, and
comfortable rooms with private bath.

Restaurants

Parque Nacional Torotoro
Several small restaurants in Torotoro village
including **Pensión La Huella**; **El Comedor**,
at the food market 2 blocks above the main
plaza (good for a typical breakfast); Doña
Elena, opposite the market, all for good
local food; Doña Rosemary's Encuentro
Torotoreño, opposite Villa Etelvina, serves
meals, drinks and has a pool table.

Villa Tunari
There are several eating places in Villa Tunari
on both sides of the main road to Santa
Cruz. The more expensive ones are on the
riverside (**San Silvestre** is recommended).
The more popular food stalls 1 block from
the bus terminal serve different fish dishes
and have also a cheap daily menu. Upstairs

at the market (breakfast and lunch) is a very
cheap option.

Festivals

Aiquile
2 Feb **La Virgen de la Candelaria**, Aiquile.
Oct/Nov **Feria del Charango**, Aiquile.

Shopping

Parque Nacional Torotoro
Rosas T'ika, *Asociación de Mujeres,*
C del Olvido, 3 blocks southwest of Plaza
Principal, 0800-1200, 1400-1800, closed Tue.
Sells beautiful, locally made textiles,
clothing and bags, mostly sheep's wool,
some of llama wool.

Transport

Parque Nacional Torotoro
Bus Trans del Norte (T7078 6818) from
Av República y C Mairana, daily at 1800;
return to Cochabamba Mon-Sat at 0600, Sun
at 1300 and 1500; US$3.50, 4-5 hrs in the dry
season, 5-8 hrs in the wet. Also minibuses
(*surubís*) from the same location (across the
street) in Cochabamba (T7144 2073, Torotoro
T7147 7601), leave when full daily 0500-1800,
US$5. There is no bus service from Sucre, it
takes 14 hrs in a private vehicle.

Inkallajta
Take a *trufi* from 0500 onwards from
6 de Agosto y Manuripi (Av República) in
Cochabamba (ask for the "Parada Pocona").
For 3 people the *trufi* will drop you off at
the entrance to the Inca ruins (US$4 pp).
Arrange with the driver to pick you up at
a specific time to return to Cochabamba.
Trufis return from Pocona to Cochabamba
when full till 1600. Taxis from Pocona charge
around US$15 one way to the ruins.

Santa Cruz &
eastern lowlands

In contrast to the highlands of the Andes and the gorges of the Yungas, eastern Bolivia is made up of vast plains stretching to the Chaco of Paraguay and the Pantanal wetlands of Brazil. Agriculture is well developed and other natural resources are fully exploited, bringing prosperity to the region. There are a number of national parks with great biodiversity, such as Amboró and Noel Kempff Mercado. Historical interest lies in the pre-Inca ceremonial site at Samaipata, the beautiful Jesuit missions of Chiquitania and, of much more recent date, the trails and villages where Che Guevara made his final attempt to bring revolution to Bolivia.

Santa Cruz *Colour map 3, B4. See map, page 456.*

Bolivia's largest city, gateway to one of the most fascinating parts of the country

Sights

The Plaza 24 de Septiembre is the city's main square with the huge **cathedral (Basílica de San Lorenzo)** ⓘ *Museum, T03-332 4683, Mon-Sat 0730-1200, 1500-2030, Sun 0700-1200, 1500-2130, US$1.50.* You can climb to a mirador in the cathedral **bell tower** ⓘ *daily 0800-1200, 1500-1900, US$0.50*, with nice views of the city. The block behind the cathedral, **Manzana Uno** ⓘ *Tue-Sat 1000-1230, 1600-2100, Sun 1600-2100*, has been set aside for rotating art and cultural exhibits. **El Casco Viejo**, the heart of the city, with its arcaded streets and buildings with low, red-tiled roofs and overhanging eaves, retains a slight colonial feel, despite the profusion of modern, air-conditioned shops and restaurants. The **Museo de Historia** ⓘ *Junín 141, T03-336 5533, Mon-Fri 0800-1200, 1500-1830, free*, has several displays including archaeological pieces from the Chané and Guaraní cultures and explorers' routes. The **Museo de Arte Contemporáneo** ⓘ *Sucre y Potosí, T03-334 0926, Mon-Fri 1000-1200, 1500-1900, free*, houses contemporary Bolivian and international art in a nicely restored old house.

Essential Santa Cruz and eastern lowlands

Finding your feet

The international airport is at Viru-Viru, 13 km from the centre of Santa Cruz, reached by taxi or micro. Regional flights operate from El Trompillo airport, south of the centre on the Segundo Anillo. Long-distance and regional buses leave from the combined bus/train terminal, Terminal Bimodal, Avenida Montes on the Tercer Anillo. There are two train lines, to Quijarro on the Brazilian border and, of much less importance, to Yacuiba on the Argentine border.

Getting around

The city has twelve ring roads, Anillos 1, 2, 3, 4 and so on, the first three of which contain most sites of interest to visitors. The neighbourhood of Equipetrol, where many upscale hotels, restaurants and bars are situated, is northwest of the centre in the Tercer (3rd) Anillo.

Medical services

Santa Cruz is an important medical centre with many hospitals and private clinics. See page 721.

Tip...

Dengue fever outbreaks are common during the wet season (December to March), take mosquito precautions.

When to go

It is hot most of the year. The rainy season runs from December to March.

Time required

One or two days for Santa Cruz itself; two or three days for Samaipata or Parque Nacional Amboró, one week for Chiquitania, two to three weeks for remote areas.

Around Santa Cruz

At Km 8 on the road to Cotoca are the **Botanical Gardens** ⓘ *micro or trufi from C Suárez Arana, 15 mins, T03-362 3101, open Mon-Fri 0900-1700, entry US$0.50*, a bit run-down but with many walking trails, birds and several forest habitats.

Parque Ecolócigo Yvaga Guazu ⓘ *Km 12.5 Doble Vía a La Guardia, taxi US$5, T03-352 7971, www.parqueyvagaguazu.org, daily 0800-1600, US$10 for 2-hr guided tour in Spanish (more for English-speaking guide)*, 14 ha of tropical gardens with native and exotic species, plants for sale, restaurant serves Sunday buffet lunch. **Biocentro Güembé** ⓘ *Km 5 Camino a Porongo, taxi US$7, T03-370 0700, www.biocentroguembe.com, daily 0830-1800, US$18.75 includes guided tour in Spanish or English*, is a resort with accommodation ($$$ range), restaurant, butterfly farm, walk-in aviary, swimming pools and other family recreation.

Listings Santa Cruz *map page 456.*

Tourist information

APAC
Av Busch 552 (2nd Anillo), T03-333 2287, www.festivalesapac.com.
Has information about cultural events in the department of Santa Cruz. See also www.destinosantacruz.com.

Fundación Amigos de la Naturaleza (FAN)
Km 7.5 Vía a La Guadria, T03-355 6800, www.fan-bo.org.

InfoTur
Sucre y Potosí, inside the Museo de Arte, T03-336 9581, Mon-Fri 0800-1200, 1500-1900. There is a departmental tourist desk at Viru-Viru airport, 0700-2000.

Municipal Tourism and Culture Office
Libertad 65, on Plaza 24 de Septiembre T03-337 8493, Mon-Sat 0900-1900, and at Plaza del Estudiante, Av Cañoto y Av Mons Rivero,

BACKGROUND

Santa Cruz

A little over 50 years ago, what is now Bolivia's largest city (population 1,566,000) was a remote backwater, but rail, road and air links ended its isolation. The exploitation of oil and gas in the Departments of Santa Cruz and Tarija and a burgeoning agribusiness sector helped fuel rapid development. Since the election of Evo Morales in 2006, however, *cruceños* have been concerned about the impact of his economic policies, perceived as favouring the highlands. There is considerable local opposition to the national government and Santa Cruz has spearheaded the eastern lowland departments' drive for greater autonomy from La Paz. The city is modern and busy, far removed from most travellers' perceptions of Bolivia. The centre still retains a bit of its former air, however, and the main plaza – 24 de Septiembre – is well cared for and a popular meeting place. During the extended lunchtime hiatus, locals (who call themselves *cambas*) take refuge in their homes from the heat or rain and the gridlock traffic eases. December to March is the hottest and rainiest time of the year.

Biblioteca Municipal, T03-337 8493, www.gmsantacruz.gob.bo, see also Dirección-Municipal-de-Cultura-Patrimonio-y-Turismo on Facebook.

SERNAP
C 9 Oeste 138, frente a la Plaza Italia, Barrio Equipetrol, T03-339 4311. Mon-Fri 0800-1200, 1400-1800.

Where to stay

$$$$ Los Tajibos
Av San Martín 455, Barrio Equipetrol, T03-342 1000, www.lostajiboshotel.com.
Set in 6 ha of lush gardens, one of several hotels in this price bracket in the city and the most traditional, all facilities including business centre, art gallery, restaurants and spa. Weekend discounts.

$$$ Cortez
Cristóbal de Mendoza 280 (2do Anillo), T03-333 1234, www.hotelcortez.com.
Traditional tropical hotel with restaurant, pool, gardens, meeting rooms, parking, good for dining and nightlife.

$$$ Royal Lodge
Av San Martín 200, Equipetrol, T03-343 8000, www.royalhotel.com.bo.

With restaurant and bar, pool, airport transfers. Excellent option for its location and price range.

$$$ Senses
Sucre y 24 de Septiembre, just off main plaza, T03-339 6666, www.sensescorp.com.
Self-styled boutique hotel in the heart of the city, minimalist decor, includes all services.

$$$ Villa Magna
Barrón 70, T03-339 9700, www.villamagna-aparthotel.com.
Fully furnished apartments with small pool, Wi-Fi, parking, attentive owner and staff, English and German spoken, from daily to monthly rates.

$$ Hotel Bolivia
C Libertad 365, T 03-333-6292, www.hotelbolivia.com.bo.
Good three-star accommodations in the primer anillo. No nonsense, very helpful, attentive service. Will hold luggage and arrange airport transfers.

$$ Bibosi
Junín 218, T03-334 8548, htlbibosi@hotmail.com.
Central, nothing fancy, electric shower, a/c, cheaper with fan, Wi-Fi in lobby, good value.

$$ Copacabana
Junín 217, T03-336 2770,
www.hotelcopacabanabolivia.com.
Very good, popular with European tour
groups, rooms cheaper without a/c, restaurant.

$$-$ Hostal Río Magdalena
Arenales 653 (no sign), T03-339 3011,
www.hostalriomagdalena.com.
Comfortable rooms, downstairs ones are dark,
with a/c or fan, small yard and pool, popular.

Santa Cruz

N

200 metres
200 yards

Where to stay 🛏
1 Bibosi *B1*
2 Copacabana *B1*
3 Cortez *A2*
4 Hostal Río Magdalena *B3*
5 Hotel Bolivia *B2*
6 Jodanga *D3*
7 Los Tajibos *A1*
8 Milán *B2*
9 Res Bolívar *B2*
10 Royal Lodge *A1*
11 Sarah *B1*
12 Senses *B2*
13 Villa Magna *B3*

Restaurants 🍴
1 Alexander Coffee *B2*
2 Café 24 & Café Lorca *B2*
3 Fridolín *B2*
4 Horno Caliente *D2*
5 Ken *B3*
6 Kiwi's *B2*
7 La Bella Napoli *D2*
8 La Casona *B2*
9 La Creperie *B2*
10 Los Hierros *A2*
11 Los Lomitos *B3*
12 Michelangelo *C2*
13 Naturalia *D3*
14 Pizzería Marguerita *B2*
15 Rincón Brasilero *B2*
16 Su Salud *B3*
17 Tapekuá *C2*
18 Vegetarian Center *B3*

Bars & clubs 🍸
19 Café Irlandés *B2*

$$-$ Jodanga
C El Fuerte 1380, Zona Parque Urbano,
Barrio Los Chóferes, T03-339 6542,
www.jodanga.com.
Good backpacker option 10 mins' walk
from Terminal Bimodal, cheaper with fan
and without bath, cheaper still in dorm,
kitchen, bar, swimming pool, billiards, DVDs,
nice communal areas, laundry, helpful owner
and multilingual staff.

$$-$ Residencial Bolívar
Sucre 131, T03-334 2500.
Includes good breakfast, cheaper with
shared bath and in dorm, lovely courtyard
with hammocks, rooms can get hot, alcohol
prohibited, popular.

$ Milán
René Moreno 70, T03-339 7500.
Some rooms with a/c, hot water, central.

$ Sarah
C Sara 85, T03-332 2425,
Facebook: HotelSarah.
Simple rooms which cost less without a/c,
screened windows, small patio, good value.

Restaurants

Av San Martín in Barrio Equipetrol, and
Av Monseñor Rivero are the areas for
upmarket restaurants and nightlife. Both
are away from the centre, take a taxi at
night. Some restaurants close Mon.

$$$-$$ La Bella Napoli
Independencia 635, T03-332 5402.
Daily 1200-2200.
Genuine Neopolitan restaurant where the
owner makes his own wine and liqueurs and
greets customers every evening. Attractive
décor, famed for pastas, pizzas and salads.

$$$-$$ La Creperie
Arenales 135, T03 333-9053.
Mon-Sat 1900-2300.
Serves crêpes, fondues, salads, pastas
and seafood.

Tip...
Santa Cruz has the best meat in
Bolivia, try a local *churrasquería* (grill).

$$$-$$ Los Hierros
Av Monseñor Rivero 300 y Castelnau.
Daily 1200-1500, 1900-2400.
Popular upmarket grill with salad bar.

$$$-$$ Michelangelo
Chuquisaca 502. Mon-Fri 1200-1430,
1900-2330, Sat evenings only.
Excellent Italian cuisine, a/c.

$$ Ken
Uruguay 730 (1er Anillo), T03-333 3728.
Open 1130-1430, 1800-2300, closed Wed.
Sushi and authentic Japanese food, popular.

$$ La Casona
Arenales 222, T03-337 8495.
Open 1130-1500, 1900-2400.
German-run restaurant, very good food.

$$ Los Lomitos
Uruguay 758 (1er Anillo), T03-332 8696.
Daily 0800-2400.
Traditional *churrasquería* with unpretentious
local atmosphere, excellent Argentine-style
beef, also pastas, sandwiches and desserts.

$$ Pizzería Marguerita
Junín y Libertad, northwest corner of the
plaza. Open 0930-2400, from 1600 on Sat-Sun.
A/c, good service, coffee, bar. Popular
with expats, Finnish owner speaks English
and German.

$$ Rincón Brasilero
Libertad 358. Daily 1130-1430, 1930-2330.
Brazilian-style buffet for lunch, pay by
weight, very good quality and variety,
popular; pizza and à la carte at night.
Recommended.

$$ Tapekuá
Ballivián y La Paz, T03-334 5905.
French and international food, good service,
live entertainment some evenings.

$$-$ Kiwi's Café Restaurant
Bolívar 208, T03-330 1410,
Facebook: KiwisCafeRestaurant.
New, inexpensive, 2 blocks from main plaza, eclectic lunches and dinners (buffalo wings, peanut soup, *picante de pollo*, etc), occasional tango lessons, popular, run by a New Zealander.

$$-$ Naturalia
Potosí 648, T03-333 4374, Facebook:
Naturalia-202835006418807.
Specializes in organic gourmet and health foods, café and deli on premises, popular. Has 2 other locations.

$$-$ Vegetarian Center
Aroma 64, entre Bolívar y Sucre.
Mon-Sat 0900-1500.
Set lunch or pay-by-weight buffet, vegan options, massive salad bar.

$ Su Salud
Quijarro 115. Mon-Thu 0800-2100,
Fri and Sun 0800-1700.
Tasty vegetarian food, filling lunches, sells vegetarian products.

Cafés
There are lots of very pleasant a/c cafés where you can get coffee, ice cream, drinks and snacks.

Alexander Coffee
Junín y Libertad near main plaza, and
Av Monseñor Rivero 400 y Santa Fe.
For good coffee and people-watching.

Café 24
Downstairs at René Moreno y Sucre,
on the main plaza. Daily 0830-0200.
Breakfast, juices, international meals, wine rack, nice atmosphere, Wi-Fi.

Café Lorca
Upstairs at Sucre 8 y René Moreno, on the
main plaza. Daily 0900-1600 for lunch,
1600-2300 for dinner.
Meals and drinks, Spanish wines, central patio, small balcony with views over plaza,

live music most nights 2030-0130, lounge Wed-Sat 1600-0300.

Fridolín
21 de Mayo 168, Pari 254, Av Cañoto y Florida,
and Monseñor Rivero y Cañada Strongest.
All good places for coffee and pastries.

Horno Caliente
Chuquisaca 604 y Moldes, also 24 de
Septiembre 653.
Salteñas 0730-1230, traditional local snacks and sweets 1530-1930. Popular and very good.

Bars and clubs

Bar Irlandés Irish Pub
3er Anillo Interno 1216, entre Av Banzer y
Zoológico), www.irishpub.com.bo.
Irish-themed pub, food available, Irish owner, live music Wed, Fri and Sat evenings. Also **Café Irlandés** (Plaza 24 de Septiembre, Shopping Bolívar), overlooking main plaza. Popular.

Kokopelli
Noel Kempff Mercado 1202 (3er Anillo
Interno). Open from 2100.
Bar with Mexican food and live music.

Med Resto Bar
Cañada Strongest y Mons Rivero (2do anillo),
T03-335 2848. Daily 1130-1500, 1830-2330.
Great local dishes, salads and grill by day, and a variety of pop, rock and tropical bands at night. Inside-outside seating, very popular with *cruceños* and foreigners alike, crowded on weekends.

Entertainment

Cinema
Cine Center, *Av El Trompillo – 2do Anillo – entre Monseñor Santiesteban y René Moreno, www.cinecenter.com.bo.*

Cultural centres with events and programmes
Centro Cultural Santa Cruz (René Moreno 369, T03-335 6941, www.culturabcb.org.bo); **Centro Simón I Patiño** (Independencia y

Suárez de Figueroa 89, T03-337 2425, www.
fundacionpatino.org), with exhibitions,
galleries, and bookstore on Bolivian cultures;
Centro Boliviano Americano (Potosí 78,
T03-334 2299, www.cba.com.bo); **Centro
Cultural Franco Alemán** (24 de Septiembre
36, on main plaza, T03-335 0142, www.
ccfrancoaleman.org); **Centro de Formación
de la Cooperación Española** (Arenales 583,
T03-335 1311, www.aecid-cf.bo).

Festivals

Cruceños are famous as fun-lovers and their
music, the *carnavalitos*, can be heard all over
South America.

Feb Of the various festivals, the brightest is
Carnaval, renowned for riotous behaviour,
celebrated for the 15 days before Lent. There's
music in the streets, dancing, fancy dress and
the coronation of a queen. Water and paint
throwing is common – no one is exempt.
**Apr/May Festival de Música Renacentista
y Barroca Americana 'Misiones de
Chiquitos'** is held in late Apr through early
May every even year (next in 2018) in Santa
Cruz and the Jesuit mission towns of the
Chiquitania. It is organized by **Asociación Pro
Arte y Cultura** (**APAC**), Av Busch 552, Santa
Cruz, T03-333 2287, www.festivalesapac.com,
and celebrates the wealth of sacred music
written by Europeans and indigenous
composers in the 17th and 18th centuries.
APAC sells books, CDs and videos and also
offers – in both Santa Cruz and the mission
towns – a schedule of musical programmes.
The festival is very popular: book hotels at
least 2-3 weeks in advance.
Festival Internacional de Teatro, also
organized by **APAC** (see above) is held every
odd year (next in 2017).
Aug and Dec Festival de la Temporada
in Santa Cruz and major towns of
Chiquitania, featuring *música misional*
with local performers.
24 Sep The local holiday of Santa Cruz
city and department.

Shopping

Handicrafts
Bolivian Souvenirs, *Shopping Bolívar,
local 10 and 11, on main plaza, T03-333 7805;
also at Viru-Viru airport*. Expensive knitwear
and crafts from all over Bolivia.
Paseo Artesanal La Recova, *off Libertad,
½ block from Plaza*. Many different kiosks
selling crafts.
Vicuñita Handicrafts, *Ingavi e Independencia,
T03-333 4711*. Wide variety of crafts from the
lowlands and the altiplano, very good.

Jewellery
Carrasco, *Velasco 23, T03-336 2841, and other
branches*. For gemstones.
RC Joyas, *Bolívar 262, T03-333 2725*. Jewellery
and Bolivian gems.

Markets
Los Pozos, *between Quijarro, Campero, Suárez
Arana and 6 de Agosto*. A sprawling street
market for all kinds of produce.
Mercado Nuevo, *at Sucre y Cochabamba*.
Siete Calles, *Isabel la Católica y Vallegrande*.
Mainly clothing.

What to do

Bird Bolivia, *T03-356 3636, www.birdbolivia.
com*. Specializes in organized birding tours,
English spoken.
Forest Tour, *Junín y 21 de Mayo, Galería
Casco Viejo, upstairs, No 115, T03-337 2042,
www.forestbolivia.com*. Environmentally
sensitive tours to Refugio los Volcanes,
birdwatching, national parks, Chiquitania
and Salar de Uyuni. English spoken.
Magri Turismo, *Velarde 49 y Irala, T03-334 4559,
www.magriturismo.com*. Long-established
agency for airline tickets and tours.
Misional Tours, *Los Motojobobos 2515, T03-
360 1985, www.misionaltours.com*. Covers all
of Bolivia, specializing in Chiquitania, Amboró,
and Santa Cruz. Tours in various languages.
Nick's Adventures, *Equipetrol 8 Este, No 11,
T7845 8046, www.nicksadventuresbolivia.com*.
Australian/Bolivian-owned company offering

tours locally and throughout Bolivia, with a strong emphasis on wildlife conservation. **Ruta Verde**, *de Mayo 318, T03-339 6470, www.rutaverdebolivia.com*. Offers national parks, Jesuit missions, Ruta del Che, Amazonian boat trips, Salar de Uyuni, and tailor-made tours, Dutch/Bolivian-owned, English and German also spoken, knowledgeable and helpful.

Transport

Air Viru-Viru, T03-338 5000, open 24 hrs, airline counters from 0600; *casa de cambio* changing cash US$ and euros at poor rates, 0630-2100; various ATMs; luggage lockers 0600-2200, US$5.50 for 24 hrs; ENTEL for phones and internet, plus a few eateries. Taxi US$10, micro from Ex-Terminal (see below), or El Trompillo, US$1, 45 mins. From airport take micro to Ex-Terminal then taxi to centre. Domestic flights with **Boliviana de Aviación (BoA)**, T03-311 6247) and **TAM** (Bolivia, T03-352 9669), to **La Paz**, **Cochabamba**, **Sucre**, **Tarija** and **Cobija**. International flights to **Asunción**, **Buenos Aires**, **Salta**, **Lima**, **Madrid**, **Miami**, **Washington**, **Santiago** and **São Paulo**.

El Trompillo is the regional airport operating daily 0500-1900, T352 6600, located south of the centre on the 2do Anillo. It has a phone office and kiosk selling drinks, but no other services. Taxi US$1.50, many micros. **TAM** has flights throughout the country, different destinations on different days.

Bus **Regional buses and vans** These leave either from behind the Terminal Bimodal (use pedestrian tunnel under the rail tracks) or from near the Ex-Terminal (the old bus station, Av Irala y Av Cañoto, 1er Anillo, which is no longer functioning).

Long distance Most long-distance buses leave from the combined bus/train terminal, **Terminal Bimodal**, Av Montes on the 3er Anillo, T03-348 8382; police check passports and search luggage here; taxi to centre, US$1.50. Terminal fee, US$0.50, left luggage US$0.50, there are ATMs and *cambios*.

To **Cochabamba**, via the lowland route, many depart 0600-0930 and 1630-2130, US$9-12. 75, *bus-cama* US$18.55, 8-10 hrs, also **Trans Carrasco** vans leave when full across the street from the Terminal Bimodal, US$20; via the old highland route, **Trans Carrasco**, depart from the main plaza in El Torno, 30 km west of Santa Cruz, daily at 1200 (from Mairana daily at 0800 and 1500), US$8, 14 hrs. Direct to **Sucre** via Aiquile, around 1600, US$13.50-18, 12-13hrs. To **Oruro**, US$15-21, 14-15 hrs, and **La Paz** between 1630-1900, US$15.50-22.75, *bus-cama* US$31.25, 15-16 hrs; change in Cochabamba for daytime travel. To **Camiri** (US$5, 4-5 hrs), **Yacuiba** (border with Argentina), US$8.50-13, 8 hrs and **Tarija**, US$18.75-27, 17-24 hrs. To **Trinidad**, several daily after 2000, 9 hrs, US$9-13. To **San José de Chiquitos**, US$7-10, 5 hrs, **Roboré**, US$7-10, 7 hrs, and **Quijarro** (border with Brazil), at 1030 and between 1700-2000, US$12-22, 8-10 hrs. Also vans to San José, leave when full, US$10, 4½ hrs. To **San Ignacio de Velasco**, US$10, 10 hrs; **Jenecherú** *bus-cama* US$18; also **Expreso San Ignacio** vans leave when full, US$20, 8 hrs.

International Terminal fee US$1.50. To **Asunción**, US$52-64, 20-24 hrs via Villamontes and the Chaco, at 1930, with **Yacyretá**, T03-362 5557, Mon, Tue, Thu, Sat; **Stel Turismo**, T03-349 7762, daily; **Pycazú**, daily, and **Palma Loma**. Other companies are less reliable. See page 467 for the route to Paraguay across the Chaco. To **Buenos Aires** daily departures around 1900, US$158, 36 hrs, several companies. To **São Paulo** via Puerto Suárez, with **La Preferida**, T03-364 7160, Mon, Wed, Fri, 2 days.

Car hire Avis, Carretera al Norte Km. 3.5, T03-343 3939, www.avis.com.bo. **A Barron's**, Av Alemana 50 y Tajibos, T03-342 0160, www.abarrons.com. Outstanding service and completely trustworthy. **IMBEX**, 3er Anillo Interno, entre Bush y N Ortiz, T03-311 1000, www.imbex.com.

Taxi About US$1-1.50 inside 1er Anillo (more at night), US$2 inside 3er Anillo, fix fare in advance. Use radio-taxis at night.

Train Ferroviaria Oriental, at Terminal Bimodal, T03-338 7300, www.fo.com.bo, runs east to **San José de Chiquitos**, **Roboré** and **Quijarro** on the Brazilian border. The **Ferrobús** (a rail-car with the fastest most luxurious service) leaves Santa Cruz Tue, Thu, Sun 1800, arriving Quijarro 0700 next day, US$29.50; **Expreso Oriental** (an express train), Mon, Wed, Fri 1320, arriving 0602, US$12.50. There is also little-used weekly train service south to **Yacuiba** on the Argentine frontier, Thu 1530, arrives 0805 next day, US$6, returns Fri 1700; buses are much faster.

West of Santa Cruz

a sacred rock, a revolutionary trail and a wildlife hotspot

The highlights of this area, known as Los Valles Cruceños, are southwest of Santa Cruz: the pre-Inca site of El Fuerte by the pleasant resort town of Samaipata, nearby Parque Nacional Amboró and the Che Guevara Trail, on which you can follow in the final, fatal footsteps of the revolutionary.

☆ Samaipata *Colour map 3, B4.*

From Santa Cruz the old mountain road to Cochabamba runs along the Piray gorge and up into the highlands. Some 120 km from Santa Cruz is Samaipata (population 10,470), a great place to relax midweek, with good lodging, restaurants, hikes and riding, and a growing ex-pat community. A two-hour walk takes you to the top of Cerro de La Patria, just east of town, with nice views of the surrounding valleys. Local *artesanías* include ceramics, paintings and sculpture. At weekends the town bursts into life as crowds of

Samaipata

To Mairana, Mataral, Comarapa, Vallegrande, Sucre & Cochabamba
To El Fuerte (9 km), Bermejo & Santa Cruz
To Cerro de la Patria
To Santa Cruz
To La Pajcha Waterfall (40 km)
To ❸ & Valleabajo

Parque Aeronáutico
Museo Arqueológico
Road Runners
Plaza
Taxis to Santa Cruz
Tucandera
Ben Verhoef

Not to scale

Where to stay		Restaurants	
1 Andoriña	5 Landhaus	1 Café 1900	6 La Mexicana
2 El Jardín	6 La Víspera	2 Chakana & La Cocina	7 Latina Café
3 El Pueblito Resort	7 Res Kim	3 El Descanso en Las Alturas	8 Tierra Libre
4 Hostal Restaurant Nómada	8 Res Paola	4 El Nuevo Turista	
		5 La Bohème	

Cruceños come to escape the city heat and to party. See www.samaipata.info. There is a Banco Unión ATM at Calle Campero s/n, between Warnes and Saavedra.

The **Museo de Arqueología** ⓘ *2 blocks east, 1 north from the plaza, Mon-Fri 0830-1200, 1400-1800, Sat-Sun 0830-1600, US$1 (for museum only, US$8 for El Fuerte and museum),* houses the tourist information office and a collection of ceramics with anthropomorphic designs, dating from 200 BC to AD 300, and provides information on the nearby pre-Inca ceremonial site commonly called El Fuerte.

> **Tip…**
> It is not permitted to walk on the rock, so visit the museum first to see the excellent model.

☆El Fuerte

Daily 0900-1630, US$8 for El Fuerte and Museum, ticket valid 4 days, Spanish- and English-speaking guides available, US$12.

El Fuerte is 9 km from Samaipata; 3 km along the highway to Santa Cruz, then 6 km up a rough, signposted road (taxi from Plaza Principal US$7.50 one way, US$15 return with two hours' wait); two to three hours' walk one way. Pleasant bathing is possible in a river on the way to El Fuerte.

This sacred structure (altitude 1990 m) consists of a complex system of channels, basins, high-relief sculptures, etc, carved out of one vast slab of rock. Some suggest that Amazonian people created it around 1500 BC, but it could be later. There is evidence of subsequent occupations and that it was the nethermost outpost of the Incas' Kollasuyo (their eastern empire). Behind the rock are poorly excavated remains of a city.

Around Samaipata

In addition to tours to El Fuerte and the Ruta del Che (see below), many other worthwhile excursions can be made in the Samaipata area. Impressive forests of giant ferns can be visited around **Cerro La Mina** and elsewhere in the Amboró buffer zone. Also **Cuevas**, 20 km east of town, with waterfalls and pools, often visited together with El Fuerte. Further east are forest and sandstone mountains at **Bella Vista/Codo de los Andes**. There is a wonderful hike up to the **Loma de Cóndores**, with many condors and nearby the the 25-m-high **La Pajcha** waterfall, 40 km south of Samaipata. **Postrervalle** is a quaint hamlet with many interesting walks and mountain bike trails. There is good birdwatching throughout the region, especially around Mataral (see below). Tour operators in Samaipata can arrange all of the above trips.

The little village of **Bermejo**, 40 km east of Samaipata on the road to Santa Cruz, provides access to the strikingly beautiful **Serranía Volcanes** region, abutting on Parque Nacional Amboró. Here is the excellent Refugio Los Volcanes ⓘ *T7688 0800, or 03-337 2042, www.refugiovolcanes.net,* a small lodge with a 15-km trail system, with good birdwatching, orchids and bromeliads. Ginger's Paradise, some 2 km from Bermejo (T6777 4772, www.gingersparadise.com), offers an organic, communal alternative, popular with backpackers (you can work to offset some room costs).

Comarapa and the old road to Cochabamba

Past Samaipata the road from Santa Cruz continues west 17 km to Mairana, a hot dusty roadside town where long-distance buses make their meal stops and there is daily service to Cochabamba (see Santa Cruz transport, page 460). It is 51 km further to Mataral, where there are petroglyphs. The paved road to Vallegrande (51 km, see below) branches south here.

Another 57 km west is Comarapa (population 15,875, altitude 1800 m), a tranquil agricultural centre halfway between Santa Cruz and Cochabamba. The town provides access to several lovely natural areas including **Laguna Verde** (12 km, taxi US$11.50 with two hours' wait, or walk back over the hills), surrounded by cloudforest bordering Parque Nacional Amboró; and the **Jardín de Cactáceas de Bolivia**, where the huge *carparí* cactus and 25 other endemic species may be seen (entry US$0.75, take a *trufi* from Comarapa to Pulquina Abajo, US$1). The *jardín* itself is run-down but there are many more impressive cacti, good walking and birdwatching throughout the area. Beyond Comarapa the road is unpaved and very scenic. It climbs through cloudforest past the village of **La Siberia** to the pass at El Churo and enters the department of Cochabamba (see page 441).

Vallegrande and La Higuera

Some 115 km south of the Santa Cruz–Cochabamba road is La Higuera, where Che Guevara was killed. On 8 October each year, visitors, most from outside Bolivia, gather there to celebrate his memory. La Higuera is reached through the town of Vallegrande (population 17,200) where, at **Hospital Nuestro Señor de Malta** ⓘ *no fee, but voluntary donation to the health station*, you can see the old laundry building where Che's body was shown to the international press on 9 October 1967. Near Vallegrande's airstrip you can see the results of excavations carried out in 1997 which finally unearthed his physical remains (now in Cuba); ask an airport attendant to see the site. Vallegrande has a small **archaeological museum** ⓘ *Mon-Fri 1000-1200, 1400-1700, US$1.50*, above which is the **Che Guevara Room** ⓘ *entry US$4.50*. Another **museum** ⓘ *T03-942 2003*, owned by René Villegas, opens on advance request.

The schoolhouse in La Higuera (60 km south of Vallegrande) where Che was executed is now a museum. Guides, including Pedro Calzadillo, headmaster of the school, will show visitors to the ravine of El Churo (or Yuro), where Che was captured on 8 October 1967.

☆**La Ruta del Che** tours organized by agencies in Santa Cruz (three days, two nights) and Samaipata (two days, one night) follow some of the last movements of Che and his band.

☆Parque Nacional Amboró *Colour map 3, B4.*

The park is administered by SERNAP, C Gabriel José Moreno 3530, Barrio Morita, Santa Cruz, T03-355 1184, see www.sernap.gob.bo and www.biobol.org. There are also park offices in Samaipata and Buena Vista.

This vast (442,500 ha) protected area lies only three hours west of Santa Cruz. Amboró encompasses four distinct major ecosystems and 11 life zones and is home to thousands of animal, plant and insect species (it is reputed to contain more butterflies than anywhere else on earth). The park is home to over 850 species of bird, including the blue-horned curassow, quetzal and cock-of-the-rock, red and chestnut-fronted macaws, hoatzin and cuvier toucans, and 130 mammals, many native to Amazonia, such as capybaras, peccaries, tapirs, several species of monkey, and jungle cats like the jaguar, ocelot and margay, and the spectacled bear. There are also numerous waterfalls and cool, green swimming pools, moss-ridden caves and large tracts of virgin rainforest. The park itself is largely inaccessible, but there is good trekking in the surrounding 195,100-ha buffer zone which is where most tours operate. The best time of year to visit the park is during April to October. You cannot enter the park without a guide, either from a tour operator, or from a community-based project. Note that there are many biting insects so take repellent, long-sleeved shirts, long trousers and good boots. There are two places to base yourself:

Samaipata (see above) to access the southern highland areas of the park, and Buena Vista (see below) for northern lowland sections.

Buena Vista

This sleeply little town is 100 km northwest of Santa Cruz by paved road (see www.buenavistabolivia.com). There's no ATM in town, but US dollars cash can be changed. There is an Amboró interpretation office one block from the plaza, T03-932 2055. Three kilometres from town is **Eco-Albergue Candelaria** ① *T7668 7071, or contact in advance through Hacienda El Cafetal (see Where to stay, below)*, a community tourism project offering cabins in a pleasant setting, activities and tours. From Buena Vista there are five tourist sites for entering the national park.

Listings West of Santa Cruz *map page 461.*

Where to stay

Samaipata

Rooms may be hard to find at weekends in high season.

$$$$-$$ El Pueblito Resort

Camino a Valle Abajo, 20 mins' walk uphill from town, T03-944 6383, www.elpueblitoresort.com.
Fully equipped cabins and rooms, pool, restaurant and bar set around a mock colonial plaza, with shops and meditation chapel.

$$ Hostal Restaurant Nómada

C Bolívar next to the museum, T7782 8132.
Most rooms have private bath, electric shower, swimming pool, restaurant, meeting rooms for 70 people.

$$ Landhaus

C Murillo uphill from centre, T03-944 6033, www.samaipata-landhaus.com.
Cabins and rooms in nice ample grounds, small pool, hammocks, parking, sauna (extra), craft shop, good breakfast available. Older rooms are cheaper and good value.

$$ La Víspera

1.2 km south of town, T03-944 6082, www.lavispera.org.
Dutch-owned organic farm with accommodation in 5 cosy cabins with kitchen, camping US$6-7 pp, breakfast and lunch available in **Café-Jardín** (daily 0800-1500), book exchange, maps for sale. A peaceful slow-paced place; owners Margarita and Pieter are very knowledgeable. They also sell medicinal and seasoning herbs.

$ Andoriña

C Campero, 2½ blocks from plaza, T03-944 6333, www.andorinasamaipata.com.
Tastefully decorated hostel, cheaper without bath, good breakfast, kitchen, bar, good views, volunteer opportunities. Dutch/Bolivian-run, enthusiastic owners Andrés and Doriña are very knowledgeable, English spoken.

$ El Jardín

C Arenales, 2 blocks from market, T7311 9461, www.eljardinsamaipata.blogspot.com.
Cheaper with shared bath and in dorm, hot water, ample gardens, camping US$3 pp, kitchen facilities, nature-friendly.

$ Residencial Kim

C Terrazas, near plaza, T03-944 6161.
Rooms with shared bath, family-run, spotless, good value.

$ Residencial Paola

C Terrazas, diagonal to the plaza, T03-944 6093.
Simple rooms, cheaper without bath, electric shower, internet (extra), kitchen and laundry facilities.

Comarapa

$ El Paraíso
Av Comarapa 396 (main road to Cochabamba), T03-946 2045.
Pleasant economical hotel, electric shower, nice garden, parking, decent restaurant, popular.

Vallegrande and La Higuera

$ Hostal Juanita
M M Caballero 123, Vallegrande, T03-942 2231.
Cheaper without bath, electric shower, good value, Doña Juanita is kind.

$ La Casa del Telegrafista
La Higuera, T7493 7807/6773 3362, casadeltelegrafista@gmail.com.
Small, welcoming French-owned *posada*, rooms with shared bath, lovely garden, great views, meals on request, camping (US$2), horseback and mountain-bike tours, US$15, also bikes for hire.

$ Residencial Vallegrande
On the plaza, Vallegrande.
Basic accommodation.

Buena Vista

$$$-$$ Hacienda El Cafetal
5.5 km south of town (taxi from plaza US$3), T03-935 2067, www.haciendaelcafetal.com.
Comfortable suites for up to 5 people, double rooms, restaurant, bar, birdwatching platform, on a working coffee plantation (tours available), with shade forest.

$$ Buenavista
700 m out of town, T03-932 2104, buenavista.hotel@hotmail.com.
Pretty place with rooms, suites and cabins with kitchen, viewing platform, pool, sauna, very good restaurant, horse riding.

$ La Casona
Av 6 de Agosto at the corner of the plaza, T03-932 2083.
Small simple rooms with fan, shared bath, electric shower, courtyard in hammocks, plants and birds, good value.

$ Quimori
1 km east of Buena Vista, T03-932 2081.
Includes breakfast, other meals with advance notice, pool, nice grounds, tours in dry season, family-run.

$ Residencial Nadia
C M Saucedo Sevilla 186, T03-932 2049.
Cheaper without bath, simple, small, family-run.

Restaurants

Samaipata

$$ El Descanso en Las Alturas
C Arteaga, uphill from plaza, opens mostly on weekends.
Wide choice including good steaks and pizzas.

$$ La Mexicana
C Rubén Terrazas near the plaza. Tue-Sun 1100-1500 and 1800-2300.
Nice restaurant/bar with very good Mexican food. Also serves breakfast Sat-Sun.

$$ Latina Café
Bolívar, 3 blocks from plaza. Fri-Tue 1800-2200, Sat-Sun also 1200-1430.
Nice upmarket restaurant/bar with very good Bolivian and international food including vegetarian. French/Bolivian-run and recommended.

$$-$ Chakana
Terrazas on plaza. Daily 0800-2300.
Bar/restaurant/café serving *almuerzos*, good snacks, salads, cakes and ice cream, outside seating, book exchange, Dutch-owned.

$$-$ Tierra Libre
Sucre ½ block from plaza. Open 1200-2200, Sun 1200-1500, closed Wed.
Nice terrace with outdoor seating, good meat and vegetarian, pleasant atmosphere.

$ Café 1900
Sucre on plaza. Daily 0800-2300.
Good set lunch, sandwiches and crêpes.

$ El Nuevo Turista
Opposite the gas station on the highway.
Good local dishes.

$ La Bohème
*Sucre y Terrazas, diagonal to plaza.
Daily 1200-2400.*
Trendy Australian-run bar for drinks
and snacks.

$ La Cocina
Sucre by the plaza. Tue-Sat 1900-2200.
Middle Eastern and Mexican fast food
with home-made breads.

Buena Vista

$$-$ La Plaza
On the plaza.
Elegant restaurant/bar with a terrace, wide
range of international dishes, good service.

$ El Patujú
On the plaza.
The only café in town, serving excellent local
coffee, teas, hot chocolate and a range of
snacks. Also sells local produce and crafts.

What to do

Samaipata
Tour operators
Samaipata has many tour operators, more
than we can list. Except as noted, all are on
C Bolívar near the museum. Most day trips
cost about US$20-25 pp in a group of 4.
Ben Verhoef Tours, *Campero 217, T03-944
6365.* Dutch-owned, English, German and
Spanish also spoken. Offer tours along
La Ruta del Che and throughout the area.
Jucumari Tours, *T944 6129, erwin-am@
hotmail.com.* Run by Edwin Acuña.
Michael Blendinger, *T03-944 6227, www.
discoveringbolivia.com.* German guide raised
in Argentina who speaks English, runs fully
equipped 4WD tours, short and long treks,
specialist in nature and archaeology.

Road Runners, *T944 6193/6294, www.
hosteltrail.com/roadrunners.* Olaf and
Frank speak English, German and Dutch,
enthusiastic, lots of information and advice.
Tucandera Tours, *T7316 7735, tucandera.
tours@hotmail.com.* Saul Arias and Elva
Villegas are biologists, excellent for nature
tours and birdwatching, English spoken,
competitive prices. Recommended.

Wine tasting
2 bodegas located outside Samaipata are
Uvairenda (www.uvairenda.com) and
Vargas (www.vitivinicolavargas.com).

Buena Vista
Amboró Travel & Adventure, *C Celso
Sandoval, ½ block from the plaza, T7663 2102,
amborotravel@hotmail.com.* Prices include
transport to and from the park, guide and
meals. Recommended.
Puertas del Amboró, *corner of the plaza,
T03-932 2059.* They also offer full packages.

Transport

Samaipata
Bus From **Santa Cruz**, **Minibus El Fuerte**,
C Arumá 90 y Av Grigotá (2ndo Anillo),
Santa Cruz, T03-359 8958, Samaipata T03-
944 6336; and **Taxis Expreso Samaipata**,
Av Omar Chávez 1147 y Soliz de Holguín,
Santa Cruz, T03-333 5067, Samaipata
T03-944 6129; both companies leave when
full Mon-Sat 0530-1900 (for Sun book in
advance), US$4.50 per person shared; or
US$22 in private vehicle, 2½ hrs. Returning
to Santa Cruz, they pick you up from your
hotel in Samaipata. Buses leaving Santa Cruz
for **Sucre** and other towns pass through
Samaipata between 1900 and 2200; tickets
can be booked with 1 day's notice through
El Nuevo Turista (see Restaurants, above).
To get to **Samaipata** from **Sucre**, buses
leave at night and arrive 0500-0600 (set
your alarm in case the driver forgets to stop
for you), stopping in Mataral or Mairana for
breakfast, about ½ hr before Samaipata.

Comarapa

To/from **Santa Cruz** with **Turismo Caballero** (T03-350 9626) and **Trans Comarapa** (T7817 5576), both on Plazuela Oruro, Av Grigotá (3er Anillo), 3 daily each, US$4.50, 6 hrs. To **Cochabamba**, 2 buses a day pass through from Mairana.

Vallegrande and La Higuera

Bus Flota **Vallegrande** has 2 daily buses morning and afternoon from Santa Cruz to **Vallegrande** via **Samaipata** (at 1130 and 1630), 5 hrs, US$5. Best to book in advance. Samaipata–Vallegrande US$3.25. From Vallegrande market, a daily bus departs 0815 to **Pucará** (45 km, US$2.50), from where there is transport (12 km) to **La Higuera**.

Taxi Vallegrande–La Higuera US$30-35.

Buena Vista

Bus and taxi Sindicato 10 de Febrero in Santa Cruz at Izozog 668 y Av Irala, 1er Anillo behind ex-terminal, T03-334 8435, 0730-1830, US$3 pp (private vehicle US$15), 1¾ hrs. Also another shared taxi company nearby, micros from Av Banzer y 3er Anillo and 'Línea 102' buses from regional section of Terminal Bimodal, US$1.50, 3 hrs. From Buena Vista, the access to the Amboró park is by gravel road, 4WD jeep or similar recommended as rivers have to been crossed. All operators and community ecolodge coordinators offer transport.

To Paraguay and Argentina

a hot, friendly city en route to the borders

South of Santa Cruz a good paved road passes through Abapó, Camiri (Hotel Premier, Avenida Busch 60, T03-952 2204, is a decent place to stay), Boyuibe, Villamontes – access for the Trans-Chaco route to Paraguay – and Yacuiba, on the border with Argentina.

Villamontes *Colour map 3, C4.*

Villamontes, 500 km south of Santa Cruz, is renowned for fishing. It holds a **Fiesta del Pescado** in August. It is a hot, friendly, spread-out city on the north shore of the Río Pilcomayo, at the base of the Cordillera de Aguaragüe. The river cuts through this range (Parque Nacional Aguaragüe) forming **El Angosto**, a beautiful gorge. The road to Tarija, 280 km west, is cut in the cliffs along this gorge. At Plaza 6 de Agosto is the **Museo Héroes del Chaco** ⓘ *Tue-Sun 0800-1200, 1400-1800, US$0.30*, with photographs, maps, artefacts, and battle models of the 1932-1935 Chaco War. There are a couple of ATMs. **Prodem** and various *cambios* are on Avenida Méndez Arcos.

Border with Paraguay From Villamontes, the road to Paraguay, almost all paved, runs east to **Ibibobo** (70 km). Motorists and bus travellers should carry extra water and some food, as climatic conditions are harsh and there is little traffic in case of a breakdown. Bolivian exit stamps are given at Ibibobo. If travelling by bus, passports are collected by driver and returned on arrival at Mcal Estigarribia (Paraguay), with Bolivian exit stamp. Paraguayan immigration and thorough drugs searches take place in Mcal Estigarribia. There are Paraguayan consulates in Santa Cruz (Avenida San Martín, Equipetrol Norte, Calle H Este Casa 8, T03-344 8989, scruzcongralpar@mre.gov.py), and Villamontes (Avenida Ingavi entre Héroes del Chaco y Cochabamba, T4672 3648, villamontesconsulpar@mre. gov.py). See Santa Cruz Transport (page 460) for international bus services. From Ibibobo to the Bolivian frontier post at Picada Sucre is 75 km, then it's 15 km to the actual border and another 8 km to the Paraguayan frontier post at **Fortín Infante Rivarola**. There are customs posts, but no police, immigration nor any other services at the border.

Yacuiba and the border with Argentina *Colour map 3, C4.*

Yacuiba is a prosperous city (population 11,000) at the crossing to Pocitos in Argentina. Hotels include **Valentín**, San Martín 3271, T04-682 2645, www.valentinhotelbolivia.com, and **París**, Comercio 1175 y Campero, T04-682 2182 (both $$). The train service from Santa Cruz is slow and poor, road travel is a better option. In Yacuiba, there are ATMs on Campero. The Argentine consul is at Santa Cruz 1540, entre Sucre y Crevaux, T04-682 2062. Passengers leaving Bolivia must disembark at Yacuiba, take a taxi to Pocitos on the border (US$0.50, beware unscrupulous drivers) and walk across to Argentina.

Listings To Paraguay and Argentina

Where to stay

Villamontes

$$$-$$ El Rancho Olivo
Av Méndez Arcos opposite the train station, 15 blocks from the centre, T04-672 2059, www.elranchoolivo.com.
Lovely rooms, frigobar, nice grounds and pool, parking, excellent restaurant.

$ Gran Hotel Avenida
Av Méndez Arcos 3 blocks east of Plaza 15 de Abril, T04-672 2828.
Helpful owner, parking.

$ Residencial Raldes
Cap Manchego 171, 1½ blocks from Plaza 15 de Abril, T04-672 2088, fernandoarel@gmail.com.
Well maintained, family-run, electric shower, cheaper with shared bath and fan, nice courtyard, small pool, parking.

Transport

Villamontes
Bus To **Yacuiba**, **Coop El Chaco**, Av Méndez Arcos y Ismael Montes, hourly 0630-1830, US$1.35, 1½ hrs. Cars from Av Montenegro y Cap Manchego, hourly or when full, 0630-1830, US$2, 1½ hrs. Long-distance buses from terminal on Av Méndez Arcos, 13 blocks east of Plaza 15 de Abril (taxi US$0.40 pp). To **Tarija** via Entre Ríos, mostly unpaved (sit on the right for best views), US$6, 10-11 hrs, several companies 1730-1930; for day travel, **Copacabana** may depart at 1030, 2-3 per week from the terminal; **Guadalupana**, Wed and Sat at 0930, from Coop El Chaco office. To **Santa Cruz**, several companies daily, US$5-8.50, some bus-cama, 7-8 hrs.

To **Asunción**, buses from Santa Cruz pass through 0200-0300, reserve a day earlier, US$35, about 15 hrs. 5 companies, offices all on Av Montenegro, either side of Av Méndez Arcos. Best are **Stel**, T04-672 3662, or Vicky Vides T7735 0934; **Yaciretá**, T04-672 2812, or Betty Borda, T7740 4111.

Yacuiba
Bus To **Santa Cruz**, about 20 companies, mostly at night, 14 hrs, US$8.50-13. To **Tarija**, daily morning and evening.

Eastern Bolivia

natural beauty, indigenous culture and Jesuit heritage

The vast and rapidly developing plains to the east of the Eastern Cordillera are Bolivia's richest area in terms of natural resources. For the visitor, the beautiful churches and traditions of the former Jesuit missions of Chiquitania are well worth a visit. Here too are some of the country's largest and wildest protected natural areas.

★Jesuit missions of Chiquitania

Nine Jesuit missions survive east of Santa Cruz, six of which – San Javier, Concepción, San Rafael, Santa Ana, San Miguel and San José de Chiquitos – have churches which are UNESCO World Heritage Sites. Many of these were built by the Swiss Jesuit, Padre Martin Schmidt and his pupils.

Besides organizing *reducciones* and constructing churches, Padre Schmidt wrote music (some is still played today on traditional instruments) and he published a Spanish-Chiquitano dictionary based on his knowledge of all the dialects of the region. He worked in this part of the then-Viceroyalty of Peru until the expulsion of the Jesuits in 1767 by order of Charles III of Spain.

San Javier (San Xavier) The first Jesuit mission in Chiquitania (1691), San Javier's church was built by Padre Schmidt between 1749 and 1752. Some of the original wooden structure has survived more or less intact and restoration was undertaken between 1987 and 1993 by the Swiss Hans Roth, himself a former Jesuit. Subtle designs and floral patterns cover the ceiling, walls and carved columns. One of the bas-relief paintings on the high altar depicts Martin Schmidt playing the piano for his indigenous choir. It is a fine 30-minute walk (best in the afternoon light) to **Mirador El Bibosi** and the small **Parque Piedra de Los Apóstoles**. There is also good walking or all-terrain cycling in the surrounding countryside (no maps, ask around), thermal swimming holes at **Aguas Calientes**, and horse riding from several hotels. Patron saint's fiesta, 3 December, but 29 June, Feast of Saints Peter and Paul, is best for viewing traditional costumes, dances and music. Tourist guides' association has an office in the **Alcaldía** ① *T7761 7902, or 7763 3203 for a guide*. Information also from the **Casa de Cultura** ① *on the plaza, T963 5149*.

Concepción The lovely town is dominated by its magnificent **cathedral** ① *0700-2000, tours 1000, 1500, donation invited*, completed by Padre Schmidt and Johann Messner in 1755 and restored by Hans Roth (1975-1982). The interior of this beautiful church has an altar of laminated silver. In front of the church is a bell-cum-clock tower housing the original bells and behind it are well-restored cloisters. On the plaza, forming part of the Jesuit complex, is the **Museo Misional** ① *Mon-Sat 0800-1200,*

Essential Jesuit missions of Chiquitos

Getting around

Access to the mission area is by bus or train from **Santa Cruz**: a paved highway runs north to San Ramón (180 km) and on north to San Javier (40 km further), turning east here to Concepción (60 km), then to San Ignacio de Velasco (160 km, of which the first 30 are paved). A paved road runs south from San Ignacio either through San Miguel or Santa Ana to meet at San Rafael for the continuation south to San José de Chiquitos. Access is also possible by the paved Santa Cruz–Puerto Suárez highway, which goes via San José de Chiquitos. By rail, leave the Santa Cruz–Quijarro train at San José and from there travel north by bus. The most comfortable way to visit is by jeep, in about five days. The route is straightforward and fuel is available.

When to go

One of the best times to appreciate this region is at the bi-annual **Festival de Música Renacentista y Barroca Americana** (next in April/May 2018), but the living legacy of the missions can be appreciated year-round.

1430-1830, Sun 1000-1230, US$3.50, which has an *artesanía* shop. The ticket also gives entry to the **Hans Roth Museum**, dedicated to the restoration process. Visit also the **Museo Antropológico de la Chiquitania** ① *16 de Septiembre y Tte Capoblanco, 0800-1200, 1400-1800, free*, which explains the life of the indigenous peoples of the region. It has a café and guesthouse. The **municipal tourist office** ① *Lucas Caballero y Cabo Rodríguez, one block from plaza, T03-964 3057*, can arrange trips to nearby recreational areas, ranches and communities. An **Asociación de Guías Locales** ① *south side of plaza, contact Ysabel Supepi, T7604 7085; or Hilario Orellana, T7534 3734*, also offers tours to local communities many of which are developing grass-roots tourism projects: eg **Santa Rita**, **San Andrés** and **El Carmen**. With a week's advance notice, they can also organize private concerts with 30 to 40 musicians. There are various restaurants in town and many places sell wood carvings, traditional fabrics and clothing.

San Ignacio de Velasco This is the main commercial and transport hub of the region, with road links to Brazil. A lack of funds for restoration led to the demolition of San Ignacio's replacement Jesuit church in 1948, the original having burnt down in 1808. A modern replica contains the elaborate high altar, pulpit and paintings and statues of saints. Tourist information office at **Casa de la Cultura** ① *La Paz y Comercio, on the plaza, T03-962 2056 ext 122, culturayturismo.siv@gmail.com, Mon-Fri 0800-1200, 1430-1830*, can help organize guides and visits to local music schools. The **Centro Artesanal** ① *Santa Cruz entre Bolívar y Oruro, Mon-Sat 0800-1930, Sun 0800-1200*, sells lovely textile and wood crafts. There is community tourism in the villages of **San Juancito**, 18 km from San Ignacio, where organic coffee is grown, and **San Rafael de Sutuquiña**, 5 km; both have artisans. **Laguna Guapomó** reservoir on the edge of San Ignacio is good for swimming and fishing. There is only one ATM in town, best take some cash.

Santa Ana, San Rafael and San Miguel de Velasco These three small towns are less visited than some others along the missions circuit. Allow at least two days if travelling independently from San Ignacio: you can take a bus to Santa Ana in the afternoon, stay overnight, then continue to San Rafael the next afternoon and return to San Ignacio via San Miguel on Tuesday, Thursday or Sunday (see Transport, page 477). A day trip by taxi from San Ignacio costs about US$65 or an all-inclusive tour can be arranged by **Parador Santa Ana** (see Where to stay, page 474). Local guides are available, US$10.

The church in Santa Ana (town founded 1755, church constructed 1773-1780, after the expulsion of the Jesuits), is a lovely wooden building. It is the most authentic of all the Jesuit *templos* and Santa Ana is a particularly authentic little village. The tourist office on the plaza can provide guides. Simple accommodation is available (see page 474).

San Rafael's church was completed by Schmidt in 1749. It is one of the most beautifully restored, with mica-covered interior walls and frescoes in beige paint over the exterior. There are restaurants near the plaza. For the tourist information office, call T03-962 4022.

The frescoes on the façade of the church (1752-1759) at San Miguel depict St Peter and St Paul; designs in brown and yellow cover all the interior and the exterior side walls. The mission runs three schools and a workshop; the sisters are very welcoming and will gladly show tourists around. There is a **Museo Etnofolclórico**, off the Plaza at Calle Betania; next door is the Municipalidad/Casa de la Cultura, with a tourist information office, T03-962 4222. San Miguel has many workshops and rivals San Ignacio for the quality of its Jesuit-inspired art.

San José de Chiquitos *Colour map 3, B5.*

One complete side of the plaza is occupied by the imposing frontage of the Jesuit mission complex of four buildings and a bell tower, begun in the mid-1740s. Best light for photography is in the afternoon. The stone buildings, in baroque style, are connected by a wall. They are the workshops (1754); the church (1747) with its undulating façade; the four-storey bell tower (1748) and the mortuary (la bóveda – 1750), with one central window but no entrance in its severe frontage. The complex and **Museo** ① *Mon-Fri 0800-1200, 1430-1800, Sat-Sun 0900-1200, 1500-1800, entry US$3*, are well worth visiting. Behind are the *colegio* and workshops, which house the **Escuela Municipal de Música**; visits to rehearsals and performances can be arranged by the tourist office. **InfoTur** ① *in the Municipio, C Velasco, ½ block from plaza, T03-972 2084, Mon-Fri 0800-1200, 1430-1830*, which has information and arranges various tours; there is internet upstairs. On Mondays, Mennonites bring their produce to San José and buy provisions. The colonies are 50 km west and the Mennonites, who speak English, German, Plattdeutsch and Spanish, are happy to talk about their way of life. There is only one ATM in town, best take some cash.

About 2 km south from San José is the 17,000 ha **Parque Nacional Histórico Santa Cruz la Vieja** ① *www.biobol.org*. It has a monument to the original site of Santa Cruz (founded 1561) and a mirador with great views. The park's heavily forested hills contain much animal and bird life. There are various trails for hiking; guides can be organized by the tourist office in San José. It gets very hot so start early, allow over one hour to get there on foot (or hire a vehicle) and take plenty of water and insect repellent. There is also good walking with lovely views at **Cerro Turubó** and the **Serranía de San José**, both outside San José.

East of San José de Chiquitos

Paving of the highway from Santa Cruz east to Brazil opened up this once-isolated region of friendly villages surrounded by natural wonders. The village of **Chochís**, 90 km east of San José de Chiquitos, is known for its sanctuary of the Virgen Asunta built by Hans Roth in 1988 (one of his few major works not connected with restoring Jesuit missions). The large sanctuary is built at the foot of an impressive red sandstone outcrop called **La Torre**, 2 km from town. Along the rail line from Chochís toward La Torre is a signed trail leading to the **Velo de Novia** waterfall, a pleasant one- to two-hour walk. A much more challenging hike climbs 800 m to the flat top of **Cerro de Chochís**, where you can camp or return to town in a long day; guide required.

Chochís is at the western end of the **Serranía de Chiquitos**, a flat-topped mountain range running east–west, north of the highway and railroad. It is filled with rich vegetation, caves, petroglyphs, waterfalls, birds and butterflies. These hills are part of the 262,000-ha **Reserva Valle de Tucavaca** (www.biobol.org) which protects unique Chiquitano dry forest and offers great hiking opportunities.

Forty kilometers east of Chochís is **Roboré**, the regional centre and transport hub. The **Oficina de Turismo** ① *Av Ejército, Parque Urbano, T7761 8280*, has information about local excursions including **Los Helechos** and **Totaisales**, two lovely bathing spots in the forest, Chochís and Santiago de Chiquitos. Roboré was founded as a garrison town in 1916 and retains a strong military presence. The local fiesta is 25 October.

Seven kilometres east of Roboré, a paved road branches northeast and in 14 km reaches the particularly friendly village of **Santiago de Chiquitos**, within the Reserva Valle de Tucavaca. Founded in 1754, Santiago was one of the last missions built in Chiquitania. There are good accommodations and more good walking to a fine mirador, natural stone arches and caves with petroglyphs; guides are available in town. A poor road continues 150 km past Santiago to **Santo Corazón**, a still-isolated former Jesuit mission town (its church was built after the missionaries were expelled) inside **Area Natural de Manejo Integrado San Matías** ⓘ *www.biobol.org*.

Aguas Calientes is 15 km east of Roboré along the rail line and highway to Brazil. The hot little village is unimpressive but nearby is a river of crystal-clear thermal water, teeming with little fish and bird life. There are several spots with facilities for bathing and camping, which is preferable to the basic accommodations in town. There are many tiny biting sand-flies, so your tent should have good netting. Soaking in the thermal water amid the sights and sounds of the surrounding forest at dawn or on a moonlit night is amazing.

☆Parque Nacional Noel Kempff Mercado
Park office in San Ignacio de Velasco, Bolívar 87 entre La Paz y Santa Cruz, T03-962 2747, turismonoelkempff@gmail.com, Mon-Fri 0830-1200, 1430-1800, lots of information, some in English; additional information from SERNAP (T03-335 2325 in Santa Cruz) and FAN, also in Santa Cruz (page 454), also www.biobol.org.

In the far northeast corner of Santa Cruz Department, Parque Nacional Noel Kempff Mercado (named after a Bolivian conservation pioneer who was killed while flying over the park), is one of the world's most diverse natural habitats. This World Heritage Site covers 1,523,446 ha and encompasses seven ecosystems, within which are 139 species of mammal (including black jaguars), 620 species of bird (including nine types of macaw), 74 species of reptile and 110 species of orchid. Highlights include the **Huanchaca** or **Caparú Plateau**, which with its 200- to 500-m sheer cliffs and tumbling waterfalls is a candidate for Sir Arthur Conan Doyle's *Lost World* (Colonel Percy Fawcett, who discovered the plateau in 1910, was a friend of Conan Doyle).

This outstanding natural area receives very few visitors. Organizing a trip requires time, money and flexibility; there is no infrastructure, visitors must be self-sufficient and take all equipment including a tent. The authorities sometimes restrict access, enquire in advance. Operators in Santa Cruz (see page 459) may be able to arrange all-inclusive tours. Otherwise, the best base is San Ignacio, which has some provisions but more specialized items should be brought from Santa Cruz. Note, though, that there is no direct access from San Ignacio. See Transport, page 478, for details.

The southwestern section of the park is reached from the village of **Florida**, where there is a ranger station and a community tourism project offering basic accommodation and guides (guide compulsory, US$25 per day). It is 65 km from Florida to the trailhead (pickup US$60 one way), which provides access to the 80-m-high **El Encanto** waterfall and the climb to the plateau; allow five to six days for the return excursion.

In the northeastern section of the park are the great **Arco Iris** and **Federico Ahlfeld** waterfalls, both on the Río Paucerna and accessible mid-December to May when water levels are sufficiently high. Access is either from the Bolivian village of **Piso Firme** or the Brazilian town of **Pimenteiras do Oeste**; in all cases you must be accompanied by a Bolivian boatman/guide, available in Piso Firme and organized by the park office in San Ignacio. It is six to seven hours by motorized canoe from Piso Firme to a shelter near the Ahlfeld waterfall, and a full day's walk from there to Arco Iris.

To Brazil
There are four routes from Santa Cruz: by air to **Puerto Suárez**, by rail or road to **Quijarro** (fully paved), by road to **San Matías** (a busy border town reported unsafe due to drug

smuggling), and via **San Ignacio de Velasco** to either Vila Bela or Pontes e Lacerda (both in Brazil). Puerto Suárez is near Quijarro and this route leads to Corumbá on the Brazilian side, from where there is access to the southern Pantanal. The San Matías and Vila Bela/Pontes roads both link to Cáceres, Cuiabá and the northern Pantanal in Brazil. There are immigration posts of both countries on all routes except Vila Bela/Pontes. If travelling this way, get your Bolivian exit stamp in San Ignacio (immigration office near **Jenecherú** bus station) and Brazilian entry stamp in Cáceres or Vilhena. There may be strict customs and drugs checks entering Brazil, no fresh food may be taken from Bolivia.

Quijarro and Puerto Suárez *Colour map 3, C6.*
The eastern terminus of the Bolivian road and railway is **Quijarro**. It is quite safe by day, but caution is recommended at night. The water supply is often unreliable. Prices are much lower than in neighbouring Brazil and there are some decent places to stay. ATMs and banks are at the border.

On the shores of Laguna Cáceres, 8 km west of Quijarro, is **Puerto Suárez**, with a shady main plaza. There is a nice view of the lake from the park at the north end of Avenida Bolívar.

Parque Nacional Otuquis, protecting the lake and extensive wetlands in the Bolivian Pantanal, is divided in two parts, both accessible from Puerto Suárez; SERNAP office: final Avenida Adolfo Rau, T03-976 3270, Puerto Suárez.

Border with Brazil The neighbourhood by the border is known as Arroyo Concepción. You need not have your passport stamped if you visit Corumbá for the day. Otherwise get your exit stamp at Bolivian immigration (see below), entry stamp at Brazilian border complex. A yellow fever vaccination may be required on either side of the border, best have it to hand. Bolivian immigration is at the border at Arroyo Concepción (0800-1200, 1400-1730 daily), or at Puerto Suárez airport, where Bolivian exit/entry stamps are also issued. There is one ATM at Arroyo Concepción, at the Hotel Pantanal. Money changers right at the border on the Bolivian side offer poor rates, better to ask around in the small shops away from the bridge; nowhere to change on the Brazilian side until Corumbá. There are Brazilian consulates in Puerto Suárez (Avenida R Otero Reich y H Suárez Abrego, T03-976 2040, cg.psuarez@itamaraty.gov.br) and Santa Cruz (Avenida Noel Kempff Mercado, Calle 9A Norte, casa 9, T03-344 7575, geral@consbras.org.bo). See Transport, page 478, for taxis from the border.

Listings Eastern Bolivia

Where to stay

San Javier

$ Alojamiento Ame-Tauná
Across from the central plaza, T03-963 5095.
Perfect location in centre of town, quiet, rooms with bath, safe parking.

$ Alojamiento San Xavier
C Santa Cruz, T03-963 5038.
Cheaper without bath, electric shower, garden, nice sitting area. Recommended.

$ Residencial Chiquitano
Av Santa Cruz (Av José de Arce),
½ block from plaza, T03-963 5072.
Simple rooms, fan, large patio, good value.

Concepción

$$ Gran Hotel Concepción
On plaza, T03-964 3031, www.
granhotelconcepcion.com.bo.

Excellent service, buffet breakfast, pool, gardens, bar, very comfortable. Highly recommended.

$$ Hotel Chiquitos
end of Av Killian, T03-964 3153, www.hotelchiquitos.com.
Colonial-style construction, ample rooms, frigobar, pool, gardens and sports fields, orchid nursery, parking. Tours available. Recommended.

$$-$ Hotel Balneario Oasis Chiquitano
S Saucedo 225, 1½ blocks from plaza, T7602 5442, www.facebook.com/ HotelYComplejoTuristicoOasisChiquitano.
Buffet breakfast, pool, nice patio with flowers.

$ Colonial
Ñuflo de Chávez 7, ½ block from plaza, T03-964 3050.
Economical place, hammocks on ample veranda, parking, breakfast available.

$ Residencial Westfalia
Saucedo 205, 2 blocks from plaza, T03-964 3040.
Cheaper without bath, German-owned, nice patio, good value.

San Ignacio de Velasco

$$$ La Misión
Libertad, on plaza, T03-962 2333, www.hotel-lamision.com.
Upmarket hotel, restaurant, meeting rooms, pool, parking, downstairs rooms have bath tubs.

$$$ Parador Santa Ana
Libertad entre Sucre y Cochabamba, T03-962 2075, www.paradorsantaana.blogspot.com.
Beautiful house with small patio, tastefully decorated, 5 comfortable rooms, good breakfast, knowledgeable owner arranges tours, credit cards accepted. Recommended.

$$ Apart Hotel San Ignacio
24 de Septiembre y Cochabamba, T03-962 2157, www.aparthotel-sanignacio.com.

Comfortable rooms, nice grounds, pool, hammocks, parking. Despite the name, no apartments or kitchenettes.

$$ San Ignacio Miguel Areiger
Plaza 31 de Julio, T03-962 2283.
In a beautifully restored former episcopal mansion, non-profit (run by diocese, funds support poor youth in the community), breakfast.

$ Residencial Bethania
Velasco y Cochabamba, T03-962 2307.
Simple rooms with shared bath, electric shower, small patio, economical and good value.

Santa Ana
Simple economical accommodation is available at **Comunidad Valenciana** (T03-980 2098).

San Rafael

$ Casa de Huéspedes
Belisario s/n, T 03-962 4241.
Clean, shared bath, good for bus connections.

San Miguel de Velasco

$$-$ Alojamiento Altiplano
Av Santa Bárbara s/n (main road), T03-962 4018.
Near the plaza, best in town, very knowledgeable staff.

San José de Chiquitos

$$$-$$ Villa Chiquitana
C 9 de Abril, 6 blocks from plaza, T7315 5803, www.villachiquitana.com.
Charming hotel built in traditional style, restaurant open to public, frigobar, pool (US$3 for non-guests), garden, parking, craft shop, tour agency. French-run.

$ Turubó
Bolívar on the plaza, T03-972 2037, hotelturubo on Facebook.
With a/c or fan, electric shower, variety of different rooms, ask to see one before checking-in, good location.

East of San José de Chiquitos
Chochís

$ Ecoalbergue de Chochís
1 km west of town along the rail line, T7263 9467; Santa Cruz contact: Probioma, T03-343 1332, www.probioma.org.bo.
Simple community-run lodging in 2 cabins, shared bath, cold water, small kitchen, screened hammock area, camping US$3.50 pp, meals on advance request.

$ El Peregrino
On the plaza, T7313 1881.
Simple rooms in a family home, some with fan and fridge, shared bath, electric shower, ample yard, camping possible.

Roboré

$$ Anahí
Obispo Santiesteban 1½ blocks from plaza, T03-974 2362.
Comfortable rooms with electric shower, nice patio, parking, kitchen and washing facilities, owner runs tours.

$$ Choboreca
Av La Paz 710, T03-974 2566.
Nice hotel, rooms with a/c. Several other places to stay in town.

Santiago de Chiquitos
There are various *alojamientos familiares* around town, all simple to basic.

$$ Beula
On the plaza, T03-313 6274, http://hotelbeula.com.
Comfortable hotel in traditional style, good breakfast, frigobar. Unexpectedly upmarket for such a remote location.

$ El Convento
On plaza next to the church, T7890 2943.
Former convent with simple rooms, one has private bath, lovely garden, hot and no fan but clean and good value.

$ Panorama
1 km north of plaza, T03-313 6286.
Simple rooms with shared bath and a family farm, friendly owners Katherine and Milton Whittaker sell excellent home-made dairy products and jams, they are knowledgeable about the area and offer volunteer opportunities.

Aguas Calientes

$$ Cabañas Canaan
Across the road from Los Hervores baths, T7467 7316.
Simple wooden cabins, cold water, fan, restaurant, rather overpriced but better than the basic places in town.

$ Camping El Tucán
1 km from town on the road to Los Hervores baths, T7262 0168, www.aguascalientesmiraflores.com.bo.
Lovely grounds with clean bathrooms, electric showers, barbecues, small pier by the river.

Quijarro

$$$-$$ Jardín del Bibosi
Luis Salazar 495, 4½ blocks east of train station, T978 2044, www.hotelbibosi.com.
Variety of rooms and prices, some with a/c, fridge, cheaper with fan and shared bath, breakfast, pool, patio, restaurant, upscale for Quijarro.

Willy Solís Cruz
Roboré 13, T7365 5587, wiland_54@hotmail.com.
For years Willy has helped store luggage and offered local information and assistance. His home is open to visitors who would like to rest, take a shower, do laundry, cook or check the internet while they wait for transport; a contribution in return is welcome. He speaks English, very helpful.

Puerto Suárez

$ Beby
Av Bolívar 111, T03-976 2700.
Private bath, a/c, cheaper with shared bath and fan, no frills, very basic.

$ Casa Real
Vanguardia 39, T03-976 3335.
A/c, frigobar, Wi-Fi and internet, parking,
tours, a decent choice.

Restaurants

San Javier

$$ Ganadero
In Asociación de Ganaderos on plaza.
Excellent steaks. Other eateries around
the plaza.

Concepción

$ El Buen Gusto
North side of plaza.
Set meals and regional specialities.

San Ignacio de Velasco

$$ Casa del Camba
24 de Septiembre y Av Santa Cruz.
Daily lunch and dinner.
Local fare as well as vegetarían, chicken
dishes and mini pizzas.

$ Club Social
Comercio on the plaza. Daily 1130-1500.
Decent set lunch.

Mi Nonna
C Velasco y Cochabamba.
Open 1700-2400, closed Tue.
Café serving cappuccino, sandwiches, salads
and pasta.

San José de Chiquitos

$$ Pizzería Romanazzi
Bolivar 1 block north of plaza, T03-972
2349 (call ahead). Daily lunch and dinner
except Sun.
Home-made pizza, and other Italian
dishes. "Unquestionably the finest pizza
in eastern Bolivia if not the country."
Recommended.

$$ Sabor y Arte
Bolívar y Mons Santisteban, by the plaza.
Tue-Sun 1800-2300.

International dishes, for innovation try their
coca-leaf ravioli, nice ambience, French/
Bolivian-run.

$$-$ Rancho Brasilero
By main road, 5 blocks from plaza.
Daily 0900-1530.
Good Brazilian-style buffet, all you can eat
grill on weekends.

East of San José de Chiquitos
Roboré
Several restaurants around the plaza, including:

$ Casino Militar
On the plaza, daily for lunch and dinner.
Set meals and à la carte.

Santiago de Chiquitos

$ Churupa
½ block from plaza.
Set meals (go early or reserve your meal in
advance) and à la carte. Best in town.

Festivals

The region celebrates the Festival de Música
Renacentista y Barroca Americana every even
year (next in 2018). Many towns have their
own orchestras, which play Jesuit-era music
on a regular basis. Semana Santa (Holy Week)
celebrations are elaborate and interesting
throughout the region.

Chiquitania
1 May Fiesta de San José, San José de
Chiquitos, preceded by a week of folkloric
and other events.
29 Jun Feast of St Peter and St Paul,
San Javier, best for viewing traditional
costumes, dances and music.
26 Jul Fiesta de Santa Ana, Santa Ana.
31 Jul Patron saint's day, San Ignacio
de Velasco, preceded by a cattle fair.
29 Sep Patron saint's day, San Miguel
de Velasco.
2nd week Oct Orchid festival, Concepción.
24 Oct Patron saint's day, San Rafael,
with traditional dancing.

3 Dec Patron saint's fiesta, San Javier.
8 Dec Fiesta de la Inmaculada Concepción.

Transport

San Javier
Bus and trufi Línea 102, T03-346 3993, from Santa Cruz Terminal Bimodal regional departures area, 2 a day, 4 hrs, US$3, continue to **Concepción**. Also **Flota 31 del Este** (poor buses, T03-334 9390, same price) and **Jenecherú**, T03-348 8618, daily at 2000, US$4.25, *bus-cama* US$5, continuing to Concepción and, on Tue, Thu, Sat, **San Ignacio**. Various taxi-*trufi* companies also operate from regional departures area, US$5, 3½ hrs.

Concepción
Bus To/from **Santa Cruz**, companies as above, US$3.55, 6½ hrs, and **Jenecherú**, as above, US$5-5.75. To **San Ignacio de Velasco**, buses pass though from Santa Cruz (many at night); **31 del Este** leaves from C Germán Busch in Concepción. Concepción to **San Javier**, 1 hr, US$1.50.

San Ignacio de Velasco
Bus and trufi From **Santa Cruz**, companies as above, plus **Trans Bolivia** (daily, T03-336 3866), from Terminal Bimodal depart 1830-2000, including **Jenecherú** (Tue, Thu, Sat, most luxurious buses, see above), US$7, *bus-cama* US$7.75, 10 hrs; returning 1800-1900. For daytime services, *trufis* from regional departures area 0900 daily (with minimum 7 passengers), US$15, 8 hrs. To **San José de Chiquitos**, see San José Transport, below. To **San Rafael** (US$2, 2½ hrs) via **Santa Ana** (US$1, 1 hr) **Expreso Baruc**, 24 de Septiembre y Kennedy, daily at 1400; returning 0600. To **San Miguel**, *trufis* leave when full from Mercado de Comida, US$1.75, 40 mins, bus US$0.75. **Trans Bolivia** and **Jenecherú** services also go to San Miguel and San Rafael (US$6.50-7.75 from Santa Cruz). To **San Matías** (for Cáceres, Brazil) several daily passing through from

Santa Cruz starting 0400, US$12, 8 hrs. To **Pontes e Lacerda** (Brazil), **Rápido Monte Cristo**, from Club Social on the plaza, Wed and Sat 0900, US$22, 8-9 hrs; returning Tue and Fri, 0630. All roads to Brazil are poor. The best option to Pontes e Lacerda is via Vila Bela (Brazil), used by **Amanda Tours** (T7608 8476 in Bolivia, T65-9926 8522 in Brazil), from **El Corralito** restaurant by the market, Tue, Thu, Sun 0830, US$28; returning Mon, Wed, Fri 0600.

San José de Chiquitos
Bus and trufi To **Santa Cruz** many companies pass through starting 1700 daily, US$7-10.55. Also *trufis*, leave when full, US$10, 3½ hrs. To **Puerto Suárez**, buses pass through 1600-2300, US$10, 4 hrs. To **San Ignacio de Velasco** via San Rafael and San Miguel, **Flota Universal** (poor road, terrible buses), Mon, Wed, Fri, Sat at 0700, US$5, 5 hrs, returning 1400; also **31 de Julio**, Tue, Thu, Sun from San Ignacio at 0645, returning 1500.

Train Westbound, the **Ferrobús** passes through San José Tue, Thu, Sat at 0150, arriving Santa Cruz 0700; **Expreso Oriental**, Tue, Thu, Sun 2305, arriving 0540. Eastbound, the **Ferrobús** passes through San José Tue, Thu, Sun 2308, arriving **Quijarro** 0700 next day; **Expreso Oriental** Mon, Wed, Fri 1930, arriving 0602 next day. See Santa Cruz, Transport (page 460) and www.fo.com.bo for fares and additional information.

East of San José de Chiquitos
Bus and trufi To **Chochís** from San José de Chiquitos, with **Perla del Oriente**, daily 0800 and 1500, US$3, 2 hrs; continuing to **Roboré**, US$1, 1 hr more; Roboré to San José via Chochís 0815 and 1430. Roboré bus terminal is by the highway, a long walk from town, but some buses go by the plaza before leaving; enquire locally. From **Santiago de Chiquitos** to Roboré, Mon-Sat at 0700, US$1, 45 mins; returning 1000; taxi Roboré–Santiago about US$15. Buses to/from Quijarro stop at **Aguas Calientes**; taxi Roboré–Aguas Calientes

about US$22 return. From Roboré to **Santa Cruz**, several companies, from US$7, 7-9 hrs; also *trufis* 0900, 1400, 1800, US$14.50, 5 hrs. From Roboré to **Quijarro** with **Perla del Oriente**, 4 daily, US$4, 4 hrs; also *trufis* leave when full, US$8, 3 hrs.

Train All trains stop in Roboré (see www. fo.com.bo), but not in Chochís or Aguas Calientes. Enquire in advance if they might stop to let you off at these stations.

Parque Nacional Noel Kempff Mercado

Road/bus All overland journeys are long and arduous, take supplies. The unpaved roads to the park turn off the Concepción–San Ignacio road at Santa Rosa de la Roca, 79 km before San Ignacio (the better route, well signed, petrol at the turn-off), or Carmen Ruiz, 47 km before San Ignacio. Florida is 200 km northeast. Paso Firme is a further 129 km, via Porvenir, on an abysmal road. A bus runs **Santa Cruz–Piso Firme** (via Santa Rosa de la Roca, not San Ignacio), **Trans Bolivia**, C Melchor Pinto entre 2do y 3er Anillo, T03-336 3866, once a week (schedule changes often), US$24, 16 hrs minimum, very rough and exhausting. Otherwise the park can be reached by hired 4WD vehicle (US$100 a day) or on a tour. For **Pimenteiras do Oeste** (Brazil) see San Ignacio Transport (above) to Pontes e Lacerda and make connections there via Vilhena. This route is no easier than on the Bolivian side. Even hiring a 4WD vehicle to get to the park via Brazil is hard-going.

Quijarro and Puerto Suárez

Air Puerto Suárez airport is 6 km north of town, T03-976 2347; airport tax US$2. Flights to **Santa Cruz** with **TAM**, 3 times a week. Don't buy tickets for flights originating in Puerto Suárez in Corumbá, these cost more.

Bus Buses from Quijarro pick up passengers in Puerto Suárez (but not Arroyo Concepción) en route to **Santa Cruz**, many companies, departures 1000-1130 and 1900-2030, *ejecutivo* US$14 and up, 8-10 hrs.

Taxi Quijarro to the border (**Arroyo Concepción**) US$1.40; to **Puerto Suárez** US$1 pp, more at night. Beware overcharging when arriving from Brazil. You will be approached by Bolivian taxi drivers who offer to hold your luggage while you clear immigration. These are the most expensive cabs (US$5 to Quijarro, US$15 to Puerto Suárez). Instead, keep your gear with you while your passport is stamped, then walk 200 m past the bridge to the **Preferida** bus office where other taxis wait (US$1.40 to Quijarro). *Colectivos* to Puerto Suárez leave Quijarro when full from Av Bolívar corner Av Luis de la Vega, US$1.

Train With paving of the highway from Santa Cruz train service is in less demand, but it remains a viable option. Ticket office in Quijarro station Mon-Sat 0730-1200, 1430-1800, Sun 0730-1100. Purchase tickets directly at the train station (passport required; do not buy train tickets for Bolivia in Brazil). The **Ferrobús** leaves Quijarro Mon, Wed, Fri 1800, arriving Santa Cruz 0700 next day; **Expreso Oriental**, Tue, Thu, Sun 1300, arriving 0540 next day. See Santa Cruz Transport (page 460) and www.fo.com.bo for fares and additional information.

Northern
lowlands

Bolivia's northern lowlands account for about 70% of national territory. Flat savannahs and dense tropical jungle stretch northwards from the great cordilleras, sparsely populated and mostly unvisited by tourists. Improved roads and frequent flights, particularly to Rurrenabaque and Trinidad, are opening up the area, and wildlife and rainforest expeditions are becoming increasingly popular. Most people head to Rurrenabaque, which gives access to two large and spectacularly diverse protected natural areas: Madidi National Park and the Pilón Lajas Biosphere Reserve. Here are several highly regarded and successful community tourism projects that allow visitors to experience life in the jungle and on the pampas.

Beni department has 53% of the country's birds and 50% of its mammals, but destruction of forest and habitat by loggers and colonists is proceeding at an alarming rate.

Caranavi to San Borja *Colour map 3, B3.*

From Caranavi (see page 390), a road runs north to Sapecho, where a bridge crosses the Río Beni. Beyond Sapecho (7 km from the bridge), the road passes through Palos Blancos (several cheap lodgings). The road between Sapecho and

Tip...

Fly from La Paz to Rurrenabaque (or vice versa) for outstanding views of the dramatic Cordillera Real.

Yucumo, three hours from Sapecho tránsito, is a good all-weather gravel surface. There are basic *hospedajes* and restaurants in **Yucumo** where a road branches northwest, fording rivers several times on its way to Rurrenabaque. Taking the eastern branch from Yucumo it is 50 km (one to two hours) to **San Borja** (see page 485).

Rurrenabaque *Colour map 3, B3.*

The charming, picturesque jungle town of Rurre (as the locals call it), on the Río Beni, is the main jumping-off point for tours in the Bolivian Amazon and pampas, from two- to four-day trips through to full expeditions. Across the river is the smaller town of San Buenaventura (canoe US$0.15). Despite its growth as a trading, transport and ecotourism centre, Rurre is a pleasant town to walk around, although the climate is usually humid. Market day is Sunday. There are two ATMs, both on Comercio near the intersection with Aniceto, but don't rely on either of them.

Jungle tours There are two types of tours from Rurrenabaque: jungle and pampas tours. See below for the latter. Jungle tours normally involve travelling by boat on the Ríos Beni and Tuichi. Lodging is either in purpose-built camps on higher-end tours, or tents at the budget end. Tours are long enough for most people to get a good feeling for life in the jungle and to experience community-run lodges. In the rainy season the jungle is very hot and humid with more biting insects and fewer animals to be seen. The best place for a one-day tour is ☆**San Miguel del Bala**, in a beautiful setting, 3 km from the entrance to Madidi. They also have overnight programmes (see Where to stay, below). Other lodges are in the Parque Nacional Madidi, reached by boat a minimum of three hours' upstream.

★Parque Nacional Madidi *Colour map 3, B2.*

Headquarters in San Buenaventura, C Libertad, about 4 blocks upriver from the plaza, T03-892 2540. US$16 entry is collected near the dock in San Buenaventura. All visitors must disembark to have their permit checked on entry to the park, just past the Estrecho de Bala. Insect repellent and sun protection are essential. See www.sernap.gob.bo.

Parque Nacional Madidi is quite possibly the most bio-diverse of all protected areas on the planet. It is the variety of habitats, from the freezing Andean peaks of the Cordillera Apolobamba in the southwest (reaching nearly 6000 m), through cloud, elfin and dry forest to steaming tropical jungle and pampas (neotropical savannah) in the north and east, that account for the array of flora and fauna within the park's boundaries. In an area roughly the size of Wales or El Salvador (1,895,750 ha) are an estimated over 1100 bird species, 10 species of primate, five species of cat (with healthy populations of jaguar and puma), giant anteaters and many reptiles. Madidi is at the centre of a bi-national system of parks that spans the Bolivia–Peru border. The Heath river on Madidi's northwestern border forms the two countries' frontier and links with the Tambopata National Reserve in Peru. To the southwest the Area Protegida Apolobamba protects extensive mountain ecosystems. It is easiest to visit the lowland areas of Madidi through Rurrenabaque.

☆**Pampas tours** In the more open terrain of the pampas you will see a lot of wildlife: howler, squirrel and capuchin monkeys, caiman, capybara, pink dolphins and a huge variety of birds. These will be seen in the gallery forest as you travel on boat trips on the slow-moving river. To see anacondas, not very likely these days, you may have to wade through knee-deep water in the wide-open pampas; wear appropriate footwear (boots may be provided). Community tourism is being developed at ☆**Santa Rosa de Yacuma**, 100 km northeast of Rurre (for information contact **FAN**, page 454). There is a fee of US$18.75 to enter the Area Protegida Municipal. All pampas tours involve a four-hour jeep ride to El Puerto de Santa Rosa, 7 km beyond Santa Rosa on the Río Yacuma. There is an *albergue* at El Puerto and boats to other lodges depart from here.

Pilón Lajas Biosphere Reserve and Indigenous Territory *Colour map 3, B3.*
HQ at Campero y Germán Busch, Rurrenabaque, T03-892 2246, crtmpilonlajas@yahoo.com, www.sernap.gob.bo, entrance fee US$18.75.

Beyond the Beni River in the southeast runs the Pilón Lajas Biosphere Reserve and Indigenous Territory (400,000 ha), home to the Tsimane and Mosetene peoples. Together with Madidi, it constitutes approximately 60,000 sq km, one of the largest systems of protected land in the neotropics. Set up under the auspices of UNESCO, Pilón Lajas has one of the continent's most intact Amazonian rainforest ecosystems, as well as an incredible array of tropical forest animal life.

Listings Madidi and Rurrenabaque

Tourist information

Rurrenabaque

Infotur municipal tourist office
Abaroa y Vaca Díez, turismorurre@hotmail.com. Mon-Fri 0800-1200, 1430-1830, Sat 0900-1100.
General information and information on tours, operators, hotels and restaurants in Spanish, English and French. Kiosks may open at the bus station and airport.

Regional tourist office
Abaroa casi Santa Cruz.
Mainly for statistics and records, but they can give general information.

Where to stay

Rurrenabaque

$$-$ Hostal Pahuichi
Comercio y Vaca Díez, T03-892 2558.
Some big rooms, cheaper with shared bath, electric shower, fan, breakfast extra, rooftop views, good.

$ Beni
Comercio y Arce, along the river, T03-892 2408.
Best rooms have a/c and TV, hot showers, cheaper with fan and without bath, kitchen facilities. Spacious, good service.

$ El Ambaibo
Santa Cruz entre Bolívar y Busch, T03-892 2107, hotel_ambaibo@hotmail.com.
Includes breakfast and airport transfer, private and shared rooms, large pool (US$2.50 for non-guests), parking, also has dorms at **Tuky**, also on Santa Cruz, T03-892 2686, Ambaibo Backpackers Hotel on Facebook.

$ El Curichal
Comercio 1490, 7 blocks from plaza, T03-892 2647, Facebook: ElCurichalhostel.
Nice courtyard, rooms with and without bath, dorms, lockers, hammocks, laundry and small kitchen facilities, pool, book exchange, games, helpful staff. Popular economy option.

$ Hostal Lobo
Upstream end of Comercio, no fixed phone.

Cheap rooms in large breezy building overlooking the river, shared bath, some double rooms, with breakfast and Wi-Fi, laundry service, *parrillada*.

$ Los Tucanes de Rurrenabaque
Arce y Bolívar, T7153 4521,
www.hotel-tucanes.com.
Big place with thatched structures, hammocks and an open communal area, rooms with and without bath. Also has **$$ La Isla resort**, on the outskirts between Av Bolívar and Av Amutari, T03-892 2127, www.islatucanes.com.

$ Oriental
Pellicioli, on plaza, T03-892 2401.
Hot showers, fan, small breakfast included, quiet, hammocks in peaceful garden, family-run, Wi-Fi in public areas. A good option.

$ Santa Ana
Abaroa entre Vaca Díez y Campero,
T03-892 2399.
A variety of rooms, all cheap and simple, laundry, pleasant hammock area in garden, no breakfast.

Jungle trips

San Miguel del Bala
45-min boat trip upriver from Rurre (office at C Comercio entre Vaca Díez y Santa Cruz), T03-892 2394, www.sanmigueldelbala.com.
This award-winning community lodge gives a good taste of the jungle, offers day trips, well-laid-out trails and has en suite cabins in a delightful setting, good restaurant with typical dishes, including vegetarian, attentive staff, bar and a pool fed by a waterfall. It is owned and operated by the indigenous Tacana community. They have a 2nd lodge in Madidi with similar attention, walks, community visits. 3 days/2 nights cost US$240 pp. Advance booking required. Highly recommended.

Parque Nacional Madidi
Berraco del Madidi is 6 hrs upriver from Rurrenabaque (office Comercio y Vaca Díez,

T03-892 2966, www.berracodelmadidi.com). This lodge is run by members of the San José de Uchupiamonas community. Fully enclosed tents with mosquito screens on covered platforms, good mattresses, clean toilets, cold showers, good kitchen with excellent food, well-run, professional, plenty of activities, US$480 for 3 days/2 nights, also longer programmes and specialist trips.
Chalalán Ecolodge is 5 hrs upriver from Rurrenabaque, at San José de Uchupiamonas, in Madidi National Park. La Paz office: Sagárnaga 189, Edif Shopping Doryan, of 23, T02-231 1451; in Rurrenabaque, C Comercio entre Campero y Vaca Díez, T03-892 2419, www.chalalan. com. This is Bolivia's top ecotourism project, founded by the Quechua Tacana community, Conservation International and the Interamerican Development Bank, and now has a well-deserved international reputation. Accommodation is in thatched cabins, and activities include fantastic wildlife-spotting and birdwatching, guided and self-guided trails, river and lake activities, and relaxing in pristine jungle surroundings. 3-day/2-night packages cost US$410 pp (US$380 with shared bath).
Madidi Jungle Eco Lodge, also run by families from the San José de Uchupiamonas community 3½ hrs from Rurre (office Av Comercio entre Vaca Díez y Campero, T7128 2697, www.madidijungle.com). Rooms around a central garden, comfortable cabins in the forest, with and without shower, hammocks, good regional food, 11 trails to explore with expert guides, other activities include tubing, handicraft-making, piranha fishing. Programmes from 1 to 5 days, US$250-280 pp for 3 days, 2 nights, flexible, responsible and excellent service.

Pilón Lajas Biosphere Reserve and Indigenous Territory

Mapajo
Mapajo Ecoturismo Indígena, Santa Cruz entre Abaroa y Comercio, Rurrenabaque,

T7113 8838, http://mapajo-ecoturismo-indigena.blogspot.co.uk.
A community-run ecolodge 3 hrs by boat from Rurrenabaque has 6 *cabañas* without electricity (take a torch), shared cold showers and a dining room serving traditional meals. You can visit the local community, walk in the forest, go birdwatching, etc. Take insect repellent, wear long trousers and strong footwear.

Restaurants

Rurrenabaque

$$ Casa del Campo
Comercio, opposite El Lobo.
Daily 0730-1400, 1800-2130.
Restaurant in a thatched building with flowers around the terrace.

$$ Juliano's
Santa Cruz casi Bolívar.
Daily 1200-1430, 1800-late.
French and Italian food, good presentation and service. Recommended.

$$ Paititi
Vaca Díez casi Bolívar.
Good Mediterranean-influenced dishes, friendly service.

$$-$ Funky Monkey
Comercio entre Santa Cruz y Vaca Díez.
Open 0900-0100.
Big pizzas, imaginative pastas, vegetarian options, grilled meats and fish, bar, lively crowd.

$$-$ Luna Lounge
Abaroa entre Santa Cruz y Vaca Diez.
Open 0800-2200.
International meals, pizza, snacks and drinks, also pool table and sports TV.

$$-$ The Angu's
Comercio entre Santa Cruz y Vaca Díez.
Pizzas, pastas, meat dishes, burgers soups and veggie options. Wi-Fi, music and sports, happy hour 1900-2200.

$ La Perla de Rurre
Bolívar y Vaca Díez. Daily 0730-2100.

Set lunch and à la carte, also breakfast and sandwiches in the morning, good food, eating outside under the mango trees.

Cafés

Café de la Jungla
Comercio y Vaca Díez. Mon-Sat 0800-1630.
Neat little café serving breakfasts, sandwiches, salads, snacks and juices, mostly local produce, Wi-Fi.

Moskkito Bar
Vaca Díez casi Abaroa. Evenings only.
Cool bar for tall jungle tales. Burgers, pizzas, rock music and pool tables.

Panadería París
Abaroa entre Vaca Díez y Santa Cruz.
Mon-Sat 0600-1200.
Delicious croissants and *pain au chocolat*, get there early, also quiches and pizzas.

What to do

Rurrenabaque

Jungle and pampas tours cost about US$80 pp plus the park fee for a typical 3-day tour by a responsible operator. Prices and quality both vary but booking in Rurre is usually cheaper than in La Paz. Much effort is being put into ensuring that all companies adhere to codes of practice that do not permit hunting, feeding animals, especially monkeys, catching caiman or handling anaconda, but there are still a few that do so. If you do not want to encourage such activities, ask in advance what is offered on the tour. Before signing up for a tour, check the Municipal Infotur office for updates and try to talk to other travellers who have just come back. Guides who belong to Agnatur (Asociación de Guías Naturalistas de Turismo Responsable), from the same community as Chalalán, have pioneered respect for wildlife here, first in Madidi and recently in the pampas. Ask for a member, or for an operator who uses them.

Some operators pool customers, so you may not go with the company you booked with. There are many more agencies in town than those listed below. Shop around and choose carefully.

Tour operators

Bala Tours, *Av Santa Cruz y Comercio, T03-892 2527, www.balatours.com.* Arranges pampas and jungle tours, singly or combined, with their own lodge in each (with bath and solar power), also specialist programmes, visits to local communities and the Guanay-Rurrenabaque route. English-speaking guides. Award-winning, services and lodges recently upgraded, top-class service. Recommended.

Donato Tours, *Vaca Díez entre Abaroa y Comercio, T7126 0919, www.donatotours.com.* Regular tours plus the opportunity to stay in a community in Pilón Lajas for 1 to 20 days.

Lipiko Tours, *Av Santa Cruz entre Bolívar y Abaroa, T02-231 5408, http://lipiko.com.* Rurre office of a company offering tours throughout Bolivia.

Madidi Expeditions, *Comercio entre Vaca Díez y Campero, T7199 8372, www.madidi expeditions.com.* Responsible tours to Madidi and the pampas, chief guide Norman is very experienced, knowledgeable and professional. Good staff. Recommended.

Madidi Travel, *Comercio y Vaca Díez, T03-892 2153, in La Paz, Linares 947, T02-231 8313, www.madidi-travel.com.* Specializes in tours to the private Serere Sanctuary in the Madidi Mosaic (details on website), minimum 3 days/2 nights, good guiding. Recommended.

Mashaquipe Tours, *Abaroa entre Pando y Arce, T03-892 2704, www.mashaquipeecotours. com.* Jungle and pampas tours run by an organization which works with communities, with lodges in both locations. They offer combined jungle and pampas tours (eg 5 days US$390 pp), also short tours. Small groups, safe, most guides speak English, a popular company.

Caranavi to San Borja

Bus See page 393 for buses in Caranavi. **Yucumo** is on the La Paz–Caranavi–Rurrenabaque and San Borja bus routes. Rurrenabaque–La Paz bus passes through about 1800. If travelling to Rurrenabaque by bus take extra food in case there is a delay (anything from road blocks to flat tyres to high river levels). **Flota Yungueña** daily except Thu at 1300 from San Borja to **La Paz**, 19 hrs via Caranavi. Also San Borja to **Rurrenabaque**, **Santa Rosa**, **Riberalta**, **Guayaramerín** about 3 times a week. Minibuses and *camionetas* normally run daily between San Borja and **Trinidad** throughout the year, US$15, about 7 hrs including 20 mins crossing of Río Mamoré on ferry barge (up to 14 hrs in wet season). Fuel available at Yolosa, Caranavi, Yucumo, San Borja and San Ignacio.

Rurrenabaque

Air Several daily flights to/from **La Paz** with **Amaszonas**, Comercio entre Santa Cruz y Vaca Diez, T03-892 2472, US$97; and 3 a week with **TAM**, Santa Cruz y Abaroa,

T03-892 2398/7113 2500. Both also fly to **Trinidad**, but not daily. Book flights as early as possible and buy onward ticket on arrival. Check flight times in advance; they change frequently. Delays and cancellations are common. Airport taxes total US$2.75 (airport and municipal taxes). Airlines provide transport to/from town, US$1.25; confirm flight 24 hrs in advance and be at airline office 2 hrs before departure.

Bus The new bus terminal is near the airport. To/from **La Paz** via Caranavi with **Flota Yungueña**, **Totaí** and **Vaca Díez**; 18-20 hrs, US$10, daily at 1030 and Sat-Mon also at 1900. See under Sorata and Cocoico, Transport, for alternative routes to Rurre. Some La Paz buses continue to **Riberalta** (US$19, 13 hrs from Rurre), **Guayaramerín** (US$20, 15 hrs) or **Cobija** (US$35, 30 hrs). Rurrenebaque–**Riberalta** may take 6 days or more in the wet season. Take lots of food, torch and be prepared to work. To **Trinidad**, with **Trans Guaya** (buses) or **Trans Rurrenabaque** (minibuses) daily, **Flota Yungueña** Mon, Wed, via **Yucumo** and **San Borja**, US$20, check that the road is open.

San Borja to Trinidad

jungle tours and river trips

San Borja, a relatively wealthy cattle-raising centre (population 40,865) with simple hotels and restaurants clustered near the plaza, is 50 km east of Yucumo. The road east from San Borja to Trinidad passes through part of the Pilón Lajas Reserve (see page 481). There are five or six river crossings and, in the wetlands, a multitude of waterfowl. At times the road can be flooded out. Another route into Beni Department is from the lowland road between Cochabamba and Santa Cruz and then by river from Puerto Villarroel.

San Ignacio de Moxos *Colour map 3, B3.*

San Ignacio de Moxos, 90 km west of Trinidad, is known as the folklore capital of the Beni Department. It's a quiet town (population 22,165) with a mainly indigenous population; 60% are Macheteros, who speak their own language. San Ignacio still maintains the traditions of the Jesuit missions with big fiestas, especially during Holy Week and the ☆**Fiesta del Santo Patrono de Moxos** (see Festivals, below).

Trinidad *Colour map 3, C3.*

The hot and humid capital of the lowland Beni Department (population 106,420, altitude 327 m) is a dusty city in the dry season, with many streets unpaved. Primarily a service centre for the surrounding ranches and communities, most travellers find themselves in the area for boats up and down the ☆**Río Mamoré**. There are two ports, Almacén and Varador, check at which one your boat will be docked. **Puerto Varador** is 13 km from town on the Río Mamoré on the road between Trinidad and San Borja; cross the river over the main bridge by the market, walk down to the service station by the police checkpoint and take a truck, US$1.75. **Almacén** is 8 km from the city. The main mode of transport in Trinidad is the motorbike (even for taxis, US$0.50 in city); rental on plaza from US$2.50 per hour, US$10 per half day. There are several ATMs on or near the central Plaza Ballivián.

About 5 km from town is the **Laguna Suárez**, with plenty of wildlife; swimming is safe where the locals swim, near the café with the jetty (elsewhere there are stingrays and alligators). Motorbike taxi from Trinidad, US$1.50.

Listings *San Borja to Trinidad*

Tourist information

Trinidad

Beni Department Tourist offices
Prefectura building, Joaquín de Sierra y La Paz, ground floor, T03-462 4831, see TurismoBeniBolivia on Facebook.

Municipal Tourism offices
Félix Pinto Saucedo y Nicolás Suárez, T03-462 1322.

Where to stay

San Ignacio de Moxos
There are some cheap *alojamientos* on and around the main plaza.

Trinidad

$$$ Campanario
6 de Agosto 80, T03-462 4733, www.hotel-campanario.com.
Rooms with a/c and frigobar, meeting room, restaurant, bar, pool.

$$ Jacaranda Suites
La Paz entre Pedro de la Rocha y 18 de Noviembre, T462 2400.
Good services, restaurant, pool, meeting rooms, internet.

$ Copacabana
Tomás M Villavicencio, 3 blocks from plaza, T03-462 2811.
Good value, some beds uncomfortable, cheaper with shared bath, helpful staff.

$ Monteverde
6 de Agosto 76, T03-462 2750.
With a/c (cheaper with fan), frigobar, owner speaks English. Recommended.

$ Residencial 18 de Noviembre
Av 6 de Agosto 135, T03-462 1272.
With and without bath, welcoming, laundry facilities.

Restaurants

Trinidad
There are several good fish restaurants in **Barrio Pompeya**, south of the plaza across river.

$$ Club Social 18 de Noviembre
N Suárez y Vaca Díez on plaza.
Good-value lunch, lively, popular with locals.

$$ El Tábano
Villavicencio entre Mamoré y Néstor Suárez.
Good fish and local fare, relaxed atmosphere.

$$ La Estancia
*Barrio Pompeya, on Ibare entre
Muiba y Velarde.*
A good choice for excellent steaks.

$ La Casona
Plaza Ballivián. Closed Tue.
Good pizzas and set lunch.

Heladería Oriental
On plaza.
Good coffee, ice cream, cakes, popular
with locals.

Festivals

San Ignacio de Moxos
Late Jul-early Aug **Fiesta del Santo
Patrono de Moxos**, is the most important
and colourful fiesta in the Bolivian Amazon
and features many traditional elements of
Beni culture, with sports, food and drink
and, above all, processions and dances
with feather headdresses, mask, wooden
machetes and huge wind instruments.

What to do

Trinidad
Most agents offer excursions to local
estancias and jungle tours. Most estancias
can also be reached independently in 1 hr
by hiring a motorbike.
Flotel Reina de Enín, *Av Comunidad Europea
624, T7391 2965, http://amazoncruiser.com.bo.*
Cruises on the Mamoré River in the Ibare-
Mamoré Reserve. Floating hotel with comfy
berths with bath, US$455 pp for 3-day/
2-night cruise includes: dolphin watching,
horse riding, visiting local communities,
jungle walks, swimming and piranha fishing.
La Ruta del Bufeo, *T7281 8317, laruta.
delbufeo on Facebook.* Specializes in river
tours for seeing dolphins.
Moxos, *6 de Agosto 114, T03-462 1141.*
Multi-day river and jungle tours with
camping. Recommended.

Paraíso Travel, *6 de Agosto 138, T03-462 0692,
paraiso@entelnet.bo.* Offers excursions to
Laguna Suárez, Rio Mamoré, camping and
birdwatching tours.

Transport

San Ignacio de Moxos
Bus The Trinidad to San Borja bus stops
at the **Donchanta** restaurant for lunch,
otherwise difficult to find transport to San
Borja. Minibus to Trinidad daily at 0730 from
plaza, also *camionetas*, check road conditions
and times beforehand.

Trinidad
Air Flights with **TAM** (Bolívar 42, T02-268
1111) to **La Paz**, **Santa Cruz**, **Cochabamba**,
Riberalta, **Guayaramerín** and other
northern destinations. To **La Paz** and
Santa Cruz with **Ecojet** (Av 6 de Agosto
146, T03-465 2617). **Amaszonas** (18 de
Noviembre 267, T03-462 2426) Mon, Wed,
Fri to **Rurrenabaque**. Airport, T03-462 0678.
Mototaxi to airport US$1.50.

Boat ☆Cargo boats down the Río Mamoré
to **Guayaramerín** take passengers, 3-4 days,
assuming no breakdowns, best organized
from Puerto Varador (speak to the Port
Captain). **Argos** is recommended as friendly,
US$25 pp, take water, fresh fruit, toilet paper
and ear-plugs; only for the hardy traveller.

Bus Bus station is on Rómulo Mendoza,
between Beni and Pinto, 9 blocks east of
main plaza. Motorbike taxis will take people
with backpacks from bus station to centre for
US$0.50. To **Santa Cruz** (10 hrs on a paved road,
US$9-13, *bus-cama* US$20) and **Cochabamba**
(US$14-20, 20 hrs), with **Copacabana**, **Mopar**
and **Bolívar** mostly overnight (*bus-cama*
available). To **Rurrenabaque**, US$20,
12-20 hrs. Enquire locally what services are
running to San Borja and **La Paz**. Similarly
to **Riberalta** and **Guayaramerín**.

Riberalta *Colour map 3, A3.*

At the confluence of the Madre de Dios and Beni rivers, Riberalta (population 97,982) is off the beaten track and a centre for brazil nut production. It's very laid back, but take care if your bus drops you in the middle of the night and everything is closed. There are places to eat on the plaza and near the airport. Change cash in shops and on street.

Guayaramerín and border with Brazil *Colour map 3, A3.*

Guayaramerín (population 39,010), 84 km from Riberalta by paved road, is a cheerful, prosperous little town on the bank of the Río Mamoré, opposite the Brazilian town of Guajará-Mirim. There are several restaurants and cafés around the plaza. It has an important Zona Libre. Passage between the two towns is unrestricted; boat trip US$1.75 (more at night).

Bolivian immigration Avenida Costanera near port; open 0800-1100, 1400-1800. Passports must be stamped here when leaving, or entering Bolivia. On entering Bolivia, passports must also be stamped at the Bolivian consulate in Guajará-Mirim. The Brazilian consulate is on 24 de Septiembre 28, Guayaramerín, T03-855 3766, open 0900-1300, 1400-1700; visas for entering Brazil are given here. To enter Brazil you must have a yellow fever certificate, or be inoculated at the health ministry (free). Exchange cash at the dock on the Bolivian side where rates are written up on blackboards, although there is an ATM at the Banco do Brasil in Guajará-Mirim; no facilities for cash.

Cobija *Colour map 3, A2.*

The capital of the lowland Department of Pando lies on the Río Acre which forms the frontier with Brazil.

A single-tower suspension bridge crosses the river to Brasiléia. As a duty-free zone, shops in centre have a huge selection of imported consumer goods at bargain prices. Brazilians and Peruvians flock here to stock up. As this is a border area, watch out for scams and cons. **Bolivian immigration** ⓘ *Miguel Farah 41 esq Av Internacional, T03-842 2081, open daily 0900-1800.* **Brazilian consulate** ⓘ *Av René Barrientos s/n, T03-842 2110, Mon-Fri 0830-1230.* There are *casas de cambio* on Avenida Internacional and Avenida Cornejo. Most shops will accept dollars or reais, and exchange money.

Listings Riberalta to Brazil

Where to stay

Riberalta
Ask for a fan and check the water supply.

$$ Colonial
Plácido Méndez 745, T03-852 3018.
Charming colonial *casona*, large, well-furnished rooms, no singles, nice gardens and courtyard, comfortable, good beds, helpful owners.

$$ Jomali
Av Nicolás Suárez, beside Banco Ganadero, T03-852 2398, www.hoteljomali.com.
Central, smart hotel with big rooms and suites, a/c, comfortable, central patio.

$ Alojamiento Comercial Lazo
NG Salvatierra 244, T03-852 2380.
With a/c, cheaper with fan, comfortable, laundry facilities, good value.

Guayaramerín

$$ San Carlos
6 de Agosto 347, 4 blocks from port,
T03-855 3555.
With a/c, hot showers, changes dollars cash and reais, swimming pool, reasonable restaurant.

$ Santa Ana 25 de Mayo 611
Close to airstrip in town, T03-855 3900.
With bath, fan, cheap and recommended.

Cobija

$$ Diana
Av 9 de Febrero 123, T03-842 2073.
A/c, TV, safe, buffet breakfast, pool.

$$ Nanijos
Av 9 de Febrero 147, T03-842 2230.
Includes breakfast, a/c, TV, *comedor* does good lunch, helpful.

$$ Triller
Av Internacional 640, T03-842 2024.
Bath, a/c (cheaper with fan), restaurant.

What to do

Riberalta
Riberalta Tours, *Av Sucre 634, T03-852 3475, www.riberaltatours.com.* Multi-day river and jungle tours, airline tickets, very helpful.

Transport

Riberalta
Air To **La Paz** and **Santa Cruz** with **Ecojet** (Av Bernardino Ochoa 966, T03-852 4837). **TAM** (Av Chuquisaca y Salvatierra, T03-852 2646) to **Trinidad**, **Santa Cruz**, **Cochabamba** and **La Paz**. Expect cancellations in the wet season.

Boat Cargo boats carry passengers along the **Río Madre de Dios**, but they are infrequent. There are no boats to Rurrenabaque.

Bus Roads to all destinations are appalling, even worse in the wet season. Several companies (including **Yungueña**) to **La Paz**, via **Rurrenabaque** and **Caranavi** daily,
35 hrs to 3 days or more, US$30. To **Trinidad** via Rurrenabaque and San Borja, 25-35 hrs. To **Guayaramerín** 7 daily, US$5, 1 hr, paved road. To **Cobija** several companies, none with daily service, 10-11 hrs.

Guayaramerín
Air Flights to **La Paz** with **Ecojet** (Sucre entre Beni y 16 de Julio, T03-855 9176). **TAM** has same services as for Riberalta. Airport is southwest of centre.

Boat Check the notice of vessels leaving port on the Port Captain's board, prominently displayed near the immigration post on the riverbank. Boats sailing up the Mamoré to **Trinidad** are not always willing to take passengers.

Bus Buses leave from General Federico Román. Same long-haul services as Riberalta, above. To **Riberalta** 1 hr, US$5, daily 0700-1730.

Cobija
Air Flights to **La Paz** and **Santa Cruz** with **Ecojet**. **TAM** (Av 9 de Febrero 49, T02-268 1111), to **La Paz** or **Trinidad** on alternating days.

Bus **Flota Yungueña** and **Flota Cobija** to **La Paz** via Riberalta and Rurrenabaque, 2-3 days or more, US$30-40. To **Riberalta** with several bus companies, depart from 2 de Febrero, most on Wed, Fri, Sun at 0600; good all-weather surface; 2 river crossings on pontoon rafts, takes 10-11 hrs.

Taxi Taxis charge US$0.75 in centre, but more expensive beyond, according to time and distance. Besides taxis there are motorbike taxis (US$0.75).

Border with Brazil
Taxis over the international bridge to **Brasiléia** are expensive. Brasiléia can also be reached by canoe, US$0.50. The bridge can be crossed on foot as well. Dress neatly when approaching Brazilian customs. From Brasiléia, **Real Norte**, has buses to **Rio Branco** and **Assis Brasil**, and **Taxis Brasileiros** run to **Rio Branco**.

This is
Ecuador

Tucked in between Peru and Colombia, this country is small enough for you to have breakfast with scarlet macaws in the jungle, lunch in the lee of a snow-capped peak and, at tea time, be eyeballed by an iguana whose patch of Pacific beach you have just borrowed.

A multitude of national parks and conservation areas emphasise the incredible variety of Ecuador. They include mangroves; an avenue of volcanoes – many of them active – striding across the equator; forests growing on the dry Pacific coast, in the clouds and under the Amazonian rains; not forgetting all the animals and birds which flourish in these habitats. In fact, as Ecuador is one of the richest places in the world for birds, with some of the planet's most beautiful species, the country is a prime birdwatching destination.

The capital, Quito, and the southern highland city of Cuenca, are two of the gringo centres of South America, bursting at the seams with language schools, tour operators and restaurants. The smaller towns and villages of Ecuador offer the most authentic experience. Indulge your senses at one of their many markets, with dizzying arrays of textiles, ceramics, carvings and other crafts, not to mention the cornucopia of fresh produce.

The exotic wildlife of the Galápagos Islands will also keep you enthralled, whether it's watching an albatross take off on its flight path, swimming with marine iguanas, sea lions and penguins, or admiring the sexual paraphernalia of the magnificent frigatebird. If the Galápagos are beyond your budget, then Isla de la Plata, in Parque Nacional Machalilla, is a more accessible alternative for seeing marine life.

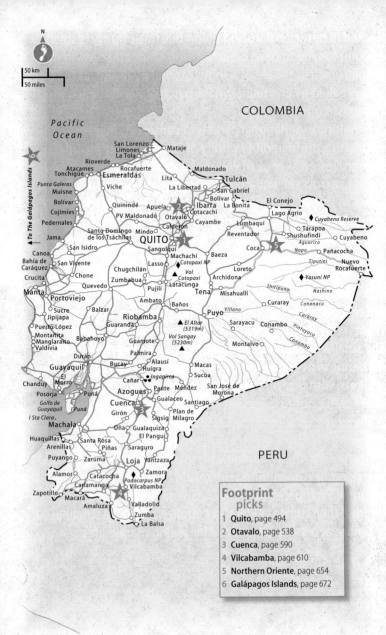

N

50 km
50 miles

Pacific
Ocean

COLOMBIA

To The Galápagos Islands

San Lorenzo
Limones   Mataje
La Tola
Rioverde
Atacames   Rocafuerte   Maldonado
Tonchigüe Esmeraldas
Punta Galeras   Lita   Tulcán
Muisne   Viche   La Libertad
Bolívar   San Gabriel
Cojimíes   Quinindé   Apuela   Bolívar La Bonita   El Conejo
Pedernales   PV Maldonado Ibarra   Lago Agrio   ◆ Cuyabeno Reserve
                Santo Domingo Otavalo Cotacachi   Lumbaquí   Tarapoa
Jama   de los Tsáchilas Mindo Calderón Cayambe Reventador Shushufindi   Cuyabeno
Canoa   San Isidro   QUITO   Baeza   Coca ⭐5 Aguarico Pañacocha
Bahía de San Vicente   Sangolquí Machachi   Loreto   Napo Nuevo
Caráquez Chone   Chugchilán Lasso Cotopaxi NP Archidona   Tiputini   Rocafuerte
Crucita   Zumbahua Pujilí Vol Tena Misahuallí   Shiripuno ◆ Yasuní NP
Manta   Portoviejo Quevedo   Cotopaxi Latacunga   Nashino
        Sucre   Ambato Baños   Puyo   Curaray Cononaco
Jipijapa Balzar Riobamba Guaranda El Altar Villano Sarayacu Conambo Curaray
Puerto López   (5319m)   Pintuyaco Conambo
Montañita Babahoyo Guamote Vol Sangay Montalvo
Manglaralto   Palmira (5230m)
Valdivia Durán Bucay Alausí Macas
Guayaquil   Cañar ● Huigra Sucúa
El Morro   ● Ingapirca   San José de
Chanduy Puná Azogues Paute Méndez Morona
Posorja   Cuenca Gualaceo Santiago
Golfo de I Puná Girón Sigsig Plan de
Guayaquil ⭐3 Oña Milagro
I Sta Clara Machala Gualaquiza
Huaquillas Santa Rosa El Pangui
Arenillas Piñas Saraguro
Puyango Zaruma   Yantzaza
Alamor Catacocha Loja Zamora
Carlamanga Vilcabamba Podocarpus NP
Zapotillo Macará ⭐4 Valladolid
Amaluza Zumba
La Balsa

PERU

⭐6 Galápagos Islands

Footprint picks

★ **Quito**, page 494

In a valley at the foot of a volcano, with a colonial centre of steep cobbled streets and fading façades, it isn't any wonder that it was the first city to be declared a UNESCO World Heritage Site.

★ **Otavalo**, page 538

The enormous Saturday market blisters with colour as the *Otavaleños* gather to sell textiles and crafts.

★ **Cuenca**, page 590

The well-preserved colonial centre of Ecuador's third city overflows with flowering plazas and pastel-coloured buildings

★ **Vilcabamba**, page 610

A favourite of expats and travellers alike, this once isolated village has nature reserves on its doorstep and wonderful places to stay and eat.

★ **Northern Oriente**, page 654

Visitors can stay deep in the rainforest in jungle lodges and experience contact with life in the tropical lowlands.

★ **Galápagos Islands**, page 672

An extraordinary collection of islands that have to be seen to be believed.

Quito

★ Few cities have a setting to match that of Quito (2850 m), the second highest capital in Latin America after La Paz. The city is set in a hollow at the foot of the volcano Pichincha (4794 m). The city's charm lies in its colonial centre – the Centro Histórico as it's known – a UNESCO World Heritage Site, where cobbled streets are steep and narrow, dipping to deep ravines. From the top of Cerro Panecillo, 183 m above the city level, there is a fine view of the city below and the encircling cones of volcanoes.

North of the colonial centre is modern Quito with broad avenues lined with contemporary office buildings, fine private residences, parks, embassies and villas. Here you'll find Quito's main nightlife and restaurant area in the district known as La Mariscal, bordered by Avenidas Amazonas, Patria, 12 de Octubre and Orellana.

Weather Quito

January	February	March	April	May	June
18°C 10°C 110mm	18°C 10°C 120mm	18°C 10°C 150mm	18°C 10°C 170mm	18°C 10°C 120mm	19°C 9°C 20mm

July	August	September	October	November	December
19°C 9°C 20mm	19°C 9°C 20mm	19°C 9°C 70mm	19°C 9°C 120mm	19°C 9°C 100mm	18°C 10°C 100mm

Best for
Colonial architecture ▪ Eating out ▪ Museums ▪ Views

Finding your feet

Most places of historical interest are in colonial Quito, while most hotels, restaurants, tour operators and facilities are in the modern city to the north. Quito is a long city stretching from north to south, with Pichincha rising to the west. Its main arteries run the length of the city and traffic congestion along them is a serious problem.

The street numbering system is based on N (Norte), E (Este), S (Sur), Oe (Oeste), plus a number for each street and each building; however, an older system is also still in use.

Getting around

Both colonial Quito and La Mariscal in modern Quito can be explored on foot, but getting between the two requires some form of public transport, using taxis is the best option. Colonial Quito is closed to vehicles Sunday 0900-1600 and main avenues across the city close Sunday 0800-1400 for the *ciclopaseo* (page 517).

There are five parallel public transit lines running north to south on dedicated lanes: the Trole, Ecovía, Metrobus, Corredor Sur and Universidades, as well as city buses. Avenida Occidental or Mariscal Sucre is a more expedite road to the west of the city. The Corredor Periférico Oriental or Simón Bolívar is a bypass east of the city. Roads through Valle de los Chillos and Tumbaco avoid the city.

Safety

For all emergencies T911. Public safety in Quito appears to have improved, however, it is still not a safe city. For further details see page 727. In colonial Quito, the main plazas and nearby streets as well as La Ronda are patrolled by officers from the Policía Metropolitana and Policía de Turismo, who speak some English and are very helpful. The top of El Panecillo is patrolled by neighbourhood brigades (see page 497); however, walking up the stairs is not recommended. In modern Quito

increased police presence has brought some improvement, but La Carolina and La Mariscal districts still call for vigilance at all hours. Plaza Foch (Calle Foch y Reina Victoria) in La Mariscal is one of the patrolled areas, but do not stray outside its perimeter at night. There have been occasional reports of 'express kidnappings', choose your taxi judiciously, see page 525. Do not walk through any city parks in the evening or even in daylight at quiet times. There have been reports of scams on long distance buses leaving Quito, especially to Baños; do not give your hand luggage to anyone and always keep your things on your lap.

Servicio de Seguridad Turística (Tourist Police) offers information and is the place to obtain a police report in case of theft. HQ at Reina Victoria N21-208 y Roca, La Mariscal, T02-254 3983, ssturistica98@gmail.com, open 24 hours; offices at: Plaza de la Independencia, Casa de los Alcaldes, Chile Oe4-66 y García Moreno, T02-295 5785, open Sunday-Wednesday 0900-2400, Thursday-Saturday 0900-0400; La Ronda, Casa de las Artes, Morales y Guayaquil, T02-295 6010, Sunday-Tuesday 0800-2300, Wednesday-Saturday 0800-0400; airport, T02-394 5000, ext 3023, Monday-Friday 0600-2400, Saturday-Sunday 0600-1800; Terminal Quitumbe, Monday-Friday 0800-0030, Saturday-Sunday 0800-1730; and Mitad del Mundo, daily 0800-1800, offers information. There is also a regular police station at Reina Victoria y Baquerizo Moreno, in La Mariscal. A report on a robbery can be filed online at www.gestiondefiscalias.gob.ec/rtourist.

When to go

Quito is within 25 km of the equator, but it stands high enough to make its climate much like that of spring in England, the days pleasantly warm and the nights cool (average low 8°C). The length of days (sunrise to sunset) is almost constant all year. See also the weather chart, opposite.

Colonial Quito

Plaza de la Independencia (Plaza Grande) Quito's revitalized colonial district is a pleasant place to stroll and admire the architecture, monuments and art. At night, the illuminated plazas and churches are very beautiful. The heart of the old city is Plaza de la Independencia or Plaza Grande, whose pink-flowered arupo trees bloom in September. It is dominated by a somewhat grim **Cathedral** ① *entry through museum, Venezuela N3-117 or off Plaza Grande, T02-257 0371, Tue-Sat, 0900-1730, no visits during Mass 0600-0900, US$3 for the museum, US$6 including cupolas, night visits to church on request,* built 1550-1562, with grey stone porticos and green tile cupolas. On its outer walls are plaques listing the names of the founding fathers of Quito, and inside are the tomb of Sucre and a famous Descent from the Cross by the indigenous painter Caspicara. There are many other 17th- and 18th-century paintings; the interior decoration shows Moorish influence. Facing the Cathedral is the **Palacio Arzobispal**, part of which now houses shops. Next to it, in the northwest corner, is the **Hotel Plaza Grande** (1930), with a baroque façade, the first building in the old city with more than two storeys. On the northeast side is the concrete **Municipio**, which fits in quite well. The low colonial Palacio de Gobierno or **Palacio de Carondelet**, silhouetted against the flank of Pichincha, is on the northwest side of the Plaza. On the first floor is a gigantic mosaic mural of Orellana navigating the Amazon. The ironwork on the balconies looking over the main plaza is from the Tuilleries in Paris. Visitors can take **tours** ① *T02-382 7700, www.presidencia.gob.ec, Mon-Fri 0900-1500, Sat 0900-2200, Sun 0900-1600, take passport or copy.* The Municipal Band plays in Plaza de la Independencia every Wednesday at 1100.

South to El Panecillo From Plaza de la Independencia two main streets, Venezuela and García Moreno, lead straight towards El Panecillo. Parallel with Venezuela is Calle Guayaquil, the main shopping street. These streets all run south from the main plaza to meet Calle Morales, better known as **La Ronda**, one of the oldest streets in the city. This narrow cobbled pedestrian way and its colonial homes with wrought iron balconies have been refurbished and house hotels, restaurants, bars, artisans' workshops, cultural centres, galleries and shops. It is a quaint corner of the city growing in popularity for a night out or an afternoon stroll (best Wednesday to Sunday). On García Moreno N3-94 is the beautiful **El Sagrario** ① *Mon-Fri, 0800-1800, Sat-Sun 1000-1400, no entry during Mass, free,* church with a gilded door. The **Centro Cultural Metropolitano** is at the corner of Espejo, housing the municipal library, a museum for the visually impaired, temporary art exhibits and the **Museo Alberto Mena Caamaño** ① *entry on C Espejo, T02-395 2300, ext 155, Tue-Sat 0900-1700, Sun 1000-1600, US$1.50.* This wax museum depicts scenes of Ecuadorean colonial history. The scene of the execution of the revolutionaries of 1809 in the original cell is particularly vivid. The fine Jesuit church of **La Compañía** ① *García Moreno N3-117 y Sucre, T02-258 1895, Mon-Thu 0930-1830, Fri 0930-1730, Sat and holidays 0930-1600, Sun 1200-1600, US$4, students US$2, visits including cupolas and nighttime visits US$6,* has the most ornate and richly sculptured façade and interior. Diagonally opposite is the **Casa Museo María Augusta Urrutia** ① *García Moreno N2-60 y*

Tip...

Because of the altitude, visitors may initially feel some discomfort and should slow their pace for the first 48 hours. The city also has a serious air pollution problem.

BACKGROUND
An ancient city

Archaeological finds suggest that the valley of Quito and surrounding areas have been occupied for some 10,000 years. The city gets its name from the Quitus, who lived here during the period AD 500-1500. By the end of the 15th century, the northern highlands of Ecuador were conquered by the Incas and Quito became the capital of the northern half of their empire under the rule of Huayna Capac and later his son Atahualpa. As the Spanish conquest approached, Rumiñahui, Atahualpa's general, razed the city, to prevent it from falling into the invaders' hands.

The colonial city of Quito was founded by Sebastián de Benalcázar, Pizarro's lieutenant, on 6 December 1534. It was built at the foot of El Panecillo on the ruins of the ancient city, using the rubble as construction material. Examples of Inca stonework can be seen in the façades and floors of some colonial buildings such as the Cathedral and the church of San Francisco. Following the conquest, Quito became the seat of government of the Real Audiencia de Quito, the crown colony, which governed current-day Ecuador as well as parts of southern Colombia and northern Peru. Beautifully refurbished, colonial Quito, is today the city's most attractive district. In 1978, Quito was the first city to be declared a UNESCO World Heritage Site.

The 20th century saw the expansion of the city to the north and south, and later to the valleys to the east. The commercial, banking and government centres moved north of the colonial centre and residential and industrial neighbourhoods sprawled in the periphery. These make up the Distrito Metropolitano, which stretches for almost 50 km from north to south.

Sucre, T02-258 0103, Tue-Fri 1000-1800, Sat-Sun 0930-1730, US$2, the home of a Quiteña who devoted her life to charity, showing the lifestyle of 20th-century aristocracy.

Housed in the fine restored, 16th-century Hospital San Juan de Dios, is the **Museo de la Ciudad** ① *García Moreno S1-47 y Rocafuerte, T02-228 3883, www.museociudadquito. gob.ec, Tue-Sun 0930-1730 (last group 1630), US$3, free entry on the last Sat of each month, English guide service US$4 per group (request ahead).* A very good museum which takes you through Quito's history from prehispanic times to the 19th century, with imaginative displays; café by the entrance overlooking La Ronda. Almost opposite on García Moreno are the convent and museum of **El Carmen Alto** ① *T02-295 5817, Wed-Sun 0930-1630, US$3, request ahead for guiding in English, small shop sells sweets and wine made in the convent.* In 2013, this beautifully refurbished cloister opened its doors to the public for the first time since 1652.

On **Cerro Panecillo** ① *Mon-Thu 0900-1700, Fri-Sun 0900-2100, US$1 per vehicle or US$0.25 per person if walking (not recommended), for the neighbourhood brigade; entry to the interior of the monument US$2,* there is a statue of the Virgen de Quito and a good view from the observation platform. Although the neighbourhood patrols the area, it is safer to take a taxi (US$6 return from the colonial city, US$10 from La Mariscal, with a short wait). There is a museum of the monastery of **San Diego** ① *Calicuchima 117 y Farfán, entrance to the right of the church, T02-317 3185, Tue-Sat 1000-1300, 1400-1700, Sun 1000-1400, US$2* (by the cemetery of the same name, just west of El Panecillo). Guided tours (Spanish only) take you to the cupolas and around four colonial patios where sculpture and painting are shown. Of special

1 Quito orientation

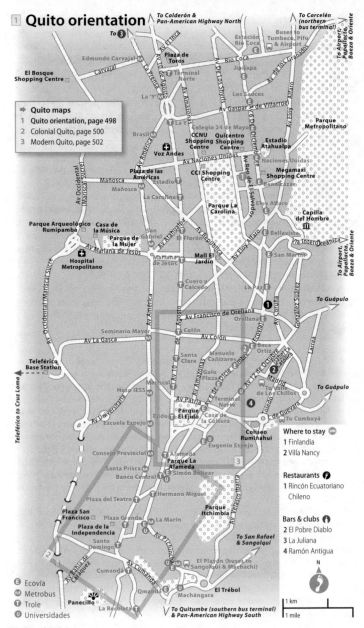

Quito maps
1 Quito orientation, page 498
2 Colonial Quito, page 500
3 Modern Quito, page 502

Where to stay
1 Finlandia
2 Villa Nancy

Restaurants
1 Rincón Ecuatoriano Chileno

Bars & clubs
2 El Pobre Diablo
3 La Juliana
4 Ramón Antigua

E Ecovía
M Metrobus
T Trole
U Universidades

1 km
1 mile

N

interest are the gilded pulpit by Juan Bautista Menacho and the Last Supper painting in the refectory, in which a *cuy* and *humitas* have taken the place of the paschal lamb.

West of Plaza de la Independencia **Plaza de San Francisco** (or Bolívar) is west of Plaza de la Independencia; here are the great church and monastery of the patron saint of Quito, **San Francisco** ① *daily 0800-1200, 1500-1800*. The church was constructed by the Spanish in 1553 and is rich in art treasures. A modest statue of the founder, Fray Jodoco Ricke, the Flemish Franciscan who sowed the first wheat in Ecuador, stands nearby. See the fine wood-carvings in the choir, a high altar of gold and an exquisite carved ceiling. There are some paintings in the aisles by Miguel de Santiago, the colonial *mestizo* painter. The **Museo Franciscano Fray Pedro Gocial** ① *in the church cloisters to the right of the main entrance, T02-295 2911, Mon-Sat 0900-1730, Sun 0900-1300, US$2*, has a collection of religious art. Also adjoining San Francisco is the **Cantuña Chapel** ① *Cuenca y Bolívar, T02-295 2911, Tue and Thu 0800-0900, Sun 0900-1000, free*, with sculptures. Note that starting in 2016 part of Plaza de San Francisco will be excavated for construction of a metro station. Not far to the south along Calle Cuenca is the excellent archaeological museum, **Museo Casa del Alabado** ① *Cuenca 335 y Rocafuerte, T02-228 0940, daily 0900-1730, US$4, guides extra*, with an excellent art shop. An impressive display of pre-Columbian art from all regions of Ecuador, among the best in the city. North of San Francisco is the church of **La Merced** ① *Chile y Cuenca, 0630-1200, 1300-1800, free*, with many splendidly elaborate styles. Nearby is the **Museo de Arte Colonial** ① *Cuenca N6-15 y Mejía, T02-228 2297, Tue-Sat 0900-1630, US$2, free concerts on the last Wed of each month at 1100*, housed in a 17th-century mansion. It has a collection of colonial sculpture and painting and temporary exhibits (free).

Southeast of Plaza de la Independencia At **Plaza de Santo Domingo** (or Sucre), southeast of Plaza de la Independencia, is the church and monastery of **Santo Domingo** ① *daily 0700-1300, 1700-1845*, with its rich wood-carvings and a remarkable Chapel of the Rosary to the right of the main altar. In the monastery is the **Museo Dominicano Fray Pedro Bedón** ① *T02-228 0518, Mon-Sat 0915-1330, 1500-1700, US$2, English speaking guides available*, with another fine collection of religious art. In the centre of the plaza is a statue of Sucre, facing the slopes of Pichincha where he won his battle against the Royalists. Just south of Santo Domingo, in the old bus station, is **Parque Qmandá** ① *Tue-Sun 0900-1300, 1500-1800, busy on weekends*, with a pool, sport fields, climbing wall, gym and activities. **Museo Monacal Santa Catalina** ① *Espejo 779 y Flores, T02-228 4000, Mon-Fri 0900-1700, Sat 0900-1200, US$2.50*, said to have been built on the ruins of the Inca House of the Virgins, depicts the history of cloistered life. Many of the heroes of Ecuador's struggle for independence are buried in the monastery of **San Agustín** ① *Chile y Guayaquil, Tue-Fri 0730-1200, 1500-1700, Sat-Sun 0800-1200*, which has beautifully painted cloisters on three sides where the first act of independence from Spain was signed on 10 August 1809. Here is the **Museo Miguel de Santiago** ① *Chile 924 y Guayaquil, T02-295 1001, Mon-Fri 0900-1230, 1400-1700, Sat 0900-1230, US$2*, with religious art.

Northeast of Plaza de la Independencia To the northeast of Plaza de la Independencia is **Plaza del Teatro** with the lovely neoclassical 19th-century **Teatro Sucre** ① *Manabí N8-131 y Guayaquil*. Further north, on Parque García Moreno, the **Basílica** ① *Carchi 122 y Venezuela, T02-228 9428, visits 0600-*

Tip...
Climb above the coffee shop in the Basílica to the top of the clock tower for stunning views.

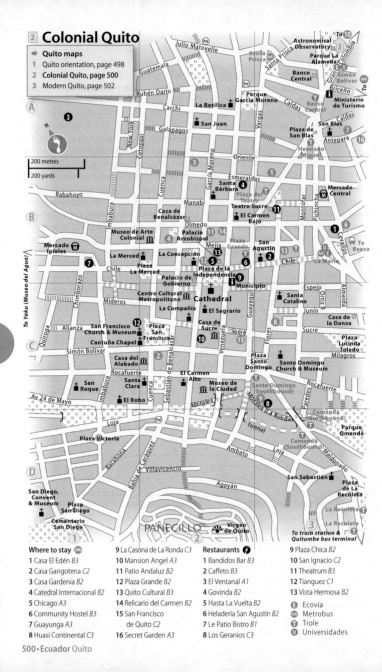

2 Colonial Quito

➡ Quito maps
1 Quito orientation, page 498
2 **Colonial Quito, page 500**
3 Modern Quito, page 502

Where to stay 🛏
1 Casa El Edén B3
2 Casa Gangotena C2
3 Casa Gardenia B2
4 Catedral Internacional B2
5 Chicago A3
6 Community Hostel B3
7 Guayunga A3
8 Huasi Continental C3
9 La Casona de La Ronda C3
10 Mansion Angel A3
11 Patio Andaluz B2
12 Plaza Grande B2
13 Quito Cultural B3
14 Relicario del Carmen B2
15 San Francisco de Quito C2
16 Secret Garden A3

Restaurants 🍴
1 Bandidos Bar B3
2 Caffeto B3
3 El Ventanal A1
4 Govinda B2
5 Hasta La Vuelta B2
6 Heladería San Agustín B2
7 Le Patio Bistro B1
8 Los Geranios C3
9 Plaza Chica B2
10 San Ignacio C2
11 Theatrum B3
12 Tianguez C1
13 Vista Hermosa B2

Ⓔ Ecovía
Ⓜ Metrobus
Ⓣ Trole
Ⓤ Universidades

1900 daily, US$2, mass at 0700, 1200 and 1800 (please be respectful); clock tower open 0900-1630 daily, US$2, is very large, has many gargoyles (some in the shape of Ecuadorean fauna), stained glass windows and fine, bas relief bronze doors (begun in 1926; some final details remain unfinished due to lack of funding). The **Centro de Arte Contemporáneo** ⓘ *Luis Dávila y Venezuela, San Juan, T02-398 8800, Tue-Sun 0900-1700, free*, in the beautifully restored Antiguo Hospital Militar, built in the early 1900s, has rotating art exhibits. To the west of the city, the **Yaku Museo del Agua** ⓘ *El Placer Oe11-271, T02-251 1100, www.yakumuseoagua.gob.ec, Tue-Sun 0900-1700, US$3, take a taxi to main entrance or enter through the parking lot at the top of C Bolívar and take the lift up*, has lovely views. This interactive museum is great for kids of all ages. Its main themes are water and climate, also a self-guided trail: *eco-ruta*. Another must for children, south of the colonial city, is the **Museo Interactivo de Ciencia** ⓘ *Tababela Oe1-60 y Latorre, Chimbacalle, T02-264 7834, Wed-Sun 0900-1630, US$3, children US$1*. East of the colonial city is **Parque Itchimbía** ⓘ *T02-228 2017, park open daily 0600-1800, exhibits 0900-1630*; a natural look-out over the city with walking and cycle trails and a cultural centre housed in a 19th-century 'crystal palace' which came from Europe, once housed the original Santa Clara market.

Modern Quito

Parque La Alameda has the oldest **astronomical observatory** ⓘ *T02-257 0765, ext 101, http://oaq.epn.edu.ec, museum Mon-Fri 1000-1700, US$3, night observations Wed and Thu 1830-1930 weather permitting*, in South America dating to 1873 (native people had observatories long before the arrival of the Europeans). There is also a splendid monument to Simón Bolívar, lakes, and in the northwest corner a spiral lookout tower with a good view.

A short distance north of Parque La Alameda, opposite Parque El Ejido and bound by 6 de Diciembre, Patria, 12 de Octubre and Parque El Arbolito, is the **Casa de la Cultura**, a large cultural and museum complex. If you have time to visit only one museum in Quito, it should be the **Museo Nacional** ⓘ *entrance on Patria, T02-222 3258, Tue-Fri 0900-1700, Sat-Sun 1000-1600, free, guided tours in English by appointment*, housed in the north side of the Casa de la Cultura. The **Sala de Arqueología** is particularly impressive with beautiful pre-Columbian ceramics, the **Sala de Oro** has a nice collection of prehispanic gold objects, and the **Sala de Arte Colonial** with religious art from the Quito School. On the east side of the complex are the museums administered by the **Casa de la Cultura** ⓘ *entrance on 12 de Octubre, T02-290 2272, ext 420, Tue-Sat 0900-1300, 1400-1645, US$2*: **Museo de Arte Moderno**, paintings and sculpture since 1830 also rotating exhibits and **Museo de Instrumentos Musicales**, an impressive collection of musical instruments, said to be the second in importance in the world. Also on the east side are an art gallery for temporary exhibits and the **Agora**, a large open space used for concerts. On the west side are halls for temporary art exhibits, in the original old building, and the entrance to the **Teatro Nacional**, with free evening performances. On the south side are the **Teatro Demetrio Aguilera Malta** and other areas devoted to dance and theatre. Near the Casa de la Cultura, in the Catholic University's **cultural centre** ⓘ *12 de Octubre y Roca, www.centroculturalpuce.org*, is the superb **Museo Jijón y Caamaño** ⓘ *T02-299 1700, ext 1078, Mon-Fri 0900-1600, free*, with a private collection of archaeological objects, historical documents and art. The interactive displays and narration in Spanish are excellent. Here too are temporary exhibits and the **Museo Weilbauer** ⓘ *T02-299 1681, www. museoweilbauer.org, Mon-Fri 0900-1700, free*, with archaeological and photo collections and a *sala tactil* where the visually impaired can touch replicas of ceramics.

3 Modern Quito

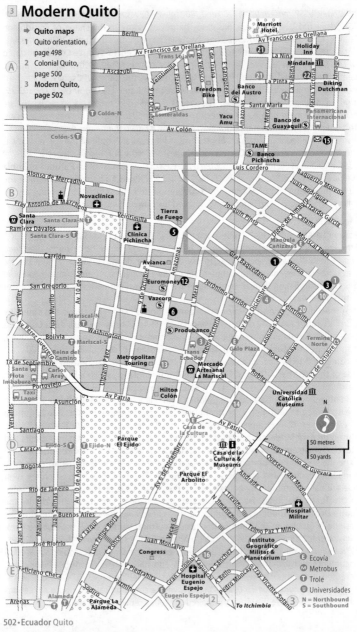

➡ Quito maps
1 Quito orientation,
  page 498
2 Colonial Quito,
  page 500
3 Modern Quito,
  page 502

Marriott Hotel
Av Francisco de Orellana
Holiday Inn
Berlín
Av Francisco de Orellana
Trans Loja
La Niña
Mindalae
J Ascázubi
Veintimilla
Freedom Bike
La Pinta
Biking Dutchman
Colón-N
Banco del Austro
Santa María
Panamericana Internacional
Yacu Amu
Banco de Guayaquil
Colón-S
Av Colón
TAME
Banco Pichincha
Luis Cordero
Baquerizo Moreno
Alonso de Mercadillo
Juan Rodríguez
Novaclínica
Joaquín Pinto
Diego de Almagro
Izardo García
Fray Antonio de Marchena
Veintimilla
Tierra de Fuego
Santa Clara
Santa Clara-N
Clínica Pichincha
Mariscal Foch
Ramírez Dávalos
Santa Clara-S
Carrión
Gral Baquedano
Wilson
San Gregorio
Avianca
Euromoney
Jerónimo Carrión
Av 6 de Diciembre
Mariscal-N
Vazcorp
Washington
Mariscal-S
Bolívar
Produbanco
Galo Plaza
Reina del Camino
Metropolitan Touring
Trans Ecuador
Terminal Norte
18 de Septiembre
Santa Flota Imbabura
Carlos Aray
Portoviejo
Mercado Artesanal La Mariscal
Roca
Taxi Lagos
Asunción
Av Patria
Hilton Colón
Universidad Católica Museums
Santiago
Casa de la Cultura
Av Patria
Caracas
Ejido-S
Parque El Ejido
Casa de la Cultura & Museums
50 metres
50 yards
Bogotá
Río de Janeiro
Parque El Arbolito
Buenos Aires
José Riofrío
Juan Montalvo
Hospital Militar
Feliciano Checa
Congress
Instituto Geográfico Militar & Planetarium
Arenas
Alameda
Hospital Eugenio Espejo
Parque La Alameda
Eugenio Espejo
To Itchimbía

E Ecovía
M Metrobus
T Trole
U Universidades
N = Northbound
S = Southbound

La Mariscal detail

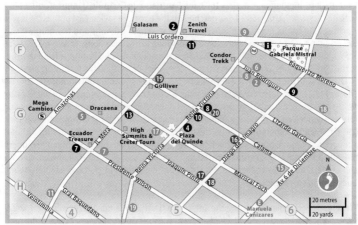

Where to stay 🛏
1 Anahi *C3*
2 Backpackers Inn *G6*
3 Café Cultura *C2*
4 Casa Helbling *C3*
5 Casa Joaquín *G4*
6 Cayman *F6*
7 City Art Hotel Silberstein *G4*
8 El Arupo *F6*
9 El Cafecito *F6*
10 Fuente de Piedra I *C3*
11 Fuente de Piedra II *H4*
12 Hostal de la Rábida *A3*
13 Hothello *C2*
14 La Cartuja *D3*
15 La Casa Sol *H6*
16 L'Auberge Inn *E2*
17 Nü House *G5*
18 Posada del Maple *G6*
19 Queen's Hostel *H5*
20 Sierra Madre *C3*
21 Travellers Inn *A3*

Restaurants 🍴
1 Baalbek *C3*
2 Chandani Tandoori *F5*
3 Chez Alain *C3*
4 Coffee Bar *G5*
5 El Hornero *B2*
6 Ethnic Coffee *C2*
7 Kallari *G4*
8 La Boca del Lobo *G5*
9 La Petite Mariscal *G6*
10 Mama Clorinda *G5*
11 Paléo *F5*
12 Sakti *C2*
13 The Magic Bean *G5*
15 Yu Su *B3*

Bars & clubs 🎵
16 Bungalow Six *G5*
17 Cherusker *H5*
18 Finn McCool's *H5*
19 No Bar *F5*
20 Selfie *G5*
21 Turtle's Head *A3*
22 Varadero *A3*

A focal point in La Mariscal, north of Parque El Ejido, is **Plaza Foch** (Reina Victoria y Foch), also called **Plaza del Quinde**, a popular meeting place surrounded by cafés and restaurants. At the corner of Reina Victoria and La Niña, is the excellent **Museo Mindalae** ⓘ *T02-223 0609 ext 101, Mon-Sat 0900-1730, US$3,* which exhibits Ecuadorean crafts and places them in their historical and cultural context, as well as temporary exhibits and a good fair-trade, non-profit shop. (For another handicrafts museum and shop, see **Folklore**, page 516.)

North of La Mariscal is the large **Parque La Carolina**, a favourite recreational spot at weekends. Around it is the banking district, several shopping malls, hotels and restaurants. In the park is the **Jardín Botánico** ⓘ *T02-333 2516, www.jardinbotanicoquito. com, Mon-Fri 1000-1700, Sat-Sun 0900-1700, US$3.50,* which has a good cross section of Andean flora. Also the **Vivarium** ⓘ *T02-227 1799, www.vivarium.org.ec, Tue-Sun 0930-1300, 1330-1730, US$3.25,* dedicated to protect endangered snakes, reptiles and amphibians, and the **Museo de Ciencias Naturales** ⓘ *T02-244 9824, http://inb.ambiente.gob.ec, Mon-Fri 0800-1300,1345-1630, US$2.* Beyond La Carolina, on the grounds of Quito's former airport, is **Parque Bicentenario** ⓘ *daily 0430-1800,* with sports fields and a great cycling track, right on the old tarmac.

Quito suburbs

East Built by indigenous slaves in 1693, the **Santuario de Guápulo** ⓘ *Mass Mon-Fri 1900, Sat 0700, Sun 0700-1200, 1600-1700*, perched on the edge of a ravine east of the city, is well worth seeing for its many paintings, gilded altars, stone carvings and the marvellously carved pulpit. The **Museo Fray Antonio Rodríguez** ⓘ *Plaza de Guápulo N27-138, T02-256 5652, Mon-Fri 0800-1200, 1400-1800, US$1.50*, has religious art and furniture, from the 16th to the 20th centuries. Guided tours (Spanish only) include a visit to the beautiful Santuario.

Overlooking the city from the northeast is the grandiose **Capilla del Hombre** ⓘ *Lorenzo Chávez E18-143 y Mariano Calvache, Bellavista, T02-244 8492, www.guayasamin.org, Tue-Sun 1000-1700, US$8, take a taxi or Jesús del Gran Poder-Bellavista bus*, a monument to Latin America conceived by the internationally famous Ecuadorean artist Oswaldo Guayasamín (1919-1999) and completed after his death. This highly recommended museum includes a collection of murals depicting the fate of Latin America from pre-Columbian to modern times and, in Guayasamín's home and studio, his works, as well as pre-Columbian, colonial and contemporary art collections. Works of art, jewellery and clothing decorated with Guayasamín's art are for sale.

West For spectacular views ride the **Teleférico** ⓘ *Av Occidental above La Gasca, T02-222 4424, daily 0800-1930, US$8.50, children and seniors US$6.50, the area below is not safe, best take a taxi (US$1.50 from América y Colón)*. The cable car is part of a complex with an amusement park, shops and food courts. It climbs to 4050 m on the flanks of Pichincha, where there are walking trails, including one to the summit of Rucu Pichincha, and horse riding just past the fence.

Parque Arqueológico y Ecológico Rumipamba ⓘ *east side of Av Occidental just north of Mariana de Jesús, Wed-Sun 0830-1600, free, some English speaking guides*, is a 32-ha park on the slopes of Pichincha, where vestiges of human occupation of several pre-Inca periods, dating from 1500 BC to AD 1500, have been found. There are walking trails in some pockets of native vegetation. Northwest of Rumipamba, in the neighbourhood of San Vicente de la Florida is **Museo de Sitio La Florida** ⓘ *C Antonio Costas y Villacrés, T02-380 3043, Wed-Sun 0800-1600, free, some English speaking guides, at north end of El Ejido-San Vicente bus line*. At this necropolis of the Quitus people, 10 17-m deep burial chambers, dating to AD 220-640, have been excavated. The elaborate dress and jewellery found in the tombs suggests most were prominent citizens.

Listings Quito *maps pages 498, 500 and 502.*

Tourist information

Empresa Metropolitana Quito Turismo/ Quito Visitor's Bureau
HQ at Parque Bicentenario (old airport), T02-299 3300, info@quito-turismo.gob.ec, www.quito.com.ec.
Has information offices with English-speaking personnel, brochures and maps, and an excellent website. They also run walking tours of the colonial city, see Rutas Turísticas, page 517.
Airport, in Arrivals area, T02-281 8363, Mon-Fri 0600-2200, Sat-Sun 0700-1900. **Bus station**, Terminal Quitumbe, T02-382 4815, daily 0800-1800. **Colonial Quito**, **El Quinde Visitors Centre**, Plaza de la Independencia, at Palacio Municipal, Venezuela y Espejo, T02-257 2445, Mon-Sat 0900-1800, Sun 1000-1700; also offer booking services and walking tours, and have storage lockers. In

the premises are also crafts and chocolate shops, tour operators and sale points for double-decker bus tours, see page 516, Mitad del Mundo, train tours and travel insurance. **La Mariscal**, at Parque Gabriela Mistral, Baquerizo Moreno y Reina Victoria, Mon-Sat 0900-1730. General information about Quito is found in www.in-quito.com. To file a complaint about services contact the **Quito Visitor's Bureau** headquarters (see above).

Ministerio de Turismo
Av Gran Colombia y Briceño, T02-399 9333 or T1-800-887476, www.ecuador.travel, www.turismo.gob.ec. Mon-Fri 0815-1700.
Offers information at their reception desk.

Sistema de Museos y Centros Culturales Quito
Calle el Placer Oe11-271, Yaku Museo del Agua, T02-251 1 100 ext 101, www.museosquito.gob.ec.
Offers useful information about museums and cultural centres throughout Quito. Good website.

Where to stay

For lodgings near the airport, see Quito suburbs, below. Near the Quitumbe bus terminal are a few simple establishments catering to short stay customers and there is one simple *hostal* (**$ Madrid**) opposite the Carcelén bus terminal, along busy Avenida Eloy Alfaro. Large international chain hotels are represented in the city and meet their international standards. For more information see: www.bestwestern. com, www.hotelquito.com (**Compass**), www.danncarltonquito.com, www. hilton.com, www.holidayinn.com, www. hiexpress.com (**Holiday Inn Express**), www.hojo.com (**Howard Johnson**), www. marriott.com, www.mercure.com, www. radisson.com, www.sheraton.com, www. swissotel.com, www.wyndham.com.

Colonial Quito

$$$$ Casa El Edén
Esmeraldas Oe 3-30 y Guayaquil, T02-228 1810, www.casaeleden.com.
Beautiful old home restored to save original murals and painted ceilings, convenient location, 6 well-appointed heated rooms, rooftop views.

$$$$ Casa Gangotena
Bolívar y Cuenca, T02-400 8000, www.casagangotena.com.
Superb location by Plaza San Francisco, luxury accommodation in beautifully refurbished classic family home with 31 rooms and suites, fine restaurant.

$$$$ La Casona de La Ronda
Morales Oe1-160 y Guayaquil, T02-228 7538, www.lacasonadelaronda.com.
Tastefully refurbished colonial house in the heart of La Ronda, comfortable rooms and suite, includes buffet breakfast, restaurant serves Ecuadorean specialities and some international dishes.

$$$$ Patio Andaluz
García Moreno N6-52 y Olmedo, T02-228 0830, www.hotelpatioandaluz.com.
Beautifully reconstructed 16th-century mansion with large arches, balconies and patios, breakfast extra, exclusive restaurant with Ecuadorean and Spanish cuisine, library, gift shop.

$$$$ Plaza Grande
García Moreno N5-16, Plaza de la Independencia, T02-251 0777, www.plazagrandequito.com.
Exclusive top-of-the-line hotel with an exceptional location, 15 suites including a presidential suite for US$2000, jacuzzi in all rooms, climate control, 3 restaurants, including **La Belle Epoque**, gourmet French cuisine and a wine cellar, mini-spa, 110/220V outlets.

$$$ Casa Gardenia
Benalcázar N9-42 y Oriente, T02-295 7936, www.hotelcasagardenia.com.

Nice 9-room B&B in a quiet location, buffet breakfast, lovely views from the terrace.

$$$ Catedral Internacional
Mejía Oe6-36 y Cuenca, T02-295 5438, www.hotelcatedral.ec.
Well-restored colonial house with 15 carpeted rooms, heaters, small patio, popular restaurant, spa.

$$$ Relicario del Carmen
Venezuela N6-43 y Olmedo, T02-228 9120, www.hotelrelicariodelcarmen.com.
Beautifully refurbished colonial house, good restaurant, cafeteria, good rooms and service, no smoking.

$$ Quito Cultural
Flores N4-160 y Chile, T02-228 8084, www.hostalquitocultural.com.
Nicely refurbished colonial house, bright, rooftop terrace with nice views, patio with plants, a bit pricey.

$$ San Francisco de Quito
Sucre Oe3-17 y Guayaquil, T02-295 1241, www.sanfranciscodequito.com.ec.
Converted colonial building, breakfast served in attractive patio or underground cloisters, restaurant, suites are particularly good value, well run by owners.

$$-$ Community Hostel
Cevallos N6-78 y Olmedo, T02-228 5108, www.communityhostel.com.
Popular hostel with 2 double rooms and dorms for 4-6 (US$10 pp), comfy beds, shared bath (may have to wait for toilet in the morning), good showers, very clean and efficient, nice sitting area, breakfast extra, kitchen facilities, helpful staff.

$$-$ Huasi Continental
Flores N3-08 y Sucre, T02-295 7327.
Colonial house, a bit dark, restaurant serves good breakfast and lunch (both extra), private or shared bath, parking, good service and value.

In between the colonial and modern cities

$$$$ Mansión del Angel
Los Ríos N13-134 y Pasaje Gándara, T02-254 0293, www.mansiondelangel.com.ec.
Luxurious hotel decorated with antiques in a beautifully renovated mansion, 14 ample rooms and a palatial suite, dinner available, nice gardens, lovely atmosphere, spa.

$$-$ Guayunga
Antepara E4-27 y León, T02-228 3127.
Attractive hostel with a few double rooms with and without bath and dorms for 3-9 (US$14 pp), breakfast extra, interior patio, rooftop terrace with great views, parking.

$$-$ L'Auberge Inn
Gran Colombia N15-200 y Yaguachi, T02-255 2912, www.auberge-inn-hostal.com.
Nice spacious rooms, duvets, private or shared bath, excellent hot water, buffet breakfast and dinner available, grill next door for lunch, spa, cooking facilities, parking, lovely garden, terrace and communal area, helpful, good atmosphere. Highly recommended.

$$-$ Secret Garden
Antepara E4-60 y Los Ríos, T02-295 6704, www.secretgardenquito.com.
Well-decorated house, some rooms small and dark, lovely rooftop terrace restaurant, private or shared bath, US$12 pp in dorm, breakfast extra, pleasant atmosphere, very popular meeting place. Ecuadorean/Australian-owned, also run a rustic lodge between Pasochoa and Cotopaxi, www.secretgardencotopaxi.com.

$ Chicago
Los Ríos N11-142 y Briceño, T02-228 1695, www.chicagohostalecuador.com.
Popular family-run hostel, small rooms, US$11 pp in dorm, cooking facilities, a good economy option.

Modern Quito

$$$$ Le Parc
República de El Salvador N34-349 e Irlanda,
T02-227 6800, www.leparc.com.ec.
Modern hotel with 30 executive suites, full
luxury facilities and service, restaurant, spa,
gym, parking.

$$$$ Nü House
Foch E6-12 y Reina Victoria, T02-255 7845,
www.nuhousehotels.com.
Modern luxury hotel with minimalist decor,
restaurant, some suites with jacuzzi, parking,
all furnishings and works of art are for sale.

$$$ Anahi
Tamayo N23-95 y Wilson, T02-250 8403,
www.anahihotelquito.com.
Very nice tastefully decorated suites, each
one is different, ample bathrooms, buffet
breakfast, safety box, fridge, terrace with
nice views, good value.

$$$ Café Cultura
Robles E6-62, T02-250 4078,
www.cafecultura.com.
A well-established hotel with ample suites,
social areas including wood-panelled library
with fireplace, restaurant, attentive service.
Planning to relocate to C Washington y Páez.

$$$ Casa Joaquín
Pinto E4-376 y JL Mera, T02-222 4791,
www.hotelcasajoaquin.com.
Nicely refurbished hotel in the heart of
La Mariscal, covered patio makes it warm,
good service, a bit pricey, Belgian-run.

$$$ Cayman
Rodríguez E7-29 y Reina Victoria, T02-256
7616, www.hotelcaymanquito.com.
Pleasant hotel, lovely dining room, cafeteria,
rooms a bit small, sitting room with fireplace,
parking, garden, very good.

$$$ City Art Hotel Silberstein
Wilson E5-29 y JL Mera, T02-515 1651,
www.cityartsilberstein.com.

10 comfortable rooms and suites in an
attractively refurbished building, includes
buffet breakfast.

$$$ Finlandia
Finlandia N32-129 y Suecia, north of centre,
T02-224 4288, www.hotelfinlandia.com.ec.
Pleasant hotel in residential area, buffet
breakfast, restaurant, spacious rooms, sitting
room with fireplace, small garden, parking,
helpful staff.

$$$ Fuente de Piedra I & II
Wilson E9-80 y Tamayo, T02-255 9775 and
JL Mera N23-21 y Baquedano, T02-252 5314,
www.ecuahotel.com.
Well-decorated modern hotels,
comfortable, some rooms are small,
nice sitting areas, pleasant.

$$$ Hostal de la Rábida
La Rábida 227 y Santa María, T02-222 2169,
www.hostalrabida.com.
Lovely converted home, bright comfortable
rooms, good restaurant for breakfast and
dinner (both extra), parking, Ecuadorean/
Italian-run. Recommended.

$$$ La Cartuja
Plaza N20-08 y 18 de Septiembre, T02-
252 3577, www.hotelacartuja.com.
In the former British Embassy, beautifully
decorated, spacious comfortable rooms,
cafeteria, parking, lovely garden, very helpful
and hospitable. Highly recommended.

$$$ La Casa Sol
Calama 127 y 6 de Diciembre, T02-223 0798,
www.lacasasol.com.
Attractive small hotel with courtyard, very
helpful, English and French spoken, also run
Casa Sol in Otavalo. Recommended.

$$$ Sierra Madre
Veintimilla E9-33 y Tamayo, T02-250 5687,
www.hotelsierramadre.com.
Fully renovated villa, comfortable rooms,
includes buffet breakfast, restaurant, nice
sun roof, English spoken.

$$$ Villa Nancy
Muros N27-94 y 12 de Octubre, T02-256 2483, www.hotelvillanancy.com.
Quaint hotel in quiet residential area, buffet breakfast, parking, homey and comfortable, helpful multilingual staff. Recommended.

$$ El Arupo
Rodríguez E7-22 y Reina Victoria, T02-255 7543, www.hostalelarupo.com.
Good hotel, cooking facilities, English and French spoken. Recommended.

$$ Hothello
Amazonas N20-20 y 18 de Septiembre, T02-256 5835, www.hotelothello.com.
Small bright hotel, tastefully decorated rooms, heating, helpful multilingual staff.

$$ Queen's Hostel/Hostal de la Reina
Reina Victoria N23-70 y Wilson, T02-255 1844.
Good small hotel, popular among travellers and Ecuadoreans, breakfast extra, cafeteria, cooking facilities, sitting room with fireplace.

$$ Travellers Inn
La Pinta E4-435 y Amazonas, T02-255 6985, www.travellersecuador.com.
In a nicely converted home, includes good breakfast, private or shared bath, parking, nice common area, bike rentals. Recommended.

$$-$ Casa Helbling
Veintimilla E8-152 y 6 de Diciembre, T02-256 5740, www.casahelbling.de.
Very good, popular hostel, spotless, breakfast extra, private or shared bath, also 6-bed dorm (US$12 pp), laundry and cooking facilities, English and German spoken, pleasant atmosphere, reliable information, luggage storage, parking. Highly recommended.

$$-$ Posada del Maple
Rodríguez E8-49 y 6 de Diciembre, T02-254 4507, www.posadadelmaple.com.
Popular hostel, private or shared bath, also 8-bed dorm (US$7 pp), cooking facilities, warm atmosphere, free tea and coffee.

$ Backpackers Inn
Rodríguez E7-48 y Reina Victoria, T02-250 9669, www.backpackersinn.net.
Popular hostel, breakfast extra, private or shared bath, adequate dorms (US$8 pp), laundry and cooking facilities.

$ Casona de Mario
Andalucía N24-115 y Galicia (La Floresta), T02-254 4036, www.casonademario.com.
Popular hostel, shared bath, laundry facilities, no breakfast, well equipped kitchen, parking, sitting room, nice garden, book exchange, long stay discounts, Argentine owner. Repeatedly recommended.

$ El Cafecito
Cordero E6-43 y Reina Victoria, T02-223 4862, www.cafecito.net.
Popular with backpackers, breakfast extra, good café including vegetarian and vegan, cheaper in dorm (US$8), 1 room with bath, relaxed atmosphere but can get noisy until 2200, Canadian-owned.

Quito suburbs

$$$$ Hacienda Rumiloma
Obispo Díaz de La Madrid, T02-254 8206, www.rumiloma.net.
Luxurious hotel in a 40-ha hacienda on the slopes of Pichincha. Sumptuous suites with lots of attention to detail, lounges with antiques, good but pricey restaurant, bar with fireplace, nice views, personalized attention from owners, ideal for a luxurious escape not far from the city.

$$$ Hostería San Jorge
Km 4 via antigua Quito-Nono, to the west of Av Mariscal Sucre, T02-339 0403, www.eco-lodgesanjorge.com.
Converted 18th-century hacienda on a 80-ha private reserve on the slopes of Pichincha, full board available, good pricey restaurant, heating, pool, sauna and jacuzzi, horse riding and birdwatching. Operates several nature reserves.

Quito airport

The **Wyndham Gran Cóndor** (www. wyndham.com) luxury hotel is 500 m from the airport terminal. A short distance further away a **Holiday Inn** (www.holidayinn.com) is due to open in early 2017 and a **Eurobuilding** (www.hoteleuro.com) is under construction. Towns near the airport with accommodation include Tababela, off highway E-35, 10 mins from the airport towards Quito (airport taxi US$10). Nearby, by the junction of E-35 and the Vía Interoceánica, is Pifo, also about 10 mins from the airport (taxi US$10). From Pifo you can go northwest to Quito, southwest to Sangolquí and points south or east to Papallacta and Oriente. Puembo, past Pifo on the Vía Interoceánica, is 20 mins from the airport (taxi US$15-20) and closer to Quito. Oyambarillo, north of the airport off E-35, is 10 mins away (taxi US$10). On E-35 to the north are Checa, about 15 mins away (taxi US$12-15), and El Quinche, about 20 mins from the airport (taxi US$15-20). The latter 2 are convenient if going to Otavalo and points north, without going to Quito. Note that taxi drivers may not be familiar with the hotels in these towns, so it is worth printing the hotel's map before travelling. Many of the hotels in this area are in rural settings where there are no restaurants. There is an expensive food court in the shopping area opposite the airport.

$$$ Hostal Su Merced
Julio Tobar Donoso, Puembo, T02-239 0251, www.sumerced.com.
Nicely refurbished 18th-century hacienda house, well-appointed rooms with bathtubs, includes traditional breakfast, restaurant, sauna, gardens, airport transfers US$15 per vehicle.

$$$ Posada Mirolindo
Vía Oyambarillo, T02-215 0363, www.posadamirolindo.com.
Pleasant rooms and cottages, includes transfers to and from the airport, breakfast provided, other meals on request.

$$ Hostería San Carlos
Justo Cuello y Maldonado, Tababela, T02-359 9057, www.hosteriasancarlos tababela.com.
Hacienda-style inn with ample grounds, restaurant, pool, jacuzzi, rooms with bath and dorms (US$20 pp), airport transfers US$5 per person.

$$ Quito Airport Suites
Alfonso Tobar 971 y Tulio Guzmán, Tababela, 1 block from the plaza, T02-359 9110 or T09-8889 9774, airporthotelquito.com.
Room price includes breakfast which can be a box breakfast in case of an early departure, dinner extra, English spoken; rooms available for day use between flights ($); luggage storage US$1 per case, per day, available to non-guests; long-term parking; airport transfers US$8 per vehicle.

$$-$ Hostal Colibrí
Pje Tobías Trujillo, 3 blocks downhill from the Tababela park, T02-215 0100, www.hostalcolibriaeropuerto.com.
Hacienda-style hotel with private rooms and dorm for 12 (US$15 pp), include breakfast, dinner extra, garden with pool and jacuzzi, plenty of information, also arrange excursions; airport transfers US$10 for 2 passengers. Recommended.

Restaurants

Eating out in Quito is excellent, varied, upmarket and increasingly cosmopolitan. There are many elegant restaurants offering Ecuadorean and international food, as well as small simple places serving set meals for US$2.50-5, the latter close by early evening and on Sun.

Colonial Quito
Many restaurants serving economical *almuerzos* (set lunches) post their daily menu at the entrance; look for them along Calles Benalcázar, García Moreno, Guayaquil and Espejo.

$$$ El Ventanal
Carchi y Nicaragua, west of the Basílica, in Parque San Juan, take a taxi to the parking area and a staff member will accompany you along a footpath to the restaurant, T02-257 2232, www.elventanal.ec. Tue-Sat 1300-1500, 1800-2230, Sun 1200-1600.
International nouvelle cuisine with a varied menu including a number of seafood dishes, fantastic views over the city.

$$$ Los Geranios
Morales Oe1-134, T02-295 6035. Mon-Thu 0900-0000, Fri-Sat 0900-0200, Sun 1000-2200.
Upscale *comida típica*, in a nicely restored La Ronda house.

$$$ Theatrum
Plaza del Teatro, 2nd floor of Teatro Sucre, T02-228 9669, www.theatrum.com.ec. Mon-Fri 1230-1500, 1900-2200, Sat-Sun 1900-2200.
Good traditional Ecuadorean cuisine in the city's most important theatre, excellent service, free transport.

$$$-$$ Hasta la Vuelta Señor
Pasaje Arzobispal, 3rd floor. Mon-Sat 1100-2300, Sun 1100-2100.
A *fonda quiteña* perched on an indoor balcony with *comida típica* and snacks, try *empanadas* (pasties) or a *seco de chivo* (goat stew).

$$ Tianguez
Plaza de San Francisco under the portico of the church. Mon-Wed 0900-1900, Thu 0900-2200, Fri-Sat 0800-2300.
International and local dishes, good coffee, snacks, sandwiches, popular, also craft shop (closes 1830), run by Fundación Sinchi Sacha.

$$ Vista Hermosa
Mejía 453 y García Moreno. Mon-Sat 1300-2400.
Good meals, drinks, pizza, live music on weekends, lovely terrace-top views of the colonial centre.

$$-$ San Ignacio
García Moreno N2-60, at Museo María Agusta Urrutia. Mon-Sat 0800-2200, Sun 0800-1600.

Good popular set lunch (US$4.50) with a choice of dishes and buffet salad bar; à la carte in the evening.

$ Govinda
Esmeraldas Oe3-115 y Venezuela. Mon-Sat 0800-1800.
Vegetarian dishes, good-value economical set lunch and à la carte snacks, also breakfast.

$ Le Patio Bistro
Chile y Chimborazo. Mon-Fri 1200-1500.
In an interior patio, choice of very good *almuerzos* (US$5).

$ Plaza Chica
Between Venezuela and Guayaquil, on an interior patio behind the Municipio. Mon-Fri 0830-1600.
Very good elegant set lunch with a choice of dishes (US$5), also coffee and pastries. Very popular, so be prepared to wait.

Cafés

Caffeto
Chile 930 y Flores. Mon-Sat 0800-1900, Sun 0815-1600.
Variety of coffees, snacks, sandwiches, sweets.

Heladería San Agustín
Guayaquil N5-59 y Chile. Mon-Fri 1000-1630, Sat-Sun 1030-1530.
Coffee, traditional home-made cakes, ices and lunch, a Quito tradition since 1858.

Modern Quito
There are at least 25 restaurants ($$$-$$) and cafés within a block of Plaza Foch. There are many restaurants serving good economical set lunches along both Pinto and Foch, between Amazonas and Cordero. A number of restaurants in La Floresta, east of La Mariscal, near Parque La Carolina and along Av Eloy Alfaro, fall outside the scope of our map.

$$$ Carmine
Catalina Aldaz N34-208 y Portugal, T02-333 2829, www.carmineristorante.com. Mon-Sat 1200-2300, Sun 1200-1800.
Creative international and Italian cuisine.

$$$ Chez Jérôme
Whymper N30-96 y Coruña, T02-223 4067,
www.chezjeromerestaurante.com.
Mon-Fri 1230-1500, 1930-2300.
Excellent traditional and modern French
cuisine, with local ingredients, good
ambiance and service.

$$$ Il Risotto
Eloy Alfaro N34-447 y Portugal, T02-224
6850 and República de El Salvador N35-79 y
Portugal, T02-224 8487. Mon-Fri 1130-1530,
1830-2300, Sat 1130-2300, Sun 1130-2200
(Eloy Alfaro); Mon-Sat 1200-2300, Sun 1200-
2200 (Rep ES).
Very popular and very good Italian cooking,
prices on Eloy Alfaro are somewhat higher.
A Quito tradition.

$$$ La Boca del Lobo
Calama 284 y Reina Victoria, T02-223 4083,
www.labocadellobo.com.ec. Sun-Wed 1700-
2330, Thu-Sat 1700-0100.
Stylish bar-restaurant with eclectic food,
drink, decor, and atmosphere, good food
and cocktails, popular, good meeting place.

$$$ La Briciola
Isabel la Católica y Salazar esquina,
T254 5157, www.labriciola.com.ec.
Daily 1200-2400.
Extensive Italian menu, excellent food,
very good personal service.

$$$ La Choza
12 de Octubre N24-551 y Cordero,
T02-223 0839. Mon-Sat 1200-1600,
1800-2130, Sun 1200-1600.
Traditional Ecuadorean cuisine, good music
and decor.

$$$ La Gloria
Valladolid N24-519 y Salazar, La Floresta,
T02-252 7855, www.lagloria.com.ec.
Daily 1200-1530, 1900-2200.
Very innovative Peruvian and international
cuisine, excellent food and service. Same
ownership as Theatrum, see Colonial Quito
Restaurants, above.

$$$ La Petite Mariscal
Almagro N24-304 y Rodríguez, T02-604 3303,
www.lapetitemariscal.com. Tue-Fri 1200-
1500, 1800-2200, Sat 1800-2200.
Upmarket European cuisine with an
Ecuadorean touch, also a good set lunch.

$$$ San Telmo
Portugal 440 y Casanova, T225 6946.
Mon-Sat 1200-2300, Sun until 2100.
Good Argentine grill, seafood, pasta, pleasant
atmosphere, great service.

$$$ Zazu
Mariano Aguilera 331 y La Pradera, T254 3559,
www.zazuquito.com. Mon-Fri 1230-1500,
1900-2300, Sat 1900-2300.
Very elegant and exclusive dinning.
International and Peruvian specialities,
extensive wine list, attentive service,
reservations required.

$$$-$$ Baalbek
6 de Diciembre N23-123 y Wilson, T02-255
2766. Sun-Tue 1200-1700, Wed-Sat 1200-2230.
Authentic Lebanese cuisine, great food and
atmosphere, friendly service.

$$ Chez Alain
Wilson E9-68 y Tamayo. Mon-Sat 1200-1530.
Choice of good 4-course set lunches,
pleasant relaxed atmosphere, monthly
dinner/show specials. Recommended.

$$ The Magic Bean
Foch E5-08 y JL Mera, daily 0800-2200 and
Portugal y Los Shyris, daily 0800-1730.
Fine coffees and natural food, more than
20 varieties of pancakes, good salads, large
portions, outdoor seating (also popular
lodging, $).

$$ Mama Clorinda
Reina Victoria N24-150 (11-44) y Calama.
Daily 1100-2300.
Ecuadorean cuisine à la carte and set meals,
filling, good value.

$$ Mr Bagel
Portugal 546 y 6 de Diciembre and Cordero
E10-55 y 12 de Octubre. Mon-Fri 0700-1500,

Sat-Sun 0730-1500 (Portugal); Mon-Fri 0730-1830, Sat-Sun 0800-1300 (Cordero).
Very popular breakfast and lunch restaurant, 17 varieties of bagels and many spreads, sandwiches, soups, salads, desserts, also take out, Wi-Fi and book exchange.

$$ Paléo
Cordero E5-36 y JL Mera. Mon-Tue 1200-1600, Wed-Sat 1200-1530, 1830-2300.
Authentic Swiss specialities such as rösti and raclette. Also good economical set lunch, pleasant ambiance. Recommended.

$$ Pekín
Whymper N26-42 y Orellana, www.restaurante-pekin.com. Mon-Sat 1200-1530, 1800-2230, Sun 1200-2000.
Excellent Chinese food, very nice atmosphere.

$$-$ El Hornero
Veintimilla y Amazonas, República de El Salvador N36-149 y Naciones Unidas and on González Suárez. Daily 1200-2300.
Very good wood oven pizzas, try one with *choclo* (fresh corn). Recommended.

$$-$ Las Palmeras
Japón N36-87 y Naciones Unidas, opposite Parque la Carolina. Daily 0900-1700.
Very good *comida Esmeraldeña*, try their hearty *viche de pescado* soup, outdoor tables, popular, good value. Recommended.

$$-$ Rincón Ecuatoriano Chileno
6 de Diciembre N28-30 y Belo Horizonte. Mon 1200-1800, Tue-Sat 1200-2000, Sun 1200-1700.
Good tasty home-cooking, Chilean specialities including *empanadas*, large portions, efficient service, some tables in back garden.

$$-$ Sakti
Carrión E4-144 y Amazonas. Mon-Fri 0830-1730.
Good-quality vegetarian food, tasty healthy breakfast, daily specials, fruit juices, great desserts (also rooms around a small garden, $$-$). Recommended.

$ Chandani Tandoori
JL Mera 1312 y Cordero. Mon-Sat 1200-2130, Sun 1200-1530.
Good authentic Indian cuisine, economical set meals, popular, good value. Recommended.

$ Yu Su
Almagro y Colón, edif Torres de Almagro. Mon-Fri 1230-1600, 1800-2000, Sat 1230-1600.
Very good sushi bar, pleasant, Korean-run, takeaway service.

Cafés

Coffee Bar
Reina Victoria y Foch. 24 hrs.
Popular café serving a variety of snacks, pasta, burgers, coffee, Wi-Fi. Very similar are **Yasuní Café**, Amazonas y Washington, and **Coffee Tov**, next to Museo Mindalae, La Niña y Reina Victoria.

Ethnic Coffee
Amazonas y Roca, Edif Hotel Mercure, local 3, www.ethniccollection.com. Mon-Fri 1000-2030.
Nice popular café with gourmet coffee as well as a wide range of desserts, meals ($$) and drinks.

Kallari
Wilson y JL Mera, www.kallari.com. Mon-Fri 0900-1830, Sat 0900-1400.
Fairtrade café, breakfast, snacks, salad and sandwich set lunches, organic coffee and chocolate, crafts, run by an association of farmers and artisans from the Province of Napo working on rainforest and cultural conservation.

Bars and clubs

Colonial Quito
In the old city, much of the nightlife is concentrated along La Ronda.

Bandidos
Olmedo y Cevallos. Mon-Sat 1600-2400.
Very popular pub, partly housed in an old chapel, serves a choice of excellent microbrews and snacks.

Modern Quito

Bungalow Six
Almagro N24-139 y Calama.
Tue-Sat 1900-0200, Sun 1200-1900.
US-style sports bar and club. Popular place to hang out and watch a game or a film, dancing later on, varied music, cover US$5 (Thu free), ladies' night on Wed, happy hour 2000-2200.

Cherusker
Pinto y Diego de Almagro esquina.
Mon-Fri 1500-2330, Fri-Sat 1500-0130.
Various microbrews and German food.

El Pobre Diablo
Isabel La Católica N24-224 y Galavis,
La Floresta, www.elpobrediablo.com.
Mon-Sat 1230-0200.
Relaxed atmosphere, friendly, jazz, sandwiches, snacks and nice meals and set lunches, live music Wed, Thu and Sat, a popular place to hang out and chill.

Finn McCool's
Almagro N24-64 y Pinto. Daily 1100-0200.
Irish-run pub, Irish and international food, darts, pool, table football, sports on TV, Wi-Fi, popular meeting place.

La Juliana
Amazonas 61-55 y El Inca, northwest of Parque La Carolina, T02-604 1569.
Thu-Sat 2130-0300.
Popular club, live 1990s Latin music, cover US$12.

No Bar
Calama E5-01 y JL Mera. Mon-Sat 1900-0300.
Good mix of Latin and Euro dance music, busy at weekends. Free drinks for women until 2200, Thu-Sat after 2200 entry US$5 with 1 free drink.

Ramón Antigua
Mena Caamaño E12-86 e Isabel la Católica, T09-6906 0262. Open 2100-0200.
Live music Fri-Sat, cover US$5-10 depending on band. Great for salsa and other hip tropical music, popular with locals.

Selfie
Calama E7-35 y Reina Victoria. Wed-Thu 1500-2400, Fri 1200-0200, Sat 1200-2400.
Popular disco attracting a young crowd, entry US$3.

Turtle's Head
La Niña E4-451 y JL Mera. Mon-Thu 1600-2400, Fri-Sat 1600-0200.
Microbrews, fish and chips, curry, pool table, darts, fun atmosphere.

Varadero
Reina Victoria N26-99 y La Pinta.
Fri-Sat 2000-0300.
Bar-restaurant, live Cuban music, attached to **La Bodeguita de Cuba** restaurant, mixed crowd.

Entertainment

There are always many cultural events taking place in Quito, often free of charge. Films are listed daily in *El Comercio*, www.elcomercio.com.

Cinema
There are several multiplexes, eg **Cinemark**, www.cinemark.com.ec and **Multicines**, www.multicines.com.ec.
Casa de la Cultura, *Patria y 6 de Diciembre, T02-290 2272, www.casadelacultura.gob.ec (click on Manifestaciones Culturales for programme).* Shows foreign films, often has documentaries, film festivals, free.
Ocho y Medio, *Valladolid N24-353 y Guipuzcoa, La Floresta, T02-290 4720.* Cinema and café, good for art films, programme available at *Libri Mundi* and elsewhere.

Dance
Casa de la Danza, *Junín E2-186 y Javier Gutiérrez, Parque San Marcos in colonial city, T02-295 5445, www.casadeladanza.org.* Run by the well-known Ecuadorean dancer Susana Reyes, is the venue for dance festivals and events. Also has **Museo del Danzante**, an exhibit about Ecuadorean folk dance and hosts other exhibits and folk

dance presentations on Thu or Sat night. Enquire ahead.

Dance schools 1-to-1 or group lessons are offered for US$4-6 per hr.
Ritmo Tropical, *Amazonas N24-155 y Calama, T02-255 7094, www.ritmotropicalsalsa.com.* Salsa, capoeira, merengue, tango and more.
Salsa y Merengue School, *Foch E4-256 y Amazonas, T02-222 0427*, also cumbia.

Ecuadorean folk ballet Ballet Andino **Humanizarte** (Casa 707, Morales 707, La Ronda, T02-257 3486. Thu 2100, Fri-Sat 2130, US$5), plays and comedies are also often in their repertoire, restaurant on the premises. **Jacchigua** (at **Teatro Demetrio Aguilera Malta**, Casa de la Cultura, 6 de Diciembre y Patria, T02-295 2025, www. jacchiguaesecuador.com. Wed at 1930). Entertaining, colourful and touristy, reserve ahead, US$30, students US$25. Other dance groups highlighting Ecuadorean traditions and folklore are **Saruymanda** (T09-8414 3747, www.saruymanda.com) and **Danzando Tierra** (at Casona del Centro de Desarrollo Comunitario de San Marcos, T09-8393 7813).

Music
Classical The **Orquesta Sinfónica Nacional** (T02-250 2815), performs at **Teatro Sucre**, **Casa de la Música**, **Teatro Escuela Politécnica Nacional**, **Teatro México**, in the colonial churches and regionally. **Casa de la Música** (Valderrama s/n y Mariana de Jesús, T02-226 7093, www.casadelamusica.ec), concerts by the Orquesta Sinfónica Nacional, Orquesta Filarmónica del Ecuador, Orquesta de Instrumentos Andinos and invited performers. Excellent acoustics.

Folk Folk music is popular in *peñas* which come alive after 2230:
Noches de Quito, *Washington E5-29 y JL Mera, T02-223 4855. Thu-Sat 2000-0300, show starts 2130.* Varied music, entry US$6.
Ñucanchi, *Av Universitaria Oe5-188 y Armero, T02-254 0967. Thu-Sat 2000-0300, show starts at 2130.* Ecuadorean and other music,

including Latin dance later in the night, entry US$8-10.

Theatre
Agora (open-air theatre), **Teatro Nacional** (large) and **Prometeo** (informal), all at Casa de la Cultura, stage plays and concerts. For upcoming events, see website listed under Cinema.
Teatro Bolívar, *Espejo 847 y Guayaquil, T02-258 2486, www.teatrobolivar.org.* Despite restoration work you can have a tour.
Teatro Sucre, *at Plaza del Teatro, T02-295 1661, www.teatrosucre.org (includes programme).* Beautifully restored 19th-century building, the city's classical theatre.

Festivals

New Year **Años Viejos**: life-size puppets satirize politicians and others. At midnight on 31 Dec a will is read, the legacy of the outgoing year, and the puppets are burnt; good at Av Amazonas, where a competition is held, very entertaining and good humoured. On New Year's day everything is shut.
6 Jan (may be moved to the weekend) Colourful **Inocentes** procesion from Plaza de Santo Domingo at 1700.
8 Mar International Women's Day, marks the start of **Mujeres en la Danza**, a week long international dance festival organized by Casa de la Danza, www.casadeladanza.org.
Mar-Apr **Música Sacra**, a 10-day religious music festival is held before and during Easter week. **Palm Sunday**, colourful procession from the Basílica, 0800-1000. The solemn **Good Friday** processions are most impressive.
24 May **Independence**, commemorating the Battle of Pichincha in 1822 with early morning cannon-fire and parades, everything closes.
Aug **Agosto Arte y Cultura**, organized by the municipality, cultural events, dance and music in different places throughout the city.
1-6 Dec **Día de Quito**. The city's main festival celebrated, commemorates the foundation of the city with elaborate

parades, bullfights, performances and music in the streets, very lively. Hotels charge extra, everything except a few restaurants shuts on 6 Dec.

25 Dec Foremost among **Christmas** celebrations is the **Misa del Gallo**, midnight Mass. Nativity scenes can be admired in many public places.

Shopping

Shops open generally 0900-1900 on weekdays, some close at midday and most shut Sat afternoon and Sun. Shopping centres are open at weekends. In modern Quito much of the shopping is done in malls. Be aware that over Christmas, Quito is crowded and the streets are packed with vendors and shoppers. For purchasing maps see Practicalities, page 717.

Bookshops
The following have a selection of books in English:
Confederate Books, *Amazonas N24-155 y Calama*. Used books.
Libri Mundi, *at Quicentro Shopping, other malls and the airport, www.librimundi.com*.
Mr Books, *Mall El Jardín, p3 and Scala and El Condado shopping centres, www.mrbooks.com*.
The English Bookshop, *Calama 217 y Almagro*. Used books sales and exchange.

Camping
Camping gas is available in many of the shops listed below, white gas is not.
Aventura Sport, *Quicentro Shopping, 2nd level*. Tents, good selection of glacier sunglasses, Ecuadorean and imported outdoor clothing and gear. The following two shops stock the same products.
Camping Sports, *Colón E6-39 y Reina Victoria*.
Equipos Cotopaxi, *6 de Diciembre N20-36 y Patria*.
Explorer, *Plaza Foch and all main shopping centres in the city*. Clothing and equipment for adventure sports.

Mono Dedo, *Rafael León Larrea N24-36 y Coruña, La Floresta, www.monodedoecuador. com*. Climbing equipment. Part of a rock climbing club, lessons.
Tatoo, *Av de los Granados y 6 de Diciembre and CC Scala in Cumbayá, www.tatoo.ws*. Quality backpacks and outdoor clothing.

Chocolate
Ecuador has exported its fine cacao to the most prestigious chocolatiers around the world for over 100 years. Today, quality chocolate is on offer in specialized shops and food stores.
Cacao & Cacao, *JL Mera N21-241 y Roca, T02-222 4951, Facebook: CacaoYCacao*. Shop and café featuring many brands of Ecuadorean chocolate and coffee.
Galería Ecuador, *Reina Victoria N24-263 y García, http://galeriaecuador.com*. Shop and café featuring Ecuadorean gourmet organic coffee and chocolate as well as some crafts.
Pacari, *Zaldumbide N24-676 y Miravalle, www.pacarichocolate.com*. Factory outlet for one of the most highly regarded manufacturers. They have won more international chocolate awards than any other company in the world. Also have an organic products market on Tue.
República del Cacao, *Reina Victoria y Pinto, Plaza Foch; Morales Oe1-166, La Ronda, Plaza de las Américas and at the airport, www. republicadelcacao.com*. Chocolate boutique and café, also sell Panama hats.

Handicrafts
There are controls on export of arts and crafts: unless they are obviously new handicrafts, you may have to get a permit from the **Instituto Nacional de Patrimonio Cultural** (Colón Oe1-93 y 10 de Agosto, T02-254 3527, offices also in other cities), before you can mail or take things home; permits cost US$5 and take time.

A wide selection can be found at the following craft markets: **Mercado Artesanal La Mariscal**, Jorge Washington, between Reina Victoria and JL Mera, daily 1000-

1800, interesting and worthwhile; **El Indio**, Roca E4-35 y Amazonas, daily 0900-1900; and **Centro de Artesanías CEFA**, 12 de Octubre1738 y Madrid, Mon-Sat 0930-1830.

On weekends, crafts are sold in stalls at **Parque El Ejido** and along the Av Patria side of this park, artists sell their paintings. There are crafts and art shops along La Ronda and souvenir shops on García Moreno in front of the Palacio Presidencial

Recommended shops with an ample selection are:

Camari, *Marchena 260 y Versalles.* Fair Trade shop run by an artisan organization.

EBD Carmal, *Amazonas N24-126 y Foch, ebdcarmal.com.* Panama and fedora hats.

Ethnic Collection, *Amazonas y Roca, Edif Hotel Mercure, www.ethniccollection.com.* Wide variety of clothing, leather, bags, jewellery and ceramic items. Also café 2 doors south.

Folklore, *Colón E10-53 y Caamaño, www.olgafisch.com.* The store of the late Olga Fisch, who for decades encouraged craftspeople to excel. Attractive selection of top quality, pricey handicrafts and rugs. Small museum upstairs includes a very good collection of pre-Columbian ceramics.

Galería Latina, *JL Mera 823 y Veintimilla. Daily.* Fine selection of alpaca and other handicrafts from Ecuador, Peru and Bolivia, visiting artists sometimes demonstrate their work.

Hilana, *6 de Diciembre N23-10 y Veintimilla.* Beautiful unique 100% wool blankets, ponchos and clothing with Ecuadorean motifs, also cotton garnments, excellent quality.

Kallari, crafts from Oriente at café, page 512.

K Dorfzaun, fine Panama hats are sold at the **República del Cacao** shops, see under Chocolate, above.

La Bodega, *JL Mera 614 y Carrión.* Recommended for antiques and handicrafts.

Mindalae, nice crafts at museum, page 503.

Productos Andinos, *Urbina 111 y Cordero.* Artisan's co-op, good selection, unusual items.

Saucisa, *Amazonas N22-18 y Veintimilla, and a couple other locations in La Mariscal.*

Very good place to buy Andean music and instruments.

Jewellery

Argentum, *JL Mera 614.* Excellent selection, reasonably priced.

Ari Gallery, *Bolívar Oe6-23, Plaza San Francisco.* Fine silver with ancestral motifs.

Taller Guayasamín, at the **Capilla del Hombre**, see page 504. Jewellery with native designs.

What to do

Birdwatching and nature

The following are specialized operators:

Andean Birding, www.andeanbirding.com; **BirdEcuador**, www.birdecuador.com; **Birdsexplore**, www.exploraves.com; **Ecuador Experience**, www.ecuador-experience.com (in French); **Mindo Bird Tours**, www.mindobirdtours.com; **Neblina Forest**, www.neblinaforest.com; **Real Nature**, www.realnaturetravel.com. **Tropical Birding**, www.tropicalbirding.com. Local birding guides are also available in Mindo.

City tours

Quito Tour Bus, *T02-245 8010, www.quitotourbus.com.* Tours on double-decker bus, stops at 11 places of interest, it starts and ends at Av Naciones Unidas, south side. You can start at any stop along the route and can alight at a site and continue later on another bus. Hourly, 0900-1600, 3-hr ride, US$15, children and seniors US$7.50, ticket valid all day. Night tour Fri, Sat and holidays at 1900, US$15, with a 1½-hr stop at La Ronda. Mitad del Mundo and Pululahua tour, Sat and Sun at 1100, US$30, children and seniors US$20, includes museum entrance fees, 7 hrs. They also offer a tour to Mitad del Mundo (without Pululahua), using a van instead of the double-decker bus, Tue, Thu 1300, US$30 pp, starts at Naciones Unidas, but can also arrange to be picked up at Plaza de la Independencia. Reservations required.

Rutas Turísticas, walking tours of the colonial city led by English- or French-speaking officers of the Policía Metropolitana start at the Plaza de la Independencia El Quinde Visitors Centre, Venezuela y Espejo, T02-257 2445. Advanced reservation and a minimum of 2 passengers required. 2 choices: **Ruta Patrimonial**, Tue-Sat at 0900, 1000 and 1400, Sun at 1100, 2½ hrs, US$15, children and seniors US$7.70, includes museum entrance fees for La Compañía, San Francisco and Museo de la Ciudad; and **Fachadas**, a daily historic buildings walking tour, at the same times, 1½ hrs, US$8; also an evening tour at 1800, US$10. On Sat 1900-2000, **Quito Eterno** (www.quitoeterno.org) a programme rescuing the city's identity, offers tours in which Quito's legenday characters guide you through their city.

Climbing, trekking and walking

The following Quito operators specialize in this area, most also offer conventional tours and sell Galápagos and jungle tours. Note that no one may climb without a licensed guide employed by an authorized agency. Independent climbers and guides are refused entry to national parks, but exceptions may be made for internationally (UIAA) certified guides and members of Ecuadorian climbing clubs.

Andes Explorer, *Tamayo N24-96 y Foch, of 801, T02-290 1493*. Good-value budget mountain and jungle trips.

Campus Adventures, *T02-234 0601, www.campus-trekking.com*. Good-value trekking, climbing and cultural tours, 8- to 15-day biking trips, tailor made itineraries. Also run **Hostería Pantaví** near Ibarra, 8 languages spoken.

Climbing Tours, *Amazonas N21-221 y Roca, T02-254 4358, www.climbingtour.com*. Climbing, trekking and other adventure sports, also tours to regional attractions, jungle tours and Galápagos. Well-established operator.

Compañía de Guías, *Valladolid N24-70 y Madrid, T02-290 1551, www.companiade guias.com*. Climbing and trekking specialists. Speak English, German, French and Italian.

Condor Trekk, *Reina Victoria N24-295 y Cordero, T02-222 6004, www.condortrekkexpeditions.com*. Climbing, trekking and fishing trips, 4WD transport, equipment rentals and sales.

Cotopaxi Cara Sur, *contact Eduardo Agama, T09-9800 2681, eagamaz@gmail.com*. Offers climbing and trekking tours, runs Albergue Cara Sur on Cotopaxi.

Gulliver, *JL Mera N24-156 y Calama, T02-290 5036, www.gulliver.com.ec*. Climbing and trekking and a wide range of economical adventure and traditional tours. Operate **Hostería Papagayo** south of Quito.

High Summits, *Pinto E5-29 y JL Mera, p2, T02-254 9358, www.climbing-ecuador.com*. Climbing specialists for over 40 years, Swiss/Ecuadorean-run.

Latitud 0°, *Mallorca N24-500 y Coruña, La Floresta, T02-254 7921, www.latitud0.com*. Climbing specialists, French spoken.

Original Ecuador, *La Tolita E18-195 y Pasaje Ninahualpa, p2, Guápulo, T02-255 9339, www.originalecuador.com*. Runs 1- to 7-day highland tours which involve walking several hours daily, also custom-made itineraries.

TribuTrek, *T09-9282 5404*. Hiking and trekking, cultural and budget tours.

Cycling and mountain biking

Quito has many bike paths and bike lanes on city streets, but mind the traffic and aggressive drivers. The city organizes a *ciclopaseo*, a cycle day, every Sun 0800-1400. Key avenues are closed to vehicular traffic and thousands of cyclists cross the city in 29 km from north to south. This and other cycle events are run by **Fundación Ciclópolis** (Equinoccio N17-171 y Queseras del Medio, T02-322 6502, www.ciclopolis. ec); they also hire bikes, US$5.60 per *ciclopaseo* (must book Mon-Fri), US$11.20 per day on other days. Rentals also from **La Casa del Ciclista** (Eloy Alfaro 1138 y República, near the *ciclopaseo* route, T02-254 0339, US$3 per hr, US$12 per day). If staying a long time in the city, sign up with **BiciQ**, to use their bikes stationed

Language schools

Quito is one of the most important centres for Spanish language study in Latin America with over 80 schools operating. There are also schools in Baños, Cuenca, Manta, Canoa and other cities. There is a great variety to choose from. Identify your budget and goals for the course: rigorous grammatical and technical training, fluent conversation skills, getting to know Ecuadoreans or just enough basic Spanish to get you through your trip.

Visit a few places to get a feel for what they charge and offer. Prices vary greatly, from US$5 to US$22 per hour. There is also tremendous variation in teacher qualifications, infrastructure and resource materials. Schools usually offer courses of four or seven hours tuition per day. Many readers suggest that four is enough. Some schools offer packages which combine teaching in the morning and touring in the afternoon, others combine teaching with travel to various attractions throughout the country. A great deal of emphasis has traditionally been placed on one-to-one teaching, but remember that a well-structured small classroom setting is also recommended.

The quality of homestays likewise varies, the cost including half board runs from US$16 to US$20 per day (more for full board). Try to book just one week at first to see how a place suits you. For language courses as well as homestays, deal directly with the people who will provide services to you, avoid intermediaries and always get a detailed receipt.

If you are short on time then it can be a good idea to make your arrangements from home, either directly with one of the schools or through an agency, who can offer you a wide variety of options. If you have more time and less money, then it may be more economical to organize your own studies after you arrive.

See What to do, Language courses, for schools in Quito and other cities. We list those for which we have received positive recommendations, but there are other good schools as well.

throughout town. **Biciacción**, www.biciaccion.org, has information about routes in the city and organizes trips outside Quito.

Mountain bike tours Many operators offer bike tours, the following are specialists:
Aries, *T09-9981 6603, www.ariesbike company.com*. 1- to 3-day tours, all equipment provided.
Biking Dutchman, *La Pinta E-731 y Reina Victoria, T02-256 8323, after hours T09-9420 5349, www.bikingdutchman.com*. 1- and several-day tours, great fun, good food, very well organized, English, German and Dutch spoken, pioneers in mountain biking in Ecuador.

Horse riding
Horse riding tours are offered on Pichincha above the gate of the *teleférico* (see page 504).

Green Horse Ranch, *see page 533*.
Ride Andes, *T09-9973 8221, www.rideandes. com*. Private and set date tours in the highlands including stays in haciendas, also in other South American countries.

Language courses
Amazonas, *www.eduamazonas.com*.
Andean Global Studies, *www.andean globalstudies.org*.
Beraca, *www.beraca.net*.
Bipo & Toni's, *www.bipo.net*.
Cristóbal Colón, *www.colonspanish school.com*.
Equinox, *www.ecuadorspanish.com*.
Instituto Superior, *www.instituto-superior.net*.
La Lengua, *www.la-lengua.com*.
Sintaxis, *www.sintaxis.net*.
South American, *www.southamerican.edu.ec*.

Universidad Católica, *T02-299 1700 ext 1388, idiomas@puce.edu.ec*. Group lessons.
Vida Verde, *www.vidaverde.com*.

Motorbiking
Freedom Bike Rental, *Juan de Velasco N26-132, T02-600 4459, www.freedombikerental.com*. Motorcycle rentals US$75-200 per day, scooter US$25, good equipment including mountain bikes, GPS, route planning, also tours.

Paragliding
Escuela Pichincha de Vuelo Libre, *Carlos Endara Oe3-60 y Amazonas, T02-225 6592 (office hours), T09-9993 1206, parapent@uio.satnet.net*. Offers complete courses for US$450 and tandem flights for US$65-US$105 (Pichincha).

Tour operators
Most operators also sell Galápagos cruises and jungle tours.
Advantage Travel, *Gaspar de Villarroel 1100 y 6 de Diciembre, T02-336 0887, www.advantagecuador.com*. Tours on the **Manatee** floating hotel on Río Napo and to Machalilla.
Andando Tours – Angermeyer Cruises, *Moreno Bellido E6-167 y Amazonas, T02-323 8631, www.andandotours.com*. Operate the *Mary Anne* sailing vessel, *Anahi* catamaran and *Passion* motor yacht, as well as land-based highland tours, see www.humbolt expeditions.com.
Andean Travel Company, *Amazonas N24-03 y Wilson, p 3, T02-222 8385, www.andeantc.com*. Dutch/Ecuadorean-owned operator, wide range of tours including trekking and cruises on the *Nemo I* catamaran and *San José* yacht.
Andes Overland, *Muros N27-94 y González Suárez, T02-512 3358, www.andesoverland.com*. A new venture that offers a 72-day tour through Bolivia, Peru, Ecuador and Colombia, offered with 2 levels of comfort. Shorter itineraries are also available. Part of an international group, which guarantees departure.

Creter Tours, *Pinto E5-29 y JL Mera, T02-254 5491, www.cretertours.com.ec*. Operate the *Treasure of Galapagos* catamaran, day tours on the *Freewind* and *Solmar* vessels and sell island-hopping tours.
Dracaena, *Pinto E4-375 y Amazonas, T02-290 6644, www.amazondracaena.com*. Runs good budget jungle tours to **Nicky Lodge** in Cuyabeno and trekking trips, popular.
EcoAndes/Unigalapagos, *JL Mera N23-36 y Baquedano, T02-222 0892, www.ecoandestravel.com*. Classic and adventure tours, volunteer opportunities Also operate hotels in Quito.
Ecoventura, *La Niña E8-52 y Almagro, T02-323 7393, www.ecoventura.com*. Operate first-class Galápagos cruises on the *Eric*, *Flamingo I*, *Letty* and *Origin* motor yachts and sell mainland tours.
Ecuador Galapagos Travels (EGT), *Veintimilla E10-78 y 12 de Octubre, Edif El Girón, Torre E, of 104, T02-254 7286, www.galapagos-cruises.ec, www.ecuadortravels.ec*. Wide range of traditional and adventure tours throughout Ecuador; tailor-made itineraries.
Ecuador Journeys, *T02-603 5548, www.ecuadorexpatjourneys.com*. Adventure tours to off-the-beaten-path destinations, day tours, treks to volcanoes, tours to expat hotspots.
Ecuador Nature, *Jiménez de la Espada N32-156 y González Suárez, T02-222 2341, www.ecuadornature.com*. Offers a variety of mainland and Galápagos tours, can arrange kosher food.
Ecuador Treasure, *Wilson E4-269 y JL Mera, T02-255 9919, 09-8901 6638, www.facebook.com/ecuador.treasure*. Daily tours, climbing, hiking, biking, trekking, horse riding and transport including a shuttle service to Lago Agrio, see page 654. Run **Chuquiragua Lodge**, near Reserva Los Ilinizas.
Enchanted Expeditions, *de las Alondras N45-102 y de los Lirios, T02-334 0525, www.enchantedexpeditions.com*. Operate the *Cachalote* and *Beluga* Galápagos vessels, sell jungle trips to Cuyabeno and highland tours. Very experienced.

Equateur Voyages Passion, *Gran Colombia N15-220 y Yaguachi, next to L'Auberge Inn, T02-322 7605, www.magical-ecuador.com.* Full range of adventure tours, run in highlands, coast and jungle. Also custom-made itineraries.

Galacruises Expeditions, *9 de Octubre N22-118 y Veintimilla, pb, T02-252 3324, www.islasgalapagos.travel.* Galápagos cruises on the *Archipel I and II* vessels and diving tours on the *Pingüino Explorer.* Also island hopping and land tours on Isabela, where they operate **Casa Isabela on the Beach.**

Galasam, *Amazonas N24-214 y Cordero, T02-290 3909, www.galasam.net.* Has a fleet of boats in different categories for Galápagos cruises, including the *Humboldt Explorer* diving yacht. City tours, full range of highland tours and jungle trips to **Siona Lodge** in Cuyabeno.

Galextur, *De los Motilones E14-58 y Charapa, T02-292 1739.* Run land-based Galápagos tours with daily sailings. Sell live aboard and diving tours on the *Astrea* motor yacht. Operate **Hotel Silberstein** in Puerto Ayora and **City Art Hotel Silberstein** in Quito. Good service.

Geo Reisen, *Shyris N36-46 y Suecia, T02-243 6081, www.georeisen-ecuador.com.* Specializing in cultural, adventure and nature tours adapted for individuals, groups or families.

Happy Gringo, *Catalina Aldaz N34-155 y Portugal, Edif Catalina Plaza, of 207, T02-512 3486, www.happygringo.com.* Tailor-made tours throughout Ecuador, Quito city tours, Otavalo, sell Galápagos, jungle and other destinations, good service. Recommended.

Klein Tours, *Eloy Alfaro N34-151 y Catalina Aldaz, also Shyris N34-280 y Holanda, T02-226 7000, www.kleintours.com.* Operate the *Galapagos Legend* and *Coral I* and *II* cruise ships. Also run community-based tours in Imbabura and highland tours with tailor-made itineraries, English, French and German spoken.

Latin Trails, T02-286 7377, www.latintrails.com. Run cruises in various Galápagos vessels including the *Seaman Journey*, *Sea Star Journey* and *Odyssey*; offer a variety of land trips in several countries and operate **Hakuna Matata Lodge** in Archidona.

Metropolitan Touring, Av de las Palmeras N45-74 y de las Orquídeas, T1800-115115, T02-298 8312, www.metropolitan-touring.com. A large organization operating in Ecuador, Peru, Chile and Argentina. Run several luxury Galápagos vessels (see pages 673 and 682), the **Finch Bay Hotel** in Puerto Ayora, **Casa Gangotena** in Quito and **Mashpi Lodge** west of Quito. Also adventure, cultural and gastronomy tours.

Positiv Turismo, Jorge Juan N33-38 y Atahualpa, T02-600 9401, www.positiv turismo.com. Cultural trips, Cuyabeno, trekking and special interest tours, Swiss-run.

Pure! Ecuador, Muros N27-94 y González Suárez, T02-512 3358, www.pure-ecuador.com. A Dutch-Ecuadorean operator offering tours throughout Ecuador and the Galápagos, trips to **Cotococha Amazon Lodge**, **Polylepis Lodge** (El Angel), **Cabras y Tunas** (Chota Valley) and tailor-made tours.

Quasar Náutica, T02-244 6996, T1-800 247 2925 (USA), www.quasarnautica.com. Offer 7- to 10-day naturalist and diving Galápagos cruises on 8- to 16-berth yachts.

Rolf Wittmer Turismo/Tip Top Travel, Foch E7-81 y Almagro, T02-2563181, www.rwittmer. com. Run first class yachts: *Tip Top III* and *IV*. Also tailor-made tours throughout Ecuador.

South America for All, T02-237 7430, www. southamericaforall.com. Specialized tours to all regions of Ecuador for the mobility and hearing-impaired traveller. Also operate in Peru and Argentina and run the **Huasquila Amazon Lodge** near Tena.

Surtrek, San Ignacio E10-114 y Caamaño, T02-250 0660, T1-866-978 7398 in the US, www.surtrek.com. Wide range of tours in all regions, helicopter and ballon flights, birdwatching, rafting, horse riding, mountain biking and jungle tours, arrange last minute

Galápagos tours, also sell domestic flights and run **Las Cascadas Lodge**.

Tierra de Fuego, Amazonas N23-23 y Veintimilla, T02-250 1418, www.ecuador tierradefuego.com. Provide transport and tours throughout the country, book domestic flight tickets, make Galápagos bookings and own and operate the *Guantanamera* yacht.

Tropic Journeys in Nature, Pasaje Sánchez Melo Oe1-37 y Av Galo Plaza, T02-240 8741, www.destinationecuador.com. Environmental and cultural tours, private day tours in Quito city, coast, highlands, lodge-to-lodge mountain treks, Chilcabamba Mountain Lodge near Cotopaxi, Amazon lodges and Galápagos land-based and multisport tours. Community-based tourism working with and donating a percentage of all profits to **Conservation in Action**. Winner of awards for responsible tourism.

Yacu Amu Experiences, Amazonas N25-23 y Colón, Edif España, of 58, T02-255 0558, www.yacuamu.com. Tailor-made adventure, nature and cultural trips for active couples, families and small groups.

Zenith Travel, JL Mera N24-264 y Cordero, T02-252 9993, www.zenithecuador.com. Good-value Galápagos cruises as well as various land tours in Ecuador and Peru. All-gay Galápagos cruises available. Multilingual service, knowledgeable helpful staff, good value.

Train rides

The lovely refurbished train station, **Estación Eloy Alfaro (Chimbacalle)**, with a railway museum and working concert hall, is 2 km south of the colonial city at Maldonado y Sincholagua, T1-800-873637, T02-265 6142, www.trenecuador.com, Mon-Fri 0800-1630. *Tren Crucero*, a luxury tourist train, runs about twice per month (but not every month) in either direction between Quito and Durán, outside Guayaquil, part of the route is run with a historic steam locomotive. The complete route takes 4 days and costs US$1393 one way; you can also take it for segments 1-3 days. The tour includes visits to places of interest and accommodation in luxury inns. See www.trenecuador.com/crucero for details. Tourist trains run Thu-Sun and holidays from Quito to **Machachi** and **El Boliche** (0800, US$39-44 includes lunch), combined transport by train one way and by bus the other. A farm is visited in Machachi. At El Boliche station is **Restaurante Nuna**, and nearby, **Area Nacional de Recreación El Boliche**, a protected area bordering Parque Nacional Cotopaxi, where the tour includes a walk. There are lovely views of Cotopaxi and Los Ilinizas. Purchase tickets in advance by phone, internet, at the station or **El Quinde Visitors Centre,** Palacio Municipal, Venezuela y Espejo. You need each passenger's passport number and age to purchase tickets. Boarding 30 mins before departure, you can visit the railway museum before boarding.

Whitewater rafting

Río Blanco/Toachi tours cost US$87. **Ríos Ecuador**, *T02-260 5828 in Quito, www.riosecuador.com*. Rafting and kayaking trips of 1-6 days, also have an office in Tena and run trips in Oriente.

Air

Details of internal air service are given under the respective destinations. Quito's **Mariscal Sucre Airport** (T02-395 4200, www.quitoairport.aero for information about current arrival and departures, airport services and airlines) is in Tababela, off Highway E-35, about 30 km northeast of the city, at 2134 m above sea level. There are ATMs and a *casa de cambio* for exchange in the arrivals level and banks and ATMs in the shopping mall across the street. Luggage storage and lockers downstairs at arrivals, www.bagparkingquito.com, US$7-15 per case per day; see also **Quito Airport Suites** hotel, page 509. The information office (arrivals level, T02-395 4200, ext 2008, open 24 hrs), will assist with hotel bookings. The

airport taxi cooperative, T02-281 8008, www.taxinquitoecuador.com, has set rates to different zones of the city; these are posted by arrivals (US$25 to La Mariscal, US$26 to colonial Quito, US$33 to Quitumbe bus station, US$26.50 to Carcelén station); taxi rates from the city to the airport are about 10% cheaper. **Aero Servicios** express bus, T02-604 3500, T1-800-237673, runs 24 hrs per day, between the new airport and the old airport in northern Quito (Parque Bicentenario), US$8, US$4 seniors and children. From Tababela, departures are hourly from 2400 to 0600 and every 30 mins the rest of the day; from Quito, departures are hourly from 1800 to 0300 and every 30 mins the rest of the day. They also offer transfers between the old airport and other locations in the city (eg.US$3.50 to/from the Mariscal, US$4 to/from the colonial city). Taking a transfer service or a taxi from the old airport to your hotel is recommended. **HATS**, T223 1824 or T09-8336 1518, shuttle bus to/from hotels in La Mariscal, US$10 pp, minimum 4 passengers. Regional buses with limited stops, run every 15 mins, 0600-2145, between the airport and Terminal Quitumbe in the south and Terminal Río Coca in the north, US$2. Private van services are good value for groups, but require advanced arrangements: **Trans-Rabbit**, T02-290 2690, www.transrabbit.com.ec, US$30 for 2 passengers, US$5 per additional person.

Note It takes at least 45 mins to reach the airport from Quito, but with traffic it can be much longer, allow enough time. There are 3 access roads to the airport: the most direct from the city centre is the Ruta Viva which starts on Av Simón Bolívar; the Vía Interoceánica originates in Plaza Argentina, northeast of La Mariscal, and goes through the suburbs of Cumbaya, Tumbaco and Puembo; and the Vía Collas, starts in Oyacoto, past the toll both along the Panamericana, north of the city. If going to the airport from other cities, take a bus that bypasses Quito along highway E-35 (available from Baños, Ambato and Ibarra), get off at the airport roundabout and take the regional bus 4.5 km from there. If coming from the east (Papallacta, Baeza or Oriente), go as far as Pifo and transfer to the regional bus there.

Bus

Local Quito has 5 parallel mass transit lines running from north to south mostly on exclusive lanes, covering almost the length of the city. There are several transfer stations where you can switch from one line to another without cost. At rush hour there are express buses with limited stops. Feeder bus lines (*alimentadores*) go from the terminals to outer suburbs. Within the city the fare is US$0.25; the combined fare to some suburbs is US$0.40. Public transit is not designed for carrying heavy luggage and is often crowded. **Trole** (T02-266 5016, Mon-Fri 0500-2345, weekends and holidays 0600-2145, plus hourly overnight service with limited stops) is a system of trolley buses which runs along Av 10 de Agosto in the north of the city, C Guayaquil (southbound) and C Flores (northbound) in colonial Quito, and mainly along Av Maldonado and Av Teniente Ortiz in the south. The northern terminus is north of 'La Y', the junction of 10 de Agosto, Av América and Av de la Prensa; south of the colonial city are important transfer stations at El Recreo and Morán Valverde; the southern terminus is at the Quitumbe bus station. Trolleys do not necessarily run the full length of the line, the destination is marked in front of the vehicle. Trolleys have a special entrance for wheelchairs. **Ecovía** (T02-243 0726, Mon-Sat 0500-2200, Sun and holidays 0600-2200), articulated buses, runs along Av 6 de Diciembre from Estación Río Coca, at C Río Coca east of 6 de Diciembre, in the north, to La Marín transfer station and on to Cumandá, east of colonial Quito. **Metrobus** (T02-346 5149, Mon-Fri 0530-2230, weekends and holidays 0600-2100) also runs articulated buses along Av de la Prensa and Av América from Terminal La Ofelia in the north to La Marín in the south. **Corredor Sur** buses run from the Seminario Mayor interchange (Av América y Colón) in the north, along Av América, Av Universitaria and Av Occidental to Terminal Quitumbe in the south; interchanges on this route are at Av Universitaria and the El Tejar and San Roque tunnels on Av Occidental; several routes branch out from Hospital del IESS station in the north. **Universidades** articulated buses run from 12 de Octubre y Veintimilla in the north to Quitumbe bus terminal. There are also 2 types of **city buses**: *Selectivos* are red, and *Bus Tipo* are royal blue, both cost US$0.25. Many bus lines go through La Marín and El Playón Ecovía/ Metrobus stations. Extra caution is advised here: pickpockets abound and it is best avoided at night. For **Quito Tour Bus**, see page 516.

Regional Outer suburbs are served by green *Interparroquial* buses. Those running east to the valleys of Cumbayá, Tumbaco and the airport leave from the Estación Río Coca (see Ecovía, above). Buses southeast to Valle de los Chillos leave from El Playón Ecovía/ Metrobus station, from Isabel la Católica y Mena Caamaño, behind Universidad Católica and from Alonso de Mercadillo by the Universidad Central. Buses going north (ie Calderón, Mitad del Mundo) leave from La Ofelia Metrobus station. Regional destinations to the north (ie Cayambe) and northwest (ie Mindo) leave from a regional station adjacent to La Ofelia Metrobus station. Buses west to Nono from the Plaza de Cotocollao, to Lloa from C Angamarca in Mena 2 neighbourhood. Buses south to Machachi from El Playón, La Villaflora and Quitumbe. Buses to Papallacta, Baeza and El Chaco leave from Chile E3-22 y Pedro Fermín Cevallos, near La Marín.

Long distance Quito has 2 main bus terminals: **Terminal Quitumbe** in the southwest of the city, T02-398 8200, serves destinations south, the coast via Santo Domingo, Oriente and Tulcán (in the north). It is served by the Trole (line 4: El Ejido–Quitumbe, best taken at El Ejido) and the Corredor Sur and Universidades buses, however it is advisable to take a taxi, about US$6, 30-45 mins to the colonial city, US$8-10, 45 mins-1 hr to La Mariscal. Arrivals and tourist information are on the ground floor. Ticket counters (destinations grouped and colour coded by region), and departures in the upper level. Left luggage (US$0.90 per day) and food stalls are at the adjoining shopping area. The terminal is large, allow extra time to reach your bus. Terminal use fee US$0.20. Watch your belongings at all times. On holiday weekends it is advisable to reserve the day before. The smaller **Terminal Carcelén**, Av Eloy Alfaro, where it meets the Panamericana Norte, serves destinations to the north (including Otavalo) and the coast via the Calacalí–La Independencia road. It is served by feeder bus lines from the northern terminals of the Trole, Ecovía and Metrobus, a taxi costs about US$5, 30-45 mins to La Mariscal, US$7, 45 mins-1 hr to colonial Quito. Ticket counters are organized by destination. See under destinations for fares and schedules; these are also listed in www.latinbus.com, where for US$3 you can also purchase tickets online for buses departing Quito. A convenient way to travel between Quitumbe and Carcelén is to take a bus bound for Tulcán, **Trans Vencedores** or **Unión del Carchi** (Booth 12), every 30 mins during the day, hourly at night, US$1, 1 hr; from Carcelén to Quitumbe, wait for a through bus arriving from the north; taxi between terminals, US$15.

All long distance buses depart from either Quitumbe or Carcelén, the following companies also have ticket sales points in modern Quito: **Flota Imbabura**, Larrea 1211 y Portoviejo, T02-256 9628, for **Cuenca**, **Guayaquil** and **Manta**; **Transportes Ecuador**, JL Mera N21-44 y Washington, T02-250 3842, hourly to **Guayaquil**; **Transportes Esmeraldas**, Santa María 870 y Amazonas, T02-250 9517, for **Esmeraldas**, **Atacames**, **Coca**, **Lago Agrio**, **Manta** and

Huaquillas. **Reina del Camino**, Larrea y 18 de Septiembre, T02-321 6633, for **Bahía**, **Puerto López** and **Manta**; **Carlos Aray** Larrea y Portoviejo, T02-256 4406, for **Manta** and **Puerto López**; **Transportes Loja**, Orellana y Jerves, T02-222 4306, for **Loja** and **Lago Agrio**, they offer transport from their office to Quitumbe for US$2.50 pp (minimum of 4 passengers); **Transportes Baños**, Santa María y JL Mera, T02-223 2752, for **Baños** and **Oriente** destinations. **Panamericana Internacional**, Colón E7-31 y Reina Victoria, T02-255 7133, ext 131 for national routes, ext 125 for international, for **Huaquillas**, **Machala**, **Cuenca**, **Loja**, **Manta**, **Guayaquil** and **Esmeraldas**.

International Buses depart from private stations; prices vary according to demand (higher in Jul-Aug and Dec); reserve ahead. **Ormeño Internacional**, from Perú, Shyris N35-52 y Portugal, of 3B, T02-245 6632, Tue, Thu and Sun to **Máncora**, US$50, 16 hrs and **Lima**, US$100, 36 hrs, with connections to other countries; Tue, Thu and Sat to **Cali**, US$80, 17 hrs and **Bogotá**, US$100, 30 hrs; every 2 weeks on Tue to **Medellín**, US$100, 30 hrs; Tue to **Caracas**, US$180-200, 2½ days. **Panamericana Internacional**, see above, to **Caracas**, on Mon; does not go into Colombian cities, but will let passengers off by the roadside (eg Popayán, Palmira for Cali, or Ibagué for Bogotá), **Rutas de América**, Selva Alegre Oe1-72 y 10 de Agosto, T02-250 3611, www.rutasenbus.com, to **Lima**, Thu and Sun; same days to **Cali**, US$60, 17 hrs, **Ibagué**, US$85, 28 hrs and **Caracas**. The route to **Peru** via Loja and Macará takes much longer than the Huaquillas route, but is more relaxed. Don't buy Peruvian (or any other country's) bus tickets here, they're cheaper outside Ecuador.

Car hire

All the main international car rental companies are at the airport. For rental procedures see Getting around, page 716. A local company is: **Simon Car Rental**,

Los Shyris 2930 e Isla Floreana, T02-243 1019, www.simoncarrental.com, good rates and service. **Achupallas Tours**, T02-255 1614, and **Trans-Rabbit**, T02-290 2690, www.transrabbit.com.ec, rent vans for 8-14 passengers, with driver, for trips in Quito and out of town.

Long-distance taxis and vans

Shared taxis and vans offer door-to-door service to some cities and avoid the hassle of reaching Quito's bus terminals. Some companies have set departures, others travel according to demand; on weekends there are fewer departures. Reserve at least 2 days ahead. There is service between Quito and Otavalo, Ibarra, Latacunga, Ambato, Riobamba, Cuenca, Baños, Puyo, Lago Agrio, Santo Domingo and Esmeraldas. For details, see Transport under the corresponding destination.

Taxi

Taxis are a cheap and efficient way to get around the city, but for safety it is important to know how to select a cab. Authorized taxis have orange license plates or white plates with an orange stripe on the upper edge; they display stickers with a unit number on the windshield, the front doors and back side-windows; the name of the company should be displayed on the back doors, the driver's photograph in the interior and they should have a working meter. Taxis with a red and blue 'Transporte Seguro' sticker on the windshield and back doors should have cameras and red panic buttons linked to the 911 emergency system. At night it is safer to use a radio taxi (*taxi ejecutivo*), ie: **Taxi Americano**, T02-222 2333; **Hot Line**, T02-222 2222; **City Taxi**, T02-263 3333. Make sure they give you the taxi number and description so that you get the correct vehicle, some radio taxis are unmarked. All taxis should use a meter, negotiate the price ahead if they refuse to use it. The minimum daytime fare is US$1.45, US$1.75 after 1900. Note the registration and the license plate numbers if you feel you have been seriously overcharged or mistreated. You may then complain to the municipal police or tourist office. To hire a taxi by the hour costs from US$8 in the city, more out of town. For trips outside Quito, agree the fare beforehand: US$70-85 a day. Outside luxury hotels cooperative taxi drivers have a list of agreed excursion prices and most drivers are knowledgeable.

Train

There is no regular passenger service. For tourist rides, see Train rides, page 521.

Mitad del Mundo

The location of the equatorial line here (23 km north of central Quito) was determined by Charles-Marie de la Condamine and his French expedition in 1736, and agrees to within 150 m with modern GPS measurements. The monument forms the focal point of **Ciudad Mitad del Mundo** ① *T02-239 4806, ext 115, 0900-1700 daily (very crowded on Sun), entry to complex and pavilions US$3.50, pavilions and planetarium US$5.50, pavilions and ethnographic museum US$6.50 (includes guided tour in Spanish or English), all the facilities US$7.50,* a leisure park built as a typical colonial town, with restaurants, gift shops, post office and travel agency. In the interior of the equatorial monument is the very interesting Museo Etnográfico, with displays about Ecuador's indigenous cultures. Each of the nations which participated in the 18th-century expedition has a pavilion with exhibits which include an interesting **model of old Quito**, about 10 m sq, with artificial day and night and an **insectarium**. The **Museo Inti-Ñan** ① *200 m north of the monument, T02-239 5122, www.museointinan.com.ec, daily 0930-1700, US$4,* is eclectic, very interesting, has lots of fun activities and gives equator certificates for visitors. Research about the equator and its importance to prehistoric cultures is carried out near Cayambe, by an organization called **Quitsato** ① *www.quitsato.org, daily 0800-1700, US$2.* Beyond Mitad del Mundo is Pululahua, see below.

> **Tip...**
> On weekends, **Quito Tour Bus**, see page 516, offers bus tours to Mitad del Mundo and Pululahua.

Papallacta

This small village high in the hills (3200 m), 64 km east of Quito, has thermal pools and walking opportunities. During the holidays and at weekends the hotels can get very busy. It is conveniently placed, 30 km east of the airport, so it is feasible to relax at the baths and go directly to the airport, without returning to the city (taxis can be arranged at the village).

☆At the **Termas de Papallacta** ① *2 km from the town of Papallacta, T02-250 4787 (Quito), www.termaspapallacta.com,* the best developed hot springs in the country, are eight thermal pools, three large enough for swimming, and four cold plunge pools. There are two public complexes of springs: the regular **pools** ① *daily 0600-2100, US$8.50,* and the **spa centre** ① *Mon-Fri 1000-1800, Sat-Sun 0900-1800, US$22 (massage and other special treatments extra).* There are additional pools at the Termas' hotel and cabins (see Where to stay, page 529) for the exclusive use of their guests. The complex is tastefully done and recommended.

In addition to the Termas there are nice municipal pools in the village of Papallacta: **Santa Catalina** ① *daily 0800-1800, US$3* and several more economical places to stay (some with pools) on the road to the Termas and in the village. On weekends and holidays all the pools and hotels are busy. The view, on a clear day, of Antisana while enjoying the thermal waters is superb. Along the highway to Quito, are several additional thermal pools. Note that Quito airport is between Quito and Papallacta.

There are several walking paths in the **Rancho del Cañón private reserve** ① *behind the Termas, US$2 for use of a short trail, to go on longer walks you are required to take a guide for US$8 pp.* To the north of this private reserve is Reserva Cayambe-Coca ① *T02-211 0370, werner.barrera@ambiente.gob.ec.* A scenic road starts by the Termas information centre, crosses both reserves and leads in 45 km to Oyacachi. A permit from Cayambe-Coca headquarters is required to travel this road even on foot, write ahead. It is a lovely two-day walk, there is a ranger's station and camping area 1½ hours from Papallacta. Reserva Cayambe-Coca is also accessed from La Virgen, the pass on the road to Quito, where there is a ranger's station. **Ríos Ecuador**, see Quito, Whitewater rafting, offer a hiking tour here which can be combined with rafting.

Refugio de Vida Silvestre Pasochoa
45 mins southeast of Quito by car, very busy at weekends; park office at El Ejido de Amaguaña, T09-9894 5704.

This natural park is set in humid Andean forest between 2700 m and 4200 m. The reserve has more than 120 species of birds (unfortunately some of the fauna has been frightened away by the noise of the visitors) and 50 species of trees. There are walks of 30 minutes to eight hours. There are picnic and camping areas. Take a good sleeping bag, food and water.

☆Western slopes of Pichincha
Despite their proximity to the capital (two hours from Quito), the western slopes of Volcán Pichincha and its surroundings are surprisingly wild, with fine opportunities for walking and birdwatching (the altitude ranges from 1200-2800 m). This scenic area known as **El Noroccidente** has lovely cloudforests and many nature reserves. The main tourist town in this region is Mindo. To the west of Mindo is a warm subtropical area of clear rivers and waterfalls, with a number of reserves, resorts and lodges.

Ecoruta Two roads go from Quito over the western Cordillera before dropping into the northwestern lowlands. The old route via **Nono** (the only town of any size along this route) and **Tandayapa**, is dubbed the Ecoruta or **Paseo del Quinde** (Route of the Hummingbird). It begins towards the northern end of Avenida Mariscal Sucre (Occidental), Quito's western ring road, at the intersection with Calle Machala. With increased awareness of the need to conserve the cloudforests of the northwest slopes of Pichincha and of their potential for tourism, the number of reserves here is steadily growing. Keen birdwatchers are no longer the only visitors and the region has much to offer all nature lovers. Infrastructure at reserves varies considerably. Some have comfortable upmarket lodges offering accommodation, meals, guides and transport. Others may require taking your own camping gear, food, and obtaining a permit. There are too many reserves and lodges to mention here.

Above Tandayapa along the Ecoruta is **Bellavista Cloud Forest Reserve** ⓘ *T02-211 6232 (lodge), 09-9416 5868 (cell phone), www.bellavistacloudforest.com*, a 700-ha private reserve rich in botany and fauna, including the olinguito (*Bassaricyon neblina*), a mammal new to science, first identified in 2013 (you can see it near the lodge most evenings). Excellent birdwatching and guides, lovely scenery including waterfalls. There are 10 km of well-maintained trails ranging from wheelchair accessible to slippery/suicidal. Day-visits including transport from Quito, two meals and guided walks arranged, restaurant open to non-guests. For lodge information, see Where to stay, below.

The new route From the Mitad del Mundo monument the road goes past **Calacalí**, also on the equator, whose plaza has an older monument to the Mitad del Mundo. Beyond Calacalí at Km 15 a road turns south to Nono and north to Yunguilla, with a community tourism project (www.yunguilla.org.ec). Another road at Km 52 goes to Tandayapa and Bellavista. The main road, with heavy traffic at weekends, continues to Nanegalito (Km 56), Miraflores (Km 62) where another road goes to the Ecoruta, the turn-off for a third road to the Ecoruta at Km 77 and the turn-off for Mindo at Km 79. Further west are San Miguel de los Bancos, Pedro Vicente Maldonado and Puerto Quito, before reaching the Santo Domingo–Esmeraldas road at La Independencia.

Pululahua ① *park office by the rim lookout, T02-239 6543, 0800-1700*, is a geobotanical reserve in an inhabited, farmed volcanic caldera. A few kilometres beyond Mitad del Mundo, off the road to Calacalí, Mirador Ventanillas, a lookout on the rim of Pululahua gives a great view, but go in the morning, as the cloud usually descends around 1300. You can go down to the reserve and experience the rich vegetation and warm micro-climate inside. From the mirador: walk down 30 minutes to the agricultural zone then turn left. There are picnic and camping areas. A longer road allows you to drive into the crater via Moraspungo. To walk out this way, starting at the mirador, continue past the village in the crater, turn left and follow the unimproved road up to the rim and back to the main road, a 15- to 20-km round trip.

At **Nanegalito**, the transport hub for this area, is the turn-off to Nanegal and the cloudforest in the 18,500-ha **Maquipucuna Biological Reserve** ① *www.maqui.org, knowledgeable guides: US$25 (Spanish), US$100 (English) per day for a group of 9*, which contains a tremendous diversity of flora and fauna, including spectacled bear, which can be seen when the *aguacatillo* trees are in fruit (around January) and about 350 species of birds. The reserve has 40 km of trails (US$10 per person) and a lodge (see below).

Next to Maquipucuna is **Santa Lucía** ① *T02-215 7242, www.santaluciaecuador.com*. Access to this reserve is 30 minutes by car from Nanegal and a walk from there. Day tours combining Pululahua, Yunguilla and Santa Lucía are available. Bosque Nublado Santa Lucía is a community-based conservation and ecotourism project protecting a beautiful 650-ha tract of cloudforest. The area is very rich in birds (there is a cock-of-the-rock lek) and other wildlife. There are waterfalls and walking trails and a lodge (see below).

At **Armenia** (Km 60), a few kilometres beyond Nanegalito, a road heads northwest through Santa Clara, with a handicrafts market on Sunday, to the village and archaeological site of **Tulipe** (14 km; 1450 m). The site consists of several man-made 'pools' linked by water channels. A path leads beside the Río Tulipe in about 15 minutes to a circular pool amid trees. The site **museum** ① *T02-285 0635, www.museodesitiotulipe.com, US$3, Wed-Sun 0900-1600, guided tours (arrange ahead for English)*, has exhibits in Spanish on the Yumbos culture and the *colonos* (contemporary settlers). There is also an orchid garden. For reserves and tours in the area, see www.tulipecloudforest.org and www.cloudforestecuador.com.

The Yumbos were traders who linked the Quitus with coastal and jungle peoples between AD 800-1600. Their trails are called *culuncos*, 1 m wide and 3 m deep, covered in vegetation for coolness. Several treks in the area follow them. Also to be seen are *tolas*, raised earth platforms; there are some 1500 around Tulipe. **Turismo Comunitario Las Tolas** ① *6 km from Tulipe, T02-286 9488*, offers lodging, food, craft workshops and guides to *tolas* and *culuncos*.

To the northwest of Tulipe are **Gualea** and **Pacto**, beyond which is $$$$ **Mashpi Lodge** and **Reserve**, www.mashpilodge.com. Back along the main road, by Miraflores, is **Tucanopy** (turn north at Km 63.5, closed Wednesday), www.tucanopy.com, a reserve with lodging, trails, canopy zip-lines and conservation volunteer opportunities. At Km 79 is the turn-off for Mindo.

Mindo Mindo, a small town surrounded by dairy farms and lush cloudforest climbing the western slopes of Pichincha, is the main access for the 19,500-ha Bosque Protector Mindo-Nambillo. The reserve, which ranges in altitude from 1400 m to 4780 m, features beautiful flora (many orchids and bromeliads), fauna (butterflies, frogs, about 450 species of birds including the cock-of-the-rock, golden-headed quetzal and toucan-barbet) and spectacular cloudforest, rivers and waterfalls. The region's rich diversity is threatened by proposed mining in the area. **Amigos de la Naturaleza de Mindo** ⓘ *9 de Octubre opposite El Quetzal Café, T02-217 0086, luisnolbertoj@yahoo.com, Tue-Sat 0900-1200, 1330-1700, entry US$2, US$40 per group for guided walk,* runs the **Centro de Educación Ambiental (CEA)** 4 km from town, a 17-ha reserve, with a shelter for 30 people. Lodging: US$25 per person full board including excursion. Arrangements have to be made in advance. During the rainy season (October to May), access to the reserve can be rough. There are also several private reserves with lodges bordering the Bosque Protector. The area has many rivers and waterfalls. Mindo also has orchid gardens, butterfly farms, a climbing wall (www. mindopuravida.com) and a microbrewery and chocolate factory. Activities include visits to waterfalls, canopy zip-lines, canyoning and tubing regattas in the rivers. The town gets very crowded with Quiteños at weekends and holidays.

West of Mindo The road continues west beyond the turn-off to Mindo, descending to the subtropical zone north of Santo Domingo de los Tsáchilas. It goes via San Miguel de los Bancos, Pedro Vicente (PV) Maldonado and Puerto Quito (on the lovely Río Caoni) to La Independencia on the Santo Domingo–Esmeraldas road. From San Miguel de Los Bancos two side-roads also go to Santo Domingo. The entire area is good for birdwatching, swimming in rivers and natural pools, walking, kayaking, or simply relaxing in pleasant natural surroundings. There are many reserves, resorts, lodgings and places to visit along the route, of particular interest to birdwatchers. There are tours from Quito, see What to do, above. See Where to stay, below, for resorts.

Listings Around Quito

Tourist Information

Municipal Tourist Information
Quito y 9 de Octubre, next to the bus station, Mindo, turismo.municipiosmb@gmail.com. Tue-Fri and Sun 0730-1300, 1430-1700.
Plenty of local information and pamphlets, map, some English spoken, very helpful.

Where to stay

Papallacta

$$$$ Guango Lodge
Near Cuyuja, 9 km east of Papallacta, T02-289 1880 (Quito), www.guangolodge.com.
In a 350 ha temperate forest reserve along the Río Papallacta. Includes 3 good meals, nice facilities, excellent birdwatching. Day visits US$5. Reserve ahead. Taxi from Papallacta US$10.

$$$$ Hotel Termas Papallacta
At the Termas complex, T06-289 5060.
Comfortable heated rooms and suites, good expensive restaurant, thermal pools set in a lovely garden, nice lounge with fireplace, some rooms with private jacuzzi, also cabins for up to 6, transport from Quito extra. Guests have access to all areas in the complex and get discounts at the spa. For weekends and holidays book 1 month in advance. Recommended.

$$$-$$ Hostería Pampallacta
On the road to Termas, T06-289 5022, www.pampallactatermales.com.
A variety of rooms with bathtubs, pools for exclusive use for guests, higher prices on the weekend, restaurant.

$$$-$$ La Choza de Don Wilson
At turn-off for Termas, T06-289 5027,
www.hosteriachozapapallacta.com.
Rooms with nice views of the valley, fancier
rooms have hot tubs and heaters, cheaper
rooms are small and heaters extra, good
popular restaurant, pools (US$5 for non-
residents), attentive.

$$ Coturpa
Next to the Santa Catalina baths in Papallacta
town, T06-289 5040, wwwhostalcoturpa.com.
A variety of rooms, some with hot tubs,
heaters, restaurant.

$$-$ El Leñador
By entrance to Termas, T06-289 5003.
Simple rooms with electric shower, skylights
make it bright and warm, restaurant,
breakfast extra.

Western slopes of Pichincha
Ecoruta

$$$$ Tandayapa Bird Lodge
T02-244 7520 (Quito), www.tandayapa.com.
Designed and owned by birders. Full board,
comfortable rooms, some have a canopy
platform for observation, large common area;
packages including guide and transport from
Quito. Not always staffed, must reserve ahead.

$$$$-$$$ Bellavista Cloud Forest
T02-361 3447 (lodge), in Quito at Jorge
Washington E7-25 y 6 de Diciembre, T02-
223 2313, www.bellavistacloudforest.com.
A dramatic lodge perched in beautiful
cloudforest, includes unique geodesic
dome. A variety of comfortable rooms with
great views ranging from large superior
rooms (completed in 2015) to rooms
with shared bath, all include 3 excellent
meals (with vegetarian options), heaters,
1 wheelchair-accessible room. Bilingual
guide service included in packages. Good
research station with dorms and kitchen
facilities (US$20 pp), camping US$9 pp.
Package tours with guide and transport
from Quito available. Guided tours to Mindo
and other reserves in the area. Restaurant
open to non-guests for breakfast and lunch.
Best booked in advance. Very good service.
Recommended.

$$$ San Jorge
T02-339 0403, www.eco-lodgesanjorge.com.
A series of reserves with lodges in bird-
rich areas. One is 4 km from Quito (see
Hostería San Jorge, page 508), 1 in
Tandayapa at 1500 m and another
in Milpe, off the new road, at 900 m.
Advanced reservations required.

The new route

$$$$ Santa Lucía
T02-215 7242, www.santaluciaecuador.com.
The lodge with panoramic views is a 1½-hr walk from the access to the reserve. Price includes full board with good food and guiding. There are cabins with private bath, rooms with shared composting toilets and hot showers and dorms ($ pp including food but not guiding).

$$$$-$$$ Maquipucuna Lodge
T02-250 7200, 09-9237 1945, www.maqui.org.
Comfortable rustic lodge, includes full board with good meals using ingredients from own organic garden (vegetarian and vegan available). Rooms range from shared to rooms with bath, hot water, electricity. Campsite is 20 mins' walk from main lodge, under US$6 pp (food extra), cooking lessons, chocolate massages.

$$$ Hostería Sumak Pakari
Tulipe, 200 m from the village, T02-286 4716, www.hosteriasumakpakari.com.
Cabins with suites with jacuzzi and rooms set in gardens, includes breakfast and museum fee, terraces with hammocks, pools, restaurant, sports fields.

$ Posada del Yumbo
Tulipe, T02-286 0121.
Up a side street off the main road. Cabins in large property with river view, also simple rooms, electric shower, pool, horse riding. Also run Restaurant **La Aldea**, by the archaeological site.

Mindo

$$$$ Casa Divina
1.2 km on the road to Cascada de Nambillo, T09-9172 5874, www.mindocasadivina.com.
Comfortable 2-storey cabins, lovely location surrounded by 2.7 forested ha, includes breakfast and dinner, bathtubs, guiding extra, US/Ecuadorean-run.

$$$$ El Monte
2 km from town on road to CEA, then opposite Mariposas de Mindo, cross river on tarabita (rustic cable car), T02-217 0102, T09-9308 4675, www.ecuadorcloudforest.com.
Beautifully constructed lodge in 44-ha property, newer cabins are spacious and very comfortable, includes 3 meals, some (but not all) excursions with a *guía nativo* and tubing, other adventure sports and horse riding are extra, no electricity, reserve in advance. Recommended.

$$$ Séptimo Paraíso
2 km from Calacalí–La Independencia road along Mindo access road, then 500 m right on a small side road, well signed, T09-9368 4417, www.septimoparaiso.com.
All wood lodge in a 420-ha reserve, comfortable, restaurant with good choice of set meals including vegetarian, warm and spring-fed pools and jaccuzi, parking, lovely grounds, great birdwatching, walking trails open to non-guests for US$10. Recommended.

$$ Caskaffesu
Sixto Durán Ballén (the street leading to the stadium) y Av Quito, T02-217 0100, caskaffesu@yahoo.com.
Pleasant *hostal* with nice courtyard, no breakfast, good coffee at café/bar, live music Wed-Sat, US/Ecuadorean-run.

$$ Dragonfly Inn
On Av Quito (main street), 1st block after bridge, T02-217 0319, www.mindo.biz.
Popular hotel, restaurant and café, comfortable rooms, also run popular apiary tours (www.thebeehivemindo.com), arrange well in advance, US$25 pp. Visa and MasterCard accepted.

$$ Hacienda San Vicente (Yellow House)
500 m south of the park, T02-217 0124.
Family-run lodge set in 200 ha of very rich forest, includes excellent breakfast, nice rooms, good walking trails open to non-guests for US$6, reservations required,

good value. Highly recommended for nature lovers.

$$ Mindo Real
Vía al Cinto (extension Av Sixto Durán) 500 m from town, T02-217 0120, www.mindoreal.com.
Cabins and rooms on ample gardens on the shores of the Río Mindo, camping US$5 pp, pool, trails.

$$-$ El Descanso
C Colibríes (1st right after Río Canchupi bridge at entrance to town), 5 blocks from Av Quito, T02-217 0213.
Nice house with comfortable rooms, cheaper in loft with shared bath, ample parking. Recommended. Good birdwatching in garden, open to non-guests for US$3, cafeteria open to the public for breakfast.

$$-$ Jardín de los Pájaros
C Colibríes, 3 blocks from Av Quito, T02-217 0159.
Family-run hostel, several types of rooms, includes good breakfast, small pool, parking, large covered terrace with hammocks, good value. Recommended.

$ Charito
C Colibríes, 2 blocks from Av Quito, T02-217 0093, hostal_charitodemindo@hotmail.com.
Family-run hostel in a wooden house, nice rooms, newer ones in back overlook the Río Canchupi, good value.

$ Rubby
5 blocks past the park along C Quito, T09-9193 1853, rubbyhostal@yahoo.com.
Family-run *hostal* on the outskirts of town, nice rooms, kitchen and laundry facilities, good value. English spoken, owner Marcelo Arias is a birding guide.

West of Mindo

$$$$ Arashá
4 km west of PV Maldonado, Km 121, T02-390 0007, Quito T02-244 9881 for reservations, www.arasharesort.com.

Resort and spa with pools, waterfalls (artificial and natural) and hiking trails. Comfortable thatched cabins, price includes all meals (world-class chef), use of the facilities (spa extra) and tours, can arrange transport from Quito, attentive staff, popular with families, elegant and very upmarket.

$$$ Selva Virgen
At Km 132, east of Puerto Quito, T02-362 9626, Quito office T02-331 7986, www.ute.edu.ec. Wed-Sun, Mon-Tue with advanced booking only.
Nice *hostería* in a 100-ha property owned by the Universidad Técnica Equinoccial (UTE). Staffed by students. Restaurant, rooms with ceiling fan and spacious comfortable cabins for 4 with fan, fridge, jacuzzi and nice porch, 3 pools, lovely grounds, part of the property is forested and has trails, facilities also open to restaurant patrons.

$$ Mirador Río Blanco
San Miguel de los Bancos, main road, at the east end of town, T02-277 0307.
Popular hotel/restaurant serving tropical dishes ($$), vegetarian options, good coffee, small rooms and ample suites overlooking the river, breakfast extra, parking, terrace with bird feeders (many hummingbirds and tanagers) and magnificent views of the river.

Restaurants

Western slopes of Pichincha
Mindo

$$$-$$ El Quetzal
9 de Octubre, 3 blocks from the park, T02-217 0034, wwwelquetzaldemindo.com. Daily 0800-2000.
Nice restaurant serving international food with vegetarian options, microbrews, local chocolate and other sweets for sale. Hourly chocolate tours 1000-1700 daily, US$10.

$$ Fuera de Babilonia
9 de Octubre y Los Ríos, 2 blocks from the park, no sign. Daily 0800-2100.

A la carte international dishes, trout, pizza, pasta, good food and nice atmosphere.

$ La Sazón de Marcelo
Av Quito past the park, opposite children's playground. Daily 0830-2100.
Set meals and à la carte including vegetarian dishes; *bandeja mindeña* a dish for 2 with trout and tilapia is one of their specialities. Very popular.

What to do

Mitad del Mundo
Calimatours, *30 m east of monument, Mitad del Mundo, T02-239 4796, www. mitaddelmundotour.com.* Tours to Pululahua and other sites in the vicinity.

Western slopes of Pichincha

Pululahua
The Green Horse Ranch, *Astrid Muller, T09-8612 5433, www.horseranch.de.* 1- to 9-day rides, among the options is a 3-day ride to Bellavista.

Mindo
Endemic Tours, *Av Quito y Gallo de la Peña, T09-9888 5801, romelly85@hotmail.com.* Bicycle rentals US$10/half day, US$15 per full day, hiking, regattas and other adventure activities.
Julia Patiño, *T09-8616 2816, juliaguideofbirds@gmail.com.* Is a English-speaking birding guide.
Mindo Xtreme Birds, *Sector Saguambi, just out of town on the road to CEA, T02-217 0188, www.mindoxtreme.com.* Birdwatching, regattas, cycling, hiking, waterfalls, horse riding, English spoken, very helpful.
Vinicio Pérez, *T09-947 6867, www. birdwatchershouse.com.* Is a recommended birding guide, he speaks some English.

Transport

Mitad del Mundo and around
Bus From Quito take a 'Mitad del Mundo' feeder bus from La Ofelia station on the Metrobus (transfer ticket US$0.15), or from the corner of Bolivia y Av América (US$0.40). Some buses continue to the turn-off for Pululahua or Calacalí beyond. An excursion by **taxi** to Mitad del Mundo (with 1 hr wait) is US$25, or US$30 to include Pululahua. Just a ride from La Mariscal costs about US$15.

Papallacta
Bus From **Quito**, buses bound for Tena or Lago Agrio from Terminal Quitumbe, or buses to Baeza from near La Marín (see page 523), 2 hrs, US$2.50. The bus and taxi stop is at El Triángulo, east of (below) the village, at the junction of the main highway and the old road through town. A taxi to Termas costs US$1 pp shared or US$2.50 private. The access to the Termas is uphill from the village, off the old road. The complex is a 40-min walk from town. To return to Quito, most buses pass in the afternoon, travelling back at night is not recommended. Taxi to Quito starts at US$50, to the airport US$40. **Transporte Santa Catalina** taxis in Papallacta, T09-8510 2556.

Refugio de Vida Silvestre Pasochoa
Bus From Quito buses run from El Playón to Amaguaña US$0.50 (ask the driver to let you off at the 'Ejido de Amaguaña'); from there follow the signs. It's about 8-km walk, with not much traffic except at weekends, or book a pick-up from Amaguaña, **Cooperativa Pacheco Jr**, T02-287 7047, about US$6.

Western slopes of Pichincha
Pululahua
Bus Take a 'Mitad del Mundo' bus from La Ofelia Metrobus terminal. When boarding, ask if it goes as far as the Pululahua turn-off (some end their route at Mitad del Mundo, others at the Pululahua Mirador turn-off,

others continue to Calacalí). It is a 30-min walk from the turn to the rim.

Tulipe

Bus From **Quito**, Estación La Ofelia, from 0615, US$1.90, 1¾ hrs: **Transportes Otavalo**, 7 daily, continue to Pacto (US$2.50, 2 hrs) and **Transportes Minas** 5 daily, continue to Chontal (US$3.15, 3 hrs). To **Las Tolas**, **Transportes Minas**, daily at 1730, US$2.50, 2½ hrs or take pick-up from Tulipe, US$5.

Mindo

Bus From **Quito**, Estación La Ofelia, **Coop Flor del Valle**, T02-217 0171, Mon-Fri 0800, 0900, 1100, 1300, 1600, Sat and Sun 0740, 0820, 0920, 1100, 1300, 1400, 1600 (last one on Sun at 1700 instead of 1600); Mindo–Quito: Mon-Fri 0630, 1100, 1345, 1500, Sat and Sun 0630, 1100 and hourly 1300-1700; US$3.10, 2 hrs; weekend buses fill quickly, buy ahead. You can also take any bus bound for Esmeraldas or San Miguel de los Bancos (see below) and get off at the turn-off for Mindo from where there are taxis until 1930, US$0.50 pp or US$3 without sharing. **Cooperativa Kennedy** to/from **Santo Domingo** 5 daily, US$5, 3½ hrs.

West of Mindo

From **Quito**, Terminal Carcelén, departures every 30 min (**Coop Kennedy** and associates) to Santo Domingo via: **Nanegalito** (US$1.90, 1½ hrs), **San Miguel de los Bancos** (US$3.15, 2½ hrs), **Pedro Vicente Maldonado** (US$3.75, 3 hrs) and **Puerto Quito** (US$4.70, 3½ hrs). **Trans Esmeraldas** frequent departures from Terminal Carcelén also serve these destinations along the Quito-Esmeraldas route.

Northern
highlands

The area north of Quito to the Colombian border is outstandingly beautiful. The landscape is mountainous, with views of the Cotacachi, Imbabura, and Chiles volcanoes, as well as the glacier-covered Cayambe, interspersed with lakes. The region is also renowned for its *artesanía*.

Quito to Otavalo

a few places worth stopping at en route

On the way from the capital to the main tourist centre in northern Ecuador, the landscape is dominated by the Cayambe volcano.

Quito to Cayambe

At **Calderón** ⓘ *getting there: take a bus at La Ofelia Metrobus terminal*, 32 km north of the centre of Quito, you can see the famous bread figurines being made. Prices are lower than in Quito. On 1-2 November, the graves in the cemetery are decorated with flowers, drinks and food for the dead. The Corpus Christi processions are very colourful.

The Pan-American Highway goes to **Guayllabamba**, home of the Quito zoo (www. quitozoo.org), where it branches, one road going through Cayambe and the second through Tabacundo before rejoining at Cajas. At 10 km past Guayllabamba on the road to Tabacundo, just north of the toll booth, a cobbled road to the left (signed Pirámides de Cochasquí) leads to Tocachi and further on to the **Parque Arqueológico Cochasquí** ⓘ *T09-9822 0686, Quito T02-399 4405, www.pichincha.gob.ec/visita-cochasqui, 0800-1600, US$3, entry only with a 1½-hr guided tour, getting there: from Terminal Carcelén, be sure to take a bus that goes on the Tabacundo road and ask to be let off at the turn-off. From there it's a pleasant 8-km uphill walk. Alternatively, from Terminal La Ofelia, take a bus to Malchinguí (hourly, US$1.50, 2 hrs) and a pickup to Cochasquí (US$3, 15 mins) or a taxi (US$6). There are also buses between Malchinguí and Cayambe which go by Cochasquí.* The protected area contains 15 truncated clay pyramids (*tolas*), nine with long ramps, built between AD 950 and 1550 by the Cara or Cayambi-Caranqui people. Festivals with dancing at the equinoxes and solstices. There is a site museum and views from the pyramids, south to Quito, are marvellous.

Opposite the park entrance is **Camping Cochasquí** ⓘ *T09-9491 9008, US$3 pp for camping, US$10 pp in cabins, meals available.*

Best for
Arts and crafts ▪ Trekking ▪ Views

Northern Ecuador

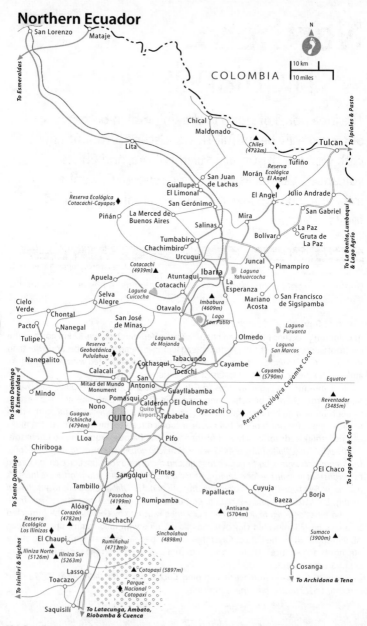

COLOMBIA

N

10 km
10 miles

To Esmeraldas

San Lorenzo
Mataje

To Ipiales & Pasto

Chical
Maldonado

Chiles (4723m)

Tulcan

Tufiño

Morán

Reserva Ecológica El Angel

Lita

San Juan de Lachas

Guallupe
El Limonal

San Gerónimo

El Angel

Julio Andrade

San Gabriel

Reserva Ecológica Cotacachi-Cayapas

La Merced de Buenos Aires

Piñán

Salinas

Mira

Bolívar

La Paz
Gruta de La Paz

To La Bonita, Lumbaqui & Lago Agrio

Tumbabiro
Chachimbiro
Urcuquí

Juncal

Pimampiro

Cotacachi (4939m)

Apuela

Atuntaqui

Ibarra

La Esperanza

Mariano Acosta

San Francisco de Sigsipamba

Selva Alegre

Cotacachi

Laguna Cuicocha

Laguna Yahuarcocha

Cielo Verde

Chontal

San José de Minas

Otavalo

Imbabura (4609m)

Lago San Pablo

Laguna Puruanta

Pacto

Nanegal

Tulipe

Lagunas de Mojanda

Olmedo

Laguna San Marcos

Nanegalito

Reserva Geobotánica Pululahua

Cochasqui

Tabacundo

Tocachi

Cayambe

Cayambe (5790m)

Calacalí

Mitad del Mundo Monument

San Antonio

Guayllabamba

Equator

Reserva Ecológica Cayambe Coca

Mindo

Pomasqui

Calderón

El Quinche

Oyacachi

Reventador (3485m)

Nono

QUITO

Quito Airport

Tababela

Guagua Pichincha (4794m)

LLoa

Pifo

Chiriboga

To Santo Domingo & Esmeraldas

To Santo Domingo

Sangolquí

Píntag

Papallacta

Cuyuja

Baeza

Borja

El Chaco

To Lago Agrio & Coca

Tambillo

Rumipamba

Pasochoa (4199m)

Antisana (5704m)

Alóag

Corazón (4782m)

Machachi

Sincholahua (4898m)

Sumaco (3900m)

Reserva Ecológica Los Ilinizas

El Chaupi

Rumiñahui (4712m)

To Isinliví & Sigchos

Iliniza Norte (5126m)

Iliniza Sur (5263m)

Lasso

Cotopaxi (5897m)

Cosanga

To Archidona & Tena

Toacazo

Parque Nacional Cotopaxi

Saquisilí

To Latacunga, Ambato, Riobamba & Cuenca

On the other road, 8 km before Cayambe, a globe carved out of rock by the Pan-American Highway is at the spot where the French expedition marked the equator (small shops sell drinks and snacks). A few metres north is **Quitsato** ⓘ *T02-361 0908, www. quitsato.org, US$2*, where studies about the equator and its importance to ancient cultures are carried out. There is a sun dial, 54 m in diameter, and **a solar culture exhibit**, with information about indigenous cultures and archaeological sites along the equator; here too there are special events for the solstices and equinoxes.

Cayambe *Colour map 1, A4.*

Cayambe, on the eastern (right-hand) branch of the highway, 25 km northeast of Guayllabamba, is overshadowed by the snow-capped volcano of the same name. The surrounding countryside consists of a few dairy farms and many flower plantations. The area is noted for its *bizcochos* (biscuits) served with *queso de hoja* (string cheese). At the Centro Cultural Espinoza-Jarrín, is the **Museo de la Ciudad** ⓘ *Rocafuerte y Bolívar, Wed-Sun 0800-1700, free*, with displays about the Cayambi culture and ceramics found at **Puntiachil**, an important but poorly preserved archaeologic site at the edge of town. There is a fiesta in March for the equinox with plenty of local music; also Inti Raymi solstice and San Pedro celebrations in June. Market day is Sunday.

Reserva Ecológica Cayambe Coca
T02-211 0370, werner.barrera@ambiente.gob.ec.

Cayambe is a good place to access the western side of Reserva Ecológica Cayambe-Coca, a large park which spans the Cordillera Oriental and extends down to the eastern lowlands. **Volcán Cayambe**, Ecuador's third highest peak, at 5790 m, lies within the reserve. It is the highest point in the world to lie so close to the equator (3.75 km north). The equator goes over the mountain's flanks. About 1 km south of the town of Cayambe is an unmarked cobbled road heading east via Juan Montalvo, leading in 26 km to the **Ruales-Oleas-Berge refuge** ⓘ *T09-5955 9765, rooms for 4-10 passengers take sleeping bag, US$14 pp with use of kitchen or US$30 with dinner and breakfast*, at 4600 m. The standard climbing route, from the west, uses the refuge as a base. There is a crevasse near the summit which can be very difficult to cross if there isn't enough snow, ask the refuge keeper about conditions. There are nice acclimatization hikes around the refuge. Otavalo and Quito operators offer tours here.

To the southeast of Cayambe, also within the reserve and surrounded by cloudforest at 3200 m is **Oyacachi** ⓘ *T06-299 1842, oyacachi@gmail.com*, a traditional village of farmers and woodcarvers, with thermal baths (US$3). Accommodation at (**$$-$**) **Cabañas Oyacachi**, T06-299 1846, www.cabanasoyacachi.com, and in family *hospedajes*. There is good walking in the area, including a two-day walk to Papallacta and a three-day walk to El Chaco in the lowlands; these require a permit from the reserve, write ahead.

Listings Quito to Otavalo

Where to stay

Cayambe

$$$ Hacienda Guachalá
South of Cayambe on the road to Cangahua, T02-361 0908, www.guachala.com.

The first hacienda in Ecuador, nicely restored, the chapel (1580) is built on top of a pre-Inca structure. Simple but comfortable rooms in older section and fancier ones in newer area, fireplaces, delicious meals, covered swimming pool, parking, attentive service, good walking, horses for rent, excursions to nearby ruins, small museum.

$$$ Jatun Huasi
Panamericana Norte Km 1.5, T02-236 3777, www.hosteriajatunhuasi.com.
US motel style, cabins with a sitting room with fireplace and frigo-bar and rooms, restaurant, indoor pool, spa, parking.

$$ Shungu Huasi
Camino a Granobles, 1 km northwest of town, T02-236 1847, www.shunguhuasi.com.
Comfortable cabins in a 6.5-ha ranch, excellent Italian restaurant with advanced reservation, heaters on request, nice setting, attentive service, offers horse riding excursions. Recommended.

$ La Gran Colombia
Panamericana y Calderón, T02-236 1238.
Modern multi-storey building, restaurant, parking, traffic noise in front rooms.

Restaurants

Cayambe

$$$ Casa de Fernando
Panamericana Norte Km 1.5. Closed Mon.
Varied menu, good international food.

$$-$ Aroma
Bolívar 404 y Ascázubi. Closed Wed.
Large choice of set lunches and à la carte, variety of desserts, very good.

Transport

Cayambe
Bus Flor del Valle, from La Ofelia, **Quito**, every 7 mins 0530-2100, US$1.50, 1½ hrs. Their Cayambe station is at Montalvo y Junín. To **Otavalo**, from traffic circle at Bolívar y Av N Jarrín, every 15 mins, US$0.95, 45 mins.

Reserva Ecológica Cayambe Coca
Road To **Volcán Cayambe**, most vehicles can go as far as the **Hacienda Piemonte El Hato** (at about 3500 m) from where it is a 3- to 4-hr walk, longer if heavily laden or if it is windy, but it is a beautiful walk. Regular pick-ups can often make it to 'la Z', a sharp curve on the road 30-mins' walk to the *refugio*. 4WDs can often make it to the *refugio*. Pick-ups can be hired by the market in Cayambe, Junín y Ascázubi, US$45, 1½-2 hrs. Arrange ahead for return transport. A milk truck runs from Cayambe's hospital to the hacienda at 0600, returning between 1700-1900. To **Oyacachi**, from the north side of Cayambe, near the Mercado Mayorista, Mon, Wed, Sat at 1500, Sun at 0800, US$2.50, 1½ hrs; return to Cayambe Wed, Fri, Sat at 0400, Sun at 1400.

Otavalo and around *Colour map 1, A4.*

a beautiful area of mountains and lakes

★Otavalo, only a short distance from the capital, is a must on any tourist itinerary in Ecuador. The Tabacundo and Cayambe roads join at Cajas, then cross the *páramo* and suddenly descend into the land of the *Otavaleños*, a thriving, prosperous group, famous for their prodigious production of woollens. The town itself, consisting of rather functional modern buildings, is one of South America's most important centres of ethno-tourism and its enormous Saturday market, featuring a dazzling array of textiles and crafts, is second to none and not to be missed. Set in beautiful countryside, the area is worth exploring for three or four days.

Otavalo
Men here wear their hair long and plaited under a broad-brimmed hat and wear white, calf-length trousers and blue ponchos. The women's colourful costumes consist of embroidered

blouses, shoulder wraps and many coloured beads. Indigenous families speak Quichua at home, although it is losing some ground to Spanish with the younger generation.

The **Saturday market** comprises four different markets in various parts of the town with the central streets filled with vendors. The *artesanías* market is held 0700-1800, based around the Plaza de Ponchos (Plaza Centenario). The livestock section begins at 0500 until 0900, outside the centre, west of the Panamericana; go west on Calderón from the town centre. The produce market, at the old stadium, west of the centre, lasts from 0700 till 1400. The *artesanías* industry is so

Tip...
Indigenous people in the market respond better to photography if you buy something first, then ask politely.

Otavalo

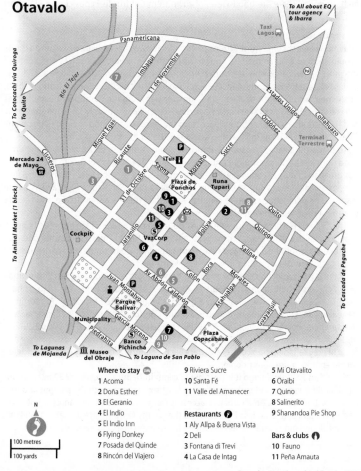

Where to stay	Restaurants	
1 Acoma	9 Riviera Sucre	5 Mi Otavalito
2 Doña Esther	10 Santa Fé	6 Oraibi
3 El Geranio	11 Valle del Amanecer	7 Quino
4 El Indio		8 Salinerito
5 El Indio Inn	**Restaurants**	9 Shanandoa Pie Shop
6 Flying Donkey	1 Aly Allpa & Buena Vista	
7 Posada del Quinde	2 Deli	**Bars & clubs**
8 Rincón del Viajero	3 Fontana di Trevi	10 Fauno
	4 La Casa de Intag	11 Peña Amauta

big that the Plaza de Ponchos is filled with vendors every day of the week. The selection is better on Saturday but prices are a little higher than other days when the atmosphere is more relaxed. Wednesday is also an important market day with more movement than other weekdays. Polite bargaining is appropriate in the market and shops. Otavaleños not only sell goods they weave and sew themselves, but they bring crafts from throughout Ecuador and from Peru and Bolivia.

The **Museo Viviente Otavalango** ① *Vía Antigua a Quiroga 1230, antigua Fábrica San Pedro, T06-292-4034, www.otavalango.org, Fri-Sun 0900-1700, call ahead at other times, US$5,* displays on all cultural aspects of Otavaleño life; live presentations of local traditions for groups. The **Museo de Tejidos El Obraje** ① *Sucre 6-08 y Olmedo, T06-292 0261, US$2, must call ahead,* shows the process of traditional Otavalo weaving from shearing to final products. There are good views of town from **Centro de Exposiciones El Colibrí** ① *C Morales past the railway line.*

Around Otavalo

Otavalo weavers come from dozens of communities. Many families weave and visitors should shop around as the less known weavers often have better prices and some of the most famous ones only sell from their homes, especially in Agato and Peguche. The easiest villages to visit are **Ilumán** (there are also many felt hatmakers in town and *yachacs*, or shamen, mostly north of the plaza – look for signs); **Agato**; **Carabuela** (many homes sell crafts including wool sweaters); **Peguche**. These villages are only 15-30 minutes away and have good bus service; buses leave from the Terminal and stop at Plaza Copacabana (Atahualpa y Montalvo). You can also take a taxi (US$2).

To reach the lovely **Cascada de Peguche**, from Peguche's plaza, facing the church, head right and continue straight until the road forks. Take the lower fork to the right, but not the road that heads downhill. There is a small campsite at the falls. From the top (left side, excellent views) you can continue the walk to Lago San Pablo. The **Pawkar Raymi** festival is held in Peguche before carnival. At the falls there is a small information centre (contributions are appreciated).

The **Ciclovía** is a bicycle path which runs along the old rail line 21 km between Eugenio Espejo de Cajas and Otavalo. Because of the slope, starting in Cajas is recommended. You can take a tour or hire a bike and take a bus bound for Quito to the bike path. This and other cycling routes described in www.otavalo.travel.

There is a network of old roads and trails between Otavalo and **Lago San Pablo**, none of which takes more than two hours to explore. It is worth walking either to or back from the lake for the views. Going in a group is recommended for safety. A good half-day excursion is via Cascada de Peguche, **Parque Cóndor** ① *on a hill called Curiloma, near the community of Pucará Alto, T06-304 9399, www.parquecondor.org, Wed-Sun 0930-1700, raptor flight demonstrations at 1130 and 1530, US$4.75, crowded on weekends,* a reserve and birds of prey rehabilitation centre, and back via **El Lechero**, a lookout by a tree considered sacred among indigenous people.

From **San Pablo del Lago** it is possible to climb **Imbabura** volcano (4630 m, a serious climb and frequently under cloud), allow at least six hours to reach the summit and four hours for the descent. An alternative access is from La Esperanza or San Clemente (see page 547). Easier, and no less impressive, is the nearby Cerro Huarmi Imbabura, 3845 m, it is not signed but several paths lead there. Take a good map, food and warm clothing.

Tourist information

Dirección de Turismo
Corner of Plaza de Ponchos, Jaramillo y Quiroga, T06-292 7230. Mon-Sat 0800-1800, Sun 0800-1200.
Local and regional information, English spoken, helpful; www.otavalo.travel is a good multilingual site.

Where to stay

Otavalo
In town
Hotels may be full on Fri night before market.

$$$ Posada del Quinde
Quito y Miguel Egas, T06-292 0750, www.posadaquinde.com.
Nicely decorated rooms with heaters, all around a lovely garden, also 2 suites with kitchenettes, very good restaurant (**Café Pachamama**, see Restaurants , page 543), parking, US-run.

$$$-$$ Acoma
Salinas 07-57 y 31 de Octubre, T06-292 6570, www.acomahotel.com.
Lovely re-built home in colonial style, parking, nice comfortable rooms, some with balcony, 1 room with bathtub, 2 suites with kitchenette.

$$$-$$ Doña Esther
Montalvo 4-44 y Bolívar, T06-292 0739, www.otavalohotel.com.
Nicely restored colonial house, a hotel for over 100 years, very good restaurant (**Arbol de Montalvo**, see Restaurants below), rooms with nice wooden floors, colourful decor, pleasant atmosphere, transfers to Quito or airport.

$$$-$$ El Indio Inn
Bolívar 9-04 y Calderón, T06-292 2922, www.hotelelindioinn.com.
Modern hotel, carpeted rooms and simple suites, restaurant, parking, use of spa US$6.50.

$$ El Indio
Sucre 12-14 y Salinas, near Plaza de Ponchos, T06-292 0060, www.hotelelindio.com.
In multi-storey building, ask for a room with balcony, simple restaurant, parking, helpful service.

$$ Riviera Sucre
García Moreno 380 y Roca, T06-292 0241, www.rivierasucre.com.
Traditional hotel with ample renovated rooms (new ones under construction in 2016), good breakfast available, cafeteria, private or shared bath, kitchen facilities, book exchange, bookshop with good selection of English and German titles, nice common areas, garden and courtyard, good meeting place. Good value and recommended.

$$-$ Rincón del Viajero
Roca 11-07 y Quiroga, T06-292 1741, www.hostalrincondelviajero.com.
Very pleasant hostel and meeting place. Simple but nicely decorated rooms, includes a choice of good breakfasts, private or shared bath, cafeteria, small parking, rooftop hammocks, sitting room with fireplace, US/Ecuadorean-run, good value. Recommended.

$$-$ Santa Fé
Roca 7-34 y García Moreno, T06-292 3640, www.hotelsantafeotavalo.com.
Modern, nice pine decoration, breakfast available, restaurant, run by indigenous Otavaleños, good value.

$$-$ Valle del Amanecer
Roca y Quiroga, T06-292 0990.
Small rustic rooms with thin walls, nice courtyard, hammocks, private or shared bath, popular.

$ El Geranio
Ricaurte y Morales, T06-292 0185, www.hostalelgeranio.com.
2 types of rooms, smaller ones with electric shower and no TV are cheaper, laundry

facilities and use of kitchen to prepare cold foods, parking, quiet, family-run, popular, runs trips. Good value, recommended.

$ Flying Donkey
Abdón Calderón 510 y Bolívar, T06-292 7812, www.flyingdonkeyotavalo.com.
Popular backpacker's hostel, rooms with private bath, US$10 pp in dorm, kitchen facilities and terrace.

Out of town

$$$$ Ali Shungu Mountaintop Lodge
5 km west of Otavalo by the village of Yambiro, T09-8950 9945, www.alishungumountaintoplodge.com.
Country inn on a 16-ha private reserve. 4 comfortable nicely decorated guesthouses for 4, each with living room, woodstove and kitchenette. Includes breakfast and dinner (vegetarian available), horse riding, US-run.

$$$$ Casa Mojanda
Vía a Mojanda Km 3.5, T09-8033 5108, www.casamojanda.com.
Comfortable cabins set in a beautiful hillside. Includes breakfast prepared with ingredients from own organic garden and short guided hike to waterfall; each room is decorated with its own elegant touch, outdoor hot tub with great views, quiet, good library, horse riding. Recommended.

$$$ Hacienda Pinsaquí
Panamericana Norte Km 5, 300 m north of the turn-off for Cotacachi, T06-294 6116, www.haciendapinsaqui.com.
Converted hacienda dating to 1790, with 30 suites, 1 with jacuzzi, restaurant with lovely dining room, lounge with fireplace, beautiful antiques, colonial ambience, gardens, horse riding.

$$$ Las Palmeras Inn
Outside Quichinche, 15 mins by bus from Otavalo, T06-266 8067, www.laspalmerasinn.com.
Cabins with terrace and fireplace in a rural setting, restaurant, parking, nice grounds

and views, pool table and ping-pong, British-owned.

$$ La Casa de Hacienda
Vía Ilumán, entrance at Panamericana Norte Km 3, then 300 m east, T06-269 0245.
Tasteful cabins with fireplace, restaurant, parking, horse riding.

$$ La Luna
On a side-road going south off the Mojanda road at Km 4, T09-9315 6082.
Pleasant hostel in nice surroundings, some rooms with fireplace, heater and private bath, others with shared bath, US$14 pp in dorm, camping US$8 pp, terrace with hammocks, pleasant dining room-lounge, transport information on hostel's website, excursions arranged, popular. Recommended.

Around Otavalo
Peguche

$$$ La Casa Sol
Near the Cascada de Peguche, T06-269 0500, www.lacasasol.com.
Comfortable rustic lodge set on a hillside. Bright cosy rooms and suites with balcony, some with fireplace, lovely attention to detail, restaurant and conference room.

$$ Aya Huma
On the railway line in Peguche, T06-269 0164, www.ayahuma.com.
In a country setting between the railway tracks and the river. Quiet, pleasant atmosphere, kitchen facilities, restaurant for breakfast and dinner, camping (US$4 pp), organizes ancestral ceremonies, Dutch/Ecuadorean-run, popular. Recommended.

Lago San Pablo

$$$$ Sacha Ji
Vía del Condor y Angel Vaca, San Pablo, T06-304 9245, www.mysachaji.com.
A wellness and yoga retreat on a hilltop overlooking Lago San Pablo and Imbabura volcano. Spacious rooms with heating,

organic gardens, restaurant, outdoor hot tub, yoga classes, horse therapy.

$$$$-$$$ Hacienda Cusín
By the village of San Pablo del Lago to the southeast of the lake, T06-291 8013, www.haciendacusin.com.
A converted 17th-century hacienda with lovely courtyard and garden, fine expensive restaurant, rooms with fireplace, sports facilities (horses, bikes, squash court, games room), library, book in advance, British-run.

$$ Green House
C 24 de Junio, Comunidad Araque, by the east shore of the lake, northwest of San Pablo del Lago, T06-291 9298, www.araquebyb.hostel.com.
Family-run *hostal*, some rooms with bath, others with detached bath, dinner on request, sitting room with fireplace, rooftop terrace with views, Quito airport pickup (US$55).

Restaurants

Otavalo

$$$-$$ Arbol de Montalvo
Montalvo 4-44 y Bolívar, in Hotel Doña Esther, T06-292 0739, www.otavalohotel.com. Tue-Thu 1800-2100, Fri-Sat 0715-2100, Sun 0715-2100.
Wide variety of dishes including excellent wood-oven pizzas.

$$$-$$ Café Pachamama
Quito y Miguel Egas, in Posada del Quinde, T06-292 0750, www.posadaquinde.com. Daily 0730-2030, reservations advised for groups over 6 people.
Pleasant relaxed setting, tasty meals with plenty of vegetarian options, good reviews.

$$$-$$ Quino
Roca 7-40 y Juan Montalvo. Mon-Sat 1000-2200.
Traditional coastal cooking, good seafood and some meat dishes, pleasant seating around patio, popular.

$$ Aly Allpa
Salinas 509 at Plaza de Ponchos. Daily 0730-2030.
Good-value set meals, breakfast and à la carte including trout, vegetarian, meat. Recommended.

$$ Buena Vista
Salinas entre Sucre y Jaramillo, p2, www.buenavistaotavalo.com. Sun-Mon 1300-2200, Wed-Thu 1000-2200, Fri 1100-2300, Sat 0900-2300.
Bistro with balcony overlooking Plaza de Ponchos. Good international food, sandwiches, salads, vegetarian options, trout, good coffee, Wi-Fi.

$$ Mi Otavalito
Sucre y Morales. Daily 1200-2100
Good for set lunch and international food à la carte. Popular with tour groups.

$$ Oraibi
Sucre y Colón. Wed-Sat 0800-2000.
Vegetarian food in nice patio setting, pizza, salads, pasta, Mexican, breakfast, Swiss-owned. Live music Fri and Sat night.

$$-$ Deli
Quiroga 12-18 y Bolívar. Daily 1130-2100.
Economical set lunch, plus good Mexican food, international and pizza à la carte, nice desserts, pleasant atmosphere, family-run, good value.

Cafés

Daily Grind
Juan Montalvo esquina Sucre, Parque Bolívar. Daily 0900-1900.
Small outdoor café with very good coffee, muffins and other treats.

La Casa de Intag
Colón 465 y Sucre. Mon-Sat 0800-1800.
Fairtrade cafeteria/shop run by Intag coffee growers and artisans associations. Good organic coffee, breakfast, pancakes, sandwiches, sisal crafts, fruit pulp and more.

La Cosecha
Jaramillo y Salinas, upstairs. Daily 0900-2000.
Great modern café and bakery overlooking
Plaza de Ponchos. Excellent coffee,
sandwiches and bagels. Recommended.

Salinerito
Bolívar 10-08 y Morales. Mon-Sat 0800-2200.
Café/deli run by the Salinas de Guaranda coop.
Good sandwiches, breakfast, pizza, coffee
and juices. A good place to buy supplies
such as cheese, coldcuts and chocolate.

Shenandoa Pie Shop
*Salinas y Jaramillo. Open 1100-2100,
Sat from 0900.*
Good fruit pies, milk shakes and ice cream,
popular meeting place, an Otavalo tradition.

Bars and clubs

Otavalo
Otavalo is generally safe but avoid deserted
areas at night. Nightlife is concentrated
at Morales y Jaramillo and C 31 de Octubre.
Peñas are open Fri-Sat from 1930,
entrance US$3.

Fauno
Morales y Jaramillo.
Café/bar, variety of cocktails, snacks.

Peña Amauta
Morales 5-11 y Jaramillo.
Good local bands, welcoming,
mainly foreigners.

Festivals

Otavalo
End of Jun **Inti Raymi** combines
celebrations of the summer solstice (21 Jun),
with the **Fiesta de San Juan** (24 Jun) and the
Fiesta de San Pedro y San Pablo (29 Jun).
These combined festivities are known as
Los San Juanes and participants are mostly
indigenous. They take place in the smaller
communities surrounding Otavalo, each
one celebrates separately on different dates,
some for a full week. The celebration begins

with a ritual bath, the Peguche waterfall
is used by Otavalo residents (a personal
spiritual activity, best carried out without
visitors and certainly without cameras). In
Otavalo, indigenous families have costume
parties, which at times spill over onto the
streets. In the San Juan neighbourhood, near
the Yanayacu baths, there is a week-long
celebration with food, drink and music.
1st 2 weeks of Sep **Fiesta del Yamor**
and **Colla Raymi**, feature local dishes,
amusement parks, bands in the plaza and
sporting events.
Oct **Mes de la cultura**, cultural events
throughout the month.
Last weekend of Oct **Mojanda Arriba** is
an annual full-day hike from Malchinguí
over Mojanda to reach Otavalo for the
foundation celebrations.

What to do

Otavalo
Horse riding
Several operators offer riding tours. Half-day
trips to nearby attractions cost US$40-50.
Full-day trips such as Cuicocha or Mojanda
run US$40-50.

Language schools
Instituto Superior de Español, *Jaramillo
6-23 y Morales, T06-292 7354, www.instituto-
superior.net.*
Mundo Andino Internacional, *Bolívar 816
y Abdón Calderón, p3, T06-292 1864, www.
mandinospanishschool.com.* Cooking classes
and other activities included.
Otavalo Spanish Institute, *31 de Octubre
476 y Salinas, p 3, T06-293 0275, www.otavalo
spanish.com.* Also offers Quichua lessons.

Mountain bikes
Several tour operators rent bikes and offer
cycling tours for US$35-70 a day trip. See also
Ciclovía, page 540. Rentals cost US$10-12 per
day. **Taller Ciclo Primaxi**, Ricaurte y Morales
and in Peguche.

Tour operators

Most tours are to indigenous communities, Cuicocha and Mojanda, US$25-35 pp.

All about EQ, *Los Corazas 433 y Albarracín, at the north end of town, T06-292 3633, www.all-about-ecuador.com*. Interesting itineraries, trekking and horse riding tours, climbing, cycling, trips to Intag, Piñán, Cayambe, Oyacachi, volunteering on organic farms. English and French spoken. Recommended.

Ecomontes, *Sucre y Morales, T06-292 6244, www.ecomontestour.com*. A branch of a Quito operator, trekking, climbing, rafting, also sell tours to Cuyabeno and Galápagos.

Runa Tupari, *Sucre y Quito, T06-292 2320, www.runatupari.com*. Arranges indigenous homestays in the Cotacachi area, also the usual tours, trekking, horse riding and cycling trips and transport.

Train rides

Beautifully restored historic train station at Guayaquil y J Montalvo, T06-292 8172, www.trenecuador.com, Wed-Sat 0800-1300, 1400-1700, Sun 0700-1300. Train ride to **Salinas** (57 km away) and back, **El Tren de la Libertad**. Departures Fri-Sun 0800, returning 1750; on Sun return from Ibarra to Otavalo is by bus. Includes stops at San Roque, Andrade Marín (with **Museo Textil**) and San Antonio de Ibarra. You can continue by bus from Salinas to **San Lorenzo**, see page 647.

see page 647.

Transport

Otavalo

Bus Terminal at Atahualpa y Ordóñez (no departures after 1930). The Ibarra Terminal offers many more destinations. To **Quito** 2 hrs, US$2.50, every 10 mins; all depart from

Tip...

Never leave anything in your car or taxi in the street. There are public car parks at Juan Montalvo y Sucre, by Parque Bolívar, and on Quito between 31 de Octubre and Jaramillo.

Terminal Carcelén in Quito, **Coop Otavalo** and **Coop Los Lagos** go into Otavalo, buses bound for Ibarra or Tulcán drop you off at the highway, this is inconvenient and not safe at night. From **Quito** or airport by taxi takes 1½ hrs, US$60 one way; shared taxis with **Taxis Lagos/Serviquito,** in Quito, Asunción Oe2-146 y Versalles, T02-256 5992; in Otavalo, Av Los Sarances y Panamericana, T06-292 3203, who run a hotel to hotel service (to/from modern Quito only) and will divert to resorts just off the highway; Mon-Sat hourly, 6 departures on Sun, 1½ hrs, US$15 pp, buy ticket at least 1 day ahead; they also go from Quito to Ibarra. Tour operators also offer transfers. Bus to **Ibarra**, every 4 mins, US$0.55, 40 mins. To **Peguche**, city bus on Av Atahualpa, every 10 mins, bus stops in front of the terminal and at Plaza Copacabana, US$0.35; taxi US$2. To **Apuela** in the Intag region, daily at 0730, 1000 and 1400, US$2.50, 2 hrs. To **Ambato** bypassing Quito, US$5.65, see Ibarra Transport (page 555), **CITA** buses from Ibarra stop along the Panamericana, enquire locally where to wait for them, and note that this is not safe after dark.

see Ibarra Transport (page 555),

Around Otavalo

Bus From Otavalo to **San Pablo del Lago** every 25 mins, more often on Sat, US$0.25, 30 mins; taxi US$4. Also buses to many nearby communities.

an area of diverse attractions and scenery

Northwest of Otavalo is Cotacachi from where a road goes west to the Cotacachi-Cayapas reserve and the subtropical Intag region. The main highway goes north to the city of Ibarra and beyond into the hot Chota Valley from where a branch road goes west to the subtropical valley of the Río Mira and the coastal town of San Lorenzo. The Panamericana reaches the border at the busy town of Tulcán, with its fantastic cemetery topiary.

Cotacachi

West of the road between Otavalo and Ibarra is Cotacachi. There is also access along a secondary road from Otavalo through Quiroga. Cotacachi, home to a growing expatriate community, produces and sells many leather goods.

The **Casa de las Culturas** ① *Bolívar 1334 y 9 de Octubre*, a beautifully refurbished 19th-century building, is a monument to peace. It houses the post office, a library, gallery and radio station. The **Museo de las Culturas** ① *García Moreno 13-41y Bolívar, T06-255 4155, Mon-Fri 0800-1300, 1400-1700, Sat-Sun 0930-1400, free*, has good displays of early Ecuadorean history and regional crafts and traditions.

Local festivals include **Inti Raymi/San Juan** in June and **Jora** during the September equinox.

☆Laguna Cuicocha

15 km from Cotacachi, visitor centre has good natural history and cultural displays, daily 0800-1700.

This crater lake (altitude 3070 m) is part of the **Reserva Ecológica Cotacachi-Cayapas**, which extends from Cotacachi volcano to the tropical lowlands on the Río Cayapas in Esmeraldas. It is a crater lake with two islands, which are closed to the public to protect the native species. There is a well-marked 8-km path around the lake, which takes four to five hours and provides spectacular views of the Cotacachi, Imbabura and, occasionally, Cayambe peaks. The best views are in the morning, when condors can sometimes be seen. There is a lookout at 3 km, two hours from the start. Take water and a waterproof jacket. There is a shorter trail which takes 40 minutes. Motor boat rides around the islands, US$3.25 per person for minimum eight persons.

To the northwest of Otavalo lies the lush subtropical region of **Intag**, reached along a road that follows the southern edge of Cuicocha and continues to the town of **Apuela**. The region's primary cloudforest is threatened by a proposed large-scale copper mine, vigorously opposed by local communities. See **Defensa y Conservación Ecológica de Intag** ① *www.decoin.org*, for local conservation and community development projects. The area's rivers will also be affected by an irrigation and hydroelectric scheme in the Piñan area, see Northwest of Ibarra, below. The **Asociación Agroartesanal de Café Río Intag (AACRI)** ① *on the main street, T06-264 8489, www.aacri.com*, a Fairtrade organic coffee grower's association, offers tours of coffee, sisal and sugar cane plantations and processing plants, also lodging and volunteer opportunities. Beyond are pleasant thermal baths at **Nangulví**. The area is rich in cloudforest and has several nature reserves. On the southwest

Tip...

Beware! Some of the berries, which grow near Laguna Cuicocha, are poisonous: do not eat them. The path around the lake is not for vertigo sufferers.

boundary of the Cotacachi-Cayapas reserve is **Los Cedros Research Station** ⓘ *2 hrs walk from the road, T06-361 2546, T09-9277 8878, www.reservaloscedros.org*, 6400 ha of pristine cloudforest, with abundant orchids and bird life. Full board in $$$ range. **Cloud Forest Adventure** (T06-301 7543, www.cloudforestadventure.com) offers accommodation, tours and volunteer opportunities in the Intag region.

Ibarra and around *Colour map 1, A4.*

Ibarra, the provincial capital, is the main commercial centre and transport hub of the northern highlands. The city has an interesting ethnic mix, with blacks from the Chota valley and Esmeraldas alongside Otavaleños and other highland *indígenas*, mestizos and Colombian immigrants.

On **Parque Pedro Moncayo** stand the Cathedral, the Municipio and Gobernación. One block away, at Flores y Olmedo, is the smaller Parque 9 de Octubre or **Parque de la Merced** after its church. Beyond the railway station, to the south and west of the centre, is a busy commercial area with several markets beyond which is the bus terminal. At the Centro Cultural Ibarra, the **Museo Regional Sierra Norte** ⓘ *Sucre 7-21 y Oviedo, T06-260 2093, Tue-Fri, 0900-1630, Sat-Sun and holidays 1000-1600*, has interesting archaeological displays about cultures of northern Ecuador, colonial and contemporary art and temporary exhibits. **Bosque Protector Guayabillas** ⓘ *Urbanización La Victoria, on the eastern outskirts of town, Tue-Sun 0900-1700*, is a 54-ha park on a hill overlooking the city which offers great views. There are trails amid the eucalyptus forest. **Virgen del Carmen** festival is on 16 July and **Fiesta de los Lagos** is in the last weekend of September.

Off the main road between Otavalo and Ibarra is **San Antonio de Ibarra**, well known for its wood carvings. It is worth seeing the range of styles and techniques and shopping around in the galleries and workshops. Further west is the town of **Atuntaqui**. On the opposite side of the Panamericana and along the rail line is Andrade Marín, home of the **Museo Fábrica Textil Imbabura** ⓘ *T06-253 0240, Wed-Sun 0900-1600, US$3, knowledgeable guides*, a good display of machinery of the most important producer and employer in the area between 1926 and 1966; included in train tours.

About 8 km from Ibarra on the road to Olmedo is **La Esperanza**, a pretty village in beautiful surroundings. Some 15 km further along, by Angochagua is the community of **Zuleta**. The region is known for its fine embroidery. West of La Esperanza, along a road that starts at Avenida Atahualpa, and also 8 km from Ibarra, is the community of **San Clemente**, which has a very good grassroots tourism project, **Pukyu Pamba**, see Where to stay, below. From either La Esperanza or San Clemente you can climb **Cubilche** volcano and **Imbabura**, more easily than from San Pablo del Lago. From the top you can walk down to Lago San Pablo (see page 540). *Guías nativos* are available for these climbs.

Ibarra to the coast The spectacular train ride from Ibarra to San Lorenzo on the Pacific coast no longer operates. A tourist train runs on a small section of this route, see pages 545 and 555.

Some 24 km north of Ibarra is the turn-off west for **Salinas**, a mainly Afro-Ecuadorean village with a Museo de la Sal, an ethnographic cultural centre and a restaurant offering local cuisine, and the very scenic road beside the Río Mira down to San Lorenzo. At 41 km from the turn-off are the villages of **Guallupe**, **El Limonal** (see Where to stay, below), and **San Juan de Lachas**, in a lush subtropical area. Ceramic masks and figurines are produced at the latter. In **Lita**, 33 km from Guallupe, there is nice swimming in the river. Beyond is the Río Chuchubi with waterfalls and swimming holes; here is **Las Siete Cascadas resort**

ⓘ *entry US$10, guide US$10 per group* (see Where to stay, page 552). It is 66 km from Lita to **Calderón**, where this road meets the coastal highway coming from Esmeraldas. Two kilometres before the junction, on the Río Tululbí, is **Tunda Loma** (see Where to stay, page 649). About 7 km beyond is San Lorenzo (see page 647).

Northwest of Ibarra Along a secondary road to the northwest of Ibarra is the town of **Urcuquí** with a basic hotel. Nearby is **Yachay**, a university and national research and technology centre, in a beautiful historic hacienda. From just south of Urcuquí, a road leads via Irunguicho towards the **Piñán lakes**, a beautiful, remote, high *páramo* region, part of the Reserva Ecológica Cotacachi-Cayapas. The local community of Piñán (3112 m) has a tourism programme (www.pinantrek.com), with a well-equipped refuge (US$12 per person, meals available), *guías nativos* (US$15 per day) and muleteers (US$12 per day, per horse). Another access to the hamlet of Piñán is via La Merced de Buenos Aires, a village reached from either Tumbabiro (see below) or San Gerónimo, near Guallupe (on the road to the coast). Along the Tumbabiro access is the community of Sachapamba, where muleteers and mules can be found. The nicest lakes, Donoso and Caricocha, are one-hour walk from the community. They can also be reached walking from either Chachimbiro (see below), Irubí or Cuellaje in the Intag area. Otavalo agencies and hotels in Chachimbiro and Tumababiro also offer trekking tours to Piñán. Note that a proposed irrigation and hydroelectric scheme will affect this beautiful area.

Beyond Urcuquí is the friendly town of **Tumbabiro**, with a mild climate, a good base from which to explore this region (several lodgings, see Where to stay, page 552); it can also be reached from Salinas on the road to the coast. Some 8 km from Tumbabiro along a side road, set on the slopes of an extinct volcano, is **Chachimbiro**, a good area for walking and horse riding, with several resorts with thermal baths. The largest one, run by the provincial government, is **Santa Agua Chachimbiro** ⓘ *T06-264 8308, www.santagua. com.ec, 0700-2000, entry to recreational pools US$5, to medicinal pools and spa US$10,* with several hot mineral pools, lodging, restaurants, zip-line and horses for riding; weekends can be crowded (see Where to stay, page 552).

North to Colombia

From Ibarra the Pan-American highway goes past Laguna Yahuarcocha (with a few hotels, a campground, see Where to stay, Ibarra, and many food stalls, busy on weekends) and then descends to the hot dry Chota valley, a centre of Afro-Ecuadorean culture. Beyond the turn-off for Salinas and San Lorenzo, 30 km from Ibarra, the highway divides. The western branch follows an older route through Mira and El Angel to Tulcán on the Colombian border, the eastern route, the Pan-American Highway, goes to Tulcán via Bolívar, San Gabriel and Huaca. A paved road between El Angel and Bolívar connects the two branches. **Note** In 2016, work on widening the eastern route was stalled and most traffic was using the western alternative. From El Angel a beautiful paved road west connects with the road between Ibarra and the coast.

Western route to Tulcán At **Mascarilla**, 1 km after the roads divide, ceramic masks are made. The women's crafts association here runs a hostel (**$ El Patio de mi Casa**, T09-9316 1621, meals available). Beyond by 16 km is **Mira** (2400 m), where fine woollens are made. This road is paved and in good condition as far as **El Angel** (3000 m), where the main plaza retains a few trees sculpted by José Franco (see Tulcán Cemetery, opposite); market day is Monday. The road north beyond El Angel goes through beautiful *páramo*. It is poor requiring a 4WD and is a great mountain bike route.

The **Reserva Ecológica El Angel** ⓘ *T06-297 7597, office in El Angel near the Municipio; best time to visit May to Aug*, nearby protects 15,715 ha of *páramo* ranging in altitude from 3400 m to 4768 m. The reserve contains large stands of the velvet-leaved *frailejón* plant, also found in the Andes of Colombia and Venezuela. Also of interest are the spiny *achupallas*, *bromeliads* with giant compound flowers. The fauna includes *curiquingues* (caracara), deer, foxes, and a few condors. From El Angel follow the poor road north towards Tulcán for 16 km to **El Voladero** ranger station/shelter, where a self-guided trail climbs over a low ridge (30 minutes' walk) to two crystal-clear lakes. Pickups or taxis from the main plaza of El Angel charge US$25 return with one-hour wait for a day trip to El Voladero. A longer route to another area follows an equally poor road to Cerro Socabones, beginning at **La Libertad**, 3.5 km north of El Angel (transport El Angel–Cerro Socabones, US$30 return). It climbs gradually to reach the high *páramo* at the centre of the reserve and, in 40 minutes, the **El Salado** ranger station. From Socabones the road descends to the village of **Morán** (lodging and guides, transport with Sr Calderón, T09-9128 4022), the start of a nice three-day walk down to Guallupe, on the Ibarra–San Lorenzo road.

Eastern route to Tulcán From Mascarilla, the Panamericana normally runs east through the warm Chota valley to El Juncal, before turning northeast to **Bolívar**, a neat little town where the houses and the interior of its church are painted in lively pastel colours; there is also a huge mural by the roadside. At the **Museo Paleontológico** ⓘ *by the north entrance to town, US$2*, remains of a mammoth, found nearby, can be seen. There is a Friday market.

Some 16 km north of Bolívar is **San Gabriel**, an important commercial centre. The 60-m-high **Paluz** waterfall is 4 km north of town, beyond a smaller waterfall. To the southeast, 11 km from town on the road to Piartal is **Bosque de Arrayanes**, a 16-ha mature forest with a predominance of myrtle trees, some reaching 20 m, taxi US$5.

East of San Gabriel by 20 km is the tiny community of **Mariscal Sucre** also known as Colonia Huaqueña, the gateway to the **Guandera Reserve and Biological Station** ⓘ *the reserve is part of Fundación Jatun Sacha. Reservations should be made at the Quito office, T02-331 7163, www.jatunsacha.org.* You can see bromeliads, orchids, toucans and other wildlife in temperate forest and *frailejón páramo*. From San Gabriel, take a taxi beyond Mariscal Sucre, one hour, then walk 30 minutes to the reserve, or make arrangements with Jatun Sacha.

Between San Gabriel and Tulcán are the towns of Huaca, site of a pre-Inca settlement and Julio Andrade, with **$$-$ Hotel Naderik**, T06-220 5433, and a Saturday market (good for horses and other large animals) and, afterwards, paddleball games. This is the beginning of the road east to La Bonita, Lumbaqui and Lago Agrio. The road follows the frontier for much of the route. Make enquiries about safety before taking this beautiful route.

Tulcán *Colour map 1, A4.*

The chilly city of Tulcán (altitude 2960 m) is the busy capital of the province of Carchi. There is a great deal of informal trade here with Colombia, a textile and dry goods fair

Tip...

Tulcán is a generally safe city, but the area around the bus terminal requires caution, especially at night. Do not travel outside town (except along the Panamericana) without advance local enquiry.

takes place on Thursday and Sunday. The eastern and western roads from the south join at Las Juntas, 2 km south of the city. In the **cemetery** ⓘ *daily 0800-1800*, two blocks from Parque Ayora, the art of topiary is taken to beautiful extremes. Cypress bushes are trimmed into archways, fantastic figures and geometric shapes in *haut* and *bas* relief. To see the stages of this art form, go to the back of the cemetery where young bushes

are being pruned. The artistry, started in 1936, is that of the late Sr José Franco, born in El Angel (see above), now buried among the splendour he created. The tradition is carried on by his sons. Around the cemetery is a promenade with fountains, souvenir and flower stalls and the **tourist office**, Unidad de Turismo ⓘ *entrance to the cemetery, T06-298 5760, daily 0800-1800, turismo@gmtulcan.gob.ec, helpful*. Write in advance to request a guided tour of the cemetery. Two blocks south is the **Museo de la Casa de la Cultura** ⓘ *Mon-Fri 0730-1300, 1500-1800*, with a collection of pre-Inca ceramics.

Border with Colombia: Tulcán–Ipiales

The border is at **Rumichaca** (stone bridge), 5 km from Tulcán. Border posts with immigration, customs and agriculture control are on either side of a concrete bridge over the Río Carchi, to the east of the natural stone bridge. This well organized border is open 24 hours. On the Ecuadorean side, next to immigration (T06-298 6169), is a tourist information office. **Colombian consulate in Tulcán** ⓘ *Bolívar entre Ayacucho y Junín, T06-298 0559, Tue-Thu 0800-1300*. Visas require three days.

Listings Otavalo to the Colombian border

Tourist information

Cotacachi

iTur Turec
Centro de Convenciones El Convento, García Moreno 13-66 y Sucre, T06-255 4122, Facebook: turecturismocotacachi for upcoming events. Mon-Fri 0900-1700, Sat 0900-1500.
Run by an association of disabled people. It provides maps, regional information, tours, rides on horse-drawn carriages and chivas (both with advanced reservations); also rents camping equipment and bicycles (US$2 per hr). On the same premises are a restaurant and cafeteria. Additional tourist information in Spanish and a city map are found in www. cotacachi.gob.ec.

Ibarra

Dirección de Turismo del Municipio
Sucre y Oviedo, T06-260 8489, www. touribarra.gob.ec. Mon-Fri 0800-1230, 1400-1730, holidays 0900-1500.
City map, pamphlets, English spoken, free Wi-Fi.

Where to stay

Cotacachi

$$$$ La Mirage
500 m west of town, T06-291 5237, www.mirage.com.ec.
Luxurious converted hacienda with elegant suites and common areas, includes breakfast and dinner, excellent restaurant, pool, gym and spa (treatments extra), beautiful gardens, tours arranged.

$$$-$$ Land of Sun
García Moreno 1376 y Sucre, T06-291 6009.
Refurbished colonial house in the heart of
town, rooms with balcony, internal ones are
cheaper, breakfast served in lovely patio,
local specialities in restaurant, request dinner
in advance, sauna, parking. Recommended.

$$ Runa Tupari
A system of homestays in nearby villages.
Visitors experience life with a indigenous
family by taking part in daily activities.
The comfortable rooms have space for 3,
fireplace, bathroom and hot shower, and
cost US$35 pp including breakfast, dinner
and transport from Otavalo. Arrange with
Runa Tupari (www.runatupari.com), or other
Otavalo tour operators.

$$-$ La Cuadra
*Peñaherrera 11-46 y González Suárez,
T06-291 6015, www.lacuadra-hostal.com.*
Modern comfortable rooms, good
matresses, private or shared bath,
no breakfast, kitchen facilities.

$ Bachita
Sucre 16-82 y Peñaherrera, T06-291 5063.
Simple place, private or shared bath, no
breakfast, quiet.

Laguna Cuicocha

$$$ Hostería Cuicocha
*Laguna Cuicocha, by the pier, T06-301 7218,
www.cuicocha.org.*
Rooms overlooking the lake, internal ones
are cheaper, includes breakfast and dinner,
restaurant, no overnight staff.

$$-$ Cabañas Mirador
*On a lookout above the pier, follow the
trail or by car follow the road to the left
of the park entrance, T09-9055 8367,
miradordecuicocha@yahoo.com.*
Rustic cabins with fireplace and modern
rooms overlooking the lake, good economical
restaurant, trout is the speciality, parking,
transport provided to Quiroga (US$5),
Cotacachi (US$5), or Otavalo (US$10); owner

Ernesto Cevillano is knowledgeable about the
area and arranges trips.

Ibarra

$$$$ Hacienda Pimán
*9 km northeast of town, Quito T02-256 6090,
www.haciendapiman.com.*
Luxuriously restored 18th-century hacienda,
price includes breakfast and dinner. All
inclusive 2- and 3-day packages with a train
ride and visit to El Angel Reserve.

$$$ Hacienda Chorlaví
*Panamericana Sur Km 4, T06-293 2222,
www.haciendachorlavi.com.*
In a historical hacienda dating to 1620,
comfortable rooms, very good expensive
restaurant, excellent *parrillada*, pool and spa,
parking, busy on weekends, folk music and
crafts on Sat.

$$$ La Estelita
Km 5 Vía a Yuracrucito, T09-9811 6058.
Modern hotel 5 km from the city, high
on a hill overlooking town and Laguna
Yahuarcocha. Rooms and suites with lovely
views, good restaurant, pool, spa, can
arrange paragliding.

$$ Montecarlo
*Av Jaime Rivadeneira 5-61 y Oviedo,
near the obelisk, T06-295 8266,
www.hotelmontecarloibarra.ec.*
Nice comfortable rooms, buffet
breakfast, restaurant, heated pool
open on weekends, parking.

$$ Royal Ruiz
*Olmedo 9-40 y P Moncayo, T06-264 4653,
www.hotelroyalruiz.com.*
Modern, comfortable carpeted rooms,
restaurant, solar-heated water, parking,
long-stay discounts.

$$-$ Finca Sommerwind
*Autopista Yahuarcocha Km 8, T09-3937 1177,
www.finca-sommerwind.info.*
A 12-ha ranch by Laguna Yahuarcocha with
cabins and campground, US$3 pp in tent,

US$5 pp for camper vans, electricity, hot shower, laundry facilities.

$ Fran's Hostal
Gral Julio Andrade 1-58 y Rafael Larrea, near bus terminal, T06-260 9995.
Multi-storey hotel, bright functional rooms, no breakfast, parking.

$ Las Garzas
Flores 3-13 y Salinas, T06-295 0985.
Simple comfortable rooms, no breakfast, sitting room.

Around Ibarra

$$$$ Hacienda Zuleta
By Angochahua, along the Ibarra-Cayambe road, T06-266 2232, www.haciendazuleta.com.
A 2000-ha working historic hacienda, among the nicest in the country. Superb accommodation and food, 15 rooms with fireplace, price includes all meals (prepared with organic vegetables, trout and dairy produced on the farm) and excursions, advance reservations required.

$$$ Pukyu Pamba
In San Clemente, T06-266-0045, 09-9916 1095, www.sanclementetours.com.
Part of a community-run programme. Nicely built cottages with hot water on family properties, cheaper in more humble family homes, price includes 3 tasty meals and a guided tour. Opportunities to participate in daily activities in the field and kitchen and learn about local traditions and celebrations. Options for hiking, horse riding and climbing Imbabura volcano.

$$ Casa Aída
In La Esperanza village, T06-266 0221.
Simple rooms with good beds, includes dinner and breakfast, restaurant, shared bath, hot water, patios, some English spoken, meeting place for climbing Imbabura.

Ibarra to the coast

$$$$ Hacienda Primavera
North of Guallupe on the road to Chical, T09-9370 8571, www.haciendaprimavera.com.
8 rooms in a beautiful forest setting, pool, includes full board, guided hiking and horse riding.

$$$ Las Siete Cascadas
Km 111, 15 km past Lita, T09-8261 1195, lily_tarupi@hotmail.com.
A-frame cabins with balconies in a 204-ha reserve, price includes full board and excursions to waterfalls and the forest, reserve well ahead.

$$-$ Parque Bambú
In El Limonal, about 600 m uphill from the main square, T06-301 6606, www.bospas.org.
Family-run farm with splendid views of the valley and many birds. Private rooms with terrace, US$14 pp in dorm, good breakfast, tasty meals available, camping U$3 pp, trekking. Run by Belgian Piet Sabbe, a permaculture landscape designer, and his daughters; Piet will share his knowledge and experience in landscape restoration and welcomes volunteers with a green thumb (arrange ahead). Recommended.

Northwest of Ibarra

$$$ Aguasavia
In Chachimbiro,15-min walk from Santa Agua complex, T06-304 8347.
Community-run modern hotel in a beautiful setting in the crater of La Viuda Volcano, includes 3 meals, rooms on ground floor with jacuzzi, thermal pools, trips.

$$$ Hacienda San Francisco
In the community of San Francisco, 5 km past Tumbabiro on the road to Chachimbiro, T06-304 8232, www.hosteriasanfrancisco.com.
Intimate family-run inn in tastefully converted hacienda stables, includes breakfast, expensive restaurant, full board packages available, small thermal pool, nice grounds, good walking, horse riding, tennis

court, excursions to Piñán, best Thu to Sun when owners are in.

$$$ Santa Agua Chachimbiro
Part of the recreational complex, T06-264 8063, in Ibarra T06-261 0250, www.santagua.com.ec.
Rooms and cabins (some with jacuzzi), includes 3 meals and access to spa and pools, restaurant, busy on weekends, reserve ahead.

$$$-$$ Hostería Spa Pantaví
7 km from Salinas, at the entrance to Tumbabiro, T06-293 4185, Quito reservations T02-234 0601, www.hosteriapantavi.com.
Stylish inn in a tastefully restored hacienda. Very comfortable rooms, decorated with the owner's original works of art, includes nice breakfast, good restaurant, pool, spa, jacuzzi, nice gardens, attentive service, bikes and horses for rent, tours. Recommended.

$ Tío Lauro
1 block from plaza, Tumbabiro, T06-293 4148.
Nice *residencial*, simple rooms, meals on request, parking, friendly owner.

North to Colombia
El Angel

$$$$ Polylepis Lodge
Abutting the reserve, 14 km from El Angel along the road to Socabones, T06-263 1819, www.polylepislodgeec.com.
Rustic cabins with fireplace by a lovely 12-ha forest, includes 3 meals (vegetarian on request) and 3 guided walks, jacuzzi.

$$ Las Orquídeas
In the village of Morán, T09-8641 6936, castro503@yahoo.com.
Mountain cabin with bunk beds, shared bath, includes 3 meals, horse riding and guide, run by Carlos Castro, a local guide and conservation pioneer.

$ Blas Angel
C Espejo, facing the roundabout by the entrance to town, T06-297 7346.

Private or shared bath, parking, a good economical option.

Eastern route to Tulcán
San Gabriel

$$ Gabrielita
Mejía y Los Andes, above the agricultural supply shop, T06-229 1832.
Modern hostel, includes breakfast, parking, best in town.

Tulcán

$$$ Palacio Imperial
Sucre y Pichincha, T06-298 0638, www.hotelpalacioimperial.com.
Modern hotel with ample rooms with wood floors, suites with jacuzzi, warm blankets, includes buffet breakfast, very popular Chinese restaurant **Chifa Pak Choy**, rooftop spa, gym, parking.

$$ Grand Hotel Comfort
Colón y Chimborazo, T06-298 1452, www.grandhotelcomfort.com.
Modern high-rise hotel with rooms and suites with jacuzzi, fridge, safety box, with breakfast, restaurant with set lunch and à la carte (closed Sat-Sun evening), parking.

$$ Sara Espíndola
Sucre y Ayacucho, on plaza, T298 6209.
Comfortable rooms, with breakfast, spa, parking, helpful.

$$-$ Los Alpes
JR Arellano next to bus station, T06-298 2235.
Best option near the bus terminal, breakfast extra, restaurant, good value.

$$-$ Torres de Oro
Sucre y Rocafuerte, T06-298 0296.
Modern, nice, restaurant, parking.

$ Florida
Sucre y Ayacucho, T298 3849.
Simple, clean, shared bath, no breakfast, a good economy option.

Restaurants

Cotacachi

A local speciality is *carne colorada* (spiced pork).

$$ D'Anita
10 de Agosto, y Moncayo. Daily 0800-2100.
Good set meal of the day, local and international dishes à la carte, popular, English spoken, good value.

$$-$ La Vaca Gorda
10 de Agosto entre Rocafuerte y Pedro Moncay. Open 1200-2200.
Grilled meats, burgers, wings, fries and beer, popular with expats.

Café Río Intag
On Plaza San Francis. Mon-Fri 0800-2000, Sat 1000-2200, Sun 1000-1800.
The best coffee, snacks, meeting place.

Ibarra

$$ Caribou
Pérez Guerrero 537 y Sucre and in Yacucalle south of the bus terminal, T06-260 5137. Mon 1700-2300, Tue-Thu 1300-2300, Fri-Sat 1300-0030.
Excellent meat specialities, including burgers, salads, bar, Canadian-owned. Recommended.

$$ El Argentino
Sucre y P Moncayo, at Plazoleta Francisco Calderón. Tue-Sun.
Good mixed grill and salads, small, pleasant, outdoor seating.

$$-$ La Cassona
Bolívar 6-47 y Oviedo. Daily.
In a nice colonial patio, international, seafood and local dishes, also set lunch.

$ Casa Blanca
Bolívar 7-83. Closed Sun.
Family-run, in colonial house with patio, good set lunches and snacks. Recommended.

Cafés and heladerías

Café Arte
Salinas 5-43 y Oviedo. Daily from 1700.
Café-bar with character, drinks, Mexican snacks, sandwiches, live music Fri-Sat night.

Café Pushkin
Olmedo y Oviedo. Open 0700-1700.
For breakfast, snacks, coffee. An Ibarra classic, very popular.

El Quinde Café
Sucre 562 y Flores.
A good place for breakfast, coffee, cake, snacks.

Heladería Rosalía Suárez
Oviedo y Olmedo.
Excellent homemade *helados de paila* (fruit sherbets made in large copper basins), an Ibarra tradition since 1896. Highly recommended.

Olor a Café
Flores y Bolívar.
Café/bar/cultural centre in a historic home, music, library.

Tulcán

$$-$ Dubai
Chimborazo. Open 1030-2200.
Set lunch, à la carte and *comida típica*, popular.

$ Bocattos
Bolívar y Panamá on Parque Ayora.
Set lunch and à la carte, Italian and Ecuadorean specialities.

$ Café Tulcán
Sucre 52-029 y Ayacucho. Open 0800-1800.
Café, snacks, desserts, juices, set lunches. A Tulcán classic.

> Tip...
> Economical meals and juices at the attractively renovated and clean Mercado Central, entrances on Boyacá, Bolívar and Sucre in Tulcán, open 0700-1700.

Bars and clubs

Ibarra

Plazoleta Francisco Calderón on Sucre y Pedro Moncayo has several café-bars with outdoor seating and a pleasant atmosphere.

Rincón de Ayer
Olmedo 9-59.
A bar with lots of character, attractively restored.

Sambuca
Oviedo 636 y Sucre.
Bar/club, the in-place among Ibarreño youth.

What to do

Ibarra

A unique form of paddle ball, *pelota nacional*, is played in the afternoon at Yacucalle, south of the bus station. Players have huge studded paddles for striking the 1-kg ball.

Paragliding
Fly Ecuador, *T06-295 3297 or T09-8487 5577, www.flyecuador.com.ec.* Tandem flight US$67-90, course US$448, arrange ahead.

Tour operators
EcuaHorizons, *Bolívar 4-67 y García Moreno, T06-295 9904.* Bilingual guides for regional tours.
Intipungo, *Rocafuerte 6-08 y Flores, T06-295 7766.* Regional tours.

Train rides

A tourist train runs from Ibarra to **Salinas**, 29 km away, Wed-Sun and holidays at 1030, returning 1600, US$15-20 one way, US$20-25 return. When there is high demand, there is also *ferrochiva* (open sided motorized railcar) service at 1030, US$15 one way, US$20 return. Purchase tickets in advance. Ibarra station at Espejo y Colón, T06-295 5050, daily 0800-1300, 1400-1630 or through T1-800-873637; you need each passenger's passport number and date of birth to purchase tickets. The ride takes 2 hrs with stops. You can continue

by bus from Salinas to **San Lorenzo**, see page 647.

Transport

Cotacachi
Bus Terminal at 10 de Agosto y Salinas by the market. Every 10 mins to/from Otavalo terminal, US$0.25, 25 mins; service alternates between the Panamericana and the Quiroga roads. To **Ibarra**, every 15 mins, US$0.50, 40 mins; service alternates between the Panamericana and Imantag roads.

Laguna Cuicocha
Pick-ups From **Otavalo** US$10. From **Cotacachi**, US$5 one way, US$10 return with short wait. From **Quiroga** US$5. Return service from the lake available from **Cabañas El Mirador**, same rates.

Los Cedros Research Station
Bus From Estación La Ofelia in Quito, **Trans Minas**, daily at 0615, 1000, 1530, 1800 to **Magdalena Alto**, US$4.50, 3½ hrs; then a 2-hr **walk**; arrange with the station for mules to carry luggage up. If the road is passable, 2 daily buses from Otavalo, pass **Chontal** on route to Cielo Verde. Take a pickup from Chontal to Magdalena Alto or it is a 5-hr walk from Chontal to Los Cedros.

Ibarra
Bus Terminal is at Av Teodoro Gómez y Av Eugenio Espejo, southwest of the centre, T06-264 4676. Most inter-city transport runs from here. There are no ticket counters for regional destinations, such as Otavalo, proceed directly to the platforms. City buses go from the terminal to the centre or you can walk in 15 mins. To/from **Quito**, Terminal Carcelén, every 10 mins, US$3, 2½ hrs. Shared taxis with **Taxis Lagos/Serviquito** (Quito address under Otavalo Transport, page 545, in Ibarra at Flores 924 y Sánchez y Cifuentes, near Parque La Merced, T06-260 6858), buy ticket at least 1 day ahead, US$15 pp, 2½ hrs. To **Tulcán**, with **Expreso Turismo**, 9 daily,

US$3, 2½ hrs. To **Otavalo**, platform 12, every 4 mins, US$0.50, 40 mins. To **Cotacachi**, platform 15, every 15 mins, US$0.50, 40 mins, some continue to **Quiroga**. To the coast, several companies, some go all the way to **San Lorenzo** US$7, 4 hrs, others only as far as **Lita**, US$4.50, 2 hrs. To **Ambato**, CITA goes via El Quinche and the Quito airport roundabout and bypasses Quito, 10 daily, US$6.50, 5 hrs. To **Baños**, Expreso Baños, also by the airport and bypasses Quito, at 0500 and 1430, US$7.50, 6 hrs. To **Lago Agrio**, Valle de Chota, at 0900, US$11.25, via La Bonita. To **Tumbabiro** via Urcuquí, **Coop Urcuquí**, hourly, US$1, 1 hr. To **Chachimbiro**, Coop Urcuquí, at 0700, 0730 and 1200, returning Mon-Fri at 1215 (Sat-Sun at 1300), 1530 and 1630, US$1.60, 1½ hrs, taxi US$40 return. Buses to La Esperanza, Zuleta and San Clemete leave from **Parque Germán Grijalva** (east of the Terminal Terrestre, follow C Sánchez y Cifuentes, south from the centre). To **La Esperanza**, every 20 mins, US$0.30, 30 mins. To **Zuleta**, hourly, US$0.60, 1 hr. To **San Clemente**, frequent, weekdays 0650-1840, Sat-Sun 0720-1500, US$0.30, 30 mins. For nearby destinations such as **San Antonio de Ibarra**, city buses run along Pérez Guerrero.

North to Colombia
Western route to Tulcán
Bus from **Ibarra** Terminal Terrestre to **Mira**, every 30 mins, US$1.25, 1 hr; to **El Angel**, hourly, US$1.75, 1½ hrs. El Angel to **Mira**, every 30 mins, US$.50, 20 mins. El Angel to **Tulcán**, US$1.75, 1½ hrs. El Angel to **Quito**, US$5, 4 hrs.

Eastern route to Tulcán
Bus From **San Gabriel** to **Tulcán**, vans and jeeps US$0.70, shared taxis US$0.95, 30 mins, all from the main plaza. From San Gabriel to **Ibarra**, buses, US$2, 2 hrs. From San Gabriel to **Quito**, buses, US$4.50, 3½ hrs. See Note, under Tulcán, below.

Tulcán
Air There is an airport, but no commercial flights were operating in early 2016.

Bus The bus terminal is 1.5 km uphill from centre; best to take a taxi, US$1.25. **Note** In 2016 most transport was going via El Angel, adding 30 mins to times indicated below (except for Lago Agrio). To **Quito**, US$5, 5 hrs, every 15 mins, service to Terminal Carcelén, some continue to Quitumbe; from Quito, service from both terminals. To **Ibarra**, 2½ hrs, US$3. **Otavalo**, US$3.75, 3 hrs (they don't go in to the Otavalo Terminal, alight at the highway turn-off where taxis are available or transfer in Ibarra). To **Guayaquil**, 20 a day, 13 hrs, US$16. To **Lago Agrio via La Bonita**, 3 a day with **Putumayo** and 2 daily with **Coop Petrolera**, US$8.75, 7 hrs, spectacular.

Border with Colombia
Bus Minivans and shared taxis (US$1 pp) leave when full from Parque Ayora (near the cemetery); private taxi US$3.50. Taxi from the bus terminal to the border US$3, shared US$1.25 pp. **Note** These vehicles cross the international bridge and drop you off on the Colombian side, where onward transport waits. Remember to cross back over the bridge for Ecuadorean immigration. *Colectivo* border–Ipiales, US$1, taxi US$6-8.

Cotopaxi, Latacunga
& Quilotoa

★ An impressive roll call of towering peaks lines the route south of Quito, appropriately called the Avenue of the Volcanoes. This area obviously attracts its fair share of trekkers and climbers, while the less active tourist can browse through the many colourful indigenous markets and colonial towns that nestle among the high volcanic cones. The Pan-American Highway's six lanes head south from Quito towards the central highlands' hub of Ambato. The perfect cone of Cotopaxi volcano is ever-present and is one of the country's main tourist attractions. Machachi and Latacunga are good bases from which to explore the region and provide access to the beautiful Quilotoa Circuit of small villages and vast expanses of open countryside.

Best for
Markets ▪ Trekking ▪ Vistas ▪ Wildlife

Machachi

In a valley between the summits of Pasochoa, Rumiñahui and Corazón, lies the town of **Machachi**, famous for its horsemen (*chagras*), horse riding trips, mineral water springs and crystal clear swimming pools. The water, 'Agua Güitig' or 'Tesalia', is bottled in a plant 4 km from the town, where there is also a sports/recreation complex with one warm and two cold pools, entry US$5. Annual highland 'rodeo', El Chagra, third week in July; tourist information office on the plaza. Just north of Machachi is Alóag, where an important road goes west to Santo Domingo and the coast.

Reserva Ecológica Los Ilinizas

Machachi is a good starting point for a visit to the northern section of the **Reserva Ecológica Los Ilinizas**. Below the saddle between the two peaks, at 4740 m, is the **Refugio Nuevos Horizontes** ⓘ *T09-8133 3483, office and café in El Chaupi, T02-367 4125, www.ilinizas-refuge. webs.com, US$15 per night, US$30 with dinner and breakfast, reserve ahead, take sleeping bag*, a shelter with capacity for 25. **Iliniza Norte** (5105 m) although not a technical climb, should not be underestimated, a few exposed, rocky sections require utmost caution. Some climbers suggest using a rope and a helmet is recommended if other parties are there because of falling rock; allow two to four hours for the ascent from the refuge. **Iliniza Sur** (5245 m) involves ice climbing despite the deglaciation: full climbing gear and experience are absolutely necessary. All visitors must register and be accompanied by an authorized mountain guide for both ascents; maximum three climbers per guide on Iliniza Norte, two per guide on Iliniza Sur.

Access to the reserve is through a turn-off west of the Panamericana 6 km south of Machachi, then it's 7 km to the village of El Chaupi, which is a good base for day-walks and climbing **Corazón** (4782 m, not trivial). A dirt road continues from El Chaupi 9 km to 'La Virgen' (statue), pickup US$15. Nearby are woods where you can camp. El Chaupi hotels arrange for horses with muleteer (US$25 per animal, one way).

☆Parque Nacional Cotopaxi *Colour map, 1, B4.*

Visitors to the park must register at the entrance. Park gates are open 0800-1500, although you can stay until 1700. Visitors arriving with guides not authorized by the park are turned back at the gate. The park administration, a small museum (open daily 0800-1530) and snack bar, are 10 km from the park gates. La Rinconada shelter and camping area are 5 km beyond, just before lake Limpio Pungo. (See also Transport section, page 564.) The museum has a 3D model of the park, information about the volcano and stuffed animals.

Cotopaxi Volcano (5897 m) is at the heart of a much-visited national park. This scenic snow-covered perfect cone is the second highest peak in Ecuador. Cotopaxi, one of the highest active volcanoes in the world, resumed activity in 2015, see box, page 574. Volcanic material from former eruptions can be seen strewn about the *páramo* surrounding Cotopaxi. The northwest flank is most often visited. Here is a high plateau with a small lake (Laguna Limpio Pungo), a lovely area for walking and admiring the delicate flora, and fauna including wild horses and native bird species such as the Andean lapwing and the Chimborazo hillstar hummingbird. The lower slopes are clad in planted pine forests, where llamas may be seen. The southwest flank, or Cara Sur, has not received as much impact as the west side. Here too, there is good walking, and you can climb Morurco (4881 m) as an acclimatization hike; condors may sometimes be seen. Just north of Cotopaxi are the peaks of Rumiñahui (4722 m), Sincholagua (4873 m) and Pasochoa (4225 m). To the southeast, beyond the park boundary, are Quilindaña (4890 m) and an area of rugged *páramos* and mountains dropping down to the jungle. The area has several large haciendas which form the Fundación Páramo (www.fundacionparamo.org), a private reserve with restricted access.

The **main entrance** to Parque Nacional Cotopaxi is approached from Chasqui, 25 km south of Machachi, 6 km north of Lasso. Once through the national park gates, go past Laguna Limpio Pungo to a fork, where the right branch climbs steeply to a parking lot (4600 m). From here it's a 30-minute to one-hour walk to the José Ribas refuge, at 4800 m (closed 2016); beware of altitude sickness. Walking from the highway to the refuge takes an entire day or more. The **El Pedregal entrance**, from the northwest, is accessed from Machachi via Santa Ana del Pedregal (21 km from the Panamericana), or from Sangolquí via Rumipamba and the Río Pita Valley. From Pedregal to the refuge car park is 14 km. There are infrequent buses to Pedregal (two a day) then the hike in is shorter but still a couple of hours. The **Ticatilín access** leads to the southwest flank. Just north of Lasso, a road goes east to the village of San Ramón and on to Ticatilín (a contribution of US$2 per vehicle may be requested at the barrier here, be sure to close all gates) and Rancho María. From the south, San Ramón is accessed from Mulaló. Beyond Rancho María is the private Albergue Cotopaxi Cara Sur (4000 m, see Where to stay, below). Walking four hours from here you reach Campo Alto (4760 m), a climbers' tent camp. Note Cotopaxi was closed to climbers in 2016 owing to volcanic activity.

Lasso

Some 30 km south of Machachi is the small town of Lasso, on the railway line and off the Panamericana. In the surrounding countryside are several *hosterías*, converted country estates, offering accommodation and meals. Intercity buses bypass Lasso.

Latacunga *Colour map, 1, B3. See map, page 560.*

The capital of Cotopaxi Province is a place where the abundance of light grey pumice has been artfully employed. Volcán Cotopaxi is much in evidence, though it is 29 km away. Provided they are not hidden by clouds, which unfortunately is all too often, as many as nine volcanic cones can be seen from Latacunga; try early in the morning. The colonial character of the town has been well preserved. The central plaza, **Parque Vicente León**, is a beautifully maintained garden (locked at night). There are several other gardens in the town including **Parque San Francisco** and **Lago Flores** (better known as 'La Laguna'). **Casa de los Marqueses de Miraflores** ⓘ *Sánchez de Orellana y Abel Echeverría, T02-281 1382, Mon-Fri 0800-1700, Sat 0900-1300, free*, in a restored colonial mansion has a modest museum, with exhibits on Mama Negra (see Festivals, page 563), colonial art, archaeology, numismatics, a library and the Jefatura de Turismo, see below.

Casa de la Cultura ⓘ *Antonia Vela 3-49 y Padre Salcedo T03-281 3247, Tue-Fri 0800-1200, 1400-1800, Sat 0800-1500, US$1*, built around the remains of a Jesuit Monastery and the old Monserrat watermill, houses a nice museum with pre-Columbian ceramics, weavings, costumes and festival masks; also gallery, library and theatre. It has week-long festivals with exhibits and concerts. There is a Saturday **market** on the Plaza de San Sebastián (at Juan Abel Echeverría). Goods for sale include *shigras* (fine stitched, colourful straw bags) and homespun wool and cotton yarn. The produce market, El Salto, has daily trading and larger fairs on Tuesday, Friday and Saturday.

Listings Cotopaxi and Latacunga *map below.*

Tourist information

Latacunga

Cámara de Turismo de Cotopaxi
*Quito 14-38 y General Maldonado,
Latacunga, T03-280 1112, www.
capturcotopaxi.com/fest.htm.
Mon-Fri 0900-1300, 1400-1700.*
Local and regional information, Spanish only.

Jefatura de Turismo
*Casa de los Marqueses, T03-280 8494.
Mon-Fri 0800-1700.*
Local and regional information and maps.

Where to stay

Machachi

$$$ La Estación y Granja
*3 km west of the Panamericana,
by railway station outside the
village of Aloasí, T02-230 9246.*

Rooms in a lovely old home and newer
section, also cabins, fireplaces, meals
available (produce from own garden),
parking, family-run, hiking access to Volcán
Corazón (guides arranged), reserve ahead.

$$$ Papagayo
*In Hacienda Bolívia, west of the
Panamericana, take a taxi fom Machachi,
T02-231 0002, www.hosteria-papagayo.com.*
Nicely refurbished hacienda, pleasant
communal areas with fireplace and library,
restaurant, jacuzzi, parking, central heating,
homey atmosphere, horse riding, biking,
tours, popular.

$$$ Puerta al Corazón
*500 m south of the train station,
T02-230 9858.*
Cosy lodge, located near the rail line
with good views of the mountains, small
restaurant, price includes dinner and
breakfast. A good base for mountain trips.

Latacunga

100 metres
100 yards

Where to stay	Restaurants
1 Central	4 Rosim	1 Café Abuela	4 Cunani
2 Endamo	5 Tiana &	2 Chifa China	5 Gamber Rosso
3 Rodelú	Tovar Expediciones	3 Chifa Dragón	6 Guadalajara Grill
	6 Villa de Tacunga		7 Parrilladas La Española

$$ Chiguac
*Los Caras y Colón, 4 blocks east
of the main park, T02-231 0396,
amsincholagua@gmail.com.*
Nice family-run hostel, comfortable rooms,
good breakfast, other meals available,
shared bath.

Reserva Ecológica Los Ilinizas

$$$-$$ Chuquiragua Lodge
*500 m before El Chaupi, then 200 m on a
cobbled road, T02-367 4046, Quito T02-603
5590, www.chuquiragualodgeandspa.com.*
Inn with lovely views, a variety of rooms
and prices, restaurant with roaring fireplace.
US$18 pp in dorm, camping US$10 pp with
hot shower (bring your own tent). Spa, horse
riding, trekking, climbing, bike tours, and
transport from Quito available, advance
booking advised.

$$-$ La Llovizna
*100 m behind the church, on the way
to the mountain, T02-367 4076.*
Pleasant hostel, sitting room with fireplace,
includes breakfast and dinner, cheaper
without meals and includes use of kitchen,
private or shared bath, ping pong, horse,
bike and gear rentals, helpful owner, guiding,
transport to Ilinizas, book in advance.

$$-$ Nina Rumy
Near the bus stop in El Chaupi, T02-367 4088.
Includes breakfast and supper, cheaper
without meals, simple rooms, private or
shared bath, hot water, family-run and
very friendly.

Parque Nacional Cotopaxi
All these inns are good for acclimatization
at altitudes between 3100 m and 3800 m.

$$$-$$ Tambopaxi
*3 km south of the El Pedregal access (1 hr drive
from Machachi) or 4 km north of the turn-off
for the climbing shelter, T02-600 0365 (Quito),
www.tambopaxi.com.*
Comfortable straw-bale mountain shelter at
3750 m. 3 double rooms and several dorms

(US$25 pp), duvets, camping US$7.50 pp,
restaurant, excellent horse riding with
advance notice.

$$ Albergue Cotopaxi Cara Sur
*At the southwestern end of the park, at the
end of the Ticatilín road, T09-9800 2681,
eagamaz@gmail.com.*
Very nice mountain shelter at 4000 m, day
use US$1. Includes breakfast and dinner,
use of kitchen, some cabins with private
bath, hot shower, transport from Quito
and climbing tours available, equipment
rental. **Campo Alto** is a very basic tent camp
(4780 m, US$8 pp), 4 hrs' walk from the
shelter, horse to take gear to Campo Alto
US$15, muleteer US$15.

Outside the park

$$$$ Hacienda San Agustín de Callo
*2 access roads from the Panamericana,
1 just north of the main park access
(6.2 km); the second, just north of Lasso
(4.3 km), T03-271 9160, Quito T02-290 6157,
www.incahacienda.com.*
Exclusive hacienda, the only place in Ecuador
where you can sleep and dine in an Inca
building, the northernmost imperial-style
Inca structure still standing. Rooms and
suites with fireplace and bathtub, includes
breakfast and dinner, horse rides, treks,
bicycles and fishing. Restaurant ($$$) and
buildings open to non-guests (US$5-10).

$$$$ Hacienda Santa Ana
*10 mins from north entrance to
Cotopaxi National Park, T02-222 4950,
www.santaanacotopaxi.com.*
17th-century former Jesuit hacienda
in beautiful surroundings. 7 comfortable
rooms with fireplaces, central heating,
great views, horse riding, hiking, trekking,
climbing. Also run **Hotel Sierra Madre**
in Quito.

$$$$ Hacienda Yanahurco
*On access road to Quilindaña, 2 hrs from
Machachi, T09-9612 7759, Quito T02-244
5248, www.haciendayanahurco.com.*

Large hacienda in wild area, rooms with fireplace or heater, includes meals, 2-4 day programmes, all-inclusive.

$$$ Secret Garden
T09-9357 2714,
www.secretgardencotopaxi.com.
Rooms and dorms (US$35 pp), includes 3 meals, hot drinks, good common areas with fireplace, indoor jacuzzi with views of Cotopaxi. Offer hiking tours, horse riding and transport (US$5 from Quito). Good value for where it is. Popular.

$$$-$$ Chilcabamba
Loreto del Pedregal, by the northern access to the National Park, T09-9946 0406,
T02-237 7098, www.chilcabamba.com.
Cabins and rooms, US$30.50 pp in dorm, magnificent views.

$$$-$$ Cuello de Luna
2 km northwest of the park's main access on a dirt road, T09-9970 0330,
www.cuellodeluna.com.
Comfortable rooms with fireplace, includes breakfast, other meals available, US$22 pp in dorm (a very low loft). Can arrange tours t.

$$$-$$ Tierra del Volcán
T09-9498 0115/0121, Quito T02-600 9533,
www.tierradelvolcan.com.
3 haciendas: **Hacienda El Porvenir**, a working ranch by Rumiñahui, between El Pedregal and the northern access to the park, 3 types of rooms, includes breakfast, set meals available, horses and mountain bikes for hire, camping, zip-line; **Hacienda Santa Rita**, by the Río Pita, on the Sangolquí-El Pedregal road, with zip-lines, entry US$6, camping US$5 pp; and the more remote, rustic **Hacienda El Tambo** by Quilindaña (limited access during volcanic activity), southeast of the park. Also offers many adventure activities in the park.

$$ Huagra Corral
200 m east of Panamericana along the park's main access road, T03-271 9729, Quito T02-380 8427, www.huagracorral.com.

Nicely decorated, restaurant, private or shared bath, heaters, convenient location, helpful, reserve ahead.

Lasso

$$$$ Hacienda Hato Verde
Panamericana Sur Km 55, by entry to Mulaló, southeast of Lasso, T03-271 9348,
www.haciendahatoverde.com.
Lovely old hacienda and working dairy farm near the south flank of Cotopaxi, tastefully restored. 10 rooms with wood-burning stoves, includes breakfast, other meals available; horse riding (for experienced riders), trekking, trip up Cotopaxi Cara Sur, charming hosts.

$$$ Hostería La Ciénega
2 km south of Lasso, T03-271 9052,
www.haciendalacienega.com.
A historic hacienda with nice gardens, rooms with heater or fireplace, good expensive restaurant.

$ Cabañas Los Volcanes
At the south end of Lasso, T03-271 9524,
maexpediciones@yahoo.com.
Small hostel, nice rooms, private or shared bath. Tours to Cotopaxi.

Latacunga

$$$ Villa de Tacunga
Sánchez de Orellana y Guayaquil, T03-281 2352.
Well-restored colonial house built of Cotopaxi pumice stone. Comfortable rooms and suites with fireplace.

$$ Endamo
2 de Mayo 438 y Tarqui, T03-280 2678.
Modern hotel with nice rooms and a small restaurant, good value.

$$ Rodelú
Quito 16-31, T03-280 0956,
www.rodelu.com.ec.
Popular hotel, restaurant, suites and rooms (some are very small, look before taking a room), breakfast included starting the 2nd day.

$$-$ Rosim
Quito 16-49 y Padre Salcedo, T03-280 2172, www.hotelrosim.com.
Centrally located, breakfast available, some carpeted rooms, quiet and comfortable. Discounts in low season.

$$-$ Tiana
Luis F Vivero N1-31 y Sánchez de Orellana, T03-281 0147, www.hostaltiana.com.
Includes breakfast, drinks and snacks available, private or shared bath, US$10 pp in dorm, nice patio, kitchen facilities, luggage store, popular backpackers' meeting place. Tour agency **Tovar Expediciones** (see What to do, below), good source of information for Quilotoa Loop.

$ Central
Sánchez de Orellana y Padre Salcedo, T03-280 2912.
A multi-storey hotel in the centre of town, breakfast available, simple adequate rooms, a bit faded but very helpful.

Machachi
Not much to choose from in town.

$$$-$$ Café de la Vaca
4 km south of town on the Panamericana. Daily 0800-1730.
Very good meals using produce from their own farm, popular.

$$-$ Pizzeria Di Ragazzo
Av Pablo Guarderas N7-107, north of centre.
Is reported good.

Latacunga
Few places are open on Sun. Many along the Panamericana specialize in *chugchucaras*, a traditional pork dish. *Allullas* biscuits and string cheese are sold by the road.

$$ Chifa China
Antonia Vela 6-85 y 5 de Junio. Daily 1030-2200.
Good Chinese food, large portions.

$$ Chifa Dragón
Amazonas y Pastaza. Daily 1100-2300.
Chinese food, large portions, popular.

$$ Gamber Rosso
Quito y Padre Salcedo, T03-281 3394. Mon-Sat 1600-2200.
Good pizzas, antipasto and lasagne.

$$ Parrilladas La Española
2 de Mayo 7-175. Mon-Sat 1230-2100.
Good grill, popular with locals.

$$-$ Guadalajara Grill
Quijano y Ordóñez y Vivero.
Economical set lunch Mon-Fri 1200-1500, good Mexican food 1800-2200.

Café Abuela
Guayaquil 6-07 y Quito, by Santo Domingo church. Closed Sun.
Pleasant cosy café/bar, nicely decorated, drinks, sweets and sandwiches, popular with university students.

Cunani
Vivero y Sanchez de Orellana. Mon-Fri 1300-2100.
Cosy café/restaurant serving home-made ravioli, *humitas* and excellent hot chocolate. Also a handicraft store.

Latacunga
23-24 Sep **La Mama Negra**, in homage to the Virgen de las Mercedes. There are 5 main characters in the parade and hundreds of dancers, some representing black slaves, others the whites. Mama Negra herself (portrayed by a man) is a slave who dared to ask for freedom in colonial times. The colourful costumes are called La Santísima Trajería.
1st or 2nd Sat in Nov (but not 2 Nov, Día de los Muertos) The civic festival of **Mama Negra**, with a similar parade, is on. It is part of the **Fiestas de Latacunga**, 11 Nov.

Shopping

Latacunga
Artesanía Otavalo, *Guayaquil 5-50 y Quito*. A variety of souvenirs from Otavalo.

What to do

Latacunga
All operators offer day trips to **Cotopaxi** and **Quilotoa** (US$50 pp, includes lunch and a visit to a market town if on Thu or Sat, minimum 2 people). Trekking trips US$80 pp per day. **Note** Many agencies require passport as deposit when renting gear.
Greivag, *Guayaquil y Sánchez de Orellana, Plaza Santo Domingo, L5, T03-281 0510, www.greivagturismo.com*. Day trips.
Neiges, *Guayaquil 6-25, Plaza Santo Domingo, T03-281 1199, neigestours@hotmail.com.* Day trips and climbing.
Tovar Expediciones, *at Hostal Tiana, T03-281 1333*. Climbing and trekking.

Transport

Machachi
Bus To **Quito**, from El Playón behind the stadium, every 15 mins to Terminal Quitumbe, every 30 mins to Villa Flora and El Trebol, all US$1, 1½ hrs. To **Latacunga**, from the monument to El Chagra at the Panamericana, US$0.75, 1 hr.

Reserva Ecológica Los Ilinizas
Bus From El Playón in Machachi, to **El Chaupi** (every 20 mins, US$0.50, ½ hr), from where you can walk to the *refugio* in 7-8 hrs. A pick-up from El Chaupi to 'La Virgen' costs US$15, from Machachi US$30. It takes 3 hrs to walk with a full pack from 'La Virgen' to the *refugio*.

Parque Nacional Cotopaxi
Main park entrance and Refugio Ribas, take a Latacunga bus from Quito and get off at the main access point, where there is a large overpass. Do not take an express bus as you can't get off before Latacunga.

At the overpass there are usually pickup trucks which go to the park, US$20 to Laguna Limpio Pungo for up to 4 passengers, or US$3 to the main park entrance where other vehicles offer half-day guided tours for US$60. From **Machachi**, pick-ups go via the cobbled road to El Pedregal and on to Limpio Pungo and the *refugio* parking lot, US$40. From **Lasso**, full day trip to the park, US$50 return, with **Cabañas los Volcanes**. From **Latacunga**, see Tour operators.

To **Cara Sur** from Quito, **Cotopaxi Cara Sur** offer transport to the **Albergue Cara Sur**, US$60 per vehicle up to 5 passengers. Alternatively take a Latacunga bound bus and get off at **Pastocalle**, and take a pick-up from there, US$15 per vehicle.

All prices subject to considerable variation, ask around and negotiate politely.

Latacunga
Air The airport is north of the centre. 1 flight a day to **Guayaquil** with TAME, Mon-Fri.

Bus Buses leave from the terminal just south of 5 de Junio. At night (1900-0700) they enter the city to pick up passengers if they have space available. **Transportes Santa** has its own terminal at Eloy Alfaro y Vargas Torres, T03-281 1659, serving **Cuenca**, US$11; **Loja**, US$15; **Machala**, US$11; **Guayaquil**, US$9.50; 4 daily to each. Other companies from main terminal: to **Quito**, every 15 mins, 2 hrs, US$2.50; also shared taxis with **Servicio Express**, T03-242 6828 (Ambato) or T09-9924 2795, US$10. To **Ambato**, 1 hr, US$1.25. To **Guayaquil**, US$8.75, 7 hrs. To **Saquisilí**, every 20 mins (see below). Through buses, which are more frequent, do not stop at Latacunga Terminal. During the day they stay on the 'Paso Lateral', the city bypass of the Panamericana, and stop at the roundabout at the road to Pujilí, taxi from town US$3. For long-haul service southbound, it may be easiest to take a local bus to Ambato and transfer there. To **Otavalo** and **Ibarra**, bypassing Quito, **Cita Express**, T03-280 9264, 12 daily from the Paso Lateral, US$5; also with

Expreso Baños. To **Baños**, US$2.25, 2 hrs, every 20 mins from the Paso Lateral. Buses on the Zumbahua, Quilotoa, Chugchilán, Sigchos circuit are given below. **Note** On Thu most buses to nearby communities leave from Saquisilí market instead of Latacunga.

Quilotoa Circuit

a challenging but rewarding hike, or bike ride

☆The popular and recommended 200-km round trip from Latacunga to Pujilí, Zumbahua, Quilotoa crater, Chugchilán, Sigchos, Isinliví, Toacazo, Saquisilí, and back to Latacunga, can be done in two to three days by bus. It is also a great route for biking and only a few sections of the loop are cobbled or rough. Hiking from one town to another can be challenging, especially when the fog rolls in. For these longer walks hiring a guide might not be unreasonable if you don't have a proper map or enough experience.

Latacunga to Zumbahua

A fine paved road leads west from Latacunga to **Pujilí** ⓘ *15 km, bus US$0.35,* which has a beautiful church. There is a good market on Sunday, a smaller one on Wednesday, and the Corpus Christi celebrations are colourful. Beyond Pujilí, many interesting crafts are practised by the *indígenas* in the **Tigua valley**: paintings on leather, hand-carved wooden masks and baskets. **Chimbacucho**, also known as Tigua, is home to the Toaquiza family, most famous of the Tigua artists. The road goes on to Zumbahua, then over the Western Cordillera to La Maná and Quevedo. This is a great paved downhill bike route. It carries very little traffic and is extremely twisty in parts but is one of the most beautiful routes connecting the highlands with the coast. Beyond Zumbahua are the pretty towns of **Pilaló** (two restaurants, small *hostal* and petrol pumps), **Esperanza de El Tingo** (two restaurants and lodging at **Carmita's**, T03-281 4657) and **La Maná** (two hotels).

Zumbahua *Colour map 1, B3.*

Zumbahua lies 800 m from the main road, 62 km from Pujilí. It has an interesting Saturday market (starts at 0600) for local produce, and some tourist items. Just below the plaza is a shop selling dairy products and cold drinks. Friday nights involve dancing and drinking. Take a fleece, as it can be windy, cold and dusty. There is a good hospital in town, Italian-funded and run. The Saturday trip to Zumbahua market and the Quilotoa crater makes an excellent excursion.

Quilotoa

Zumbahua is the point to turn off for a visit to Quilotoa, a volcanic crater filled by a beautiful emerald lake. From the rim of the crater (3850 m) several snowcapped volcanoes can be seen in the distance. The crater is reached by a paved road which runs north from Zumbahua (about 12 km, three- to five-hours' walk). There's a 300-m drop down from the crater rim to the water. The hike down takes about 30 minutes (an hour or more to climb back up, mind the altitude). The trail starts at the village of Quilotoa, up the slope from the parking area, then, down a steep canyon-like cut. You can hire a mule to ride up from the bottom of the crater (US$10), best arrange before heading down. There is a basic hostel by the lake and kayaks for rent (US$5 per hour). Everyone at the crater tries to sell the famous naïve Tigua pictures and carved wooden masks, so expect to be besieged (also by begging children). To the southeast of the crater is the village of **Macapungo**, which runs the **Complejo Turístico**

Shalalá, see Where to stay, below. The Mirador Shalalá platform offers great views of the lake. To hike around the crater rim takes 4½ to six hours in clear weather. Be prepared for sudden changes in the weather, it gets very cold at night and can be foggy. Never deviate from the trail. For a shorter loop (three to four hours), start on the regular circuit going right when you reach the rim by Quilotoa village and follow it to Mirador Shalalá, a great place for a picnic; then backtrack for about five minutes and take the path down to the lake. To return, follow a path near the lake until you reach the large trail which takes you back up to Quilotoa village. If you are tired, you can hire a horse to take you up.

Chugchilán, Sigchos and Isinliví

Chugchilán, a lovely scenic village, is 16 km by paved road from Quilotoa. An alternative to the road is a five- to six-hour walk around part of the Quilotoa crater rim, then down to Guayama, and across the canyon (Río Sigüi) to Chugchilán, 11 km. Outside town is a cheese factory and nearby, at Chinaló, a woodcarving shop. The area has good walking.

Continuing from Chugchilán the road, being paved in 2016, runs to **Sigchos**, the starting point for the Toachi Valley walk, via Asache to San Francisco de las Pampas (0900 bus daily to Latacunga). There is also a vehicle road to Las Pampas, with two buses from Sigchos. Southeast of Sigchos is **Isinliví**, on the old route to Toacazo and Latacunga. It has a fine woodcarving shop and a pre-Inca *pucará*. Trek to the village of Guantualó, which has a fascinating market on Monday. You can hike to or from Chugchilán (five hours), or from Quilotoa to Isinliví in seven to nine hours.

From Sigchos, a paved road leads to **Toacazo** ($$ **La Quinta Colorada**, T03-271 6122, www.quintacolorada.com, price includes breakfast and dinner) and on to Saquisilí.

Saquisilí

Some 16 km southwest of Lasso and 4 km west of the Panamericana is the small but very important market town of Saquisilí. Its Thursday market (0500-1400) is famous throughout Ecuador for the way in which its seven plazas and some streets become jam-packed with people, the great majority of them local *indígenas* with red ponchos and narrow-brimmed felt hats. The best time to visit the market is 0900-1200 (before 0800 for the animal market). Be sure to bargain, as there is a lot of competition. This area has colourful Corpus Christi processions.

Listings Quilotoa Circuit

Where to stay

Latacunga to Zumbahua

$$ La Posada de Tigua
3 km east of Tigua-Chimbacucho,
400 m north of the road, T03-305 6103,
posadadetigua@yahoo.com.
On a working dairy ranch, 6 rooms, wood-burning stove, includes tasty home-cooked breakfast and dinner, pleasant family atmosphere, horse riding, trails, nice views.

Zumbahua

$ Cóndor Matzi
Overlooking the market area, T09-8906 1572
or T03-281 2953 to leave message.
Basic but best in town, shared bath, hot water, dining room with wood stove, kitchen facilities, try to reserve ahead, if closed ask at **Restaurante Zumbahua** on the plaza.

$ Richard
Opposite the market on the road in to town,
T09-9015 5996.

Basic shared rooms and 1 shower with hot water, cooking facilities, parking.

Quilotoa

$$ Complejo Shalalá
In Macapungo, T09-6917 3990, on Facebook.
Community-run lodge in a lovely 35-ha cloudforest reserve. Nice cabins, 1 with wheelchair access, includes breakfast and dinner, restaurant, trails.

$$ Quilotoa Crater Lake Lodge
On the main road facing the access to Quilotoa, T03-305 5816, http:// quilotacraterlodge.hlsecuador.com.
Somewhat faded hacienda-style lodge, includes breakfast and dinner, dining room, views.

Humberto Latacunga, a good painter who also organizes treks, runs 3 good hostels, T09-9212 5962, all include breakfast and dinner: $$ **Hostería Alpaca**, *www. alpakaquilotoa.com*, the most upmarket, rooms with wood stoves; $$ **Cabañas Quilotoa**, *on the access road to the crater,* private or shared bath, wood stoves; $$ **Hostal Pachamama**, *at the top of the hill by the rim of the crater,* private bath.

> **Tip...**
> Quilotoa hotels are all expensive for what they offer, and polite bargaining is appropriate.

Chugchilán

$$$$-$$$ Black Sheep Inn
Below the village on the way to Sigchos, T03-270 8077, www.blacksheepinn.com.
A lovely eco-friendly resort which has received international awards. Includes 3 excellent vegetarian meals, private and shared bath, US$35 pp in dorms, spa, water slide, zip-line, arrange excursions.

$$ El Vaquero
Just outside town on the road to Quilotoa, T03-270 8003, www.hostalelvaquero.com.

Variety of rooms with bath, great views, heaters in common areas, includes generous dinner and breakfast, helpful owners, transport to Quilotoa available (US$20).

$$ Hostal Cloudforest
At the entrance to town, T03-270 8016, www.cloudforesthostal.com.
Simple popular family-run hostel, sitting room with wood stove, includes dinner and great breakfast, restaurant open to public for lunch, private or shared bath, also dorm, parking, very helpful, great value.

$$ Hostal Mama Hilda
On the road in to town, T03-270 8015, www.mamahilda.com.
Pleasant family-run hostel, warm atmosphere, large rooms some with wood stoves, includes good dinner and breakfast, private or shared bath, camping, parking, arrange trips.

Sigchos

$$ Hostería San José de Sigchos
1.5 km south of town, Quito T02-240 19 68, www.sanjosedesigchos.com.
Comfortable rooms on a 150 ha working hacienda with heated pool, spa, restaurant, karaoke, horse riding, day visit US$8.

$ Jardín de los Andes
Ilinizas y Tungurahua, T03-271 2114.
Basic but quite clean and friendly.

Isinliví

$$$ Llullu Llama
T09-9258 0562, www.llullullama.com.
Farmhouse with cosy sitting room with wood stove, tastefully decorated rooms, cheaper in dorm, shared ecological bath. Also cottages with bath, fireplace and balcony. All include good hearty dinner and breakfast. Warm and relaxing atmosphere, a lovely spot. Recommended.

$ Taita Cristóbal
T09-9137 6542, taitacristobal@gmail.com.
Simple economy hostel with rooms and dorms, includes dinner and breakfast.

Saquisilí

$$ Gilocarmelo
*By the cemetery, 800 m from town
on the road north to Guaytacama,
T09-9966 9734, T02-340 0924.*
Restored hacienda house in a 4 ha property.
Plain rooms with fireplace, restaurant, pool,
sauna, jacuzzi, nice garden.

$ San Carlos
Bolívar opposite the Parque Central.
A multi-storey building, electric shower,
parking, good value, but watch your
valuables. Will hold luggage for US$1
while you visit the market.

Transport

Zumbahua
Bus Many daily on the Latacunga–Quevedo
road (0500-1900, US$1.50, 1½ hrs). Buses
on Sat are full, get your ticket on Fri. A
pick-up truck can be hired from Zumbahua
to **Quilotoa** for US$5-10 depending on
number of passengers; also to **Chugchilán**
for around US$30. On Sat mornings there are
many trucks leaving the Zumbahua market
for Chugchilán which pass Quilotoa. Pick-up
Quilotoa–Chugchilán US$25.

Taxi Day-trip by taxi to Zumbahua, Quilotoa,
and return to **Latacunga** is about US$60.

Quilotoa
Bus From the terminal terrestre in
Latacunga **Trans Vivero** daily at 1000, 1130,
1230 and 1330, US$2.50, 2 hrs. Note that this
leaves from Latacunga, not Saquisilí market,
even on Thu. Return bus direct to Latacunga
at 1300. Buses returning at 1400 and 1500 go
only as far as Zumbahua, from where you can
catch a Latacunga bound bus at the highway.
Also, buses going through Zumbahua bound
for Chugchilán will drop you at the turn-off,
5 mins from the crater, where you can also
pick them up on their way to Zumbahua
and Latacunga. Taxi from Latacunga, US$40
one way. For **Shalalá**, **Trans Ilinizas** from

Tip...
Note that throughout this region,
buses leave when full, sometimes
ahead of schedule.

Latacunga to **Macapungo** at 1300, US$2, or
go to Zumbahua and take a pick-up from
there, US$5. From Macapungo it is a 30-min
walk to the cabins.

Chugchilán
Bus From **Latacunga**, daily at 1130 (except
Thu) via Sigchos, another bus, also at 1130,
goes via Zumbahua; on Thu from **Saquisilí
market** via Sigchos around 1130, US$3.25,
3 hrs. Buses return to Latacunga at at 0330
via Sigchos, at 0400 via Zumbahua. On Sun
there are extra buses to Latacunga leaving
0600, 0900, 1100 and 1200. There are extra
buses going to Zumbahua Wed 0600, Fri
0600 and Sun between 0900-1000; these
continue towards the coast. Milk truck to
Sigchos around 0900. On Sat also pick-ups
going to/from market in Zumbahua and
Latacunga. From **Sigchos**, through buses as
above, US$0.75, 1 hr. Pick-up hire to Sigchos
US$20, up to 5 people, US$5 additional
person. Pick-up to **Quilotoa** US$25, up to
5 people, US$5 additional person. Taxi from
Latacunga US$50; to **Isinliví**, taxi US$30.

Sigchos
Bus From **Latacunga** almost every hour,
0930-1600; returning to Latacunga most
buses leave Sigchos before 0700, then at
1430 (more service on weekends); US$2,
2 hrs. From **Quito** direct service Mon-Sat
at 1400 (more frequent Sun) with **Reina de
Sigchos**; also Fri 1700 with **Illinizas**; US$3.75,
3 hrs. To **La Maná** on the road to Quevedo,
via Chugchilán, Quilotoa and Zumbahua,
Fri at 0500 and Sun at 0830, US$4.50, 6 hrs
(returns Sat at 0730 and Sun at 1530). To **Las
Pampas**, at 0330 and 1400, US$3.25, 3 hrs.
From Las Pampas to **Santo Domingo**, at
0300 and 0600, US$3.25, 3 hrs.

Isinliví

From **Latacunga** daily (except Thu), via Sigchos at 1215 (**14 de Octubre**) and direct at 1300 (**Trans Vivero**), on Thu both leave from Saquisilí market around 1100, on Sat the direct bus leaves at 1100 instead of 1300, US$2.25, 2½ hrs. Both return to Latacunga 0300-0330, except Wed at 0700 direct, Sun 1245 direct and Mon 1500 via Sigchos. Buses fill quickly, be early. Connections to Chugchilán, Quilotoa and Zumbahua can be made in Sigchos. Bus schedules are posted on www.llullullama.com.

Saquisilí

Bus Frequent service between **Latacunga** and Saquisilí, US$0.50, 20 mins; many buses daily to/from **Quito** (Quitumbe), 0530-1300, US$2.50, 2 hrs. Buses and trucks to many outlying villages leave from 1000 onwards. Bus tours from Quito cost US$45 pp, taxis charge US$80, with 2 hrs wait at market.

Ambato   *Colour map 1, B3.*

service and transport hub of the area

Almost completely destroyed in the great 1949 earthquake, Ambato lacks the colonial charm of other Andean cities, though its location in the heart of fertile orchard-country has earned it the nickname of 'the city of fruits and flowers'. It is also a transport hub and the principal commercial city of the central highlands, with a large Monday market and smaller ones Wednesday and Friday.

Sights

The modern cathedral faces **Parque Montalvo**, where there is a statue of the writer Juan Montalvo (1832-1889), whose **house** ⓘ *Bolívar y Montalvo, T03-282 4248, US$1, Mon-Fri 0800-1200, 1400-1800,* can be visited. The **Museo de la Provincia** in the Casa del Portal (built 1900), facing Parque Montalvo, has a photo collection.

Northeast of Ambato is the colonial town of **Píllaro**, gateway to **Parque Nacional Los Llanganates**, a beautiful rugged area (for tours see **Sachayacu Explorer**, page 580). The town is known for its colourful festivals: a *diablada* (devils' parade) 1-6 January and Corpus Christi.

Ambato to Baños

To the east of Ambato, an important road leads to **Salasaca**, where the *indígenas* sell their weavings; they wear distinctive black ponchos with white trousers and broad white hats. Further east, 5 km, is **Pelileo**, the blue jean manufacturing capital of Ecuador with good views of Tungurahua. There are opportunities for cultural tourism, walking and paragliding in the area (contact Patricio Cisnero at **Blue Land Adventures** ⓘ *T03-283 0236, bluelandsalasaca@yahoo.com.ar*). From Pelileo, the road descends to Las Juntas, where the Patate and Chambo rivers meet to form the Río Pastaza. About 1 km east of Las Juntas bridge, the junction with the road to Riobamba is marked by a large sculpture of a macaw and a toucan (locally known as Los Pájaros – the lower bird was destroyed by the volcano). It is a favourite volcano watching site. The road to Baños then continues along the lower slopes of the volcano.

Eight kilometres northeast of Pelileo on a paved side-road is **Patate**, centre of the warm, fruit growing Patate valley. There are excellent views of Volcán Tungurahua from town. The fiesta of **Nuestro Señor del Terremoto** is held on the weekend leading up to 4 February, featuring a parade with floats made with fruit and flowers.

Ambato to Riobamba and Guaranda

After Ambato, the Pan-American Highway runs south to Riobamba (see page 580). About half way is **Mocha**, where guinea pigs (*cuy*) are bred for the table. You can sample roast *cuy* and other typical dishes at stalls and restaurants by the roadside, **Mariadiocelina** is recommended. The highway climbs steeply south of Mocha and at the pass at **Urbina** there are fine views in the dry season of Chimborazo and Carihuayrazo.

To the west of Ambato, a paved road climbs through tilled fields, past the *páramos* of Carihuayrazo and Chimborazo to the great Arenal (a high desert at the base of the mountain), and down through the Chimbo valley to Guaranda (see page 581). This spectacular journey reaches a height of 4380 m and vicuñas can be seen.

Listings Ambato

Tourist information

Ministerio de Turismo
*Guayaquil y Rocafuerte, Ambato,
T03-282 1800. Mon-Fri 0800-1700.*

Where to stay

$$$ Florida
*Av Miraflores 1131, T03-242 2007,
www.hotelflorida.com.ec.*
Pleasant hotel in a nice setting, restaurant with good set meals, weekend discounts.

$$$ Mary Carmen
*Av Ceballos y Martínez, T03-242 0908,
www.hotelboutiquemc.com.*
Very nice boutique hotel with gym, spa and parking.

$$$ Roka Plaza
*Bolívar 20-62 y Guayaquil, T03-242 3845,
www.hotelrokaplaza.com.*
Small stylish hotel in a refurbished colonial house in the heart of the city, sushi restaurant.

$$-$ Colony
*12 de Noviembre 124 y Av El Rey,
near the bus terminal, T03-282 5789.*
A modern hotel with large rooms, parking, spotless.

$$-$ Pirámide Inn
Cevallos y Mariano Egüez, T03-242 1920.
Comfortable hotel, cafeteria, English spoken.

Ambato to Baños
Salasaca and Pelileo

$$ Runa Huasi
*In Salasaca, 1 km north off main highway,
T09-9984 0125, www.hostalrunahuasi.com.*
Simple hostel, includes breakfast and fruit, other meals on request, cooking facilities, nice views, guided walks.

$ Hostal Pelileo
Eloy Alfaro 641, T03-287 1390.
Shared bath, hot water, simple.

Patate

$$$$-$$$ Hacienda Manteles
*In the Leito valley on the road to El Triunfo,
T09-9213 5309, Quito T 02-603 9415,
www.haciendamanteles.com.*
Converted hacienda with views of Tungurahua and Chimborazo, includes breakfast, dinner, snacks, walk to waterfalls, hiking and horse riding. Reserve ahead.

$$$ Hacienda Leito
*On the road to El Triunfo, T03-306 3196,
www.haciendaleito.com.*
Classy hacienda with spacious rooms and great views of Tungurahua.

$$$ Hostería Viña del Río
*3 km from town on the old road to Baños,
T03-287 0314, www.hosteriavinadelrio.com.*
Cabins on a 22-ha ranch, restaurant, pool, spa and mini golf, US$7 for day use of facilities.

$ Hostal Casa del Valle
Juan Montalvo y Ambato, 2 blocks from plaza, T09-8150 1062.
A good simple place right in town.

Restaurants

$$$-$$ Ali's Parrillada y Pizzeria
Bolivar entre JL Mera y Martínez, also in Ficoa neighbourhood and opposite Mall de los Andes. Open 1030-2230.
Good pizzas and international meat dishes.

$$$-$$ La Fornace
Cevallos 1728 y Montalvo. Open 1100-2200.
Wood oven pizza. Opposite is **Heladería La Fornace**, Cevallos y Castillo. Snacks, sandwiches, ice cream, very popular.

$$ El Alamo Chalet
Cevallos 1719 y Montalvo.
Open 0800-2300 (2200 Sun).
Ecuadorean and international food. Set meals and à la carte, Swiss-owned, good quality.

$$-$ Govinda's
Cuenca y Quito. Mon-Sat 0800-2030, Sun 0800-1600.
Vegetarian set meals and à la carte, also a meditation centre (T03-282 3182).

$ Roho Wine
Quito 924 y Bolívar. Mon-Sat 1200-1530.
Good set meals.

Cafés

Crème Brulée
Juan B Vela 08-38 y Montalvo.
Daily 0900-2100.
Very good coffee and pastries.

Pasterlería Quito
JL Mera y Cevallos. Daily 0700-2100.
Coffee, pastries, good for breakfast.

Festivals

Feb/Mar Ambato has a famous festival, the **Fiesta de frutas y flores**, during carnival when there are 4 days of festivities and parades (best Sun morning and Mon night). Must book ahead to get a hotel room.

Shopping

Ambato is a centre for leather: shoe shops on Bolívar; jackets, bags, belts on Vela between Lalama and Montalvo. Take a bus up to the leather town of Quisapincha for the best deals, every day, but big market on Sat.

What to do

Train rides
An *autoferro* runs from Ambato to **Urbina** and back via **Cevallos**, Fri-Sun at 0800, US$17. The train station is at Av Gran Colombia y Chile, near the Terminal Terrestre, T03-252 2623; Wed-Sun 0800-1630.

Transport

Bus The main bus station is on Av Colombia y Paraguay, 2 km north of the centre. City buses go there from Plaza Cevallos in the centre, US$0.25. Buses to **Quito**, 3 hrs, US$3.25; also door to door shared taxis, US$12, with **Servicio Express**, T03-242 6828 or T09-9924 2795 and **Delux**, T09-3920 9827or 09-8343 0275. Buses to **Cuenca**, US$10, 6½ hrs. To **Guayaquil**, 6 hrs, US$7.50. To **Riobamba**, US$1.50, 1 hr. To **Guaranda**, US$2.50, 3 hrs. To **Ibarra**, via the Quito airport and bypassing Quito, **CITA**, 8 daily, 5 hrs, US$6.25. To **Santo Domingo de los Tsáchilas**, 4 hrs, US$5. To **Tena**, US$6.25, 4½ hrs. To **Puyo**, US$3.75, 2½ hrs. To **Macas**, US$8.75, 5½ hrs. To **Esmeraldas**, US$10, 8 hrs. **Note** Buses to **Baños** leave from the Mercado Mayorista and then stop at the edge of town, 1 hr, US$1.10. Through buses do not go into the terminal, they take the Paso Lateral bypass road.

Baños
& Riobamba

Baños and Riobamba are both good bases for exploring the Sierra and their close proximity to high peaks gives great opportunities for climbing, cycling and trekking (but check about Tungurahua's volcanic activity before you set out). The thermal springs at Baños are an added lure and the road east is a great way to get to the jungle lowlands. Riobamba and Alausí offer the opportunity to ride the train on the famous section of the line from the Andes to Guayaquil, around the Devil's Nose.

Baños and around   *Colour map 1, B4.*

a busy place popular with tourists from near and far

Baños is nestled between the Río Pastaza and the Tungurahua volcano, only 8 km from its crater. Baños bursts at the seams with hotels, *residenciales*, restaurants and tour agencies. Ecuadoreans flock here on weekends and holidays for the hot springs, to visit the Basílica and enjoy the local *melcochas* (toffees), while escaping the Andean chill in a sub-tropical climate (wettest in July and August). Foreign visitors are also frequent; using Baños as a base for trekking, organizing a visit to the jungle, making local day trips or just plain hanging out.

Sights
The **Manto de la Virgen** waterfall at the southeast end of town is a symbol of Baños. The **Basílica** attracts many pilgrims. The paintings of miracles performed by Nuestra Señora del Agua Santa are worth seeing. There are various thermal baths in town, all charge US$2 unless otherwise noted. The **Baños de la Virgen** ① *0430-1700*, are by the waterfall. They get busy so best visit very early morning. Two small hot pools open evenings only (1800-2200, US$3). The **Piscinas Modernas** ① *Fri-Sun and holidays 0900-1700*, with a water slide, are next door. **El Salado baths** ① *daily 0500-1600, weekends also 1800-2100, US$3*, several hot pools, plus icy cold river water, repeatedly destroyed by volcanic debris (not safe when activity is high), 1.5 km out of town off the Ambato road. The **Santa Ana baths** ① *Fri-Sun and holidays 0900-1700*, have hot and cold pools in a pleasant setting, just east of town on the road to Puyo. All the baths can be very crowded at weekends and holidays; the brown

Best for
Hot springs ▪ Relaxing ▪ Spas ▪ Trekking

colour of the water is due to its high mineral content. The **Santa Clara baths** ① *C Velasco Ibarra behind Parque Montalvo, Mon-Fri 1400-2100, Sat-Sun 1000-2100, US$4*, are not natural springs but have clean heated pools as well as a nice large cold pool for swimming laps.

As well as the medicinal baths, there are various spas, in hotels, as independent centres and massage therapists. These offer a combination of sauna, steam bath (Turkish or box), jacuzzi, clay and other types of baths, a variety of massage techniques (Shiatsu, Reiki, Scandinavian) and more.

Around Baños

There are many interesting **walks** in the Baños area. The **San Martín shrine** is a 45-minute easy walk from town and overlooks a deep rocky canyon with the Río Pastaza thundering below. Beyond the shrine, crossing to the north side of the Pastaza, is the **Ecozoológico San Martín** ① *T03-274 0552, 0800-1700, US$2.50*, with the **Serpentario San Martín** ① *daily 0900-1700, US$2*, opposite. Some 50 m beyond is a path to the **Inés María waterfall**, cascading

Baños

Where to stay 🛏		
1 Alisamay B1	11 La Floresta C2	23 Villa Santa Clara C4
2 Apart-Hotel Napolitano A4	12 La Petite Auberge C3	24 Volcano C4
3 Casa del Molino Blanco C1	13 Los Pinos B4	
4 El Belén B2	14 Luna Runtún A3	**Restaurants** 🍴
5 El Oro B1	15 Plantas y Blanco C3	1 Ali Cumba C3
6 Finca Chamanapamba A4	16 Posada del Arte C4	2 Café Blah Blah B2
7 Hostal Ilé C3	17 Princesa María B1	3 Café Honey B2
8 Isla de Baños C2	18 Puerta del Sol B4	4 Café Hood C4
9 La Casa Verde A4	19 Samari A4	5 Casa Hood C3
10 La Chimenea C4	20 Sangay C4	6 El Castillo C4
	21 Santa Cruz C3	7 Jota Jota C3
	22 Transilvania B3	8 Mariane C2

9 Pancho's C2	**Bars & clubs** 🍸
10 Rico Pan B2	14 Buena Vista B3
11 Sativa C3	15 Ferchos B3
12 Swiss Bistro C3	16 Jack Rock B3
13 Taberna Armenia C2	17 Leprechaun B3
	18 Peña Ananitay B3

ON THE ROAD

Tungurahua and Cotopaxi volcanoes: active again

In 1999, after over 80 years of dormancy, Tungurahua became active again and remains so; its last eruptive activity was in March 2016. The volcano can be quiet for weeks or months between bursts of energy. Baños continues to be a safe destination unless the level of eruptive activity greatly increases. The summit of the volcano is closed to climbers but all else is normal and tourists regularly hike from Pondoa to the old refuge at 3800 m.

In 2015, after 135 years of tranquility, it was Cotopaxi's turn. The eruption in August 2015 was small and activity diminished in early 2016. The volcano is only putting out mild vapour columns with some gas being expulsed near the summit. Visitors may travel freely about Parque Nacional Cotopaxi and may hike up to the refuge at 4800 m. Climbing to the summit is being considered, but a new route must be made, since the old one is heavily crevassed and unsafe. Camping is permitted. There are six huge sirens with digital messages along the tourist route in case the volcano should have a surprise reactivation. Also under surveillance is Cayambe, which showed signs of increased activity in 2016. See the daily posts from the National Geophysical Institute of the Escuela Politécnica Nacional in Quito, www.igepn.edu.ec.

down, but polluted. Further, a *tarabita* (cable car) and zip-lines span the entrance to the canyon. You can also cross the Pastaza by the **Puente San Francisco** road bridge, behind the kiosks across the main road from the bus station. From here a series of trails fans out into the hills, offering excellent views of Tungurahua from the ridge-tops in clear weather. A total of six bridges span the Pastaza near Baños, so you can make a round trip.

On the hillside behind Baños are a series of interconnecting trails with nice views. It is a pleasant 45-minute hike to the **statue of the Virgin**; go to the south end of Calle JL Mera, before the street ends, take the last street to the right (Misioneros Dominicanos) at the end of which are stairs leading to the trail. A steep narrow path continues along the ridge, past the statue. Another trail also begins at the south end of JL Mera and leads to the **Hotel Luna Runtún**, continuing on to the village of Runtún (five- to six-hour round-trip). Yet another trail starts at the south end of Calle Maldonado and leads in 45 minutes to the **Bellavista cross**, from where you can also continue to Runtún.

The scenic road to **Puyo** (58 km) has many waterfalls tumbling down into the Pastaza. Many *tarabitas* (cable cars) and zip-lines span the canyon offering good views. By the Agoyán dam and bridge, 5 km from town, is **Parque de la Familia** ① *0900-1700, entry free, parking US$1*, with orchards, gardens, paths and domestic animals. Beyond, the paved road goes through seven tunnels between Agoyán and Río Negro. The older gravel road runs parallel to the paved road, directly above the Río Pastaza, and is the preferred route for cyclists who, coming from Baños, should only go through one tunnel at Agoyán and then stay to the right avoiding the other tunnels. Between tunnels there is only the paved road, cyclists must be very careful as there are many buses and lorries. The area has excellent opportunities for walking and nature observation.

At the junction of the Verde and Pastaza rivers, 17 km from Baños is the town of **Río Verde** with snack bars, restaurants and a few places to stay. The Río Verde has crystalline green water and is cold but nice for bathing. The paved highway runs to the north of town, between it and the old road, the river has been dammed forming a small lake where rubber rafts are rented for paddling. Near the paved road is **Orquideario** ⓘ *0900-1700, closed Wed, US$1.50*, with nice regional orchids. Before joining the Pastaza the Río Verde tumbles down several falls, the most spectacular of which is **El Pailón del Diablo** (the Devil's Cauldron). Cross the Río Verde on the old road and take the path to the right after the church, then follow the trail down towards the suspension bridge over the Pastaza, for about 20 minutes. Just before the bridge take a side trail to the right (signposted) which leads you to **Paradero del Pailón**, a nice restaurant, and viewing platforms above the falls (US$1.50). The **San Miguel Falls**, smaller but also nice, are some five minutes' walk from the town along a different trail. Cross the old bridge and take the first path to the right, here is **Falls Garden** (US$1.50), with lookout platforms over both sets of falls. Cyclists can leave the bikes at one of the snack bars while visiting the falls and return to Baños by bus.

Listings Baños and around *map page 573.*

Tourist information

iTur
Oficina Municipal de Turismo, at the Municipio, Halflants y Rocafuerte, opposite Parque Central, Baños, T03-274 0483. Mon-Fri 0800-1230, 1400-1730.

Where to stay

Baños has plenty of accommodation but can fill during holiday weekends.

$$$$ Luna Runtún
Caserío Runtún Km 6, T03-274 0882, www.lunaruntun.com.
A classy hotel in a beautiful setting overlooking Baños. Includes dinner, breakfast and use of pools (spa extra), very comfortable rooms with balconies and superb views, lovely gardens. Good service, English, French and German spoken, tours, nanny service.

$$$$ Samari
Vía a Puyo Km 1, T03-274 1855, www.samarispa.com.
Upmarket resort opposite the Santa Ana baths, nice grounds, tastefully decorated hacienda-style rooms and suites, pool and spa (US$24.50 for non-residents, daily 0800-2000), fine upmarket restaurant.

$$$$-$$$ Sangay
Plazoleta Isidro Ayora 100, next to waterfall and thermal baths, T03-274 0490, www.sangayspahotel.com.
Traditional Baños hotel with spa, buffet breakfast, good restaurant specializes in Ecuadorean food, pool and spa open to non-residents 1600-2100 (US$10), parking, tennis and squash courts, games room, car hire, disco, attentive service, mid-week discounts, British/Ecuadorean-run. Recommended.

$$$ Apart-Hotel Napolitano
C Oriente 470 y Suárez, T03-274 2464, napolitano-apart-hotel@hotmail.com.
Large comfortable apartments with kitchen, fireplace, pool and spa, garden, parking. A bit pricey, daily rentals or US$600 per month.

$$$ Finca Chamanapamba
On the east shore of the Río Ulba, a short ride from the road to Puyo, T03-274 2671, www.chamanapamba.com.
2 nicely finished wooden cabins in a spectacular location overlooking the Río Ulba and just next to the Chamanapamba waterfalls, very good café-restaurant serves German food.

$$$ La Floresta
Halflants y Montalvo, T03-274 1824, www.laflorestahotel.com.
Nice hotel with large comfortable rooms set around a lovely garden, excellent buffet

breakfast, wheelchair accessible, craft and book shop, parking, attentive service. Warmly recommended.

$$$ Posada del Arte
Pasaje Velasco Ibarra y Montalvo, T03-274 0083, www.posadadelarte.com.
Cosy inn, restaurant with vegetarian options, pleasant sitting room, more expensive rooms have fireplace, terrace, US-run.

$$$ Volcano
Rafael Vieira y Montalvo, T03-274 2140, www.volcano.com.ec.
Spacious modern hotel, large rooms with fridge, some with views of the waterfall, buffet breakfast, restaurant, heated pool, massage, nice garden.

$$$-$$ Isla de Baños
Halflants 1-31 y Montalvo, T03-274 0609, www.isladebanios.com.
Well-decorated comfortable hotel, includes European breakfast and steam bath, spa operates when there are enough people, pleasant garden.

$$ Alisamay
Espejo y JL Mera, T03-2741391, www.hotelalisamay.com.
Rustic hotel, nice cosy rooms with balconies, includes breakfast and use of spa, gardens with pools.

$$ Casa del Molino Blanco
Misioneros Dominicanos y JL Mera, T03-274 1138, www.casamolinoblanco.com.
Located in a quiet area, with bath, US$11 pp in dorm, spotlessly clean, includes buffet breakfast, German spoken.

$$ Hostal Ilé
12 de Noviembre y Montalvo, T03-274 2699, www.facebook.com/hostalile.
Rustic feel with lots of wood, ample comfortable rooms, Mexican restaurant.

$$ La Casa Verde
In Santa Ana, 1.5 km from town on Camino Real, a road parallell and north of the road to Puyo, T03-274 2671, www.lacasaverde.com.ec.
Spacious hotel decorated in pine, the largest rooms in Baños, laundry and cooking facilities, very quiet, New Zealand-run.

$$-$ El Belén
Reyes y Ambato, T03-274 1024, www.hotelelbelen.com.
Nice hostel, cooking facilities, spa, parking, helpful staff.

$$-$ La Petite Auberge
16 de Diciembre y Montalvo, T03-274 0936, www.lepetit.banios.com.
Rooms around a patio, some with fireplace, good French restaurant, parking, quiet.

$$-$ Los Pinos
Ricardo Zurita y C Ambato, T03-274 1825.
Large hostel with double rooms and dorms (US$9-10 pp), includes breakfast (and dinner Mon-Wed), spa, kitchen and laundry facilities, pool table Argentine-run, great value.

$$-$ Puerta del Sol
Ambato y Arrayanes (east end of C Ambato), T03-274 2265.
Modern hotel, better than it looks on the outside, large well-appointed rooms, includes breakfast, pleasant dining area, laundry facilities, parking.

$ El Oro
Ambato y JL Mera, T03-274 0736.
With bath, laundry and cooking facilities, good value, popular. Recommended.

$ La Chimenea
Martínez y Rafael Vieira, T03-274 2725, www.hostalchimenea.com.
Nice hostel with terrace café, breakfast available, private or shared bath, US$8 pp in dorm, small pool, jacuzzi extra, parking for small cars, quiet, helpful and good value. Recommended.

$ Plantas y Blanco
12 de Noviembre y Martínez, T03-274 0044, www.plantasyblanco.com.
Pleasant popular hostel decorated with plants, private or shared bath, US$9-10 pp in dorm, excellent breakfast available, rooftop

cafeteria, steam bath, classic films, good restaurant (open 1700-0100), bakery, French-owned, good value. Recommended.

$ Princesa María
Rocafuerte y Mera, T03-274 1035.
Spacious rooms, US$8 pp in dorm, laundry and cooking facilities, parking, popular budget travellers' meeting place, helpful and good value.

$ Santa Cruz
16 de Diciembre y Martínez, T03-274 3527, www.santacruzbackpackers.com.
Large rooms, US$10.50 pp in dorm, fireplace in lounge, small garden with hammocks, kitchen facilities, mini pool on roof.

$ Transilvania
16 de Diciembre y Oriente, T03-274 2281, www.hostal-transilvania.com.
Multi-storey building with simple rooms, includes breakfast, US$8.50 pp in dorm, Middle Eastern restaurant, nice views from balconies, large TV and movies in sitting room, pool table, popular meeting place.

$ Villa Santa Clara
12 de Noviembre y Velasco Ibarra, T03-274 0349, www.hotelvillasantaclara.com.
Nice cabins in a quiet location, breakfast available, laundry facilities, wheelchair accessible, garden, spa, parking.

Around Baños

$$$ Miramelindo
Río Verde, just north of the paved road, T03-249 3004, www.miramelindo.banios.com.
Lovely hotel and spa, well-decorated rooms, good restaurant, pleasant gardens include an orchid collection with over 1000 plants.

$$ Hostería Río Verde
Between the paved road and town, T03-249 3007 (Ambato), www.hosteriarioverde.com.
Simple cabins in a rural setting, includes breakfast and use of spa, large pool, restaurant specializes in trout and tilapia.

$$$ Mariane
On a small lane by Montalvo y Halflants. Mon-Sat 1300-2200.
Excellent authentic Provençal cuisine, generous portions, lovely setting, popular, slow service. Highly recommended. **Hotel Mariane** (**$$**) at the same location, very clean and pleasant.

$$$ Swiss Bistro
Martínez y Alfaro. Daily 1200-2230.
International dishes and Swiss specialities, Swiss-run.

$$$ Taberna Armenia
Pastaza y Montalvo. Fri-Mon 1600-2400.
Upmarket restaurant serving mostly meat dishes, including llama. Russian owner, very friendly, professional and good quality.

$$ Café Hood
Montalvo y Vieira. Thu-Tue 1200-2200.
Mainly vegetarian but also some meat dishes, excellent food, English spoken, always busy. Also rents rooms.

$$ Casa Hood
Martínez between Halflants and Alfaro. Open 1200-2200.
Largely vegetarian, juices, milkshakes, varied menu including Indonesian and Thai, good set lunch and desserts. Travel books and maps sold, book exchange, cinema, cultural events, nice atmosphere. Popular and recommended.

$$ Sativa
Martínez y Eloy Alfaro. Open 1100-2200.
Wholesome food, some organic ingredients from their own garden.

$ El Castillo
Martínez y Rafael Vieira, in hostel. Open 0800-1000, 1200-1330.
A favourite for a good filling set lunch.

Cafés

Ali Cumba
12 de Noviembre y Martínez.
Daily 0800-2000.
Excellent breakfasts, salads, good coffee (filtered, espresso), muffins, cakes, home-made bread, large sandwiches, book exchange. Danish/Ecuadorean-run.

Café Blah Blah
Halflants y Martínez. Daily 0800-2000.
Cosy, popular café serving very good breakfasts, coffee, cakes, snacks and juices.

Café Honey
Maldonado y Rocafuerte at the Parque Central. Daily 0900-2100.
Fine modern café with all kinds of coffees, teas and pastries, very good.

Jota Jota
Martínez y Halflants. Tue-Sun to 1000-2200.
Great choice of coffees and cocktails, book exchange. German-run.

Pancho's
Rocafuerte y Maldonado at Parque Central. Daily 1530-2200.
Hamburgers, snacks, sandwiches, coffee, large-screen TV for sports and other events.

Rico Pan
Ambato y Maldonado at Parque Central. Mon-Sat 0700-1900, Sun 0700-1300.
Good breakfasts, hot bread (including whole wheat), fruit salads and pizzas, also meals.

Bars and clubs

Eloy Alfaro, between Ambato and Oriente has many bars including:

Buena Vista
Alfaro y Oriente.
A good place for salsa and other Latin music.

Ferchos
Alfaro y Oriente. Tue-Sun 1600-2400.
Café-bar, modern decor, snacks, cakes, good varied music, German-run.

Jack Rock
Alfaro y Ambato.
A favourite traveller hangout.

Leprechaun
Alfaro y Oriente.
Popular for dancing, bonfire on weekends, occasional live music.

Entertainment

Chivas, open-sided buses, cruise town playing music, they take you to different night spots and to a volcano lookout when Tungurahua is active.

Peña Ananitay, *16 de Diciembre y Espejo.* Bar, good live music and dancing on weekends, no cover.

Festivals

During Carnival and Holy Week hotels are full and prices rise.

Oct Nuestra Señora de Agua Santa. Daily processions, bands, fireworks, sporting events and partying through the month.
15 Dec Verbenas. A night-time celebration when each barrio hires a band and parties.
16 Dec The town's anniversary, with parades, fairs, sports, cultural events leading up to this date.

Shopping

Look out for jaw-aching toffee (*melcocha*) made in ropes in shop doorways, or the less sticky *alfeñique*.

Handicrafts
Crafts stalls at Pasaje Ermita de la Vírgen, off C Ambato, by the market. Tagua (vegetable ivory made from palm nuts) crafts on Maldonado y Martínez. Leather shops on Rocafuerte between Halflants and 16 de Diciembre.
Centro Naturista, *Eloy Alfaro y Oriente.* Health foods and alternative medicine.
Latino Shop, *Ambato y Alfaro and 4 other locations.* For T-shirts.

Librería Vieira – Arte Ilusion, *Halflants y Martínez*. Bookstore with a café, Wi-Fi, nice meeting place.

What to do

Adventure sports are popular in Baños, including mountaineering, white water rafting, canyoning, canopying and bridge jumps. Safety standards vary greatly. There is seldom any recourse in the event of a mishap so these activities are at your own risk.

Bus tours

The *chivas* (see Entertainment) and a **double-decker bus** (C Ambato y Halflants, T03-274 0596, US$6) visit waterfalls and other attractions. Check destinations if you have a specific interest such as El Pailón falls.

Canopying or zip-line

Involves hanging from a harness and sliding on a steel cable. Prices vary according to length, US$10-20. Cable car, US$1.50.

Canyoning

Many agencies offer this sport, rates US$30 half day, US$50 full day.

Climbing and trekking

There are countless possibilities for walking and nature observation near Baños and to the east. Tungurahua has been officially closed to climbers since 1999. Operators offer trekking tours for about US$45 per day.

Cycling

Many places rent bikes, quality varies, US$5-10 per day; check brakes and tyres, find out who has to pay for repairs, and insist on a helmet, puncture repair kit and pump. The following have good equipment:
Carrillo Hermanos, *16 de Diciembre y Martínez*. Rents mountain bikes and motorcycles (reliable machines with helmets, US10 per hr).
Hotel Isla de Baños, rentals, US$10 per day.

Horse riding

There are many places, but check their horses as not all are well cared for. Rates around US$8-10 per hr (minimum 2 hrs), US$40 per day. The following have been recommended: **Antonio Banderas** (Montalvo y Halflants, T03-274 2532). **Hotel Isla de Baños** (see above), 3½ hrs with a guide and jeep transport costs US$35 pp, English and German spoken. **José & Two Dogs** (Maldonado y Martínez, T03-274 0746), flexible hours.

Language schools

Spanish schools charge US$7-9 per hr, many also offer homestays. **Baños Spanish Center** (www.spanishcenter.banios.com). **Home Stay Baños** (T03-274 0453). **Mayra's** (www.mayraspanishschool.com). **Raíces** (www.spanishlessons.org).

Paragliding

See www.aeropasion.net; US$60 per day.

Puenting

Many operators offer this bungee-jumping-like activity from the bridges around Baños, US$10-20 per jump, heights and styles vary.

Tour operators

There are many tour agencies in town, some with several offices, as well as 'independent' guides who seek out tourists on the street (the latter are generally not recommended). Quality varies considerably; to obtain a qualified guide and avoid unscrupulous operators, it is best to seek advice from other travellers who have recently returned from a tour. We have received some critical reports of tours out of Baños, but there are also highly respected and qualified operators here. Most agencies and guides offer trips to the jungle (US$50-70 per day pp). There are also volcano-watching, trekking and horse tours, in addition to the day-trips and sports mentioned above. Several companies run tours aboard a *chiva* (open-sided bus). The following agencies and guides have received positive recommendations but the list is not exhaustive and there are certainly others.

Expediciones Amazónicas, *Oriente 11-68 y Halflants*, T03-274 0506.

Geotours, *Ambato y Halflants, next to Banco Pichincha*, T03-274 1344, www.geotoursbanios. com. Offer good rafting trips and paragliding for US$60.

Imagine Ecuador, *16 de Diciembre y Montalvo*, T03-274 3472, www. imagineecuador.com.

Natural Magic, *Martínez y 16 de Diciembre*, T095-879 6043, www.naturalmagic.travel.

Sachayacu Explorer, *Bolívar 229 y Urbina, in Píllaro*, T03-287 5316 or T09-8740 3376, www.treasureoftheincas.com. Trekking in the Llanganates, jungle tours in Huaorani territory, Yasuní and as far as Peru, English spoken.

Wonderful Ecuador, *Maldonado y Oriente*, T03-274 1580, www.wonderfulecuador.org. Good for whitewater rafting.

Whitewater rafting

Fatal accidents have occurred, but not with the agencies listed above. Rates US$30 for half-day, US$70 for full-day. The Chambo, Patate and Pastaza rivers are all polluted.

Transport

Bus City buses run from Alfaro y Martínez east to Agoyán and from Rocafuerte by the

> **Tip...**
> Note that buses from Quito to Baños are the target of thieves, take a shared taxi or bus to Ambato and transfer there.

market, west to El Salado and the zoo. The long distance bus station is on the Ambato–Puyo road (Av Amazonas). It gets very busy on weekends and holidays, buy tickets in advance. To **Rio Verde** take any Puyo-bound bus, through buses don't go in the station, 20 mins, US$0.65. To **Quito**, US$4.25, 3 hrs, frequent service; going to Quito sit on the right for views of Cotopaxi; also shared taxis US$20, with **Autovip**, T02-600 2582 (Quito) or 09-9629 5406 and **Delux**, T09-3920 9827 or 09-8343 0275. To **Ambato**, 1 hr, US$1.10. To **Riobamba**, some buses take the direct Baños–Riobamba road but most go via Mocha, 1½ hrs, US$2.50. To **Latacunga**, 2 hrs, US$2.25. To **Otavalo** and **Ibarra** direct, bypassing Quito, **Expreso Baños**, at 0400 and 1440, US$6, 5½ hrs. To **Guayaquil**, 1 bus per day and 1 overnight, US$10, 6-7 hrs; or change in Riobamba. To **Puyo**, 1½ hrs, US$2.40. Sit on the right. You can cycle to Puyo and take the bus back (passport check on the way). To **Tena**, 3½ hrs, US$6. To **Misahuallí**, change at Tena. To **Macas**, 4½ hrs, US$9 (sit on the right).

Riobamba and around

colourful markets and mountains to climb

☆Guaranda and Riobamba are good bases for exploring the Sierra. Riobamba is the bigger of the two and is on the famous railway line from Quito to Guayaquil. Many indigenous people from the surrounding countryside can be seen in both cities on market days. Because of their central location Riobamba and the surrounding province are known as 'Corazón de la Patria' – the heartland of Ecuador – and the city boasts the nickname 'La Sultana de Los Andes' in honour of lofty Mount Chimborazo.

Riobamba *Colour map 1, B3.*

The capital of Chimborazo Province has broad streets and many ageing but impressive buildings. The main square is **Parque Maldonado** around which are the **Cathedral**, the

Municipality and several colonial buildings with arcades. The **Cathedral** has a beautiful colonial stone façade and an incongruously modern interior. Four blocks northeast of the railway station is the **Parque 21 de Abril**, named after the Batalla de Tapi, 21 April 1822, the city's independence from Spain. The park, better known as **La Loma de Quito**, affords an unobstructed view of Riobamba and Chimborazo, Carihuairazo, Tungurahua, El Altar and occasionally Sangay. It also has a colourful tile tableau of the history of Ecuador; ask about safety before visiting. **Convento de la Concepción** ⓘ *Orozco y España, entrance at Argentinos y J Larrea, T03-296 5212, Tue-Sat, 0900-1230, 1500-1730, US$5*, has a religious art museum. **Museo de la Ciudad** ⓘ *Primera Constituyente y Espejo, at Parque Maldonado, T03-294 4420, Mon-Fri 0800-1230, 1430-1800, free*, in a beautifully restored colonial building, has an interesting historical photograph exhibit and temporary displays.

Riobamba is an important **market centre** where people from many communities congregate. Saturday is the main day when the city fills with colourfully dressed *indígenas* from all over Chimborazo, each wearing their distinctive costume; trading overflows the markets and buying and selling go on all over town. Wednesday is a smaller market day. The 'tourist' market is in the small **Plaza de la Concepción or Plaza Roja** ⓘ *Orozco y Colón, Sat and Wed only, 0800-1500*, is a good place to buy local handicrafts and authentic *indígena* clothing. The main produce market is **San Alfonso**, Argentinos y 5 de Junio, and also sells clothing, ceramics, baskets and hats. Other markets in the colonial centre are **La Condamine** ⓘ *Carabobo y Colombia, daily*, largest market on Fridays, **San Francisco** and **La Merced**, near the churches of the same name.

Guano ⓘ *getting there: buses leave from the Mercado Dávalos, García Moreno y New York, every 15 mins, US$0.30, last bus back at 1900, taxi US$5*, is a carpet-weaving, sisal and leather working town, 8 km north of Riobamba. Many shops sell rugs and you can arrange to have these woven to your own design.

Guaranda *Colour map 1, B3.*

This quaint town, capital of Bolívar Province, proudly calls itself 'the Rome of Ecuador' because it is built on seven hills. There are fine views of the mountains all around and a colourful market. Locals traditionally take an evening stroll in the palm-fringed main plaza, **Parque Libertador Simón Bolívar**, around which are the Municipal buildings and a large stone **Cathedral**. Towering over the city, on one of the hills, is an impressive statue of **El Indio Guaranga**; museum (free) and art gallery. There is also a small local museum at the **Casa de la Cultura** ⓘ *Sucre entre Manuela Cañizares y Selva Alegre.*

Market days are Friday (till 1200) and Saturday (larger), when many indigenous people in typical dress trade at the market complex at the east end of Calle Azuay, by Plaza 15 de Mayo (9 de Abril y Maldonado), and at Plaza Roja (Avenida Gen Enríquez). Carnival in Guaranda is among the best known in the country. **Tourist office**: **Oficina Municipal de Turismo** ⓘ *García Moreno entre 7 de Mayo y Convención de 1884, T03-298 0321, www.guaranda.gob.ec (in Spanish), Mon-Fri 0800-1200, 1400-1800.* Provides information in Spanish and maps.

> **Tip...**
> Although not on the tourist trail, there are many sights worth visiting in the province, for which Guaranda is the ideal base. Of particular interest is the highland town of Salinas, with its community development projects (accommodations and tours available, see Where to stay, below), as well as the *subtrópico* region, the lowlands stretching west towards the coast.

Reserva Faunística Chimborazo

Information from Ministerio del Ambiente, Avenida 9 de Octubre y Duchicela, Quinta Macají, Riobamba, T03-261 0029, ext110, Mon-Fri 0800-1300, 1400-1700. Ranger station T03-302 7358, daily 0800-1700.

The most outstanding features of this reserve, created to protect the camelids (vicuñas, alpacas and llamas) which were re-introduced here, are the beautiful snow-capped volcanos of **Chimborazo** and its neighbour **Carihuayrazo**. Chimborazo, inactive, is the highest peak in Ecuador (6310 m), while Carihuayrazo, 5020 m, is dwarfed by its neighbour. Day visitors can enjoy lovely views, a glimpse of the handsome vicuñas and the rarefied air above 4800 m. There are great opportunities for trekking on the eastern slopes, accessed from **Urbina**, west of the Ambato–Riobamba road, and of course climbing Ecuador's highest peak. Horse riding and trekking tours are offered along the Mocha Valley between the two peaks and downhill cycling from Chimborazo is popular.

To the west of the reserve runs the Vía del Arenal which joins San Juan, along the Riobamba–Guaranda road, with Cruce del Arenal on the Ambato–Guaranda road. A turn-off from this road leads to the main park entrance and beyond to the **Refugio Hermanos Carrel**, a shelter at 4800 m, from where it is a 45-minute walk to **Refugio Whymper** at 5000 m. The Carrel shelter has 32 dorm beds, shared bath, no shower, US$30 pp including dinner and breakfast, lunch available (US$6), no cooking facilities. The Whymper refuge normally opens only 0900-1600; book in advance if you want to spend the night, prices as above for a minimum of four people, with meals in the Carrel refuge. Contact T09-7908 4401, refugioschimborazo@gmail.com.

The access from Riobamba (51 km, paved to the park entrance) is very beautiful. Along the Vía del Arenal past San Juan are a couple of small indigenous communities which grow a few crops and raise llamas and alpacas. They offer lodging and *guías nativos*, the area is good for acclimatization The *arenal* is a large sandy plateau at about 4400 m, to the

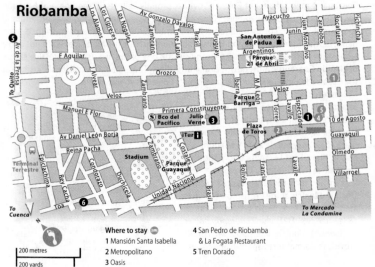

Riobamba

200 metres
200 yards

Where to stay 🛏
1 Mansión Santa Isabella
2 Metropolitano
3 Oasis
4 San Pedro de Riobamba & La Fogata Restaurant
5 Tren Dorado

west of Chimborazo, just below the main park entrance. It can be a harsh, windy place, but it is also very beautiful; take the time to admire the tiny flowers which grow here. This is the best place to see vicuñas, which hang around either in family groups, one male and its harem, or lone males which have been expelled from the group.

Climbing Chimborazo At 6310 m, this is a difficult climb owing to the altitude. Climbers must go with a certified guide working for an operator who has a special permit (*patente*). Rope, ice-axe, helmet and crampons must be used. It is essential to have at least one week's acclimatization above 3500 m. Chimborazo can be climbed all year round but the weather is unpredictable. It is best to avoid late July

Tip...
Climbers arriving at the Chimborazo park entrance without a guide and tour operator or with services not authorized by the ministry are turned back at the gate; exceptions are made for members of alpine clubs. Apply for an entry permit at the Ministerio del Ambiente in Riobamba.

and August, when it can be very windy and the risk of rock fall increases. Deglaciation is making the climb more difficult and ice pinnacles, *penitentes*, sometimes prevent climbers reaching the main, Whymper summit.

The Devil's Nose Train
This spectacular ride is popular with Ecuadorean and foreign tourists alike. Tourist trains run between Alausí and Sibambe, the most scenic part of the trip including the **Devil's Nose**, as well as Riobamba-Alausí and Riobamba-Colta. For details see What to do, page 588.

Alausí *Colour map 1, B3.*
This picturesque town perched on a hillside is where many passengers join the train for the amazing descent over *La Nariz de Diablo* to Sibambe. There is good walking, a Sunday market and a **Fiesta de San Pedro** on 29 June.

Restaurants
1 Café París
2 Helados de Paila
3 Jamones La Andaluza & Naranjo's
5 Mónaco Pizzería
6 Zen Wei

Parque Nacional Sangay
Riobamba provides access to the central highland region of **Sangay National Park** ⓘ *information from Ministerio del Ambiente, see Reserva Chimborazo, above,* a beautiful wilderness area with excellent opportunities for trekking and climbing. A spectacular road, good for downhill biking, runs from Riobamba to Macas in the Oriente, cutting through the park. Near Cebadas (with a good cheese factory) a branch road joins from **Guamote**, a quiet, mainly indigenous town on the Pan-American highway, which comes to life during its colourful Thursday market. At **Atillo**, south of Cebadas, an area of lovely *páramo* dotted with lakes, there is lodging (US$7 per person) and restaurant at **Cabaña Saskines** (T03-301 4383, atillosaskines@ hotmail.com). **Sangay** (5230 m) is an active

volcano, access to the mountain takes at least three days and is only for those who can endure long, hard days of walking and severe weather. Climbing Sangay can be dangerous even when volcanic activity seems low and a helmet to protect against falling stones is vital, November to January is a good time to climb it. Agencies in Quito and Riobamba offer tours or you can organize an expedition independently. A guide is essential; porters can be hired in the access towns of **Alao** and **Guarguallá**. The latter has a **community tourism project** ① *T03-302 6688, T09-9121 3205, accommodation in Guarguallá Chico US$15 pp, US$23.50 pp with dinner and breakfast (reserve in advance), kitchen facilities US$5 per group. Guías nativos, US$40 per day plus US$110 for ascent; porters and horses US$20 per day.* Also in Sangay National Park is the beautiful **El Altar** volcano (5315 m), whose crater is surrounded by nine summits. The most popular climbing and trekking routes begin beyond Candelaria at **Hacienda Releche** (see **Hostal Capac Urcu, Where to stay**).

Listings Riobamba and around *map page 582.*

Tourist information

iTur
Av Daniel León Borja y Brasil, Riobamba, T03-296 3159. Mon-Fri 0830-1230, 1430-1800.
Municipal information office, English spoken.

Where to stay

Riobamba

$$$$-$$$ Abraspungo
Km 3 on the road to Guano, T03-236 4275, www.haciendaabraspungo.com.
Nice country hotel, comfortable rooms, includes buffet breakfast, excellent restaurant, parking, attentive service. Recommended.

$$$$-$$$ La Andaluza
16 km north of Riobamba along the Panamericana, T03-294 0002, www.hosteriaandaluza.com.
An old hacienda, rooms with heaters and roaring fireplaces, includes buffet breakfast, good restaurant, lovely views, good walking.

$$$ Mansión Santa Isabella
Veloz 28-48 y Carabobo, T03-296 2947, www.mansionsantaisabella.com.
Lovely restored house with pleasant patio, comfortable rooms most with bathtub, duvets, includes buffet breakfast, restaurant serves set lunches and à la carte, bar in stone

basement, parking, attentive service, British/Ecuadorean-run. Recommended.

$$$ San Pedro de Riobamba
Daniel L Borja 29-50 y Montalvo, opposite the train station, T03-294 0586.
Elegant hotel in a beautifully restored house in the centre of town, ample comfortable rooms, bathtubs, cafeteria, parking, covered patio, reservations required. Recommended.

$$ Rincón Alemán
Remigio Romero y Alfredo Pareja, Ciudadela Arupos del Norte, T03-260 3540, www.hostalrinconaleman.com.
Family-run hotel in a quiet residential area north of the centre, laundry and cooking facilities, parking, fireplace, sauna, gym, garden, terrace, good views, German spoken.

$$ Tren Dorado
Carabobo 22-35 y 10 de Agosto, near station, T03-296 4890, www.hoteltrendorado.com.
Modern hotel with nice large rooms, buffet breakfast available (starting 0730, open to non-guests), restaurant, reliable hot water, good value. Recommended.

$$-$ Oasis
Veloz 15-32 y Almagro, T03-296 1210, www.oasishostelriobamba.com.
Small, quiet, family-run hostel, laundry facilities, some rooms with kitchen and fridge, shared kitchen for the others, parking,

nice garden, Wi-Fi US$1 per day, popular with backpackers. Recommended.

$ Metropolitano
Daniel L Borja y Lavalle, near the train station, T03-296 1714.
One of the oldest hotels in Riobamba, built in 1912 and nicely restored. Ample rooms, convenient location, no breakfast.

Guaranda

$$$ La Colina
Av Guayaquil 117, on the road to Ambato, T03-298 0666, www.complejolacolina.com.
Nicely situated on a quiet hillside overlooking the city. Bright spacious rooms, nice views, gardens, parking, tours available.

$$-$ Bolívar
Sucre 704 y Rocafuerte, T03-298 0547, http://hotelbolivar.wordpress.com.
Pleasant hotel with courtyard, small modern rooms, best quality in the centre of town. Restaurant next door open Mon-Fri for economical breakfasts and lunches.

$ El Marquez
10 de Agosto y Eloy Alfaro, T03-298 1053.
Pleasant hotel with family atmosphere, newer rooms with private bath are clean and modern, older ones with shared bath are cheaper, parking.

$ La Casa de las Flores
Pichincha 402 y Rocafuerte, T03-298 5795.
Renovated colonial house with covered courtyard and flowers, private bath, hot water, simple economical rooms.

$ Oasis
Gen Enriquez y Garcia Moreno, T03-298 3762.
Modern multi-storey building with large, bright and clean rooms.

Salinas

$$ Hotel Refugio Salinas
45 min from Guaranda, T03-221 0044, www.salinerito.com.
Pleasant community-run hotel, economical meals on request, private or shared bath, dining/sitting area with fireplace, visits to community projects, walking and horse riding tours, packages available, advance booking advised.

$$-$ La Minga
By the main plaza, T09-9218 8880, www.laminga.ec.
Simple rooms with bath and dorms, meals on request, offer full board packages including tour.

Reserva Faunística Chimborazo
The following are all good for acclimatization; those in Urbina can be reached by autoferro from either Riobamba or Ambato.

$$$ Chimborazo Lodge
Operated by Expediciones Andinas, see tour operators below.
Comfortable cabins in a beautiful location on the south flank of Chimborazo, includes dinner and breakfast, advance booking required.

$ Casa Cóndor
In Pulinguí San Pablo, Vía del Arenal, T03-301 3124, T09-8650 8152.
Basic community-run hostel, dinner and breakfast available, use of cooking facilities extra, tours in the area.

$ Posada de la Estación
Opposite Urbina train station, T09-9969 4867.
Comfortable rooms with heaters, shared bath, meals available or cooking facilities (US$5 per group), wood stoves, magnificent views, trips and equipment arranged, tagua workshop, helpful. Also run $ **Urcu Huasi**, cabins at 4150 m, 10 km (2½ hrs walking) from Urbina, in an area being reforested with polylepis trees.

Alausí

$$$ El Molino
Sucre N141 y Bolívar, T03-293 1659, http://hotelelmolino.com.ec/.

Comfortable rooms in a restored historical home, one block from station, pleasant common areas, includes buffet breakfast.

$$$ La Quinta
Eloy Alfaro 121 y M Muñoz, T03-293 0247, www.hosteria-la-quinta.com.
Well-restored old house along the rail line to Riobamba. Pleasant atmosphere, restaurant, gardens, excellent views, not always open, reserve ahead.

$$$ Posada de las Nubes
On the north side of the Río Chanchán, 7 or 11 km from Alausí depending on the route, best with 4WD, pick-up from Alausí US$7, T03-302 9362 or T09-9315 0847, www.posadadelasnubes.com.
Rustic hacienda house in cloudforest at 2600 m. Rooms are simple to basic for the price, some with bath, includes dinner and breakfast, hiking and horse riding, advance booking required.

$$ Gampala
5 de Junio 122 y Loza, T03-293 0138, www.hotelgampala.com.
Nicely refurbished modern rooms and 1 suite with jacuzzi ($$$), restaurant and bar with pool table.

$$ La Posada del Tren
5 de Junio y Orozco, T03-293 1293.
Nice, modern, with parking.

$$-$ San Pedro
5 de Junio y 9 de Octubre, T03-293 0196, hostalsanpedro@hotmail.com.
Simple comfortable rooms, a few cheaper rooms in older section, restaurant downstairs, parking, nice owner.

Parque Nacional Sangay

$ Hostal Capac Urcu
At Hacienda Releche, near the village of Candelaria, T03-301 4067.
Basic rooms in small working hacienda. Use of kitchen (US$10 per group) or meals prepared on request, rents horses for the trek to Collanes, US$40 per horse, plus US$40 per muleteer, round trip. Also runs the *refugio* at Collanes (same price), by the crater of El Altar: thatched-roof rustic shelters with solar hot water. The *refugio* is cold, take a warm sleeping bag. Rubber boots are indispensable for the muddy trail.

Guamote

$$ Inti Sisa
Vargas Torres y García Moreno, T03-291 6529, www.intisisa.org.
Basic but pleasant guesthouse, part of a community development project, most rooms with bath, US$23.75 pp in dorm, includes breakfast, other meals available, dining room and communal area with fireplace, horse riding and cultural tours to highland villages, reservations necessary.

Restaurants

Riobamba
Many places close after 2100 and on Sun.

$$ Mónaco Pizzería
Av de la Prensa y Francisco Aguilar. Mon-Fri 1500-2200, Sat-Sun 1200-2200.
Delicious pizza and pasta, nice salads, good food, service and value. Recommended.

$ La Fogata
Daniel L Borja y Carabobo, opposite the train station. Wed-Mon 0730-2115, Tue 0730-1500.
Simple but good local food, economical set meals and breakfast.

$ Naranjo's
Daniel L Borja 36-20 y Uruguay. Tue-Sun 1200-1500.
Excellent set lunch, friendly service, popular.

$ Zen Wei
Princesa Toa 43-29 y Calicuchima. Mon-Sat 1200-1500.
Oriental restaurant serving economical vegetarian and vegan set meals.

Cafés and bakeries

Café París
Daniel L Borja y Juan Montalvo.
Mon-Sat 0800-2200.
Small popular meeting place serving excellent coffees and snacks.

Helados de Paila
Espejo y 10 de Agosto. Daily 0900-1900.
Excellent home-made ice cream, coffee, sweets, popular.

Jamones La Andaluza
Daniel L Borja y Uruguay. Daily 0830-2300.
Indoor and outdoor seating, good set lunches, coffee, sandwiches, salads, variety of cold-cuts and cheeses, tapas.

La Abuela Rosa
Brasil y Esmeraldas. Mon-Sat 1600-2100.
Cafetería in grandmother's house serving typical Ecuadorean snacks. Nice atmosphere and good service.

Guaranda
Most places close on Sun.

$$$-$$ Pizza Buon Giorno
Sucre at Parque Bolívar. Tue-Sun 1100-2200.
Pizza and salads.

$$ La Bohemia
Convención de 1884 y 10 de Agosto.
Mon-Sat 0800-2100.
Very good economical set meals and pricier international dishes à la carte, nice decor and ambiance, very popular. Recommended.

$$ La Estancia
García Moreno y Sucre. Mon 1200-1500,
Tue-Sat 1200-2100.
Excellent buffet lunch for quality, variety and value, à la carte in the evening, nicely decorated, pleasant atmosphere, popular.

$$-$ Chifa Gran Cangrejo Rojo
10 de Agosto y Convención de 1884.
Open 1100-2200.
Good Chinese food.

Cafés

Cafetería 7 Santos
Convención de 1884 y Olmedo.
Mon-Sat 1000-2200.
Pleasant café and bar with open courtyard. Good coffee and snacks, fireplace, live music Fri and Sat, popular.

Salinerito
Plaza Roja. Daily 0800-1300, 1430-1900.
Salinas cheese shop also serves coffee, sandwiches and pizza.

Alausí

$$ El Mesón del Tren
Ricaurte y Eloy Alfaro. Tue-Sun
0700-0930, 1200-1430.
Good restaurant, popular with tour groups, breakfast, set lunch and à la carte.

$$ Bukardia
Guatemala 107. Open 1300-2200, closed Wed.
Meat specialities, snacks and drinks.

$ Flamingo
Antonio Mora y 9 de Octubre.
Open 0700-2000, closed Sat.
Good economical set meals. Also run **Ventura Hostal ($$-$)**, simple.

Bars and clubs

Riobamba

La Rayuela
Daniel L Borja 36-30 y Uruguay.
Mon-Sat 1200-2200, Sun 1200-1600.
Trendy bar/restaurant, sometimes live music on Fri, sandwiches, coffee, salads, pasta.

San Valentín
Daniel L Borja y Vargas Torres. Mon-Thu
1800-2400, Fri-Sat 1800-0200.
Very popular bar, good pizzas and Mexican dishes.

Entertainment

Riobamba

Casa de la Cultura, *10 de Agosto y Rocafuerte*, *T03-296 0219*. Cultural events, cinema on Tue. **Super Cines**, *at El Paseo Shopping, Vía a Guano*. 12 screens, some with 3-D.

Festivals

Riobamba

Dec-Jan **Fiesta del Niño Rey de Reyes**, street parades, music and dancing, starts in Dec and culminates on 6 Jan.
Apr **Independence** celebrations around 21 Apr lasting several days, hotel prices rise.
29 Jun **Fiestas Patronales** in honour of San Pedro.
11 Nov Festival to celebrate the 1st attempt at independence from Spain.

Shopping

Riobamba
Camping gear

Some of the tour operators listed below hire camping and climbing gear; also **Veloz Coronado** (Chile 33-21 y Francia, T03-296 0916, after 1900). **Marathon Explorer** (Multiplaza mall, Av Lizarzaburu near the airport). High-end outdoor equipment and clothing. **Protección Industrial** (Rocafuerte 24-51 y Orozco, T03-296 3017). Outdoor equipment, rope, fishing supplies, rain ponchos.

Handicrafts

Crafts sold at Plaza Roja on Wed and Sat. **Almacén Cacha** (Colón y Orozco, next to the Plaza Roja). A cooperative of indigenous people from the Cacha area, sells woven bags, wool sweaters, and other crafts, good value (closed Sun-Mon).

What to do

Riobamba
Mountain biking

Guided tours with support vehicle average US$50-60 pp per day.

Julio Verne, *see Tour operators*. Very good tours, equipment and routes.
Pro Bici, *Primera Constituyente 23-51 y Larrea, T03-295 1759, www.probici.com*. Tours and rentals.

Tour operators

Most companies offer climbing trips (US$240 pp for 2 days to Chimborazo or Carihuayrazo), trekking (US$100 pp per day) and day-hikes (US$50-60 pp).
Andes Trek, *Esmeraldas 21-45 y Espejo, T03-2951275, www.goandestrek.com*. Climbing and trekking, transport, equipment rental. Also runs an office and hostel in Quito.
Expediciones Andinas, *Vía a Guano, Km 3, across from Hotel Abraspungo, T03-236 4278, www.expediciones-andinas.com*. Climbing expeditions run by Marco Cruz, a guide certified by the **German Alpine Club**, operate **Chimborazo** Lodge (see Where to stay, above). Recommended.
Incañán, *Brasil 20-28 y Luis A Falconí, T03-294 0508, http://incanian2011.blogspot.com*. Trekking, cycling and cultural tours.
Julio Verne, *Brasil 22-40 between Daniel L Borja and Primera Constituyente, T03-296 3436, www.julioverne-travel.com*. Climbing, trekking, cycling, jungle and Galápagos trips, transport, equipment rental, English spoken, Ecuadorean/Dutch-run, very conscientious and reliable. Uses official guides. Highly recommended.

The Devil's Nose Train

The Devil's Nose Train departs from Alausí, Tue-Sun at 0800, 1100 and 1500 (the latter only if there are enough passengers), 2½ hrs return, US$30, includes a snack and folklore dance. Riobamba to Alausí, Tue-Fri 0630, arriving 1040 to connect to 1100 Devil's Nose Train; Alausí to Riobamba, Tue-Fri 1245, connecting from 1100 Devil's Nose Train, arriving Riobamba 1745; US$50 one way Riobamba–Alausí or vice versa, US$68 including Devil's Nose. *Autoferro* from Riobamba to Colta (Thu-Sun at 1200, US$15), dress warmly. Purchase tickets well in advance for weekends and holidays at any train station (Riobamba, T03-296 1038, Mon-Fri 0800-1630, Sat-Sun 0700-1200; Alausí, T03-293 0126, Tue-Sun 0700-1530), through the call centre (T1800-873637) or by email (info@trenecuador.com, then you have to make a bank deposit). Procedures change frequently, so enquire locally and check www.trenecuador.com.

Transport

Riobamba
Bus **Terminal Terrestre** on Epiclachima y Av Daniel L Borja for all long-distance buses including to Baños and destinations in Oriente. **Terminal Oriental**, Espejo y Cordovez, only for local services to Candelaria and Penipe. **Terminal Intercantonal**, Av Canónigo Ramos about 2.5 km northwest of the Terminal Terrestre, for Guamote, San Juan and Cajabamba (Colta). Taxi between terminals US$1.50-2. To **Quito**, US$4.75, 4 hrs, about every 30 mins; also shared taxis with: **Montecarlo Trans Vip**, T03-296 8758 or T09-8411 4114, 7 daily, US$18 (US$5 extra for large luggage) and **Delux**, T09-3920 9827 or T09-8343 0275, every 2 hrs, US$20. To **Guaranda**, US$2.50, 2 hrs (sit on the right). To **Ambato**, US$1.50, 1 hr. To **Alausí**, see below. To **Cuenca**, 8 a day via Alausí, 5½ hrs, US$8. To **Guayaquil** via Pallatanga, frequent service, US$7, 5 hrs, spectacular for the first 2 hrs. To **Baños**, 2 hrs, US$2. To **Puyo** US$4, 4 hrs. To **Macas** via Parque Nacional Sangay, 8 daily, 4 hrs, US$6.25 (sit on the left).

Guaranda
Bus Terminal at Eliza Mariño Carvajal, on road to Riobamba and Babahoyo; if you are staying in town get off closer to the centre. Many daily buses to: **Ambato**, US$2.50, 2 hrs. **Riobamba**, see above. **Babahoyo**, US$3.75, 3 hrs, beautiful ride. **Guayaquil**, US$5, 5 hrs. **Quito**, US$6.25, 5 hrs.

Reserva Faunística Chimborazo
There are no buses to the shelters. Take a tour or arrange transport with a Riobamba tour operator (US$35 one way, US$45 return with wait) or take a Riobamba–Guaranda bus, alight at the turn-off for the refuges and walk the remaining steep 8 km (5 km taking short cuts) to the 1st shelter. For the eastern slopes, take a trekking tour, arrange transport from an agency or take a bus between Riobamba and Ambato, get off at the turn-off for **Posada La Estación** and Urbina and walk from there.

Alausí
Bus To **Riobamba**, 1½ hrs, US$2.50, 84 km. To **Quito**, from 0600, 8 a day, 6 hrs, US$7.50, often have to change in Riobamba. To **Cuenca**, 4 hrs, US$6.25. To **Ambato** hourly, 3 hrs, US$3.75. To **Guayaquil**, 4 a day, 4 hrs, US$6.25. **Coop Patria**. Colombia y Orozco, 3 blocks up from the main street; **Trans Alausí**, 5 de Junio y Loza. Many through buses don't go into town, but have to be caught on the highway, taxi from town US$1.

Parque Nacional Sangay
To **Atillo** from Parque La Dolorosa, Puruhá y Primera Constituyente, 15 daily 0400-1845, US$2.50, 2 hrs. Also Riobamba–**Macas** service goes through Atillo, see above. To **Alao**, from Parque La Dolorosa, hourly 0700-2300, US$1.50, 1½ hrs. To **Guarguallá Grande** from Parque La Dolorosa daily at 1345 (return to Riobamba at 0545), US$2 (Grande), 2 hrs; also a milk truck from La Dolorosa to Guargualla at 0530, US$2. To **Candelaria**, from Terminal Oriental, daily 0600, 0800, 1100, 1500 and 1700, US$1.25, 1½ hrs. Alternatively, take a bus from the same terminal to Penipe, every 30 mins, US$0.40, 40 mins, and hire a pickup truck from there to Candelaria, US$15, 40 mins.

Cuenca
& around

★ Founded in 1557 on the site of the Inca settlement of Tomebamba, much of Cuenca's colonial air has been preserved, with many of its old buildings renovated. Its cobblestone streets, flowering plazas and pastel-coloured buildings with old wooden doors and ironwork balconies make it a pleasure to explore. The climate is spring-like, but the nights are chilly. In 1999 Cuenca was designated a UNESCO World Heritage Site. It is home to the largest expat retiree community in Ecuador. The surrounding area is known for its crafts.

Cuenca Colour map 1, C3.

Inca remains, colonial buildings, museums

Sights

On the main plaza, **Parque Abdón Calderón**, are the Old Cathedral, **El Sagrario** ⓘ *Mon-Fri 0900-1730, Sat-Sun 0900-1300, US$2*, begun in 1557, and the immense 'New' **Catedral de la Inmaculada**, started in 1885. The latter contains a famous crowned image of the Virgin, a beautiful altar and an exceptional play of light and shade through modern stained glass. Other churches which deserve a visit are **San Blas**, **San Francisco** and **Santo Domingo**. Many churches are open at irregular hours only and for services. The church of **El Carmen de la Asunción**, close to the southwest corner of La Inmaculada, has a flower market in the tiny **Plazoleta El Carmen** in front. There is a colourful daily market in **Plaza Rotary** where pottery, clothes, guinea pigs and local produce, especially baskets, are sold. Thursday is the busiest.

Museo del Monasterio de las Conceptas ⓘ *Hermano Miguel 6-33 entre Pdte Córdova y Juan Jaramillo, T07-283 0625, Mon-Fri 0900-1830, Sat and holidays 1000-1300, US$3*, in a cloistered convent founded in 1599, houses a well displayed collection of religious and folk art, in addition to an extensive collection of lithographs by Guayasamín.

Pumapungo ⓘ *C Larga y Huayna Capac, T07-283 1521, Mon-Fri 0830-1730, Sat 1000-1400*, is a museum complex on the edge of the colonial city, at the actual site of Tomebamba excavations. Part of the area explored is seen at **Parque Arqueológico Pumapungo**. The **Sala Arqueológica** section contains all the Cañari and Inca remains and artifacts found

Essential Cuenca

Finding your feet

The **Terminal Terrestre** is on Avenida España, 15 minutes' ride northeast of the centre, T07-284 2633. The **airport** is five minutes beyond the Terminal Terrestre, T07-286 2203, www.aeropuertocuenca.ec. Both can be reached by city bus, but best take a taxi at all hours (US$1.50-2.50 to the centre). The **Terminal Sur** for regional buses within the province is by the Feria Libre El Arenal on Avenida Las Américas. Many city buses pass here.

The city is bounded by the Río Machángara to the north and the Ríos Yanuncay and Tarqui to the south. The Río Tomebamba separates the colonial heart from the newer districts to the south. Avenida Las Américas is a ring road around the north and west of the city and the *autopista*, a multi-lane highway bypasses the city to the south.

Getting around

The narrow streets of colonial Cuenca are clogged with cars on weekdays, detracting from the area's considerable charm. It is hoped that a new tram system projected for completion in 2017 will help alleviate the congestion. See Transport, page 599, for further details.

Safety

Though safer than Quito or Guayaquil, routine precautions are advised. Outside the busy nightlife area around Calle Larga, the city centre is deserted and unsafe after 2300, taking a taxi is recommended. The river banks are OK while university students are around, until about 2200. The Cruz del Vado area (south end of Juan Montalvo), the Terminal Terrestre and all market areas are not safe after dark.

at this site. Other halls in the premises house the **Sala Etnográfica**, with information on different Ecuadorean cultures, including a special collection of *tsantsas* (shrunken heads from Oriente), the **Sala de Arte Religioso**, the **Sala Numismática** and temporary exhibits. There are also book and music libraries, free cultural videos and music events. Three blocks west of Pumapungo, **Museo Manuel Agustín Landívar** ⓘ *C Larga 2-23 y Manuel Vega, T07-282 1177, Mon-Fri 0800-1300, 1500-1800, Sat 0900-1300, free*, is at the site of the small Todos los Santos ruins, with Cañari, Inca and colonial remains; ceramics and artifacts found at the site are also displayed.

Museo de las Culturas Aborígenes ⓘ *C Larga 5-24 y Hermano Miguel, T07-283 9181, Mon-Fri 0900-1800, Sat 0900-1200, US$4, craft shop*, the private collection of Dr J Cordero Íñiguez, has an impressive selection of pre-Columbian archaeology. **Museo Remigio Crespo Toral** ⓘ *C Larga 7-25 y Borrero, Mon-Fri 1000-1730, Sat 1000-1600, Sun 1000-1300, free*, in a beautifully refurbished colonial house, has important history, archaeology and art collections. **Museo del Sombrero** ⓘ *C Larga 10-41 y Gral Torres, T07-283 1569, Mon-Fri 0900-1800, Sat 0900-1500, Sun 0930-1330*, shop with all the old factory machines for hat finishing.

On Plaza San Sebastián is **Museo Municipal de Arte Moderno** ⓘ *Sucre 1527 y Talbot, T07-283 1027, Mon-Fri 0830-1300, 1500-1830, Sat-Sun 0900-1300, free*, has a permanent contemporary art collection and art library. It holds a biennial international painting competition and other cultural activities. Across the river from the Museo Pumapungo, the **Museo de Artes de Fuego** ⓘ *Las Herrerías y 10 de Agosto, T07-288 3061, Mon-Fri 0900-1300, 1500-1800, free except for special events*, has a display of wrought iron work and pottery. It is housed in the beautifully restored Casa de Chaguarchimbana. At the University of Cuenca is an **Orquideario** ⓘ *Av Víctor Manuel Albornoz, Quinta de Balzay,*

Mon-Fri, 0800-1200, 1400-1800. South of city, accessed via Avenida Fray Vicente Solano, beyond the football stadium, is **Turi church**, orphanage and mirador; a tiled panorama explains the magnificent views.

Listings Cuenca *map page 594.*

Tourist information

General information from www.cuenca.com.ec. To locate an establishment see www.ubicacuenca.com.

Cámara de Turismo
Terminal Terrestre, T07-284 5657.
Mon-Sat 0800-1300, 1500-1800.
Information about the city, including city and long-distance bus routes; also at the airport.

Ministerio de Turismo
Sucre y Benigno Malo, on Parque Calderón next to the Municipio, T07-282 1035. Mon-Fri, 0800-2000, Sat 0830-1730, Sun 0900-1600.
Helpful.

Where to stay

$$$$ Carvallo
Gran Colombia 9-52, entre Padre Aguirre y Benigno Malo, T07-283 2063, www.hotelcarvallo.com.ec.
Combination of an elegant colonial-style hotel and art/antique gallery. Very comfortable rooms all have bath tubs, buffet breakfast, cafeteria.

$$$$ Mansión Alcázar
Bolívar 12-55 y Tarqui, T07-282 3918, www.mansionalcazar.com.
Beautifully restored house, a mansion indeed, central, very nice rooms, restaurant serves gourmet international food, lovely gardens, quiet relaxed atmosphere.

$$$$ Oro Verde
Av Ordóñez Lazo, northwest of the centre towards Cajas, T07-409 0000, www.oroverdehotels.com.
Elegant hotel, buffet breakfast, excellent international restaurant (buffet Sun lunch), small pool, parking.

$$$$ Santa Lucía
Borrero 8-44 y Sucre, T07-282 8000, www.santaluciahotel.com.
A stylish renovated colonial house, very nice comfortable rooms, excellent Italian restaurant, safe deposit box.

$$$ Inca Real
Gral Torres 8-40 entre Sucre y Bolívar, T07-282 3636, www.hotelincareal.com.ec.
Refurbished colonial house with comfortable rooms around patios, breakfast available, good Spanish restaurant, parking.

$$$ La Casona
Miguel Cordero 2-124 y Alfonso Cordero, near the stadium, T07-410 3501, www.lacasonahotel.com.ec.
Attractive refurbished family home in a residential area, comfortable carpeted rooms, buffet breakfast, restaurant, parking.

$$$ Mercure El Dorado
Gran Colombia 787 y Luis Cordero, T07-283 1390, www.eldoradohotel.com.ec.
Elegant modern hotel, rooms have safe and mini-bar, buffet breakfast, cafeteria, spa, gym, business centre, parking.

$$$ Posada del Angel
Bolívar 14-11 y Estévez de Toral, T07-284 0695, www.hostalposadadelangel.com.
A nicely restored colonial house, comfortable rooms, good Italian restaurant, parking, patio with plants, some noise from restaurant, English spoken, helpful staff. Recommended.

$$$ Victoria
C Larga 6-93 y Borrero, T07-283 1120, www.hotelvictoriaecuador.com.
Elegant refurbished hotel overlooking the river, comfortable modern rooms, excellent expensive restaurant, nice views.

$$$-$$ Casa Ordóñez
Lamar 8-59 y Benigno Malo, T07-282 3297,
www.casa-ordonez.com.
Well-renovated colonial house with wood floors and 3 inner patios, attractively decorated rooms and common areas, down comforters, no smoking.

$$ Casa del Barranco
Calle Larga 8-41 y Luis Cordero, T07-283 9763,
www.casadelbarranco.com.
Tastefully restored colonial house, some rooms with lovely views over the river, cafeteria overlooking the river.

$$ Casa del Río
Bajada del Padrón 4-07 y C Larga, T07-282 9659, hostalcasadelrio@hotmail.com.
Pleasant quiet *hostal* on El Barranco overlooking the river, private or shared bath, breakfast available, nice views, attentive service.

$$ Colonial
Gran Colombia 10-13 y Padre Aguirre, T07-284 1644.
Refurbished colonial house with beautiful patio, carpeted rooms.

$$ El Príncipe
J Jaramillo 7-82 y Luis Cordero, T07-284 7287, www.hotelprincipe.com.ec.
A refurbished 3-storey colonial house, comfortable rooms around a nice patio with plants, restaurant, parking.

$$ La Orquídea
Borrero 9-31 y Bolívar, T07-282 4511,
www.laorquidea.com.ec.
Refurbished colonial house, bright rooms, fridge, low season and long term discounts, good value.

$$ La Posada Cuencana
Tarqui 9-46 y Bolivar, T07-282 6831,
www.laposadacuencana.com.ec.
Small family-run hotel with beautiful colonial-style rooms.

$$ Macondo
Tarqui 11-64 y Sangurima, T07-284 0697,
www.hostalmacondo.com.

Nice restored colonial house, large rooms, buffet breakfast, cooking facilities, pleasant patio with plants, garden, very popular, US-run. Highly recommended.

$$ Milán
Pres Córdova 989 y Padre Aguirre, T07-283 1104, www.hotelmilan.com.ec.
Multi-storey hotel with views over market, restaurant, popular.

$$ Posada Todos Santos
C Larga 3-42 y Tomás Ordóñez, near the Todos Santos Church, T07-282 4247.
Tranquil hostel decorated with murals, good views of the river, very good, attentive service, English spoken, group discounts.

$ Hogar Cuencano
Hermano Miguel 436 y C Larga, T07-283 4941, celso3515@yahoo.com.
Well-furnished family-run central *hostal*, private or shared bath, US$10 pp in dorm, cafeteria, breakfast available, cooking facilities.

$ La Cigale
Honorato Vasquez 7-80 y Cordero, T07-283 5308, www.hostallacigale.com.
Very popular hostel with private rooms and dorms (US$8 pp), breakfast available, very good restaurant ($$-$), hostel can be noisy until midnight.

$ Turista del Mundo
C Larga 5-79 y Hermano Miguel, T07-282 9125, esperanzab65@gmail.com.
Popular hostel with comfortable rooms, private or shared bath, no breakfast, cooking facilities, nice terrace, very helpful.

$ Yakumama
Cordero 5-66 y Honorato Vásquez, T07-283 4353, www.hostalyakumama.com.
Popular hostel, 2 private rooms and dorms with 2-6 beds US$7.50-10 pp, restaurant with Ecuadorean and Swiss dishes, bar, patio with plants and lounging area, terrace with skate ramp, can get noisy.

Restaurants

There is a wide selection and fast turnover of restaurants. Most places are closed on Sun evening. There are cheap *comedores* at the Mercados 9 de Octubre and 10 de Agosto.

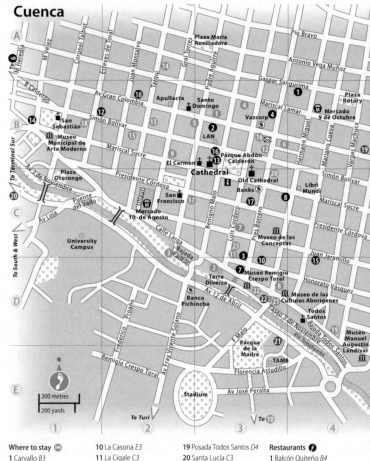

Cuenca

$$$ Tiestos
J Jaramillo 4-89 y M Cueva, T07-283 5310. Tue-Sat 1230-1500, 1830-2200, Sun 1230-1500.

9 Mixx Gourmet *C5*
10 Moliendo Café *D3*
11 Monte Bianco *C5*
12 Pedregal Azteca *B1*
13 Raymipampa *B3*
14 San Sebas *B1*
15 Tiestos *D4*
16 Tutto Freddo *B3*
17 Viejo Rincón *C3*
18 Villa Rosa *B2*

Bars & clubs 🕐
19 La Mesa Salsoteca *B4*
20 MalAmado *C1*
21 Rue *D3*
22 Wunderbar *D3*

Superb international cuisine prepared on *tiestos*, shallow clay pans, comfortable feel-at-home atmosphere, very popular, reserve ahead.

$$$ Villa Rosa
Gran Colombia 12-22 y Tarqui, T07-283 7944, www.restaurantevillarosa.com. Mon-Fri 1230-1530, 1830-2200.
Very elegant restaurant in the centre of town, excellent international and Ecuadorean food and service. A meeting place for business people.

$$$-$$ Balcón Quiteño
Sangurima 6-49 y Hermano Miguel, and Av Ordóñez Lazo 311 y los Pinos, T07-283 1928. Daily 1000-0100.
Good Ecuadorean and international food and service, 1960s decor. Popular with locals after a night's partying.

$$$-$$ El Carbón
Borrero 10-69 y Lamar, in Hotel Cuenca, T07-283 3711, www.hotelcuenca.com.ec. Daily 0700-2300.
Excellent charcol-grilled meat served with a choice of fresh salads, seafood, wide choice of dishes and breakfasts, large portions enough for 2.

$$$-$$ El Maíz
C Larga 1-279 y C de los Molinos, T07-284 0224. Mon-Sat 1100-1600, 1830-2100.
Good traditional Ecuadorean dishes with some innovations, salads.

$$$-$$ Mangiare
Estévez de Toral 8-91 y Bolívar, at Posada del Angel, T07-282 1360. Mon-Sat 1200-1500, 1730-2230, Sun 1200-1500.
Excellent Italian food, home-made pasta, good value, very popular with locals.

$$$-$$ Pedregal Azteca
Esteves de Toral 8-60 y Bolívar, T07-282 3652. Tue-Sat 1200-1500, 1830-2300, Sun 1200-1500.
Nicely decorated restaurant with very good authentic Mexican food.

$$ Café Eucalyptus
Gran Colombia 9-41 y Benigno Malo.
Mon-Fri 1700-2300 or later, Sat 1900-0200.
A pleasant restaurant, café and bar in an elegantly decorated house. Large menu with dishes from all over the world. British-owned, popular. Recommended.

$$ Cesare's
Honorato Vásquez 6-83 y Borrero,
T09-9814 9651. Mon-Sat 1700-2200.
Mediterranean and international food, popular with expats.

$$ Raymipampa
Benigno Malo 8-59, at Parque Calderón.
Mon-Fri 0830-2300, Sat-Sun 0930-2230.
Good typical and international food in a nice central location, inexpensive set lunch on weekdays, fast service, very popular, at times it is hard to get a table.

$$-$ Viejo Rincón
Pres Córdova 7-46 y Borrero.
Mon-Fri 0900-2100, Sat 0900-1500.
Tasty Ecuadorean food, very good economical set lunch and à la carte, popular.

$ Good Affinity
Capulíes 1-89 y Gran Colombia.
Mon-Sat 0930-1530.
Very good vegetarian food, vegan options, cheap set lunch, nice garden seating.

$ Grecia
Gran Colombia y Padre Aguirre.
Mon-Sat 1200-1500.
Good quality and value set lunch and à la carte.

$ Moliendo Café
Honorato Vásquez y Hermano Miguel.
Mon-Sat 0900-2100.
Tasty Colombian food including set lunch, friendly service.

Cafés

Goza
C Larga y Borrero, Plaza de la Merced. Mon-Thu 0800-2200, Fri-Sat 0800-2400, Sun 0800-2200.

Very popular café/restaurant with a varied menu; one of the few places in Cuenca with outdoor seating and open Sun evening.

Maria's Alemania
Hermano Miguel 8-09 y Sucre.
Mon-Fri 0730-1800.
Excellent bakery and cafeteria, wide variety of whole-grain breads.

Mixx Gourmet
Parque San Blas 2-73 y Tomás Ordoñez.
A variety of fruit and liquor flavoured ice cream, popular. Several others nearby.

Monte Bianco
Bolívar 2-80 y Ordóñez and a couple of other locations.
Good ice cream and cream cakes, good value.

San Sebas
San Sebastián 1-94 y Sucre, Parque San Sebastián. Tue-Sun 0830-1500.
Outdoor café, popular for breakfast, good selection of giant sandwiches and salads.

Tutto Freddo
Bolívar 8-09 y Benigno Malo and several other locations. Daily 0900-2200.
Good ice cream, crêpes, pizza, sandwiches and sweets, reasonable prices, popular.

Bars and clubs

Calle Larga is a major destination for night life, with lots of bars with snacks and some restaurants. Av 12 de Abril, along the river near Parque de la Madre, and to the west of the centre, Plaza del Arte, Gaspar de Sangurima y Abraham Sarmiento, opposite Plazoleta El Otorongo, are also popular. Most bars open Wed-Thu until 2300, Fri-Sat until 0200.

La Mesa Salsoteca
Gran Colombia 3-36 entre Vargas Machuca y Tomás Ordóñez (no sign).
Latin music, salsa, popular among travellers and locals, young crowd.

MalAmado
C San Roque y Av 12 de Abril.

Pleasant atmosphere, good music, food, a good place for dancing, US$10-15.

Rue

at Parque de la Madre, Av 12 de Abril. Tue-Sat 2200-0200.
Nice bar/restaurant with outdoor seating, no cover charge.

Wunderbar

Entrance from stairs on Hermano Miguel y C Larga. Mon-Fri 1100-0200, Sat 1500-0200.
A café-bar-restaurant, drinks, good coffee and food including some vegetarian. Nice atmosphere, book exchange, German-run.

Entertainment

Cinemas

Multicines, *Av José Peralta*. Complex of 5 theatres and food court, also at Mall del Río.

Dance classes

Cachumbambe, *Remigio Crespo 7-79 y Guayas, p2, T07-288 2023*. Salsa, merengue and a variety of other rhythms, group and individual classes.

Festivals

Mar/Apr **Good Friday**. There is a fine procession through the town to the Mirador Turi.

12 Apr **Foundation of Cuenca**.

May-Jun **Septenario**, the religious festival of Corpus Christi, lasts a week.

Oct-Dec **Bienal de Cuenca**, an internationally famous art competition. The next one is due 21 Oct to 31 Dec, 2016. Information from Bolívar 13-89, T07-283 1778, www.bienaldecuenca.org.

3 Nov **Independence of Cuenca**, with street theatre, art exhibitions and night-time dances all over the city.

24 Dec **Pase del Niño Viajero**, probably the largest and finest Christmas parade in all Ecuador. Children and adults from all the barrios and surrounding villages decorate donkeys, horses, cars and trucks with symbols of abundance. Little children in colourful indigenous costumes or dressed up as Biblical figures ride through the streets accompanied by musicians. The parade starts at about 1000 at San Sebastián, proceeds along C Bolívar and ends at San Blas about 5 hrs later. In the days up to, and just after Christmas, there are many smaller parades.

Shopping

Books

BC Carolina, *Hermano Miguel 4-46 y C Larga*. Good selection of English books for sale and exchange. Friendly service.

Librimundi, *Hermano Miguel 8-14 y Sucre, www.librimundi.com*. Nice bookshop with good selection and a café/reading area.

Camping equipment

Bermeo Hnos, *Borrero 8-35 y Sucre, T07-283 1522*.

Explorer, *at Mall del Río*. Sporting goods, clothing.

Tatoo/Cikla, *Av Remigio Tamariz 2-52 y Federico Proaño, T07-288 4809, www.tatoo.ws*. Good camping, hiking, climbing and biking gear. Also rent bikes.

Several other shops near the university, on or near Av Remigio Crespo. Equipment rental from **Apullacta**, see Tour operators.

Handicrafts

There are many craftware shops along Gran Colombia, Benigno Malo and Juan Jaramillo alongside Las Conceptas. There are several good leather shops in the arcade off Bolívar between Benigno Malo and Luis Cordero. *Polleras*, traditional skirts worn by indigenous women are found along Gral Torres, between Sucre and Pres Córdova, and on Tarqui, between Pres Córdova and C Larga. For basketwork, take a 15-min bus ride from the Feria Libre (see Markets, below) to the village of **San Joaquín**.

Arte, Artesanías y Antigüedades, *Borrero y Córdova*. Textiles, jewellery and antiques.

Artesa, *L Cordero 10-31 y Gran Colombia,*
several branches. Modern ceramic tableware,
can visit Eduardo Vega's studio on the hill
just below El Turi.

Centro Artesanal Municipal 'Casa de la
Mujer', *Gral Torres 7-33.* Crafts market with
a great variety of handicrafts.

Colecciones Jorge Moscoso, *J Jaramillo 6-80*
y Borrero. Weaving exhibitions, ethnographic
museum, antiques and crafts.

El Barranco, *Hermano Miguel 3-23 y Av 3 de*
Noviembre. Artisans' cooperative selling a
wide variety of crafts.

El Otorongo, *3 de Noviembre by Plaza*
Otorongo. Exclusive designs sold at this
art gallery/café.

El Tucán, *Borrero 7-35.* Good selection.
Recommended.

Galápagos, *Borrero 6-75.* Excellent selection.

La Esquina de las Artes, *12 de Abril y Agustín*
Cueva. Shops with exclusive crafts including
textiles; also cultural events.

Jewellery
Galería Claudio Maldonado, *Bolívar 7-75.*
Has unique pre-Columbian designs in silver
and precious stones.

Unicornio, *Gran Colombia y Luis Cordero.*
Good jewellery, ceramics and candelabras.

Markets
Feria Libre, *Av Las Américas y Av Remigio*
Crespo, west of the centre. The largest market,
also has dry goods and clothing, busiest
Wed and Sat.

Mercado 9 de Octubre, *Sangurima y*
Mariano Cueva. Busiest on Thu. Nearby at
Plaza Rotary (Sangurima y Vargas Machuca),
crafts are sold, best selection on Thu. Note
this area is not safe.

Mercado 10 de Agosto, *C Larga y Gral Torres.*
Daily market with a prepared foods and
drinks section on the 2nd floor.

Panama hats
Manufacturers have displays showing the
complete hat making process, see also
Museo del Sombrero, page 591.

Homero Ortega P e Hijos, *Av Gil*
Ramírez Dávalos 3-86, T07-280 1288,
www.homeroortega.com. Good quality.

K Dorfzaun, *Gil Ramírez Dávalos 4-34, near*
bus station, T07-286 1707, www.kdorfzaun.
com. Mon-Fri 0800-1600. Good quality and
selection of hats and straw crafts, nice styles,
good prices. English-speaking guides.

What to do

Language courses
Rates US$6-7 per hr shared lessons,
US$8-12 per hr private.

Centro de Estudios Interamericanos
(CEDEI), *Gran Colombia 11-02 y General Torres,*
T07-283 9003, www.cedei.org. Spanish and
Quichua lessons, immersion/volunteering
programmes, also run the attached **Hostal**
Macondo. Recommended.

Estudio Internacional Sampere, *Hermano*
Miguel 3-43 y C Larga, T07-284 2659,
www.sampere.es. At the high end of
the price range.

Sí Centro de Español e Inglés, *Bolívar*
13-28 y Juan Montalvo, T09-9918-8264,
www.sicentrospanishschool.com. Good
teachers, competitive prices, homestays,
volunteer opportunities, helpful and
enthusiastic, tourist information available.
Recommended.

Tours
Day tours to Ingapirca or Cajas run about
US$50 pp, to Gualaceo or Chordeleg US$55.
Trekking in Cajas about US$60-100 pp per
day, depending on group size.

Apullacta, *Gran Colombia 11-02 y Gral Torres,*
p 2, T07-283 7681, www.apullacta.com. Run
city and regional tours (Cajas, Ingapirca,
Saraguro), also adventure tours (cycling,
horse riding, canopy, canyoning), sell jungle,
highland and Galápagos trips; also hire
camping equipment.

Metropolitan Touring, *Sucre 6-62 y Borreo,*
T07-284 3223, www.metropolitan-touring.com.
A branch of the Quito operator, also sells
airline tickets.

TerraDiversa, *C Larga 8-41 y Luis Cordero, T07-282 3782, www.terradiversa.com.* Lots of useful information, helpful staff. Ingapirca, Cajas, community tourism in Saraguro, jungle trips, horse riding, mountain biking and other options. The more common destinations have fixed departures. Also sell Galápagos tours and flights. Recommended.

Van Service, *T07-281 6409, www.vanservice. com.ec.* City tours on a double-decker bus. The 1¾-hr tour includes the main attractions in the colonial city and El Turi lookout. US$8, hourly departures 0900-1900 from the Old Cathedral. Also hire cars and vans with driver.

Transport

Air Airport is about a 20-min ride northeast of the centre. To **Quito** with **LATAM** (Bolívar 9-18, T07-283 8078) and **TAME** (Florencia Astudillo 2-22, T07-288 9581). Also to **Guayaquil** with TAME.

Bus City buses US$0.25. For the local **Baños**, city buses every 5-10 mins, 0600-2230, buses pass the front of the Terminal Terrestre, cross the city on Vega Muñoz and Cueva, then down Todos los Santos to the river, along 12 de Abril and onto Av Loja. A tram system is under construction and expected to start operating in 2017. Note that many streets are closed due to the construction, taxis have to take detours, traffic is chaotic, allow extra time.

Regional Buses to nearby destinations leave from **Terminal Sur** at the Feria Libre on Av Las Américas. Many city buses pass here but it is not a safe area.

Long distance The **Terminal Terrestre** is on Av España, 15 mins by taxi northeast of centre. Take daytime buses to enjoy scenic routes. To **Riobamba**, 5½ hrs, US$8. To **Baños** (Tungurahua), transfer in Riobamba. To **Ambato**, 6½ hrs, US$10. To **Quito**,

Terminal Quitumbe, US$12-15, 8-9 hrs. To **Alausí**, 4 hrs, US$6; all Riobamba-and Quito-bound buses pass by, but few enter town. To **Loja**, 4 hrs, US$7.50, see www.viajerosinternacional.com; transfer here for Vilcabamba.To **Saraguro**, US$5.40, 2½ hrs. To **Machala**, 3½ hrs, US$6, sit on the left, wonderful scenery. To **Huaquillas**, 5 hrs, US$8 To **Guayaquil**, via Cajas and Molleturo, 4 hrs, or via Zhud, 5 hrs, both US$8. To **Macas** via Paute and Guarumales or via Gualaceo and Plan de Milagro, 6-7 hrs, US$11; spectacular scenery but prone to landslides, check in advance if roads are open. To **Gualaquiza**, in the southern Oriente, via Gualaceo and Plan de Milagro or via Sígsig, 6 hrs, US$8.75.

International To **Chiclayo** (Peru) via Tumbes, **Máncora** and **Piura**, with **Super Semería**, at 2200, US$20, 11 hrs (US$17 as far as Piura or Máncora); also with **Azuay** at 2130; and **Pullman Sucre**, connecting with CIFA in Huaquillas; or go to Loja and catch a bus to Piura from there.

Long-distance taxis and vans **Río Arriba**, Del Batán 10-25 y Edwin Sacoto, near Feria Libre, T07-404 1790, to **Quito**, daily at 2300, US$25, 6½ hrs, from Quito, Páez N20-64 y Washington, T02-252 1336, at 1700; to **Guayaquil**, hourly 0400-2200, US$12, 3 hrs, several other companies nearby. To **Loja**, **Elite Tours**, Remigio Crespo 14-08 y Santa Cruz, T07-420 3088, also **Faisatur**, Remigio Crespo y Brazil, T07-404 4771, US$12, 3 hrs; taxi US$60. To **Vilcabamba**, van service daily at 1330 from **Hostal La Cigale**, Honorato Vásquez y Luis Cordero, US$15, 5 hrs, reserve ahead.

Car rental **Bombuscaro**, España 11-20 y Elia Liut, opposite the airport, T07-286 6541. Also international companies.

Taxi All taxis are required to use meters, US$1.50 is the minimum fare; approximately US$2 from the centre to the bus station; US$2.50 to airport; US$5 to Baños.

Around Cuenca

sulphur baths, Inca remains, lakes and hiking

Baños

There are sulphur baths at Baños, with a domed, blue church in a delightful landscape, 5 km southwest of Cuenca. These are the hottest commercial baths in Ecuador, entry US$3-10. Above **Hostería Durán** (see Where to stay) are four separate complexes of warm baths with spa and lodging, **Agapantos** (www.agapantos.com, T07-289 2493), **Rodas** (www.hosteriarodas.com), **Durán** (www.hosteriaduran.com) and **Piedra de Agua** (www.piedradeagua.com.ec). The latter two are better maintained and more exclusive.

Ingapirca *Colour map 1, B3.*
Open 0800-1800, US$6, including museum and tour in Spanish; bags can be stored, small café.

Ecuador's most important Inca ruin, at 3160 m, lies 8.5 km east of the colonial town of **Cañar** (*hostales* in **$** range). Access is from Cañar or **El Tambo**. The Inca Huayna Capac took over the site from the conquered Cañaris when his empire expanded north into Ecuador in the third quarter of the 15th century. Ingapirca was strategically placed on the Capac Ñan, the Great Inca Road that ran from Cuzco to Quito, see Inca Trail, below. The site shows typical imperial Cuzco-style architecture, such as tightly fitting stonework and trapezoidal doorways. The central structure may have been a solar observatory. Nearby is a throne cut into the rock, the **Sillón del Inca** (Inca's Chair) and the **Ingachugana**, a large rock with carved channels. A 10-minute walk away from the site is the **Cara del Inca**, or 'face of the Inca', an immense natural formation in the rock looking over the landscape. On Friday there is an interesting indigenous market at Ingapirca village.

A tourist *autoferro* (bus on rails) runs from El Tambo 7 km to the small Cañari-Inca archaeological site of **Baños del Inca** or **Coyoctor** ① *site open daily 0800-1700, US$1; 5 daily departures Wed-Sun, US$8, includes entry to El Tambo museum and Coyoctor site, excursion lasts 2 hrs*, a massive rock outcrop carved to form baths, showers, water channels and seats overlooking a small amphitheatre. There is an interpretation centre with information about the site, a hall with displays about regional fiestas and an audiovisual room with tourist information about all of Ecuador.

Inca Trail to Ingapirca

The three-day hike to Ingapirca starts at **Achupallas** (lively Saturday market, one hostel), 25 km from Alausí (see page 583). The walk is covered by three 1:50,000 *IGM* sheets, Alausí, Juncal and Cañar. The Juncal sheet is most important, the name Ingapirca does not appear on the latter, you may have to ask directions near the end. Also take a compass and GPS. Good camping equipment is essential. Take all food and drink with you as there is nothing along the way. A shop in Achupallas sells basic foodstuffs. There are persistent beggars the length of the hike, especially children. Tour operators in Riobamba offer this trek for about US$360 per person (two passengers, less for a larger group), three days, with everything included; tours from Cuenca cost about US$520 per person (group of two).

East of Cuenca

Northeast of Cuenca, on the paved road to Méndez in the Oriente, is **Paute**, with a pleasant park and modern church. South of Paute, **Gualaceo** is a rapidly expanding modern town set in beautiful landscape, with a charming plaza and Sunday market. The iTur ① *at the Municipio, Gran Colombia y 3 de Noviembre, Parque Central, T07-225 5131, Mon-Fri 0800-1300, 1400-1700*, is very helpful, English spoken. A scenic road goes from Gualaceo to Limón in Oriente. Many of Ecuador's 4000 species of orchids can be seen at **Ecuagénera** ① *Km 2 on the road to Cuenca, T07-225 5237, www.ecuagenera.com, Mon-Fri 0730-1600, Sat0730-1700, Sun 0900-1700, US$5 (US$3 pp for groups of 3 or more)*.

South of Gualaceo is **Chordeleg**, a touristy village famous for its crafts in wood, silver and gold filigree, pottery and panama hats. At the **Museo Municipal** ① *C 23 de Enero, Mon-Fri 0800-1300, 1400-1700, Sat-Sun 1000-1600*, is an exhibition hall with fascinating local textiles, ceramics and straw work, some of which are on sale at reasonable prices. It's a good uphill walk from Gualaceo to Chordeleg, and a pleasant hour downhill in the other direction. South of Gualaceo, 83 km from Cuenca, **Sígsig**, an authentic highland town where women can be seen weaving hats 'on the move'. It has a Sunday market, two *residenciales* and an archaeology museum. A scenic road goes from Sígsig to Gualaquiza in Oriente, paved as far a Chigüinda, two-thirds of the way.

Parque Nacional Cajas

The park office is at Laguna Sorocucho, T07-237 0127, Mon-Fri 0800-1600. Entry free, overnight stay US$4 per night (see Where to stay, below).

Northwest of Cuenca, Cajas is a 29,000-ha national park with over 230 lakes. The park is being diligently conserved by municipal authorities both for its environmental importance and because it is the water supply for Cuenca. The *páramo* vegetation, such as chuquiragua and lupin, is beautiful and the wildlife interesting. Cajas is very rich in birdlife; 125 species have been identified, including the condor and many varieties of hummingbird (the violet-tailed metaltail is endemic to this area). On the lakes are Andean gulls, speckled teal and yellow-billed pintails. On a clear morning the views are superb, even to Chimborazo, some 300 km away.

There are two access roads. The paved road from Cuenca to Guayaquil via Molleturo goes through the northern section and is the main route for Laguna Toreadora, the visitors' centre and Laguna Llaviuco. Skirting the southern edge of the park is a gravel secondary road, which goes from Cuenca via San Joaquín to the Soldados entrance and the community of Angas beyond. (See Transport, page 604.) There is nowhere to stay after the *refugio* at Laguna Toreadora (see Where to stay, below) until you reach the lowlands between Naranjal and La Troncal.

The park offers ideal but strenuous walking, at 3150-4450 m altitude, and the climate is cold and wet. There have been deaths from exposure. The best time to visit is from August to January, when you may expect clear days, strong winds, night-time temperatures to -8°C and occasional mist. From February to July temperatures are higher but there is much more fog, rain and snow. Arrive in the early morning if possible since it can get very cloudy, wet and cool after about 1300. It is best to get the *IGM* maps in Quito (Chaucha, Cuenca, San Felipe de Molleturo, and Chiquintad 1:50,000) and take a compass and GPS. It is easy to get lost.

Listings Around Cuenca

Where to stay

Baños
There are also a couple of cheap *residenciales* in town.

$$$ Caballo Campana
Vía Misicata-Baños Km 4, on an alternative road from Cuenca to Baños (2 km from Baños, taxi US$5 from the centre of Cuenca), T07-412 8769, www.caballocampana.com.
Nicely rebuilt colonial hacienda house in 28 has with gardens and forest, heated rooms, suites and cabins, includes buffet breakfast, Ecuadorean and international cuisine, horse riding and lessons, sports fields, discounts for longer stays.

$$$ Hostería Durán
Km 8 Vía Baños, T07-289 2485, www.hosteriaduran.com.
Includes buffet breakfast, restaurant, parking, has well-maintained, very clean pools (US$3-7 for non-residents), gym, steam bath, transport from Cuenca, camping.

Ingapirca
There are a couple of simple places in the village. Also good economical meals at **Intimikuna**, at the entrance to the archaeological site.

$$$ Posada Ingapirca
500 m uphill from ruins, T07-221 7116, for reservations T07-283 0064 (Cuenca), www.grupo-santaana.net.
Converted hacienda, comfortable rooms, heating, includes typical breakfast, excellent but pricey restaurant and bar with fireplace, good service, great views.

$$-$ Cabañas del Castillo
Opposite the ruins, T09-9998 3650, cab.castillo@hotmail.com.
3 simple cabins, heating, restaurant with fireplace.

El Tambo
This is the nearest town to Ingapirca on the Panamerican Highway.

$ Chasky Wasy
Montenegro next to Banco del Austro, 1 block from the park, T09-9883 0013.

Nice hostel with ample rooms, no breakfast, parking nearby.

$ Sunshine
Panamericana y Ramón Borrero, at north end of town, T07-223 3394.
Simple, family-run, not always staffed, private or shared bath, restaurant nearby, traffic noise.

Inca Trail to Ingapirca

$ Ingañán
Achupallas, T03-293 0663.
Basic, with bath, hot water, meals on request, camping.

East of Cuenca
Paute

$$$$ Hostería Uzhupud
Km 32 Vía a Paute, T07-370 0860, www.uzhupud.com.
Set in the beautiful Paute valley 10 km from town, deluxe, relaxing, rooms at the back best views, swimming pools and sauna (US$15 for non-residents), sports fields, horse riding, gardens, lots of orchids. Recommended.

$ Cutilcay
Abdón Calderón, by the river, T07-225 0133.
Older basic hostel, private or shared bath, no breakfast.

Gualaceo

$$ Peñón de Cuzay
Sector Bullcay El Carmen on the main road to Cuenca, T07-217 1515.
In one of the weaving communities, spa and pool, no breakfast. Fills on weekends, book ahead.

$ Hostal El Jardín
On the corner next to bus terminal.
Very clean ample rooms with private or shared bath, no breakfast, a simple decent place.

Parque Nacional Cajas
There is a *refugio* at **Laguna Toreadora** (US$4 pp, reserve ahead at T07-283 1900), cold (take sleeping bag), cooking facilities, and camping at **Laguna Llaviuco**. Other shelters in the park are primitive.

$$$$-$$$ Hostería Dos Chorreras
Km 21 Vía al Cajas, sector Sayausí, T07-404 3108, www.hosteriadoschorreras.com.
Hacienda-style inn outside the park. Heating, restaurant serves excellent fresh trout, buffet breakfast, reservations advised, horse rentals with advanced notice.

Transport

Ingapirca
Bus Direct buses **Cuenca** to Ingapirca with **Transportes Cañar** Mon-Fri at 0900 and 1220, Sat-Sun at 0900, returning 1300 and 1545, US$3.50, 2 hrs. Buses run from Cuenca to Cañar (US$2.15) and El Tambo (US$2.50) every 15 mins. From **Cañar**, corner of 24 de Mayo and Borrero, local buses leave every 15 mins for Ingapirca, 0600-1800, US$0.75, 30 mins; last bus returns at 1700. The same buses from Cañar go through **El Tambo**, US$0.75, 20 mins. If coming from the north, transfer in El Tambo. Pick-up taxi from Cañar US$10, from El Tambo US$6.25.

Inca Trail to Ingapirca
From **Alausí to Achupallas**, small buses and pickups leave as they fill between 1100 and 1600, US$1.50, 1 hr. Alternatively, take any bus along the Panamericana to **La Moya**, south of Alausí, at the turn-off for Achupallas, and a shared pick-up from there (best on Thu and Sun), US$0.50. To hire a pick-up from Alausí costs US$12-15, from La Moya US$10.

East of Cuenca
Bus From Terminal Terrestre in Cuenca: to **Paute**, every 15 mins, US$1.50, 1 hr; to **Gualaceo**, every 15 mins, US$1, 50 mins; to **Chordeleg**: every 15 mins from Gualaceo, US$0.35; 15 mins or direct bus from Cuenca,

US$1.50, 1 hr; to **Sigsig**, every 30 mins via Gualaceo, US$2.15, 1½ hrs.

Parque Nacional Cajas
Bus From Cuenca's Terminal Terrestre take any **Guayaquil** bus that goes via Molleturo (not Zhud), US$2, 30 mins to turn-off for Llaviuco, 45 mins to Toreadora. **Coop**

Occidental to Molleturo, 8 a day from the Terminal Sur/Feria Libre, this is a slower bus and may wait to fill up. For the Soldados entrance, catch a bus from Puente del Vado in Cuenca, daily at 0600, US$2.15, 1½ hrs; the return bus passes the Soldados gate at about 1600.

Cuenca to the Peruvian border
impressive scenery on the way to and beyond an Andean indigenous community

From Cuenca various routes go to the Peruvian border, fanning out from the pleasant city of Loja, due south of which is Vilcabamba, famous for its invigorating climate and lovely countryside.

South to Loja
The Pan-American Highway divides about 20 km south of Cuenca. One branch runs south to Loja, the other heads southwest through Girón, the Yunguilla valley (with a small bird reserve, see www.fjocotoco.org) and Santa Isabel (several hotels with pools and spas; cloudforest and waterfalls). The last stretch through sugar cane fields leads to Pasaje and Machala. The scenic road between Cuenca and Loja undulates between high, cold *páramo* passes and deep desert-like canyons.

Saraguro *Colour map 1, C3.*
On the road to Loja is this old town, where the local people, the most southerly indigenous Andean group in Ecuador, dress all in black. The men are notable for their black shorts and the women for their pleated black skirts, necklaces of coloured beads and silver *topos*, ornate pins fastening their shawls. The town has a picturesque Sunday market and interesting Mass, Easter and Christmas celebrations. Traditional festivities are held during solstices and equinoxes in surrounding communities, Inti Raymi (19-21 June) being the most important. Necklaces and other crafts are sold near the church. Saraguro has a community tourism programme with tours and homestay opportunities with indigenous families (US$33 pp full board). Contact **Fundación Kawsay** ⓘ *18 de Noviembre y Av Loja, T07-220 0331, www.turismosaraguro.com*, or the **Oficina Municipal de Turismo** ⓘ *C 10 de Marzo y Av Loja, T07-220 0100 ext 18, Mon-Fri 0800-1200, 1400-1800.* See also www.saraguro.org. **Bosque Washapampa** ⓘ *entry US$3*, 6 km south has good birdwatching.

Loja *Colour map 1, C3.*
This friendly, pleasant highland city, encircled by hills, is an important transport hub, of particular interest to travellers on route to and from Peru. If spending any time in the area then the small town of Vilcabamba, 40 km to the south (see below), is a more interesting place to hang out but Loja makes a practical overnight stop with all facilities and services.

Housed in a beautifully restored house on the main park is the **Centro Cultural Loja** home of the **Museo de la Cultura Lojana** ⓘ *10 de Agosto 13-30 y Bolívar, T07-257 0001, Mon-Fri 0830-1700, Sat-Sun 1000-1600, free*, with well-displayed archaeology, ethnography, art, and history halls and temporary exhibits. **Parque San Sebastián** at Bolívar y Mercadillo and the adjoining Calle Lourdes preserve the flavour of old Loja and are worth visiting. Loja is famed for its musicians and has a symphony orchestra. Cultural evenings with music and dance are held at Plaza San Sebastián, on Thursday 2000-2200. The **Museo de Música** ⓘ *Valdivieso 09-42 y Rocafuerte, T07-256 1342. Mon-Fri 0830-1300, 1500-1800, free*, honours 10 Lojano composers.

Parque Universitario Francisco Vivar Castro (Parque La Argelia) ⓘ *on the road south to Vilcabamba, Tue-Sun 0800-1700, US$1, city bus marked 'Capulí-Dos Puentes' to the park or 'Argelia' to the Universidad Nacional and walk from there*, has trails through the forest to the *páramo*. Across the road is the **Jardín Botánico Reynaldo Espinosa** ⓘ *Mon-Fri 0730-1230, 1500-1800, Sat-Sun 1300-1800, US$1*, which is nicely laid out. On a ridge to the west of the city is the largest wind farm in Ecuador.

Parque Nacional Podocarpus
Headquarters at Cajanuma entrance, T07-302 4862. Limited information from Ministerio del Ambiente in Loja, Sucre 04-55 y Quito, T07-257 9595, parquepodocarpus@gmail.com, Mon-Fri 0800-1700. In Zamora at Sevilla de Oro y Orellana, T07-260 6606. Their general map of the park is not adequate for navigation, buy topographic maps in Quito.

Podocarpus (950 m to 3700 m) is one of the most diverse protected areas in the world. It is particularly rich in birdlife, including many rarities, and includes one of the last major habitats for the spectacled bear. The park protects stands of *romerillo* or podocarpus, a native, slow-growing conifer. Podocarpus is divided into two areas, an upper premontane section with many lakes, spectacular walking country, lush cloudforest and excellent birdwatching; and a lower subtropical section, with remote areas of virgin rainforest and unmatched quantities of flora and fauna. Both zones are wet (wellies are recommended) but there may be periods of dry weather October to January. The upper section is also cold, so warm clothing and waterproofs are indispensable year-round.

Entrances to the upper section: at Cajanuma, 8 km south of Loja on the Vilcabamba road, from the turn-off it is a further 8 km uphill to the guard station; and at San Francisco, 23 km from Loja along the road to Zamora. Entrances to the lower section: Bombuscaro is 6 km from Zamora, the visitor's centre is a 30-minute walk from the car park. **Cajanuma** is the trailhead for the demanding eight-hour hike to **Lagunas del Compadre**, a series of beautiful lakes set amid rock cliffs, camping is possible there (no services). Another trail from Cajanuma leads in one hour to a lookout with views over Loja. At **San Francisco**, the *guardianía* (ranger's station) operated by Fundación Arcoiris, offers nice accommodation (see below). This section of the park is a transition cloudforest at around 2200 m, very rich in birdlife. This is the best place to see podocarpus trees: a trail (four hours return) goes from the shelter to the trees. The **Bombuscaro** lowland section, also very rich in birdlife, has several trails leading to lovely swimming holes on the Bombuscaro River and waterfalls; Cascada La Poderosa is particularly nice.

Conservation groups working in and around the park include: **Arcoiris** ⓘ *Macará 11-25 y Azuay, T07-2561830, www.arcoiris.org.ec*, and **Naturaleza y Cultura Internacional** ⓘ *Av Pío Jaramillo y Venezuela, T07-257 3691, www.natureandculture.org*.

Routes to the Peruvian border
Of all the crossings from Ecuador to Peru, by far the most efficient and relaxed is the scenic route from Loja to Piura via Macará (see below). Other routes are from Vilcabamba to La Balsa (see page 611), Huaquillas on the coast (page 627) and along the Río Napo in the Oriente (see page 655). There are smaller border crossings at Lalamor/Zapotillo, west of Macará, and Jimbura, southeast of Macará. The latter has immigration but no customs service. If arriving with a vehicle, cross at one of the other border posts.

Leaving Loja on the main paved highway going west, the airport at **La Toma** (1200 m) is reached after 35 km. La Toma is also called **Catamayo**, where there is lodging. At Catamayo, where you can catch the Loja-Macará-Piura bus, the Pan-American Highway divides: one branch runs west, the other south.

On the western road, at San Pedro de La Bendita, a road climbs to the much-venerated pilgrimage site of **El Cisne**, dominated by its large incongruous French-style Gothic church. Vendors and beggars fill the town and await visitors at festivals (see page 608). Continuing on the western route, **Catacocha** is spectacularly placed on a hilltop. Visit the Shiriculapo rock for the views. There are pre-Inca ruins around the town; small archaeological **Museo Hermano Joaquín Liebana** ⓘ *T07-268 3201, 0800-1200, 1400-1800*. From Catacocha, the road runs south to the border at Macará.

Another route south from Catamayo to Macará is via **Gonzanamá**, a small city (basic *hostales*), famed for the weaving of beautiful *alforjas* (multi-purpose saddlebags), and **Cariamanga**, a regional centre (various hotels and services). From here the road twists along a ridge westwards to **Colaisaca**, before descending steeply through forests to **Utuana** with a nature reserve (www.fjocotoco.org) and **Sozoranga** (one hotel), then down to the rice paddies of **Macará**, on the border. There is a choice of accommodation here and good road connections to Piura in Peru.

Macará–La Tina The border is at the international bridge over the Río Macará, 2.5 km from town, taxi US$1.50. There are plans to build a border complex, in the meantime, immigration, customs and other services are housed in temporary quarters. The border is open 24 hours. Formalities are straightforward, it is a much easier crossing than at Huaquillas. In Macará, at the park where taxis leave for the border, there are money changers dealing in soles, but no changers at the bridge. On the Peruvian side, minivans and cars run to Sullana (US$5 pp) but it is much safer to take a bus from Loja or Macará directly to Piura. **Peruvian consulate in Loja** ⓘ *Zoilo Rodríguez 03-05, T07-258 7330, Mon-Fri 0900-1300, 1500-1700*.

Listings Cuenca to the Peruvian border

Tourist information

iTur
José Antonio Eguiguren y Bolívar, Parque Central, Loja, T07-257 0407 ext 202. Mon-Fri 0800-1300, 1500-1800, Sat 0800-1600.
Local information and map, monthly cultural agenda, English spoken, helpful.

Ministerio de Turismo
Bernardo Valdivieso y 10 de Agosto, Ed Colibrí, p2, Loja, T07-257 2964. Mon-Fri 0815-1700.
Regional information for Loja, Zamora and El Oro.

Where to stay

Saraguro

$$ Achik Huasi
On a hillside above town, T07-220 0058, or through Fundación Kawsay, T07-220 0331.
Community-run *hostería* in a nice setting, private bath, hot water, parking, views, tours, taxi to centre US$1.

$ Saraguro
Loja 03-2 y A Castro, T07-220 0286.
Private or shared bath, hot water, no breakfast, nice courtyard, family-run, basic, good value.

Loja

International chain hotels include **Howard Johnson** (www.hojo.com)

$$$$ Grand Victoria

B Valdivieso 06-50 y Eguiguren, ½ a block from the Parque Central, T07-258 3500, www.grandvictoriabh.com.
Rebuilt early 20th-century home with 2 patios, comfortable modern rooms and suites, restaurant, small pool, spa, gym, business centre, frigobar, safety box, parking, long-stay discounts.

$$ Bombuscaro

10 de Agosto y Av Universitaria, T07-257 7021, www.bombuscaro.com.ec.
Comfortable rooms and suites, includes buffet breakfast, cafeteria, parking, good service.

$$ Libertador

Colón 14-30 y Bolívar, T07-256 0779, www.hotellibertador.com.ec.
A very good hotel in the centre of town, comfortable rooms and suites, includes buffet breakfast, good restaurant, indoor pool (open to non-guests Sat-Sun 1000-1700, US$5), spa, parking.

$ Londres

Sucre 07-51 y 10 de Agosto, T07-256 1936.
Economical hostel in a well-maintained old house, shared bath, hot water, no breakfast, basic, clean.

$ Real Colón

Colón 15-54 entre 18 de Noviembre y Sucre, T07-257 7826.
Modern centrally located multi-storey hotel, parking, decent value for this price range.

$ Vinarós

Sucre 11-30 y Azuay, T07-258 4015, hostalvinaros@hotmail.com.
Pleasant hostel with simple rooms, private bath, electric shower, no breakfast, good value.

Parque Nacional Podocarpus

At **Cajanuma**, there are cabins with beds for US$4, bring warm sleeping bag, stove and food. At San Francisco, the *guardianía* (ranger's station), operated by **Fundación Arcoiris** offers rooms with shared bath, hot water and kitchen facilities, US$8 pp if you bring a sleeping bag, US$12 if they provide sheets. Ask to be let off at Arcoiris or you will be taken to Estación San Francisco, 10 km further east. At **Bombuscaro** there are cabins with beds US$4 and an area for camping (note that it rains frequently).

Routes to the Peruvian border
Catamayo

$$ MarcJohn's

Isidro Ayora y 24 de Mayo, at the main park, T07-267 7631, granhotelmarcjohns@hotmail.com.
Modern multi-storey hotel, rooms with fan or a/c, includes breakfast from 0700 or set dinner, restaurant, attentive service.

$$ Rosal del Sol

A short walk from the city on the main road west of town, T07-267 6517.
Ranch-style building, comfortable rooms with fan, restaurant not always open, small pool, parking, includes airport transfer, welcoming owner.

$ Reina del Cisne

Isidro Ayora at the park, T07-267 7414.
Simple adequate rooms, hot water, cheaper with cold water, fan, no breakfast, pool, gym, parking, good value.

Macará

$ Bekalus

Valdivieso y 10 de Agosto, T07-269 4043.
Simple hostel, a/c, cheaper with fan, cold water, no breakfast.

$ El Conquistador

Bolívar y Abdón Calderón, T07-269 4057.
Comfortable hotel, some rooms are dark, request one with balcony, includes simple breakfast Mon-Sat, electric shower, a/c or fan.

Restaurants

Saraguro

Several restaurants around the main plaza serve economical meals.

$$$ Shamuico
10 de Marzo, next to the touristinformation office, at the main park, T07-220 0509. Wed-Sun 1230-2100.
Gourmet European-Ecuadorean fusion cuisine, run by a Saraguro-born chef who trained in Spain. Live music some Fri and Sat.

$ Tupay
10 de Marzo y Vivar, at the main park. Sun-Fri 0700-2200.
Very good set meals, also breakfast.

Loja

$$$ Riscomar
Rocafuerte 09-00 y 24 de Mayo, T07-257 4965, www.riscomarloja.com. Tue-Sat 1000-1600, 1900-2200, Sun 1000-1600.
Extensive choice of good seafood and meat dishes.

$$ Lecka
24 de Mayo 10-51 y Riofío, T07-256 3878. Mon-Fri 1700-2230.
Small quaint restaurant serving German specialities, very good food, friendly German-Ecuadorean owners. Recommended.

$$ Mama Lola
Av Salvador Bustamante Celi y Santa Rosa, T07-2614381. Mon-Sat 1200-2200, Sun 1200-1600.
Popular place for typical *lojano* specialities such as *cecina* and *cuy*.

$$-$ Casa Sol
24 de Mayo 07-04 y José Antonio Eguiguren. Daily 0830-2330.
Small place serving breakfast, economical set lunches and regional dishes in the evening. Pleasant seating on balcony.

$$-$ Pizzería Forno di Fango
24 de Mayo y Azuay, T07-258 2905. Tue-Sun 1200-2230.
Excellent wood-oven pizza, salads and lasagne. Large portions, home delivery, good service and value.

$ Angelo's
18 de Noviembre y José Félix de Valdivieso, at Hotel Floy's. Mon-Sat 0700-1500, 1800-2100.
A choice of good quality set meals, also breakfast, pleasant atmosphere, quiet (no TV), friendly service.

Cafés

Biscuit & Co.
24 de Mayo y Rocafuerte. Mon-Sat 1100-2100.
Nice café with good sandwiches, snacks, sweets and coffee. French-Ecuadorean run.

Jugo Natural
José A Eguiguren14-20 y Bolivar, near the main park. Mon-Fri 0700-1900, Sat 0800-1800, Sun 0800-1400.
Small popular café with a choice of fresh fruit juices, snacks (try their *empanadas*), coffee, salads, vegetarian soups and lunches, cake, ice-cream.

Festivals

Loja
Aug-Sep Fiesta de la Virgen del Cisne, thousands of faithful accompany the statue of the Virgin in a 3-day 74-km pilgrimage from El Cisne to Loja cathedral, beginning 16 Aug. The image remains in Loja until 1 Nov when the return pilgrimage starts. Town is crowded Aug-Sep.

What to do

Loja
Birdsexplore, *Lourdes 14-80 y Sucre, T07-258 2434, T09-8515 2239, www.exploraves.com.* Specializes in birdwatching tours throughout Ecuador, overnight trips to different types of forest, about US$150 pp per day. Pablo

Andrade is a knowledgeable English-speaking guide.

Saraguro
Bus To **Cuenca** US$5.40, 2½ hrs. To **Loja**, US$2.10, 1½ hrs. Check if your bus leaves from the plaza or the Panamericana.

Loja
Air The airport is at La Toma (Catamayo), 35 km west (see Routes to the Peruvian border, page 605): taxi from airport to Catamayo town US$2, to Loja shared taxi US$5 pp, to hire US$20 (cheaper from Loja) eg with Jaime González, T07-256 3714 or Paul Izquierdo, T07-256 3973; to Vilcabamba, US$40. There are 1-2 daily flights to **Quito** and **Guayaquil** with **TAME** (24 de Mayo y E Ortega, T07-257 0248).

Bus All buses leave from the Terminal Terrestre at Av Gran Colombia e Isidro Ayora, at the north of town, 10 mins by city bus from the centre; left luggage; US$0.10 terminal tax. Taxi from centre, US$1.50. To **Cuenca**, almost every hour (www.viajerosinternacional.com), 4 hrs, US$7.50. Van service with **Elite Tours**, 18 de Noviembre 01-13, near Puerta de la Ciudad, T07-256 0731 and **Faisatur**, 18 de Noviembre y Av Universitaria, T07-258 5299, US$12, 3 hrs; taxi US$60. **Machala**, 10 a day, 5-6 hrs, US$7 (3 routes, all scenic: via Piñas, for **Zaruma**, partly unpaved and rough; via Balsas, paved; and via Alamor, for **Puyango petrified forest**). **Quito**, Terminal Quitumbe, regular US$17; **Transportes Loja** *semi-cama* US$21, 12 hrs. **Guayaquil**, US$12 regular US$15 *semi-cama*, 8 hrs. To **Huaquillas**,

US$7.50, 6 hrs direct. To **Zumba** (for Peru, paved to Palanda), 10 daily including **Sur Oriente** at 0500 to make connections to Peru the same day and **Cariamanga** at 0900, US$10, 7 hrs; **Nambija** at 2400 direct to the border at La Balsa (only in the dry season), US$12.50, 8 hrs. To **Catamayo** (for airport) every 15 mins 0630-1900, US$1.30, 1 hr. To **Macará**, see below. To **Piura (Peru)**, Loja **Internacional**, via Macará, at 0700 and 2300 daily, US$14, 8-9 hrs including border formalities. Also **Unión Cariamanga** at 2400. To **Zamora**, frequent service, 1½-2 hrs, US$3.

Parque Nacional Podocarpus
For **Cajanuma**, take a Vilcabamba bound bus, get off at the turn-off, US$1, it is a pretty 8-km walk from there. Direct transport by taxi to Cajanuma, about US$10 (may not be feasible in the rainy season) or with a tour from Loja. You can arrange a pickup later from the guard station. Pickup from Vilcabamba, US$20. To the **San Francisco section**, take any bus between Loja and Zamora, make sure you alight by the Arcoiris *guardanía* and not at Estación Científica San Francisco which is 10 km east. To the **lower section**: **Bombuscaro** is 6 km from Zamora, take a taxi US$6 to the entrance, then walk 1 km to the visitor's centre.

Routes to the Peruvian border
Macará
Bus **Transportes Loja** and **Cariamanga** have frequent buses, daily from Macará to **Loja**; 5-6 hrs, US$7.50. Direct Loja-**Piura** buses can also be boarded in Macará, US$5 to Piura, 3 hrs.**Transportes Loja** also has service to **Quito**, US$19, 15 hrs, and **Guayaquil**, US$14, 8 hrs.

a beautiful, tranquil area popular with tourists and expats

★Vilcabamba *Colour map 1, C3.*

Once an isolated village, Vilcabamba (population around 5000) is today a colourful and eclectic cross between a resort town and a thriving expatriate community. It is popular with travellers and a good place to stop on route between Ecuador and Peru. The whole area is beautiful, with an agreeable climate. There are many nice places to stay and good restaurants. The area offers many great day-walks and longer treks, as well as ample opportunities for horse riding and cycling. A number of lovely private nature reserves are situated east of Vilcabamba, towards Parque Nacional Podocarpus. Trekkers can continue on foot through orchid-clad cloudforests to the high *páramos* of Podocarpus. Artisans from all over Latin America sell their crafts in front of the school on weekends and there is an organic produce market by the bus terminal on Saturday morning, in addition to the regular Sunday market. **Craig's Book Exchange** ⓘ *in Yamburara, 1 km east of town, follow*

Vilcabamba

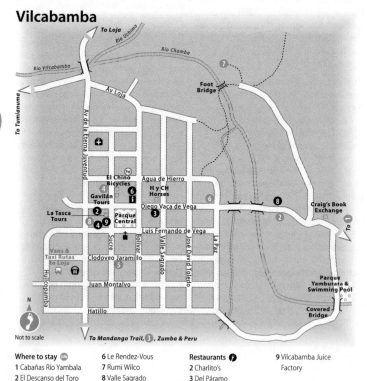

Not to scale

Where to stay 🛏
1 Cabañas Río Yambala
2 El Descanso del Toro
3 Izhcayluma
4 Jardín Escondido
5 Las Margaritas
6 Le Rendez-Vous
7 Rumi Wilco
8 Valle Sagrado

Restaurants 🍴
2 Charlito's
3 Del Páramo
4 La Baguette
6 Natural Yogurt
8 Shanta's
9 Vilcabamba Juice Factory

Diego Vaca de Vega, has 2500 books in 12 languages and a small art gallery and pottery studio.

Rumi Wilco ⓘ *10-min walk northeast of town, take C Agua de Hierro towards C La Paz and turn left, follow signs, US$2 valid for three visits*, is 40-ha private nature reserve with several signed trails.

Tip...
There are several ATMs by the iTur office and the church. Not all cards are accepted, however.

Many of the trees and shrubs are labelled with their scientific and common names. There are great views of town from the higher trails, and it is a very good place to go for a walk. Over 100 species of birds have been identified here. Volunteers are welcome. **Sacred Sueños** ⓘ *1½-hr walk in the hills above town, T09-8931 3698, www.sacredsuenos.wordpress. com*, is a grassroots permaculture community which accepts volunteers, two weeks' minimum commitment.

Climbing **Mandango**, 'the sleeping woman' mountain is a scenic half-day walk. The signed access is along the highway, 250 m south of the bus terminal. Be careful on the higher sections when it is windy and enquire beforehand about public safety. South of Vilcabamba, 45 km on the road to Zumba is the 3500 ha bird and orchid rich **Reserva Tapichalaca** ⓘ *T07-250 5212, www.fjocotoco.org, entry US$15*, with a lodge ($$$).

Border with Peru: La Balsa

Many daily buses run on the scenic road from Loja via Vilcabamba to **Zumba** (see Loja, Transport, page 609), 112 km south of Vilcabamba. It is a 1½-hour rough ride by *ranchera* (open-sided bus) from Zumba to the border at La Balsa; there is a control on the way, keep your passport to hand. La Balsa is just a few houses on either side of the international bridge over the Río Canchis; there are simple eateries, shops, money changers (no banks here or in Zumba), and one very basic hotel on the Peruvian side. It is a relaxed border, Ecuadorean customs and immigration are officially open 24 hours. The Peruvian border post is open 0800-1300, 1500-2000; entering Peru, visit immigration and the PNP office (see page 606 under Macará–La Tina for Peru's consulate in Loja). On the Peruvian side mototaxis run to **Namballe**, 15 minutes away, and cars run to Namballe and **San Ignacio** when full, two hours, from where there is transport to **Jaén**. This is a faster, more direct route between Vilcabamba and **Chachapoyas** (see the Chacapoyas to Ecuador section, page 160) than going via the coast. Parts are rough but it can be done in two days; best take the bus passing Vilcabamba around 0600.

Listings Vilcabamba to Peru *map page 610.*

Tourist information

iTur
Diego Vaca de Vega y Bolívar, on the corner of the main plaza, Vilcabamba, T07-264 0090. Daily 0800-1300, 1400-1800.
Has various pamphlets, helpful, Spanish only.

Where to stay

Vilcabamba

$$ Cabañas Río Yambala
Yamburara Alto, 4 km east of town (taxi US$4), T09-9106 2762, www.vilcabamba-hotel.com.
Cabins with cooking facilities in a beautiful tranquil setting on the shores of the Río Yambala, private or shared bath, hot water, sauna, weekly and monthly rates available. No shops or restaurants nearby, bring food.

Tours to Las Palmas private nature reserve. Family-run, English spoken.

$$-$ Izhcayluma
2 km south on road to Zumba, T07-302 5162, www.izhcayluma.com.
Popular inn with comfortable rooms and cabins with terrace and hammocks. Very good buffet breakfast available, excellent restaurant with wonderful views, private or shared bath, also dorm US$9.50 pp, very nice grounds, pool, massage centre, yoga centre and lessons, lively bar, billiards, ping-pong, bird observation platform, walking trails, map and route descriptions, English and German spoken, helpful. Highly recommended.

$$-$ Las Margaritas
Sucre y Clodoveo Jaramillo, T07-264 0051.
Small family-run hotel with comfortable well-furnished rooms, includes good breakfast, intermittent solar-heated water, parking, pool, garden.

$$-$ Le Rendez-Vous
Diego Vaca de Vega 06-43 y La Paz, T09-9219 1180, www.rendezvousecuador.com.
Very comfortable rooms with terrace and hammocks around a lovely garden. Private or shared bath, pleasant atmosphere, attentive service, French and English spoken. Recommended.

$$-$ Rumi Wilco
10-min walk northeast of town, take C Agua de Hierro towards C La Paz and turn left, follow the signs from there, www.rumiwilco.com.
Cabins in the Rumi Wilco reserve. Lovely setting on the shores of the river, very tranquil, private or shared bath, laundry facilities, fully furnished kitchens, discounts for long stays and volunteers, camping US$4 pp, friendly Argentine owners, English spoken. Recommended.

$ Hostal Taranza
1 km from the main park on the way to Yamburara, T07-302 5144, erenatomauricio@gmail.com.
Brightly painted hostel, economical rooms, private or shared bath, cooking facilities, terrace, hammocks, pool, parking.

$ Jardín Escondido
Sucre y Diego Vaca de Vega, T07-264 0281.
Various types of rooms around a lovely patio and garden, most with private bath, breakfast available, restaurant (Mon-Sat 0800-2200) has set lunches and international and Mexican food, live music some Sat nights, small pool, organizes excursions. English and Italian spoken. New management in 2016.

$ Valle Sagrado
Av de la Eterna Juventud y Luis Fernando de Vega, T07-264 0142, miriantaday@outlook.com.
Simple economical rooms around a large garden, private or shared bath, electric shower, laundry and cooking facilities, breakfast extra, restaurant (open 0800-2200), parking, family-run.

Border with Peru

$$-$ Emperador
Colón y Orellana, Zumba, T07-230 8063.
Rooms with private bath, a/c, no breakfast.

$ San Luis
12 de Febrero y Brasil, Zumba, T07-230 8017.
Rooms on top floor are nicer, private or shared bath, no breakfast, attentive service.

Restaurants

Vilcabamba
Around the Parque Central are many café/bar/restaurants with pleasant sidewalk seating; too many to list, see map, page 610.

$$$-$$ The Lion's Bear
Diego Vaca de Vega y Valle Sagrado,
T09-5929 4323. Thu-Mon 1200-2100.
Fine European cuisine, especially French,
weekly menu according to seasonal
ingredients, live music Fri-Mon. British/
French-run.

$$ Izhcayluma
At the hotel of the same name, see above.
Daily 0800-2000.
Excellent international food, German
specialities and several vegetarian options,
served in a lovely open-air dining room
with gorgeous views and attentive service.
Highly recommended.

$$ Shanta's
Off Av Loja, 700 m north of the main park,
T09-5949 1012. Wed-Sat 1300-2100, Sun
1300-2000.
Excellent pizza, trout, filet mignon and
cuy (with advance notice). Also pasta and
vegetarian options, good fruit juices and
drinks. Nicely decorated rustic setting,
pleasant atmosphere and attentive service.
Recommended.

$ Charlito's
Diego Vaca de Vega y Sucre. Tue-Sun 1130-2100.
Salads, pasta, pizza, soup, sandwiches
with tasty home-made wholemeal bread,
microbrews and other drinks.

$ Natural Yogurt
Bolívar y Diego Vaca de Vega.
Mon Sat 0800-2100.
Very popular economical restaurant,
breakfast, home-made yoghurt, a variety of
savoury and sweet crêpes, pasta, Mexican
dishes, hamburgers, vegetarian options.

$ Urku Warmi
Sucre 10-30 y Diego Vaca de Vega.
Tue-Sun 1200-1930.
Vegetarian food, also desserts.

$ Vilcabamba Juice Factory
Sucre y Luis Fernando de Vega, Parque
Central. Tue-Sat 0800-1600, Sun 0800-1400.

Healthy juices, soups and salads, vegan food
available, waffles on weekends, run by a
naturopath, sells natural food products,
very popular with expats.

La Baguette
Diego Vaca de Vega y Av de la Eterna
Juventud. Wed-Sat 0700-1700, Sun 0700-1400.
French bakery and café, great bread and
pastries, crêpes, selection of breakfasts.
Recommended.

What to do

Vilcabamba
See Where to stay, above, for more options.

Cycling
El Chino, *Sucre y Diego Vaca de Vega, T09-*
8187 6347, chinobike@gmail.com. Mountain
bike tours (US$25-35), rentals (US$2-3 per
hr, US$10-15 per day) and repairs. Also see
La Tasca Tours, below.

Horse riding
Prices pp for group of 2: 2 hrs US$20, half day
US$30, full day with snack US$45, overnight
trips US$70 per day all included.
Gavilán Tours, *Sucre y Diego Vaca de Vega,*
T07-264 0256 or 09-8133 2806 (Gavin Moore),
gavilanhorse@yahoo.com. Run by a group of
experienced horsemen.
H y CH, *Diego Vaca de Vega y Valle Sagrado,*
T09-9152 3118. Alvaro León, good horses
and saddles.
La Tasca Tours, *Sucre at the plaza, T09-8556*
1188, latascatours@yahoo.com. Horse and
bike tours with experienced guides, René
and Jaime León.
Vilcabamba Exploring, *Diego Vaca de Vega*
y Bolívar, T09-9020 8824. Julio Ocampo, horse
riding tours, also guided hike to waterfall.

> **Tip...**
> Try the local microbrew, **Sol del Venado**,
> which is served by many establishments.

Language courses

Spanish classes with **Marta Villacrés** (T09-9751 3311).

Massage

Beauty Care, *Diego Vaca de Vega y Valle Sagrado, T09-8122 3456. Daily 0800-1200, 1400-1800.* Karina Zumba, facials, waxing, Reiki, massage 1 hr US$20.

Shanta's, *see Restaurants, above, T09-8538 5710, by appointment only.* Lola Encalada, very good 1½-hr therapeutic massage US$31, also does waxing. Recommended.

Transport

Vilcabamba

Loja to Vilcabamba, a nice 1-hr bus ride; from Loja's Terminal Terrestre, **Vilcabambaturis** mini-buses, every 15-30 mins, 0545-2115, US$1.65, 1 hr; or *taxirutas* (shared taxis) from José María Peña y Venezuela, 0600-2000, US$2.25, 45 mins; taxi, US$20. To **Loja**, vans and shared taxis leave from the small terminal behind the market. For **Parque Nacional Podocarpus**, taxis charge US$20 each way, taking you right to the trailhead at Cajanuma. To **Cuenca** vans at 0800 from **Hostería Izhcayluma**, US$15, 5 hrs, Cuenca stop at Hostal La Cigale. To **Zumba** buses originating in Vilcabamba pass Vilcabamba about 1 hr after departure and stop along the highway in front of the market (1st around 0600, next 1000), US$8.25, 5-6 hrs. To Catamayo airport, taxi US$40, 1½ hrs. To **Quito** (Quitumbe) **Transportes Loja** (tickets sold for this and other routes at Movistar office, Av de la Eterna Juventud y Clodoveo Jaramillo) at 1900, with a stop in Loja, US$22.50, 13-14 hrs.

Border with Peru

Terminal Terrestre in Zumba, 1 km south of the centre. From Zumba to **La Balsa**, *rancheras* at 0800, 1430 and 1730, US$2.25, 1-1½ hrs. From La Balsa to Zumba at 1200, 1730 and 1900. Taxi Zumba-La Balsa, US$30. To **Loja**, see above. In Zumba, petrol is sold 0700-1700.

Guayaquil
& south to Peru

Guayaquil is hotter, faster and louder than the capital. It is Ecuador's largest city, the country's chief seaport and main commercial centre, some 56 km from the Río Guayas' outflow into the Gulf of Guayaquil. Industrial expansion continually fuels the city's growth. Founded in 1535 by Sebastián de Benalcázar, then again in 1537 by Francisco de Orellana, the city has always been an intense political rival to Quito. Guayaquileños are certainly more lively, colourful and open than their Quito counterparts. Since 2000, Guayaquil has cleaned-up and 'renewed' some of its most frequented downtown areas, it boasts modern airport and bus terminals, and the Metrovía transit system.

Thriving banana plantations and other agro-industry are the economic mainstay of the coastal area bordering the east flank of the Gulf of Guayaquil. The Guayas lowlands are subject to flooding, humidity is high and biting insects are fierce. Mangroves characterize the coast leading south to Huaquillas, the main coastal border crossing to Peru.

Best for
Birdlife ■ Hotels ■ Museums ■ Sightseeing

Essential Guayaquil

Finding your feet

José Joaquín de Olmedo international airport is 15 minutes north of the city centre by car. Not far from the airport is the **Terminal Terrestre** long distance bus station. Opposite this station is Terminal Río Daule, an important transfer station on the Metrovía rapid transit system.

A number of hotels are centrally located in the downtown core, along the west bank of the Río Guayas, where you can get around on foot. The city's suburbs sprawl to the north and south of the centre, with middle-class neighbourhoods and some very upscale areas in the north, where some elegant hotels and restaurants are located, and poorer working-class neighbourhoods and slums to the south. Road tunnels under Cerro Santa Ana link the northern suburbs to downtown.

Getting around

Metrovía is an integrated transport system of articulated buses running on exclusive lanes. The buses can be packed and so should be avoided if you are carrying a lot of belongings. The taxis are efficient, but although drivers should use the meter, they do not always do so. See also Transport, page 624.

Safety

The Malecón 2000, parts of Avenida 9 de Octubre, Las Peñas and Malecón del Estero Salado are heavily patrolled and reported safe. The rest of the city requires precautions. Do not go anywhere with valuables, for details see page 727. Parque Centenario is also patrolled, but the area around it requires caution. 'Express kidnappings' are of particular concern in Guayaquil; do not take a taxi outside the north end of the Malecón 2000 near the MAAC museum, walk south along the Malecón as far as the Hotel Ramada, where there is a taxi stand; whenever possible, call for a radio taxi.

When to go

From May to December the climate is dry with often overcast days and pleasantly cool nights, whereas the rainy season from January to April is oppressively hot and humid.

Guayaquil *Colour map 1, B2.*

a lively city with fine hotels and restaurants

A wide, tree-lined waterfront avenue, the Malecón Simón Bolívar runs alongside the Río Guayas from the Palacio de Cristal, past Plaza Olmedo, the Moorish clock tower, by the imposing Palacio Municipal and Gobernación and the old Yacht Club to Las Peñas.

Sights

The riverfront along this avenue is an attractive promenade, known as **Malecón 2000** ① *daily 0700-2400*, where visitors and locals can enjoy the fresh river breeze and take in the views. There are gardens, fountains, childrens' playgrounds, monuments, walkways and an electric vehicle for the disabled (daily 1000-2000, US$2). You can dine at upmarket restaurants, cafés and food courts. Towards the south end are souvenir shops, a shopping mall and the **Palacio de Cristal** (prefabricated by Eiffel 1905-1907), originally a market and now a gallery housing temporary exhibits.

At the north end of the Malecón is an **IMAX** large-screen cinema, and downstairs the **Museo Miniatura** ① *Tue-Sun 0900-2000, US$1.50*, with miniature historical exhibits.

Beyond is the **Centro Cultural Simón Bolívar**, better known as **MAAC, Museo Antropológico y de Arte Contemporaneo** ① *T04-230 9400, daily 0900-1630, free,* with excellent collections of ceramics and gold objects from coastal cultures and an extensive modern art collection.

North of the Malecón 2000 is the old district of **Las Peñas**, the last picturesque vestige of colonial Guayaquil with its brightly painted wooden houses and narrow, cobbled main street (Numa Pompilio Llona). It is an attractive place for a walk to **Cerro Santa Ana**, which offers great views of the city and the mighty Guayas. It has a bohemian feel, with bars and restaurants. A large open-air exhibition of paintings and sculpture is held here during the **Fiestas Julianas** (24-25 July). North of La Peñas is **Puerto Santa Ana**, with a luxury hotel, upmarket apartments, a promenade and three museums: to the romantic singer Julio Jaramillo, to beer in the old brewery, and to football.

By the pleasant, shady **Parque Bolívar** stands the **Cathedral** (Chimborazo y 10 de Agosto), in Gothic style, inaugurated in the 1950s. In the park are many iguanas and it is popularly referred to as Parque de las Iguanas. The nearby **Museo Municipal** ① *in the Biblioteca Municipal, Sucre y Chile, Tue-Sat 0900-1700, free, city tours on Sat, also free,* has

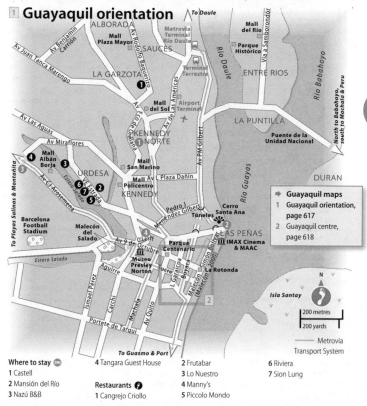

1 Guayaquil orientation

→ **Guayaquil maps**
1 Guayaquil orientation, page 617
2 Guayaquil centre, page 618

Metrovía Transport System

Where to stay
1 Castell
2 Mansión del Río
3 Nazú B&B
4 Tangara Guest House

Restaurants
1 Cangrejo Criollo
2 Frutabar
3 Lo Nuestro
4 Manny's
5 Piccolo Mondo
6 Riviera
7 Sion Lung

paintings, gold and archaeological collections, shrunken heads, a section on the history of Guayaquil and a good newspaper library.

Between the Parque Bolívar and the Malecón is the **Museo Nahim Isaías** ① *Pichincha y Clemente Ballén, T04-232 4283, Tue-Fri 0830-1630, Sat-Sun 0900-1600, free*, a colonial art museum with a permanent religious art collection and temporary exhibits.

② Guayaquil centre

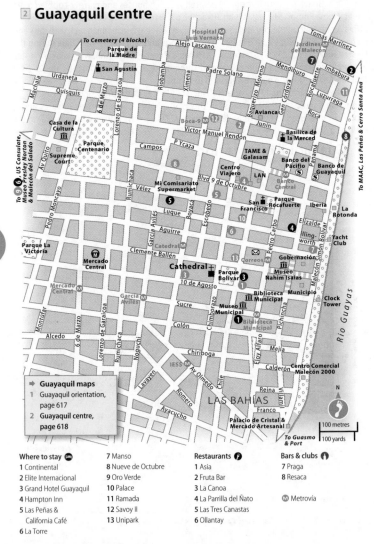

Where to stay 🛏
1 Continental
2 Elite Internacional
3 Grand Hotel Guayaquil
4 Hampton Inn
5 Las Peñas & California Café
6 La Torre
7 Manso
8 Nueve de Octubre
9 Oro Verde
10 Palace
11 Ramada
12 Savoy II
13 Unipark

Restaurants 🍴
1 Asia
2 Fruta Bar
3 La Canoa
4 La Parrilla del Ñato
5 Las Tres Canastas
6 Ollantay

Bars & clubs 🍸
7 Praga
8 Resaca

Ⓜ Metrovía

Avenida 9 de Octubre, the city's main artery, runs west from the Malecón. Halfway along it is **Parque Centenario** with a towering monument to the liberation of the city erected in 1920. Overlooking the park is the museum of the **Casa de la Cultura** ⓘ *9 de Octubre 1200 y P Moncayo, T04-230 0500,*

Tip...
Outside downtown, addresses are hard to find; ask for a nearby landmark to help orient your driver.

Mon-Fri 0900-1800, Sat 0900-1500, free, English-speaking guides available, which houses an impressive collection of prehispanic gold items in its archaeological museum; and a photo collection of old Guayaquil.

West of Parque Centenario, the **Museo Presley Norton** ⓘ *Av 9 de Octubre y Carchi, T04-229 3423, Tue-Sat 0900-1700, free,* has a nice collection of coastal archeology in a beautifully restored house. At the west end of 9 de Octubre are **Plaza Baquerizo Moreno** and the **Malecón del Estero Salado**, another pleasant waterfront promenade along a brackish estuary. It has various monuments, eateries specializing in seafood, and rowing boats and pedal-boats for hire.

Around the city

Parque Histórico Guayaquil ⓘ *Vía Samboron-dón, near Entrerríos, T04-283 2958, Wed-Sun 0900-1630, free; CISA buses to Samborondón leave from the Terminal Terrestre every 20 mins, US$0.25.* The park recreates Guayaquil and its rural surroundings at the end of the 19th century. There is a natural area with native flora and fauna, a traditions section where you can learn about rural life, an urban section with old wooden architecture, and eateries. A pleasant place for a family outing.

Botanical Gardens ⓘ *Av Francisco de Orellana, in Ciudadela Las Orquídeas (bus line 63), T04-289 9689, daily 0800-1600, US$3, guiding service for up to 5 visitors US$10 (English available).* There are over 3000 plants, including 150 species of Ecuadorean and foreign orchids (most flower August to December). One area emulates the Amazon rainforest and has monkeys and other animals. It is northwest of the city.

Bosque Protector Cerro Blanco ⓘ *Vía a la Costa, Km 16, T09-8622 5077 (Spanish), fundacionprobosque@ymail.com, http://bosquecerroblanco.org, US$4, additional guiding fee US$10-15 depending on trails visited, camping US$20 for group of 8, lodge available.* The reserve, run by **Fundación Pro-Bosque**, is set in tropical dry forest with an impressive variety of birds (over 200 species), many reptiles and with sightings of monkeys and other mammals. Unfortunately it is getting harder to see the animals due to human encroachment in the area. Reservations required during weekdays, for groups larger than eight at weekends, and for birders wishing to arrive before or stay after normal opening hours (0800-1600). Take a **CLP** bus from the Terminal Terrestre, a **Cooperativa Chongón** bus from Antepara y 10 de Agosto (hourly) or a taxi (US$8-10). On the other side of the road, at Km 18 is **Puerto Hondo**, where there are **rowboat trips** ⓘ *through the mangroves are offered, T09-9140 0186, US$15 for a group of 7, 1 hr, reserve ahead.*

Area Nacional de Recreación Isla Santay ⓘ *www.islasantay.info, open 0600-1800, bicycle rental US$4.* On the Río Guayas, opposite downtown Guayaquil is this Ramsar wetland rich in fauna and flora. Two pedestrian draw bridges (open 0600-2100) link the island with the mainland, one from Calle El Oro, south of Malecón 2000, the second from the city of Durán; a boardwalk/cycle path joins the two. By the local village, 2.8 km from the Guayaquil bridge and 5.3 km from the Durán bridge, is the Eco Aldea, with a crocodile breeding centre (open 0600-1700), a cabin and restaurant run by the local community. Boat service to the Eco Aldea from **Cooperativa las Palmeras** ① *T09-8654 7034, US$4 pp return, minimum 10 passengers, depart from the Yacht Club.*

Reserva Ecológica Manglares Churute ① *Free entry, camping and use of basic cabins; boat tour US$20-40, depending on group size (2-4 hrs recommended), arrange several days ahead through the Dirección Regional, Ministerio del Ambiente in Guayaquil, Parque de los Samanes, Bloque 7, north of the city, T04-372 9066. Buses (CIFA, Ecuatoriano Pullman, 16 de Junio) leave the Terminal Terrestre every 30 mins, going to Naranjal or Machala; ask to be let off at the Churute information centre. The reserve can also be reached by river.* Heading east then south from Guayaquil, 22 km beyond the main crossroads at Km 50 on the road to Machala, lies this rich natural area with five different ecosystems created to preserve mangroves in the Gulf of Guayaquil and forests of the Cordillera Churute. Many waterbirds, monkeys, dolphins and other wildlife can be seen. There is a trail through the tropical forest (1½ hours' walk) and you can also walk (one hour) to Laguna Canclón or Churute, a large lake where ducks nest. Near the park is **Monoloco Lodge** ($), www.monoloco.ec, tours available.

Listings Guayaquil *maps pages 617 and 618.*

Tourist information

Centro de Información Turística del Municipio
Clemente Ballén y Pichincha, at Museo Nahim Isaías, T04-232 4182, ext 26. Mon-Fri 0830-1630, turismo.guayaquil.gob.ec (in Spanish). Has pamphlets and city maps. There are also information booths at the Malecón 2000 by the clock tower (irregular hours), and at the Terminal Terrestre.

Immigration
Av Río Daule, near the bus terminal, T04-214 0002.

Ministerio de Turismo
Subsecretaría del Litoral, Av Francisco de Orellana y Justino Cornejo, Edif Gobierno del Litoral, p 8 and counter on the ground floor, Ciudadela Kennedy, T04-268 4274, www.ecuador.travel. Mon-Fri 0900-1700. Information about the coastal provinces of Ecuador and whale watching regulations.

Where to stay

Guayaquil has some of the best top-class accommodation in Ecuador.

For major chain hotels see: www.hilton.com (**Hilton Colón** and **Hampton Inn**, both excellent), www.oroverdehotels.com (**Oro Verde** and **Unipark**), www.hotelcontinental.com.ec, www.hojo.com (**Howard Johnson**), www.hdoral.com (**Best Western**), www.marriott.com, www.sheraton.com www.sonesta.com/guayaquil and www.wyndham.com (with excellent location and views of the river). There are several mid-range ($$) hotels on Junín between Gen Córdova and Escobedo but decent economy places are few and far between; the latter are concentrated around Parque Centenario, not a safe area.

$$$$ Mansión del Río
Numa Pompilio Llona 120, Las Peñas, T04-256 6044, www.mansiondelrio-ec.com. Elegant boutique hotel in a 1926 mansion, period European style, river view, buffet breakfast, airport transfers, 10 mins from city centre.

$$$ Castell
Av Miguel H Alcivar y Ulloa, by Parque Japonés, Kennedy Norte, T04-268 0190, www.hotelcastell.com.
Modern comfortable hotel in a quiet location in the north of the city, includes buffet breakfast, restaurant, a/c, convenient for the airport (taxi US$2.50).

$$$ Grand Hotel Guayaquil
Boyacá 1600 y 10 de Agosto, T04-232 9690, www.grandhotelguayaquil.com.
A traditional Guayaquil hotel, central, includes buffet breakfast, good restaurants, pool, gym and sauna.

$$$ Nazú B&B
Ciudadela La Cogra, Manzana 1, Villa 2, off Av Carlos Julio Arosemena Km 3.5 (taxi from bus terminal or airport US$6-8, Metrovía '28 de Mayo' stop, best without luggage), T04-220 1143, www.nazuhouse.com.
Lovely suburban guesthouse with a variety of rooms and suites with a/c, includes dinner and breakfast, pool, parking, terrace with views of the city, English and German spoken.

$$$ Palace
Chile 214 y Luque, T04-232 1080, www.hotelpalaceguayaquil.com.ec.
Modern hotel, includes buffet breakfast, restaurant, 24-hr cafetería, traffic noise on Av Chile side, good value for business travellers.

$$$ Ramada
Malecón 606 e Imbabura, T04-256 5555, www.hotelramada.com.
Excellent location right on the Malecón, rooms facing the river are more expensive, includes buffet breakfast, restaurant, a/c, pool, spa.

$$ La Torre
Chile 303 y Luque, p 13-15, T04-253 1316.
Popular hotel in a downtown office tower, long flight of stairs to get into the building, comfortable rooms, cafetería, a/c, nice views,

reasonably quiet for where it is, popular, advance booking advised, good value.

$$ Las Peñas
Escobedo 1215 y Vélez, T04-232 3355.
Nice hotel in a refurbished part of downtown, ample modern rooms, cafetería, a/c, quiet despite being in the centre of town, good value. Recommended.

$$ Manso
Malecón 1406 y Aguirre, upstairs, T04-252 6644, www.manso.ec.
Nicely refurbished hostel in a great location opposite the Malecón. Rooms vary from fancy with a/c, private bath and river view, to simpler with shared bath and fan, and 3-4-bed dorms (US$17 pp), English spoken.

$$ Tangara Guest House
Manuela Sáenz y O'Leary, Manzana F, Villa 1, Ciudadela Bolivariana, T04-228 4445, www.tangara-ecuador.com.
Comfortable hotel in a nice area by the university and near the Estero Salado, a/c, fridge, low season discounts, convenient for airport and bus terminal but also along the flight path, so it is noisy.

$$-$ Elite Internacional
Baquerizo Moreno 902 y Junín, T04-256 5385.
Completely refurbished old downtown hotel, comfortable rooms with a/c and hot water, some rooms remodeled in 2015, parking.

$$-$ Savoy II
Junín 627 y Boyacá, T04-231 0206.
Central location, simple rooms with a/c and hot water.

$ Nueve de Octubre
9 de Octubre 736 y García Avilés, T04-256 4222.
Busy 8-storey hotel in a central location. Simple functional rooms, those facing the street are larger but noisy, restaurant, private bath, cold water, a/c, cheaper with fan, parking extra. Fills early and does not accept reservations. Good value.

Restaurants

Main areas for restaurants are the centre with many in the larger hotels, around Urdesa and the residential and commercial neighbourhoods to the north.

$$$ Cangrejo Criollo
Av Rolando Pareja, Villa 9, La Garzota, T04-262 6708. Mon-Sat 0900-0100, Sun 0900-2300.
Excellent, varied seafood menu.

$$$ Lo Nuestro
VE Estrada 903 e Higueras, Urdesa, T04-238 6398. Daily 1200-2300.
Luxury restaurant with typical coastal cooking, good seafood platters and stuffed crabs, colonial decor.

$$$ Manny's
Av Miraflores 112 y C Primera, Miraflores, T04-220 2754; also in Urdesa and Kennedy. Daily 1000-2400.
Well known crab house with specialities such as *cangrejo al ajillo* (crab in garlic butter), good quality and value.

$$$-$$ La Parrilla del Ñato
VE Estrada 1219 y Laureles in Urdesa; Av Francisco de Orellana opposite the Hilton Colón; Luque y Pichincha downtown; and several other locations, T04-268 2338. Daily 1200-2300.
Large variety of dishes, salad bar, also pizza by the metre, good quality, generous portions. Try the *parrillada de mariscos*, available only at the Urdesa and Kennedy locations. Recommended.

$$$-$$ Piccolo Mondo
Bálsamos 504 y las Monjas, Urdesa, T04-238 7079. Mon-Sat 1230-2330, Sun 1230-2200.
Very exclusive Italian restaurant since 1980, the best in food and surroundings, good antipasto.

$$$-$$ Riviera
VE Estrada 707 y Ficus, Urdesa, and Mall del Sol, T04-288 3790. Daily 1230-2330.
Extensive Italian menu, good pasta, antipasto, salads, bright surroundings, good service.

$$$-$$ Sion Lung
VE Estrada 621 y Ficus, Urdesa, also Av Principal, Entre Ríos, T04-288 8213. Daily 1200-2230.
Chinese food, a variety of rice (*chaulafán*) and noodle (*tallarín*) dishes.

$$ Asia
Sucre 321 y Chile, downtown, also VE Estrada 508 y Las Monjas, Urdesa and in shopping centres in the north. Daily 1100-2130.
Chinese food, large portions, popular.

$$ La Canoa
Hotel Continental, Chile y 10 de Agosto. Open 24 hrs.
Rare regional dishes, with different specials during the week, a Guayaquil tradition.

$$-$ Manso
Malecón 1406 y Aguirre, at the hotel. Mon-Fri 1230-2200, Sat 1830-2200.
Small dining area serving innovative set lunches, à la carte dishes and snacks. Tables overlooking the river are nice.

$ Ollantay
Tungurahua 508 y 9 de Octubre, west of downtown.
Good vegetarian food.

Cafés and snacks

California
Escobedo 1215 y Vélez, below Hotel Las Peñas. Mon-Sat 0700-2000, Sun 0800-1500.
Good and popular for breakfast, snacks, drinks, sweets and à la carte meals.

Fruta Bar
Malecón e Imbabura, VE Estrada 608 y Monjas, Urdesa.
Excellent fruit juices and snacks, unusual African decor, good music.

Las Tres Canastas
Vélez y García Avilés and several other locations.
Breakfast, snacks, safe fruit juices and smoothies.

Bars and clubs

Guayaquil nightlife is not cheap. There are clubs and bars in most of the major hotels, as well as in the northern suburbs, especially at the Kennedy Mall. Also in vogue are the Las Peñas area, and the Zona Rosa, bounded by the Malecón Simón Bolívar and Rocafuerte, C Loja and C Roca. Both these areas are considered reasonably safe but always take a radio taxi back to your hotel.

La Paleta
Escalón 176, Las Peñas. Tue-Sat from 2000.
Good music, great drinks and snacks. US$10-15 cover Fri and Sat, popular, reserve.

Praga
Rocafuerte 636 y Mendiburo.
Tue-Sat from 1830.
US$10-16 cover, live music Fri-Sat. Pleasant atmosphere, several halls, varied music.

Resaca
Malecón 2000, at the level of Junín.
Daily 1130-2400.
Lovely setting, live tropical music Fri-Sat night. Also serves set lunches on weekdays, regional dishes and pricey drinks.

Entertainment

Cinema
Cinemas are at the main shopping centres and cost US$4-8. The IMAX Cinema, Malecón 2000, projects impressive films on its oversize screen.

Theatre
Centro Cívico, *Quito y Venezuela*. Excellent theatre/concert facility, home to the Guayaquil Symphony which gives free concerts.

Festivals

24-25 Jul The foundation of Guayaquil. **9-12 Oct** The **city's independence**. Both holidays are lively and there are many public events; cultural happenings are prolonged throughout Oct.

Shopping

There are many shopping malls (eg **Malecón 2000**, south end of Malecón and the huge **San Marino**, Av Francisco de Orellana y L Plaza Dañín) which are noisy but have a/c for cooling off on hot days.

Camping equipment
Casa Maspons, *Ballén 517 y Boyacá*.
Camping gas.

Handicrafts
Mercado Artesanal del Malecón 2000, *at the south end of the Malecón*. Has many kiosks selling varied crafts.
Mercado Artesanal, *Baquerizo Moreno between Loja and J Montalvo*. Greatest variety, almost a whole block of stalls with good prices.
In Albán Borja Mall are: **El Telar** with a good variety of *artesanías* and **Ramayana**, with nice ceramics. **Mall del Sol**, near the airport, also has craft shops.

What to do

Boat tours
The gulf islands and mangroves can be visited on tours from Guayaquil, Puerto Hondo or Puerto El Morro.
Isla Puná, the largest of the islands has a community tourism programme, contact the village of **Subida Alta**, T09-9156 4562.
Capitan Morgan, *Muelle Malecón y Sucre*. 1-hr tours on the river with nice city views, Tue-Fri at 1600, 1800 and 1930, Sat and Sun at 1230, 1400, 1600, 1800 and 1930, Fri and Sat also at 2130; US$7. Also 2-hr party cruises, Thu 2130-2330, Fri-Sat from 2330-0200, US$15, with live music, open bar and dancing.
Cruceros Discovery, *Muelle Malecón y Tomás Martínez*. 1-hr river cruises, US$7, Tue-Fri from 1600, Sat-Sun from 1300, and party trips.

Tour operators
A 3-hr city tour costs about US$14 pp in a group. See **Guayaquil Visión** for bus tours

of the city. Tours to coastal haciendas offer a glimpse of rural life.

Centro Viajero, *Baquerizo Moreno 1119 y 9 de Octubre, of 805, T04-230 1283, T09-9235 7745 24-hr service, www.centroviajero.com.* Custom-designed tours to all regions, travel information and bookings, flight tickets, car and driver service, well informed about options for Galápagos, helpful, English, French and Italian spoken. Recommended.

Galasam, *Edif Gran Pasaje, 9 Octubre 424, ground floor, T04-230 4488, www.galasam. com.ec.* Galápagos cruises, city tours, tours to reserves near Guayaquil, diving trips, also run highland and jungle tours and sell flight tickets.

Guayaquil Visión, *ticket booth at Olmedo y Malecón, T04-292 5332, www.guayaquilvision. com.* City tours on a double-decker bus, US$6-17 depending on route, departs from Plaza Olmedo and the Rotonda, Malecón at the bottom of 9 de Octubre. Also tours to attractions outside the city and night-time party tours.

La Moneda, *Av de las Américas 406, Centro de Convenciones Simón Bolívar, of 2, T04-292 5660, www.lamoneda.com.ec.* City and coastal tours, whale watching, also other regions.

Metropolitan Touring, *Francisco De Orellana, Edif. World Trade Center, CC Millenium Galery, PB, T04-263 0900, www.metropolitan-touring.com.* High-end land tours and Galápagos cruises.

Train rides

The train station is in Durán, across the river from Guayaquil, T04-215 4254, reservations T1800-873637, www.trenecuador.com, Mon-Fri 0800-1630, Sat-Sun 0730-1530. For information on the luxury *Tren Crucero* from Durán to Quito, see page 521. Combined train/bus day trips to Bucay, 88 km away, cost US$25. 2 similar itineraries depart Thu-Sun and holidays at 0800 and return at 1800; snack included. Tickets are also sold at the railcar in Malecón 2000, Malecón y Aguirre, Wed-Fri 1000-1600, Sat-Sun 1000-1530.

see page 521

Transport

Transport

Air José Joaquín de Olmedo is a modern airport with all services including banks (change only cash euros at poor rates) and luggage storage. The information booth outside international arrivals (T04-216 9000, open 24 hrs) has flight, hotel and transport information. It is 15 mins to the city centre by taxi, US$5, and 5-10 mins to the bus terminal, US$3. Fares from the airport to other areas are posted at exit doors and on www.taxiecuadorairport.com. Official airport taxis are more expensive but safer than those out on the street. It is along line 2 of the Metrovía, but neither the Metrovía nor buses to the centre (eg Línea 130 'Full 2') are safe or practical with luggage. For groups, there are van services such as **M&M**, T04-216 9294, US$15 to centre.

Many flights daily to **Quito** (sit on the right for the best views) and **Galápagos**, see page 673, with **Avianca** (Junín 440 y Córdova, T04-231 1028, T1-800-003434), **LATAM** (Gen Córdova 1042 y 9 de Octubre, and in Mall del Sol, T1-800-101075) and **TAME** (9 de Octubre 424 y Chile, T04-268 9127 and Galerías Hilton Colón, T04-268 9135 or T1-700-500800). **TAME** also flies to **Esmeraldas** and **Loja**.

Bus Metrovía (T04-213 0402, www. metrovia-gye.com.ec, US$0.25) is an integrated system of articulated buses on exclusive lanes and *alimentadores* (feeder buses) serving suburbs from the terminuses. Line 1 runs from the Terminal Río Daule, opposite the Terminal Terrestre, in the north, to the Terminal El Guasmo in the south. In the city centre it runs along Boyacá southbound and Pedro Carbo northbound. Line 2 goes from the Terminal Río Daule along Av de las Américas past the airport, then through the centre and on to Integración Pradera in the southern suburbs. Line 3 goes from the centre (transfer points to line 1at Biblioteca Municipal and IESS; to line 2 at Plaza La Victoria) along C Sucre to the northwest as far as Bastión. Provides access to neighbourhoods such as Urdesa, Miraflores, and Los Ceibos. The Metrovía is a good way of getting around without luggage or valuables. You need a prepaid card to board. **City buses** (US$0.25) are only permitted on a few streets in the centre; northbound buses go along Rumichaca or the Malecón, southbound along Lorenzo de Garaicoa or García Avilés. Buses and Metrovía get very crowded at rush hour.

Taxi Using a radio taxi, such as **Samboroncar**, T04-284 3883, or **Vipcar**, T04-239 3000, is recommended. Short trips costs US$2.50, fares from the centre to Urdesa, Policentro or Alborada are around US$4-5. Taxis are supposed to use a meter, but not all drivers comply.

Long distance The **Terminal Terrestre**, just north of the airport, is off the road to the Guayas bridge. The Metrovía, opposite the bus station, and many city buses (eg Línea 84 to Parque Centenario) go from to the city centre but these are not safe with luggage; take a taxi (US$3-4). The bus station doubles as a shopping centre with supermarket, shops, banks, post office, calling centres, internet, food courts, etc. Incoming buses arrive on the ground floor, where the ticket offices are located. Regional buses depart from the 2nd level and long distance (interprovincial) buses depart from the 3rd level. The terminal is very large, so you need to allow extra time to get to your bus. Check the board at the entrance for the location of the ticket counters for your destination, they are colour-coded by region.

Several companies to **Quito**, 8 hrs, US$12.50, US$15for express buses which go at night; also non-stop, a/c services, eg **Transportes Ecuador**, Av de las Américas y Hermano Miguel, opposite the airport terminal, T04-292 5139. To **Cuenca**, 4 hrs via Molleturo/Cajas, 5 hrs via Zhud, both

US$8, both scenic; also hourly van service, 0500-2100, with **Río Arriba**, Centro de Negocios El Terminal, Bloque C, of 38, Av de las Américas y entrada a Bahía Norte, T09-8488 9269, US$12, 3 hrs, reserve ahead; several others at the same address, departures every 30-40 mins. **Riobamba**, 5 hrs, US$6.25. To **Santo Domingo de los Tsáchilas**, 5 hrs, US$6.25. **Manta**, 4 hrs, US$5. **Esmeraldas**, 8 hrs, US$10. To **Bahía de Caráquez**, 6 hrs, US$6.25. To **Ambato**, 6 hrs, US$7.50. Frequent buses to **Playas**, 2 hrs, US$3.25; and to **Salinas**, 2½ hrs, US$4.75. To **Santa Elena**, 2 hrs, US$3.25, change here for **Puerto López**. To **Montañita** and **Olón**, CLP, at 0520, 0620, 0900, 1300, 1500 and 1640, 3¼ hrs, US$7.25. For the Peruvian border, to **Huaquillas** direct, 4½-5 hrs, US$7.50; van service with **Transfrosur**, Chile 616 y Sucre, T04-232 6387, hourly 0500-2000, Sun 0700-2000, 4 hrs, US$13.50; to **Machala**, 3 hrs, US$5, also hourly vans with **Oro Guayas**, Luque y García Avilés, T04-252 3297, US$12, 3 hrs. To **Zaruma**, 8 buses daily, US$8.25, 6 hrs. To **Loja**, with **Trans Loja**, 8 daily, US$12, 9-10 hrs.

International (Peru) CIFA, T04-213 0379, www.cifainternacional.com, from Terminal Terrestre to **Tumbes** 8 daily, 6 hrs, US$10 *ejecutivo*, US$15 *bus-cama*; to **Piura** via **Máncora** (9 hrs, same price as Piura), *ejecutivo* service at 0720, and 2100, 10-11 hrs, US$15; and *bus-cama* at 1950 and 2330, US$20; also with **CIVA**, daily at 2130, *semi-cama* US$17, *cama* US$20. To **Chiclayo** with **Super Semería**, at 2200 daily, US$25, 12 hrs. To **Lima** with **Cruz del Sur**, of 88, T04-213 0179, www.cruzdelsur.com.pe, Tue, Wed, Fri, Sun at 1400, US$85 *semi-cama*, US$120 *cama* (including meals), 27 hrs (stops in Trujillo). With **Ormeño**, Centro de Negocios El Terminal (near Terminal Terrestre), Of C34, T04-213 0847, Tue, Thu, Sun at 1200 to **Lima**, US$60.

a few beaches, a lovely town and some archaeological sites

Machala

The capital of the province of El Oro (altitude 4 m) is a booming agricultural town in a major banana producing and exporting region. It is unsafe, somewhat dirty and oppressively hot. For the tourist, the only reasons for stopping here are to go to the beautiful tranquil uplands of El Oro, and to catch a through **CIFA** bus to Peru (also runs from Guayaquil) for the beaches around Máncora. **Tourist office** ⓘ *25 de Junio y 9 de Mayo, Municipio, iturmachala@hotmail.com, Mon-Fri 0800-1300, 1430-1730, Spanish only.* Some 30 km south along the road to Peru is **Santa Rosa** with the regional airport.

Puerto Bolívar

Puerto Bolívar, on the Estero Jambelí among mangroves, is a major export outlet for over two million tonnes of bananas annually. From the old pier canoes cross to the beaches of **Jambelí** (every 30 minutes, 0730-1500, US$4 return) on the far side of the mangrove islands which shelter Puerto Bolívar from the Pacific. The beaches are crowded at weekends, deserted during the week and not very clean. Boats can be rented for excursions to the **Archipiélago de Jambelí**, a maze of islands and channels just offshore, stretching south between Puerto Bolívar and the Peruvian border. These mangrove islands are rich in birdlife (and insects for them to feed on, take repellent), the water is very clear and you may also see fish and reefs.

☆Zaruma

Southeast from Machala is the delightful old gold-mining town of Zaruma (118 km). It is reached from Machala by paved road via Piñas, by a scenic dirt road off the main Loja–Machala road, or via Pasaje and Paccha on another scenic dirt road off the Machala–Cuenca road.

> **Tip...**
> The Zaruma area has virtually no tourists and is well worth a visit.

   Founded in 1549, Zaruma is perched on a hilltop, with steep, twisting streets and painted wooden buildings. The **tourist office** ⓘ *in the Municipio, at the plaza, T07-297 3533, Mon-Fri 0800-1200, 1400-1800, Sat 0900-1600,* is friendly and helpful. They can arrange for guides and accommodation with local families. Next door is the small **Museo Municipal** ⓘ *Wed-Fri 0800-1200, 1400-1800, Sat 0900-1600, Sun 0900-1300, free,* it has a collection of local historical artifacts.

   The Zaruma area has a number of prehispanic archaeological sites and petroglyphs. Tours with **Oroadventure** ⓘ *at the Parque Central, T07-297 2761,* or with English-speaking guide **Ramiro Rodríguez** ⓘ *T07-297 2523, kazan_rodríguez@yahoo.com.* Zaruma is also known for its excellent Arabica coffee freshly roasted in the agricultural store basement, the proud owner will show you around if the store isn't busy. On top of the small hill beyond the market is a public swimming pool (US$1), from where there are amazing views over the hot, dry valleys. For even grander views, walk up **Cerro del Calvario** (follow Calle San Francisco); go early in the morning as it gets very hot. At **Portovelo**, south of Zaruma, is the largest mine in the area. Its history is told inside a mine shaft at the **Museo Magner Turner** ⓘ *T07-294 9345, daily 0900-1730, US$2.* There are also archaeological pieces; the owner is knowledgeable about sites in this region.

Piñas and around

Piñas, 19 km west of Zaruma, along the road to Machala is a pleasant town which conserves just a few of its older wooden buildings. Northwest of Piñas, 20 minutes along the road to Saracay and Machala, is **Buenaventura**, to the north of which lies an important area for bird conservation, with over 310 bird species recorded, including many rare ones. The Jocotoco Foundation (www.fjocotoco.org) protects a 1500-ha forest in this region, with 13 km of trails, entry US$15, lodge $$$$, advance booking required.

Bosque Petrificado Puyango

110 km south of Machala, west of the Arenillas–Alamor road, T07-293 2106 (Machala), bosquepuyango@hotmail.com, 0900-1700, US$1.

At Puyango, a dry-forest reserve, a great number of petrified trees, ferns, fruits and molluscs, 65 to 120 million years old, have been found. Over 120 species of birds can be seen. There is a camping area, no accommodation in the village, but ask around for floor space or try at the on-site information centre. If not, basic accommodation is available in **Las Lajas**, 20 minutes north (one residencial) and **Alamor**, 20 km south (several hotels, eg $ **Rey Plaza**, T07-268 0256).

Huaquillas

The stiflingly hot Ecuadorean border town of Huaquillas is something of a shopping arcade for Peruvians. The border runs along the Canal de Zarumilla and is crossed by two international bridges, one at the western end of Avenida La República in Huaquillas and a second newer one further south.

Border with Peru: Huaquillas-Tumbes

The best way to cross this border is on one of the international buses that run between Ecuador and Peru. Border formalities are only carried out at the new bridge, far outside the towns of Huaquillas (Ecuador) and Aguas Verdes (Peru). There are two border complexes called CEBAF *(Centro Binacional de Atención Fronteriza)*, open 24 hours, on either side of the bridge; they are about 4 km apart. Both complexes have Ecuadorean and Peruvian customs and immigration officers so you get your exit and entry stamps in the same place. There is a **Peruvian Consulate in Machala** ⓘ *Urb Unioro, Mz 14, V 11, near Hotel Oro Verde, T07-298 5379, Mon-Fri 0830-1300, 1500-1730.* If crossing with your own vehicle, you have to stop at both border complexes for customs and, on the Ecuadorean side, you also have to stop at the customs *(aduana)* post at Chacras, 7 km from the Ecuadorean CEBAF, on the road to Machala. If you do not take one of the international buses, the crossing is inconvenient. See details on page 132. A taxi from Huaquillas to the Ecuadorean CEBAF costs US$2.50, to the Peruvian CEBAF US$5. See Peru chapter for transport to Tumbes and beyond. Banks do not change money in Huaquillas. Many street changers deal in soles and US$ cash. Do not change more US$ than you need to get to Tumbes, where there are reliable *cambios*, but get rid of all your soles here as they are difficult to exchange further inside Ecuador. Only clean, crisp US$ bills are accepted in Peru. Those seeking a more relaxed crossing to or from Peru should consider Macará (see page 606) or La Balsa (see page 611).

Where to stay

Machala

$$$$ Oro Verde
Circunvalación Norte in Urbanización Unioro, T07-298 5444, www.oroverdehotels.com.
Includes buffet breakfast, 2 restaurants, nice pool (US$13 for non-guests), beautiful gardens, tennis courts, full luxury. Best in town.

$$ Oro Hotel
Sucre y Juan Montalvo, T07-293 0032, www.orohotel.com.
Includes breakfast, pricey restaurant, a/c, fridge, parking, nice comfortable rooms but those to the street are noisy, helpful staff. Recommended.

$ San Miguel
9 de Mayo y Sucre, T07-292 0474.
Good quality and value, some rooms without windows, hot water (request), no meals, a/c, cheaper with fan, fridge, helpful staff.

Zaruma

$$ Hostería El Jardín
Barrio Limoncito, 10-min walk from centre (taxi US$1.50), T07-297 2706.
Lovely palm garden and terrace with views, internet, parking, comfortable rooms, breakfast extra, family-run. Recommended.

$$-$ Roland
At entrance to town on road from Portovelo, T07-297 2800.
Comfortable rooms (some are dark) and nicer more expensive cabins around pool, no breakfast, parking.

$$-$ Zaruma Colonial
Sucre y Sesmo, T07-297 2742, on Facebook.
Colonial style hotel, ample rooms, those to the back have mountain views, no meals.

$ Blacio
C Sucre, T07-297 2045.
Modern, ask for rooms with balcony, no meals.

$ Romería
On the plaza facing the church, T07-297 3618.
Old wooden house with balcony, a treat, restaurant downstairs.

Huaquillas

$$$$ Hillary Nature Resort
Km 1 Vía Arenillas-Alamor, 25 km east of Huaquillas, T07-370 0260, www.hillaryresort.com.
Luxury resort and spa. Ample rooms with all amenities, pool, 2 restaurants, several meeting rooms and convention facilities for 600 people.

$$-$ Hernancor
1 de Mayo y 10 de Agostso, T07-299 5467, grandhotelhernancor@gmail.com.
Nice rooms with a/c, includes breakfast, parking.

$$-$ Sol del Sur
Av La República y Chiriboga, T07-251 0898, www.soldelsurhotel.com.
Attractive rooms, includes breakfast, a/c, small bathrooms, parking.

$ Vanessa
1 de Mayo y Hualtaco, T07-299 6263.
A/c, internet, fridge, parking, pleasant.

Restaurants

Machala
The best food is found in the better hotels.

$$ Mesón Hispano
Av Las Palmeras y Sucre.
Very good grill, attentive service, outstanding.

$ Chifa Gran Oriental
25 de Junio entre Guayas y Ayacucho.
Good food and service, clean. Recommended.

Zaruma

$$ Amalsi
C Pichincha s/n. Mon-Sat 1100-2100.
Good pizzas, hamburgers and meals.

$$-$ 200 Millas
Av Honorato Márquez, uphill from bus station.
Good seafood.

$ Cafetería Uno
C Sucre.
Good for breakfast and Zaruma specialities, best *tigrillo* in town.

Transport

Machala

Air The regional airport is at Santa Rosa, 32 km south of Machala. 1 or 2 flights a day to **Quito** with TAME (Montalvo entre Bolívar y Pichincha, T07-293 0139).

Bus There is no Terminal Terrestre. Do not take night buses into or out of Machala as they are prone to hold-ups. To **Quito**, with **Occidental** (Buenavista entre Sucre y Olmedo), 10 hrs, US$10, 8 daily, with **Panamericana** (Colón y Bolívar), 7 daily. To **Guayaquil**, 3 hrs, US$6, hourly with **Ecuatoriano Pullman** (Colón y Rocafuerte), **CIFA** (Bolívar y Guayas) and **Rutas Orenses** (Tarqui y Rocafuerte), half-hourly; also hourly vans with **Oro Guayas**, Guayas y Pichincha, T07-293 4382, US$15, 3 hrs. There are 3 different scenic routes to **Loja**, each with bus service. They are, from north to south: via **Piñas** and **Zaruma**, partly paved and rough, via **Balsas**, fully paved; and via **Arenillas** and **Alamor**, for **Puyango** petrified forest. Fare to **Loja**, US$7, 5-6 hrs, several daily with **Trans Loja** (Tarqui y Bolívar). To **Zaruma**, see below. To **Cuenca**, half-hourly with **Trans Azuay** (Sucre y Junín), 3½ hrs, US$6. To **Huaquillas**, with **CIFA**, direct, 1½ hrs, US$2.50, every 20 mins. To **Piura**, in Peru, with **CIFA**, at 1100, 2300 and 2400, US$10-15, 6 hrs, via **Máncora**, US$9-1400, 5 hrs and **Tumbes**, 6 daily, US$5, 3 hrs.

Zaruma

Bus To/from Machala with Trans Piñas or **TAC**, half-hourly, US$4.50, 3 hrs. To **Piñas**, take a Machala bound bus, US$1.25, 1 hr. To

Guayaquil, 8 buses daily US$8.25, 6 hrs. To **Quito**, 5 daily, US$13.75, 12 hrs; to **Cuenca**, 3 daily (**Trans Azuay** at 0730, US$8.75, 6 hrs and **Loja**, 4 daily, US$6.25, 5 hrs (may have to change at Portovelo).

Puyango

Puyango is west of the Arenillas-Alamor highway: alight from bus at turn-off at the bridge over the Río Puyango. Bus from **Machala**, Trans Loja at 0930 and 1300, **CIFA** at 0600, US$3.50, 2½ hrs. From **Loja**, Trans Loja 0900, 1400 and 1930, US$7, 5 hrs. From **Alamor**, Trans Loja at 0730, 1000 and 1300, US$1.50, 1 hr. From **Huaquillas**, CIFA at 0500, **Trans Loja** at 0740 and **Unión Cariamanga** at 1130, US$2.50, 1½ hrs. You might be able to hire a pick-up from the main road to the park, US$3. Pick-up from Alamor to Puyango US$25 return, including wait.

Huaquillas

Bus There is no Terminal Terrestre, each bus company has its own office, many on Teniente Cordovez. If you are in a hurry, it can be quicker to change buses in Machala or Guayaquil. To **Machala**, with CIFA (Santa Rosa y Machala), direct, 1½ hrs, US$2.50, every 20 min; via Arenillas and Santa Rosa, 2 hrs, every 10 mins. To **Quito**, with **Occidental**, every 2 hrs, 12 hrs, US$12.50; with **Panamericana**, 11½ hrs, 3 daily via Santo Domingo; 2 daily via **Riobamba** and **Ambato**, 12 hrs. To **Guayaquil**, frequent service with **CIFA** and **Ecuatoriano Pullman**, 4½-5 hrs, US$7.50, take a direct bus; van service to downtown Guayaquil with **Transfrosur**, C Santa Rosa y Machala, T07-299 5288, hourly 0500-2000, Sun 0700-2000, 4 hrs, US$13.50. To **Cuenca**, 8 daily, 5 hrs, US$7.50. To **Loja**, 6 daily, 6 hrs, US$7.50.

> **Tip...**
> There may be military checkpoints on the roads in this border area, so keep your passport to hand.

Pacific
lowlands

This vast tract of Ecuador covers everything west of the Andes and north of the Guayas delta. Though popular with Quiteños and Guayaquileños, who come here for weekends and holidays, the Pacific lowlands receive relatively few foreign visitors, which is surprising given the natural beauty, diversity and rich cultural heritage of the coast. Here you can surf, watch whales, visit archaeological sites, or just relax and enjoy some of the best food this country has to offer. Parque Nacional Machalilla protects an important area of primary tropical dry forest, pre-Columbian ruins, coral reef and a wide variety of wildlife. Further north, in the province of Esmeraldas, there are not only well-known party beaches, but also opportunities to visit the remaining mangroves and experience two unique lifestyles: Afro-Ecuadorean on the coast and indigenous Cayapa further inland. Coastal resorts are busy and more expensive from December to April, the *temporada de playa*.

Best for
Archaeology ■ Natural beauty ■ Relaxing ■ Wildlife

ON THE ROAD
2016 earthquakes

On 16 April 2016 an earthquake measuring 7.8 on the Richter scale struck the coast of Manabí near Pedernales. Over 650 people were killed and nearly 5000 were injured, with heavy property damage from Manta north to Muisne. In the aftermath of the tragedy, considerable assistance was provided by both Ecuadoreans and the international community. Reconstruction began promptly, but another major earthquake, of 5.8 magnitude, struck the coast off Esmeraldas province on 19 December. Although few people died, there was extensive property damage. Many of the affected areas lived from tourism and tourists can play an important role in the economic recovery of the region. There may be specific opportunities for volunteers and anybody can help just by visiting.

We have tried to reflect the state of affairs after the earthquakes in this section, but there will be many changes and advance enquiry is advised before travelling between Manta and San Lorenzo. Conditions on other parts of the coast and elsewhere in Ecuador are reported to be normal. The Galápagos Islands were not affected by either earthquake.

Guayaquil to Puerto López
quiet beaches, popular resorts and small fishing villages

Southwest of Guayaquil is the beach resort of Playas and, west of it, the Santa Elena Peninsula, with Salinas at its tip. From the town of Santa Elena, capital of the province of the same name, the coastal road stretches north for 737 km to Mataje on the Colombian border; along the way are countless beaches and fishing villages, and a few cities. Puerto López is the perfect base for whale watching and from which to explore the beautiful Parque Nacional Machalilla.

Playas and Salinas *Colour map 1, B1/B2.*
The beach resorts of Playas and Salinas remain as popular as ever with vacationing Guayaquileños. The paved toll highway from Guayaquil divides after 63 km at El Progreso (Gómez Rendón). One branch leads to **Playas** (General Villamil), the nearest seaside resort to Guayaquil.

Playas Bottle-shaped ceibo (kapok) trees characterise the landscape as it turns into dry, tropical thorn scrub. In Playas a few single-sailed balsa rafts, very simple but highly ingenious, can still be seen among the motor launches returning laden with fish. In high season (*temporada* – December to April), and at weekends, Playas is prone to severe crowding, although the authorities are trying to keep the packed beaches clean and safe (thieving is rampant during busy times). Out of season or midweek, the beaches are almost empty especially north towards Punta Pelado (5 km). Playas has six good surf breaks. There are showers, toilets and changing rooms along the beach, with fresh water, for a fee. Many hotels in our $$-$ ranges. Excellent seafood and typical dishes from over 50 beach cafés (all numbered and named). Many close out of season. **Tourist office** ⓘ *on the Malecón, Tue-Fri 0800-1200, 1400-1800, Sat-Sun 0900-1600.*

Salinas and further south Salinas, surrounded by miles of salt flats, is Ecuador's answer to Miami Beach. **Turismo Municipal** ⓘ *Eloy Alfaro y Mercedes de Jesús Molina, Chipipe, T04-293 0004, Tue-Fri 0800-1700, Sat 0800-1400*. There is safe swimming in the bay and high-rise blocks of holiday flats and hotels line the seafront. More appealing is the (still urban) beach of Chipipe, west of the exclusive Salinas Yacht Club. In December-April it is overcrowded, its services stretched to the limit. Even in the off season it is not that quiet. The ocean all along the south shore of the Santa Elena peninsula is a marine reserve. Built on high cliffs, 8 km south of La Libertad, is **Punta Carnero**, with hotels in the $$$-$$ range. To the south is a magnificent 15-km beach with wild surf and heavy undertow, there is whale watching in season.

North to Puerto López

The '**Ruta del Spondylus**' north to Puerto López in the province of Manabí parallels the coastline and crosses the Chongón-Colonche coastal range. Most of the numerous small fishing villages along the way have good beaches and are slowly being developed for tourism. Beware of rip currents and undertow.

Valdivia

San Pedro and Valdivia are two unattractive villages which merge together. There are many fish stalls. This is the site of the 5000-year-old Valdivia culture. Many houses offer 'genuine' artefacts (it is illegal to export pre-Columbian items from Ecuador). Juan Orrala, who makes excellent copies, lives up the hill from the **Ecomuseo Valdivia** ⓘ *open daily, US$1.50*, which has displays of original artefacts from Valdivia and other coastal cultures. There is also a handicraft section, where artisans may be seen at work, and lots of local information. At the museum is a restaurant and five rooms with bath to let. Most of the genuine artefacts discovered at the site are in museums in Quito and Guayaquil.

Manglaralto *Colour map 1, B2.*

Located 180 km northwest of Guayaquil, this is the main centre of the region north of Santa Elena. There is a tagua nursery; ask to see examples of worked 'vegetable ivory' nuts. It is a nice place, with a quiet beach, good surf but little shade. **Pro-pueblo** is an organization working with local communities to foster family-run orchards and cottage craft industry, using tagua nuts, *paja toquilla* (the fibre Panama hats are made from), and other local products. They have a craft shop in town (opposite the park), an office in San Antonio south of Manglaralto, T04-278 0230, and headquarters in Guayaquil, T04-268 3569, www.propueblo.com. **Proyecto de Desarrollo Ecoturístico Comunitario** ⓘ *contact Paquita Jara T09-9174 0143*, has a network of simple lodgings with local families (US$9 per person), many interesting routes into the Cordillera Chongón Colonche and whale-watching and island tours.

Montañita and Olón

About 3 km north of Manglaralto, **Montañita** has mushroomed into a major surf resort, packed with hotels, restaurants, surf-board rentals, tattoo parlours and craft/jewellery vendors. The murder of two tourists in Montañita in 2016 focused media attention on public safety here and a 'clean-up' was promised by the authorities. At the north end of the bay, 1 km away, is another hotel area with more elbow-room, Baja Montañita (or Montañita Punta, Surf Point). Between the two is a lovely beach where you'll find some of the best surfing in Ecuador. Various competitions are held during the year. At weekends in season, the town is full

> **Tip...**
> There is an ATM at **Banco Bolivariano** in Montañita and one other but they do not always work, so take cash.

Ecuador has an outstanding array of protected natural areas including a system of 50 national parks and reserves administered by the Ministerio del Ambiente (T02-398 7600, www.ambiente.gob.ec). Entry to all national protected areas is currently free except for Parque Nacional Galápagos. Some parks can only be visited with authorized guides. Contact park offices in the cities nearest the parks, they have more information than the ministry in Quito.

of Guayaquileños. Beyond an impressive headland and a few minutes north of Montañita is **Olón**, with a spectacular long beach, still tranquil but starting to get some of the overflow from Montañita. Nearby is **El Cangrejal**, a 7-ha dry tropical forest with mangroves.

Ayampe to Salango
North of Montañita, by **La Entrada**, the road winds up and inland through lush forest before continuing to the tranquil village of **Ayampe**. Tourism is growing here, with many popular places to stay at the south end of the beach, but the village retains an especially peaceful atmosphere, carefully safeguarded by the local community. The surfing here is very good. North of Ayampe are the villages of **Las Tunas**, **Puerto Rico** and **Río Chico**. There are places to stay all along this stretch of coast. Just north of Río Chico is **Salango**, with an ill-smelling fish processing plant, but worth visiting for the excellent **Salango archaeological museum** ① *at the north end of town, daily 0900-1200, 1300-1700, US$1*, housing artefacts from excavations right in town. It also has a craft shop and, at the back, nice rooms with bath in the $ range. There is a place for snorkelling offshore, by Isla Salango.

Puerto López *Colour map 1, B2.*
This pleasant fishing town is beautifully set in a horseshoe bay. The beach is best for swimming at the far north and south ends, away from the fleet of small fishing boats moored offshore. The town is popular with tourists for watching humpback whales from approximately mid-June to September, and for visiting Parque Nacional Machalilla and Isla de la Plata.

Tip...
Banco Pichincha is situated in a large building at south end of Malecón. It has the only ATM in town, so it is best to take some cash.

Parque Nacional Machalilla
Park office in Puerto Lópe, C Eloy Alfaro y García Moreno, daily 0800-1200, 1400-1600.

The park extends over 55,000 ha, including Isla de la Plata, Isla Salango, and the magnificent beach of **Los Frailes** and preserves marine ecosystems as well as the dry tropical forest and archaeological sites on shore. The beach is clean and well cared for, but gets busy on weekends and holidays. At the north end of Los Frailes beach is a trail through the forest leading to a lookout with great views and on to the town of Machalilla (don't take valuables). The land-based part of the park is divided into three sections which are separated by private land, including the town of Machalilla. The park is recommended for birdwatching, especially in the cloudforest of Cerro San Sebastián (see below); there are also howler monkeys, several other species of mammals and reptiles.

About 5 km north of Puerto López, at Buena Vista, a dirt road to the east leads to **Agua Blanca** (park kiosk at entry). Here, 5 km from the main road, in the national park, amid hot, arid scrub, is a small village and a fine, small **archaeological museum** ① *0800-1800, US$5 for a 2-hr guided tour of the museum, ruins (a 45-min walk), funerary urns and sulphurous lake, horses can be hired, camping is possible and there's a cabin and 1 very basic room for rent above the museum for US$5 pp; pick-up from Puerto López US$8*, containing some fascinating ceramics from the Manteño civilization. **San Sebastián**, 9 km from Agua Blanca, is in tropical moist forest at 800 m; orchids and birds can be seen and possibly howler monkeys. Although part of the national park, this area is administered by the Comuna of Agua Blanca, which charges an entry fee; you cannot go independently. It's five hours on foot or by horse. A tour to the forest costs US$40 per day including guide, horses and camping (minimum two people), otherwise lodging is with a family at extra cost.

Puerto López

About 24 km offshore is **Isla de la Plata**. Trips are popular because of the similarities with the Galápagos. Wildlife includes nesting colonies of Waved Albatross (April to November), frigates and three different booby species. Whales can be seen from June to September, as well as sea lions. It is also a pre-Columbian site with substantial pottery finds, and there is good diving and snorkelling, as well as walks. Take a change of clothes, water, precautions against sun and seasickness (most agencies provide snorkelling equipment). You can only visit with a tour and staying overnight is not permitted.

Puerto López to Manta

North of Machalilla, the road forks at **Puerto Cayo**, where whale-watching tours may be organized July-August. One road follows the coast, partly through forested hills, passing Cabo San Lorenzo with its lighthouse. The other route heads inland through the trading centre of **Jipijapa** to **Montecristi**, below an imposing hill, 16 km before Manta. Montecristi is renowned as the centre of the panama hat industry. Also produced are varied straw- and basketware, and wooden barrels which are strapped to donkeys for carrying water. Ask for José Chávez Franco, Rocafuerte 203, where you can see panama hats being made. Some 23 km east of Montecristi is **Portoviejo**, capital of Manabí province, a sweltering unsafe commercial city.

Not to scale

Where to stay 🛏
1 Itapoa
2 La Terraza
3 Mandála
4 Máxima
5 Nantu
6 Sol Inn
7 Victor Hugo

Restaurants 🍴
1 Bellitalia
2 Carmita
3 Patacón Pisao

Where to stay

Salinas

$$$ El Carruaje
Malecón 517, T04-277 4282.
Comfortable rooms, some with ocean view, all facilities, good restaurant, electric shower, a/c, fridge, parking.

$$ Francisco I and II
Enríquez Gallo y Rumiñahui, T04-277 4106; Malecón y Las Palmeras, T04-277 3751.
Both are very nice, comfortable rooms, restaurant, a/c, fridge pool.

$$ Travel Suites
Av 5 Y C 13, T04-277 2856, miltoninnhotel@hotmail.com.
Modern, a/c, kitchenette with fridge, very good value in low season.

$$-$ Porto Rapallo
Av Edmundo Azpiazu y 24 de Mayo, T04-277 1822.
Modern place in a quiet area, hot water, a/c, cheaper with fan, good value.

Valdivia

$$ Valdivia Ecolodge
At Km 40, just south of San Pedro.
Screened cabins without walls in a nice location above the ocean, fresh and interesting. Restaurant, pool and access to nice bathing beach.

Manglaralto
See also **Proyecto de Desarrollo Ecoturístico Comunitario**, page 632.

$$-$ Manglaralto Sunset
1 block from the Plaza, T09-9440 9687, manglaralto_beach@yahoo.com.
Nice modern place, comfortable rooms with a/c, hammocks, cafeteria bar, electric shower, parking.

Montañita
There are many places to stay in town; the quieter ones are at Montañita Punta. Prices are negotiable in low season.

$$$-$$ Balsa Surf Camp
50 m from the beach in Montanita Punta, T09-8971 4685.
Very nice spacious cabins with terrace, hammocks in garden, fan, parking, surf classes and rentals, small well-designed spa, French/Ecuadorean-run. Recommended.

$$ La Casa del Sol
In Montañita Punta, T09-6863 4956, www.casadelsolmontanita.com.
A/c, some rooms are dark, fan, restaurant/bar, surf classes and rentals, yoga drop-in.

$$ Pakaloro
In town at the end of C Guido Chiriboga, T04-206 0092.
Modern 4-storey building with lots of wood, ample rooms with balcony and hammock, fan, shared kitchen, nice setting by the river, good value.

$$ Rosa Mística
Montañita Punta, T09-9798 8383, www.rosamisticahostal.com.
Tranquil place, small rooms, cheaper ones away from beach, a/c, garden.

$$-$ La Casa Blanca
C Guido Chiriboga, T09-9918 2501.
Wooden house, rooms with bath, mosquito nets, hammocks, good restaurant and bar. A Montañita classic, in the heart of the action.

$$-$ Las Palmeras
Malecón at south end of town, T09-8541 9938.
Reasonably quiet, fan, laundry, family-run, English spoken.

$$-$ Sole Mare
On the beach at the north end of Montañita Punta, T04-206 0119.
In a lovely setting on the beach, fan, garden, parking, run by an attentive father-and-son,

both called Carlos, English spoken, good value. Recommended.

Olón

$$$ Samai
10 mins from town by taxi (US$5), T09-462 1316, www.samailodge.com.
Rustic cabins in a natural setting, great views, restaurant/bar, pool, jacuzzi, advance booking required.

$$ Isramar
Av Sta Lucia, ½ block from beach, T04-278 8096.
Rooms with bath and fan, small garden, restaurant/bar, friendly owner Doris Cevallos.

$$-$ La Mariposa
A block from the beach, near church, T09-8017 8357, www.lamariposahostal.com.
3-storey building, nice ocean views from top floor, Italian-run, English and French also spoken, good value.

Ayampe to Salango
Ayampe

$$ Finca Punta Ayampe
South of other Ayampe hotels, Quito T09-9189 0982, www.fincapuntaayampe.com.
Bamboo structure high on a hill with great ocean views, restaurant, hot water, mosquito nets, helpful staff.

$$-$ Cabañas de la Iguana
Ayampe, T05-257 5165, www.hotelayampe.com.
Cabins for 4, mosquito nets, cooking facilities, quiet, relaxed family atmosphere, knowledgeable and helpful, organizes excursions, good choice.

Las Tunas–Puerto Rico

$$$-$$ La Barquita
By Las Tunas, 4 km north of Ayampe, T05-234 7051, www.hosterialabarquita.com.
Restaurant and bar are in a boat on the beach with good ocean views, rooms with

fan and mosquito nets, pool, nice garden, games, tours, Swiss-run.

Salango

$$ Islamar
On a hilltop south of Salango, T09-9385 7580, www.hosteria-islamar.com.ec.
Ample comfortable cabins, restaurant, lovely views of Isla Salango, camping in your own tent US$10 pp, parking for motor-homes. Offers paragliding and diving, Swiss/Ecuadorean-run, advance booking advised.

Puerto López

$$$ La Terraza
On hill overlooking town (moto-taxi US$0.50), T09-8855 4887, www.laterraza.de.
Spacious cabins, great views over the bay, gardens, restaurant (only for guests), crystal-clear pool and jacuzzi, parking, German-run.

$$$ Victor Hugo
North along the beach, T05-230 0054, www.victorhugohotel.com.ec.
Ample rooms with bamboo decor, balconies.

$$ Mandála
Malecón at north end of the beach, T05-230 0181, www.hosteriamandala.info.
Nice cabins decorated with art, fully wheelchair accessible, gorgeous tropical garden, good restaurant only for guests, fan, mosquito nets, games, music room, Swiss/Italian-run, English spoken, knowledgeable owners. Highly recommended.

$$ Nantu
Malecón at north end of the beach, T05-230 0040, www.hosterianantu.com.
Ample modern well-maintained rooms, a/c, small pool and garden, restaurant and bar overlooking the beach.

$$-$ Itapoa
On a lane off Abdón Calderón, between the Malecón and Montalvo, T09-9314 5894.
Thatched cabins around large garden, hot water, cheaper in dorm, includes breakfast

on a lovely terrace overlooking the sea, family-run, English spoken.

$ Máxima
González Suárez y Machalilla, T05-230 0310, www.hotelmaxima.org.
Cheaper with shared bath, mosquito nets, laundry and cooking facilities, parking, modern, English spoken, good value.

$ Sol Inn
Montalvo entre Eloy Alfaro y Lascano, T05-230 0248, hostal_solinn@hotmail.com.
Bamboo and wood construction, private or shared bath, hot water, fan, laundry and cooking facilities, garden, pool table, popular, relaxed atmosphere.

Puerto López to Manta
There are other places to stay but many close out of season.

$$ Luz de Luna
5 km north of Puerto Cayo on the coastal road, T09-9708 8613 Quito T02-249 3825, www.hosterialuzdeluna.com.
On a clean beach, comfortable spacious rooms with balcony, a/c, cheaper with fan, cold water in cabins, shared hot showers available, mosquito nets, pool.

$$ Puerto Cayo
South end of beach, Puerto Cayo, T05-238 7119, T09-9752 1538.
Good restaurant, a/c or fan, comfortable rooms with hammocks and terrace overlooking the sea.

Restaurants

Salinas
A couple of blocks inland from the Malecón are food stalls serving good ceviches and freshly cooked seafood.

$$$ La Bella Italia
Malecón y C 17, near Hotel El Carruaje.
Good pizza and international food.

$$$-$$ Amazon
Malecón near Banco de Guayaquil, T04-277 3671.
Elegant upmarket eatery, grill and seafood specialities, good wine list.

$$ Oyster Catcher
Enríquez Gallo entre C 47 y C 50. Oct-May.
Restaurant and bar, friendly place, safe oysters, enquire here about birdwatching tours with local expert Ben Haase.

$ El Mayquito
Av 2 y C 12.
Simple, friendly place with good food.

Montañita

$$$-$$ Tikilimbo
Opposite Hotel Casa Blanca.
Good quality, vegetarian dishes available.

$$ Hola Ola
In the center of town.
Good international food and bar with some live music and dancing, popular.

$$ Marea Pizzeria Bar
10 de Agosto y Av 2. Open evenings only.
Real wood-oven pizza, very tasty. Recommended.

$$ Rocío
10 de Agosto y Av 2, inside eponymous hotel.
Good Mediterranean food.

Salango

$$ El Delfín Mágico.
T09-9114 7555.
Excellent, order meal before visiting museum because all food is cooked from scratch, very fresh and safe.

Puerto López

$$$ Bellitalia
North toward the river, T09-9617 5183. Mon-Sat 1800-2100.
Excellent authentic Italian food, home-made pasta, attentive owners Vittorio and Elena. Reservations required. Recommended.

$$ Carmita
Malecón y General Córdova.
Tasty fish and seafood,
a Puerto López tradition.

$$ Patacón Pisao
Gen Córdova, half a block from the malecón.
Colombian food, giant *patacones* and *arepas*.

What to do

Salinas
Ben Haase, *at Museo de Ballenas, Av Enríquez Gallo 1109 entre C47 y C50, T04-277 7335, T09-8674 7607.* Expert English-speaking naturalist guide runs birdwatching tours to the Ecuasal salt ponds, US$50 for a small group. Also whale watching and trips to a sea lion colony. **Fernando Félix**, *T04-238 4560, T09-7915 8079.* English-speaking marine biologist, can guide for whale watching and other nature trips, arrange in advance.

Montañita
Surfboard rentals all over town from US$4 per hr, US$15 per day.

Language courses
Montañita Spanish School, on the main road 50 m uphill outside the village, T04-206 0116, www.montanitaspanishschool.com.

Ayampe to Salango
Ayampe
Otra Ola, *beside Cabañas de la Iguana, www. otraola.com.* Surf lessons and board rental, yoga and Spanish classes. Enthusiastic Canadian owners.

Puerto López
Language courses
La Lengua, *Abdón Calderón y García Moreno, east of the highway, T09-233 9316 or Quito T02-250 1271, www.la-lengua.com.*

Whale watching
Puerto López is a major centre for trips from Jun to Sep, with many more agencies than we can list. Whales can also be seen elsewhere, but most reliably in Puerto López. There is a good fleet of small boats (16-20 passengers) running excursions, all have life jackets and a toilet, those with 2 engines are safer. All agencies offer the same tours for the same price. Beware touts offering cheap tours to "La Isla", they take you to Isla Salango not Isla de la Plata. In high season: US$40 pp for whale watching, Isla de la Plata and snorkelling, with a snack and drinks, US$25 for whale watching only (available Jun and Sep). Outside whale season, tours to Isla de la Plata and snorkelling cost US$40. Trips depart from the pier (US$1 entry fee) around 0800 and return around 1700. Agencies also offer tours to the mainland sites of the national park. A day tour combining Agua Blanca and Los Frailes costs US$25 pp plus US$5 entry fee. There are also hiking, birdwatching, kayaking, diving (be sure to use a reputable agency) and other trips.
Aventuras La Plata, *on Malecón, T05-230 0189, www.aventuraslaplata.com.* Whale-watching tours.
Cercapez, *at the Centro Comercial on the highway, T05-230 0173.* All-inclusive trips to San Sebastián, with camping, local guide and food at US$40 pp per day.
Exploramar Diving, *Malecón y Gral Córdova, T05-230 0123, www.exploradiving.com.* Quito based, T02-256 3905. Have 2 boats for 8-16 people and their own compressor. PADI divemaster accompanies qualified divers to various sites, but advance notice is required, US$120 pp for all-inclusive diving day tour (2 tanks). Also diving lessons. Recommended.
Palo Santo, *Malecón y Abdón Calderón, T05-230 0312, palosanto22@gmail.com.* Whale-watching tours.

Transport

Playas
Bus Trans Posorja and **Villamil** to **Guayaquil**, frequent, 2 hrs, US$3.25; taxi US$25.

Salinas

Bus To **Guayaquil**, **Coop Libertad Peninsular (CLP)**, María González y León Avilés, every 5 mins, US$4.75, 2½ hrs. For **Montañita**, **Puerto López** and points north, transfer at La Libertad (not safe, take a taxi between terminals) or Santa Elena. From La Libertad, every 30 mins to Puerto López, US$5, 2½ hrs; or catch a Guayaquil–Olón bus in Santa Elena.

Manglaralto

Bus To **Santa Elena** and **La Libertad**, US$1.50, 1 hr. Transfer in Santa Elena for Guayaquil. To **Guayaquil** direct, see Olón, below. To **Puerto López**, 1 hr, US$2.

Montañita and Olón

Bus Montañita is just a few mins south of Olón, from where **CLP** has direct buses to **Guayaquil** at 0445, 0545, 1000, 1300, 1500, 1700 (same schedule from Guayaquil), US$7.50, 3 hrs; taxi US$90; or transfer in Santa Elena, US$2, 1½ hrs. To **Puerto López**, **Cooperativa Manglaralto** every 30 mins, US$2.50, 45 mins.

Puerto López

Mototaxis all over town, US$0.50 pp.

Bus Bus terminal 2 km north of town. To **Santa Elena** or **La Libertad**, every 30 mins, US$5, 2½ hrs. To **Montañita** and **Manglaralto**, US$3.25, 1 hr. To **Guayaquil**, direct with **Cooperativa Jipijapa** via Jipijapa, 10 daily, US$5.75, 4 hrs; or transfer in Olón or Santa Elena. Pick-ups for hire to nearby sites are by the market, east of the highway. To/from **Manta**, direct, hourly, US$3.75, 2½ hrs; or transfer in Jipijapa. To **Quito** with **Reina del Camino**, office in front of market, daily 0800 and 2000; and **CA Aray** at 0500, 0900 and 1900, 9 hrs, US$16. To **Jipijapa**, **Cooperativa Jipijapa**, every 45 mins, US$2, 1 hr.

Parque Nacional Machalilla

Bus To Los Frailes: take a bus towards Jipijapa (US$0.75), mototaxi (US$5), or a pick-up (US$8), and alight at the turn-off just south of the town of Machalilla, then walk for 30 mins. No transport back to Puerto López after 2000 (but check in advance). **To Agua Blanca**: take tour, a pick-up (US$7), mototaxi (US$10 return with 2 hrs wait) or a bus bound for Jipijapa (US$0.75); it is a hot walk of more than 1 hr from the turning to the village. **To Isla de la Plata**: the island can only be visited on a day trip. Many agencies offer tours, see Puerto López, above.

Puerto López to Manta

Bus From Jipijapa (terminal on the outskirts) to **Manglaralto** (2 hrs, US$2.50), to **Puerto López** (1 hr, US$1.25, these go by Puerto Cayo), to **Manta** (1 hr, US$1.25), to **Quito** (10 hrs, US$9).

Manta and Bahía de Caráquez
busy centres separated by wildlife and sporting opportunities

These are two quite different seaside places: Manta a rapidly growing port city, prospering on fishing and trade; Bahía de Caráquez a relaxed resort town and a pleasant place to spend a few days. It is proud of its 'eco' credentials. Just beyond Bahía, on the other side of the Río Chone estuary, is the popular resort village of Canoa, boasting some of the finest beaches in Ecuador.

Manta and around *Colour map 1, B2.*
Ecuador's second port after Guayaquil is a busy town that sweeps round a bay filled with all sorts of boats. A constant sea breeze tempers the intense sun and makes the city's *malecones* pleasant places to stroll. At the gentrified west end of town is Playa

Murciélago, a popular beach with wild surf (flags indicate whether it is safe to bathe), with good surfing from December to April. Here, the Malecón Escénico has a cluster of bars and seafood restaurants. It is a lively place especially at weekends, when there is good music, free beach aerobics and lots of action. Beyond El Murciélago, along the coastal road are San Mateo, Santa Marianita, San Lorenzo and Puerto Cayo, before reaching Machalilla and Puerto López. The **Museo Centro Cultural Manta** ① *Malecón y C 19, T05-262 6998, Mon-Fri 0900-1630, Sat-Sun 1000-1500, free,* has a small but excellent collection of archaeological pieces from seven different civilizations which flourished on the coast of Manabí between 3500 BC and AD 1530. Three bridges join the main town with **Tarqui**, which was flattened in the April 2016 earthquake. Manta has public safety problems, enquire locally about the current situation.

Crucita

A rapidly growing resort, 45 minutes by road from either Manta or Portoviejo, Crucita is busy at weekends and holidays when people flock here to enjoy ideal conditions for paragliding, hang-gliding and kite-surfing. The best season for flights is July to December. There is also an abundance of sea birds in the area. There are many restaurants serving fish and seafood along the seafront. A good one is **Motumbo**, try their *viche*, they also offer interesting tours and rent bikes.

North to Bahía

About 60 km northeast of Manta (30 km south of Bahía de Caráquez) are **San Clemente** and, 3 km south, **San Jacinto**. The ocean is magnificent but be wary of the strong undertow. Both get crowded during the holiday season and have a selection of *cabañas* and hotels. Some 3 km north of San Clemente is **Punta Charapotó**, a high promontory clad in dry tropical forest, above a lovely beach. Here are some nice out-of-the way accommodations and an out-of-place upmarket property development.

☆Bahía de Caráquez and around *Colour map 1, B2.*

Set on the southern shore at the seaward end of the Chone estuary, Bahía has an attractive riverfront laid out with parks along the Malecón which goes right around the point to the ocean side. The beaches in town are nothing special, but there are excellent beaches nearby between San Vicente and Canoa and at Punta Bellaca (the town is busiest July-August). Bahía has declared itself an 'eco-city', with recycling projects, organic gardens and ecoclubs. Tricycle rickshaws called 'eco-taxis' are a popular form of local transport and keep the streets blissfully quiet. Information about the eco-city concept can be obtained from **Río Muchacho Organic Farm** in Canoa (see below) or the **Planet Drum Foundation** ① *www.planetdrum.org.* **Museo Bahía de Caráquez** ① *Malecón Alberto Santos y Aguilera, T05-269 2285, Tue-Sat 0830-1630, free,* has an interesting collection of archaeological artefacts from prehispanic coastal cultures, a life-size balsa raft and modern sculpture. Bahía is a port for international yachts, with good service at **Puerto Amistad** ① *T05-269 3112.* There was significant earthquake damage in April 2016.

The Río Chone estuary has several islands with mangrove forest. The area is rich in birdlife, and dolphins may also be seen. **Isla Corazón** has a boardwalk through an area of protected mangrove forest and there are bird colonies at the end of the island which can only be accessed by boat. The village of **Puerto Portovelo** is involved in mangrove reforestation and runs an ecotourism project (tour with *guía nativo* US$6 per person). You can visit independently, taking a Chone-bound bus from San Vicente or with an agency. Visits here are tide-sensitive, so even if you go independently, it is best to check with the agencies about the best time to visit. Inland near Chone is **La Segua** wetland, very rich in birds; Bahía agencies offer tours here. **Saiananda** ① *5 km from Bahía along the bay, T05-239 8331, owner Alfredo Harmsen, biologist, reached by taxi or any bus heading out of town, US$2*, is a private park with extensive areas of reforestation and a large collection of animals, a cactus garden and spiritual centre. Also offer first-class accommodation ($$ including breakfast) and vegetarian meals served in an exquisite dining area over the water.

San Vicente and Canoa *Colour map 1, B2.*

On the north side of the Río Chone, **San Vicente** is reached from Bahía de Caráquez by a long bridge. Some 17 km beyond, **Canoa**, once a quiet fishing village with a splendid 200-m-wide beach, has grown rapidly and is increasingly popular with Ecuadorean and foreign tourists. It was badly damaged in the April 2016 earthquake. There is no ATM in Canoa, but in San Vicente at Banco Pichincha. The beautiful beach between San Vicente and Canoa is a good walk, horse or bike ride. Horses and bicycles can be hired through several hotels. Surfing is good, particularly during the wet season, December to April. In the dry season there is good wind for windsurfing. Canoa is also a good place for hang-gliding and paragliding. Tents for shade and chairs are rented at the beach for US$3 a day. About 10 km north of Canoa, the **Río Muchacho organic farm** (www.riomuchacho. com, see What to do, page 645) accepts visitors and volunteers, it's an eye-opener to rural coastal (*montubio*) culture and to organic farming.

North to Pedernales *Colour map 1, A2.*

The coastal road cuts across Cabo Pasado to **Jama** (1½ hours; cabins and several *hostales*), then runs parallel to the beach past coconut groves and shrimp hatcheries, inland across some low hills and across the Equator to **Pedernales**, a market town and crossroads with nice undeveloped beaches to the north. It was heavily damaged in the 2016 earthquake. A poor unpaved road goes north along the shore to Cojimíes. The main coastal road, fully paved, goes north to Chamanga, El Salto and Esmeraldas. Another important road goes inland to El Carmen; it divides at Puerto Nuevo: one branch to Santo Domingo de los Tsáchilas, another to La Concordia. The latter is the most direct route to Quito.

Santo Domingo de los Tsáchilas

In the hills above the western lowlands, Santo Domingo, 129 km from Quito, is an important commercial centre and transport hub. It is capital of the eponymous province. The city is big, noisy and unsafe, caution is recommended at all times in the market areas, including the pedestrian walkway along 3 de Julio and in peripheral neighbourhoods. Sunday is market day, shops and banks close Monday instead. It was known as 'Santo Domingo de los Colorados', a reference to the traditional red hair dye, made with *achiote* (annatto), worn by the indigenous Tsáchila men. Today the Tsáchila only wear their indigenous dress on special occasions. There are less than 2000 Tsáchilas left, living in eight communities off the roads leading from Santo Domingo towards the coast. Their lands make up a reserve of some 8000 ha. Visitors interested in their culture are welcome at the **Complejo Turístico Huapilú**, in the Comunidad Chigüilpe, where there is a small but interesting museum (contributions expected). Access is via the turn-off east at Km 7 on the road to Quevedo, from where it is 4 km. Tours are run by travel agencies in town. The Santo Domingo area also offers opportunities for nature trips and sports activities, such as rafting.

Tourist information

Ministerio de Turismo (Paseo José María Egas 1034 (Av 3) y C 11, Manta, T05-262 2944, Mon-Fri 0900-1230, 1400-1700); **Dirección Municipal de Turismo** (C9 y Av 4, Manta, T05-261 0171, Mon-Fri 0800-1700); and **Oficina de Información ULEAM** (Malecón Escénico, Manta, T05-262 4099, daily 0900-1700); all helpful and speak some English.

Where to stay

Manta and around
All streets have numbers; those above 100 are in Tarqui (those above C110 are not safe).

$$$$ Oro Verde
Malecón y C 23, T05-262 9200,
www.ororverdehotels.com.
Includes buffet breakfast, restaurant, pool, all luxuries.

$$$ Vistalmar
C M1 y Av 24B, at Playa Murciélago, T05-262 1671, www.hosteriavistaalmar.com.
Exclusive hotel overlooking the ocean. Ample cabins and suites tastefully decorated with art, a/c, pool, cabins have kitchenettes, gardens by the sea. A place for a honeymoon.

$$$-$$ Donkey Den
In Santa Marianita, 20 mins south of Manta, T09-9723 2026, www.donkeydenguesthouse.com.
Nice rooms right on the beach where kite-surfing is popular, private or shared bath, dorm for 5 US$15 pp, cooking facilities, breakfast available, popular with US expats, taxi from Manta US$10.

$$ Manakin
C 20 y Av 12, T05-262 0413.
A/c, comfortable rooms, small patio, nice common areas.

$$ YorMar
Av 14 entre C 19 y C 20, T05-262 4375, www.hostalyormar.com.ec.

Attractive rooms with small kitchenette and patio, a/c, parking.

$ Centenario
C 11 No 602 y Av 5, enquire at nearby Lavamatic Laundry, T05-262 9245.
Pleasant hostel in a refurbished old home in the centre of town. Shared bath, hot water, fan, cooking facilities, nice views, quiet location, good value.

Crucita

$$-$ Cruzita
Towards the south end of beach, T05-234 0068.
Pleasant hostel right on the beach with great views, meals on request, cold water, fan, small pool, use of kitchen in the evening, parking, good value. Owner Raul Tobar offers paragliding flights and lessons. Recommended.

$$-$ Hostal Voladores
At south end of beach, T05-234 0200, www.parapentecrucita.com.
Simple but nice, restaurant, private bath, chaeper with shared bath, hot water, small pool, sea kayaks available. Owner Luis Tobar offers paragliding flights and lessons.

North to Bahía
San Jacinto and San Clemente

$$ Hotel San Jacinto
On the beach between San Jacinto and San Clemente, T05-267 2516, www.hotelsanjacinto.com.
Older refurbished place with a pleasant location right by the ocean, restaurant, hot water, fan.

Punta Charapotó

$$-$ Peñón del Sol
On the hillside near Punta Charapotó, T09-9941 4149, penondelsol@hotmail.com.

Located on a 250 ha dry tropical forest reserve, meals on request, shared bath, cold water, lovely atmosphere, great views, camping possible.

$ Sabor de Bamboo
On the ocean side of the road to Punta Charapotó, T09-8024 3562, see Facebook.
Nice simple wooden cabins with sea breeze, cold water, restaurant and bar, music on weekends, wonderfully relaxed place, friendly owner Meier, German and English spoken.

Bahía de Caráquez

$$$ La Piedra
Circunvalación near Bolívar, T05-269 0780, www.hotellapiedra.com.ec.
Modern hotel with access to the beach and lovely views, good expensive restaurant, a/c, pool, good service, bicycle rentals for guests.

$$ La Herradura
Bolívar e Hidalgo, T05-269 0446, www.laherradurahotelecuador.com.
Older well-maintained hotel, restaurant, a/c, cheaper with fan and cold water, nice common areas, cheaper rooms are good value.

$ Bahía Hotel
Malecón y Vinueza, T05-269 1880, http://ecuavacation.com.
A variety of different rooms, those at the back are nicer, a/c, cheaper with fan, parking.

Canoa

There are over 60 hotels in Canoa.

$$$ Hostería Canoa
1 km south of town, T09-9995 5401, www.hosteriacanoa.com.
Comfortable cabins and rooms, good restaurant and bar, a/c, pool, sauna, whirlpool.

$$-$ Baloo
On the beach at south end of the village, T05-258 8155, www.baloo-canoa.com.
Wood and bamboo cabins, restaurant, private or shared bath, British-run. Nice quiet location but a little run down.

$$-$ La Vista
On the beach towards the south end of town, T09-9228 8995.
All rooms have balconies to the sea, palm garden with hammocks, good value. Recommended.

$ Casa Shangrila
On main road 200 m north of bridge, T09-9146 8470, http://casashangrila.com.
Inland, away from the buzz of the centre but only 5 min walk from a nice quiet stretch of beach. Rooms with fan and private bath, hot water, nice garden, small pool, attentive service, good value.

$ Coco Loco
On the beach toward the south end of town, T09-9243 6508, www.hostalcocoloco.weebly.com.
Pleasant breezy hotel with nice views, café serves breakfast and snacks, bar, private or shared bath, also dorm, hot showers, cooking facilities, surfboard rentals, party atmosphere, excellent horse riding, English spoken, popular.

North to Pedernales
Jama

$$$$-$$$ Punta Prieta Guest House
By Punta Prieta, T09-8039 5972, Quito T02-286 2986, www.puntaprieta.com.
Gorgeous setting on a headland high above the ocean with access to pristine beaches. Meals available, comfortable cabins and suites with fridge, balcony with hammocks, nice grounds.

Pedernales

There are many other hotels in all price ranges.

$$ Agua Marina
Jaime Roldós 413 y Velasco Ibarra, T05-268 0491.
Modern hotel, cafeteria, a/c, pool, parking.

$$ Cocosolo
On a secluded beach 20 km north of Pedernales (pickups from main park

US$1, 30 mins), T09-09-9940 6048,
http://cocosololodge.com.
A lovely hideaway set among palms. Cabins
and rooms, camping possible, restaurant,
horses for hire, French and English spoken.

Santo Domingo de los Tsáchilas

$$$$ Tinalandia
*16 km from Santo Domingo, on the road to
Quito, poorly signposted; look for a large
rock painted white; T09-9946 7741, Quito
T02-244 9028, www.tinalandia.com.*
Includes full board, nice chalets in cloudforest
reserve bordering on Bosque Protector
Tanti, great food, spring-fed pool, good
birdwatching, advance booking required.

$$$ Zaracay
*Av Quito 1639, 1.5 km from the centre,
T02-275 0316, www.hotelzaracay.com.*
Restaurant, gardens and swimming pool
(US$5 for non-guests), parking, good rooms
and service. Advance booking advised,
especially on weekends.

$ Safiro Internacional
29 de Mayo 800 y Loja, T02-276 0706.
Comfortable modern hotel, cafeteria,
hot water, a/c, good value.

Restaurants

Manta and around
Restaurants on Malecón Escénico serve
local seafood.

$$ Club Ejecutivo
Av 2 y C 12, top of Banco Pichincha building.
First-class food and service, great view.

$$ El Marino
Malecón y C 110, Tarqui. Open for lunch only.
Classic fish and seafood restaurant, for
ceviches, *sopa marinera* and other delicacies.

Bahía de Caráquez

$$ Puerto Amistad
*On the pier at Malecón y Vinueza.
Mon-Sat 1200-2400.*

Nice setting over the water, international
food and atmosphere, popular with yachties.

$$-$ Arena-Bar Pizzería
*Riofrío entre Bolívar y Montúfar, T05-269
2024. Daily 1700-2330.*
Restaurant/bar serving good pizza, salads
and other dishes, nice atmosphere, also take-
away and delivery service. Recommended.

$$-$ Muelle Uno
*By the pier where canoes leave for San
Vicente. Daily 1000-2400.*
Good grill and seafood, lovely setting over
the water.

$ Doña Luca
*Cecilio Intriago y Sergio Plaza, towards the tip
of the peninsula. Daily 0800-1800.*
Simple little place serving excellent local
fare, ceviches, *desayuno manabita* (a
wholesome breakfast), and set lunches.
Friendly service, recommended.

Canoa

$$ Amalur
Behind the soccer field. Daily 1200-2100.
Fresh seafood and authentic Spanish
specialities, attentive service.

$$-$ Surf Shak
At the beach. Daily 0800-2400.
Good for pizza, burgers and breakfast, best
coffee in town, Wi-Fi, popular hangout for
surfers, English spoken.

What to do

Manta and around
Delgado Travel, *Av 6 y C 13, T05-262 2813,
vtdelgad@hotmail.com.* City and regional
tours, whale-watching trips, Parque Nacional
Machalilla, run **Hostería San Antonio** at
El Aromo, 15 km south of Manta.

Language courses
Academia Sur Pacífico, *Av 24 y
C 15, Edif Barre, p3, T05-267 9206,
www.surpacifico.k12.ec.*

Bahía de Caráquez
Language courses
Sundown, *at Sundown Inn, in Canoa, on the beach, 3 km toward San Vicente, contact Juan Carlos, T09-9364 5470, www.ecuadorbeach. com.* US$7.50-9 per hr.

Canoa
Surfboard rentals US$5 per hr.
Canoa Thrills, *at the beach next to Surf Shak, www.canoathrills.com.* Surfing tours and lessons, sea kayaking. Also rent boards and bikes. English spoken.
Río Muchacho Organic Farm, *J Santos y Av 3 de Noviembre, T05-302 0487, www. riomuchacho.com.* Bookings for the organic farm and ecocity tours. Also has an ecolodge ($ pp) with meals at US$5. Hikes from Canoa to Río Muchacho and around Río Muchacho. Knowledgeable and helpful with local information. Recommended.

Transport

Manta and around
Air Eloy Alfaro airport. **TAME** (T05-390 5052), **Avianca** (T05-262 8899) and **LATAM** to **Quito** several daily.

Bus Most buses leave from the terminal on C 7 y Av 8 in the centre. A couple of companies have their own private terminals nearby. To **Quito** Terminal Quitumbe, 9 hrs, US$10. **Guayaquil**, 4 hrs, US$5, hourly. **Esmeraldas**, 3 daily, 10 hrs, US$10. **Santo Domingo**, 7 hrs, US$7.50. **Portoviejo**, 45 mins, US$1, every 10 mins. **Jipijapa**, 1 hr, US$1.25, every 20 mins. **Bahía de Caráquez**, 3 hrs, US$3.75, hourly.

Crucita
Bus Run along the Malecón. There is frequent service to **Portoviejo**, US$1.25, 1 hr and **Manta**, US$1.50, 1½ hrs.

North to Bahía
Bus From San Clemente to **Portoviejo**, every 15 mins, US$1.50, 1¼ hrs. To **Bahía de Caráquez**, US$0.75, 30 mins, a few start in

San Clemente in the morning or wait for a through bus at the highway. Mototaxis from San Clemente to Punta Charapotó, US$0.75.

Bahía de Caráquez
Boat Motorized canoes (*lanchas* or *pangas*) cross the estuary to **San Vicente**, from the dock opposite C Ante, US$0.50.

Bus The Terminal Terrestre is at the entrance to town, 3 km from centre, taxi US$2. To **Quito** Terminal Quitumbe, **Reina del Camino** at 0620, 0800, 2145 and 2220, 8 hrs, US$12.50. To **Santo Domingo**, 5 hrs, US$7.50. To **Guayaquil**, hourly, 6 hrs, US$8.75. To **Portoviejo,** 2 hrs, US$2.50. To **Manta**, 3 hrs. US$3.75. To **Puerto López**, change in Manta, Portoviejo or Jipijapa.

Canoa
Bus To/from **San Vicente**, every 30 mins, 0600-1900, 30 mins, US$0.75; taxi US$5. Taxi to/from Bahía de Caráquez, US$7. To **Pedernales**, every 30 min 0600-1800, 2 hrs, US$3.25. To **Quevedo**, 4 daily, where you can get a bus to **Quilotoa** and **Latacunga**. To **Quito**, direct with **Reina del Camino** at 2145, US$12.50, 6 hrs; or transfer in Pedernales or Bahía.

Pedernales
Bus To **Santo Domingo**, every 15 mins, 3½ hrs, US$5, transfer to Quito. To **Quito** (Quitumbe) direct **Trans Vencedores**, 7 daily via Santo Domingo, US$7.75, 5 hrs; also starting in Jama at 0815 and 2300. To **Chamanga**, hourly 0600-1700, 1½ hrs, US$2.50, change there for **Esmeraldas**, 3½ hrs, US$4.50. To **Bahía de Caráquez**, shared vans from Plaza Acosta 121 y Robles, T05-268 1019, 7 daily, US$5.75.

Santo Domingo de los Tsáchilas
Bus The bus terminal is on Av Abraham Calazacón, at the north end of town, along the city's bypass. Long distance buses do not enter the city. Taxi downtown, US$1, bus US$0.25. A major hub with service

throughout Ecuador.To **Quito** via Alóag US$3.75, 3 hrs; via San Miguel de los Bancos, 5 hrs; also **Sudamericana Taxis**, Cocaniguas y Río Toachi, p 2, T02-275 2567, door to door shared taxi service, frequent departures via Alóag or Los Bancos, 0400-1900, US$15-17,

3-4 hrs. To **Ambato** US$5, 4 hrs. To **Loja** US$16.25, 11 hrs. To **Guayaquil** US$6.25, 5 hrs. To **Esmeraldas** US$3.75, 3 hrs. To **Atacames**, US$5, 4 hrs. To **Manta** US$7.50, 7 hrs. To **Bahía de Caráquez** US$6.25, 6 hrs. To **Pedernales** US$5, 3½ hrs.

Northern lowlands

a lush area with an interesting cultural mix

A mixture of palm lined beaches, mangroves (where not destroyed for shrimp production), tropical rainforests, Afro-Ecuadorean and Cayapa indigenous communities characterize this part of Ecuador's Pacific lowlands as they stretch north to the Colombian border.

North to Atacames

North of Pedernales the coastal highway veers northeast, going slightly inland, then crosses into the province of Esmeraldas near **Chamanga** (San José de Chamanga, population 4400), a village with houses built on stilts on the freshwater estuary. It was devastated in the April 2016 earthquake. The town is 1 km from the highway. Inland and spanning the provincial border is the **Reserva Ecológica Mache-Chindul**, a dry forest reserve.

North of Chamanga by 31 km and 7 km from the main road along a paved side road (this intersection is not a safe place to wait) is **Mompiche** with a lovely beach and one of Ecuador's best surfing spots. There is an international resort complex and holiday real-estate development 2 km south at Punta Portete. The beach is being gradually eroded by the sea and a break-water has been built near the town. The nearest banks and ATMs are far away in Atacames and Pedernales. Take sufficient cash. The main road continues through El Salto, the crossroads for **Muisne**, a town on an island with a beach (strong undertow) and a few hostels.

The fishing village of **Tonchigüe** is 25 km north of El Salto. South of it, a paved road goes west and follows the shore to **Punta Galera**, along the way is the secluded beach of **Playa Escondida** (see Where to stay, below). Northeast of Tonchigüe by 3 km is Playa de **Same**, with a beautiful, long, clean, grey sandy beach, safe for swimming. The accommodation here is mostly upmarket, intended for wealthy Quiteños, but it is wonderfully quiet in the low season. There is good birdwatching in the area and some of the hotels offer whale watching tours in season. Ten kilometres east of Same and 4 km west of Atacames, is **Súa**, a friendly little beach resort, set in a beautiful bay (damaged in the April 2016 earthquake).

Atacames *Colour map 1, A2.*

One of the main resorts on the Ecuadorean coast, Atacames, 30 km southwest of Esmeraldas, is a real party town during the high season (July-September), at weekends and national holidays. Head instead for Súa or Playa Escondida (see above) if you want peace and quiet.

After the damage caused by the April 2016 earthquake, the area around Atacames and Esmeraldas was badly affected by a second major earthquake in December 2016. At the time of writing (January 2017) it is not known what services are open.

Esmeraldas *Colour map 1, A2.*

Capital of the eponymous province, Esmeraldas is a place to learn about Afro-Ecuadorean culture and some visitors enjoy its very relaxed swinging atmosphere. Marimba groups can be seen practising in town, enquire about schedules at the tourist office. A bridge connects the city to Tachina, where the airport is located. Ceramics from La Tolita culture (see below) are found at the **Museo y Centro Cultural Esmeraldas** ⓘ *Bolívar y Piedrahita, US$1, English explanations.* Despite its wealth in natural resources, Esmeraldas is among the poorest provinces in the country. Shrimp farming has destroyed much mangrove, and timber exports are decimating Ecuador's last Pacific rainforest.

Insect-borne diseases including malaria are a serious problem in many parts of Esmeraldas province, especially in the rainy season (January to May). Most *residenciales* provide mosquito nets (*toldos* or *mosquiteros*), or buy one in the market near the bus station. Esmeraldas also suffered in the December 2016 earthquake. It is not yet known what services are closed.

North of Esmeraldas

From Esmeraldas, the coastal road goes northeast to Camarones and Río Verde, with a nice beach, from where it goes east to **Las Peñas**, once a sleepy seaside village with a nice wide beach, now a holiday resort. With a paved highway from Ibarra, Las Peñas is the closest beach to any highland capital, only four hours by bus. Ibarreños pack the place on weekends and holidays. From Las Peñas, a secondary road follows the shore north to **La Tola** (122 km from Esmeraldas) where you can catch a launch to Limones. Here the shoreline changes from sandy beaches to mangrove swamp; the wildlife is varied and spectacular, especially the birds. The tallest mangrove trees in the world (63.7 m) are found by **Majagual** to the south. To the northeast of La Tola and on an island on the northern shore of the Río Cayapas is **La Tolita**, a small, poor village, where the culture of the same name thrived between 300 BC and AD 700. Many remains have been found here, several burial mounds remain to be explored and looters continue to take out artefacts to sell.

Limones (also known as Valdez) is the focus of traffic downriver from much of northern Esmeraldas Province, where bananas from the Río Santiago are sent to Esmeraldas for export. The Cayapa people live up the Río Cayapas and can sometimes be seen in Limones, especially during the crowded weekend market, but they are more frequently seen at Borbón (see below).

Borbón and further north

Borbón, upriver from La Tola at the confluence of the Cayapas and Santiago rivers, is a lively, dirty, busy and somewhat dangerous place, with a high rate of malaria. The local fiestas with marimba music and other Afro-Ecuadorean traditions are held the first week of September.

From Borbón, the coastal road goes northeast towards **Calderón** where it meets the Ibarra-San Lorenzo road. Along the way, by the Río Santiago, are the nature reserves of **Humedales de Yalare**, accessed from **Maldonado**, and Playa de Oro (see below). From Calderón, the two roads run together for a few kilometres before the coastal road turns north and ends at **Mataje** on the border with Colombia. The road from Ibarra continues to San Lorenzo.

San Lorenzo *Colour map 1, A3.*

Hot and humid San Lorenzo stands on the Bahía del Pailón, which is characterized by a maze of canals. It is a good place to experience the Afro-Ecuadorean culture including marimba music and dances. There is a local festival 6-10 August and groups practice throughout the year; ask around. At the seaward end of the bay are several beaches without facilities, including San Pedro (one hour away) and Palma Real (1¾ hours). Note that this is a tense border area with many

Tip…
Arrive in San Lorenzo prepared! Expect to be mobbed by children wanting a tip to show you to a hotel or restaurant. Also take insect repellent.

police and other patrols, but also armed civilians and much contraband activity. Enquire about current conditions with the police or Navy (Marina). From San Lorenzo you can visit several natural areas; launches can be hired for excursions, see Transport, page 651. There are mangroves at **Reserva Ecológica Cayapas-Mataje**, which protects islands in the estuary northwest of town. **Reserva Playa de Oro** ⓘ *www.touchthejungle.org, see Where to stay, page 649*, has 10,406 ha of Chocó rainforest, rich in wildlife, along the Río Santiago. Access is from **Selva Alegre** (a couple of basic *residenciales*), off the road to Borbón.

Border with Colombia: San Lorenzo–Tumaco

The Río Mataje is the border with Colombia. From San Lorenzo, the port of Tumaco in Colombia can be reached by a combination of boat and land transport. Because this is a most unsafe region, travellers are advised not to enter Colombia at this border. Go to Tulcán and Ipiales instead.

Listings Northern lowlands

Tourist information

iTur
Bolívar y 9 de Octubre, Esmeraldas, T06-272 3150.

Ministerio de Turismo
Mejía y Sucre, p 4, Esmeraldas, T06-245 2242. Mon-Fri 0900-1200, 1500-1700.

Oficina Municipal de Turismo
On the road into Atacames from Esmeraldas, T06-273 1912. Mon-Fri 0800-1230, 1330-1600.

Where to stay

North to Atacames
Mompiche
There are several economical places in the town. Camping on the beach is not safe.

$ Gabeal
300 m east of town, T09-9969 6543, http://hosteriagabeal.wixsite.com/turismoecuador.
Lovely quiet place with ample grounds and beachfront. Bamboo construction with ocean views, balconies, small rooms, cabins

and dorms (U\$10 pp), camping (US\$5 pp) breakfast available, discounts in low season. Rooms 6 to 10 are good choices.

Tonchigüe to Punta Galera

\$\$\$-\$\$ El Acantilado
By the cliff, T06-302 7620, www.elacantilado.net.
Comfortable rooms, pool, nice views, gardens, good restaurant, path to the beach. Also operate a camping area at Tongorachi, US\$30 pp including 3 meals prepared in the community, a private development project.

\$\$ Playa Escondida
10 km west of Tonchigüe and 6 km east of Punta Galera, T06-302 7496, T09-9650 6812, www.playaescondida.com.ec.
A charming beach hideaway set in 100 ha with 500 m beachfront stretching back to dry tropical forest. Run by Canadian Judith Barett on an ecologically sound basis. Nice rustic cabins overlooking a lovely little bay, excellent restaurant, private showers, shared composting toilets, camping US\$10 pp,

good birdwatching, swimming and walking along the beach at low tide. Also offers volunteer opportunities.

$$-$ La Terraza
On same beach, T06-247 0320,
pepo@hotmail.es.
Pleasant rooms and cabins for 3-4 with balconies, hammocks and large terrace, spacious, hot water, a/c, fan, mosquito net, some rooms have fridge, good restaurant open in season, Spanish-run.

Súa

$$ Buganvillas
On the beach, T06-247 3008, see Facebook.
Nice, room 10 has the best views, pool, helpful owners.

$ Chagra Ramos
On the beach, T06-247 3106.
Ageing hotel with balconies overlooking the beach, restaurant, cold water, fan, parking, good service.

Atacames
Prices rise on holiday weekends, discounts may be available in low season. There are many more hotels than we can list.

$$$ Juan Sebastián
Towards the east end of the beach,
T06-273 1049, www.hoteles-embassy.com/
juansebastian/en/index.php.
Large upmarket hotel with cabins and suites, restaurant, a/c, 3 pools (US$5 for non-guests), fridge, parking, popular with Quiteños.

$$ Carluz
Behind the stadium, T06-273 1456,
www.hotelcarluz.com.
Good hotel in a quiet location. Comfortable suites for 4 and apartments for 6, good restaurant, a/c, fan, pool, fridge, parking.

$$ Cielo Azul
Towards the west end of the beach,
near the stadium, T06-273 1813,
www.hotelcieloazul.com.

Restaurant, fan, pool, fridge, rooms with balconies and hammocks, comfortable and very good.

Esmeraldas
Hotels in the centre are poor; better to stay in the outskirts.

$$ Apart Hotel Esmeraldas
Libertad 407 y Ramón Tello, T06-272 0622,
http://aparthotelesmeraldas.net.
Good restaurant, a/c, fridge, parking, excellent quality.

$$ Perla Verde
Piedrahita 330 y Olmedo, T06-270 4024,
www.hotelperlaverde.ec.
Good rooms with a/c and fridge. Check website for post-earthquake situation.

North of Esmeraldas
Las Peñas

$$$-$$ Cabañas Mikey
By the beach, north end, T06-279 3101, http://
laspeñasesmeraldas.com/cabanas_mikey.html.
Cabins with kitchenettes, private bath, hot water, pool.

San Lorenzo

$$$ Playa de Oro
On the Río Santiago, upriver from Borbón,
contact Ramiro Buitrón at Hotel Valle del
Amanecer in Otavalo, T06-292 0990,
www.touchthejungle.org.
Basic cabins with shared bath, includes 3 meals and guided excursion. Advance booking required.

$$ Tunda Loma
Km 17 on the road to Ibarra (taxi from
San Lorenzo US$5), T06-278 0367.
Beautifully located on a hill overlooking the Río Tululbí. Wood cabins, includes breakfast, restaurant, warm water, fan, organizes tubing trips on the river and hikes in the forest.

$$-$ Castillo Real
Camilo Ponce y Esmeraldas, T06-278 0152,
see Facebook.

Rooms with private bath and a/c, cheaper with fan, good restaurant, parking.

Restaurants

North to Atacames
Mompiche
Several other places serve cheap set meals.

$$ La Facha
Between the main street and Hotel Gabeal.
Great sea food and vegetarian (try their veggie burgers), very creative and recommended. Argentine chef.

$ Comedor Margarita
On main street, 2 blocks from the beach. Daily from 0730.
Basic *comedor* serving tasty local fare, mostly fish and seafood.

Same

$$$ Seaflower
By the beach at the entrance road.
Excellent international food.

$$-$ Azuca
By south entrance to village, T09-8882 9581, Facebook: Same-Azuca-Restaurant.
Good creative food, also rents cheap rooms with shared or private bath.

Súa

$ Kikes
On the Malecón, T09-9355 8406.
Good local food, generous portions, good value, also rents rooms.

Atacames
The beach is packed with bars and restaurants offering seafood, too many to list.

$$ Da Giulio
Malecón y Cedros. Weekdays 1700-2300, weekends from 1100.
Spanish and Italian cuisine, good pasta.

$$-$ La Ramada
On the Malecón.
Specializes in ceviches and *encebollados*, good value.

Esmeraldas
There are restaurants and bars on the Malecón at Las Palmas beach offering regional specialities.

$$ Chifa Asiático
Cañizares y Bolívar, T06-272 6888.
Chinese and seafood, a/c, excellent.

$$ El Chacal
Manabí y Alfaro, T06-272 4436, Facebook: La-Casa-Del-Chacal. Open 1700-2300.
Tasty à la carte meals, popular with locals.

$$-$ Ceviche Maranatha
Quito y Olmedo, T09-415 0681.
Good ceviche and other seafood.

$$-$ Parrilladas el Toro
Olmedo y 9 de Octubre, T06-272 3610, Facebook: parrilladaeltoro.
Popular meat and seafood grill.

Transport

North to Atacames
Bus Hourly from **Chamanga** to **Esmeraldas**, US$4.50, 3½ hrs, and to **Pedernales**, US$2.50, 1½ hrs. **Mompiche** to/from **Esmeraldas**, 8 a day, US$3.75, 3 hrs, the last one from Esmeraldas about 1630. To **Playa Escondida**: take a *ranchera* or bus from Esmeraldas or Atacames for Punta Galera or Cabo San Francisco, 5 a day, US$2.50, 2 hrs. A taxi from Atacames costs US$15 and a pick-up from Tonchigüe US$6.25. To **Súa** and **Same**: Buses every 30 mins to and from **Atacames**, 15 mins, US$0.50. Make sure it drops you at Same and not at Club Casablanca.

Atacames
Bus To **Esmeraldas**, every 15 mins, US$1, 1 hr. To **Guayaquil**, US$11.25, 8 hrs, **Trans Esmeraldas** at 0830 and 2245. To **Quito**, various companies, about 10 daily, US$10,

7 hrs. To **Pedernales**, **Coop G Zambrano**, 4 daily, US$5, 4 hrs or change in Chamanga.

Esmeraldas

Air The Airport is along the coastal road heading north. A taxi to the city centre costs US$3, buses to the Terminal Terrestre from the road outside the airport pass about every 30 mins. If heading north towards San Lorenzo, you can catch a bus outside the airport. **TAME** (at Centro Comercial Multiplaza, Maldonado entre Estupiñán y Manabí, T06-272 5203), 1-2 daily flights to **Quito**; to **Guayaquil**, 1 daily Mon, Wed, Fri.

Bus *Terminal terrestre* by Redondel CODESA, taxi to town US$3, to airport US$6. **Trans-Esmeraldas** (recommended) and **Panamericana** have *servicio directo* or *ejecutivo* to Quito and Guayaquil, a better choice as they are faster buses and don't stop for passengers along the way. Frequent service to **Quito** via Santo Domingo or via Calacalí, US$8.75, 6 hrs; ask which terminal they go to before purchasing ticket; also shared vans via Los Bancos with **Esmetur Express**, Espejo y Eloy Alfaro, T06-271 3488 or T09-9226 0857, 4 vehicles daily, 5 hrs, US$30, US$10-20 extra to/from the beaches. To **Ibarra**, 9 hrs, US$12.50, via Borbón. To **Santo Domingo**, US$3.75, 3 hrs. To **Ambato**, 6 a day, US$10, 8 hrs. To **Guayaquil**, hourly, US$10, *directo*, 8 hrs. To **Bahía de Caráquez**, via Santo Domingo, US$10, 9 hrs. To **Manta**, US$10, 10 hrs. **La Costeñita** and **El Pacífico**, both on Malecón, to/from **La Tola**, 8 daily, US$4.75, 3 hrs. To **Borbón**, frequent service, US$4.50, 3 hrs. To **San Lorenzo**, 8 daily, US$5.75, 4 hrs. To **Súa**, **Same** and **Atacames**, every 15 mins from 0630-2030, to Atacames US$1, 1 hr. To **Chamanga**, hourly 0500-1900, US$4.50, 3½ hrs, change here for points south.

North of Esmeraldas

Ferry There are launches between **La Tola** and **Limones** which connect with the buses arriving from Esmeraldas, US$3.75, 1 hr, and 3 daily Limones-**San Lorenzo**, 2 hrs US$3. You can also hire a launch to **Borbón**, a fascinating trip through mangrove islands, passing hunting pelicans, approximately US$10 per hr.

Borbón

Bus To **Esmeraldas**, US$4.50, 3 hrs. To **San Lorenzo**, US$2, 1 hr.

San Lorenzo

Bus Buses leave from the train station or environs. To **Ibarra**, 10 daily, US$5, 4 hrs. To **Esmeraldas**, via Borbón, 8 daily, US$5.75, 4 hrs.

Ferry Launch service with **Coopseturi**, T06-278 0161; and **Costeñita**, both near the pier. All services are subject to change and cancellation. To **Limones**, 4 daily, US$3, 2 hrs. To **La Tola**, US$6, 4 hrs. To **Palma Real**, for beaches, 2 daily, US$3, 2 hrs. To hire a boat for 5 passengers costs US$20 per hr.

The
Oriente

East of the Andes the hills fall away to tropical lowlands. Some of this beautiful wilderness remains unspoiled and sparsely populated, with indigenous settlements along the tributaries of the Amazon. Large tracts of jungle are under threat, however: colonists are clearing many areas for agriculture, while others are laid waste by petroleum development. For the visitor, the Ecuadorean jungle, especially the Northern Oriente, has the advantage of being easily accessible and infrastructure here is well developed. The eastern foothills of the Andes, where the jungle begins, offer a good introduction to the rainforest for those with limited time or money. Further east lie the few remaining large tracts of primary rainforest, teeming with life, which can be visited from several excellent (and generally expensive) jungle lodges. Southern Oriente is as yet less developed for tourism, it offers good opportunities off the beaten path but is threatened by large mining projects.

Best for
Adventure sports ▪ Jungle lodges ▪ Wildlife

Essential Oriente

There are commercial flights from Quito to Lago Agrio, Coca and Macas; and from Guayaquil to Coca via Latacunga. From Quito, Macas and Shell, light aircraft can be chartered to any jungle village with a landing strip. Western Oriente is also accessible by scenic roads which wind their way down from the highlands. Quito, via Baeza, to Lago Agrio and Coca, Baños to Puyo, and Loja to Zamora are fully paved, as is the entire lowland road from Lago Agrio south to Zamora. Other access roads to Oriente include: Tulcán to Lago Agrio via Lumbaqui, Riobamba to Macas, and roads from Cuenca to Macas and Gualaquiza.

Getting around

Some roads are narrow and tortuous and subject to landslides in the rainy season, but all have regular bus service and all can be travelled in a 4WD or in an ordinary car with good ground clearance. Deeper into the rainforest, motorized canoes provide the only alternative to air travel.

Jungle travel without a guide is not recommended. Access to national parks and reserves is controlled, some indigenous groups prohibit the entry of outsiders, navigation in the jungle is difficult, and there are dangerous animals. For your own safety as well as to be a responsible tourist, the jungle is not a place to wander off on your own. See below for tours.

Jungle tours

These fall into four basic types: lodges, guided tours, indigenous ecotourism and river cruises. When staying at a jungle lodge, you will need to take a torch (flashlight), insect repellent, protection against the sun and a rain poncho. See also Lodges on the Lower Napo (page 658) and the Upper Napo (page 666). All jungle lodges must be booked in advance. **Guided tours** of varying length are offered

Tip...

There may be police and military checkpoints in the Oriente, so always have your passport handy.

by tour operators, who should be licensed by the Ecuadorean **Ministerio de Turismo**. Tour operators are mainly concentrated in Quito, Baños, Puyo, Tena, Misahuallí, Coca, and, to a lesser extent, Macas and Zamora.

A number of indigenous communities and families offer **ecotourism** programmes in their territories. These are either community-controlled and operated, or organized as joint ventures between the indigenous community or family and a non-indigenous partner. These programmes usually involve guides who are licensed as *guías nativos* with the right to guide within their communities. You should be prepared to be more self-sufficient on such a trip than on a visit to a jungle lodge or a tour with a high-end operator. Take a light sleeping bag, rain jacket, trousers (not only shorts), long-sleeve shirt for mosquitoes, binoculars, torch, insect repellent, sunscreen and hat, water-purifying tablets, and a first aid kit. Keep everything in waterproof stuff-sacks or several plastic bags to keep it dry. Ask if rubber books are provided.

River cruises offer an appreciation of the grandeur of Amazonia, but less intimate contact with life in the rainforest. Passengers sleep and take meals onboard comfortable river boats, stopping to visit local communities and the jungle.

Safety

A yellow fever vaccination is required. Anti-malarial tablets are recommended, as is an effective insect repellent. In the province of Sucumbíos, enquire about public safety before visiting sites near the Colombian border.

When to go

Heavy rain can fall at any time, but it is usually wettest from March to September.

waterfalls, cloudforests, lagoons and wildlife

Much of the Northern Oriente is taken up by the Parque Nacional Yasuní, the Cuyabeno Wildlife Reserve and most of the Cayambe-Coca Ecological Reserve. The main towns for access are Baeza, Lago Agrio and Coca.

Quito to the Oriente

From Quito to Baeza, a paved road goes via the **Guamaní pass** (4064 m). It crosses the Eastern Cordillera just north of **Volcán Antisana** (5705 m), and then descends via the small village of **Papallacta** (hot springs, see page 526) to the old mission settlement of Baeza. The trip between the pass and Baeza has beautiful views of the glaciers of Antisana (clouds permitting), high waterfalls, *páramo*, cloudforest and a lake contained by an old lava flow.

Baeza *Colour map 1, A4.*

The mountainous landscape and high rainfall have created spectacular waterfalls and dense vegetation. Orchids and bromeliads abound. Baeza, in the beautiful Quijos valley, is about 1 km from the main junction of roads from Lago Agrio and Tena. The town itself is divided in two parts: a faded but pleasant **Baeza Colonial** (Old Baeza) and **Baeza Nueva** (New Baeza), where most shops and services are located. The trail/road from Baeza Vieja to Las Antennas has nice views, two hours return. There are excellent kayaking and rafting opportunities in the area, tours offered by Casa de Rodrigo (see Where to stay, below) and operators in Quito and Tena.

Beyond Baeza

From Baeza a road heads south to Tena, with a branch going east via Loreto to Coca, all paved. Another paved road goes northeast from Baeza to Lago Agrio, following the Río Quijos past the villages of **Borja** (8 km from Baeza, very good *comedor* Doña Cleo along the highway, closed Sunday) and **El Chaco** (12 km further, basic accommodation) to the slopes of the active volcano **Reventador**, 3560 m. Check www.igepn.edu.ec and enquire locally about volcanic activity before trekking here; simple $ Hostería El Reventador at the bridge over the Río Reventador; Ecuador Journeys offers tours, see page 519. Half a kilometre south of the bridge is signed access to the impressive 145-m **San Rafael Falls** (part of **Reserva Ecológica Cayambe-Coca**), believed to be the highest in Ecuador. It is a pleasant 45-minute hike through cloudforest to a *mirador* with stunning views of the thundering cascade. Many birds can be spotted along the trail, including cock-of-the-rock, also monkeys and coatimundis. A large hydroelectric project has been built nearby. Although access to the falls is not restricted, the turbines use up to 70% of the water in the Río Quijos, leaving the remainder to go over the falls.

Lago Agrio *Colour map 1, A5.*

The capital of Sucumbíos province is an old oil town which now lives mainly from commerce with neighbouring Colombia. The name comes from Sour Lake, the US headquarters of Texaco, the first oil company to exploit the Ecuadorean Amazon in the 1970s. It is also called Nueva Loja or just 'Lago'. If taking a Cuyabeno tour from Lago Agrio, it is worth leaving Quito a couple of days early, stopping en route at Papallacta, Baeza and San Rafael falls (see above).

Tip...

Lago Agrio is 30 km from the Colombian border, the crossing here is not safe and routine precautions are advised in town as well; best return to your hotel by 2200.

Cuyabeno Wildlife Reserve

This large tract of rainforest, covering 603,000 ha, is located about 100 km east of Lago Agrio along the Río Cuyabeno, which eventually drains into the Aguarico. In the reserve are many lagoons and a great variety of wildlife, including river dolphins, tapirs, three species of caimans, ocelots, 11 species of monkeys and some 680 species of birds. This is among the best places in Ecuador to see jungle animals. The reserve is deservedly popular and offers a more economical jungle experience than many other areas in Oriente.

Access to most lodges is by paved road from Lago Agrio via Tarapoa as far as the bridge over the Río Cuyabeno, where there is a ranger station and visitors must register. Nobody is allowed to enter the reserve without a tour. From the bridge, transport is mainly by motorized canoe; **Magic River** also offers a worthwhile paddling alternative, see Cuyabeno jungle lodges, below. Most tours include a visit to a local Siona community.

The reserve can be visited year-round but the dry season (January-February) can bring low water levels and generally less wildlife, although certain species may be easier to see at this time. In order to see as many animals as possible and minimally impact their habitat, seek out a small tour group which scrupulously adheres to responsible tourism practices. Cuyabeno is close to the Colombian border and there have, in the past, been occasional armed robberies of tour groups. Do not take unnecessary valuables. Most Cuyabeno tours are booked through Quito agencies or online, see Cuyabeno jungle lodges, below.

Coca *Colour map 1, A5.*

Officially named **Puerto Francisco de Orellana**, Coca is a hot, noisy, bustling city at the junction of the Ríos Payamino and Napo, which has experienced exceptionally rapid growth from petroleum development. It is the capital of the province of Orellana and, for tourists, a launch pad to visit the lower Río Napo and jungle areas accessed from the Vía Auca, a road running south from the city. The view over the water is nice, and the riverfront **Malecón** can be a pleasant place to spend time around sunset; various indigenous groups have craft shops here. Hotel and restaurant provision is adequate but heavily booked and ironically for an oil-producing centre, petrol supplies are erratic.

Jungle tours from Coca The **lower Río Napo**, **Parque Nacional Yasuní** and **Huaorani Reserve**, all accessed from Coca, offer some of the finest jungle facilities and experiences in Ecuador. Wildlife in this area is nonetheless under threat, insist that guides and fellow tourists take all litter back and ban all hunting. Many tours out of Coca are booked through agencies in Quito but there are also a few local operators (see below).

The paved road to Coca via Loreto passes through **Wawa Sumaco**, where a rough road heads north to **Sumaco National Park**; 7 km along it is $$$$ **Wildsumaco** ⓘ *T06-301 8343, Quito office T02-333 1633, www.wildsumaco.com, reservations required,* a comfortable birdwatching lodge with full board, excellent trails and over 500 birds including many rare species. Just beyond is the village of **Pacto Sumaco** from where a trail runs through the park to the *páramo*-clad summit of **Volcán Sumaco** (3732 m), six to seven days round-trip. Local guides must be hired, there are three nice shelters along the route and a community-run hostel in the village (T06-301 8324, www.sumacobirdwatching.com).

Coca to Nuevo Rocafuerte and Iquitos (Peru)

Pañacocha is halfway between Coca and Nuevo Rocafuerte, near a magnificent lagoon. Here are a couple of lodges (see Lodges on the Lower Napo, in Where to stay, below) and Coca agencies also run tours to the area (see Jungle tours, in What to do, below). Entry to Pañacocha reserve US$10. There are basic places to stay and eat in Pañacocha village.

Following the Río Napo to Peru is rough, adventurous and requires plenty of time and patience. There are two options: by far the more economical is to take a motorized canoe from Coca to **Nuevo Rocafuerte** on the border. This tranquil riverside town has simple hotels, eateries, a phone office and basic shops. It can be a base for exploring the endangered southeastern section of **Parque Nacional Yasuní**; local guides are available. Ecuadorean immigration is two blocks from the pier, next to the Municipio. Peruvian entry stamps are given in **Pantoja**, where there is a decent municipal *hospedaje*, $ **Napuruna**. Shopkeepers in Nuevo Rocafuerte and Pantoja change money at poor rates; soles cannot be changed in Coca. In addition to immigration, you may have to register with the navy on either side of the border so have your passport at hand. See Transport, page 660, for Coca–Nuevo Rocafuerte boat services and onward to Pantoja and Iquitos. See also Iquitos Transport, page 330.

The second option for river travel to Iquitos is to take a tour with a Coca agency, taking in various attractions on route, and continuing to Iquitos or closer Peruvian ports from which you can catch onward public river transport. These tours are expensive and may involve many hours sitting in small, cramped craft; confirm all details in advance.

Listings Northern Oriente

Tourist information

Lago Agrio

iTur
Av Quito y 20 de Junio, in the Parque Recreacional, T06-283 3951, iturlagoagrio@hotmail.com. Mon-Fri 0800-1700.

Coca

iTur
Chimborazo y Amazonas, by the Malecón, T06-288 0532, www.orellanaturistica.gob.ec. Mon-Sat 0730-1630.

Ministerio de Turismo
Quito y Chimborazo, Ed Azriel Shopping, T06-288 1583.
The place to file any complaints regarding a jungle lodge or tour.

Where to stay

Baeza

$$-$ Gina
Jumandy y Batallón Chimborazo, just off the highway in the old town, T06-232 0471, restaurantgina@hotmail.com.

Hot water, parking, pleasant, popular restaurant.

$$-$ Quinde Huayco
By the park in the old town, T06-232 0649.
Nice ample rooms, garden, restaurant, quiet location away from the main road.

$ La Casa de Rodrigo
In the old town, T09-232 0467, rodrigobaeza1@yahoo.com.
Modern and comfortable, hot water, cheaper with shared bath, kitchen facilities, friendly owner offers rafting trips, kayak rentals and birdwatching. Good value and recommended.

$ Samay
Av de los Quijos, in the new town, T06-232 0170.
Very well-maintained older place with private or shared bath, hot water, friendly, family-run, good value.

Around Baeza

$$$$ Cabañas San Isidro
Near Cosanga, 19 km south of Baeza, T02-289 1880 (Quito), www.cabanasanisidro.com.
A 1200-ha private nature reserve with rich birdlife, comfortable accommodation and

warm hospitality. Includes 3 excellent meals, reservations required.

$$ Hostería El Reventador
On main highway next to bridge over the Río Reventador, turismovolcanreventador@yahoo.com.
Meals on request, hot water, pool, simple rooms, busy at weekends, a bit run-down and mediocre service but well located for San Rafael Falls and Volcán Reventador.

Lago Agrio

$$$ Gran Hotel de Lago
Km 1.5 Vía Quito, T06-283 2415, granhoteldelago@grupodelago.com.
Restaurant, a/c, pool, parking, cabins with nice gardens, quiet. Recommended and often full.

$$ Arazá
Quito 536 y Narváez, T06-283 1287, www.hotel-araza.com.
Nice comfortable rooms, restaurant, a/c, pool, fridge, parking. Recommended.

$$ El Cofán
12 de Febrero 3915 y Quito, T06-283 0526, elcofanhotel@yahoo.es.
Restaurant, a/c, fridge, parking, older place but well maintained.

$$ Lago Imperial
Colombia y Quito, T06-283 0453, hotellagoimperial@hotmail.com.
A/c, some rooms with hot water, ample common areas, pool, patio, restaurant, central location, good value.

$$-$ Gran Colombia
Quito y Pasaje Gonzanamá, T06-283 1032, hgrancolombia@yahoo.es.
With a/c, cheaper with fan and cold water, more expensive rooms in back are quieter and better, indoor parking, central.

$$-$ Oasis
9 de Octubre y Orellana, T06-283 0879.
Modern hotel away from centre, a/c, cheaper with fan, very clean, includes breakfast.

$ Casa Blanca
Quito 228 y Colombia, T06-283 0181.
Simple adequate rooms with electric shower and fan.

Cuyabeno Wildlife Reserve
Lodges
There are over a dozen lodges operating in Cuyabeno, more than we can list. The following are all recommended. Prices range from US$300-475 pp for 5 days/4 nights, including transport from Lago Agrio, accommodation, all meals and guiding. A small community fee is charged separately.

Caiman Lodge
T09-9161 0922, www.caimanlodge.com.
On Quebrada La Hormiga near the lagoon. Well maintained lodge with an observation tower.

Cuyabeno Lodge
Operated by Neotropic Turis, Quito T02-292 6153, www.neotropicturis.com.
On the lagoon. This was the first lodge in the reserve, operating since 1988. Very well organized and professional. Ample grounds, comfortable accommodation in several price categories, observation tower, and paddle canoes for use of guests.

Guacamayo Ecolodge
Operated by Ara Expeditions, Quito, T02-290 4765, www.guacamayoecolodge.com.
On the Río Cuyabeno near the lagoon. Well maintained lodge with an observation tower.

Magic River
Quito T02-262 9303, www.magicrivertours.com.
On the Río Cuyabeno downstream from the lagoon. Specialize in paddling trips (great fun and wildlife watching without engine noise) which spend the first night in a tent camp in the jungle. Friendly atmosphere at the lodge, good food and service.

Nicky Lodge
Operated by Dracaena, Quito T02-290 6644, www.amazondracaena.com.

On the lower Río Cuyabeno near it's confluence with the Aguarico, far from all the other lodges. Good wildlife including some species not easily seen elsewhere.

Siona Lodge
Booked through Galasam, Quito T02-290 3909, www.galasam.net.
On the lagoon. Comfortable lodge with very good infrastructure.

Tapir Lodge
Quito T02-380 1567, www.tapirlodge.com.
On the Río Cuyabeno downstream from the lagoon. Known for high-quality guiding.

Coca
Coca hotels are often full, best book in advance.

$$$ Heliconias
Cuenca y Amazonas, T06-288 2010, heliconiaslady@yahoo.com.
Spotless rooms, ample grounds, upmarket restaurant, includes buffet breakfast, pool and gym (US$5 for non-guests). Large new section under construction in 2016. Recommended.

$$$-$$ El Auca
Napo y García Moreno, T06-288 1554, www.hotelelauca.com.
Restaurant, a/c, parking, a variety of different rooms and mini-suites. Comfortable, nice garden with hammocks, English spoken. Popular, central, but can get noisy.

$$$-$$ Río Napo
Bolívar entre Napo y Quito, T06-288 0872, www.hotelrionapo.com.
Modern rooms with a/c, good but a bit overpriced.

$$ La Misión
By riverfront 100 m downriver from the bridge, T06-288 0260, hotelamision@hotmail.com.
A larger hotel, restaurant, disco on weekends, a/c and fridge, pool (US$3 for non-guests), parking, a bit faded but still adequate.

$$ Omaguas
Quito y Cuenca, T06-288 2436, h_omaguas@hotmail.com.
Very clean rooms with tile floors, a/c, restaurant, parking, attentive service.

$$-$ Amazonas
12 de Febrero y Espejo, T06-288 0444, hosteriacoca@hotmail.com.
Nice quiet setting by the river, away from centre, restaurant, electric shower, a/c, cheaper with fan, parking.

$$-$ San Fermín
Quito 75-04 y Bolívar, T06-288 0802, alexandragalarza@amazonwildlife.ec.
Variety of different rooms, some with a/c, cheaper with fan, ample parking, popular and busy, good value, owner organizes tours. Recommended.

$ Santa María
Rocafuerte entre Quito y Napo, T09-9761 7034.
Small adequate rooms with a/c or fan, private bath, cold water, good economy option.

Jungle tours from Coca
Lodges on the Lower Napo
All Napo lodges count travel days as part of their package, which means that a '3-day tour' spends only 1 day actually in the jungle. All prices given below are per person based on double occupancy, including transport from Coca. Most lodges have fixed departure days from Coca (eg Mon and Fri) and it is very expensive to get a special departure on another day. For lodges in Cuyabeno, see page 657; for lodges on the Upper Napo, see page 666, for southern Oriente lodges see page 667.

Amazon Dolphin Lodge
Quito T02-250 3225, www. amazondolphinlodge.com.
On Laguna de Pañacocha, 4½ hrs downriver from Coca. Special wildlife here includes Amazon river dolphins and giant river otters as well as over 500 species of birds. May be closed in dry season (Jan-Feb). Cabins with private bath, US$600 for 4 days.

Napo Wildlife Center

Quito T02-600-5893, USA T1-866-750-0830, UK T0-800-032-5771, www.ecoecuador.org.
Operated by and for the local Añangu community, 2½ hrs downstream from Coca. This area of hilly forest is rather different from the low flat forest of some other lodges, and the diversity is slightly higher. There are big caimans and good mammals, including giant otters, and the birdwatching is excellent with 2 parrot clay-licks and 2 canopy towers, 32 m and 50 m high. US$1100 for 4 days. Recommended.

La Selva

Quito T02-255 0995, www. laselvajunglelodge.com.
An upmarket lodge and spa, 2½ hrs downstream from Coca on a picturesque lake. Surrounded by excellent forest, especially on the far side of Mandicocha. Bird and animal life is exceptionally diverse. Many species of monkey are seen regularly. A total of 580 bird species have been found, one of the highest totals in the world for a single elevation. Comfortable cabins, excellent meals, massage treatments available at extra cost. High standards, canopy tower, most guides are biologists. US$1215 for 4 days.

Sacha

Quito T02-256 6090, www.sachalodge.com.
An upmarket lodge 2½ hrs downstream from Coca. Very comfortable cabins, excellent meals. The bird list is outstanding; the local bird expert, Oscar Tapuy (Coca T06-2881486), can be requested in advance. Canopy tower and 275-m canopy walkway. Several species of monkey are commonly seen. Nearby river islands provide access to a distinct habitat. US$1050 for 4 days.

Sani

Quito T02-243 2813, www.sanilodge.com.
All proceeds go to the Sani Isla community, who run the lodge with the help of outside experts. It is located on a remote lagoon which has 4- to 5-m-long black caiman. This area is rich in wildlife and birds, including many species such as the scarlet macaw which have disappeared from most other Napo area lodges. There is good accommodation and a 35-m canopy tower. An effort has been made to make the lodge accessible to people who have difficulty walking; the lodge can be reached by canoe (total 3½ hrs from Coca) without a walk. US$953 for 4 days. Good value, recommended.

Lodges in the Reserva Huaorani

Otobo's Amazon Safari

www.rainforestcamping.com.
8-day/7-night camping expeditions in Huaorani territory, access by road from Coca then 2-day motorized canoe journey on the Ríos Shiripuno and Cononaco. All meals and guiding included. Excellent jungle with plenty of wildlife. US$200 pp per night.

Shiripuno

Quito T02-227 1094, www.shiripunolodge.com.
A lodge with capacity for 20 people, very good location on the Río Shiripuno, a 4-hr canoe ride downriver from the Vía Auca. Cabins have private bath. The surrounding area has seen relatively little human impact to date. US$400 for 4 days, plus US$20 entry to Huaorani territory.

Coca to Nuevo Rocafuerte and Iquitos

$ Casa Blanca

Malecón y Nicolás Torres, T06-238 2184.
Rooms with a/c or fan, nice, simple, welcoming. There are a couple of other basic places to stay in town.

Restaurants

Baeza

$$-$ Kopal

50 m off the main road opposite the old town.
Good pizza, nice atmosphere, closes early.

$ El Viejo

East end of Av de los Quijos, the road to Tena in the new town. Daily 0700-2100.
Good set meals and à la carte.

Lago Agrio

There are good restaurants at the larger hotels (see above).

$$-$ D'Mario
Av Quito 2-63. Daily 0630-2200.
Set meals and à la carte, generous portions, popular, meeting place for Cuyabeno groups.

$$-$ La Casanostra
Guayaquil 500 y 9 de Octubre. Mon 1200-1500, Tue-Sat 1200-1500, 1830-2230.
Nice quiet place with open-air seating, good set lunch, à la carte at night.

$ El Buen Samaritano
12 de Febrero y Venezuela. Sun-Fri 0700-1930.
Cheap and simple vegetarian restaurant.

Coca

$$ Fuego y Carne
Fernando Roy y Amazonas.
Upmarket for Coca, good grill and Italian dishes.

$$-$ Pizza Choza
Rocafuerte entre Napo y Quito. Daily 1800-2200.
Good pizza, nice atmosphere.

$ La Casa del Maito
Espejo entre Quito y Napo. Daily 0700-2300.
Simple place serving *maitos* and other local specialities, good food, hopelessly chaotic service, go early before it gets crowded.

$ Media Noche
Napo y Rocafuerte (no sign). Daily 1700-2400.
Only chicken in various dishes, large portions, quick service, very popular, a Coca institution.

$ Ocaso
Eloy Alfaro entre Napo y Amazonas. Mon-Sat 0630-2030, Sun 0630-1400.
Simple set meals and à la carte.

Papa Dan's Bar
Napo y Chimborazo.
A landmark watering-hole by the Malecón. Several other bars nearby.

What to do

Coca
Jungle tours
See also page 655.

Amazon Travel, *Amazonas y Espejo, in Hotel Safari, T06-288 1805, www.ecuador travelamazon.com.* Patricio Juanka runs jungle tours throughout the region, very knowledgeable and helpful.

Luis Duarte, *at Casa del Maito (see Restaurants, above), T06-288 2285, cocaselva@hotmail.com.* Regional tours and trips to Iquitos.

Sachayacu Explorer, *in Píllaro near Baños (see page 569), T03-287 5316.* Although not based in Coca, experienced jungle guide Juan Medina offers recommended jungle tours and trips to Iquitos. Advance arrangements required.

Wildlife Amazon, *Robert Vaca at Hotel San Fermín (see Where to stay, above), T06-288 0802, www.amazonwildlife.ec.* Jungle tours and trips to Iquitos.

River cruises on the lower Río Napo
Manatee, *operated by Advantage Travel, Quito T02-336 0887, www.manateeamazonexplorer. com.* This 30-passenger vessel sails between Pompeya and Pañacocha, US$986 for 4 days. First-class guides, excellent food, en suite cabins. They also operate similar cruises onboard the 40-passenger luxury vessel **Anakonda** (www.anakondaamazoncruises. com), US$1800 for 4 days.

Coca to Nuevo Rocafuerte and Iquitos
Juan Carlos Cuenca, *Nuevo Rocafuerte, T06-238 2257.* Is a *guía nativo* who offers tours to Parque Nacional Yasuní, about US$60 per day.

Transport

Baeza
Bus Buses to and from **Tena** pass right through town. If arriving on a **Lago Agrio** bus, get off at the crossroads (La "Y") and

walk or take a pick-up for US$0.25. From **Quito**, Mon-Sat at 1130, 1245, 1520, 1645, with **Trans Quijos**, T02-295 0842, from Chile E3-22 y Pedro Fermín Cevallos (near La Marín, an unsafe area at night), US$4, 3 hrs. These continue to Borja and El Chaco. To Quito from El Chaco Mon-Sat at 0330, 0430, 0600, 0800, pass Baeza about 20 mins later.

Lago Agrio

Air Airport is 3 km southeast of the centre, taxi US$1.50. **TAME** (Orellana y 9 de Octubre, T06-283 0113) flies once or twice a day to **Quito**. Book several days in advance. If there is no space available to Lago Agrio then you can fly to **Coca** instead, from where it is only 2 hrs by bus on a good road.

Bus Terminal terrestre, Manuela Sáenz y Progreso, 8 blocks north of Av Quito, taxi US$1.25. To **Quito** Terminal Quitumbe, frequent service with several companies (**Trans Baños** is good), US$10, 7-8 hrs; most buses go via Reventador and El Chaco, but may take the slightly longer route via Coca if there are disruptions. To **Baeza** 5 hrs, pay fare to Quito. To **Tena**, US$8.75, 6 hrs. **To Tulcán** via La Bonita, US$8.75, 7 hrs. Several companies offer service direct to **Guayaquil**, without stopping in Quito, US$17.50, 14 hrs, as well as other coastal cities. To **Coca,** every 15 mins 0800-1830, US$3.75, 2 hrs.

Coca

Air Flights to **Quito** with **TAME** (C Quito y Enrique Castillo, T06-288 0768) and **Avianca** (at the airport T06-288 1742), several daily, fewer on weekends, reserve as far in advance as possible.

Bus Long distance buses, including those to Lago Agrio, depart from the modern Terminal Terrestre, 3 km north of centre, taxi US$1.50. A small terminal on 9 de Octubre serves only regional destinations. **Hotel San Fermin** (T06-288 0802, see above) will purchase bus tickets from Coca for a small commission. To **Quito** Terminal Quitumbe, US$12.50, 7 hrs via Loreto, 9 hrs via Lago Agrio, several daily. To **Baeza**, pay fare to Quito, 5 hrs. To **Tena**, US$8.75, 4 hrs. To **Baños**, US$12.50, 7 hrs. To **Riobamba**, US$13.50, 9 hrs. To **Guayaquil**, US$20, 15-16 hrs.

River Down the Río Napo to **Nuevo Rocafuerte** on the Peruvian border, 50-passenger motorized canoes leave Coca daily except Sat, 0700, 10-12 hrs; returning at 0500, 12-14 hrs; US$15. Details change, enquire locally, buy tickets at the dock a day in advance and arrive early for boarding. **Transportes Fluvial Orellana**, T06-288 2582, cfluvialorellana@yahoo.es, and 2 others.

From Nuevo Rocafuerte boats can be hired for the 30 km trip down river to the Peruvian border town of **Pantoja**, US$60 per boat, try to share the ride. Departure dates of riverboats from **Pantoja to Iquitos** are irregular, about once a month, be prepared for a long wait. Try to call Iquitos or Pantoja from Coca, or check with Luis Duarte at **Casa del Maito** restaurant (see above), to enquire about the next sailing; full details are given under Iquitos, Transport, page 330. For the journey, take a hammock, cup, bowl, cutlery, extra food and snacks, drinking water or purification, insect repellent, toilet paper, soap, towel, cash dollars and soles in small notes; soles cannot be purchased in Coca.

Central and southern Oriente
a whitewater rafting centre and off-the-beaten-track exploration

Quito, Baños, Puyo, Tena and Puerto Misahuallí are all starting points for central Oriente. Further south, Macas, Gualaquiza and Zamora are the main gateways. All have good road connections.

Archidona

Archidona, 65 km south of Baeza and 10 km north of Tena, has a striking, small painted church and not much else. Tours can be arranged to a private reserve on **Galeras Mountain** where there is easy walking as well as a tougher trek, the forest is wonderful; contact Elias Mamallacha, T09-8045 6942, mamallacha@yahoo.com.

Tena and around *Colour map 1, B4.*

Relaxed and friendly, Tena is the capital of Napo Province. It occupies a hill above the confluence of the Ríos Tena and Pano, there are nice views of the Andean foothills often shrouded in mist. Tena is Ecuador's most important centre for whitewater rafting and also offers ethno-tourism. It makes a good stop en route from Quito to points deeper in Oriente. The road from the north passes the old airstrip and market and heads through the town centre as Avenida 15 de Noviembre on its way to the bus station, nearly 1 km south of the river. Tena is quite spread out. A couple of pedestrian bridges and a vehicle bridge link the two halves of town.

Tena

Where to stay
1 Austria
2 Christian's Palace
3 Gran Sumaco
4 La Casa del Abuelo
5 Limoncocha
6 Los Yutzos

Restaurants
1 Café Tortuga & Adventure River Amazonas Tours
2 Chuquitos & Río y Fuego
3 Guayusa Lounge
4 La Fogata
5 Pizzería Bella Selva
6 The Marquis

Misahuallí *Colour map 1, B4.*

This small port, at the junction of the Napo and Misahuallí rivers, is perhaps the best place in Ecuador from which to visit the 'near Oriente', but your expectations should be realistic. The area has been colonized for many years and there is no extensive

Tip...
Beware the troop of urban monkeys by the plaza, who snatch food, sunglasses, cameras, etc.

virgin forest nearby (except at **Jatun Sacha** and **Liana Lodge**, see Lodges on the Upper Río Napo, page 666). Access is very easy however, prices are reasonable, and while you will not encounter large animals in the wild, you can still see birds, butterflies and exuberant vegetation – enough to get a taste for the jungle.

There is a fine, sandy beach on the Río Misahuallí, but don't camp on it as the river can rise unexpectedly. A narrow suspension bridge crosses the Río Napo at Misahuallí and joins the road along the south shore. At Chichicorumi, outside Misahuallí, is **Kamak Maki** ① *US$3, T09-9982 7618, www.museokamakmaki.com*, an ethno-cultural museum run by the local Kichwa community.

Puyo *Colour map 1, B4.*

The capital of the province of Pastaza feels more like a lowland city anywhere in Ecuador rather than a typical jungle town. Visits can nonetheless be made to nearby forest reserves and tours deeper into the jungle can also be arranged from Puyo. It is the junction for road travel into the northern and southern Oriente (80 km south of Tena, 130 km north of Macas), and for traffic heading to or from Ambato and Riobamba via Baños; all on paved roads. The Sangay and Altar volcanoes can occasionally be seen from town.

Omaere ① *T06-288 3174, Tue-Sun 0900-1700, US$3, access by footbridge off the Paseo Turístico, Barrio Obrero,* is a 15.6-ha ethnobotanical reserve located in the north of Puyo. It has three trails with a variety of plants, an orchidarium and traditional indigenous homes. **Yana Cocha** ① *3 km from Puyo, 500 m off the road to Tena, T06-288 5641, daily 0800-1700, US$3,* is a rescue centre with good conditions for the animals, and you can see them close up. There are other private reserves of varying quality in the Puyo area and visits are arranged by local tour operators (see page 670). You cannot however expect to see large tracts of undisturbed primary jungle here.

Macas *Colour map 1, B4.*

Capital of Morona-Santiago province, Macas is situated high above the broad Río Upano valley. It is a pleasant tranquil place, established by missionaries in 1563. **Sangay volcano** (5230 m) can be seen on clear mornings from the plaza, creating an amazing backdrop to the tropical jungle surrounding the town. The modern cathedral, with beautiful stained-glass windows, houses the much-venerated image of La Purísima de Macas. Five blocks north of the cathedral, at Don Bosco y Riobamba, the **Parque Recreacional,** which also affords great views of the Upano Valley, has a small orchid collection. The Sunday market on 27 de Febrero is worth a visit. **Fundación Chankuap** ① *Soasti y Bolívar, T07-270 1176, www.chankuap.org,* sells a nice variety of locally produced crafts and food products. **Ministerio de Turismo** ① *Bolívar y 24 de Mayo, T07-270 1480, Mon-Fri 0800-1700.* Macas provides access to **Parque Nacional Sangay** ① *Macas office, Juan de la Cruz y Guamote, T07-270 2368, Mon-Fri 0800-1300, 1400-1700.* The lowland area of the park has interesting walking with many rivers and waterfalls. See also Sangay Transport (page 589) for notes on the road from Macas to Riobamba.

Macas to Gualaquiza

South of Macas lies one of Ecuador's least touristed areas, promising much to explore. **Sucúa**, 23 km from Macas, is the administrative centre of the Shuar indigenous people who inhabit much of southern Oriente. The town has most services and some attractions nearby; enquire at the **Tourist Office** in the Municipio. **Logroño**, 24 km further south, has a large limestone cave nearby; to visit contact Mario Crespo, T07-391 1013. It is another 31 km to (Santiago de) **Méndez**, a crossroads with a modern church. A paved road descends from Cuenca via Paute and Guarumales to Méndez, and another road heads east from Méndez via Patuca to Santiago and San José de Morona, near the Peruvian border. Some 26 km south of Méndez is **Limón** (official name General Leónidas Plaza Gutiérrez), a busy, friendly place, surrounded by impressive hills. From Limón the road climbs steeply 10 km to **Plan de Milagro**, another crossroads, where a great road for birdwatching (partly paved), descends from Cuenca via Gualaceo. Next are **Indanza**, 5 km south, then **San Juan Bosco**, 16 km further, with striking views of Cerro Pan de Azucar (2958 m) rising abruptly out of the jungle, before the road reaches Gualaquiza, 55 km ahead.

Gualaquiza *Colour map 1, C3.*

A pleasant town with an imposing church on a hilltop, Gualaquiza's pioneer-settlement charm is threatened by large mining projects in the area. Fortunately, tourism offers an alternative as there are also lovely waterfalls, good rivers for tubing, caves, and undeveloped archaeological sites nearby. Information and tours from the **Oficina Municipal de Turismo** ① *García Moreno y Gonzalo Pesántez, Mon-Fri 0730-1230, 1330-1630*, and from Leonardo Matoche at **Canela y Café**.

At Gualaquiza a rough road forks northwest to climb steeply to Cuenca via **Sígsig**. The road south from Gualaquiza passes El Pangui and Yantzaza (55 km), 8 km south of which is **Zumbi**, with basic hotels on the plaza. At Zumbi, a bridge crosses the Río Zamora and a side road goes southeast to Guayzimi and the beautiful **Alto Nangaritza** region, with **Reserva El Zarza**. The upper Río Nangaritza flows through Shuar territory and a magnificent jungle-covered gorge with 200-m-high walls. There are also oilbird caves and other natural attractions. There is bus service to the area from Zamora, and tours are available form **Cabañas Yankuam** (see Where to stay, page 668) and Zamora tour operators. South of Zumbi, the broad valley of the Río Zamora becomes progressively narrower, with forested mountains and lovely views. It is 35 km to Zamora.

Zamora *Colour map 1, C3.*

The colonial mission settlement of Zamora, at the confluence of the Ríos Zamora and Bombuscaro, today has a boom-town feeling due to large mining and hydroelectric projects in the area. It is reached by road from Gualaquiza (see above) or Loja, 64 km away. The road from Loja is beautiful as it wanders from *páramo* down to high jungle, crossing mountain ranges of cloudforest, weaving high above narrow gorges as it runs alongside the Río Zamora. The town itself is hilly, with a pleasant climate and a nice linear park along the river. It gives access to the **Alto Nangaritza** (see above) and is the gateway to the lowland portion of **Parque Nacional Podocarpus** (see page 605). Between town and the park is **Copalinga**, a bird-rich private reserve (see Where to stay, page 668). There are two private orchid collections that can be visited: **Pafinia** ① *Av del Ejército Km 2*, run by Marco Jiménez, mmjimenez473@gmail.com; and another belonging to **Padre Stanislau** ① *Av del Ejército, Cumbaratza, across from Hotel El Arenal.*

Tourist information

Tena

iTur and Ministerio de Turismo
Malecón, sector El Balnerio, T06-288 8046.
Mon-Fri 0730-1230, 1400-1700.

Puyo

iTur
Francisco de Orellana y 9 de Octubre, T06-288
5122. Daily 0800-1700. Also at Treminal
Terrestre, T06-288 5122, Wed-Sun 0900-1600.

Zamora
Ministerio de Turismo
José Luis Tamayo y Amazonas.
Mon-Fri 0815-1700, English spoken.

Unidad de Turismo
Municipio, Diego de Vaca y 24 de Mayo,
by the plaza, Zamora, T07-305 9386.
Mon-Fri 0800-1230, 1400-1730.

Where to stay

Archidona

$$$$-$$$ Hakuna Matata
Vía Shungu Km 3.9, off the road between
Tena and Archidona, T06-288 9617,
www.hakunamat.com.
Comfortable cabins in a lovely setting by the
Río Inchillaqui. Includes 3 meals, walks, river
bathing and horse riding.

$$$ Huasquila
Vía Huasquila, Km 3.5, Cotundo, T02-237 6158,
T09-8764 6894, www.huasquila.com.
Wheel chair accessible bungalows and
Kichwa-style cabins, includes breakfast,
various packages, full board available,
jungle walks, caving, rock art.

$$$ Orchid Paradise
2 km north of town, T06-288 9232.
Cabins in nice secondary forest with lots
of birds. Full board or cheaper with only
breakfast, owner organizes tours in the area.

$$-$ Hoteles Palmar del Rio
Circunvalacion E45 y Transversal 16, T06-
287 7001; more economical branch on main
street 4 blocks south of plaza, T06-287 7000;
www.hotelespalmardelrio.com.
Clean pleasant rooms with fan and parking.
Premium branch has pool, sauna, restaurant
and tour agency, includes breakfast.

Tena

$$$-$$ Los Yutzos
Augusto Rueda 190 y 15 de Noviembre,
T06-288 6769.
Comfortable rooms and beautiful grounds
overlooking the Río Pano, quiet and family-
run. A/c, cheaper with fan, parking.

$$ Christian's Palace
JL Mera y Sucre, T06-288 6047.
Restaurant, a/c, cheaper with fan, pool,
parking, modern and comfortable.

$$ La Casa del Abuelo
JL Mera 628, T06-288 6318,
www.tomas-lodge.com.
Nice quiet place, comfortable rooms and
suites, small garden, hot water, ceiling fan,
parking, tours. Recommended.

$$-$ Austria
Tarqui y Díaz de Pineda, T06-288 7205.
Spacious rooms, with a/c, cheaper with fan,
ample parking, quiet, good value.

$$-$ Gran Sumaco
Augusto Rueda y 15 de Nov, T06-288 8434,
www.hostalgransumaco.net.
Nice hotel in a good location, quiet, clean,
bright, ample rooms, many with balcony and
views. A/c, cheaper with fan, very good value.

$ Limoncocha
Sangay 533, Sector Corazón de Jesús,
on a hillside 4 blocks from the bus station,
ask for directions, T06-284 6303,
www.hostallimoncocha.com.
Concrete house with terrace and hammocks,
some rooms with a/c, private or shared

bath, US$7 pp in dorm, hot water, fan, laundry and cooking facilities, breakfast available, parking, German/Ecuadorean-run, enthusiastic owners organize tours. Out of the way in a humble neighbourhood, nice views, pleasant atmosphere, good value.

Misahuallí

$$$$ El Jardin Aleman
Jungle lodge on shores of Río Mishualli, 3 km from town, T06-289 0122, www.eljardinaleman.com.
Comfortable rooms with bath, hot water. Price includes 3 meals and river tour, set in protected rainforest.

$$$$ Hamadryade
Behind the Mariposario, 4 km from town, T09-8590 9992, www.hamadryade-lodge.com.
Luxury lodge in a 64-ha forest reserve, 5 designer wood cabins, packages include breakfast, dinner and excursions, French chef, pool, lovely views down to the river.

$$$ Hostería Misahuallí
Across the river from town, T06-289 0063, www.hosteriamisahualli.com.
Cabins for up to 6 in a nice setting, includes breakfast, other meals on request, electric shower, fan, pool and tennis court.

$$ Cabañas Río Napo
Cross the suspension bridge, then 100 m on the left-hand side, T06-289 0071, www.cabanasrionapo.blogspot.com.
Nice rustic cabins with thatch roof, private bath, hot water, ample grounds along the river, Swiss/Kichwa-run, enthusiastic.

$$ El Paisano
Rivadeneyra y Tandalia, T06-289 0027, www.hostalelpaisano.com.
Restaurant, hot water, mosquito nets, small pool, helpful.

$$-$ Banana Lodge
500 m from town on road to Pununo, T06-289 0190, www.bananalodge.com.
Nicely decorated hostel, ample rooms, huge garden with hammocks, breakfast available,

cooking facilities, parking, US$4 for campervans, Russian/Ecuadorean-run.

$ Shaw
Santander on the Plaza, T06-289 0163, hostalshaw@hotmail.com.
Good restaurant, hot water, fan, simple rooms, annexe with kitchen facilities and small pool, operate their own tours, English spoken, very knowledgeable. Good value. Recommended.

Lodges on the Upper Río Napo

Casa del Suizo
Quito T02-256 6090, www.casadelsuizo.com.
On north shore at Ahuano, resort with capacity for 200, comfortable rooms, well-tended grounds, pool, gift shop, great views. Swiss/Ecuadorean-owned. US$125 pp per night.

Cotococha Amazon Lodge
Km 10 on the road from Puerto Napo to Ahuano, shore of Río Napo, T02-2234336 (Quito office), www.cotococha.com.
Comfortable cabins. Packages with meals, entrance fees and local guides, excursions by dug-out canoe. US$440 for 4 days.

Jatun Sacha Biological Station
East of Ahuano and easily accessible by bus, Quito T02-243 2240, www.jatunsacha.org.
A 2500-ha reserve for education, research and tourism. 507 birds, 2500 plants and 765 butterfly species have been identified. Basic cabins with shared bath, cold water, good self-guided trails, canopy tower. US$30 per night, day visit US$6, guiding US$30 per group. Good value.

Liana Lodge
On Río Arajuno near confluence with the Napo, Tena T06-301 7702, www.amazoonico.org.
Comfortable cabins with terraces and river views on a 1700-ha reserve. *Centro de rescate* has animals on site. US$265 for 4 days. Also arranges stays at **Runa Wasi**, next door; basic cabins run by the local Kichwa community, US$32 pp per night with 3 meals, guiding extra; US$380 for 4-day package.

Yachana
Quito T02-252 3777, www.yachana.com.
Near the village of Mondaña, 2 hrs
downstream from Misahuallí or 2½ hrs
upstream from Coca, also accessible by
road (about 6 hrs from Quito). On a 2500 ha
reserve, 14 cabins on a bluff overlooking the
Río Napo. Proceeds help support community
development projects. US$366-456 for
4 days. Recommended.

Puyo

$$$$ Altos del Pastaza Lodge
access from Km 16 of Puyo-Macas road,
Quito T09-9767 4686.
Attractive lodge in 65-ha reserve overlooking
the Río Pastaza, pool. Don't expect much
wildlife, but a nice place to relax, 1- to 4-day
packages include meals and walking tours.

$$$$ Las Cascadas Lodge
Quito T02-250 0530, www.surtrek.com.
First-class lodge 40 km east of Puyo, 8 rooms
with terraces, includes full board, activities
and transport from/to Quito, waterfalls;
3- and 4-day packages US$434-650.

$$$ El Jardín
Paseo Turístico, Barrio Obrero, T03-288 6101,
www.eljardinrelax.com.ec.
Nice rooms and garden, good
upmarket restaurant.

$$ Delfín Rosado
Ceslao Marín y Atahualpa, T03-288 8757.
Pool, modern rooms with a/c, parking.

$$ Las Palmas
20 de Julio y 4 de Enero, 5 blocks
from centre, T03-288 4832,
hostal_laspalmas_puyo@yahoo.com.
Comfortable modern rooms with
fridge, parking.

$ Colibrí
Av Manabí entre Bolívar y Galápagos,
T03-288 3054.
Hot water, private bath, parking, away from
centre, simple but nice, good value, offers
tours. Recommended.

$ San Rafael
Tte Hugo Ortiz y Juan de Velazco, 1½ blocks
from bus station, T03-288 7275.
Good choice for late arrivals or early
departures. Clean rooms with private bath,
hot water, good value.

Southern Oriente jungle lodges

Kapawi
Quito T02-600 9333, www.kapawi.com.
A top-of-the-line lodge located on the Río
Capahuari near its confluence with the
Pastaza, not far from the Peruvian border.
Run by the local Achuar community and
accessible only by small aircraft and motor
canoe. The biodiversity is good, but more
emphasis is placed on ethno-tourism here than
at other upmarket jungle lodges. US$1350
for 4 days includes transport from Quito.

Macas

$$$ Arrayán y Piedra
Km 7 Vía a Puno, T07-304 5949,
arrayanypiedra@hotmail.com.
Large resort-style lodging, nice rooms,
pool and spa, ample grounds, restaurant
with very good food, but variable service.

$$ Cabañas del Valle
Av 29 de Mayo, 1.5 km from town,
T07-232 2393.
Comfortable rooms, pool, parking,
sports areas.

$$ Casa Blanca
Soasti 14-29 y Sucre, T07-270 0195.
Hot water, small pool, modern and
comfortable, very helpful, good value, often
full, book in advance. Recommended.

$$ Nivel 5
Juan de la Cruz y Amazonas, T07-270 1240.
Nice modern multi-storey hotel, hot water,
fan, pool, parking, helpful staff.

Macas to Gualaquiza
Sucúa
There are several other hotels ($) in town.

$$ Arutam
Vía a Macas Km 1, north of town, T07-274 0851.
Restaurant, pool and sauna, parking, modern comfortable rooms, nice grounds, sports fields, well suited to families.

$$ Lucelinda
1 km vía a Cuenca, T07-274 2118.
Comfortable rooms with fans, large clean pool, good restaurant.

Méndez

$ Interoceánico
C Quito on the plaza, T07-276 0245.
Hot water, parking, smart, good value.

Limón

$ Dream House
Quito y Bolívar, T07-277 0166.
With restaurant, shared bath, hot water, adequate.

San Juan Bosco

$ Antares
On the plaza.
Restaurant, hot water, indoor pool, simple functional rooms, helpful owner.

Gualaquiza

$ Gran Hotel
Orellana y Gran Pasaje, T07-278 0722.
Modern concrete building, hot water, fan, parking, small rooms, some windowless.

$ Wakis
Orellana 08-52 y Domingo Comín, T07-278 0138.
Older simple place with small rooms, private or shared bath, hot water, parking, enthusiastic owner speaks English.

Alto Nangaritza

$$ Cabañas Yankuam
3 km south of Las Orquideas, T07-260 5739 (Zamora), www.lindoecuadortours.com.

Rustic cabins, includes breakfast, other tasty meals on request, private or shared bath, good walking in surrounding jungle-clad hills, organizes trips up the Río Nangaritza. Family-run. Reservations required.

Zamora
In addition to those listed below, there are several other hotels in town.

$$$ Copalinga
Km 3 on the road to the Bombuscaro entrance of Parque Nacional Podocarpus, T09-9347 7013, www.copalinga.com.
Nice comfortable cabins with balcony in a lovely setting, includes very good breakfast, other delicious meals available if arranged in advance, more rustic cabins with shared bath are cheaper, excellent birdwatching, walking trails. Belgian-run, English, French and Dutch spoken, attentive service, reserve 3 days ahead. Highly recommended.

$$ Samuria
24 de Mayo y Diego de Vaca, T07-260 7801, hotelsamuria@hotmail.com.
Modern bright hotel, comfortable well furnished rooms, a/c, cheaper with fan, restaurant, parking.

$$ Wampushkar
Diego de Vaca y Pasaje Vicente Aldeán, T07-260 7800.
Nice modern hotel, ample rooms, a/c, cheaper with fan, hot water, parking, good value.

$ Betania
Francisco de Orellana entre Diego de Vaca y Amazonas, T07-260 7030, hotel-betania@hotmail.com.
Modern, functional, breakfast available, private bath, hot water.

Restaurants

Tena

$$$ The Marquis
Amazonas entre Calderón y Olmedo.
Daily 1200-1600, 1800-2200.
Upmarket restaurant serving good steaks.

$$ Chuquitos
García Moreno by the plaza.
Mon-Sat 0700-2100, Sun 1100-2100.
Good food, à la carte only, seating on a
balcony overlooking the river. Pleasant
atmosphere, attentive service, popular
and recommended. **Araña Bar** downstairs,
Mon-Thu 1700-2400, weekends to 0200.

$$ Pizzería Bella Selva
Malecón south of the footbridge;
2nd location on east side. Daily 1100-2300.
Pizza and pasta.

$$ Río y Fuego
JL Mera y García Moreno.
Daily 0730-1100, 1700-2300.
Good breakfast and dinner. Asian and
international dishes, Vietnamese/
Ecuadorean-run.

$$-$ Guayusa Lounge
Juan Montalvo y Olmedo. Tue-Sat 1500-2300.
Light meals, snacks and cocktails, good
meeting place, US-run.

$ La Fogata
Serafín Guetiérrez entre Rafaela Segala and
Av Napo. Daily 1200-2200.
Tasty set meals, large portions, good value.

Café Tortuga
Malecón south of the footbridge.
Mon-Sat 0700-1930, Sun 0700-1330.
Juices, snacks, book exchange, handy bus time-
table, Wi-Fi, nice location, friendly Swiss owner.

Misahuallí

$$$ El Jardín
300 m past bridge to Ahuano.
Daily 1200-1600, 1800-2200.
Variety of dishes, beautiful garden setting.

$$ Parrilería Fasage
1 block from the plaza near Hotel El Paisano.
Daily 1200-2400.
Good quality grill.

$$-$ Bijao
On the plaza. Wed-Sun 0900-2200.
Good set meals and *comida típica* à la carte.

> **Tip...**
> In Puyo, there are several cheap
> *comedores* serving local dishes on
> Calle San Francisco near 10 de Agosto.

Puyo

$$$-$$ Lagarto Juancho
Orellana y Sangay. Mon-Sat 1800-2400.
Ecuadorean *comida típica*, large portions,
very clean.

$$ Pizzería Buon Giorno
Orellana entre Villamil y 27 de Febrero.
Mon-Sat 1200-2300, Sun 1400-2300.
Good pizza, lasagne and salads, pleasant
atmosphere, very popular. Recommended.

El Fariseo Café
Atahualpa entre 27 de Febrero y General
Villamil. Mon-Sat 0700-2200.
Good cakes and the best coffee in town.

Escobar Café
Atahualpa y Orellana. Mon-Sat 0630-2400.
Good for early breakfast, sandwiches, bar at
night, attractive bamboo decor.

Macas

$$ Junglab
Bolívar entre Guamote y Amazonas,
T07-270 2448. Tue-Sun 1200-2230.
Delicious creative meals using local produce.

$$-$ La Italiana
Soasti y Sucre. Mon-Sat 1200-2300.
Great pizzas, pasta and salads.

$ La Choza de Mama Sara
10 de Agosto y 9 de Octubre.
Mon-Sat 0830-2100.
Traditional Macabeo cuisine such as
ayampacos and *yuca* and palm tamales,
served for breakfast. Also a choice of set
lunches, good value.

$ Rincón Manabita
Amazonas y 29 de Mayo. Mon-Fri 0700-2200,
Sat-Sun 0700-1600.

Good breakfasts and a choice of set meals which are delicious and filling. Also à la carte.

Zamora

$ Agape
Sevilla de Oro y Pje San Francisco.
Mon-Fri for lunch only.
Good set lunch and à la carte.

$ Asadero Tío Bolo
Alonso de Mercadillo, across from the riverside park. Tue-Sat 1830-2130.
Small place with good grill, friendly service, very popular, go early.

Spiga Pan
Av del Maestro y Pío Jaramillo.
Daily 0730-2230.
Great bakery with a variety of hot bread, cream cakes and fresh fruit yoghurt.

What to do

Tena
Rafting tours cost US$40-80 per day, safety standards vary between operators. Avoid touts selling tours on the street.
Adventure River Amazonas (ARA), *Francisco de Orellana 280 y 9 de Octubre, on the malecón, T06-288 8648, www.river amazonas.com.* Rafting, adventure sports and community cultural tours. Ecuadorean/ French run.
Caveman Tours, *no storefront, T09-8420 0173, www.cavemanecuador.com.* Water sports and tours.
Limoncocha, *at Hostal Limoncocha (see Where to stay, above).* Rafting, kayaking and jungle, English and German spoken.
Ríos Ecuador, *Tarqui 230 y Díaz de Pineda, T06-288 6727; plans to move in 2016 to Hostal Tena Ñaui, Via a las Antenas, 10 mins from centre, T06-288 7188, www.riosecuador.com.* Rafting and kayaking.
River People, *no storefront, T09-8356 7307, www.riverpeopleecuador.com.* Rafting and kayaking.

Misahuallí
Jungle tours (US$45-80 pp per day) can be arranged by most hotels as well as:
Ecoselva, *Santander on the plaza, T06-289 0019, www.ecoselvapepetapia.com.* Recommended guide Pepe Tapia speaks English and has a biology background. Well organized and reliable. Bike rentals, US$10 per day.
Runawa Tours, *in La Posada hotel, on the plaza, T06-289 0031.* Owner Carlos Santander, tubing, kayak and jungle tours.
Teorumi, *between the plaza and malecón, T06-289 0203, www.teorumi misahualli.com.* Offers tours to the Shiripuno Kichwa community.

Puyo
Selvavida Travel, *Ceslao Marín y Atahualpa, T03-288 9729, www.selvavidatravel.com.* Specializes in rafting and Parque Nacional Yasuní.

Macas
Tours to indigenous communities and lowland portions of Parque Nacional Sangay, cost about US$50 per day.
Insondu, *Bolívar y Soasti, T07-270 2533.*
Real Nature Travel Company, *no storefront, T07-270 2674, www.realnaturetravel.com.* Run by RhoAnn Wallace and professional bird-watching guide Galo Real, English spoken.
Tsuirim Viajes, *Don Bosco y Sucre, T09-9357 9003.* Owner Leo Salgado.

Zamora
Cabañas Yankuam, *see page 668.*
Offer tours to the Alto Nangaritza.
Wellington Valdiviezo, *T09-9380 2211, lindozamoraturistico@gmail.com.* Tours to the Alto Nangaritza, Shuar communities, adventure sports, visits to shamans. Contact in advance.

Tena

Bus Run-down Terminal Terrestre on 15 de Noviembre, 1 km from the centre (taxi US$1). To **Quito**, US$7.50, 5 hrs. To **Ambato**, via Baños, US$6.25, 4½ hrs. To **Baños**, US$6, 3½ hrs. To **Riobamba**, US$7.50, 5½ hrs. To **Puyo**, US$3.75, 2 hrs. To **Coca and Lago Agrio**, fares given above. To **Misahuallí**, see below. To **Archidona**, from Amazonas y Bolívar by market, every 20 mins, US$0.35, 15 mins.

Misahuallí

Bus Buses run from the plaza. To **Tena**, hourly 0600-1900, US$1.25, 45 mins. Make long-distance connections in Tena. To **Quito**, 1 direct bus a day at 0830, US$8.75, 5 hrs.

River No scheduled passenger service, but motorized canoes for 8-10 passengers can be chartered for touring.

Puyo

Air The nearest airport to Puyo is at Shell, 13 km. Military flights to jungle villages are not open to foreigners, but light aircraft can be chartered starting around US$300 per hr.

Bus Terminal Terrestre on the outskirts of town, a 10- to 15-min walk from the centre; taxi US$1. To **Baños**, US$2.50, 1½ hrs. To **Ambato**, US$3.75, 2½ hrs. To **Quito**, US$6.25, 5 hrs via Ambato; shared taxis with **Autovip**, T02-600 2582 or 09-9629 5406, US$40, 8 daily, fewer on weekends or **Delux**, T09-3920 9827or 09-8343 0275, every 2 hrs, US$25. To **Riobamba**, US$5, 3½ hrs. To **Tena**, see above. To **Macas**, US$6.25, 2½ hrs. To **Coca**, US$11.25, 8hrs. To **Lago Agrio**, US$15, 11 hrs.

Macas

Air Small modern airport within walking distance at Cuenca y Amazonas. To **Quito**, Mon, Wed and Fri with **TAME** (office at airport T07-270 4940). Sit on left for best views of Volcán Sangay. Air taxis to jungle villages, US$600 per hr for 9 passengers.

Bus Terminal Terrestre by the market. To **Puyo**, see above. To **Baños**, US$9, 4½ hrs. To **Quito**, via Puyo, Baños and Ambato, US$10, 8 hrs. To **Riobamba** through Parque Nacional Sangay, a beautiful ride, 6 daily, US$6.25, 4 hrs. To **Cuenca**, US$11, 6-7 hrs, via Guarumales and Paute or via Plan de Milagro and Gualaceo. To **Gualaquiza**, US$8, 8 hrs, where you can get a bus to Zamora and Loja (see below). To **Sucúa**, hourly, US$1.25, 30 min. To **9 de Octubre**, for **PN Sangay**, US$2, 45 mins.

Gualaquiza

Bus To **Macas**, see above. To **Cuenca**; via Sígsig, 4 daily, US$8.75, 6 hrs; or via Plan de Milagro and Gualaceo. To **Zamora**, US$4.50, 3½ hrs. To **Loja**, US$7.50, 5½ hrs.

Alto Nangaritza

To **Las Orquídeas**, with **Trans Zamora**, from Zamora at 0400, 0645, 1115 and 1230, US$4.75, 3½ hrs; from Yantzaza at 0440, 0740, 1150 and 1310, US$3.25, 3½ hrs; with **Unión Yantzaza**, from Yantzaza at 0430, 0930, 1130, 1430 and 1630; from Loja at 1415, 1510, US$7.75, 5½ hrs.

Zamora

Bus Leave from Terminal Terrestre. To **Loja**, frequent service, 1½-2 hrs, US$3; to **Gualaquiza**, US$4.50, 3½ hrs, where you can transfer for Macas.

Galápagos
Islands

★ A trip to the Galápagos Islands is an unforgettable experience. The islands are world renowned for their fearless wildlife but no amount of hype can prepare the visitor for such a close encounter with nature. Here you can snorkel with penguins, sea lions and the odd hammerhead shark, watch giant 200-kg tortoises lumbering through cactus forest and enjoy the courtship display of the blue-footed booby and magnificent frigatebird, all in startling close-up.

Lying on the equator, 970 km west of the Ecuadorean coast, the Galápagos consist of six main islands, 12 smaller islands and over 40 islets. The islands have an estimated population of 27,000, but this does not include many temporary inhabitants. Santa Cruz has 16,600 inhabitants, with Puerto Ayora the main city and tourist centre. San Cristóbal has a population of 7900 with the capital of the archipelago, Puerto Baquerizo Moreno. The largest island, Isabela, is 120 km long and forms over half the total land area of the archipelago, some 2500 people live there, mostly in and around Puerto Villamil on the south coast. Floreana, the first island to be settled, has about 160 residents.

Best for
Scenery ▪ Swimming ▪ Walking ▪ Wildlife

Essential Galápagos Islands

Finding your feet

Airports at **Baltra**, across a narrow strait from Santa Cruz, and **Puerto Baquerizo Moreno**, on San Cristóbal, receive flights from mainland Ecuador. The two islands are 96 km apart and on most days there are local flights in light aircraft between them, as well as to **Puerto Villamil** on Isabela. There is also speedboat service between Puerto Ayora (Santa Cruz) and the other populated islands. There are no international flights to Galápagos.

Avianca, **LATAM** and **TAME** all fly from Quito and Guayaquil to Baltra or San Cristóbal. Baltra receives more flights but there is at least one daily to each destination. You can arrive at one and return from the other. You can also depart from Quito and return to Guayaquil or vice versa, but you may not buy a one-way ticket. The return airfare varies considerably, starting at about US$500 from Quito, US$350 from Guayaquil (2016 prices); lower fares may be available if you purchase in advance. See also Fees and inspections, page 678.

Buses meet flights from the mainland at Baltra: some run to the port or *muelle* (10 minutes, no charge) where the cruise boats wait; others go to Canal de Itabaca, the narrow channel which separates Baltra from Santa Cruz. It is 15 minutes to the Canal, free, then you cross on a small ferry, US$1. On the other side, buses (US$2, may involve a long wait while they fill) and pickup truck taxis (US$18 for up to four passengers) run to Puerto Ayora, 45 minutes. For the return trip to the airport, buses leave the Terminal Terrestre on Avenida Baltra in Puerto Ayora (2 km from the pier, taxi US$1) at 0700, 0730 and 0830 daily. See also Transport, page 690.

Getting around

Emetebe Avionetas, Boyacá 916 y Victor Manuel Rendón, next to Hotel City Plaza, Guayaquil, T04-230 4245, www.emetebe.com.ec, see Transport for local offices, offers inter-island flights in light aircraft. Two daily flights except Sun between **Puerto Baquerizo Moreno** (San Cristóbal), **Baltra** and **Puerto Villamil** (Isabela). All fares US$165 one way; baggage allowance 25 lbs.

Lanchas (speedboats with three large engines for about 20 passengers) operate daily between Puerto Ayora and each of Puerto Baquerizo Moreno, Puerto Villamil, and Puerto Velasco Ibarra (Floreana); US$30 one way, two hours or more depending on the weather and sea. Tickets are sold by several agencies in Puerto Baquerizo Moreno, Puerto Ayora, and Puerto Villamil; purchase a day before travelling. This can be a wild ride in rough seas, life vests provided, take drinking water.

When to go

The Galápagos climate can be divided into a hot season (December-May), when there is a possibility of heavy showers, and the cool or *garúa* (mist) season (June to November), when the days generally are more cloudy and there is often rain or drizzle. July and August can be windy, force four or five. Daytime clothing should be lightweight. (Clothing generally, even on 'luxury cruises', should be casual and comfortable.) At night, however, particularly at sea and at higher altitudes, temperatures fall below 15°C and warm clothing is required. The sea is cold July to October; underwater visibility is best January to March. Ocean temperatures are usually higher to the east and lower at the western end of the archipelago. Despite all these climatic variations, conditions are generally favourable for visiting Galápagos throughout the year.

High season for tourism is June to August and December to January, when last-minute arrangements are generally not possible. Some boats may be heavily booked throughout the year and you should plan well in advance if you want to travel on a specific vessel at a specific time.

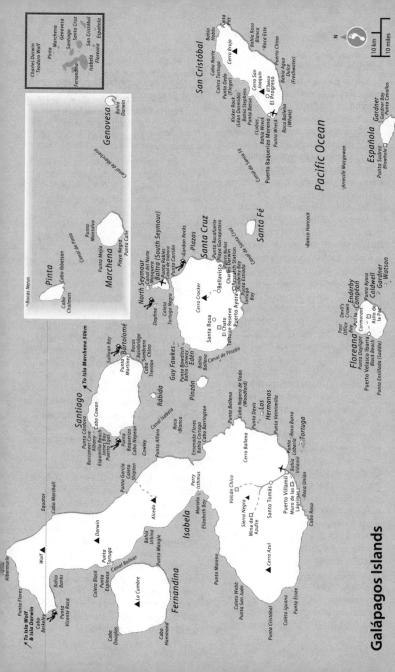

Galápagos Islands

Santa Cruz: Puerto Ayora *See map, page 676.*

Santa Cruz is the most central of the Galápagos islands and the main town is Puerto Ayora. About 1.5 km from the pier is the **Charles Darwin Research Station** ⓘ *at Academy Bay, www.darwinfoundation.org, office Mon-Fri 0700-1600, visitor areas 0600-1800 daily, free.* A visit to the station is a good introduction to the islands. Collections of several of the rare sub-species of giant tortoise are maintained on the station as breeding nuclei, together with tortoise-rearing pens for the young. The **Centro Comunitario de Educación Ambiental** ⓘ *west end of Charles Binford, Mon-Fri 0730-1200, 1400-1700, Sat morning only, free,* has an aquarium and exhibits about the Galápagos Marine Reserve.

There is a beautiful beach at **Tortuga Bay**, 45 minutes' easy walk (2.5 km each way) west from Puerto Ayora on an excellent cobbled path through cactus forest. Start at the west end of Calle Charles Binford; further on there is a gate where you must register, open 0600-1800 daily, free. Make sure you take sun screen, drinking water, and beware of the very strong undertow. Do not walk on the dunes above the beach, which are a marine tortoise nesting area. At the west end of Tortuga Bay is a trail to a lovely mangrove-fringed lagoon, with calmer warmer water, shade, and sometimes a kayak for rent.

Las Grietas is a lovely gorge with a natural pool at the bottom which is splendid (crowded on weekends) for bathing. Take a water taxi from the port to the dock at Punta Estrada (five minutes, US$0.60). It is a 10-minute walk from here to the **Finch Bay hotel** and 20 minutes further over rough lava boulders to Las Grietas – well worth the trip.

The Puerto Ayora-Baltra road goes through the agricultural zone in the highlands. The community of **Bellavista** is 7 km from the port, and **Santa Rosa** is 15 km beyond. The area has National Park visitor sites, walking possibilities and upmarket lodgings. **Los Gemelos** are a pair of large sinkholes, formed by collapse of the ground above empty magma chambers. They straddle the road to Baltra, beyond Santa Rosa. You can take a taxi (US$15 return with wait) or airport bus all the way; otherwise take a bus to Santa Rosa, then walk one hour uphill. There are several **lava tubes** (natural tunnels) on the island. Some are at **El Mirador**, 3 km from Puerto Ayora on the road to Bellavista. Two more lava tubes are 1 km from Bellavista. They are on private land, it costs US$3-5 (US$10 with torch) to enter the tunnels (bring a torch) and it takes about 30 minutes to walk through them. Tours to the lava tubes can be arranged in Puerto Ayora.

The highest point on Santa Cruz Island is **Cerro Crocker** at 864 m. You can hike here and to two other nearby 'peaks' called **Media Luna** and **Puntudo**. The trail starts at Bellavista where a rough trail map is painted as a mural on the wall of the school. The round trip from Bellavista takes six to eight hours. A permit and guide are not required, but a guide may be helpful. Always take food, water and a compass or GPS.

Another worthwhile trip is to the **El Chato Tortoise Reserve**, where giant tortoises can be seen in the wild during the dry season (June to February). In the wet season the tortoises are breeding down in the arid zone. Follow the road that goes past the Santa Rosa school to 'La Reserva'. At the end of the road (about 3 km) you reach a faded wooden memorial to an Israeli tourist who got lost here. Take the trail to the

> **Tip...**
> A recommended bilingual website is **www.galapagospark.org**. It describes each visitor site and gives details of guides and tourist vessels operating in the islands, but these are not always up to date.

Puerto Ayora

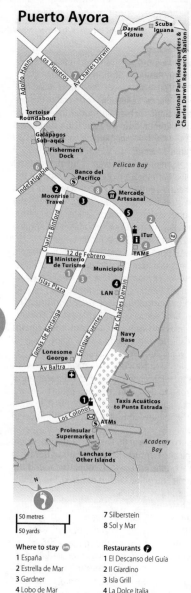

Where to stay
1 España
2 Estrella de Mar
3 Gardner
4 Lobo de Mar
5 Los Amigos
6 Peregrina
7 Silberstein
8 Sol y Mar

Restaurants
1 El Descanso del Guía
2 Il Giardino
3 Isla Grill
4 La Dolce Italia
5 La Garrapata

right (west) for about 45 minutes. There are many confusing trails in the reserve itself; take food, water and a compass or GPS. If you have no hiking experience, horses can sometimes be hired at Santa Rosa or arrange a tour from Puerto Ayora.

Tortoises can also be seen at **Cerro Mesa** and at several private ranches, some of which have camping facilities; eg **Butterfly Ranch** ① *Hacienda Mariposa, entry US$3, camping US$25 pp including breakfast, access at Km 16, just before Santa Rosa, walk 1 km from here, make previous arrangements at Moonrise Travel.*

San Cristóbal: Puerto Baquerizo Moreno

Puerto Baquerizo Moreno, on San Cristóbal island, is the capital of the archipelago. Electrical energy here is provided by wind generators in the highlands, see www. eolicsa.com.ec. The town's attractive *malecón* has many shaded seats shared by tourists, residents and sea lions. The **cathedral** ① *on Av Northía y Cobos, 0900-1200, 1600-1800*, has interesting artwork combining religious and Galápagos motifs.

To the north of town, opposite **Playa Mann** (suitable for swimming), is the Galápagos National Park highly informative visitor centre or **Centro de Interpretación** ① *T05-252 0138, ext 123, daily 0700-1700, free.* A good trail goes from the Centro de Interpretación to the northeast through scrub forest to **Cerro Tijeretas**, a hill overlooking town and the ocean, 30 minutes away. From here a rougher trail continues 45 minutes to **Playa Baquerizo**. Frigatebirds nest in this area; there are sea lions on the beaches below. To go back from Cerro Tijeretas, if you take the trail which follows the coast, you will end up at **Playa Punta Carola**, a popular surfing beach, too rough for swimming. To the south of Puerto Baquerizo Moreno, 30 minutes' walk past the stadium and high school (ask for directions), is **La Lobería**, a popular beach with sea lions, marine iguanas, many bathers at weekends, and a rough trail leading to beautiful cliffs with birds, overlooking the sea.

Four buses a day run the 6 km inland from Puerto Baquerizo Moreno to **El Progreso**, US$0.50, 15 minutes, then it's a 2½-hour walk to **El Junco lake**, the largest body of fresh water in Galápagos. Pick-up trucks to El Progreso charge US$3, or you can hire them for touring: US$25 to El Junco (return with wait), US$50 continuing to the beaches at **Puerto Chino** on the other side of the island, past a man-made tortoise reserve. Camping is possible at Puerto Chino with a permit from the National Park, take all supplies. At El Junco there is a path to walk around the lake in 20 minutes. The views are lovely in clear weather but it is cool and wet in the *garúa* season. Various small roads fan out from El Progreso and make for pleasant walking. **Jatun Sacha** (www.jatunsacha.org) has a volunteer centre on an old hacienda in the highlands beyond El Progreso, working on eradication of invasive species and a native plant nursery; US$15 taxi ride from town, take repellent.

Boats go to **Punta Pitt** at the northeast end of San Cristóbal where you can see all three species of booby. Off the northwest coast is **Kicker Rock** (León Dormido), the basalt remains of a volcanic plug; many seabirds, including nazca and blue-footed boobies, can be seen around its cliffs (five-hour trip, including snorkelling, recommended).

Isabela: Puerto Villamil

This is the largest island in the archipelago, formed by the coalesced lava flows of six volcanoes. Five are active and each has (or had) its own separate sub-species of giant tortoise. Isabela is also the island which is changing most rapidly, driven by growing land-based tourism. It remains a charming place but is at risk from uncontrolled development. Most residents live in Puerto Villamil. In the highlands, there is a cluster of farms at Santo Tomás. There are several lovely beaches right by town, but mind the strong undertow and ask locally about the best spots for swimming and surfing.

It is 8 km west to **Muro de las Lágrimas**, built by convict labour under hideous conditions. It makes a great day-hike or hire a bicycle (always take water). Short side-trails branch off the road to various attractions along the way, and a trail continues from the Muro to nearby hills with lovely views. Inland from the same road, 30 minutes from town, is the **Centro de Crianza**, a breeding centre for giant tortoises surrounded by lagoons with flamingos and other birds. In the opposite direction, 30 minutes east toward the *embarcadero* (pier) is **Concha de Perla Lagoon**, with a nice access trail through mangroves and a small dock from which you can go swimming with sea lions and other creatures. Tours go to **Las Tintoreras**, a set of small islets in the harbour where white-tipped reef sharks and penguins may be seen in the still crystalline water (US$35 per person). There are also boat tours to **Los Túneles** at Cabo Rosa (US$80 per person, a tricky entrance from the open sea), where fish, rays and turtles can be seen in submerged lava tunnels.

Sierra Negra Volcano has the second-largest basaltic caldera in the world, 9 km by 10 km. Visits are only permitted with a guide. It is 19 km (US$20, 30 minutes) by pickup truck to the park entrance (take passport and National Park entry receipt), where you start the 1½-hour hike to the crater rim at 1000 m. It is a further 1½ hours' walk along bare brittle lava rock to **Volcán Chico**, with several fumaroles and more stunning views. You can camp on the crater rim but must take all supplies, including water, and obtain a permit the day before from the National Park office in Puerto Villamil. A tour including transport and lunch costs about US$50 per person. Highland tours are also available to **La Cueva de Sucre**, a large lava tube with many chambers; be sure to take a torch if visiting on your own. A bus to the highlands leaves the market in Puerto Villamil at 0700 daily, US$0.50, ask the driver for directions to the cave and return times.

ON THE ROAD
Information and advice

Fees and inspections A US$20 fee is collected at Quito or Guayaquil airport, where a registration form must be completed. It is best to pre-register on line at www.gobierno galapagos.gob.ec, or ask your tour operator to do so for you. Bags are checked prior to flights to Galápagos, no meat, dairy products, fresh fruit or vegetables may be taken. On arrival, every foreign visitor must pay a US$100 National Park fee in cash only. Be sure to have your passport to hand at the airport and keep all fee receipts throughout your stay in the islands. Bags are checked again on departure, as nothing may be taken off the islands. Puerto Villamil charges a US$5 port fee on arrival in Isabela.

What to take A remedy for seasickness is recommended. A good supply of sun block and skin cream to prevent windburn and chapped lips is essential, as are a hat and sunglasses. You should be prepared for dry and wet landings, the latter involving wading ashore; keep photo equipment and other delicate items in a waterproof stuff-sack or plastic bags. The animals are so tame that you will take far more photos than you expected; if you run out of memory cards they can be bought in Puerto Ayora, but best to take your own. Snorkelling equipment is particularly useful as much of the sea-life is only visible under water. The cheaper boats may not provide equipment or it may be of poor quality. If in doubt, bring your own. Good sturdy footwear is important, boots and shoes soon wear out on the abrasive lava terrain. Always take US$ cash to Galápagos as there are few ATMs and they may not always work. ATMs on Puerto Ayora, Puerto Baquerizo, no banks or ATMs in Puerto Villamil, but there is **MoneyGram**, in La Isla supermarket for international funds transfer. The ATM withdrawal limit is US$300-500 per day. There are no cash advances on credit cards.

Tipping A ship's crew and guides are usually tipped separately. Amounts are often suggested onboard or in agencies' brochures, but these should be considered in light of the quality of service received.

Problems Raise any issues first with your guide or ship's captain. Serious complaints are rare but may filed with **iTur** or **Ministerio de Turismo** offices in Puerto Ayora or Puerto Baquerizo Moreno, see Tourist information in Listings, below.

Choosing a tour There are various options for visiting Galápagos but by far the best is the traditional **live-aboard cruise** (*tour navegable*), where you travel and sleep on a yacht, tour boat or cruise ship. These vessels travel at night, arriving at a new landing site each day. Cruises range from three to 14 nights, seven is recommended. All cruises begin with a morning flight from the mainland on the first day and end on the last day with a midday flight back to the mainland. The less expensive boats are normally smaller and less powerful so you see less and spend more time travelling; also the guiding may be mostly in Spanish. The more expensive boats have air conditioning, hot water and private baths. All boats have to conform to certain minimum safety standards; more expensive boats are better equipped. Boats with over 20 passengers take quite a time to disembark and re-embark people, while the smaller boats have a more lively motion, which is important if you are prone to seasickness. Note also that there may be limitations for vegetarians on the cheaper boats. The least expensive boats (economy class) cost up to US$200 per person per day and a few of these vessels are dodgy. For around US$250-600 per day (tourist and tourist superior class) you will be on a better, faster boat which can travel more quickly. Over US$600 per day are the first-class and luxury brackets, with far more comfortable and spacious cabins and better service and cuisine.

The table on page 682 lists tourist vessels; for dive boats see page 688. The sailing vessels listed also have motors and many frequently operate under engine power. Captains, crews and guides regularly change on all boats. Many overseas agencies sell cruises in the Galápagos Islands. Some are listed in Tour operators, page 730.

Island-hopping is another option for visiting Galápagos, whereby you spend a night or two at hotels on some of the four populated islands, travelling between them in speedboats. You cover less ground than on a cruise, see fewer wildlife sites, and cannot visit the more distant islands. Island-hopping is sold in organized packages but visitors in no rush can also travel between and explore the populated islands independently and at their leisure. **Day tours** (*tour diario*) are yet another alternative, based mostly out of Puerto Ayora. Some take you for day-visits to National Park landing sites on nearby unpopulated islands, such as Bartolomé, Seymour, Plazas and Santa Fe (US$85-180), and can be quite good. Others go for the day to the populated islands of Isabela or Floreana, with no stops permitted along the way. The latter require at least four hours of speedboat travel and generally leave insufficient time to enjoy visitor sites; they are not recommended. All forms of land-based tourism have grown rapidly, with a considerable impact on the Islands.

None of the above options is cheap, with the flight from the mainland and entry fees alone amounting to about US$600. Galápagos is such a special destination for nature-lovers however, that most agree it is worth saving for and spending on a quality tour. If nature is not your great passion and you are looking mainly for an exotic cruise or beach holiday, then your money will go further and you will likely have a better experience elsewhere.

Booking a tour in advance You can book a Galápagos cruise in several different ways: 1) online; 2) from either a travel agency or directly though a Galápagos wholesaler in your home country; 3) from one of the many agencies found throughout Ecuador, especially in Quito (see page 516) but also in other tourist centres and Guayaquil (page 623); or 4) from local agencies, mostly in Puerto Ayora but also in Puerto Baquerizo Moreno. The trade-off is always between time and money: booking from home is most efficient and expensive, last-minute arrangements in Galápagos are cheapest but most time-consuming (and the cost of staying in Puerto Ayora is high), while Quito and Guayaquil are intermediate. It is not possible to obtain discounts or make last-minute arrangements in high season (see When to go, page 673). Surcharges may apply when using a credit card to purchase tours on the islands, so take sufficient cash if looking for a last-minute cruise. Also, if looking for a last-minute sailing, it is best to pay your hotel one night at a time since hoteliers may not refund advance payments. Especially on cheaper boats, check carefully about what is and is not included (eg drinking water, snorkelling equipment, etc).

Basic rules

Do not touch any of the animals, birds or plants. Do not transfer sand, seeds or soil from one island to another. Do not leave litter anywhere; nor take food on to the uninhabited islands, which are also no-smoking zones. There is increasingly close contact between people and sea lions throughout Galápagos. Never touch them however, and keep your distance from the male 'beach-masters', they have been known to bite. Always take food, plenty of water and a compass or GPS if hiking on your own. It is easy to get lost. Also watch out for the large-spined opuntia cactus and the poisonwood tree (*manzanillo*) found near beaches, contact with its leaves or bark can cause severe skin reactions.

Floreana: Puerto Velasco Ibarra

Floreana is the island with the richest human history and the fewest inhabitants, most living in Puerto Velasco Ibarra. You can reach the island with a day-tour boat from Puerto Ayora, but these do not leave enough time to enjoy the visit. A couple of days stay is recommended, but you must be flexible in case there isn't enough space in boats returning to Puerto Ayora. Services are limited, one shop has basic supplies and there are a handful of places to eat and sleep, none is cheap. Margaret Wittmer, one of the first settlers on Floreana, died in 2000, but you can meet her daughter and granddaughter.

La Lobería is a beautiful little peninsula (which becomes an island at high tide), 15 minutes' walk from town, where sea lions, sea turtles, marine iguanas and various birds can be seen. The climate in the highlands is fresh and comfortable, good for walking and birdwatching. A *ranchera* runs up to **Asilo de La Paz**, with a natural spring and tortoise area, Monday to Saturday 0600 and 1500, returning 0700 and 1600; Sun 0700 returning 1000. Or you can walk down in three to four hours, detouring to climb **Cerro Allieri**.

Post Office Bay, on the north side of Floreana, is visited by tour boats. There is a custom (since 1792) for visitors here to place unstamped letters and cards in a barrel, and deliver, free of charge, any addressed to their own destinations.

BACKGROUND
Unconnected islands

The Galápagos have never been connected with the continent. Gradually, over many hundreds of thousands of years, animals and plants from over the sea somehow migrated there and as time went by they adapted themselves to Galápagos conditions and came to differ more and more from their continental ancestors. Unique marine and terrestrial environments, due to the continuing volcanic formation of the islands in the west of the archipelago and its location at the nexus of several major marine currents, have created laboratory-type conditions where only certain species have been allowed access. The formidable barriers which prevent many species from travelling between the islands, has led to a very high level of endemism. A quarter of the species of shore fish, half of the plants and almost all the reptiles are found nowhere else. In many cases different forms have evolved on the different islands. Charles Darwin recognized this speciation within the archipelago when he visited the Galápagos on the *Beagle* in 1835 and his observations played a substantial part in his formulation of the theory of evolution.

This natural experiment has been under threat ever since the arrival of the first whaling ships and even more so since the first permanent human settlement. New species were introduced and spread very rapidly, placing the endemic species at risk. Quarantine programmes have since been implemented in an attempt to prevent the introduction and spread of even more species, but the rules are not easy to enforce. There have also been campaigns to eradicate some of the introduced species on some islands, but this is inevitably a very slow, expensive and difficult process.

One striking feature of the islands is the tameness of the animals. The islands were uninhabited when they were discovered in 1535 and the animals still have little instinctive fear of man.

Plant and animal species are grouped into three categories. **Endemic species** are those which occur only in the Galápagos and nowhere else on the planet. Examples of Galápagos endemics are the Galápagos marine and Galápagos land iguana, Galápagos fur sea lion, flightless cormorant and the 'daisy tree' (*Scalesia pedunculata*). **Native species** make their homes in the Galápagos as well as other parts of the world. Examples include all three species of boobies, frigate birds and the various types of mangroves. Although not unique to the islands, these native species have been an integral part of the Galápagos ecosystems for a very long time. **Introduced species** on the other hand are very recent arrivals, brought by man, and inevitably the cause of much damage. They include cattle, goats, donkeys, pigs, dogs, cats, rats and over 500 species of plants such as elephant grass (for grazing cattle), and fruit trees. The unchecked expansion of these introduced species has upset the natural balance of the archipelago. Any domestic animals must now be neutered before they can be brought to the islands. The number of tourists also has grown steadily: from 11,800 in 1979, to 68,900 in 2000, to over 224,755 in 2015. From 2007 to 2010, Galápagos was on the UNESCO list of endangered World Heritage Sites. Although it is now off the list, promoting environmental conservation and sustainable development in the face of growing tourism and population has proven to be an ever greater challenge.

Galápagos tourist vessels

Name	Type	Capacity	Website	Class
Galapagos Legend	CS	100	kleintours.com	L
Silver Galapagos	CS	100	silversea.com	L
Xpedition	CS	100	galapagosxpedition.co.uk	L
Nat Geo Endeavour	CS	96	expeditions.com	L
Eclipse	CS	48	oagalapagos.com	L
Nat Geo Islander	CS	48	expeditions.com	L
Isabela ll	CS	40	metropolitan-touring.com	F
Coral I	MY	36	kleintours.com	F
Evolution	MV	32	galapagosxpeditions.com	L
La Pinta	CS	48	metropolitan-touring.com	L
Galaven	MY	22	various	TS
Coral II	MY	20	kleintours.com	F
Eric	MY	20	ecoventura.com	F
Flamingo I	MY	20	ecoventura.com	F
Letty	MY	20	ecoventura.com	F
Monserrat	MY	20	monserrat-cruise.info	TS
Grace	MY	18	galapagosexpeditions.com	L
Aída María	MY	16	aidamariatravel.com	TS
Amigo I	MY	16	various	E
Anahi	MC	16	andandotours.com	F
Angelito	MY	16	cometatravel.com	TS
Archipel I	MY	16	galacruises.com	TS
Archipel ll	MC	16	galacruises.com	F
Athala ll	MC	16	various	L
Beluga	MY	16	enchantedexpeditions.com	F
Cachalote	2mSCH	16	enchantedexpeditions.com	F
Cormorant Evolution	MC	16	haugancruises.com	TS
Daphne	MY	16	various	TS
Darwin	MY	16	vigaltravel.com	TS
Eden	MY	16	aidamariatravel.com	TS
Estrella del Mar I	MY	16	gadventures.com	TS
Floreana	MY	16	yatefloreana.com	TS
Fragata	MY	16	yatefragata.com	TS
Galaxy I	MC	16	galagents.com	T
Galaxy ll	MC	16	galagents.com	T
Golondrina	MY	16	golondrinaturismo.com	T
Grand Odyssey	MY	16	galapagosgrandodyssey.com	F
Guantanamera	MY	16	ecuadortierradefuego.com	T
Integrity	MY	16	various	L
Majestic	MY	16	gadventures.com	F
Mary Anne	3mBarq	16	andandotours.com	F

Name	Type	Capacity	Website	Class
Millennium	MC	16	galapagosexperience.net	F
Nemo III	MC	16	nemogalapagoscruises.com	T
Ocean Spray	MC	16	haugancruises.com	L
Odyssey	MC	16	galapagosodyssey.com	F
Origin	MY	20	origingalapagos.com	L
Petrel	MC	16	haugancruises.com	T
Queen Beatriz	MC	16	peakdmc.com	L
Queen of Galapagos	MC	16	gadventures.com	L
Reina Silvia	MY	16	reinasilvia.com	F
San José	MY	16	various	F
Santa Cruz	CS	90	metropolitan-touring.com	F
Seaman Journey	MC	16	galapagosjourneycruises.com	F
Sea Star Journey	MY	16	latintrails.com	F
Stellamaris	MY	16	galasam.net	F
Tip Top III	MY	16	rwittmer.com	F
Tip Top IV	MY	16	rwittmer.com	F
Treasure of Galapagos	MC	16	treasureofgalapagos.com	F
Xavier	MY	16	various	TS
Yolita II	MY	16	yolitayacht.com	TS
King of the Seas	MY	14	various	E
Nemo I	MC	14	nemogalapagoscruises.com	T
Samba	SV	14	galapagosexperience.net	TS
Beagle	2mSch	13	galapagosexperience.net	F
Nemo II	MC	12	nemogalapagoscruises.com	F
Passion	MY	12	andandotours.com	TS
New Flamingo	MY	10	various	E

Type Key

CS = Cruise Ship
MY = Motor Yacht
MV = Motor Vessel
MC = Motor Catamaran
2mSch = 2-masted Schooner
3mSch = 3-masted Schooner
3mBarq = 3-masted Barquentine
SV = Sailing Vessel

Class Key

L = Luxury Class
F = First Class
TS = Tourist Superior Class
T = Tourist Class
E = Economy Class

Tourist information

Santa Cruz

iTur
Av Charles Darwin y 12 de Febrero, Puerto Ayora, T05 252 6153 ext 22. Mon-Fri 0730-1230, 1400-1730, Sat-Sun 1600-1930.
Has information about Puerto Ayora and Santa Cruz Island.

Ministerio de Turismo
Charles Binford y 12 de Febrero, Puerto Ayora, T05-252 6174. Mon-Fri 0830-1300, 1430-1730.
An administrative office but receives complaints about agencies and vessels.

San Cristóbal

Ministerio de Turismo
12 de Febrero e Ignacio Hernández, Puerto Baquerizo Moreno, T05-252 0704. Mon-Fri 0830-1230, 1400-1730.
Operates as in Santa Cruz, above.

Municipal tourist office
Malecón Charles Darwin y 12 de Febrero, Puerto Baquerizo Moreno, T05-252 0119 ext 120. Mon-Fri 0730-1230, 1400-1800.
Downstairs at the Municipio.

Isabela

Municipal tourist office
By the park, Puerto Villamil, T05-252 9002, ext 113. Mon-Fri 0730-1230, 1400-1700.
Has local information.

Where to stay

Santa Cruz
Puerto Ayora

$$$$ Angemeyer Waterfront Inn
By the dock at Punta Estrada, T05-252 6561, www.angermeyer-waterfront-inn.com.
Gorgeous location overlooking the bay south of the centre. Includes buffet breakfast, restaurant, comfortable modern rooms and apartments, some with kitchenettes, a/c, attentive service. Spa, pool and gym are planned for 2017.

$$$$ Silberstein
Darwin y Piqueros, T05-252 6277, Quito T02-225 0553, www.hotelsilberstein.com.
Modern and comfortable with lovely grounds, pool in tropical garden, a/c, buffet breakfast, restaurant (see page 686), bar, spacious rooms and common areas, very nice.

$$$$ Sol y Mar
Darwin y Binford, T05-252 6281, www.hotelsolymar.com.ec.
Right in town but with a priviledged location overlooking the bay. Inculdes buffet breakfast, restaurant, bar, pool, jacuzzi and use of bicycles.

$$$ España
Berlanga y 12 de Febrero, T05-252 6108, www.hotelespanagalapagos.com.
Pleasant and quiet, spacious rooms, a/c, small courtyard with hammocks, good value.

$$$ Jean's Home
Punta Estrada, T05-252 6446, T09-9296 0347, gundisg@hotmail.es.
Comfortably refurbished home in a lovely out-of-the-way location (short water taxi ride south of town), a/c, family-run, English and German spoken.

$$$ Lobo de Mar
12 de Febrero y Darwin, T05-252 6188, Quito T02-250 2089, www.lobodemar.com.ec.
Modern building with balconies and rooftop terrace, great views over the harbour. A/c, small pool, fridge, modern and comfortable, attentive service.

$$$ Peregrina
Darwin e Indefatigable, T05-252 6323, peregrinagalapagos@yahoo.com.
Away from the centre of town, a/c, nice rooms and common areas, small garden, family-run, homey atmosphere.

$$ Estrella de Mar
by the water on a lane off 12 de Febrero, T05-252 6427.
Nice quiet location with views over the bay. A/c, fan, fridge, spacious rooms, sitting area.

$$-$ Gardner
Berlanga y 12 de Febrero, T05-252 6979, hotelgardner@yahoo.com.
Comfortable rooms, cheaper with fan, kitchen facilities, breakfast available, good value.

$$-$ Los Amigos
Darwin y 12 de Febrero, T05-252 6265.
Small place, basic rooms with shared bath, cold water, fan, laundry facilities, good value.

Highlands of Santa Cruz

$$$$ Galápagos Safari Camp
T09-8296 8228, www.galapagos safaricamp.com.
Luxury resort with a central lodge and comfortable, en suite tents. Includes breakfast and dinner, swimming pool, organizes tours and activities.

$$$$ Semilla Verde
T05-301-3079, www.gps.ec.
Located on a 5 ha property being reforested with native plants, comfortable rooms and common areas, includes breakfast, other meals available or use of kitchen facilities, British/Ecuadorean-run, family atmosphere.

San Cristóbal
Puerto Baquerizo Moreno

$$$$ Miconia
Darwin e Isabela, T05-252 0608, www.hotelmiconia.com.
Restaurant, a/c, small pool, large well-equipped gym, modern if somewhat small rooms, some with fridge.

$$$ Blue Marlin
Española y Northia, T05-252 0253, www.bluemarlingalapagos.ec.
Ample modern rooms are mostly wheelchair accessible, bathtubs, a/c, pool, fridge.

$$$ Casablanca
Mellville y Darwin, T05-252 0392, www.casablancagalapagos.com.
Large house with terrace and views of harbour. Each room is individually decorated by the owner who has an art gallery on the premises.

$$ Casa de Nelly
Tijeretas y Northia, T05-252 0112, casadenellygalapagos.com.
3-storey building, quiet, bright comfortable rooms, a/c, kitchen facilities, family-run.

$$ Mar Azul
Northia y Esmeraldas, T05-252 0139.
Nice comfortable lodgings, electric shower, a/c and fan, fridge, kitchen facilities, pleasant. Same family runs 2 more expensive hotels.

$ San Francisco
Darwin y Villamil, T05-252 0304.
Simple rooms with private bath, cold water, fan, kitchen facilities, good value.

El Progreso

$$ Casa del Ceibo
Pto Baquerizo Moreno T05-252 0248.
A single unique room in the branches of a huge kapok tree. Private bath, hot water, US$1.50 to visit, advance booking required.

Isabela
Puerto Villamil
Many hotels have opened in recent years.

$$$$ Albemarle
On the beachfront in town, T05-252 9489, www.hotelalbemarle.com.
Attractive Mediterranean-style construction, restaurant, bright comfortable rooms with wonderful ocean views, a/c, small pool.

$$$$ La Casa de Marita
At east end of beach, T05-252 9238, www.galapagosisabela.com.
Tastefully chic, includes breakfast, other meals on request, a/c and fridge, very comfortable, each room is slightly different, some have balconies. A little gem and recommended.

$$$ Casa Isabela on the Beach
On the beachfront in town, T05-252 9103,
casitadelaplaya@hotmail.com, Quito office:
Galacruises, www.islasgalapagos.travel.
Pleasant house on the beach, rooms with a/c,
nice ocean views.

$$$ La Laguna
Los Flamencos y Los Petreles, T05-349 7940,
www.gruposanvicentegalapagos.com.
Pleasant rooms with a/c, attractive balconies
and common areas, jacuzzi.

$$$ San Vicente
Cormoranes y Pinzón Artesano, T05-252 9140,
www.gruposanvicentegalapagos.com.
Very popular and well organized hotel which
also offers tours and kayak rentals, includes
breakfast, other meals on request or use of
cooking facilities, a/c, jacuzzi, rooms a bit
small but nice, family-run.

$$ Hostal Villamil
10 de Marzo y Antonio Gil, T05-252 9180,
www.gruposanvicentegalapagos.com.
A/c, kitchen and laundry facilities, small patio
with hammocks, family-run and very friendly,
good value. Recommended.

$$ The Jungle
Off Antonio Gil at the west edge of town,
T05-301 6690.
Nice rooms with a/c, beach views, meals on
request, secluded non-central location.

Highlands of Isabela

$$ Campo Duro
T09-8545 3045, refugiodetortugasgigantes@
hotmail.com.
Camping (tents provided), includes breakfast
and dinner, nice ample grounds, giant
tortoises may be seen (US$2 to visit), friendly
owner. Taxi from Pto Villamil, US$7.

Floreana: Puerto Velasco Ibarra

$$$$ Lava Lodge
Book through Tropic Journeys in Nature,
www.destinationecuador.com.
Wooden cabins on the beach a short distance
outside town, family-owned, full board, kayak,
snorkel and SUP equipment, guided tours to
wildlife and historic sites, popular with groups.

$$$ Hostal Santa María
Opposite the school, T05-253 5022.
Nice modern rooms with private bath, hot
water, fan, fridge, screened windows, friendly
owner Sr Claudio Cruz.

$$$ Hotel/Pensión Wittmer
Right on Black Beach, T05-253 5013.
Lovely location, simple comfortable rooms,
electric shower, fan, very good meals
available, family-run, German spoken,
reservations required.

Santa Cruz: Puerto Ayora

$$$ Il Giardino
Charles Darwin y Charles Binford, T05-252
6627. Open 0800-2230, closed Tue.
Very good international food, service and
atmosphere, excellent ice cream, very
popular, book in advance.

$$$ Isla Grill
Charles Darwin y Tomás de Berlanga,
T05-252 4461. Tue-Sun 1200-2200.
Upmarket grill, seafood and pizza.

$$$ La Dolce Italia
Charles Darwin y 12 de Febrero.
Daily 1100-1500, 1800-2200.
Italian and seafood, wine list, a/c, pleasant
atmosphere, attentive owner.

$$$-$$ La Garrapata
Charles Darwin between 12 de Febrero and
Tomás de Berlanga. Mon-Sat 0900-2200.
Good food, attractive setting and nice music.

$$$-$$ Silberstein
Darwin y Piqueros, T05-252 6277.
Serves a good range of both Ecuadorian
and international cuisine. Lovely setting
with tables, inside and outside, some
overlooking the pool area. In eponymous
hotel; see page 684.

$$ Kiosks
Along Charles Binford between Padre Herrera and Rodríguez Lara.
Tasty local fare, including a variety of seafood, outdoor seating, lively informal atmosphere, busy at night. Also beside the fishermen's dock at Pelican Bay, evenings only.

$ El Descanso del Guía
Charles Darwin y Los Colonos. Daily 0645-1945.
Good set meals, very popular with locals.

San Cristóbal: Puerto Baquerizo Moreno

$$$-$$ La Playa
Av de la Armada Nacional, by the navy base.
Daily 0930-2330.
Varied menu, fish and seafood.

$$$-$$ Olimpio
Northía y Isabela. Closed Sun.
Attractive restaurant, international food.

$$$-$$ Rosita
Ignacio de Hernández y General Villamil.
Daily 0930-1430, 1700-2230.
Old-time yachtie hangout, good food, large portions, nice atmosphere, à la carte and economical set meals. Recommended.

$$ Descanso del Marinero
Northia y Española. Wed-Mon 0800-2100.
Ceviches and seafood, outdoor seating.

$ Mi Grande
Villamil y Darwin, upstairs.
Popular for set meals and good breakfast.

$ Several simple places serving economical
set meals on Northia between Española and 12 de Febrero. Also Sun lunch up at El Progreso, good *comida del campo*.

Mockingbird Café
Española y Hernández. Mon-Sat 0730-2330, Sun from 0930.
Fruit juices, brownies, snacks, internet.

Sabor Cuencano
Northía y Isabela. Closed Sun.
Good popular bakery.

Isabela: Puerto Villamil
$$$-$$ Various outdoor restaurants around the plaza feature seafood on the menu: **Cesar's**, **Los Delfines** and **Encanto de la Pepa**, which is very good.

$$-$ Isabela Grill
16 de Marzo y Flamencos.
Good choice for set lunch, dinner and à la carte.

$ El Faro
Las Fragatas ½ block from Plaza.
Daily 1200-1400, 1800-1930.
Simple set lunch, grill at night, popular.

Floreana: Puerto Velasco Ibarra
$$$-$$ Meals available at hotels or from a couple of restaurants catering to tour groups, all require advance notice.

$$ Lelia Restaurante
Opposite the school, T05-253 5041.
Good home cooking. Friendly owner also has 2 rooms for rent.

$ The Devil's Crown
100 m from the dock on road to the highlands.
Set lunch and dinner most days, ask in advance.

Shopping

Santa Cruz: Puerto Ayora
There is an attractive little **Mercado Artesanal** (craft market) at Charles Darwin y Tomás de Berlanga. **Proinsular**, opposite the pier, is the largest and best-stocked supermarket in Galápagos.

San Cristóbal: Puerto Baquerizo Moreno

Galamarket
Isabela y Juan José Flores.
A modern well-stocked supermarket.

> **Tip...**
> Most items can be purchased on the islands but at a higher price than in mainland Ecuador. Do not buy anything made of black coral as it is an endangered species.

Dive boats

Name	Type	Capacity	Website	Class
Aggressor III	MY	16	aggressor.com	L
Astrea	MY	16	various	TS
Deep Blue	MY	16	various	F
Galapagos Sky	MY	16	galapagossky.com	L
Humbolt Explorer	MY	16	galasam.net	F
Pingüino Explorer	MY	16	galacruises.com	TS
Encantada	2mSch	12	scubagalapagos.com	T
Nortada	MY	8	galapagosnortada.com	F

Type Key	Class Key
MY = Motor Yacht	L = Luxury Class
2mSch = 2-masted Schooner	F = First Class
	TS = Tourist Superior Class
	T = Tourist Class

What to do

Santa Cruz: Puerto Ayora
Cycling
Mountain bikes can be hired from travel agencies in town. Prices and quality vary, about US$15-20 for 3 hrs.

Diving
Only specialized diving boats are allowed to do diving tours. It is not possible to dive as part of a standard live-aboard cruise nor are dive boats allowed to call at the usual land visitor sites when they are diving. Some dive boats, however, might offer a week of diving followed by a week of cruising to land sites. For a list of dive boats, see table, opposite. National Park rules prohibit collecting samples or souvenirs, spear-fishing, touching animals, or other environmental disruptions. Experienced dive guides can help visitors have the most spectacular opportunities to enjoy the wildlife. There are several diving agencies in Puerto Ayora, Baquerizo Moreno and Villamil (see Tour operators, below) offering courses, equipment rental, and dives; prices and quality vary. On offer in Puerto Ayora are diving day trips (2 dives, US$175-250) and daily tours for up to 1 week in the central islands. There is a hyperbaric chamber in Puerto Ayora at **Centro Médico Integral**, Marchena y Hanny, T05-252 4576, www.sssnetwork.com. Check if your dive operator is affiliated with this facility or arrange your own insurance from home. To avoid the risk of decompression sickness, divers are advised to stay an extra day on the islands after their last dive before flying to the mainland, especially to Quito at 2840 m above sea level.

Dive Center Silberstein, *opposite Hotel Silberstein, T05-252 6028, www. divingalapagos.com.* Day tours in nice comfortable boat for up to 8 guests, English-speaking guides, good service, dive courses and trips for all levels of experience. Island-hopping dive tours and 8-day diving cruises are also organized.
Nautidiving, *Av Charles Darwin, T05-252 7004.* Offers day-trips to central islands as well as longer trips.
Scuba Iguana, *Charles Darwin near the research station, T05-252 6497, www.scuba*

iguana.com. Matías Espinoza runs this long-time reliable and recommended dive operator. Courses up to PADI divemaster.

Snorkelling

Masks, snorkels and fins can be rented from travel agencies and dive shops, US$5 a day, deposit required. Las Grietas is a popular place to snorkel near Puerto Ayora.

Surfing

There is surfing at Tortuga Bay and at other more distant beaches accessed by boat. Look for the surf club office at Pelican Bay. There is better surfing near Puerto Baquerizo Moreno on San Cristóbal. The **Lonesome George** agency rents surfboards, see below.

Tour operators

Lonesome George, *Av Baltra y Enrique Fuentes, T05-252 6245, lonesomegrg@yahoo. com*. Run by Victor Vaca. Sells tours and rents:

bicycles (US$3 per hr), surf-boards (US$30 per day) snorkelling equipment and motorcycles.
Moonrise Travel, *Av Charles Darwin y Charles Binford, T05-252 6348, www.galapagos moonrise.com*. Last-minute cruise bookings, day-tours to different islands, bay tours, flights, enquire about horse riding at ranches, run guesthouse in Punta Estrada and rent chalets by Playa de los Alemanes. Owner Jenny Devine is knowledgeable and helpful.
Zenith Travel, *JL Mera N24-264 y Cordero, Quito, T02-252 9993, www.zenithecuador.com*. Good-value Galápagos cruises. All-gay Galápagos cruises available. Multilingual service, knowledgeable helpful staff, good value.

San Cristóbal: Puerto Baquerizo Moreno

Cycling

Bike rentals cost US$3 per hr, US$15 per day.

Diving

There are several dive sites around San Cristóbal, most popular being Kicker Rock, Roca Ballena and Punta Pitt, full day about US$200, see Tour operators, below.

Kayaking

Rentals US$10 per hr; from **Islander's Store** (Av J Roldós, above cargo pier, T05-252 0348); and **Galápagos Eco Expedition** (Av de la Armada, next to La Playa restaurant).

Surfing

There is good surfing in San Cristóbal, the best season is Dec-Mar. Punta Carola near town is the closest surfing beach; other spots are Canon and Tongo Reef, past the navy base. There is a championship during the local fiesta, the 2nd week of Feb.

Tour operators

Canon Point, *Armada Nacional y Darwin*. Rents bikes, skate boards and surfboards.
Chalo Tours, *Darwin y Villamil*, T05-252 0953, *chalotours@hotmail.com*. Specializes in diving and snorkelling.
Sharksky, *Darwin y Villamil*, T05-252 1188, *www.sharksky.com*. Highlands, diving, snorkelling, island-hopping, last-minute cruise bookings and gear rental. Also has an office on Isabela. Swiss/Ecuadorean-run, English, German and French spoken, helpful.
Wreck Bay Dive Center, *Darwin y Wolf*, T05-252 1663, *www.wreckbay.com*. Reported friendly and respectful of the environment.

Puerto Villamil

Hotels also arrange tours. Kayak rentals at **Hotel San Vicente**.
Galápagos Dive Center, *16 de Marzo y Cormoranes*, T05-301 6570. Dive trips, diving gear sale and rental.

Galapagos Native, *Cormoranes y 16 de Marzo*, T05-252 9140, *www.gruposanvicente galapagos.com*. Mountain biking downhill from Sierra Negra, full day including lunch, US$42. Also rentals: good bikes US$3 per hr, US$20 per day; snorkelling gear US$5 per day; surf boards US$4 per hr.
Isabela Dive Center, *Escalecias y Alberto Gil*, T05-252 9418, *www.isabeladivecenter.com.ec*. Diving, land and boat tours.

Transport

Santa Cruz: Puerto Ayora

Airline offices Avianca, Rodríguez Lara y San Cristóbal, T05-252 6798. **Emetebe**, Darwin y Berlanga, T05-252 4978, Baltra airport T05-252 4755. **LATAM**, Av Charles Darwin e Islas Plaza, T1-800-101075. **TAME**, Av Charles Darwin y 12 de Febrero, T05-252 6527.

Sea *Lanchas* (speedboats) depart daily from the pier near the volleyball courts (see map) for the following islands: **San Cristóbal** at 1400; **Isabela** at 0730 and 1400; **Floreana** at 0700; all fares US$30.

Pick-up truck taxis These may be hired for transport throughout town, US$1. A *ranchera* runs up to the highlands from the **Tropidurus** store, Av Baltra y Jaime Roldóss, 2 blocks past the market: to **Bellavista** US$0.50, 10 mins; **Santa Rosa** US$1, 20 mins. For airport transfers, see page 673.

Water taxis (*taxis acuáticos*) From the pier to Punta Estrada or anchored boats, US$0.60 during the day, US$2 at night.

Yacht agents All yachts must use an agent by law. **Galápagos Ocean Services** (Peter Schiess), Charles Darwin next to Garrapata restaurant, T09-9477 0804, *www. gos.ec*. **Naugala Yacht Services** (Jhonny Romero), T05-252 7403, *www.naugala.com*.

Background

History

Theories regarding the arrival of human beings in South America are constantly being revised as new archaeological discoveries force reassessments of old models. After the Pleistocene Ice Age, 8000-7000 BC, rising sea levels and climatic changes introduced new conditions as many mammal species became extinct and coastlands were drowned. A wide range of crops was brought into cultivation and camelids and guinea pigs were domesticated. It was originally thought that people turned from hunter-gathering in small nomadic groups to a village-based existence between 2500-1500 BC, but evidence form the coast of central Peru has radically altered that view.

It is indisputable that in this region settled life developed rapidly. The abundant wealth of marine life produced by the Humboldt Current, especially north of today's Lima, boosted population growth and a shift from nomadic to settled farming in this area. The introduction of sophisticated irrigation systems encouraged higher productivity and population growth, leading to organized group labour which could be devoted to building and making textiles from cotton. Evidence from Caral, Aspero and other sites in the Huaura, Supe, Pativilca and Fortaleza river valleys prove that this process happened much earlier than previously imagined. Caral dates from 2627 BC (other sites have older dates) and is a monumental construction. It flourished for some 500 years and appears to have been a city with primarily a religious, rather than a warlike purpose. The archaeological finds point to Caral and neighbouring sites predating the development of pottery in this region, but artefacts show cultural links with other communities, even as far as the Amazon. Almost contemporaneous with Caral was Ventarrón, a city in Lambayeque, northern Peru, with a temple containing the oldest murals discovered in the Americas. In the central Andes near Huánuco, also in what is now Peru, more advanced architecture was being built at Kotosh. There is evidence of a pre-ceramic culture here, too, but some of the earliest pottery from the site's later phases was found, showing signs of influence from southern Ecuador and the tropical lowlands. Radiocarbon dates of some Kotosh remains are from 1850 BC and Japanese archaeological excavations there in the 1960s revealed a temple with ornamental niches and friezes.

Andean and Pacific Coastal Civilizations

Chavín and Sechín

For the next 1000 years or so up to c900 BC, communities grew and spread inland from the north coast and south along the north highlands. Farmers still lived in simple adobe or rough stone houses but built increasingly large and complex ceremonial centres. As farming became more productive and pottery more advanced, commerce grew and states began to develop throughout central and north-central Peru, with the associated signs of social structure and hierarchies.

Around 900 BC a new era was marked by the rise of two important centres; Chavín de Huántar in the central Andes and Sechín Alto, inland from Casma on the north coast, both now in Peru. The chief importance of Chavín de Huántar was not so much in its highly advanced architecture as in the influence of its cult, coupled with the artistic style of its ceramics and other artefacts. The founders of Chavín may have originated in the tropical lowlands, as some of its carved monoliths show representations of monkeys and felines.

The Chavín cult

This was paralleled by the great advances made in this period in textile production and in some of the earliest examples of metallurgy. The origins of metallurgy have been attributed to some gold, silver and copper ornaments found in graves in Chongoyape, near Chiclayo, which show Chavín-style features. But earlier evidence has been discovered at Kuntur Wasi (some 120 km east of the coast at Pacasmayo) where 4000-year old gold has been found, and in the Andahuaylas region, dating from 1800-900 BC. The religious symbolism of gold and other precious metals and stones is thought to have been an inspiration behind some of the beautiful artefacts found in the central Andean area.

The cultural brilliance of Chavín de Huántar was complemented by its contemporary, Sechín, with which it may have combined forces, Sechín being the military power that spread the cultural word of Chavín. The Chavín hegemony broke up around 500 BC, soon after which the Nazca culture began to bloom in southern Peru. This period, up to about AD 500, was a time of great social and cultural development. Sizable towns of 5-10,000 inhabitants grew on the south coast, populated by artisans, merchants and government and religious officials.

Paracas-Nazca

Nazca origins are traced back to about the second century BC, to the Paracas Cavernas and Necropolis, on the coast in the national park near Pisco in Peru. The extreme dryness of the desert here has preserved remarkably the textiles and ceramics in the mummies' tombs excavated. The technical quality and stylistic variety in weaving and pottery rank them among the world's best, and many of the finest examples can be seen in the museums of Lima. The famous Nazca Lines are a feature of the region. Straight lines, abstract designs and outlines of animals are scratched in the dark desert surface forming a lighter contrast that can be seen clearly from the air. There are many theories of how and why the lines were made but no definitive explanation has yet been able to establish their place in South American history. There are similarities between the style of some of the line patterns and that of the pottery and textiles of the same period. Alpaca hair found in Nazca textiles, however, indicates that there must have been strong trade links with highland people.

Moche culture

Nazca's contemporaries on the north coast were the militaristic Moche who, from about AD 100-800, built up an empire whose traces stretch from Piura in the north to Huarmey, in the south. The Moche built their capital outside present day Trujillo. The huge pyramid temples of the Huaca del Sol and Huaca de la Luna mark the remains of this city. Moche roads and system of way stations are thought to have been an early inspiration for the Inca network. The Moche increased the coastal population with intensive irrigation projects. Skilful engineering works were carried out, such as the La Cumbre canal, still in use today, and the Ascope aqueduct, both on the Chicama River. The Moche's greatest achievement, however, was its artistic genius. Exquisite ornaments in gold, silver and precious stones were made by its craftsmen. Moche pottery progressed through five stylistic periods, most notable for the stunningly lifelike portrait vases. A wide variety of everyday scenes were created in naturalistic ceramics, telling us more about Moche life than is known about other earlier cultures. Spectacular Moche tombs, discovered at Sipán since 1987, have included semi-precious stones brought from Chile and Argentina, and seashells from Ecuador. The Moche were great navigators.

The cause of the collapse of the Moche Empire around AD 600-700 is unknown, but it may have been started by a 30-year drought at the end of the sixth century, followed by one of the periodic El Niño flash floods (identified by meteorologists from ice thickness in the Andes) and finished by the encroaching forces of the Huari Empire. The decline of the Moche signalled a general tipping of the balance of power in Peru from the north coast to the south sierra.

Huari-Tiwanaku

The ascendant Huari-Tiwanaku movement, from AD 600-1000, combined the religious cult of the Tiwanaku site in the Titicaca basin, with the military dynamism of the Huari, based in the central highlands. The two cultures developed independently but they are generally thought to have merged compatibly. Up until their own demise around AD 1440, the Huari-Tiwanaku had spread their empire and influence across much of south Peru, north Bolivia and Argentina. They made considerable gains in art and technology, building roads, terraces and irrigation canals across the country. The Huari-Tiwanaku ran their empire with efficient labour and administrative systems that were later adopted by the Incas. Labour tribute for state projects practised by the Moche were further developed. But the empire could not contain regional kingdoms who began to fight for land and power. As control broke down, rivalry and coalitions emerged, the system collapsed and the scene was set for the rise of the Incas.

Chachapoyas and Chimú cultures

After the decline of the Huari Empire, the unity that had been imposed on the Andes was broken. A new stage of autonomous regional or local political organizations began. Among the cultures corresponding to this period were the Chachapoyas in northern highlands and the Chimú. The Chachapoyas people were not so much an empire as a loose-knit 'confederation of ethnic groups with no recognized capital' (Morgan Davis *Chachapoyas: The Cloud People*, Ontario, 1988). But the culture did develop into an advanced society with great skill in road and monument building. Their fortress at Kuélap was known as the most impregnable in the Peruvian Andes. The Chimú culture had two centres. To the north was Lambayeque, near Chiclayo, while to the south, in the Moche valley near present-day Trujillo, was the great adobe walled city of Chan Chán. Covering 20 sq km, this was the largest prehispanic Peruvian city. Chimú has been classified as a despotic state that based its power on wars of conquest. Rigid social stratification existed and power rested in the hands of the great lord Siquic and the lord Alaec. These lords were followed in social scale by a group of urban couriers who enjoyed a certain degree of economic power. At the bottom were the peasants and slaves. In 1450, the Chimú kingdom was conquered by the Inca Túpac Yupanqui, the son and heir of the Inca ruler Pachacútec.

Northern Andes

What is today Ecuador was a densely populated region with a variety of peoples. One of the most important of these was the **Valdivia culture** (3500-1500 BC) on the coast, from which remains of buildings and earthenware figures have been found. A rich mosaic of cultures developed in the period 500 BC to AD 500, after which integration of groups occurred. In the mid-15th century, the relentless expansion of the Inca empire reached Ecuador. The **Cañaris** resisted until 1470 and the Quitu/Caras were defeated in 1492. Further north, most of the peoples who occupied Colombia were primitive hunters or nomad agriculturists, but one part of the country, the high basins of the Eastern Cordillera, was densely occupied by **Chibcha** people who had become sedentary farmers. Their staple foods were maize and the potato, and they had no domestic animal save the dog; the use they could make of the land was therefore limited. Other cultures present in Colombia in the pre-Columbian era were the **Tayrona**, **Quimbaya**, **Sinú** and **Calima**. Exhibits of theirs and the Chibcha's (Muisca's) goldwork can be seen at the Gold Museum in Bogotá and other cities.

Southern Andes

Although there was some influence in southern Bolivia from cultures such as Tiwanaku, most of the southern Andes was an area of autonomous peoples, probably living in fortified settlements by the time the Incas arrived in the mid-15th century.

The Amazon

Archaeological evidence from the Amazon basin is more scanty than from the Andes or Pacific because the materials used for house building, clothing and decoration were perishable and did not survive the warm, humid conditions of the jungle. Large earthworks and mounds of ceramics have been discovered in the department of Beni, in the northern jungle of Bolivia, suggesting an important civilization inhabited this area around AD 1000. Although such structured societies developed in the Amazon Basin and population was large, no political groupings of the scale of those of the Andes formed. The Incas made few inroads into the Amazon so it was the arrival of Europeans in the 16th century which initiated the greatest change in this region.

The Inca Dynasty

The origins of the Inca Dynasty are shrouded in mythology and shaky evidence. The best known story reported by the Spanish chroniclers talks about Manco Cápac and his sister rising out of Lake Titicaca, created by the sun as divine founders of a chosen race. This was in approximately AD 1200. Over the next 300 years the small tribe grew to supremacy as leaders of the largest empire ever known in the Americas, divided into the four quarters of Tawantinsuyo, all radiating out from Cuzco: Chinchaysuyo, north and northwest; Cuntisuyo, south and west; Collasuyo, south and east; Antisuyo, east.

At its peak, just before the Spanish Conquest, the Inca Empire stretched from the Río Maule in central Chile, north to the present Ecuador-Colombia border, contained most of Ecuador, Peru, west Bolivia, north Chile and northwest Argentina. The area was roughly equivalent to France, Belgium, Holland, Luxembourg, Italy and Switzerland combined, 980,000 sq km. For a brief description of Inca Society, see box, page 234.

The first Inca ruler, Manco Cápac, moved to the fertile Cuzco region, and established Cuzco as his capital. Successive generations of rulers were fully occupied with local conquests of rivals, such as the Colla and Lupaca to the south, and the Chanca to the northwest. At the end of Inca Viracocha's reign the hated Chanca were finally defeated, largely thanks to the heroism of one of his sons, Pachacútec (Pachacuti Inca Yupanqui), who was subsequently crowned as the new ruler.

From the start of Pachacútec's own reign in 1438, imperial expansion grew in earnest. With the help of his son and heir, Topa Inca, territory was conquered from the Titicaca basin south into Chile, and all the north and central coast down to the Lurin Valley. In 1460-1471, the Incas also laid siege to the Chimú. Typical of the Inca method of government, some of the Chimú skills were assimilated into their own political and administrative system, and some Chimú nobles were even given positions in Cuzco.

Perhaps the pivotal event in Inca history came in 1527 with the death of the ruler, Huayna Cápac. Civil war broke out in the confusion over his rightful successor. One of his legitimate sons, Huáscar, ruled the southern part of the empire from Cuzco. Atahualpa, Huáscar's half-brother, governed Quito, the capital of Chinchaysuyo. In 1532, soon after Atahualpa had won the civil war, Francisco Pizarro arrived in Tumbes with 167 conquistadores, a third of them on horseback. Atahualpa's army was marching south, probably for the first time, when he clashed with Pizarro at Cajamarca. Francisco Pizarro's only chance against the formidable imperial army he encountered at Cajamarca was a bold stroke. He drew Atahualpa into an ambush, slaughtered his guards and many of his troops, promised him liberty if a certain room were filled with treasure, and finally killed him on the pretext that an Inca army was on its way to free him. Pushing on to Cuzco, he was at first hailed as the executioner of a traitor: Atahualpa had ordered the death of Huáscar in 1533, while himself captive of Pizarro, and his victorious generals were bringing the defeated Huáscar to see his half-brother. Panic followed when the conquistadores set about sacking the city, and they fought off with difficulty an attempt by Manco Inca to recapture Cuzco in 1536.

The Spanish Conquest

Pizarro's arrival in Peru had been preceded by Columbus' landfall on the Paria Peninsula (Venezuela) on 5 August 1498 and Spanish reconaissance of the Pacific coast in 1522. Permanent Spanish settlement was established at Santa Marta (Colombia) in 1525 and Cartagena was founded in 1533. Gonzalo Jiménez de Quesada conquered the Chibcha kingdom and founded Bogotá in 1538. Pizarro's lieutenant, Sebastián de Belalcázar, was sent north through Ecuador; he captured Quito with Diego de Almagro in 1534.

Gonzalo Pizarro, Francisco's brother, took over control of Quito in 1538 and, during his exploration of the Amazon lowlands, he sent Francisco de Orellana to prospect downriver. Orellana did not return, but drifted down the Amazon, finally reaching the river's mouth in 1542, the first European to cross the continent in this way. Belalcázar pushed north, founding Pasto, Cali and Popayán (Colombia) in 1536, arriving in Bogotá in 1538. Meanwhile, wishing to secure his communications with Spain, Pizarro founded Lima, near the ocean, as his capital in 1535. The same year Diego de Almagro set out to conquer Chile. Unsuccessful, he returned to Peru, quarrelled with Pizarro, and in 1538 fought a pitched battle with Pizarro's men at the Salt Pits, near Cuzco. He was defeated and put to death. Pizarro, who had not been at the battle, was assassinated in his palace in Lima by Almagro's son three years later.

Treasure hunt

As Spanish colonization built itself around new cities, the *conquistadores* set about finding the wealth which had lured them to South America in the first place. The great prize came in 1545 when the hill of silver at Potosí (Bolivia) was discovered. Other mining centres grew up and the trade routes to supply them and carry out the riches were established. The Spanish crown soon imposed political and administrative jurisdiction over its new empire, replacing the power of the *conquistadores* with that of governors and bureaucrats. The Viceroyalty of Peru became the major outlet for the wealth of the Americas, but each succeeding representative of the Kingdom of Spain was faced with the twofold threat of subduing the Inca successor state of Vilcabamba, north of Cuzco, and unifying the fierce Spanish factions. Francisco de Toledo (appointed 1568) solved both problems during his 14 years in office: Vilcabamba was crushed in 1572 and the last reigning Inca, Túpac

Amaru, put to death. For the next 200 years the Viceroys closely followed Toledo's system, if not his methods. The Major Government – the Viceroy, the *Audiencia* (High Court), and *corregidores* (administrators) – ruled through the Minor Government – indigenous chiefs put in charge of large groups of natives: a rough approximation to the original Inca system.

Towards Independence and thereafter

Significant dates

1780	A rebellion led by Túpac Amaru II in **Peru** fails, as does a second revolt in 1814.
1820	José de San Martín, with help from English admiral Lord Cochrane, lands in southern **Peru**.
1821	**Peruvian** independence is declared by San Martín.
1822	Presidencia de **Quito** wins independence from Spain at the Battle of Pichincha after two years of revolt.
	San Martín goes into voluntary exile after meeting Simón Bolívar in Guayaquil. Bolívar and Antonio José de Sucre continue the liberation struggle in **Peru**.
1824	Battles of Junín and Ayacucho: after the latter the Spanish are finally defeated in **Peru**.
1825	Independence of **Bolivia** declared on 6 August. Simón Bolívar is president until January 1826 when Sucre assumes the role.
1826	Spain's last stronghold in **Peru**, the Real Felipe fortress in Callao, capitulates.
1830	**Ecuador** opts for independence from the Gran Colombia confederation. Government thereafter is dominated by various elites. Two principal figures were Gabriel García Moreno (president 1860-1865, 1869-1875), an arch-conservative dictator, and the liberal Eloy Alfaro (1895-1901 and 1906-1911). Both were assassinated.
1836	President Andrés Santa Cruz (in office 1829-1839) tries to reunite **Bolivia** with Peru; Argentina and Chile intervene to overthrow him.
1864-1866	**Peru** and Spain go to war over the guano-rich Chincha Islands. Peru is victorious.
1879-1883	War of the Pacific: **Bolivia** aligns with **Peru**, which loses the war to Chile. Bolivia loses its coastal provinces and its outlet to the sea while Peru loses its southern province.
1903	Brazil annexes the **Bolivian** state of Acre.
1924	Víctor Raúl Haya de la Torre founds the Alianza Popular Revolucionaria Americana (APRA), which becomes one of the predominant political parties in **Peru**.
1932	APRA seizes power in Trujillo, **Peru**, which leads to many deaths.
1932-1935	War of the Chaco in which **Bolivia** loses three-quarters of its Chaco territory to Paraguay.
1936	The army seizes power in **Bolivia**, leading to a series of unstable military governments.
1948	General Manuel Odría seizes power and outlaws APRA in **Peru**.
1951	Movimiento Nacionalista Revolucionario is elected to power in **Bolivia**, but a coup prevents it taking office.

1952	A popular revolution in **Bolivia** overthrows the military in April; Víctor Paz Estenssoro and MNR take power; mines are nationalized; universal suffrage is introduced; large estates are broken up and redistributed.
1962	Haya de la Torre wins **Peruvian** elections but is prevented from taking office by the military. In 1963 Fernando Belaúnde Terry is elected president.
1964	After 12 years of MNR rule, vice president General René Barrientos seizes power in **Bolivia** ushering in a series of military governments, including those of Coronel Hugo Banzer (1971-1978) and General Luis García Meza (1980-1981), renowned for brutality and links to the cocaine trade.
1968	In **Peru** a coup is led by General Juan Velasco Alvarado which brings about wide-ranging land reform and nationalizations. There is fierce opposition from the business sector and landholders, but also from unions and *campesinos* in response to the military's crackdown on dissent.
1975	Velasco retires as president of **Peru**.
1979	Jaime Roldós takes office as president of **Ecuador** after decades of alternating military and civilian rule (eg between 1931 and 1948 there were 21 governments).
1980	**Peru** returns to democracy. Belaúnde Terry is re-elected president. His term of office is marked by the rise of Sendero Luminoso and the Movimiento Revolucionario Túpac Amaru (MRTA).
1982	Democratic elections in **Bolivia** bring Hernán Siles Zuazo to power. Civilian rule continues thanks to various alliances and coalitions, including a return to power of Banzer in 1997.
	President Roldós of **Ecuador** dies in an air crash.
1985	Alán García Pérez is elected as **Peru's** first APRA president. At the end of his term of office in 1990, Peru is bankrupt and APRA discredited. Sendero Luminoso and MRTA actions are at their height.
1990	Alberto Fujimori defeats novelist Mario Vargas Llosa in the **Peruvian** elections. Fujimori has no established political framework and so, lacking congressional or senate support, he dissolves congress and suspends the constitution two years later.
1992	Abimael Guzmán and Víctor Polay of Sendero Luminoso and MRTA respectively are arrested.
1993	A new **Peruvian** constitution is drawn up.
1995	Fujimori is re-elected president of **Peru**.
1996	Abdalá Bucaram elected president of **Ecuador**; he lasts six months.
	MRTA take 490 hostages in the Japanese Embassy in **Lima**. Fujimori takes personal control of the situation and, after six months, all the hostages bar one (who died of heart failure) are freed and all the terrorists killed.
1998	Jamil Mahuad becomes president of **Ecuador**. He signs a peace treaty to end the long-running border dispute with **Peru**. The country suffers economic and political chaos after a series of bank failures. The US dollar is adopted as national currency.
2000	Mahuad ousted by **Ecuadorean** indigenous groups and the military. The coup lasts three hours. Gustavo Noboa takes office.
	Peru is thrown into crisis when Vladimiro Montesinos, the head of the National Intelligence Service and a close aide of Fujimori is caught on film offering a bribe to a congressman to switch allegiance to Fujimori's coalition. A vast web of criminality and corruption is uncovered.

In November, Fujimori fled to Japan from where he texts his resignation to Congress.

2001   Banzer resigns from the **Bolivian** presidency because of ill health. His term had been marked by austerity and violent protests.

Montesinos is captured in Venezuela and returned to **Peru** to stand trial. He is convicted of multiple charges. Meanwhile Alejandro Toledo is elected president.

2002   Gonzalo Sánchez Lozada returns to power in **Bolivia** (he had been president 1993-1997), but faces huge economic challenges. Mass demonstrations force his eventual resignation in 2003.

Ecuadorean coup leader Coronel Lucio Gutiérrez is elected president. Mass demonstrations sweep him from office in 2005.

2005   Evo Morales is elected president in **Bolivia** in December.

Fujimori flies to Chile vowing that he will be exonerated and will be able to stand for the presidency of Peru in 2006. Chile imprisons him for seven months and Fujimori is extradited to **Peru** in 2006; he stands trial on a number of occasions and is eventually sentenced to 25 years in prison in 2009.

2006   Morales sends troops into the **Bolivian** gas fields.

Rafael Correa elected president of **Ecuador**.

Alan García is re-elected president of **Peru**.

2007   A new **Bolivian** constitution is approved by the Constituent Assembly.

2009   Clashes between indigenous protestors and police at Bagua Grande in **Peru** over oil-drilling rights lead to 50 deaths.

2009 and 2013   Correa is re-elected president of **Ecuador**.

2009 and 2014   Morales is re-elected president of **Bolivia**.

2011   Ollanta Humala, who lost to García in 2006, defeats Keiko Fujimori (Alberto's daughter) in the **Peruvian** presidential election.

2012   Julian Assange of WikiLeaks takes refuge in the **Ecuadorean** Embassy in London.

2016   Morales' bid to stand for re-election in **Bolivia** in 2019 is defeated in a referendum.

In **Peru**, Keiko Fujimori again loses the presidential race, this time to Pedro Pablo Kuczynski.

2017   Elections to be held in **Ecuador** on 19 February.

People

Note Statistics, unless indicated otherwise, are taken from The CIA World Factbook, 2015-16 estimates. GDP per capita is measured at purchasing power parity (PPP).

Peru

Population in 2016 was 30.7 million. Population growth was 0.96%; infant mortality rate 19.0 per 1000 live births; literacy rate 94.5%; GDP per capita US$12,200 (2015).

Peruvian society is a mixture of native Andean peoples, Afro-Peruvians, Spanish, immigrant Chinese, Japanese, Italians, Germans and, to a lesser extent, indigenous Amazon tribes. The first immigrants were the Spaniards who followed Pizarro's expeditionary force. Their effect, demographically, politically and culturally, has been enormous. Peru's black community is based on the coast, mainly in Chincha, south of Lima, and also in some working-class districts of the capital. Their forefathers were originally imported into Peru in the 16th century as slaves to work on the sugar and cotton plantations on the coast. Large numbers of poor Chinese labourers were brought to Peru in the mid-19th century to work in virtual slavery on the guano reserves on the Pacific coast and to build the railroads in the central Andes. The Japanese community, now numbering some 100,000, established itself in the first half of the 20th century. Like most of Latin America, Peru received many emigrés from Europe seeking land and opportunities in the late 19th century. The country's wealth and political power remains concentrated in the hands of this small and exclusive class of whites, which also consists of the descendants of the first Spanish families.

The **indigenous population** is put at about three million Quechua and Aymara in the Andean region and 200,000-250,000 Amazonian people from 40-50 ethnic groups. In the Andes, there are 5000 indigenous communities but few densely populated settlements. Their literacy rate is the lowest of any comparable group in South America and their diet is 50% below acceptable levels. About two million *indígenas* speak no Spanish, their main tongue being Quechua; they are largely outside the money economy. Many indigenous groups are under threat from colonization, development and road-building projects.

Bolivia

Population in 2016 was 11.0 million. Population growth was 1.6%; infant mortality rate 36.4 per 1000 live births; literacy rate 95.7%; GDP per capita US$6,500 (2015).

Of the total population, some two-thirds are indígena, the remainder being mestizo, European and other. The racial composition varies from place to place: indígena around Lake Titicaca; more than half *indígena* in La Paz; three-quarters mestizo or European in the Yungas, Cochabamba, Santa Cruz and Tarija, the most European of all. There are also about 17,000 blacks, descendents of slaves brought from Peru and Buenos Aires in 16th century, who now live in the Yungas. Since the 1980s, regional tensions between the 'collas' (altiplano dwellers) and the 'cambas' (lowlanders) have become more marked. Less than 40% of children of school age attend school even though it is theoretically compulsory between seven and 14.

The most obdurate of Bolivian problems has always been that the main mass of population is, from a strictly economic viewpoint, in the wrong place, the poor Altiplano and not the potentially rich Oriente; and that the *indígenas* live largely outside the monetary system on a self-sufficient basis. Since the land reform of 1952 isolated communities continue the old life but in the agricultural area around Lake Titicaca, the valleys of Cochabamba, the Yungas and the irrigated areas of the south, most peasants now own their land, however small the plot may be. Migration to the warmer and more fertile lands of the east region has been officially encouraged. At the same time roads are now integrating the food-producing eastern zones with the bulk of the population living in the towns of the Altiplano or the west-facing slopes of the Eastern Cordillera.

The **highland indígenas** are composed of two groups: those in La Paz and in the north of the Altiplano who speak the guttural Aymara and those elsewhere, who speak Quechua (this includes the *indígenas* in the northern Apolobamba region). Outside the big cities many of them speak no Spanish. In the lowlands are some 150,000 people in 30 groups, including the Ayoreo, Chiquitano, Chiriguano, Garavo, Chimane and Mojo. The lowland *indígenas* are, in the main, Guaraní. About 70% of Bolivians are Aymara, Quechua or Tupi-Guaraní speakers. The first two are regarded as national languages, but were not, until very recently, taught in schools.

Ecuador

Population in the 2010 census was 14.5 million (estimates for 2016 are 16.1 million). Population growth was 1.31%; infant mortality rate 16.9 per 1000 live births; literacy rate 94.5%; GDP per capita US$11,300 (2015).

Roughly 50% of Ecuador's people live in the coastal region west of the Andes, 45% in the Andean Sierra and 5% in Oriente. Migration is occurring from the rural zones of both the coast and the highlands to the towns and cities, particularly Guayaquil and Quito, and agricultural colonization from other parts of the country is taking place in the Oriente. There has also been an important flux of mostly illegal migrants out of Ecuador, seeking opportunities in the USA and Spain (officially put at 300,000 – probably an underestimate). Meanwhile, Colombian refugees and migrants are becoming an important segment of Ecuador's population. The national average population density is the highest in South America.

There are 900,000 Quichua-speaking highland indígenas and about 120,000 lowland indígenas. The following groups maintain their distinct cultural identity: in the Oriente, Siona, Secoya, Cofán, Huaorani, Zápara, Kichwa del Oriente, Shiwiar, Achuar and Shuar; in the Sierra, Otavalo, Salasaca, Puruhá, Cañari and Saraguro; on the coast, Chachi (Cayapa), Tsáchila (Colorado), Awa (Cuaiquer) and Epera. Many Amazonian communities are fighting for land rights in the face of oil exploration and colonization.

Culture

Music

The pipes of the Andes: Peru, Bolivia and Ecuador

For many, the sprightly pan-pipe and *charango* music of the Andes is synonymous with pre-Columbian South America. Yet while bamboo pipes or *siku*, and split-reed *quena* flutes have been used to make music in the Andes (together with conches and various percussion instruments) for thousands of years, contemporary Andean music is in reality a recent invention, born of a meeting between the indigenous past and the *nueva canción* movement in the late 1950s and early 1960s. Marching bands of pan pipes swapping notes and melodic lines, accompanied by drum troupes and singers delighted the conquistadores. And the music of the Incas and their contemporaries thrives today in remote communities from southern Colombia to Bolivia, where it is played, as it probably always was, at rituals and key community events. Singing styles, melodies and modes vary from village to village, as do the instruments used, with the more traditional villages only playing percussion and woodwind.

Were it not for the rise of left-wing politics in the 1950s Andean music would probably only have trickled out onto the world stage. But as discontent with dictatorship and the ruling elite grew after the Second World War and the Cuban revolution, so South American intellectuals looked to solidarity with the people. And with this came a rediscovery of their artistic and musical traditions. After the Bolivian revolution of 1952, indigenous Bolivians were granted suffrage, land was re-distributed and the new, left-wing administration created a governmental department of folklore, one of whose functions was the organization of traditional music festivals. This climate and the influence of Argentine and Chilean groups like **Urubamba** and **Quilapayún** inspired a renaissance in Andean music in La Paz. In 1965 a singer and percussionist called Edgar 'Yayo' Joffré formed **Los Jairas**, who were arguably the first world-music band, made up of enthusiastic middle-class intellectuals, traditional Andean musicians, a virtuoso classical guitarist called **Alfredo Domínguez** and the influential French-Swiss flute player**Gilbert Favre** (simply called 'El Gringo' by the Bolivian public). Los Jairas found a regular haunt in the **Peña Naira** in La Paz, where they re-invented Andean music and became a national sensation.

Joffré's melodies and lyrics were imbued with wistful almost operatic melancholy and were accompanied by Ernesto Cavour's flamenco-tinged *charango* and Favre's lilting *quena* flute. All that was missing were the pan-pipes. These were added by numerous imitators from La Paz to Quito. The most successful were **Los K'jarkas**, a Cochabamba-based trio of brothers who both consolidated and built-upon Los Jairas' model. They retained the melancholic melodies and evocations of pastoral landscapes, adding traditional costume, a stylized logo borrowing motifs from Tiwanaku and a few up-tempo numbers drawing on Andean dance rhythms like the *huayno* and the *saya*. Los K'jarkas' fame spread throughout the Andean world, spawning a mini-musical revolution among the Quichua people of Ecuador whose *cachullapi* and *yumbo* dances are an interesting fusion of marching band, modern Andean and traditional Inca music. In 2017, Los K'jarkas continue to perform and record new albums and among their most popular successors is Ch'ila Jatun, a group of K'jarkas' children.

In a *peña* in La Paz and Cuzco today what you'll hear is little more than a footnote to Los Jairas and Los K'jarkas, but music in Peru, Ecuador and Bolivia has diversified. Singers like **Emma Junaro** have taken the Andean sound and the *nueva canción* to produce a new, politically sensitive singer-songwriter genre known as *canto nuevo*. Singers like **Susana Baca** have brought the music of African Peru to the attention of the world, through a series of stunning albums and mesmerizing shows, and in the shanty towns of Lima and the lowlands of eastern Peru and Ecuador *chicha* music has established itself as the new vernacular sound of the poor urban majority.

Arts and crafts

Handicrafts

South America has an abundance of different traditional handicrafts that have developed over time and although there are regional variations, many have flourished right across the continent. The distinctive crafts often show a mixture of indigenous, European and later also African influences.

Textiles and weaving

Textiles have been of utmost importance throughout South America from an economic, as well as a social and spiritual-religious perspective. Traditional weaving goes a long way back, with cultures such as the Incas inheriting 3000 years of weaving skills. These skills were to be exploited in colonial times, in large-scale *mitas*, textile workshops, and the Spaniards were soon exporting cloth to Europe. For the native population, textiles were also used for rituals and ceremonies. These items often had intricate designs and patterns, such as those of the Aymara people of the islands of Lake Titicaca, who have carried on their traditions to this day. Different communities wear different traditional outfits, some introduced by the conquistadors, some of more ancient origin, and what a person wears often indicates where they come from.

The use of materials, designs and motifs varies widely, with llama, alpaca, vicuña or sheep's wool mostly used in the Andean countries. There are many areas that are rich in weaving, knitting and embroidery traditions, making everything from tapestries and decorative blankets, to every item of clothing imaginable.

Jewellery and metalwork

Copper, gold and platinum were all mined before the arrival of the Spaniards and although many of the objects of the early civilizations were functional, intricately ornate jewellery and ceremonial knives have been found at archaeological sites, particularly in Peru. Precious and semiprecious stones were often used in ceremonial costumes and at burials, since metal objects on their own were not considered of worth. The conquistadors were amazed by the wealth they saw and this seemingly endless thirst for gold and silver led to some of the most appalling exploitations of the local population. The longstanding traditions of jewellery-making continue and many modern day artisans are inspired by traditional, native methods to create new and different motifs.

Pottery

Pottery is perhaps the oldest craft in South America with extensive ceramic archaeological findings. Pre-Columbian pottery often carried highly spiritual significance and the Nazca, Moche and Inca cultures all used such ceramics. The pre-Hispanic techniques survive although communities often mix ancient and modern production processes.

Land &
environment

The whole of Peru's west seaboard with the Pacific is desert on which rain seldom falls. From this coastal shelf the Andes rise to a high Sierra which is studded with groups of soaring mountains and gouged with deep canyons. The highland slopes more gradually east and is deeply forested and ravined. Eastward from these mountains lie the vast jungle lands of the Amazon basin.

The **Highlands** (or Sierra), at an average altitude of 3000 m, cover 26% of the country and contain about 50% of the people, mostly indigenous, an excessive density on such poor land. Here, high-level land of gentle slopes is surrounded by towering ranges of high peaks including the most spectacular range of the continent, the Cordillera Blanca. This has several ice peaks over 6000 m; the highest, Huascarán, is 6768 m and is a mecca for mountaineers. There are many volcanoes in the south. The north and east highlands are heavily forested up to a limit of 3350 m: the grasslands are between the forest line and the snowline, which rises from 5000 m in the latitude of Lima to 5800 m in the south. Most of the Sierra is covered with grasses and shrubs, with Puna vegetation (bunch grass mixed with low, hairy-leaved plants) from north of Huaraz to the south. Here the indigenous graze llamas, alpacas and sheep providing meat, clothing, transport and even fuel from the animals' dung. Some potatoes and cereals (*quinua, kiwicha* and *kañiwa*) are grown at altitude, but the valley basins contain the best land for arable farming. Most of the rivers which rise in these mountains flow east to the Amazon and cut through the plateau in canyons, sometimes 1500 m deep, in which the climate is tropical. A few go west to the Pacific including the Colca and Cotahuasi in the south, which have created canyons over 3000 m deep.

The **coast**, a narrow ribbon of desert 2250 km long, takes up 11% of the country and holds about 45% of the population. It is the economic heart of Peru, consuming most of the imports and supplying half of the exports. When irrigated, the river valleys are extremely fertile, creating oases which grow cotton throughout the country, sugar cane, rice and export crops such as asparagus in the north, grapes, fruit and olives in the south. At the same time, the coastal current teems with fish and Peru has in the past had the largest catch in the world.

The **jungle** covers the forested eastern half of the Andes and the tropical forest beyond, altogether 62% of the country's area, but with only about 5% of the population who are crowded on the river banks in the cultivable land – a tiny part of the area. The few roads have to cope with dense forest, deep valleys, and sharp eastern slopes ranging from 2150 m in the north to 5800 m east of Lake Titicaca. Rivers are the main highways, though navigation is hazardous. The economic potential of the area includes reserves of timber, excellent land for rubber, jute, rice, tropical fruits and coffee and the breeding of cattle. The vast majority of Peru's oil and gas reserves are also east of the Andes.

A harsh, strange land, with a dreary grey solitude except for the bursts of green after rain, Bolivia is the only South American country with no coastline or navigable river to the sea. It is dominated by the Andes and has five distinct geographical areas. The **Andes** are at their widest in Bolivia, a maximum of 650 km. The Western Cordillera, which separates Bolivia from Chile, has high peaks of 5800 m-6500 m and a number of active volcanoes along its crest. The Eastern Cordillera also rises to giant massifs, with several peaks over 6000 m in the Cordillera Real section to the north. The far sides of the Cordillera Real fall away very sharply to the northeast, towards the Amazon basin. The air is unbelievably clear – the whole landscape is a bowl of luminous light.

The **Altiplano** lies between the Cordilleras, a bleak, treeless, windswept plateau, much of it 4000 m above sea-level. Its surface is by no means flat, and the Western Cordillera sends spurs dividing it into basins. The more fertile northern part has more inhabitants; the southern part is parched desert and almost unoccupied, save for a mining town here and there. Nearly 70% of the population lives on it; over half of the people live in towns. **Lake Titicaca**, at the northern end of the Altiplano, is an inland sea of 8965 sq km at 3810 m, the highest navigable water in the world. Its depth, up to 280 m in some places, keeps the lake at an even all-year-round temperature of 10° C. This modifies the extremes of winter and night temperatures on the surrounding land, which supports a large Aymara indigenous population, tilling the fields and the hill terraces, growing potatoes and cereals, tending their sheep, alpaca and llamas, and using the resources of the lake. The **Yungas** and the **Puna** are to the east of the Altiplano. The heavily forested northeastern slopes of the Cordillera Real are deeply indented by the fertile valleys of the Yungas, drained into the Amazon lowlands by the Río Beni and its tributaries, where cacao, coffee, sugar, coca and tropical fruits are grown. Further south, from a point just north of Cochabamba, the Eastern Cordillera rises abruptly in sharp escarpments from the Altiplano and then flattens out to an easy slope east to the plains: an area known as the Puna. The streams which flow across the Puna cut increasingly deep incisions as they gather volume until the Puna is eroded to little more than a high remnant between the river valleys. In these valleys a variety of grain crops and fruits is grown.

The **tropical lowlands** stretch from the foothills of the Eastern Cordillera to the borders with Brazil, Paraguay and Argentina. They take up 70% of the total area of Bolivia, but contain only about 20% of its population. In the north and east the Oriente has dense tropical forest. Open plains covered with rough pasture, swamp and scrub occupy the centre. Before the expulsion of the Jesuits in 1767 this was a populous land of plenty; for 150 years Jesuit missionaries had controlled the area and guided it into a prosperous security. Decline followed but in recent years better times have returned. Meat is now shipped from Trinidad, capital of Beni Department, and from airstrips in the area, to the urban centres of La Paz, Oruro, and Cochabamba. Further south, the forests and plains beyond the Eastern Cordillera sweep down towards the Río Pilcomayo, which drains into the Río de la Plata, getting progressively less rain and merging into a comparatively dry land of scrub forest and arid savannah. The main city of this area is Santa Cruz de la Sierra, founded in the 16th century, now the second city of Bolivia and a large agricultural centre.

The Andes, running from north to south, form a mountainous backbone to the country. There are two main ranges, the Central Cordillera and the Western Cordillera, separated by a 400-km long Central Valley, whose rims are about 50 km apart. The rims are joined together, like the two sides of a ladder, by hilly rungs, and between each pair of rungs lies an intermont basin with a dense cluster of population. These basins are drained by rivers which cut through the rims to run either west to the Pacific or east to join the Amazon. Both rims of the Central Valley are lined with the cones of more than 50 volcanoes. Several of them have long been extinct, for example, Chimborazo, the highest (6310 m). At least eight, however, are still active including Cotopaxi (5897 m), which had several violent eruptions in the 19th century and comparatively minor activity in 2015; Pichincha (4794 m), which re-entered activity in 1998 and expelled a spectacular mushroom cloud in October 1999; Sangay (5230 m), one of the world's most active volcanoes, continuously emitting fumes and ash; Tungurahua (5016 m), active since 1999; and Reventador (3562 m), which has erupted several times since 2002; and Cayambe which re-entered activity in 2016. Earthquakes too are common.

The **sierra**, as the central trough of the Andes in known, is home to about 47% of the people of Ecuador, the majority of whom are mestizos. Some communities live at subsistence level, others have developed good markets for products using traditional skills in embroidery, pottery, jewellery, knitting, weaving, and carving. The **costa** is mostly lowland at an altitude of less than 300 m, apart from a belt of hilly land which runs northwest from Guayaquil to the coast, where it turns north and runs parallel to the shore to Esmeraldas. In the extreme north there is a typical tropical rain forest, severely endangered by uncontrolled logging. The forests thin out in the more southern lowlands and give way to tropical dry forest. The main agricultural exports come from the lowlands to the southeast and north of Guayaquil. The heavy rains, high temperature and humidity suit the growth of tropical crops. Bananas, cacao and mango are grown here while rice is farmed on the natural levees of this flood plain. The main crop comes from the alluvial fans at the foot of the mountains rising out of the plain. Coffee is grown on the higher ground. Shrimp farming was typical of the coast until this was damaged by disease in 1999; it continues, but at the same scale. The Guayas lowland is also a great cattle-fattening area in the dry season. South of Guayaquil the rainfall is progressively less, mangroves disappear and by the border with Peru, is semi-arid.

The **Oriente** is east of the Central Cordillera where the forest-clad mountains fall sharply to a chain of foothills (the Eastern Cordillera) and then the jungle through which meander the tributaries of the Amazon. This east lowland region makes up 36% of Ecuador's total territory, but is only sparsely populated by indigenous and agricultural colonists from the highlands. In total, the region has only 5% of the national population, but colonization is now proceeding rapidly owing to population pressure and in the wake of an oil boom in the northern Oriente. There is gold and other minerals in the south. The **Galápagos** are about 1000 km west of Ecuador, on the Equator, and are not structurally connected to the mainland. They mark the junction between two tectonic plates on the Pacific floor where basalt has escaped to form massive volcanoes, only the tips of which are above sea level. Several of the islands have volcanic activity today. Their isolation from any other land has led to the evolution of their unique flora and fauna.

Practicalities

Getting there

Most international flights to the region arrive at Lima (LIM, page 37), Quito (UIO, page 522), Guayaquil (GYE, page 616, good if visiting only the coast or Galápagos), La Paz (LPB, page 349) or Santa Cruz (VVI, page 454) with the first three receiving by far the majority. There are direct flights to all three countries from **Europe**, though in many cases the choice of departure point is limited to Madrid and one or two other cities (Paris or Amsterdam, for instance). Peru became better connected in 2016 with **British Airways'** new direct service from London Gatwick to Lima. **Air Europa** ① *T087 1423 0717, www.aireuropa.com*, specializes in flights to Latin America from European airports.

Alternatively, connections can be made in the USA (Miami, or other gateways), Buenos Aires, Rio de Janeiro or São Paulo. **Main US gateways** are Miami, Houston, Dallas, Atlanta and New York. On the west coast, Los Angeles has direct flights to Lima. If buying airline tickets routed through the USA, check that US taxes are included in the price. Flights from **Canada** are mostly via the USA although there are direct flights from Toronto to Lima with **Air Canada**, and to Bogotá with **Air Canada** and **Avianca**. Likewise, flights from **Australia** and **New Zealand** are best through Los Angeles, except for the **LATAM** route from Sydney and Auckland to Santiago, and **Qantas'** non-stop route Sydney–Santiago, from where connections can be made. Within **Latin America** there is plenty of choice on local carriers and some connections on US or European airlines. Enquire about open-jaw flights (arriving at one airport and leaving from another). For departure tax, see page 728.

TRAVEL TIP
Packing for Peru, Bolivia and Ecuador

Everybody has their own preferences, but a good principle is to take half the clothes and twice the money that you think you will need. Listed here are those items most often mentioned. These include an inflatable travel pillow and strong shoes (footwear over 9½ British size or 42 European size is difficult to find in South America). You should also take waterproof clothing and waterproof treatment for leather footwear. Earplugs are vital for long bus trips or in noisy hotels. Also important are flip flops, which can be worn in showers to avoid athlete's foot, and a sheet sleeping bag to avoid sleeping on dirty sheets in cheap hotels.

Other useful items include: a clothes line, a nailbrush, a vacuum flask, a water bottle, a universal sink plug, string, a Swiss Army knife, an alarm clock, candles (for power cuts), a torch/flashlight, pocket mirror, a padlock for the doors of the cheapest hotels (or for tent zip if camping), a small first-aid kit, sun hat, lip salve with sun protection, contraceptives, waterless soap, dental floss (which can also be used for repairs), wipes and a small sewing kit. Always carry toilet paper, especially on long bus trips. The most security conscious may also wish to include a length of chain and padlock for securing luggage to bed or bus/train seat, and a lockable canvas cover for your rucksack. Don't forget cables and adaptors for recharging phones, laptops and other electrical equipment. If you wear contact lens, bring lens solution because it can be difficult to find in Bolivia and Peru. Ask for it in a pharmacy, rather than in an optician's. Always take out a good travel insurance policy.

Most airlines offer discounted fares on scheduled flights through agencies which specialize in this type of fare (see Tour operators, page 730). If you buy discounted air tickets always check the reservation with the airline concerned to make sure the flight still exists. Peak times are 7 December-15 January and 10 July-10 September. If you intend travelling during those times, book as far ahead as possible. Special offers may be available February-May and September-November.

Getting around

There are one or two daily direct flights between Lima and each of Quito, Guayaquil and La Paz with **LATAM** and **Avianca**, among others. When flying between Ecuador and Bolivia however, you must make a connection in Lima or Bogotá. **Peruvian Airlines** flies direct daily between La Paz and Cuzco, which can be a convenient part of a tourist itinerary. A potentially economical option (but check first as prices fluctuate) is to travel by land from either Ecuador or Bolivia to just inside Peru (eg to Tumbes, Piura or Juliaca) and then take a domestic flight with a Peruvian airline. If you're thinking of buying a ticket online, bear in mind that some airlines require a locally issued credit card or local ID to make a purchase. You will get the best advice from an authorized agent (such as **Journey Latin America** in the UK).

Peru

Air With the exception of a very few regional connections, such as between Cuzco and La Paz (Bolivia), all international flights arrive at Jorge Chávez Airport near Lima. Carriers serving the major cities are **Star Perú** ⓘ *T01-705 9000, www.starperu.com,* **LATAM** ⓘ *T01-213 8200, www.latam.com,* **Avianca** ⓘ *T01-511 8222, www.avianca.com,* and **Peruvian Airlines** ⓘ *T01-716 6000, www.peruvianairlines.pe.* For destinations such as Andahuaylas, Ayacucho, Cajamarca, Jauja, Huánuco, Huaraz and Cuzco, flights are offered by **LC Perú** ⓘ *T01-204 1313, www.lcperu.pe.*

Flights start at about US$100 one-way anywhere in the country from Lima, but prices vary greatly between airlines, with **LATAM** being the most expensive for non-Peruvians. Prices often increase at holiday times (Semana Santa, May Day, Inti Raymi, 28-29 July, Christmas and New Year), and for elections. During these times and the northern hemisphere summer, seats can be hard to come by, so book early. Internal flight prices are fixed in US dollars (but can be paid in soles) and have 18% tax added.

Flight schedules and departure times often change and delays are common. In the rainy season cancellations occur. Flights into the mountains may well be put forward one hour if there are reports of bad weather. Flights to jungle regions are also unreliable. Always allow an extra day between national and international flights, especially in the rainy season. Flights must be reconfirmed at least 24 hours in advance. You can do this online or in the town you will be leaving from. Be at the airport well ahead of your flight.

Bus Good-quality bus services radiate out from Lima in every direction. But travelling overland takes time, so if you're on a short visit, try to stick to one area or consider flying. Services along the coast to the north and south as well as inland to Huancayo, Ayacucho and Huaraz are generally good, but on long-distance journeys it is advisable to pay a bit extra and travel with a reliable company. Whatever the standard of service, accidents and hold-ups on buses do occur, especially at night; it's best to travel by day whenever possible, both for safety and to enjoy the outstanding views. All major bus companies operate modern buses with two decks on inter-departmental routes. The first deck is called *bus cama*, the second *semi-cama*. Both have seats that recline, *bus cama* further than *semi-cama*. These buses usually run late at night and are more expensive than ordinary buses which tend to run earlier in the day. Many buses have toilets and show movies. Each company has a different name for its regular and *cama* or *ejecutivo* services. **Cruz del Sur, Móviltours, Oltursa, Ittsa** and **Ormeño** are among the better bus lines and cover most of the country. **Cruz del Sur**, generally regarded as a class above the others, accepts Visa cards and gives 10% discount to ISIC and Under 26 cardholders (you may have to insist). There are many smaller but still excellent bus lines that run only to specific areas. You can book online and find good deals for an increasing number of companies. For bus lines, see page 69. For a centralized information and booking site, visit www.busportal.pe.

Some bus terminals charge a usage fee of about US$0.50 which you pay at a kiosk before boarding. Many also charge a small fee for the toilet. Take a blanket or warm jacket when travelling in the mountains. Where buses stop it is possible to buy food on the roadside. With the better companies you will get a receipt for your luggage, which will be locked under the bus. On local buses watch your luggage and never leave valuables on the luggage rack or floor, even when on the move. If your bus breaks down and you are transferred to another line and have to pay extra, keep your original ticket for a refund from the first company.

Combis operate between most small towns on one- to three-hour journeys. This makes it possible, in many cases, just to turn up and travel within an hour or two. Combis can be minibuses of varying age and comfort, or slightly more expensive, faster but often overfilled car *colectivos*, called *autos*, or *cars*. These usually charge twice the bus fare. They leave only when full. They go almost anywhere in Peru; most firms have offices. Book one day in advance and they might pick you up at your hotel or in the main plaza.

Car The Pan-American Highway runs north–south along the coast. Travelling east, great steps have been taken to improve the road links between the Pacific and the highlands, including the completion of the fully paved Carretera Interoceánica, which runs from the Pacific port of Ilo to Puerto Maldonado and on to the Brazilian border. However, more minor roads in the highlands and jungle regions can be poor and may be impassable during or after the rainy season. Each year these roads are affected by heavy rain and mud slides, especially on the east slopes of the mountains. Check with locals (not with bus companies, who only want to sell tickets), as accidents are common during the rainy season.

You must be over 21 years old to drive a car in Peru. If renting a car, your home driving licence will be accepted for up to six months; you must be over 25 to hire a car. Car hire rates tend to be very expensive but tourist offices and hotels should know of the cheapest companies. Always check that the vehicle you rent has a spare wheel, toolkit and functioning lights etc. The **Touring y Automóvil Club del Perú** ① *T01-611 9999, www.touringperu.com.pe*, has offices in several provincial cities and offers help to tourists.

If bringing in your own vehicle you must provide proof of ownership; a *libreta de pasos por aduana* or *carnet de passages* is accepted and recommended, although not officially required. You cannot officially enter Peru with a vehicle registered in someone else's name. On leaving Peru there is no check on the import of a vehicle. All vehicles are required to carry Peruvian insurance (SOAT, Seguro Obligatorio para Accidentes de Tránsito) and spot checks are frequent, especially in border areas. SOAT can be purchased for as little as one month (US$10) at larger border crossings, but only during office hours (Monday-Friday 0800-1800).

Availability of fuel varies around the country and the price depends on the octane rating. Unleaded is widely available along the Pan-American Highway and in large cities but rarely in the highlands or jungle. Prices range from US$4.70-6.45 per gallon for petrol/gasoline and US$5 for diesel.

Tolls, US$1.50-3.70, are charged on most major paved roads.

Hitchhiking Hitchhiking is difficult. Freight traffic has to stop at the police *garitas* outside each town and these are the best places to try (also toll points, but these are further from towns). Drivers usually ask for money but don't always expect to get it. In mountain and jungle areas you usually have to pay drivers of lorries, vans and even private cars; ask the driver first how much they are going to charge, and then check with locals.

River On almost any trip to the Amazon Basin, a boat journey will be required at some point, either to get you to a jungle lodge, or to go between river ports. Large passenger and cargo vessels are called *lanchas*; smaller faster craft are called *rápidos* or *deslizadores* (speedboats). *Yates* are small to medium wooden *colectivos*, usually slow, and *chalupas* are small motor launches used to ferry passengers from the *lanchas* to shore. Jungle lodges invariably have their own motorized canoes with a canopy for transporting guests. On *lanchas* you can pay either to sling your hammock on deck, or for a berth in a cabin sleeping two to four people. Bear in mind that it's safer to club together and pay for a cabin in which to lock your belongings, even if you sleep outside in a hammock. A hammock is essential. A double hammock, of material (not string), provides one person with a blanket. Board the boat many hours in advance to guarantee hammock space. If you're going on the top deck, try to be first down the front; take some rope for hanging your hammock, plus string and sarongs for privacy. On all boats, hang your hammock away from lightbulbs (they aren't switched off at night and attract all sorts of strange insects) and away from the engines, which usually emit noxious fumes. Guard your belongings from the moment you board. There is very little privacy; women travellers can expect a lot of attention. There are basic washing and toilet facilities, but the food is rice, chicken and beans (and whatever can be picked up en route) cooked in river water. Stock up on drinking water, fruit, tinned food and snacks before boarding. Vegetarians must take their own supplies. There is usually a bar on board. Take plenty of prophylactic enteritis tablets; many contract dysentery on the trip. Also take insect repellent and a good book or two. *Rápidos* carry life jackets and have bathrooms; a simple breakfast and lunch are included in the price.

Taxi Taxi prices are fixed in the mountain towns, about US$1-1.50 in urban areas. Fares are not fixed in Lima although some drivers work for companies that do have standard fares. Ask locals what the price should be and always set the price beforehand; expect to pay US$3-5 in the capital. The main cities have taxis that can be hired by phone, which charge a little more, but are reliable and safe. Many taxi drivers work for commission from hotels. Choose your own hotel and find a driver who is willing to take you.

Taxis at airports are more expensive; seek advice about the price in advance. In some places it is cheaper to walk out of the airport to the main road and flag down a cab, but this may not be safe, especially at night (never do so in Lima).

Another common form of public transport is the mototaxi, a three-wheel motorcycle with an awning covering the double-seat behind the driver. Fares are about US$1.

Train There are three main railway lines. PerúRail ① *T084-581414, www.perurail.com*, and Inca Rail ① *T084-581860, www.incarail.com*, run services on the Cuzco–Machu Picchu line.

PerúRail also runs operates trains on the Puno–Cuzco line. The other railway that carries passengers is the line from Lima to Huancayo, with a continuation to Huancavelica in the Central Highlands. The service runs on an irregular basis; the FCCA ⓘ *T01-226 6363, www. fcca.com.pe*, will have the latest schedule. Train services may be cut in the rainy season.

Bolivia

Air All of the following offer internal air services. **Boliviana de Aviación (BoA)** ⓘ *T02-211 0793, www.boa.bo*, flies to São Paulo, Buenos Aires, Salta, Madrid and Barcelona and Buenos Aires; **Amaszonas** ⓘ *T901-10 5500, www.amaszonas.com*, flies to Cuzco, Asunción (with connections to Ciudad del Este and Montevideo) and Iquique. Both also fly to other domestic South American destinations. **TAM** ⓘ *T268111, www.tam.bo*, the civilian branch of the Bolivian Air Force, flies to the main cities as well as several smaller and more remote destinations. **Amaszonas** flies to all main cities from Santa Cruz and between La Paz and Sucre, Rurrenabaque and Uyuni. **Ecojet** ⓘ *T901-105055, www.ecojet.bo*, flies to La Paz, Santa Cruz, Cochabamba, Sucre, Tarija, Trinidad, Riberalta, Guajaramerín and Cobija. Many flights radiate from La Paz, Santa Cruz or Cochabamba. Make sure you have adequate baggage insurance.

Bus Buses ply most of the main roads. Inter-urban buses are called *flotas*, urban ones *micros* or *minibuses* (vans); *trufis* are shared taxis. Larger bus companies run frequent services and offer air-conditioning, TV and other mod cons. You can usually buy tickets with reserved seats a day or two in advance. Alternatively, savings may sometimes be obtained by bargaining for fares at the last minute, although not at peak travel times like national holidays. A small charge is made for use of bus terminals; payment is before departure.

In the wet season, bus travel is subject to long delays and detours, at extra cost, and cancellations are not uncommon. On all journeys, take some food, water and toilet paper. It is best to travel by day, not just to enjoy the scenery and avoid arriving at night, but also for better road safety. Bus companies are responsible for any items packed in the luggage compartment or on the roof, but only if they give you a ticket for each bag.

Car A relatively small (but growing) percentage of Bolivian roads are paved, the rest are gravel-surfaced or earth. Any road, whatever its surface, may be closed in the rainy season (December–March). The main paved road axis of Bolivia runs from the Peruvian border at Desaguadero (also Copacabana) via La Paz and Oruro to Cochabamba and Santa Cruz, continuing to the Brazilian border at Arroyo Concepción. Some sections, such as La Paz–Oruro, are dual carriageway; others are in the process of being made so. Other paved roads connect the La Paz–Oruro highway with Tambo Quemado on the Chilean border, continuing paved to Arica. From Potosí there are paved, or soon-to-be-paved, roads to Uyuni, to Villazón (on the Argentine border) via Tupiza and to Aguas Blancas (also on the Argentine border) via Camargo and Tarija. As well as the main route to Brazil mentioned above, paved routes from Santa Cruz go to Trinidad and to Yacuiba on the Argentine border. The Trans-Chaco highway, from Santa Cruz to Asunción (Paraguay) branches off the Yacuiba road at Villamontes; it is mostly paved. Road improvement projects continue in many areas. The remainder of Bolivia's roads are either gravel or earth, notoriously narrow and tortuous in the highlands, notoriously prone to wash-outs in the lowlands.

Road tolls vary from US$0.50 to US$2.45 for journeys up to 100 km. On toll roads you are given a receipt at the first toll; keep it at hand as it is asked for at subsequent toll posts. The **Administradora Boliviana de Carreteras (ABC)** has a useful website, www.abc. gob.bo, with daily updates of road conditions, including any roadblocks due to social unrest (click on 'Servicios' and then 'Transitabilidad'); toll-free phone for emergencies T800-107222. Always carry spare petrol/gas and supplies and camping equipment if going off major roads. Your car must be able to cope with altitude and freezing temperatures. Take great care on the roads, especially at night. Too many truck drivers are drunk and many vehicles are driven with faulty headlights. Stalled trucks without lights are a common cause of accidents.

To bring a private vehicle into Bolivia you must have an International Driving Permit, the vehicle's registration documents (in your name, or with a notarized letter of authorization from the owner plus approval from the Bolivian consulate in the country of origin) and your passport. On entry you must get temporary admission from customs (free of charge) and surrender the documention departure (maximum 90 days). A carnet de passages en douane is not required, but insurance is compulsory. It is called SOAT and can be bought locally. Generally the police are helpful to foreign motorists, but stop you often and ask to see your documents, a complete first aid kit, triangle and fire extinguisher. There are restrictions on which vehicles may drive in La Paz, depending on license plate number and day of the week. The national motoring organization is the **Automóvil Club Boliviano** ⓘ *www.acbbolivia.com.bo.*

The minimum age for hiring a car is 25. Rental companies may only require your licence from home, but police ask to see an international licence. Rental of a small car costs about US$370 per week; a small 4WD vehicle US$505-550 per week.

Especial, 85 octane containing lead, costs around US$0.54 per litre (it may cost more in remote areas). Diesel costs about the same. Higher octane premium, US$0.70 per litre, is only available in La Paz, if at all. There may be fuel shortages, especially in border areas, so keep your tank full.

Train The western highland railway is operated by **Ferroviaria Andina (FCA)** ⓘ *www.fca. com.bo*. There are passenger trains to Villazón from Oruro, via Atocha, Tupiza and Uyuni. There are plans to reopen the La Paz to Arica line to passenger services. The eastern lowland line is run by **Ferroviaria Oriental** ⓘ *www.fo.com.bo*, with services from Santa Cruz east to the Brazilian border and south to the Argentine border at Yacuiba.

Ecuador

Air If you are short of time, it's worth opting for a few flights. Airlines operating within Ecuador include: **Avianca** ⓘ *T1-800-003434, www.avianca.com*, serving Quito, Guayaquil, Coca, Manta and Galápagos and international routes to Bogotá and Lima; **LATAM** ⓘ *T1-800-000527, www.latam.com*, with flights to Quito, Guayaquil, Cuenca and Galápagos and international routes to Miami, New York, Madrid, Cali, Medellín, Lima, Santiago and Buenos Aires; and **TAME** ⓘ *T1-700-500800, www.tame.com.ec*, serving Quito, Guayaquil, Cuenca, Latacunga, Loja, Coca, Lago Agrio, Esmeraldas, Manta and Santa Rosa (Machala), as well as international flights to Bogotá, Cali, Caracas, New York and Lima.

Bus Bus travel is generally more convenient and regular than in other Andean countries. Several companies use comfortable air-conditioned buses on their longer routes; some companies have their own stations, away from the main bus terminals, exclusively for these better buses. In Quito, the bus terminals are very far from the city centre. Bus company information and itineraries for some major routes are found in http://latinbus.

com, where tickets for some major routes can also be purchased online for a small fee. In 2017, bus fares were approximately US$1.50 per hour of travel time. Throughout Ecuador, travel by bus is safest during the daytime.

Car An excellent network of paved roads runs throughout most of the country. Maintenance of major highways is franchised to private firms, who charge tolls of US$1.15. Roads are subject to damage during heavy rainy seasons and some roads on the coast of Manabí were damaged in the 2016 earthquake. Always check road conditions before setting out.

> **Tip...**
> Driving during the day is safer, especially on mountain roads. It's best to stay off the road altogether at the beginning and end of busy national holidays.

Unfortunately, better roads have meant higher speeds and more serious accidents. Bus and truck drivers in particular are known for their speed and recklessness.

To bring a foreign vehicle or motorcycle into the country, its original registration document (title) in the name of the driver is required. If the driver is not the owner, a notarized letter of authorization is required. All documents must be accompanied by a Spanish translation. A 90-day permit is granted on arrival, extensions are only granted if the vehicle is in the garage for repairs. No security deposit is required and you can enter and leave at different land borders. Procedures are generally straightforward but it can be a matter of luck. Shipping a vehicle requires more paperwork and hiring a customs broker. The port of Guayaquil is prone to theft and is particularly officious. Manta and Esmeraldas are smaller and more relaxed, but receive fewer ships. A valid driver's licence from your home country is generally sufficient to drive in Ecuador and rent a car, but an international licence is helpful.

To rent a car you must be 21 and have an international credit card with embossed numbers. Surcharges may apply to clients aged 21-25. You may be asked to sign two blank credit card vouchers, one for the rental fee itself and the other as a security deposit, and authorization for a charge of as much as US$5000 may be requested against your credit card account if you do not purchase the local insurance. The uncashed vouchers will be returned to you when you return the vehicle. Make sure the car is parked securely at night. A small car suitable for city driving costs around US$550 per week including unlimited mileage, tax and full insurance. A 4WD or pickup truck (recommended for unpaved roads) costs about US$1400 a week. Drop-off charges are about US$125.

There are two grades of petrol, 'Extra' (82 octane, US$1.48 per US gallon) and 'Super' (92 Octane, US$1.98-2.30). Both are unleaded. Extra is available everywhere, while 'Super' may not be available in more remote areas. Diesel fuel (US$1.03) is notoriously dirty and available everywhere.

Hitchhiking Public transport in Ecuador is so abundant that there is seldom any need to hitchhike along the major highways. On small out-of-the-way country roads however, the situation can be quite the opposite, and giving passers-by a ride is common practice and safe, especially in the back of a pick-up or truck. A small fee is usually charged, check in advance.

Taxi In cities, all taxis must in principle use meters. At especially busy times or at night drivers may nonetheless refuse to do so, in which case always agree on the fare before you get in. Shared taxis and vans are available on some routes.

Train For more information contact **Empresa de Ferrocarriles Ecuatorianos** ⓘ *T1-800-873637, www.trenecuador.com*. A series of tourist rides have replaced regular passenger services along the spectacular Ecuadorean railway system, extensively restored in recent years. Some trains have two classes of service, standard and plus; carriages are fancier in the latter and a snack is included. On some routes, an *autoferro*, a motorized railcar, runs instead of the train. The following routes are on offer: Quito to El Boliche (Cotopaxi and Machachi); Riobamba to Alausí; Alausí to Sibambe via the Devil's Nose; Ambato to Urbina; Riobamba to Urbina or Colta; Otavalo and Ibarra to Salinas; El Tambo to Coyoctor near Ingapirca; Durán (outside Guayaquil) to Bucay; and the **Tren Crucero**, an upmarket all-inclusive tour of up to four days along the entire line from Quito to Durán. Details are given under What to do, in the corresponding cities.

Vans and shared taxis These operate between major cities and offer a faster, more comfortable and more expensive alternative to buses. Some provide pick-up and drop-off services at your hotel.

Maps and guidebooks

Peru

The **Instituto Geográfico Nacional** in Lima sells a selection of maps, see page 65. Another official site is **Ministerio de Transporte** ⓘ *Jr Zorritos 1203, Lima centre, T01-615 7800, www.mtc.gob.pe*. Lima 2000's *Mapa Vial del Perú* (1:2,200,000) is probably the most correct road map available.

A good tourist map of the Callejón de Huaylas and Cordillera Huayhuash, by Felipe Díaz, is available in many shops in Huaraz, including **Casa de Guías**. *Alpenvereinskarte Cordillera Blanca Nord 0/3a* and *Alpenvereinskarte Cordillera Blanca Süd 0/3b* at 1:100,000 are the best maps of that region, available in Huaraz, Caraz and Lima, but best bought outside Peru. *Cordillera Huayhuash map*, 1:50,000 (The Alpine Mapping Guild, 2nd ed, 2004) is recommended, available in Huaraz at **Café Andino**, see page 79.

Bolivia

Good maps of Bolivia are few and far between, and maps in general can be hard to find. **Instituto Geográfico Militar** (IGM, see page 368). Many IGM maps date from the 1970s and their accuracy is variable; prices also vary, US$4.50-7 a sheet. **Walter Guzmán Córdova** makes several travel and trekking maps, available from some bookshops in La Paz. The **German Alpine Club** (Deutscher Alpenverein) ⓘ *www.alpenverein.de*, produces two maps of Sorata-Ancohuma-Illampu and Illimani, but these are not usually available in La Paz.

Ecuador

Instituto Geográfico Militar (IGM) ⓘ *Senierges y Telmo Paz y Miño, east of Parque El Ejido, Quito, T02-397 5100, ext 2502, www.geoportaligm.gob.ec, Mon-Thu 0730-1600, Fri 0700-1430, take ID*, sell country and topographic maps in a variety of paper and digital formats for US$3-7. Maps of border and sensitive areas are 'reservado' (classified) and not available for sale without a permit. Buy your maps here, because they are rarely available outside Quito.

Essentials A-Z

Accident and emergency

Peru
Emergency medical attention (Cruz Roja) T115. **Fire** T116. **Police** T105, for police emergencies nationwide (does not work in all locations). **Tourist Police**, Jr Moore 268, Magdalena, 38th block of Av Brasil, Lima, T01-460 1060/0844 daily 24 hrs, T0800-22221 nationwide toll-free. They are friendly, helpful and speak English and some German.

Bolivia
Ambulance T165 in La Paz, T161 in El Alto. **Fire** 119. **Police** T110. Robberies should be reported to the **Policía Turística**, they will issue a report for insurance purposes but stolen goods are rarely recovered. In cities which do not have a Policía Turística report robberies to the **Fuerza Especial de Lucha Contra el Crimen (FELCC)**, Departamento de Robos. In La Paz, see page 349.

Ecuador
Emergencies T911. **Police** T101.

Children *See also Health, page 720.*

Travel with children can bring you into closer contact with South American families and, generally, presents no special problems. In fact the path is often smoother for family groups as officials tend to be more amenable where children are concerned.

Food
Food can be a problem if the children are picky eaters. It is easier to take food such as biscuits, drinks and bread on longer trips than to rely on meal stops. Avocados are safe and nutritious for babies as young as 6 months and most older children like them too. A small immersion heater and jug for making hot drinks is invaluable, but remember that electric current varies. Try and get a dual-voltage one (110v and 220v).

Hotels
In all hotels, try to negotiate family rates. If charges are per person, always insist that 2 children will occupy 1 bed only, therefore counting as 1 tariff. If rates are per bed, the same applies. You can often get a reduced rate at cheaper hotels. Sometimes when travelling with a child you will be refused a room in a hotel that is 'unsuitable'. On river boat trips, unless you have large hammocks, it may be more comfortable and cost effective to hire a 2-berth cabin for 2 adults and a child.

Transport
People contemplating overland travel in South America with children should remember that a lot of time can be spent waiting for public transport. Even then, buses can be delayed on the journey. Travel on trains allows more scope for moving about, but trains are few and far between these days. In many cases trains are luxurious and much more expensive than buses. If hiring a car, check that it has rear seat belts.

On all long-distance buses you pay for each seat, and there are no half-fares if the children occupy a seat each. For shorter trips it is cheaper, if less comfortable, to seat small children on your knee. There may be spare seats which children can occupy after tickets have been collected. In city and local tour buses, small children generally do not pay a fare, but are not entitled to a seat when paying customers are standing. On sightseeing tours you should always bargain for a family rate; often children can go free. All civil airlines charge half for children under 12, but some military services don't have half-fares, or have younger age limits. Note that a child travelling free on a long trip is not always covered by the operator's travel insurance; it is advisable to pay a small premium to arrange cover.

Disabled travellers

In most of South America, facilities for the disabled are severely lacking. For those in wheelchairs, ramps and toilet access are limited to some of the more upmarket, or most recently built hotels. Pavements are often in a poor state of repair or crowded with street vendors. Most archaeological sites, even Machu Picchu, have little or no wheelchair access. Visually or hearing-impaired travellers are also poorly catered for, but there are experienced guides in some places who can provide individual attention. There are also travel companies outside South America who specialize in holidays which are tailor-made for the individual's level of disability.

Some moves are being made to improve the situation and Ecuador's former vice-president (until 2013, and presidential candidate in 2017) Lenín Moreno, himself a paraplegic, made huge strides in providing assistance at all levels to people with disabilities. At street level, Quito's trolley buses are supposed to have wheelchair access, but they are often too crowded to make this practical.

PromPerú has initiated a programme to provide facilities at airports, tourist sites, etc. While disabled South Americans have to rely on others to get around, foreigners will find that people are generally very helpful.

The **Global Access – Disabled Travel Network** website, www.globalaccessnews. com/index, is useful. Another informative site, with lots of advice on how to travel with specific disabilities, plus listings and links, belongs to the **Society for Accessible Travel and Hospitality**, www.sath.org.

Electricty

Peru
220 volts AC, 60 cycles throughout the country, except Arequipa (50 cycles). Most 4- and 5-star hotels have 110 volts AC. Plugs are American flat-pin or twin flat and round pin combined.

Bolivia
220 volts 50 cycles AC. Sockets usually accept both continental European (round) and US-type (flat) 2-pin plugs. There are also some 110-volt sockets; when in doubt, ask.

Ecuador
AC, 110 volts, 60 cycles. Sockets are for twin flat blades, sometimes with a round earth pin.

Festivals and public holidays

Public holidays common to all
3 countries include:
1 Jan **New Year's Day**
Feb/Mar **Carnaval**
Mar/Apr **Semana Santa (Holy Week)**
1 May **Labour Day**
1 Nov **Todos los Santos (All Souls' Day)**;
see box, page 19
25 Dec **Christmas Day**

Peru
28-29 Jul **Independence (Fiestas Patrias)**
1 Aug **National Day of the Alpaca**, with events in major alpaca-rearing centres across the country
8 Oct **Battle of Angamos**
8 Dec **Festividad de la Inmaculada Concepción**

Bolivia
2 Feb **Virgen de la Candelaria**, in rural communities in Copacabana, Santa Cruz departments
3 May **Fiesta de la Invención de la Santa Cruz**, various parts
May/Jun **Corpus Christi**, a colourful festival
2 Jun **Santísima Trinidad** in Beni Department

24 Jun **San Juan**, bonfires throughout all Bolivia

29 Jun **San Pedro y San Pablo**, at Tiquina, Tihuanaco and throughout Chiquitania

16 Jul **La Paz Municipal Holiday**

25 Jul **Fiesta de Santiago** (St James), Altiplano and lake region

5-7 Aug **Independence**

14-16 Aug **Virgen de Urkupiña**, Cochabamba, a 3-day Catholic festivity mixed with Quechua rituals and parades with folkloric dances

16 Aug **San Roque**, patron saint of dogs; the animals are adorned with ribbons and other decorations

24 Sep **Santa Cruz Municipal Holiday**

Ecuador

24 May **Battle of Pichincha, Independence**

May/Jun **Corpus Christi**

10 Aug **First attempt to gain the Independence of Quito**

9 Oct **Independence of Guayaquil**.

3 Nov **Independence of Cuenca**

6 Dec **Foundation of Quito**.

Health

See your GP or travel clinic at least 6 weeks before departure for general advice on travel risks and vaccinations. Try phoning a specialist travel clinic if your own doctor is unfamiliar with health in the region. Make sure you have sufficient medical travel insurance, get a dental check, know your own blood group and, if you suffer a long-term condition such as diabetes or epilepsy, obtain a **Medic Alert** bracelet (www.medicalert.org.uk).

Vaccinations and anti-malarials

Confirm that your primary courses and boosters are up to date. It is advisable to vaccinate against polio, tetanus, typhoid, hepatitis A and, for more remote areas, rabies. Yellow fever vaccination is obligatory for most areas. Cholera, diphtheria and hepatitis B vaccinations are sometimes advised. Specialist advice should be taken on the best antimalarials to take before you leave.

Health risks

The major risks posed in the region are those caused by insect disease carriers such as mosquitoes and sandflies. The key parasitic and viral diseases are malaria, South American trypanosomiasis (Chagas' disease) and dengue fever. Be aware that you are always at risk from these diseases. **Malaria** is a danger throughout the lowland tropics and coastal regions. **Dengue fever**, which is widespread, is particularly hard to protect against as the mosquitoes can bite throughout the day as well as night (unlike those that carry malaria). Cases of the **chikungunya virus**, transmitted by the same mosquito that carries dengue, are increasing in the region. Cases of the **Zika virus**, similarly spread, have been reported too.

Try to wear clothes that cover arms and legs and also use effective mosquito repellent. Mosquito nets dipped in permethrin provide a good physical and chemical barrier at night. **Chagas' disease** is spread by faeces of the triatomine, or assassin bugs, whereas sandflies spread a disease of the skin called **leishmaniasis**.

Some form of **diarrhoea** or intestinal upset is almost inevitable, the standard advice is always to wash your hands before eating and to be careful with drinking water and ice; if you have any doubts about the water then boil it or filter and treat it. In a restaurant buy bottled water or ask where the water has come from. Food can also pose a problem, be wary of salads if you don't know whether they have been washed or not.

There is a constant threat of **tuberculosis** (TB) and although the BCG vaccine is available, it is still not guaranteed protection. It is best to avoid unpasteurized dairy products and try not to let people cough and splutter all over you.

One of the major problems for travellers in the region is **altitude sickness**. It is essential to get acclimatized to the thin air of the Andes before undertaking long treks or arduous activities. The altitude of the Andes means that strong protection from the sun is always needed, regardless of how cool it may feel.

Another risk, especially for campers and young children, is the **hanta virus**, which is carried by some riverine and forest rodents. Symptoms are a flu-like illness, which can lead to complications. Try as far as possible to avoid rodent-infested areas, especially close contact with rodent droppings.

Medical services

Peru

Arequipa Clinic Arequipa SA, Puente Grau y Av Bolognesi, T054-599000, www. clinicarequipa.com.pe. Fast and efficient with English-speaking doctors and all hospital facilities.
Paz Holandesa, Villa Continental, C 4, No 101, Paucarpata, T054-432281, www. pazholandesa.com. Dutch and English spoken, 24-hr service. Highly recommended.

Cuzco Hospital Regional, Av de la Cultura, T084-231640, www.hospitalregionalcusco. gob.pe.
Clínica Pardo, Av de la Cultura 710, T084-256976, T989-431050 (24 hrs), www. clinicapardo-cusco.com. Open 24 hrs daily, highly regarded and expensive, works with international insurance companies, some English-speaking staff.
Clínica SOS, Urb La Florida 0-3, T084-984-662599, www.sos-mg.com. Open 24 hrs daily, excellent service, emergency doctors speak good English.

Iquitos Clínica Ana Stahl, Av la Marina 285, T065-250025, www.clinicaanastahl.org.pe.

Lima Clínica Anglo Americana, Alfredo Salazar 350, San Isidro, T01-616 8900, www. angloamericana.com.pe. Stocks yellow fever and tetanus.
Clínica Internacional, Jr Washington 1471 y Paseo Colón (9 de Diciembre), T01-619 6161, www.clinicainternacional.com.pe. Good,

clean and professional, consultations up to US$35, no inoculations.
Instituto de Medicina Tropical, Av Honorio Delgado 430, near the Pan American Highway in the Cayetano Heredia Hospital, San Martín de Porres, T01-482 3910, www. upch.edu.pe/tropicales. Good for check-ups after jungle travel; samples taken Mon-Fri 0815-1300 and 1400-1500.
International Health Department, at Jorge Chávez airport, T01-517 1845. Daily 24 hrs for vaccinations.
Trujillo Clínica Peruano Americana, Av Mansiche 810, T044-242400. English spoken, good.

Bolivia

La Paz Laboratorios Illimani, Edif Alborada p 3, of 304, Loayza y Juan de la Riva, T02-231 7290, www.laboratoriosillimani.com. Open 0900-1230 and 1430-1700. Fast, efficient, hygienic.
Ministerio de Desarrollo Humano, Secretaría Nacional de Salud, Av Arce, near Radisson Plaza. Yellow fever shot and certificate, rabies and cholera shots, malaria pills; bring your own syringe.

Pharmacies Daily papers list pharmacies on duty (*de turno*). **Sumaya** (Dr Orellana), Linares 339 esq Sagárnaga, T02-242 2342, or 7065 9743. Good English-speaking doctor; for more severe cases the same doctor runs the **Clínica Lausanne**, Av Los Sargentos, esq Costanera in Bajo LLojeta, close to upper side of Obrajes. Very helpful, recommended.

Santa Cruz Santa Cruz is an important medical centre with many hospitals and private clinics.
Clínica Foianini, Av Irala 468, T03-336 2211, www.clinicafoianini.com. Among the better regarded and more expensive hospitals.
Hospital Santa Bárbara, Ayacucho y R Moreno, Plazuela Libertad, T04-645 1900, Hospital-SantaBarbara on Facebook. Public hospital.
San Juan de Dios, Cuéllar y España. The public hospital.

Sucre Hospital Cristo de las Américas, Av Japón s/n, T04-643 7084, www.hsjd.org. Private hospital.

Ecuador

Cuenca Hospital Monte Sinaí, Miguel Cordero 6-111 y Av Solano, near the stadium, T07-288 5595, www.hospitalmontesinai.org. Several English-speaking physicians.
Hospital Santa Inés, Av Daniel Córdova y Agustín Cueva, T07-282 7888. Dr Jaime Moreno Aguilar speaks English.

Galápagos Islands Hospital Oskar Jandl, Av Northía y Quito, Pto Baquerizo Moreno, San Cristóbal.
Hospital República del Ecuador, Av Baltra, Pto Ayora, Santa Cruz, T05-252 7439.

Guayaquil Clínica Alcívar, Coronel 2301 y Azuay, T04-372 0100, emergencies T1700-101010, www.hospitalalcivar.com.
Clínica Guayaquil, Padre Aguirre 401 y General Córdova, T04-256 3555, www.clinicaguayaquil.com. Dr Roberto Gilbert speaks English and German.
Clínica Kennedy, Av del Periodista y Callejón 11-A, T1800-536 6339, www.hospikennedy.med.ec. Reliable; also has branches in Ciudadela La Alborada and Vía Samborondón. It has many specialists and a very competent emergency department.

Ibarra Instituto Médico de Especialidades, Egas 1-83 y Av Teodoro Gómez de La Torre, northern highlands, T06-295 5612.

Latacunga Clínica Latacunga, Sánchez de Orellana 11-79 y Marqués de Maenza, central highlands, T03-281 0260. Open 24 hrs.

Loja Hospital-Clínica San Agustín, 18 de Noviembre 10-72 y Azuay, T07-257 0314, www.hospitalclinicasanagustin.com.

Quito Clínica Pichincha, Páez 22-160, T02-299 8700, emergencies T02-299 8777, http://hcp.com.ec. Good but expensive.
Hospital Metropolitano, Mariana de Jesús y Nicolás Arteta, T02-399 8000, http://hospitalmetropolitano.org/en. Very professional and recommended, but expensive.
Hospital Vozandes, Villalengua Oe 2-37 y Av 10 de Agosto, emergencies T02-226 2142, www.hospitalvozandes.org. Quick and efficient, fee based on ability to pay, a good place to get vaccines.

Websites

www.cdc.gov Centres for Disease Control and Prevention (USA).
www.fitfortravel.scot.nhs.uk Fit for Travel (UK), a site from Scotland providing a quick A-Z of vaccine and travel health advice requirements for each country.
www.itg.be Institute for Tropical Medicine, Antwerp.
www.nathnac.org National Travel Health Network and Centre.
www.nhs.uk/nhsengland/healthcareabroad Department of Health advice for travellers.
www.who.int World Health Organization.

Books

Dawood, R, editor, *Travellers' health,* 5th ed, Oxford: Oxford University Press, 2012.
Johnson, Chris, Sarah Anderson and others, *Oxford Handbook of Expedition and Wilderness Medicine,* OUP 2008.
Wilson-Howarth, Jane. *The Essential Guide To Travel Health: don't let Bugs Bites and Bowels spoil your trip,* Cadogan 2009, and *How to Shit around the World: the art of staying clean and healthy while travelling,* Travelers' Tales, US, 2011.

Internet

Public access to the internet is widespread. In large cities an hour in a cyber café will cost between US$0.50 and US$2. Speed varies enormously, from city to city, café to café. Away from population centres, service is slower and more expensive. Remember that for many South Americans a cyber café provides their only access to a computer, so it can be a very busy place and providers can get overloaded. See also Telephone and Wi-Fi, page 728.

Language

Without some knowledge of Spanish you will become very frustrated and feel helpless in many situations. English, or any other language, is absolutely useless off the beaten track. Not all the locals speak Spanish; you will find that some people in the more remote highland parts of Bolivia and Peru, and lowland communities in Amazonia, speak only their indigenous languages (Quichua in Ecuador, Quechua in Peru and Bolivia, also Aymara in southern Peru and Bolivia), though at least one person in each village usually speaks Spanish. Some initial study or a beginner's Spanish course is strongly recommended, as is a pocket phrasebook and dictionary.

Quito has the most language schools in all price ranges. Other language study centres include Cuenca, as well as Cuzco and Arequipa in Peru, Sucre and Cochabamba in Bolivia. See under Language schools in the What to do sections in Listings for details. The following international agencies arrange language classes, homestays, educational tours and volunteer opportunities.

AmeriSpan, T215-531 7917 (worldwide), T1-800-511 0179 (USA), www.amerispan. com. Offers Spanish immersion programmes, educational tours, volunteer and internship positions in Peru and Ecuador.
Cactus, T0845-130 4775 (UK), +44-1273 830960 (international), www. cactuslanguage.com. Has courses in Peru.
Spanish Abroad, T1-888-722 7623, or T602-778 6791, www.spanishabroad.com. Also runs courses in Peru, Bolivia and Ecuador.

LGBT travellers

South America is hardly well known for its gay-friendliness, but recent years have seen a shift in public opinion and attitudes. There is still a definite divide between the countryside and cities, but at least in the latter there are now more gay bars and organizations springing up. The legal framework is also changing and homosexuality is now legal in Peru, Bolivia and Ecuador. That said, it is still wise to use caution and avoid overt displays of affection in public, especially in rural areas.

Lima and Quito have active gay communities and there are local and international organizations which can provide information. Cuzco also has a gay scene. Useful websites include **www. gayecuador.com** and **www.quito gay. net** for Ecuador. For Peru, see **http://lima. queercity.info**, **www.deambiente.com/ web** and **www.gayperu.com** (the last 2 in Spanish only).

Local customs and laws

Appearance

There is a natural prejudice in all countries against travellers who ignore personal hygiene and have a generally dirty and unkempt appearance. Most Latin Americans, if they can afford it, devote great care to their clothes and appearance; it is appreciated if visitors do likewise. Buying clothing locally can help you to look less like a tourist. As a general rule, it is better not to wear shorts in official buildings, upmarket restaurants or cinemas.

Courtesy

Remember that politeness – even a little ceremoniousness – is much appreciated. Men should always remove any headgear and say "*con permiso*" when entering offices, and be prepared to shake hands (this is much more common in Latin America than in Europe or North America); always say "*Buenos días*" (until midday) or "*Buenas tardes*" and wait for a reply before proceeding further. Always remember that the traveller from abroad has enjoyed greater advantages in life than most Latin American minor officials and should be friendly and courteous in consequence. Never be impatient. Do not criticize situations in public; the officials may know more English than you think and they can certainly interpret gestures and facial expressions. Be judicious about talking politics with strangers. Politeness can be a liability, however, in some situations; most Latin Americans are disorderly queuers. In commercial transactions (eg buying goods in a shop), politeness should be accompanied by firmness, and always ask the price first (arguing about money in a foreign language can be difficult).

Politeness should also be extended to street traders. Saying "*No, gracias*" with a smile is better than an arrogant dismissal. Whether you give money to beggars is a personal matter, but your decision should be influenced by whether a person is begging out of need or trying to cash in on the tourist trail. In the former case, local people giving may provide an indication. On giving money to children, most agree don't do it. There are times when giving food in a restaurant may be appropriate, but find out about local practice.

Money

Withdrawing cash from an ATM with a credit or debit card is by far the easiest way of obtaining money, but always have a back-up plan. ATMs are common, but cannot always be relied on and have been known to confiscate valid cards. The affiliations of banks to the Plus and Cirrus systems change often, so ask around. Always bring some US dollar bills, travellers' cheques (TCs, although these are increasingly hard to exchange), or both. US dollar notes are often worn and tatty in Ecuador, but will only be accepted in Peru and Bolivia if they are in good condition. Low-value US dollar bills are very useful for shopping: shopkeepers and *casas de cambio* give better exchange rates than hotels or banks. Some banks (few in Ecuador) and the better hotels will normally change TCs

for their guests (often at a poor rate); some may ask to see a record of purchase before accepting. Take plenty of local currency, in small denominations, when making trips off the beaten track. Frequently, the rates of exchange on ATM withdrawals are the best available but check if your bank or credit card company imposes handling charges. Whenever possible, change money at a bank or *casa de cambio* rather than money changers on the street. Change any local currency before you leave the country or at the border.

For purchases, credit cards of the Visa and MasterCard groups, American Express (Amex), and Diners Club can be used. Transactions using credit cards are normally at an officially recognized rate of exchange; but may be subject to a surcharge of 8-12% and/or sales tax. For ATM locations, see www.visalatam.com, www.mastercard.com and www.americanexpress.com.

Another option is to take a prepaid currency card. There are many on offer, from, for example, **Caxton**, **FairFX**, **Travelex**, banks and other organizations. It pays to check their application fees and charges carefully.

Peru *US$1 = S/3.34; €1 = S/3.55 (Jan 2017)*
Currency The sol (s/) is divided into 100 céntimos. Notes in circulation are: S/200, S/100, S/50, S/20 and S/10. Coins: S/5, S/2, S/1, S/0.50, S/0.20, S/0.10 and S/0.05 (being phased out). Some prices are quoted in dollars (US$) in more expensive establishments, to avoid changes in the value of the sol. A large number of forged US dollar notes (especially US$20 and larger bills) are in circulation. There are also many forged soles coins and notes. Posters in public places explain what to look for.

Cost of travelling The average budget is US$45-60 pp a day for living fairly comfortably, including transport. Your budget will be higher the longer you stay in Lima and Cuzco and depending on how many internal flights you take. Rooms range from

US$7-11 pp for the most basic *alojamiento* to US$20-40 for mid-range places, to over US$90 for more upmarket hotels (more in Lima or Cuzco). Living costs in the provinces are 20-50% below those in Lima and Cuzco. The cost of using the internet is generally US$0.35-0.70 per hr, but where competition is not fierce, rates are higher.

Bolivia *US$1 = Bs6.96. €1 = Bs7.70 (Jan 2017)*
The currency is the boliviano (Bs), divided into 100 centavos. There are notes for 200, 100, 50, 20 and 10 bolivianos, and 5, 2 and 1 boliviano coins, as well as 50, 20 and (rare) 10 centavos. Bolivianos are often referred to as pesos; expensive items, including hotel rooms, may be quoted in dollars. ATMs are not always reliable and, in addition to plastic, you must always carry some cash. Most ATMs dispense both Bs and US$.

Cost of travelling Bolivia is cheaper to visit than most neighbouring countries. Budget travellers can get by on US$20-25 per person per day for 2 travelling together. A basic hotel in small towns costs as little as US$6-12 pp, breakfast US$1.50-2, and a simple set lunch (*almuerzo*) around US$2.50-3.50. For around US$35-40, though, you can find much better accommodation, more comfortable transport and a wider choice in food. Prices are higher in the city of La Paz; in the east, especially Santa Cruz and Tarija; and in Pando and the upper reaches of the Beni. The average cost of using the internet is US$0.50 per hr.

Ecuador
The US dollar (US$) is the official currency of Ecuador. Only US$ bills circulate. US coins are used alongside the equivalent size and value Ecuadorean coins. Ecuadorean coins have no value outside the country. Many establishments are reluctant to accept bills larger than US$20 because of counterfeit notes or lack of change. There is no substitute for cash-in-hand when travelling in Ecuador; US$ cash in small denominations

is by far the simplest and the only universally accepted option. Other currencies are difficult to exchange outside large cities and fetch a poor rate.

Cost of living/travelling Despite dollarization, prices remain modest by international standards and Ecuador is still affordable for even the budget traveller. A daily travel budget is about US$65-80 pp based on 2 travelling together fairly comfortably, but allow for higher costs in main cities and resorts. A basic travel budget, using hotels with shared bath, simple meals, no flights and no tours would be US$25-30 a day. Internet use is about US$0.50-1 per hr, US$2 in the Galápagos. Bus travel is cheap, about US$1.50 per hr, flights cost almost 10 times as much for the same route.

Opening hours

Peru
Banks Mon-Fri 0900-1800, Sat 0900-1230. Outside Lima and Cuzco banks may close 1200-1500 for lunch. **Government offices** Jan-Mar Mon-Fri 0830-1130; Apr-Dec Mon-Fri 0900-1230 and 1500-1700, but these hours change frequently. **Other offices** 0900-1700; most close on Sat. **Shops** 0900 or 1000-1230 and 1500 or 1600-2000. In the main cities, supermarkets do not close for lunch and Lima has some that are open 24 hrs. Some are closed on Sat and most are closed on Sun.

Bolivia
Banks and offices Normally open Mon-Fri 0900-1600, Sat 0900-1300, but may close for lunch in small towns. **Shops** Mon-Fri 0830-1230, 1430-1830 and Sat 0900-1200. Opening and closing in the afternoon are later in lowland provinces.

Ecuador
Banks Mon-Fri 0900-1700. **Government offices** Variable hours Mon-Fri, some close for lunch. **Other offices** 0900-1230 and

1430-1800. **Shops** 0900-1900; close at midday in smaller towns, open till 2100 on the coast.

Post

Postal services vary in efficiency and prices are quite high; pilfering is frequent. All mail, especially packages, should be registered. Some countries have local alternatives to the post office. Check before leaving home if your embassy will hold mail, and for how long, in preference to the Poste Restante/General Delivery (Lista de Correos) department of a country's post office. If there seems to be no mail at the Lista under the initial letter of your surname, ask them to look under the initial of your forename or your middle name. Remember that there is no W in Spanish; look under V, or ask. To reduce the risk of misunderstanding, use title, initial and surname only. If having items sent to you by courier (such as DHL), do not use poste restante, but an address such as a hotel: a signature is required on receipt.

Peru

The central Lima post office is on Jr Camaná 195 near the Plaza de Armas. Mon-Fri 0730-1900, Sat 0730-1600. Poste Restante is in the same building but is considered unreliable. In Miraflores the main post office is on Av Petit Thouars 5201 (same hours). There are many small branches around Lima and in the rest of the country, but they are less reliable. For express service: **EMS**, next to central post office in downtown Lima, T01-533 2020.

Bolivia

The main branches of post offices in La Paz, Santa Cruz and Cochabamba are best for sending parcels. DHL and FedEx have offices in major cities.

Ecuador

There is no surface mail to or from Ecuador, but a lower priority SAL/APR service is available at slightly lower cost.

Safety

Seek security advice before you leave from your own consulate rather than from travel agencies. You can contact the **British Foreign and Commonwealth Office**, Travel Advice Unit, www.fco.gov.uk/en/travel-and-living-abroad, and see www.gov.uk/travelaware for some basic precautions or see the **US State Department's Bureau of Consular Affairs**, Overseas Citizens Services, T1-888-407 4747 (from overseas: T202-501 4444), www.travel.state.gov, or the **Australian Department of Foreign Affairs**, T+61-2-6261 3305, www.smartraveller.gov.au.

Peru

The following notes should not hide the fact that most Peruvians are hospitable and helpful. The police presence in Lima and Cuzco, and to a lesser extent Arequipa and Puno, has been greatly stepped up. Nevertheless, be aware that assaults may occur in Lima and centres along the gringo trail. Also watch for scammers who ask you, "as a favour", to change dollars into (fake) soles and for strangers who shake your hand, leaving a chemical which will knock you out when you next put your hand to your nose. Outside the Jul-Aug peak holiday period, there is less tension, less risk of crime, and more friendliness.

Although certain illegal drugs are readily available, anyone carrying any is almost automatically assumed to be a drug trafficker. If arrested on any charge the wait for trial in prison can take a year and is very unpleasant. If you are asked by the narcotics police to go to the toilets to have your bags searched, insist on taking a witness. **Drug use or purchase is punishable by up to 15 years' imprisonment. There are a number of foreigners in Peruvian prisons on drug charges.** Tricks employed to get foreigners into trouble over drugs include slipping a packet of cocaine into the money you are exchanging, being invited to a party or somewhere involving a taxi ride, or simply being asked on the street if you want to buy cocaine. In all cases, a plain clothes 'policeman' will discover the planted cocaine, in your money, at your feet in the taxi, and will ask to see your passport and money. He will then return them, minus a large part of your cash. Do not get into a taxi, do not show your money, and try not to be intimidated. Beware also thieves dressed as policemen asking for your passport and wanting to search for drugs; **searching is only permitted if prior paperwork is done**.

Many places in the Amazon and in Cuzco offer experiences with Ayahuasca or San Pedro, often in ceremonies with a shaman. These are legal, but always choose a reputable tour operator or shaman. Single women should not take part. There are plenty of websites for starting your research. See also under Iquitos, page 328.

For up-to-date information contact the **Tourist Police** (see Accident and emergency, above), your embassy or consulate, or fellow travellers.

Bolivia
Violent crime is less common in Bolivia than some other parts of South America. The largest cities (Santa Cruz, El Alto, La Paz and Cochabamba) call for the greatest precautions. The countryside and small towns throughout Bolivia are generally safe.

Tricks and scams abound. Fake police, narcotics police and immigration officers – usually plain-clothed but carrying forged ID – have been known to take people to their 'office' and ask to see documents and money; they then rob them. Legitimate police do not ask people for documents in the street unless they are involved in an accident, fight, etc. If approached, walk away and seek assistance from as many bystanders as possible. Never get in a vehicle with the 'officer' nor follow them to their 'office'. Many of the robberies are very slick, involving taxis and various accomplices. Also if smeared or spat on, walk away, don't let the good

Samaritan clean you up, they will clean you out instead.

Take only radio taxis, identified by their dome lights and phone numbers. Always lock the doors, sit in the back and never allow other passengers to share your cab. If someone else gets in, get out at once.

Civil disturbances, although less frequent in recent years, remain part of Bolivian life. It can take the form of strikes, demonstrations in major cities and roadblocks (*bloqueos*), some lasting a few hours, others weeks. Try to be flexible in your plans if you encounter disruptions and make the most of nearby attractions if transport is not running. You can often find transport to the site of a roadblock, walk across and get onward transport on the other side. Check with locals first to find out how tense the situation is.

Road safety This should be an important concern for all visitors to Bolivia. Precarious roads, poorly maintained vehicles and frequently reckless drivers combine to cause many serious, at times fatal, accidents. Choose your transport judiciously and don't hesitate to pay a little more to travel with a better company. Look over the vehicle before you get on; if it doesn't feel right, look for another. If a driver is drunk or reckless, demand that they stop at the nearest village and let you off. Also note that smaller buses, although less comfortable, are often safer on narrow mountain roads.

Ecuador
Public safety is an important concern throughout mainland Ecuador; Galápagos is generally safe. Armed robbery, bag snatching and slashing, and holdups along the country's highways are among the most significant hazards. 'Express kidnapping', whereby victims are taken from ATM to ATM and forced to withdraw money, is a threat in major cities, and fake taxis (sometimes yellow official-looking ones, sometimes unmarked *taxis ejecutivos*) are often involved. Radio taxis are usually safer.

Secure your belongings at all times, be wary of con tricks, avoid crowds and congested urban transport, and travel only during the daytime. It is the larger cities, especially Guayaquil, Quito, Cuenca, Manta, Machala, Esmeraldas, Santo Domingo, and Lago Agrio which call for the greatest care. Small towns and the countryside in the highlands are generally safer than on the coast or in the jungle. The entire border with Colombia calls for precautions; enquire locally before travelling there.

If robbed, a report can be filed online at www.gestiondefiscalias.gob.ec/rtourist. See also Safety, page 495.

Although much less frequent than in the past, sporadic social unrest remains part of life in Ecuador and you should not overreact. Strikes and protests are usually announced days or weeks in advance, and their most significant impact on tourists is the restriction of overland travel. It is usually best to wait it out rather than insisting on keeping to your original itinerary.

In Ecuador, drug sales, purchases, use or growing is punishable by lengthy imprisonment.

Ecuador's active volcanoes are spectacular, but have occasionally threatened nearby communities. The **National Geophysics Institute** provides daily updates at www.igepn.edu.ec.

Tax

Peru
Airport tax US$31 on international flight departures; US$9.40 on internal flights (when making a domestic connection in Lima, you don't have to pay airport tax; contact airline personnel at baggage claim to be escorted you to your departure gate). Regional airports have lower departure taxes. Both international and domestic airport taxes should be included in the price of flight tickets, not paid at the airport. 18% state tax is charged on air tickets; it is included in the price of the ticket.
VAT/IGV 18%.

Bolivia
Airport tax International departure tax of US$25 is included in tickets at La Paz, Cochabamba and Santa Cruz airports Domestic tax is also included in tickets at these airports, but at all others an airport tax of US$1-2.50, depending on airport, is charged.
VAT/IVA 13%.

Ecuador
International and domestic departure tax is included in the ticket price.
VAT/IVA 14%. It may in principle be reclaimed on departure if you keep official invoices with your name and passport number; don't expect a speedy refund or bother with amounts under US$100. High surtaxes applied to various imported items make them expensive to purchase in Ecuador.

Telephone and Wi-Fi

Peru
International phone code: +51. Easiest to use are the independent phone offices, *locutorios*, all over Lima and other cities as well as coin-operated payphones, but mobile (cellular) phones are by far the most common form of telecommunication. You can easily purchase a SIM card (*un chip*) for US$5.50 (much more at Lima airport) for either of the 2 main mobile carriers: **Claro** and **Movistar**. You must show your passport. The chips work with many foreign mobile phones, but enquire about your unit before purchasing. Mobile phone shops are everywhere; look for chip signs with the carrier's logo. You get a Peruvian mobile phone number and can purchase credit (*recarga*) anywhere for as much or as little as you like. Calls cost about US$0.20 per min and only the caller pays.

Mobile phone numbers (*celulares*) have 9 digits, landlines (*fijos*) have 7 digits in Lima, 6 elsewhere, plus an area code (e g 01 for Lima, 084 for Cuzco). When calling a landline from a mobile phone, you must include the area code. The numbering system for digital phones is as follows: for Lima mobiles, add 9 before the number, for the departments of La Libertad 94, Arequipa 95, Piura 96, Lambayeque 97; for other departments, add 9 – if not already in the number – and the city code (for example, Cuzco numbers start 984). Note also that some towns are dominated by Claró, others by Movistar (the 2 main mobile companies). As it is expensive to call between the two you should check, if spending some time in one city and using a mobile, which is the best account to have.

Free Wi-Fi is standard at even the most basic hotels in tourist areas and at better hotels everywhere. Some cafés and public areas also have connectivity. Skype and similar services on Wi-Fi-enabled devices are the most economical form of international communication from Peru.

Bolivia

International phone code: +591. Equal tones with long pauses: ringing. Equal tones with equal pauses: engaged. IDD prefix: 00. Calls from public *cabinas* are expensive. Equal tones with long pauses: ringing. When dialling a number from a landline, there is no need to add the 0 in an area code, unless calling from outside that area. Cellular numbers have no city code, but carry a 3-digit prefix starting with a 6 or 7. Mobile phone service is offered by 3 main companies, **Entel** (with the most extensive coverage), **Tigo** and **Viva**. They have shops everywhere and you can buy a SIM card (*un chip*) for your phone or tablet if you would rather use local services than your home provider. Ask at a shop if a local SIM is compatible with your device and what the best package will be. There are call centres as well if you wish to make a call on a phone or local mobile.

Wi-Fi coverage is best in major towns and cities but all internet access is generally slow throughout Bolivia. Free Wi-Fi is standard in most hotels. Many places, such as cafés and

restaurants in tourist areas, also have Wi-Fi; just ask for the code.

Ecuador

International phone code: +593. There are independent phone offices, *cabinas*, in most cities and towns, but mobile (cellular) phones are by far the most common form of telecommunication. You can purchase a SIM card (*un chip*) for US$5 for either of the 2 main mobile carriers: **Claro** and **Movistar**; in principle an Ecuadorean *cédula* (national ID card) is required but a passport is sometimes accepted or ask an Ecuadorean friend to buy a *chip* for you. The *chips* work with many foreign mobile phones, but enquire about your unit before purchasing. Mobile phone shops are everywhere, look for the carrier's logo. You get an Ecuadorean mobile phone number and can purchase credit (*recarga*) anywhere for as much or as little as you like. Calls cost about US$0.20 per min and only the caller pays.

Mobile phone numbers have 10 digits starting with 09, landlines (*fijos*) have 7 digits plus an area code (eg 02 for Quito, 04 for Guayaquil). When calling a landline from a mobile, you must include the area code.

Skype, **WhatsApp** and similar services on Wi-Fi-enabled devices are the most economical form of international communication from Ecuador. Cyber cafés are common in the cities and towns of Ecuador but are gradually being replaced by widespread Wi-Fi access. Wi-Fi is available in most hotels, at many cafés and in some public places.

Time

Peru GMT -5.
Bolivia GMT -4.
Ecuador GMT -5 (Galápagos, -6).

Tipping

Peru
Restaurants: service is included in the bill, but tips can be given directly to the waiter

for exceptional service. **Taxi drivers**: none (bargain the price down, then pay extra for good service). If going on a trek or tour, it is customary to tip the guide as well as the cook and porters.

Bolivia

Up to 10% in restaurants is very generous; Bolivians seldom leave more than a few coins. Tipping is not customary for most services (eg taxi drivers) though it is a reward when service has been very good. Guides expect a tip as does someone who has looked after a car or carried bags.

Ecuador

In restaurants 10% may be included in the bill. In cheaper restaurants, tipping is uncommon but welcome. It is not expected in taxis. Airport porters, US$1 per bag.

Tour operators

Amazing Peru and Beyond, T1-800-704 2915, www.amazing peru.com. Wide selection of tours in Latin America.
Andean Trails, T0131-467 7086 (UK), www.andeantrails.co.uk. Small group trekking, biking and jungle tours in the Andes and Amazon.
Aston Garcia, T01740-582007 (UK), www.astongarciatours.com. Tailor-made tours in Ecuador and Peru.
Audley Travel, T01993-838000 (UK), www.audleytravel.com. Tailor-made trips to South America.
Condor Travel, T01-615 3000 (Peru), T1-855-926 2975 (US), www.condortravel.com. A full range of tours, including custom-made, and services in Bolivia, Ecuador and Peru (offices in each country), with a strong commitment to social responsibility.
Discover South America, T01273-921655 (UK), T1-917-200-9277 (US), www.discoversouthamerica.co.uk. British/Peruvian-owned operator offering tailor-made and classic holidays. Specialist in off-the-beaten-track destinations in Peru.

Dragoman, T01728-861133 (UK), www.dragoman.co.uk. Overland adventures.
Enchanted Adventures, www.enchanted adventures.ca. Ready-made and custom tours focusing on socially and environmentally responsible travel.
Fairtravel4u, Jan van Gentstraat 35, 1755 PB Petten, The Netherlands, T0226-381729, www.fairtravel4u.org. Tailor-made travel experiences in Ecuador, Peru and Bolivia.
Galápagos Classic Cruises with **Classic Cruises** and **World Adventures**, T020-8933 0613 (UK), www.galapagoscruises.co.uk. Specialize in individual and group travel including cruises, diving and land-based tours to the Galápagos, Amazon, Ecuador and Peru.
HighLives, T020-8144 2629 (UK), www.highlives.co.uk. Specialists in luxury tailor-made travel to Bolivia and South America.
Journey Latin America, T020-8747 8315 (UK), www.journeylatinamerica.co.uk. Deservedly well regarded, this excellent long-established company runs adventure tours, escorted groups and tailor-made tours to Argentina and other destinations in South America. Also offers cheap flights and expert advice. Well organized and very professional. Recommended.
Journeyou, T0-808- 134-9965 (UK), T1-855-888-2234 (US), www.journeyou.com. Pre-packaged tours and tailor-made itineraries to suit individual travel dates and budget.
Last Frontiers, T01296-653000 (UK), www.lastfrontiers.com. South American specialists offering tailor-made itineraries, family holidays, honeymoons and Galápagos cruises.
Latin American Travel Association, www.lata.org. For useful country information and listings of UK tour operators specializing in Latin America. Also has the **LATA Foundation**, www.latafoundation.org, supporting charitable work in Latin America.
Metropolitan Touring, T020-3371 7096 (UK), T1-888-572-0166 (US), www.metropolitan-touring.com. Long-established Ecuadorean company with tours in Ecuador and Peru.

Neblina Forest Tours, T02-239 3014 (Ecuador), www.neblinaforest.com. Birdwatching and cultural tours with a fully South American staff.

Oasis Overland, T01963-530113 (UK), www.oasisoverland.co.uk. Small-group trips to Peru and Bolivia as well as overland tours.

Rainbow Tours, T020-7666 1260 (UK), www.rainbowtours.co.uk. Tailor-made travel in Peru, Boliva and Ecuador.

Reef and Rainforest, T01803-866965 (UK), www.reefandrainforest.co.uk. Tailor-made and group wildlife tours.

Select Latin America, T020-7407 1478 (UK), www.selectlatinamerica.co.uk. Tailor-made holidays and small group tours.

South America Adventure Tours, T0845-463 3389 (UK), www.southamericaadventure tours.com. Specialize in personalized adventure tours in Ecuador and Peru.

SouthAmerica.travel, www.southamerica. travel, T0800-011 9170 (UK), T1-800-747 4540 (US and Canada). Experienced company offering luxury tours to South America and discount flights.

Steamond, T020-7730 8646 (UK), www. steamondtravel.com. Organizing all types of travel to Latin America since 1973, very knowledgeable and helpful.

Steppes Latin America, T 01285-601 495 (UK), www.steppestravel.co.uk. Luxury tailor-made itineraries for destinations throughout Latin America.

Tambo Tours, T1-888-2-GO-PERU (246-7378), www.tambotours.com. Long-established adventure and tour specialist with offices in Peru and the US. Customized trips to the Amazon and archaeological sites of Peru, Bolivia and Ecuador.

Tribes Travel, T01473-890499 (UK), www. tribes.co.uk. Tailor-made tours from ethical travel specialists.

Vaya Adventures, T1-(800)-342 -1796 (US), www.vayaadventures.com. Customized, private itineraries throughout South America.

Peru

Tourism promotion and information is handled by **PromPerú**. Their main office is at Jorge Basadre 610, San Isidro, Lima, T01-421 1627, www.promperu.gob.pe, Mon-Fri 0900-1800. See also www.peru.travel. PromPerú runs an information and assistance service, **i perú**, T01-574 8000 (24 hrs). There is also a 24-hr office at Jorge Chávez airport and other offices throughout the country.

There are tourist offices in most towns, either run by the municipality, or independently. Outside Peru, information can be obtained from Peruvian embassies/consulates. **Indecopi**, T01-224 7777 (in Lima), T0800-44040 (in the provinces), www.indecopi.gob.pe, is the government-run consumer protection and tourist complaints bureau. They are friendly, professional and helpful.

National parks

Peru has 68 national parks and protected areas. For information see **Servicio Nacional de Areas Naturales Protegidas por el Estado** (Sernanp), Calle Diecisiete 355, Urb El Palomar, San Isidro, Lima, T01-717 7500, www.sernanp. gob.pe. Mon-Fri 0830-1730.

Useful websites

www.caretas.com.pe The most widely read weekly magazine, *Caretas* (in Spanish).

www.peruthisweek.com Informative guide and news service in English for people living in Peru.

www.peruviantimes.com The *Andean Air Mail & Peruvian Times* internet news magazine.

www.terra.com.pe TV, entertainment and news (in Spanish).

Bolivia

The **Viceministerio de Turismo**, C Mercado, Ed Ballivián, p 18, has an informative website, www.bolivia.travel, in English. **InfoTur** offices are found in most departmental capitals (addresses are given under each city), at international arrivals in El Alto airport (La Paz) and Viru Viru (Santa Cruz). In La Paz at Mariscal Santa Cruz y Colombia.

National parks

Parks are administered by the **Servicio Nacional de Areas Protegidas (SERNAP)**, Francisco Bedregal 2904 y Victor Sanjinés, Sopocachi, T02-242 6268, www.sernap. gob.bo, an administrative office with limited tourist information. Better are Sernap's regional offices; addresses are given in the text under relevant towns.

Involved NGOs include: **Fundación para el Desarrollo del Sistema Nacional de Areas Protegidas**, Prolongación Cordero 127, across from the US Embassy, La Paz, T02-211 3364/243 1875, www.fundesnap.org; **Fundación Amigos de la Naturaleza (FAN)**, Km 7.5 Vía a La Guadria, Santa Cruz, T03-355 6800, www.fan-bo.org; **Probioma**, C 7 Este 29, Equipetrol, Santa Cruz, T03-343 1332, www.probioma.org.bo.

See also **www.biobol.org**, a portal in English with information on Bolivia's protected areas, and the **World Conservation Society**'s site, https://bolivia. wcs.org/en-us.

Ramsar's website, www.ramsar.org, has details of protected wetlands, including the Llanos de Moxos (Ríos Blanco, Matos and Yata), which covers 6.9 million ha, making it the largest protected wetland in the world.

Useful websites

www.bolivia.com News, tourism, entertainment and information on regions. In Spanish.

www.bolivia-online.net Travel information about La Paz, Cochabamba, Potosí, Santa Cruz and Sucre. In Spanish, English and German.

http://lanic.utexas.edu/la/sa/bolivia Database on various topics indigenous to Bolivia, by the University of Texas, USA. It's an interesting resource but is no longer being updated.

www.noticiasbolivianas.com All the Bolivian daily news in one place. In Spanish.

Ecuador

Ministerio de Turismo, Av Gran Colombia and Briceño, Quito, T02-399-9333, www. ecuador.travel. Local offices are given in the text. The ministry has a Public Prosecutors Office, where serious complaints should be reported. Outside Ecuador, tourist information can be obtained from Ecuadorean embassies.

National parks

Ecuador has an outstanding array of protected natural areas including a system of 43 national parks and reserves administered by the **Ministerio del Ambiente**, Madrid 1159 y Andalucía, T398 7600, www.ambiente. gob.ec/areas-protegidas-3/. Entry to national protected areas is free except for the Galápagos. Some parks can only be visited with authorized guides. For information on specific protected areas, contact park offices in the cities nearest the parks, they have more information than the ministry.

Useful websites

www.ecuador.travel A good introduction.
www.ecuador.com, **www.paisturistico. com** and **www.explored.com.ec** (the latter 2 in Spanish) General guides with information about activities and national parks.
www.ecuadorexplorer.com, **www. ecuador-travel-guide.org** and **www. ecuaworld.com** Travel guides in English.
www.trekkinginecuador.com For hiking information.

Visas and documentation

Peru

Tourist cards No visa is necessary for citizens of EU countries, most Asian countries, North and South America, and the Caribbean, or for citizens of Andorra, Belarus, Finland, Iceland, Israel, Liechtenstein, Macedonia, Moldova, Norway, Russian Federation, Serbia and Montenegro, Switzerland, Ukraine, Australia, New Zealand

and South Africa. A Tourist Card (TAM – Tarjeta Andina de Migración) is free on flights arriving in Peru, or at border crossings for visits up to 183 days. The form is in duplicate, the original given up on arrival and the copy on departure. A new tourist card must be obtained for each re-entry. If your tourist card is stolen or lost, get a new one from **Migraciones**, Digemin, Av España 734, Breña, Lima, T01-200 1000, www. migraciones.gob.pe, Mon-Fri 0830-1300.

Tourist visas For citizens of countries not listed above (including Turkey), visas cost US$37.75 or equivalent, for which you require a valid passport, a departure ticket from Peru (or a letter of guarantee from a travel agency), 2 colour passport photos, 1 application form and proof of economic solvency. Tourist visas are valid for 183 days. In the first instance, visit the Migraciones website (as above) for visa forms.

Keep ID, preferably a passport, on you at all times. You must present your passport when reserving travel tickets. To avoid having to show your passport, photocopy the important pages of your passport – including the immigration stamp, and have it legalized by a Notario Público.

Once in Peru tourists may not extend their tourist card or visa under any circumstances. It's therefore important to insist on getting the full number of days to cover your visit on arrival (it's at the discretion of the border official). If you plan to return to Peru later in your trip then don't ask for much more than you will need, as the full number of days you are granted (not the days you actually stay) is deducted from your 183-day limit. If you exceed your limit, you'll pay a US$1-per-day fine.

Bolivia
A passport only, valid for 6 months beyond date of visit, is needed for citizens of almost all Western European countries, Japan, Canada, South American countries (except Guyana and Suriname), Mexico, Costa Rica,

Panama, Australia and New Zealand. Most others require a visa issued in advance at a Bolivian consulate. US citizens need a visa which can be obtained in advance at consulates, or on arrival at international airports or land borders; US$160 cash fee plus various requirements including a return or onward ticket and yellow fever vaccination certificate. Israeli citizens need a visa which, in principle, must be issued at a consulate but exceptions may be made at the land borders at Kasani and Villazón; 648 bolivianos cash fee (US$93) and much paperwork. Always allow extra time to obtain a visa. Some nationalities must gain authorization from the **Bolivian Ministry of Foreign Affairs**, which can take 6 weeks. All regulations are subject to change and it is best to check current requirements before leaving home.

Tourists are usually granted 90 days stay on entry. If you are given less time, then you can apply for a free extension (ampliación) at immigration offices in all departmental capitals, up to a maximum stay of 90 days per calendar year (180 days for nationals of Andean nations). If you overstay, the current fine is Bs20, roughly US$3 per day. Be sure to keep the green paper with entry stamp inside your passport, you will be asked for it when you leave. You can get further information, including for student and work visas, from the **Dirección General de Migración** in La Paz, at Camacho 1480, T02-211 0960, www.migracion.gob.bo. Mon-Fri 0830-1230 and 1430-1830, but make sure you go early. Allow 48 hrs for visa extensions.

Ecuador
All visitors to Ecuador must have a passport valid for at least 6 months and an onward or return ticket, but the latter is seldom asked for. Citizens of Afghanistan, Bangladesh, Cuba, Eritrea, Ethiopia, Kenya, Nepal, Nigeria, Pakistan, Senegal and Somalia require a visa to visit Ecuador, other tourists do not require a visa unless they wish to stay more than 90 days. Upon entry all visitors must

complete an international embarkation/
disembarkation card. Keep your copy, you
will be asked for it when you leave.

Note You are required by Ecuadorean
law to carry your passport at all times.
Whether or not a photocopy is an acceptable
substitute is at the discretion of the
individual police officer, having it notarized
can help. Tourists are not permitted to work
under any circumstances.

Length of stay Tourists are granted
90 days upon arrival and there are no
extensions except for citizens of the Andean
Community of Nations. Visitors are not
allowed back in the country if they have
already stayed 90 days during the past
12 months. If you want to spend more time
studying, volunteering, etc, you can get
a purpose specific visa (category '12-IX',
about US$200 and paperwork) at the end of
your 90 days as a tourist. There is no fine at
present (subject to change) for overstaying
but you must request an exit permit 48 hrs
before departure and may be barred from
returning to Ecuador.

Dirección Nacional de Migración
(immigration) has offices in all provincial
capitals. If your passport is lost or stolen then,
after it has been replaced by your embassy,
you will have go to an immigration office to
obtain a *movimiento migratorio* (a certificate
indicating the date you entered Ecuador) in
order to be able to leave the country.

Visas for longer stays are issued by the
Ministerio de Relaciones Exteriores
(Foreign Office), through their diplomatic
representatives abroad.

Immigration Dirección Nacional de
Migración, Amazonas N32-171 y República,
Quito, T02-243 9408, www.ministeriointerior.
gob.ec/migracion, Mon-Fri 0800-1200 and
1500-1800.

Weights and measures

Peru Metric.
Bolivia Metric, but some old Spanish
measures are used for produce in markets.
Ecuador Metric, US gallons for petrol,
some English measures for hardware
and weights and some Spanish measures
for produce.

Footnotes

Index

*Entries in **bold** refer to maps*

FOOTPRINT

Features

About the authors

Robert and Daisy Kunstaetter

Daisy was born and raised in Ecuador. She attended university in Canada, where she met Robert and they planned a year of travels together. South America soon captured both their imaginations and the 'year' proved elastic, stretching from 1983 to the present. Along the way they became correspondents for the Footprint *South American Handbook*, and later authors and cartographers of *Ecuador*, *Peru* and *Bolivia*. Trekking is another of their passions, and they have written trekking guides to Ecuador and Peru. Robert and Daisy live in Ecuador and have yet to tire of trekking, travelling or writing. South America continues to capture their imaginations.

Ben Box

One of the first assignments Ben Box took as a freelance writer in 1980 was subediting work on the *South American Handbook*. The plan then was to write about contemporary Iberian and Latin American affairs, but in no time at all the lands south of the Rio Grande took over, inspiring journeys to all corners of the subcontinent. Ben has contributed to newspapers, magazines and learned tomes, usually on the subject of travel, and became editor of the *South American Handbook* in 1989. He has also been involved in Footprint's Handbooks on *Central America & Mexico*, *Caribbean Islands*, *Brazil*, *Peru*, *Cuzco & the Inca Heartland*, *Bolivia*, *Peru*, *Bolivia and Ecuador* and *Jamaica*. On many of these titles he has collaborated with his wife and Footprint Caribbean expert, Sarah Cameron.

Having a doctorate in Spanish and Portuguese studies from London University, Ben maintains a strong interest in Latin American literature. In the British summer he plays cricket for his local village side and year round he attempts to achieve some level of self-sufficiency in fruit and veg in a rather unruly country garden in Suffolk.

Acknowledgements

The authors wish to thank the following:
In Peru, Chris Benway, Alberto Cafferata, Kristof De Rynck, Rob Dover, Leo Duncan, Ricardo Espinosa, John and Julia Forrest, Peter Frost, Klaus Hartl, Carlos Manco, Humberto Medrano, Gerardo Pinto, Julio Porras, William Reyes and Martijn Steijn.
In Bolivia, Saúl Arias, Geoffrey Groesbeck, Alistair Matthew, Fabiola Mitru, Jedily Murillo, Derren Patterson, Ana Gabriela Sánchez, Mariana Sánchez, Martin Stratker and Remy van den Berg.
In Ecuador, Andrés Bermeo, Jeaneth Barrionuevo, Jean Brown, Popkje van der Ploeg, Michael Resch, Peter Schramm and Iván Suárez.

We should also like to thank for their invaluable support during the preparation of this book the team at Footprint who put the book together: Jo, Emma, Kevin and Angus, and the travellers who have written to Footprint and who are acknowledged in the *South American Handbook*, 2017 edition.

Credits

Footprint credits
Editor: Jo Williams
Production and layout: Emma Bryers
Maps: Kevin Feeney
Colour section: Angus Dawson

Publisher: Felicity Laughton
Marketing: Kirsty Holmes
Advertising and content partnerships:
Debbie Wylde

Photography credits
Front cover: Christian Vinces/
Shutterstock.com
Back cover top: Ammit Jack/
Shutterstock.com
Back cover bottom: Ali Cole/
Shutterstock.com
Inside front cover: CaseyFrench.

Colour section
Page 1: CaseyFrench. **Page 2**: Gabor Kovacs
Photography/Shutterstock.com. **Page 4**:
Mikadun/Shutterstock.com, CaseyFrench.
Page 5: CaseyFrench, Adalbert Dragon/
Shutterstock.com. **Page 6**: LOOK-foto/
Superstock.com, Jess Kraft/Shutterstock.
com, CaseyFrench. **Page 7**: Noradoa/
Shutterstock.com, Angela N Perryman/
Shutterstock.com, Alberto Loyo/
Shutterstock.com, Don Mammoser/
Shutterstock.com. **Page 10**: CaseyFrench.
Page 11: saiko3p/Shutterstock.com.
Page 12: CaseyFrench. **Page 13**: The
Editors/Shutterstock.com, Mint Images/
Superstock.com. **Page 14**: mageBROKER/
Superstock.com. **Page 15**: sunsinger/
Shutterstock.com, flocu/Shutterstock.com.
Page 16: CaseyFrench.

Duotones
Page 32: Nika Lerman/Shutterstock.com.
Page 344: Vadim Petrakov/Shutterstock.com.
Page 490: Ecuadorpostales/Shutterstock.com.

Publishing information
Footprint Peru, Bolivia & Ecuador
5th edition
© Footprint Handbooks Ltd
May 2017

ISBN: 978 1 911082 19 4
CIP DATA: A catalogue record for this book
is available from the British Library

® Footprint Handbooks and the
Footprint mark are a registered
trademark of Footprint Handbooks Ltd

Published by Footprint
5 Riverside Court
Lower Bristol Road
Bath BA2 3DZ, UK
T +44 (0)1225 469141
footprinttravelguides.com

Distributed in the USA by
National Book Network, Inc.

Printed in India by Replika Press Pvt Ltd

Every effort has been made to ensure that
the facts in this guidebook are accurate.
However, travellers should still obtain advice
from consulates, airlines, etc about travel
and visa requirements before travelling.
The authors and publishers cannot
accept responsibility for any loss, injury
or inconvenience however caused.

Footprint Mini Atlas
Peru, Bolivia & Ecuador

	National highway including Pan-American Highway
	Paved road
	Unpaved all weather including unpaved Pan-American Highway
	Seasonal unpaved road, track
	Rail

Altitude in metres
4000
3000
2000
1000
500
200
0
Neighbouring Country

See page 674
ECUADOR
Galápagos Islands

500 km
500 miles

Map 1 Ecuador

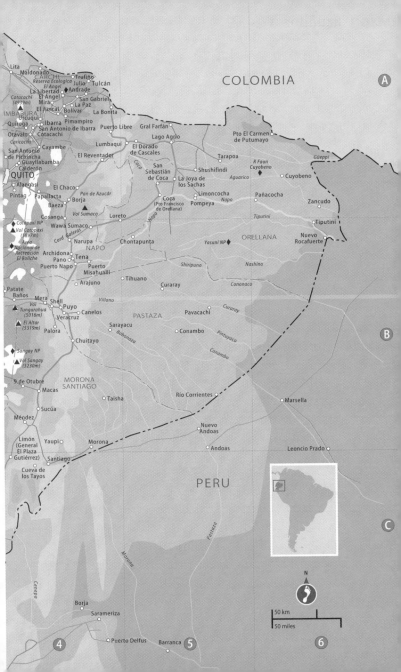

Colour map index

Footprint story

It was 1921

Ireland had just been partitioned, the British miners were striking for more pay, and the Federation of British Industry had an idea. Exports were booming in South America – how about a handbook for businessmen trading in that far-away continent? The Anglo-South American Handbook was born that year, written by W Koebel, the most prolific writer on Latin America of his day.

1924

Two editions later, the book was 'privatized', and in 1924, in the hands of Royal Mail, the steamship company for South America, it became The South American Handbook, subtitled 'South America in a nutshell'. This annual publication became the 'bible' for generations of travellers to South America and remains so to this day. In the early days travel was by sea and the Handbook gave all the details needed for the long voyage from Europe. What to wear for dinner; how to arrange a cricket match with the Cable & Wireless staff on the Cape Verde Islands, and a full account of the journey from Liverpool up the Amazon to Manaus: 5898 miles without changing cabin!

1939

As the continent opened up, the South American Handbook reported the new Pan Am flying boat services and the fortnightly airship service from Rio to Europe on the Graf Zeppelin. For reasons still unclear but with extraordinary determination, the annual editions continued throughout the Second World War.

1970s

Many more people discovered South America and the backpacking trail started to develop. All the while the Handbook was gathering fans, including literary vagabonds such as Paul Theroux and Graham Greene (who once sent some updates addressed to "The publishers of the best travel guide in the world, Bath, England").

1990s

During the 1990s the company set about developing a new travel guide series using this legendary title as the flagship. By 1997 there were over a dozen guides in the series and the Footprint imprint was launched.

2000s

The series grew quickly and there were soon Footprint travel guides covering more than 150 countries. In 2004, Footprint launched its first thematic guide: Surfing Europe, packed with colour photographs, maps and charts. This was followed by further thematic guides such as Diving the World, Snowboarding the World, Body and Soul Escapes, Travel with Kids and European City Breaks.

2017

Today we continue the traditions of the last 96 years that have served legions of travellers so well. We believe that these help to make Footprint guides different. Our policy is to use authors who are genuine experts and who write for independent travellers; people possessing a spirit of adventure, looking to get off the beaten track.

 footprinttravelguides.com

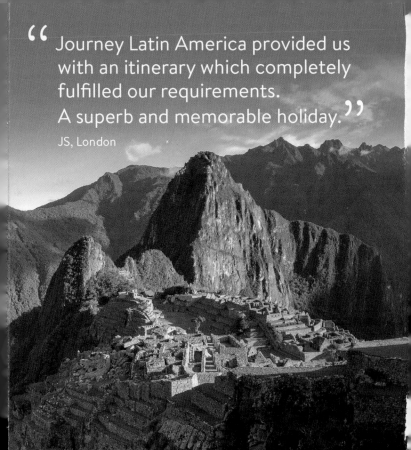